Tanzania

written and researched by

Jens Finke

ROUGH GUIDES

www.roughguides.com

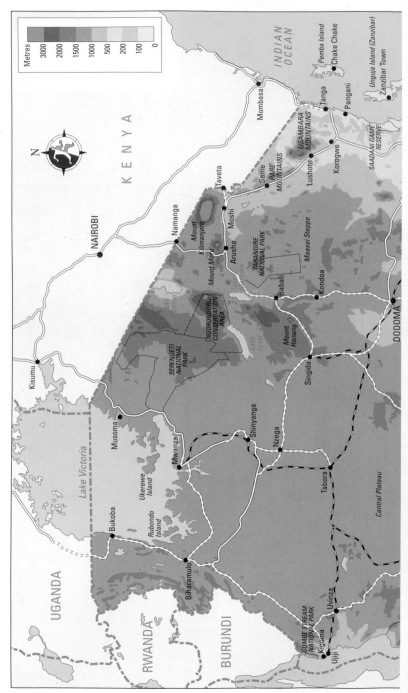

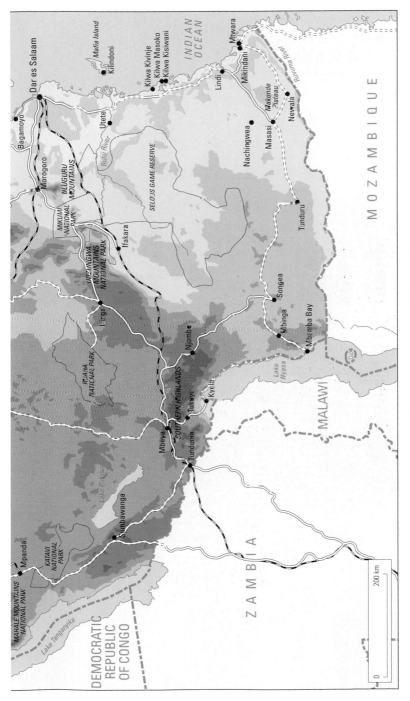

iii

Introduction to
Tanzania

Lying just south of the equator, Tanzania is East Africa's largest country, and an immensely rewarding place to visit. Filling the brochures are several world-famous attractions: the plains of the Serengeti, Ngorongoro Crater, snow-capped Mount Kilimanjaro (Africa's highest mountain) and Zanzibar, with its idyllic palm-fringed beaches and historic Stone Town. Yet there's a whole lot more to Tanzania than these obvious highlights. Almost everywhere you go you'll find interesting wildlife and inspiring landscapes (over forty percent of the country is protected in some form or other) ranging from forest-covered volcanic peaks to dusty savanna populated by elephants, antelopes, lions, leopards and cheetahs. Tanzania is one of the four most naturally diverse nations on earth: it contains Africa's second-largest number of bird species (around 1500), the continent's biggest mammal population and three-quarters of East Africa's plant species (over ten thousand). Add to this the country's rich ethnic diversity, some superb hiking and other activities like snorkelling and diving, and you have the makings of a holiday of a lifetime.

For all its natural diversity, Tanzania's best asset is its people: friendly, welcoming, unassumingly proud and yet reserved – you'll be treated with uncommon warmth and courtesy wherever you go, and genuine friendships are easily made. The best known tribe are the Maasai, a pastoralist cattle-herding people who inhabit the region around the safari parks in the

v

Fact file

• Tanzania was **created in 1964** by the union of mainland Tanganyika (former German East Africa) and Zanzibar, which was an Omani colony for several centuries before the British made it a protectorate. Covering 945,203 square kilometres, Tanzania is bigger than Kenya and Uganda combined, almost four times the size of the UKand twice that of California. The population is estimated at 33 million, growing annually at a rate of 2.8 percent. Population density is generally thin, apart from in the urban sprawl of Dar es Salaam and around the shoreline of Lake Victoria – one of the most densely populated regions on earth.

• Tanzania is among the **world's poorest countries**, with an average annual income below $200. Half the population live in poverty and lack access to safe water; one in six children die before the age of five; and life expectancy, albeit high by African standards, is falling – it's now under 50 years. Tanzania's foreign debt, currently around $7 billion, is a crippling burden on the economy: in 2002, forty percent of the Tanzanian government's revenue was used to service external debts – almost twice the country's budget for education and health. Tanzania receives over $1 billion annually in aid. Fortunately, these depressing statistics do not paint the full picture or reflect traditional modes of life, much of which – such as subsistence agriculture and cattle herding – carries on outside the official economy.

• Tanzania has been a **multi-party democracy** since 1995, although the ruling CCM party still receives the lion's share of media coverage. Zanzibar remains semi-autonomous and has its own parliament.

north, yet there are at least 127 other tribes in Tanzania, perhaps not as visually colourful as the red-robed, spear-carrying Maasai warriors, but with equally rich traditions, histories, customs, beliefs and music, much of which survive despite the ravages of colonialism, modernity and Christianity. For many years, only those with months on their hands had the privilege of really getting to know these people, but since 1995, an award-winning cultural tourism programme has broken new ground in enabling tourists, even those with little time or limited budgets, to experience for themselves local life in an intimate and inevitably fascinating way.

Where to go

Many visitors make a beeline for Tanzania's best-known protected areas, encompassed by the so-called **Northern Safari Circuit**. For many, the enormous volcanic caldera of **Ngorongoro Crater** is the highlight, providing a year-round haven for wildlife in a glorious setting and also the starting point for a wild hike through the Crater Highlands and past Tanzania's only active volcano, **Ol Doinyo Lengai**, to **Lake Natron**, an immense soda lake that appeals to flamingos and desert fanatics alike. The **Serengeti**, west of Ngorongoro, needs no introduction: its well-documented annual migration of over a million wildebeest, zebra and antelope provides one of the world's most awesome wildlife spectacles. Less-well-known northern parks include **Tarangire**, fantastic for elephants, whose size is amply complemented by forests of gigantic baobabs; **Lake Manyara**, at the foot of a particularly spectacular section of the Rift Valley escarpment; and **Arusha National Park**, which contains the country's second-highest mountain, **Mount Meru**. The main base for Northern Circuit safaris is the attractive town of **Arusha**, home to hundreds of safari companies and with a good handful of cultural tourism programmes within easy reach.

Hey, Mzungu!

Mzungu (plural *wazungu*) is a word you'll hear all over East Africa – children, especially, take great delight in chanting the word whenever you're around. Strictly speaking, a *mzungu* is a European, although Afro-Europeans and Afro-Americans need not feel left out, being known as *mzungu mwafrikano*. The term was first reported by nineteenth-century missionaries and explorers, who flattered themselves to think that it meant wondrous, clever or extraordinary.

The real meaning of the word is perhaps more appropriate. Stemming from *zungua*, it means to go round, to turn, to wander, to travel, or just to be tiresome. However weary you may grow of the *mzungu* tag, you should at least be grateful that the Maasai word for Europeans didn't stick: inspired by the sight of the trouser-wearing invaders from the north, they christened the newcomers *iloridaa enjekat* – those who confine their farts.

East of the Northern Circuit parks lie the **Northern Highlands**, dominated by the snow-capped **Mount Kilimanjaro** (5891m), the challenging ascent of which is one of the classic African adventures. Further east, Kilimanjaro's foothills give way to the much older granite formations of the **Pare** and **Usambara Mountains**, the repository of some of earth's

most biologically diverse rainforests, especially at **Amani Nature Reserve** near the coast, which well deserves its nickname of "the Galapagos of Africa".

Much of **central Tanzania** is dry and semi-arid woodland, and natural attractions are fewer. **Dodoma**, Tanzania's capital, is a hot and dusty planned city, though it makes a good starting point for excursions to the fabulous prehistoric rock paintings of the **Irangi Hills**, the oldest of which date back some 18,000 years. **Morogoro** is the liveliest of central Tanzania's towns, and offers hikers access to the **Uluguru Mountains**, another place with high species diversity. Heading south, the **Udzungwa Mountains** provide similar riches: the eastern flanks are especially good for primates, while the centre and west are bird-watchers' paradise. **Iringa**, to the west, is one of Tanzania's more attractive towns and gateway to **Ruaha National Park**, whose wealth of wildlife is the equal of the Northern Circuit parks, but without the crowds.

The **far south**, for long ignored, has recently been opened to tourism through a number of cultural tourism programmes. The mountainous towns of Mbeya and Tukuyu are the bases for hikes and day-trips in the **Southern Highlands**, with its rainforests and crater lakes. The highlight for many visitors to the region is **Lake Nyasa**, the southernmost of the Rift Valley lakes and home to hundreds of species of colourful cichlid fish; a trip in the weekly ferry along the Tanzanian side of the lake offers one of the country's classic journeys, as well as a convenient way of entering neighbouring Malawi.

North from here is the immense **Lake Tanganyika** the world's longest (and second-deepest) freshwater lake and scene of another unforgettable ferry ride aboard the vintage *MV Liemba*. The lakeshore provides the scenic setting for two remote nature reserves – **Mahale Mountains** and **Gombe Stream** national parks – both of which are home to troops of chimpanzees. Access to either is from the harbour town of **Kigoma**, close to **Ujiji**, where Stanley uttered his famous words, "Dr Livingstone, I presume?"

Northwest Tanzania is dominated by the shallow **Lake Victoria**, the world's second-largest freshwater lake. The views are magnificent, and the lake's southwestern corner contains the little-known **Rubondo Island National Park**, which harbours a number of endangered species and immense colonies of birds. There are three main towns on the Tanzanian part of the lake, each with its own distinctive personality and attractions: **Musoma** in the east; the burgeoning city of **Mwanza** in the south; and **Bukoba** in the west, which is connected to Mwanza by ferry and provides overland access to Uganda.

The **Indian Ocean** coastline offers an altogether different Tanzanian experience. The most obvious attractions are the idyllic beaches and outstanding coral reefs – paradise for scuba-divers. Especially recommended for diving and snorkelling is the island paradise of **Zanzibar**, one of Africa's most famous and enticing destinations, comprising the islands of **Unguja** and **Pemba**, which have idyllic beaches and multicoloured coral reefs aplenty. There's a whole lot more to Zanzibar than beaches and tropical languor, however. The archipelago's capital, **Stone Town**, is one of the world's most fascinating cities, centred on an Arabian-style labyrinth of narrow, crooked alleyways, packed with nineteenth-century mansions, palaces and bazaars. South from Zanzibar, the remote **Mafia Archipelago** has its own share of historical ruins, as well as stunning coral reefs which offer superlative snorkelling and diving.

On the mainland coast, the biggest settlement is **Dar es Salaam**, the country's former capital and still its most important city. Though it's usually only visited en route to Zanzibar, Dar is well worth spending some time in, especially for its exuberant nightlife and music – East Africa's liveliest. Tanzania's **north coast** features a series of beach resorts, the coastal **Saadani Game Reserve** and three towns which were involved in the nineteenth-century slave trade with Zanzibar – **Tanga**, **Pangani** and atmospheric **Bagamoyo**, which preserves a wealth of haunting old buildings and ruins. Tanzania's **south coast** is much wilder and less accessible.

Historical colour is provided by the ruins of the island-state of **Kilwa Kisiwani** – at its height the wealthiest and most important of the Swahili coastal trading towns. In the far south are a trio of towns: workaday **Mtwara** and **Lindi**, and the smaller **Mikindani**, like Bagamoyo an attractively tumbledown reminder of the slave trade.

Ujamaa

With 128 officially recognized tribes – plus a few more forgotten by the census people – Tanzania boasts more distinct cultures than any other country in Africa apart from Congo (which is two and a half times as big). Yet unlike Congo, Tanzania remains a peaceful oasis amidst the continent's wars. Although Tanzania's borders were drawn up in the interests of colonial Europe rather than along socio-cultural lines, the country is unique in having successfully forged a healthy sense of unity within those artificial borders – and one which encompasses both tribal and national identities. Undoubtedly, part of the reason for this success is that none of the nation's tribes comes close to forming a majority (the biggest, the Sukuma, comprises no more than thirteen percent of the population), while the brutal period of German colonization also played a part, in that the Germans introduced Kiswahili as the national language, so that every tribe could converse with every other. More than anything, however, Tanzania's uncommon unity owes its existence to the country's first president, Julius Nyerere, and his experiment in African socialism, known as *Ujamaa*, or "togetherness". Although economically disastrous, *Ujamaa* threw everyone together during the 1960s and 1970s, when over eighty percent of the rural population were moved from their ancestral lands and relocated in collective villages. *Ujamaa* is Nyerere's lasting legacy to the Tanzanian people, and for this reason alone, he deserves his unofficial title of *Babu ya Taifa*, the Father of the Nation.

When to go

Tanzania's **climate** can be divided into two rainy seasons and two dry seasons. The coast and lakeside regions are almost always hot and humid; highland regions have a more temperate climate; the semi-arid central plateau is hot and dry. Much of the country's climate, especially the eastern half and the coast, is controlled by the Indian Ocean's **monsoon winds** – the dry, northeast monsoon (*kaskazi*) blowing from December to March, the moist southeast monsoon (*kusi*) from April to November. The **"long rains"** (*masika*) fall from March to May, and are hot and wet. The lighter **"short rains"** (*mvuli*), usually lasting a month, come between October and December (usually late Nov and early Dec). The end of both rainy seasons is heralded by winds and mosquitoes. June can be rainy or dry. The period from July to October is dry, and starts cold, before becoming progressively warmer and more humid. December to February is usually also dry. At high altitudes, however, it can rain at almost any time. Western Tanzania, while broadly following the sequence outlined above, has a scattered rainfall pattern influenced by the presence of lakes Victoria, Tanganyika and Nyasa, and is always humid.

Temperatures are determined largely by altitude, though tropical humidity on the coast and by the lakes makes the air feel hotter than it really is. You can reckon on a drop of

6°C (or 11°F) for every 1000m you climb from sea level. However, daytime temperatures in most places average 22–30°C. The hottest period is from November to February; the coolest from May to August.

The main **tourist seasons** tie in with rainfall patterns: the biggest influxes are in December and January and, to a lesser extent, July and August. **Dry-season travel** has a number of advantages, not least of which is the ability to actually move around the country – many roads become impassable during the rains. The dry season is also better for spotting wildlife, when animals congregate around the diminishing water sources. July and August are probably the best months overall for **game-viewing**. October to January (especially Nov) has the clearest seas for **snorkelling and diving**. But the **rainy seasons**, except for March to May when your travelling options are severely hampered, shouldn't deter you unduly: the rains usually come only in short afternoon or evening cloudbursts, and the landscape is strikingly green and fresh even if the skies are cloudy. There are bonuses, too, in the lack of tourists: hotel and other prices are reduced, and people generally have more time for you.

The month of **Ramadan** (see p.51 for dates) has little effect on travel in mainland Tanzania, but isn't the best time to visit Zanzibar, as most restaurants close by day and the mood in Stone Town, especially, isn't at its best.

Tanzania's average temperatures and rainfall

	Jan	Feb	Mar	Apr	May	Jun	Jul	Aug	Sep	Oct	Nov	Dec
Dar es Salaam (sea level)												
°C	31	31	31	30	29	29	28	28	28	29	30	31
mm	75	75	125	275	300	60	50	25	50	55	75	100
Kigoma (altitude 781m)												
°C	27	28	28	27	27	26	28	27	28	28	27	27
mm	120	115	150	155	60	5	0	0	10	50	130	140
Mbeya (altitude 1700m)												
°C	23	23	23	23	22	21	21	22	25	27	27	25
mm	190	160	160	120	20	5	0	0	5	20	50	130

23

things not to miss

It's not possible to see everything that Tanzania has to offer in one visit, and we don't suggest you try. What follows is a selective taste of the country's highlights – outstanding scenery, exciting wildlife, memorable hikes – arranged in five colour-coded categories. All highlights have a page reference to take you straight into the guide, where you can find out more.

01 Serengeti Page **456** •
The legendary Serengeti is home to Africa's highest density of plains game and the scene of one of the greatest wildlife spectacles on Earth each year, when over a million animals set off on their annual migration.

02 Usambara Mountains Page **349** •
Part of an ancient chain of mountains formed twenty million years ago, the Usambara Mountains are home to ancient rainforests which contain an astonishing number of rare plant and animal species.

03 Seafood, Zanzibar Page **637** • Seafood features prominently in Swahili cooking, especially in Zanzibar, where all fish, prawns, squid and lobster are served with subtle spicings and blended with sauces.

04 Stone Town Page **615** • Stone Town's labyrinthine network of narrow streets is magically atmospheric, with a wealth of opulent nineteenth-century palaces, Persian baths and – in a poignant reminder of the sources of the town's wealth – cramped underground cells in which slaves were kept before being auctioned at the nearby market.

05 Scuba-diving Page **52** • The coral reefs off Tanzania's coast at Zanzibar and Mafia Island offer some of the world's finest scuba-diving.

06 Mount Kilimanjaro Page **324** • Africa's highest mountain and the world's tallest free-standing volcano, Kilimanjaro draws hikers from all over the world – although fewer than a third of them get to Uhuru Peak at the very top.

07 Kilwa Kisiwani Page **200** • The spectacular ruins of the island city-state of Kilwa Kisiwani – for many centuries the most successful of a chain of coastal trading centres – are testimony to the immense riches that were made first from gold, then from ivory and slaves.

08 Ngorongoro Conservation Area Page **447** • The enormous caldera of an extinct volcano provides the spectacular setting for Ngorongoro's abundant plains game and their predators – close-up encounters with lions, buffaloes and rhinos are virtually guaranteed.

09 Maasai Page **434** • One of Africa's best-known tribes, the cattle-herding Maasai inhabit northern Tanzania and southern Kenya. For many safari-goers, the Maasai are no more than the providers of picturesque photo-opportunities, but a series of cultural tourism programmes based in Arusha now provide much more enlightening – and respectful – encounters with the Maasai and their culture.

10 **Maji Moto springs, Lake Manyara** Page **437** •
The Rift Valley, a gigantic continental fault that runs from Lebanon to Mozambique, is at its most spectacular in East Africa, and the sulphurous springs which emerge along the shore of Lake Manyara testify to the continuing subterranean volcanic activity which runs beneath it.

11 **Makonde carvings** Page **232** • The Makonde tribe of southern Tanzania are famed for their abstract woodcarvings, including remarkable "trees of life" which perfectly illustrate the archetypal African concepts of remembrance and continuity.

12 **Tarangire National Park** Page **419** • In the dry season Tarangire is the best place in all Africa for seeing elephants – though even these mighty beasts are dwarfed by the park's huge baobab trees, many of them over a thousand years old.

13 **Nightlife in Dar es Salaam** Page **105** • *Muziki ya dansi* – dance music – is all the rage in Dar es Salaam. The city's nightlife is East Africa's liveliest, with both Congolese imports and home-grown talents performing nightly in dozens of venues.

14 **Mount Meru** Page **402** • Looming over Arusha, Mount Meru offers a taste of many of Tanzania's varied wildlife habitats, plus a spectacular volcanic crater, the east side of which was blown to smithereens in a series of catastrophic explosions 250,000 years ago.

15 **Tingatinga painting** Page **387** • Tingatinga painting uses bold and bright bicycle paints to illustrate its eye-catching and humorous designs, many of which are based on *sheitani* spirit mythology.

16 **Hiking in the Udzungwa Mountains** Page **298** • The forest-covered Udzungwa Mountains date back millions of years and offer hikers eyeball-to-eyeball encounters with primates and hundreds of species of bird.

17 **Indian Ocean flights** Page **37** • Any flight from the mainland to Zanzibar or Mafia Island offers an unforgettable bird's-eye panorama of the coral reefs of the Indian Ocean.

18 **Forodhani Gardens, Stone Town** Page **637** • Stone Town's waterfront Forodhani Gardens are a paradise for street-food enthusiasts, with a bewildering array of seafood, snacks and even roast bananas covered in melted chocolate – and all for no more than a dollar or two.

19 **Chimpanzees at Gombe Stream and Mahale Mountains** Page **532** • Since the 1960s, studies of wild chimp populations at Mahale Mountains and Gombe Stream national parks in western Tanzania have shed light on many fascinating aspects of chimp life, such as their use of tools and medicinal plants, along with some less attractive traits, including murder and warfare.

20 Beaches, Zanzibar

Page **681** • There's no better place to relax after a hot and dusty safari than on Zanzibar's beaches, especially at Nungwi in the north or along the east coast, where there's plenty of accommodation to suit all tastes and pockets.

21 Bull-fighting, Pemba

Page **699** • The two centuries of Portuguese occupation of the Swahili coast left few visible reminders. An enjoyable exception are the annual bull-fighting festivals held on Pemba Island – as in the Portuguese version, the bull is not killed, just mightily annoyed.

22 Lake Nyasa

Page **595** • Arguably Tanzania's prettiest lake, little-known Lake Nyasa offers unspoilt beaches, crystal-clear waters ideal for snorkelling and unforgettable views from the weekly ferry which plies down the Tanzanian side of the lake.

23 Kondoa-Irangi rock paintings

Page **257** • The craggy Irangi Hills of central Tanzania are home to a remarkable complex of painted rock shelters, the oldest dating back some 18,000 years old.

xvi

The wildlife of East and Southern Africa

This field guide provides a quick reference to help you identify the larger mammals likely to be encountered in East and Southern Africa. It includes most species that are found throughout these regions, as well as a limited number whose range is more restricted. Straightforward photos show easily identified markings and features. The notes give you clear pointers about the kinds of habitat in which you are most likely to see each mammal; its daily rhythm (usually either nocturnal or diurnal); the kind of social groups it usually forms; and general tips about sighting it on safari, its rarity and its relations with humans. For further details and background, see p.722.

✳ HABITAT   ◑ DAILY RHYTHM   ♉ SOCIAL LIFE   ✓ SIGHTING TIPS

Baboon *Papio cynocephalus*

❀ open country with trees and cliffs; adaptable, but always near water

◑ diurnal

❦ troops led by a dominant male

✓ common; several subspecies, including Yellow and Olive in East Africa and Chacma in Southern Africa; easily becomes used to humans, frequently a nuisance and occasionally dangerous

Eastern Black and White Colobus
Colobus guereza

❀ rainforest and well-watered savannah; almost entirely arboreal

◑ diurnal

❦ small troops

✓ troops maintain a limited home territory, so easily located, but can be hard to see at a great height; not found in Southern Africa

Patas Monkey *Erythrocebus patas*

❀ savannah and forest margins; tolerates some aridity; terrestrial except for sleeping and lookouts

◑ diurnal

❦ small troops

✓ widespread but infrequently seen; can run at high speed and stand on hind feet supported by tail; not found in Southern Africa

Vervet Monkey *Cercopithecus aethiops*

❀ most habitats except rainforest and arid lands; arboreal and terrestrial

◑ diurnal

❦ troops

✓ widespread and common; occasionally a nuisance where used to humans

❀ HABITAT   ◑ DAILY RHYTHM   ❦ SOCIAL LIFE   ✓ SIGHTING TIPS

White-throated or Sykes' Monkey/Samango
Cercopithecus mitis/albogularis

 forests; arboreal and occasionally terrestrial

 diurnal

families or small troops

✓ widespread; shyer and less easily habituated to humans than the Vervet

Aardvark Orycteropus afer

open or wooded termite country; softer soil preferred

nocturnal

solitary

✓ rarely seen animal, the size of a small pig; old burrows are common and often used by warthogs

Spring Hare Pedetes capensis

 savannah; softer soil areas preferred

 nocturnal

 burrows, usually with a pair and their young; often linked into a network, almost like a colony

✓ fairly widespread rabbit-sized rodent; impressive and unmistakable kangaroo-like leaper

Crested Porcupine
Hystrix africae-australis

adaptable to a wide range of habitats

nocturnal and sometimes active at dusk

family groups

✓ large rodent (up to 90cm in length), rarely seen, but common away from croplands, where it's hunted as a pest

Bat-eared Fox Otocyon megalotis

🌼 open country

◑ mainly nocturnal; diurnal activity increases in cooler months

🌱 monogamous pairs

✓ distribution coincides with termites, their favoured diet; they spend many hours foraging using sensitive hearing to pinpoint their underground prey

Blackbacked Jackal Canis mesomelas

🌼 broad range from moist mountain regions to desert, but drier areas preferred

◑ normally nocturnal, but diurnal in the safety of game reserves

🌱 mostly monogamous pairs; sometimes family groups

✓ common; a bold scavenger, the size of a small dog, that steals even from lions; black saddle distinguishes it from the shyer Side-striped Jackal

Hunting Dog or Wild Dog
Lycaon pictus

🌼 open savannah in the vicinity of grazing herds

◑ diurnal

🌱 nomadic packs

✓ extremely rare and rarely seen, but widely noted when in the area; the size of a large dog, with distinctively rounded ears

Honey Badger or Ratel
Mellivora capensis

🌼 very broad range of habitats

◑ mainly nocturnal

🌱 usually solitary, but also found in pairs

✓ widespread, omnivorous, badger-sized animal; nowhere common; extremely aggressive

African Civet *Civettictis civetta*

 prefers woodland and dense vegetation

 mainly nocturnal

 solitary

✓ omnivorous, medium-dog-sized, short-legged prowler; not to be confused with the smaller genet

Common Genet *Genetta genetta*

 light bush country, even arid areas; partly arboreal

 nocturnal, but becomes active at dusk

 solitary

✓ quite common, slender, cat-sized omnivore, often seen at game lodges, where it easily becomes habituated to humans

Banded Mongoose *Mungos mungo*

 thick bush and dry forest

 diurnal

 lives in burrow colonies of up to thirty animals

✓ widespread and quite common, the size of a small cat; often seen in a group, hurriedly foraging through the undergrowth

Spotted Hyena *Crocuta crocuta*

 tolerates a wide variety of habitat, with the exception of dense forest

 nocturnal but also active at dusk; also diurnal in many parks

 highly social, usually living in extended family groups

✓ the size of a large dog with a distinctive loping gait, quite common in parks; carnivorous scavenger and cooperative hunter; dangerous

 HABITAT   DAILY RHYTHM   SOCIAL LIFE   ✓ SIGHTING TIPS

Caracal Caracal caracal

⚘ open bush and plains; occasionally arboreal

◖ mostly nocturnal

🐐 solitary

✓ lynx-like wild cat; rather uncommon and rarely seen

Cheetah Acionyx jubatus

⚘ savannah, in the vicinity of plains grazers

◖ diurnal

🐐 solitary or temporary nuclear family groups

✓ widespread but low population; much slighter build than the leopard, and distinguished from it by a small head, square snout and dark "tear mark" running from eye to jowl

Leopard Panthera pardus

⚘ highly adaptable; frequently arboreal

◖ nocturnal; also cooler daylight hours

🐐 solitary

✓ the size of a very large dog; not uncommon, but shy and infrequently seen; rests in thick undergrowth or up trees; very dangerous

Lion Panthera leo

⚘ all habitats except desert and thick forest

◖ nocturnal and diurnal

🐐 prides of three to forty; more usually six to twelve

✓ commonly seen resting in shade; dangerous

⚘ HABITAT ◖ DAILY RHYTHM 🐐 SOCIAL LIFE ✓ SIGHTING TIPS

Serval Felis serval

 reed beds or tall grassland near water

● normally nocturnal but more diurnal than most cats

✿ usually solitary

✓ some resemblance to, but far smaller than, the cheetah; most likely to be seen on roadsides or water margins at dawn or dusk

Rock Hyrax or Dassie
Procavia capensis

 rocky areas, from mountains to isolated outcrops

● diurnal

✿ colonies consisting of a territorial male with as many as thirty related females

✓ rabbit-sized; very common; often seen sunning themselves in the early morning on rocks

African Elephant
Loxodonta africana

✿ wide range of habitats, wherever there are trees and water

● nocturnal and diurnal; sleeps as little as four hours a day

✿ almost human in its complexity; cows and offspring in herds headed by a matriarch; bulls solitary or in bachelor herds

✓ look out for fresh dung (football-sized) and recently damaged trees; frequently seen at water holes from late afternoon

Black Rhinoceros
Diceros bicornis

❀ usually thick bush, altitudes up to 3500m

◑ active day and night, resting between periods of activity

✻ solitary

✓ extremely rare and in critical danger of extinction; largely confined to parks where most individuals are known to rangers; distinctive hooked lip for browsing; small head usually held high; bad eyesight; very dangerous

White Rhinoceros Ceratotherium simum

❀ savannah

◑ active day and night, resting between periods of activity

✻ mother/s and calves, or small, same-sex herds of immature animals; old males solitary

✓ rare, restricted to parks; distinctive wide mouth (hence "white" from Afrikaans wijd) for grazing; large head usually lowered; docile

Burchell's Zebra Equus burchelli

❀ savannah, with or without trees, up to 4500m

◑ active day and night, resting intermittently

✻ harems of several mares and foals led by a dominant stallion are usually grouped together, in herds of up to several thousand

✓ widespread and common inside and out-side the parks; regional subspecies include granti (Grant's, East Africa) and chapmani (Chapman's, Southern Africa, left)

Grevy's Zebra Equus grevyi

❀ arid regions

◑ largely diurnal

✻ mares with foals and stallions generally keep to separate troops; stallions sometimes solitary and territorial

✓ easily distinguished from smaller Burchell's Zebra by narrow stripes and very large ears; rare and localized but easily seen; not found in Southern Africa

❀ HABITAT ◑ DAILY RHYTHM ✻ SOCIAL LIFE ✓ SIGHTING TIPS

Warthog Phacochoerus aethiopicus

🌸 savannah, up to an altitude of over 2000m

🌓 diurnal

🐾 family groups, usually of a female and her litter

✓ common; boars are distinguishable from sows by their prominent face "warts"

Hippopotamus
Hippopotamus amphibius

🌸 slow-flowing rivers, dams and lakes

🌓 principally nocturnal, leaving the water to graze

🐾 bulls are solitary, but other animals live in family groups headed by a matriarch

✓ usually seen by day in water, with top of head and ears breaking the surface; frequently aggressive and very dangerous when threatened or when retreat to water is blocked

Giraffe Giraffa camelopardalis

🌸 wooded savannah and thorn country

🌓 diurnal

🐾 loose, non-territorial, leaderless herds

✓ common; many subspecies, of which Maasai (*G. c. tippelskirchi*, right), Reticulated (*G. c. reticulata*, bottom l.) and Rothschild's (*G. c. rothschildi*, bottom r.) are East African; markings of Southern African subspecies are intermediate between *tippelskirchi* and *rothschildi*

African or Cape Buffalo
Syncerus caffer

✿ wide range of habitats, always near water, up to altitudes of 4000m

◑ nocturnal and diurnal, but inactive during the heat of the day

✿ gregarious, with cows and calves in huge herds; young bulls often form small bachelor herds; old bulls are usually solitary

✓ very common; scent much more acute than other senses; very dangerous, old bulls especially so

Hartebeest Alcelaphus buselaphus

✿ wide range of grassy habitats

◑ diurnal

✿ females and calves in small, wandering herds; territorial males solitary

✓ hard to confuse with any other antelope except the topi/tsessebe; many varieties, distinguishable by horn shape, including Coke's, Lichtenstein's, Jackson's (left), and Red or Cape; common, but much displaced by cattle grazing

Blue or White-bearded
Wildebeest Connochaetes taurinus

✿ grasslands

◆ diurnal, occasionally also nocturnal

✿ intensely gregarious; wide variety of associations within mega-herds which may number over 100,000 animals

✓ unmistakable, nomadic grazer; long tail, mane and beard

Topi or Tsessebe Damaliscus lunatus

✿ grasslands, showing a marked preference for moist savannah, near water

◑ diurnal

✿ females and young form herds with an old male

✓ widespread, very fast runners; male often stands sentry on an abandoned termite hill, actually marking the territory against rivals, rather than defending against predators

Gerenuk *Litocranius walleri*

 arid thorn country and semi-desert

 diurnal

solitary or in small, territorial harems

✓ not uncommon; unmistakable giraffe-like neck; often browses standing upright on hind legs; the female is hornless; not found in Southern Africa

Grant's Gazelle *Gazella granti*

wide grassy plains with good visibility, sometimes far from water

diurnal

small, territorial harems

✓ larger than the similar Thomson's Gazelle, distinguished from it by the white rump patch which extends onto the back; the female has smaller horns than the male; not found in Southern Africa

Springbok *Antidorcas marsupalis*

arid plains

seasonally variable, but usually cooler times of day

highly gregarious, sometimes in thousands; various herding combinations of males, females and young

✓ medium-sized, delicately built gazelle; dark line through eye to mouth and lyre-shaped horns in both sexes; found only in Botswana, Namibia and South Africa

Thomson's Gazelle *Gazella thomsoni*

 flat, short-grass savannah, near water

diurnal

gregarious, in a wide variety of social structures, often massing in the hundreds with other grazing species

✓ smaller than the similar Grant's Gazelle, distinguished from it by the black band on flank; the female has tiny horns; not found in Southern Africa

Impala Aepyceros melampus

⚘ open savannah near light woodland cover

◑ diurnal

🌱 large herds of females overlap with several male territories; males highly territorial during the rut when they separate out breeding harems of up to twenty females

✓ common, medium-sized, no close relatives; distinctive high leaps when fleeing; the only antelope with a black tuft above the hooves; males have long, lyre-shaped horns

Red Lechwe Kobus leche

⚘ floodplains and areas close to swampland

◑ nocturnal and diurnal

🌱 herds of up to thirty females move through temporary ram territories; occasionally thousand-strong gatherings

✓ semi-aquatic antelope with distinctive angular rump; rams have large forward-pointing horns; not found in East Africa

Common Reedbuck
Redunca arundinum

⚘ reedbeds and tall grass near water

◑ nocturnal and diurnal

🌱 monogamous pairs or family groups in territory defended by the male

✓ medium-sized antelope, with a plant diet unpalatable to other herbivores; only males have horns

Common or Defassa Waterbuck
Kobus ellipsiprymnus

⚘ open woodland and savannah, near water

◑ nocturnal and diurnal

🌱 territorial herds of females and young, led by dominant male, or territorial males visited by wandering female herds

✓ common, rather tame, large antelope; plant diet unpalatable to other herbivores; shaggy coat; only males have horns

⚘ HABITAT   ◑ DAILY RHYTHM   🌱 SOCIAL LIFE   ✓ SIGHTING TIPS

Kirk's Dikdik *Rhincotragus kirki*

 scrub and thornbush, often far from water

 nocturnal and diurnal, with several sleeping periods

🐾 pairs for life, often accompanied by current and previous young

✓ tiny, hare-sized antelope, named after its alarm cry; only males have horns; not found in Southern Africa except Namibia

Common Duiker *Sylvicapra grimmia*

 adaptable; prefers scrub and bush

 nocturnal and diurnal

 most commonly solitary; sometimes in pairs; occasionally monogamous

✓ widespread and common small antelope with a rounded back; seen close to cover; rams have short straight horns

Sitatunga *Tragelaphus spekei*

 swamps

🌓 nocturnal and sometimes diurnal

🐾 territorial and mostly solitary or in pairs

✓ very localized and not likely to be mistaken for anything else; usually seen half submerged; females have no horns

---

Nyala *Tragelaphus angasi*

🌸 dense woodland near water

🌓 primarily nocturnal with some diurnal activity

🐾 flexible and non-territorial; the basic unit is a female and two offspring

✓ in size midway between the Lesser Kudu and Bushbuck, and easily mistaken for the latter; orange legs distinguish it; only males have horns; not found in East Africa

🌸 HABITAT   🌓 DAILY RHYTHM   🐾 SOCIAL LIFE   ✓ SIGHTING TIPS

Bushbuck Tragelaphus scriptus

✿ thick bush and woodland close to water

◑ principally nocturnal, but also active during the day when cool

 solitary, but casually sociable; sometimes grazes in small groups

✓ medium-sized antelope with white stripes and spots; often seen in thickets, or heard crashing through them; not to be confused with the larger Nyala; the male has shortish straight horns

Eland Taurotragus oryx

✿ highly adaptable; semi-desert to mountains, but prefers scrubby plains

◑ nocturnal and diurnal

✿ non-territorial herds of up to sixty with temporary gatherings of as many as a thousand

✓ common but shy; the largest and most powerful African antelope; both sexes have straight horns with a slight spiral

Greater Kudu
Tragelaphus strepsiceros

✿ semi-arid, hilly or undulating bush country; tolerant of drought

◑ diurnal when secure; otherwise nocturnal

✿ territorial; males usually solitary; females in small troops with young

✓ impressively big antelope (up to 1.5m at shoulder) with very long, spiral horns in the male; very localized; shy of humans and not often seen

Lesser Kudu Tragelaphus imberbis

✿ semi-arid, hilly or undulating bush country; tolerant of drought

◑ diurnal when secure; otherwise nocturnal

 territorial; males usually solitary; females in small troops with young

✓ smaller than the Greater Kudu; only the male has horns; extremely shy and usually seen only as it disappears; not found in Southern Africa

✿ HABITAT ◑ DAILY RHYTHM ✿ SOCIAL LIFE ✓ SIGHTING TIPS

Gemsbok *Oryx gazella gazella*

 open grasslands; also waterless wastelands; tolerant of prolonged drought

nocturnal and diurnal

highly hierarchical mixed herds of up to fifteen, led by a dominant bull

✓ large antelope with unmistakable horns in both sexes; subspecies gazella is one of several similar forms, sometimes considered separate species; not found in East Africa

Fringe-eared Oryx
Oryx gazella callotis

 open grasslands; also waterless wastelands; tolerant of prolonged drought

nocturnal and diurnal

highly hierarchical mixed herds of up to fifteen, led by a dominant bull

✓ the *callotis* subspecies is one of two found in Kenya, the other, found in the northeast, being *Oryx g. beisa* (the Beisa Oryx); not found in Southern Africa

Roan Antelope *Hippotragus equinus*

tall grassland near water

nocturnal and diurnal; peak afternoon feeding

small herds led by a dominant bull; herds of immature males; sometimes pairs in season

✓ large antelope, distinguished from the Sable by lighter, greyish colour, shorter horns (both sexes) and narrow, tufted ears

Sable Antelope *Hippotragus niger*

open woodland with medium to tall grassland near water

nocturnal and diurnal

territorial; bulls divide into sub-territories, through which cows and young roam; herds of immature males; sometimes pairs in season

✓ large antelope; upper body dark brown to black; mask-like markings on the face; both sexes have huge curved horns

Grysbok Raphicerus melanotis

✿ thicket adjacent to open grassland

◗ nocturnal

✻ rams territorial; loose pairings

✓ small, rarely seen antelope; two sub-species, Cape (*R. m. melanotis*, South Africa, left) and Sharpe's (*R. m. sharpei*, East Africa); distinguished from more slender Steenbok by light underparts; rams have short horns

Oribi Ourebia ourebi

✿ open grassland

◗ diurnal

✻ territorial harems consisting of male and one to four females

✓ localized small antelope, but not hard to see where common; only males have horns; the Oribi is distinguished from the smaller Grysbok and Steenbok by a black tail and dark skin patch below the eye

Steenbok Raphicerus campestris

✿ dry savannah

◗ nocturnal and diurnal

✻ solitary or (less often) in pairs

✓ widespread small antelope, particularly in Southern Africa, but shy; only males have horns

Klipspringer Oreotragus oreotragus

✿ rocky country; cliffs and kopjes

◗ diurnal

✻ territorial ram with mate or small family group; often restricted to small long-term territories

✓ small antelope; horns normally only on male; extremely agile on rocky terrain; unusually high hooves, giving the impression of walking on tiptoe

Contents

Using this Rough Guide

We've tried to make this Rough Guide a good read and easy to use. The book is divided into six main sections, and you should be able to find whatever you want in one of them.

Colour section

The front colour section offers a quick tour of Tanzania. The **introduction** aims to give you a feel for the place, with suggestions on where to go. We also tell you what the weather is like and include a basic country fact file. Next, our author rounds up his favourite aspects of Tanzania in the **things not to miss** section – whether it's great food, amazing sights or a special hotel. Right after this comes a full **contents** list.

Basics

The Basics section covers all the **pre-departure** nitty-gritty to help you plan your trip. This is where to find out which airlines fly to your destination, what paperwork you'll need, what to do about money and insurance, about internet access, food, security, public transport, car rental – in fact just about every piece of **general practical information** you might need.

Guide

This is the heart of the Rough Guide, divided into user-friendly chapters, each of which covers a specific region. Every chapter starts with a list of **highlights** and an **introduction** that helps you to decide where to go, depending on your time and budget. Likewise, introductions to the various towns and smaller regions within each chapter should help you plan your itinerary. We start most town accounts with information on arrival and accommodation, followed by a tour of the sights, and finally reviews of places to eat and drink, and details of nightlife. Longer accounts also have a directory of practical listings. Each chapter concludes with **public transport** details for that region.

Contexts

Read Contexts to get a deeper understanding of what makes Tanzania tick. We include a brief history, articles about **wildlife** and **music**, and a detailed further reading section that reviews dozens of **books** relating to the country.

Language

The **language** section gives useful guidance for speaking **Swahili** and pulls together all the vocabulary you might need on your trip, including a comprehensive menu reader. Here you'll also find a glossary of words and terms peculiar to the country.

Index + small print

Apart from a **full index**, which includes maps as well as places, this section covers publishing information, credits and acknowledgements, and also has our contact details in case you want to send in updates and corrections to the book – or suggestions as to how we might improve it.

Map and chapter list

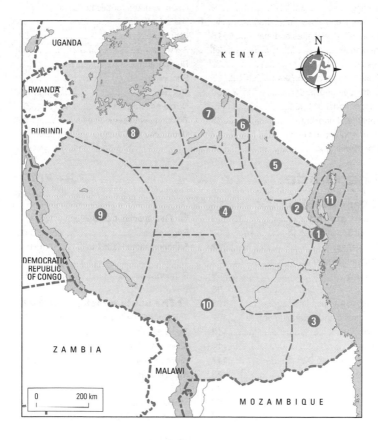

3

Contents

Colour section   i–xxxii

Basics   7–72

The Guide   73–706

Contexts

Language

Index and small print

Map symbols

maps are listed in the full index using coloured text

Regional Maps

-----	International border
---	Chapter division boundary
▰▰▰	Motorway
═══	Major tarred road
═══	Minor tarred road
───	Untarred road
-----	Footpath
▬▬▬	Railway
───	Coastline/river
– –	Ferry route
───	Wall
✕	International airport
✗	Domestic airport
◆	Point of interest
▲	Mountain peak
峠	Mountain range
◷	Crater
峡	Gorge
岩	Reef rocks
瀧	Waterfall
∿	Spring
沼	Swamp
↯	Viewpoint
◠	Cave
∴	Ruins
⚲	Lighthouse
⚑	Church
⛺	Campsite
⌂	Hut
⌂	Ranger post
⊠—⊠	Gate
⊼	Picnic site

▨	National park/nature reserve
◡	Glacier
▱	Forest
◺	Mangrove swamp
▨	Coral reef
▦	Beach

Town Maps

═══	Tarred roads
-----	Untarred roads
ⓘ	Information office
⊠	Post office
◐	Telephone office
@	Internet access
⊙	Statue
★	Transport stop
⊞	Hospital
🕌	Mosque
▬	Sikh temple
▲	Hindu temple
⛽	Petrol station
T	Toilets
⍓	Coconut plantation
■	Building
⊞	Church
▯	Market
⬭	Stadium
⊡	Christian cemetery
⊓	Muslim cemetery
▨	Park

Basics

Basics

Getting there

Flying to Tanzania is the only practical way to reach the country from outside eastern and southern Africa – there are a reasonable number of direct and one-stop flights from Europe and other parts of Africa to Dar es Salaam, though it can be difficult to find direct flights into Zanzibar from anywhere other than mainland Tanzania and Kenya.

A much more challenging – and rewarding – option would be to make your way to Tanzania **overland** (see p.14), though this is currently only practicable from Kenya, Uganda or southern Africa. There are also a few **ferry routes** into the country, either from Malawi over Lake Nyasa or from Zambia and Burundi across Lake Tanganyika; there are currently no international ferries on Lake Victoria or on the Indian Ocean. Coming from southern Africa, it's also possible to make the journey by **train** (p.14).

Tanzania has three **international airports**: **Dar es Salaam**, **Zanzibar** and **Kilimanjaro**, the last close to Tanzania's safari capital, Arusha. The regional airport at **Mwanza** also receives flights from Nairobi via Kilimanjaro. Flying into Kilimanjaro from the north, try to get a seat on the left of the plane: if you arrive by day, you might (cloud permitting) get an unforgettable view of Africa's highest mountain. Those on the opposite aisle can console themselves with the view of northern Kenya's Lake Turkana – the world's largest permanent desert lake – about an hour's flight north of Kilimanjaro.

Buying a ticket

When **buying a ticket**, your first stop should be the discount agents listed on pp.11–13, these often offer scheduled flight tickets at substantially **discounted rates**, though they may carry restrictions (like not being able to change flight dates). Always ask what **refund** you'll get if anything goes wrong and find out how easy it will be to **change your flight dates** once you've got your ticket.

In terms of **fares**, departures in July, August and December are the most expensive. Some agents also have special discounted fares for **students and under-26s**. If you want to travel onwards from Tanzania

and only need a one-way flight, check the cancellation charge for cashing in the unused half of a return ticket, as this might work out much cheaper than buying a single. You may be able to fly out to Tanzania and back from somewhere else (an "open-jaw" ticket).

If Tanzania is just one stop on a multi-continent trip you might consider a **round-the-world (RTW)** plane ticket. As a general rule you'll have to select your itinerary and stopover cities in advance, travelling in a single direction, either eastbound or westbound (most tickets don't allow backtracking). You set a date for the first outbound flight in advance, and then reserve the others as you go, completing the entire journey within either six months or a year. Tanzania seldom features on RTW tickets, however: most routes go through Nairobi, Johannesburg or Harare, and make their way across southern or eastern Africa from there. Tickets including Nairobi and Johannesburg start at £1500/$2500. Conditions and available routings are constantly changing, so your best sources of advice are the various flight agents listed on pp.11–13.

Booking flights online

The websites of many airlines and discount travel agents allow you to book your tickets **online**, cutting out the costs of agents and middlemen. Good deals can also often be found through discount or auction sites.

Online booking agents and general travel sites

Ⓦ**www.bridgetheworld.com** One-off flights or tailor-made round-the-world itineraries, with good deals aimed at the backpacker market.
Ⓦ**www.cheapflights.com** Flight deals, plus links to travel agents and other travel sites.

Ⓦ **www.cheaptickets.com** Discount flight specialists.

Ⓦ **www.deckchair.com** Bob Geldof's online venture, drawing on a wide range of airlines.

Ⓦ **www.ebookers.com** Low fares on an extensive selection of scheduled flights.

Ⓦ **www.etn.nl/discount.htm** A hub of consolidator and discount agent web links, maintained by the nonprofit European Travel Network.

Ⓦ **www.expedia.com** Discount airfares, all-airline search engine and daily deals.

Ⓦ **www.flightcentre.com.au** Major online ticketer in Australia and New Zealand.

Ⓦ **www.flynow.com** Large range of discounted tickets, travel info and reservations; official South African Airways agent.

Ⓦ **www.gohop.com** Irish company selling discounted and round-the-world tickets.

Ⓦ **www.hotwire.com** Bookings from the US only. Last-minute savings of up to forty percent on regular published fares. Travellers must be at least 18 and there are no refunds, transfers or changes allowed. Log-in required.

Ⓦ **www.lastminute.com** Good last-minute holiday package and flight-only deals.

Ⓦ **www.priceline.com** Bookings from the US only. Name-your-own-price website that has deals at around forty percent off standard fares. You cannot specify flight times (although you can specify dates), and tickets are non-refundable, non-transferable and non-changeable.

Ⓦ **www.skyauction.com** Bookings from the US only. Auctions tickets and travel packages using a "second bid" scheme. The best strategy is to bid the maximum you're willing to pay, since if you win you'll pay just enough to beat the runner-up, regardless of your maximum bid.

Ⓦ **www.travelocity.com** Discounted web fares and cheap car rental, accommodation and lodging. Provides access to SABRE, the most comprehensive central reservations system in the US.

Ⓦ **www.travelshop.com.au** Australian website offering discounted flights, packages, insurance and online bookings.

Ⓦ **www.uniquetravel.com.au** Australian site with a good range of packages and good-value flights.

Flights from the UK and Ireland

The only **direct flights from the UK** to Tanzania are with British Airways from London Heathrow to Dar, although there are plenty of one-stop flights via various European, Middle Eastern and African

cities; there are also direct flights daily with KLM from Amsterdam to Kilimanjaro, continuing to Dar. Coming **from Ireland** it's possible to buy a through ticket with British Airways from Belfast or Dublin. Flight **times** to Tanzania are around ten to fourteen hours, depending on the route taken and stops made, if any, though because of the small time difference (Tanzania is two hours ahead of Britain in summer; three hours ahead in winter) you at least won't experience jet lag.

The cheapest non-discounted fares are currently with British Airways. Airlines to watch for special discounted fares are Egyptair, Ethiopian Airlines (a reputable carrier, often forgotten by agents) and, especially, Emirates. Low-season discounts offered by these airlines have been known to bring the price of a return flight down to under £400.

Airlines

British Airways UK ☎ 0845/77 333 77, Republic of Ireland ☎ 1800/626 747, Ⓦ www.ba.com. Three weekly flights from Heathrow to Dar, with connecting flights from Belfast and Dublin. Return fares range from £460 to £800 (€800–1400 from Dublin) in low/high season.

Egyptair UK ☎ 020/7734 2343 or 7734 2395, Republic of Ireland ☎ 01/370 011, Ⓦ www.egyptair.com.eg. Weekly flights from London to Dar via Cairo.

Emirates UK ☎ 0870/243 2222, Ⓦ www.emiratesairline.com. Daily flights from London to Dubai, from where there are four flights weekly on to Dar. Low-season returns average £550; high-season fares start at £750.

Ethiopian Airlines UK ☎ 020/8987 7000, Ⓦ www.flyethiopian.com. Daily flights from London to Addis Ababa, from where there are three to five connections weekly on to Kilimanjaro, Dar and (sometimes) Zanzibar. A London–Dar return goes for around £470 in low season, £650 in high.

Kenya Airways UK ☎ 01784/888 222, Ⓦ www.kenya-airways.com. Twice-weekly flights from London to Nairobi, from where there are daily connections on to Kilimanjaro and Dar. Fares range from £600 in low season to £850 in high.

KLM UK ☎ 0870/507 4074, Ⓦ www.klm.com. Daily flights from Amsterdam to Dar via Kilimanjaro, though fares are expensive, with an unrestricted return (low or high season) from £1200.

South African Airways UK ☎ 020/7312 5000, Ⓦ www.flysaa.com. Daily flights from London to Dar

via Johannesburg, from £850 return.
Swiss UK ☎0845/601 0956, ⊛www.swiss.com.
The new incarnation of Swissair, and one of the
cheapest carriers to Tanzania at present, with low-
season returns from London to Dar via Zürich (3
weekly) for £490, and high-season fares from
around £850.

Discount flight and travel agents

Africa Travel Shop London ☎020/7387 1211,
ⓔafricatravel@easynet.co.uk. Helpful and
resourceful Africa travel agents; they also act as
agents for a number of overland truck companies.
Apex Travel Dublin ☎01/241 8000,
⊛www.apextravel.ie. Flight specialist.
Aran Travel International Galway ☎091/562
595, ⊛homepages.iol.ie/~arantvl/aranmain.htm.
Good-value flights to all parts of the world.
Joe Walsh Tours Dublin ☎01/676 3053,
⊛www.joewalshtours.ie. General budget fares
agent.
McCarthy's Travel Cork ☎021/427 0127,
⊛www.mccarthystravel.ie. General flight agent.
North South Travel Chelmsford
☎01245/608291, ⊛www.northsouthtravel.co.uk.
Friendly and competitive travel agency offering
discounted fares worldwide – profits are used to
support projects in the developing world, especially
the promotion of sustainable tourism.
Quest Travel London ☎0870/442 2699 or
020/8547 3322, ⊛www.questtravel.com.
Specialists in round-the-world and discount fares.
Rosetta Travel Belfast ☎028/9064 4996,
⊛www.rosettatravel.com. Flight and holiday deals.
Soliman Travel London ☎020/7244 6855,
ⓔinfo@soliman.prestel.co.uk. Particularly good on
Egyptair flights.
Somak Travel London ☎020/8903 8526,
⊛www.somak.co.uk. Good deals on BA and Kenya
Airways.
STA Travel UK ☎0870/1600 599,
⊛www.statravel.co.uk. Worldwide specialists in low-
cost flights, including round-the-world tickets, and
tours for students and under-26s, though other
customers are welcome. Over two dozen UK branches.
Trailfinders London ☎020/7628 7628, Dublin
☎01/677 7888, ⊛www.trailfinders.com. One of
the best-informed and most efficient agents for
independent travellers, with ten branches in the
British Isles; their quarterly magazine is worth
scrutinizing for round-the-world routes.
Travel Cuts London ☎020/7255 2082,
⊛www.travelcuts.co.uk. Specializes in budget,
student and youth travel, and round-the-world
tickets.

usit NOW Belfast ☎01232/324073, Dublin
☎01/602 1600, ⊛www.usitnow.ie. Student and
youth specialists, with seven branches in Ireland.
World Express Travel London ☎020/7 434
1654. Official UK consolidators for Kenya Airways
and Ethiopian Airlines.

Tour operators in the UK

All the following agencies offer safaris, at
prices considerably higher than those
offered in Tanzania itself – however, you may
find it's a small price to pay to avoid the
potential hassle and pitfalls of arranging
something yourself (covered on pp.58–59).
See also overland tour operators listed on
p.15.
Abercrombie and Kent ☎020/7559 8746,
⊛www.abercrombiekent.com. UK arm of the
upmarket US long-haul specialists, specializing
mainly in Northern Circuit safari packages with
accommodation in lodges and tented camps.
Itineraries are flexible if you have the money – count
on around £250 a day.
Exodus Expeditions (see p.000). Primarily an
overland outfit, but also offer walking tours of Mount
Kenya and Kilimanjaro (17 days from £1750,
including flight) and a camping tour of western Kenya
and Tanzania (15 days from £670, excluding kitty).
Hayes and Jarvis ☎0870/333 1952,
⊛www.hayesandjarvis.co.uk. Large, long-
established and experienced operator, whose wide-
ranging options stretch from budget self-catering
and no-frills safaris to luxury escorted tours.
IntoAfrica UK ☎0114/255 5610,
⊛www.intoafrica.co.uk. If you can't stand the idea
of the colonial-style safaris that clutter up most
brochures, this is the one for you. A Tanzanian-British
outfit (the headquarters are in Arusha), IntoAfrica
promotes fair-trade safaris, walks and mountain
hikes, tailor-made to suit your needs and all making
good use of Tanzania's cultural tourism programme
as well as their own community-based projects.
Count on around £100 per day.
Kuoni ☎01306/740888 or 743000,
⊛www.kuoni.co.uk. Reputable long-haul holiday
operator with lots of experience. Despite its large
size, the approach remains flexible and personal, and
they have dedicated Africa specialists. Good choice
of safaris and coastal destinations.
Pulse Africa ☎020/8995 5909,
⊛www.africansafari.co.za. Small and upmarket
operator offering "tailor made safaris for the
discerning travellers".
Simply Tanzania Tour Company ☎020/8986
0615, ⊛www.simplytanzania.freeserve.co.uk.

Recommended Tanzania specialist covering less-travelled areas, including the southern highlands, and a lot of cultural tourism. Fourteen-day packages from £1500.

Tanzania Odyssey ☎020/7471 8780, ⓦ www.tanzaniaodyssey.com. Tanzania specialists, acting as agents for reputable local companies. Their Northern Circuit safaris, mostly in the Serengeti, go for £150–250 per person in a couple; Kilimanjaro climbs cost upwards of $1000.

Tribes ☎01728/685971, ⓦ www.tribes.co.uk. Off-the-beaten-track agency that pays more than just lip-service to community involvement, with a range of luxurious yet adventurous trips away from the tourist circus with the focus as much on local communities as on wildlife. Their annual fourteen-day Maasai trip in June is recommended (maximum six people; £2685 excluding flights), while for £1600 their more general, fourteen-day game-viewing safari compares well even with Arusha's prices.

Flights from the US and Canada

There are no direct flights **from North America** to East Africa: you're going to have to change planes and, quite possibly, airlines too. The fastest routes are from New York via London on British Airways, or via Amsterdam on Northwestern Airlines and KLM, though even on these, the total journey time is likely to be at least twenty hours.

Fares on these flights can be extremely expensive, however, rising to $5000 and above. An alternative is to fly to a different African destination and continue from there: possibilities include Addis Ababa (Ethiopian Airlines) and Cairo (Egyptair) – the latter is accessible by direct flights from New York. Unless time is a big consideration, you're likely to make an overall saving by flying to London, stopping over for a day or two, and picking up a last-minute flight from there. Return flights from New York to London can be had for around $500 (try Virgin Atlantic, ⓦ www.virgin-atlantic.com).

Airlines

British Airways ☎1-800/247-9297, ⓦ www.ba.com. Daily flights from the US and Canada, but a through ticket to Dar es Salaam starts at well over $3000.
EgyptAir ☎1-800/334-6787, ⓦ www.egyptair.com.eg.

Ethiopian Airlines ☎1-800/445-2733, ⓦ www.flyethiopian.com.
KLM/Northwest US ☎1-800/225-2525, ⓦ www.klm.com. Daily flights to Dar with connections from JFK on Northwestern, but extremely expensive.
South African Airways ☎1-800/722-9675, ⓦ www.flysaa.com.
Swiss ☎1-800/221-4750, ⓦ www.swiss.com.
Virgin Atlantic ☎1-800/862-8621, ⓦ www.virgin-atlantic.com. One of the cheapest trans-Atlantic carriers, with return fares from New York to London for around $500.

Discount flight agents

Air Brokers International ☎1-800/883-3273, ⓦ www.airbrokers.com. Consolidator and specialist in round-the-world tickets.
Airtech ☎1-877/247-8324 or 212/219-7000, ⓦ www.airtech.com. Standby seat broker; also deals in consolidator fares and courier flights.
Council Travel ☎1-800/226-8624, ⓦ www.counciltravel.com. Nationwide organization that mostly, but by no means exclusively, specializes in student/budget travel. Flights from the US only.
High Adventure Travel ☎1-800/350-0612 or 415/912-5600, ⓦ www.airtreks.com. Round-the-world tickets. The website features an interactive database that lets you build and price your own round-the-world itinerary.
Skylink US ☎1-800/247-6659 or 212/573-8980, Canada ☎1-800/759-5465, ⓦ www.skylinkus.com. Consolidator.
STA Travel ☎1-800/777-0112 or 1-800/781-4040, ⓦ www.sta-travel.com. Worldwide specialists in independent travel.
Travel Cuts Canada ☎1-800/667-2887, US ☎1-866/246-9762, ⓦ www.travelcuts.com. Canadian student-travel organization.
Worldtek Travel ☎1-800/243-1723, ⓦ www.worldtek.com. Discount travel agency for worldwide travel.

Tour operators

Abercrombie & Kent US ☎1-800/323-7308, ⓦ www.abercrombiekent.com. Leading upmarket operator with over thirty years' experience organizing African safaris, and with a comprehensive programme in Tanzania. Reckon on around $350 per day.
African Adventure Company US ☎1-800/882-WILD or 954/781-3933, ⓦ www.africa.adventure.com. Huge range of tours.

Africa Travel Centre US ☎ 800/361-8024, ⓦ www.africatvl.com. Mainly lodge and tented-camp safaris. Prices are around $300–450 per day, excluding flights.

Holbrook Travel US ☎ 904/377-7111, ⓦ www.holbrooktravel.com. Top-quality natural history tours and safaris.

Thomson Safaris US ☎ 1-800/235-0289, ⓦ www.thomsonsafaris.com. A huge and long-established Tanzania specialist. Two-week camping safaris in the Northern Circuit go for around $4000 (including airfare), whilst accommodation in lodges adds another $1000. Most of their clients travel around in convoys of several vehicles - perhaps not the romance you're looking for.

Wilderness Travel US ☎ 1-800/369-2794 or 510/548-0420, ⓦ www.wildernesstravel.com. Small group expeditions to game parks led by an experienced guide, including walking; upwards of $1500–2000 per week excluding airfare.

Worldwide Adventures Canada ☎ 1-800/387-1483 or 416/221-3000, ⓦ www.worldwidequest.com. Better value and more off-beat than most, with a sixteen-day walking trip through northern Tanzania (Kilimanjaro, Ngorongoro and Tarangire) costing just under US$3000.

Flight from Australia and New Zealand

There are no direct flights **from Australia and New Zealand** to Tanzania – all require a stopover either in Asia, southern Africa or the Middle East. From Australia, the best deals are on Gulf Air via Singapore and Bahrain, and Egyptair via Bangkok and Cairo. More direct but more expensive would be to go via Harare with Air Zimbabwe (A$2300–3000/NZ$2500–3000) or to Johannesburg on Qantas (A$2500–3000) and change there.

Airlines

Air New Zealand Australia ☎ 13 24 76, New Zealand ☎ 0800/737 000, ⓦ www.airnewzealand.com. Has a convoluted routing from New Zealand to Johannesburg.

Air Zimbabwe Australia ☎ 02/8272 7822, New Zealand ☎ 09/309 8094, ⓦ www.airzimbabwe.com. Twice-weekly flights from Perth and Sydney to Harare, connecting with onward flights (3 weekly) to Dar.

Egyptair Australia ☎ 02/9232 6677, ⓦ www.egyptair.com.eg.

Gulf Air Australia ☎ 02/9244 2199, New Zealand ☎ 09/308 3366, ⓦ www.gulfairco.com.

Qantas Australia ☎ 13 13 13, New Zealand ☎ 09/661 901, ⓦ www.qantas.com.au. Low-season economy returns from Sydney to Johannesburg cost A$2830 (high-season A$3482).

Travel agents and tour operators

Abercrombie & Kent Melbourne ☎ 03/9699 9766; Auckland ☎ 09/358 4200, ⓦ www.abercrombiekent.com.au. Long-established, upmarket operator selling its own exclusive holidays.

The Adventure Travel Company New Zealand ☎ 09/379 9755, ⓦ www.adventuretravel.co.nz. Agent for Gecko's (see below).

Adventure World Auckland ☎ 09/524 5118, Sydney ☎ 1800/221931, Perth ☎ 09/221 2300, ⓦ www.adventureworld.co.nz. Accommodation, car rental, discounted airfares and a varied selection of tours.

Africa Travel Centre Auckland ☎ 09/520 2000, Sydney ☎ 02/9267 3048. Accommodation, car rental, scuba-diving and a comprehensive range of safaris.

Gecko's Holidays Sydney ☎ 02/9290 2770, Melbourne ☎ 03/9662 2700, ⓦ www.geckos.com.au. Eight-day Northern Circuit safaris from around A$1600.

STA Travel Sydney ☎ 02/9212 1255 or 1800/637444, Melbourne ☎ 03/9347 4711, Auckland ☎ 09/366 6673, Wellington ☎ 04/385 0561, Christchurch ☎ 03/379 9098, ⓦ www.statravel.com. Worldwide specialists in independent travel.

Flights from neighbouring countries

The main African carriers operating to and from Tanzania are Kenya Airways (see p.10), Ethiopian Airlines (p.10) and the ever-unreliable Air Tanzania (see below). Fares from neighbouring African countries are relatively expensive.

Air Malawi ⓦ www.africaonline.co.ke/airmalawi. Twice-weekly flights from Lilongwe and Blantyre to Dar.

Air Tanzania (ATC) ⓦ www.airtanzania.com. Flights to Dar es Salaam from Bujumbura (1 weekly), Entebbe (4 weekly), Johannesburg (2 weekly), Kigale (1 weekly), Luanda (1 weekly), Lubumbashi (2 weekly), Lusaka (3 weekly), Mauritius (2 weekly), Mombasa via Zanzibar (9 weekly), Comoros (2 weekly), plus flights from Nairobi to Mwanza via Kilimanjaro (3 weekly).

Air Zimbabwe ⓦ www.airzimbabwe.com. Flights to Dar from Bulawayo (2 weekly) and Harare (3 weekly).

Travelling overland or by boat to Tanzania

Travelling to Tanzania **overland** – whether by public transport, driving yourself, hitching or even walking – is obviously peppered with potential pitfalls, but is also without any doubt the most satisfying way of reaching the country, offering daily contact with ordinary people, many of whom will rarely have talked to a European or North American before.

Feasible routes are liable to change as Africa's borders open and close in the wake of various conflicts. The ongoing conflicts in Burundi, Sudan, northern Uganda and Congo show no signs of stopping, however, and mean that the overland routes from North and West Africa are closed for the time being, unless you fly part of the way. Crossing the border from **Kenya** is a formality, however, whilst travel overland is also possible from **Mozambique**, **Malawi**, **Zambia** and **Rwanda**. There are also some weekly **ferries** into Tanzania on the western lakes: from Nkhata Bay in Malawi across Lake Nyasa (Lake Malawi) to Mbamba Bay and Itungi Port; from Mpulungu in Zambia along Lake Tanganyika to Kigoma; and from Bujumbura in Burundi to Kigoma. There are currently no ferries from Kenya or Uganda on Lake Victoria, nor to Kenya along the coast.

It is still possible to get to East Africa **by boat** from Europe – a romantic idea, though it will cost you considerably more than a standard airfare. Strand Voyages (Charing Cross Shopping Concourse, The Strand, London WC2N 4HZ ☎ 020/7836 6363, ⓦ www.strandtravel.co.uk) are the main agents in Britain for passenger-carrying cargo ships. There are no scheduled services, so it's a matter of contacting them to find out when the next sailing is. It takes approximately 28 days from the UK to Dar es Salaam, through the Mediterranean and via the Suez Canal and Djibouti. The price is around £2200/$3300 one-way.

Overland routes from northern and southern Africa

There are several overland routes to Tanzania **from South Africa**, all of them currently reported safe (despite recent unrest in Zimbabwe). The easiest way to make this journey is on one of dozens of trips by overland truck (see opposite for a list of operators): this guarantees you plenty of company and, though rushed, is a pretty good way of ticking off the main sights en route. Much more rewarding would be to go it alone by public transport – it's possible to bus-hop all the way to Tanzania from South Africa. There's also a **railway** from Cape Town to Dar es Salaam, passing through Botswana, Zimbabwe and Zambia.

The overland route from Europe to Tanzania **south via Egypt, Sudan and Ethiopia** isn't currently safe thanks to the civil war in Sudan. Travel in Ethiopia itself is usually fine, and the Ethiopian border with Kenya at Moyale is passable with a minimum of fuss; the next few hundred kilometres to Isiolo are prone to bandit attacks, but after that it's plain sailing along good tarmac all the way to Tanzania.

Overland tour operators

The **overland** trips through Africa offered by the companies listed opposite generally use a converted truck, taking a set number of weeks (or months) to travel overland across all or a part of Africa. The classic trans-Africa trip traditionally went from the UK to Cape Town via Nairobi, but wars in Congo and Sudan, as well as the continuing problems in Burundi and Rwanda, mean that travellers now have to fly from Cameroon to Nairobi. As a result, Nairobi is now the main base for the southern continuations of these trips, and a good place to join up with a tour, heading down to South Africa via Tanzania.

All the operators listed opposite do the Nairobi to Cape Town run (5–8 weeks) via Tanzania; in addition, check the "Tour operators" and "Discount agents" listings on pp.11–13. A number of other, smaller (and potentially cheaper) operators also advertise regularly in *BBC Wildlife* magazine or in the classified columns of the national dailies – but check out any less-established company carefully before signing up. When getting quotes, find out whether flights are included, and how much your contribution to the communal "kitty" will be, as this can add up to thirty percent to the total cost (unless stated otherwise, prices quoted below include the kitty, but exclude flights). Your fellow passengers will tend to be around 25 years old and very much in road-trip mentality: not everyone's cup of tea – you'll either love or loathe it.

Overland tour operators in the UK

Absolute Africa ☎020/8742 0226, ⊛www.absoluteafrica.com. A wide range of trips lasting up to 77 days, with departures every two or three weeks from Nairobi. Zanzibar and Pemba can also be included as optional extras. Approximately £20 a day including kitty.

Africa Travel Shop ☎020/7387 1211, ✉africatravel@easynet.co.uk. A helpful agent for a number of the operators listed on this page.

African Trails ☎020/8742 7724, ⊛www.africantrails.co.uk. A seven-week Nairobi to Cape Town trip (including Tanzania and Uganda) goes for under £900.

Bukima Adventure Tours ☎0870/757 2230, ⊛www.bukima.com. Long-established overlanders, pricier than most, offering a bumper twelve-week trip from Nairobi to Cape Town (£2200).

Dragoman ☎01728/861133, ⊛www.dragoman.co.uk. Friendly company with good trucks and competitive prices: Itineraries include three-week East Africa tours; six-week East Africa to the Cape trips (around £2000); plus longer journeys. Most start in Nairobi, but it's okay to join in Tanzania.

Encounter Overland ☎020/7370 6951, ⊛www.encounter-overland.com. Respected operator offering one- to eight-week trips through East and southern Africa. Offers lots of choices, including a massive UK to Cape Town run for £3400.

Exodus Expeditions ☎020/8675 5550, ⊛www.exodustravels.co.uk. Long-established operators offering a wide variety of options, including three-week overland trips from Nairobi to the Cape (from £790 excluding kitty) and a 22-day round trip exploring the Kenyan, Tanzanian and Ugandan Rift Valley from Nairobi (from £1000 excluding kitty).

Guerba Expeditions ☎01373/826611, ⊛www.guerba.com. The acknowledged Africa experts, though nowadays they concentrate equally on shorter trips.

Kumuka Expeditions ☎020/7937 8855, ⊛www.kumuka.com. Three different overland trips from Nairobi to Harare or vice versa (5–10 weeks), and a seven-week spin down to the Cape for around £1800.

Phoenix Expeditions ☎01509/881818, ⊛www.phoenixexpeditions.com. Well-equipped outfit offering a fourteen-week overland trip from Istanbul to Nairobi via Cairo (from £1650, including Cairo-Addis Ababa flight but excluding kitty), plus trips through East and southern Africa, including an eight-week Nairobi–Cape Town trip (around £1500).

Truck Africa ☎020/7731 6142, ⊛www.truckafrica.com. Personal but professional outfit which gets enthusiastic reviews. They run a big trans-Africa expedition from London to Kenya (20 weeks; £2650), East Africa trips from Nairobi and the usual Nairobi–Cape run for £1130.

Red tape and visas

At present, citizens of most nationalities need a visa to enter Tanzania, the exceptions being Kenyans, Ugandans and – curiously – Irish. Rules regarding visas have a habit of changing frequently, however, so check beforehand with the nearest Tanzanian embassy, consulate or high commission, and don't rely on information posted on Tanzania's official websites, as it's often years out of date. You'll also need to make sure that your passport is valid for six months beyond the end of your stay.

Visas

Visas can be obtained in person or by post from any Tanzanian embassy, consulate or high commission (see below). Visas normally take 24 hours to process, require two passport-size photos and – sometimes – an **air ticket** out of the country. Standard fees for a three-month single-entry visa are £38 for Britons and around $50 for citizens of the US and Canada. Multiple-entry visas cost about double. Note that Tanzanian diplomatic missions are closed on Tanzanian public holidays (see p.51).

Apart from South Africans, West Africans, Indians and Pakistanis, visas can also be obtained – and are actually cheaper ($20) – when you arrive. It's best not to rely on this if you're arriving at night, however, since there might not be any officials around to issue a visa. In addition, although the process is generally hassle-free, visitors from countries with Tanzanian missions may have to satisfy immigration why they didn't get a visa before arriving, potentially leaving you at the mercy of bribe-seeking officials.

There are **immigration posts** at Tanzania's three international airports (Kilimanjaro, Dar es Salaam and Zanzibar) and at major land borders. Anticlockwise, these are: Horohoro, Taveta, Namanga and Sirari (all with Kenya),

Mutukala (Uganda), Rusumu (Rwanda), Kabanga (Burundi), Kasesya and Tunduma (Zambia), Mwandenga (Malawi) and Kalambo (Mozambique). Note that both soliciting and giving **bribes** is illegal (though you'd never guess it) – kicking up a fuss is the best way to set a rogue officer to rights. **Payment** for visas is in US dollars or sterling equivalent, though officials do sometimes accept other currencies – but don't rely on this.

On arrival your passport will be stamped to show your permitted **length of stay** – currently three months for pretty much everyone. In spite of the newly resurrected East African Community, crossing over to Kenya and Uganda requires a new visa for each country, and – officially at least – it's not possible to re-enter Tanzania on the same visa unless it's multiple-entry.

Tanzanian embassies, consulates and high commissions

Opening hours for **visa applications** are usually Monday to Friday 10am to 12.30pm. Processing takes 24 hours, although the high commission in London offers same-day processing for an extra £5. There's no Tanzanian diplomatic representation in Australia, New Zealand or Ireland.

Yellow fever vaccination certificates

Although mainland Tanzania has now officially stopped checking **yellow fever vaccination certificates** at airports, the situation on the ground is confused, and you may still be asked to present a certificate. Certificates are also needed to enter the country overland, and Zanzibar still insists on the formality, however you arrive. It's therefore well worth getting yourself a jab – and a certificate – before you leave. You also need to remember to allow ten days from the date of your inoculation for the certificate to be valid.

Canada 50 Range Rd, Ottawa, Ontario K1N 8J4
℡1-613/232-1500, ℻1-613/232-5184.
Kenya 4th floor, Continental House, PO Box
47790, Nairobi ℡02/331056, ℻02/218269.
Mozambique PO Box 4515, Maputo
℡01/490110-3.
South Africa 845 Goont Ave, PO Box 56572,
Arcadia, Pretoria 0007 ℡012/342 4371.
Uganda Kagera Rd, Kampala ℡041/556 755.
UK 43 Hertford St, London W1Y 8DB ℡020/7499
8951, ℻020/7491 9321,
✉visa@tanzania-online.gov.uk.
US 2139 R St NW, Washington DC 20008
℡1-202/939-6125, ℻1-202/797-7408.
Zambia Ujamaa House, 5200 UN Ave, PO Box
31219, Lusaka ℡01/253320.

Entering Zanzibar

Whilst visitors flying directly to **Zanzibar** from
outside Tanzania complete the same procedures outlined above (as with mainland
Tanzania, you can buy a visa on arrival),
entry procedures for visitors coming from
mainland Tanzania by plane or ferry are a
farce. In theory, given that Zanzibar is part of
the United Republic of Tanzania, your
Tanzanian visa is perfectly valid so long as
you remain within your allotted three months.
In practice, however, many arriving visitors
go through the rigmarole of filling in forms
identical to those they already completed
when they arrived in mainland Tanzania. A
few travellers have even reportedly been
given a two-week time limit to their stay in
Zanzibar – this has no legal basis, but is
guaranteed to make things awkward with
corrupt immigration officials if you overstay.
This can be avoided either by graciously
telling the officer that you would like to
spend all of the time remaining on your
Tanzanian visa in beautiful Zanzibar (flattery,
and a few Kiswahili words beyond *Jambo*,
can work wonders). The alternative, if you've
arrived **by ferry** from Dar es Salaam, is simply to ignore immigration altogether, some-

thing that many visitors do quite by accident,
as you actually have to track them down at
the port.

If you're crossed **from Mombasa** in Kenya
by dhow, however, you'll definitely need to
visit customs and immigration on arrival.

Extending your stay

Although they exist in theory, in practice it's
almost impossible to obtain a six-month
tourist visa, so if you plan to stay longer than
three months, you'll have to leave the country and then re-enter on a new visa (unless
you're happy paying an extortionate $400
for a two-month extension at the immigration offices in Arusha or Dar). This is most
easily done from Arusha, which is only a
couple of hours away from Namanga on the
Kenyan border. The border officials may be a
little suspicious if you return an hour or two
later, however, so it might be worth spending a day or two in Kenya before heading
back – in any case, you'll have to fork out
$50 for a Kenyan visa, even if it's only for an
hour's stay. This system works fine once or
twice, but the officials will get, well, officious
if you start making a habit of it, as obviously
you should by then have applied for a residence permit.

Customs and duty-free

The **duty-free allowance** for visitors entering Tanzania is one litre of spirits, 200 cigarettes, 50 cigars or 250g of tobacco and
250ml of perfume. Unless you're carrying a
real mountain of gear, items for personal
use, like binoculars, cameras and laptops,
pose no problem with **customs**. At worst
you'll just have to sign (and pay) a bond
which is redeemed when you leave the
country with all your stuff. If you're taking
items into Tanzania as presents, however,
you're likely to have to pay duty if you
declare them.

Information, websites and maps

The embassies listed on p.17 have a few government-produced brochures to hand out, but aren't much help otherwise, while the Tanzanian Tourist Board has no overseas offices.

Maps

The best general **map of Tanzania** is Harms IC Verlag's *Tanzania, Rwanda and Burundi* (1:1,400,000), published in 2001 (ⓦ www.harms-ic-verlag.de), which is detailed, accurate and has good inset town plans of Arusha and Dar es Salaam. A good alternative is Nelles-Verlag's of *Tanzania, Rwanda Burundi* (1:1,500,000), though it's becoming dated. For **Zanzibar**, the best map is Harms IC Verlag's *Zanzibar*, which shows Unguja at 1:100,000 and has insets of Pemba (1:250,000) and Stone Town. You can forget most other maps of Zanzibar, as they're more decorative than practical. The exception is Giovanni Tombazzi's *Zanzibar at Sea*, an attractive compilation of painted maps showing the best dive sites off Pemba and Unguja.

The best **maps for hiking** are the series of 1:50,000 sheets available at the Government's Mapping & Surveys Department in Dar es Salaam (see p.116). Unfortunately, the most popular sheets (Usambaras, Kilimanjaro, Arusha and the national parks) are currently out of stock, though it may be possible to buy photocopies. Most of the sheets were produced between 1959 and 1962, so whilst the topographical detail remains more or less accurate (don't expect the forest cover to be as extensive though), things like roads and villages will have changed. The office also has regional maps at 1:250,000, and an excellent road map of Dar es Salaam.

The **national parks** are covered by two series of maps. The best and newest – once again – are those produced by Harms IC Verlag (in collaboration with TANAPA). At the time of writing only Lake Manyara and Ngorongoro were available, but Arusha National Park, Kilimanjaro, Tarangire and Serengeti were imminent. You can find them in Tanzania at the TANAPA headquarters and Ngorongoro Tourist Information office in Arusha (see p.373), and at better bookshops – buy them in advance, as there's no guarantee you'll find them at the park gates. Alternatively, Giovanni Tombazzi's beautifully painted national parks maps (available from Ma.Co. Editions, PO Box 1797, Arusha ☎0741/ 326914 or 0742/400002, ⓔmaco@ ark.eoltz.com) come with a dry-season version on one side and wet-season on the other (showing the changes of vegetation and illustrations of commonly seen plants and trees) and make lovely souvenirs, though they can be out of date for roads, many of which were washed away during the 1998 El Niño floods.

If you're doing more in Africa than visiting Tanzania alone, you'll probably want one or more of the Michelin series (ⓦwww. michelin-travel.com), still the best all-purpose travel maps for Africa; #955 (1:4,000,000) covers Central and Southern Africa. Tanzania comes out small at this scale but with surprising detail.

Map outlets

In the UK and Ireland

Easons Bookshop 40 O'Connell St, Dublin 1 ☎01/873 3811, ⓦwww.eason.ie.

John Smith and Sons 26 Colquhoun Ave, Glasgow G52 4PJ ☎0141/552 3377, ⓦwww.johnsmith.co.uk.

National Map Centre 22–24 Caxton St, London SW1H 0QU ☎020/7222 2466, ⓦwww.mapsnmc.co.uk.

Newcastle Map Centre 55 Grey St, Newcastle upon Tyne NE1 6EF ☎0191/261 5622, ⓦwww.traveller.ltd.uk.

Stanfords (ⓦwww.stanfords.co.uk) 12–14 Long Acre, London WC2E 9LP ☎020/7836 132; c/o British Airways, 156 Regent St, London W1R 5TA ☎020/7434 4744; 29 Corn St, Bristol BS1 1HT ☎0117/929 9966. Maps can be ordered by phone or via ⓔ sales@stanfords.co.uk.

The Travel Bookshop 13–15 Blenheim Crescent, London W11 2EE ☎020/7229 5260, ⓦwww.thetravelbookshop.co.uk.

In the US and Canada
Elliot Bay Book Company, 101 S Main St, Seattle, WA 98104 ☎206/624-6600 or 1-800/962-5311, ⓦwww.elliotbaybook.com.
GORP Adventure Library online only ☎1-800/754-8229, ⓦwww2.gorp.com.
Rand McNally 444 N Michigan Ave, Chicago, IL 60611 ☎312/321-1751; 150 E 52nd St, New York, NY 10022 ☎212/758-7488; 595 Market St, San Francisco, CA 94105 ☎415/777-3131; plus around thirty stores across the US (call ☎1-800/333-0136 ext 2111 or check ⓦwww.randmcnally.com for your nearest store).
Travel Books & Language Center 4437 Wisconsin Ave, Washington, DC 20016 ☎1-800/220-2665, ⓦwww.bookweb.org/bookstore/travellers.
World Wide Books and Maps 1247 Granville St, Vancouver V6Z 1G3 ☎604/687-3320, ⓦwww.worldofmaps.com.

In Australia and New Zealand
Mapland 372 Little Bourke St, Melbourne ☎03/9670 4383, ⓦwww.mapland.com.au.
The Map Shop 6 Peel St, Adelaide ☎08/8231 2033, ⓦwww.mapshop.net.au.
Mapworld 173 Gloucester St, Christchurch ☎03/374 5399, ⓕ03/374 5633, ⓦwww.mapworld.co.nz.
Perth Map Centre 1/884 Hay St, Perth ☎08/9322 5733, ⓦwww.perthmap.com.au.
Specialty Maps 46 Albert St, Auckland ☎09/307 2217, ⓦwww.ubd-online.co.nz/maps.

Tanzania online

The following are some of the more informative and interesting **websites** on Tanzania. Websites specific to places and tribes are mentioned in the guide.

Official websites

Tanzania Tourist Board
ⓦwww.tanzania-web.com. The official line on tourism, but nowhere near as comprehensive as it could be.
Tanzanian Embassies
ⓦwww.tanzania-online.gov.uk; ⓦwww.tanzania embassy-uk.org. More of the same.

The United Republic of Tanzania ⓦwww.tanzania.go.tz. The official national website, aimed mainly aimed at businesses.

News, current affairs and magazines

Africanews ⓦwww.peacelink.it/afrinews.html. Part of an NGO dedicated to peace in Africa, with a monthly online journal.
allAfrica.com ⓦhttp://allafrica.com/tanzania. Comprehensive and up-to-date news round-up.
Amnesty International ⓦwww.amnesty.org/ailib. What the government won't tell you, and so especially useful for the background to Zanzibar's political woes.
Arusha Times ⓦwww.arushatimes.co.tz. News and some laughs from up north.
BBC News – Africa ⓦhttp://news.bbc.co.uk/hi/english/world/africa. Reliable daily coverage of Africa, with a useful search function for older news stories.
The East African ⓦwww.nationaudio.com/eastafrican. One of Africa's leading weeklies and by far the most authoritative news source on East Africa.
IPP Media ⓦwww.ippmedia.com. Home of Tanzania's *Guardian* newspaper and the Kiswahili *Nipashe*.
Newafrica ⓦwww.newafrica.com/news. Tons of current news links (all on the same site), including good coverage of East Africa, and a seachable archive.

Travel advisories, portals, newsgroups and general sites

The Index on Africa ⓦwww.afrika.no. A useful portal with over 2000 good-quality links.
Newafrica ⓦwww.newafrica.com. Especially strong on Tanzania and East Africa, with links to pretty much everything you might need.
rec.travel.africa The best and busiest newsgroup for seeking advice from fellow travellers and self-appointed experts about travel practicalities.
soc.culture.african A mix of stuff on various cultural topics.
UK Foreign & Commonwealth Office ⓦwww.fco.gov.uk/travel. Reliable travel safety advice.
US Government ⓦhttp://travel.state.gov/travel–warnings.html. More comprehensive and detailed than the British version, and equally accurate. Also has up-to-date visa info.
Zanzibar Travel Network ⓦwww.zanzibar.net. A good portal dedicated to Zanzibar with loads of links and sections on tourism and arts.

Tourism

There are dozens of safari companies on the web; URLs for recommended companies are given in our reviews on p.124 (Dar), and p.396 (Arusha). Don't necessarily believe the recommendations given in newsgroups, which are used by several dodgy companies to plug themselves.

All About Zanzibar ⓦwww.
allabout zanzibar.com. Enormous, comprehensive and accurate travel resource for Zanzibar, with lots of background reading and an accommodation reservations service.

Into Tanzania ⓦwww.intotanzania.com.
Comprehensive resource about mainland Tanzania, with loads of reviews, advice and a hotel and safari booking service.

Tanzania Association of Cultural Tourism Operators ⓦwww.tourismtanzania.org. Home page of Tanzania's pioneering and award-winning cultural tourism programme (see p.405).

Tanzania Odyssey ⓦwww.tanzaniaodyssey.com. Mid-range UK-based specialist tour operator for Tanzania and Zanzibar whose website contains dozens of downloadable scans of hotel brochures.

People and culture

Africanhiphop ⓦwww.africanhiphop.com.
Hiphop across the continent, with news, reviews and some (difficult to find) MP3s.

Clouds FM ⓦwww.cloudsfm.com. Dar es Salaam's hippest radio station, with a bunch of interviews, articles and a live radio feed through RealAudio.

East African Music Page ⓦhttp://hometown.
aol.com/dpaterson/eamusic.htm. Devoted to popular East African music, with lots of essays, plus discographies and CDs for sale.

The Internet Living Swahili Dictionary
ⓦwww.yale.edu/swahili. Online English–Swahili dictionary, lots of language resources and excellent links covering East and Central Africa.

Kanga Writings ⓦwww.glcom.com/hassan/
kanga.html. Dozens of popular Kiswahili sayings found on women's kangas, together with their English translation and meaning.

Kiswahili Slang Dictionary ⓦhttp://members.
tripod.com/chumvi/Kiswahili–slang–dictionary.htm.
The title says it all.

The Rockers ⓦwww.africaonline.co.tz/rockers.
Music magazine with a bit of football thrown in, too, with the accent on hiphop, rap and R&B.

Swahili Coast ⓦwww.swahilicoast.com. Online version of one of Tanzania's best glossy mags, covering mainly Zanzibar and the mainland coast.

Tingatinga and his Followers
ⓦwww.art-bin.com/art/atingae.html. A thoughtful essay about Eduardo Tingatinga and the art form named after him, with plenty of images.

Traditional Music & Cultures of Kenya
ⓦwww.bluegecko.org/kenya. Although this principally covers Kenya's tribes, the Maasai, Kuria, Makonde and Digo (who can also be found in Tanzania) are represented, and there are hundreds of images and hours of soundclips.

Zanzibar International Film Festival
ⓦwww.ziff.or.tz. The home site of the fantastic annual Zanzibar International Film Festival.

Insurance

It's essential to take out an insurance policy before travelling to cover against theft, loss, illness or injury. Before paying for a policy, however, it's worth checking whether you are already covered: some all-risks home insurance policies may cover your possessions when overseas, and many private medical schemes include cover when abroad. In Canada, provincial health plans usually provide partial cover for medical mishaps overseas, while holders of official student/teacher/youth cards in Canada and the US are entitled to meagre accident coverage and hospital in-patient benefits. Students will often find that their student health coverage extends during the vacations and for one term beyond the date of last enrolment.

After exhausting the possibilities above, you might want to contact a specialist travel insurance company, or consider the travel insurance deal offered by Rough Guides (see box). A **typical policy** usually provides cover for the loss of baggage, tickets and – up to a certain limit – cash or cheques, as well as cancellation or curtailment of your journey. Most of them exclude so-called **dangerous sports** unless an extra premium is paid: in Tanzania this can mean wildlife trekking and any kind of mountaineering or scuba-diving, though probably not jeep safaris. Many policies can be chopped and changed to exclude coverage you don't need – for example, sickness and accident benefits can often be excluded or included at will. If you do take **medical coverage**, check whether benefits will be paid as treatment proceeds or only after you return home, and whether there is a 24-hour medical emergency number. When securing **baggage cover**, make sure that the per-article limit – typically under £500 – will cover your most valuable possession. If you need to make a claim, you should keep receipts for medicines and medical treatment; in the event you have anything stolen, you must obtain an official statement from the police.

Rough Guides travel insurance

Rough Guides offers its own travel insurance, customized for our readers by a leading UK broker and backed by a Lloyds underwriter. It's available to anyone, of any nationality and any age, travelling anywhere in the world.

There are two main Rough Guide insurance plans: **Essential**, for basic, no-frills cover; and **Premier** – with more generous and extensive benefits. Alternatively, you can take out **annual multi-trip insurance**, which covers you for any number of trips throughout the year (with a maximum of 60 days for any one trip). Unlike many policies, the Rough Guides schemes are calculated by the day, so if you're travelling for 27 days rather than a month, that's all you pay for. If you intend to be away for the whole year, the Adventurer policy will cover you for 365 days. Each plan can be supplemented with a "Hazardous Activities Premium" if you plan to indulge in sports considered dangerous, such as skiing, scuba-diving or trekking. For a policy quote, call the Rough Guide Insurance Line on UK freefone ℡0800/015 09 06; US freefone ℡1-866/220 5588, or, if you're calling from elsewhere ℡+44 1243/621 046. Alternatively, get an online quote or buy online at ⓦwww.roughguides.com/insurance.

Health

Tanzania isn't a particularly dangerous place healthwise, and with sensible precautions you're unlikely to suffer anything more than minor tummy troubles – though this is just as well, given the country's lack of well-equipped hospitals. For further information, the *Rough Guide to Travel Health* offers a comprehensive and practical account of the health problems which travellers encounter worldwide.

Inoculations

No **inoculations** are required for passengers arriving by air from Europe, Australia or North America, and health checks at Kilimanjaro and Dar es Salaam airports were officially stopped in 2001. Entering overland, though, you may well be required to show a **yellow fever vaccination certificate**, and if you fly on an airline that stops en route in Africa, you should also have the jab in case the rules change. Remember that a yellow fever certificate only becomes valid ten days after you've had the jab. You should also start taking malaria tablets before departure and have **tetanus** and **polio** boosters, while doctors usually recommend **typhoid** jabs.

For **hepatitis A**, Havrix is now commonly prescribed – it lasts for ten years if you have a second, booster jab within six months. The much cheaper gamma-globulin (or immunoglobulin) shots are only effective for a few months, if at all. The disease itself is debilitating, taking up to a year to clear. To reduce the risk of contracting hepatitis, be extra careful about cleanliness and, in particular, about contaminated water – a problem wherever a single cistern holds the whole water supply in a cockroach-infested toilet/bathroom, as often happens in Zanzibar.

In **Britain** your first source of advice and probable supplier of jabs and prescriptions is your GP. Family doctors are often well informed and are likely to charge you a (relatively low) flat fee for routine injections. However, for yellow fever and other exotic shots you'll normally have to visit a specialist clinic.

Medical resources for travellers

UK and Ireland

British Airways Travel Clinic 156 Regent St, London W1 ☎ 020/7439 9584 (Mon–Fri 9.30am–5.15pm, Sat 10am–4pm; no appointment required). Offer a wide variety of usual and unusual vaccinations (including plague, anthrax and rabies), as well as anti-malarial tablets and various hardware. There are more than thirty similar BA Travel Clinics around the UK – phone ☎ 01276/685040 for the address of your nearest one.

Hospital for Tropical Diseases Healthline ☎ 0839/337733. User-friendly service offering comprehensive advice via phone or fax.

Malaria Helpline, London School of Hygiene and Tropical Medicine ☎ 0891/600350. Advice on malaria prevention.

MASTA (Medical Advisory Service for Travellers Abroad) London School of Hygiene and Tropical Medicine. Operates a pre-recorded 24-hour Travellers' Health Line (UK ☎ 0906/822 4100, 60p per min; Republic of Ireland ☎ 01560/147 000, 75p per min) giving written information tailored to your journey by return of post.

Trailfinders Immunization clinics (no appointments necessary) at 194 Kensington High St, London ☎ 020/7938 3999.

Travel Clinic Hospital for Tropical Diseases, Mortimer Market, Capper St, London WC1E 6AU ☎ 020/7388 9600, ⊕ www.thehtd.org/travelclinic.html (Mon–Fri 9am–5pm). Advice and low-cost inoculations, plus a series of useful fact sheets. With a referral from your GP, they can also give you a complete check-up on your return.

Travel Medicine Services, PO Box 254, 16 College St, Belfast 1 ☎ 01232/315220.

Tropical Medical Bureau, Grafton St Medical Centre, Dublin 2 ☎ 01/671 9200. Pre-trip medical advice and help afterwards in the event of problems.

US and Canada

Centers for Disease Control and Prevention
ⓦ www.cdc.gov. Publish a very informative booklet – "Health Information for International Travel" – and run a 24-hour phone line (☎ 404/332-4555) giving details on jabs, bugs and general advice.
Travelers Medical Center 31 Washington Square, New York, NY 10011 ☎ 212/982-1600. Offers a consultation service on immunizations and disease treatment.
Travel Medicine 351 Pleasant St, Suite 312, Northampton, MA 01060 ☎ 1-800/872-8633. Sells first-aid kits, mosquito netting, water filters and other health-related travel products.

Australia and New Zealand

Auckland Hospital Park Rd, Grafton, New Zealand ☎ 09/797 440.
Travellers' Medical and Vaccination Centres 428 George St, Sydney ☎ 02/9221 7133; 393 Little Bourke St, Melbourne ☎ 03/9602 5788; 29 Gilbert Place, Adelaide ☎ 08/8267 3544; 247 Adelaide St, Brisbane ☎ 07/3221 9066; 1 Mill St, Perth ☎ 09/321 1977.

Cholera

You're most unlikely to catch cholera, although there's always a small risk throughout Tanzania, and isolated outbreaks of the water-borne disease are a regular occurrence. Outbreaks usually coincide with heavy rains, as flooding mixes sewage with drinking water; areas lacking basic sanitation and sewerage systems are most at risk. The symptoms of cholera are fever and chronic diarrhoea; most attacks are relatively mild, and clear up naturally after a few days, though if left untreated, the sudden and severe dehydration caused by the disease can sometimes be fatal.

Treatment is surprisingly simple: lots of oral rehydration therapy (salt and sugar in water) or, in severe cases, rehydration fluid administered through a drip. Antibiotics (usually tetracycline or doxycycline) can also help, but are not essential. The best way to avoid catching cholera is to exercise the usual caution over water and uncooked fruit and vegetables. The cholera **vaccine** is widely considered completely ineffective and most places no longer offer it.

Malaria

Despite worldwide attempts to eradicate **malaria**, the disease remains endemic in tropical Africa and accounts for at least one in seven deaths among children under five in Tanzania, as well as remaining the biggest cause of death amongst adult Africans after AIDS.

The disease is caused by a parasite carried in the saliva of female *Anopheles* mosquitoes, which tend to bite in the evening and at night and can be distinguished from other mosquitoes by their rather eager, head-down position. Malaria has a variable incubation period of a few days to several weeks, so you can develop the disease some time after you've actually been bitten. Malaria is not infectious, but it can be very dangerous and sometimes even fatal if not treated quickly. The destruction of red blood cells caused by the *Plasmodium falciparum* strain of malaria prevalent in East Africa can lead to **cerebral malaria** (blocking of the brain capillaries) and is also the cause of a nasty complication called **blackwater fever**, in which the urine is stained by excreted blood cells.

Malaria is most prevalent in low-lying areas and around large bodies of water, meaning along the coast, on Zanzibar and around lakes. The risk of contracting the disease decreases as you gain altitude and becomes non-existent over 1800m. Unless you're taking malarone, or are spending an extended period in the northern or southern highlands, don't break your course of prophylactics, as it's vital to keep your parasite-fighting level as high as possible. The disease is present all year around but the risk of infection increases during the rains, peaking in April.

Avoiding bites

The best way to avoid contracting malaria is to **avoid getting bitten**. You can greatly reduce bites by sleeping under a **mosquito net** (if you don't already have one, you can pick one up for Tsh2000–5000) and burning **mosquito coils**, which are readily available in Tanzania (but don't use Cock Brand or Lion coils, which are said to contain DDT and are banned in many countries).

After dark, always cover exposed flesh with something strong: look for a product with at least fifty percent Deet (diethyltoluamide). The idea of soaking wrist and ankle sweat bands with Deet seems a good one, but is fiddly in practice; the stuff gets everywhere and corrodes most artificial materials, especially plastic. If you're bringing your own mosquito net, it's worth impregnating it with insecticide as well.

If you don't like all this synthetic protection, there are now some good, **natural alternatives** based on the flower-extract, pyrethrum. Other supposedly effective repellants (though none appears to have been clinically tested) include vitamin tablets, citronella or lemongrass oil (be careful: too much and you'll sting your face) and even Avon "Skin-so-soft" bath oil – not that they market it as such.

Prophylactics

Before leaving for Tanzania you should get a prescription for a course of **anti-malaria tablets** (the oft-promised vaccine has yet to materialize). Anti-malarials are freely available in the US; in the UK you'll need a private prescription – your doctor or clinic will advise you about which to take. Make sure you keep to the prescribed regime. Prophylactic drugs are rarely used by Tanzanians themselves, and outside larger towns you're unlikely to find any that are effective.

Tanzania is a chloroquine-resistant area, so the drug most often prescribed is **mefloquine** (trade name **Lariam**), which is expensive, and can cause nasty psychological side effects ranging from mild depression to full-blown hallucinations and paranoia. Although the manufacturers claim that the risks are minimal compared to the dangers of contracting malaria, figures indicate that about a quarter of patients taking Lariam are likely to suffer mild bouts of nausea or dizziness, and reports from travellers suggest that the official count of one in ten thousand experiencing neuro-psychiatric problems such as depression and sleep disturbances is grossly underestimated. The manufacturers advise against taking mefloquine for periods of over two months (which means one month's travel). In addition, it's unsuitable for pregnant women, people with liver or kidney problems, epileptics, or infants under 3 years. The dose is one 250mg tablet per week, starting two weeks before entering a malarial zone and continuing for at least two weeks after leaving. Some travellers report that side

effects can be minimized by taking half a tablet at four-day intervals, though this hasn't been clinically tested.

If you can't or won't take Lariam, a combination of **chloroquine** (2 weekly) and **proguanil** (2 daily) provides a reasonable level of protection, although chloroquine on its own is virtually useless. Take the first pills a week before arriving, and the last four weeks after returning. The dose is best taken at the end of the day, and never on an empty stomach, or it will make you feel nauseous.

There are two other alternatives. The antibiotic **doxycycline** is recommended by some doctors if you have trouble with Lariam, but the major side effect is that it causes an exaggerated sensitivity to sunlight, both for eyes and skin. It can also cause thrush in women, reduces the effectiveness of contraceptive pills and is unsuitable for children or during pregnancy. Tablets are taken daily, starting one day before arrival and ending four weeks after you leave.

The newcomer to this inglorious pharmacopoeial collection is **Malarone**, a combination of atovaquone and 100mg of proguanil hydrochloride. The known side effects are benign compared to the competition, and Malarone also currently offers the fullest protection of any anti-malarial – its newness means that no strains of malaria resistant to it have yet developed. In addition, you only need to start taking the tablets one day before entering a malarial zone, and for just seven days after. The disadvantage is that it costs a bomb, cannot be used by children, and can only be prescribed for a maximum of four weeks.

Treatment

If you get malaria, you'll probably know it. Common symptoms include waves of flu-like fever, shivering and headaches, while joint pain is also characteristic, and some people also have diarrhoea after the first week. If you think you've caught malaria, get to a doctor as soon as possible and have a **blood test** to determine whether you've got malaria and to identify the strain (note that using Lariam can lead to an inconclusive result). There's a welter of competing remedies, while the confusion isn't helped by drugs being sold under several brand names. **Sulfadoxine pyrimethamine (SP;** sold under various names including Fansidar, Malostat, Falcidin, Crodar, Laridox and Metakelfin), has long been used by Tanzanians. SP, under the name Fansidar, is sold in the UK. Severe side effects from SP are rare, but you shouldn't take it if you're allergic to sulphur. An alternative treatment is **amodiaquine hydrochloride** (brand names: Basoquin, CAM-AQ1, Camoquin, Flavoquin, Fluroquine and Miaquin) – take 600mg to start, then 200mg after six hours, and 400mg daily on each of the two following days. Do not administer amodiaquine to children as it can be toxic. **Lariam** is also an effective alternative if you haven't been taking it as a prophylactic, though you'll need to have brought the tablets with you, as the drug is unavailable in Tanzania. Lastly, note that **chloroquine** is now virtually useless in treating the *falciparum* strain of malaria.

All these treatments will leave you feeling completely shitty, so you might dose up on painkillers to help ease the worst of the discomfort. Take plenty of fluids, and keep eating (but avoid milk-based products).

HIV and AIDS

Sexually transmitted diseases are widespread in Tanzania, particularly in the larger towns, and the **HIV virus** is alarmingly prevalent and spreading all the time. It's very easily passed between people suffering relatively minor, but ulcerous, sexually transmitted diseases, and the very high prevalence of these is thought to account for the high incidence of heterosexually transmitted HIV. According to the Ministry of Health, one in ten people in the country are now infected with HIV. Areas along the Tanzam highway from Zambia to Dar es Salaam via Mbeya, Iringa and Morogoro, as well as tourist areas like Moshi and Arusha, are especially badly affected, with infection rates topping twenty percent. Standard advice is to avoid sexual contact or use a condom. Several seemingly reliable brands, including Salama, are sold in pharmacies throughout the country.

Water and bugs

In most places in Tanzania the tap water is considered safe to drink by locals, though most tourists choose to give it – and ice – a wide berth. If you're only staying a short time, it makes sense to be scrupulous: if bottled or purified water (usually around Tsh500–700 for a litre and a half) isn't available, either purify your drinking water with tablets or (better) iodine, or boil it for half an hour. For longer stays, think of **re-educating your stomach** rather than fortifying it; it's virtually impossible to travel around the country without exposing yourself to strange bugs from time to time. Take it easy at first, don't overdo the fruit (and wash it in clean water) and be very wary of salads served in cheap restaurants, as well as the pre-cooked contents of their ubiquitous display cabinets.

Should you have a **serious stomach upset**, 24 hours of sweet, black tea and nothing else may rinse it out. The important thing is to replace your lost fluids. If you feel the need, you can make up a **rehydration mix** with four heaped teaspoons of sugar or honey and half a teaspoon of salt in a litre of water (or just bring some pre-mixed sachets with you in your medicine bag). Flat Coca Cola is quite a good tonic; avoid coffee, strong fruit juice, and alcohol. If it seems to be getting worse – or you have to travel a long distance – any chemist should have anti-diarrhoea remedies, but these shouldn't be overused. Stay right away from the popular Kaomycin, though, which is actually designed for use on sheep and goats, and can actually encourage diarrhoea. And avoid jumping for antibiotics at the first sign of trouble: they annihilate what's nicely known as your "gut flora" (most of which you want to keep) and don't work on viruses. Most upsets resolve themselves after two or three days. If you continue to feel bad, see a doctor.

Injuries, bites and stings

Take more care than usual over minor **cuts and scrapes**. In the tropics, the most trivial scratch can quickly become a throbbing infection if you ignore it. Take a small tube of antiseptic with you, or apply alcohol or iodine.

Otherwise, there are all sorts of potential bites, stings and rashes which rarely, if ever, materialize. **Dogs** are usually sad and skulking, posing little threat. **Scorpions and spiders** abound but are hardly ever seen unless you deliberately turn over rocks or logs:

Medicine bag

There's no need to take a mass of drugs and remedies you'll probably never use. Various items, however, are immensely useful, especially on a long trip, and well worth buying in advance.

On a local level, if you're interested in herbal and other natural remedies, you'll find a wealth of medicines in markets or by consulting traditional doctors (look under "Alternative medicines and therapies" in the Yellow Pages (*Kurasa za Njano*), or just ask around).

Alcohol swabs Medi-swabs are invaluable for cleaning wounds, insect bites and infections.

Antibiotics Ciproxin or Bactrim are good in a lower bowel crisis. Amoxil (amoxycillin) is a broad-spectrum antibacterial drug useful against many infections. Flagyl (metronizadole) is the recommended treatment for giardia and amoebic dysentry. Ampicillin is fine for people allergic to penicillin and works wonders on severe toothaches. All these antibiotics should only be used, however, if you can't see a doctor.

Antihistamine cream To treat insect bites.

Antiseptic cream Cicatrin and Bacitracin are good, but creams invariably squeeze out sooner or later so avoid metal tubes. Bright red or purple mercurochrome liquid, or iodine, is good for drying wounds.

Aspirin Good for mild pain relief and relieving fevers. Not to be taken if bleeding wounds take long to heal.

Codeine phosphate This is the best emergency anti-diarrhoeal pill, though in some countries may only be available on prescription. Immodium is also useful.

Iodine tincture or **water-purifying tablets** (chlorine-based) Chlorine tastes horrific; iodine is pleasant in comparison, is much cheaper, and can also be used to disinfect wounds instead of alcohol. Some people are allergic to chlorine, others to iodine (especially if seafood gets to you); neither are recommended for long-term use.

Lip-salve/chapstick Invaluable for dry lips.

Sticking plaster, steri-strip wound closures, sterile gauze dressing, micropore tape You don't need much of this stuff. If you use it up, supplies can be replenished in any pharmacy.

Vitamin tablets Handy if you're going to be on the road for a long time.

Zinc oxide powder Useful anti-fungal powder.

scorpion stings are painful but almost never fatal, while spiders are mostly quite harmless.

Snakes are common but, again, the vast majority are harmless. To see one at all, you'd need to search stealthily; walk heavily and they obligingly disappear. Victims of venomous snake bites should be hospitalized as quickly as possible, but whatever you do don't panic: most snake bite deaths are caused by shock rather than the venom itself. Venomous snake bites are usually treated with hydrocortisone and an anti-inflammatory and, in an emergency, with adrenaline injections. Local medicine, especially *jiwe ya punju* ("snake bite medicine

stone"), apparently works very well if applied to the wound immediately after the bite as it sucks up moisture and, hence, the venom; you can buy it in markets everywhere. Another local remedy, from the bark of a shrub, is called *mkingiri*.

Other complaints

Bilharzia (schistosomiasis) is a dangerous but curable disease which comes from tiny flukes (schistosomes) that live in freshwater snails and which, as part of their life cycle, leave their hosts and burrow into animal (or human) skin to multiply in the bloodstream. The symptoms are difficult to diagnose properly: a rash or itchy skin appears a few days after infection, and you may also feel severe fatigue and pass blood. After that you won't experience any further symptoms until a month or two later, when fever, chills, coughs and muscle aches may kick in. If left untreated, internal organs including the liver, intestines, lungs and bladders can be permanently damaged, and paralysis is also known, although all these effects are thankfully rare. The snails only favour stagnant water, and the chances of picking up bilharzia are small. The usual recommendation is never to swim in, wash with, or even touch, fresh lake water that can't be vouched for. Sea water is fine, as are well-maintained swimming pools. Early symptoms include severe fatigue and passing blood.

Fungal infections can be avoided by not using used soap in cheap hotels, or towels if unwashed, badly washed or still damp. Antifungal cream is the best treatment for infections; alternatively, douse affected skin in iodine. Many people get occasional **heat rashes**, especially at first on the coast. A warm shower (to open the pores) and cotton clothes should help. It's important not to overdose on **sunshine** in the first week or two. The powerful heat and bright light can mess up your system, and a hat and sunglasses are strongly recommended. Some people **sweat** heavily and lose a lot of salt. If this applies to you, sprinkle extra salt on your food. Salt tablets are a waste of money – a spoonful of table salt works just as well.

Finally, make sure you get a thorough **dental check-up** before leaving home, and take extra care of your teeth while in Tanzania. Stringy meat, acidic fruit and sugary tea are some of the hazards. There are reliable dentists in Arusha, Dar es Salaam, Dodoma and Stone Town. For acute **toothache**, the antibiotic Ampicillin works well, plus paracetamol for pain. Diclofenac helps reduce swellings. If you have a history of tooth inflammation or a dodgy tooth take a course of the analgesic and anti-inflammatory nimesulida (brand name Aulin) with you.

Costs, money and banks

Tanzanian's currency, the Tanzanian shilling (abbreviated to "Tsh"), is a colonial legacy based on the old British currency (people still occasionally refer to them by their old English slang name, "bob"). Notes come in denominations of Tsh200, 500, 1000, 5000 and 10,000 (a Tsh2000 note is also being introduced); coins are denominated in Tsh5, 10, 20, 50, 100 and 200 varieties. The shilling is a soft currency, and has depreciated steadily in value over the years, to your advantage. As of spring 2002, exchange rates were Tsh1300 to £1, and Tsh900 to US$1.

Most prices in Tanzania are given in **Tanzanian shillings**. However, you'll also see prices quoted in **US dollars**, especially for tourist services such as safaris, park entry fees and car rental. Throughout this guide we've quoted prices in whichever currency you're most likely to encounter them in. In addition, almost all the country's more expensive hotels and lodges charge non-Tanzanians ("non-residents") in dollars, though you're legally entitled to pay in shillings, albeit at inferior rates of exchange.

What to take

US dollars are widely accepted and generally rapidly changed. There's little difference between rates for cash and travellers' cheques. Higher denominations ($100) attract better rates, but avoid $500 bills, which are understandably treated with suspicion, given the risk of forgery. It's also best to avoid **pounds sterling**: although widely accepted, the exchange rate is bad relative to dollars, and even worse for travellers' cheques. Some overseas banks and exchange bureaux at airports stock Tanzanian shillings – rates aren't too bad (and are actually better than those offered in Arusha).

Travellers' cheques

Travellers' cheques are the safest way to carry money, and the marginally lower exchange rates are a small price to pay for your peace of mind, as cash can't be replaced if lost or stolen. Both American Express and Thomas Cook travellers' cheques are widely accepted, though at the time of research some banks were refusing American Express cheques on the grounds that stolen cheques were a problem.

All Tanzanian banks, and an increasing number of forex bureaux, need to see your passport and the **purchase receipt** you received when you bought the cheques (the one that includes the cheques' serial numbers). The importance of keeping your receipt in a safe place and in a legible state cannot be overstated; make photocopies and stash them away.

Credit cards and ATMs

Visa and **American Express** cards are widely accepted for tourist services such as upmarket hotels and restaurants, flights, safaris and car rental; Mastercard, Diners Club and JCB cards are less useful. There's usually a mark-up of five to ten percent but, as establishments are charged a fixed percentage of their transactions, this is obviously negotiable. A credit card can be particularly useful for leaving deposits for car rental.

Branches of Barclays Bank and Standard Chartered give **cash advances** in shillings (no charge) and US dollars or sterling (1 percent charge) on Visa, Mastercard and JCB. You can usually withdraw up to your card limit, although large transactions may entail an interrogation to screen for potential fraud. Note, however, that your credit card company will charge you for the service: anything up to four percent including a "conversion fee" included in the exchange rate.

Also useful are the 24-hour **ATMs** at branches of Barclays and Standard Chartered in Dar es Salaam, Arusha, Mwanza and Mbeya, where you can withdraw cash up to a maximum of Tsh400,000 per day. The machines accept cards with Visa, Visa Electron, Mastercard, Plus or Cirrus symbols, but unreliable electronic communications mean that they shouldn't be relied on. Obviously, **security** is a concern if you're using ATMs; although most are inside the bank, they're visible from the street, so if you're wary get a friend to come along and look out for you. The actual exchange rate you'll be charged for ATM withdrawals depends on the day that the advance is processed by the credit card company, so it's something of a lottery, and you'll also have to pay a cash advance fee.

Credit card abuse is uncommon, but is bound to rise as the use of credit cards increases. If you're paying a sum in shillings by credit card, make sure that the voucher specifies the currency before you sign. In addition, fill in any empty boxes on the slip with zeroes, and be especially careful not to let the card leave your sight (for example in hotels and restaurants) to ensure that only one slip is filled in.

Changing money

You can **exchange** hard currencies in cash or travellers' cheques at banks and foreign exchange bureaux ("forex") all over the country, including at the international airports, and also at most large hotels (though for substantially poorer rates). In theory you should keep exchange receipts until you leave the country, though they're rarely – if ever – asked for.

Exchange rates are pretty uniform, the exceptions being Dodoma, Stone Town and, especially, Arusha, where you'll receive ten to fifteen percent less for your money than elsewhere. Try to avoid carrying Tsh5000 or 10,000 notes as they're difficult to change in small villages, bars and some restaurants. Requesting smaller notes when changing money in a bank or forex doesn't always work; it seems to depend on the cashier's mood.

Forex bureaux (usually open Mon–Fri 9am–4.30pm, Sat 9am–noon or later, occasionally on Sun mornings) are invariably the fastest and most convenient way of changing money, usually taking little more than five minutes and rarely charging commission or other fees – although not all will change travellers' cheques. You'll find plenty in Arusha and Dar es Salaam, and a handful in Moshi and in Stone Town in Zanzibar.

Branches of **banks** in major towns and cities are usually open Monday to Friday 8.30am to 4pm and Saturday 8.30am to 1pm. Rural branches open Monday to Friday

8.30am to 12.30pm and Saturday 8.30 to 10.30am. Always ask first what **commission and charges** will be deducted, as they vary mysteriously even within branches of the same bank (you shouldn't pay more than 2 percent). **Standard Chartered** is fastest for changing money, but only has branches in Dar, Arusha, Mwanza and Mbeya. The best of the rest is the **National Bank of Commerce** (NBC), which averages between 30 and 45 minutes to change travellers' cheques. The ubiquitous **National Microfinance Bank** is reliable, but queues are long and things take forever. **CRDB** is the only bank you should actively avoid: staff are consistently obstructive, service is slow, they're a pain with travellers' cheques, and some of their branches charge outrageous commission. If a clerk is being unhelpful or otherwise difficult, a polite but firm demand to see the manager can work miracles.

Lastly, **do not change money on the street**, whether in a city or at border crossings. There's no need for a black market, and although touted street rates may be marginally better than bank or forex rates, you're guaranteed to get swindled.

Money transfers

The easiest way of sending money to Tanzania is via **Western Union** – transferred funds can be picked up at any branch of the Tanzania Postal Bank, which are usually found in or near the post offices of larger towns; the most reliable is the main branch at the TTCL Building in Dar, off Samora Avenue (☎022/213 2821, ℱ022/211 0449, ℮tpb.wunion@africaonline.com).

Alternatively, **MoneyGram** (🖳www .moneygram.com) claim to be able to transfer money within ten minutes. Funds can be collected at the National Bureau de Change in Dar es Salaam (☎022/211 5575, ℱ022/211 2350).

Costs

Tanzania can be very expensive if you want to rent a car or go on safari, but very cheap if you don't, especially if you avoid staying too long in the main tourist areas of Dar es Salaam, Arusha and (particularly) Zanzibar, where even "budget" accommodation averages $16–20 a night for a double. On the mainland, solo budget travellers can scrape by on around $10 a day, while couples can survive on even less. For $20–50 a day you can stay in good hotels and enjoy a few luxuries, whilst for upmarket travellers the sky really is the limit – if you really want to part from your cash as quickly as possible you'll even find a few hotels charging over $1000 a night.

Obviously, safaris and activities like hiking, snorkelling and scuba-diving, will significantly hike up your budget. For a standard budget **camping safari**, count on a minimum of $80–90 per person per day. Mid-range camping or lodge safaris go for between $120 and $200 per person per day, and top-end trips range from $200 up to $500 a day. **Scuba-diving** courses cost around $70–100 per person per day (not including accommodation).

Getting around by **bus and daladala** is very cheap (rarely more than Tsh1000 for an hour's journey). Unfortunately, they can't drive you around the game parks, and renting a vehicle – and paying for fuel – will add

Seasons and prices

Rates at Tanzania's mid- and top-range accommodation options fall significantly out of high season, and **beach resort hotels** and **safari lodges** have separate low-, mid- and high-season tariffs. Low-season rates can be anything from a third to a half of the high-season tariff.

Low season: From Easter until the end of June or mid-July (coinciding with the long rains, or the "Green Season", as some hotels prefer to call it).

Mid season: July to the end of November or mid-December (coinciding with the short rains). July and August are sometimes considered high season.

High season: Early- or mid-December to Easter (hot and sunny weather, until the long rains break in March). Extra supplements may be charged over Christmas and New Year.

around $80–150 a day to your costs, though this isn't so cripplingly expensive if shared between two or more people.

With the exception of food, most things in Tanzania are **bargainable**, especially anything that a tourist might want – like accommodation, safaris and souvenirs.

An **International Student Identity Card (ISIC)** entitles you to cheaper airline deals, but won't get you discounts on much in Tanzania itself apart from reduced rates at a handful of museums. There are no student rates for park entry fees, accommodation or transport.

Getting around

The usual way of getting around Tanzania is by bus: though they can be slow and uncomfortable (and driving standards are pretty horrendous), they reach pretty much every part of the country, and are a good way of mixing with the locals. Alternatively, two railway lines cross the country, both originating in Dar: one runs south to New Kapiri Mposhi in Zambia, the other heads west to Kigoma and Mwanza. All three western lakes – Victoria, Tanganyika and Nyasa (Malawi) – have ferry services, and on the coast boats connect Dar es Salaam to Zanzibar, and to Mtwara in the far south; there's also a weekly passenger boat from Tanga to Zanzibar. Finally, air travel is a relatively affordable option if you're in a hurry.

Tanzania's main traffic artery is the tarmac Tanzam Highway, which runs across the country from Zambia though Mbeya, Iringa, Morogoro to Dar es Salaam, and then up to Tanga, Moshi and Arusha. Apart from this, however, Tanzania's **roads** are in a pitiful state, and often become impassable in the rains. In general, roads are worst along the south coast and in the far south, centre, west and northwest. We've given descriptions of road conditions in the relevant sections of the guide, but be aware that conditions can change radically in just half a year, and another El Niño – which in East Africa translates into catastrophic flooding and washed-out roads – is due any time.

Whether you're travelling by bus or driving, you'll quickly appreciate the reality behind Tanzania's abysmal **road safety record**, one that would be much worse were there any more tarmac. The main causes of accidents are speeding and reckless driving (encouraged by irresponsible timetables). The most **dangerous routes** are from Arusha to Moshi, and along the Tanzam Highway south of Iringa, especially down to Songea.

Buses, minibuses and pick-ups

In towns of any size, you'll find a whole crowd of **buses**, **minibuses** and **pick-ups** hustling for business. Buses and large minibuses (Toyota DCMs, also called Coasters) cover the whole country, getting you close to almost anywhere you might want to go, at least in the dry season, though in the rains, getting stranded for hours or days at a time isn't unheard of. The main routes are served by flashy **"video coaches"** – these are reasonably reliable and generally leave on time (6am is usual). Off the main routes you'll find smaller **"country bus"** companies operating a single battered Leyland or DCM. These are much less predictable and are prone to frequent breakdowns, so don't expect to get anywhere in a hurry. For security reasons – mainly to avoid the risk of bandit attack – buses are forbidden from travelling between 10pm and 4am, so if you're on a long-distance bus (especially in the west, northwest and centre) you'll either have to sleep on the bus or break your journey.

Safety is a nagging concern on fast tarmac, given the country's appalling road safety record: always seek unbiased local advice before buying a ticket. Tanzania's **safest bus**

Drugging

Long a problem in Kenya, the drugging of bus passengers in order to rob them is also on the rise in Tanzania. The ruse involves someone befriending a traveller (locals are as much at risk as tourists) and then offering some kind of food or drink laced with powerful knock-out drugs. By the time victims wake up (sometimes in hospital), their luggage, money and other valuables will have disappeared. The simple way to avoid falling victim is not to accept food, cigarettes or drink from strangers, even if this might offend. You should also take care on ferries and trains, where the same trick might be used.

company is Scandinavian Express (although even they have been known to speed). Other companies with decent reputations include Fresh ya Shamba and Royal Coach. **Companies to avoid** include Abood, Coaster, Hood, Takrim and Tawfiq. Public vehicles at the smaller end of the spectrum also have a gruesome safety record and their drivers, on the whole, possess a breathtaking lack of road sense; this is especially true of DCM minibuses along main routes, most notoriously between Arusha and Moshi, where fatal crashes are common. If you do have to travel on one of these vehicles, try to sit at the back; it's also a good idea to wear sunglasses if your face is near a front window – they sometimes shatter.

There are dozens of competing bus companies: in most towns, all services depart from the main bus station (usually called the "bus stand", or *stendi*), which is also usually where the various companies' ticket offices are located. On lesser travelled routes, or for seats with safer companies along the main tarmac roads, you generally need to **reserve seats** a day in advance (and arrive at least thirty minutes before departure, or you may find your seat gets sold to someone else). **Tickets** usually have seat numbers indicated: when buying your ticket, it's worth considering which side will be shadier, since the combination of a slow, bumpy ride, dust and fierce sun can be trying. On rough roads choose a seat in the middle or front of the bus – away from the axles – to avoid the worst of the bumps.

Fares tend to be around Tsh1000 for an hour's journey (approximate journey times are given in "Travel details" at the end of each chapter). Attempts to overcharge tourists are rare. **Baggage charges** aren't normally levied unless you're transporting commercial goods, though plenty of touts will try and convince you otherwise.

Except for some Scandinavian Express coaches, most buses lack **toilets** – instead, buses stop every few hours for passengers to scurry into the bush to relieve themselves (bring toilet paper). You don't have to bring mountains of food for the journey: there's plenty available from hawkers at bus stations and villages, and most long-distance buses also stop for lunch at a roadside restaurant.

Pick-ups

In rural areas things are less predicable, and transport is mainly by **pick-up**. These can be anything from small saloon cars to Land Rovers, minibuses (the most dangerous) or (most commonly) open-backed pick-up trucks, the best of which are fitted with wooden benches and canvas roofs. On the downside, pick-ups tend to be extremely crowded, deeply uncomfortable on bottoms (though locals seem strangely immune) and often break down. Despite this, they can be an enjoyable way of getting about, giving you close contact – literally – with local people, and often offering the most convenient (indeed sometimes the only) means of reaching smaller places off the main roads. They're also cheap – even the longest journey shouldn't cost more than Tsh3000. Don't hand over any money before you set off, though; or, if the pick up does get going, wait until you've left town before paying. This isn't a question of being ripped off but too often the first departure is just a cruise around town rounding up passengers and buying petrol (with your money) and then back to square one – a rigmarole which could go on for hours.

Hitching

Hitching is how the majority of rural Tanzanians get around, though because of

...eapness of buses, travellers don't try ...ch. If you do hitch, you'll usually be ...pected to pay something, whether you ...ave down a pick-up, a lorry or a private vehicle with a spare place. Private vehicles off tarmac are comparatively rare and usually full.

Hitching **techniques** need to be fairly exuberant; a modest thumb is more likely to be interpreted as a friendly, or even rude, gesture than a request for a lift. Beckon the driver to stop with your whole arm.

Urban transport: daladalas and taxis

Daladalas (usually Toyota Hiace minivans) are the standard way of getting around large Tanzanian towns. Fares are a pretty uniform Tsh150 for a short journey, rising up to Tsh400 for longer rides. Daladalas run along pre-determined routes, often – but not always – colour-coded, and destinations are clearly marked on the fronts of vehicles, though place-name abbreviations may need some working out. Daladalas have the advantage of being plentiful and reasonably quick; the downside is that they can get amazingly crowded: 25 people in a vehicle with just twelve seats is common.

When boarding a vehicle at a main **daladala terminal** (known as the "stage" or "stand") always choose a vehicle that's full and about to leave, or you'll have to wait inside until they are ready to go – sometimes for hours. Beware also of drivers who fill their car with young touts pretending to be passengers (spot them by the lack of luggage), who mysteriously disappear when you've bought a ticket. Competition is intense and people will lie unashamedly to persuade you the vehicle is going "just now".

Rather more comfortable are **taxis**, which are also the only safe way of getting around late at night. They lack meters, however, so always settle on a fare before getting in. A ride around town costs Tsh1000–2000, though drivers will invariably try for more – haggle hard and, if you get nowhere, try another driver.

Car rental

Renting a car has definite advantages. With the exceptions of Udzungwa Mountains National Park (no vehicles allowed) and

Mahale Mountains and Gombe (accessed by boat), Tanzania's **wildlife parks** are all open to private rented vehicles, and there's a lot to be said for the freedom of having your own wheels, though unless there are more than two of you, it won't save you money over one of the cheaper camping safaris. You're also required to leave a hefty deposit, roughly equivalent to the anticipated bill. Credit cards are useful for this, but you'll need to trust the company.

You have three main options if you want to rent a car. The easiest, if it's only for a day or two, is to rent a **taxi**: up to Tsh40,000 for a full day is reasonable. Bear in mind though that most taxis are battered old saloons, and although there's little left to break, rough roads are not exactly their strength.

Alternatively, there are plenty of **car rental companies** – recommended outfits are listed on p.121 (Dar), p.390 (Arusha) and p.643 (Stone Town). Given Tanzania's awful roads, most companies insist you hire one of their drivers as well – no bad thing, especially as they tend to double as safari guides with the unerring ability to spot things like a leopard's tail dangling from a tree a mile away. Very few multinational car rental companies have any kind of presence in Tanzania. Avis (Ⓦ www.avis.com) have an agent in Dar, while Hertz (Ⓦ www.hertz.com) have agents in Dar and Arusha, though neither operation is particularly outstanding.

Choosing a vehicle

High **clearance** is pretty much essential, thanks to the dire state of many roads, even in dry weather. A **four-wheel-drive** (4WD) is also useful, and essential for wildlife parks, mountainous areas and on minor roads during the long rains – non-4WDs will be turned back at the gates of most parks, regardless of the season. 4WD **Land Rovers** and **Toyota Land Cruisers** are the most widely available vehicles. There's little to choose between them, though the Land Rover's springs are easier to repair than a Land Cruiser's coils; the newer Land Rovers, like the 110 series, also have Turbo Direct Injection (TDI), which gives more power and makes them more economical on tarmac. One or two rental companies still have diminutive **Suzuki jeeps**, which are light, rugged and capable of amazing feats. Don't expect them to top more than their legal limit

Buying a second-hand car

If you're going to be in Tanzania for some time, buying a second-hand vehicle in Arusha or Dar es Salaam is a possibility, though prices are inflated and you'll need to be mechanically confident. Rental companies sometimes have vehicles to dispose of, and the *Guardian* carries lots of ads, as does *Advertising in Dar*, a freesheet that you can also find in Arusha and on the internet at ⓦ www.advertisingdar.co.tz. The price of a used Land Rover 110 TDI in good condition shouldn't be more than $5000.

of 80kph, however, and beware of their notorious tendency to fall over on bends or on the dangerously sloping gravel hard shoulders that line many roads.

Costs

Hiring a decent 4WD with driver averages $100 per day from Dar es Salaam and $130 from Arusha. Self-drive is $15–25 cheaper. Saloon cars, for use within cities, towns and on tarmac, cost around $70 a day self-drive, or $50–60 on Zanzibar. Rates are always cheaper by the week, and many firms are prepared to negotiate a little as well, especially off-season.

Always check the insurance details and pay the daily **collision damage waiver (CDW)** premium, which is sometimes included in the price: even a small bump could be very costly otherwise. **Theft protection waiver (TPW)** should also be taken. However, even with these, you'll still be liable for **excess liability**, which can be anything from $100 to $2000 – as a rule of thumb, high excess liability is the trademark of dodgy companies hoping for punters to crash so they can earn some quick cash. Lastly, always check whether VAT is included or you'll be stung for an extra twenty percent.

Fuel is available everwhere except the very smallest villages, and also along major highways, though it's still worth filling up before heading out on a long drive. Fuel gets more expensive the further inland or away from a major town you get. A litre of Super starts at around Tsh600 in Dar es Salaam, rising to over Tsh1000 in some of the national parks. You should get 10–14km per litre out of a Land Rover TDI, depending on its condition, less in a Land Cruiser. If you're intending to do a lot of driving in a remote area you should definitely carry spare fuel in cans.

Before setting off

Don't automatically assume your rental vehicle is roadworthy: **check out the vehicle** before signing anything, and insist on a test drive – it's amazing how many vehicles "fresh from the mechanic" have weak brakes, dodgy clutches, leaky radiators or wobbly wheels. Things to check include wheel tread, a full complement of wheel nuts (many cars have wheels held on with only two or three) and cracks in the gearbox and engine mounts (you'll have to get under the car to check this). The vehicle should also have at last one spare tyre (with good tread and no punctures), preferably two.

If you're planning to spend any time off tarmac, the carburettor intake has to be close to roof height to avoid clogging things up with splashed muddy water and dust; most safari vehicles are customized with a "chimney" for this purpose. Ensure you have a spanner that fits *all* the wheel nuts, as well as the spare tyre if it's mounted, as different nut sizes are sometimes used, and you'll also need a jack. A working mileometer is also helpful even if you're not paying by the kilometre, as navigating using map distances is often the only way to avoid missed turnings.

Other items you should carry, certainly for longer drives, are a shovel for digging your way out of mud or sand, a machete (*panga*), small bottles of engine oil and brake fluid (which can also be used as clutch fluid), a spare fan belt and possibly brake pads, tow rope, spare fuel and plenty of drinking water. Finally, try if you can to stay close to the place you rented the car from for the first day and night, as the first day's drive will give you a chance to spot any mechanical problems without the hassle of being miles from anywhere.

Regulations and fines

Officially, traffic drives on the left, although on rough roads you'll find people driving on whichever side of the road has fewer potholes (or mud pools in the rains). The **speed limit** is 50kph in populated areas and between 80kph and 120kph on major highways. Drivers must be 25 to 70 years old and have held a licence for at least two years. Zanzibar requires a valid **international driving licence** which must be endorsed by the police on arrival. If you don't have one, a temporary permit can be obtained on production of your national licence. On the mainland, an international driving licence is recommended but not legally required. You may also be asked to produce a **PSV (passenger service vehicle) licence**, which is usually displayed in one of the windows of rental vehicles. Note that some certificates restrict the vehicle's movements to a particular region, and this will leave you open to an array of spot fines should you stray outside the region(s) on the permit. Check this out with the company before you leave.

Police checkpoints are generally marked by low strips of spikes across the road with just enough room to slalom round. Always slow down, and stop if signalled. The usual reason given if you're pulled over is that you were speeding, although Tanzania's notoriously corrupt traffic police are quite capable of finding something, *anything*, wrong with your car (broken wing mirror, flat spare tyre). Tourists are not immune – and indeed are favoured by some bent cops. Do not, under any account, let them keep your passport or driving licence. **Spot fines** are Tsh20,000, less if you're happy foregoing the official receipt (i.e. a bribe). This might reduce the fine to under Tsh10,000.

Incidentally, the barriers slung across roads outside smaller towns and villages are maintained by local authorities for the purpose of extracting taxes from commercial vehicles. You should be let through without any payment.

Driving hazards and etiquette

When driving, expect the unexpected: rocks, ditches, potholes, animals and people on the road, as well as lunatic drivers. It's accepted practice to honk your horn stridently to warn pedestrians and cyclists of your approach. Beware also of **speed bumps**. These are sometimes signposted, but more usually the first you'll know of them is when your head hits the roof. They are found both in rural areas, wherever a busy road has been built through a village, and on the roads in and out of nearly every large town. **Be especially wary of buses** – which seldom slow down for anything – and also be careful when overtaking heavy vehicles, even more so when passing lorries groaning uphill: sometimes a line of them churning out diesel fumes can cut off your visibility without warning – extremely dangerous on a narrow mountain road.

It's common practice to flash oncoming vehicles, especially if they're leaving you little room or their headlights are blinding you, and to signal right to indicate your width and deter drivers behind you from overtaking. Left-hand signals are used to say "Please overtake" – but don't assume that a driver in front who signals you to overtake can really see whether the road ahead is clear.

If you **break down** or have an **accident**, the first thing to do is pile bundles of sticks or foliage at fifty-metre intervals behind and in front of your car. These are the red warning triangles of Africa, and their placing is always scrupulously observed (as is the wedging of a stone behind at least one wheel). When you have a puncture, as you will, get it mended straight away so that you're never without a spare tyre – it's very cheap (Tsh500) and can be done almost anywhere there are vehicles. Spare parts, tools and proper equipment are rare off the main routes, though local mechanics (*fundis*) can work miracles with minimal tools. Many are especially knowledgeable about diesel-powered Land Rovers; Land Cruisers and petrol engines are trickier. Always settle on a price before work begins.

Foreign-registered vehicles

If you're arriving overland in your own vehicle, a **carnet de passage** is highly recommended to avoid a potentially time-consuming paper chase when you eventually leave the country. With a *carnet*, you'll have to pay a one-off road fund tax ($5) and $20 for a one-month foreign-vehicle permit. Without a *carnet* you'll have to leave a deposit equivalent to the tax payable on cars, including VAT, which can be several thousand dollars. The deposit is paid back when you leave the country, although arranging this with the authorities can be a hassle.

Tips and tricks for rough roads

Rough roads should be treated with respect and patience. Driving in the dry season is rarely too difficult, and following the most worn vehicle tracks should see you through without any problems. Driving in the rains, however, is a challenge that you'll either love or hate. The following tips should come in useful.

Driving on loose sand and mud, always keep your speed down to minimize skidding and give yourself more time to deal with a skid if your car loses traction. On a consistently slippery surface your steering needs constant play to avoid sliding. In other words, even if you're driving in a straight line, repeatedly move the steering wheel a small distance left and right – you'll feel the increased traction between the ground and the wheels (though, obviously, too much play and the car will begin lurching).

If you do start sliding to one side, try to avoid the natural reaction of steering in the opposite direction; instead, steer briefly in the direction of the slide to bring the car back under control, then gradually steer the car back to its correct course. If you do inadvertently steer in the opposite direction, be ready to turn the wheel abruptly in the opposite direction when the car regains traction or you risk spinning out of control or ricocheting in the opposite direction. Deflating tyres a bit can also help, though this is a pain if you then have to drive 200km to the nearest foot pump.

Whereas slippery roads are mentally tiring over a long period of time, the art of crossing mud pools is a more immediately nerve-wracking experience. First off, get out of the car and use a stick (or your feet) to gauge the depth. If the depth is less than about 50cm you should be fine (if it's more than that and you're inexperienced, turn back, as there might be worse to come). The usual rule is to make a line straight through the centre, as the surface under the water is more likely to be hard and settled than at the edges, which can get treacherously muddy. If there are tyre tracks, you're best off following them both into and out of the pool. The crossing itself is easiest in second gear at a slow but steady speed (too fast and you'll drench the car in mud). Some drivers recommend first gear, but the disadvantage is that you risk getting stuck much faster should you run into difficulty (spinning wheels when you're stuck just gets you stuck even more). For deeper or muddier pools, engage four-wheel-drive first.

The most treacherous of wet season driving hazards is black cotton soil, called *kindiga* in Kiswahili (areas of *kindiga* are called *mbuga*). *Kindiga* quickly becomes waterlogged and has little traction, forming a perilous trap which should be completely avoided in the rains. If you have no choice, a combination of the techniques described above might help you through. The problem is that at low speed the vehicle may lack the momentum to get through particularly tricky sections, whilst at higher speed you run the risk of losing control and ending up in a ditch.

If you do get stuck and aren't completely off the beaten track, the next lorry along should be able to haul you out. Local villagers may also be willing to help you out, whether from the goodness of their hearts or (more likely) the prospect of payment.

Trains

Tanzania has two railways: the **Central Line**, which runs west from Dar es Salaam to Kigoma and Mwanza; and the **Tazara Line**, which heads southwest across the country and into Zambia. There are no passenger services along the lines from Dar es Salaam to Arusha or to Tanga, and the connection to Kenya was discontinued years ago after a dispute over rolling stock.

The Central Line

The main section of the **Central Line**, running 1254 kilometres from Dar es Salaam to

Train security

Overnight trains are obvious targets for opportunistic thieves. If you have a compartment, keep it locked when you're asleep or outside, or ensure that there's always someone there to look after bags. Be especially careful when the train pulls in at main stations, especially Dodoma and Tabora on the Central Line. You should also be wary of people looking for a spare seat in second-class (all genuine passengers should have a numbered ticket corresponding to a particular compartment) and of passengers without bags – they may leave with yours. If you really get suspicious stay awake until the ticket inspector comes round. In third-class you'll probably have to stay awake all night or else stash your valuables out of reach (in a bag under your seat hemmed in by other people's bags, for example). All this is not to say that you should be paranoid, but just that you shouldn't drop your guard.

Kigoma on the shores of Lake Tanganyika, was laid by the Germans just before World War I. The line isn't in the best condition: derailings involving freight trains are common, and a disastrous accident in 2002 claimed 281 lives when a train's brakes failed. Nonetheless, the line remains safer than road transport. A branch was added north **to Mwanza** on Lake Victoria in the 1920s. There are four trains a week to Mwanza and Kigoma apiece. The line splits at **Tabora**. There are also two other less important branches: one south **to Mpanda** (services from Tabora three times weekly), and one north **to Singida** (three weekly trains from Dodoma).

There are three classes of ticket. **First-class** is in compartments with just two berths – ideal for couples. **Second-class** is in compartments with six berths each. Compartments are segregated by sex unless you book and pay for the whole lot, and both kinds have wash basins, bed linen and blankets. **Third-class** consists of open carriages of reserved seats, but can become extremely crowded and uncomfortable, what with all the suitcases, boxes, baskets, chickens, children and *mama kubwas* ("big ladies"). All trains have a dining car (though this mainly sees use as a bar), and food can also be ordered from a roving waiter – Tsh1500 gets you a simple but filling meal of chips, rice or *ugali* with beef, chicken or fish; breakfast goes for Tsh1000. On long journeys the train stops at trackside villages whose inhabitants set up stalls where you can sample some of the best "street" food in the country, featuring anything from stews with rice or *ugali* to tangerines, pineapples and other seasonal fruit. You might also like to take some supplies of your own, just in case.

It's important to **make reservations**, especially if you want a first-class compartment during busy periods, such as Christmas and New Year. Ticket offices take bookings several weeks ahead, and travel agents can do the work for you, albeit for a hefty supplement. For an idea of **prices**: Dar to Kigoma costs Tsh32,700/24,200/9200 (1st/2nd/3rd class); Tabora to Kigoma is Tsh18,000/14,400/Tsh5700 and the exhausting run from Dar to Mwanza costs Tsh44,600/32,600/12,300.

Delays are frequent, so don't count on arriving at your destination at the scheduled time. The impending privatization of the Tanzania Railways Corporation may change things for the better, or – if British Rail's sorry tale is an example – might just make things worse.

The Tazara Line

If you thought the Central Line was unreliable, the **Tazara Line** – or Mukuba ("Copper") Express – that runs from Dar es Salaam to New Kapiri Mposhi in northern Zambia is a total shambles. The line, which is the northernmost extension of the railway from Cape Town, was constructed in the 1960s to provide an outlet for Zambian copper exports without going through the racist regimes of Southern Rhodesia and South Africa. Whilst outbound **schedules** from Dar are reasonably reliable, northbound services from Zambia, or from Mbeya in southern Tanzania, are notoriously capricious, so much so that even stationmasters along the way often have little idea when the next train is due. On the positive side, the route passes through some especially beautiful and wild landscape, including part of the Selous Game Reserve (antelopes, buffaloes and giraffes are frequently seen).

At the time of writing there were only three trains a week from Dar es Salaam: one all the way to New Kapiri Mposhi (38hr, in theory), the other two terminating in Mbeya (19hr). **Fares** from Dar to Mbeya are currently Tsh22,200 first-class, Tsh14,700 second-class and Tsh8300 third-class, whilst a first-class ticket to New Kapiri Mposhi costs Tsh47,600. First-class compartments have four berths, second-class six, and third-class is a predictably heaving mass of humanity. There's also a dining car.

Air

Tanzania has a number of reasonably priced **internal air services** and it's well worth seeing the country from above at least once: the flight from Dar or Stone Town to Pemba, over spice and coconut plantations, reefs, sandbanks and creeks, is especially beautiful. Flight schedules are given at the end of each chapter. The best local airlines – all operating propeller planes – are Coastal Travels, Precisionair and ZanAir, which can usually be relied on to keep to their schedules. Both Coastal Travels and Precisionair use some single-engine planes for less busy routes, worth bearing in mind if mono-props give you the heebie-jeebies, although these companies have good reputations regarding safety. The other main carriers are the increasingly irregular Eagle Air and the perennially unreliable Air Tanzania Corporation (ATC) – aptly nicknamed "Any Time Cancellation".

Fares for non-Tanzanians are invariably quoted in dollars, but you may be able to wangle cheaper shilling fares for less touristic destinations like Mwanza, Bukoba and Tabora. Fares from Dar es Salaam are currently: Arusha ($170–180); Zanzibar ($50); Mafia Island ($50); Selous Game Reserve ($120); and Ruaha National Park ($300). An airport tax of $6 (Tsh5000) is payable on all domestic flights starting from the mainland; the tax on domestic departures from Zanzibar is Tsh2000 – these taxes are sometimes included in the ticket.

Charter flights – mainly useful for getting to remoter national parks in a hurry – are offered by several companies in Zanzibar,

Dar es Salaam and Arusha, including Precisionair and ZanAir (see the "Listings" sections of these towns for details). **Prices** depend on the destination and the type of aircraft. A twelve-seater from Arusha to Kigoma works out at around $4000, equating to $330 per person if you can fill every seat. Smaller aircraft and shorter distances are much cheaper: a five-seat Cessna from Dar to Zanzibar, for example, shouldn't be more than $300.

Ferries

On the **coast**, there are daily ferries between Dar es Salaam, Stone Town (Unguja) and Pemba. The slower boats take four to five hours from Dar to Stone Town; faster hydrofoils complete the journey in ninety minutes. There's also at least one ferry weekly between Dar and Mtwara in the far south, constituting the only connection to that region – other than flying – during the long rains. There are no longer any ferries to Mafia Island, Tanga or to Mombasa in Kenya, although the weekly cargo boat from Tanga to Pemba does carry passengers.

On **Lake Victoria**, steamers sail several times a week between Mwanza, Bukoba and various minor Tanzanian islands. The ferry service to Port Bell in Uganda has been suspended for several years, while an invasion of water hyacinth – which snarls up propellers – has put paid to ferries to Kisumu in Kenya. On **Lake Tanganyika**, there are two weekly ferries from the railhead at Kigoma, one to Bujumbura in Burundi, the other along the eastern lakeshore to Mpulungu in northern Zambia. This latter run is something special, aboard a vessel – the *MV Liemba* – which is a pre-World War I relic. On **Lake Nyasa**, a weekly ferry runs from Itungi Port to Mbamba Bay on the Tanzanian side (24hr), then across the lake to Nkhata Bay in Malawi, where you can connect with other Malawian ferries.

Dhows

Though discouraged by the authorities, getting a passage on a commercial **dhow** is a legal and feasible – if adventurous –way of getting along parts of the coast and from the mainland to Zanzibar. Be aware, however, that travelling by dhow is considered risky: dhows do occasionally capsize, and there's little chance of being rescued should that happen.

The main hassle if you want to take a dhow to Zanzibar is dealing with the **paperwork**, something not helped by vague immigration rules and corrupt officials. An exit stamp is needed when leaving the mainland; though free in theory, this may cost anything from the price of a soda to $35, depending on the official you're dealing with.

Journey times given in this book are very approximate, so take plenty of food and water and remember that although the thought of a dhow trip is undeniably romantic, the reality can be rather different, with choppy seas, cramped seating and rudimentary toilet facilities.

The main ports for catching **dhows to Zanzibar** are Bagamoyo, Pangani and Tanga. Finding something in Dar es Salaam is virtually impossible. Dhow-hopping **along the south coast** of Tanzania is also a possibility if you're not in a hurry. The nearest main port to Dar is at Kisiju, 90km south of the city, from where you can get to Mafia Island or south to Songo Songo Island. From there, with luck, you'll find an onward connection to Kilwa Kivinje (or sometimes Kilwa Kisiwani), and then on to Lindi and Mtwara. From Mtwara, dhows occasionally head on to Mozambique.

Cycling

Tanzania's climate and varied terrain make it challenging **cycling** country. Given time, you can cycle to parts of the country that would be hard to visit by any other means except on foot, and of course people will treat you in a completely different way – as a traveller rather than a tourist. And what would take several days to hike can be cycled in a matter of hours. Most towns have bicycle shops which sell both trusty Indian and Chinese three-speed roadsters, as well as mountain bikes (though many of these also have only three gears).

Bringing your own bicycle by air is fairly straightforward, but check with your airline in advance in terms of what you'll be charged and whether they have any special packing requirements. Few airlines will insist your bike be boxed or bagged, but it's best to turn the handlebars into the frame and tie them down, invert the pedals and deflate the tyres. Whatever you take – and a mountain bike is best – it will need low gears and strongly built wheels; you should also carry some essential spare parts, lights (the front light can also double as a torch) and a U-bolt cycle lock. Rented bikes can be locked with a padlock and chain in a length of hosepipe which you can buy in any market.

Buses always carry bicycles for about half-fare (even if flagged down at the roadside), and trucks will often give you a lift for a small payment; trains also take bikes for a low fixed fare. You'll need to consider the **seasons**, however; you won't make much progress on dirt roads during the rains when chain sets and brakes become totally jammed with sticky mud. Obviously, you also need to be cautious when **cycling on main roads**. A mirror is essential and, if the pavement is broken at the edge, give yourself plenty of space and be ready to leave the road if necessary – local cyclists wisely scatter like chickens at the approach of a bus. That said, cycle tourists are still a novelty in Tanzania: drivers often slow down to look and you'll rarely be run off the road.

If you don't want to arrange your own trip, the US-based Bicycle Africa (4887 Columbia Drive South, Seattle, WA 98108-1919 USA ☎ & ℱ 206/767-0848, ⊕ www.ibike.org/bikeafrica) offer a seventeen-day **cycling holiday** for $1490 plus airfare, which includes visits to Zanzibar, Tanga, Usambaras and a hike up Kilimanjaro (without bikes, needless to say) The total cycling distance is 420km, mostly on paved roads. Trips leave in February, July and August, and you'll need to bring your own bike. In Tanzania itself, the East African Safari & Touring Company in Arusha (p.397) should be able to arrange some short cycling trips (a week or so) around northern Tanzania.

Accommodation

Tanzania has a wide range of accommodation to suit all tastes and pockets, ranging from cheap local guest houses to luxury lodges and tented camps in the bush. Camping is possible on the mainland (but not on Zanzibar), though prices for a pitch are often more than you would pay in a decent guest house. Zanzibar's hotels are expensive by mainland standards, with the cheapest double rooms generally starting at around $20, though this should be bargainable, especially in low season.

Some accommodation terms

A **lodge** is a designer hotel or country house, usually situated in a game park. A **banda** is traditionally a cheap thatched cottage or chalet; the round ones are called "rondavels". Upmarket versions can be found in tourist lodges in the bush. A **tented camp** is a kind of hotel in the bush, using large tents, or *bandas*, often with a solid bathroom plumbed in at the back. A **hoteli** is usually a cheap restaurant, rarely a hotel.

Nomenclature can be confusing when it comes to describing types of room. **Single** rooms have just one bed, though some hotels will let couples use a single for the same price as a solo traveller. Rooms with two beds are normally called **twins**, as

---

Accommodation price codes

All accommodation listed in this guide has been graded according to the **price codes** given below, based on the cost of a **standard double or twin room** charged at non-resident (tourist) rates. For dormitory accommodation, hostels and campsites (which charge per person), exact prices have been given where possible.

Except in Zanzibar, cheap hotels quote their rates in Tanzanian shillings (Tsh). More upmarket places quote their rates in US dollars, although rooms can also be paid for in shillings at the hotel's (often inferior) exchange rate – it's useful to know that the law that required tourists to pay in dollars was repealed a few years ago. Note that hotels nearly always have two tariffs, one for tourists and one for Tanzanian residents (which are always quoted in shillings and are invariably much cheaper).

Prices vary according to the season at some park lodges and in most tourist- or luxury-class accommodation on the coast. Elsewhere, tariffs don't change with the time of year, though it should be possible to bargain the price down when things are slow. As a rough guide, facilities in each category are as follows.

Price code ❶ covers very basic guest houses with shared (or "common") bathrooms. Price codes ❷–❹ include progressively more comfortable guest houses or lower-end hotels with private showers and toilets, with breakfast included. Price codes ❺–❼ denote tourist-class hotels or lodges, often with half- or full-board. At the top end of the price range (❽–❾) are luxury hotels and lodges with full board and special facilities.

❶ Under $5 (under Tsh4500)
❷ $5–10 (Tsh4500–9000)
❸ $10–20 (Tsh9000–18,000)
❹ $20–40 (Tsh18,000–36,000)
❺ $40–70 (Tsh36,000–63,000)

❻ $70–100 (Tsh63,000–90,000)
❼ $100–150 (Tsh90,000–135,000)
❽ $150–250 (Tsh135,000–215,000)
❾ Over $250 (over Tsh215,000)

opposed to a **double**, which has one large bed suitable for couples. At least this is the theory, although confusingly many hotels use the word "double" for twin-bed rooms, and "single" for rooms with one bed, even when it's big enough for a whole family. Wherever possible, we've made the distinction clear in our hotel reviews.

The self-explanatory **long-drop** (or "squat loo") is the kind of non-flushing toilet found in some guest houses and in most downmarket *bandas* and campsites. We've used the term **box net** to describe mosquito nets which are either draped around a rectangular frame or suspended from four points. This type of net is superior to the standard (or round) mosquito net, hung from a single point, since there's more room inside box nets and thus less chance that you'll come into contact with the net (and the hungry mosquitoes on the other side).

Hostels

There are no youth hostels in Tanzania. Their role is filled instead by a number of cheap **church-run hostels**, notably the Moravian Church in the south of the country, the Salvation Army and YWCA in Dar, and the Lutheran Church elsewhere. There are no membership requirements. Revellers and night owls should look elsewhere, however, as there's usually a curfew and the atmosphere can be a cloying contrast to the livelier – and sleazier – guest houses.

Guest houses

Nearly every town in Tanzania has at least one clean and comfortable **guest house** (known as *gesti* or, in more rural areas, *nyumba ya kulala wageni* – "house for sleeping guests"). These vary from mud shacks with water from a well to little multi-storey buildings containing rooms with private bathrooms, plus a bar and restaurant. Guest houses themselves are usually fairly quiet, though street noise and the proximity of mosques might wake you up earlier than you want. Still, if the place seems noisy in the afternoon, it will probably become cacophonous during the night, so ask for a room away from the source of the din. This applies especially to Wednesday, Friday and Saturday nights, when most discos operate.

You should rarely have to pay more than

Tsh6000 for a double (Tsh4000 for a single, which can sometimes be shared by a couple sleeping together), often much less – it's always worth trying to bargain, especially if a place doesn't seem particularly busy. Be aware that room prices aren't always a good indication of the standard of an establishment, and it's worth checking several places, testing the electricity, size of mosquito nets (it's amazing how many don't cover the whole bed), hot water (if any) and asking to see the toilets; you won't cause offence by saying no thanks. It's a good idea to bring toilet paper, a towel and soap, as well as pillow cases and two thin cotton sheets (a *kanga* or *kitenge* will do) to replace the ubiquitous nylon sheets, many of which are too small for the beds.

Security is also an important factor: obviously, the more the establishment relies on its bar for income, the less secure it will be (you could bring your own padlock, though it won't fit all doors). Leaving valuables in rooms is usually safe enough – but don't leave them lying around too temptingly and try to take the key with you when you go out. If you do decide to leave stuff with the management, ensure you get an **itemized receipt** for *everything* you leave, including banknote serial numbers – rumours circulate of real notes being replaced by forgeries.

If you're **driving**, some lodgings have lock-up yards where you can park – helpful in avoiding mysteriously deflated tyres and lost wing mirrors and wipers. Don't leave anything inside a car at any time of the day or night.

Hotels and lodges

More **expensive hotels** are distinctly variable. At the top of the range are the big tourist establishments (known as **lodges** in the game parks). Some are extremely good value; others are shabby and overpriced, so check carefully before splurging. It's worth reserving in advance at the more popular establishments, especially from December to February.

As a rule, expect to pay anything from Tsh8000 to Tsh30,000 for a decent double or twin room in a **town hotel**, with private bathroom, electricity, hot water, and breakfast included. Singles usually cost around seventy percent of a double. Out of the towns and on the coast, top-range hotels

Eco-friendly accommodation: myth and reality

Most of the lodges and tented camps in Tanzania's wildlife areas nowadays claim to be "eco-friendly". Although some are genuine about this, many have simply appropriated the "ecotourism" tag for business purposes. For a start, however eco-friendly they may claim to be, it's worth remembering that the very existence of a lodge or hotel inevitably has a negative impact on the environment, no matter how many safeguards are used. Equally, although many establishments boast that they are built entirely from natural or local materials, the very scale of many of these places means that the collection of materials for their construction was itself a huge blow to the environment: many coastal lodges, for instance, are constructed from a mixture of endangered tropical hardwoods, mangrove poles and coral ragstone, all of which continue to be exploited in a wholly unsustainable fashion. In short, don't believe the hype, and if a really ecologically sound holiday is important to you, steer clear of the big tourist places and stay instead in local guest houses.

We've tried, so far as possible, to mention ecological factors in our reviews, and have also excluded establishments that were built or are maintained in ways that damage the environment. The main exception to this rule – reluctantly so – are most of the lodges around the rim of the Ngorongoro Crater. These have been accused for many years of un-ecological practices, but cannot practically be excluded due to the huge number of tourists who stay there. We've also excluded a number of lodges, tented camps and safari companies that, in our opinion, operate unethically. All this is not to say that all the hotels and companies reviewed in this guide are guaranteed to be ethical –and feedback from travellers is always welcome.

On the positive side, a recent and very encouraging trend in lodges and tented camps outside national parks has been to involve local communities as owners and managers, as well as staff; these places are noted in the guide.

and lodges are normally quoted in dollars and on a half- or full-board basis, and prices can go right into orbit ($80–$300 is usual, with a few places costing over $1000). Most of these hotels cut their prices in low season (April–June, see the box on p.29), and many also have much lower rates for Tanzanian residents, which you might be able to wangle if you can do a good enough impression of a seasoned expatriate.

Tanzania's **mid-range** hotels vary from the slightly grand but faded to newer establishments catering to the country's emerging middle class. A few are fine – either delightfully decrepit or bristlingly smart and efficient – but most are boozy and uninteresting. In general, it adds more colour to your travels to mix the cheapest lodgings with the occasional night of luxury.

Camping

Tanzania has enough **campsites** to make carrying a tent worthwhile, and it's cheap too, at around $3–5 per person for a pitch, sometimes less. Camping rough is often a viable option, too. **Campsites** in the national parks are usually very basic, though a handful of privately owned sites have more in the way of facilities. In rural areas, hotels will often let you camp discreetly in their grounds.

There are **public campsites** in most of Tanzania's national parks; they're not cheap ($20 per person), but they don't require advance booking. The national parks also have some **special campsites**: these are restricted sites which you can reserve on an exclusive basis for your private use, though they cost double a standard pitch. Some sites are especially attractive and often get fully booked up to a year in advance, but they are all quite devoid of facilities. To book them, either write to the warden in charge of the park (addresses are given in the guide), or visit or write to TANAPA's headquarters in Arusha (p.394). Reliable travel agents can book things for you, though they'll charge a premium and are likely to push their own safaris as part of the deal. The locations of both kinds of campsite are liable to change every few years to avoid damaging the environment. Incidentally, you're no longer allowed to collect **firewood** in the parks; some parks provide firewood for campers, others insist that you use gas cartridges (available in Arusha and Dar es Salaam).

Camping rough depends on whether you can find a suitable space; note that any form of camping is officially illegal in Zanzibar (though a handful of hotels allow it in their grounds). In the more heavily populated highland districts on the mainland, you should ask someone before pitching a tent – a fire may worry local people and delegations armed with *pangas* sometimes turn up to see who you are. Out in the wilds, hard or thorny ground is likely to be the only obstacle (a foam sleeping mat is a good idea if you don't mind the bulk). During the dry seasons, you'll rarely have trouble finding wood for a fire, so a stove is optional, but don't burn more fuel than you need and take care to put out the fire (or embers) completely before leaving: wildfires put lives and livelihoods at risk. A torch is another useful piece of equipment.

Safety

Camping out is generally pretty safe, but there are some places you should avoid. Don't camp right by the road, in dried-out riverbeds, or on trails used by animals going to water, and avoid areas where cattle-rustling is prevalent (anywhere on the fringes of Maasailand, for example), and anywhere on the Kenyan border: border clashes between different clans of the same tribe are common, especially in Kuria-land (north of Musoma), and north of Lake Natron, where Somali bandits have been operating over the last decade and a half. Things have been calm there for a couple of years, but there are no guarantees. In addition, sleeping out on any but the most deserted of Indian Ocean beaches is an open invitation to robbers.

On the subject of **animals**, if you're way out in the bush, lions and hyenas are very occasionally curious of fires, but will rarely attack unless provoked. Nonetheless, take local advice about lions, which have taken to terrorizing some districts, especially Kondoa and Babati north of Dodoma, and Songea and Tunduru in the far south. Usually more dangerous are **buffalo**, which you should steer well clear of (especially old solitary males), and lake- or river-side **hippo**, who will attack if they fear that you're blocking their route back to water.

Eating and drinking

Not surprisingly, perhaps, Tanzania has no great national dishes: the living standards of the majority of people don't allow for frills and food is generally plain and filling. That said, so long as you're adventurous and know what to look for, you could be pleasantly surprised.

In cheaper places, **lunch** is typically served from noon to 2pm, and **dinner** no later than 8pm; at other times you may only have fare from the dreaded display cabinet to choose from. Having said that, restaurants learning more towards expatriates and tourists tend to stay open all day.

Tanzanian food

In terms of culinary culture, only **the coast** has developed a distinctive style of regional cooking, influenced by its contact with Indian Ocean trade and dominated by seafood and rice, flavoured with coconut, tamarind and exotic spices. This is most memorably sampled in the fantastic open-air market held every evening at Forodhani Gardens in Stone Town. You can also find some very good fresh fish around the lakes, where another speciality is **dagaa** – tiny freshwater sardines that are fried in palm oil and eaten whole.

Wherever you are, you'll never go hungry. In any **hoteli** (a small restaurant, not a hotel), there are always a number of predictable dishes intended to fill you up as cheaply as possible, often for well under Tsh1000. **Rice** and **ugali** (a stiff cornmeal porridge) are the national staples, eaten with chicken, goat, beef, or vegetable stew, various kinds of spinach, beans and sometimes fish. Meals are usually served in a metal platter with hollows for each dish, so you can mix things as you wish.

Portions are usually gigantic, and half-portions (*nusu*) aren't much smaller. But even in small towns, more and more **cafés** are appearing where most of the menu is fried – chips, eggs, fish, chicken, burgers and more chips. Indeed, chips have spawned one species of junk food that's peculiarly Tanzanian: **chipsi mayai** (meaning "chips-eggs"): a Spanish-style omelette with chips replacing the boiled potatoes. **Snacks**,

which can easily become meals, include samosas (*sambusa*), chapatis, miniature kebabs (*kababu*) and roasted corn cobs (*mahindi*). **Andazi** – sweet, puffy, deep-fried dough cakes – are made before breakfast and served until evening time, when they've become cold and solid.

The standard blow-out feast for most Tanzanians is a huge pile of **nyama choma** (roast meat). *Nyama choma* is usually eaten at a purpose-built *nyama choma* bar, with beer and music (live or otherwise) as the standard accompaniment, along with optional *ugali* and spinach. You go to the kitchen or a booth and order by weight (half a kilo is plenty) direct from the butcher's hook; you can also order grilled plantain (*ndizi*) at the same time – two per person is enough. There's usually a choice of goat, beef or mutton as well as chicken. After roasting, the meat is brought to your table on a wooden platter and chopped into bite-size pieces with a sharp knife. The better places also bring you a small bowl of **homemade chilli sauce** (*pilipili hoho*) – at their best, these are subtle and fresh, and laced with plenty of tomato, onion and lemon or vinegar. The more basic places simply cut up a green chilli pepper for you; these vary in strength from moderately hot to incendiary.

You'll usually find plenty of foodstalls out on the streets – especially around bus stations and at night – selling small skewers of grilled meat (goat is tastiest, and you'll also sometimes find beef) called **mishkaki** (or *mishikaki*), served with salt and (optional) chilli. Other commonly available street food includes grilled **cassava** (*muhogo*) doused with a watery chilli sauce – it's usually mouth-drying, though it can occasionally be deliciously moist. Other popular choices include grilled corn cobs (*mahindi*) and – you've guessed it – chips.

Fruit in Tanzania is a delight. Bananas,

Being invited to eat at home

If you're invited to a meal at someone's home, do accept – it's something of an honour both for you and for the people whose home you visit. In any case, the food is likely to be much, much better than what you'll find in an average *hoteli*. Taking small gifts for the family is in order. Elder men often appreciate tobacco, whether "raw" (a piece of a thick, pungent coil that you can buy in markets everywhere) or a couple of packets of filterless Sigara Nyota cigarettes, nicknamed *sigara ya babu* – grandfather's cigarettes. Women appreciate anything that helps keep down their household expenses, be it soap, sugar, tea or a few loaves of bread. Kids, of course, adore sweets – but give them to the mother to hand out or you'll end up getting mobbed. Make sure you leave a big hole in your stomach before coming: your hosts will probably make a huge play out of the fact that you're not eating enough, even if you've just gobbled up twice what anyone else has.

Before eating, one of the girls or women of the house will appear with a bowl, soap and a jug of hot water to wash your hands with. Food is eaten by hand from a communal bowl or plate – though you may be presented with a plate and cutlery, it's best to try to eat with your hand: the gesture will be valued. When eating, use only your right hand. *Ugali* is eaten by taking a small piece with your fingers and rolling it in the palm of your hand to make a small ball. The ball is then dipped in sauce and popped into your mouth. And, finally, don't worry about making a mess – your hosts will be surprised if you don't.

---

avocados, papayas and pineapples can be found in markets all year round; mangoes and citrus fruits are more seasonal. Look out for passion fruit (both the familiar shrivelled brown variety and the sweeter and less acidic smooth yellow ones), tree tomatoes, custard apples and guavas – all distinctive and delicious. On the coast, roasted **cashew nuts** (*korosho*) are cheap, especially in the south around Lindi, Mtwara and Masasi, where they're grown and processed, while **coconuts** are filling and nutritious, going through several satisfying changes of condition (all edible) before becoming the familiar hairy brown nuts.

Breakfast

The first meal of the day varies widely. Stock **hoteli fare** consists of a cup of sweet *chai* and a doorstep of white bread, thickly spread with margarine, occasionally with scrambled eggs or an omelette. At the other extreme, if you're staying in a **luxury hotel** or lodge, breakfast is usually a lavish expanse of hot and cold buffets that you can't possibly do justice to. In the average **mid-priced hotel**, you'll get an English-style "full breakfast" – greasy sausage, bacon, eggs and baked beans, with instant coffee (in a pot) and soggy toast.

Cheaper than either, and usually tastier, is **supu** – a light broth made from bony pieces of meat, chicken or fish. It may contain sweetmeats, can be spicy, and serves as a great hangover cure; it's usually eaten with chapati or rice. Other good and filling traditional breakfasts include *uji* (especially in Moshi), a porridge or gruel made of millet; and *mtori* (in Arusha and westwards), a light banana soup.

Restaurants

Eating out is not a Tanzanian tradition and few Tanzanians would consider it cheap. Standard tourist restaurants charge Tsh4000–5000, whilst fancier establishments can charge anything upwards of Tsh15,000 for a large spread of international-style dishes. The main concentration of these kinds restaurants (including Indian, Chinese and Italian) is, predictably, in the tourist areas of Arusha, Moshi, Dar es Salaam and Zanzibar, with a few more in Dodoma, Iringa, Mbeya, Morogoro and Mwanza. Outside these places you're limited to whatever the local *hotelis* happen to have prepared that day. The **bigger hotels and lodges** usually have buffet lunches (about $12–15), which can be great value if you're really hungry.

Vegetarians

If you're **vegetarian**, tourist-class hotels usually have a meat-free pasta dish available each day, and you can also eat remarkably well at Indian and Chinese restaurants (found in Arusha, Moshi, Dar es Salaam and Zanzibar). Local *hotelis* have plenty of choice, too, and not only the insidious chips and omelettes: most can be relied upon to supply beans and vegetables, and the better ones may be able to rustle up a salad.

Most Tanzanian staples are vegetarian, like *ugali*, cassava, *uji*, roast corn cobs, and all manner of bananas (*ndizi*), whether grilled, boiled, stewed (as in *mtori*), roasted or just plain. Many of these are served with *supu* – not the early morning broth, but a sauce. This can be vegetarian but is more likely to be based on a meat stock.

If you eat fish, you'll be in paradise in Zanzibar. Elsewhere, fish is generally limited to *tilapia*, dried and trucked in from the lakes in the west, which can be good depending on how it's cooked. Lastly, don't forget Tanzania's glorious fruits; mangoes, bananas and coconuts can be found almost everywhere, and there are always seasonal specialities in each region.

Non-alcoholic drinks

The national beverage is **chai** – tea. Universally drunk at breakfast and as a pick-me-up at any time, it's a weird variant on the classic British brew: milk, water, lots of sugar and tea leaves, brought to the boil in a kettle and served scalding hot. Its sweetness must eventually cause diabolical dental damage, but it's curiously addictive and very reviving. Instant **coffee** – fresh is rare – is normally available in *hotelis* as well (together with powdered milk), but it's expensive (ironically, given that Tanzania is a major coffee-producer) and so not as popular as tea. Moshi is probably the best place for coffee; the Arabica from Kilimanjaro is delightfully subtle and absolutely world class.

Soft drinks (called sodas; large half-litre bottles are called *bonge*) are usually very cheap, and crates of Coke and Fanta find their way to the wildest corners of the country, though, uncooled, they're pretty disgusting. Krest bitter lemon is a lot more pleasant, and Krest also makes an Indian tonic and a ginger ale, though they're watery and insipid – Stoney Tangawizi has more of a punch. You can also get plain soda water. There are fresh **fruit juices** available in the towns, especially on the coast. Passion fruit, the cheapest, is excellent, though nowadays it's likely to be watered-down concentrate; you'll also find orange juice, pineapple and sometimes tamarind juice (*mkwaju*) mixed with water – very refreshing, and worth seeking out.

Ordinary bottled **mineral or spring water** is expensive, but can be bought almost everywhere. **Tap water** (see p.25) is usually quite drinkable, but seek local advice.

Alcoholic drinks

Tanzania has a strong drinking culture, inherited from the tradition of elders sharing drinks while sorting out the affairs of the day. Most tourists drink in bars; hard-up locals patronize *pombe* houses to partake of rough-and-ready local brews.

Beer and cider

Tanzanian **beer** is generally good. Prices vary according to where you drink it: from around Tsh650 for a half-litre bottle in local dives up to Tsh1500 in poshier establishments. Safari (5.5 percent), Kilimanjaro (4.5 percent) and Tusker (4.2 percent) are the biggest selling **lagers**; other brands include Kibo Gold (5.2 percent) and the more expensive Castle Lager (5 percent). You can also find Pilsner Ice and Pilsner Extra, which apparently make your breath smell sweeter to the missus when you stagger back late. Everyone adopts a brand, even though you can't reliably tell the difference between any of them, and certainly not after you've drunk a few. More distinctive brews include Ndovu (4.2 percent), which has a sickly-sweet smell which isn't to everyone's liking, and the infamous Bia Bingwa (7 percent) whose name means "Hero Beer", possibly because a few of these will see you flat out on the ground like Samson. A similarly lethal concoction found in Dar and Moshi is called, for no apparent reason, The Kick.

There are also two **stouts**: a head-thumping version of Guinness which, at 7.5 percent, owes more to soya sauce in texture and flavour than pure genius; and Castle Milk Stout (6 percent), a milder and more palatable competitor from South Africa. Alternatively, you could always try one of the country's two **fake ciders**: 49er and Redds Cool, both sickly-sweet concoctions of fermented malt, sugar and artificial flavourings that have never been near a real apple.

There are two points of **beer etiquette** worth remembering. First, never take your bottle out of the bar (bottles carry deposits and this is considered theft). Second, in local bars, men buy each other beers and accumulate them on the table in a display of mutual generosity. When they've drunk enough, each customer takes his unopened presents back to the bar and stores them for the next day.

Pombe

Unlike Kenya, where home-brewing and distilling is illegal, things are much laxer in Tanzania – to the extent that Kenyan revellers living near the border have got into the habit of sneaking over to Tanzania for a cheap piss-up before staggering back into the arms of the Kenyan police. You can sample **pombe** (home-brewed beer) all over the country and under many different names: the versions available are as varied in taste and colour as their ingredients, which may include fermented sugar cane (*boha*), maize and honey (*kangara*), bananas and sorghum (*rubisi*), bamboo juice (*ulanzi*), barley (*busa*) or just millet, all sometimes mixed with herbs and roots for flavouring and/or to kick off the process of fermentation. The results are frothy and deceptively strong, and can cause you to change your plans for the rest of the day.

On the coast, merely lopping off the growing shoot at the head of a coconut tree produces a naturally fermented **palm wine** called *tembo*. The drink remains popular despite the majority of people on the coast being Muslim, though there's usually a furtive discretion about *tembo* drinking sessions. Still, keep the Kiswahili proverb in mind: "If the maker of *tembo* is praised for his wine, he adds water to it" (*mgema akisifiwa tembo hulitia maji*).

Whilst *tembo* and *pombe* are generally quite safe – and indeed still play an important part in traditional festivities – the same cannot be said for traditional spirits – **chang'aa** – treacherous and frequently contaminated firewaters that regularly kill drinking parties en masse, filling a niche in the East African press currently occupied in the West by crack cocaine.

Spirits and liqueurs

Most bars stock a limited range of **spirits**, invariably including some dodgy local whiskies and vodkas. By far the most popular bottled spirit is the homegrown and very drinkable **Konyagi** (35 percent), something between weird gin and lukewarm water with a kick. It's generally drunk to get drunk, often with bitter lemon, Indian tonic or soda water. The recently introduced Konyagi Ice is a mix of Konyagi and bitter lemon. **Liqueurs**, where you can find them, are pretty much the same as anywhere else in the world, though it's worth seeking out a chocolate and coconut liqueur called Afrikoko, and the South African Amarula, similar to Bailey's.

Wines

Tanzania produces some quite palatable **wines**, notably in West Usambara. These are produced by the Benedictine Fathers in Sakharani near Soni under the name Sakharani Usambara (see p.355); quality varies from average to good. You can buy it in Lushoto, and in supermarkets or wine shops in Dar es Salaam, Arusha and even Stone Town in Zanzibar. Rather less tempting are the trio of wines produced by Tanganyika Vineyards in Dodoma, purveyors of what is widely considered to be among the world's worst plonk. Choose from Makutapora Rosé, Makutapora Red and Chenin Blanc.

Other alternatives worth trying are **papaya wine** and **banana wine** – look out for the latter especially in Moshi, Arusha (where you can visit the Meru Banana Wine factory; see p.385) and Lushoto (whose Doshi Banana Wine is produced by the Catholic Mission of the Montessori Sisters; see p.354). Both are an acquired taste, but it's one you might get used to quickly, since the stuff is both potent and much cheaper than imported wine.

Post, phones and email

Keeping in touch by post and telephone is easy if not fantastically reliable. Things do go missing, however – use a courier if you need to send valuables. Tanzania's telephone network is improving, though it's still expensive for anything other than local calls – no surprise, then, that Tanzanians have embraced mobile phones and the internet with gusto.

Mail

There are **post offices** in all Tanzanian towns and throughout rural areas; opening times are generally Monday to Friday 8am to 4.30pm and Saturday 9am to noon. You'll also find branches of international **courier companies** like DHL and TNT in major towns and cities; they're a good deal more reliable for parcels and valuables than the postal system.

Poste restante is fairly reliable in major towns like Arusha, Dar es Salaam, Dodoma, Iringa, Mbeya, Morogoro and Mwanza. Make sure people writing to you mark your surname clearly; it's also worth looking under your first (and any other) names. You may have to show your passport to collect mail, and there's a fee of Tsh200 for every item received. Smaller post offices will also hold mail, but your correspondent should mark the letter "To Be Collected". Parcels can be received, too, but expect to haggle over import duty when they're opened. Ask the sender to mark packages "Contents to be re-exported from Tanzania", which might be helpful in your discussions.

Sending mail

Prepaid **aerograms** are the cheapest way of writing home, but can be difficult to find. If you want speedy delivery for small **parcels**, it's worth paying a little extra for EMS express; there's a branch at most post offices. **Airmail** takes about five days to Europe and ten days to North America and Australasia. **Stamps** can be bought at post offices and large hotels. Sending a postcard by airmail costs Tsh400 to Europe, Tsh500 to North America and Australasia. Airmailed letters under 20g cost Tsh600 to Europe and Tsh800 elsewhere; letters up to 50g cost Tsh1500 to Europe, Tsh1800 elsewhere.

Addresses in Tanzania

All addresses in Tanzania have a post office box number (PO Box or SLP, its Kiswahili equivalent) except out in the sticks, where some are just given as "Private Bag" or "PO", followed by the location of the post office. There's no home delivery service. In large towns, business and office addresses are usually identified by the "House" or "Building" in which they're situated.

Surface mail isn't significantly cheaper, and is unreliable.

The cheapest way to send **parcels** is via surface mail, but this is achingly slow (three to four months is the norm), and there are frequent reports of things going missing – you can minimize the risk by wrapping the parcel like your grandmother wrapped Christmas presents (think Egyptian mummy). Parcels must be no more than 105cm long and the sum of the three sides less than 200cm; they must also be wrapped in brown paper and tied with string. Take whatever you want to send unwrapped to the post office, as the contents have to be checked by a customs officer prior to posting. A 15–20kg parcel to Europe costs Tsh37,000, slightly more to the Americas or Australasia. **Airmail parcels** are much quicker and more reliable, but also shockingly expensive. The basic cost is Tsh8000 for the first 500g (Tsh9000 elsewhere) plus Tsh2500/3000 for each additional 200g. Registering the parcel costs Tsh500 more, and using the express service adds another Tsh600.

The advent of email has largely kicked **faxes** into oblivion. Still, if you need one, the larger post offices have them, and you can also find machines in private telephone offices.

Telephones

Tanzania's terrestrial telephone network is run by Tanzania Telecom – or **TTCL**. There are also five mobile phone operators. The terrestrial network is gradually getting more reliable, though there are times when valid numbers just won't work. Most of the country is now covered by automatic direct dial telephone exchanges, but there are still a large number of manual exchanges in operation in more remote areas. For these numbers (generally two or three digits), dial the national operator (☎100) and give them the location and the number (e.g. "Kilwa Masoko 18"). The dialling tone is a continuous purring; a high-pitched interrupted tone means the number is engaged; a high-pitched continuous tone means there's no service for the number. It's not possible to make international **collect calls** (reverse-charge) from Tanzania.

You can **phone abroad** from any **TTCL office**; these are invariably found in or close to the main post offices of towns and larger rural settlements; opening hours vary widely. You pay in advance for a specified number of minutes (minimum three) and get your money back if you fail to get through, but not if the conversation ends up taking less time than you expected or if you get through to an answerphone – all very user-unfriendly. You shouldn't have a problem getting a connection to the UK, but be prepared to wait – sometimes for hours – for a connection to anywhere else, including the US.

Useful phone numbers

At present, TTCL is in the process of changing all telephone numbers to a standardized seven digits, though there are still a lot of four- and six-digit numbers in use; if these don't work, check with the local telephone office on how to convert them or ring **directory enquiries** on ☎135.

Country codes

Phoning abroad from Tanzania you'll need to dial ☎000 (unless you're ringing Kenya and Uganda) followed by the relevant country code (see below), followed by the subscriber's area code (minus the initial 0) and the number itself. **Phoning Tanzania from abroad**, the country code is ☎255.

- ☎ Australia 61
- ☎ Canada 1
- ☎ Ireland 353
- ☎ New Zealand 64
- ☎ UK 44
- ☎ US 1

Area codes

Area codes aren't needed when you're calling from within the same area. The exception is mobile telephone codes (☎0741, 0742, 0743, 0744 and 0747), which should be dialled wherever you are.

- ☎ 022 Dar es Salaam
- ☎ 023 Coast (Bagamoyo, Lindi, Masasi, Mtwara, Newala)
- ☎ 024 Zanzibar (Unguja, Pemba)
- ☎ 025 West and south (Kigoma, Kyela, Mbeya, Mpanda, Sumbawanga)
- ☎ 026 Centre (Dodoma, Ifakara, Iringa, Kondoa, Morogoro, Tabora)
- ☎ 027 North (Arusha, Moshi, Pangani, Pare, Tanga, Usambaras)
- ☎ 028 Northwest (Bukoba, Musoma, Mwanza)

Useful numbers

- ☎ 100 Operator (English)
- ☎ 135 Directory enquiries
- ☎ 112 Emergency services (but don't expect them to come in a hurry)

Much more convenient are the direct-dial **cardphones** (*simu ya kadi*) found outside most TTCL offices and in some bus stations, bars and hotels. The pre-paid cards (*kadi ya simu*) can in theory be bought at TTCL offices and in shops close to call boxes, though in practice they're often out of stock. They're sold in units of 40 (Tsh2000), 100 (Tsh5000) and 150 (Tsh7500). Cardphones also accept **charge cards** issued by international telephone companies. Some places still have **coin-operated call boxes**, though these are slowly being replaced by cardphones, and you'll need a good handful of Tsh100 coins to get anywhere.

Also convenient are a growing number of **private telephone bureaus**; charges here are rarely much higher than TTCL's, and in fact can sometimes be significantly cheaper. Cheapest of the lot, however, is **internet calling**, currently offered by a handful of internet cafés in Dar es Salaam and Arusha, which cuts the price of calls by up to seventy percent, albeit at the expense of low sound quality, drop-outs and a stuttering line.

Standard **costs** for local calls are relatively inexpensive at Tsh275 for three minutes. National calls aren't too bad either at Tsh740–1220 for three minutes; ringing a mobile costs Tsh1765 for three minutes. International rates, however, are painful: currently Tsh3325 per minute outside Africa, with only a small discount for longer calls. Calling from Zanzibar is much cheaper at around Tsh1800–2000 a minute. Using hotel phones should be avoided at all costs: you could end up paying anything up to $43 a minute to the US.

Some **useful words** include: phone (noun) *simu*; phone (verb) *kupiga simu*; phone book *kitabu cha simu*; phone number *namba ya simu*.

Internet and email

Given the expense and unreliability of other forms of communication, the use of the **internet and email** in Tanzania is rocketing. Most of Tanzania's larger towns are blessed with surprisingly fast broadband internet connections, and the proliferation of internet cafés may come as a surprise. At the same time, prices for internet access are well below what you would pay in Europe, averaging Tsh500 per hour in Dar, and Tsh1000 per hour elsewhere. Details of internet access are given in the "Listings" sections of major towns.

The media

Tanzania is a nation absorbed in its press, with many lively and outspoken newspapers, though, unfortunately for the visitor, most are in Kiswahili. The leading English-language daily is the The Guardian (and Sunday Observer), whose independence relies on the financial and political clout of tycoon Reginald Mengi. The Guardian's main competitor is the stodgy, government-owned Daily News (and Sunday News), strong on eastern and southern African news and with some syndicated international coverage, but spoiled by its slavish bias in favour of the ruling CCM party, which becomes outrageous around election time. There's also the daily Business News – though a more tedious read would be difficult to find.

Rest of the **weekly publications** is *The East African*, whose relatively weighty, conservatively styled round-up of the week's news in Kenya, Uganda and Tanzania is shot through with an admirable measure of justified cynicism. Its reporters and columnists are consistently incisive, articulate and thought-provoking, and it also carries the cream of the foreign press's news features – all in all a superb publication. A less substantial but equally impartial weekly is *The African*, combining an admirably combative and occasionally scurrilous editorial line with syndicated articles from Britain's *Guardian* newspaper. *The Express* is more downmarket but still entertaining. *The Financial Times* is almost totally occupied by business news.

Of the **foreign press**, the *Daily Telegraph*, *USA Today* and the *International Herald Tribune* get to all sorts of expatriate bastions. *Time* and *Newsweek* are widely hawked and, together with old copies of *The Economist*, filter through many hands before reaching street vendors (availability largely depends on what passengers left on the plane when arriving). Sunday and daily papers such as *The Times*, *Express* and *Mail* (and, more occasionally, the *Guardian*) can usually be found in Arusha and Dar or, a few days further on, at one or two other stores around the country.

One of the best of the locally published **magazines**, *Kitingoma* is the place for music fans, with loads on Tanzanian and Congolese bands; *Femina* is a women's magazine with the balls to address issues like AIDS and wife-beating directly; *Tantravel*, published by the tourist board, carries interesting features as well as saccharine holiday blurb; and *Tanzania Wildlife*, published in both English and Kiswahili (*Kakakuona*), contains superb in-depth articles on wildlife, ecology, people and conservation. All these magazines are published quarterly.

Radio and TV

Zanzibari **radio and television** are particularly noxious examples of state control. Much more enlightening are mainland Tanzania's stations. The government-run Radio Tanzania broadcasts mainly in Kiswahili but is good for getting to know traditional music. The station is now facing competition from several emerging independent networks, most of them based on a diet of imported soul and home-grown rap, dance and hiphop. These include the mellow Radio Free Africa (Arusha 89.0FM, Dar 98.6FM, Mbeya 88.8FM, Mwanza 89.8FM and nationwide at 1377KHz), Kiss FM (Arusha 89.9FM, Dar 89.0FM, Mbeya 96.4FM, Mwanza 88.7FM), and Clouds FM (Arusha 98.6FM, Dar 88.4FM). The **BBC World Service** is on 101.4FM in Dar and 105.60–105.80FM in Arusha. Elsewhere you can catch it on 21.47, 17.88, 15.42 or 6.135MHz. **Voice of America** can be picked up on shortwave at 21.49, 15.60, 9.525 or 6.035MHz, and also provides newsfeeds for several local FM stations.

Tanzanian **television**, much of it imported, is mainly in Kiswahili, but also has English programmes. Tanzania was the last country in the world to establish a national TV station, when the digital TVT (Television Tanzania) was launched in 2000. It currently only broadcasts to Dar es Salaam, so you'll usually find most TV sets tuned to ITV (Independent Television), which screens a number of locally produced soap operas as well as a whole lot of syndicated American sit-coms – though it can be shamelessly pro-government despite the "independent" moniker. There are also a trio of regional channels: Mwanza-based Star Television around Lake Victoria, Burudani Television in Arusha and Abood TV in Morogoro. **Satellite TV** is ubiquitous in upmarket bars, restaurant and hotels, and includes the usual diet of CNN newscasts, the Discovery Channel, DSTV and other favourites.

Opening hours, public holidays and festivals

In larger towns, major shops and tourist services are usually open Monday to Friday from 8.30am to 12.30pm, and from 2pm to between 5pm and 7pm; they also open on Saturday mornings. Museums are open daily from 9.30am to 5pm or 6pm. Government offices have earlier hours, usually Monday to Friday 7.30am to 2.30pm (or 8am to 3pm). Post offices generally open Monday to Friday 8am to 4.30pm and Saturday 9am to noon. Banks in major towns and cities open Monday to Friday 8.30am to 4pm and Saturday 8.30am to 1pm; rural branches close at 12.30pm weekdays, and at 10.30am on Saturday. In rural areas, many small shops double as *hotelis* or *chai* kiosks, and may open at almost any hour.

Public holidays

Both Christian and Muslim **public holidays** are observed, as well as secular national holidays. Government offices, banks, post offices and other official establishments are closed at these times. **Public holidays with fixed dates** are as follows: January 1 (New Year); January 12 (Zanzibar Revolution Day); April 26 (Union Day between Zanzibar and Tanganyika); May 1 (Workers' Day); July 7 (Industrial Day); August 8 (Farmers' Day); December 9 (Independence Day); December 25 (Christmas); December 26 (Boxing Day). If a holiday falls on a weekend the holiday is taken the following Monday. Another special day, if not yet a holiday, is 17 October, which marks the death of Tanzania's much-loved first President, Julius Nyerere.

Public holidays with variable dates are: Good Friday, Easter Sunday and Monday, and the Islamic festivals of Idd al Fitr, Idd al Haj and Maulidi (see dates below).

Islamic festivals

The lunar Islamic Hegira calendar is followed in Muslim communities throughout Tanzania. The Muslim year has either 354 or 355 days, so dates recede in relation to the Western calendar by ten or eleven days each year. Precise dates for Islamic festivals are impossible to give, especially as things depend on the sighting of the moon; if the sky is cloudy, things are put on hold for another day.

Only the month of fasting, **Ramadan**, will have much effect on your travels. This holy month is observed by all Muslims, who may not eat, drink or smoke between dawn and dusk during the whole of the month. Visiting the coast and (especially) Zanzibar during this month might leave a slightly strange impression, as most stores and restaurants are closed by day, though the evenings are much livelier than usual, and stores and restaurants stay open late. Public transport and official businesses continue as usual, however, and you can usually find a discreet non-Muslim restaurant serving food, but you'll offend sensibilities if you're seen eating, drinking or smoking on the street by day. **Idd al Fitr** (or *Fitri*), the two to four day holiday that follows the sighting of the new moon at the end of Ramadan, is a great time to be in Zanzibar, with feasting, merrymaking and firecrackers. Another good time to be on the coast or in Zanzibar is for **Maulidi al Nebi** (*Maulidi* for short), the Prophet Muhammad's birthday. Also fascinating, so long as the sight of blood leaves you unfazed, is the **Idd al Haj** (*Idd al-Adha*) – the one-day feast of the sacrifice – during which every family with the means sacrifices a sheep or goat to commemorate the unquestioning willingness of Ibrahim (Abraham) to sacrifice his son Ishmael (Isaac) for the love of God. Rooms fill up quickly for these festivals, so arrive a few days early or book in advance.

Approximate dates for these events over the next few years are as follows:

Idd al-Haj February 12, 2003; February 2, 2004; January 21, 2005; January 10, 2006; December 31, 2006.

Maulidi 14 May, 2003; 2 May, 2004; 21 April, 2005; 11 April, 2006.

Start of Ramadan 6 November, 2002; 27 October, 2003; 15 October, 2004; 4 October, 2005;

51

24 September, 2006.
Idd al-Fitr 6 December, 2002; 26 November,

2003; 14 November, 2004; 3 November, 2005; 24
October, 2006.

Outdoor activities

Tanzania has a huge but largely untapped potential for outdoor activities, including hiking, diving, snorkelling and birding. For information about cycling, see p.38; safaris are covered on p.55.

Hiking

Hiking gives you unparalleled contact with local people and nature, and you'll sometimes come across animals out in the bush. Don't ignore the dangers, however, and stay alert – especially in the far south and in the region between Dodoma and Arusha, where lion attacks are frequently reported.

Regulations restricting walking in **national parks and nature reserves** have recently been eased, making hiking safaris a real – and exciting – possibility, so long as you're accompanied by a guide (and sometimes an armed ranger). Parks which allow access on foot are: Arusha, Kilimanjaro, Udzungwa Mountains, Katavi, Mahale Mountains, Gombe, Selous and Ngorongoro. Other superb hiking areas include the rainforest at Amani Nature Reserve in East Usambara, the Uluguru Mountains, both the Pare Mountains and West Usambara, the Southern Highlands and Mount Hanang, near Babati to the south of Arusha. If you prefer **organized walking safaris**, a number of safari companies in Arusha (p.395) and Moshi (p.334) can sort things out.

Diving

There are excellent **scuba-diving** reefs along much of Tanzania's 800-kilometre coastline, though unless you've plenty of money and time to arrange a long trip, you're limited to places within easy reach of dive centres.

Pemba is generally reckoned the country's best dive centre, offering vertiginous drop-offs, largely unspoiled reefs and a stupendous variety of marine life; Misali Island is a particular gem. The waters around **Unguja** are shallower and sandier, and visibility is less, especially outside the November-to-March peak season. On the plus side, the corals here are excellent, there are many sheltered sites suitable for novices, and there are also a few wrecks within reach. Often forgotten, but also good, are the handful of islands off the coast **north of Dar es Salaam**, though some of the reefs here were badly damaged in the 1990s by dynamite fishing. There are also some good coral-fringed islets off **Bagamoyo**. To the south of Dar, the reefs around **Mafia Island** rival Pemba's, and are reckoned by some connoisseurs to be among the world's most beautiful. Accommodation is pricier here than elsewhere, however, but few visitors leave disappointed. In the far south, the newly created **Mnazi Bay–Ruvuma Estuary Marine Park** on the border with Mozambique is barely known, though the reefs here are in superb condition.

Diving is possible all year round, although the *kusi* **monsoon** (strongest June–Sept) is accompanied by choppy seas and strong currents that make the more exposed reefs inaccessible. There can also be strong winds in December and January. **Visibility** is best from November to March, before the long rains set in. Except for the east coast of Pemba, you'll always find good reefs for **beginners** (and most dive centres offer PADI-certified courses), whilst **experienced divers** can enjoy night dives, drift dives and deep drop-offs. On any dive you can expect to see a profusion of colourful tropical fish in extensive coral gardens, together with giant groupers, Napoleon wrasse and larger pelagic gamefish, including barracuda, kingfish, tuna and wahoo. Dolphins are frequently sighted, as are marine turtles (mainly green and hawksbill), blue spotted rays, manta rays and sometimes even whale sharks.

PADI dive courses

The Professional Association of Diving Instructors – **PADI** for short – is the leading international scuba-diving association, and sets the minimum standards for scuba-diving lessons. Pupils are given certification on completing courses which is recognized worldwide. The following PADI courses are offered by most of Tanzania's dive centres.

Discover Scuba (half-day): a quick introduction for novices, including a couple of sheltered dives, one normally in a swimming pool. Average cost $50–70.

Scuba Diver (2 days): a basic course (including three dives) which allows you to dive down to 12m and also counts towards the Open Water qualification. Around $200.

Open Water Course (4–5 days): a comprehensive diving course that gives you the right to dive to 18m with any qualified diver. Includes four dives plus a lot of theory (there's even an exam to pass). Around $350.

Advanced Open Water (3–5 days): the next stage on from Open Water, covering different diving conditions and including five dives (including one deep dive and a navigation dive). Around $250.

Rescue Diver (3 days): the next step up from Advanced Open Water, offering tuition on how to take care of other divers in emergencies. $350–400.

Divemaster (45 days): the biggie, which qualifies you to work as a professional dive guide – you'll have to do a minimum of sixty dives and ingest a massive amount of theory. $650–850.

Blue whales, though rarely seen, are sometimes heard on their northward migration towards the end of the year.

Costs vary between dive centres. A standard dive for qualified divers averages $40 ($50 for night dives), increasing to $70 if they involve a long boat ride. Things work out cheaper if you buy a package, usually six or ten dives, which can bring the price down to $25 a dive. If you're learning to dive, tuition costs are given in the box above.

Unless otherwise stated, the **dive centres** reviewed in this book were PADI-accredited at the time of writing, but it's worth checking out the official list on PADI's website at Ⓦ www.padi.com. **Safety** is obviously important, and many operators will refuse to take you down further than 25–27m, given the lack of decompression facilities in Tanzania – the nearest decompression chambers are in Mombasa (Kenya) and South Africa. Nonetheless, one or two companies do offer deeper dives, but only for very experienced divers. Most dive centres are based in mid to upper-range hotels: though you're not obliged to stay there, some places have little in the way of alternative cheap accommodation nearby.

Dive boats vary greatly. Some are state-of-the-art inflatables equipped with oxygen,

radio and powerful engines; others are converted dhows; whilst many are just normal boats with outboard motors. There are also a couple of live-aboard operators in Nungwi (Unguja) and Pemba. You don't need to bring your own **equipment**, though there's often a discount of about ten percent if you do. In-house equipment is usually fine, though bringing specialist gear like dive computers is a good idea as hiring can be expensive, if you can even find what you want. The warm water of the western Indian Ocean means that wetsuits aren't essential, although most companies routinely offer them and some recommend a thin wetsuit from June to September. At the time of writing, Tanzania's only dive centre with **Nitrox facilities** (enabling deeper and longer dives, averaging 40min at 30m) was the Jangwani Seabreeze Dive Centre north of Dar es Salaam (p.128). For **further information**, Anton Koornhof's *The Dive Sites of Kenya and Tanzania* (New Holland) is highly recommended, and also covers a good number of snorkelling sites.

Snorkelling

If the idea (or cost) of scuba-diving scares you, **snorkelling** is an excellent and cheap way of discovering the fantastic underwater world of East Africa. Snorkelling is possible virtually everywhere off the coast, and whilst some reefs are close enough to swim out to (especially off Unguja), it's worth getting a boat to reach the more beautiful but less accessible reefs. All the dive sites mentioned above, with the exception of eastern Pemba, have shallow reefs suitable for snorkelling: **Chumbe Island** and **Mnemba Atoll** off Unguja, and **Misali Island** off Pemba are especially recommended. There are also good snorkelling reefs off **Pangani** and **Ras Kutani** on the mainland, as well as fresh water snorkelling at the north end of **Lake Nyasa** near Matema, remarkable for its extraordinary number of colourful cichlid fish species.

It's definitely worth bringing your own gear if you plan to do much snorkelling, since It costs anywhere between Tsh1000 and Tsh9000 to rent snorkelling equipment for a

day. The price of **renting a boat** is equally variable: some fishermen will happily take you out for Tsh2000 per person, while dive centres and beach hotels might charge fifteen times as much.

Birding

Tanzania boasts over 1100 **bird species**, including endangered species and several dozen endemics (species unique to Tanzania, and often only found in a particular forest or mountain range). The best time for birding is from November to March, when resident species are joined by Eurasian and Palearctic winter migrants. It's impossible to recommend one area over another, as every place has something special. Highlights include Tarangire National Park, which contains over 350 recorded species. For endemics, the rainforest at Amani Nature Reserve in East Usambara is the place to

---

Responsible diving and snorkelling

Coral reefs are among the most fragile ecosystems on earth, consisting of millions of individual living organisms, called polyps. Solid though it seems, coral is extremely sensitive, and even a small change in sea temperature can have disastrous effects – even now, many sections of Tanzania's reefs show the scars of the mass coral bleaching that followed the 1997–98 El Niño event, which killed up to ninety percent of coral in places. You can minimize the impact that you have on a reef when diving or snorkelling by following the following common-sense rules.

Dive and swim carefully. Never touch the corals. Some polyps can die merely by being touched, and all suffocate if covered with silt or sand stirred up by a careless swipe of fins (flippers). For this reason, some companies don't provide fins for snorkellers. If you do wear fins, always be aware of where your feet are, and use your hands to swim when you're close to anything. If you're inexperienced, keep your distance from the coral to avoid crashing into it if you lose your balance. If you haven't scuba-dived for a while, take a refresher course and practice your buoyancy control in a swimming pool first.

Do not touch, handle or feed anything. This is both for your own safety (many corals and fish are poisonous or otherwise dangerous) and to avoid causing stress to fish and interrupting feeding and mating behaviour. Although several companies encourage it, do not feed fish. In some species, feeding encourages dependence on humans and upsets the natural balance of the food chain.

Do not take anything. Collecting shells, coral and starfish for souvenirs disrupts the ecosystem and is illegal, both in Tanzania and internationally. Getting caught will land you in serious trouble. Similarly, do not buy shells, corals or turtle products. With no market, people will stop collecting them. Taking a beautiful seashell might also deprive a hermit crab of a home, and certainly deprives other visitors of the pleasure of seeing it after you.

When mooring a boat, ensure you use established mooring points to avoid damaging corals. If there are no buoys, drop anchor well away from the reef and swim in.

head for, while other Eastern Arc Mountain ranges – like Uluguru and Udzungwa – also contain endemics. Close to Udzungwa, the Kilombero floodplain has also turned up some endemics.

A recommended Tanzanian company for avid twitchers is the East African Safari and Touring Company in Arusha (p.397), which has enthusiastic guides and includes Tarangire, Udzungwa, Uluguru Mountains, the Usambaras and Ruaha National Park in its itineraries (around $120–180 per person per day). A good website on Tanzanian birding is the Birding & Beyond Safaris site at Ⓦwww.tanzaniabirding.com, which has a comprehensive bird checklist and information on endemics.

Safaris

Tanzania has a higher percentage of protected wildlife areas than any other country on earth, with 27 percent of its land given over to eleven national parks, thirty-eight game reserves and numerous forest reserves – as well as some forty "wildlife management areas" and several other kinds of protected area.

The country's **national parks** are administered by the refreshingly efficient **TANAPA** (Tanzania National Parks Authority). The parks are total sanctuaries: there are no settlements other than tourist lodges and tented camps, and the exploitation of wildlife and other resources is not allowed. Flanking the national parks are a series of government-run **game reserves** that act as a protective buffer for the parks, at least in theory. Human activity in these areas is tolerated, although the exact extent of this activity depends on the corruptibility of the politicians and officers in charge. Trophy hunting by tourists is allowed here and in the **wildlife management areas**. The **Ngorongoro Conservation Area**, meanwhile, has its own special status which gives privileges to Maasai pastoralists – in theory, at least, though in practice they have been gradually driven out by the openly antagonistic park administrators.

All parks and a handful of reserves are open to private visits as well as organized safaris. A few – notably the Serengeti, Lake Manyara and Tarangire national parks, plus the Ngorongoro Conservation Area – have been extensively developed for tourism and have plenty of graded tracks, signposts, lodges and the rest. There's virtually no kind of **public transport** inside any of the parks, apart from buses from Dar or Morogoro to Iringa (which cut through Mikumi National Park); the Tazara railway (which skirts the northern fringes of Selous); and the road between Mpanda and Sumbawanga (which goes through Katavi). There's also a weekly bus between Mwanza and Arusha that goes through Serengeti and Ngorongoro, although the legal status of this isn't clear, and it may be suspended in future.

Entry fees

Park entry fees are charged per person per day, so if you stay overnight you have to pay for two days. Game reserves charge per 24 hour period (so if you arrive in the afternoon you can stay overnight and leave the next morning). Prices are fixed in dollars, and tourists must pay in hard currency (travellers' cheques are accepted).

You're meant to pay in advance at the park gate for the entire length of your stay, though in practice it's possible to pay for extra days on leaving if you've stayed longer than you originally intended. Fees vary according to the popularity and uniqueness of the park. The most expensive are the duo containing chimpanzees: Gombe ($100) and Mahale Mountains ($50). Next down are Kilimanjaro and Serengeti ($30), followed by Arusha, Lake Manyara and Tarangire ($25) Entrance to Katavi, Mikumi, Ruaha, Rubondo and Udzungwa, as well as Selous, costs $15. Entrance fees for children range from $5 to $20

National Parks

Arusha Contains a range of habitats up the slopes of beautiful Mount Meru (4566m), plus a wealth of wildlife.

Gombe Stream On the shore of Lake Tanganyika, famous for its chimpanzees, and also contains some gorgeous groundwater forest.

Katavi Little-visited park best known for its seasonal floodplains and large concentrations of plains game, including one of Africa's largest buffalo populations, and over 400 bird species.

Kilimanjaro Africa's highest mountain (5892m) – an exhausting five- or six-day hike to the top.

Lake Manyara Smallest of the Northern Circuit parks, famous for its flocks of flamingoes.

Mahale Mountains Several chimpanzee communities and an impressive mountain range on the shore of Lake Tanganyika.

Mikumi Lots of wildlife in a mixture of habitats, mainly *miombo* woodland and swamp. Frequent sightings of elephants.

Ngorongoro Conservation Area Gorgeous scenery in one of the world's largest unbroken volcanic craters, plus lots of plains game, including rhinos.

Ruaha One of Tanzania's wildest and most remote parks, consisting of undulating *miombo* woodland plateau broken by isolated hills and the Great Ruaha River valley.

Rubondo Island A paradise for bird-watchers in Lake Victoria; also contains an introduced colony of chimpanzees.

Serengeti The biggest concentration of wild mammals on earth, and scene of the famous annual plains game migration. Lions and hyenas are frequently seen.

Tarangire Great for elephants and gigantic baobab trees, plus lots of other wildlife and birds.

Udzungwa Mountains Fantastic hiking terrain through steep-sided rainforest; great for primates.

Reserves

Amani Nature Reserve Part of the East African Arc mountains, covered in incredibly biodiverse rainforests.

Jozani Forest Nature Reserve One of Zanzibar's few remaining patches of indigenous forest.

Lukwika–Lumesule Game Reserve Isolated park along the Ruvuma River in the far south; mainly migratory plains game.

Mkomazi Game Reserve Mainly low-lying plains, with migratory game from Kenya's Tsavo complex.

Msanjesi Game Reserve Close to Lukwika–Lumesule, with mainly migratory plains game.

Ngesi Forest Nature Reserve A patch of indigenous forest on Pemba Island.

Pugu Hills Conservation Area The closest forest to Dar, with nature trails.

Rondo Forest Reserve Rarely visited hill forest near Lindi.

Saadani Game Reserve Coastal reserve, with a combination of big game – including elephants – and forests, mangroves and river estuary.

Selous Game Reserve Mainly used for trophy hunting, though a small part in the north, including the fabulous Rufiji River floodplain, is reserved for "photographic tourism".

Protected marine areas

Chumbe Island Coral Park Stunning coral reefs for snorkelling, plus unique coastal forest cover.

Kilwa Marine Reserve Little-visited area of reefs, mangroves, salt flats and estuaries, with historic ruins nearby.

Mafia Island Marine Park One of the world's finest scuba-diving sites.

Misali Island Nature Reserve Off Pemba Island, with brilliant diving, decent snorkelling and some interesting nature trails.

Mnazi Bay–Ruvuma Estuary Marine Park Superb and unspoilt coral reefs and the mangrove-lined Ruvuma estuary.

Park regulations and etiquette

Driving Most parks have a speed limit of 50kph; 25kph is recommended. Keep only to authorized tracks and roads; off-road driving is illegal and causes irreparable damage to fragile vegetation. Please ask your driver to stay on the designated tracks, even if it means you won't get the best photographs, as he's only doing what he thinks you want. Driving is not allowed between 7pm and 6am.

Do not disturb So much is made of spotting the "Big Five" – elephant, lion, leopard, cheetah and rhino – that many safari drivers are encouraged to drive off-road in search of classic close-up shots. In fact, watching a family of warthogs can be much more rewarding than crowding around a pissed-off leopard. If you really need to eyeball animals, bring a pair of binoculars or watch a documentary: animals deserve the same respect you would accord visiting people in their own homes. Harassment disturbs feeding, breeding and reproductive cycles, and the presence of too many vehicles distresses the animals – cheetahs, for instance, only hunt during the day and, if surrounded by vehicles, will be deprived of a meal. Be quiet when viewing, ask the driver to switch off the engine, keep a minimum distance of 25m and do not, under any circumstance, get out of your vehicle.

Do not feed animals Feeding wild animals upsets their diet and leads to unnecessary dependence on humans. Habituated baboons, especially, can become violent if refused handouts.

Take only memories Do not uproot, pick, cut or damage any plant, and take care putting out campfires and cigarettes; don't chuck them out of your window – dozens of bush fires are started this way every year. Littering is equally stupid.

Vehicles of less than two tons are charged Tsh5000 ($30 if foreign-registered), though plans are afoot to massively increase these fees. The services of an **official guide** – optional if you're driving on main routes, obligatory if you're planning to get off the beaten track – is $10 for a few hours (nothing fixed), or $15 outside normal working hours. If the guide accompanies you on a walk, the cost is $20; an armed ranger – obligatory for walking in some areas – costs the same.

Apart from expensive lodges and tented camps, the only roofed **accommodation** is in park-run *bandas* or resthouses, costing $20–50 per person. **Campers** have to stay either in a recognized campsite ($20 per person) or in a "special campsite" ($40; see p.41). **Bookings** for special campsites and park-run accommodation can be made through the Office of the Director, Tanzania National Parks, TANAPA Complex, Dodoma Rd, Arusha (PO Box 3134, Arusha; ☎027/250 3471, ✉tanapa@habari.co.tz). Alternatively, write directly to the Warden in Charge at each park: addresses are given in the text.

Choosing a safari company

A number of **recommended operators** are reviewed on p.395 (Arusha; mainly for the northern wildlife areas) and p.124 (Dar es Salaam; for the centre and south), but it's notoriously difficult to find a company that's absolutely consistent. The companies reviewed in this book have pretty good records, but even they turn up the occasional duff trip. In any case, unless you have the luxury of a long stay, your choice will probably be limited by what's available at the time you arrive, though you may be able to use this to your advantage, as many companies discount unsold seats at the last minute. You could also try for a student discount – or in fact any other discount you can think of.

Bear in mind that a "four-day safari" actually means three nights, and that most of the first and last days are likely to be spent driving to and from the parks, so you'll actually only get two full days in wildlife areas. In terms of **group size**, the smaller the group, the more expensive the safari; on most trips you're likely to find yourself travelling with up to eight other people. For some people this

Be extremely careful when **choosing a safari company**, especially at the budget end. Of over 300 companies operating from Arusha and Dar es Salaam, only 120 are official licensed – which means that the rest are operating illegally if they take you inside a national park. We've only included the most reputable operators in our reviews (see pp.124–125); if you choose to go with a company that hasn't been reviewed (a new set-up, for example), the travellers' grapevine is the best way to get the latest recommendations. The following advice will also help you avoid getting stung.

Flycatchers A "flycatcher" is the nickname for a tout who approaches tourists on the street, in bus stations, train stations, airports and even hotels, with offers of cheap safaris, money changing, drugs and pretty much anything else a tourist might conceivably want. The advice is simple: never buy a safari from a company touted by flycatchers: 95 percent of flycatchers represent illegal or otherwise disreputable outfits, and any company worth its reputation does not use flycatchers. Likewise, be extremely wary of any company offering you a free ride from the airport, whether they're Tanzanian or European, and no matter how professional their appearance or smooth their patter.

Check the blacklist The tourist board offices in Arusha (p.373) and Dar es Salaam (p.81) maintain a blacklist of safari operators which you should consult before handing over any money. Be sure to check the telephone or PO box numbers of your choice against those in the blacklist, as companies have an unsurprising tendency to change names as soon as they're blacklisted. Note, however, that the blacklist is far from comprehensive, and some blacklisted companies mysteriously disappear from the list after a few months of "punishment".

Booking ahead When booking from abroad, dozens of people get ripped off every year by paying hefty deposits to phantom or otherwise bad companies. If you book before coming, you're strongly advised to use one of the companies reviewed in this book. If the company isn't listed, contact the Tanzania Tourist Board to ask whether the company is registered and licensed, and (if yes) since when.

TALA licences A safari company is legally required to possess a valid TALA licence to take visitors into national parks or to Ngorongoro (the licence is not required if tours do not enter the parks). Demand to see the licence certificate, which should show both the current year and the correct company name (con-artists rent licences from each other) – don't accept a photocopy. And make sure that they really are the company they claim to be by checking that their physical address matches the one given in our review: there have been cases of con-artists using the names of reputable operators to get clients. The deadline for paying for licences, incidentally, is June, so there might be cases where the operator is using last year's licence: in these cases check with the tourist board. And remember that a licence doesn't necessarily guarantee quality – although the reputable companies will always be licensed, there's nothing stopping dodgy outfits from obtaining a licence in their first year (before the complaints roll in and they get blacklisted), and being blacklisted doesn't cause the licence to become invalid.

How long have they been around? Although a handful of perfectly decent operations start up every year, so do dozens of sham outfits. So, if a company has been established for more than two years you stand a better chance of avoiding duds. Ask how long they've been running and whether they changed their name recently – usually the sign of a blacklisted company. If you really want to be careful, take a note of the PO box numbers of blacklisted companies and compare them to those of your choice – while a blacklisted company will often change its name, physical address and phone number, the PO Box number usually remains the same. These tricks will exclude one or two genuine companies, but it's better than being conned.

Internet The existence of a company website is not everything it's cracked up to be. While many reputable companies have an Internet presence, not all do – some like to preserve the allure of word-of-mouth exclusivity, others say they have enough clients already. There have also been cases in the past where phantom companies have set up websites, leaving hapless punters to arrive at the airport with no one to meet them, no safari, and a whole lot of money down the drain. In similar vein, don't believe everything you read in newsgroups, forums and bulletin boards – a number of blacklisted and phantom companies have become quite sophisticated at plugging themselves (and rubbishing the opposition) with fake postings. Some people advise against using companies that have Hotmail or Yahoo addresses; although this seems unfair on companies without a private connection, it does get rid of a lot of dodgy outfits.

Appearances Companies whose offices comprise just a desk and a chair in a rented room should be avoided. And no electricity means unpaid bills, which means you should look elsewhere. The local nickname for these jokers is "briefcase companies".

Off-road driving Driving off-road in Tanzania's parks is illegal and destructive. Plenty of companies do it though, even some of the bigger ones. To check a company's morals, ask them innocently whether it would be possible to drive off-road for that perfect shot of a lion or leopard.

Comments book Don't believe everything you read in a comments book – few companies will show you complaints, and no one will ask a dissatisfied punter to sign their comments book. Ripped-out pages are a dead give-away for something they don't want you to read. Try asking them what kind of complaints they receive (there isn't a single safari company that doesn't receive complaints from time to time). If they say they never receive complaints, well... You could also try asking them about their complaints or refunds procedure.

Vehicles Find out how many vehicles the company owns – this will tell you whether they can offer prompt back-up if your vehicle gives up halfway through a safari. In addition, you should check out the vehicle you'll be travelling in: apart from getting an idea of its roadworthiness (see p.33), it's worth knowing that safari vehicles are legally obliged to display their company name and logo on each of the front doors, plus a visible vehicle licence in the name of the company. These measures aren't foolproof but they will weed out a few bad apples.

Who's really running the safari? Many companies accept bookings for safaris that are actually being run by another firm. If it's someone else, book it there instead – you'll save on commission, and getting redress if things go wrong will be easier than having to deal with a middleman. For the same reasons, you should check whether the vehicle you'll be using will be rented from another company.

TATO, ATTO and AATTO Many companies are members of tour and safari operators' organizations like TATO (Tanzania Association of Tour Operators; PO Box 6162, Arusha ℡027/250 6430; ⓦwww.safari.cc/tato) and ATTO (Association of Tanzanian Travel Operators; ℡027/254 4318). Don't pay too much heed to alleged membership of these: the logos are easily faked, and in any case the organizations have very little clout. TATO is the most respected, and although its membership list contains one or two bad apples (and a good number of hunting companies too), the list is by and large pretty respectable – you can see it at ⓦwww.safari.cc/tato.memlist.html.

doesn't matter, and indeed the larger operators (catering almost exclusively to US tour groups) are commonly seen in convoys of half a dozen vehicles. Nonetheless, group relations among the passengers can assume surprising significance in a very short time.

Types of safari

Before arranging the details, think about whether you want comfort or a more authentic experience. Taking internal flights as part of your trip — a so-called **"air safari"** – will add enormously to the cost and comfort of your trip and give you spectacular views, though in return you'll be left with a less intimate feel for Africa. On the other hand, long bumpy drives can be completely exhausting, while hours of your time may pass in a cloud of dust.

A standard **lodge safari** takes you from one game park lodge to another, using minibuses with lift-up roofs for picture-taking – make sure you get a window seat and ask how many passengers the vehicle will be carrying. The alternative to a standard lodge safari is a **camping safari**, also in a minibus, where the crew – or you, if it's a budget trip – put up your tents at the end of the day. You'll have to be prepared for a degree of discomfort with this kind of trip: you may not get a shower every night, the food won't be as lavish and the beer won't be so cold.

When going on a safari, it's important not to take too passive an attitude. Although some of the itinerary may be fixed, it's not all cast in stone, and daily routines may be altered to suit you and your fellow travellers – if you want to go on an early game drive, for example, don't be afraid to suggest you skip breakfast, or take sandwiches. As long as they know there will be reasonable tips at the end of the trip, most staff will go out of their way to help. **Tipping**, however, can often cause days of argument and misunderstanding. Groups are usually expected to organize themselves to give collective gratuities on the last day; good companies make suggestions in their briefing packs.

Costs

The cheapest reliable **budget safaris** go for between $85 and $120 per day, which includes park fees, transport (usually in a minivan) and accommodation in tents. The choice of operators is vast, with over 250 companies at the last count, though only around a hundred of these are licensed, and only half again are anything close to reliable.

As the competition in Arusha becomes more cut-throat, some budget camping operators, the majority illegal, are pushing safaris at the very bottom of the market. Any safari that is offered at much less than $80 per day is likely to be cutting corners: you won't be entering parks every day, and you'll be camping outside them to save money. If the operator is honest about this, that's fine – but if they claim otherwise, look elsewhere. See the box on pp.58–9 for more advice on avoiding bad companies.

Most **mid-range** operators ($120–$200 per day) offer pretty decent safaris, and may even offer accommodation in a lodge, rather than under canvas. The better safaris use 4WD Land Cruisers or even an open-sided lorry rather than minivans; these offer a more intimate bush experience, but visibility can be hampered in the rear seats. Try to establish what the maximum group size is and the type of vehicle that will be used, and be aware that maximum group sizes may become irrelevant if you end up travelling in a convoy of half a dozen vehicles, as frequently happens with the larger operators.

Although many companies offer **"tailor-made" safaris**, the hefty premium these tours attract seems hard to justify (although there are a handful of exceptional outfits whose expertise justifies the cost). You'll also be treated to luxurious touches like champagne breakfasts, fly-camps in the bush (set up in advance of your arrival by a support crew), and expert expat guides (who seem to model themselves on the white hunter types in *Out of Africa*). The main disadvantages to such Hemingwayesque capers are the cost (up to $1000 a day) and the almost total exclusion of Tanzanians from both the safari and its profits – most of these outfits are owned by Europeans and South Africans.

Complaints

First off, it's best to avoid **complaints** by choosing a reputable company – you've only yourself to blame if a $75 safari bought off the street turns sour. Also, be understanding about things outside a company's control – like bad weather, a lack of animals, and breakdowns caused by unforeseeable things like broken fuel-injection pumps, which even the best mechanics cannot predict. For justified complaints, the best operators (in all price ranges) should at least offer a partial refund or a replacement trip.

Should the operator not be forthcoming, there's unfortunately very little you can do to get a refund. You can, however, make things awkward for them in future. Alerting the tourist board may result in the company being blacklisted, and TATO can expel errant members – not that this castigation is worth much. Some people have even set up web-pages warning of their experiences and written to newsgroups, bulletin boards and the like, but the best way to get revenge is to write to the guidebooks: we're at ⊛ www.roughguides.com.

Photography

Tanzania is immensely photogenic, and if you take photography seriously the temptation is to takes loads of equipment. Remember, however, that SLR cameras and lenses are heavy, relatively fragile and eminently stealable. Except in the game parks (where some kind of telephoto is essential if you want pictures of animals rather than savanna), you don't really need cumbersome lenses. It's often easier and less intrusive to take a small compact.

Whatever you decide to take, **insure it** (if ordinary travel insurance won't cover it, check the insurers who advertise in photo magazines) and make sure you have a dust-proof camera bag. Take spare **batteries** – flashy, hyper-automated cameras are completely useless without juice (SLRs, in contrast, will usually work without a battery, it's just the light meter that goes dead). **Film** is not especially expensive, but bring all the slide and black-and-white film you'll need, as these can be difficult to find in Tanzania. Keep film cool by stuffing it inside a sleeping bag, or else wrapping it in newspaper or a (dry) towel. If you're away for some time, posting it home seems a good idea but is risky, even if registered: better to leave it with a reliable hotel or friend in Arusha or Dar. Processing in Tanzania has improved with the introduction of automatic machines (1hr service is not uncommon), but be aware that even machines can mess up your film, especially when cutting and mounting slides. A few places in Arusha have a decent enough reputation (see p.391). Prices for developing and printing 35mm film is on a par with the UK, but APS costs a fortune: typically Tsh700 for developing, Tsh1500 for the index, and Tsh200 (L), Tsh300 (H) and Tsh700 (P) for the prints.

Subjects

Animal photography is principally a question of patience: if you can't get close enough, don't waste your film, and always turn off the engine when taking photos from a vehicle. The question of **photographing people** is more tricky: you should never take pictures of people without asking their permission. The Maasai – Tanzania's most photographed people – are usually prepared to do a deal (at monopoly prices), and in some places you'll even find professional posers making a living at the roadside. If you're motivated to take a lot of pictures of people, you might consider lugging along a Polaroid camera – most people will be very pleased to have a snap. Or you could have a lot of photos of you and your family printed up with your address on the back, which should at least raise a few laughs when you try the exchange.

One thing is certain: if you won't accept that some kind of interaction and exchange is warranted, you won't get many pictures. Promising to send the subject a copy of the photo when you get home might work, but is decreasingly popular with subjects who look on the photo call as work and have fixed rates. Blithely aiming at strangers is arrogant; it won't make you any friends and

61
■

it may well get you into trouble. Note also that in Islamic areas, popular belief equates the act of taking a picture with stealing a piece of someone's soul.

It's also a bad idea to take pictures of anything that could be construed as strategic, including any military or police building, prisons, airports, harbours, bridges and His Excellency the President. It all depends who sees you, of course – but protesting your innocence won't appease small-minded officials.

Shopping

Woodcarvings are ubiquitous in Tanzania, including walking sticks, Maasai spears and figurines, combs, animals and (especially) the intricate and abstract Makonde carvings, named after the largest tribe of southern Tanzania and northern Mozambique – though they're nowadays more likely to have been made by craftsmen of the Zaramo tribe around Dar es Salaam. See p.232 for more about the Makonde and the woodcarving tradition.

Also well worth buying are the colourful **Tingatinga paintings**, found anywhere there are tourists; see the box on p.387. Also ubiquitous are **tie-dye batiks**, annoyingly so in Arusha, where you'll have reams of them shoved under your nose by street vendors. The country's distinctive **toys** also make good souvenirs: most worthwhile are the beautifully fashioned buses, cars and lorries made out of wire – you'll rarely find these for sale, but you might commission one if you have time.

Other frequently seen items include a huge variety of **sisal baskets**, **beadwork** and **soapstone carvings** imported from Kisii in Kenya (though the bowls and plates are for decoration only, since the dye that is used in their manufacture can be toxic). **Traditional crafts** – weapons, shields, drums, musical instruments, stools, headrests and metal jewellery – are common as well, but much more expensive. With the notable exception of Makonde "helmet masks", **masks** are mostly reproductions based on central and western African designs, and even the oldest-looking examples may have been made specifically for the tourist market, no matter how much congealed cow dung appears to fill the crevices.

Textiles, notably a profusion of printed women's wraps in cotton (*kanga*) and the heavier-weave men's loincloths, are really good buys on the coast, and older ones represent collectable items worth seeking out.

Kangas are always sold in pairs and are printed with intriguing Swahili proverbs. Most of them are manufactured in the Far East, although there's a growing demand for locally produced cloth and patterns.

Lastly, remember that purchasing or exporting **ivory**, **turtleshell** (often called "tortoiseshell"), **seahorses** and **seashells** encourages the destruction of wildlife and is in any case strictly illegal, both in Tanzania and abroad – penalties include heavy fines or even imprisonment. Similarly, avoid anything like animal skins or game trophies; possession of these is illegal in Tanzania without the requisite paperwork, and may be completely illegal in other countries.

Bargaining

Bargaining is an important skill to learn in Tanzania, since every time you pay an unreasonable price for goods or services, you contribute to local inflation. You're expected to knock most negotiable prices down by at least half: souvenirs are sometimes offered at a first price which is ten times what the vendor is prepared to accept. The bluffing on both sides is part of the fun; don't be shy of making a big scene, and once you get into it, you'll rarely end up paying more than the going rate for transport or accommodation. Where prices are marked, they are generally fixed.

Trouble

Tanzania is a largely safe and peaceful country: crime levels are low, and outside the main tourist areas, you're unlikely to come across much hassle either. If you stick to the following common-sense precautions, you're unlikely to run into trouble.

There are a few places in the country's larger towns and cities that should be avoided at night, and sometimes by day – these are mentioned in the guide. More general areas that you should be wary of, if not avoid completely, are parts of the **northwest** close to Burundi and Rwanda, and **Loliondo** and the area around Lake Natron, which saw a spate of bandit attacks by Somali gunmen in the 1990s. These fizzled out after a spectacular police chase over the border into Kenya, but you should be aware that the region is by its very nature difficult to control and things could start up again at any time.

The only other substantial risks on the mainland are some stretches of **beach**, especially north of Dar (including Bagamoyo), where valuables often disappear from the beach or occasionally get grabbed. Local hotels routinely advise their guests not to walk unaccompanied on the beach, or to carry valuables.

Wherever you are, avoid **political rallies and demonstrations** – the infamously bloody police crack-down on demonstrations in Zanzibar and Dar es Salaam in January 2001 was the worst political violence that Tanzania has ever experienced, and political unrest is a constant theme in Zanzibar, especially on Pemba and in the Ng'ambo area of Zanzibar Town (and also be aware that publicly airing your own opinions about Tanzanian politics isn't always such a great idea either).

Hassle

There's virtually no **hassle** outside the main tourist centres of Arusha, Moshi, Dar es Salaam and Zanzibar. In these places, your **appearance** goes a long way to determining the extent to which you'll attract attention. It's impossible not to look like a tourist – local expats are known by all – but you *can* dress down and look like you're been travel-ling for months, so that people will assume you're streetwise. Avoid wearing anything brand-new, especially white clothes (apart from businessmen's shirts, no one wears whiter-than-white in Tanzania), and make sure your shoes aren't overly shiny. Some tourists swear by sunglasses to avoid making unwanted eye-contact; while this usually works, it still marks you out as a tourist and also puts a barrier between you and everyone else, not just hasslers.

Beggars and street children

Beggars are fairly common in the touristy parts of Arusha, rare in Moshi and Dar es Salaam and virtually non-existent elsewhere. The curious exception is Dodoma, whose capital status seems to attract down-and-outs. Most beggars are visibly destitute; many are cripples, lepers or homeless mothers with children, and they are harassed by the police and often rounded up. Some have regular pitches; others keep on the move. Tanzanians often give to the same beggar on a regular basis in fulfilment of the Islamic requirement to give alms to the poor. A Tsh100 coin suffices.

Much more common, especially in Arusha, are the hundreds of **street children**, many of them glue-sniffing boys aged 8–14. They're responsible for much of the city's petty crime and are mostly ignored by Tanzanians. Pitiful as they are, they offer a disturbing insight into one of the realities of Tanzanian life. The children are forced onto the streets by a variety of reasons, most commonly to escape physical abuse and domestic violence. Others come from homes decimated by AIDS. With no prospect of employment (the situation is chronic enough for adults), the children's only option is the street.

Some people argue that giving street children money encourages a culture of dependency (the logic being that the supposedly rich pickings to be made on the streets will only encourage more kids to join them). If you want to help, it's probably best either to give food or to donate money to one of charitable organizations working with street children: particularly active Children for Children's Future in Arusha (PO Box 10826; ☎027/250 0428, ✉ccfarusha@hotmail.com).

Misunderstandings

It's very easy to fall prey to **misunderstandings** in your relations with people (usually boys and young men) who offer their services as guides, helpers or "facilitators" of any kind. You should absolutely never assume anything is being done out of simple kindness. It may well be, but, if it isn't, you must expect to pay something. If you have any suspicion, it's invariably best to confront the matter head on at an early stage and either apologize for the offence caused by the suggestion, or agree a price. What you must never do, as when bargaining, is enter into an unspoken contract and then break it by refusing to pay for the service. If you're being bugged by someone whose "help" you don't need, just let them know you can't pay anything for their trouble. It may not make you a friend, but it always works, and it's better than a row and recriminations.

Driving

For tips on avoiding hassle with the police when **driving**, see p.34. It's never a good idea to leave even a locked car unguarded if it has anything of value in it – in towns, there's usually someone who will guard it for you for a tip (Tsh500 is enough). While **driving at night** in a town or city – especially Arusha and Dar es Salaam – local advice is to keep the doors locked and windows up to avoid grab-and-run incidents.

Car-jackings and armed hold-ups – though still rare – are on the rise, especially at night (never a good time to be driving). Areas to be wary of are Arusha, and – more seriously – remoter parts of the northwest along the borders with Burundi and Rwanda, where armed incursions from rebel factions and other bandits have been reported in the past. Other roads along which armed robberies have been reported are the unsurfaced seventy-kilometre stretch between

Tanga and the Kenyan border, and the highways between Morogoro and Mikumi, and between Chalinze and Segera (part of the road between Dar and Moshi), which was targeted by highway bandits before the road was resurfaced. You should be extremely wary of stopping for anyone along these stretches outside villages. In Zanzibar, be aware that robberies at **fake police roadblocks** have also recently been reported.

Trouble with the police

Though you might sometimes hear stories of extraordinary kindness and of occasional bursts of efficiency that would do credit to any constabulary, in general the **Tanzanian police** are notoriously corrupt, and it's usually best to steer clear of them. If you have official business with the police, then politeness, smiles and handshakes always help. Treat even the most offensively corrupt cop with respect (greeting him with "Shikamoo, Mzee" helps a lot). Having said this, in unofficial dealings the police can go out of their way to help you with food, transport or accommodation, especially in remote outposts. Try to reciprocate. Police salaries are low – no more than Tsh40,000 a month – and they rely on unofficial income to get by. Only a brand-new police force and realistic salaries could alter a situation which is now entrenched.

Drugs

If you spend any time in Dar or Arusha, you'll probably be offered drugs, usually by fly-catchers also offering batiks, dodgy safaris and money change. **Grass** (*bhangi*) is widely smoked and remarkably cheap. However, it's also officially illegal, and the authorities do make some effort to control it: if you're caught in possession, you'll be hit with a heavy fine and deported, at the very least. Anything harder than marijuana is rarely sold and will obviously get you in much worse trouble if you're caught in possession.

The use of and attitudes to grass vary considerably, but you should be very discreet if you're going to indulge, and watch out who you get high with. Never buy marijuana on the street – you're guaranteed to be ripped off or shopped to the police, who may or may not be amenable to bribes. There are also a number of **scams** associated with buying drugs, the most common one being approached by fake policemen shortly after buying, who will shake you down for everything you have.

Another drug you might be offered is **miraa** (*qat* or *khat*), a mild herbal stimulant grown in central Kenya that is especially popular with Somali and Yemeni immigrants. The leaves are chewed for ages and then spat out: *miraa* is traditionally used by people in drought-prone areas as it suppresses hunger, and also keeps you awake at night and so is favoured by East African lorry drivers. The drug is legal is Kenya but illegal in Tanzania.

Bribes

Unless you're driving a car, police are rarely out to solicit **bribes** from tourists, though there have been cases of them taking advantage when the law's not totally clear: swimming at Coco Beach after the man-eating shark scare of 2000 earned one policeman Tsh20,000 from a traveller who hadn't noticed the "no swimming" signs by the roadside, which in any case were in Kiswahili. Another paid a bribe of $200 for "soliciting prostitutes" after asking a woman the time in Dar es Salaam. If approached by policemen asking for money for alleged offences, insist on identification before going to a police station to make any payments.

If you know you've done something wrong and are expected to give a bribe, wait for it to be hinted at and haggle over it as you would any payment; Tsh2000 or so is often enough to oil small wheels, though traffic police may expect something more substantial from tourists. Be aware, of course, that bribery is illegal – if you know you've done nothing wrong and are not in a rush, refusing a bribe will only cost a short delay until the cop gives up on you and tries another potential source of income. If you're really getting nowhere, you can always kick up a loud fuss – it usually works wonders.

Unseemly behaviour

Be warned that failure to observe the following points of **Tanzanian etiquette** can get you arrested or put you in a position where you may be obliged to pay a bribe. Stand in cinemas and on other occasions when the national anthem is playing. Stand still when the national flag is being raised or lowered in your field of view. Don't take photos of the flag or the president. Pull off the road completely when scores of motorcycle outriders appear, then get out and stand by your vehicle (for it is he, or else the burly chief of police). Never tear up a banknote, of any denomination, and don't urinate in public.

Robbery and theft

Your chances of being **robbed** in Tanzania are pretty slim, but you should nonetheless be conscious of your belongings and never leave anything unguarded even for a second. In addition, you should be careful of where you walk, at least until you've got the pack off your back and are settled in somewhere. You should also be very careful in bus stations, especially when arriving. If you can't help walking around with valuables and are in a town for more than a couple of days, vary your route and schedule to avoid creating temptation. Note also that there are always more **pickpockets** about at the end of the month, when people are carrying the salaries they've just been paid. Finally, beware of **doping scams** on public transport; see box on p.31 for more details.

Muggings

The best way to avoid being **mugged** is to not carry any valuables, especially anything visible. It should go without saying that you don't wear dangling earrings or any kind of chain or necklace, expensive-looking sunglasses or wristwatches; even certain brands of sports shoes (sneakers) can be tempting. Similarly, try to avoid carrying valuables in those handy off-the-shoulder day bags or even small rucksacks, as these provide visible temptation. Old plastic bags (nicknamed "Rambos", courtesy of the dim-witted action hero whose likeness is printed on millions of them) are a much less conspicuous way of carrying cameras. If you clearly have nothing on you, you're unlikely to feel, or be, threatened.

If you do get mugged, don't resist, since knives and guns are occasionally carried. It will be over in an instant and you're unlikely to be hurt. If you are robbed, you'll have to go to the nearest police station for a statement to show your insurance company, though you may well be expected to pay a

Carrying money safely

First off, carry as little cash as possible and put whatever money you are carrying in several different places: a money belt tucked under your trousers or skirt is invisible and thus usually secure for travellers' cheques, passports and large amounts of cash. The best money belts are cotton or linen, as nylon ones can cause skin irritations if you sweat a lot. For the same reason, wrap up your things in a plastic bag before placing them in the belt. Make sure that your money belt lies flat against your skin; the voluminous "bum bags" worn back-to-front by many tourists over their clothing invite a mugging, and are only one step short of announcing your stash with flashing neon lights. Equally dumb are pouches hanging around your neck, and ordinary wallets are a disaster.

Put the rest of your money – what you'll need for the day or your night out – in a pocket or somewhere more accessible: somewhat perversely, you're safer with at least some money to hand, as few muggers will believe you have nothing on you whatsoever.

"little something" for it. You can usually forget about enlisting the police to try and get your stuff back.

As angry as you may feel about being robbed, it's worth trying to understand the desperation that drives men and boys to risk their lives for your things. Thieves caught red-handed are usually mobbed – and often killed – so when you shout "Thief!" ("*Mwizi!*" in Kiswahili), be ready to intercede once you've retrieved your belongings.

Theft from hotel rooms

Thefts from locked hotel bedrooms are extremely rare, except in a handful of backpackers' lodgings in Arusha. Petty pilfering by hotel staff is also uncommon. Other than – judiciously – depositing valuables with the hotel management, the best way to avoid either scenario is not to leave things lying about openly. Burying stuff in the bottom of your rucksack and closing all bags deters temptation, and hiding stuff between a mattress and bed frame is also usually safe – at least judging by the amount of accumulated grime under most hotel mattresses.

Cons and scams

An incredible number of newly arrived visitors get **ripped off** during their first day or two, perhaps because, with pale skin, new luggage and clean shoes, they stick out a mile. Most scams are confidence tricks, and though there's no reason to be paranoid (indeed, one or two scams play on a tourist's paranoia), a healthy sense of cynicism is helpful.

Ferry tickets

The process of buying **ferry tickets** between Dar es Salaam and Stone Town is a firm favourite with scammers both on the mainland and in Zanzibar. The scam basically involves someone selling you a ferry ticket at the discounted rates available to Tanzanians or bona fide residents. If you fall for it, you may well be let on the ferry, whence – cometh the ticket inspector, bent policeman and assorted heavies – you'll be made to buy another ticket at the full tourist price plus a bribe to smooth things over. A variation on this scam is to be offered a ticket at the discounted price paid by tourists travelling with overland trucks. The ticket inspector has a list of these clients, and if you're not on it, it's the same outcome.

An even cruder scam is to be sold a ticket for a ferry departure that doesn't even exist – especially the "night ferry" from Dar to Stone Town (there isn't one, though there *is* an overnight sailing in the opposite direction). All these scams are easily avoided by buying your ticket at the tourist rate and either at the ferry company's office at the port or from a reputable travel agent. Make sure that the company selling you the ticket is the one operating the service, though, or you run the risk of being sold a ticket for a nonexistent boat.

Although we've received no reports about the same scam being tried on **bus tickets**, it's probably only a matter of time before it is.

Money-changers

Another old favourite is the offer to **change money** on the street at favourable rates. Given that the Tanzanian shilling is floated freely against hard currencies, there's no possible reason for a black market to exist, so it doesn't take a genius to realize that by changing money on the street you're just setting yourself up to get ripped off.

In its most obvious form, the money-changer simply dashes off with your money, sometimes aided by the timely appearance of a "police officer". Much more subtle – and common – is to trick you by sleight of hand: the scammer lets you count the shilling notes, takes your money, then proceeds to roll up the shillings and tie them with a rubber band. When you open the bundle it's been switched for one containing only low-value notes or even paper.

In addition, if you're entering the country overland, be aware that there are no regulations saying that visitors need to have Tanzanian shillings to be allowed in: it's just a line that con-men feed you.

School fees

Approaches in the street from "school children" or "students" with sponsorship forms (only primary education is free, and even then, books, uniforms, even furniture have to be bought) and from "refugees" with long stories are not uncommon and probably best shrugged off. Some, unfortunately, may be genuine.

A variation of the scam relies entirely on people's belief in the paranoid republic. As you leave the "student" with a sigh of relief, a group of heavies surround you and claim to be police, interested in the discussion you've been having with that "subversive" or "Sudanese terrorist" (or whoever), and the funds you provided him. A large fine is demanded. You can tell them to go to hell, or suggest you all go to the police station.

Finally, one last totally blatant scam that still catches people out: if you're grabbed by a man who has just picked up a wad of money in the street and seems oddly willing to share it with you in a convenient nearby alley, you'll know you're about to be robbed …

Customs and beliefs

Tanzanians are known for their tactfulness and courtesy, qualities that are highly valued right across the social spectrum and by all the nation's tribes. The desire to maintain healthy relationships with both neighbours and strangers epitomizes the peaceful and non-tribalistic nature of Tanzanian society, and expresses itself in the warm welcome given to visitors. As such, you'll be treated as an honoured guest by many people, and if you make the effort, you'll be welcomed to a side of Tanzania that too few tourists see.

Appearance and behaviour

There are no hard and fast rules about public behaviour so long as you respect local customs, cultural and religious beliefs. Apart from **indecent dress**, a few things are generally considered offensive: these include **public displays of intimacy** (though a couple holding hands is fine); **immodesty**, both verbal and material (don't flaunt wealth); and open displays of **bad temper and impatience**, which will not endear you to anyone. There are exceptions to this, of course: if you're a woman being pestered by a man, for instance, expressions of anger will usually result in embarrassed bystanders coming to your rescue. Lastly, it is insulting and invasive to **take photographs** of people without their permission. Always ask, and respect people if they refuse or ask for money in return.

Dress

Tanzanians make an effort to appear well dressed, and so should you. The simple rule is to wear comfortable and decent clothes; they should also be clean, within reason. Although Islamic moral strictures tend to be generously interpreted, in Muslim majority areas – mainly the coast and Zanzibar – men and women should **cover up** when not on a beach frequented by tourists. This means long trousers for men, and a long dress, skirt, *kanga* or trousers for women. Sleeves don't have to be too long, only enough to cover your shoulders. There's no need for head gear, though you'll probably be wearing a sun hat anyway. Although people are far too polite to admonish strangers, tourists who ignore the dress code – which is posted up in pretty much every hotel in Zanzibar – are considered with scorn. The other very good reason for covering up is simple: you'll attract much less hassle from touts and flycatchers, and won't be treated as a dumb tourist.

Sadly, gross ignorance or wilful disregard of local customs by tourists appears to be on the increase, especially in Zanzibar as it switches onto mass tourism. The idea seems to be that spending a fortune on a two-week beach holiday also buys you the right to ignore local feelings and traditions. It doesn't.

Greetings

Lengthy **greetings** – preferably in Kiswahili – are extremely important in Tanzania, and people will value your efforts to master them. Elderly men and women are invariably treated with great deference. The word for greeting anyone older than you is *Shikamoo*, best followed by an honorific title: *Babu* (grandfather) for an elderly man, *Bibi* (grandmother) for an elderly woman, *Baba* (father) for a man, *Mama* (mother) for a woman and *Mwalumi* for a teacher. The standard acknowledgement is *Marahaba*. It certainly doesn't hurt to show the same deference yourself to older men and woman. And when you're addressed with *Shikamoo* – often by children in rural areas – do respond with the requisite *Marahaba* (pulling a silly face goes down a storm, too). For some **commonly used phrases** when greeting acquaintances, see the "Language" section on p.761.

As well as the verbal greeting, younger women do a slight curtsy when greeting elders, while men invariably shake hands both at meeting and parting. Among younger people especially there are a number of more elaborate handshakes that anyone will be happy to teach you. You should always use your right hand to shake or to give or receive anything. Incidentally, if someone's hands are wet or dirty when you meet, they'll offer their wrist instead. It's impolite to discuss a man's work or financial standing unless you know him well.

Gifts

When invited into someone's home, it's usual to bring small presents (see box on p.44) for the family if you've been invited to lunch or dinner. If you're staying longer, slightly more elaborate presents are in order. Increase the amount of practical presents you bring (a few of kilos of sugar, more tea), and bring a *kanga* or *kitenge* for the mother and grandmother. Ballpoint pens and writing pads will always find a use, and the kids will be fascinated by books (Tanzania's literacy rate, though down from a peak of 90 percent-plus which it reached in the 1980s, is still high by African standards). Most bookshops sell gorgeously illustrated children's books in Kiswahili. For other gift ideas, ask your host before coming – and insist beyond their polite insistence that the only presents you need to bring is your own presence.

Lastly, when **on safari** do not give coins, sweets or pens to children: it encourages begging, as you'll notice in the chorus of "*Mzungu* give me money/pen/sweet" that accompanies you anywhere where tourists ignoring this rule have been in the past. If you really want to give something, hand it to an adult who will share it out, or – even better – make a donation to the local school. If you'll be travelling or staying for some time and really want to prepare, get a large batch of photos of you and your family with your address on the back. You'll get lots of mail.

Sexuality

Machismo, in its fully fledged Latin varieties, is rare in Tanzania, and male egos are usually softened by reserves of humour. Women's groups flourish across the country, but are concerned more with improvement of incomes, education, health and nutrition than social or political emancipation, though this is changing.

Sexual mores in Tanzania are refreshingly hedonistic and uncluttered, nor is prostitution the rigid, secretive transaction it is in the West. Unfortunately, the downside of this openness is that sexually transmitted diseases, including the HIV virus, are rife. Surveys have revealed that at least one in ten Tanzanians carries the HIV virus; the real figure is possibly much higher, and four out of five deaths among 25- to 35-year-olds are now AIDS-related. It goes without saying that casual sex without a condom is a deadly gamble and you should assume any sexual contact to be HIV-positive. Despite this, female **prostitution** still flourishes in the towns.

Among tourists, enough arrive expecting sexual adventures to make flirtatious pestering a fairly constant part of the scene, irritating or amusing as it strikes you. And if you're a woman looking for a holiday affair, Zanzibar and – to a lesser extent – Arusha seem to be the places (though be aware that your lover does this for a living; the sight of them in the local bank waiting for bankers' drafts from Europe is instructive).

Attitudes to **gays** are rather hard to pin down. While there is no gay scene as such, male homosexuality is an accepted undercurrent on the coast. Gigolos and male prostitutes – far fewer and more secretive than their female counterparts – are limited mostly to Arusha and Dar es Salaam. *Msenge* is Kiswahili for gay man. Elsewhere, homosexuality *seems* scarce enough not to be an issue. On the statute books, however, it remains illegal, and punishable by up to fourteen years in jail.

Religion

The majority of mainland Tanzanians have converted to **Christianity** – if sometimes only in name. Varieties of Catholicism and Protestantism are dominant but, as with Kenya, there are also many minor **Christian sects** and churches, often based around the teaching of local prophets and preachers. Broad-based **Sunni Islam** dominates the coast and Zanzibar, and is in the ascendant throughout the country. Many towns have several mosques (or, on the coast, dozens). The Aga Khan's Ismaili sect is also influential, with powerful business interests. Unless you're given permission, mosques should only be entered by Muslims. **Hindu** and **Sikh** temples are found in most large towns, and there are adherents of **Jainism** and the **Bahai** faith, too.

Indigenous religion (mostly based around the idea of a supreme god and intercession between the living and the spirit worlds by deceased ancestors) survives in more mountainous and otherwise remote terrain, as well as among pastoralists like the Maasai and Barbaig, but is increasingly under threat from Christian missionaries, thanks to whom much of the cumulative wisdom, customs and traditional music of neighbouring Kenya has already been destroyed.

Sexual harassment

Women, whether travelling alone or together, may come across occasional **persistent hasslers** but seldom much worse. Universal rules apply: if you suspect ulterior motives, turn down all offers and stonily refuse to converse, though you needn't fear expressing your anger if that's how you feel. You will be left alone – eventually. Really obnoxious individuals are usually on their own, fortunately. A useful trick if you're unmarried and travelling alone is to wear a "wedding" ring (silver ones feel safer than gold in terms of tempting robbery). For this to work it would be helpful to take along a picture of a burly male friend à la Mike Tyson with a suitably husband-like message written on the back as "proof". These tactics are hardly necessary except on the coast, particularly in Zanzibar. Blonde women suffer more, though cutting your hair short or dyeing it seems drastic, and anyway you'll still look like a tourist.

Travellers with disabilities

Although by no means easy, Tanzania doesn't pose insurmountable problems for people with disabilities. While there is little government involvement in improving access, staff in the tourist industry – not to mention passers-by – will usually help where necessary. Wheelchair-users will find that many hotels have ground-floor rooms, while a number on the coast have ramped access walks to public areas, and larger hotels in Arusha and Dar es Salaam have elevators. Safari vehicles can usually manage wheelchair-users. If you're looking for an all-in tour, contact the upmarket specialists Abercrombie & Kent (see pp.11–12), who have some experience in working with disabled passengers.

Attitudes to disabled people in Tanzania are generally good – there are always willing hands to help you over any obstacle. **Getting around** the cities, however, is difficult in a wheelchair: there is little ramping of pedestrian areas, and pavements are often blocked by parked cars. Taxis are invariably small saloon cars.

Safari vehicles have superb springing, an advantage somewhat offset by the skills of the average safari driver, so taking a pressure cushion is a wise precaution. Even then, off-road trips can be very arduous, especially on the awful roads in and around Selous and in any other parks outside the Northern Safari Circuit, where flying in is recommended. If you're determined, however, any of the luxury lodges and tented camps should be accessible, with help, making a proper safari quite feasible, especially if you fly. Only on the most adventurous trips, with temporary camps set up in the bush, and long-drop toilets, would wheelchair-users really have problems.

The 36-hour sleeper **trains** from Dar es Salaam to Kigoma or Mwanza sound improbable but, again, are possible. On these, though, you would have to be carried – which might prove difficult – from your cabin (first-class is the only feasible choice) to the toilets and dining car, as the corridors are very narrow. Your wheelchair would go in the luggage van, too, so expect a delay in retrieving it on arrival. With the exception of the "luxury" **coaches** which ply between Arusha, Dar and Mbeya, other public transport in Tanzania isn't at all wheelchair-friendly.

Contacts for travellers with disabilities

In the UK and Ireland

Holiday Care ☎01293/774 535, Minicom ☎01293/776 943, ⓦwww.holidaycare.org.uk. Provides free lists of accessible accommodation abroad, and information on financial help for holidays.
Irish Wheelchair Association ☎01/833 8241, ⓕ833 3873, ⓔiwa@iol.ie. Useful source of information about travelling abroad with a wheelchair.
Tripscope ☎0845/7585 641, ⓦwww.justmobility.co.uk/tripscope. Telephone information service offering free advice on transport for those with a mobility problem.

In the US and Canada

Access-Able ⓦwww.access-able.com. Useful website for travellers with disabilities.
Directions Unlimited ☎1-800/533-5343 or 914/241-1700. Tour operator specializing in customized tours for people with disabilities.
Mobility International USA Voice and TDD ☎541/343-1284, ⓦwww.miusa.org. Information and referral services, access guides, tours and exchange programmes. Annual membership $35 (includes quarterly newsletter).
SATH (Society for the Advancement of Travelers with Handicaps) ⓦwww.sath.org. Non-profit educational organization.
Travel Information Service ☎215/456-9600. Telephone-only information and referral service.
Twin Peaks Press ☎360/694-2462 or 1-800/637-2256, ⓦwww.twinpeak.virtualave.net. Publisher of the *Directory of Travel Agencies for the Disabled* ($19.95), listing more than 370 agencies

worldwide; *Travel for the Disabled* ($19.95); and *Wheelchair Vagabond* ($19.95), loaded with personal tips.

Wheels Up! ☎1-888/389-4335, ⊛www.wheelsup.com. Provides discounted airfare, tour and cruise prices for disabled travellers, publishes a free monthly newsletter and has a comprehensive website.

In Australia and New Zealand

ACROD (Australian Council for Rehabilitation of the Disabled) ☎02/9554 3666. Provides lists of travel agencies and tour operators for people with disabilities.

Disabled Persons Assembly ☎04/801 9100. Resource centre with lists of travel agencies and tour operators for people with disabilities.

Directory

Clothes Bring loose cotton clothes, comfortable flip-flops (or suede shoes, plus boots for the highlands), and at least one really warm sweater or a jacket. See the "Mount Kilimanjaro" section (pp.330–331) for advice on what you need at high altitudes. Don't bring mounds of clothes, though: cheap clothes are available in markets throughout the country.

Contraceptives Condoms are available from town pharmacies and supermarkets. Oral contraceptives need a prescription from a doctor, and you'll have to pay. It's far wiser to bring all you'll need.

Electricity Like Britain, most of Tanzania uses square three-pin plugs on 220–240V, at least in theory: in practice, unstable supplies, power surges and drop-offs widen the range considerably; Arusha's supply varies from 160V to 200V. If you're using sensitive electronic equipment like a laptop, ensure that it or the transformer accepts the whole of this range. A few places use thick round two-pin plugs, though adapters can easily be bought for about Tsh500. Only fancier hotels have outlets or shaver points in the rooms. Apart from the unstable current, Tanzania is also subjected to frequent power cuts (blackouts). Things are worse at the end of particularly dry spells, when reservoirs are too low to adequately power the nation's hydroelectric stations. At these times, power rationing is common. Many rural places are not connected to the national grid, so electricity in these places – if any – is powered by local oil-fired power stations or else by private generators belonging to hotels and businesses.

Laundry There are no laundromats in Tanzania and it's usually easiest to wash your own clothes: you can buy packets of soap powder, and things dry fast. Beware of New Blue Omo – it's very strong and wrecks clothes if you use it for long. Otherwise, there's often someone wherever you're staying who will be prepared to negotiate a laundry charge.

Time Tanzania is three hours ahead of Greenwich Mean Time all year round, which means two hours ahead of Britain during the summer and three in winter; seven or eight hours ahead of US Eastern Standard Time; and 6.5–7.5 hours behind Australian time. Remember that the hours in "Swahili time" run from 6am to 6pm rather than noon to midnight, so that 7am and 7pm western time equate to 1 o'clock in Swahili (*saa moja*), whilst midnight and noon are *saa sita* (six o'clock). It's not as confusing as it first sounds – just add or subtract six hours to work out Swahili time (or read the opposite side of your watch). People and things are usually late in Tanzania, though trains heading out from Dar nearly always leave right on time, and buses often depart punctually as well. In more remote areas, though, if a driver tells you he's going somewhere "today", it doesn't necessarily mean he expects to arrive today.

Tipping The average salary for a Tanzanian is about $40 (Tsh36,000) a month. If you're staying in tourist-class establishments, and travelling a lot, you will often have to tip staff. In expensive hotels, Tsh1000 wouldn't be out of place for portering a lot of luggage, but Tsh500 is adequate. For small services, Tsh200–500 is more than welcome. In the very humblest establishments, tipping is not the custom. Note that on safaris, tips are considered almost part of the pay; expectations vary widely, though anything less than $10 per person would be considered stingy.

Toilets Carry toilet paper – which you can buy in most places – as few cheap hotels provide it. Public toilets (*Wanawake* = Women; *Wanaume* = Men) are invariably disgusting, as are those in cheaper guest houses. Public buildings and hotels are unlikely to turn you away if you ask to use their facilities.

Work Unless you've lined up a job or voluntary work before leaving for Tanzania, you have little chance of getting employment. Wages are extremely low – school teachers earn about $80 a month – and there's serious unemployment in the towns. Particular skills are sometimes in demand – mechanics at game park lodges, for example – but the employer will need good connections to arrange the required papers. It's illegal to obtain income in Tanzania while staying on a tourist visa.

Guide

Guide

Dar es Salaam and around

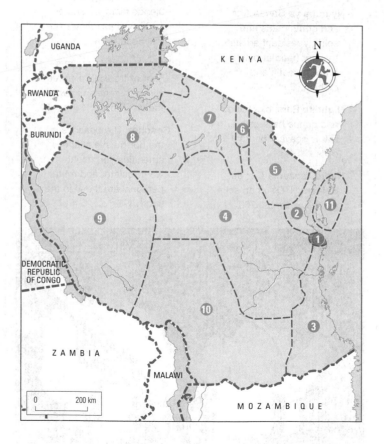

CHAPTER 1   # Highlights

* **National Museum** Small but perfectly formed, covering every angle on Tanzanian culture and history, from prehistoric hominid fossils through colonization to Independence. See p.94

* **Nyumba ya Sanaa** Arts and crafts made and sold by resident artists; try your hand at painting, drawing, batik and etching. See p.95

* **Nightlife** Bars, nightclubs and dance halls galore, Dar is heaven for night owls. See p.107

* **Radio Tanzania Dar es Salaam** RTD's shop sells copies of almost 200 archive recordings of traditional and modern music; a national treasure. See p.109

* **Gezaulole** A traditional fishing village whose community-based cultural tourism programme blends history, culture and beaches, all at minimal cost. See p.133

* **Pugu Forest** A rare remnant of tropical rainforest within a stone's throw of the city. See p.135

* **Beaches** The beaches in the north have all the amenities you might want; quieter and more personal are those in the south. See p.126 and p.131

Dar es Salaam
and around

From a moribund settlement of three thousand people, **DAR ES SALAAM** ("Dar" for short) has grown in little over a century to become one of Africa's largest cities. Its present population, estimated at close to four million, has an annual growth rate of almost ten percent, thanks to massive immigration from rural areas, and over seventy percent of its inhabitants live in non-planned housing, often little more than slums. Their nickname for the city is **Bongo**, meaning "smart" or "clever", suggesting the skills that are needed to survive in an urban expanse of this size.

Dar es Salaam remains Tanzania's industrial and commercial heart, in spite of having lost its capital status to Dodoma in 1974. Most of the country's large businesses are located here, and much of its wealth is based on a lively import

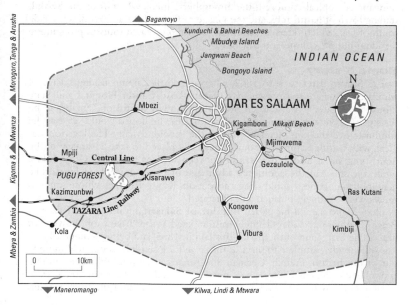

trade conducted through the city's port – East Africa's largest – which also handles most of Tanzania's agricultural and mineral exports, as well as transit goods bound for central Africa. This commercial ethos expresses itself best in the city's colourful shops and markets, especially in Kariakoo, where you're likely to find anything from trussed-up chickens to illegal drugs, and dodgy electronics imported from the Far East to magical charms and concoctions sold by traditional healers.

Barely a century old, the city remains true to the old cliché of being a "melting pot", a vibrant blend of traditional tribal cultures and immigrant communities from Europe and Asia. In the centre, European-planned streets, Neoclassical facades and Gothic churches jostle for elbowroom with hawkers, pedlars and women dressed in shrouding black *buibuis*, whilst Europeans, Asians and wealthy Tanzanians drive by in air-conditioned 4WDs. In the predominantly Asian area west of the centre, Indian traders lord it over colourful reams of cloth, spices and tourist trinkets, whilst in the harbour you can still see wooden dhows whose design hasn't changed for a thousand years bobbing up and down alongside freighters and oil tankers. For all its incongruities, everything seems to fit: Dar es Salaam is a cosmopolitan city. But what really sets it apart from most other African metropolises is its characteristically gentle and laid-back feel: the word you're likely to hear more than other is *karibu* – welcome.

For the visitor, the city's attractions may be difficult to pin down, but for all that, missing out on Dar would be a shame, as not only does it boast all the modern amenities and services unobtainable elsewhere in the country, but it's also home to a handsome collection of museums and cultural attractions as well as being a mecca for lovers of **East African music**, eclipsing even Nairobi in the number and quality of live acts on offer. For many, though, Dar's northern **beaches** are the main draw – and if the prospect of the fully fledged holiday resorts north of the city puts you off, there's an almost undeveloped stretch of coast to the south. Other attractions around Dar include **Pugu Forest** – a rare remnant of tropical rainforest; the atmospheric medieval ruins of the Swahili trading town of **Kunduchi**; and the village of **Gezaulole**, an easy daladala ride south of Dar, which offers an excellent community-based tourism programme blending history, culture and beaches.

Some history

Dar es Salaam dates back to 1862, when the small Zaramo fishing village of **Mzizima** – where the present-day Ocean Road Cancer Hospital and State House are located – was chosen by **Sultan Seyyid Majid** of Zanzibar to be the site of his new summer palace, which in time he hoped would serve as the administrative and commercial centre of the Busaidi dynasty. The location was ideal, with its fine natural harbour strategically placed to take advantage of the flourishing **slave and ivory trade** between the coast and the Great Lakes, while the site had the additional advantage of being untroubled by warlike neighbouring tribes, unlike Bagamoyo and Kilwa Kivinje, whose caravan routes were routinely pillaged and disrupted.

Sultan Majid named his palace **Bandur ul Salaam**, meaning the "Palace of Peace", a phrase nowadays happily mistranslated as the "haven" or "heaven" of peace. The first stone of the palace was laid in 1865, and by September 1867 it was sufficiently complete to serve as the stage for a lavish banquet held in honour of the British, French, German and American consuls, whose economic and military influence the sultan openly courted. Hadhramaut Arabs from Yemen were invited to develop coconut plantations around the small hamlet, and with the arrival of Indian merchants buying slaves in exchange for imported goods the fledgling city seemed set to flourish. Unfortunately, the sultan died in 1870 – ironically from a broken neck sustained in a fall in his new palace – before his plans could be fully realized. His successor, Sultan Barghash, had little interest in the site and soon abandoned the project. Economically, too, the city seemed to have been stillborn: in 1873, the British forced Barghash to sign a decree prohibiting the slave trade by sea, and three years later they banned the trade on the mainland, effectively robbing Dar es Salaam of its essential purpose.

Decline was swift: the traders left, the dhows returned to Bagamoyo and Kilwa Kivinje, and Dar became little more than a small village with an outsize palace. So it remained for fourteen years until, in 1887, the **German East Africa Company** established a station there. Four years later, with the German colonization of Tanganyika in full swing, the capital of German East Africa (Deutsch Ostafrika) was transferred from Bagamoyo to Dar and the construction of the city resumed in earnest. The renascent city attracted Benedictine and Lutheran missionaries, who built churches and the Kaiserhof Hotel (now the New Africa), hoping to use the city as a base from which to continue the evangelization of East Africa. In 1894, Dar es Salaam's newfound importance was confirmed by the surveying of the **Mittelland Bahn** – the present-day Central Line railway – which was to connect the city with Lake Tanganyika. Begun in 1905, the 1250-kilometre railway line finally arrived in Kigoma on the shore of Lake Tanganyika nine years later, becoming the colony's primary commercial conduit and allowing trade to flourish.

Unfortunately for the Germans, **World War I** resulted in their expulsion by Allied forces in September 1916. The new British overlords retained Dar as their commercial and administrative centre and began construction of the modern city proper, dividing it into three racially segregated "classes". **Usunguni** (now comprising the city centre east of Azikiwe Street), was designated for Europeans, and benefited from asphalt streets, shady trees, stone buildings, a hospital, a botanical garden inherited from the Germans, and other amenities. The more compact **Uhindini** area, to the west of Usunguni, was reserved for Asian immigrants brought by the British to work as coolies in the construction of the new colony, and its Indian shops and bazaars still form the city's retailing centre. Lastly, the **Uswahilini** district, between the Asian area and the swampy floodplain of the Jangwani River, was left open to Africans. This area, of which Kariakoo was the heart, lacked – and in many parts still lacks – even the most basic of facilities.

As the city and its African population grew, the **Tanganyika African Association**, an ethnically diverse welfare agency and social club, was founded in Dar in 1927 to advocate the betterment of the African lot, and soon spread to rural communities, where it ultimately merged with the Tanganyika African National Union (TANU) to become the driving force behind the successful push for independence after World War II. Throughout this period, the city expanded relentlessly, seeing the advent of a new hospital complex, a technical institute, a university and the country's high court. Following **independence**, Dar became the capital of Tanganyika, and after the 1964 union of Tanganyika and Zanzibar, the capital of Tanzania.

The failure of Julius Nyerere's collectivist *Ujamaa* policy (see p.718) and the consequent collapse of the country's economy led to a reverse in the city's fortunes, however. By the 1970s Dar's economy had fallen into the doldrums, not helped by the loss of its capital status to Dodoma in 1974. Yet the city today is a far cry from its run-down state in the early 1980s. The election of the reformist president, **Ali Hassan Mwinyi**, in 1985 ushered in a new era of economic liberalization which continues to this day. Dar's former potholed streets have been patched up, new highways have been built, and the city's basic infrastructure – although still far from adequate for the majority – is being developed with the aid of loans from the World Bank, the IMF and other international agencies.

Arrival and information

Arriving in Dar, particularly by ferry or bus, can be a chaotic experience, especially given the disorienting attention of hustlers and touts peddling the services of dubious safari companies. If you're at all nervous about the city (though there's actually little reason to be – read the box "Avoiding trouble" opposite), you're best off taking a taxi to your hotel.

For information on **moving on from Dar**, see p.117.

By air

Dar es Salaam's **airport** lies 15km southwest of the city, 25 minutes away by road. **International flights** use terminal 2, which has a bar, an expensive restaurant, car-rental agencies, a post office, telephones and a tourist office (though it's of only limited use). You can change money and travellers' cheques either side of immigration. Avoid the safari operator offices here unless the companies are reviewed on p.124, as some are blacklisted, and be wary of the safari touts in the arrivals hall: the majority of these represent decidedly dodgy operators, no matter how polished their presentation and patter may appear. Don't feel pressurized into accepting anything, and if you're offered a free lift into town, remember that you're under no obligation to buy a safari from them in return. Most **domestic flights** use Terminal 1, a fifteen-minute walk from Terminal 2, whose facilities are limited to a snack bar, toilet and charter airline offices.

Taxis charge around Tsh10,000 to the city centre or Msasani Peninsula, although this can be haggled down to as little as Tsh5000 depending on your bargaining skills. Fares to the northern beach resorts of Jangwani, Bahari and Kunduchi start at Tsh20,000, though these too can be talked down. **Daladalas** to the city (Tsh150) run past the start of the slip road to the international terminal, a 500-metre walk away.

By bus

Arriving by bus is a relatively simple affair thanks to the new **bus station** at Ubungo, 8km west of the city along Morogoro Road, at which most services now arrive. The terminal itself is relatively calm, though there are still enough hawkers and touts to keep you on your toes – watch your bags and pockets, especially outside the station.

Taxis can be hired inside the terminal and charge around Tsh5000 to the city centre. It's much cheaper to catch a **daladala** to Kariakoo or Posta (Tsh150), though clambering aboard one with a bulging backpack won't endear you to your fellow passengers. Note that the buses of some companies – including Akamba, Royal, Tawfiq and Takrim – still finish at their old terminals in Kariakoo and Kisutu districts, which are much closer to the main budget hotels on and around Libya Street. Scandinavian Express services pass through Ubungo before finishing up at their terminal on Msimbazi Street, close to the Kariakoo hotels and a ten to fifteen-minute walk from Libya Street.

Avoiding trouble

Dar es Salaam is a relatively **safe** city in spite of its size. Nonetheless, there are a number of hazards you should be aware of. Most obviously, offers of marijuana and money-changing on the street should be refused (these tricksters hang out along Samora Avenue near the clock tower, and in front of the post office) – you're pretty much guaranteed to get conned or worse (this scam now seems to have acquired a time lapse whereby the victim is tailed for a few hours before being stung). Equally, all safari touts should be given a wide berth: any operator worth its salt shouldn't need to tout for trade. For the lowdown on scams involving ferry tickets, see p.66.

As to **specific areas**, you should definitely be on your guard between Bibi Titi Mohamed Street and Kariakoo and Magomeni. The attendant poverty, shadowy corners and lack of *askaris* are an invitation to muggers, although there have been few reported incidents. Be equally careful along Ocean Road, even by day, especially along the beach or on the path running beside it, which at certain points is invisible from the road. That said, unless you're carrying valuables, you should have nothing to worry about. Lastly, beware of pickpockets and bag-snatchers at all the main transport terminals, especially Ubungo bus station and around the ferry port, both of which can be disorienting for new arrivals.

By train

Coming from Zambia or the southwest, the **TAZARA Line** terminates 5.5km west of the city centre at the Tazara Station, on the corner of Nelson Mandela Expressway and Nyerere Road. There are lots of daladalas outside here, serving both the city and the coast immediately to the south of Dar (Tsh150), and there are also taxis, which shouldn't cost more than Tsh4000 into the centre. Trains on the **Central Line** from Mwanza and Tabora terminate at **Central Railway Station**, right by the harbour in the centre of the city. The Stesheni daladala stand, one block east of the station along Sokoine Drive, has services to the south and the west as well as to Kariakoo, from where there are daladalas to almost every corner of the city. There are also plenty of taxis outside the station.

By sea

The **ferry terminal**, where boats arrive from Zanzibar, Pemba and Mtwara, is on Sokoine Drive, 500m east of the Central Railway Station. Daladalas pass by frequently until around 10pm, heading south or on towards Kariakoo. Alternatively, it's perfectly safe to walk from here into the city.

Information

Dar's **tourist office** (Mon–Fri 8am–4pm, Sat 8am–1pm; ☎022/213 1555 or 212 0373, ⊜safari@ud.co.tz) is on the ground floor of Matasalamat Mansions on Samora Avenue, four blocks southwest of the Askari Monument. They have useful lists of the main hotels together with phone numbers and prices, a register of blacklisted safari operators (though it's not comprehensive), train timetables and some brochures. The maps in this book will be sufficient for most purposes, but if you need a really comprehensive plan of the city the excellent *Dar es Salaam City Map and Guide* ($5) is available in better bookshops (see p.113) and the government map office (see p.116).

For information about **forthcoming events**, pick up a copy of the monthly *What's Happening in Dar es Salaam* (also available online at ⓦ www.whatsindar.com) or the bi-monthly *Dar es Salaam Guide*. Both are free, and can also be found at major travel agents, the better bookshops, and at the *Royal Palm, Sea Cliff* and *Ocean Breeze* hotels. If you're spending more than a few days in Dar it's worth investing in *Dar es Salaam: A Dozen Drives around the City* (Mkuki na Nyota Publishers), by Laura Sykes and Uma Waide, which describes not only drives but also a number of walks in and around the city, and is packed with tons of fascinating background information.

City transport

Despite periodic complaints in the press about dangerous driving, dirty uniforms and unsociably loud music, Dar es Salaam's **public transport** is surprisingly efficient and will get you almost anywhere within a twenty-kilometre radius of the city for only a few hundred shillings. The set fare for **daladalas** is usually Tsh150. In addition, there are **taxis** almost everywhere, even after midnight, and in the city centre at least you'll probably grow tired of hearing the persistent chorus of hisses accompanied by "taxi, taxi".

Daladalas

Dar's **daladalas** – shared minibuses – appeared when the city's decrepit bus service was opened to competition in the 1980s. As a result, there are now literally thousands of licensed daladalas that together cover almost every corner of the city. Services run from 5am to 9 or 10pm, and the vehicles are usually battered old Hiace minibuses or slightly larger Dynacruisers or Toyota DCMs. The system is actually fairly well organized: each daladala is **colour coded** (the thick band painted around the middle) according to the route, and the terminals that it runs between are clearly marked in big letters on the front, together with details of which route it goes by if there are alternatives. The standard **fare** for all but the longest journeys to the outskirts is Tsh150; you're issued a ticket on board, and you're unlikely to be ripped off, especially if you give a Tsh200 coin instead of a big banknote. The only hassle you're likely to encounter is at the main terminals, where you'll have to contend with turnboys competing to get you onto their vehicle. If there are several daladalas going the same way, choose the one that seems fullest, since it's most likely to leave first.

Most daladalas start and finish at one of the two main terminals, called stands or *stendi*, in the city centre. The first of these, **Posta**, covers the section of Azikiwe Street between Ghana and Garden avenues. The second, **Kariakoo**, lies a couple of kilometres to the west along Msimbazi Street. The busiest routes out of the city have services from both stands.

Other city-centre stands are **Kivukoni** (or "Ferry"), by the ferry and fish market at the east end of Kivukoni Front, and **Stesheni**, one block east of Central Railway Station off Sokoine Drive, which are where most southbound services depart from. Outside the city centre, you may find yourself having to change at Mwenge or Ubungo stands if there's no direct service to where you're going. **Mwenge**, 9km northwest of the city at the junction of Bagamoyo and Sam Nujoma roads, has daladalas heading north, whilst **Ubungo**, a few hundred metres beyond the main bus terminal at the junction of Morogoro and Sam Nujoma roads, covers the western outskirts and the university. There are plenty of daladalas from the city centre to both these stands.

Taxis

Taxis can be found almost everywhere, especially outside major hotels, road junctions and nightclubs. Licensed cabs are usually white and carry white number plates; others risk being pulled up by the police at your inconvenience. Trips within the city shouldn't cost more than Tsh1500, and journeys to the outskirts average Tsh2000–2500, while a ride to the airport shouldn't set you back more than Tsh8000. For longer journeys, one hour's hire costs around Tsh5000, while a full day will set you back around Tsh30,000. Obviously, all these prices depend on how well you can bargain. if you're not in the mood, you could end up paying anything up to fifty percent more.

Accommodation

Dar has a wide choice of **accommodation**, ranging from basic guest houses and Christian-run hostels to a growing number of business-class hotels and beach resorts aimed squarely at the international market. **Prices** are higher than elsewhere in mainland Tanzania, and cheap rooms – anything under Tsh10,000 a double - are often little more than a bed in a cell.

The main area for **budget accommodation** is the cluster of hotels in the Asian-dominated Mchafukoge and Kisutu areas, both within walking distance of the centre. A popular alternative is to head to Mikadi or Mjimwema beaches south of the city (see p.132), while the beach hotels north of the city (see p.127) are also worth considering. The nearest **campsites** are also at Mikadi and Mjimwema beaches (see p.132), and there are less accessible pitches at *Jangwani Seabreeze Lodge* (see p.127) and *Silver Sands Beach Resort* (see p.129), both over 20km to the north, and at *Pugu Hills Resort* in Pugu Forest (see p.136), 25km to the southwest.

For **long-term accommodation**, try to get hold of the weekly *Advertising Dar* freesheet, available at hotels on the Msasani Peninsula, at A Novel Idea bookshop (see p.113), and online at Ⓦ www.advertisingdar.co.tz It usually contains a page of announcements for flats and houses to rent, most of them at ludicrously inflated prices, but you might strike lucky (Tsh70,000 a month is a bargain).

All the following places to stay are marked on the **maps** on p.84 or on p.90 (Northern Dar).

City centre: east from Maktaba Street

The area between Maktaba/Azikiwe Street and Ocean Road (equivalent to the old European quarter of Uzunguni) benefits from wide streets and plenty of trees. It contains an odd blend of backpackers' hostels (the best of which is the *YWCA*) and good luxury accommodation like the *Royal Palm Hotel* and *New Africa Hotel*.

Embassy Garden Ave ☏022/211 7084, Ⓔ embassy@raha.com. Mid-range place that has clearly seen better days, though the slightly tatty rooms are still adequate, and come with a/c and fridges (the more expensive ones also have TVs). The small swimming pool and 24hr room service are a big bonus, and there's also a restaurant, bar and safe parking. Breakfast included. ❻

Holiday Inn Dar es Salaam Garden Ave ☏022/213 7575, Ⓦ www.holiday-inn.com. Brand-new five-storey hotel crammed into a small plot beside the Botanical Gardens. The 152 double rooms (including some with disabled facilities) come with satellite TV, telephone, a/c, safe, bathtub, and local art on the walls. Facilities include a curio shop, internet and travel centre, swimming pool, gym, and a bar and restaurant. Buffet breakfast included. ❼

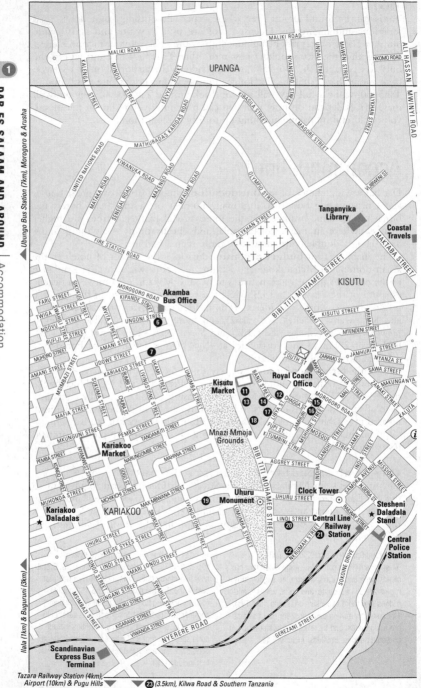

Msasani Peninsula, Northern Beach Resorts & Bagamoyo ▲

UPANGA

Tanganyika
Library

Coastal
Travels

KISUTU

Akamba
Bus Office

❻

❼

Kisutu
Market

Royal Coach
Office

❶❶
❶❸ ❶❹ ❶❷
❶❼ ❶❺
❶❻
❶❽

Mnazi Mmoja
Grounds

Kariakoo
Market

Kariakoo
Daladalas

KARIAKOO

❶❾

Uhuru
Monument

Clock Tower

Stesheni
Daladala
Stand

❷❶
❷❷
❷❸

Central Line
Railway
Station

Central
Police
Station

ℹ

Ilala (1km) & Buguruni (3km) ▲

Scandinavian
Express Bus
Terminal

Tazara Railway Station (4km),
Airport (10km) & Pugu Hills ▲   ▼ ❷❸ (3.5km), Kilwa Road & Southern Tanzania

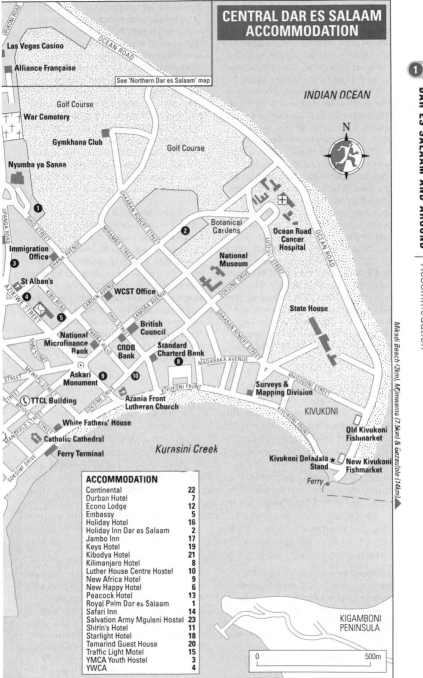

CENTRAL DAR ES SALAAM ACCOMMODATION

DEVCON ROAD

OCEAN ROAD

Las Vegas Casino

Alliance Française

See 'Northern Dar es Salaam' map

INDIAN OCEAN

Golf Course

War Cemetery

Gymkhana Club

Golf Course

N

Nyumba ya Sanaa

UPANGA ROAD

OHIO STREET

❶

SHAABAN ROBERT STREET

MITAMBO STREET

❷

Botanical Gardens

Ocean Road Cancer Hospital

OCEAN ROAD

LUTHULI STREET

Immigration Office

GHANA AVENUE

SERENGETI AVENUE

National Museum

❸

St Alban's

AZIKIWE STREET

KIBO ROAD

GARDEN AVENUE

OHIO STREET

WCST Office

SAMORA AVENUE

SOKOINE DRIVE

SHAABAN ROBERT STREET

State House

❹

❺

PAMBA ROAD

British Council

National Microfinance Bank

SIMU STREET

CNDB Bank

Standard Chartered Bank

❽

MADARAKA AVENUE

MAGOGONI STREET

Surveys & Mapping Division

STREET

MKWEPU STREET

Askari Monument

❾

❿

SOKOINE DRIVE

KIVUKONI FRONT

KIVUKONI

BRIDGE STREET

TTCL Building

Azania Front Lutheran Church

KIVUKONI FRONT

MANSFIELD STREET

White Fathers' House

Catholic Cathedral

Old Kivukoni Fishmarket

SOKOINE DRIVE

Ferry Terminal

Kurasini Creek

Kivukoni Daladala Stand

New Kivukoni Fishmarket

Ferry

Mikadi Beach (2km), Mjimwema (7.5km) & Gezaulole (14km)

KIGAMBONI PENINSULA

0   500m

ACCOMMODATION

Continental	22
Durban Hotel	7
Econo Lodge	12
Embassy	5
Holiday Hotel	16
Holiday Inn Dar es Salaam	2
Jambo Inn	17
Keys Hotel	19
Kibodya Hotel	21
Kilimanjaro Hotel	8
Luther House Centre Hostel	10
New Africa Hotel	9
New Happy Hotel	6
Peacock Hotel	13
Royal Palm Dar es Salaam	1
Safari Inn	14
Salvation Army Mgulani Hostel	23
Shirin's Hotel	11
Starlight Hotel	18
Tamarind Guest House	20
Traffic Light Motel	15
YMCA Youth Hostel	3
YWCA	4

Kilimanjaro Hotel Kivukoni Front ☎0742/332100 or 0741/667664. A huge and exceedingly dilapidated 1960s monolith whose staff seem genuinely surprised to see any guests. The rooms have huge beds, balconies overlooking the harbour, a/c and fridges, and musty carpets smelling of boot polish – some also have TVs, but forget the phones (they don't work), while the swimming pool hasn't seen water for years. Even so, all in all the price is perfectly reasonable. There's also a self-service canteen. Breakfast included. ❺

Luther House Centre Hostel Sokoine Drive ☎022/212 0734. The unusually gloomy staff set the mood for this long-established and safe – though overpriced – backpackers' haunt run by the Lutheran Church. The rooms, all with private bathroom, are adequate if not sparkling, with box nets, a chair, table, and cotton sheets. The beds are narrow, though, and the whirring of water pumps may bug you at night. Good restaurant. ❹

New Africa Hotel Azikiwe St ☎022/211 7050 or 211 7051, ⊛www.newafricahotel.com. Large and classy establishment with a touch of Art Deco, and recently refurbished to the same luxurious standard as the *Royal Palm*. All rooms have a/c, satellite TV, a minibar, hairdryer and telephone, and amenities include smoking and non-smoking floors, room service, a business centre and two restaurants, though there's no swimming pool. Breakfast included. ❽

Royal Palm Dar es Salaam Ohio St ☎022/211 2416, ⊛www.royalpalmdar.com. Dar's leading hotel (it was formerly the *Sheraton*), with 251 luxurious rooms, all with a/c, satellite TV and safe. Amenities include two restaurants, a business centre, safari offices, swimming pool, a sauna and a gym. No single rates. Breakfast included. Rooms from ❾

YMCA Youth Hostel Upanga Rd ☎ & ⒻO22/213 5457. This has all the charm of an army blockhouse, in spite of its small courtyard garden, and the staff are amazingly grumpy. The rooms, all with shared bathrooms, are becoming ragged, but are clean and have nets and fans. There's also secure parking and a cafeteria (you'll need to preorder) and they also sell beer. Breakfast included. ❸

YWCA, corner Maktaba St and Ghana Ave, entrance on Ghana Ave ☎0741/622707. One of Dar's few budget choices that comes heartily recommended (at least if you don't mind the racket from the Posta daladala stand between 6am and 10pm). It's cheap by Dar standards, has big reductions for singles, is clean and friendly (well, excepting the kitchen staff), and also takes single men and couples. There's also a laundry service and a good cheap restaurant, and the 11pm curfew isn't a problem as the *askari* will let you in at any time. Also has two-bed flats for Tsh10,000 per flat. Breakfast included. ❷

City centre: Kisutu and Mchafukoge

The predominantly Asian areas of **Kisutu** and **Mchafukoge**, bounded by Maktaba Street to the east and Bibi Titi Mohamed Street to the north and west, contain the main concentration of Dar's budget hotels, as well as a few out-of-place mid-range choices. Prices have been rising steadily, with most half-decent rooms now costing upwards of Tsh10,000, but you can still find a basic room for about half that, though it's likely to be a horrible fleapit. The hotels around Libya Street are the best for meeting fellow travellers (for which reason the area is also favoured by a number of irritating if harmless safari touts), and several bus companies serving Moshi, Arusha and Mombasa (Royal Coach, Scandinavian, Tawfiq and Takrim) stop nearby after passing through Ubungo bus terminal. There are plenty of *askaris* around should you be carrying luggage, and walking around at night shouldn't pose any problems so long as you're sensible.

Continental, Nkrumah St ☎ 022/213 1470, Ⓔhotcont@intafrica.com. A decent if unexciting mid-range option near Central Railway Station. All rooms have private bathroom and a/c, satellite TV, a minibar and phone. There's also 24hr room service, two restaurants and a bar that plays Indian music. ❹

Econo Lodge Down a nameless side street off Libya St ☎022/211 6048 or 211 6049,

Ⓔeconolodge@raha.com. A quiet and rather plain four-storey Muslim hotel with linoleum floors and a TV on each level (but no lift). The rooms have decent bathrooms and phone, but the beds are narrow, there are no mosquito nets and the nylon sheets aren't always clean. Most rooms have fans, the better ones have balconies, and the most expensive have a/c. Breakfast included. ❸–❹

Holiday Hotel Jamhuri St, opposite Chagga St

022/212 0675. Given the inflated prices of the *Jambo Inn* and *Safari Inn*, this is now the number-one backpackers' choice in the city, with reasonable rooms (some with private bathroom) and good security. The staff aren't particularly helpful, but you can't really complain at the price. ❷

Jambo Inn Libya St ☎022/211 4293, ℉022/211 3149. A popular backpackers' haunt, and good value for single travellers, though it's a tad overpriced for doubles. There's a mixed bag of rooms (and those facing the road can be noisy), so ask to see a selection: some are past their best, with small beds, nylon sheets and fans but no nets (rooms are sprayed instead); others are perfectly adequate, with good-sized nets, and more expensive rooms have a/c. A mediocre breakfast is included. ❸

Kibodya Hotel, corner Uhuru St and Nkrumah St ☎022/211 7856. The large bar which occupies the ground floor makes for a distinctly intimidating atmosphere, especially for women, but the rooms themselves (all doubles) are OK, and come with bathrooms and fans. ❷

Peacock Hotel Bibi Titi Mohamed St ☎022/212 0334, ⓦwww.peacock-hotel.co.tz. Facing Mnazi Mmoja Grounds, this modern seven-storey hotel caters mainly to African and Asian businessmen. The staff are friendly and efficient, and the rooms are good – if overpriced compared to places like *The Courtyard* (see p.88) – with immense beds, a/c, satellite TV and phone; those higher up or in the new wing are bigger, brighter and more expensive. Facilities include an internet café, secure parking, a bar and a pricey but bad restaurant. Free airport transfer, and breakfast included. ❻–❼

Safari Inn off Band St, signposted off Libya St ☎022/211 9104, ℮safari-inn@mailcity.com. Another long-established backpackers' haunt, as reflected in its steadily increasing rates (though again, single rooms are much cheaper). The small rooms are bright and airy, with big double beds

("No women of immoral turpitude" though), fans and nets, though the bathrooms are smelly and the atmosphere isn't the most welcoming. Pricier rooms have a/c, and there's an internet café downstairs. Breakfast included. ❸

Shirin's Hotel Entrance at the back of Kisutu Market, off Bibi Titi Mohamed St ☎022/212 4068. A dark and down-at-heel Asian-run high-rise which wouldn't be mentioned were it not one of the cheapest places in town. The tatty rooms have undersized nylon sheets, fans but no nets, electricity and cleanish Western-style toilets – fine if you're used to cheap guest houses, but be careful walking back late at night. ❷

Starlight Hotel Bibi Titi Mohamed St, also accessible from Libya St ☎022/211 9387 or 211 9388, ℮starlight@cats-net.com. An eight-storey business-class monolith with 150 rooms, some overlooking Mnazi Mmoja Grounds. It's older than the *Peacock* and getting frayed, but at almost half the price is very good value. All rooms come with private bathroom, both a/c and fan, hot water, TV, phone and fridge, but the beds are small and there are no nets. Amenities include a bureau de change, gift shop and restaurant. Breakfast included. ❺

Tamarind Guest House Lindi St, near Mnazi Mmoja Grounds ☎& ℉022/211 3629. One of Dar's cheapest, and perfectly decent at that, offering a choice of rooms with private or shared bathrooms. ❶–❷

Traffic Light Motel Jamhuri St, close to Morogoro Rd ☎022/212 3438. Outwardly unappetizing, thanks to a courtyard which seems to be a venue for men doing nothing very much in particular, but if you can cope with the atmosphere it's OK, with a choice of rooms with private or shared bathrooms, and plenty of ripped linoleum. All rooms have fans and nets, and the small beds have clean cotton sheets. ❷

West of the centre: Kariakoo

Over the last decade, a growing number of multi-storey hotels have sprung up in **Kariakoo** between Msimbazi Street and Lumumba Road to the west of Mnazi Mmoja Grounds; most of them offer much better value for money than more central options. The following is a selection of the cheaper choices; there are several more expensive ones – such as *Ricki Hill*, at the corner of Kipata Street and Lumumba Street, and the *Valley View*, at the corner of Kongo Street and Matumbi – which are overpriced at around $40–60 a night. Note that walking around Kariakoo at night isn't recommended, unless you're feeling confident and are unencumbered by valuables.

Durban Hotel, Udowe St, just off Lumumba St ☎022/218 0555, ℮durbanhotel@nyezi.co.tz. A cool and calm mid-range choice, offering good rooms with private bathrooms and either fans or a/c, plus a handful of suites ($45). The restaurant makes up for its bland appearance with some marvellous food, and breakfast is included. ❹

DAR ES SALAAM AND AROUND | Accommodation

Keys Hotel, 13 Uhuru St, just west of Mnazi Mmoja Grounds ☎ 022/218 3033, ✉ abcclick@raha.com. Big place offering excellent-value rooms with private bathroom as well as suites, which are still good value despite costing twice as much. It also has a large restaurant and bar, and breakfast is included. Rooms ❷, suites ❹

New Happy Hotel Ungoni St, just off Lumumba St ☎ 022/218 0505. Good-value rooms on the eastern edge of Kariakoo, all with fans, though many of the beds lack nets. There's also an attractive rooftop bar, plus a restaurant-cum-bar on the ground floor. ❷

North of the centre: Upanga

The strip of waterfront from Ocean Road to the Msasani Peninsula, including the Upanga area south of Selander Bridge, contains a good number of midrange options, most of them modern and well run. All have restaurants, and a handful also have nightclubs. Frequent daladalas run up Ali Hassan Mwinyi Road from Posta to Kawe, Mwanan/Nyamala and Mwenge and, less frequently, from Stesheni to Mwananyamala/Nyamala.

The Courtyard Ocean Rd ☎ 022/213 0130, ✉ courtyard@raha.com. With its bougainvillea-festooned wooden balconies, this three-storey hotel looks like part of New Orleans rebuilt around a small swimming pool in, yes, a courtyard. The location is odd, flanked by high-rise, low-cost housing, and the nearby beach isn't recommended for swimming because of pollution, but no matter – service and standards are high. Standard rooms (twin or double) have a/c, telephone, satellite TV, bathtubs, coffee tray, safe and minibar, but smell of bug spray (no nets); the more expensive rooms are larger but otherwise identical. Other amenities include a very good restaurant (the *Langi-Langi*; see p.104), snack bar, bar, room service and travel desk. Breakfast included. ❼–❽

Etienne's Hotel Ocean Rd (no phone). A rather run-down hotel that has clearly seen better days, as suggested by the ancient (but empty) bottles of champagne and cognac adorning its attractive pub-like bar. The rooms (twins only) have fans but lack nets, and offer a perfectly adequate refuge from the noise and bustle of the city centre. There's also a beer garden at the back. Breakfast included. ❸

Palm Beach Hotel 305 Ali Hassan Mwinyi Rd, on the left before Selander Bridge ☎ 022/213 0985, ⊛ www.pbhtz.com. A rather shabby 1950s hotel in desperate need of renovation, but which nonetheless remains popular. Its 28 rooms are large but tatty, with small nets, no fans, few remaining TVs (most were stolen long ago) and battered a/c units. Some have fridges and bathtubs (allegedly with hot water); cheaper ones share bathrooms. There are no palm trees or beach, incidentally, but there is an excellent restaurant and a popular bar. Breakfast included. ❹

North of the city: Msasani Peninsula

Msasani Peninsula and Oyster Bay, roughly 6km north of the city centre, are Dar's upmarket residential districts. To get to Msasani from the city, catch a daladala from Posta to Masaki marked "via A. H. Mwinyi" or "No. 13". These go all the way around the peninsula, running up Touré Drive past the *Oyster Bay*, *Golden Tulip* and *Sea Cliff* hotels, returning along Chole Road on the west side and passing close to *Smokies Tavern* and the *Hotel Karibu*. A taxi to the peninsula from the city costs Tsh4000–6000 depending on exactly where you're going.

Golden Tulip Dar es Salaam, Touré Drive ☎ 022/260 0288, ✉ goldentuliptanzania @afsat.com. This huge Arabian-style resort is one of the city's slickest upmarket beach hotels, if you ignore the fact that you can't currently swim in the ocean here because of sharks. The spacious standard rooms all have balconies with sea views, satellite TV, minibar and marble bathrooms, and facilities include Dar's largest swimming pool, poolside bar and grill, a jacuzzi with sea view, fitness area, shopping mall, coffee shop and the *Sanaa Restaurant*, which does a good range of Tanzanian dishes. Breakfast included. ❽

Karibu Haile Selassie Rd ☎022/260 1767 or 260 1768, ℮karibursvn@hotmail.com. Recently refurbished, standard four-star hotel, with clean and well-maintained rooms, all with satellite TV, a/c and minibar. There's a swimming pool and poolside bar, two restaurants, and a popular Saturday disco. ❹

Oyster Bay Hotel Touré Drive, Msasani Peninsula ☎022/260 0352 or 260 0353, ℗www.tanzaniantravel.com. Thoroughly idiosyncratic, if overpriced, place facing Coco Beach (but on the wrong side of the road), with every inch of its shady grounds crammed with sculptures, duck and fish ponds, a bar, bird cages, walkways, bridges, an old car halfway up a tree, sun loungers, a 1km jogging track, squash court and even a golf course. Other facilities include a freeform swimming pool, jacuzzi and sauna, seafood restaurant and safari office. Rooms vary greatly: some are cramped with furniture and rather musty; others are stylish and have sea views; all have TV, fridge, a/c and phone. There are also three large cottages each with a private pool and optional self-catering. ❽

Q-Bar and Guest House Off Haile Selassie Rd ☎022/260 2150 or 0744/282474, ℮qbar@hotmail.com. A modern hotel typical of a number of mid-range choices on Msasani with the difference that they also offer cheap bed space in a "backpackers' room" at $12 per person. Standard rooms have satellite TV and a/c, and there's a live band in the bar every Friday. Breakfast included. ❺

Sea Cliff Hotel Touré Drive ☎022/260 0300 or 260 0381, ℗www.hotelseacliff.com. Perched on the northern tip of the peninsula, this 86-room hotel is a graceless thatched concrete block from the outside but very stylish inside. You've a choice of double or twin rooms, all spotless, with a/c, satellite TV, minibar, coffee percolator, telephone and bathtub. For $20 more you get a sea view, but forget the expensive "executive suites", which are little different. Amenities include expensive bars and restaurants, a pastry shop, safari office, shopping centre, gymnasium and swimming pool. The downside is that there's no beach (it's on a cliff, of course), and the almost entirely *wazungu* clientele. Breakfast included. ❽–❾

Outside the city

As well as the places listed below, accommodation outside Dar can be found at the Pugu Hills (p.136); at the beaches north of the city at Jangwani (p.127), Kunduchi and Bahari (p.129); and south of the city at Mikadi and Mjimwema (p.132) and Ras Kutani (p.136).

Salvation Army Mgulani Hostel 3.5km down Kilwa Rd, Mgulani ☎022/285 1467, ℮david_burrows@tnz.salvationarmy.org. If you don't mind catching a daladala into town (or a taxi back at night), this is excellent value for single travellers, and also offers the singularly rousing pleasure of waking up to the Sally's oom-pah-pah band and the police force's combo next door. There are 68 rooms in individual bungalows, all with private bathrooms and fans, and most with box nets. The canteen is nothing special, though, and you'll need to pre-order; there's cheaper food at the roadside bars on Nelson Mandela Expressway nearby. To get there, catch a daladala from Kariakoo, Stesheni or Posta to Bayala, Temeke or Rangi Tatu marked "via Kilwa Road". Breakfast included. ❸

The City

Central Dar is a patchwork of influences, from the vibrant **Asian district** to the more sedate European quarter of **Uzunguni**, although to find any authentically African streetlife you'll have to head to **Kariakoo Market**, just west of the centre. In general it's the contrasting flavours of these different districts which provide the city's main interest, since conventional tourist attractions are thin on the ground, while the city's low-rise colonial structures are rapidly being replaced by modern high-rises, including the recently completed 25-storey Mafuta House on Azikiwe Street – Tanzania's tallest building. For a bird's-eye **view** of the city, get to the top of the *Kilimanjaro Hotel* or the *New Africa Hotel* (head for the restaurant on the ninth floor).

A number of travel agents (p.123) offer guided **city tours**, usually consisting of a half-day ride around the main sights, but at around $70 (or $100 for a full

Jangwani, Kunduchi & Bahari Beaches & Bagamoyo

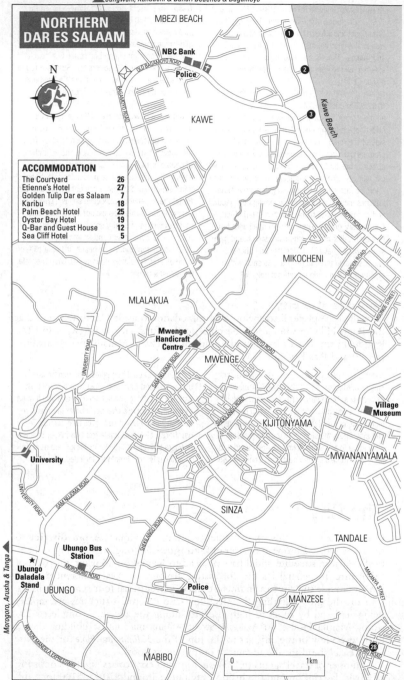

NORTHERN DAR ES SALAAM

MBEZI BEACH

NBC Bank

Police

N

KAWE

ACCOMMODATION

The Courtyard	26
Etienne's Hotel	27
Golden Tulip Dar es Salaam	7
Karibu	18
Palm Beach Hotel	25
Oyster Bay Hotel	19
Q-Bar and Guest House	12
Sea Cliff Hotel	5

Kawe Beach

MIKOCHENI

MLALAKUA

Mwenge Handicraft Centre

MWENGE

Village Museum

KIJITONYAMA

MWANANYAMALA

University

SINZA

TANDALE

Ubungo Bus Station

Ubungo Daladala Stand

Police

UBUNGO

MANZESE

MABIBO

0   1km

Morogoro, Arusha & Tanga

Tazara Train Station, Airport & Mgulani

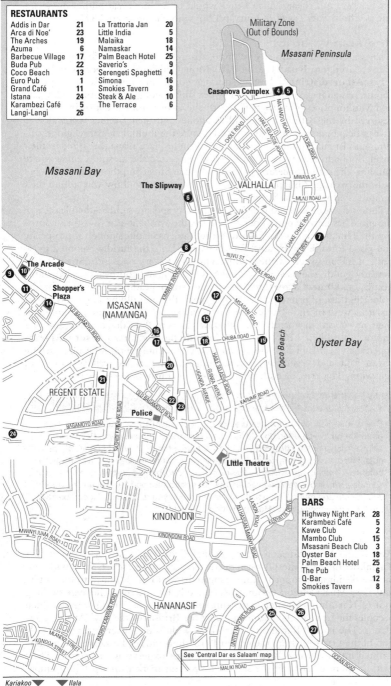

RESTAURANTS

Addis in Dar	21	La Trattoria Jan	20
Arca di Noe'	23	Little India	5
The Arches	19	Malaika	18
Azuma	6	Namaskar	14
Barbecue Village	17	Palm Beach Hotel	25
Buda Pub	22	Saverio's	9
Coco Beach	13	Serengeti Spaghetti	4
Euro Pub	1	Simona	16
Grand Café	11	Smokies Tavern	8
Istana	24	Steak & Ale	10
Karambezi Café	5	The Terrace	6
Langi-Langi	26		

Military Zone
(Out of Bounds)

Msasani Peninsula

Casanova Complex 4 5

Msasani Bay

The Slipway 6

VALHALLA

MA-ANDO ROAD
CHOLE ROAD
HAILE SELASSIE ROAD
TOURE DRIVE
MWAYA ST.
MLALI ROAD
CHAKE CHAKE ROAD
TOURE DRIVE

7

RUVU ST.
KAOLE ROAD
MSASANI ROAD

8

The Arcade
9 10

11

Shopper's Plaza
14

MSASANI
(NAMANGA)

12

15

16
17

18

CHUBA ROAD

19

Coco Beach

Oyster Bay

20

OLD BAGAMOYO ROAD
NIMWEZI AVENUE
HAILE SELASSIE ROAD
UGANDA AVENUE
GUINEA AVENUE E.
KATUME ROAD

21

REGENT ESTATE

22
23

Police

24

KASHIM KAWAWA ROAD
OLD BAGAMOYO ROAD

BAGAMOYO ROAD

Little Theatre

LA IBON ROAD
AL HASSAN MWINYI ROAD
KENYATTA DRIVE

KINONDONI

MWINYI JUMA ROAD

KINONDONI ROAD

BARS

Highway Night Park	28
Karambezi Café	5
Kawe Club	2
Mambo Club	15
Msasani Beach Club	3
Oyster Bar	18
Palm Beach Hotel	25
The Pub	6
Q-Bar	12
Smokies Tavern	8

HANANASIF

KASHIM KAWAWA ROAD
MLANDIZI ROAD
KONDOA STREET

25 26

27

UNITED NATIONS ROAD

See 'Central Dar es Salaam' map

MALIKI ROAD

OCEAN ROAD

Kariakoo ▼   ▼ *Ilala*

day) they're not cheap. Much better would be to hire a car with a driver for the day from Easy Travel & Tours (p.124), who charge around $25.

The Asian district

The western end of the city centre – a rough triangle bounded by Sokoine Drive, Morogoro Road and Bibi Titi Mohamed Street – is occupied by the city's **Asian district**, a bustling quarter containing hundreds of shops, tea rooms, restaurants, goldsmiths and sweet shops, along with Hindu, Sikh, Jain and Muslim places of worship. This is the heart of historical **Uhindini**, the area reserved by the British for the Indian coolies and their families who came to Dar to help build the modern city, and despite the multiplicity of religions, cultures and languages, the individual communities have managed to retain their strong individual characters. You're not allowed into the mosques unless you're Muslim (the main concentration is on Mosque Street and the streets off it), but both the Sikh and Hindu communities will be happy to show you around their temples: start on Kisutu Street.

There's no real centre to the district, nor any specific sights – the pleasure of the place lies in unexpected details, such as the wrought-iron swastikas adorning the Hindu temples on **Kisutu Street** (an auspicious symbol of prosperity and good fortune for Hindus, Buddhists and Jain), the luridly coloured pyramids of Indian sweets (Temeke Confectionary Bakery on Kisutu Street is particularly good), the *paan* shops (see box below), and the beautiful balconied houses on **Uhuru Street**, which is well worth heading to anyway for the colourful blaze of printed cloth *kitenge* panels that are sold by shops and hawkers at its western end – watch for the *mama kubwas* ("big ladies") squinting at their reflections in mirrors and window panes as they drape one ream after another over their hefty shoulders. In addition, don't miss **Kisutu Market** (open daily) on Bibi Titi Mohamed Street, an atmospheric little place selling cheap fruit and vegetables, honey, beans and pulses, as well as baskets of squawking chickens, dried fish and some gorgeously pungent herbs.

Dar's paan shops

One of the most distinctive features of Dar es Salaam's Asian area are the Indian **paan shops**, which often double as tobacconists and corner shops. *Paan* is essentially a mildly narcotic dessert: you choose from a range of sweet spices, chopped nuts, bits of vegetable, syrup and white lime, which are then wrapped in a hot, sweet betel leaf (*mtambuu*), which is the mildly narcotic bit – it tastes as exotic as it sounds. *Paan* is chewed and sucked but not swallowed: pop the triangular parcel in your mouth and munch, then spit out the pith when you're finished. A good place to try it is the Shehenai Paan House on Mrima Street.

Kariakoo

West of the Asian district, on the far side of the Mnazi Mmoja Grounds, lies **Kariakoo**, the city's most African district: a dusty grid of streets lined with low, mud-walled houses topped with corrugated-iron roofs. Bounded to the east by the grassy Mnazi Mmoja Grounds, Kariakoo is dominated by the huge swelling roof of **Kariakoo Market** (daily sunrise–sunset), East Africa's largest, which occupies the heart of the area set aside by the British for the city's African population. The name "Kariakoo" dates from World War I, when, after the expulsion of the Germans from the city in 1916, thousands of Tanzanians were conscripted into the hated British **Carrier Corps** to serve as war porters. Their barracks were erected on the site of the present market on a patch of empty ground that had been earmarked for a ceremonial park in honour of Kaiser Wilhelm II. After the war, Kariakoo (along with Ilala district further to the west) was left to the African population. No amenities were provided – and indeed many parts of the area still lack the most basic of facilities – but in spite of the poverty, Kariakoo exudes a solid sense of community that manages to combine both tribal and national identities. In many ways, the district is like a microcosm of the country, and its pan-Tanzanian nature has resulted in one of the most fascinating and headily colourful markets in Africa. In it, and in the maze of shops and stalls surrounding it, you'll find everything from exotic fruits, vegetables and fish to freshly cooked meat, aromatic spices, herbs and coffee, handicrafts, textiles, local brews (*pombe*), and children's toys made from wire and recycled tin cans. Old men sell medicinal herbs, potions and powders in little bottles salvaged from hospitals, as well as bundles of tree bark, dried lizards and seashells with curative properties. Elsewhere, great squawking bundles of trussed-up chickens create a clamour, whilst in other parts of the market you might be offered marijuana, snuff tobacco or dodgy imported electronics. What's most striking though is the care with which everything is displayed, whether pieces of cloth rolled into tight cones and propped up on the ground, oranges and other fruits balanced atop one other, or fresh flowers artistically inserted between mounds of coconuts. Visitors are welcome, of course, but take precautions against pickpockets.

The Askari Monument, Kivukoni Front and the fish market

The eastern edge of the Asian district merges almost imperceptibly with the broad planned streets of **Uzunguni** district, the area of Dar in which the Germans (and subsequently the British) settled after taking control of the city. The centre of this area – the roundabout between Samora Avenue and Maktaba Street four blocks east of the tourist office – is marked by the **Askari Monument**. The first statue on this spot was erected in 1911 and depicted Hermann von Wissmann – the soldier, explorer and governor who played a key role in the German development of the city. The present statue, designed by James Alexander Stevenson and cast in bronze, was erected in 1927 to commemorate the African soldiers and members of the Carrier Corps who lost their lives in the war, depicting an *askari* standing with his rifle at the ready.

Heading 300m southeast from the monument along Maktaba Street brings you to Sokoine Drive, which is where many of Dar es Salaam's first buildings, erected during Sultan Majid's rule in the 1860s, were concentrated. Though most have long since disappeared, a notable exception is the **White Fathers' House**, near the corner with Bridge Street, which served as the sultan's harem until being put to more holy uses by the Society of Missionaries of Africa, a Roman Catholic organization founded by Europeans in Algeria in 1868, who founded their first East African mission in Zanzibar in 1878.

Nearby, **St Joseph's Metropolitan Cathedral**, consecrated in 1897, is a major city landmark and a good place to experience Dar's vibrant church music (*kwaya*), best heard during Sunday Mass. The cathedral is notable for its twin confessionals facing the altar, one in Baroque style, the other in Gothic. The squat, whitewashed **Azania Front Lutheran Church**, 200m to the east, is unmissable thanks to its fanciful tower, which looks like it should really be adorning a Rhineland castle. The church *kwaya* rivals that of St Joseph's.

Heading east along the bay, **Kivukoni Front** leads east past a number of graceful German colonial buildings, most adorned with wooden balconies, which are nowadays occupied by various government ministries and offices. At the eastern end of Kivukoni Front is the ferry (*kivuko*) terminal for Kigamboni (p.132) and, almost opposite, the open-air **Kivukoni Fish Market** – not that you need directions to get there: the smell is unmistakeable. Unsurprisingly, this is the best place in Dar, indeed probably the best place along the entire coast, for seafood, with red snapper, kingfish, barracuda, squid, crabs, lobster and prawns all usually available – if you fancy something cooked, come here for lunch or, even better, for dinner. There's also a fruit-and-veg section. A new market enclosure and landing jetty are currently being constructed with Japanese help, though hopefully these won't detract too much from the market's earthy charm.

Ocean Road

The **beach** starts just up from Kivukoni Fish Market, a small part of which is enclosed by the members-only **Tanganyika Swimming Club** (see p.117). There's nothing to stop you swimming just outside the club, of course, but you may be interested to know that the pipeline which stretches out into the ocean carries most of the city's effluent with it. In theory, coastal currents carry the sewage out to sea, but you never know. The nearest really clean stretches of sand are at Coco Beach (p.96) and Mikadi or Mjimwema beaches (p.132). Still, heading up Ocean Road from Kivukoni you'll see a few brave souls stripping off for a dip, though most people are content to sit around and feel the breeze, or else wander out onto the extensive sandflats which appear at low tide.

The big, white, heavily guarded building on your left, opposite a similarly guarded jetty, is the **State House**. Originally dating from German times, it was damaged by British shelling during World War I and partially reconstructed during 1919–22. Its ornate structure blends elements of African and Arabian architecture, and currently houses the Office of the President – which means no photography. Next to it is the newly renovated **Ocean Road Cancer Hospital**, built in 1886 as the German Malaria Research Laboratory. This was where **Richard Koch**, who in 1905 was awarded a Nobel Laureate for his discovery of tuberculin (wrongly believed to be the cure for TB), developed the standard laboratory method for preparing pure bacterial strains: the Koch Method. Using his method, he went on to discover that flea-infested rats were responsible for the bubonic plague, and that the tsetse fly was the vector for sleeping sickness.

The National Museum and Botanical Gardens

A five-minute walk from the Cancer Hospital on Shaaban Robert Street is Tanzania's **National Museum** (daily 9.30am–6pm; entry $3, photography $4). Established in 1940 as the King George V Memorial Museum, this is rather smaller than you'd expect for a national showcase, but worth a visit nonetheless, since it briefly covers pretty much every aspect of Tanzanian culture and history, from prehistoric hominid fossils through to colonialism and independence. The exhibits of tribal culture are especially fascinating, and it's a pity that no one has ever bothered to expand them, seeing that many of Tanzania's traditional cultures are now on the verge of disappearing.

The **Entrance Hall** is currently occupied by temporary (and usually excellent) exhibitions of photographs or paintings, and by a dusty Rolls Royce which was used by colonial governors and Nyerere. To the left of the entrance, the **Hall of Man** succinctly traces mankind's evolution with displays of stone tools, a cast of the famous Laetoli footprints found at Ngorongoro (p.455), and reproductions of fossilized hominid skulls from Olduvai Gorge and elsewhere, including the 1,750,000-year-old partial skull of *Australopithecus boisei*, whose impressive jaw led to it being dubbed "Nutcracker Man". Don't miss the hilarious letter from an irate newspaper reader in 1958 fuming about the "hideous" suggestion that man might have evolved from animals.

The **History Room** upstairs is something of a hotchpotch, with fragmentary displays on the colonial period, short biographies of nineteenth-century explorers, mementos from the Abushiri War and Maji Maji Uprising, a nineteenth-century Portuguese ship's figurehead, photographs tracing the road to independence, the original Uhuru Torch that was planted on top of Kilimanjaro on December 9, 1961, and bits of moon rock from the Apollo missions. Part of the room is dedicated to finds from the medieval coastal trading town of Kilwa Kisiwani (p.200), including glazed Chinese porcelain removed from graves, Indian trading beads, oil lamps, pottery, stone friezes and coins.

In the older building at the rear of the grounds, the **Marine Biology Hall** contains a large collection of seashells (including a truly enormous clam), but with the exception of a sewn-bark river canoe from the Kwere people, the dusty plaster casts of fish and jars of pickled marine life aren't exactly riveting. Much better is the adjacent **Ethnography Room**, which contains some real gems. The grotesque clay figurines from the Pare and Sambaa tribes, which were used in male and female initiation ceremonies, are as bizarre as they are abstract. The beaded leather skirt from Lake Eyasi is strikingly beautiful, as is the carved door from the Fipa tribe, made from a single piece of wood incised with geometric zigzags and concentric circles. Kids will adore the brilliant wooden bicycle, of which similar examples – fully functional – can still be seen in parts of the country. The musical instruments, too, are a delight, including an intricately carved wooden ceremonial horn from the Kimbu tribe, a giant Nyamwezi drum made from a hollow tree trunk, and a gorgeous-sounding Zaramo xylophone.

There's a small **cafeteria** in one of the outbuildings selling sodas and excellent cheap lunches for around Tsh600. Lastly, don't forget to look through the books on sale at the entrance desk, most of which you won't find anywhere else: Fidelis Masao's booklet on the prehistoric rock art of Kondoa and Singida is especially recommended.

The **Botanical Gardens** (daily sunrise–sunset; free), opposite the museum at the eastern end of Samora Avenue, date from German times and offer a shady oasis of peace and a wonderful escape from the city. The gardens are reasonably well tended, and contain dozens of species of palm trees and fern-like cycads, as well as a raucous population of peacocks. If you're in luck, the explanatory leaflet (Tsh500) covering the plants and the garden's history may have been reprinted – ask at the gardener's office.

Nyumba ya Sanaa

Nyumba ya Sanaa (the "House of Arts"; also known as the Nyerere Cultural Centre; shops Mon–Fri 8am–8pm, Sat & Sun 8am–4pm; workshops Mon–Fri 8am–3pm; ☎022/212 0344 or 213 3960), on Upanga Road next to the *Royal Palm Hotel*, is a unique arts centre in which over a hundred artists, most of them young, create and sell their work. The huge range of items on sale are generally of a very high quality and include jewellery, textiles, pottery and ceramics, woodcuts, etchings, Tingatinga and other paintings – some of them truly outstanding – and the inevitable Makonde woodcarvings (see the box on p.232). You can also try your own hand at painting, drawing, batik and etching (ring ahead, or apply at the centre). **Traditional dances** are performed most Fridays at 7.30pm (and occasionally on other days), and there's a small bar selling alcohol and sodas, plus a cafeteria which is open for lunch.

North from the centre

Heading north from the city, Ali Hassan Mwinyi Road crosses the mangrove-lined Msimbazi Creek at the mouth of the Jangwani River before reaching the **Msasani Peninsula**, the city's most affluent residential district. On the west side of the road here is **Kinondoni** district, home to the city's most vibrant nightlife, while a short distance further on is **Msasani Village**, another lively nightlife venue. Further north from here the suburbs thin out, though there are still a couple of attractions, including the **Mwenge Handicraft Centre** and the **Village Museum**.

Msasani Peninsula and Bongoyo Island

Some 6km north of Dar is the **Msasani Peninsula**, a crooked finger of land that protrudes inquisitively into the Indian Ocean. With the exception of the fishing village of Msasani itself, 8km from the centre of Dar and now completely engulfed by the city, the peninsula seems to have been uninhabited until the arrival of the Europeans, who set up their homes from home in the Oyster Bay area on the peninsula's eastern side. The peninsula is now the address of choice for diplomats, civil servants, NGOs and the otherwise rich and privileged, their homes surrounded by buzzing electric fences and guarded by armed *askaris*, many of them Maasai, whilst the wealth of their owners is equally evident in the small but growing number of upmarket restaurants and bars. Most of the mansions and beachfront establishments were constructed after the economic liberalization (and attendant corruption) that followed President Mwinyi's election in 1985. It's actually still illegal to build on the beach, though you'd never guess it judging by the number of hotels and luxury apartments to shooting up all over the place.

Things acquire a more human face on the southwestern part of the peninsula, where the mansions give way to the more earthy district of **Msasani Village** (also called Namanga), which manages to blend a host of cheap eateries, bars and street-food joints with a handful of posh restaurants and nightclubs. **Public transport** to and around the peninsula is limited, as most of its residents have yet to step inside a daladala – see p.88 for details.

The peninsula's first proper beach is **Coco Beach**. This used to be the main draw for the masses, attracting a refreshingly Tanzanian crowd compared to the almost exclusively *wazungu*-frequented resorts further north. Sadly, swimming and sunbathing here have been banned since October 2000 following a spate of **shark attacks** – see the box opposite. **Food and drink** is limited to the *Coco Beach Restaurant*, attractively situated on a small breezy headland, and the bars and restaurants at the *Oyster Bay Hotel* (p.89), overlooking the beach.

Given the ban on swimming at Coco Beach, the beautiful stretch of sand surrounding the uninhabited **Bongoyo Island** – 6km north of the peninsula - is even more popular that it was, especially at weekends, when it gets crammed with picnickers. Ferries leave daily from The Slipway on the west side of Msasani Peninsula at 9.30am, 11.30am and 1.30pm, returning from the island at 12.30pm, 2.30pm and 5pm. The Tsh5500 return fare includes the entry fee to the island. Snacks and drinks are available on the island.

The Mwenge Handicraft Centre and Village Museum

Further north are a couple of cultural attractions which are invariably included in organized tours of Dar, though both are also accessible by public transport. The **Mwenge Handicraft Centre** (daily 8am–6.30pm) is 12km from the city on Sam Nujoma Road in Mwenge. There are frequent daladalas to

Shark attacks at Coco Beach

For reasons as yet unknown, in January 2000 **sharks** began migrating north from Mozambique and South Africa to the Tanzanian coast, to which they had never previously ventured. The gruesome deaths of five swimmers off Coco Beach the same year in a series of attacks terrorized beach-goers and led to the government prohibiting swimming on Coco Beach (as well as, strangely enough, sunbathing or even walking on the beach). The killer shark (or sharks), which at the time of writing had yet to be caught or chased away, apparently settled behind Bongoyo Island, attracted to this part of the coast – some say – by the city's nutritious sewage.

The story of the sharks and attempts to capture them became something of a soap opera, much enlivened by the appearance of **Dr Taratonga** of the Kunduchi Beach Marine Research Institute, who was introduced on the National Television Network as a "warrior and marine science consultant". "You should expect to see a man-eating fish and then a fight between me and the fish," he announced, as crowds waited eagerly to watch the impending drama on huge screens set up in the city's Mnazi Mmoja Grounds. "But don't think it doesn't eat women. Unfortunately, it does," he added, before slipping into a dapper chain-mail suit which an assistant proceeded to stab with a knife to demonstrate its efficacy.

Sadly, when the crunch came, the "man-eating fish" was nowhere to be seen. The next development came when **Hugo "Grub" van Lawick** – owner of a deep-sea fishing-safari outfit – claimed that he had caught the killer shark. Unfortunately, the Zambezi River Shark he hooked is not believed to have been the man-eater, and a post-mortem showed no traces of human flesh in the shark's stomach. Meanwhile, local astrologer **Sheikh Yahya Hussein** – always ready with a word to say on anything of national importance – insisted that the deaths had been caused a fairy spirit or demon appearing in the shape of a fish, suggesting that an offering be made to appease the spirits of the dead. The government's offering was a $5000 "monitoring station" equipped with satellite antennae and fast patrol boats, though predictably enough, nothing ever came of this.

Mwenge terminal from both Posta and Kariakoo, leaving you with a 600-metre walk. The centre, founded in 1984, comprises almost a hundred shops, most of them selling identical Makonde woodcarvings, reproductions of studded Zanzibari chests, soapstone carvings from Kisii in Kenya, and Zambian malachite. Spend some time looking around, however, and you'll turn up some more unusual items, including traditional wooden stools, bao games, Christian idols, masks, sisal baskets and bags, coconut shredders, batiks, cow bells, Makonde masks and some paintings.

Heading 3km back towards the city along Bagamoyo Road, the **Village Museum** in Kijitonyama (daily 9.30am–6pm; $4) nicely complements a visit to the carvers (to reach the museum, take a daladala to Mwenge and get off at Makumbusho). The museum was founded in 1966 in an attempt to preserve some of the architectural and associated material traditions of traditional Tanzanian societies, and in so doing educate future generations about their heritage. Spread out over the open-air site are sixteen replicas of houses built in the architectural styles of different tribes, each furnished with typical household items and utensils, and surrounded by small plots of local crops and animal pens. Although laudable, the aims of the museum became grimly ironic in the years following its establishment, when Nyerere embarked on his economically disastrous policy of "Villagization" (see p.718), in which the majority of rural Tanzanians were forcibly moved out of their villages to begin new lives as collective labourers in planned townships. By the time the experiment collapsed in the mid-1970s, the Tanzanian economy was in ruins.

Traditional crafts and arts, such as carving, weaving and pottery, are demonstrated by resident "villagers", whilst a blacksmith explains the intricacies of his craft, which has existed in East Africa for at least two millennia. The finished products are sold in the museum shop, which also stocks books and other souvenirs. There's a small café serving drinks and Tanzanian food, and performances of **traditional dance** (Weds–Sun 2pm–6pm). Early March and early November are also good times to visit, when the museum hosts three-day **cultural festivals** (or "ethnic days") dedicated to a particular Tanzanian tribe or region, featuring song and dance, recitals of oral history and poetry, and traditional food.

Eating

Dar es Salaam has no shortage of **places to eat**, with plenty of high-quality establishments to stimulate even the most jaded of palates. The larger **hotels** all have restaurants, often several, some offering eat-all-you-want lunchtime buffets, others rotating through alternating theme nights. Although not cheap (upwards of Tsh10,000 per head is the norm), you're pretty much guaranteed good food and, anyway, where else in Tanzania could you find Swiss fondue or a Mongolian barbecue? Don't expect much in the way of **seafood**, however, unless you're dining in one of the more upmarket places or, at the other end, sampling the rough-and-ready delights of Kivukoni's fish market (see p.94).

There's a good range of **top-end restaurants** at which you can eat well for Tsh5000–10,000, so long as you're happy adding a taxi fare to the bill, as most places are north of the centre. In this price bracket you'll find dozens of Chinese, Indian and Italian places, plus more unusual culinary experiences like Ethiopian, Japanese, Malaysian, Irish, Hungarian and even Croatian fare. More affordable and less fancy are **mid-range restaurants** in the Tsh3000–5000 range, which you can find more or less everywhere, and which serve mainly European- and Indian-inspired food – but choose carefully here as quality and standards of hygiene are far from uniform. If this is still too expensive, there's a host of smaller basic restaurants and **cafés** throughout the city dishing up filling Indian, Swahili and European dishes for around Tsh1000–2500. Most restaurants are closed on Sundays.

Almost all the **local bars and nightclubs** provide large and filling portions of *nyama choma* (roast meat), *chipsi mayai* (chip omelettes), *ndizi* (fried or grilled plantain) and, more rarely, *ugali* (cornmeal porridge). The busier the place, the better the food, and the meat is often superior to anything you'll find even in a tourist hotel.

Markets

For your own supplies, any of the city's **markets** are great places to stock up in. Apart from Kariakoo (p.92), Kivukoni (p.94) and Kisutu (p.92), **Ilala Market**, to the west of Kariakoo on Uhuru Street, is worth a visit, selling greens and fresh and dried fish, along with second-hand clothes and shoes – most daladalas from Kivukoni and Kariakoo to Buguruni run straight past the entrance. Another good market is the open-air one at **Manzese Mitumba**, 7km along Morogoro Road; catch a daladala from Posta or Kariakoo towards Ubungo. Sprawling along both sides of the highway, this is livelier than Ilala and in addition to food offers everything from the finest domestic wares, second-hand clothes and shoes to TVs. As with Kariakoo, don't take any valuables

Street food

You won't find much traditional Tanzanian fare on the menus of Dar's posher restaurants. Out on the streets, however, you'll find some truly superb and often dirt-cheap local food, especially around markets and transport terminals. **Kariakoo Market** (p.92) is unbeatable for freshly roasted meat, whilst **Kivukoni Fish Market** (p.94) has some of the finest grilled fish on the coast, which can be bought straight from the fishermen who pull up their boats on the beach 50m away. Stretching westwards from Kivukoni Market along Kivukoni Front towards the *Kilimanjaro Hotel* are hawkers aplenty peddling **snacks** such as samosas, rice cakes, roasted maize cobs, mangoes (which are peeled for you), and delicious roast cassava doused in light chili sauce, a far cry from the usual mealy, mouth-drying tuber. For fuller **meals**, try one of the *mama ntilies* in the Swedish-built buildings on Kivukoni Front between Ohio Street and Azikiwe Street, who dish out rice and *ugali* with stew, fried fish or *mishkaki* (skewers of grilled goat meat), all for under Tsh1000. In addition, *mama* (and some *baba*) *ntilies* at the west end of Garden Avenue serve full meals, as do a handful of stalls at the north end of Zanaki Street. To cap a meal on the move, look for the **coffee vendors** in the late afternoon and evenings, especially in the Asian district and at the daladala stands, who sell scalding Turkish-style coffee in small porcelain cups.

as pickpockets abound. If you want an overview of the place before diving in, walk up onto the pedestrian footbridge. In the city centre, **fruit stalls** can be found at the top end of Zanaki Street, north of Jamhuri Street. **Delicatessen** items are sold by Melela Bustani at The Slipway shopping centre on Msasani Peninsula (Mon, Tues, Thurs & Fri 10am–5.30pm, Sat 10am–3pm), including a wide range of conserves, cheeses and smoked meats. Should the meat in the markets put you off (though it is, in fact, freshly slaughtered), try Choice Meats on Maktaba Street, which also has sausages, halal meat and beef jerky (*biltong*). **Supermarkets** are listed on p.113.

City centre: east from Maktaba Street

99'ers Steak House *Royal Palm Hotel*, Ohio St ℡022/211 2416. Small and comfortable restaurant decorated with Tanzanian art and carvings, whose candlelight dinners were a romantic novelty prior to power rationing. Dishes include South African and Angus beef, grilled quail, barbecued spare ribs, grilled jumbo prawns, tuna and salmon. Mon–Sat evenings only. Licensed.

Bandari Grill *New Africa Hotel*, Azikiwe St ℡022/211 7050. Daytime offerings include full English breakfasts and lunchtime buffets (Mon–Fri; Tsh10,000). In the evening (when the none-too-exciting Graffiti Band plays) you can choose from Indian dishes, flambéed meat and prawns, or splash out on one of the special themed buffets – the "Seafood Extravaganza" (Weds; Tsh12,000) is especially good. Licensed.

Baraza Restaurant *Holiday Inn*, Garden Ave. A swish venue specializing in Swahili seafood, with mains from Tsh4500 to 10,000. Live music by the poolside on Sunday afternoons is planned. Licensed.

Chinese Restaurant Basement, NIC Investments House, Samora Ave. This unforgettably named place looks like a cafeteria but serves up some delicious quasi-Chinese meals and snacks with not a pinch of MSG in sight. There's not a huge choice, but a full meal won't cost more than Tsh4000 and a vegetable stir-fry with rice goes for just Tsh2000. Closed Sun.

Chuo Cha Mafunzo ya Utalii (Forodhani) Kivukoni Front. One of the few central restaurants serving up decent local dishes, though the choice is very limited. Portions are big, and the food perfectly acceptable as well as cheap, with nothing over Tsh2000. See also the review under Bars (p.105). Open Mon–Fri lunchtimes only. Licensed.

City Garden Corner of Garden Ave and Pamba Rd. Plenty of shaded outdoor seating under trees and parasols, plus a friendly atmosphere and generally good and reasonably priced food, both Tanzanian and European, as well as snacks and soft drinks.

Dar Shanghai, *Luther House Hostel*, Sokoine Drive. Relatively cheap and unquestionably tasty Chinese and Tanzanian food with little or no MSG. Full meals cost from Tsh2500 to 5000. Closed Sun during the day.

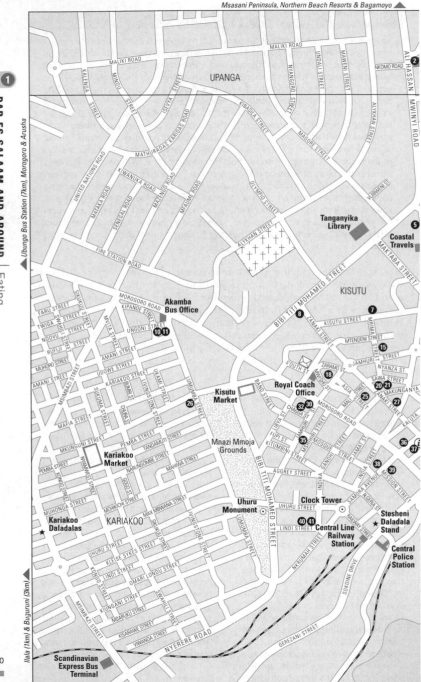

Msasani Peninsula, Northern Beach Resorts & Bagamoyo ▲

UPANGA

MALIKI ROAD

MALIKI ROAD

NKOMO ROAD

KALENGA STREET

MINDU STREET

ISEVYA STREET

NYANGORO STREET

UINDALI STREET

MAWENI STREET

ALI HASSAN MWINYI ROAD

MATHURADAS KARIDAS ROAD

UNITED NATIONS ROAD

KIWANUKA ROAD

MATAKA ROAD

SENEGAL ROAD

MALENGO ROAD

MZUME ROAD

RIBASILA STREET

MAGORE STREET

ALYKHAN STREET

OLYMPIO STREET

YUSRNANI ST

Tanganyika Library

❺

Coastal Travels

MAKTABA STREET

FIRE STATION ROAD

ALYKHAN STREET

KISUTU

BIBI TITI MOHAMED STREET

MOROGORO ROAD

KIPANDE STREET

Akamba Bus Office

❽

KISUTU STREET

ZANAKI STREET

MRIMA STREET

FARU STREET

SIKUKUU STREET

TWIGA STREET

SWAHILI STREET

NDOVU STREET

MVITA STREET

UNGONI STREET

❿ ⓫

MTENDENI STREET

❼

⓯ STREET

RUFIJI STREET

AMANI STREET

UDOWE STREET

SOUTH ST

NYANZA ST

MUHORO STREET

KARIAKOO STREET

UKAMI STREET

ZARAMO ST.

MNGSO ST.

JAMHURI STREET

AMANI STREET

LIVINGSTONE STREET

MSIMBAZI STREET

RUMBI ST

⓲

ASIA ST

SAWA STREET

MAKUNGANYA

MAFIA STREET

SUKUMA STREET

CHURO ST

Kisutu Market

BAND STREET

Royal Coach Office

MOROGORO ROAD

MANI ST

ZANAKI STREET

❿ ⓴ ㉑

㉕

㉗

KALUTA

MKUNGUNI STREET

TANDAMUTI STREET

㉖

CHAGGA ST

BIBI TITI MOHAMED STREET

Kariakoo Market

NYAMWEZI STREET

NARUNGOMBE STREET

MAHIWA STREET

PEMBA STREET

Mnazi Mmoja Grounds

㉜ ㉚

FUPI ST.

MOSQUE ST

LUMUMBA STREET

LIBYA ST

GANDHI STREET

JAMAT ST

INDIA STREET

㊱ ⓘ

㊲

KONGO STREET

GOGO ST

MCHIKICHI STREET

KITUMBINI STREET

㉟

㊳

MISSION STREET

KARIAKOO

MAX MBWANA STREET

SIKUKUU STREET

AGGREY STREET

㊴

PEMBA STREET

MUHONDA STREET

Uhuru Monument

Clock Tower

SAMORA AVENUE

ALGERIA ST

Stesheni Daladala Stand

Kariakoo Daladalas ★

UHURU STREET

UHURU STREET

UNUMBA STREET

RAILWAY STREET

KLEI SE SYKES STREET

LINDI STREET

㊵ ㊶

Central Line Railway Station

Central Police Station

KIONGO STREET

LINDI STREET

LIVINGSTONE STREET

BIBI TITI MOHAMED STREET

NKRUMAH STREET

OMARI LONDU STREET

KIUNGANI STREET

SWAHILI STREET

MDARUKU STREET

SWAHILI ST

SOKOINE DRIVE

MSIMBAZI STREET

KISARAWE STREET

VIWANDA STREET

NYERERE ROAD

GEREZANI STREET

Scandinavian Express Bus Terminal

Tazara Railway Station (4km); Airport (10km) & Pugu Hills ▼   ▼ Kilwa Road & Southern Tanzania

Ubungo Bus Station (7km), Morogoro & Arusha ▲

Ilala (1km) & Buguruni (3km) ▲

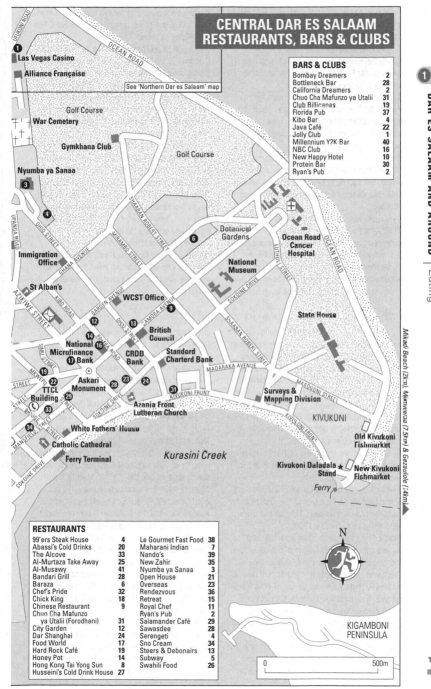

CENTRAL DAR ES SALAAM
RESTAURANTS, BARS & CLUBS

Las Vegas Casino

Alliance Française

See 'Northern Dar es Salaam' map

Golf Course

War Cemetery

Gymkhana Club

Golf Course

Nyumba ya Sanaa

Botanical Gardens

Ocean Road Cancer Hospital

National Museum

Immigration Office

St Alban's

WCST Office

British Council

State House

National Microfinance Bank

CRDB Bank

Standard Charterd Bank

MADARAKA AVENUE

Askari Monument

TTCL Building

Surveys & Mapping Division

KIVUKONI

Azania Front Lutheran Church

White Fathers' House

Old Kivukoni Fishmarket

Catholic Cathedral

Ferry Terminal

Kurasini Creek

Kivukoni Daladala Stand

New Kivukoni Fishmarket

Ferry

Mikadi Beach (2km), Mjimwema (7.5km) & Gezaulole (14km)

BARS & CLUBS

Bombay Dreamers	2
Bottleneck Bar	28
California Dreamers	2
Chuo Cha Mafunzo ya Utalii	31
Club Billicanas	19
Florida Pub	37
Kibo Bar	4
Java Café	22
Jolly Club	1
Millennium Y2K Bar	40
NBC Club	16
New Happy Hotel	10
Protein Bar	30
Ryan's Pub	2

RESTAURANTS

99'ers Steak House	4	Le Gourmet Fast Food	38
Abassi's Cold Drinks	20	Maharani Indian	7
The Alcove	33	Nando's	39
Al-Murtaza Take Away	25	New Zahir	35
Al-Musawy	41	Nyumba ya Sanaa	3
Bandari Grill	28	Open House	21
Baraza	6	Overseas	23
Chef's Pride	32	Rendezvous	36
Chick King	18	Retreat	15
Chinese Restaurant	9	Royal Chef	11
Chuo Cha Mafunzo		Ryan's Pub	2
ya Utalii (Forodhani)	31	Salamander Café	29
City Garden	12	Sawasdee	28
Dar Shanghai	24	Serengeti	4
Food World	17	Sno Cream	34
Hard Rock Café	19	Steers & Debonairs	13
Honey Pot	14	Subway	5
Hong Kong Tai Yong Sun	8	Swahili Food	26
Husseini's Cold Drink House	27		

N

0   500m

KIGAMBONI PENINSULA

Food World Maktaba St. A good place for breakfast, snacks and full meals, and handily placed close to the Askari Monument, with CNN news on the TV in the morning.

Honey Pot Pamba Rd. Cheap snacks and light meals (under Tsh1000) – popular at lunchtimes with office workers. Closed Sun.

Nyumba ya Sanaa (Nyerere Cultural Centre) Upanga Rd. The cafeteria here has a choice of three Tanzanian dishes each day, costing Tsh2500 for beef or fish, and Tsh3800 for prawns. Open daily for lunch only.

Overseas Restaurant Monte Carlo Casino, corner of Ohio St and Sokoine Drive. Chinese and Korean dishes, specializing in seafood and using halal meat; the steamed fish and crab are both good. Licensed.

Sawasdee New Africa Hotel, Azikiwe St ☎022/211 7051. Rooftop Thai restaurant with fantastic views over the harbour and famous buffets, including seafood on Tuesday and Friday nights (Tsh12,000). The Thai chefs dish up pretty genuine fare, characteristically aromatic and delicious – the prawn and ginger soup is excellent –

and there's a good wine list too. Ideal for a romantic tête-à-tête. Open evenings daily, plus Sat & Sun noon–3pm. Licensed.

Serengeti Royal Palm Hotel, Ohio St. "Neptune's Kingdom" is the fishy name for Thursday evening's theme, where the all-you-can-eat seafood buffet (Tsh15,000) includes lobster, crab claws, smoked sailfish and prawns. By complete contrast, Friday's "British Pub Night" offers bangers and mash, steak and Guinness pie and fish and chips served in newspaper. Licensed.

Steers & Debonairs CDTF Building, corner of Samora Ave and Ohio St. The Islamic South African fast-food chain Steers offers the usual junk food plus toasted sandwiches, salads, milk shakes, juices and great toffee ice cream – a kind of halal-meets-McDonald's concept which works surprisingly well. Debonairs next door has (overpriced) pizzas, and both also do takeaways.

Subway Peugeot House, corner of Bibi Titi Mohamed St and Upanga St. Part of the American chain, serving up salads and low-fat sandwiches, including some 12-inch monsters on Italian or wheat bread.

City centre: Kisutu and Mchafukoge

Abassi's Cold Drinks Zanaki St. A good place for breakfast, with a wide selection of refreshing fruit juices and snacks like samosas and rice cakes.

The Alcove Samora Ave. Long-established upmarket Indian and Chinese restaurant with variable cooking – sometimes it's excellent, at other times it's just bland and overpriced. Full meals go for around Tsh8000–10,000 (though vegetarian mains cost under Tsh4800), and watch out for VAT. Closed Sun lunchtime. Licensed.

Al-Murtaza Take Away Asia St. Cheap meals and snacks including a great lunchtime chicken pilau, and chicken biriani on Sundays.

Al-Musawy Restaurant Corner of Indira Gandhi St and Lindi St. No-frills snacks like andazi doughnuts, samosas and chapatis. The fish and chips are a filling bargain at Tsh1000.

Chef's Pride Chagga St. Busy establishment packed with families and couples at weekends, and attracting a fair share of tourists as well. There's an embarrassment of choice, and most of it's freshly cooked, whether Zanzibari-style fish in coconut, biriani curry or tender roast chicken. It also serves up fast-food favourites and great breakfast combos for Tsh1200. Nothing much over Tsh2000.

Chick King Jamhuri St (open daily). Fast food à la 1970s, with all the tattered formica tables and wonky plastic chairs you could wish for, plus an

ever-decreasing choice of greasy pre-fried food (their claim to provide the best fried chicken in town presumably alludes to a long-gone golden age). Having said that, it's handy for a quick bite.

Hard Rock Café, corner Mkwepu St and Makunganya St. This sneaky imitation of the US chain does mainly Italian food, with dishes going for Tsh4000–6000. Closed Sat & Sun. Licensed.

Hong Kong Tai Yong Sun Corner of Bibi Titi Mohamed St and Zanaki St. Some of the best Chinese food in the city, but you'll pay through the nose. Most dishes cost Tsh6500 and up, excluding rice or starters, and the Tsh3500 lunchtime specials are really too small to fill you up. Still, it's good for a treat. Closed Sun lunchtime. Licensed.

Husseini's Cold Drink House Corner of India St and Zanaki St. Simple meals (chips or rice with everything) and snacks, including tasty Scotch eggs, as well as juices and ice cream.

Le Gourmet Fast Food Samora Ave. Good snacks and cheap Tanzanian lunches, mostly under Tsh1500, including ugali with ox liver. The stews are good, but the fried stuff less so. Open Mon–Fri 7am–6pm only.

Maharani Indian Restaurant Kisutu St. Highly recommended, with fresh and tasty food including a huge vegetarian choice, either à la carte (around Tsh2500) or in the famous lunchtime buffet, a bargain at Tsh3000. Closed Tues evenings. Licensed.

Nando's Lehmann's Building, corner of Samora Ave and Mission St. The Tanzanian branch of the Portuguese-themed South African halal barbecue chicken chain, together with four similarly shiny fast-food joints – *Pizza Inn*, *Chicken Inn*, *Creamy Inn* (ice cream) and *Gold Reef* (seafood, including hot fish subs). Prices are reasonable, but not cheap.

New Zahir Restaurant, Mosque St. Reasonable curries and birianis for Tsh1800, plus some Tanzanian dishes, though hygiene is questionable. Get there early at lunchtimes to be sure of a table. Closed Fri 12.20–1.20pm for prayers.

Open House Sewa St. Large and imposing place with attentive walters, pressed tablecloths, icy a/c and an extensive Indian and Chinese menu, with most mains around Tsh5000 (watch out for VAT), plus pizzas (around Tsh3000). The Chinese shredded chicken and chicken tikka masala are both excellent, but the noodles are really just spaghetti.

Rendezvous Restaurant Samora Ave ☎022/211 1102. Long-established city-centre joint with an a/c interior, uninspiring snacks and more appetiz-ing mains (Tsh2600–4000) – try the *mishkaki* meat skewers and sizzling platters in the evenings (Tsh3800 for meat, fish or chicken). Closed all day Thurs and Sun evenings. Licensed.

Retreat Mrima St ☎022/212 8048. Don't be put off by the stark cafeteria-like dining room, since this vegetarian place serves up seriously good South Indian food, plus a small selection of more average Chinese dishes heavy on cornflour and MSG. A full meal with drinks shouldn't cost more than Tsh5000. No smoking.

Salamander Café corner of Samora Ave and Mkwepu St. A good central option, with a street-corner verandah, offering a variety of snacks, pas-tries, juices with sugar and boiled water (the tangy tamarind – *ukwaju* – is very refreshing) and deli-cious full meals for under Tsh2000. They also do a self-serve breakfast until noon. Closed Sun after 2pm.

Sno Cream Mansfield St. Scrummy ice creams at European prices served up in a f-f-freezingly cold interior. There's another branch at the north end of Alykhan Rd.

West of the centre: Kariakoo

Royal Chef Lumumba St, around the corner from *New Happy Guest House*. This is run by the folks from *Chef'o Pride*, and it shows in the tasty food, with enough choice to please all palates and priced to suit all pockets, with an attractive street-side verandah to boot. Most meals cost Tsh1000–1500, and even the T-bone steaks and prawn dishes are little more than Tsh3000. Licensed.

Swahili Food Restaurant Corner of Lumumba St and Mkunguni St. Very tasty and reasonably priced Tanzanian food, with most dishes under Tsh2000. There are also outside tables facing the street, and an internet café. Licensed.

North of the centre: Mikocheni and Kawe

The following restaurants are marked on the map on p.90.

Addis in Dar 35 Ursino St, off Migombani St, Regent Estate ☎0741/266299. If you've never eaten Ethiopian food before, don't miss this oppor-tunity. The basic staple is *njera*, a huge soft pan-cake that you share with your partner, from which you tear bits off to eat with a variety of highly spiced sauces and stews. They also brew an excellent cup of coffee. A little pricey, but recom-mended. They also sell bright and colourful Ethiopian art and some beautiful silverwork. Open Mon–Sat lunchtimes and evenings only. Catch a cab. Closed Sun. Licensed.

Euro Pub Off Bagamoyo Rd, Kawe ☎022/261 7371 or 261 7365. Air-conditioned, German-style pub with prices to match. The wide menu includes steaks, Mexican fajitas and seafood, with most dishes costing Tsh6000–10,000. Mon–Fri open evenings only, Sat & Sun 11am–11pm. Grab a cab or a purple daladala marked "via Old Bagamoyo Rd" from Posta to Kawe and ask to be dropped off at the signpost on Old Bagamoyo Road, from where it's a 500-metre walk. Licensed.

Grand Café Old Bagamoyo Rd ☎0741/553623 A recommended little Tanzanian-run place modelled after a French bistro, with candlesticks and care-fully pressed tablecloths, plus a/c inside and out-door tables. It majors on Mexican food, especially fajitas (from Tsh6500), but also has a Chinese menu and seafood, with dishes from around Tsh6000. Mon–Fri 5–11pm, Sat & Sun 11am–11pm. Licensed.

Istana Ali Hassan Mwinyi Rd, opposite Gapco ☎022/265 0156. Welcoming and friendly place serving a small range of spicy Malaysian, Chinese and Indian dishes, most for under Tsh4500. Meals are dished up on banana leaves, if you like, and served at tables in garden huts – try the *nasi lemak* (steamed coconut rice). It's also famous for its eat-all-you-like nightly buffets (Tsh5000), with Indian food on Sundays, Chinese on Tuesdays, and a good choice of seafood on Saturdays. Open evenings daily, plus Sun noon–3pm. Licensed.

Namaskar 1st floor, Shopper's Plaza, Old Bagamoyo Rd ☏0741/338411. Outstanding vegetarian restaurant with a massive choice of freshly cooked South Indian, Mughlai and Punjabi dishes for around Tsh2500–3500. If you're really hungry, go for the *dosa*, a thinly rolled tube of fried lentil and rice flour which is almost as long as the tables. Closed Wed.

Saverio's Old Bagamoyo Rd, opposite the Arcade, Namanga. Delicious wood-oven pizzas (under Tsh3500) plus seafood, steaks and an ice-cream parlour. It's deservedly popular, though this also makes for somewhat shirty service. Closed Mon. Licensed.

Steak & Ale The Arcade, Old Bagamoyo Rd, Namanga. Designed to look like an English country pub. The T-bone and rump steaks (Tsh6000–12,000 depending on the quality of the meat) satisfy any appetite, though the chicken, fish and seafood are better value at Tsh4000–4500. There's live music on Friday nights, when things get busy. Open daily, evenings only. Licensed.

North of the centre: Upanga

Langi-Langi At *The Courtyard Hotel*, Ocean Rd ☏022/213 0130. Classy French, Indian and continental cuisine in a sophisticated ambience, with a popular Sunday brunch (11.30am–3pm; Tsh8000, including use of the swimming pool. Licensed.

Palm Beach Hotel, 305 Ali Hassan Mwinyi Rd. A popular and recommended outdoor restaurant, set under tall shady trees and boasting a huge menu covering everything from Indian, vegetarian and seafood dishes to specialities like Russian meat dumplings, pork bratwurst, kofta kebabs and grilled octopus. It's also very good value for money, with grills going for Tsh1000–2500, and most other meals for Tsh2500–4500. Licensed.

Ryan's Pub Las Vegas Casino ☏022/212 7298. Tasty Irish offerings – beef and Guinness pie, lamb with mint sauce, Irish stew – plus some decidedly un-Irish food such as savoury crepes stuffed with onion and mushrooms, and shrimps topped with cheese. Mains cost Tsh3000–5000 in the restaurant, or there's a less extensive menu (including snacks) in the bar. Restaurant daily 6.30–10.30pm; bar daily 12.30–3pm & 5–10pm. Licensed.

North of the city: Msasani Peninsula

All the following are licensed.

Arca di Noe' Kimweri Ave, Namanga ☏022/266 7215. Posh seafood and pizzeria joint in a big *makuti*-thatched building. Closed Tues lunchtime.

The Arches *Oyster Bay Hotel*, Touré Drive, Msasani Peninsula. This idiosyncratic hotel's main restaurant has a good reputation for seafood, but it's expensive, with starters at around Tsh4000, mains from Tsh8000 and wine at Tsh10,000 a bottle.

Azuma The Slipway, Msasani Peninsula ☏022/260 0893. Authentic if expensive Japanese and Indonesian cuisine, with full meals for Tsh10,000 and up, plus lunchtime specials for around Tsh7000 – the *sashimi* is superb. Closed all day Mon, and Sat & Sun evenings.

Barbecue Village just off Kimweri Ave, Namanga T022/266 7927. A flashy hotchpotch of styles – Indian, Chinese and continental – with seafood buffets every Friday and Saturday, including lobster, crab masala and seafood fondue, and barbecues the rest of the time. Tues–Sun evenings only.

Buda Pub, Kimweri Ave, Namanga Ave, Namanga. Good little place (open evenings only) with attentive service, substantial portions and a huge, mainly Hungarian menu, with plenty of fresh mushrooms and inventive stews – the stuffed cabbage leaves are truly great.

Karambezi Café *Sea Cliff Hotel*, Touré Drive, Msasani Peninsula. This beautifully located restaurant (open 24hr) has fine Indian Ocean views and seats right on the cliff edge. The huge menu includes pizzas, steaks, fish and other European dishes (Tsh3000–6000); there's also an excellent Mongolian barbecue and salad buffet for Tsh7500 on Tuesday, Thursday and Sunday evenings, accompanied by cheesy solo guitar music.

La Trattoria Jan Kimweri Ave, Namanga. Consistently good and reasonably priced food, with live music (including the incomparable Dr Remy Ongala) Thursday to Saturday. Cars are guarded by Maasai *askaris*. Recommended.

Little India *Sea Cliff Hotel*, Touré Drive, Masasani Peninsula ☏022/260 0380. Fine, if expensive, North Indian dining, with a tandoori night on Wednesday. Open evenings only.

Malaika At the *Karibu Hotel*, Haile Selassie Rd, Msasani Peninsula. Continental, Chinese and Indian cuisine, with a poolside buffet for Tsh6000 on Sundays.

Serengeti Spaghetti Casanova Complex, next to the *Sea Cliff Hotel*, Touré Drive, Msasani Peninsula Italian restaurant in a vast, *makuti*-roofed complex, with good-value pasta at Tsh3800, tasty pizzas (up to Tsh5000), real espresso and occasional live music on Fridays. Bar open 8am–11pm, food from 4pm; closed Thurs.

Simona Restaurant Kimweri Ave, Namanga ℡022/266 6935 or 0741/411640. Perhaps Africa's only Croatian restaurant, frequently recommended for its seafood, and with a well-stocked bar. The ambience is upmarket, but it's not overly expensive. Live music Wed–Sat; closed Sun evenings.

Smokies Tavern Off Chole Rd, Msasani village ℡0742/780567. One of the city's best places for

meat and fish: the evening buffets offer an embarrassment of choice, from smoked sailfish, crab claws, prawns and lemon fish to sizzling chicken, beef in tarragon sauce and grilled vegetable kebabs. Daily 5pm–midnight; also Sat & Sun lunchtimes.

The Terrace The Slipway, Msasani Peninsula ℡0741/330200. A good terrace bar and Italian restaurant with superb views over Msasani Bay, and not too expensive at around Tsh6000 for a meal. Evenings only; closed Tues.

Drinking and nightlife

The predominantly Muslim city of Dar es Salaam isn't at first glance the most promising place for **bars** or **nightlife**, and indeed if you stay only in the centre, you could probably count the bars on one hand and the clubs on the other. But if you head out into the suburbs – places like Kariakoo, Sinza, Ilala, Magomeni, Kinondoni, Manzese and Mwenge – you'll discover a wealth of **clubs** and **dance halls** brimming over with people dancing to live bands or drowning their sorrows in any one of a thousand bars. If the local scene isn't to your liking, more upmarket areas like the Msasani Peninsula have more than their fair share of places, too, as glitzy, brash or downright expensive as you like, though these also attract a lot of prostitutes on the prowl.

Taxis are the usual way to get around, although you can get to most places by daladala before 9pm or 10pm, when services stop for the night – details are given in the reviews where appropriate. Taxi rides rarely cost more than Tsh2000 around the city centre, and even the longest ride (say out to Sinza) shouldn't cost more than Tsh5000. Getting back is no problem as even the smallest bar or club will have a few cars waiting outside for customers, even at the most unsociable hours.

The following places are just a tiny selection of what's available – with time (and a strong liver) you could probably spend an entire year of weekends out and about without having to go to the same place twice.

Bars

See also the list of live music venues (see p.109), most of which also operate as normal bars when not hosting bands.

City centre

The following bars are marked on the map on p.100.

Bottleneck Bar First floor, *New Africa Hotel*, Azikiwe St. An upmarket sports bar with two 48-inch TV screens, an extensive snack menu, and a wide range of drinks (including cocktails).

Chuo Cha Mafunzo ya Utalii (Forodhani) Kivukoni Front. The most attractive of the city-centre options, housed in a beautiful colonial-era building facing the harbour, with seating indoors in wood-panelled splendour, outside on the shady verandah or on the first-floor terrace. It's run by the Hotel & Tourism Training Institute, so

service can be rather sketchy at times, but drinks are cheap, and there's good food too (see p.99). Mon–Fri until 8pm, Sat until 4pm; closed Sun.

Florida Pub Mansfield St. Known for having the city's prettiest, haughtiest and most useless barmaids – pay for your drinks straight off as they're also not averse to overcharging. There's Castle Lager on tap, a mute TV, two pool tables, reasonable food (Tsh1500–3000) and arctic a/c.

Kibo Bar *Royal Palm Hotel*. Upmarket sports bar

with satellite TV and European-style bites like pasta and stuffed baguettes.

Java Café Corner of Mkwepu St and Makunganya St, opposite *Hard Rock Café*. Pleasant afternoon refuge for a drink or snack, with rickety tables on a covered streetside verandah, Indian food, *nyama choma* and an internet café in the pipeline. Closes 8pm.

Jolly Club Next to the Las Vegas Casino, Ufukoni St. A great local place with seats in a shady garden, desperate prostitutes, *nyama choma*, chips and other junk food and occasional live music on Wednesdays and either Friday or Saturday night.

Millennium Y2K Bar Lindi St. Friendly local bar close to the city centre, with tables in a courtyard at the back and on the street-front verandah at night. There's a pool table, cheerful Congolese music, full meals until around 4pm and snacks and *mishkaki* meat skewers thereafter.

NBC Club Pamba Rd. Famous unmarked bar in the business and banking district of the city centre with two distinct sections, one inside with a TV, the other outside with a popular dartboard. Good soup, *nyama choma* and *ndizi* (grilled plantain) available.

New Happy Hotel Ungoni St, off Lumumba St near Morogoro Rd. This guest house's rooftop bar is popular with locals, with a good atmosphere and great views. The grilled goat meat is succulent, but beware of being overcharged – it's best to pay for your drinks as you order them.

Protein Bar Jamhuri St, near the *Holiday Hotel*. Currently Kisutu's only bar, with boisterous barmaids and an agreeable mix of seasoned drunkards and the occasional backpacker. Open late.

Ryan's Pub Las Vegas Casino, Ali Hassan Mwinyi Rd ☏ 022/212 7298. Dar's first Irish bar (it had to happen), but alas still no real Guinness, though the lively and friendly atmosphere makes up for this, helped along with satellite TV, tasty food (see p.104) and live music on Wednesdays, Fridays and Saturdays.

Outside the centre

The following bars are marked on the map on p.90.

Highway Night Park 4km along Morogoro Rd at Magomeni-Mapipa. Dar's most infamous streetside dive, open 24hr, with live music some evenings (free entry) and dancers every night (including an acrobatic couple of polio victims on Sundays). Gets packed around midnight when the music really gets going. Food available here and in any number of neighbouring kiosks and basic restaurants.

Karambezi Café *Sea Cliff Hotel*, Touré Drive, Msasani Peninsula. A lovely view over the beach and ocean, and open 24hr, but you pay through the nose and the clientele is almost entirely *wazungu*.

Kawe Club 650m off Old Bagamoyo Rd, Kawe ☏ 0741/325791. An old colonial club established in 1952 by the Tanganyika Packers (lapsed purveyors of corned beef), now totally dilapidated and run by a cheerful bunch of young Tanzanian rap fans. The beach is the main attraction, but there's also a wonderful broken piano and an equally sorry-looking flint snooker table in the old lounge. Live music is planned for weekend nights (ring beforehand) and there's chips with chicken or beef if you're hungry. Catch a daladala to Kawe from Posta or Kariakoo.

Msasani Beach Club 550m off Old Bagamoyo Rd, Kawe. Cavernous and very run-down place, mostly used for wedding receptions, with a large bar area and a scrubby garden fronting the beach with tables under parasols. No food except chicken. Catch a daladala to Kawe from Posta or Kariakoo. Daily until 10pm.

Oyster Bar *Karibu Hotel*, Haile Selassie Rd, Msasani Peninsula. Upmarket *wazungu* sort of place with English premier league matches and movies on a large TV.

Palm Beach Hotel Ali Hassan Mwinyi Rd. This has two bars: a wonderfully relaxing one in the front under trees, and the *Palm Beach Club* (formerly *Sugar Ray's*) round the back, which currently functions as a sports bar but may well have live music or discos in future.

The Pub The Slipway, Msasani Peninsula. Calm place with a cool a/c interior, outdoor seating on the patio under parasols, sport and music on satellite TV, aromatic coffee and continental food (mains Tsh3500–4500).

Q-Bar Next to *Karibu Hotel*, Haile Selassie Rd, Msasani Peninsula. This upmarket place is busiest on Fridays, when the disco attracts the same kind of crowd as *Smokies* and *Blue Palms*, including the prostitutes. Happy hour daily 5–7pm; cocktail nights on Wed, Thurs & Sat from 7.30pm.

Smokies Tavern Off Chole Rd, Msasani village. Lively on Thursdays, when the expats pile in for the buffet dinner (8pm onwards) featuring fabulous smoked sailfish and a live if not overly exciting band. At other times it's pretty quiet, despite its attractive rooftop terrace overlooking the bay and good food (p.105) – though the drinks are unreasonably expensive.

Nightclubs

Entrance fees average Tsh1500–4000, depending on the night of the week. Some places admit women for free; others are free for all at weekdays.

Blue Palms Garden Rd, Mikocheni. Bright and cheerful bar, at its busiest on Wednesday and Saturday nights, when it gets packed with prostitutes and their prospective punters, but the atmosphere is light and not oppressive. There's sometimes live music from Tuesdays to Thursdays (free), and busy discos on Fridays and Saturdays (Tsh2000–3000). Food available. Closed Mon.

Bombay Dreamers Las Vegas Casino complex, corner of Ali Hassan Mwinyi Rd and Ufukoni St. One of Dar's more unusual nightspots, an Indian-themed nightclub that combines cabaret, live music and dancing every evening from 9pm, and has an equally individual door policy: couples and women are charged admission at weekends to discourage prostitutes.

California Dreamers Las Vegas Casino complex, corner of Ali Hassan Mwinyi Rd and Ufukoni St. Along with *Club Bilicanas*, this is Dar's flashiest disco, with a good lighting and sound system, dancy modern music and a Chinese restaurant should you get the munchies. Daily from 9pm; entrance Tsh3000–4000.

Club Aqua Kimweri Ave, Namanga, 50m from *La Trattoria Jan*. Named after the weirdly fascinating fish tank under the bar, the main attraction here – apart from the fact that it stays open so late – is the loud nightly disco of mainly Congolese and Tanzanian tunes, which get pumping around 10pm. It's most popular Fri–Sun, when the prostitutes turn out in force. There's a small choice of continental dishes (Tsh2000–4500), and pool tables outside. Daily until 5am; free.

Club Bilicanas In the same building as the *Hard Rock Café*, but accessed from Simu St at the back. Right in the city centre, this is Dar's foremost, brashest and most popular nightclub (you'll have to pay to get in), with good lighting and sound. Wednesday features mainly African tunes; the rest of the week offers a more cosmopolitan mix.

Mambo Club, facing the *Karibu Hotel*, Haile Selassie Rd, Msasani Peninsula. "Dar best clubbing in town" quips the blurb about this pleasingly flashy African place, which has discos every Friday and Sunday, and occasional talent nights.

Silent Club (also known as New Silent Club or Silent Inn), Sam Nujoma Rd, Mwenge. Lively and friendly venue on account of the large student population from the university nearby, with reggae on Wednesdays, a disco and occasional live bands on Saturdays (and sometimes Tues), and a family show on Sunday evenings.

The Slipway Msasani Peninsula. This upmarket shopping centre hosts an outdoor disco on Fridays which is popular with well-to-do Europeans and Indians.

Tazara Club Kilimani Rd, off Bagamoyo Rd just north of Selander Bridge, Kinondoni. A great place on Saturdays, when it heaves with sweaty bodies dancing to Congo's latest craze (currently Mayemu). Sometimes has live bands at weekends.

Live music and entertainment

Dar is the best place in East Africa for catching live music. There are over twenty professional **dance bands** in the city, most of them playing three to six times a week on an ever-changing circuit of clubs and dance halls around the suburbs. At weekends (Saturday night and Sunday afternoon) the bands usually play on their home turf, generally a bar, club or social hall run by the same people who own the instruments the bands play on. For up-to-date **listings**, the best source is the Kiswahili *Nipashe* newspaper, which sometimes carries a page of announcements covering the following week's events. The weekend edition of *Uhuru* also has a small boxed listing on the inside back page for gigs that weekend. For information about more upmarket places see the listings in either the *Dar es Salaam Guide* or *What's Happening in Dar* booklets. If you're around in July or August, it's worth coinciding with the annual **Summer Jam Festival**, which attracts big-name bands from all over East Africa. It's held at a number of venues around the city including FM Club, Mango Garden,

△ Dar Es Salaam

Ambassador Plaza and Leaders Club. For more information, visit Ⓦ www.cloudsfm.com.

Big names to look out for include the legendary DDC Mlimani Park Orchestra; their great rivals the OTTU Jazz Band (formerly Juwata Jazz); 1960s twist-kings Shikamoo; Dr Remy Ongala, with or without his band Super Matimila; the mellow sounds of Vijana Jazz; the guitar-rich Mchinga Sound; the pro-government TOT; Skuta One Theatre (SOT); African Stars, with their eminently danceable "Twanga Pepeta" style; and their stable-mates the African Revolution Band. For reviews of these and other bands, and a history of the Tanzanian music scene, see p.749.

For something completely different, search out a **taarab** (or *tarabu*) band. *Taarab* is *the* definitive musical expression of coastal Swahili culture, in its modern incarnation a strange blend of synthesizers, Bantu drum beats, twangy guitar and high-pitched Indo-Arabian singing. It's danced almost entirely by women, who shuffle along on their feet while shaking their bottoms rhythmically in a complex pelvic movement called *kukata kiuno*, meaning "to cut the waist". **Traditional music** (*ngoma*; see p.749) is best caught at the Village Museum (see p.97; Wed–Sun 2–5pm; $4) or at Nyumba ya Sanaa (see p.95; Fri at 7.30pm).

Many venues are known by more than one name – we've given both where this is the case. **Entrance fees** aren't normally more than Tsh3000.

Amana Club (OTTU Social Club), Uhuru St, Ilala, past Kawawa Rd. A long-established social hall run by the Organization of Tanzanian Trade Unions, this is a superb place to be on Sunday, when home boys the OTTU Jazz Band draw the masses and the dancing goes on almost without stop from 4pm to midnight (Tsh1000). There's also *taarab* on Wednesdays (Tsh3000).

Bar es Salaam next to *Arca di Noe'*, Kimweri Ave, Namanga. Some of the best live music in town, with live bands (Wed–Sat from around 8pm, Sun from 6pm) currently featuring Tatu Nane (Wed) and Dr Remy Ongala (Sat). There's also a "cultural night" every other Wednesday featuring dance, theatre and music. Good cocktails, plus barbecues and a menu heavy on seafood. Daily noon until late.

City Ambassador Hotel, Morocco Rd, Kinondoni. Good local place hosting lesser-known bands. Saturday is the main night, with Kilimanjaro Connection strumming their *njenje* dance style into the early hours.

Hiphop, rap and reggae

Hiphop, rap and R&B are the poor cousins of Dar's thriving dance band scene, although each of these styles has gained in popularity over the last few years. The scene is constantly changing: much of the music remains underground and performances are difficult to locate, not helped by the fact that even the big names only perform a dozen times or so a year. The university is probably the best place to start your quest.

The big names in **hiphop** are Underground Souls, who released their first single, *Battlefield*, in 1998 to became an instant success, and Sos-B, who had a similar baptism with their single *KKZ* (*Kukuru kakara zako*). Another popular combo, Afro Reign, combine rap in both English and Kiswahili with R&B. For hardcore **rap**, the granddaddies are Kwanza Unit ("First Unit"), formed by veterans K. B. C. and Rhymson around 1990. Other crews worth checking out include E-Attack, De-Plow-MaTz – most of whom are the sons of Tanzanian diplomats, as it happens, and prefer their audiences to be seated – and Gangstas With Matatisu (GWM), who perform from time to time at *Hotel Kilimanjaro*'s rooftop. Details of upcoming hiphop events, if any, are posted on ⓦ www.africanhiphop.com, which also carries a round-up of groups that have been most active over the last year or so. **Reggae** is surprisingly under-represented: the main outfits are Roots & Culture, Jhiko Man and Ras Inno. The reggae Sunsplash festival has been held a few times in Tanzania: you might find details on ⓦ http://reggaefestivalguide.com.

Club La Petite (Lango La Jiji), Magomeni. Hosts a *taarab* group on Sundays from around 4pm; a good day out for families.

DDC Kariakoo (DDC Social Hall, Kariakoo), Narungombe St, off Msimbazi St, Kariakoo. This vast concrete hangar is Dar es Salaam's oldest African bar, and home turf of the famous DDC Mlimani Park Orchestra (who play here Sun 4–10.30pm).

FM Club (DDC Lang'ata), Kinondoni Rd, Kinondoni. A popular venue most nights, with Congolese-influenced FC Academia performing most Saturdays, and a Sunday afternoon talent show sponsored by Times 100.5 FM radio station which has become a well-known place to spot upcoming musicians.

Leaders Club, Kinondoni. A major venue which has been favoured of late for big one-off music industry functions. It's also the home base of TOT on Saturdays, whilst Sunday afternoons and evenings feature veteran musicians from Zaita Musica, Achigo Sounds and the late Maquis du Zaire.

Lions Club (or Lions Hotel) Off Shekilango Rd, Sinza. One of Dar's leading venues, especially on Fridays, when legendary twist-kings Shikamoo still pull the punters in. On Saturdays or Sundays the resident Tango Stars band play their "Lolela First" version of *Ndombolo*. A taxi from town costs around Tsh4000.

Mango Garden (Mango Club), Mwinyijuma Rd. Along with the *Lions Club*, one of the best places on Friday, with the African Stars belting out their "Twanga Pepeta" style of Ndombolo (8pm–2am; Tsh500) in a friendly and unhustly atmosphere, with lots of dancing and cheap drinks. Saturday features more of the same, or else the highly recommended OTTU Jazz Band.

Max Motel Ilala. A great place for live music, with the Juju Sound Band playing a lively mixture of dance tunes on Wednesday, African Revolution on Thursday, *taarab* on Saturdays (especially popular with women) and the Afri Swezi Band on Sundays.

Oyster Bay Police Mess, Toure Drive, Oyster Bay, Msasani Peninsula. Sunday is the day to come here, with laid-back veterans Shikamoo Jazz playing from mid-afternoon.

Ryan's Pub Las Vegas Casino, Ali Hassan Mwinyi Rd. Irish-themed bar catering mainly to the monied crowd, with live bands on Wednesdays, Fridays and Saturdays (9pm–2am).

Sine Club Beach (Beach Compound), Old Bagamoyo Rd, between Tanesco and Kawe village. Popular with locals at weekends, with good food and bands on Sundays from mid-afternoon, when it's especially popular with local families; you can even swim here at high tide. Daladalas from Posta and Kariakoo to Kawe run here until around 9–10pm; get off at Warioba.

The Slipway Msasani Peninsula. This upmarket shopping centre hosts live bands on Sundays, and one-off events midweek including rap and hip-hop festivals – check press for details.

Tiger Motel Bagamoyo Rd, 21km north of the city along Bagamoyo Road. Normally a stuffy and rather formal venue, this place performed a volte face in 2001 by booking the immensely popular African Revolution Band as their Sunday residents. **The Tilt** The Arcade, Old Bagamoyo Rd. Open daily from 10am till midnight, except on Fridays, when a packed house dances till dawn to the sound of the Inafrika Band (from 10.30pm; Tsh1500). Sundays feature Ndombolo copycats Diamond Sound (from 8pm; Tsh2000).

Vijana Social Club (New Vijana Club or Vijana Hostel), next to *Mango Garden*, Mwinyinjuma Rd, Kinondoni. Home turf of Vijana Jazz, who perform on Sundays from 3pm onwards. Saturday nights feature African Stars.

Film, theatre and the arts

With the exception of the Euro African Film Festival (Nov) and the Art in Tanzania festival (Dec), **cultural events** in Dar are pretty thin on the ground. **Theatre** is limited to the Little Theatre, off Haile Selassie Road near Ali Hassan Mwinyi Road, home of the Dar es Salaam Players who put on a production roughly once a month. The plays cater mainly for English-speaking expats and the Europhile Tanzanian elite, though the Christmas pantos are always a laugh. Details are given in *What's Happening in Dar*.

Film

There's only one proper **cinema** in Dar (The Avalon), though several other venues put on weekly screenings. If you're fed up with the usual fare of blurry kung-fu, soppy Bollywood flicks or gung-ho American B-movies, try to catch the annual two-week **European Film Festival**, held at various venues (including the British Council and the Alliance Française) in the second and third weeks of November. Contact the tourist office for more information, or check schedules in the free *Dar es Salaam Guide* or *What's Happening in Dar* booklets closer to the time.

Avalon Cinema Zanaki St. Bollywood movies. Tickets cost Tsh3600–4200.
British Council Samora Ave. Free screenings of British movies at 6.30pm on Wednesdays.
Club Aqua Kimweri Ave, Namanga. Shows mainly US movies on Monday and Tuesday nights. Tsh2000 admission (includes popcorn). Take a taxi.
La Trattoria Jan Kimweri Ave, Namanga. Shows Italian movies on Wednesday at 9.30pm. Take a taxi.
Mambo Club, opposite the *Karibu Hotel*, Haile Selassie Rd, Msasani Peninsula. This popular nightclub screens movies on Saturdays: the program starts 6.30pm, the movie at 7.30pm. The nearest daladala route is the Masaki run from Posta marked "via A.H. Mwinyi" or "No.13", which runs along Touré Drive. Take a taxi back.

The Slipway Msasani Peninsula. Outdoor screenings of Hollywood films at 7.30pm on Tuesday. The Tsh1000 entry fee is refundable on food and drinks. The Masaki daladala from Posta ("via A.H. Mwinyi" or "No.13") runs close by on Chole Rd. Take a taxi back.
US Marine House Msasani Peninsula. An unlikely venue, with its passport check and metal detector, this shows Hollywood films on an outdoor video projection screen on Thursday at 8pm (Tsh1000, including a drink). Drinks, burgers, hot dogs and hash browns are available. Take a taxi.
Wet 'n' Wild Kunduchi Beach (see p.130). Shows an English-language film on Saturday at 6pm and an Indian one on Sunday at 6pm. Catch a Mwenge–Tegeta daladala displaying a number 7.

Galleries and exhibitions

The annual **Art in Tanzania** exhibition provides a major showcase for modern Tanzanian artists. Held over the first three weeks of December at the Alliance Française (see below; Mon–Sat 9am–6pm), the event assembles works by around fifty painters, cartoonists, photographers and sculptors. For details, contact the tourist office or check the listings in *What's Happening in Dar* or the *Dar es Salaam Guide*. The superb exhibition catalogue ($10) can be found in Dar's better bookshops (see p.113) or obtained direct from the publishers: East African Movies, 1st floor, 1085–1195 Nkrumah St opposite Home Butchery ☎022/212 1472.

The **Alliance Française**, off Ali Hassan Mwinyi Rd next to the Las Vegas Casino complex (☏022/211 9415), and the **Russian–Tanzanian Cultural Centre** on Upanga Rd (☏022/213 6577) both regularly host art exhibitions and other cultural events, and are always worth a visit. Other places that put on occasional events include Nyumba ya Sanaa (see p.95); the Village Museum (see p.97); the American Cultural Centre in the Peugeot House Building, corner Bibi Titi Mohamed St and Upanga St (☏022/211 7174); and the Iranian Cultural Centre, Ali Hassan Mwinyi Rd (☏022/211 5932).

Shopping

Given the city's size and cosmopolitan nature, you can find pretty much anything you might need in Dar, either in the centre or in several modern shopping centres on the outskirts. The usual souvenirs you'll see elsewhere in Tanzania can also be found, and although the choice isn't as wide as in Arusha, prices can be lower. For **food markets**, see p.98; for **recorded music**, see the box on p.109.

Souvenirs

Although the choice of **souvenirs** isn't as wide as in Arusha, Dar has a handful of excellent curio shops, as well as the Mwenge Carvers (see p.96) and Nyuma ya Sanaa (see p.95), which is *the* place to buy **contemporary art**. Apart from the shops listed below, you'll find souvenir stalls throughout the city: the ones on Bridge Street opposite the Tanzania Curio Shop have a great selection of **Makonde carvings**. There are stalls outside the *YMCA* on Upanga Road, but the vendors are pushy and also double as dope dealers and money-changers. Give a wide berth to the ones selling **seashells** and other marine curios, sometimes under the guise of medicine (ground seahorses are said by Japanese to be as potent as Viagra), since the collecting of seashells, even empty ones, has a direct and damaging impact on coral reef ecology. In any case, the export of seashells is illegal. For the colourful **kitenge and kanga cloths** worn by women (see box opposite), the section of Uhuru Street between the clock tower and Bibi Titi Mohamed Street, spilling up Bibi Titi Mohamed to Libya Street, is excellent, with dozens of shops and hundreds of street vendors to choose from.

Acacia Gallery The Slipway, Msasani Peninsula. Beautifully handcrafted wooden objects, paintings by local artists and nice earrings (though most of them are from Kenya).

Artizan Casanova Complex, next to the *Sea Cliff Hotel*, Touré Drive, Msasani Peninsula. Good selection of handicrafts from all over Africa, but the prices reflect the upmarket location.

Karibu Art Gallery Bagamoyo Rd, Mbezi Beach area. A recommended place offering a huge choice of souvenirs at very reasonable prices (marked, but still negotiable), with no sales patter or pressure to buy. Choose from Tingatinga paintings, carvings from the Makonde, Zaramo and Kamba (Kenya), Kisii soapstones (also Kenyan), and some marvellous Makonde *Mapiko* helmet masks (see p.232), a bargain at Tsh10,000. Metre-tall *sheitani*

(spirit) sculptures go for Tsh75,000, and you can sometimes see the carvers at work in the gallery grounds. Performances of traditional music are held Saturdays 3–5pm, and there's a bar round the back. Frequent daladalas run throughout the day along Bagamoyo Road from Mwenge to Tegeta. Closed Tues.

Karibu Arts & Crafts Samora Ave. Run by the same people as the Karibu Art Gallery – the choice is much smaller, but the prices are the same and discounts are possible on larger purchases. Closed Sat afternoon and Sun.

Morogoro Stores (Tingatinga Art Centre), Haile Selassie Rd, Msasani Peninsula. Famous for Tingatinga paintings (it was here that Eduard Tingatinga first sold his work); other handicrafts are also available, from canvases to crockery.

Kangas and kitenges

The colourful printed cotton wraps worn by most Tanzanian women are called **kangas** (the name means "guinea fowl", as one of the first designs was a series of light polka dots on a dark background that resembled that bird's plumage). A double-pane *kanga* is called a **doti**, and is often cut in two, one part being worn around the body, the other around the head or shoulders. *Kangas* were introduced to Tanzania by Portuguese merchants in the mid-nineteenth century, though it was only at the start of the twentieth century that they began to acquire the **proverbs and riddles** (*neno*, literally statements) which are now such a characteristic feature of the design. The proverb is a way of making public sentiments that would be taboo expressed in any other form. So, for instance, a wife wishing to reprimand her husband for infidelity or neglect might buy a *kanga* for herself with the proverb, "The gratitude of a donkey is a kick" (*Fadhila ya punda ni mateke*), while one reading "A heart deep in love has no patience" (*Moyo wa kupenda hauna subira*) might be bought for a woman by her lover, expressing his desire to get married.

Similar to a *kanga*, but without the proverb or riddle, is a **kitenge**, made of thicker cloth and as a double-pane; their size also makes them ideal for use as bedlinen. **Prices** for simple *kangas* range from Tsh2000 to Tsh4000 depending on the design and where you buy it, while *doti* and *kitenges* go for Tsh4000–7000. Women will be happy to show you some ways of tying it. For more ideas, winkle out a copy of *Kangas: 101 Uses*, by Jeanette Hanby and David Bygott.

Tanzania Curio Shop Corner of Bridge St and Mansfield St. Attractively poky little store selling a mixture of pure kitsch, malachite figurines, modern and antique Zanzibari silver (the dagger sheaths and heavy necklaces are especially attractive), coins and some beautiful reproduction Zanzibari chests. Closed Sat afternoon and Sun

Bookshops

Dar's best **bookshop** is A Novel Idea at The Slipway, Msasani Peninsula (Mon–Sat 10am–7pm, Sun noon–6pm), which has a lavish choice of imported coffee-table books, novels, academic tomes, guidebooks and maps, though it's poor on Tanzanian-published titles. Prices are in sterling, and VISA and Mastercard are accepted for a five percent surcharge. Other bookshops with similar but smaller stocks include At the Green, Shopper's Plaza, Old Bagamoyo Road (there's another branch on Jamhuru Street, just west of Morogoro Road, which is mainly useful for European and American magazines); and the bookshop at the *Royal Palm Hotel*, Ohio Street. For Tanzanian-published books, Tepusa Bookshop on Mshihiri Street is outstanding, with a wide choice of African novels and poetry in English, and some lovely children's books. Other bookshops are very poorly stocked, though you may turn up the occasional worthwhile find. Try the New Text Book Centre on Nkrumah Street; the Tanzania Publishing House on Samora Avenue one block west of the Askari Monument; and the University Bookshop, out of town in the university campus on University Road. There are also second-hand bookstalls throughout the city centre, especially along Samora Avenue on both sides of the Askari Monument, at the corner of Samora Avenue and Mkwepu Street, and – with the best choice of Tanzania-related works – Sokoine Drive between Ohio Street and Pamba Road, and around the corner on Pamba Road itself.

Supermarkets

The two branches of Score, one in JM Mall (Lehman's Building), Samora Avenue, the other on Lumumba Street facing Mnazi Mmoja Grounds (both Mon–Fri 9am–6pm, Sat 10am–3pm) are recommended. Imalaseko

Supermarket, Pamba House, corner of Garden Avenue and Pamba Road (Mon–Fri 9am–7pm, Sat 9.30am–4pm, Sun 10am–4pm) has a wide if expensive selection of goods, including nappies and other baby stuff. There's another branch (daily 8am–9pm) on Bagamoyo Road opposite the temptingly named *Viagra Inn*. Smaller city-centre supermarkets include Royal Supermarket on Samora Avenue, just east of Askari Monument, and Shrijee Supermarket on Mtendeni Street (both daily 9am–9pm).

Shopping Centres

The handful of modern **shopping centres** on the outskirts of the city are no competition for the markets in terms of atmosphere or price, but they do stock a fairly good range of products that many *wazungu* cannot live without.

The Arcade Old Bagamoyo Rd. Includes a couple of bars, restaurants, a pharmacy, ice-cream parlour, and Hakuna Matata Travels.

Casanova Complex North end of Touré Drive, Msasani Peninsula. Has a small bookshop, fashion boutiques, a hairdresser, sports shop and a handicrafts shop.

Shoppers Plaza Old Bagamoyo Rd. Toy shop, health club, internet café, Standard Chartered bank with a 24hr Visa-card ATM, photographic supplies,

pharmacy, supermarket, bookshop, opticians and coffee shop.

The Slipway Msasani Peninsula. Dar's finest, this upmarket shopping centre includes a great bookshop (A Novel Idea), commercial art galleries, restaurants, bars, juice bar and ice-cream parlour, bakery, delicatessen, internet café and Visa cashadvance services. There are movie screenings on Tuesday nights in an open-air pavilion, and daily scheduled boat cruises to Bongoyo Island.

Listings

Air charters African Joint Air Services, Bibi Titi Mohamed St ☎022/211 7018; Aviazur, Airport terminal 1 ☎022/284 3075, ✉aviazur@africaonline.co.tz; Coastal Travels, 107 Upanga Rd, near the *YMCA*, and at Airport terminal 1☎022/211 7959, ✉safari@coastal.cc; Flightlink, Airport terminal 1 ☎ 022/284 3073, ✉flightlink_ltd@yahoo.com; General Aviation Services, Airport terminal 1 ☎022/284 2080, ☎022/284 3313; Mbuyu Aviation, c/o Selous Safari Company (see p.125); Precisionair, Maarifa House, Ohio St ☎022/213 0800; Sky Tours, Airport terminal 1 ☎022/211 7730, ✉skytours@cctz.com; Tanzania Air Services (Tanzanair), *Royal Palm Hotel*, Ohio St ☎022/211 3151, ✉tanzanair@raha.com; ZanAir, Airport terminal 1 ☎0741/605230, ⊛www.zanair.com.

Airlines (domestic) Air Tanzania Corporation (ATC), ATC House, corner of Ohio St and Garden Ave ☎022/211 0245, ✉commercial@airtanzania.com; Coastal Travels, 107 Upanga Rd ☎ 022/211 7959, ✉safari@coastal.cc (also at the airport ☎022/284 3293 or 0741/325673); Eagle Air, Samora Ave by the Askari Monument ☎022/212 7411, ✉eagleair@africaonline.co.tz; Precisionair, Maarifa House, Ohio St ☎022/213 0800, ✉information@precisionairtz.com; ZanAir, Airport Terminal 1 ☎0741/605230, ✉zanair@zitec.org.

Airlines (international) Air India, corner of Bibi Titi Mohamed St and Ali Hassan Mwinyi Rd ☎022/215 2642 or 022/215 2643; Air Malawi, TDFL Building, Ohio St ☎022/212 2019 or 212 4820; Air Tanzania Corporation (ATC), ATC House, corner of Ohio St and Garden Ave ☎022/211 0245, ✉commercial@airtanzania.com; Air Zimbabwe, c/o Easy Travel & Tours, Avalon House ☎022/211 4479; British Airways, *Royal Palm Hotel*, Ohio St ☎022/211 3820, ✉britishairways@cats-net.com; Egyptair, Matasalamat Mansions, corner of Samora Ave and Zanaki St ☎022/211 3333, ☎022/211 2344; Emirates, ground floor, Haidery Plaza, corner of Upanga St and Kisutu St ☎022/211 6100, ☎022/211 6273; Ethiopian Airlines, TDFL Building, Ohio St ☎022/211 5875, ☎022/211 5875; Gulf Air, Raha Towers, corner of Bibi Titi Mohamed St and Ali Hassan Mwinyi Rd ☎022/213 7852, ☎022/211 1304; Kenya Airways, Peugeot House, corner of Bibi Titi Mohamed St and Upanga St ☎022/211 3336, ✉fredk@intafrica.com; KLM, Peugeot House, corner of Bibi Titi Mohamed St and Upanga St ☎022/211 5012; South African Airways, Raha Towers, Bibi Titi Mohamed St ☎022/211 7044, ✉sunshine@raha.com; Yemenia Airways, TDFL Building, Ohio St ☎022/212 6036.

Airport information For flight times and informa-

tion call ☎022/284 4239 or 284 4211.
Ambulance ☎112 for emergencies. Knight Support (☎022/276 0087 or 276 0088) run a more reliable private ambulance service.
American Express c/o Rickshaw Travels (open daily) at the *Royal Palm Hotel*, Ohio St ☎022/213 7275, ✉amex@twiga.com; advances are made in the form of travellers' cheques.
Banks and exchange Don't change money on the street as you're almost guaranteed to get ripped off (not on the rate, but by sleight of hand). Most foreign exchange bureaux (forex) are located along Samora Avenue and India Street, especially between Morogoro Road and Bridge Street (generally Mon–Fri 8.30am–4/5pm, Sat 8.30am–1pm), and whilst they're handy for changing cash quickly at reasonable rates, they're pretty lousy for travellers' cheques, if they accept them at all. One exception is Crown Forex, corner of India and Zanaki streets, though you'll need to produce your purchase receipt to change them. You'll get better travellers' cheque rates at banks; the best are the National Bureau de Change, Samora Ave, which doesn't charge commission and doesn't need your purchase receipt, and the NBC Foreign Branch, corner of Jamhuri St and Azikiwe St, which also waives commission but requires the receipt. National Microfinance Bank, at the corner of Samora Avenue and Pamba Road, gives marginally inferior rates but doesn't require your purchase receipt. Standard Chartered charges swingeing commission on travellers' cheques, but has 24hr Visa and Mastercard ATMs: they have branches at NIC Life House, at the corner of Sokoine Drive and Ohio Street; International House, on the corner of Garden Avenue and Shaaban Robert Street; JM Mall, Samora Avenue; and Shopper's Plaza, on Old Bagamoyo Road. Barclays Bank also has 24hr Visa-card ATMs at the TDFL Building on Ohio Street and at The Slipway on Msasani Peninsula. If you don't have a PIN number, cash advances (up to $500 a week into either shillings or dollars) on Visa, Mastercard, Delta and JCB cards can be arranged through Coastal Travels (Mon–Fri 9am–4pm, Sat 9am–1pm) at 107 Upanga Rd near the *YMCA*. The Local Currency office (Coastal Travels) at Airport terminal 2 has a similar service (daily 7am–9pm) ☎022/284 2866, as does the Cash Assistance Point office at The Slipway on Msasani Peninsula (Tues–Sun 10am–7pm) ☎022/260 1337. On Sundays, you can change cash in the morning at one of the forex bureaux in the IPS Building at the corner of Samora Avenue and Azikiwe Street. If you miss these, one of the big hotels might oblige, but don't count on it; otherwise, the airport is your only choice. Western

Union Money Transfers can be collected at the Tanzania Postal Bank, TTCL Building, Samora Avenue (Mon–Fri 8.30am–6pm, Sat 8.30am–2pm) ☎022/213 2821,
✉tpb.wunion@africaonline.com.
Birding The Wildlife Conservation Society of Tanzania (WCST), Garden Ave, corner of Ohio St ☎022/211 2518, ✉wcst@africaonline.co.tz, organizes a bird walk from their office every Friday at 7.30am.
Car rental See p.121.
Courier services DHL, 12b Nyerere Rd ☎022/286 1000 or 0744/781153, ℻022/286 2703, plus branches at The Arcade, on Old Bagamoyo Rd, and at Peugeot House, corner of Bibi Titi Mohamed St and Upanga St. There's also a Fedex office in Peugeot House.
Dentists Nordic Dental Clinic, Valhalla Estate, Msasani Peninsula ☎022/211 8295; Dr Rahim, Aga Khan Hospital ☎022/211 5151; Dr Mushtaq Dhirani, Osman Towers, Zanaki St ☎022/213 0884; Dr Shabbir Mohmedali, Asia St ☎022/211 6630.
Embassies and consulates Most embassies and consulates are concentrated in Upanga and the Msasani Peninsula north of the city. When complete sometime around 2003, European House, on the corner of Mirambo Street and Garden Avenue, will house the embassies of Germany, the Netherlands and the UK. Embassies and consulates currently located in the city include: Burundi, 1007 Lugalo Rd, Upanga ☎022/211 7615 or 0742/341777, ℻022/212 1499; Canada, 38 Mirambo St ☎022/211 2831 or 211 2832, ℻022/211 4542 or 211 6896; DR Congo, Maliki Rd, Upanga ☎022/215 0282; Ireland, 1131 Msasani Rd, Msasani Peninsula ☎022/266 6211 or 266 6348, ℻022/266 7214 or 266 7852; Kenya, NIC 12th floor, Investments House, Samora Ave ☎022/211 2811 or 211 2955, ℻022/266 6834 or 211 3098; Malawi, 38 Ali Hassan Mwinyi Rd ☎022/211 3238 or 022/211 3239, ℻022/211 3360; Mozambique, 25 Garden Ave ☎022/211 6502, ℻022/211 6502; Rwanda, 32 Ali Hassan Mwinyi Rd ☎022/211 7631, ℻022/211 5889; Uganda, Extelcoms House, Samora Ave ☎022/211 7646 or 211 7667, ℻022/211 2913 or 211 2974; UK, Social Security House (Hifadhi House), Samora Ave ☎022/211 2953 or 211 7659, ℻022/211 2951; US, temporarily at 140 Msese Rd, Kinondoni ☎022/266 6010 or 266 6011, ℻022/266 6701 (a new embassy is being constructed at the Drive-In Cinema, Old Bagamoyo Rd); Zambia, corner of Ohio St and Sokoine Drive ☎022/211 8481 or 211 8482, ℻022/211 2974 or 211 2977 (visa applications on Mon, Weds & Fri only).

1

Football At the end of 2001, after years of being forced to play in Morogoro and elsewhere thanks to hooliganism at their home matches, Dar's two big rivals – Simba and Yanga – once again took the field at the National Stadium, Nelson Mandela Rd, Mgulani. Catch a daladala from Kariakoo, Stesheni or Posta to Bagala, Temeke or Rangi Tatu marked "via Kilwa Road" and walk the remaining 1km, or catch one to Mgulani from Tazara.

Hospitals and clinics In a medical emergency, the best hospital is the modern Aga Khan Hospital, Ocean Rd at Ufukoni St ☏ 022/211 4096 or 211 5151. Other hospitals include the TMJ Hospital, Old Bagamoyo Rd, Mikocheni ☏ 022/270 0007 or 270 0008; Oyster Bay Hospital, Haile Selassie Rd, Msasani Peninsula ☏ 022/260 0015 or 260 0929; and Mikocheni Mission Hospital, Regent Estate ☏ 022/270 0021. Recommended clinics include Nordic Clinic, Valhalla Estate, Msasani Peninsula ☏ 0741/325569 (24hr) or 022/260 1650, which also has a good dentist; and the Oyster Bay Medical Clinic, Oyster Bay Hotel Shopping Centre, Touré Drive, Msasani Peninsula ☏ 022/266 7932. For Chinese medicine, head to the Chintan Chinese Traditional Medicine Clinic, corner of Jamhuru Rd and Morogoro Rd ☏ 0741/337586.

Immigration The Immigration Department (Wizara ya mambo ya ndani) is opposite Posta House at the corner of Ohio St and Ghana Ave (PO Box 9143) ☏ 022/212 6811, ☏ 022/211 3297, but is only useful for work visas and permits. For extending tourist visas, your only option is to leave the country – see p.17 for full details.

Internet and email access Dar has well over a hundred internet cafés, so you should be able to find one within a block or two of wherever you are in the centre. The biggest concentration is on Jamhuri St and Samora Ave. Rates average Tsh500–1000 per hour (printing costs Tsh300–500 per page, with the cheaper outlets clustered along the western end of Jamhuri St and in the Kisutu area. Good places include the Millennium Internet Café, Jamhuri St (daily 8am–midnight; Tsh500 per hour), which is reliable and has internet phone facilities (though they really should invest in some new keyboards); Cyberspot, on the same street (daily 8am–midnight; Tsh1000 per hour) is more expensive but has fast and well-maintained machines and soft drinks for sale.

Language courses KIU Ltd, Salvation Army complex, Kilwa Rd ☏ 022/285 1509 or 0744/271263, ☏ kiu@raha.com (Mon–Fri 8am–3.30pm) offers a variety of Kiswahili courses at various levels, both intensive and part-time. A three-week course comprising four hours a day costs Tsh125,000; intensive training with a personal tutor costs Tsh3800

per hour. Occasional courses are also held at Nyuma ya Sanaa (four weeks), and at the Russian Tanzanian Cultural Centre on Upanga Rd (twelve weeks). Catch a daladala from Posta or Kariakoo to Temeke or Rangi Tatu marked "via Kilwa Rd" and get off at Mgulani, just before the radio mast.

Libraries Tanzania's main public library, also housing the National Archives, is the Tanganyika Library (also known as Central Library), Maktaba Complex, Bibi Titi Mohamed St (Mon–Sat 9am–6pm). Daily membership costs Tsh500. The British Council Library is at the corner of Samora Ave and Ohio St (Tues–Fri 10am–6pm, Sat 9.30am–1pm; ☏ 022/211 6574, ☏ www.britishcouncil.org/tanzania). Temporary monthly membership costs Tsh7000. The Alliance Française, off Ali Hassan Mwinyi Rd next to Las Vegas Casino complex (☏ 022/211 9415), has a good collection of French books in a chilly a/c interior. Membership costs Tsh10,000 (Tsh6000 students). Both the Alliance and British Council screen endless satellite news programmes (no membership required). The Wildlife Conservation Society of Tanzania (WCST; ☏ 022/211 2518), on Garden Ave near Ohio St, has an outstanding library on environmental and ecological matters (Mon–Fri 8.30am–4.30pm; membership required in theory if not always in practice.

Maps The government's Surveys & Mapping Division on Kivukoni Front ☏ 022/212 4575 (Mon–Fri 8am–3.30pm) sells 1:250,000 regional maps and 1:50,000 topographical maps covering the entire country (Tsh4000), mostly dating from 1959–62 – especially useful if you're planning to do some hiking off the beaten track, though they've run out of the more popular sheets. They also have a excellent road map of Dar es Salaam (Tsh5000), and 1:2500 sheets covering major towns and urban areas, although at the last check only Dar es Salaam was in stock. For up-to-date maps of the national parks, head to one of the bigger bookshops in Dar or Arusha, or go to the TANAPA headquarters in Arusha (p.394).

Opticians Two excellent opticians with everything you'll need for spectacles or contact lenses are Eyeline, Sewa St ☏ 022/212 1869, and Vision Plus, Shopper's Plaza, Old Bagamoyo Rd ☏ 022/270 0841.

Pharmacies The best stocked pharmacy in the city centre is Mansoor Daya Chemists (Mon–Fri 8.30am–12.30pm & 2–5pm) in the IPS Building, corner of Samora Ave and Azikiwe St. Also good is Makunganya Pharmaceuticals, Makunganya St ☏ 022/212 1642 (Mon–Fri 8.30am–5pm, Sat 8.30am–2pm). Further out, there's Phoenix Pharmacy at the Arcade, Old Bagamoyo Rd, and

Zeam Pharmaceuticals in Shoppers Plaza on the same road.

Photography Number One Color Lab, Haidery Plaza, corner of Upanga St and Kisutu St, is well equipped and also has a one-hour developing service, but if you need anything other than simple prints, you'd be better off waiting until you get home.

Police In an emergency dial ☎112, but don't expect a quick response. To report a theft and get paperwork done for an insurance claim, go to the Central Police Station on Sokoine Drive near the railway station (☎022/211 5507 of 0741/322999).

Post The main post office ("Posta") is on Maktaba St facing the Posta daladala stand. There are smaller offices at Sokoine Drive near Mkwepu St, and in other parts of the city, often lodged in converted shipping crates. There's a customs officer in the main post office's parcels division for the paperwork.

Safaris See p.123.

Sport Hash House Harriers organize weekly runs on Mondays at 5.30pm, followed by – or sometimes preceded by – the imbibing of vast quantities of beer. The venue changes weekly; look for details in the *What's Happening in Dar es Salaam* listings booklet, or ring them on ☎0741/784813 or 0741/327506. More serious runs are organized by the Hare and Tortoise Running Club, including a 5km time-trial on Thursdays at 5.30pm leaving from outside the Little Theatre, and a 10km run from the *Oyster Bay Hotel*, Touré Drive, Masani Peninsula, at 7am on Saturdays. The annual Dar es Salaam Marathon is held at the end of February; the annual Dar es Salaam Terry Fox Run is in early October; for details ring ☎022/211 7313. Modern gyms include the FitZone Health Club, Ghuba Rd, off Touré Drive, Msasani Peninsula (☎022/260 1953) and Elite City in Acacia House, Samora Ave (☎022/212 2079). The *Oyster Bay Hotel* (see p.89) has an extremely short golf course in its crowded grounds (the longest hole is 170 yards), but the manifold obstacles – trees, bedrooms, guests, the bar, sculptures – provide a challenge. The course

at the Gymkhana Club on Ghana Ave (☎022/213 8445) is more conventional, located on both sides of the avenue, but its "greens" are made from sand and engine oil, and membership is expensive. For something even less strenuous, the Cosmic Bowling Alley at *Sea Cliff Hotel*, Touré Drive, Msasani Peninsula, has a state-of-the-art computerized alley (Tues–Sun 11.30am–2am).

Swimming pools You should be able to use the pools at the *Embassy*, *Karibu*, *Oyster Bay*, *Royal Palm* and *Sea Cliff* hotels so long as you also buy a meal or some drinks. The *Kilimanjaro Hotel*'s pool is usually dry. Forget the Tanganyika Swimming Club, on Ocean Rd just up from Kivukoni Market, whose steep Tsh49,000 annual membership entitles you to swim in the murky waters next to the harbour entrance.

Telephones There are coin and cardphones throughout the city centre and in all the shopping centres. Most are run by TTCL (coin and cards) or Mobitel (cards only). The companies use different cards: buy them at street kiosks. For operator-assisted calls, the main TTCL telephone office is on Bridge St, off Samora Ave (Mon–Fri 7.45am–midnight, Sat & Sun 8.30am–midnight).

Tide tables Helpful for timing visits to the beach, these are published in *What's Happening in Dar es Salaam* and the *Dar es Salaam Guide*, both free (see p.81).

Worship The Hindu, Sikh, Jain and Muslim communities in the Asian district are happy to welcome members of their faith. The main Christian churches are: the Azania Front Lutheran Church, next to the Luther House Centre (English-language service Sun 5.30pm); St Alban's Anglican Church, corner of Azikiwe St and Ghana Ave (English services Mon, Wed & Fri 6.30am, Sun 8.15am); the Catholic St Joseph's Metropolitan Cathedral (Sun morning); the Pentecostal Church, Kinondoni Rd (English service Sun 9am); and the Baptist Church at the International School of Tanganyika, United Nations Rd, Upanga (Sun 10.15am).

Moving on from Dar

Dar es Salaam lies at the hub of Tanzania's road, rail and air networks, so you can get to pretty much anywhere else in the country from here in just one or two hops.

By train

Two passenger train lines converge in Dar. The **TAZARA Line** begins at the space-age TAZARA station (☎022/286 0344 or 0742/771416), 5.5km from the city centre at the corner of Nelson Mandela Expressway and Nyerere Road and served by frequent daladalas from Kariakoo, There are currently two weekly services to Mbeya via Fuga and Kisaki (both handy for Selous), Mang'ula (for the Udzungwa National Park) and Ifakara. There's also a weekly "express" service which continues on to New Kapiri Mposhi in Zambia. Unfortunately, the TAZARA line's schedules are notoriously unreliable, and can change on an almost monthly basis. Dar's tourist office (p.81) or any decent travel agent (p.123) are the best sources of current information, as the station itself is closed when there are no trains.

In spite of its often badly maintained tracks, the **Central Line**, which connects Dar with Kigoma and Mwanza, is much more dependable, with four weekly departures for either destination. The line passes Morogoro and Dodoma before branching at Tabora. Trains to Mwanza currently leave Dar at 5pm on Tuesday, Wednesday, Friday and Sunday; those to Kigoma leave at the same time on Tuesday, Thursday, Friday and Sunday. Services depart from Central Railway Station, on the corner of Railway and Gerezani streets (ticket office Mon–Fri 8am–1pm & 2–5pm, Sat & Sun 8am–1pm, and from two hours prior to departures; ☎022/211 7833 or 0744/262659).

There are no longer any passenger train services to Tanga, Moshi, Arusha or Kenya.

Train services from Dar

To	Duration
TAZARA Line	
Fuga	3hr 40min–4hr 40min
Kisaki	4hr 20min–5hr 15min
Makambako	14hr 15min–17hr 20min
Mang'ula	6hr 20min–7hr 45min
Mbeya	18hr 40min–22hr 50min
New Kapiri Mposhi, Zambia	38hr
Tunduma	21hr 45min
Central Line	
Dodoma	14hr 35min
Kigoma	38hr 25min
Morogoro	6hr 35min
Mwanza	38hr 35min
Singida (change at Dodoma or Manyoni)	26hr
Tabora	25hr 25min

By bus

Dozens of bus companies operate services out of Dar, almost all of which pass through **Ubungo Bus Station** on their way in and out of the city. The bus station is 8km from the centre along Morogoro Road; the ticket offices are in two rows of booths just outside the bus station gate under an enormous billboard displaying schedules and the corresponding ticket office number – note that information about bus times given here is subject to change. It's best to buy your **ticket** the day before when you're unencumbered by luggage, and when you'll also have a wider choice of seats. If you can't do this, arrive early at

Bus services from Dar

Most bus services peter out by midday or early afternoon, so "hourly" in the table below refers to services up to that time. Asterisks denote routes that are open in the dry season only; during the rains (usually Nov or Dec, and most of March–May) these routes are often closed for days, weeks or even months at a time. Buses that do attempt these routes in the rains are subject to lengthy delays, often meaning days rather than hours.

To	Frequency	Duration
Arusha	At least 10 daily	9–11hr
Dodoma	Hourly	6–8hr
Ifakara	2 daily	7hr
Iringa	Hourly	7–8hr
Kampala	3 daily	26hr
Kyela	4 daily	13hr
Lindi	2–3 daily*	22–28hr
Lushoto	3 daily	5hr
Mahenge	1 daily*	12hr
Mang'ula	2 daily	6hr
Mbeya	10 daily	11–12hr
Mohoro	3 daily	7hr
Mombasa	3 daily	12hr
Morogoro	1–2 hourly	2hr 45min
Moshi	Hourly	8–9hr
Mtwara	2–3 daily*	24–30hr
Musoma (via Kenya)	2 daily	27hr
Mwanza (via Kenya)	2 daily	30hr
Mwanza (via Singida)	4 daily*	35hr+
Nachingwea	1 daily*	25–32hr
Nairobi	4 daily	14hr
Newala	5–7 weekly*	26hr+
Njombe	4 daily	9hr
Singida	2 daily*	24hr
Songea	2 daily	13hr
Tanga	5–6 daily	6hr

Ubungo, as the first buses to almost everywhere leave at around 6am. Make sure you buy your ticket from a bona fide company office, not from some guy on the street (unless it's the ticket man and you're next to the bus), or you'll get ripped off. Similarly, if a tout escorts you to the ticket office, make sure his presence doesn't increase the fare.

Some companies also have offices in town (see below for recommended operators) where you can also board their buses: the time given on your ticket usually refers to departure from Ubungo (generally thirty minutes after it's left the town centre offices). Tickets generally cost around Tsh1000 for each hour's travel, with the exception of services from Dar to the south coast, which cost around Tsh600 per hour. Note that if you're taking the "short cut" to Mwanza, Musoma or Bukoba via Nairobi, you'll need to cough up $50 for a Kenyan visa if you don't already have one.

The company with the best and safest reputation is **Scandinavian Express Services**, which runs daily to Arusha, Nairobi, Mwanza, Mikumi, Morogoro, Iringa, Mbeya, Songea and Kyela. Their terminal is at the junction of Msimbazi Street and Nyerere Road (☎022/218 4833 or 0741/325474), and they charge a slight premium for a tout-free bus station, free onboard sodas and biscuits, comfortable modern buses with speed-limiters and somewhat saner drivers than usual. Similar standards and buses are maintained by **Royal Coach**, who cover Moshi and Arusha twice a day. Their office is at the corner of Libya and Mwisho streets (☎022/212 4073). Also relatively safe, but with ageing buses, is **Fresh ya Shamba**, on Nkrumah Street next to the *Kibodya Hotel* (☎022/213 1535 or 0741/531959). The Kenyan company **Akamba** (for Arusha, Nairobi, Mwanza, Kampala and Kenyan destinations) also has a reasonable reputation. Their office is next to the *Royal Chef* restaurant on Lumumba Street. **Companies to avoid** include Air Msae, Hood, Tawfiq and Takrim. Dar Express, who run to Arusha, gets mixed reviews.

By boat

Passenger ferries connect Dar with Stone Town (roughly hourly), Mkoani on Pemba (5 weekly), and Mtwara (1–2 weekly). There are no longer any services to Tanga, Mombasa, Mafia Island or Kilwa. All ferries leave from **Dar es Salaam Ferry Terminal** in the centre of town on Sokoine Drive, behind the ferry ticket offices. It's virtually impossible nowadays to arrange a **dhow** passage from Dar itself, although there's usually a dhow or two leaving daily for Kilindoni on **Mafia Island** from Kisiju village, 90km south of the city (see p.188 for more details). The trip takes anything from eight to twelve hours.

The first ferries for **Zanzibar** leave Dar at 7.30am, and continue roughly hourly from then until 4.15pm. The crossing takes 75 to 90 minutes. **Fares** are $35 for a one-way second-class ticket (including $5 port tax) and $40 for first class (where available). The cheaper and slower exception is the *MV Flying Horse* (4–5hr; $25). If you're really broke, there's a weekly **government boat** (5–6hr, $10 including tax) to Stone Town that none of the touts or offices will tell you about; the downside is its bad state of repair, lack of shade, food or

---

Ferry companies in Dar

Ticket offices in Dar are bunched together outside the ferry terminal on Samora Avenue, in the centre of town. The ferry port is behind them.

Azam Marine ☎022/212 3324 or 0741/303308, ✉azam@cats-net.com. Operates several fast catamarans called *MV Sea Bus* (they are distinguished by numbers). Daily sailings at 4.15pm, often with early morning departures too.
Megaspeed Liners ☎0741/326414. Operates the slick *MV Sepideh* catamaran (daily). The *Sepideh's* 7.30am run on Mon, Wed, Fri and Sun continues on to Pemba ($75), taking an

extra 2.5hr, and returns the same day.
Mkunazini Shipping Enterprises. Operates the *MV Aziza*; at the time of writing sailings were once a week from Dar to Pemba via Stone Town.
Sea Express ☎022/213 7049. Operates several boats, including the *MV Sea Star I*, *MV Sea Star II* and *MV Flying Horse*. The first ferry from Dar to Stone Town sets sail at 7.30am, the last at 4.15pm.

drinks, and an infamously unreliable schedule. The office is about 100m to the right of the other ferry company offices, through the gate and down the ramp. The guards at the gate, incidentally, will try any angle to get a bribe - just remember that you, like the locals, don't have to pay anything to get into the harbour.

The only reliable boat to **Mtwara** is the *MV Safari* (☎022/212 4506), whose booking office is just to the west of the Zanzibar ones. It currently sails from Dar at 8am on Tuesday, taking 22 hours to reach Mtwara ($25) - it fills up quickly, so book several days ahead. A new boat, the *MV Aziza*, joined the route in December 2001 (it also sails to Zanzibar and Pemba 1–2 times a week), but had no fixed schedule at the time of writing. The *MV Zahara* is currently impounded on account of its parlous state of repair – it used to leave on Sunday (first class Tsh10,500, second class Tsh7500, third class Tsh6500), though will probably return to service sometime in the future.

Double-check fares and times with each of the company offices before buying a ticket, and ensure that the **$5 port tax** is included. For an extra $5, most travel agents (see p.123) can buy the ticket for you. **Advance bookings** are not normally necessary, even during the peak tourist season (July–Aug). Whichever boat you choose, be aware of the various **scams** connected with buying ferry tickets (see p.66).

By plane

Dar es Salaam International Airport is 15km southwest of the city, 25 minutes by road. Most domestic **flights** take off from Terminal 1, though some Precisionair flights leave from Terminal 2 – check beforehand. A departure **tax** of $6 is levied on non-Tanzanians if not already included in the price of the ticket. You can book directly tickets with the relevant airline (see p.114) or via a travel agent (see p.123). Airline codes used in the box on p.122 are: EA (Eagle Air), CT (Coastal Travels), ATC (Air Tanzania Corporation), PA (Precisionair) and ZA (ZanAir). Where there's more than one airline flying to a destination, the one with most frequent flights is listed first. To get to the airport from the city, catch a daladala from Kariakoo to P/Kajiungeni, PG/Kwalala or Vingunguti, or a daladala from Ubungo to G/Uboto. Alternatively, catch a taxi: the fare is easier to bargain down when departing than arriving, since there's lots of competition between taxis in the centre, so Tsh5000–7000 is reasonable.

By car

First, read the section on car rental in Basics (see p.32). Prices in Dar are reasonable compared to prices in Arusha, but still expensive in international terms. Self-drive is rarely offered; instead, companies often include a driver in the price. You're fully insured if you take a driver in case of accident, but do take care with the small print if you're driving yourself - especially regarding the excess liability, which is what you'll have to pay in case of a serious accident. Check also whether VAT and fuel are included, and what the daily mileage allowance is (120km is usual; if you average more than that, there's a per-kilometre charge to pay). The following prices include VAT and insurance. If you're driving your own vehicle and need **repairs**, head to CMC on Maktaba Street, near Bibi Titi Mohamed Street (☎022/213 0453).

Avis c/o Executive Rentals, Nyerere Rd, also at the *New Africa Hotel* ☎022/286 1214, ©avis@raha.com. An a/c self-drive Kia Sportage costs $70/day including 150km free mileage; hiring a driver adds $15 per day. A Land Cruiser with driver costs $105 per day including 150km free mileage. Prices exclude fuel. You're fully covered in case of an accident.

Domestic flights from Dar

To	Operator	Departures	Duration
Arusha	EA	2 weekly	1hr 30min
Arusha (via Zanzibar)	PA, CT	2 daily	2hr 30min
Bukoba (via Shinyanga & Mwanza)	PA, EA	5 weekly	5hr 15min
Dodoma	EA	2 weekly	1hr 30min
Kagera	EA	2 weekly	3hr 50min
Kigoma	ATC, PA	3 weekly	3hr
Kilimanjaro	EA, ATC	2–3 daily	1hr 10min
Kilwa	EA	2 weekly	50min
Lindi	ATC, EA	1 daily	1hr–1hr 15min
Mafia Island	EA	3 weekly	30–45min
Marifa (via Zanzibar)	PA	5 weekly	1hr 25min
Mombasa (via Zanzibar)	ATC	6 weekly	1hr
Mtwara	EA, ATC	6 weekly	1hr 10min
Mtwara (via Lindi)	ATC, EA	3 weekly	1hr 40min
Musoma (via Kilimanjaro)	EA	2 weekly	2hr 50min
Musoma (via Arusha)	EA	2 weekly	3hr 40min
Mwanza	ATC, PA	1–2 daily	3hr
Mwanza (via Shinyanga)	PA, ATC, EA	5 weekly	3hr 40min
Nachingwea	EA	2 weekly	70min–2hr 10min
Pemba	CT, ZA	1–2 daily	45min
Ruaha National Park	CT	3 weekly	3hr 10min
Selous Game Reserve	CT	1–2 daily	45min
Shinyanga	ATC, EA	5 weekly	3hr
Tabora	PA, EA	4 weekly	2hr–2hr 45min
Zanzibar	CT, ATC, PA, EA	2–4 daily	20min

Business Rent-a-Car Rickshaw Travels, *Royal Palm Hotel*, Ohio St ☎022/212 2852 or 0744/604958, ✉business@raha.com; also at Peugeot House, Bibi Titi Mohamed St and Upanga St, and the *Sea Cliff Hotel*, Touré Drive, Msasani Peninsula. No self-drive. Cheap, efficient and reliable: a Land Cruiser with driver costs $102 per day including 120km free mileage and fuel.
Evergreen Nkrumah St, next to M. D. Motors ☎022/218 3345 or 0741/324538, ✇www.cats-net.com/evergreen. Self-drive is only possible within Dar. A Land Cruiser with driver costs $115 per day including 120km free mileage and fuel. They may also have Suzuki Vitaras available for around $20 per day less.
Fourways Travel 3rd floor, Acacia House, Samora Ave ☎022/213 1735,

✉fourways@africaonline.co.tz. Self-drive is rarely available, and there are no fixed prices. A 4WD with driver should cost around $100 per day with unlimited mileage, but you'll have to bargain hard and watch the excess liability arrangement.
Savannah Tours *Royal Palm Hotel*, Ohio St ☎022/212 0269 or 0741/600738, ✇www.savannahsafaris.com. As the agent for Hertz, Savannah offer self-drive Toyota and Nissan 4WDs for $180 per day self-drive including 100km free mileage, collision damage and theft waiver (you're liable for $350 excess). Fuel not included.
Skylink Rent-A-Car TDFL Building, Ohio St ☎022/211 5381 or 0741/323152, ✉skylink@cats-net.com. No self-drive. A Land Cruiser with driver costs $125 per day including 120km free mileage and fuel.

Travel agents

The following reputable agents all handle reservations for planes, ferries, trains and some buses, and can also arrange car rental, hotel bookings and short trips to Zanzibar.

Ami Travel Bureau Corner of Samora Ave and Mkwepu St ℡022/211 5777 or 211 5778.

Easy Travel & Tours 1st floor, Avalon House, Zanaki St ℡022/212 3526 or 212 1747, ⓦwww.easytravel.co.tz.

Hakuna Matata Travels The Arcade, Old Bagamoyo Rd ℡022/270 0231 or 0742/784737, ⓔhakunamatata@raha.com.

Hit Holidays Travel & Tours Bibi Titi Mohamed St, opposite Magore St ℡022/211 9024 or 0741/324552, ⓔhittours@ud.co.tz.

Kearsleys Travel and Tours Branches at Makunganya St and at the *Holiday Inn* ℡022/211 5026, ⓦwww.kearsley.net.

Walji's Travel Corner India St and Zanaki St ℡022/211 0321, ⓦwww.waljistravel.com.

Worldlink Travel & Tours Libya St ℡022/211 6026, ⓔworldlink@raha.com.

Safaris from Dar

If you're looking to arrange a **Northern Circuit safari** (Serengeti, Ngorongoro, Lake Manyara and/or Tarangire), you're best off heading to Arusha (see p.393), which is where these trips depart from, and where there's much more choice. You might consider booking in Dar if you're short of time, but bear in mind that you'll have to trek back to Dar to get anything done should things go wrong. Prices for Northern Circuit safaris arranged in Dar are generally $5–10 more per day.

Where Dar's operators come into their own is for **Southern Circuit safari trips**, which include the Selous Game Reserve, Mikumi National Park and Ruaha National Park. Unfortunately, there are only a handful of **budget operators** that can be wholeheartedly recommended, whereas there are dozens of unreliable companies and assorted con-artists: read the reviews below carefully, and if you decide to go with another company, follow our advice on how to choose a reliable operator (see pp.58–59). The cheapest option is to go on a **camping safari**, though at upwards of $100 per person per day, these are relatively pricey compared to the Northern Circuit, certainly given that Mikumi, Ruaha and Udzungwa can all be visited under your own steam (see below). **Mid-range and upmarket** Southern Circuit safaris, with accommodation in lodges or luxury tented camps, cost around $200 per person per night.

With the exception of Mikumi, road transport to the parks takes the best part of a day, potentially making a **two-day safari** an exhausting and unsatisfying experience. The alternative is to book a **flying safari**, though these cost upwards of $250–300 per person per day. If you have money for a **longer trip** lasting over a week or so, some companies are be happy to include lesser-known destinations in southern Tanzania in your itinerary (minimum 7–10 days), such as the Kilwas, Mikindani and Mtwara.

Arranging your own safari

To arrange your own transport, consult the reviews of car-rental agencies on p.121 or the list of air-charter operators on p.114. The cheapest way to see **Mikumi**, apart from catching a bus through the park to Iringa or further south (the drivers rarely pause for photographs) would be to catch a bus to Mikumi village and hire a car with a driver there (p.283). Similarly, **Ruaha National Park** works out a great deal cheaper if you hire a car and driver in Iringa (p.576). If your driver doesn't know the park too well, you can always hire an official guide at the park gate.

It's a slightly different story with **Selous** (p.290). Getting to the reserve under your own steam is possible, but there's no car rental anywhere near the reserve, so you'll be limited to hiring an official ranger-gude for walks in the reserve. In addition, you don't need to go on an organized safari to reach the fantastic hiking terrain in the **Udzungwa Mountains National Park** and the **Uluguru Mountains**, since both are easy to get to by public transport.

Safari operators

The importance of choosing a reliable and reputable **safari operator** cannot be over-emphasized – full details of how to do this are given on pp.58–59. There's a reasonable choice of mid- and upper-range operators, but unfortunately, it's almost impossible to wholeheartedly recommend any of Dar's **budget safari companies** – even the more established ones can sometimes come up with truly dreadful trips, with bad cars, ignorant guides or just plain dangerous drivers. It's not as though there's no choice – you'll probably be assailed by offers from different companies – but unfortunately telling good from bad is no easy matter, with even the official TALA licence meaning little in terms of quality or reliability (it's available to anyone with $2000). Be especially suspicious of the companies operating in and around Dar's budget guest houses in Kisutu, and those touting themselves at the airport, some of whom are little more than paper companies with scant regard for the quality of their services. Bearing this in mind, it might be safer to avoid the budget companies altogether and spend an extra $20 per day for more reliable service and peace of mind.

The following companies are all licensed and have reasonable reputations, and most are members of TATO (Tanzanian Association of Tour Operators; see p.59), which gives some leverage in case of serious complaints. As ever, talking with other travellers is really the only foolproof way to get current recommendations.

A Tent with a View Safaris 3rd floor, Sido Small Business Centre, Bibi Titi Mohamed St next to Tritel (PO Box 40525) ☎022/215 1106 or 0744/323318, ⊛www.saadani.com. Reputable company specializing in affordable trips to Saadani Game Reserve (see p.155 for prices), where they run the only camp. They also own the *Sable Mountain Lodge* in Selous (p.295; $120–170 per day all inclusive). Other trips cover less well-trodden areas of southern and western Tanzania, including Uluguru, Udzungwa, Katavi National Park and Lake Tanganyika.

Coastal Travels 107 Upanga Rd, near the *YMCA* (PO Box 3052) ☎022/211 7959 or 0741/800285 (toll free), ⊛www.coastal.cc. A reliable and long-established company specializing in flying safaris using their own planes, especially to the Southern Circuit parks and reserves, and a combination of Serengeti and the infrequently visited Rubondo Island National Park in Lake Victoria. They operate a lodge in Ruaha (the *Mdonya Camp*) and can also tailor safaris to Zanzibar and the Northern Circuit. Member of TATO.

Easy Travel & Tours (Vintage Safaris) First floor, Avalon House, Zanaki St (PO Box 1428)

☎022/212 3526 or 212 1747, ⊛www.easy travel.co.tz. Large and reputable operator offering a wide range of both Northern and Southern Circuit safaris, as well as holiday packages to Zanzibar. Their four-night Selous Rail Safari ($710–810) is a speciality. Camping safaris cost $90–130 per day for the Northern Circuit, slightly less for the Southern Circuit.

Elephant Adventures Nkrumah St (PO Box 12988) ☎0741/350601. A newish budget company that receives a mix of rave reports and occasional scathing criticism. They specialize in extended trips in southern Tanzania and might be worth checking out, but keep your sense of cynicism intact.

Eurotan Safaris Pamba House, Pamba Rd (PO Box 7950) ☎022/213 8198 or 0741/612213, ⓔeurotan@hotmail.com. Long-established German company purporting to specialize in everything, the majority of whose clients come pre-booked from Europe. They have a reliable reputation, and offer a four-night Selous trip which includes a "boat tour along the Rufiji, decorated by Hippos and Crocodiles jumping up and down". Upwards of $120 per day.

Family Travel & Tour Services Jued Mall, near Shoppers Plaza, Old Bagamoyo Rd (PO Box 456) ☎0741/785291, ✉ftts@raha.com. Mid-range operator specializing in Selous, with guests staying at their *Hidden Paradise* campsite, 7km outside the reserve. Camping safaris cost $150–200 per day; lodge safaris are $200–270.

Foxtreks (PO Box 10270) ☎0741/327706, ⓦwww.tanzaniasafaris.info. A mid-range to upmarket operator offering quality safaris based around their own lodges: *Lazy Lagoon Island* near Bagamoyo, *Mufundi Highland Lodge* in southern Tanzania, *Fox's Safari Camp* at Mikumi and *Ruaha River Lodge* at Ruaha. Expect to pay upwards of $200 per day.

Hippotours & Safaris Nyumba ya Sanaa, Ohio St, next to the *Royal Palm Hotel* (PO Box 13824) ☎022/212 8662 or 0744/267706, ⓦwww.hippo-tours.com. A reliable operator which owns the *Rufiji River Camp* in Selous – their special four-day fly-in excursion departs twice a month and costs $820. They also do road safaris (around $190–260 per day) including accommodation in lodges or tented camps.

JMT African Heart Expeditions *Safari Inn*, off Band St, signposted off Libya St (PO Box 21844) ☎022/212 4503 or 0744/282251, ⓦwww.african-heart.com. Belgian-run outfit specializing in Northern Circuit camping safaris ($100–150 per day). Lodge safaris cost around $165–260 per day. In the south, they mainly cover Selous and Mikumi, but their "budget" trips are pricey at $125–190 per day. Better value is the $120 one-night camping trip to an elephant hole in Simanjiro Plain east of Tarangire, which leaves weekly between June and September. Member of TATO.

Klipspringer Behind *Chef's Pride*, Chagga St (PO Box 38062) ☎022/266 7704, ✉klipspringersafari@yahoo.com. One of the cheaper budget companies, and receives very mixed feedback – their reputation isn't helped by the fact that they use a blacklisted Arusha-based company for their Northern Circuit safaris. They're probably best outside the parks, as they offer a wide range of cultural and activity-oriented trips such as canoeing, hiking, visits to local communities (all around $100 per day), and a day-trip to the Pugu Hills (see p.135) for $60. TALA licensed.

Leopard Tours Haidery Plaza, corner of Upanga St and Kisutu St (PO Box 979) ☎022/211 9754 or 211 9756, ⓦwww.leopard-tours.com. One of the largest mid-range operators, with another branch in Arusha, specializing in lodge and tented camp safaris ($155–215 per day); they also run more unusual trips featuring Gombe National Park in the far west ($200–300 per day including the flight from Dar). Member of TATO.

Safari Scene Next to Shoppers Plaza, Old Bagamoyo Rd (PO Box 40525) ☎022/270 1497 or 0741/323318, ⓦwww.safariscene.com. A marketing and information centre for several lodges and tented camps in south and west Tanzania, offering virtual tours of several lodges, expert and unhurried advice, and a booking service for safaris.

Savannah Tours *Royal Palm Hotel*, Ohio St (PO Box 20517) ☎022/212 0269 or 0741/600738, ⓦwww.savannahsafaris.com. A long-established company specializing in six- or seven-day lodge-based Southern Circuit safaris (roughly $200–270 per day), plus an adventurous thirteen-day trip ($2200–3000) to the seldom-visited Katavi National Park in the far west of Tanzania, via Mikumi and Ruaha, though a lot of the journey consists of backtracking. Member of TATO.

Selous Safari Company Nyerere Rd (PO Box 1192) ☎022/211 1728, ⓦwww.selous.com. Upmarket operator specializing in flying safaris using their lodges in Ruaha, Selous and Ras Kutani. A typical five-night jaunt goes for around $2000, eight days for $3000.

Takims Holidays Tours & Safaris Mtendeni St (PO Box 20350) ☎022/211 0346, ⓦwww.takimsholidays.com. Offer a huge range of safaris in minibuses or Land Cruisers, all equipped with HF radio, fridge, binoculars and reference books. Their longer trips are better value, with a four-night safari to Mikumi and Selous staying at lodges or tented camps costing around $1000. A two-night trip to Selous in similar accommodation costs $680 ($820 if flying). No camping safaris. Member of TATO.

North of Dar

The beaches north of the city – **Kunduchi**, **Jangwani** and **Bahari** – are mainland Tanzania's busiest and most developed, and the resorts here offer all the amenities and standards you'd expect at the price (generally $100 and upwards for a double room), but there's little that's recognizably Tanzanian about them, and you're likely to see and meet as many *wazungu* as locals. For many visitors, the resort areas represent little more than sun, sand, sea and, even in the AIDS era, sex. That said, most of the development is low key and well spaced out, with few if any buildings higher than three storeys. The downside of beach tourism in the developing world is startlingly obvious, however: security is a major concern, with frequent reports of muggings both on the beaches and along the access roads. Most hotels routinely advise guests not to stray outside the usually well-guarded hotel compounds, nor to walk on the beach beyond the hotel strip without an *askari*. If you choose to ignore their advice – and plenty of visitors do – read the section on "Trouble" in Basics (p.63). You can, of course, have a wonderful time basking on the beaches doing nothing very much, but if you get bored with this there's the deeply atmospheric ruined medieval trading town of **Kunduchi**, south of Kunduchi and Bahari beach resorts, to explore.

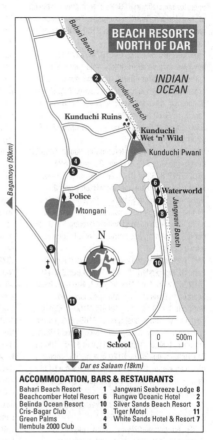

BEACH RESORTS NORTH OF DAR

INDIAN OCEAN

Kunduchi Ruins

Kunduchi Wet 'n' Wild

Kunduchi Pwani

Waterworld

Jangwani Beach

Police

Mtongani

N

School

Bagamoyo (50km)

Bahari Beach

Kunduchi Beach

Dar es Salaam (18km)

0   500m

ACCOMMODATION, BARS & RESTAURANTS

Bahari Beach Resort	1
Beachcomber Hotel Resort	6
Belinda Ocean Resort	10
Cris-Bagar Club	9
Green Palms	4
Ilembula 2000 Club	5
Jangwani Seabreeze Lodge	8
Rungwe Oceanic Hotel	2
Silver Sands Beach Resort	3
Tiger Motel	11
White Sands Hotel & Resort	7

Jangwani Beach

The most developed and accessible of the resort strips is **JANGWANI BEACH**, 21km north of the city. Apart from the beach itself, the main attraction is the **coral reef**, some 7km out to sea, whose six- to forty-metre drop makes it ideal for scuba-diving – see the box on p.128. Jangwani's other attraction, especially for families, is **Waterworld** (daily 10am–6pm; Tsh2500), 250m beyond the *White Sands Hotel & Resort*, which has several water flumes, four pools, beach volleyball, basketball, snooker tables and paddle boats.

Arrival and accommodation

Frequent **daladalas** run throughout the day from Mwenge in Dar along Bagamoyo Road to Tegeta, passing the turn-off to Jangwani Beach. However, there's no public transport from the turn-off to the beach so, given the real risk of muggings, your only option is to take a taxi from the junction (Tsh2500–5000 depending on your bargaining skills). Once in Jangwani, the *Beachcomber Hotel Resort* hires cars with drivers at a very reasonable $32 for a full day, or $20 for half a day.

With the exception of the **campsite** at the *Jangwani Seabreeze Lodge* ($7.50 per person; tent hire may be available for $10), Jangwani's accommodation is expensive and limited, with the cheapest doubles starting at around $90 half-board for a double room.

Beachcomber Hotel Resort, 4.5km off Bagamoyo Rd ☎022/264 7772, ⓦwww.beachcomber.co.tz. Jangwani's newest package hotel, and a good place for families. It's pleasingly informal, with an airy and cheerful design, friendly staff and comfortable rooms, all with a/c. Amenities include a swimming pool, children's activities, a health club with sauna and gym ($8/day), massage and internet café. Water sports can be arranged, and boat trips are planned. The only gripe is the narrow beach, which is flanked by unsightly breakwaters, though it extends north into wide sand banks on which you can walk if accompanied by an *askari*. Rates include transfer from Dar. Half-board ❼ full board ❽

Belinda Ocean Resort, 2.8km off Bagamoyo Rd, signposted off on the left ☎ 022/264 7552, ⓔmekon@ud.co.tz. A modern and attractive hotel somewhere in style between a Roman villa and a Swahili townhouse, with nice decorative touches like Makonde sculptures built into the staircases. The sixteen rooms are clean and cool, and come with a/c, fans, large box nets, satellite TV, telephone and bathtubs; upper rooms have balconies, though the views aren't great. The staff are friendly and efficient, and there's a swimming pool in the cramped gardens. The big drawback is the location, 300m from the beach, though some beachside *bandas* are planned. Breakfast included. ❻

Jangwani Seabreeze Lodge, 3.8km from Bagamoyo Road ☎022/264 7215 or 0741/320875, ⓔjangwani@afsat.com. Long-established German-run hotel with a vaguely macho ambience (upmarket prostitutes frequent the bars and the street outside). Like the *Belinda*, it's on the wrong side of the road, though there's a beachfront annexe opposite with a beer garden (live music Wed & Sat). The 34 rooms in the main building, mostly doubles, are a mixed bunch, though all have box nets, satellite TV, a/c and fan, minibar and safe. Facilities and activities include a Finnish sauna (Tsh15,000), two swimming pools and various water sports. A laugh if beer figures prominently in your plans, but families should steer clear. Breakfast included. ❼

White Sands Hotel & Resort, 400m along from *Jangwani Seabreeze Lodge* on the beach ☎022/264 7621 or 264 7622, ⓦwww.hotelwhite-sands.com. The largest and best equipped of Jangwani's hotels, and excellent value for money if you don't mind the slightly formal air. The beachfront location is good, and the 88 bedrooms are all sea-facing, though some views are obscured by trees – get a room on the top away from the main building. Rooms have a/c, satellite TV, large beds, fans, nets and verandahs. There's a large octagonal pool, and activities and entertainment include diving, water sports, day-trips to Mbudya Island, live bands (Tues–Fri evenings), traditional dancing (Sat) and Barry White barbecue theme nights. Rates include breakfast and transfer from Dar. ❼

Eating and drinking

Jangwani's only **restaurants** and **bars** are in the hotels and at Waterworld, and with the exception of the hotel bistros and snack bars, you won't find a full meal for much under Tsh7000. The *Beachcomber Hotel Resort* specializes in Indian and Chinese dishes – the ginger-spiced chicken is especially succulent. The *Jangwani Seabreeze Lodge* serves mainly north and central European food, with lots of pork, dumplings and stews, plus a special eat-all-you-can spare ribs and mash evening on Wednesdays (Tsh5800; from 7pm), accompanied by live music. The *Belinda Ocean Resort* has a good à la carte menu, whilst *White Sands Hotel* has some Romanian specialities, thanks to the nationality of its chef.

Scuba-diving around Dar

First, read the section on diving in Basics (p.62). Most of Dar's **diving sites** are located north of the city along a double chain of coral reefs, with the main concentration lying off Jangwani and Bahari beaches. The coral is in mixed condition, with many of the interior reefs having been extensively damaged by dynamite fishing, while others suffered from the worldwide coral bleaching phenomenon that accompanied the 1997–98 El Niño event. Still, the corals are recovering well, and after a successful and ongoing campaign by the Marine Action Conservation Trust (MACT), explosions from dynamite fishing are now infrequently heard. The trust is also involved in a coral transplanting programme around Mbudya Island, grafting live coral from healthier parts of the reef onto concrete bases.

The best dive sites are on the ocean-facing reefs 7km offshore. **Fungu Yasini** ("Sand Bank") is the easiest to visit. Its wide variety of coral is home to crocodile fish, rays, pufferfish, lobsters, eels, lion fish, sea cucumbers, and a worryingly large population of the destructive crown-of-thorns starfish, which feed on coral. Much of the reef has also been damaged by dynamite fishing so there are few large fish other than the occasional barracuda. In contrast, the depth of the **Big T Reef** (also known as Mbudya Patches) further out has enabled it to survive dynamite fishing better, so you're more likely to see large game fish like kingfish, tuna and occasionally, bull and white-tipped reef sharks. Whales have occasionally been spotted, and heard – listening to their eerily powerful song through the water must rank as one of the world's most bewitching experiences. The reef is 45 minutes by *ngalawa* outrigger or fifteen minutes by speedboat, but diving should only be attempted in calm seas as there are strong currents and swells: you stand a better chance of good weather in the morning.

Trips to either reef are offered by two PADI-accredited scuba-diving schools on Jangwani Beach. Best equipped, with Nitrox facilities, is the **Jangwani Seabreeze Dive Centre**, based at *Jangwani Seabreeze Lodge* (☏0744/783241, ℮seabreeze@afsat.com), which offers four- or five-day Open-Water courses with four dives for $320, and single dives at $40 ($50 at night). Their three-day Scuba Diver course ($200) includes two open-water dives and gets you a licence for depths up to 12m, which can be upgraded to a full Open-Water qualification. A five-dive Advanced Open Water course costs $250. Day-trips to dive sites around Zanzibar can also be arranged, as can parasailing ($20 for 20min). **Blue Chip Diving**, based at *White Sands Hotel & Resort* (☏0741/325483, ℮bluechip@intafrica.com), is slightly more expensive for the Open-Water course ($350) but cheaper for individual dives ($35), and also runs a single-dive "Discover Scuba" course for $50. They can also supply equipment for underwater photography and night dives. There's also a rarely undertaken **wreck dive** on the thirty-metre German freighter *Schlammerstadt* in Oyster Bay, which was towed out and scuttled in 1908 after it caught fire inside Dar harbour. The top of wreck lies just three metres below sea level. Either of the PADI schools can arrange a dive there.

Kunduchi and Bahari beaches

Slightly over a kilometre further along Bagamoyo Road from the turning for Jangwani Beach, a signposted right turn takes you to two more beaches. **KUNDUCHI BEACH** takes its name from a fishing village and the nearby ruins of a Swahili trading town. **BAHARI BEACH** is the northern continuation of Kunduchi Beach, and at its furthest point lies some 28km from Dar. The beaches here are pretty similar to that at Jangwani, but there are far fewer hotels, and some good cheap accommodation.

Arrival

The easy but expensive way to reach the beaches is by **taxi**: seasoned bargainers might get the fare from Dar down to Tsh8000, but Tsh12,000 is more usual (Tsh20,000 from the airport). You'll find it harder bargaining for the ride back into town as there's less competition. Cheaper but more fiddly is **public transport**. You have two options: catch a Tegeta-bound daladala from Mwenge in Dar, and get off at the turn-off to Kunduchi on the Bagamoyo Road, from where it's a Tsh2000 taxi ride to the beach; alternatively, catch a daladala from Mwenge to Mtongani, which is about 1km towards the beaches from Bagamoyo Road, from where the cab fare shouldn't be more than Tsh1500, or a bicycle taxi – if you can find one – only a few hundred shillings. **Car rental** can be arranged at the *Bahari Beach Hotel*, but it's much cheaper doing a deal in Dar.

Accommodation

Although there are only three **hotels** on Kunduchi and Bahari beaches (with a fourth in the making), they offer a range of accommodation to suit all pockets. If you're **camping**, the best choice is the site at the *Silver Sands Beach Resort* ($3 per person plus $2 per vehicle), which has good security, clean showers and the use of the hotel facilities included in the price. The run-down campsite at the *Rungwe Oceanic Hotel* next door (Tsh1000 per person) seems far from secure.

Bahari Beach Hotel 4.5km off Bagamoyo Rd; the turn-off is 1.1km beyond the one for the *Silver Sands Beach Resort* ☏022/265 0475, ℮bbhbuz@intafrica.com. The shotgun-toting *askaris* may or may not reassure you, but they certainly don't set the mood for a holiday resort. Given the heavy security, almost the only genuinely local thing here is the coral ragstone and *makuti* thatch used in the two-storey accommodation rondavels. The 100 rooms each have box nets, telephone, local TV and ocean-facing balconies, but facilities are limited to a swimming pool, tennis court and jogging circuit. There are no water sports at present, but jet-skiing, surfing and boat rides are planned, as is a small golf course. In the meantime, it's a thoroughly lacklustre option. Breakfast included. ➏

Rungwe Oceanic Hotel 4.5km off Bagamoyo Rd; turn right after 3.2km and then left at the *Silver Sands Beach Resort* (no phone). It's amazing that this severely dilapidated structure is still standing, never mind in business. The management in their wisdom consider ten rooms to be habitable, the rest having been consigned to dereliction. Despite their tatty outward appearance, broken locks and sagging rusty roofs, the beds are reasonably clean, albeit covered by too-small nets, and the fans work. No sea views, which is no bad thing as the beach is spoilt by abandoned concrete sewerage pipes. Security seems far from adequate, though perhaps given the lack of clientele the thieves stay away as well. Recommended for those with hardly any money, a twisted sense of humour and little to lose. No single rates. ➌

Silver Sands Beach Resort 4km off Bagamoyo Rd; turn right after 3km ☏022/265 0567, ℮silversands@africaonline.co.tz. In a breezy beachfront location, this is the oldest of the north coast hotels, still going strong after four decades and offering very good value for this part of the coast. There's a choice of "standard" rooms (with fans) and "deluxe" rooms, which have a/c but are otherwise nothing special, plus bunk beds in a dorm ($7 per person). Facilities are limited to a swimming pool and some excursions, by far the best being the trip to Kunduchi-Pwani village and the Kunduchi ruins, followed by a dhow trip to Mbudya Island for snorkelling ($15 per person). The hotel boasts 400m of beachfront, though there's not too much of it extending out to sea thanks to erosion, which a number of unsightly breakwaters are attempting to stem. Credit cards accepted. Breakfast included. ➏

Eating, drinking and nightlife

You'll need a taxi to get to these places if you want to avoid the possibility of being mugged.

Bahari Beach Hotel (see p.129). Huge restaurant with a steel-vaulted *makuti* roof serving lunch and dinner à la carte – the admission fee (Tsh1500) is recouped against the price of your meal. Musicians and snake dancers entertain diners on Wednesdays.
Cris-Bagar Club Near the Bagamoyo Rd junction. This is the main local club on this stretch of the beach, and is worth checking out on weekend nights. There's the usual bar food available (mainly grilled meat and bananas).

Green Palms. 2km off Bagamoyo Rd. A bar and restaurant with seating in shady *bandas* surrounded by bushes and low trees, good for an afternoon drink.
Ilembula 2000 Club 2km off Bagamoyo Rd. Deceptively rough from the outside, it's actually a lively and friendly nightspot that gets packed at weekends when dance tunes reign.

Kunduchi Wet 'n' Wild

At the south end of Kunduchi Beach, next to Kunduchi Pwani village, is **Kunduchi Wet 'n' Wild** (Tues–Sun 9am–6.30pm; Tsh3600), East Africa's largest water park. With a spaghetti-like arrangement of 22 water chutes and tubes, a 1000-square-metre main pool and fake river, this is very much tailored towards the affluent minority, and successfully manages to exclude anything that might spoil the Disney-like illusion. Past the heavy gate security, you'll also find slot machines, pool tables, a go-kart track (Tsh4000 for 5min), beach buggies (Tsh2000 for 5min), a miserable horse for rides and several restaurants. Jet-skiing is planned, as well as a huge resort-style hotel. Access for visitors without their own transport is by daladala from Mwenge either to Kunduchi (with "7/20" displayed in the window) or to Tegeta ("via Bagamoyo Road"). If you're driving or cycling, the turn-off is next to the police station in Mtongani; the water park is just under 2km along.

Kunduchi ruins

Just 600m north of Wet 'n' Wild are the infrequently visited but exceedingly atmospheric ruins of the Swahili trading town of **KUNDUCHI**, comprising a sixteenth-century mosque and various other ruined buildings set in a grove of baobab trees and bushes, together with graves dating from the eighteenth and nineteenth centuries. Little is known about the history of Kunduchi other than, like Kaole, Kilwa, Tongoni and other ruined coastal settlements, it was part of the medieval Swahili trading empire. Some of the graves bear distinctive obelisk-like pillars mounted on their heads, a style that's typical of the coast, whilst other tombs are made of ornately carved coral ragstone inset with Chinese blue-and-white celadon porcelain bowls, one of the few sites where you can still see the bowls in their original settings. Different theories have been advanced to explain the presence of this porcelain. One suggests that the bowls were merely decorative, while another claims that they were indicators of the deceased's wealth and standing in the community. Either way, their presence is visible proof that East Africa was once part of a vast trading network that stretched as far afield as China.

Unfortunately, the site is a popular hang-out for muggers: the easiest and safest way to reach it is by car, but if you have a day to spare the combined trip with Mbudya Island organized by the *Silver Sands Beach Resort* is highly recommended – see p.129. If you can't find the site, ask for *magofu* – the "ruins" or "charmed place". There are two access roads. The easiest to follow is from Wet 'n' Wild (see above), where you leave the tarmac and continue north. After 400m you come to a small crossroads under a tree. Dar es Salaam's university marine labs are on the right beside a water tower, whilst the main track veers off to the left. Ignore the track and continue 200m straight into the wood.

Less easy is the 2km route from the signs for Seamic and ESAMRDC Labs on the main Kunduchi Road, for which you really need a local guide. If you're walking, a police escort from Mtongani village is advisable. Although it's an informal arrangement, the *askari* will expect a decent tip (around Tsh2000 should do). There's a hut for the guard-cum-curator at the site, but he's usually absent.

Mbudya Island

Snorkelling conditions are best around the uninhabited **Mbudya Island**, 3km off Kunduchi and Bahari beaches. The coral surrounds most of the island, with the reefs barely 15m offshore at low tide. The three main reefs here are **Mbudya North**, which is good for night dives but otherwise nothing special; the **"Coral Gardens"** (Mbudya West) which has staghorn and lettuce coral, but has been damaged by dynamite fishing, dragnets and careless anchoring; and the **"Octopus Gardens"** (Mbudya East), which has lots of moray eels but few if any octopus, despite its name. The reefs are now belatedly protected as part of a marine reserve which also encloses Bongoyo, Pangavini and Fungu Yasini islands. The **fee** structure for using the island is currently something of a mess: officially, rates are $10 for non-Tanzanians, but currently only Tsh500 is charged, if at all. In any case, the fee should be included in the cost of the boat trips to the island on *ngalawa* outriggers which are offered by most of the hotels. Of these, the best value is the daily "ferry" run by the *White Sands Hotel & Resort* on Jangwani Beach (see p.127; Tsh3000 per person). An attractive alternative is offered by the *Silver Sands Beach Resort* on Kunduchi Beach (see p.129), combining a walk to Kunduchi ruins with snorkelling at Mbudya. You can usually stay on the island as long as you want. There are plenty of shady casuarina, baobab and palm trees, which are also home to the endangered coconut crab (see p.651). Barbecued fish, sodas and sometimes beer are sold by enterprising locals, hence the island's nickname, "Mini Bar". Equally enterprising are the petty thieves and muggers: the mainland hotels post guards on the island, but take care not to leave stuff unattended.

Snorkelling gear can be rented from the Jangwani Seabreeze Dive Centre and the *White Sands Hotel & Resort* on Jangwani Beach, and from the *Silver Sands Beach Resort* at Kunduchi Beach. The cost is $5 for a mask and snorkel. Fins (flippers) are not usually included, primarily for fear of the damage they can inadvertently cause by suffocating coral polyps with sand that's been kicked up.

South of Dar

The beaches south of Dar are much less frequented than those to the north, and the nearest – **Mikadi** and **Mjimwema** – are just a short ferry and daladala ride away from the city. Thankfully, the south coast has yet to see the kind of investment being sunk into Jangwani and Kunduchi, and the only real facilities at present are a handful of rooms and campsites, and – 25km further south at **Ras Kutani** – a couple of searingly expensive lodges. It seems inevitable that multi-million-dollar development will happen sooner or later, so enjoy it while you can. If the stress of hanging around on beaches and in bars gets to you, the community-run cultural tourism programme at **Gezaulole** village makes for a refreshing and humanizing change.

For something completely different, there's the easy day-trip from Dar to the **Pugu Hills**, 25km southwest of the city, which contain rare remnants of coastal monsoon forest whose lush vegetation and relatively cool climate makes a pleasant break from the sweltering heat and humidity of the coast.

Mikadi and Mjimwema beaches

Just to the south of Dar, Mikadi and Mjimwema are a very different prospect from the northern resorts, with only a handful of cheap rooms and campsites to their name. **MIKADI BEACH** is currently the main stop on the coast for trans-Africa truck tours, and can be a lot of fun if you're happy slipping into road-trip mentality. A few kilometres further south is the village of **MJIMWEMA**, which is much more peaceful, with rather fewer dazed and dreadlocked *wazungu* wandering around. It also benefits from a safer beach, not only hygienically (the water is marginally less murky than at Mikadi) but also security-wise, as the locals have yet to be swamped by tourists bent on booze, sex and the Big Five.

Practicalities

To reach Mikadi and Mjimwema you'll first have to catch the **ferry** (*kivuko*) from Dar to the Kigamboni Peninsula, which sails every thirty minutes or so between 4am and 1am from the east end of Kivukoni Front by the fish market (Tsh100 per person, Tsh1000 per car; 10min). The terminal in Dar is surprisingly orderly, so the seething mass of confusion that greets you at Kigamboni is something of a shock. Watch your bags and pockets, and don't allow yourself to be harried by daladala touts. There are frequent **daladalas** (6am–8pm; Ts150) from Kigamboni to both Mikadi and Mjimwema, and hourly runs to Gezaulole (see opposite). You could also catch a cab, which shouldn't cost more than Tsh1500 to Mikadi or Tsh2000 to Mjimwema. A word of warning: if you're considering walking the 2km to Mikadi, don't – **muggings** of unsuspecting tourists are all too common.

Mikadi is good for those wanting to meet fellow travellers; Mjimwema is ideal for getting away from them. The *Genda Yeka* and the *Kipepeo* (see below) are the only places serving **food** where you don't need to pre-order; for a **drink**, try the *Barracuda Beach Resort* at Mjimwema village, on a cliff with a lovely view over the ocean.

Accommodation
Accommodation is limited to the following three places.

Genda Yeka Beach Village, Mjimwema village, 300m beyond *Kipepeo* ☎0742/786229. Set in the ruins of a colonial governor's residence, this place is as strange as it is likeable, with no electricity, friendly if completely disorganized management, and a nice 150m stretch of beach which is safe to walk on unaccompanied. The rooms are in large thatched *bandas* but lack toilets and bathrooms,

and are way overpriced if you don't bargain. Camping is better value at $5 per person. There's also a bar, plus a restaurant specializing in seafood (meals Tsh3000–4000). Boats to Sinda Island (bring your own snorkelling gear) can be arranged, and are a bargain at $15 for four people. Lifts from Dar are possible from *Chef's Pride* (p.102), who run the place. ❹

Kipepeo Beach Camp, Mjimwema village, 7.5km south of Kigamboni, then 1.3km along a dirt track ☎ 0744/276178, ⊛ www.kipepeocamp.com. Spread out along 400m of beach, Kipepeo ("butterfly") is a friendly, intimate and recommended alternative to the *Mikadi Beach Campsite*. With a ban on overland trucks, and good relations with local villagers, there's no need for armed guards, and walking on the beach is no problem. There are ten gorgeous tent pitches right on the beach under thatched shelters (Tsh2000 per person), plus nine simple but comfortable two-bed *bandas* with large nets but no power (❸) and six bunks in the main house (Tsh5000 per person). The bar and restaurant serve snacks and full meals (around Tsh3500), and a great English breakfast for Tsh2500. They can pick you up from Dar if you ring in advance.

Mikadi Beach Campsite, Mikadi Beach, 2km south of Kigamboni ☎ 022/282 0485, ⓔ mikadibeach@yahoo.com. Mikadi is a major stopover for overlanders on the Nairobi to Cape Town run, and in its way is as anachronistic as the neo-colonial game lodges at the opposite end of the scale. Local relations are strained, as evidenced by the shotgun-toting *askaris*, and the beach is dangerous to walk along beyond the campsite. In any case, the water isn't too clean, thanks to Dar's proximity. The bar (open most nights till 1am) is the main attraction, with US rock, techno, and even a Slush Puppy machine. Food is limited to snacks and a set dinner if ordered in the morning. Most people camp (Tsh2000 per person), but there are also a dozen basic thatched *bandas* on stilts (❸), the best on the beach, containing mattresses and smallish nets. Boat trips can be arranged (Tsh65,000).

Gezaulole

Some 14km south of Kigamboni is the typical coastal settlement of **GEZA-ULOLE**, whose 4500 inhabitants survive through fishing and the cultivation of rice, sweet potatoes, mushrooms, maize and cassava. The whole place would be unremarkable were it not for its community-based **cultural tourism programme**, one of eighteen in Tanzania (see p.405), which allows visitors to combine the hedonistic pleasures of beach, dhow and snorkelling trips with local history, culture and village life. The price is very reasonable, with a half-day tour costing Tsh4500 (Tsh6000 for a couple), and a full day with meals Tsh6500 (Tsh9500 for a couple). The price includes a guide but excludes boat or bicycle rental. Although you can visit the village without hiring a guide, you'll miss much if you don't and you'll understandably be seen by villagers as something of a scrooge, given that proceeds from the programme go directly towards helping them. The programme has already financed the refurbishment of the primary school – next in line are the provision of a clean and reliable water supply and the construction of a dispensary.

Guided walks

Gezaulole's history is well presented in the cultural programme's **Historical Places and Beach Walk**, which covers a number of historically important sites. The village's first inhabitants were Zaramo fishermen who used the site as a *dago* (temporary camp). After a while they decided to stay permanently and so – according to legend – went to their soothsayer for advice. He chillingly ordered that a young virgin be buried alive in sacrifice, and added, "then *gezaulole* (try and see) whether you can stay here". The walk includes the unfortunate girl's tomb, as well as some early Muslim graves nestling – as in so many other coastal sites – in the shade of a large old baobab tree.

Gezaulole remained a village until the arrival of the Omani Arabs in the sixteenth century, when it changed its name to Mbwamaji and became a destination for ivory, hide and slave caravans travelling from the interior. Sadly the ruins of the **slave depot** are now on privately owned land and cannot be visited, whilst the 400-year-old Arab **mosque** which for years lay in ruins has recently been rebuilt, much to the anguish of archeologists. Mbwamaji changed its name back to Gezaulole in the early 1970s, when it became one of Tanzania's first collective agricultural villages under Nyerere's disastrous policy of *Ujamaa*, or "Villagization" (see p.719), during which the old tag of "try and see" once more became appropriate.

With the ivory and slave caravans now long since gone, Gezaulole survives on agriculture and fishing as well as the small-scale harvesting of seaweed by women. Because of its *Ujamaa* past, Gezaulole's present population is now very mixed, comprising not only Zaramo but Chagga from around Kilimanjaro, Nyamwezi, Sukuma and Matumbi from the far west, Makonde from the south, and Ngindo from central Tanzania. This unusual cosmopolitan aspect of village life is explored by the **Village Life Walk**, which combines visits to local farms, tie-dyers, woodcarvers, an elderly female potter and women making mats and baskets. You can also have henna tattoos painted on your skin.

Sinda and Latham Islands

The **dhow trips** with local fishermen, also arranged by the tourism programme, are excellent value at Tsh5000 per person (minimum two people), and are the only way of visiting the uninhabited **Sinda Island**, 14km offshore, which has some superb snorkelling reefs. You'll have to bring your own snorkelling gear, but there's no time limit so you can stay as long as you like. You might also be able to arrange a lift to **Latham Island**, further south, some 26km offshore from Ras Kutani, which has a massive reef and a completely unspoilt beach. There's no vegetation or people, but the island offers brilliant diving if you have your own equipment.

Practicalities

Access to Gezaulole is quickest if you take the ferry from Dar to Kigamboni, and then catch a daladala to Gezaulole (ones running to Kimbiji also pass by); daladalas run roughly hourly between 7am and 6pm. The all-weather road from Kigamboni to Gezaulole is attractive, passing through a chain of small villages set amidst thick coconut, banana and mango plantations. On arrival, head for the cultural tourism programme's base at *Akida's Garden*, signposted 1km east of the village, where you'll find the project co-ordinator, the energetic and helpful Akida Mohammed Nzambah (☎022/211 2518, ✆wcst@africaonline.co.tz). He can also arrange **bicycle** rental (Tsh1000 a day) – a great way to get around.

If you want **to stay** in the village, *Kali Mata Ki Jai's House* has two basic but adequate rooms (❶), one with four beds and the other with two, each with wonky raffia furniture, mosquito nets and cleanish sheets. Lodgings with other local families can be arranged through Akida. There are two **campsites**, one at *Akida's Garden* (Tsh1000 per person plus Tsh2000 for a night watchman; tents are available for Tsh1000), the other at the *Kia Beach Campsite*, on the beach about 1km down the path from *Akida's*. The beach is beautiful and clean, with plenty of white sand, but the campsite itself was closed at the time of writing. For **eating**, a good restaurant is the *Upendo*, in the village, whose *kisamvu* – cassava pounded in leaves, cooked in coconut milk and served with *ugali* – is absolutely delicious.

Ras Kutani

The *murram* road which heads southeast from Gezaulole is usually in very bad condition, and frequently gets washed away altogether in the rains, rendering road access impossible over the slippery black cotton soil. This shouldn't be a problem for most visitors, since the only place of note is the promontory of **RAS KUTANI**, 30km south of Dar, which has two (soon to be three) extremely expensive and exclusive **tourist lodges** complete with their own airstrips. The area badly needs some sanely priced accommodation, especially as the location is one of the coast's most beautiful, with kilometres of fine sandy beaches and crystalline waters protected by two coral reefs close to the shore, the nearest barely 600m away. Dynamite fishing has decreased in recent years, but the effect of previous assaults is visible at Ras Kutani headland itself, where much of the cliff has collapsed into the sea as a result of stronger ocean currents unleashed against the coast by the destruction of protective coral. Without your own vehicle, transport is by air. The fifteen-minute flight from Dar is operated by Easy Travel & Tours (see p.124) and costs $180 one-way for a three-seater aircraft, or $240 for a five-seater. The lodges can book the flight for around $75 per person.

Accommodation

Ras Kutani has two very pricey **lodges**, with a third one in the offing, though their barbed wire and electric fences provide an unsettling atmosphere of neocolonial exclusion, despite the beauty of the setting.

Protea Hotel Amani Beach ☎0741/410033, ⓦwww.protea-hotels.co.za. An "exotic and tranquil hideaway in a country of proud, peaceable and welcoming people" gushes the brochure, somewhat ironically given the total exclusion of locals from the lodge and its profits. That said, this Swahili-Arab themed place, set in extensive woodland grounds, offers stylish accommodation in two-room cottages on a baobab-studded lawn, complete with a/c, satellite TV and big Zanzibari four-poster beds. Facilities include a tennis court, horse-riding (Tsh40,000/hr), a large freshwater swimming pool by the beach and surfboards, but no boat trips. Full board ⑨

Ras Kutani (reserve through the Selous Safari Company; see p.125) ☎022/211 3220, ⓦwww.selous.com. Situated on an inlet close to a freshwater lagoon and coastal forest, this is more expensive than the *Amani* and is shrouded in even more Colditz-like security, but has the edge with its rustic feel and wilder gardens, plus a good range of water sports, horse-riding (Tsh50,000/hr) and walks with an armed *askari*. The fifteen bedrooms are huge and attractive, with bamboo walls, reed mats, open *makuti* roofs and spacious beds and hammocks. No children under 4. Full board ⑨

The Pugu Hills

Ten million years ago the entire coast of East Africa – from Mozambique in the south to Somalia in the north – was covered with a thick belt of forest. The constant climate over this period, influenced by the Indian Ocean monsoon system, led to the development of a diverse ecosystem rich in endemic plants and animals. Sadly, over the last few centuries most of the coastal forests have disappeared, leaving only a few isolated patches which are now under intense pressure from a vastly increased human population. The most studied – and indeed the most disturbed – of Tanzania's coastal forests covers the **Pugu Hills**, roughly 25km southwest of Dar es Salaam. Fifty years ago it extended to within

10km of the city and was home to lions, cheetahs, hippos and black-and-white colobus monkeys, all of which have since disappeared. Despite official protection in the form of the forest reserves of Pugu and Kazimzumbwi, the forest's destruction continues unabated: by 1995, clearance for farmland and tree-felling for building materials, domestic fuel and charcoal had left just four square kilometres of natural forest in "reasonable condition". Accidental wild-fires, started in neighbouring farms to clear stubble, haven't helped matters either. Despite all of this, however, Pugu still contains an astonishing biodiversity, including over 120 tree species and 120 types of birds. The most commonly seen animals include giant elephant shrews, monkeys, bush pigs, suni antelopes and mongooses. Leopards, hyenas and pangolins also inhabit the area, but are rarely seen.

Practicalities

There are two approaches to the Pugu Hills. The first and most obvious is via **Kisarawe Village**, which is where the main gate to the **forest reserve** (entrance Tsh2500) is situated. There's also an office for the WCST (Wildlife Conservation Society of Tanzania), who you should contact in advance in Dar es Salaam (p.115) for up-to-date information, though their map and brochures were out of print at the time of writing. There's also a short nature trail at Kisarawe. **Daladalas** to Kisarawe run from Kariakoo or Buguruni. **Daladalas** to Msata also go through Kisarawe; the last one returns to Dar around 6pm. Should you get stuck, there are rooms at *Kiki's Hotel* near the forest gate in Kisarawe. If you're **driving**, head down Nyerere Road (formerly Pugu Road), turn right at the airport and continue for 14km.

The alternative approach is to head to the **Pugu Hills Resort** on the south-eastern flank of the hills (weekends and holidays only), whose Tsh1000 entrance fee lets you use their swimming pool. There's also a restaurant (meals cost Tsh5000; you're not allowed to bring your own food), and several camp-sites (Tsh3000 per person). The resort is the best base for short **hikes** around the reserves, and staff can provide detailed directions to a number of attractions, including a reservoir, a sacred cave, and a viewpoint over Dar es Salaam. To get to the resort, turn left at the Oryx petrol station before reaching Kisarawe, then take the next right and turn right again along a narrow dirt road. Daladalas can drop you at the turn-off onto the dirt road, from where it's a twenty-minute walk.

The north coast

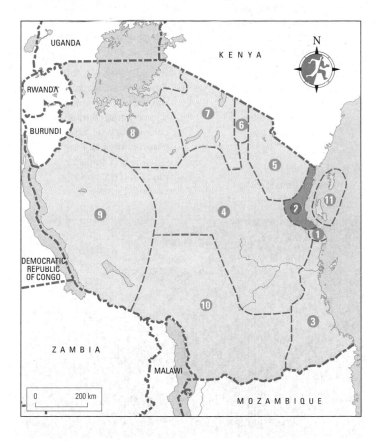

CHAPTER 2

Highlights

✳ **Bagamoyo** The infamous transit point for the nineteenth-century slave and ivory trades, but now at the heart of Tanzania's contemporary arts scene. See p.140

✳ **Freedom Village** Bagamoyo's Catholic Mission was founded in 1868 and the story of slavery and Christianity in Tanzania is adroitly told in the museum. See p.145

✳ **Bagamoyo College of Arts** Weekly arts performances, an annual arts festival and hands-on tutorials for visitors. See p.148

✳ **Kaole** The ruins of a medieval trading town, dating from the height of the Shirazi trading civilization, and now partly reclaimed by mangroves and the ocean. See p.150

✳ **Saadani Game Reserve** Where bush meets beach; a unique shoreline wilderness combining marine, savanna, forest and riverine environments, together with the historic village of Saadani. See p.152

✳ **Amboni caves** A great day-trip from Tanga: winding passageways, dripping stalactites, colonies of bats, an assortment of unlikely legends and a nearby forest and hot-water springs. See p.166

The north coast

North of Dar es Salaam the beach resorts give way to a string of little-visited fishing villages interspersed by mangrove forests and sweeping sandy beaches, backed by a narrow fertile plain crossed by seasonal streams and the Ruvu, Wami and Pangani rivers. The main towns, all of historical significance, are Bagamoyo, Tanga and Pangani. **Bagamoyo** is easily visited on a day-trip from Dar, although it's worth a stay of several days. Wallowing in its infamous past as the coast's foremost slaving port, Bagamoyo is also the place where a host of explorers and missionaries set off into the African interior. Historic buildings from the slaving and colonial periods abound, including East Africa's first Catholic mission and a fort which served as the departure point for slaves being shipped out to Zanzibar. A few kilometres away the ruins of the medieval Swahili trading centre of **Kaole** give a taste of what life was like almost eight centuries ago.

North of Bagamoyo, a strip of coastline is protected as the **Saadani Game Reserve**, the only such coastal sanctuary in East Africa, which provides ample opportunities for spotting elephant, lion, leopard, zebra, antelopes giraffe and buffalo, as well as a plethora of birds and marine and riverine wildlife. Further north, at the mouth of the Pangani River, the delightful and laid-back fishing village and coconut-processing centre of **Pangani** blends the attractions of nearly deserted beaches with atmospherically decrepit Swahili and colonial architecture. It's one of the nicest places on the coast to chill out for a few days of *dolce far niente*, and there's also an excellent cultural tourism programme here offering river cruises, dhow and snorkelling trips and historical tours.

Despite having Tanzania's second-busiest harbour, **Tanga**, 50km north of Pangani on the main road into Kenya, has preserved a distinctly small-town feel. The beaches aren't brilliant and the town has clearly seen better days, but Tanga's proximity to the Amani Nature Reserve and Usambara Mountains (both covered in Chapter 5), as well as to Pangani, makes it an ideal base, while closer to hand there are the limestone caves at **Amboni** and the extensive Swahili ruins at **Tongoni** and **Toten Island** to explore.

The north coast is one of Tanzania's easier regions to travel around. **Transport** to the main towns is plentiful, and the main road up the coast from Dar es Salaam to Tanga is good tarmac. The drawback is that for the most part the road passes around 100km inland. A more direct coastal road from Dar to Tanga via Bagamoyo, Saadani and Pangani has been on the drawing board for years, but at present the only all-weather stretch is from Dar to Bagamoyo – the continuation to Saadani will remain impassable until the rope-pulled Wami River ferry, which was washed away in the 1998 El Niño floods, is replaced.

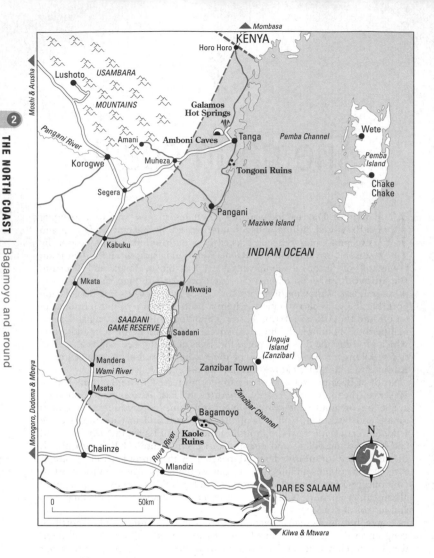

The road from Tanga into Kenya is also in an abysmal state, disintegrating every rainy season into a barely passable swill of mud.

Bagamoyo and around

Set on a beautiful, mangrove-fringed bay 72km north of Dar es Salaam, the attractive town of **BAGAMOYO** makes a popular day-trip from Dar, but has enough of interest to reward a longer stay. Though now little more than a large village, relying on fishing, coconuts and, to an increasing extent, tourism for its survival, Bagamoyo's peaceful atmosphere conceals a very different past, when

Bagamoyo: lay down my heart

The name **"Bagamoyo"** derives from the words *bwaga* (to put or throw down) and *moyo* (heart). As the exact meaning of Kiswahili depends on the context in which it is spoken, two theories have developed about the name. The first contends that the words were uttered by slaves on reaching the coast, where the impending sea voyage to Zanzibar signalled the end of any lingering hopes of escape. For them, Bagamoyo meant "crush your heart". An alternative and more likely explanation is that the words were spoken by caravan porters arriving on the coast after their arduous journey from the interior. In this context, *bwaga moyo* would have meant a place to "lay down the burden of your heart" – an expression of relief. This second theory is supported by the existence of other places called Bagamoyo, one near Tanga, the other on the northern boundary of Rungwa Game Reserve in central Tanzania, both of which lay on caravan routes, and by a song that was sung by porters on the 1200km Ujiji–Bagamoyo route.

Be happy, my soul, let go all worries
soon the place of your yearnings is reached
the town of palms, Bagamoyo.
Far away, how was my heart aching
when I was thinking of you, my pearl
you place of happiness, Bagamoyo.

it was one of the richest and most important cities in East Africa. Its wealth stemmed from its role as a major conduit for the ivory and slave trade, being the place from which thousands of slaves were transported annually to the market in Zanzibar, whose lights can been seen twinkling over the water on clear nights. Bagamoyo is also Tanzania's **arts capital** and home to one of East Africa's leading arts colleges, as well as a number of artists' co-operatives.

For those with more time, there's bird-watching and hippo-spotting in the **Ruvu River delta** plus the ruins of **Kaole**, a few kilometres to the south, which provide a vivid insight into medieval times, when the Shirazi trading civilization was at its height. And of course Bagamoyo has all the ingredients of a good **beach holiday**, with sandy shores, snorkelling trips and an increasingly broad choice of accommodation. Unfortunately, beach security is a real concern: if the need to be watched over by hotel *askaris* turns you off, look elsewhere.

Some history

Bagamoyo's proximity to Zanzibar, 42km away across the Zanzibar Channel, is the key to the town's historical importance. During the eighteenth and nineteenth centuries, much of the Tanzanian coastline was ruled by the Omani Sultanate from Zanzibar, whose trading links with Arabia, Asia and Europe created one of the wealthiest dynasties ever seen in Africa. For much of this time, their riches came from the export of goods from the mainland, especially **slaves and ivory**, which were exchanged for cotton, beads and other manufactured goods. An estimated 769,000 slaves were transported from the East African coast during the nineteenth century. Many of them passed through Bagamoyo, which served as the major caravan terminus for routes coming from Lake Tanganyika and Lake Victoria, both over 1000km away.

Given its trading links, Bagamoyo was the logical starting and ending point for many European explorations of the continent. Stanley, Burton, Speke and Grant all passed through, as did a number of Christian missionaries and, most famously, the body of David Livingstone. In the 1880s, following the ground-work laid by the explorers and missionaries, the European **colonization** of East Africa began in earnest, and for the Germans – who had been accorded the territories now comprising Tanganyika, Burundi and Rwanda – Bagamoyo was an obvious choice for the capital of German East Africa. It was a status it enjoyed for less than a decade, however, as the **Abushiri War** of 1888–89, aimed against both Arab and German rule, prompted the Germans to move their capital to Dar es Salaam in 1891. Bagamoyo continued as provincial capital, but with the slave and ivory trades at an end and its shallow harbour eclipsed by new facilities at Dar es Salaam, Tanga and Mombasa, the town entered a long period of economic decline, and has nowadays effectively reverted to being the fishing village it once was.

Arrival and information

Bagamoyo is easily reached by road from Dar es Salaam. Other routes are difficult and unreliable, and the dhow trade has virtually ceased. Frequent **buses** and **daladalas** leave Dar's Kariakoo and Mwenge terminals for Bagamoyo throughout the day. The journey takes about ninety minutes – more during the rains – but the road surfacing that's currently under way should reduce the trip to under an hour. The alternative route **from Msata** (see p.155) in the west on the A14 highway is more difficult, and becomes impassable during the rains. If you're loaded down with luggage, take a **taxi** once you've arrived both for security reasons and because the nearest beach hotel is a good fifteen minutes' walk away. You'll find plenty of taxis at the daladala stand.

The nearest thing to a **tourist office** is the Roman Catholic Mission Museum (see p.145), which should have a fold-out map and town guide available, and sells a small range of booklets relating to the history of Bagamoyo, slavery and Catholicism – *Bagamoyo: a pictorial essay* by Jesper Kirknaes and John Wembah-Rashid (which you can also buy at the *Badeco Beach Resort*) is recommended. For further information, speak with the charming Father John Henschel at the mission.

Accommodation

The main tourist **hotels** are spread out along the beach north of town, but there's little here that could be described as cheap, so budget travellers without tents are limited to the **guest houses** in the town centre. **Camping** (Tsh3000 per person including breakfast) is possible in the grounds of the *Badeco Beach Resort*, which has a grassy area with limited shade.

Town centre

Moyo Mmoja Guest House A few hundred metres east from the post office ☎023/244 0236, ✉ moyommoja@hotmail.com. About ten minutes from the beach, this is the best of the budget hotels. There's a big garden and a kitchen for guests, but only three rooms (one with a private bathroom), so book ahead. Profits fund the adjacent children's home. ❷

Pop Juice Guest House Msata Rd ☎023/244 0318. A perfectly decent cheapie, with basic rooms sharing squat loos and showers. ❶
Vatican Guest House Dunda Rd (no phone). Similar to *Pop Juice*, with the advantage of having some rooms with private bathroom. ❶

Beach

The following hotels all include breakfast in their rates.

Badeco Beach Resort ☎023/244 0018, ☏023/244 0154. A long-standing favourite in need

of an overhaul, with twelve rather dark rooms, the cheapest with shared bathrooms and no fans, more

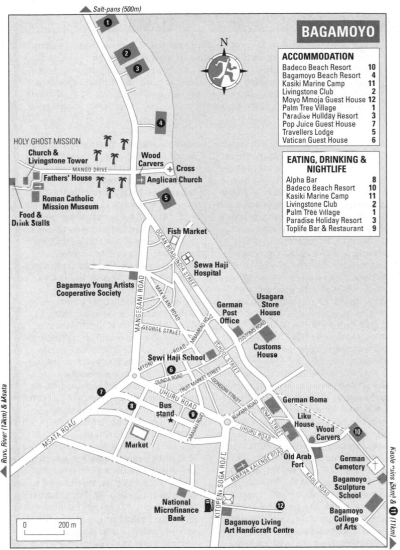

BAGAMOYO

Salt-pans (500m)

N

ACCOMMODATION

Badeco Beach Resort	10
Bagamoyo Beach Resort	4
Kasiki Marine Camp	11
Livingstone Club	2
Moyo Mmoja Guest House	12
Palm Tree Village	1
Paradise Holiday Resort	3
Pop Juice Guest House	7
Travellers Lodge	5
Vatican Guest House	6

EATING, DRINKING & NIGHTLIFE

Alpha Bar	8
Badeco Beach Resort	10
Kasiki Marine Camp	11
Livingstone Club	2
Palm Tree Village	1
Paradise Holiday Resort	3
Toplife Bar & Restaurant	9

HOLY GHOST MISSION
Church & Livingstone Tower
Wood Carvers
Cross
MANGO DRIVE
Fathers' House
Anglican Church
Roman Catholic Mission Museum
Food & Drink Stalls

Fish Market

Sewa Haji Hospital

Bagamoyo Young Artists Cooperative Society

OCEAN ROAD/INDIA STREET
MANGESANI ROAD
MAKVLANI ROAD
MBAMAYO ROAD
GEORGE STREET
MTONI ROAD
SCHOOL STREET

German Post Office

Usagara Store House

CUSTOMS ROAD

Customs House

Sewi Haji School
DUNDA ROAD
UHURU ROAD
FRUIT MARKET STREET
GONGONI STREET
BLUMANI ROAD
BOMA STREET

German Boma

Liku House
Wood Carvers

Ruvu River (12km) & Msata

MSATA ROAD
Bus stand
Market
CARAVAN ROAD
UHURU ROAD

KITOPENI SOGA ROAD
MWANA KALENSE ROAD
KAOLE ROAD

Old Arab Fort

German Cemetery

Bagamoyo Sculpture School

Kaole ruins (5km) & (11km)

National Microfinance Bank
Bagamoyo Living Art Handicraft Centre

Bagamoyo College of Arts

0   200 m

Dar es Salaam (65km)

---

expensive ones with toilet, shower and a/c. Only two rooms have sea views, there's no swimming pool and water sports are limited to dhow hire at a negotiable price, though safaris can be arranged The grounds contain the place where the Germans hanged opponents of colonial rule. ❸–❹
Bagamoyo Beach Resort ☎023/244 0341 or 0744/565196, ✉bbr@ud.co.tz. French-managed place with a welcoming atmosphere and efficient staff, making it a popular choice with families.

There's a wide choice of rooms, so ask to see a selection. The eighteen standard rooms are set well back from the beach and getting tatty, but have large box nets, comfy beds and big patios; more expensive rooms have a/c and are better kept. There are also some cheap *bandas* on the beach which lack bathrooms or fans but have fantastic views. Amenities include a swimming pool, boat trips, sailing, windsurfing and motor-boat rental. ❷–❹

143

Beach safety

Bagamoyo's beaches may be most people's idea of a tropical paradise, but unfortunately **security** is a major concern, so, heed the warnings given by your hotel about not walking unaccompanied on the beach, as reports of *panga*-point robberies of tourists are wearyingly familiar. The hotels should be able to provide an *askari* to keep an eye on you, though he'll appreciate a tip. As ever, don't take any valuables (which includes flashy sunglasses and running shoes) and if you *are* held up, don't resist.

Kasiki Marine Camp 11km south of Bagamoyo at Mbegani ⓣ 0744/278590, ⓔ kasiki@africaonline.co.tz. Set in a former coconut and pineapple plantation, this laid-back place is run by a couple of Italian ladies and has a reputation for outstanding food (see p.147). The location, on a small bluff overlooking Lazy Lagoon, is pleasing, but mangroves restrict swimming to one or two clearings on a silty beach. The accommodation itself is unexceptional, with six smallish rooms, some much better than others, though all have private bathrooms with hot water, fans and electricity. Activities are limited to dhow trips around the lagoon. Transport from Bagamoyo is free if you stay a few days, otherwise $9. Closed mid-April to June. ⑤, full board ⑦

Lazy Lagoon Island Lodge 20km south of Bagamoyo by road; access also possible by plane ⓦ www.lazylagoon.info (reserve through Foxtreks in Dar; see p.125). This upmarket place consists of twelve wooden thatched *bandas* on the beach of on a nine-square-kilometre private island. Each *banda* comes with en-suite bathroom, solar-powered water and light, and a large verandah. There's also a restaurant and a bar with panoramic views, a swimming pool and sea bathing. The price includes boat transfer, kayaking, windsurfing, sailing and snorkelling, but excludes dhow trips and excursions. Full board ⑧

Livingstone Club ⓣ 023/244 0059, ⓦ www.livingstone-club.com. An impressive two-level entrance sets the tone for Bagamoyo's classiest hotel, combining modern comforts with attractive Swahili style. Accommodation is in colourful two-room bungalows, all with a/c, minibar, fan, box net, a safe and verandah, though some of them stink of air freshener. The beach, unfortunately, is narrow and

bounded by mangroves. Water sports include canoeing, windsurfing, boat excursions, snorkelling and a PADI diving school, and there's also a tennis court, two swimming pools, a Jacuzzi, and mountain bikes for guests' use. Overall an excellent choice. ⑥

Palm Tree Village ⓣ 023/244 0245 or 244 0246, ⓕ 023/244 0247. Not the most exciting choice (and the palm trees have yet to grow tall enough to give much shade), though the big, bright and airy en-suite rooms are attractive enough, and some come with huge, four-poster Zanzibari beds. There are also five self-catering family cottages for the same price. The downside is no water sports (there's only a swimming pool), no alcohol during Ramadan, and a rather lifeless atmosphere. ⑤

Paradise Holiday Resort ⓣ 023/244 0136 or 244 0137, ⓦ www.paradiseresort.net. Shoehorned into a rather narrow plot, this Somali-run place is nothing special at the price, though the welcome is friendly. The rooms, in thatched chalets, are small, far from the sea and look towards the car park or gardens, though they do have satellite TV and a/c. The pool also lacks views, and there are no water sports other than snorkelling. ⑥

Travellers Lodge ⓣ 023/244 0077, ⓕ 023/244 0154. Run by an engagingly eccentric German and South African couple, this is the best mid-range place in Bagamoyo, with large and attractive balconied rooms, most with a/c, and three cheaper rooms sharing bathrooms. The main attraction is the large beach and the fantastic carved wooden decor of the restaurant and coffee lounge, much of which was evidently inspired by copious tokes of marijuana. There's a bar in the garden. The main drawback is the lack of water sports, but these are apparently in the offing. Busy at weekends, so book ahead. ④

The Town

Bagamoyo's rich history is embodied in a wealth of buildings dating from the slaving era and subsequent German colonization – many of them ruined, all of them photogenic, especially with the slender coconut trees and glimpses of the ocean that frame most views. It's perfectly safe to walk around the town centre, but be wary of areas with a lot of tree or mangrove cover, especially along the shoreline, as muggings do occur. Read the box on "Beach Safety" opposite and leave valuables in your hotel.

Holy Ghost Mission and Museum

At the north end of town in what used to be a slave-worked coconut plantation, the Catholic **Holy Ghost Mission** occupies a collection of whitewashed buildings whose plain appearance belies their historical importance. Also called Freedom Village, the mission was founded in 1868 by the French Holy Ghost Fathers, whose priests were instructed to spend as much as they could afford on buying slaves their freedom. The first transport of ransomed slaves, fifty boys, arrived on December 10, 1868 from Zanzibar. Eleven months later, 46 girls arrived, and by 1872 the village housed over 300 children and young adults. Of course, the former slaves were expected to embrace the new religion, but the priests were open-minded enough to tolerate those who continued to follow their traditional beliefs. Although the immediate impact of the mission was limited to the freedom of a few hundred souls, the moral boost given to the anti-slavery movement by this pioneering mission could be said to have heralded the beginning of the end of the East African slave trade. In 1873, Sultan Barghash, under pressure from the British, reluctantly abolished the slave trade between Zanzibar and the mainland, although the trade continued illicitly for several decades more.

The **church** itself, built in the midst of the 1872 cholera epidemic, is now the oldest Catholic building in East Africa and attracts a variety of pilgrims from all over the region. It is dominated by a squat tower – the so-called **Livingstone Tower** – topped with a combination of arches and pinnacles resembling a mitre and named after the explorer-cum-missionary David Livingstone, whose preserved body was laid out here for a night on February 24, 1874, having been carried by foot on an epic eleven-month journey from Chitambo, in present-day Zambia, by his servants Susi and Chuma. The following morning it was carried to the shore to be taken to Zanzibar and hence on to England, where Livingstone was buried as a national hero in London's Westminster Abbey.

The colonnaded, three-storey **Fathers' House** facing the church was completed in 1873, and in 1876 a small chapel (also called the Grotto) was erected in the centre of Freedom Village and dedicated to Our Lady of Lourdes, who had made her miraculous appearance in France in 1858. Over the following years, especially during a second cholera outbreak during the Abushiri War (see p.154), Freedom Village's population increased as people sought refuge, and it is from these refugees that many of Bagamoyo's present-day inhabitants are descended.

The story of the mission and its fight against the slave trade is told in the **Roman Catholic Mission Museum** (daily 10am–5pm; free, but donations welcome), housed in the newly renovated Sisters' House of 1876. There's a small collection of woodcarvings, books and booklets for sale, and plenty of material documenting not only the arrival and progress of Christianity, but also much of Bagamoyo's pre-history, with extensive explanations in English. Other items on display include Indian and Arab door frames and a sewing machine, along with shackles, chains and whips which were used to restrain slaves, though even these are not as disturbing as the photographs of slaves tied together with chains around their necks.

The big baobab tree outside the mission office was planted in 1868. Look carefully at its base and you'll see a short piece of metal **chain** protruding. This has nothing to do with slavery. Instead, the story goes that sometime after 1895 a certain Madame Chevalier, who had been running a dispensary in Zanzibar, came to the Bagamoyo mission as a volunteer. She fastened a chain around the tree in order to tie her donkey to it, and eventually forgot all about it. Since then, the tree's circumference has swelled by over seven metres, engulfing all but a foot or so of the chain.

The Anglican church

At the junction of the Holy Ghost Mission's driveway and Ocean Road are a cluster of pushy woodcarvers and a small **Anglican church**. A sign over the church door reads, "Through this door David Livingstone passed", a particularly fine example of linguistic sophistry, since although Livingstone did indeed pass through it, at that time the door was 1200km away on the shores of Lake Tanganyika. It was donated by an Anglican parish in 1974 following the construction of the present church, which is thought to occupy the site of the tree under which Livingstone's body was laid whilst awaiting the high tide to carry him to Zanzibar. Set in a small garden by the shore is a **stone cross**, not without its own touch of sophistry: though the inscription reads "First Cross of the RC Church in East Africa planted 17.6.1868", the cross itself is entirely modern.

South along Ocean Road to Liku House

Five minutes' walk south along Ocean Road from the Anglican church brings you to the fish market and the **Sewa Haji Hospital**, built in 1895 by the Indian trader and philanthropist Sewa Haji on the principle that it would admit people of any race or religion. Some 500m further south along Ocean Road is the old **German Post Office** and, just inland, the three-storey **Sewa Haji School**, another of the Indian philanthropist's gifts, built in 1896 and donated to the German government on condition that it remained multi-racial. Close by on the shore are two more colonial buildings from: the **Customs House** and the **Usagara Store House**, erected as a military depot during the Abushiri War.

Continuing south along Ocean Road brings you to the half-wrecked **German Boma**, one of Bagamoyo's most imposing buildings. Flanked by twin crenellated towers, this has a heavily defensive feel despite the arabesque arches of its balconies. It was built in 1897 to replace Liku House (see below) as the seat of the German regional administration. Part of the facade has collapsed and the roof was carried off years ago, though the building is now being restored.

Just south of the Boma, **Liku House** was built in 1885 and served as the headquarters of German East Africa until 1891, when the capital was transferred to Dar es Salaam. It continued functioning as the regional headquarters until 1897, when the offices were moved to the Boma. The building currently houses the immigration department (Ofisi ya Mkuu Wilaya). Liku House is known for its connection with **Emin Pasha**, a Silesian Jew, originally called Eduard Schnitzer, who adopted a Turkish name and Muslim way of life while serving as the Ottoman governor of northern Albania during 1870–74. In 1878 he was appointed *pasha* (governor) of Equatoria by the British governor-general of the Sudan, General Charles Gordon, though he later had to be reluctantly "rescued" (against his own wishes) from the "mad Mullah's hordes" by Henry Morton Stanley following the Mahdist uprising. Evidently in need of another journalistic scoop to cap his meeting with Livingstone, Stanley subsequently published *In Darkest Africa, or The Quest, Rescue and Retreat of Emin, Governor of Equatoria*. Together with their sizeable entourage (albeit reduced to 196 from an original

708), Stanley and Emin Pasha arrived in Bagamoyo in December 1889. To celebrate their safe passage, the Germans threw a lavish party at Liku House, at which Emin Pasha became so carried away that, in the words of Evelyn Waugh, he accidentally took "a header off the balcony". He recovered from his fractured skull, but was murdered two years later in the Congo.

Old Arab Fort

Just south of Liku House, at the turn-off for the *Badeco Beach Resort*, is the **Old Arab Fort**, a large whitewashed and unadorned building. Its serene location, set amidst beautiful old palm trees overlooking the Indian Ocean, is rendered grimly ironic thanks to its nineteenth-century history as a holding place for slaves awaiting transportation to Zanzibar. According to popular belief, the fort was the first stone building in Bagamoyo, although this isn't strictly true: the foundations are indeed some of the oldest in town, and belonged to a military garrison built by Omani Arabs, but the fort itself was totally remodelled and fortified during Sultan Barghash's reign at the end of the nineteenth century. It subsequently served as a German military camp, a customs office and police headquarters, and is now undergoing extensive restoration. When complete, it should once again be open to the public; in the meantime it may be possible to gain admission if you show the workers a ticket from the Kaole ruins, which in theory is also valid for the fort.

The highlight of the visit used to be when visitors were led out of the fort along the same route followed by blindfolded slaves after they had been released from their small, dark and overcrowded cells. The path follows a winding circuit around the open courtyard, then heads up a treacherously steep flight of stairs to the upper level of the fort, from where the slaves were led back down along another stairway and out of the fort to the waiting dhows. The disorienting procedure was intended to deter any last-minute attempts at escape. Legend has it that a tunnel connected the fort with the beach, but no evidence of this has been found.

The German Cemetery and the "Hanging Tree"

A short walk east of the fort are a couple of poignant memorials to the bloody Abushiri War of 1888–89 (see p.154), in which thousands of Africans died. The **German Cemetery**, down a path next to the *Badeco Beach Resort*, contains the graves of eight German soldiers who lost their lives during the uprising and over the following years when the colonial Schutztruppe was almost constantly engaged in quelling resistance. The African dead are commemorated by a small plinth just inside the gate to the hotel which reads: "Here is the place where the German colonialists used to hang to death revolutionary Africans who were opposing their oppressive rule." Popularly called the Hanging Tree, the site was actually a scaffolded gallows and is believed to have been where the leader of the rebellion, Abushiri ibn Salim al-Harthi, was executed in December 1889.

Eating

The beach hotel restaurants offer a good range of **food**, though at tourist prices. You'll find cheaper and more basic fare in town.

Badeco Beach Resort Specializes in fish, and is good value at under Tsh4000 for whatever the day's catch is. Grilled fish or meat cost around Tsh5000, and shellfish goes for Tsh7000–10,000.
Kasiki Marine Camp 11km south of Bagamoyo ☎0744/278590. Delicious Italian cooking (most mains are around Tsh6000) with enticing touches like home-made pesto, brilliant ice cream and excellent coffee. You can arrange to be picked up from Bagamoyo for $9. Open noon–3pm for non-guests; closed mid-April to June.

Arts and crafts in Bagamoyo

Bagamoyo is Tanzania's leading centre for the **modern arts**, having the Bagamoyo College of Arts plus a number of artists' collectives to its name, as well as an annual **Bagamoyo Art Festival**. This takes places over five days in late September and early October (contact the arts college for exact dates), showcasing theatre, music, dance and the plastic arts, and featuring both college students and artists and performers from abroad, notably Scandinavians (the college was partly funded with Norwegian money).

Bagamoyo College of Arts

Founded in 1981, the esteemed **Bagamoyo College of Arts** (Chuo Cha Sanaa) teaches drama, acrobatics, plastic arts and both African and European music and dance. The school is on Kaole Road about 900m south of the Boma (Mon–Sat 8am–3pm; PO Box 32; ☎023/244 0032). Walking here is considered risky if you're carrying any kind of valuables, so catch a taxi, or contact the college to arrange for a student to escort you.

Free performances are held on the last Friday, Saturday or Sunday of each month except during Ramadan (ring beforehand for exact dates). At other times (weekdays only) you're welcome to watch the fine art, sculpture and women's handicraft classes, where you can also buy items. For a more hands-on experience, $5 an hour gets you a personal tutor in whatever takes your fancy, from wood sculpture and dance to lessons in how to play the lyre (*iritungu*), Zaramo xylophone (*marimba*), drums and bamboo flute (*felembi amwanzi*). Long-term foreign students are also welcome; the fees aren't fixed, but shouldn't be prohibitively expensive.

Bagamoyo Sculpture School

Just north of the Bagamoyo College of Arts, the Swedish-supported **Bagamoyo Sculpture School** (PO Box 89; ⓦwww.svetan.org/skulp/schol/school.html) offers free tuition and accommodation to Tanzanian students. The school is also open to paying foreign students; courses range from a few lessons to a whole nine months, and short group courses can be arranged during the school break (Aug–Oct). Examples of the students' work, including life-size heads in wood, clay or cement, plus knives, combs and candleholders, are on sale in the school shop.

Livingstone Club Italian-owned and it shows, with what some consider the best cappuccino in Tanzania along with great pasta (Tsh3000–4000; Tsh5000 with lobster), plus slightly more expensive meat dishes, as well as a three-course set menu for around Tsh11,000.

Palm Tree Village Very good full English breakfast, and they rustle up some pretty decent main courses, too. Meat dishes cost around Tsh4000 (try the pepper steak), and grilled prawns or half a lobster go for around Tsh7000.

Paradise Holiday Resort Another good hotel restaurant, with cheaper à la carte dishes than

other places and plenty of choice, especially if you're after seafood or the ubiquitous Italian fare. Most mains cost around Tsh3500–4500, and they lay on a buffet lunch whenever there's a conference.

Roman Catholic Mission The small area with thatched *bandas* at the rear of the mission buildings is good for cheap lunches and soft drinks.

Toplife Bar & Restaurant Corner Uhuru and Caravan roads. Good cheap local food – dishes like *ugali*, rice with grilled meat skewers (*mishkaki*) or stewed goat, fish or chicken won't cost more than Tsh1500–2000.

Drinking and nightlife

Despite the town's diminutive size, there's a reasonable selection of **bars** both in the centre and at the beach hotels. The most popular local joint is the friendly and relaxed *Toplife Bar & Restaurant*. *Alpha Bar* sometimes has discos, as does the *Livingstone Club* (weekends except during Ramadan). The *Badeco Beach Resort* also used to hold discos, though these had been stopped at the time of

Bagamoyo Young Artists Cooperative Society

The **Bagamoyo Young Artists Cooperative Society** (BYACSO), on Mangesani Road (PO Box 67; ☎ 023/244 0277), is an inspired collective comprising mainly former students of the sculpture school. Starting off by producing life-size heads in both wood and cement (the entrance is marked by two cement sculptures of Nyerere), some of the collective's members have gained the confidence to progress to much more abstract – not to mention surreal – work, with deeply expressive, fluid and often grotesque results. Of the artists, Dula Bute is outstanding. Also worth checking out are Abdallah Ulimwengu, Mohamed Maulidi, Rama Marunda, Zakaria Mweru and Mwandale Mwanyekwa.

You're welcome to drop by, but they prefer visitors in the evening when they're not so busy. The price of their work depends as much on the finish as the size and the theme of the object. Expect to pay between Tsh150,000 and Tsh200,000 for a well-finished life-size wooden head, or Tsh50,000–80,000 for a cement cast. There are plenty of cheaper alternatives, too, starting with key rings at Tsh1000. Avoid objects made from the endangered African blackwood tree (ebony) – the co-operative is aware of the problem and has pioneered sculpture in several other kinds of wood, including coconut, which has a coarse but unusually hard grain.

Bagamoyo Living Art Handicraft Centre

Facing the post office, the **Bagamoyo Living Art Handicraft Centre** (BLACC; daily 9am–4.30pm; PO Box 163; ☎ 023/244 0141) is a locally run NGO established in 1996 by the Association of Women Artists in Tanzania (AWATA) with the aim of training disadvantaged women in handicraft and business skills. Their showroom sells a variety of items including pottery and ceramics, textiles, embroidery, basketry and clothes. You're welcome to visit the women at work, and there's a shop where you can buy their crafts. The centre has little outside support and is a laudable venture, currently training around sixty women a year.

writing; the hotel's bar remains open and is liveliest between Thursday and Sunday. If you're into **live music**, ask around for Mlutso Frontline (or Mrema Lugodi Traditional Sounds), who occasionally perform traditional dances (*ngomas*) in the town's bars – a fascinating fusion of modern and traditional styles fronted by veteran Hamis W. Digallu on the Zaramo xylophone accompanied by rappers and other musicians from the arts college.

Listings

Banks The National Microfinance Bank, on the road opposite the post office, changes travellers' cheques and isn't too fussy about seeing proof of purchase. The commission is around Tsh2000 per $100. Some of the beach hotels might change money if you're desperate.

Hospital The district hospital is on India St (☎ 023/244 0008). For a doctor, ask at the Huruma Dispensary, near the *MM Guest House* in the centre of town.

Language classes Kiswahili lessons with a personal tutor are given at the arts college for $5 an hour.

Pharmacy The Roman Catholic Mission has a well-stocked pharmacy, or try Huruma Dispensary near the *MM Guest House* in the centre of town.

Police The police station (☎ 023/244 0026) is at the corner of Caravan St and Boma St.

Post The post office (Mon–Fri 8am–5pm) is on Kitopeni Soga Road.

Swimming pools The cheapest pool is at the Livingstone Club, which charges Tsh2000 if you're not taking a meal. Other hotels may or may not be happy with day guests using their pools – it largely depends on who's at reception and how much you're willing to pay.

149

Moving on from Bagamoyo

Leaving Bagamoyo, if you're heading north in the dry season, it's quickest to go straight to **Msata** rather than backtrack to Dar. In reasonable weather, this route is covered by occasional daladalas, a journey of around two hours – they're best caught in the morning, but check at the daladala stand near the water tower the evening before you plan to leave.

By dhow to Zanzibar

Given Bagamoyo's proximity to **Zanzibar**, it's a wonder that there isn't any regular transport to the island. If you want to try to get a passage on a dhow, the manager of the *Bagamoyo Beach Resort* can help you out. Alternatively, talk to local boat owners and captains headed to Kizimkazi at the southern tip of Zanzibar. If you strike a deal, you'll need first to visit the district commissioner to clear formalities, then the customs officer in Liku House to get an exit stamp. The trip usually takes six to eight hours by motorized dhow: bring everything you'll need.

Kaole

The ruins of the once prosperous Shirazi town of **KAOLE**, 5km south of Bagamoyo, provide a fascinating and atmospheric complement to the historical sights of Bagamoyo. Founded in the thirteenth century, the ruins include what is thought to be the oldest mosque on the East African mainland, as well a collection of unusual pillar tombs. The town went into decline following the arrival of the Portuguese, and by the time the Omanis gained control of Bagamoyo in the eighteenth century, Kaole had been abandoned. Kaole's original name was Pumbuji, but was renamed "Kalole" by the Zaramo after the town's desertion, meaning "go and see" what had been left behind. The attribution is similar to that of Gezaulole, south of Dar es Salaam (p.133), which means "try and see". No one knows for sure the reasons why the town was deserted, but the fact that much of it has now been reclaimed by sea and mangroves suggests environmental change as a possible cause.

There's **no public transport** to the site, and given the risk of being mugged if you walk, you'll need either to take a taxi (up to Tsh5000 for a return trip) or rent a bicycle. Either way, head for the modern village of Kaole, 4km south of Bagamoyo, which is notable for a couple of glaringly phallic **pillar tombs** on the right-hand side of the road as you come in, all quite different from the pillar tombs found in the main archeological site.

The archeological site

The **archeological site** itself (daily 8am–5.30pm; Tsh1500) is 1km beyond Kaole village. The entrance fee includes admission to a small but interesting **museum** (and is also valid for entry to the Arab Fort in Bagamoyo) – this contains pottery shards, oil lamps and other artefacts, some of them Chinese. There are two helpful guides who appreciate a small tip for their services. The museum office sells beautiful ocean shells, but bear in mind that the trade in these is illegal both in Tanzania and internationally.

Once you've seen the museum, the first stop is the thirteenth-century **mosque**, which was excavated from its sandy tomb in 1958 by the archeologist Neville Chittick. Although the ceiling of the building collapsed long ago, probably before the second mosque to the east of the site was erected in the fifteenth century, the fact that most of the walls are still standing attests to the strength of the coral, lime and sand mortar which was typical of the time – the *mihrab* (the alcove indicating the direction of Mecca) is especially well pre-

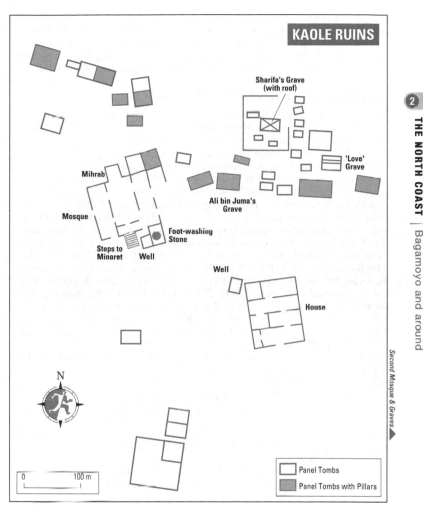

KAOLE RUINS

Sharifa's Grave
(with roof)

'Love'
Grave

Mihrab

Ali bin Juma's
Grave

Mosque

Foot-washing
Stone

Steps to
Minaret   Well

Well

House

N

Second Mosque & Graves ▶

0   100 m

Panel Tombs

Panel Tombs with Pillars

served. Outside, the steps up the wall were used by the muezzin for calling the faithful to prayer. Next to these is a well for ablutions which still contains water, its freshness proved by the frogs which have taken up residence in it. Beside the well is a much burnished stone which was used for washing feet.

Beside the mosque, and spread out throughout the site, are twenty-two **tombs**, some with tall pillars rising from their headstones, a feature found in many other sites in East Africa. These "pillar tombs" date from the fourteenth to nineteenth centuries, and the most intact one bears traces of an Arabic inscription recording Ali ibn Jumaa, who died in 1270 aged 55 (the date relates to the Muslim Hegira calendar, equating to around 1854 of the Christian era). The pillar has five depressions which formerly held Chinese porcelain bowls. Sadly, three were stolen, and the other two are now in the National Museum in Dar es Salaam.

Also worth looking out for is the remarkable **Sharifa's grave**, the "hut tomb" of a holy woman who is still venerated by local women who pray to her for help and leave small offerings in a small metal bowl inside the tomb (which, like the pillar tomb, was originally decorated with Chinese porcelain bowls). There's a similar hut tomb on Toten Island in Tanga Bay (see p.169). Lastly, note the small cluster of **"love graves"** – single structures containing two graves laid side by side which are believed to contain married couples who drowned at sea.

The Ruvu and Wami Rivers

The road to Msata, which is mostly graded, heads west out of Bagamoyo and then down into the **Ruvu River delta**, a reedy saltbush marshland which offers superb bird-watching. Amazingly, even the swamp isn't enough to deter human habitation, as shown by the tiny houses perched improbably above it on stilts. **Bird-watching** and **hippo-spotting** are possible: although there are no organized tours, the owner of the *Bagamoyo Beach Resort* (see p.143) might be able to arrange a guide and a vehicle. Alternatively, rent a bicycle in town (there's no formal outlet – just ask anyone with a bike), and then hire a local once at the river to track down wildlife (the word for hippo is *kiboko*; birds are *ndege*) – be cautious of hippos, however, as they can be extremely dangerous. You'll need a tent if you plan on doing anything more than a day-trip, since there are no guest houses in any of the small villages dotted about the delta. The Ruvu River itself, 10km from Bagamoyo, is now spanned by the narrow **Federici Bridge**. The rope-pulled ferry which it replaced is still moored here but is earmarked to be moved to the Wami River further north (where it will finally give direct road access from Bagamoyo to the Saadani Game Reserve).

For a longer trip (ideally by private vehicle), turn right 3.5km beyond the bridge to follow the old road to Saadani, which leads 65km to the south bank of the **Wami River**. Elephant, hippo, lion and buffalo abound here, as you might notice from their tracks in the dry mud (don't even dream of doing this trip in the rains). The tiny and friendly village at the end of the road on the south bank of the Wami River, tantalizingly close to Saadani Game Reserve on the opposite bank, doesn't see many visitors, especially since the rope-pulled ferry across the river was washed away in the 1998 El Niño floods (it now lies on its side 50m downstream from its steel guiding cable). Until the new ferry arrives from the Ruvu River, the only thing you can really do here is head on a few more kilometres towards the beach, which you'll share with a handful of sea-cucumber fishermen, an odd dhow and nothing and no one else. The drive here from Bagamoyo takes around seven or eight hours, which means that camping on the beach is the only way to avoid having to drive back at night.

Saadani Game Reserve

Located 45km north of Bagamoyo, the 500-square-kilometre **SAADANI GAME RESERVE** is one of the most fascinating, and least visited, of Tanzania's game parks, and East Africa's only coastal wildlife refuge. Its unique ecosystem combines marine, terrestrial and fluvial environments, which, together with the historic village of **Saadani** itself, makes for an attractive as well as unusual destination. Created in 1969, the reserve includes the botanically rich Zaraninge Forest Reserve and the former Mkwaja Cattle Ranch, whose remaining cattle were sold in June 2000.

Apart from the ocean coast, the reserve contains three distinct environments: the plains near the coast, characterized by swamps; the low, undulating hills behind; and the Wami River, on the reserve's southern boundary. The **plains**

△ Woman in doorway, Bagamoyo

and swamps are home to around thirty species of large mammal, although many are both rare and shy, thanks in part to the reserve's previous use as a hunting ground; these include warthog, elephant, buffalo, zebra and enormous herds of giraffe, as well as antelopes: hartebeest, wildebeest, waterbuck, dik dik, eland, oryx and the rare Roosevelt and Roan sables. Predators are represented by lions and hard-to-spot leopards. Although touted as a place to see big game on the beach, such sightings are rare, as few animals need venture to the coast except perhaps during the rains, when salt licks can become flooded, though you may well see waterbuck there during the day and, after nightfall, mongooses in search of crabs. The **Wami River** attracts some fabulous birdlife, as well as hippos, crocodiles and colobus monkeys, whilst the low hills are covered with rare remnants of coastal forest. The **best time to visit** is from June to September, when the animals converge towards the river. The reserve is also home to some herbivores which were released into the wild when the reserve's former zoo was closed in 1977. Of these, eland and zebra adapted best, though neither population has grown large enough to endanger the previous ecological balance.

Bwana Heri and the Abushiri War

The small and tranquil village of **Saadani**, in the heart of the reserve, was formerly an important harbour town and slave-trading centre which, under the charismatic leadership of the legendary slave trader **Bwana Heri**, played an important role in the Abushiri War. During the nineteenth century, Saadani – under the control of the Zigua tribe – was one of only a few mainland coastal towns to retain its political independence from the Omani sultans, growing wealthy on the slave trade with Zanzibar. A missionary writing in 1877 mentioned seeing slave caravans passing daily into Saadani, each with around a hundred children in chains. The profits from the trade were used to buy firearms from Zanzibar, which further served to strengthen Saadani's independence. Bwana Heri, who ruled Saadani from the early 1870s, achieved considerable power in this way, and also enjoyed considerable influence with the chiefs of the hinterland, especially with his own Zigua and the Nyamwezi tribe from the Central Plateau (see p.542), becoming a valued ally of European traders and missionaries hoping to travel into the interior.

All this changed with the arrival, in 1884, of a young German, **Karl Peters**, who set off from Saadani in November 1884 to make a series of bogus treaties with tribal chiefs which effectively gave Peters control of their land. Nonetheless, it was not until 1888 that Bwana Heri and the coastal people saw their political and economic power directly threatened, when the sultan of Zanzibar granted the Germans the right to extract customs duties on the mainland coastal strip. With local passions already inflamed by what many perceived as German arrogance (notably the desecration of mosques; see box on p.175), armed resistance was formed under the leadership of Bwana Heri in Saadani and Abushiri ibn Salim al-Harthi at Pangani, and the Germans were quickly expelled from much of the coast, signalling the beginning of the **Abushiri War**.

The German response took time to arrive, but was brutal when it did. In April 1889, **Major Hermann von Wissmann** and his army (the majority of whom were Nubians and Zulus) quickly recaptured the towns north of Dar es Salaam. In June 1889 Saadani was bombarded and taken, and Bwana Heri was forced to flee inland, where he built a series of forts. These, however, were destroyed one after the other by Wissmann, and Bwana Heri finally surrendered at Saadani in April 1890. Perhaps because of his previous hospitality to Wissmann, whom he had treated as an honoured guest in 1883, he was spared the fate of Abushiri (who was hanged at Bagamoyo), and was even left in control of Saadani. In March 1894 he tried to rise again, but once more was defeated.

Indigenous migratory mammals like sable antelope, kudu, buffalo and elephant seasonally pass beyond the reserve and its protection, which is a constant worry for ecologists, as poaching is more difficult to control outside the reserve. The most acute threats to the ecosystem however are destructive land use practices around its margins, and hunting for meat, especially around the dams in the former Mkwaja Ranch and in the west of the reserve, which game scouts have dubbed "Kosovo" on account of the abundance of firearms. New regulations allowing limited hunting by villagers using a quota system may improve the situation, although local communities have so far gained little from the reserve (indeed, they suffer crop damage from wildlife) and relations with the authorities are strained.

Getting to the reserve

Charter **flights** are operated by Easy Travel & Tours in Dar es Salaam (see p.124). The 35-minute hop **from Dar** costs $400 one-way for a three-seater aircraft, or $450 for a five-seater. Flights **from Zanzibar** take thirty minutes and cost $420 one-way for a five-seater. There may well be scheduled flights in future – ask at Easy Travel, or with A Tent with a View Safaris, also based in Dar (see p.124). You'll be picked up by someone from your lodge on arrival.

Much cheaper is the scheduled **car service** run by A Tent with a View Safaris on Wednesdays, Fridays and Sundays. Seats cost $25 each way. You're not obliged to stay at their tented camp, though unless you're camping, this is the only option. With your **own transport**, road access is dictated by the seasons: the dirt roads to the reserve frequently become impassable after heavy rains (most of March–May, and occasionally Nov–Jan), and the roads within the reserve, although recently regraded, are also liable to become impassable, especially around Saadani village. The direct route **from Bagamoyo** over the Wami River has been closed since 1998, when the rope-pulled ferry was washed away, though there are plans to replace it with the old ferry from Ruvu River. The alternative route from Bagamoyo (around 4hr) involves heading west to **Msata** on the A14 and then north to Mandera 2km beyond the Wami River. From here, turn right onto a signposted dirt road to Saadani, a two-hour, 58-kilometre drive in reasonable weather. A more adventurous alternative is to follow the coast down **from Pangani**, for which 4WD is recommended. From Pangani, cross the river and follow the main track, which takes you past the Sakura sisal estates to the former Mkwaja Ranch. Pass through Mikocheni village and, after 5km, turn right on to a graded road. Follow this for 3km, where there's a smaller track – the old Bagamoyo road – leading off to the south at a bend. From here it's about an hour to Saadani village.

Accommodation

Accommodation options are limited to a luxurious tented camp and a couple of basic if atmospheric campsites. The *Saadani Safari Camp* (book through either A Tent with a View Safaris or Safari Scene in Dar – see p.124–125; full board ❾), right on the beach 1km north of Saadani village, enjoys a location of unequalled beauty. There are ten luxurious beachfront *bandas*. Facilities include a bar and library, a restaurant specializing in prawns, and a treehouse behind the camp overlooking a waterhole.

Much more basic, but equally charming, are the reserve's two **campsites**. The *Saadani Village Camp Site* is run by the Saadani Conservation and Development Programme. For information and payment, ask at the reserve headquarters in the village. There's no running water, but local boys can fetch some for a small tip. The camp's lack of wildlife is amply compensated for by its proximity to the historic village, and the gorgeous snacks sold by kids in the evenings, including *kashata* coconut biscuits and goat milk biscuits. For a more remote location and the bonus of a nature trail with the chance of sighting black-and-white colobus and blue monkeys, head to *Kiwandi Camp* in the centre of Zaraninge Forest, for which you'll need your own transport. The camp is run by the WWF, whose project manager you should contact first. Turn off the Saadani–Mandera road outside the reserve and follow the WWF signs for Zaraninge Forest. The headquarters are about twenty minutes beyond the campsite.

Exploring the reserve

Entrance fees are $20 for 24 hours; you pay at the reserve headquarters in Saadani village unless you're staying at the *Saadani Safari Camp*. The best source of **information** is online at Ⓦ http://wildlife-programme.gtz.de/wildlife/tourism_saadani.html.

The reserve has a multitude of **drives**; a ranger is recommended if you're not on an organized safari (see below). Both the northern and southern sections are accessed from a crossroads about 5km west of Saadani village on the road to Mandera. Without your own transport, the best way around the reserve is on one of the safaris arranged by the *Saadani Safari Camp* and the reserve headquarters. A classic **game drive** costs $30 for a few hours and covers a variety of habitats. A more intimate – though at times nerve-wracking – way to experience the reserve is on a **walking safari** ($15); the **boat safaris** ($35) are also recommended. The boat heads down the coast before entering the Wami River, whose estuarine mangroves are often frequented by large flocks of flamingos. In the river itself, look out for the pink backs of hippo lounging about in the water, and the log-like forms of Nile crocodile in the reeds along either bank – one particularly intrepid croc swam across the Zanzibar Channel a few years back, much to everyone's surprise. High above in the forest canopy you might, if you're lucky, catch glimpses of black-and-white colobus monkeys.

Commonly seen **animals** include waterbuck, vervet monkeys and warthogs – the abundance of warthogs is thought to be the result of local Islamic beliefs which hold both them and the mainly nocturnal bushpigs to be a form of swine and so *haram* – forbidden. Liechtenstein's hartebeest, with their S-shaped horns and funny appearance (they look like they're wearing trousers), are also seen relatively frequently. The most numerous predators are leopards, though lions are more visible thanks to the nocturnal leopard's preference for dense bush.

The reserve attracts a wide variety of **birdlife**, including several endemic species. Marine and freshwater birds can be seen fishing along the ocean shore and in the dams of Mkwaja Ranch to the north, one of the more eye-catching species being the fish eagles which perch up in the trees waiting for prey to be carried up on the high tide. Waders include the woolly-necked stork, yellow-billed stork, open-billed stork, common sand piper and grey heron. Birds of prey include palmnut and white-backed vultures, yellow-billed kites, and various species of eagle. The acacia woodlands are a good place for the colourful lilac-breasted roller, fork-tailed drongos, grey hornbills, bee-eaters, flocks of Meyer's parrots and red-cheeked cordonbleus.

Marine wildlife includes dozens of species of fish, jellyfish and several kinds of crabs, prawns and shrimps. Small sharks can also be found, though these are believed to content themselves with a diet of prawns rather than humans. Bottle-nosed dolphins are common off the southern coast of the reserve, and humpback whales have been reported passing through the Zanzibar Channel in October and November. The proximity of the silty Wami River means that some species, such as the sea catfish, have adapted to the muddy flats. Another remarkable local species is the green sea turtle: a conservation project was established in 1993 at Madete Beach, 13km south of Mkwaja village, to protect their favourite hatching ground.

The reserve's **northern sector** sustains a small population of around fifty elephants, though you'll be lucky to spot more than a couple, as their memories of poaching are still fresh. Two rare types of antelope can also be found in the north: greater kudu, which are well camouflaged and rarely seen (they spend much of the day resting in the shadow of bushes); and sable antelope, found mainly in and to the west of Mkwaja South. They're smaller and lighter in colour than the common sable, and have shorter horns, which for a long time led zoologists to class them as a separate species.

The **southern sector** of the reserve, which comprises dense acacia woodland, is best for wildlife during the dry season (July–Oct), when many animals migrate south to the perennial waters of the Wami River. The giraffes here tend to keep away from humans, but can be seen gliding between the acacia trees and around Saadani village. Closer to the river, Eastern Bohor reedbuck can be seen in reedbeds near swamps, whilst bushbuck are quite common, though they hide by day in dense bush alongside the river. In the river itself, hippopotamuses abound, easily given away by their blubbery pink hulks peeking up above the water. They live in groups of up to 35, although they can also be found in smaller groups in small creeks and isolated waterholes far to the north of the river, notably Madete Hippo Pool.

Tanga and around

Located on a large, pear-shaped bay 200km due north of Dar es Salaam (but 350km by road), **TANGA** is Tanzania's second busiest port and the country's third largest town, with a population of around 200,000. Despite the town's size it's a refreshingly friendly and laid-back place, and surprisingly safe – in many respects, Tanga resembles Lindi on the south coast, with which it shares a similar feeling of decaying grandeur. In Tanga's case, decline started when its economy was eclipsed by that of Dar es Salaam in the early twentieth century, and was accelerated by the collapse of world sisal prices after World War II, when synthetics took away much of the demand for what is still the region's major cash crop. By 1999 Tanga had slipped from being the country's second most powerful economic region to the sixteenth.

The beaches are disappointing, since much of Tanga Bay is lined with mangroves, and there's not a whole lot to see in Tanga itself either, but an aimless wander around town is always fun. For those interested in history, the mangrove-fringed **Toten Island**, in the middle of Tanga Bay, is home to ruins and graveyards from medieval times, while the excursion to the **Amboni Caves** and **Galamos Sulphur Springs** makes another good day-trip. Tanga also serves as a springboard for longer trips to the wonderful beaches at the historic village of **Pangani**, 54km to the south; to the atmospheric fourteenth-century ruins of the Swahili trading town of **Tongoni** en route; and to the fantastic rainforest at **Amani Nature Reserve** in the East Usambaras (see p.361).

Some history

Tanga was founded in the fourteenth century by Persian traders, but little remains of this period except for the graves and ruined mosques on Toten Island and Tongoni, and the town's name – which is Persian for "green valley" or "road beside a mountain". Tanga remained small until the eighteenth century, when it was occupied by **Omani Arabs**, under whose tutelage the town grew within a century into a major entrepôt for slaves and ivory, which were shipped on to the Omani capital in Zanzibar. The town's trading links began to attract German missionaries, who started operating here in 1876, and by the early 1880s the town and its harbour had become a major centre for the **German conquest** of the interior. By 1888 the Germans had effectively become rulers of the region, although in the same year their brutal and often tactless rule led to the spontaneous uprising which became known as the Abushiri War (see box on p.154).

Following the end of the war in 1889, the Germans imposed a "protectorate" and began the military conquest of the hinterland. As their regional headquarters, Tanga looked set to prosper, especially when construction began on a railway linking Tanga with Moshi and the Kilimanjaro region. The driving force behind Tanga's renaissance was **sisal**, a major source of fibre for making ropes and sacks, which had been introduced to Tanzania by the German botanist Richard Hindorf in 1892. Despite only 62 of the 1000 plants originally taken from Florida surviving the journey, sisal proved to be spectacularly well adapted to the land and climate – by 1908 there were over ten million sisal plants in Tanzania, and at its height the region was producing 250,000 tonnes of sisal fibre a year (compared to 20,000 tonnes in 2000). The plantations, which stretch westwards from Tanga along much of the plains edging the Usambara mountains, still constitute the region's major export crop.

Tanga saw **World War I**'s first land engagement in East Africa when, on November 2, 1914, General Aitken rashly issued the order that "Tanga is to be taken tonight." Some 2000 Allied troops, mostly Indian, fought a pitched battle against 1000 Germans and their well-trained *askaris*, who were lying in wait on the other side of the railway cutting. Although some Allied forces fought their way as far in as the town centre, others were ambushed at the railway, were stung by bees or got lost in the plantations and long grass. The battle was a disaster for the British, who after three days and 795 casualties were forced to retreat to Mombasa. The Germans were finally ejected in 1917, and under **British rule** the railway connecting Tanga with the Central Line was finally completed. With sisal already proving its worth, Tanga's harbour was expanded in anticipation of a massive export trade, and the interwar years saw the town's heyday. Goans, Indians and Greeks – as well as Swahili and British merchants and administrators – descended on the town in the expectation that it would rival both Dar es Salaam and Mombasa in importance. Sadly, the invention of synthetic textiles such as nylon after World War II caused the sisal market to collapse, and the town entered a period of rapid decline from which it still shows precious little sign of emerging.

Arrival and information

Tanga is well connected with the rest of the country by good tarmac roads, although the unsurfaced road to Pangani can become impassable during the long rains (March–May), and is tricky during the short rains (usually Nov). The **bus stand** is a ten-minute walk from the town centre along Pangani Road. It's relatively hassle-free as far as bus stations go, and buses park in clearly defined

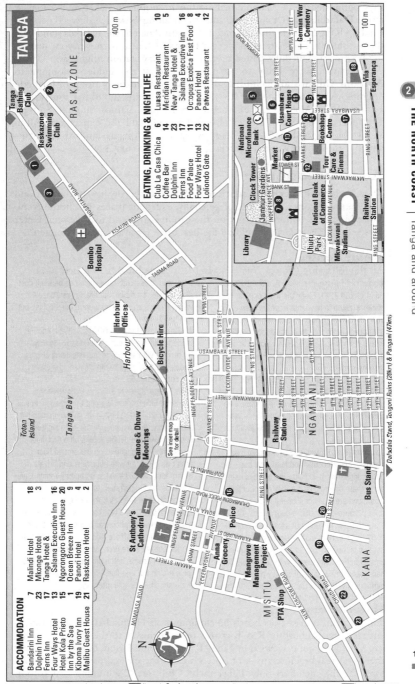

ACCOMMODATION

Bandarini Inn	7
Dolphin Inn	23
Ferns Inn	17
Four Ways Hotel	13
Hotel Kola Prieto	15
Inn by the Sea	1
Kiboma Ivory Inn	19
Malibu Guest House	21
Malindi Hotel	18
Mkonge Hotel	3
Salama Executive Inn	16
Ngorongoro Guest House	20
Ocean Breeze Inn	9
Panori Hotel	4
Raskazone Hotel	2

EATING, DRINKING & NIGHTLIFE

Club La Casa Chica	6
Coffee Bar	14
Dolphin Inn	23
Ferns Inn	17
Food Palace	11
Four Ways Hotel	13
Loliondo Gate	22
Luasa Restaurant	10
Meridian Restaurant	5
New Tanga Hotel & Salama Executive Inn	16
Octopus Exotica Fast Food	8
Panori Hotel	4
Patwas Restaurant	12

THE NORTH COAST | Tanga and around

159

bays signposted by destination, making the attentions of ticket touts easier to resist. **Daladalas** generally come into town along New Korogwe Road and head up Ring Street before cutting up Pangani Road to the daladala stand near the bus station. There are no passenger **trains** to Tanga, whatever your map or the prehistoric schedules pasted up in Dar's railway station might say.

On arrival you're likely to be met by one of the guides belonging to **Amboni Culture and Guiding Promoters**, a self-help group of formerly unemployed youths. The usual fee is Tsh5000 per guide (up to five tourists) for a visit to the Amboni Caves, Tongoni ruins or Galamos Sulphur Springs. Transport and entry fees cost extra, and the guide will also expect a tip. All in all it's a pretty good idea which deserves support, so long as standards are maintained – though they're not "official", whatever they may say.

Accommodation

There's plenty of **accommodation** in Tanga, especially in the budget and moderate categories, with lots of generally excellent places to choose from. More luxurious options are thin on the ground and tend to have seen better days – the *Mkonge Hotel* should be the best once renovations are complete.

Town centre

All the following (except *Four Ways Hotel*) include breakfast in their rates.

Bandarini Inn Independence Ave ☎027/264 6674 or 264 7221. Easily the most popular backpackers' place in town, not least because of the charming Indian owner and the superb views from the ocean-facing top-floor rooms (some with private bathrooms). It's temporarily closed at present, but should have reopened by the time this book hits the shelves. ❷

Ferns Inn Usambara St, near Ring St ☎027/264 6276. Run by a sweet Goan, this has nine clean twin-bed rooms with fans and nets, some with bathrooms, though the ones with a/c are way overpriced. There's a bar, and food is available (p.163). ❷–❸.

Four Ways Hotel Market St (no phone). Four rooms above a popular and loud local bar – the better ones have balconies, and all have nets, fans and private bathrooms, but they're not entirely clean, and are really only useful if you're looking for a place to crash after a boozy night. ❶

Hotel Kola Prieto India St, close to Custom Rd ☎027/264 4206. Tanga's best business-class hotel, this modern four-storey affair has 24 clean and attractive rooms, each with carpet, big double beds, satellite TV (some also have phones) and bathrooms with hot water. The rooms with fans are a bargain; those with a/c (which can be loud) cost almost twice as much, but are still reasonable value. There's a formal restaurant (no alcohol), but no lift. ❸–❹

Malindi Hotel Ring St ☎0741/332984. Another modern four-storey affair offering excellent value for money, with sixteen rooms (including singles, doubles and twins), all with clean cotton sheets. A/c costs extra. ❸

New Tanga Hotel & Salama Executive Inn Corner of Eckernforde Ave and Chumbageni Police Rd ☎027/264 6030 or 264 4631. Recommended choice attached to a popular bar, with eighteen spotless twin and double rooms off a first-floor terrace (the three singles on the ground floor aren't as good), all with nets, fans and private bathrooms; a/c costs extra. Some bathrooms have bathtubs. No single rates. ❷

Ocean Breeze Inn Clock Tower St, facing the market ☎027/264 3441. This modern and potentially good-value option was being rebuilt at the time of writing; staff are sleepy and not everything works, but there are great sea views from some rooms, and private bathrooms and fans throughout (plus a/c on the first floor). A bar and restaurant are planned. No single rates. ❷

Ras Kazone

Tanga's main tourist-class hotels lie along and off Hospital Road in the affluent residential suburb of **Ras Kazone**, on a peninsula to the east of the centre. Most have good views over Tanga Bay and Toten Island, but unfortunately there's no real beach to speak of (the nearest is the cleared patch of mangrove forest at the members–only Tanga Yacht Club; see "Swimming" on p.164).

Frequent daladalas run up and down Hospital Road from the main stand (Tsh150). Room rates in all the following places include breakfast.

Inn by the Sea 1.5km along Hospital Rd ⓣ027/264 4614. Perched on a low cliff among lush bougainvillea hedges, this rather tatty establishment sees little trade, while the rooms (no singles; a/c extra) are well past their prime, especially the saggy beds. Even so, at the price this is the best value of the bayside hotels, and you can swim in the sea. There's also a restaurant and a bar selling soft drinks. ❷–❸

Mkonge Hotel 1250m down Hospital Rd past Bombo Hospital ⓣ & ⓕ027/264 3440. Tanga's only international-class resort, set in baobab-studded lawns by the bay, though the fringing mangroves inhibit swimming. The main building is an oddly attractive hulk dating from the happier days of the sisal industry; less enticing is the tatty 1970s accommodation wing (currently under renovation), although its large, newly refurbished rooms are cheerfully furnished and equipped with a/c, TV and fridge, and the better ones have fine views over the bay and Toten Island. No single rates. ❻

Panori Hotel 3km from the centre ⓣ027/264 6044, ⓕ027/264 7425. The location is poor, being close to a stretch of beach owned by the military and over 1km from Tanga Bathing Club and public transport, but the welcome is hospitable, and all rooms have private bathrooms and a/c, though the smell of bug spray is pervasive. The better rooms, in the New Wing, have parquet floors, TV and big bathrooms; those in the cheaper Old Wing are small, dingy and way overpriced. There's also a bar and a good, if expensive, restaurant. ❸–❹

Raskazone Hotel 200m off Hospital Rd near Tanga Bathing Club, 2km from the centre ⓣ & ⓕ027/264 3897. Offers a warm reception if you can actually find anyone around, though rooms (with either fan or a/c) are slightly faded and the nets are too small to cover the beds. The food is good, however, and there's the bonus of an unusual garden with (dry) pools and artificial waterfalls adorned with sculptures of monsters and wildlife. ❸–❹

Misitu and Kana

The **Misitu** and **Kana** areas, just east of the railway south of Ring Street, have a number of decent budget-range guest houses, as well as some popular bars and nightclubs. Walking around with a backpack is safe by day. The hotels are a ten-to-twenty-minute walk west of the bus and daladala stands; alternately, if you're arriving in Tanga by public transport, you could ask the driver to let you off in Misitu by the Mangrove Management Project office. From here, cross the road, and take the path over the railway by the large mango tree. The *Ngorongoro Guest House* is about 300m along on the left, with the others down the road to your right.

Dolphin Inn Just east of the railway tracks on the signposted road to Pangani ⓣ027/264 5005 or 0744/294564. Probably the best hotel in this district, this modern and efficiently run establishment has thirteen rooms with nets, fans, tiled bathrooms, big beds and cotton sheets. There's also a hair salon. Breakfast included. ❷

Kiboma Ivory Inn 8th St ⓣ027/264 3578. Very good value, with clean double rooms (sharing bathrooms) and a handful of more expensive singles with private bathroom. Also has a quiet bar and restaurant with local dishes. ❶

Malibu Guest House 8th St ⓣ027/264 7251. This is the same price as *Kiboma Ivory Inn* with the bonus of breakfast included, though not all rooms have bathrooms. Staff are reasonably friendly once you get past the language barrier, and there's a restaurant (but no alcohol). ❶

Ngorongoro Guest House 8th St ⓣ027/264 3512. An excellent budget choice with large, clean rooms with private bathroom, fans, cold showers, huge comfortable beds with cotton sheets and suitably sized nets. There's also a quiet bar, but the food is pretty average and the fish truly awful. Breakfast included. ❷

The Town

Apart from the harbour, there's no real focus to the older, colonial part of town, with most restaurants, hotels and businesses more or less evenly spread out over the four or five blocks inland from the bay. At times the place can feel almost deserted, incomprehensibly so until you realize that the main commercial centre is now located in the grid of colourful, crowded streets and haphazard structures around the bus station, 1km inland across the railway tracks, where the bulk of the population live and work.

In the colonial centre, though, there's little to dispel the gently mouldering atmosphere, with a wealth of colonial-era buildings gradually succumbing to woodworm and verdigris. An aimless wander is always rewarding, as most streets contain a least a handful of beautiful and photogenic old buildings. Although few if any buildings survive from the Omani period, the Omani legacy can be seen in the carved wooden balcony screens, or **masharabiyya**, that grace the first floors of some buildings. These decorative devices were designed to protect the modesty of the houses' inhabitants, while letting in light and giving a view onto the street.

The German period is perhaps best represented by the neo-Gothic **Usambara Court House** on Usambara Street. Formerly the German Governor's House, this is currently derelict, although it's being very slowly restored – it now has a new roof, though the rest of the building is still boarded up. Other reminders of German times include the **clock tower** of 1901, close by on Independence Avenue, and the German **obelisk** in the adjacent Jamhuri Gardens. Its three surviving plaques commemorate marines who died in the Abushiri War, though the inscriptions have been partly disfigured with some rather tardy graffiti along the lines of "Germans Go Home". The subsequent wars that the Germans were almost constantly engaged in are recalled by the **German War Cemetery**, at the corner of Swahilli and Mpira streets, which contains the graves of 48 African solders and porters and sixteen German solders, including that of Tom von Prince, who commanded the German army's bitter but ultimately successful 1894–98 campaign against Chief Mkwawa of the Hehe (see "Kalenga" on p.570).

The British period, which coincided with the town's heyday between the two world wars, is represented by the attractive green-and-white gabled **railway station** on Ring Street, dating from 1930. For steam train enthusiasts, it's the sidings to the south and east of here that will bring on the euphoria: dozens of rusty steam locomotives and carriages occupy most of the shuntings and sheds. There shouldn't be any problem walking around the area, but be very careful with your camera – a lone tourist would be an easy target, and the railway itself is still used for freight and so may be considered a sensitive target by overzealous policemen.

The cosmopolitan aspect of British rule is also reflected in the dozens of buildings throughout the town whose architectural style was influenced by Asians brought over by the British as coolies, who later became merchants and traders. The 1930 **Vila Esperança** (Villa of Hope) at the east end of Ring Street is a particularly fine example of this cross-cultural pollination, gracefully combining Goan and Art Deco styles with a hint of Portuguese. Its name reflects the wealth and high aspirations that Tanga enjoyed in the interwar years, before the collapse of the sisal market brought a sudden end to the town's golden age.

If you need a rest, there are two small parks: **Jamhuri Gardens**, overlooking the bay, benefits from a sea breeze and a children's playground, whilst two blocks inland, **Uhuru Park** has a few surviving benches under the trees arranged around a bizarre missile-like monument celebrating independence.

Eating

Street food in the town centre is restricted to a handful of fruit stalls, coconut-juice vendors and peanut and cashew pedlars rhythmically marking their presence with seed rattles. The area around the bus station has much more choice, and the narrow beach beside the canoe and dhow moorings just east of St Anthony's Cathedral is the best place for fried fish. For your own supplies, the small **market** between Market Street and Independence Avenue is reasonable. The Anna Grocery on Chumbageni Police Road may not look like much but stocks occasional treats like feta cheese and pork. As for **restaurants**, there's not a huge amount of choice, but what there is is generally good, and you can also find *nyama choma* and *chipsi mayai* in most of Tanga's bars.

Coffee Bar Corner of Usambara St and India St. Cheap and filling local dishes like *ugali* with fish, with tables on a wide verandah outside.

Ferns Inn, Usambara St, near Ring St. Friendly Goan-run place offering chips with meat, fish or squid (all under Tsh1000), prawns (Tsh1500) and curried or roast octopus (Tsh1000).

Food Palace Market St ☎027/264 6816. Always popular with expats and Asians, the menu here isn't particularly extensive but the food itself is reliably good, including pizzas and Indian (try the *nylon bhajia*, potato slices in batter), and there's a famous outdoor barbecue in the evening. It's good value, too, with most mains under Tsh2500. Closed Mon evening.

Luasa Restaurant Just up the side street opposite Globe Net Works internet café, off Market St. Very cheap eats, and popular with local office workers at lunchtimes.

Meridian Restaurant At the back of Nasaco House, corner of Independence Ave and Custom St. Friendly and laid-back place which functions mainly as a bar and disco (see p.164), but which is

open during the day for reliably good *nyama choma*, *pilau*, *ndizi* and *chipsi mayai*, when the TV attracts the locals.

Octopus Exotica Fast Food In the shipping crate next to the *Bandarini Inn* on Independence Ave. Serves up some truly delicious and cheap food, including octopus, prawns, kingfish and curry rice. Open daily from 6pm.

Panori Hotel 3km from town in Ras Kazone (a taxi costs Tsh2000). Offers a wide selection of dishes, notably seafood, though at between Tsh4500 and Tsh7500 for mains it's not cheap. Also has a pleasant shaded garden and a well-stocked bar with satellite TV.

Patwas Restaurant Mkwakwani St. Now almost forty years old, this famous Indian-run place is located in a bright and breezy old factory, and still serves up some of the best juices (Tsh400) and milk shakes (Tsh800) in Tanzania, as well as reasonably priced curries (up to Tsh2500 – avoid the dodgy salad) and other snacks, but make sure they're fresh, as some sit around for days. Closed Sun.

Drinking and nightlife

You'll find plenty of **drinking** holes throughout the town centre and in the suburbs. For something a bit different, the Majestic Cinema on Mkwakwani Street is a fun place to escape to, especially on Monday, Thursday and Sunday, when they screen genuine Bollywood movies complete with singing, dancing and slushy endings (5.45pm & 9.15pm; Tsh500–700); distinctly less rousing Hollywood video screenings are shown on other days (6.15pm & 9.15pm; Tsh300).

Bars

Apart from the following, there are also sleepy **bars** at the *Mkonge, Raskazone* and *Panori* hotels in Ras Kazone, and at the distinctly livelier *Meridian Restaurant* (see p.164).

Coffee Bar Corner of Usambara St and India St. Nice sleepy bar for an afternoon drink, with TV inside and tables on a wide verandah outside. Also serves decent food (see above).

Ferns Inn, Usambara St. Quiet place with seats outside in a small garden by the road. Live traditional music is planned, *Mungu akipenda* – God willing.

Four Ways Hotel Market St. Large local dive on the first floor, especially busy on Wed and Fri–Sun when it rocks to cheerful Tanzanian and Congolese sounds. Food is limited to *nyama choma* and chip omelettes.

New Tanga Hotel & Salama Executive Inn Corner of Eckernforde Ave and Chumbageni Police Rd. One of the most popular town-centre bars, large and not too noisy, with as many women as men thanks to the unthreatening atmosphere. There's also passable *nyama choma*, a restaurant,

satellite TV, dartboard and pool table, while a disco and live-music venue is planned on an adjacent plot.

Nightlife

The main focus of Tanga's **nightlife** is a cluster of lively bars and clubs in the Misitu and Kana areas between the railway and bus station. Taxis from town cost around Tsh1000. It might also be worth asking whether the *Mkonge Hotel's* weekend discos have started up again.

Club La Casa Chica Top floor, Sachak House, Independence Ave. Near the *Meridian*, this popular, western-style disco keeps out the rabble with its Tsh2000 entry fee (Tsh3000 for couples), though it has the worrying appearance of a fire trap. Wed & Fri–Sun from 9pm.

Dolphin Inn Around the corner from *Loliondo Gate*. A popular alternative to the *Loliondo* judging from the quantity of gold jewellery adorning the matron; also serves good *nyama choma*.

Loliondo Gate Facing the railway tracks in Misitu/Kana. This two-storey affair is by far the most popular nocturnal venue at present, and its

fresh *nyama choma* and Watangatanga Band (Wed & Fri–Sun from around 8pm; Tsh500 entrance) attract plenty of inebriated revellers of both sexes.

Meridian Restaurant At the back of Nasaco House, corner of Independence Ave and Custom St. The place to be on Wednesday and weekend nights when this otherwise dozy restaurant comes alive with discos on its verandah (from 9pm; Tsh1000 for men, women free). The packed crowd covers all ages, and the music is a lively mix of local rap, Congolese jingles and old Tanzanian twist; there's good, simple food too.

Listings

Banks The National Microfinance Bank, corner of Sokoine Ave and Clock Tower St, changes travellers' cheques fairly speedily (count on around 30min). The NBC, corner of Bank St and Sokoine Ave, and CRDB, at the corner of Independence Ave and Clock Tower St, are much the same in terms of speed, but are more likely to want to see the original purchase agreement.

Bicycle rental Bicycles can be rented at the street corner opposite the post office; at the main market square; on New Korogwe Rd by the PTA shop close to the Mangrove Management Project office; and just west of the port gate on the road leading to the dhow moorings. They shouldn't cost more than Tsh2000–3000 a day, or Tsh200 an hour.

Bookshops and newspapers Bookshop Centre on Guinea St has some English-language novels by African authors and a small selection of second-hand English novels. For Tanzanian newspapers, there's a good stall opposite the National Microfinance Bank on Market St.

Car repairs Akhtar Service, next to BP, has Land Rover spares.

Hospitals The largest is Bombo Hospital, 800m along Hospital Rd (℡027/264 2997). Private clinics include the Fazal Memorial Hospital on Independence Ave (℡027/2646895), and Tanga Medicare Centre Hospital on the same avenue (℡027/264 6920), which also has a dental clinic.

Internet access Globe Net Works, Market St (Mon–Fri 8.30am–1pm & 2.30–9pm, Sat 8.30am–4pm, Sun 10am–2pm) charges Tsh2000 per hour; there's a less reliable internet café on Independence Ave, in the small shopping centre opposite the children's playground in Jamhuri Gardens.

Library Tanga Library (George V Memorial Library), in a lovely Arab-inspired building on Independence Ave, is surprisingly well stocked (Mon–Fri 9am–6pm, Sat 9am–2pm; daily membership Tsh500, annual membership Tsh3000).

Police The main police station is off Independence Ave near Tanga library.

Post The general post office is on Independence Ave (Mon–Fri 8am–12.45pm & 2–4.30pm, Sat 9am–noon). The DHL agent is Karimjee Travel, Nasaco House, corner of Independence Ave and Custom St ℡027/264 6523.

Shopping Apart from the small produce market between Market St and Independence Ave, the main market area is in the streets behind the bus station. There's also a lively clothes market on the west side of Pangani Rd, south of the railway beside some old locomotive sheds. Woodcarvers sell their work in stalls at the northwest corner of the market square.

Swimming Tanga lacks a public swimming pool, but there are two swimming clubs along Hospital Rd: the Raskazone Swimming Club (Tsh500), next

By bus and daladala

Most **bus** services depart early in the morning, with the last ones generally leaving shortly after noon. Several buses run daily to Dar es Salaam, Morogoro, Moshi, Arusha and Pangani, while Air Shengena run an exhausting midweek service to Sumbawanga in the southwest of the country (roughly 24hr), passing through Morogoro, Iringa and Mbeya. Mombasa is served by three buses a day (8.30am, 11am & 2pm) and by a night bus coming from Dar run by the notoriously reckless Tawfiq. Kenyan visas are easily obtained at the border (currently $50 for most nationalities). Bus **tickets** can be bought on the day of departure from the bus conductor, but it's best to get them the day before – and vital if you're heading for Mombasa or Dar – from the offices around the edges of the station. There are frequent **daladalas** to Muheza for connections to the Amani Nature Reserve, and to Mombo for Lushoto in the West Usambara. Less frequent daladalas run directly to Lushoto and Pangani.

If you're heading **to Kenya**, note that the road from Tanga up to Horo Horo near the Kenyan border is in an atrocious state – it can take up to four hours to cover the 70km, depending on the rains. This lamentable state of affairs undoubtedly aided a spate of armed bandit attacks on buses heading into Kenya in 2001 (fortunately, no one was injured) – a decent road is long, long overdue. It's best to get a bus all the way to Mombasa, as otherwise there's a long 8km walk through no-man's land between Horo Horo and the Kenyan border post at Lunga Lunga.

By dhow

Tanga's **harbour** isn't the most user-friendly place on earth. The men hanging around waiting for casual labour can seem threatening, and you may even have trouble entering the place without paying a little *chai* to the guard on the gate. The best tactic is just to stride in with a purposeful air and, if stopped, explain that you have an appointment with the harbour master or the director of immigration, both of whom you will indeed be seeing.

Mega-speed's comfortable **MS Sepideh** catamaran ferry formerly ran once a week to Pemba, Zanzibar and Dar es Salaam, and to Mombasa in Kenya, but the service was suspended during the violent aftermath of the 2000 elections in Pemba and Zanzibar, and looks unlikely to resume – ask at the port or at one of the travel agents in town (see p.166). In the meantime, the only fairly regular passenger service to Pemba is the wooden **MV Baracuda**, which sails roughly once a week (usually Monday night) to Mkoani, arriving the next day. There's no fixed schedule, however, so ask at the Harbour Office or decipher the chalked-up sign propped up at the harbour gate announcing the next sailing. The fare varies, at least for *wazungu*, so it's a matter of bargaining with the captain: it's usually around $15–25. The alternative is to arrange a passage on one of the frequent **commercial dhows**, who should settle for much less, depending on your bargaining skills. Bring enough food and water for the journey. Travelling by dhow or on the *MV Baracuda*, there are a few **formalities** to complete. First off, pay a visit to the harbour master and the port manager (℡027/264 3078) to find out which boats are going where, and when. The only payment to them might be a harbour tax – this shouldn't be more than around $5.

The other critical formality, if you're heading to Pemba or Kenya, is to obtain an exit stamp from the **immigration office** after clearing your baggage with **customs** (both are also in the port complex). Unfortunately, actually getting the stamp is by far the biggest headache you'll come across. Officially there's no charge for it, but in practice this depends on the (lack of) honesty of the officer. If you're lucky, a small tip will suffice, but some officials make such high demands that many travellers simply give up. If this is what happens, consider heading to Pangani (p.169) to arrange your passage to Nungwi in Zanzibar from there. Note that under no circumstances should you have to pay the **arrival tax** for Zanzibar before setting foot on the islands.

to *Inn by the Sea*, with a tiled platform over the bay as well as a bar and restaurant, and the similar Tanga Bathing Club, 300m further along. You can also reach the ocean from the roadside between the two clubs, down some short steep paths to a very narrow strip of sand, though being close to the town and still within the bay, the water is less than crystal clear. The closest clean stretch of shoreline is a few kilometres to the east of town at the end of Eckernforde Ave.

Telephones The TTCL office is at the post office on Independence Ave, with both operator-assisted calls and a phone booth.

Travel agents Coco Travel & Tours, Bandari House, Independence Ave ℡027/264 4332 or 264 4141, ℮cocotravel@cats-net.com, handle airline ticketing and some hotel reservations, and were also the agents for the *MS Sepideh* ferry to Mombasa, Pemba and Zanzibar before the service was suspended. Other travel agents include H. A. Travel Services, also in Bandari House (PO Box 748) ℡027/264 7907, ℱ027/264 6528; and Karimjee Travel, Nasaco House, corner of Independence Ave and Custom St (PO Box 1563) ℡027/262 1099 or 264 6534, ℱ027/264 5132.

Around Tanga

There are a number of rewarding half-day trips in the vicinity of Tanga. Natural attractions include educational visits to nearby mangrove forests, as well as the amazing limestone **Amboni Caves**, which can be combined with a soak in the **Galamos Sulphur Springs**. For a glimpse into Tanga's medieval past, a visit to the ruins and Shirazi tombs of the Swahili trading town of **Tongoni** is well worth the effort, while there are more Shirazi ruins on **Toten Island**, just off Tanga in the middle of the bay, though getting to the island can be a hassle.

It's well worth taking a **guide** for Tongoni, Amboni and Galamos, as the access roads are poorly marked, if at all — if one hasn't already adopted you, ask at Tour Care on Mkwakwani Street next to the Majestic Cinema, which is the base for Amboni Culture and Guiding Promoters (PO Box 1021 ℡027/264 3546 or 0741/211091). The Tsh5000 fee for a group of up to five people is perfectly reasonable (transport and admission fees cost extra), but don't expect them to be too knowledgeable about the sites.

The Amboni Caves

With their winding passageways and galleries, dripping stalactites, weirdly shaped stalagmites, bat colonies and assortment of unlikely legends, the limestone **Amboni Caves** (Mapango ya Amboni) are for many visitors one of the highlights of Tanzania. The caverns are thought to have formed during the Bathonian Period (176–169 million years ago), when sea levels were much higher than they now are, leading to inland limestone deposits. The caves cover

---

Mangrove forests around Tanga

Tanga's **mangroves** have been heavily depleted over last few decades for use as building poles and fuel, as well as for the wood-intensive practice of boiling sea water to obtain salt. Working to counteract this trend is the **Zonal Mangrove Management Project** on New Korogwe Rd (PO Box 1449; ℡027/264 2684; Mon–Fri 7.30am–3.30pm), whose aims include protecting and replanting mangroves, and finding sustainable alternatives to mangrove use. They also help educate local communities about the importance of the forests, explaining their role as fish nurseries and filters for the fish-rich offshore reefs, and their function in preventing coastal erosion. The project is happy to arrange trips to existing or replanted mangroves and have two boats in Tanga and one in Pangani; you're expected to pay for fuel and, of course, a tip or donation would be appreciated – talk to the Zonal Mangrove Officer.

an area of approximately fifteen square kilometres, making them the most extensive known cave complex in East Africa, and contain at least ten networks of caverns and passageways, one or two of which can be visited. There's no light, and even with a torch (the guide will have one) it takes a few minutes for your eyes to adjust to the obscurity. Bats (*popo*) live in the caves in colonies numbering tens of thousands, hanging upside down in enormous bunches for most of the day. If you hang around the entrance at sunset, you'll see clouds of the creatures fluttering out of the caves to feed. In most of the chambers the ground is very soft, the millennial product of accumulated bat droppings, which support numerous other animals including crickets, moths and spiders.

One cavern was allegedly used as a hide-out by a pair of local Robin Hoods during the 1950s Mau Mau insurrection in Kenya – Osale Otango (or Otayo) and Paulo Hamis – who, according to local legend, used to rob from the Europeans to give to the Africans. Otango was shot dead by the British in 1958. Your guide will probably show you the **Mombasa Road Cavern**, which is said to go all the way to the Kenyan port, and other passages which are rumoured to lead to Nairobi and Kilimanjaro. The last of these rumours originates from the tale of two Europeans who tried to explore the caves after World War II. They disappeared without trace, but their dog was found dead a few months later 400km away outside another cave near Kilimanjaro. Sadly, these stories were scotched by a German-Turkish survey in 1994, which concluded that the longest of the caves extended no further than 900m from the entrance.

Of more genuine significance is the **Chamber of the Spirits** (*Mzimuni*), which is sacred to local people, who believe it to be inhabited by a force, represented by a snake, which can grant fertility to childless women, who come here to pray and leave offerings like food, money, flowers, goats and chickens. The floor of the chamber is littered with bottles, flags, charcoal and the remains of food. Another cavern, containing the chillingly named **Lake of No Return** (not always included in tours), is said to have been the place where the Digo tribe threw albino babies, which were believed to be a bad omen. Other attractions you might be shown include a miniature Mount Kilimanjaro (10m tall) and two natural "statues", one of the Virgin Mary, the other of the Statue of Liberty.

The patch of **riverine forest** above and around the caves is also of great interest, affording good bird- and butterfly-watching, as well as the chance to see members of a rare population of black-and-white colobus monkeys.

Practicalities

The caves are located near **Kiomoni village**, 8km north of Tanga off the Mombasa road, and are open daily from 9am to 4pm. The Tsh1500 entrance fee includes a guided tour, but tips are appreciated. The caves can be reached either on any **daladala** headed from Tanga to Mombasa or Horo Horo, or by **taxi**, though you'll need to bargain doggedly to get a realistic fare, since you'll probably be quoted Tsh14,000 or up for the return trip – a more reasonable fare would be around Tsh8000. The best way to get to the caves, however, is by **bicycle**, which you can rent from several places in Tanga (see p.164). The ride there takes around an hour at an easy pace.

A **campsite** has recently been opened outside the caves, part of a community ecotourism project from which locals will profit directly. Work currently in progress includes the environmental protection and management of the surrounding riverine forest and wetlands, microfinance ventures and studies on the impact of tourism on the bat population of the caves.

Some 3km east from the Amboni Caves are the **Galamos Sulphur Springs**. The track from the Mombasa road is very poorly marked and becomes impassable in the rains, so a guide comes in useful – the springs are in any case usually tacked onto guided tours of the caves. Named after a Greek sisal planter named Christos Galamos, the springs are rarely visited and the small spa beside them has been derelict for years. It's possible to bathe in the hot, green and stinky waters, which are believed to relieve arthritis and cure skin ailments. Coming from Amboni, you have to cross the **Sigi River** by dugout canoe – your guide will arrange this for you. Crocodiles are sometimes found in the river here, depending on the Indian Ocean tide: high tide tends to push the crocs upriver. Needless to say, don't swim in the river (though the springs are fine).

Tongoni

The atmospheric ruins of **Tongoni** (meaning "deserted village") lie just off the Pangani road about 20km south of Tanga. Comprising a mosque and over forty graves, the ruins are all that remain of a small but prosperous town which peaked shortly after being founded in the fourteenth and fifteenth centuries.

Although much smaller than contemporary ruins at Kilwa Kisiwani (p.200), Tongoni contains the largest collection of **Shirazi tombs** in East Africa, an indication of the prosperity it enjoyed before the arrival of the Portuguese disrupted the trading routes on which coastal towns like Tongoni depended. The settlement of Tongoni was mentioned by Vasco da Gama in April 1498 en route to India, when one of his ships ran aground on Mtangata (or Tangata) shoal near present-day Tongoni. Before they set sail they were visited by "Moors" from Tongoni who brought oranges which, according to da Gama, were better than those in Portugal. During the return voyage the following year his fleet spent fifteen days here, during which they scuttled one of their ships, as disease had reduced the fleet's manpower, and obtained domestic fowl from Mtangata in exchange for shirts and bracelets. According to later Portuguese sources, Tongoni was still a power to be reckoned with during the seventeenth century, when its rulers were friendly to the Portuguese, as they shared an enmity against Mombasa, which had become the most powerful sultanate on the coast.

To get to Tongoni, catch a Pangani-bound **bus** from Tanga and get off at the modern village of Tongoni, from where the ruins are a ten-minute walk towards the shore – you'll need to ask for directions. Leave early in the morning to be sure of having enough time to explore the site at your leisure; the last bus back from Pangani passes Tongoni around 4pm, but it would be unwise to rely on it, especially as there's no accommodation nearby. The site is open daily from 9am to 4pm, and entrance costs Tsh1500. There's a caretaker on site, although he's not very knowledgeable – the 1975 booklet *A Guide to Tongoni Ruins* by A. A. Mturi, published by the Antiquities Department, has more information, though at the last check it was only available (bizarrely enough) in the bookshop at Olduvai Gorge in Ngorongoro. Once you've paid, you're free to explore the site on your own.

The ruins

The bulk of **the town** appears to have been situated to the north and west of the mosque, where the foundations of stone walls and a considerable quantity of pottery have been found, although much has been reclaimed by the ocean. The ruined **mosque** was cleared and excavated in 1958, revealing glazed blue *sgraffito* shards from the fifteenth century and a large amount of nineteenth-century pottery in the *mihrab* which archeologists speculate may have been used as offerings. Although the building measured just 12m by 13m, it was large for its time, though nowadays you'll need a lively imagination to picture what it might have looked like 600 years ago. The roof disappeared long since and the east wall has collapsed, leaving only the remaining pillars, coral ragstone walls and the finely arched *mihrab*. On the south side is a transverse room the same size as the mosque, which was probably used by women. To the west is an extra structure which may have been a verandah (*baraza*), with windows in its west wall serving as ventilation. On the east you can still see coral stone bosses which were used for standing on when performing ablutions; a pillar tomb stands next to the ablution area.

Tongoni's **graveyard**, surrounding the mosque on three sides, contains over forty **Shirazi tombs** (many more have evidently succumbed to coastal erosion). About half of the tombs have been dated to the fourteenth century, when the Shirazi–Swahili civilization was at its height. These are characterized by their pillars, some square, others octagonal, which are contemporary with the mosque, though only one of them still stands intact. As with Kunduchi and Kaole, the recesses in a number of these pillars originally held Chinese or Islamic ceramic bowls, of which no trace remains. Other tombs bear traces of fine relief work, all testifying to the town's former riches. The extent of Tongoni's trading links were shown by one tomb which bore an imported glazed tile with a Persian inscription – the only example of Persian script ever found in East Africa – though this has scandalously been "lost".

The other tombs are rather crude in comparison, and date from Tongoni's brief revival in the eighteenth and nineteenth centuries, when it was occupied by migrants from Kilwa who rebuilt the houses and renamed the place *Sitahabu*, meaning "better than there". From this period dates the walled double enclosure near the tomb whose pillar has collapsed onto the east wall of the mosque. It is revered by local people, especially barren women, who make offerings at the base of the grave, claiming the tomb belongs to a descendant of the Prophet Muhammad.

Toten Island

Should Tongoni have woken the sleeping archeologist in you, the mangrove-fringed **Toten Island** in the middle of Tanga Bay facing Tanga is the site of another cluster of **Shirazi ruins**. The island's name comes from the German word for "dead ones", alluding to the numerous graves it contains. Although the island is barely 1km from Tanga, getting there can be awkward – it's a matter of arranging boat or canoe hire with the fishermen on the beach just east of St Anthony's Cathedral (this shouldn't cost more than Tsh3000 per person for the return journey). There are no facilities on the island and you'll have to trudge through the mangroves to get ashore. The sites themselves are very overgrown and you'll be lucky to find the two mosques that were briefly surveyed in the 1960s, never mind the third mosque which was reported by the Germans but has not been found since.

Pangani and around

Located at the mouth of the Pangani River 54km south of Tanga, the small and historic trading town of **PANGANI** is one of Tanzania's most underrated coastal destinations, boasting attractive sandy beaches, a friendly and laid-back

Pangani and Rhapta

According to some, Pangani's origins can be traced back almost two thousand years to the trading centre of **Rhapta**, which was mentioned in the *Periplus of the Erythraean Sea* (c.130–140 AD), a commercial guide which vividly recounts the considerable trade which flourished along the coast at that time. A fuller account of Rhapta, based on a report by the Phoenician geographer Marinus of Tyre about the journey of a Greek merchant named Diogenes, was given in Claudius Ptolemy's *Geography*, written a century or so later, in which the metropolis of "Rhaptum" marked the end of the known world. Beyond it, according to Ptolemy, lived *anthropophagoi* – cannibals. The identification of Pangani with Rhapta is given credence by Diogenes' claim to have "travelled for a twenty-five days journey [from Rhapta] and reached a place in the vicinity of the two great lakes and the snowy mountains from where the Nile draws its sources". Although doubted by experts, who consider 25 days too short a time to have reached Lake Victoria (700km distant) or Lake Tanganyika (1200km), never mind the Ruwenzori Mountains, the account nonetheless has a ring of truth to it: the very mention of two great lakes and snowy mountains at the very least proves that knowledge of the interior – and of the source of the Nile, which is indeed fed by the Ruwenzori Mountains via Lake Victoria – was a great deal more advanced in those times than it was in the nineteenth century.

atmosphere, and a wealth of atmospherically decaying colonial buildings dating from the time of the slave trade and German occupation. The town is also home to a community-based **cultural tourism programme** which offers a variety of guided walks and river cruises, plus snorkelling trips on an outrigger dhow and visits to fossilized dinosaur remains – a perfect place for a few days of blissful languor to the chorus of "good morning teacher" from local kids, no matter what time it is.

Arrival and information

There are two roads to Pangani, one from Muheza (see p.361) on the A14 highway, the other from Tanga via Kirare. Neither is surfaced and both require 4WD in the rains, especially the Muheza road, which frequently becomes impassable thanks to its waterlogged black cotton soil. Five daily **buses** lurch along the bumpy road **from Tanga** at roughly two-hour intervals from 8am to 4pm, returning from Pangani between 6.30am and 3pm. Buy your ticket early to be assured of a seat, as standing for the three- to five-hour journey is definitely not recommended.

The road itself winds some distance inland through sparsely populated marshland interspersed with small farming communities and ragged coconut groves, ideal territory for herons and other waders. If you're staying at one of the beach hotels north of Pangani, ask the conductor to drop you at the appropriate turning; otherwise stay on the bus until it reaches the ferry slipway by the river in town. If you're heading to one of the resorts south of the river, the midday *Shakila* bus from Tanga arrives in Pangani around 3–4pm and continues to the fishing village of **Kipumbwi** to the south, though the village itself unfortunately has no accommodation. **From Muheza**, there's one bus daily during the dry season (2–3hr) and a couple of daladalas, but the latter are unpredictable and sometimes don't run at all. The Muheza road joins the Tanga road 3km north of Pangani; get off here for the beach hotels, which are to the north.

Information

You may well be met off the bus by guides, not all of them trustworthy. Ignore them as politely as you can and head 100m east to the **Tourist Information Centre** (Mon-Sat 7.30am–4pm; PO Box 89 ☎027/263 0008 or 263 0011), which provides official guides and reliable advice about accommodation and restaurants. They can also arrange performances of traditional dancing on request, but the main purpose of the centre is to co-ordinate the town's highly recommended **cultural tourism programme**. The programme is part of a nationwide network of community-based initiatives intended to benefit local communities. In Pangani's case, the profits go to an educational trust which supports the district's neglected schools (there are currently 28 for a population of 44,000) and to build a hostel for schoolgirls who would otherwise be unable to afford both school fees and boarding.

The programme arranges a number of excellent **guided walks**, including a two-hour historical tour of Pangani, and an extensive agricultural and nature walk (which can be split into two separate walks), combining visits to local farmers, the coconut-processing area at the mouth of the river and the German fort on the opposite bank, sisal estates and the 200- to 300-million-year-old fossilized remains of dinosaurs, concluding with dinner in a local home. The walking tours cost Tsh6000 for the first person and Tsh3000 for each additional person up to a maximum of five (larger groups are assigned additional guides); the price includes guide fees and Tsh1000 per person for educational projects. Details of two boat trips organized by the programme are given on pp.177–78.

Accommodation

The **town centre** options are all pretty basic. Mid-range places are spread out along the coast **north of town** and are relatively accessible, whereas for the more upmarket options **south of town** you'll ideally have your own transport. Four hotels allow **camping** in their grounds; rates include the use of toilets and showers. *Pangadeco* is the only central option, with an attractive plot right by the beach under plenty of shade (Tsh5000 per tent); *Tinga Tinga Resort*, 3km to the north, is better value at Tsh2000 for a pitch on the cliff edge. Some 2km further north, *Argovia Tented Lodge* has (expensive) space for Tsh5000 per

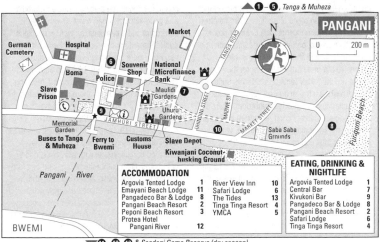

ACCOMMODATION

Argovia Tented Lodge	1
Emayani Beach Lodge	11
Pangadeco Bar & Lodge	8
Pangani Beach Resort	2
Peponi Beach Resort	3
Protea Hotel Pangani River	12
River View Inn	10
Safari Lodge	6
The Tides	13
Tinga Tinga Resort	4
YMCA	5

EATING, DRINKING & NIGHTLIFE

Argovia Tented Lodge	1
Central Bar	7
Kivukoni Bar	9
Pangadeco Bar & Lodge	8
Pangani Beach Resort	2
Safari Lodge	6
Tinga Tinga Resort	4

person, whilst least accessible but in the nicest location is the *Peponi Beach Resort* (Tsh4000 per person), 17km north of town, which also has tents for hire (Tsh4000).

Note that Pangani's **water supply** comes from two badly maintained boreholes: do not drink the tap water as there have been cholera outbreaks in the past, though, having said that, it's a rare day when the water supply actually functions at all.

Town centre

Pangadeco Bar & Lodge 1km east of the ferry at Funguni Beach (no phone). Pangani's best budget choice, on a large breezy beachside plot with plenty of tall trees, shaded seating and views over the ocean. Rooms are excellent value so long as you don't mind the saggy beds, and the Western-style shared toilets are reasonably clean, while the showers have Pangani's only guaranteed running water. There's also a good bar and food is available, but check the price before ordering. ❶
River View Inn Jamhuri St, 500m east of the ferry ☎027/263 0121. A reasonable standby, though it's well past its prime, with nine basic and not totally clean rooms sharing grubby showers and squat loos. The nets and sheets in the larger doubles are too small, and slightly annoying young men hang around the bar (soft drinks only). ❶

Safari Lodge ☎ Pangani 13. Pangani's only accommodation with private bathrooms – a fact reflected in the price – with Western-style toilets (but no lid or paper), shower and linoleum floors, though some rooms lack nets. The larger and more expensive rooms have a/c, huge beds and sofas, and there's also a bar and restaurant – see p.176. ❷–❸

North coast

The following hotels are all signposted off the Tanga road. Whilst they advertise themselves as "beach" hotels, all occupy cliff-top locations, and the beaches below get covered at high tide. The water is clearer the further north you go. With the exception of the *Peponi Beach Resort*, all are within easy cycling distance of town, while the *Tinga Tinga* and *Pangani Beach Resort* are close enough to walk to. All except the *YMCA* include breakfast, but other meals are invariably expensive.

Argovia Tented Lodge 5km north of Pangani on Mkoma Bay ☎0741/511600 or 0744/260277, ⊛www.argovia-lodge.com. This good-value and pleasingly idiosyncratic Swiss-run place is the best on the coast north of Pangani, set in a breezy location with a stylish blend of traditional architecture and quirky modern touches. The cheaper rooms are in bunker-like, prefabricated *bandas* with narrow twin beds and shared bathrooms. More expensive but more attractive (though they lack views) are the luxury tents on platforms under *makuti* roofs, each with a small verandah, box nets, table fans and attached bathroom. There's a swimming pool, a very good restaurant and a raft 1km out for swimming and sunbathing, while snorkelling trips can be arranged. ❹–❺
Pangani Beach Resort 3km north of Pangani on Mkoma Bay ☎ 027/263 0088. Ten clean if slightly musty and smallish rooms (no singles) in a motel-like environment, all featuring private bathrooms (with showers and Western toilets), small twin beds and a/c. No excursions – go to *Tinga Tinga* next door or the tourist office. ❸

Peponi Beach Resort 17km north of Pangani; coming from Tanga, get off 1km before Kigombe village and follow the signpost for 500m ☎0741/540139, ⊛www.peponiresort.com. A welcoming and well-run place offering comfortable and good-value two-bed *bandas* (with private bathroom) and a campsite, as well as delicious and reasonably priced food. The shady beach is beautiful, there are mangroves nearby, and *ngalawa* dhow snorkelling trips can be arranged. The main disadvantage is its isolation, meaning you're pretty much stuck there until you leave. ❹
Tinga Tinga Resort 3km north of Pangani on Mkoma Bay ☎027/263 0022 or c/o ACTAL Tanga ☎027/264 3419. Long-established place with ten clean and very large circular rooms in semi-detached bungalows, all with twin beds, good bathrooms, plenty of furniture, fans and electricity, though they lack ocean views and nets (they're sprayed instead). There's no pool, however, and both the food and snorkelling trips are expensive – the fishing trips in local canoes and bicycle rental are better value. Single rates negotiable. ❹

YMCA 5km north of Pangani at Mkoma Bay
☎027/263 0044. Next to the *Argovia*, this place is
getting pretty run down and sees little trade,
although the four large rooms are acceptable and
good value; the better ones have private bathrooms
(with showers and Western toilets), nets, twin beds,
electricity, and verandahs with ocean views. There
are no activities – arrange these at the *Argovia* or
the tourist office. Simple food is available if ordered
well in advance. No single rates. ❷

South coast

Facing Pangani across the river is the village of **BWEMI**, to which a ferry
(Tsh100) and small local boats cross frequently between dawn and dusk. The
Protea Hotel lies within walking distance of Bwemi; onward public transport to
the *Emayani Beach Lodge* is limited to the noon bus from Tanga to Kipumbwi,
which passes through the centre of town between 3pm and 4pm. Breakfast is
included in the rates of all the places below.

Emayani Beach Lodge 10km south of Pangani –
turn left at the Ushongo Hotels signpost ☎027/263
0045 or c/o Serengeti Select Safaris in Arusha
(☎027/254 4222). Set in a coconut grove on the
beach with tidal pools, there are plenty of activities
here including snorkelling, bird-watching in nearby
mangroves, river trips, windsurfing and catamaran
sailing. The twelve thatched bungalows face the
beach; all have private bathrooms and nets. There's
also a gift shop, bar and restaurant. ❼
Protea Hotel Pangani River On the bluff above
the river estuary ☎0741/324422,
℮0741/410099, ⓦwww.proteahotels.com.
"Where colonial tradition blends with modern hoo
pitality" runs the blurb for this South African-
owned resort, a claim given an ironic twist by the
armed guards and electric fences that surround
the place. If you can cope with this, there are
wonderful views over the river, town and ocean,
expansive lawns, a lovely pool and luxurious a/c
accommodation in cheerful modern style. The
beach consists of a number of small sandy coves
along the craggy shoreline. Optional game drives
to Saadani. ❽
The Tides 16km south of Pangani
☎0741/325812, ⓦwww.thetideslodge.com. An
intimate and frequently recommended place,
classy but unostentatious, in a lovely beachfront
location among palm trees. Accommodation is in
seven thatched chalets, and there's also a beachside bar and an excellent open-sided restaurant.
Activities include windsurfing and waterskiing,
kayaking, river cruises, snorkelling, and game
safaris to Saadani (book ahead). Free pick-up from
Pangani is included. Closed May. Full board: low
season ❼, high season ❽

The Town

A walk in Pangani is always a pleasure – there are picturesque tumbledown
buildings more or less everywhere, local children are invariably delighted to
greet you (as are adults, for that matter), and the town's quiet and laid-back
atmosphere makes for a pleasurably relaxing stroll at any time of day. All of
which could hardly offer a greater contrast to Pangani's murky nineteenth-
century history, when it served as a major slaving entrepôt – the town's very
name, derived from the word *panga*, meaning to cut or divide, refers to the way
in which auctioneers would separate slaves into groups before sale.

Although Pangani is small enough to be walked around in an hour or so, it's
sombre past is best understood as part of the cultural tourism programme's **historical walk** (see p.171).

The Boma and around

At the west end of town, the **Boma** – with its attractive carved doors – was
built in 1810 by Mohamed Salim Breki, who decided that burying a live slave
in each of its corners would ensure strong foundations (a belief that was also
current in Zanzibar – see p.630). The roof was added by the Germans, who
used the building as their first district office, which remains its function today.

The **Slave Prison**, just to the southwest, was built by the Germans to house
recalcitrant slaves (as well as tax evaders) – although the slave trade between the

THE NORTH COAST | Pangani and around

2

mainland and Zanzibar was officially abolished in 1873, slavery itself continued well into the British period, and was only completely eradicated in the 1920s. After this time, the building served as the district hospital, and is presently used as government offices and, once more, as a prison. There are plans to turn a couple of rooms into a local museum – ask at the Tourist Information Centre.

The first Europeans to visit Pangani were the Portuguese in 1498, when a ship belonging to Vasco da Gama's fleet, the *São Rafael*, called in. The Portuguese met a chief called Makumba at Pangani's original centre at **Kumba**, 200m west of the Boma, and were well received and given food and water. The site of Kumba is now covered by the overgrown **German Cemetery**, containing several dozen graves. A handful were completely excavated a few years ago by locals in the belief that the Germans had buried treasure there, and most of the others have been vandalized. Some apparently date from the Abushiri War, but have lost their inscriptions.

The riverfront

Some 200m east of the Slave Prison, the small **memorial garden** facing the ferry slipway (where most guided walks start) contains an irregular pillar commemorating the handful of Germans who died in the Abushiri War (surprisingly, no memorial exists to the thousands of African victims). Following the expulsion of the Germans by the British on July 23, 1916, the plaque was replaced with one celebrating the British victory. This was recently stolen and hidden (not without justification) by a local madman, though the tourist office has now recovered it and plans to remount it. Next to the pillar, there's a very battered column celebrating independence, whilst the modern era is marked by a huge electricity pylon.

The main building that survives from the German period is the **Customs House**, on Jamhuri Street, five minutes' walk to the east along the riverfront. This imposing edifice took four years to build, opening in 1916 just before the Germans were kicked out. It's now used as a warehouse for coconuts, most of them from the Mauya plantations across the river – a legacy of the slave trade when cheap labour was plentiful – which constitute Pangani's main source of income. The Customs House's minor claim to fame is that the famous poet **Shaaban Robert** (see p.746) worked here as a customs official in the 1930s: his broken and rusty typewriter still sits in the office.

Almost next door, the **Slave Depot**, now derelict and close to collapse, used to have a whipping platform where slaves were punished, and a tunnel which led to the river for ferrying blindfolded slaves to the dhows. A particularly gruesome story about the building concerns the request of a slave-owner's wife to see an unborn baby inside a woman's womb, for which a pregnant slave had her stomach sliced open while still alive.

The beach

Some 400m further east along Jamhuri Street is the Kiwanjani coconut husking ground, beyond which you can either follow the coast as it curls north into Funguni Beach and the ocean proper, or follow the road a few hundred metres along to the *Pangadeco Bar & Lodge*, which also has access to the **beach**. Although the water doesn't look too enticing (the brown colour comes from the silt gathered along the river's 400km journey), it's apparently safe to bathe here. You should, however, be extremely cautious of the river currents to your right, as the Pangani pushes its waters out a good few kilometres before losing itself in the ocean. Local advice is to swim to the left of the beach, away from the river. At low tide you can walk almost 1km out to sea over the sandflats,

Pangani and the Abushiri War

Pangani's location at the mouth of Tanzania's second longest river, with its easy access to the interior, made it an obvious base from which to launch the German conquest of Tanganyika. In August 1888, a few days before the Muslim feast of Idd al-Hajj, **Emil von Zelewski** of the German East Africa Company appeared at the court of Abdulgawi bin Abdallah, the Omani governor of Pangani. To everyone's consternation, Zelewski proceeded to insult the governor by telling him that in few days' time he, Zelewski, and not Abdulgawl would be the sultan's highest representative on the coast. True to his word, a few days later a small force of German soldiers entered Abdulgawi's quarters and removed the sultan's flag, taking it back to the German East Africa Company station house. Tensions rose, and the next day one hundred German marines landed and entered the mosque with their shoes and a hunting dog in their search of Abdulgawi, whom, not content with having humiliated, they now wanted to arrest.

The mosque's desecration (the very presence of non-Muslims, as well as dogs, would have been seen as such) not only turned people against the Germans, but undermined the credibility of the Omani rulers, who had failed to protect this sacred place from profanity. Deliberately or not, Zelewski further eroded Omani standing by breaking open the prison and releasing its inmates. By early September, local rage at both Omani impotence and the arrogant German presence had reached a point where the Germans had to be locked up by the Omanis in their company house for protection against the mob. They eventually slipped out to Zanzibar in the same week that they were expelled from Tanga. By end of September, the Germans had been killed or expelled from all but two coastal enclaves – Dar and Bagamoyo.

The expulsion of the Germans, however, did nothing to placate local feelings against the Omanis, who now faced open rebellion. Having no military means of their own for putting down the rebellion, the Omans tried to persuade the Germans to return and help restore Omani rule, even if only in diluted form. But by then the rebellion had turned into a fully fledged war against both Germans and Omanis, the **Abushiri War**, led in most towns by high-ranking Shirazis. The leader of the Pangani rebellion – by whose name the war is now known – was **Abushiri ibn Salim al-Harthi**, a wealthy Arab who united Arab traders and local tribes in a common effort to remove the Germans and the Omanis. By November, however, he had lost control of the rebellion and was forced to flee with a rump force to Bagamoyo, where he began a six-month siege of the town in a futile attempt to expel the Germans. In Pangani, the rebellion continued until July 1889, when it was brutally put down by German artillery. Abushiri was eventually captured by the Germans and hanged in Bagamoyo in December 1889. He was buried in an unmarked grave, some believe at Pangani, either in the grounds of the *Pangadeco Bar & Lodge*, or else in one of the mass graves which have recently been uncovered in the grounds of the Boma.

but keep an eye on the tide. It's apparently safe to walk up the beach to the *Pangani Beach Resort* (around 3km), but don't tempt fate by taking valuables or sports shoes.

Eating

Apart from the rather pricey **hotel restaurants** north of town (which you'll need your own transport to reach in the evenings), eating out in Pangani itself is pretty limited, and unless you're content with chips or rice with fried chicken or fish, you're advised to order early for local specialities like prawns, lobster, octopus, parrotfish or kingfish. The cheapest eats are at the **foodstalls** along Jamhuri Street near the ferry and from the *mama ntilies* in the Saba Saba Grounds (also called Kizota) near the mouth of the river, where rice or *ugali* with fried fish costs under Tsh600. If you're lucky you might also find grilled octopus (*pweza*), and there's also a bar here. For your own supplies, the **market** lies 100m along the street heading north from *Central Bar*.

Argovia Tented Lodge 5km north of Pangani. Slightly pricey but very good food, with light lunches at $5 and the full works at $12 for lunch or $15 for dinner (advance notice required for non-guests). There's the added bonus of genuine espresso and European and South African wines.
Central Bar Town centre. For good, cheap and filling portions of *nyama choma*, grilled chicken and *chipsi mayai*, this is definitely the place, and it stays open late. Open evenings only.
Pangadeco Bar & Lodge Funguni Beach. An unbeatable location, with plenty of tables under creaking trees in the gardens, but without at least two hours' notice you're only likely to find the usual chip omelettes, fried chicken and perhaps fried fish. Pre-ordered meat, fish or octopus cost around Tsh1700, with prawns up to Tsh2500 depending on the season.
Safari Lodge Town centre. The town's main mid-range restaurant, and reasonably priced too, with most meat dishes at around Tsh2500 and fish going for Tsh2500–3500, all with fresh salad.

Bars and nightlife

You'll find plenty of people, including Muslims, downing the beers and *konyagi*s in the town's three main **bars**, and the atmosphere is both friendly and tolerant. Indeed, this seems to be a source of constant exasperation for the elderly muezzin of the mosque near the *Safari Lodge*, who is famous locally for his unusually blunt early morning exhortations to the faithful, starting with a strident series of loudspeakered "Amka!" ("Wake up!"), followed by a litany of colourful curses which invariably include the line "If you sleep now, your bed will be your coffin and your sheets shall be your grave clothes!"

The bars are all open until around 11pm on weekdays, later at weekends. *Central Bar* is the main venue, especially at night, with cold drinks, seats on a

---

Moving on from Pangani

Leaving Pangani, the first **buses** and **daladalas** for both Tanga and Muheza leave between 6am and 6.30am. You should definitely catch one of these if you're heading to Muheza or south to Dar, to be sure of finding onward transport. Both the bus and daladala to Muheza arrive in time to catch the early buses from Tanga to Dar; spare seats are reserved on these for passengers getting on in Muheza, so buy your onward ticket as soon as you arrive. The last bus to Tanga departs at 1pm, but it's best not to rely on it.

If you're **driving**, there's an adventurous and infrequently travelled route south of Pangani into Saadani Game Reserve (see p.155 for details). If you have problems, though, you might have to spend a night or two waiting for assistance. Note that the southern continuation of the route from Saadani to Bagamoyo has been impassable since 1998 when the rope-pulled ferry over the Wami River was washed away.

Getting a passage from Pangani on a **dhow to Zanzibar** (either to Mkokotoni or, more usually, Nungwi village, both at the northern tip of Unguja) is relatively straightforward, with at least two motorized dhows sailing each week, taking four hours if things run smoothly. Talk with Iddi Chagutwi at the *Pangadeco Bar & Lodge*, who's knowledgeable about the paperwork and can arrange things with the captains. The cost varies between Tsh8000 and Tsh15,000 per person depending on the number of passengers. A word of caution: apart from the risk of capsizing (slight, but it *can* happen), obtaining an exit stamp from the immigration office on the first floor of the district commissioner's office in the old Boma is essential as it gives you two days of semi-official grace to get from Nungwi or Mkokotoni to Stone Town to complete the formalities. The permit doesn't cost anything, but the offer of a soda or a beer wouldn't go amiss.

street corner verandah, a dartboard, *nyama choma* evenings, satellite TV inside and cheerful music. Also good, primarily on account of its location, is the *Pangadeco Bar & Lodge* on Funguni Beach, with cold beers available from mid-afternoon, shaded seats in the gardens, food available if you order in advance, and of course the beach within a stone's throw. *Safari Lodge* is more run-of-the-mill, with reliably cold drinks and shaded outdoor seating which provides a nice quiet place for an afternoon drink. **Discos** are held on Wednesday and Friday to Sunday nights at the community centre's *Kivukoni Bar* between the bank and the ferry slipway.

Listings

Banks The National Microfinance Bank, 100m from the ferry, accepts both cash and travellers' cheques.

Bicycle rental This can be arranged via the tourist office; at the bicycle shop on Uhindini (Indian) St; or at *Tinga Tinga Resort* to the north of town. The cost is Tsh1000 per day or Tsh100–200 per hour.

Hospital The reasonably well-equipped district hospital is 200m west of the *Safari Lodge*.

Post office The post office is on the same block as the tourist office, about 100m east of the ferry.

Shopping For souvenirs, try the unnamed shop opposite the *Safari Lodge* – it sells baskets, earthenware bowls and coconut shredders called *kibau cha mbuzi* ("goat board"), which resemble small lecterns. It's also worth a rummage through the tailors' shops on Uhindini (Indian) St, many of whose buildings date from the 1870s, when Calcutta linen was the economic mainstay of the immigrant Indian community.

Telephones The TTCL office is 200m west of the ferry on the riverfront.

Around Pangani

The cultural tourism programme's **Coconut Sunset Cruise** (Tsh20,000 up to eight people; 1–2hr) starts at Kiwanjani by the river mouth, where a team of around fifty workers dehusk giant mounds of coconuts with sharp iron crowbars, leaving behind a surreal debris of tens of thousands of coconut husks which are carried out to sea whenever the river floods. The dehusked coconuts are then stored in the Customs House before being transported by road to Dar es Salaam and other markets. The vast plantations in the area constitute about half of Tanzania's production.

Boarding the boat on the beach, the cruise heads up the Pangani River and past mangroves and coconut plantations. The mangroves are rich in birdlife, especially pied kingfishers, which are most active just before dusk. If you're lucky you might also see colobus monkeys and crocodiles, though the latter are less common since the El Niño floods of 1991 and 1997–98 widened the estuary and caused the waters to become more saline. Your best chance of spotting them is around midday, which is a bit awkward as most river cruises take place over the two hours before sunset, starting around 4pm, when it's cooler and you've more chance of spotting other wildlife. The tour concludes with juice from a freshly picked coconut (*madafu*) as the sun sets over the river.

Maziwe Island Marine Reserve

Maziwe Island, 8km southeast of Pangani, is a prime example of the effects of both mangrove clearance and rising sea levels. Until the 1960s the island was totally wooded with casuarina trees and fringed with mangroves, while its beaches served as East Africa's single most important nesting ground for three species of endangered marine turtles: the Olive Ridley turtle, green turtle and hawksbill turtle. By 1976, however, the last casuarina had been felled, and the final blow to the island's ecology came during the 1978–79 war with Idi Amin's Uganda, when the remaining mangroves were cleared away for security reasons, given the island's proximity to Pangani, Zanzibar and Pemba. Sadly, the mangroves have not rerooted, and the ensuing erosion means that the island is now submerged at high tide. The beaches are still being eroded, especially during the southeastern monsoon, though the island's disappearance is attributed by fishermen to rising sea levels.

The surrounding live **coral reef** has also been badly damaged by dynamite fishing and careless anchoring, though there are still some beautiful coral heads providing food and shelter for dozens of beautiful tropical fish species (including moray eels, the poison-barbed lion fish, butterfly fish, clownfish, starfish and octopus), plus the attraction of a school of dolphins which can be seen feeding regularly a few hundred metres out. Bring plenty of sun cream and a T-shirt for swimming or you'll get cooked to a cinder.

Heading out from Pangani, notice the **German fortress** at the mouth of the estuary on the south bank of the river, half-hidden by heavy tree cover and bush. A few kilometres out, you cross the unusually well-defined border between the brown estuarine waters and the clear blue of the ocean, a boundary which is also marked by a line of floating coconut husks and other debris from Pangani.

The trip out to the island by *ngalawa* dhow outrigger (90min sailing each way) costs Tsh10,000–40,000 for the boat, depending on its size, plus Tsh1500 per person for a mask and snorkel. A park fee of $6 per person may also be asked for. The trip can be arranged through the cultural tourism programme or the *Pangadeco Bar & Lodge*.

Travel details

Buses and daladalas

The bus companies Hood, Tashriff, Takrim and Tawfiq have particularly bad reputations for reckless driving and should be avoided. The long rains, when some services cease, are usually from March to May. Services may also be cancelled at times during the short rains (usually Nov, and sometimes Oct or Dec), though rarely for more than a day or two.

Bagamoyo to: Dar (hourly; 90min); Msata (1–2 daily except in the rains; 2–3hr).

Pangani to: Muheza (2 daily except in the rains; 2–3hr); Tanga (5 daily; 3–5hr).

Tanga to: Arusha (3–4 daily; 6hr); Dar (hourly until 2pm; 5–6hr); Korogwe (hourly; 90min); Lushoto (every 2hr until mid-afternoon; 3hr); Mombasa (4 daily; 4–7hr); Mombo: (hourly; 2hr); Morogoro (every 2hr until noon; 5–6hr); Moshi (3–4 daily; 5hr); Muheza (every 30min; 45min); Pangani (5 daily; 3–5hr).

Dhows

For information on catching dhows to Pemba or Zanzibar, see the boxes under Bagamoyo (p.150), Pangani (p.165) and Tanga (p.176).

The south coast

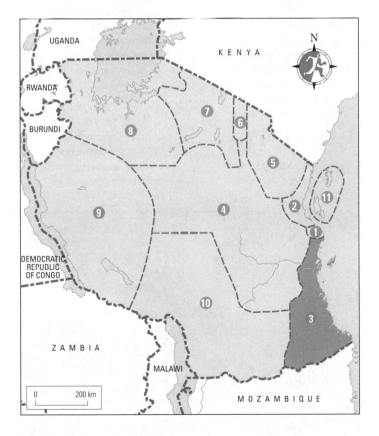

CHAPTER 3

Highlights

✳ **Kilwa Kisiwani** In medieval times the wealthiest city on the Swahili coast, this ruined medieval island state is one of Africa's most impressive and histori- cally significant sites. See p.200

✳ **Kilwa Kivinje** Atmospheric and very tumbledown nineteenth- century slaving harbour whose rise signalled the demise of Kilwa Kisiwani. See p.208

✳ **Mafia Archipelago** A little- visited marine park pro- tects superb coral reefs, justly famed for superb scuba diving. See p.186

✳ **Mikindani** Another old slaving port with plenty of ruins, pleasantly laid- back atmosphere and one of Tanzania's nicest hotels. See p.226

✳ **Mnazi Bay-Ruvuma Estuary Marine Park** Newly established, along the border with Mozambique, this offers superb beaches, snorkelling and scuba- diving. See p.224

✳ **Makonde carvings** The Makonde tribe of south- ern Tanzania are famed for their abstract wood- carvings, including remarkable "trees of life". See p.232

The south coast

T he **south coast** is one of Tanzania's most fascinating and unspoilt regions, containing a wealth of infrequently visited natural and historical attractions, as well as beaches to dream about, although the lack of infrastructure and facilities makes exploring it a challenge. Road access from Dar is determined by the state of the **Rufiji River**, which floods its delta every year, cutting off the southern regions from the rest of Tanzania. The delta itself contains East Africa's largest mangrove forest, and would be a paradise for bird-watchers were travelling around not so difficult. Some 25km offshore from the delta, **Mafia Island** is home to some of the southern coast's best beaches, as well as the stunning coral reefs of the **Mafia Island Marine Park**, which is justly famed for its superb diving.

Beyond the delta, the first settlements of note are the three Kilwas. The first of these is the atmospherically tumbledown town of **Kilwa Kivinje**, steeped in the history of nineteenth-century slaving and colonialism. To the south, **Kilwa Masoko** is the main base for visitors to the area, with several decent guest houses, but the main reason to come here is the nearby island of **Kilwa Kisiwani**, whose ruined medieval city ranks among Africa's most impressive historical sites. Further south are the pleasant harbour towns of **Lindi** and **Mtwara**, although a more atmospheric place to stay is **Mikindani**, just north of Mtwara, a fishing village which retains a number of historic buildings, and whose German Boma was recently converted into one of Tanzania's most attractive hotels. It's also the best base from which to explore the newly established **Mnazi Bay-Ruvuma Estuary Marine Park**, along the border with Mozambique.

Inland from Lindi and Mtwara lies the **Makonde Plateau**, home of the famous woodcarving tribe. The main town here is **Newala**, its relatively cool climate a boon to those wearied by the coast's heat and humidity. All these towns have regular transport to the cashew-nut trading centre of **Masasi**, but the road beyond towards Lake Nyasa and Malawi is exceedingly hard going, and – like the road from Dar – becomes impassable during the rains. Settlements along this stretch are few and far between, and the delights of travelling in the back of a rickety lorry replace the only slightly more comfortable experience of the bus ride down from Dar.

The generally abysmal roads explain why the coast has so far been ignored by developers, and if creature comforts are important to you, best look elsewhere. The roads will leave you battered and bruised, luxuries like electricity and running water are rare outside the major towns, and few places have more than a handful of rudimentary hotels. The main problem for visitors, however, is **transport**. The flooding of the Rufiji River cuts off the road south during

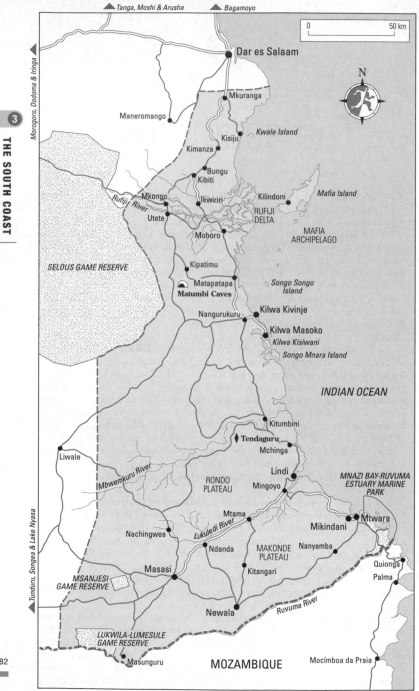

the long rains (March/April to May/June) and for several days at a time towards the end of the short ones (Nov or Dec), making flying or the weekly ferry from Dar to Mtwara your only options. Even when the roads are open, the bus journey from Dar to Mtwara takes at least 24 hours, so breaking the journey at Kilwa is advisable. The new bridge across the Rufiji River has fuelled hope that the road may finally be upgraded, but this won't happen until at least 2005, when the new tarmac section south of the bridge is scheduled for completion. For the time being, however, any trip along the south coast retains a heady, dusty and bone-rattling aura of adventure.

The Rufiji River delta and Mafia archipelago

The estuarine delta of Tanzania's largest river, the **Rufiji**, is one of the country's most important and sensitive ecological areas, containing East Africa's largest mangrove forest as well as seasonally flooded woods, saline swamps, tidal marshes and sandbanks. This largely unspoiled wilderness forms an integral part of a much larger ecosystem running from the western woodlands of the Selous Game Reserve (covered in Chapter 4) to the coral reefs around Mafia Island, 25km offshore. The reefs, which are supported by fresh water and nutrients filtered through the Rufiji's mangroves, enclose what is probably East Africa's most diverse marine environment, offering near-perfect conditions for diving and snorkelling (see box on pp192–193).

Unfortunately, neither area is easy to explore. **Road access** to the floodland south of the Rufiji is subject to the rains, whilst the Mafia archipelago is only reachable by **plane** unless you have the patience – and resilience – to brave the dhow crossing from Kisiju, 90km south of Dar. Still, both areas more than repay the practical inconveniences and cost of getting there and around.

The Rufiji River delta

The **Rufiji River delta** is one of East Africa's most beautiful and ecologically significant areas, though it's also every bit as hot, swampy and mosquito-infested as you might imagine. The delta contains seasonally flooded woods alive with the sound of frogs, birds and cicadas, along with East Africa's largest **mangrove forest**, covering some 5300 square kilometres, which acts as a gigantic sump, supplying the fragile reefs offshore with nutrients whilst protecting them against siltation. The delta and its floodplain support a population of over 150,000 people, the majority subsisting on cultivation, fishing and mangrove-pole extraction. During the long rains, the river can increase in width by up to fifteen kilometres: the silt carried by the floods fertilizes the land on either side of the river and feeds innumerable small lakes and pools in which a number of unique **fish** species have been found, while the waters around the mangroves themselves are an important breeding ground for prawns and shrimps. Commonly seen **birds** include the plain-backed sunbird, longbills and lovebirds, and the majestic African fish eagle. Rarer species include the African pitta, found north of the river, and Livingstone's flycatcher, to the south.

Unsurprisingly, the delta's natural wealth has attracted the gaze of big industry, and the area is coming under increasing pressure from logging and fishing companies, something that the new $25 million **Rufiji River Bridge**, East Africa's longest, is likely to facilitate. The discovery of oil reserves north of the river also raises cause for concern. The greatest threat to the delta's environment came in the 1990s, however, when an Irish businessman proposed a $200 million **prawn farm**, the world's largest, which would have destroyed 1100 square-kilometre of mangrove forest, degraded and polluted the land and water supply on which 33,000 villagers depend and displaced 6000 people. Despite the condemnation of the National Environmental Management Council, the government approved the project, prompting an international outcry. Local people took the company to the High Court and, after a four-

The Königsberg's last stand

The Rufiji delta was the site of the German cruiser **Königsberg**'s last stand during World War I, the end of a pursuit by the British navy which lasted eleven months, tying down twenty ships and ten aircraft and using nearly 40,000 tons of coal. The importance of the *Königsberg* lay in the fact that it was Germany's only warship in the Indian Ocean at the outbreak of the war, and as such was able to threaten British supply routes from Kenya, Zanzibar, Aden and India. A day after war was declared, the *Königsberg*, under the command of Captain Max Looff, captured a British freighter, the *City of Winchester*, off the coast of Oman, which was scuttled five days later. Despite taking on the *Winchester*'s coal supply, the *Königsberg*'s reserves were low, and at the beginning of September Looff was forced to seek shelter in the Rufiji delta to await further supplies from Dar es Salaam. The choice of the delta was astute: the British considered its channels to be unnavigable to larger vessels, not knowing that the Germans had charted the delta just before the war. After two weeks, sufficient coal supplies had been brought from Dar es Salaam and the cruiser slipped out on another mission, sinking *HMS Pegasus* at Zanzibar on September 20 with the loss of 38 lives, before engine failure once more forced the *Königsberg* into the delta.

It took the British a further five weeks to discover the cruiser's hiding place, 8km upriver, after which a blockade was mounted to prevent her escape. Several attempts were made to bombard the ship using aircraft, but they were so unreliable that their main preoccupation appeared to be staying aloft. The much mythologized gentlemanly aspect of World War I was aptly demonstrated at the end of the year: "We wish you a Happy Christmas and a Happy New Year; we hope to see you soon," the *HMS Fox* signalled to the *Königsberg*. "Thanks, same to you," replied Looff, "if you wish to see me, I am always at home."

The stand-off lasted until July 1915, when a couple of brief battles aided by reconnaissance planes flying from the recently captured Mafia Island finally damaged the *Königsberg* beyond repair. The cruiser was scuttled on 11 July and sank into the mud, remaining visible until 1962, when the wreck was salvaged and the remains cut up for scrap. The largest surviving relics are a pair of four-inch guns which were unmounted before the ship was sunk and used in Von Lettow Vorbeck's subsequent land campaign. One now stands outside Fort Jesus in Mombasa, the other in Pretoria.

3

THE SOUTH COAST | The Rufiji River delta

year battle, the project was finally abandoned in 2001, to the jubilation of the villagers and environmentalists alike.

It's possible **to visit the delta by boat** from Mafia Island, but this needs to be arranged in advance, either with the *Chole Mjini* lodge (p.189) or with local boatmen in Kilindoni, who occasionally sail into the delta to collect mangrove poles. It isn't always plain sailing, in any sense of the word, as the sea can become rough, especially when the monsoon changes direction between July and August. The best chance for calm seas is during the northerly *kaskazi* monsoon (Nov–March). On the mainland you might be able to hire a boat in Mohoro (see below), but all these possibilities are very hit and miss.

South from Dar to Mohoro

Until the roads south of the new bridge are surfaced, the north bank of the Rufiji is as far as you can travel by road from Dar during the rains. For much of the journey the tarmac is in such a pitiful state that drivers prefer making their own tracks in the bush on either side rather than risk the road itself. There's a string of settlements along the way which have small markets, bars, simple restaurants and hawkers aplenty selling mangoes, coconuts, smoked fish and improbably giant jackfruit. Basic **guest houses** (❶) can be found at **Kimanza**, 80km south of Dar (*Kilwa Guest House*) and **Bungu**, 40km further on (*Nyamwimbe Guest House*), which also has a reliable petrol supply.

Straddling the junction of the roads from Dar to Lindi and Utete, the bustling market village of **KIBITI** is the busiest settlement between Dar and Kilwa; you can **change money** at the National Microfinance Bank, and there's also a petrol station. The *Zebra Bar & Restaurant* here does brilliant *ugali* and fish and there are **rooms**, some with private bathrooms, at the *Victoria Guest House* (no phone; ❶), signposted 300m off the Lindi road – it's not the most welcoming place in the world, but is secure.

Ikwiriri and Ndundu Ferry

Beyond Kibiti, a good tarmac road drops down into the Rufiji floodplain, heading 28km to the large town of **IKWIRIRI**. A road is currently being built from Ikwiriri to the new bridge, but until the continuation south of the bridge is complete, the only way over from here is along the old dirt road to the ferry (*kivuko*) over the Rufiji River at **Ndundu**, 10km beyond Ikwiriri, which takes two buses or four vehicles at a time (sailings 6.30am–6.30pm; every 30–60min; Tsh2000 for a car including occupants, Tsh100 for pedestrians). The ferry is reliable in the dry season, but flooding and strong currents can cause hold-ups of several days in the rains, and also make things more dangerous (the ferry isn't overly stable). A number of *mama ntilies* by the slipway sell fried chicken and fish, chip omelettes and smoked catfish. Should you have to **stay**, there's the basic *Jimmy's Guest House* in Ikwiriri (❶).

The Ndundu Ferry to Mohoro

Over on the south side of the river, the tricky 55-kilometre haul through thick and swampy flood forest is the main reason why the road to Kilwa and Mtwara becomes impassable in the rains. Here and there you pass tiny settlements placed in small isolated clearings where the ground rises just a metre or two above the swamps, but for the most part the forest canopy is almost complete, and provides a haven for plentiful birdlife, including pretty sunbirds.

The small Muslim village of **MOHORO**, 30km south of the ferry, is the first place of any size beyond the river. Set on a creek which feeds the southernmost branch of the delta (which means it gets infested with mosquitoes towards the end of the rains), the village has plenty of *chai* shops (but no petrol), and very basic, dirt-cheap **rooms** at the *6-Hotel* (❶), with nets, shared long-drops, and a large water barrel to shower with. Bear in mind that the 61km south of Mohoro are very rough and muddy, so if you're driving and arrive in the evening you should stay the night. The same applies if you're heading north, as the ferry stops running at 6.30pm. The first bus back to Dar leaves Mohoro at 6.30am. Mohoro is a great place from which to head off into the delta by boat, although you officially need a permit from the district commissioner in Utete; you could try asking at the village clinic, where they have a number of boats. For **forest walks**, the tiny roadside Forest Office on the road out towards Kilwa may oblige with an unofficial guide; a generous tip would be in order.

The Mafia archipelago

Lying 25km off the Rufiji delta, the **Mafia archipelago** – consisting of **Mafia Island** (where you arrive), the smaller islands of **Chole**, **Juani** and **Jibondo**, and a host of minor isles and atolls – is surrounded by one of the world's richest marine habitats, much of it protected as the **Mafia Island Marine Park**. The coral reefs here are among the world's most enthralling diving areas, while the archipelago's **beaches** provide an additional draw, as do the mangroves that cover much of the coast.

Mafia's attractions are not all marine, however: **wildlife** includes duiker antelopes, monkeys, wild pigs, bushbabies and black-and-rufous elephant shrews, all of which might be seen in the few remnants of coastal forest which dot the islands, and there are even some hippos, whose ancestors were presumably swept out to sea by the Rufiji's floods. **Birdlife** is plentiful too, with some 130 species, including falcons, fish eagles and waders. Historical interest is provided by a number of **ruins**, notably at Kua on Juani Island and Chole Mjini on Chole Island. Awkward **access** means that Mafia sees little tourism outside the main diving and sports-fishing seasons (Nov–March), so at other times you're likely to be pretty much the only visitor.

Some history

Excavations of Iron Age forges suggest that Mafia's earliest inhabitants were Bantu farmers who crossed over from the mainland no later than 200 AD, and from whom the present-day Mbwera tribe are believed to be descended. Around this time, the still-to-be-located mainland port and metropolis of **Rhapta** (possibly near Pangani, see box on p.170) was governed by a Yemenite people called the Ma'afir, who probably also ruled over Mafia, giving a possible source for the archipelago's name. An alternative is *maafya*, meaning "healthy place" in Kiswahili, but the most likely derivation is from the Arabic *morfiyeh* (archipelago), which appears misspellt as *monfiyeh* on sixteenth-century Portuguese charts.

The archipelago's geographical position made it a natural stopover for Arab and Persian dhows plying the ancient trade routes between Arabia and East Africa. Finds of pottery, coins and glassware indicate that Mafia was a regular part of the monsoon-driven Indian Ocean trading network which, in its heyday, stretched as far as Malaysia, Indonesia and even Ming-dynasty China. Following the **conquest** of Mafia by the Portuguese captain Duarte Lemos in

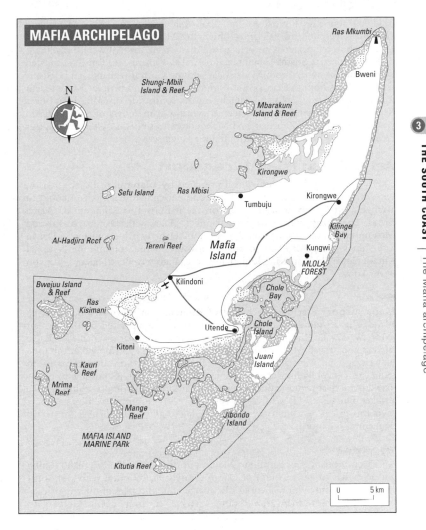

MAFIA ARCHIPELAGO

1508, Mafia's fortunes entered a long period of decline, culminating in the destruction of Kua, the island's main town, by the cannibalistic Sakalava of Madagascar in 1829. The archipelago's fortunes revived briefly after 1840 under the control of the Zanzibari **Busaidi dynasty**, whose slaving and ivory trading interests left a indelible impression, not least in the establishment of slave-worked coconut plantations on Mafia Island, most of which survive today. But the days of the slave trade were numbered and the balance of power was shifting towards Europe; in 1890, the year Britain imposed a protectorate over Zanzibar, Sultan Seyyid Ali was forced to sell Mafia to Germany for four million marks.

Britain seized Mafia from Germany in 1915 for use as a base against the cruiser *Königsberg* (see p.184), after which the archipelago became a backwater.

Trade is nowadays limited to the small-scale export of fish, seaweed and coconuts. Despite this fall into obscurity, Mafia's present-day population reflects the archipelago's historic past. Apart from the Mbwera, inhabitants include Shirazis, Shatiri Hadhramaut Arabs, Omanis, Indians, assimilated descendants of traders from Madagascar and the Comoros Islands, and descendants of slaves from the Yao, Nyasa, Ngindo and Pokomo peoples. More recent immigrants include Pakistani Baluchi on the south side of Mafia Island near Kitoni, who arrived in the nineteenth century as members of an expedition sent by the sultan of Zanzibar, and Makonde, who settled in Utende village as recently as 1991, having fled Mozambique's civil war.

Arrival and island transport

The Mafia archipelago is most easily reached **by plane** from Dar es Salaam, but with plenty of patience – and a strong enough stomach – you could to arrange a lift **by dhow** from Kisiju on the mainland to Kilindoni on Mafia Island. The **ferry**, which used to connect Mafia with Dar es Salaam and Mtwara, ceased operation years ago but it might be worth enquiring in Dar in case things change. It's best to change **money** before coming: the National Microfinance Bank in Kilindoni claims to change travellers' cheques, but you never know.

By air

Mafia airport is at the beach end of Kilindoni on the west side of Mafia Island. The 35-minute scheduled flight from Dar is operated by Precisionair (Mon, Wed & Fri–Sun; $55), and currently returns to Dar via Zanzibar. Eagle Air has also served Mafia in the past, but flights had been stopped at the time of writing (and were, in any case, unreliable). Both companies are prone to reduce or cancel flights during the long rains. Flying out, it's possible to negotiate a good deal with the pilot or agent at the airport if you don't already have a ticket. The *Kinasi Lodge*'s five-seater Cessna also flies in several times a week; their top price for a one-way ticket is Tsh40,000; you might get a discount depending on your bargaining skills.

By dhow

An adventurous way of getting to Mafia is by dhow from the mainland fishing village of **Kisiju**, 90km south of Dar. You might have to deal with petty officialdom in Kisiju, who will try to discourage you with tales of missing or capsized boats, most of them true (if rare) – see p.37 for more details. **Getting to Kisiju** from Dar involves catching a bus towards Kibiti, Utete, Lindi, Mtwara or Masasi. Get off at Mkuranga, 46km south of Dar, where crowded and uncomfortable pick-ups run the remaining 45km to Kisiju along a sandy and bumpy road (2hr 30min). Several dhows sail to and from Kilindoni each day or night, depending on the tides, sometimes stopping en route at Kwale and Kome Islands, 1km and 10km from Kisiju respectively. **Sailing times** depend on weather conditions and the tide, as the sandbar at the river mouth allows passage only at high tide, so you may well have to spend the night in Kisiju. There are a handful of rudimentary guest houses, but the village has a reputation for pickpockets and petty thieves, so take care. One last piece of advice: empty your bowels in Kisiju unless you fancy testing the cantilevered contraptions over the side of the vessels.

Motorized dhows are quickest (8-12hr) so long as the engines don't give out, but they're usually grimy. Sailing dhows take up to 24 hours, longer if the winds aren't right or the sea's rough: take more than enough food and water for the journey. **Fares** depend on what you arrange with the captain: locals pay upwards of Tsh2500–3500 for space on a sailing dhow or Tsh5000 on a motorized one.

Island transport

Public transport on Mafia Island is limited to a handful of **daladalas**, the main one of interest to tourists being the daily run between Kilindoni and Utende (Mon–Sat only), close to the Chole Bay beach hotels. It leaves Utende around 7am, and returns from Kilindoni at around 1pm. The Chole Bay hotels (see below) can arrange transport to meet flights. If you're not being picked up, you could try catching a lift with one of these vehicles (Tsh12,000–15,000 to Chole Bay). Alternatively, *Lizu's Hotel* in Kilindoni can help you find a vehicle (same price), and can also fix you up with a **bicycle** should you be immune to the wearying heat and humidity. Transport to Chole, Juani and Jibondo islands is from Chole Bay – see p.191.

Accommodation and information

West is best if you're on a budget, with **Kilindoni** offering the archipelago's only cheap accommodation, though options are confined to a handful of basic guest houses. Mafia's **beach hotels** are located on the eastern side of the island, within the marine park boundaries, and are decidedly upmarket: three of them face **Chole Bay**, 14km east of Kilindoni and about 2km beyond Utende village; the fourth is on **Chole Island**, 1km offshore from Chole Bay. Chole Bay's sandy beaches and warm, reef-protected waters are ideal for swimming and water sports, and the islands of Chole, Juani and Jibondo are all within easy reach. Room rates include transport from the airport: check in advance exactly what else is included in terms of excursions and water sports. Rates increase by fifty percent during Christmas and New Year, and all the places below except the *Mafia Island Lodge* are closed in April and May during the long rains.

A $10 **entry fee** (currently with no time limit, but slated to become per 24-hour period) is collected by the beach hotels on the behalf of the marine park, within which they're situated. The hotels can fill you in about most things regarding the park, but for more specialized information – and to pay the entry fee if you're not staying at the hotels – contact the **marine park headquarters** at Utende, just behind the *Mafia Island Lodge* (Mon–Fri 7.30am–3.30pm; ℡023/240 2690 extension 116, ✉mimpmafia@raha.com).

Camping is possible on the beaches – the glorious stretch of sand either side of Kilindoni is an obvious place to aim for – but seek local advice about safety. You'll need permission from the marine park headquarters in Utende if you want to camp inside the park, which includes Chole Bay.

Kilindoni

Bismillah Hotel 50m from the *New Lizu* in an unmarked blue building. Much more basic even than the *New Lizu*, with pretty horrid shared long-drops and bucket showers, but it's safe, and all rooms have ceiling fans – make sure you get one with a mosquito net, though. The *Kijuju Guest House*, 300m from the *New Lizu* along the Utende road, is very similar. ❶

New Lizu Hotel In the town centre ℡023/240 2683. The only rooms in Kilindoni with private

bathroom, though they're overpriced, given that most lack mosquito nets (they do at least have fans). ❷

Chole Bay and Chole Island

Chole Mjini At the northern tip of Chole Island, ⓦwww.cholemjini.com (reserve through Safari Scene in Dar; see p.125). One of Tanzania's most characterful hotels, with five treehouses on stilts (plus one at ground level). Each has two floors with a double bed on each level, and a bucket shower and composting toilet in a straw shelter at the base. Facilities include a comfy lounge, bar and restaurant, and scuba-diving. There's no electricity and no beach, though beaches can easily be combined with the daily snorkelling or boat trips included in the rates. Local communities receive $10 per guest per night for development projects. Full board ❾

Kinasi Lodge Chole Bay ☏024/223 8220 or 284 4238, ⊛www.mafiaisland.com. Relaxed and classy with twelve large and airy *makuti*-roofed bungalows, each sleeping two, set on a hill facing the bay. Views are best from the three sea-facing bungalows with king-size beds. The open-plan lounge area is a delight, with a bar, satellite TV and a superb reference library. Other facilities include Mafia's only swimming pool (guests only), hammocks slung between palm trees, a silty mangrove-flanked beach and lots of activities (most at additional cost) including snorkelling, diving, excursions and guided walks. Full board ❾

Mafia Island Lodge Chole Bay ☏ & ℻022/211 6609. Uninspiring socialist-era government hotel that's clearly past its best, the saving graces being the fact that it's three times cheaper than the competition and that it has the best sea views. The forty rooms, most of them musty and in need of a refit, are built of coral ragstone; the better ones in the new wing (#1–10) have good views over the bay, but only the "VIP" suites have double beds. All have a/c, hot water, fans and nets. Facilities are limited to a bar and seafood restaurant, a gift shop, and a number of overpriced excursions. The lodge is due to be privatized, so prices (and standards) may increase substantially. Half and full board ❻

Pole Pole Bungalow Resort Chole Bay ⊛www.polepole.com (reserve through Safari Scene in Dar; see p.125). This intimate Italian-run hotel is the most stylish and expensive of Chole Bay's hotels, with attentive service and excellent food. There are five (soon to be ten) exquisitely designed ocean-facing bungalows on stilts, each sleeping two or three people. Although a patch of mangroves was cleared to make the beach (as at Kinasi), the lodge is run on sound principles and helps with local development projects. Activities revolve around an experienced PADI diving centre (which also offers snorkelling), and rates include half-day boat trips within the bay; excursions elsewhere cost extra. Full board ❾ ($400)

Eating and drinking

Mafia's best **restaurants** are at the Chole Bay hotels, all of whom welcome day guests for meals. Seafood is the predictable – and usually delicious – speciality; meals cost upwards of $12–15. Reservations are needed for *Kinasi Lodge*: you can radio them for free from the airport. In Kilindoni, food is available at the *New Lizu Hotel*, but unless you order well in advance for things like octopus, prawns or lobster, it's limited to the standard fried fish and rice you can find almost anywhere else in Tanzania – they're also prone to overcharge *wazungu*. Much better is *Al-Watan*, just around the corner on the Utende road and run by a couple of friendly women who – if you order early enough – can prepare all manner of dishes. Also good are the foodstalls along the Utende road, by the market and at the harbour, where you can find various kinds of fish, octopus (*pweza*) and grilled goat meat. The only **bar** in town is at *New Lizu Hotel*, a spartan and deeply uninspiring place; much more atmospheric are the hotel bars at Chole Bay, though you'll pay around Tsh2000 for a beer.

Kinasi Nature Trail

Winding along the beach that stretches south from *Kinasi Lodge* on Chole Bay, the **Kinasi Nature Trail** (2hr) is a good way to explore the mangrove ecosystem and associated coastal forest, and also provides good opportunities for bird-watching – with patience you're likely to spot fish eagles and lilac-breasted rollers, whilst the shoreline is good for black kites, crab plovers and low-tide waders. Some of the plants are labelled and correspond to a free pamphlet available from *Kinasi Lodge*, who can provide knowledgeable guides.

Mafia Island

The low-lying **Mafia Island** is by far the largest of the archipelago's islands, measuring some 55km from northeast to southwest. Much of the island is covered by coconut plantations and other crops, of which pineapples and cassava are easiest to distinguish. The main town and major port is **KILINDONI**, on the southwest coast, a scruffy and dozy little place for most of the time (especially during the rains), though it does boast a stunning **beach**, an attractively poky market and an equally tiny but animated harbour; it's also useful for mundane things like its bank, post office, telephones and pharmacy. If you can coincide with a **full moon**, however, the place really comes into life, when an age-old ritual **procession** takes place through the town's streets. The evening starts just after the full moon is seen rising in the east, with drumming announcing the start of the festivities. Over the next few hours, pretty much the whole town joins the milling crowd, headed by dozens of women singing to the rhythms of a brass band and drummers following behind, as local kids dash around in an excited frenzy. The music itself bears a resemblance to traditional Swahili *taarab*, not only in terms of its rhythm and melody, but in the fact that it is women who control the words and therefore the mood of the occasion.

Although the new moon is important in Islam, marking the months of the Hegira calendar, the importance of the full moon appears to have its roots in pre-Islamic times, and so is denigrated as "voodoo" by some. Whatever, the respect that locals have for more orthodox Islam (they're all Muslim, for that matter) is evident in that the procession falls silent as it moves past the Friday Mosque on the Utende road, only to pick up with even more exuberance on the other side.

Ras Kisimani

Ras Kisimani – the "Headland of the Wells" – is Mafia Island's westernmost point, and as such proved useful in the past as a major port to the mainland. Much of the headland, together with the town of Kisimani, was washed away by a cyclone in 1872. Locals say that Kisimani, together with its rival Kua, were destroyed because of their wickedness. Potsherds and other remnants occasionally still turn up on the sandy beach, the oldest of which date to the twelfth century. *Pole Pole Bungalow Resort* runs trips to Kisimani for \$40 per person (minimum four).

Chole Island

Just 1.5km east of Mafia Island's Utende Point, the tiny and lushly vegetated **Chole Island** is the archipelago's oldest continuously inhabited settlement, having taken over Kua's mantle as Mafia's capital when the latter was sacked in 1829. Under Busaidi rule, Chole gained notoriety as one of East Africa's main slave-trading centres, so much so that for a time the main island of Mafia was known as Chole Shamba – Chole's Farm – as its slave-worked coconut plantations were planted and owned by slavers from Chole. But the boom was not to last. The slave trade was nearing its end and Chole soon fell into an irreversible decline – all that now remains of the wealthy nineteenth-century town is a picturesque collection of ruins overgrown with the twisted roots of strangling fig trees and thick undergrowth inhabited by timid monitor lizards.

Access to Chole Island is by **boat**. Small local outriggers, basking in the grandiose title of ferries, shuttle between the beach in front of the *Mafia Island Lodge* and the island; the ten-minute trip costs Tsh50 for locals but Tsh200–500

Snorkelling and diving in Mafia Island Marine Park

Established in 1995, **Mafia Island Marine Park** encloses 822 square kilometres of coastline, reefs and mangroves. The park includes **Chole Bay**, the islands of **Chole**, **Jibondo** and **Juani**, and a narrow strip running up much of the eastern shore of Mafia Island which covers most of the unbroken fringing reef, as well as the last remnants of Mafia's evergreen coastal forests. In this area can be found over 400 species of fish, 53 genera of both hard and soft corals – including giant table corals, huge stands of blue-tipped staghorn, whip corals and delicate seafans – 140 forms of sponge, seven mangrove species, 134 species of marine algae, breeding grounds for hawksbill and green turtles and a sea-grass area that is home to the highly endangered dugong.

Although the establishment of the park halted much of the destruction that previously threatened the area, the fate of the archipelago's marine turtles and dugongs remains a major concern. **Green** and **hawksbill turtles** nest at various sites on the archipelago, migrating from as far away as South Africa and Aldabra Atoll in the Seychelles. However, their populations have declined dramatically over the last two decades, a direct result of the introduction of *jarife* shark nets for fishing (which have also greatly reduced shark and ray populations), and subsequent habitat damage by the use of beach seine nets and dynamite fishing. Until recently, female turtles were also traditionally hunted during their nesting periods, while their eggs were taken by fishermen for food. Mafia's **dugongs** – the apparent inspiration of seafarers' tales of mermaids, possibly because of the sight of their blubbery breasts bobbing on the water – are in an even more desperate situation, and thought to be close to extinction in Africa. They breed – or used to breed – in the shallow sea-grass beds of the Majira Channel to the west and south of Mafia Island, but sadly, *jarife* nets are also used to hunt dugong. Even today, a dugong carcass is worth about $80 to fishermen, which represents a fortune. Although efforts are being made to eliminate the use of *jarife*, the handful of dugongs that are accidentally caught are pretty much all that researchers ever see of their subjects. For more information on the **Mafia Island Turtle & Dugong Conservation Programme**, contact the WWF office near the park headquarters in Utende (©wwfmafia@raha.com).

In addition, the mass coral bleaching that followed the **1997–98 El Niño event** in places killed – according to one controversial report, at least – up to ninety percent of Mafia's corals. El Niño caused a temporary rise in ocean temperature that killed off large numbers of symbiotic algae called *zooxanthellae*, without which the coral polyps also died. Although still far from returning to the fluorescent colours they enjoyed before El Niño, the archipelago's corals appear to have recovered well, and are still rated by many as among the beautiful in the world.

For details of park **fees** and **information**, see p.189.

Snorkelling

The isolated coral outcrops inside the warm shallow waters of **Chole Bay** – which range in depth from 2m to 8m and boast an underwater visibility of up to 40m – are perfect for snorkelling and attract a great number of colourful tropical marine life including lion fish, damselfish, angelfish, sponges, sea cucumbers, crabs and other crustaceans. Other good snorkelling areas include **Okuta Reef** around Jibondo Island, the **Blue Lagoon** south of Juani Island, and **Kifinga Bay**, on the east coast of Mafia Island, which is also a nesting site for green turtles. **Kitutia Reef** (see below)

for tourists. Alternatively, the Chole Bay hotels can arrange a motorboat for about $10. The boats land next to a church-like building on the beach, erected in the 1990s as a fish market but now used as a place where locals sell Chole's high-quality woven mats, made from the fronds of Mafia Island's

also has good snorkelling within swimmable distance of a lovely beach. **Snorkelling gear** can be rented from the Chole Bay hotels for around $5 a day; there's no equipment for sale or rent in Kilindoni. **Access** to the reefs is by *mashua* dhow or *ngalawa* outrigger, which can be hired on the beach facing the *Mafia Island Lodge*. These shouldn't cost more than $10 per person for a few hours, though sailing times mean that only Chole Bay and the Blue Lagoon are feasible to visit this way unless you leave early in the morning; this needs arranging in advance and a measure of luck with tides and winds. More reliable access, especially to locations further out, is provided by *Pole Pole Bungalow Resort* and *Kinasi Lodge*: both charge $45 per person for a full day's snorkelling at Kitutia Reef with lunch (minimum four people).

Diving

Mafia has two PADI-accredited **dive centres**. The one at the *Pole Pole Bungalow Resort*, jointly run with *Chole Mjini*, charges $35 a dive ($50 at night) plus $12 for equipment. The centre at the *Kinasi Lodge* offers a similarly wide range of dives at slightly lower prices, with $35 for a dive within Chole Bay including equipment, and $40 outside the bay; they also arrange trips to little-known reefs around Songo Songo Island, a little over halfway to Kilwa. Both centres offer Open Water courses for $350 and tuition up to Dive Master; *Pole Pole* also offers assistant instructor certification. Diving conditions are best, with calmer seas, weaker currents and better visibility, during the northerly *kaskazi* monsoon (Oct/Nov to Feb/March). Sharks, especially white-tipped, black-tipped and grey reef, are most commonly seen from November to January, whilst whales can occasionally be spotted – or heard – from November to December. Even at the best of times, however, visibility is generally poor on outgoing tides thanks to organic and granular matter in the water.

The following are some of the most popular diving reefs.

Kinasi Pass Wall Between Chole Bay and the open sea, this is a long-standing favourite, with dense coral formations at depths of 6–26m and especially good coral cover between 10m and 15m, with a wealth of marine life including groupers up to 2m in length, large shoals of snappers, stingrays and ribbontail rays, moray eels, Napoleon wrasse, humphead parrotfish and occasional biggies like white-tipped reef and tiger sharks, barracuda and turtles. The reef is usually seen on a drift dive, although you can catch the slack between ebb and flow tides.

Chole Wall Situated inside Kinasi Pass northeast of Chole Island, this goes down to 18m and is best on incoming tides. It has fewer big fish than Kinasi Pass Wall, but the coral is in pristine condition and you may see turtles close up.

Kitutia Reef At the southern tip of the archipelago surrounding a tidal sandbank, Kitutia is visited as a day-trip by motorboat with a picnic lunch on the sandbank. Diving is mainly on the seaward side, and whilst there isn't a great variety of marine life, there's a good range of corals which are slowly recovering from the effects of dynamite fishing and the El Niño bleaching.

Ras Kisimani Less frequently dived are the reefs off Ras Kisimani to the west of the archipelago, which are awkward and expensive to get to. The best are the relatively shallow Sefu Reef (average depth 12m), 15km northwest of Kilindoni, which offers good chances of seeing large schools of barracuda and other big game fish; and Belami Reef (average 17m depth), 4km west of Ras Kisimani, which has the added attractions of an exposed sandbank surrounded by coral heads (bommies) teeming with fish, and its proximity to Ras Kisimani itself (see p.191).

phoenix palm (*mkindu*). These colourful, naturally dyed mats have been made for centuries and come in two forms: large, rectangular floor mats (*mikela*) or oval prayer mats (*misuala* or *misali*).

Immediately behind the market and in the lee of a glorious stand of frangipani trees is Chole's most impressive ruin, consisting of a coral ragstone facade and associated foundations, which served as the **residence** of the German governor of Mafia between 1892 and 1913 when the island's capital was moved to Kilindoni, since it offered a better anchorage for the newly introduced steamboat service. Prior to German colonization, the house was apparently owned by a rich Omani slave-trader, and it is from this period that Chole's other ruins date. The old **prison**, almost next door amidst a fantastic tangle of fig-tree roots, has weathered the years somewhat better, with its eight small cells – said to have held up to fifty inmates each – still intact, though missing their roofs. The inmates were (presumably) mostly slaves, as the free population of Chole would never have needed so large a jail. Further along the broad "Market Street", which in the nineteenth century is said to have had lantern street lights arrayed along its length (something that's difficult to imagine now), a series of rectangular stumps within a low wall are said to have been the tethering pillars of the slave market, although some say the structure was actually just a warehouse. The ruins of a Hindu temple further on have, like the prison, acquired an impressive encrustation of fig-tree roots, which appear to be the only things keeping the walls upright. For those with more time, a mosque, various wells and other stone houses can also be seen.

Among Chole's other curiosities are its protected colonies of giant *Pteropus*, or **Comoros fruit bats** (also called flying foxes), that roost in big mango trees and which – unlike their cave-dwelling cousins – rely on eyesight rather than sonar for navigation. The colonies are included as part of the locally managed **Bat Trail** (1hr 30min), whose winding pathways provide an ideal way of experiencing the island's lush vegetation. There's a Tsh1000 entry charge in theory, although this isn't currently levied. Leaflets detailing the trail and other walks can be picked up at the *Chole Mjini* lodge, and the local kindergarten – which the lodge can direct you to – has an exhaustive bird list. For more information, *The Chole Booklet* (Tsh5000), by Dudley Iles and Christine Walley, available at the *Chole Mjini* lodge, offers an excellent guide to the island's history and wildlife.

Juani Island

Separated from Chole Island by a narrow waterway, **Juani** is the archipelago's second largest island, and is frequently visited by hotel guests as a half-day trip by *mashua* dhow to see the mangrove-lined Kua Channel at the south end of the island, and the ruins of Kua, believed to have been the base of the sultanate of Kilwa. Half-day trips, usually circumnavigating Juani Island via the Kua Channel, are offered by both the *Pole Pole Bungalow Resort* and *Kinasi Lodge* and cost around $15–20 per person.

The island's wildlife includes feral pigs (introduced by the Portuguese), monkeys and the diminutive blue duiker antelope, but the main attraction is undoubtedly the atmospheric **Kua ruins**, believed by locals to be haunted, which languish almost forgotten on the west side of the island among a dense tangle of undergrowth studded with baobab trees. Excavations in 1955 unearthed a rectangular grid of streets, along with Chinese and Indian coins from the thirteenth and fourteenth centuries. Kua appears to have covered about 1.5 square kilometres, and its ruins include a two-storey palace dating from the eighteenth century, two graveyards, at least fifteen houses and seven mosques, the oldest of which dates back to the fourteenth century. It's impossible to give a ruin-by-ruin description of the place, as what you see will depend on the state of the vegetation.

According to legend, Kua was founded by **Bashat**, a son of the Shirazi founder of Kilwa, early in the eleventh century. The archipelago's position between Kilwa and Zanzibar made Kua an important trading town, and before long, Arab traders were given the right to build their own settlement on the northern side of town; according to legend, they later seized power and began to rule unfairly.

Kua's rivalries were not confined to Shirazis and Arabs, but also between Kua, which was allied to Kilwa on the mainland, and Kisimani (see p.191), which was linked to Zanzibar. Legend tells of the launching of a *jahazi* dhow at Kisimani. The people of Kua were invited over for the celebrations, but on arriving, the children of Kua's elite were bound and laid on the ground in front of the dhow. The dhow was launched over their backs, killing the children. The people of Kua took their time to exact revenge. At Kua, they built a beautifully decorated chamber deep underground. When five or ten years had passed, they invited the people of Kisimani for a wedding. The people of Kisimani, having assumed that the Kua had forgiven them for killing their children, arrived unsuspecting. The wedding feast was held in the underground chamber. One by one, the people of Kua left the feast, until only an old man – who had volunteered to sacrifice himself – remained to entertain the guests. The entrance to the chamber was sealed off, and the occupants died.

Historians still debate the catastrophe that subsequently overtook Kua. According to one story, at the start of the nineteenth century Kua was ruled by a very harsh queen. Some opponents of the queen travelled to Madagascar, where they sought help from the Sakalava people. The Sakalava agreed to help overthrow the queen on condition that they be allowed to rule Kua, but when they arrived, in 1829, with a force of eighty canoes, they proceeded to sack the entire town regardless of allegiance, allegedly eating many of its inhabitants in the process. A good proportion of the three thousand survivors were sold into slavery, and by 1840 the last inhabitants had deserted Kua to start new lives on Kome Island, halfway between Mafia and Kisiju on the mainland.

Jibondo Island

About an hour's sail south of Chole, **Jibondo Island** is the most traditional of the archipelago's settlements, and most of its two thousand inhabitants engage in fishing, especially for sharks, and octopus baiting. The beaches facing the open ocean are important turtle-nesting sites – seaweed farming was introduced by NGOs in 1992 as an alternative source of income to killing turtles. Jibondo's craftsmen are famed for their skill in boat building without the use of iron, or even nails. With the onset of modern boats, their art is gradually becoming obsolete, although ongoing repairs and the small-scale construction of *mashua* dhows keeps some in business. A trip to Jibondo is usually included with a snorkelling trip from one of the Chole Bay hotels, and costs around $20 per person in a group of four.

The Kilwas

Some 140km south of the Rufiji delta are the **KILWAS**, three settlements of exceptional historical interest whose atmospheric ruins represent a wide sweep of East African coastal history, from the dizzy heights of the Swahili and Shirazi trading civilization to the darker days of slavery and the uprisings against German rule. At the neck of the Kilwa peninsula, **Kilwa Kivinje** ("Kilwa of the Casuarina Trees") was a major slave-trading centre and later a German garrison; nowadays little more than a fishing village, its historical core is in a severely dilapidated if picturesque state. At the peninsula's southern tip, the modern town of **Kilwa Masoko** ("Kilwa of the Market") is the regional headquarters and the main base for travellers, as well as boasting a couple of beautiful deserted beaches. It also offers easy access to the oldest and most fas-

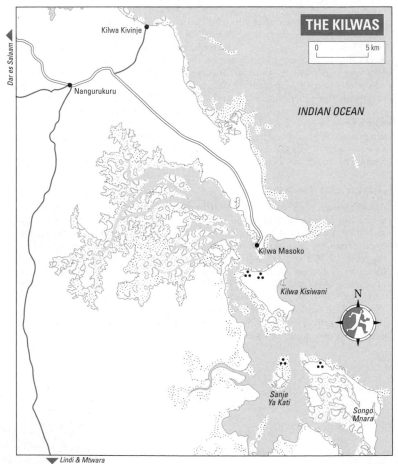

cinating of the Kilwas, **Kilwa Kisiwani** ("Kilwa of the Island"), situated on an island of the same name a couple of kilometres off the coast. Once one of Africa's wealthiest towns, Kilwa Kisiwani is now a UNESCO World Heritage Site and contains the world's most extensive and best-preserved Swahili ruins. There are similar if smaller sites on the nearby islands of **Songo Mnara** and **Sanje ya Kati**.

Kilwa Masoko

For the handful of visitors who manage to make it down here, the small town of **KILWA MASOKO** is a handy base, with several cheap and clean – if basic – hotels and a couple of attractive, huge and completely undeveloped beaches. **Jimbiza Beach** on the east side of town is closest, but **Masoko Pwani Beach**, a five-kilometre hike to the northeast, is more secluded. The daily **market**, under the mango trees on the north side of town, is always fun and continues well into the night, though the selection of fresh produce is generally limited. But the main reason for coming here is to visit the ruins of **Kilwa Kisiwani**, on the mangrove-rimmed island of the same name, some 2km from Kilwa Masoko's harbour.

The first thing that strikes you about Kilwa Masoko is its overpowering lethargy. Given the strength-sapping heat and humidity, siestas are unavoidable, and you'll see people sleeping almost anywhere, even flat out on the ground in front of their shops. Some locals say that the listlessness is a legacy of slavery; a more certain reminder of that trade can be seen in the dark skin of many of Kilwa's inhabitants, some of whom – from the Ngoni, Machinga, Mwera, Matumbi, Ngindo and Yao tribes – descend from slaves. People also seem rather reserved in their dealings with *wazungu*, and the long stares that greet you can feel unsettling at first, though once people get to recognize you, Kilwa is as welcoming as anywhere in the country.

Telephone number changes

Kilwa Masoko and Kilwa Kivinje were set to acquire an automated telephone exchange sometime in 2002, so the phone numbers given here will change. Check with the nearest TTCL office or contact directory enquiries on ⓣ135.

Arrival and information

During the long rains (March–May) and towards the end of the short ones (usually early Dec; sometimes late Nov or Jan), the plains immediately south of the Rufiji River become flooded, completely cutting off road access to Kilwa and the rest of the south coast. During the rest of the year, one or two rickety old **buses** ply the bumpy road from Dar every day, leaving at 6.30am from Ubungo bus station. It's an extremely rough journey, hot and dusty, and takes upwards of fourteen hours, including an extensive lunch break during which the bus gets repaired. Things should improve once the bridge over the Rufiji is completed and if – a big if – the road south of the river is finally upgraded. Alternatively, you could catch a bus from Dar to Lindi, Mtwara, Nachingwea or Masasi and get off in **Nangurukuru**, from where daladalas cover the remaining 30km throughout the day (Tsh700).

If you're **driving** during or close to the rains, check the state of the road with every driver you meet, and keep an eye on the weather. If it looks like raining,

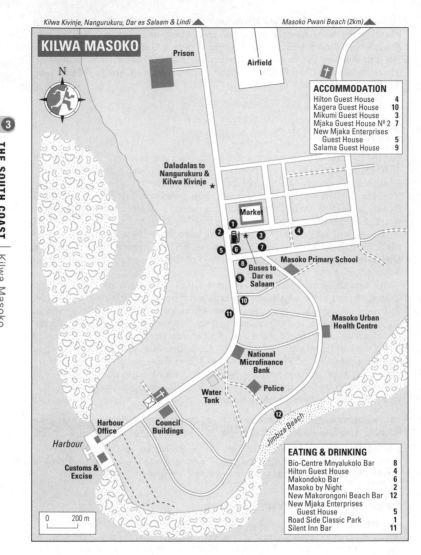

KILWA MASOKO

Prison

Airfield

N

ACCOMMODATION

Hilton Guest House	4
Kagera Guest House	10
Mikumi Guest House	3
Mjaka Guest House Nº 2	7
New Mjaka Enterprises Guest House	5
Salama Guest House	9

Daladalas to
Nangurukuru &
Kilwa Kivinje ★

Market

❶ ❷ ❸ ❹
❺ ❻ ❼
❽ Buses to
Dar es
❾ Salaam

Masoko Primary School

❿
⓫

Masoko Urban
Health Centre

National
Microfinance
Bank

Police

Water
Tank

⓬

Jimbiza Beach

Harbour
Office

Council
Buildings

Harbour

Customs &
Excise

0   200 m

EATING & DRINKING

Bio-Centre Mnyalukolo Bar	8
Hilton Guest House	4
Makondoko Bar	6
Masoko by Night	2
New Makorongoni Beach Bar	12
New Mjaka Enterprises Guest House	5
Road Side Classic Park	1
Silent Inn Bar	11

get out quick or be prepared to stay in Kilwa for at least an extra day after the rains stop to give the road time to dry out (or two days after a particularly heavy downpour). There are two petrol stations in Nangurukuru and one in Kilwa Masoko on the main road opposite *Masoko by Night Bar*. Fill up here, as the next fuel isn't guaranteed until Lindi in the south or Kibiti in the north. Another option would be to catch the weekly **ferry** from Dar to Mtwara (see p.220) and hope that the road back up to Kilwa is passable. **Flights** between Dar and Kilwa are unpredictable, and services can be suspended for long periods. At the time of writing, Eagle Air (see p.122) were flying twice weekly (Mon & Fri) from Dar, and once weekly (Fri) from Lindi. The airport is just north of Kilwa Masoko, within walking distance of the hotels.

Buses **to Dar** leave at daily at 5am from beside the market. Heading south **to Lindi**, **Mtwara** or **Masasi**, you'll have to catch a daladala to Nangurukuru and wait for a bus from Dar. Arrive as early as possible, since buses from Dar don't always have spare seats; if it looks like you'll be stuck for the night, Nangurukuru has a basic guest house, but you'd be better off at Kilwa Kivinje, whose equally basic guest houses at least have the advantage of an atmospheric location. For information on moving on from the Kilwas by dhow, see the box on p.210.

There's no tourist office in Kilwa Masoko. For advice about **local excursions** contact Daniel Masasi at the *Bio-Centre Mnyalukolo Bar*. The **Antiquities Department**, in the council buildings opposite the post office (Mon–Fri 7.30am–3.30pm; ☎ Kilwa Masoko 16, 19 or 60), dispenses permits and practical advice on getting to the archeological sites of Kilwa Kisiwani, Songo Mnara and Sanje ya Kati. **Bicycle hire**, which can be arranged informally with almost any local bike owner, is handy for getting to Masoko Pwani beach, and – if the 58km round trip doesn't faze you – to Kilwa Kivinje. Alternatively, the trip by daladala costs Tsh700 cach way.

Accommodation

There's a number of perfectly decent budget guest houses in Kilwa Masoko, but nothing fancy. Low water pressure means that showers only work intermittently, and electricity is equally erratic. **Camping** is possible in the grounds of the house belonging to Daniel Masasi, the owner of the *Bio-Centre Mnyalukolo Bar*. It's right on the beach two houses down from *New Makorongoni Beach Bar*. The price is negotiable but shouldn't be more than Tsh2500 per person, including use of a bathroom.

Of the **guest houses**, two stand out: the *Hilton Guest House*, 200m east of the market and bus stop (☎ Kilwa Masoko 114; ●) is friendly, clean and safe, its rooms equipped with fans and electricity, the more expensive of which have bathrooms with clean long-drops, but the downside is that the bed sheets and mosquito nets are too small – use plenty of repellent. On the way into town at the west end of the road leading to the *Hilton*, the *New Mjaka Enterprises Guest House* (☎ Kilwa Masoko 89; ●) is the main alternative, also offering a choice of self-contained or shared facilities in concrete *bandas*. It benefits from a better restaurant, but buses revving up in the morning will disturb light sleepers. If it's full, they have an annexe on a nearby side street. Cheaper and more basic (all ●), with shared squat loos and bucket showers, are the *Salama Guest House* (☎ Kilwa Masoko 86), and *Kagera Guest House* (☎ Kilwa Masoko 89), both on the main road, and *Mikumi Guest House* (☎ Kilwa Masoko 49), on the same street as the *Hilton*.

Eating and drinking

Kilwa Masoko isn't the most gastronomically well-endowed place on earth, and few restaurants have more than a sackful of rice in their larders. Still, there are a handful of half-decent places at which you might strike lucky. The *Bio-Centre Mnyalukolo Bar* is the best of the **restaurants**, though you'll need to order the day before to sample *kamba* (prawns or lobster), *ngisi* (squid) or delicious *pweza* (octopus), either stewed or grilled. More pedestrian is the pre-fried fish and chicken served up at the *New Mjaka Enterprises Guest House*, which is at least reliable, unlike the *Hilton Guest House*'s restaurant, which rarely has anything

Excursions from Kilwa Masoko

Apart from the historical attractions of Kilwa Kisiwani, Songo Mnara and Sanje ya Kati, Kilwa Masoko also serves as a base for a number of infrequently visited natural attractions. The person to talk to about arranging trips is Daniel Masasi at *Bio-Centre Mnyalukolo Bar*. Possible excursions include trips to the **Kilwa Marine Reserve**, one of the few places where the endangered dugong might be seen, and a number of rivers – notably the **Nyange** and **Ukuli** – which have hippo and untouched riverine forests. The best place for hippo, though, is **Mutonyange Lake** on the way to Lindi. To get there, turn off the main road at Kiranjeranje and head west 17km to Makangaga. Park there and ask for the village chairman (*mwenyekiti wa kijiji*), who should be able to provide someone to guide you the remaining 3km to the lake. The lake itself contains literally thousands of hippo – legend has it that should you try to hunt them, you'll never be seen again.

Another excellent destination, though again you'll need your own transport, is the large **cave complex** in the Matumbi Hills, which saw service as a hide-out during the 1905–7 Maji Maji Uprising – it's now used a place for catching porcupines, whose quills have medicinal and ritual significance. The local name for the caves varies according to which entrance is used: choose from Nang'oma, Anduli, Nakitala or Nakinduguyu. To get there from Kilwa Masoko, head back towards Dar and turn west at Matapatapa, 53km north of Nangurukuru. The main entrance to the caves is at Kipatimu near Nandembo village, 60km further on. For more information, see Peter Marwan's *The Caves in the Matumbi Hills and their Importance to the Native People* (Ⓦwww.karst.net/Forschung/tanzania_e.htm).

other than chapatis, tea, *andazi* or eggs. For coconut juice and grilled dorado, try the **market**.

Kilwa has several **bars**, one or two of which might even be described as lively at the weekend. The *New Makorongoni Beach Bar*, overlooking Jimbiza beach, sells alcohol and *nyama choma*, and plays cheerful music. In the centre, the popular *Bio-Centre Mnyalukolo Bar* vies with the *Makondoko Bar* opposite for evening trade. Open latest is *Masoko by Night*, where the barmaids appear to double as prostitutes. Other choices include the large *Road Side Classic Park*, with its shaded outdoor seating, and the *Silent Inn Bar*, which has a nice view of the sea inlet to the west, but only sells sodas.

Kilwa Kisiwani

Two kilometres across the water south of Kilwa Masoko are the spectacular ruins of the medieval city-state of **KILWA KISIWANI**, located on the northern shore of a small, mangrove-fringed island of the same name. At its height, Kilwa Kisiwani was the single most important trading centre on the East African coast, and the ruins here include several mosques, a fourteenth-century palace (in its time the largest stone structure in sub-Saharan Africa), dozens of Shirazi graves atmospherically set in groves of giant baobabs, and a well-preserved Omani fortress.

Some history

The oldest archeological remains at Kilwa Kisiwani date from the ninth century, part of an extensive settlement that pre-dated the arrival of the Arabs. According to legend, the **Sultanate of Kilwa** was founded in 975 by a Shirazi trader named Hassan bin Ali, who is said to have bought the island from the ruling chief for a quantity of cloth. Early Arab chronicles are clear that the inhabitants were Africans rather than Arabs or Asians, although the ruling class came to be dominated by immigrants from Perdia and, later, from Arabia.

Kilwa reached its apogee in the fourteenth century, from when the bulk of the surviving ruins date. Kilwa's riches lay in its control of the **gold trade** from the Monomotapa kingdom in Zimbabwe: by 1300, Monomotapa's entire production was passing through Kilwa en route to Arabia, India and Europe. The most famous visitor to Kilwa during this period was the renowned Moroccan traveller **Ibn Battuta**, who in 1332 wrote that "Kilwa is amongst the most beautiful of cities and elegantly built". At the height of the gold trade, Kilwa boasted sub-Saharan Africa's largest stone building, its largest mosque and first mint. The ruling class lived in stone houses with indoor plumbing, wore silk and fine cotton, and ate off Chinese porcelain. The general population presumably lived in less durable mud-and-thatch dwellings, much as they do now, as only the palaces and mosques have survived.

The **arrival of the Portuguese** in 1498 marked the end of Kilwa's first golden age and triggered a long period of decline. Their first visit was innocuous enough, when Vasco da Gama's flotilla pulled into Kilwa's harbour on its way to discovering the sea route to India. They found a flourishing and powerful city, exporting not only gold and slaves but silver, precious stones, ivory, myrrh, animal skins, frankincense and ambergris, receiving spices and metal goods in exchange. But it was the gold trade that incited **Vasco da Gama's return** in 1502. After calling briefly at Sofala and Mozambique, da Gama sailed once more into Kilwa, this time ostensibly to avenge the "unfriendly" welcome that the ruler, Amir Ibrahim, had accorded Pedro Álvares Cabral a couple of years earlier (Cabral, with the characteristic tact of the conquistadors, had refused to meet the sultan, had threatened war, and then proposed that Kilwa, which at the time was the most important Islamic settlement in sub-Saharan Africa, convert to Christianity). Da Gama threatened to burn the city and kill its inhabitants unless he was paid sufficient tribute. The amir submitted and Kilwa effectively became a Portuguese possession.

In 1505 came the turn of the even more militaristic **Dom Francisco d'Almeida**, who had been made viceroy of the newly conquered territories of India. He quickly took a liking to the town: "Kilwa, of all the places I know in the world, has the best port and the fairest land that can be." Despite his fine words, d'Almeida set about plundering the town and triggering the collapse of much of the old coastal trading network, so much so that by 1513 the Portuguese saw no more reason to remain in Kilwa, and left. With its trading links destroyed, the town's fortunes nose-dived, brought to a brutal and gruesome end in 1587 by the massacre of forty percent of its population by the marauding **Zimba tribe**. Believed to have come from the Zambezi area, little more is known of the Zimba other than their cannibalistic habits.

The city's fortunes revived at the start of the eighteenth century, following the expulsion of the Portuguese from the African coast north of Mozambique. Kilwa gradually fell under **Omani control**, with slaves replacing gold as the coast's major commodity, and the following century saw a renaissance in Kilwa's fortunes, mostly though trade with the French. The latter part of this period also saw the establishment of Kilwa's semi-independent **ash-Shirazi dynasty**, whose first sultan was installed in 1776. The new sultan almost immediately signed a treaty with a French slave-trader, Jean-Vincent Morice, for the annual purchase of at least 1000 slaves. It was under the Shirazis that the present Gereza fort was constructed, but the upturn was not to last long. In 1842, Kilwa was captured by Zanzibar and the following year the last Shirazi sultan was exiled to Muscat. With its trade eclipsed by the new mainland slaving centre of Kilwa Kivinje, Kilwa Kisiwani was finally abandoned and collapsed into the ruins that are now all that survives of the city.

Visiting the site

Visitors to Kilwa Kisiwani need a **permit** (Tsh1500 or $2) from the Antiquities Department in Kilwa Masoko (see p.199), where you can also borrow a sketch map of the site. While you're there, ask to see or buy a copy of John Sutton's fascinating *Kilwa: A History of the Ancient Swahili Town* (also available from the British Institute in Eastern Africa in Nairobi on ⓔ britinst@insightkenya.com or biea@britac.ac.uk). Another book worth seeking out in libraries is Neville Chittick's *Kilwa, an Islamic Trading City on the East African Coast* (Nairobi, 1974).

There are two ways of getting from Kilwa Masoko to Kilwa Kisiwani. The romantic option is to catch a local *mashua* **dhow** from Kilwa Masoko's harbour. Most of these leave in the morning, though you may strike lucky in the afternoon. If there are other passengers on the boat, it shouldn't cost more than Tsh300 each way, assuming you can get the captain to charge you the going rate (even *wazungu* shouldn't pay more than Tsh1000 after bargaining), but if you want the dhow to yourself – as the captain is likely to assume you do – you'll pay anything from Tsh5000 to Tsh10,000 for the return trip. Less romantic is the **motorboat** owned by the Antiquities Department, which costs Tsh20,000 for the return trip (Tsh50,000 to Songo Mnara). You could also ask Daniel Masasi at the *Bio-Centre Mnyalukolo Bar* whether he's managed to get a boat; he was talking of Tsh10,000 a day. There's a Tsh200 harbour tax at Kilwa Masoko; pay at the hut just inside the gate.

Dhows usually drop you at the Gereza, where the captain will locate a **guide**. You're then shown around as many ruins as you want, and finish up (if you can face the walk) 2km east of the Gereza at Husuni Kubwa, where you're picked up for the return to Kilwa Masoko. Officially there are two guides, but it's the *askari* who usually takes people around, though his grasp of English is as limited as his knowledge of the sites; he'll expect a tip (Tsh1000 will suffice). Of the guides, Juma Meli has an excellent reputation, speaks good English and has a dhow which is handy for visiting Songo Mnara and Sanje ya Kati (no fixed price). You can usually find him near the harbour in Kilwa Masoko.

If you fancy spending the night on the island, the Antiquities Department maintains a very basic **rest house**, equipped with beds and tattered sheets and nets. The *askari* can help collect water from a nearby well (it's safe to drink). The price is negotiable with the *askari*, but shouldn't be more than Tsh2000 per person. **Camping** is possible around the rest house – again, there's no fixed price.

The ruins

The **ruins** are scattered in and around the present-day settlement of Kilwa Kisiwani on the north side of the island, whose simple mud houses provide a stark contrast to the wealthy city that Kilwa once was. The bulk of the ruins, comprising the heart of the old city and the Gereza fort (where the boat deposits you), are in the northwest and cover little more than one square kilometre. Husuni Kubwa and Husuni Ndogo are 2km to the east, accessed by narrow footpaths wending between dusty plots of irrigated farmland, cashew plantations, shady mango groves and acacia and baobab thickets where, with a keen eye, you may spot bee-eaters and bulbuls.

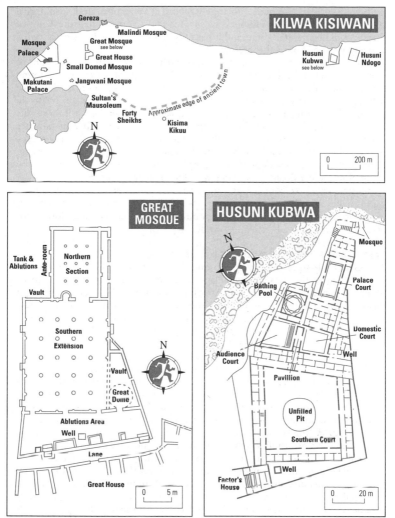

Adapted from John Sutton (1998), in Azania 33. Reproduced by permission of the British Institute in East Africa.

The Gereza

The crenellated **Gereza** (also known as the fort or the prison) is Kilwa's most prominent building; boats from Kilwa Masoko drop you on the beach beside it. Built of coral limestone blocks, the Gereza occupies a commanding position, with unobstructed views over the harbours of both Kilwa Kisiwani and Kilwa Masoko, and sweeping vistas over the open ocean. Parts of the northern walls have crumbled into the waves, but the Gereza is otherwise in remarkably fine condition. Its name comes from the church (in Portuguese, *igreja*) which it once contained, and it's said that construction of the complex took less than three weeks: in the florid words of Francisco d'Almeida, writing to the king of

Portugal in 1505: "We built a fortress which if it were possible I would give years of my life for Your Highness to see, for it is so strong that the King of France could be awaited there, and it has lodgings in very fine houses for twice as many people as are left there now."

He was exaggerating its strength, however: when the Omanis gained control they had to rebuild the entire fortress with the exception of the tower foundations, and this is the building you see today. In keeping with its defensive nature, there is only one entrance, though the door and frame are relatively modern. Above the entrance is a slot for muskets, and there are still more slits arranged along the parapet. The courtyard inside has a number of benches along the walls, and spyholes from the middle level of the surrounding three-storey edifice. If you look up, you might still see a young baobab growing improbably on the tower's platform, though it's likely to be removed when the restoration project finally gets under way. The best-preserved rooms are in the southeast corner, on your left as you enter. The chamber set in the southern wall is believed to have been a gunpowder magazine. In the northeast corner, excavations have unearthed several cannonballs and musket shot, along with over 3000 trading beads.

The Great Mosque and Great House

The **Great Mosque** (or Friday Mosque) lies just to the south of the Gereza on the edge of the present-day village in an area now frequented by goats. Once the largest mosque in East Africa, it would have been at the heart of medieval Kilwa. It was excavated between 1958 and 1960 by Neville Chittick, who reconstructed parts of it and also somewhat carelessly left behind his own traces in the form of a short length of railway and an upturned carriage, which was used to clear debris during the excavations.

The mosque is a beautiful building, and the play of light and shadow on the mildewed archways and walls makes it supremely photogenic. Its architecture reflects Kilwa's rising prosperity over the centuries. The roofless **northern section** is the older, built in the twelfth century when the gold trade was in its infancy. Its flat, coral-concrete roof was supported by nine sixteen-sided wooden columns set in rows of three, on top of which were laid three beams running north–south. As the wood rotted away long ago, the only clues to this are the gaps left in the masonry into which the beams and pillars would have fitted.

As Kilwa prospered in the fourteenth-century, the riches generated by the gold trade were reflected in the mosque's large **southern extension**, which was given an elaborately domed and vaulted roof supported by thin, octagonal stone pillars. Though elegant, they were unable to bear the weight of the roof, part of which collapsed in 1350. The pillars were subsequently replaced with coral limestone blocks, most of which still stand today. Some of the original stone pillars lie discarded by the eastern wall, and the domes are nowadays home to a small colony of bats.

At the southern end of the mosque is a porch which was used as the **ablutions area** by the faithful before entering the prayer hall. It was equipped with a well, a water trough, a bench and a piece of round sandstone where visitors would wash their feet before entering the mosque. At the eastern side of the ablutions area, a narrow door gave onto a large room under a single dome, which may have been used by the sultan for his prayers. On the south side of the ablutions area is the **Great House**, a complex of buildings, now much overgrown (look for the huge fig tree growing into the walls), which apparently dates from the fourteenth century and included many dwellings and courts.

Next to the mosque is a very deep well. If you peer down, you'll see two **underground passages** leading off it about halfway down. The one on the eastern side leads to the Gereza and may have been used for moving slaves, whilst the one to the west heads to the Makutani Palace – a strange conjunction of privilege and servitude.

The Small Domed Mosque

The **Small Domed Mosque**, 150m southwest of the Great Mosque across open grassland, is the best preserved of Kilwa's medieval buildings, with more than half of the original roof surviving intact, and it's certainly the most attractive. It dates from the middle of the fifteenth century when Kilwa's prosperity was at its height, though the thick fortifying buttresses supporting the walls from the outside bear a distinctly defensive air, perhaps foreshadowing the arrival of the Portuguese and the city's subsequent demise. Although the mosque's floor is now level with the land (which has been raised due to the collapse of the surrounding houses), it's thought that the mosque was originally raised on a platform 1.6m above the ground and surrounded by a plastered pavement, which would have made it an impressive landmark.

The first thing that strikes you is the partly broken octagonal pillar that projects upwards from the central dome, which suggests comparison with the pillar tombs found at other sites, such as Kaole and Kunduchi. **Inside**, the mosque is an architectural gem. As with the Great Mosque, the African influence is visible in the overall form of the building, which is based on a rectangular prayer hall with a roof supported on numerous pillars, rather than on the contemporary Arabian "pavilion" style featuring arcaded courtyards. The central dome was inlaid with circles of green-glazed ceramic bowls, some of which can still be seen, while some of the other surviving domes bear traces of blue paint. There's also an elegant *mihrab* in the north wall – like the domes, it's now home to a colony of easily startled bats. The **ablutions area** to the southwest is more complex than that in the Great Mosque, and contains a latrine and two water tanks. Like the Great Mosque, there are also some large flat circular stones which were used for scrubbing feet.

The Makutani Palace and around

At the western end of town next to the ocean is the **Makutani Palace**. The palace's name means a "gathering place", hinting at the traditional African mode of rule in which a state's affairs were run by a council of elders rather than just a king or sultan. With the exception of the enclosing perimeter walls, however, much of the original fifteenth-century structure was demolished at the end of the eighteenth century to provide building material for the new palace – still largely intact – which occupies the south side of a roughly triangular area adjacent to the northeastern wall of the old palace, surrounded with enormous defensive outer walls which open only onto the shore.

The old palace consists of a **residential section** to the west and barracks or store rooms around a large **courtyard** to the east. The rusty cannon barrel in the courtyard adds to the impression that defence was a prime concern, as does the water cistern, which would have proved invaluable during a siege. Both wings of the palace had long, narrow rooms, their width limited by the length of the mangrove poles from which the ceilings were made. The reception rooms and living quarters were on the upper two floors, the latter north-facing and provided with toilets, as your guide will inevitably point out. The decor of the rooms is hinted at by traces of pink plaster which can be seen halfway up the walls of the corridor connecting the stores with the palace antechamber.

△ Gereza Fort

While you're wandering around, have a closer look at the coral ragstone walls, some of which contain incredibly intricate natural patterns of cream and grey.

A few hundred metres southeast of the palace are the scanty remains of the **Jangwani Mosque**, which is of interest mainly to archeologists on account of the unique ablutionary water jars set into its walls just inside the main entrance. Passing the mosque, at low tide you can cut across the salt-crusted sands of the inlet just to the south to reach the so-called **Forty Sheikhs Cemetery**, part of which has been eroded by sea. Like the vast majority of Shirazi grave sites, the tombs here nestle in groves of baobabs, including one of the biggest you're ever likely to see. The presence of the trees is explained by the legend that when a sultan died, a pair of baobab saplings would be planted at either end of his grave; these would eventually grow together, effectively making the tomb part of the tree. The story certainly fits the atmosphere of the place, at once overpoweringly sacred and meditative.

Husuni Kubwa

Built on a protruding rocky spur high above the fringing mangroves 2km east of the Gereza, **Husuni Kubwa** (The Great Palace) was in its time the largest permanent building in sub-Saharan Africa, and remains one of the most enigmatic constructions on the Swahili coast. Walking along the footpath from the Gereza and the village, the undergrowth suddenly clears as your eyes meet a grey maze of courtyards, hallways, galleries, staircases and rooms up to three storeys high. Excavations suggest that the construction was never fully completed, nor lived in by more than three generations of sultans before the dynasty moved to the Makutani Palace. No one really knows why the building was abandoned, especially as the cliff-top location was ideal, benefiting from continuous sea breezes and a commanding position over the ocean and the channel running between the mainland and the island.

An inscribed plaque found in the palace lauded the praises of Sultan "al-Malik al-Mansur" ("the conquering ruler") al-Hasan ibn Sulaiman, which dates the bulk of the palace's construction to the 1320s, though its location outside the city has prompted much inconclusive speculation. The very size and ornateness of the building illustrates in spectacular fashion the wealth that was being made from the gold trade – if you've seen the display on Kilwa in the National Museum in Dar (see p.95), with its Chinese porcelain bowls, elaborately engraved friezes, oil lamps, pottery and coins, it shouldn't be too difficult to imagine the opulence of the palace in the mid-fourteenth century An inscription from the palace, also in the National Museum, reads: "Your good fortune is always new and with you, all days are festivals. Your Creator is glorious and protects you from destruction."

The palace complex had two main parts: the palace itself in the north, and a rectangular commercial section to the south, which is the first area you reach if walking here from the Gereza. Walking down a flight of steps, you pass a well and enter the large **Southern Court**, enclosed by a double range of rooms. No roof was found during the excavations, and as the walls of the rooms are uncommonly thick, they may have been intended to carry another storey. Near the centre of the courtyard is a large irregular pit which was used either as a quarry or may have been intended to form a large cistern.

North of the Southern Court is the **Palace** itself, occupying the north- and west-facing tip of the headland. Entering from the southern court, you pass through the **Domestic Court**, which is surrounded by terraces. To the west is the **Pavilion** in which the sultan would have received visitors and conducted public business. A short flight of steps below the Pavilion on the western edge of the complex is the **Audience Court**, flanked by wide terraces which may also have been used for receptions and dances and which offer a fine view westwards over the coast and harbour. The niches in the walls here were possibly used for oil lamps.

North of the Audience Court is the octagonal **Bathing Pool**, set in an unroofed square enclosure; it's been estimated that this would have needed 80,000 litres of water to fill, which – given the lack of channels – would necessarily have had to be hauled by hand from the well next to the Domestic Court by an army of slaves or servants. The scale and opulence of palace fittings like these suggest why the site might have been abandoned prematurely, since the running costs of such a grandiose building must have been very much at the mercy of trading conditions, not just in the vicinity of Kilwa, but at Sofala too.

North of the Bathing Pool and through the rectangular **Palace Court**, steps lead down to a landing creek in the mangroves where most dhows collect passengers before returning to Kilwa Masoko.

West of Husuni Kubwa, and separated from it by a deep gully, **Husuni Ndogo** (Small Palace) is believed to have been constructed in the fifteenth century, though archeologists are at a loss to explain much about the building. With the exception of its outer walls and turrets, it contains virtually no internal structures, and dense thorny shrubs render access difficult.

Songo Mnara and Sanje ya Kati

To the south of Kilwa Kisiwani are several more islands, including Songo Mnara and Sanje Ya Kati, both of which contain Shirazi ruins. Those at **Songo Mnara** are the most impressive, mostly dating from the fourteenth and fifteenth centuries and comprising an extensive palace complex, at least four mosques and dozens of graves and houses, all surrounded by a defensive wall. **Sanje ya Kati**, formerly known as Shanga, is 3km to the west and contains the foundations of oblong houses and a tenth-century mosque, although they're little more than rubble.

You need a special **permit** from the Antiquities Department in Kilwa Masoko to visit Songo Mnara (Tsh1500 or $2; see p.199), but it's unclear whether you need one just to visit Sanje ya Kati (it should be covered by the Songo Mnara permit in any case). If the cost of hiring a boat (see p.202) is prohibitive, Songo Mnara is also accessible by irregular *mashua* **dhow ferries** sailing between Kilwa Masoko and Pende; you'll have to wade through the water to get ashore. The journey to Pende costs Tsh700 for locals, though non-Kiswahili speakers will probably pay more. Be sure to double-check arrangements for your pick-up on the return trip, as there are no facilities on the island if you get stuck. Songo Mnara has a **guide** who will expect a tip (and may put you up for a night).

Kilwa Kivinje

Facing the ocean on the neck of Kilwa peninsula, 29km north of Kilwa Masoko, is the totally dilapidated but charming town of **KILWA KIVINJE**, a fascinating and rarely visited destination. In its brief period of prosperity in the mid-nineteenth century, the town was one of the main terminuses of the southern slave and ivory caravan route from Lake Nyasa, replacing Kilwa Kisiwani, which had been all but abandoned. Later on it became a garrison town for the Germans, and played a role in suppressing both the Abushiri War and the Maji Maji Uprising.

With slaving long gone and road access from the rest of the country cut off for much of the year, Kilwa Kivinje is nowadays little more than a large fishing village, and most of its historical buildings, the majority of which date from the German and British periods, are rapidly crumbling away. Whilst there are no outstanding sights (the ruined courthouse facing the fishing harbour comes closest), Kilwa Kivinje is a great place just to wander around and absorb the atmosphere – wander around the streets radiating from the market and you'll come across some beautiful balconies and carved doors, the latter invariably in better condition than the houses they guard. There's no problem in terms of security.

Apart from the ruins and the somnolent **market** (a good place to buy coconuts, mangoes and herbal remedies), there's not actually all that much to see or do, though if you're around on a Friday you may be lucky enough to see an **Islamic wedding** – joyous processions of singing women accompanied by people carrying gifts and waving green branches (a universal symbol of fertility and blessing) in the air. If it's **beaches** you're after, Kilwa Kivinje isn't the best place, as mangroves line much of the coast, although at low tide the sea goes out almost 1km, making for fine walks along the shore.

KILWA KIVINJE

INDIAN OCEAN

EATING & DRINKING
Al-Mahmouda Hotel	3
Boys Corner Hotel	7
Former Dolphin Restaurant	5
Kivulini Beach Bar	1
Sea Breeze Bar	4

Commercial Harbour

Slipway

Fishing Harbour

Foodstalls

Courthouse

Covered Market

Market

Daladalas to Nangurukuru & Kilwa Masoko

German Memorial

N

ACCOMMODATION
Four Ways Guest House	8
New Sudi's Guest House	6
Savoye Guest House	2
Unnamed guesthouse	9

0   200 m

Mbukwa Grocery

Police Station (500m), Maji Maji Memorial (1km), Nangurukuru & Kilwa Masoko ▼

Arrival and accommodation

There are no direct **buses** to Kilwa Kivinje from Dar es Salaam, so you're best off heading to Kilwa Masoko first and then catching a daladala for the journey back up the peninsula. Alternatively, you could skip Kilwa Masoko by getting off at Nangurukuru and catching a **daladala** from there – though if you get stuck there's only one exceedingly grubby guest house to stay in. All daladalas drop off passengers in Kilwa Kivinje opposite the German memorial. Note that most road maps of Tanzania get this area totally wrong – the road from Nangurukuru to Kilwa Masoko *doesn't* go through Kilwa Kivinje, but passes it 6km inland. **Leaving** Kilwa Kivinje, board the bus in Kilwa Masoko if you're aiming for Dar. Heading south, you have no choice but to go to Nangurukuru and wait for a spare seat on a bus coming from Dar. Drivers should note that there's no **petrol** at Kilwa Kivinje, so fill up at Nangurukuru or Kilwa Masoko.

There are four cheap and basic **guest houses** in Kivinje (all ❶). By far the most pleasant, if you don't mind doing without electricity and a private bathroom, is the *Savoye Guest House* (☎ Kilwa Kivinje 4), beside the commercial harbour, which has cleanish rooms with mosquito nets, shared bathrooms and friendly owners, though they don't speak English. Otherwise, there's the grotty *Four Ways Guest House* by the market, with dark and dingy but exceptionally cheap rooms with electricity; and the similar if even grubbier *New Sudi's Guest House*, which is accessed through a small bar. Equally basic but more atmospheric than any of these is the unnamed guest house on the little triangular square west of the market (it's on the second floor). Despite the modern facade, it's an old construction with thick walls, and still retains residual decoration (such as stuccowork and carved window frames) from more glorious times past.

Dhows from Kilwa Kivinje

Kilwa Kivinje is one of the few remaining places on the coast where catching a **dhow** along the coast is a real possibility (for general advice on catching dhows, see p.37). The first place to head for is the harbour, which has two distinct areas separated by a clump of mangroves. The eastern harbour is for fishing boats, the western one for commercial dhows. As is the case along the whole of the south coast, your best chance of arranging lifts is between November and March or April. **Fishing dhows** will rarely give you a lift, as few of them land anywhere, though you could try to arrange an overnight trip with them to near Songa Songa, where they bait fish at night with lanterns, returning home at the crack of dawn. More promising if you actually want to get somewhere are the **cargo dhows** moored in the commercial harbour, which will usually take passengers for a fee. There are no fixed schedules, and the price depends on how wealthy the captain thinks you are. It's worth asking locally about the seaworthiness and the character of the skipper of any boat you decide to go in.

There are boats to **Songa Songa** most days, some continuing to **Mafia Island**. Songa Songa itself has connections northwards, and occasionally all the way to **Zanzibar**, though you'll need an exit stamp to make this trip (ask at the regional offices in Kilwa Masoko; you'll need to be extremely patient). Failure to do this will land you in hot water with the Zanzibari authorities, who will require convincing explanations (or a bribe) to overlook your unorthodox entry. You'll also need to bring your own food and water. Heading south, there are less frequent dhows to **Lindi** – ask around, but be prepared to have to wait a few days or longer. There are no boats between Kilwa Masoko and Kilwa Kivinje.

The Town

The bulk of Kilwa Kivinje's nineteenth-century buildings lie along a couple of sandy streets flanking the shore, just back from the two harbours. Many of these structures date from Kilwa Kivinje's short but prosperous golden age in the middle of the nineteenth century, when it was chosen by the Zanzibar Omanis to replace Kilwa Kisiwani as the major terminus for the southern **slave route** from Lake Nyasa. Slaves, ivory and other goods were transported along this route from the interior to Zanzibar, or directly to Madagascar and the French colonies of the Bourbon Islands (now Réunion) and Îles Maurice – it's estimated that over 20,000 slaves were exported annually from Kilwa Kivinje during the 1860s.

Following the abolition of the slave trade in the 1870s (slavery itself only disappeared in the 1920s, however), decline was inevitable, and was swiftly followed by **German colonization** in 1888. On the strength of the town's trading links with the interior, Kilwa Kivinje was an obvious choice for the colony's southern headquarters. German rule was harsh and unforgiving, and their occupation – which lasted less than three decades – saw the German *schutztruppen* almost constantly engaged in quelling rebellions and uprisings all over the country. The **former courthouse**, an imposing two-storey building facing the fishing harbour, dates from this time. The **cannon** mounted on a replica carriage outside is from Omani times, and there are two more, unmounted cannons a few metres away on the grimy beach, which only appear at low tide.

Under German rule, Kilwa Kivinje played a part in two major confrontations: the Abushiri War of 1888–89 and the Maji Maji Uprising of 1905–6. Some 500m along the road to Nangurukuru from the fishing harbour in a square on the left is a small **German memorial**, with four cannons planted point downwards at its corners. It commemorates two Germans who were killed during the Abushiri War in September 1888, defending, according to the inscription, "the house of the German East Africa Company in a heroic fashion". Locals have another version of the story: the Germans, they say, had been hunting warthogs or wild boar, and after the hunt had skinned the animals and prepared the meat. Unfortunately for them, the meat was stolen by a local inhabitant, who proceeded to eat it with his family and friends. On discovering that what they had just eaten was a kind of pork and thus *haram* (forbidden), the good Muslim thieves returned to lynch the hapless Germans.

Kilwa put up strong resistance during the rebellion, and was one of the last places to be "pacified" when its leader, **Hassan bin Omari Makunganya**, was captured in November 1895 and hanged from a mango tree. The tree has disappeared but the site of the hanging is still known as Mwembe-Kinyonga, "hangman's mango tree". It's located 1.5km further along the Nangurukuru road on the right, and is marked with another obelisk put up after independence to commemorate both Makunganya and other local fighters who were hanged during the Maji Maji Uprising. The rebellion began in the Matumbi Hills near Kilwa, in the village of a soothsayer named **Kinjikitile**. Kinjikitile claimed to have discovered a spring from which magic water (*maji*) flowed. If sprinkled on a person, he said, the water would protect the wearer from bullets. Within months, word of the charm had spread and the entire south of the country rose up in arms against the Germans. Kinjikitile himself was one of the first victims of the German reprisal, and was hanged by troops from Kilwa. Surmounting the obelisk is a wooden statue of an old man, possibly Kinjikitile or Makunganya, though both his arms have broken off. The much-eroded painted inscription reads: *Mashujaa Walio Nyongwa na Mjerumani Vita Nya Maji Maji* ("concerning brave people hanged by the Germans in the war of Maji Maji"). German rule ended during World War I, when they were ejected by British troops. If you look around the beach at the top of the slipway in the commercial harbour, you can still see a thick, armour-plated **gun hatch**. Where it comes from, nobody knows, though it's most likely to have turned up here sometime during World War I.

Eating and drinking

Kilwa Kivinje doesn't exactly roll out the carpet when it comes to food. Indisputably the best bites in town are at the ramshackle **foodstalls** on the beach facing the old courthouse, which serve up delicious grilled fish and squid, and also sell seasonal fruit. The ducks waddling around here don't appear to feature on anyone's menu, though. As to proper **restaurants**, the best of the bunch – which doesn't mean an awful lot – is the *Kivulini Beach Bar*, facing the mangroves at the northwest end of the port, which also has reasonably cool beers. You could also ask at the French-run fish-processing company occupying the former *Dolphin Restaurant*: they're planning to open a relatively swish restaurant almost next door, mainly so that they can have decent breakfasts. Other choices are little more than eat houses: try *Al-Mahmouda Hotel*, to the left of the ruined courthouse looking from the beach, which offers cheap basic fare and is popular with locals; or the unnamed *hoteli* to the right of the courthouse, whose smoky atmosphere and grilled fish attracts old men. For breakfast, the best place is the friendly and dirt-cheap *Boys Corner Hotel* beside the market, with *andazi* doughnuts, scalding hot sweet tea, chapatis and *ugali* with sauce.

Beers and sodas are easy to come by. The coldest are at *Mbukwa Grocery*, the bamboo construction 1km back along the road to Nangurukuru on the left, which also does snacks (mainly egg and chip omelettes). Cool beers are also served at *Kivulini Beach Bar* near the port. The *Sea Breeze Bar* has warm beers in small thatched huts near the harbour inside a bamboo fence, but their food is abysmal.

Lindi, Mtwara and Mikindani

It must be said that the port towns of **Lindi and Mtwara**, whilst pleasant enough, aren't much of a draw in themselves, although if you've just arrived from Kilwa or have braved the overland route east from Lake Nyasa, they'll feel like veritable oases of civilization. As a bonus, both have access to some beautiful beaches, and Mtwara is also the base for visiting the newly established **Mnazi Bay–Ruvuma Estuary Marine Park**, right on the border with Mozambique. Much more attractive is the former slave-trading town of

Mikindani, sitting on a bay just north of Mtwara, with its picturesque ruins, a palpable sense of history and a variety of walks and day-trips offered by a local NGO.

Lindi and around

Founded in the eighteenth century as a caravan terminus on the slave and ivory route from Lake Nyasa, the Indian Ocean port of **LINDI** ("Deep Channel") is now the capital of one of Tanzania's most impoverished regions, suffering both from geographical isolation and the decline in the world market for cashew nuts, the region's major cash crop. There's a justified feeling of injured pride, too, at being ignored by the government, whilst neighbouring Mtwara has matured into the south coast's most important trading centre and port, at Lindi's expense.

The feeling of abandonment is most obviously and mundanely expressed in Lindi's crumbling infrastructure. After the rains, especially, when clouds of mosquitoes and flies descend on town, it's hard to imagine that Lindi was home to a thriving expatriate community as recently as the 1950s. Most of the *wazungu* cleared out after Independence and nowadays only a handful of expats remain, mostly NGO workers and missionaries. Few people speak English, but the locals are unfailingly friendly and the town itself is enjoyable enough, with a host of attractive buildings dating from the first half of the twentieth century and a lovely location, nestled on Lindi Bay at the mouth of the Lukuledi River, flanked by hills on its landward side and by the ocean on the other.

Arrival and accommodation

The **roads** from Dar es Salaam and Songea are in a dreadful state, and are impassable for much of the year during the rains. There are no longer any

---

Dhows from Lindi

Lindi has two harbours: the fenced-in **commercial harbour**, and the informal **fishing harbour**, 500m to the south past the NBC Bank, which is basically a strip of beach where local women sell fresh or grilled fish. If you want to catch a lift in a dhow, you'll have to talk your way into the commercial harbour. Ask to be shown the Office of the Dhow Registrar (Mon–Fri 8am–4pm; ☏023/220 2162), which is the building on your right as you enter the harbour. The officer can tell you which dhows are due when, and – if any are in port – where they're headed to. The next step is to come to an arrangement with a dhow captain, after which the registrar will write your name on the passenger manifest and ask for payment of the Tsh200 harbour tax, and Tsh800 per item of "non-personal" luggage (exactly what this means is vague). Once through these formalities, you have to see the Customs & Excise officer; if you're sailing to a Tanzanian destination this is just a formality and no fee should be levied. For general advice on travelling by dhow, see p.37.

The most frequent dhow connection is with **Kilwa Masoko** (which, bizarrely enough, exports boatloads of dried fish to Lindi). Dhows also sometimes go to **Kilwa Kivinje** and **Mafia**, though it's often quicker to take the first dhow headed north and proceed from there. In addition, there are occasional cargo boats (not dhows) to and from **Dar**, **Zanzibar** and **Mozambique**. There are no regular dhows to Mozambique or Mtwara. The peak period for dhows is from November to March or April, when the road from Dar es Salaam is often impassable.

ferries, either, which means that during the rains the only access is **via Mtwara** (which is connected to Dar by plane and ferry), from where there are frequent buses and daladalas (Tsh1800). These arrive at the bus stand in the middle of town between Makongoro Road and Msonobar Street. During the dry season there are at least a couple of **buses** from Dar every day, and buses to Mtwara, Masasi, Newala and Nachingwea also pass through. If you're **driving**, have the car checked out before heading back up north or westwards to Lake Nyasa: ask for mechanics (*fundis*) at the bus stand.

If you've flown, the **airport** is 6km from town back towards Kilwa – you'll have to take a taxi or hitch a lift. Flights are operated by Eagle Air (to and from Dar on Mon, Wed & Sun; to Kilwa on Fri; ℡023/220 2717), whose office is by the bus station on Uhuru Avenue, and by the unreliable Air Tanzania (to and from Dar on Sat; ℡023/220 2537), on Karume Street at the back of the Tanzania Revenue Authority building.

You should **change money** before coming to Lindi, as cashing travellers' cheques is almost impossible without a proof of purchase receipt, and even then the transaction can take (literally) hours. The only banks in town are NBC, in the former *Lindi Beach Hotel* south of the harbour, and CRDB, near the clock tower roundabout facing the market.

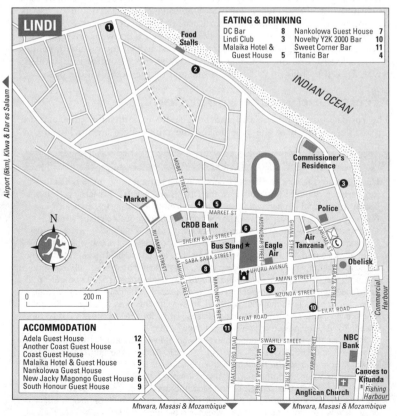

LINDI

Airport (6km), Kilwa & Dar es Salaam

INDIAN OCEAN

Food Stalls

EATING & DRINKING

DC Bar	8	Nankolowa Guest House	7
Lindi Club	3	Novelty Y2K 2000 Bar	10
Malaika Hotel &		Sweet Corner Bar	11
Guest House	5	Titanic Bar	4

Commissioner's Residence

Market

MOBET STREET

MARKET ST

Police

CRDB Bank

SHEIKH BADI STREET

RUTAMBA STREET

JAMHURI STREET

SABA SABA STREET

MAKONDE STREET

Bus Stand ★

Eagle Air

MSONOBAR STREET

Air Tanzania

GHANA STREET

ARUSHA ST

Obelisk

UHURU AVENUE

AMANI STREET

NZUNDA STREET

BARAZA STREET

Commercial Harbour

EILAT ROAD

MAKONGORO ROAD

SWAHILI STREET

MSONOBAR STREET

GHANA STREET

KARUME STREET

NBC Bank

Canoes to Kitunda

Fishing Harbour

Anglican Church

N

0   200 m

ACCOMMODATION

Adela Guest House	12
Another Coast Guest House	1
Coast Guest House	2
Malaika Hotel & Guest House	5
Nankolowa Guest House	7
New Jacky Magongo Guest House	6
South Honour Guest House	9

Mtwara, Masasi & Mozambique ▼   ▼ *Mtwara, Masasi & Mozambique*

Accommodation

Lindi has a wide choice of cheap **accommodation**, plus a couple of slightly more upmarket places. There's no campsite, though, and camping on the beach would be inviting trouble.

Adela Guest House Swahili St ☎023/220 2571. A welcoming and safe budget option with dozens of cell-like rooms sharing showers and squat loos, clean if stained sheets, large box nets and quiet fans. The *askari* appreciates a tip if you've got a car for him to look after. ❶

Another Coast Guest House Jamhuri St ☎023/220 2423. The rooms here are fresher than at the *Coast Guest House*, but the ocean view is partially obscured by buildings on the opposite side of the road. ❶

Coast Guest House On the beach near the top of Makongoro Rd ☎023/220 2423. Currently the only beachside option, though only the front two rooms have sea views, and these are through wire mesh windows. The rooms, all sharing bathrooms, are slightly musty and have box mosquito nets and fans, but little else. There's a choice of large double beds or two small single ones. ❶

Malaika Hotel & Guest House Market Ave (no phone). Lindi's best and most expensive accommodation, albeit overpriced and still a tad basic. All rooms have a private shower and Western style

toilet, ceiling fans and large box nets, and there's also an "executive room" containing an enormous bed (too large for its net), a desk and a pleasingly horrendous three-piece suite. ❷–❸

Nankolowa Guest House Rutamba St ☎023/220 2727. A longstanding favourite which fills the gap between the town's cheap options and the *Malaika*, with which it compares favourably in terms of price. It's safe and friendly, and rooms are clean, with a choice of single, double or twin beds (more expensive ones have private bathrooms), but some are musty and there are no mosquito nets (rooms are sprayed instead). Breakfast included. ❷

New Jacky Magongo Guest House Corner of Makongoro Rd and Sheikh Badi St. Cheap, reasonably clean, and in a handy location next to the bus stand. ❶

South Honour Guest House Amani St (no phone). Similar to the nearby *Adela*, but not as nice or as friendly, and more pricey to boot, though it's still not exactly expensive. Single rooms only, but these can be shared by a mixed-sex couple. ❶

The Town

The centre of town comprises the grid of streets bounded by Jamhuri Street in the west, Market Street and the Stadium in the north, the harbour to the east and Eilat Street in the south. Throughout the centre, especially along the tarmacked central section of the main thoroughfare, **Ghana Street**, you'll find two- or three-storey shops and buildings inscribed with the names of their original owners (mostly Indian traders) and the date of their construction (mainly 1930s–1950s).

Despite the loss of its economic importance, the town centre retains a lively and bustling air, best experienced around the bus stand and at the main **market** at the west end of Market Avenue. Heading east from here takes you to the Chinese-built Stadium, from where a left turn along Makongoro Road heads up to the beach. Turning right at the roundabout marked by a small lighthouse, follow the coast road back into town. This is a pleasantly green part of town, and was favoured by colonial Europeans for their residences and offices, most of them now in ruins. The highlight here is the marvellously dilapidated **Commissioner's Residence**, its flags and bunting now replaced by festoons of ivy. Another reminder of the colonial period is the **obelisk** in the garden outside the commercial harbour, 400m to the south. Although the obelisk has lost its plaques, its similarity to the two obelisk monuments in Kilwa Kivinje suggests that it commemorates Germans who died during the Maji Maji Uprising. Heading south from the commercial habour, you reach the small **fishing harbour**, which also has a small market. Just behind this is the **Anglican Church**, a clumsy attempt at the formal proportions of Neoclassicism, not helped by the battleship-grey cement.

Local beaches

The town-centre **beaches** are mainly used by fishing boats, and for the most part are lined with houses, offering you neither privacy nor – if you're a woman – much chance to respect local Islamic sensibilities. More suitable are the beaches north of town, which get better the further you go. The nearest, **Mtema beach**, is about 4km away in a beautiful sheltered cove, but a quarry on the headland beside it has turned the water brown. Better, if you have time, would be to catch a motorized **canoe ferry** (Tsh200) across the Lukuledi River to the small farming village of **Kitunda**, from where a thirty-minute walk along the coast gets you to a beautiful sheltered beach. The canoes leave from Lindi's fish market, south of the harbour, and take about five minutes to cross the river. It should also be possible to hire a whole canoe (with its owner) to explore the wide river estuary, which contains a number of secluded beaches and bays, mangroves, outlandish limestone formations, crocodiles and the small island of **Kisiwa cha Popo** ("Island of Bats"), which – as its name suggests – serves as a daytime roost for fruit bats.

Eating and drinking

Lindi has a handful of half-decent restaurants, but what's really recommended is the row of **street vendors** inside the bus stand who rustle up roast or fried chicken, eggs and chips to hungry travellers. There's the bonus of chairs and tables arranged out in front, so you can sit out in the street at night under the stars watching the world go by in the flickering light of the *kibatari* oil lamps. Waitresses from nearby bars bring sodas and beers, and the atmosphere is very friendly, with kids dancing about to the music which blares out from surrounding stores. Other street food can be found at kiosks at the fishing harbour (you might find some prawns if you're lucky) and facing the beach just north of *Coast Guest House*, which are especially good for grilled fish.

Lindi is one of the few Tanzanian towns where you can still walk around at night without having to worry about security, even when one of the town's frequent power cuts is in full swing. There are plenty of **bars** to choose from, though for a different drinking experience you could also try the bars inside the bus stand, which have tables set up outside at night.

DC Bar Corner of Uhuru Ave and Makonde St. A cavernous bar owned by the district council and housed in a large courtyard and what looks like an old warehouse. It gets lively at weekends, and occasionally hosts live bands.

Lindi Club (also known as the NBC Club) On the shore east of the stadium. Set in a large plot on the beach, it seems only a matter of time before this gently mouldering colonial club begins to welcome fig trees and creepers into its walls, though old photographs of Greek expats at play in the 1950s still commemorate the days before decline set in. Quiet most of the time, it makes a peaceful and breezy place for lunch (though book early in the morning to ensure there's food, especially if you want to try their fish or prawns). Things are livelier in the evenings, when *nyama choma* and the usual fare (chips, eggs) take over, and there are occasional dances at weekends.

Malaika Hotel & Guest House Market Ave. The best restaurant in town, with great breakfasts (a Tanzanian-style full monty goes for Tsh1000), but arrive early for lunch or dinner as the food is generally gone by 8.30pm. Portions are generous and cost Tsh1000 for *pilau* or stewed meat and bananas, and there's a special biriani for Tsh2000.

Nankolowa Guest House Rutamba St. Enjoys a good reputation and has an extensive menu to choose from, with most dishes under Tsh2500 (served until 9pm), but order early to give them enough time to prepare things.

Novelty Y2K 2000 Bar Corner of Eilat Rd and Karume St. Lindi's biggest, newest and currently most popular bar – it gets especially busy on Friday and Saturday nights.

Sweet Corner Bar Corner of Makongoro Rd and Eilat Rd. A quiet little *nyama choma* joint with tables outside and beer for sale.

Titanic Bar Market Ave. Good place if you want to hit the beers and sink without a trace.

South and west of Lindi

You'll need your own transport and, ideally, to hire an experienced driver if you want to explore the virtually unknown region **around Lindi**. The roads are tough going even in the dry season, and in the rains commonly become impassable.

Tendaguru Hills and Rondo Forest Reserve

An infrequently visited target for a leisurely two-day (or perhaps a rushed one-day) trip are the **Tendaguru Hills**, 110km northwest of Lindi, which contain the richest deposit of **late Jurassic fossils** in Africa. During the late Jurassic period (approximately 150 million years ago) land "bridges" still existed between the various post-Gondwanan continents – as proved by the considerable similarities between Tendaguru's dinosaur fossils and those found at the Morrison Formation in the western USA. The site was "discovered" by a German mining engineer, Bernhard Sattler, in 1907, whilst searching for garnet. Locals were already well acquainted with the gigantic fossilized bones that protruded from the ground, saying that they were the remains of a man-eating ogre whose toes had been slit open by warriors to release people that had been eaten. The scientific excavation – and officially sanctioned plunder – of the site began in April 1909 under the direction of Professor Werner Janensch and Edwin Hennig of the Museum für Naturkunde in Berlin, which still houses their finds. During the three-and-a-half years of excavations, an astonishing 225,000kg of fossils were removed by hand by up to five hundred labourers working simultaneously, to be swiftly packed off to Berlin. Of the dozens of vertebrate species uncovered, including a mammal, crocodiles, sharks and bony fish, pterosaurs and dinosaurs, the prize was the nearly complete skeleton of the giant sauropod, *Brachiosaurus brancai* – at 12m in height, the largest dinosaur ever to have been reconstructed (it now stands in the Berlin museum).

Practicalities are a pain. Officially, visitors first have to contact the Natural Resources Officer (Afisa ya Maliasili; ☏023/222 0501 or 222 0336) at the regional headquarters in Lindi (Mkoa wa Lindi) for permission. Access is the main problem as there's no public transport, so you'll have to hire a vehicle (the Land Rover pick-up drivers in Lindi should be happy to do a deal). The trip takes seven to eight hours each way, depending on the road and the weather, and you'll need to take a guide. Arriving at the site, you'll see the trenches dug by researchers and slowly come to recognize the litter of smaller fossil fragments scattered about the place. There are no facilities at the site, which was recently vandalized by illicit fossil hunters who hired several dozen vehicles packed with workers for a swift overnight excavation.

The **Rondo Forest Reserve**, 77km due west of Lindi, is another challenging excursion off the beaten track, and could conceivably be combined with Tendaguru over three days, so long as you're totally self-sufficient and have adequate 4WD transport. The reserve's eighteen square kilometres of semi-deciduous coastal forest sits on the Rondo Plateau, and offers birders the possibility of spotting the rare East Coast akalat, spotted ground thrush and the Rondo green barbet.

Mingoyo

For those without their own vehicle, there are only two onward options from Lindi served by public transport: westwards towards **Masasi** (covered on p.235), or south to **Mtwara**. The tarmac has now almost completely disappeared along the 26km from Lindi to **MINGOYO**. Also called Mnazi Moja

(One Palm Tree), Mingoyo is a scruffy village straddling the junction of the roads from Lindi, Mtwara and Masasi, and the busiest place on all these routes. It's nothing special in itself, although the persistent hawkers peddling a variety of tasty snacks (mainly seafood, mangoes, cashew nuts and huge king prawns) warrant a short stop. Should you find yourself stranded here – which is unlikely given the plentiful transport connecting the three towns – there are two **guest houses** (both ❶), the better of which is the *Makala Guest House and Bar*. The alternative is the *Apex Guest House*, just down the Mtwara road on the edge of a valley stuffed with coconut palms.

Mtwara and around

Twelve kilometres south of Mingoyo, the dirt road finally gives way to tarmac, which runs the remaining 70km to **MTWARA**, close to the border with Mozambique and 108km south of Lindi. Dubbed "Siberia" by civil servants thanks to its isolation from the rest of Tanzania, this modern town is something of an anomaly, and testimony to the failure of the "Groundnut Scheme", a grand plan for Mtwara's development which the British put into action after World War II. Unfortunately, they seem not once to have considered whether the soil was suitable for growing groundnuts (peanuts) – it was not – and the project collapsed amidst colossal losses and bitter recriminations. The 211-kilometre railway from Mtwara to Nachingwea that had been built as part of the scheme was ripped up, leaving only the empty spaces which nowadays intersperse Mtwara's broad streets to bear witness to the grandiose and short-sighted dreams of the past.

The cashew-nut economy that replaced the Groundnut Scheme has been the victim of fickle market prices, making the Mtwara region a net importer of food and a favoured base for dozens of NGOs and aid organizations. Still, things are looking up despite the woeful state of the cashew market. The recent introduction of a vehicle-carrying ferry over the Ruvuma River on the border with Mozambique promises to open new markets for trade, as does the development of the "Mtwara Development Corridor" from Dar es Salaam, which has come a step closer to realization with the completion of the Rufiji River Bridge (the long-mooted "Unity Bridge" over the Ruvuma River into Mozambique is still just talk). In addition, in anticipation of Mtwara being declared a free port, six million dollars have recently been spent on modernizing the harbour, Tanzania's third busiest, while a survey began in 2000 amid hopes that the Mtwara–Nachingwea Railway might be resurrected.

For visitors, Mtwara's modern origins mean that it lacks even a single building or sight of note. It does, however, sit on one of Tanzania's most beautiful stretches of coastline, while the recently established **Mnazi Bay-Ruvuma Estuary Marine Park** to the south offers superlative swimming, snorkelling and miles of sandy beaches. The town is also a handy (and cheap) springboard for visiting Mikindani, 11km to the north.

Arrival

The **bus** journey from Dar es Salaam takes 24 hours on average, though journeys of several days are not unheard of if the roads are bad, the Rufiji is flooded or the bus breaks down; services cease completely during heavy rains (meaning most of March–May, and occasionally Nov–Jan). A private 4WD can cover the distance in around eighteen hours in good conditions, but it's a

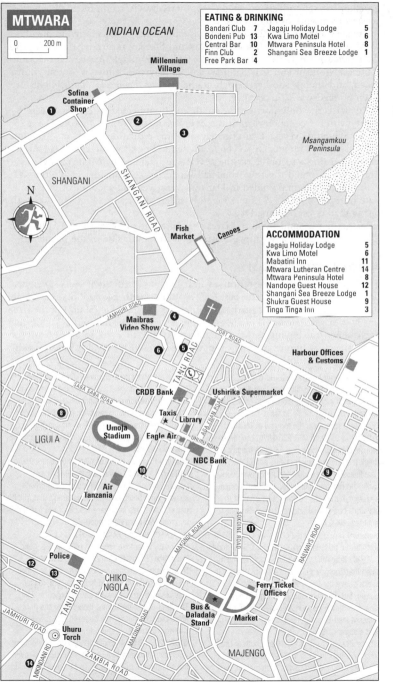

MTWARA

INDIAN OCEAN

0 — 200 m

EATING & DRINKING

Bandari Club	7	Jagaju Holiday Lodge	5
Bondeni Pub	13	Kwa Limo Motel	6
Central Bar	10	Mtwara Peninsula Hotel	8
Finn Club	2	Shangani Sea Breeze Lodge	1
Free Park Bar	4		

Millennium Village

Sofina Container Shop ①

②

③

Msangamkuu Peninsula

SHANGANI

SHANGANI ROAD

N

Fish Market

Canoes

ACCOMMODATION

Jagaju Holiday Lodge	5
Kwa Limo Motel	6
Mabatini Inn	11
Mtwara Lutheran Centre	14
Mtwara Peninsula Hotel	8
Nandope Guest House	12
Shangani Sea Breeze Lodge	1
Shukra Guest House	9
Tinga Tinga Inn	3

JAMHURI ROAD

Maibras Video Show ④

PORT ROAD

⑥ ⑤

Harbour Offices & Customs

SABA SABA ROAD

TANU ROAD

CRDB Bank

Ushirika Supermarket

AGA KHAN ROAD

⑧

Taxis ★ Library

Umoja Stadium

Eagle Air

UHURU ROAD

LIGUIA

NBC Bank

⑨

⑩

Air Tanzania

MAKONDE ROAD

SOKOINE ROAD

⑪

RAILWAYS ROAD

Police

⑫

⑬

CHIKO NGOLA

Ferry Ticket Offices

TANU ROAD

MAKONDE ROAD

Bus & Daladala Stand ★

Market

JAMHURI ROAD

Uhuru Torch

ZAMBIA ROAD

MIKINDANI RD

MAJENGO

▼ *Airport (6km), Mikindani, Mnazi Bay-Ruvuma Estuary Park, Lindi, Masasi, Mozambique & Newala (A19)*

gruelling drive, and an overnight stop at Kilwa is recommended whether you're driving or coming by bus.

Mtwara's **airport** (☎023/233 3845) is 6km south of town. Air Tanzania flies to Mtwara from Dar on Tuesday, Friday and Sunday, returning the same day; their office is on TANU Road (☎023/233 3417). Eagle Air covers the same route on Monday, Thursday, Saturday and Sunday; their office is just off Uhuru Road, and there's another branch at the *Mtwara Peninsula Hotel*. Flights are often booked weeks in advance.

Mtwara is the only port on the south coast connected to Dar es Salaam by **ferry**, with a weekly service on the *MV Safari* (☎022/212 4506 in Dar; $25; 22hr), which leaves Dar on Tuesday at 8am, returning north at 10am on Thursday. It fills up quickly, so you're advised to book several days ahead. At the time of writing, a second ferry, the *MV Aziza*, operated by Mkunazini General Traders, had joined the route, but had yet to fix its schedules, while the *MV Zahara* had been impounded in Dar for over a year on account of its parlous state of repair. The ticket offices for all boats are in the broad square just north of the market off Sokoine Road.

For getting around town, **taxis** can be hired at the corner of TANU and Uhuru roads, and there's also a taxi rank on the south side of the bus stand.

Accommodation

There are no decent **guest houses** near the bus stand, so if you're weighed down with luggage you're best off heading north along Sokoine Road between the stand and the market to either the *Mabatini Inn* (500m) or the better *Shukra Guest House* (1km). Most of the decent places fill up quickly during the cashew-nut buying season (roughly mid-Nov to Feb), so arrive early or book ahead by phone. Mtwara's **tap water** is unsafe to drink thanks to sediment contamination.

Jagaju Holiday Lodge TANU Rd ☎023/233 3380. A friendly place, although little English is spoken, with a choice of rooms with or without bathroom (all have nets and fans). ❶–❷

Kwa Limo Motel Off the top end of TANU Rd ☎023/233 3570, ⓕ023/233 3538. The fifteen self-contained doubles here all have fridges, but check the nets for holes, sheets and pillows for cleanliness, and see whether the shower works. Sadly, the manager isn't averse to overcharging *wazungu*, but on the positive side, it's next to Mtwara's busiest bar and restaurant. Breakfast included. ❷–❸

Mabatini Inn Signposted off Sokoine Rd, 500m north of the bus stand ☎023/233 4025. A friendly if slightly tatty family-run place with that musty smell that seems so characteristic of Mtwara. It doesn't have the best rooms, and bathrooms are shared, but the bedrooms have big box nets and fans, and they play good African music in the adjacent lean-to bar (though this might disturb light sleepers). ❶

Mtwara Lutheran Centre 100m south of Uhuru Torch roundabout ☎ & ⓕ023/233 3294. One of the nicest choices in Mtwara, with a quiet and gentle atmosphere, and a wide choice of clean rooms, all with box nets and standing fans (some also have bathrooms) – recommended so long as you don't plan on crawling back late after a night on the town, as there's a curfew. African food and soft drinks are also available, and breakfast is included. ❶–❷

Mtwara Peninsula Hotel West of Umoja Stadium ☎023/233 3638. Mtwara's best and priciest option. Though the standard rooms (with private shower, new beds, nets and fans) aren't that much better than those in cheaper places, for a few dollars more you can get a good-value "superior" room with a/c and TV. Safe parking. ❹

Nandope Guest House West off TANU Rd, near the police station ☎023/233 3362. One of Mtwara's best budget choices, with simple, colourful rooms painted in Rastafarian colours, reasonably clean shared showers and enclosed parking. The long drops are smelly, though, and the nets are a tad too tight for the beds. ❶

Shangani Sea Breeze Lodge Shangani ☎023/233 3819. A recommended choice right on the coast (though you'll need sandals to walk over the sharp coral to the water, and the sea comes right up to the wall at high tide). The rooms have rattly fans, nets and electric plugs; some also have private bathrooms (same price). ❷

Shukra Guest House Railways Rd, signposted on Port Rd opposite the Pax Filling Station ☎023/233 3822. One of the town's better cheapies, and more peaceful than the nearby *Mabatini Inn*. Most rooms (shared bathrooms only) are huge and contain either a large double bed or two smaller twins, all with nets. ❶

Tinga Tinga Inn Shangani ☎023/233 3146. A popular option (so arrive early), with colourful paintings in the entrance, and large rooms with shared bathrooms, box nets, fans and electric sockets. ❷

The town and beaches

Mtwara's expansive modern layout means that it isn't overly conducive to walking – not that there's an awful lot to see. You could always hire a **bicycle**: there's nothing formal, so it's a matter of asking around and arranging something privately - it shouldn't cost more than Tsh2000 a day. The liveliest area is the district around the **market** near the bus station (but don't bring any valuables), but the rest of town is pretty somnolent. In the town centre, probably the most interesting architectural sights are the terraces of two-storey concrete stores which face one another on **Aga Khan Road**, the town's main commercial drag. Dating from the 1950s to 1970s, these pillared shopfronts are the modern equivalent of the traditional balconied Swahili townhouses you can still see in Mikindani, Kilwa Kivinje and elsewhere.

The town's main beach is in the suburb of **Shangani**, a couple of kilometres north of town. There's no public transport so you'll have to walk, take a bike or grab a cab. The beach consists of fine gravel and sand. The water is pretty clean and is popular with locals at weekends, though the beach can get covered in seaweed. Swimming is best at high tide, as low tide exposes a coral plateau which goes out several hundred metres. Children will love rummaging around in the exposed pools in search of crabs and other animals, but bring sandals or flip-flops as the corals are sharp. The Sofina Container Shop, just back from the beach, has drinks. You might also want to ask whether construction of **Millennium Village**, at the east end of the beach, is complete. This rather fantastical project aims to create Mtwara's answer to Dar es Salaam's upmarket The Slipway shopping centre - though it probably won't be as flashy, the Comoros-born Finnish TV chef involved in the project has a reputation for fun and inventive food.

With more time, you could head across the bay entrance to the much more attractive beach at **Msangamkuu** – the "Big Sand" – a giant sandspit across the harbour entrance on the western tip of Msimbati Peninsula. Regular canoe ferries (around Tsh300) make the crossing throughout the day from the jetty behind the Catholic church. People have camped here in the past without problems, but a recent marine research expedition was robbed of pretty much everything it possessed, so camping is no longer recommended unless you have nothing to lose. There are more beaches at the Mnazi Bay–Ruvuma Estuary Marine Park (see p.224)

Eating

For your own supplies, the **market** near the bus station is good, though most *wazungu* tend to shop at the Ushirika Supermarket, at the north end of Aga Khan Road. Prices are high compared to the rest of Tanzania, especially during the rains. For **eating out**, any of the bars and local *hotelis* are likely to serve up perfectly acceptable *nyama choma* (one excellent example is the nameless place on TANU Road, 50m north of Uhuru Road on the right, serving up

Dynamite fishing

Of the dozens of aid programmes operating from Mtwara, one in particular stands out. Funded by the Finnish and Tanzanian governments, **RIPS** – the Rural Integrated Project Support – is one of the few programmes to have successfully applied a "help yourself" ideology to local problems, rather than relying on the ineffectual handouts. One of the project's major successes has been the elimination of **dynamite fishing**, which by the mid-1990s had become the favoured means of a few mainly young fishermen to get rich quick. The explosions killed or stunned everything around, leaving the fishermen with the easy task of simply gathering whatever floated to the surface. However, the explosions damaged the fragile coral reefs, which in turn increased coastal erosion and led to the disappearance of many larger species of fish, as well as chasing out of the bay fish shoals which had been the mainstay of many local women. RIPS organized a meeting of concerned locals and produced a video of the resulting debate. The video was played back at subsequent meetings with fishermen, and each time their own comments were filmed and added to the video, creating a dynamic forum for debate. In May 1998, it all paid off and the fishermen finally handed over their stocks of dynamite. If the staff aren't too busy, they'll be happy to show you this video and some others, many of them as inspiring as they are beautifully produced – speak to Flora, the media producer. The organization is based on the 2nd floor, Bodi ya Korosho Tanzania Building (Cashew Nut Board), TANU Rd (PO Box 113) ☎023/233 3268 or 233 3449, ✉rips.mtwara@africaonline.co.tz.

local dishes for under Tsh1000). For real restaurants, your choice is pretty much limited to the following.

Bandari Grill In the *Mtwara Peninsula Hotel*. Not especially cheap for its standard Western and Indian fare, with mains at around Tsh3500–5000, and it doesn't always have meat, but they can rustle up lasagne whenever they have mince, and the a/c is arctic.

Finn Club Shangani ☎023/233 3020. This club in the heart of affluent Shangani is the prime haunt of local expatriates and has one of the best restaurants in Mtwara, with full meals for around Tsh2500–4000. The menu isn't particularly inspired, but both the fish and (especially) the chicken are good, and they also have lobster if you want to splurge.

Jagaju Holiday Lodge TANU Rd. Simple eats in the bar at the side of the guest house – the grilled fish is best.

Kwa Limo Motel Off the top end of TANU Rd. The row of double-parked Land Rovers outside testifies to *Kwa Limo*'s popularity with expatriates. There's a wide choice of food at reasonable prices (generally under Tsh2500), including banana soup.

Shangani Sea Breeze Lodge Shangani. This has a limited choice of food if you pre-order a couple of hours ahead, but the main attraction is the idyllic beachfront location.

Bars and nightlife

There are plenty of **bars** to choose from, and a more unusual distraction in the form of the Maibras Video Show, located at the junction of Shangani Road and Port Road, where you can watch awful karate movies or pirated Hollywood flicks in a box-like room full of excitable locals.

Bandari Club Port Rd. Mtwara's main nightspot, this lively and friendly place has a live band on Wed, Fri and Sat nights and Sun afternoons, with plenty of dancing. Tsh500 entry.

Bondeni Pub 100m from *Nandope Guest House*. A popular bar which also has basic rooms (❶) if you can't face the walk back to your hotel.

Central Bar TANU Rd. A pleasant place for a drink

in the basement of a modern house hidden behind four fern trees.

Free Park Bar Port Rd, next to Maibras Video Show. Nothing special, but a handy stopover to and from the ferry to Msangamkuu beach if you're walking.

Kwa Limo Motel Off the top end of TANU Rd. Mtwara's biggest bar, with plenty of outdoor

The **bus and daladala stand** is at the bottom of Sokoine Road near the market. Destinations for the various services are clearly marked on chalkboards by the parking bays, together with their Kiswahili departure times. The first buses for **Dar es Salaam** (Tsh12,000) leave around 5–6am, with a second flurry between 9am and 10am. Most of these, such as Ilala Bus, originate in Newala. There are hourly departures for **Lindi** via **Mikindani** throughout the day. Other destinations covered daily include **Newala, Masasi** and **Nachingwea**. For the **Kilwas**, catch a Dar-bound bus as far as Nangurukuru and get a daladala from there. During the rains, road transport runs only to Lindi, Masasi and (sometimes) Nangurukuru.

For information about **flights and ferries from Mtwara**, see p.220.

By road or sea to Mozambique

The only official border crossing between Tanzania and **Mozambique** is at the mouth of the Ruvuma River, 40km southeast of Mtwara beyond the village of **Kalambo**, where a landing craft carries vehicles across the river, the first time that Tanzania and Mozambique have been directly connected by road. Several pick-ups and Land Rovers cover the 35km of rough *murram* road from Mtwara to Kalambo throughout the day (Tsh2000, for locals at least), but it's best to catch one early in the morning in case you're delayed in Kalambo or at the river. Kalambo is where you complete customs and immigration formalities, in that order – as a tourist you'll need to obtain a Mozambique visa in advance. (When arriving from Mozambique, go to immigration first: a valid *carnet* for drivers is highly recommended – see p.34 – as you'll otherwise be escorted into Mtwara to pay a hefty deposit). Kalambo has plenty of bars and *hotelis* but no accommodation – more reason to arrive early.

Transport from Mtwara waits for its passengers to finish their paperwork before struggling on across the remaining 5km of floodplain to the river itself, assuming the road is passable: the irregularly repaired narrow causeway frequently gets washed away. There are a handful of lean-tos down by the jetty selling warm sodas, tea and beer, but nothing else as yet. The ferry operates at high tide (in effect, for a few hours twice in every 24hr) and occasionally runs at night. It costs Tsh500 for passengers and Tsh5000 for a car. There should also be boys taking people over in canoes.

Once in Mozambique, clear customs and immigration at **Namoto**, 8km south of the river and connected to it by *chapas* (daladalas), which run from early morning to around 5pm. There's also a daily pick-up that goes all the way from the river to Mocímboa da Praia (200,000 meticals); ask in Kalambo about the departure time. There's no bank in Namoto, but you'll find informal money-changers both there and in Kalambo: in December 2001, 10,000 Mozambican meticais were worth Tsh400. The first major town in Mozambique is **Quionga**, 20km south of the river. The road to here, and the 30km continuation to Palma, is tricky sand, but the remaining 85km to the main coastal town of **Mocímboa da Praia** is good dirt. The disastrous floods of 2000 and 2001 may however have washed away sections of this road – ask any drivers you meet about conditions.

There are neither ferries nor regular passenger-carrying **boats** to Mozambique, but with some luck you could find a **commercial dhow** headed for Mocímboa da Praia (at least 48hr) or Pemba (not to be confused with Pemba Island in Zanzibar or Pemba village near Mikindani), which leave roughly every two days from the dhow wharf by the fish market. Alternatively, enquire at the harbour office (Mon–Fri 8am–5pm; ✆023/233 3243) in the main port complex about the cargo-carrying **motorboat** to Pemba, which leaves once or twice a month. You should clear customs formalities in the main port complex in any case, and the immigration office (Ofisi ya Mkuu wa Mkoa) is in the regional administration buildings on TANU Road.

seating under shady trees. It's always popular, both in the daytime, when it catches a bit of a sea breeze, and at night – though it's next to a bug-infested pool which reeks during the rains.

Mtwara Peninsula Hotel A huge *makuti* roof was being built at the time of writing, and both discos and *nyama choma* were planned.

Shangani Sea Breeze Lodge Right on the coast, the somnolent bar here is a lovely place to drop in during the afternoon, with a great view of the ocean despite the chicken-wire fence.

Listings

Banks Two banks change money. The most helpful is NBC on Uhuru Rd, which may occasionally change travellers' cheques without seeing the purchase receipt (but don't count on it). The CRDB on Tanu Rd can be awkward, and insists on seeing purchase receipts.

Car rental The *Kwa Limo Motel* has a Land Rover for rent (in theory only for use within Mtwara, though you might be able to negotiate something); it costs Tsh500 per kilometre or Tsh45,000 for 12hr with unlimited mileage.

Immigration The immigration office is on the ground floor of the Regional Administration Block on TANU Rd.

Library The "Mtwara Intellectual Service Station", also known as the public library, is on Uhuru Rd (Mon–Fri 9.30am–6pm, Sat 9am–2pm; temporary membership Tsh500 per day).

Newspapers The grocery opposite the library does a roaring trade in local newspapers every afternoon, though they can be a day late. The post office opens on Sunday evenings to distribute

newspapers arriving on the flight from Dar.

Pharmacy Bus Stand Pharmacy, in the bus stand (☎023/233 3359).

Post office The post office is on the corner of TANU Rd and Uhuru Rd. Mail is sent to Dar three times a week.

Souvenirs There's a stall next to the *Jagaju Holiday Lodge* at the top of TANU Rd which sells Makonde woodcarvings, and another at the top of Aga Khan Rd facing the Ushirika Supermarket.

Sports The annual Tsh10,000 membership at the *Finn Club* (bring two passport photos) gives you use of their tennis court and swimming pool. These are free if you can get a member to sign you in.

Telephones The TTCL office is in the side of the post office building (Mon–Fri 7.45am–4.30pm, Sat 9am–12.30pm). There are cardphones outside the office, and also at the bus stand and in the bar at the *Kwa Limo Motel*. Cards can be bought in all three locations.

Mnazi Bay–Ruvuma Estuary Marine Park

Formally established in 2000, **Mnazi Bay–Ruvuma Estuary Marine Park** covers a large part of the land and ocean east of Mtwara between the mouth of the Ruvuma River and Msangamkuu Peninsula, encompassing a network of estuarine, mangrove, shore, peninsular, island and coral-reef environments. The last offer superb snorkelling and diving, especially on **Ruvula Reef**, off the north end of Msimbati Peninsula, which slopes very steeply right up to the shore. To arrange **scuba-diving**, contact *Ten Degrees South Lodge* in Mikindani (see p.227), who run the only PADI-accredited dive centre between Mafia Island and Mozambique.

Msimbati Beach, on the east shore of Msimbati Peninsula, is one of Tanzania's most beautiful, with two kilometres of white sand, fringing palm trees, warm water and coral reefs just offshore. A word of caution: there's a dangerous **undertow** here at spring tide, and a few people get swept away every year, so seek local advice; **snorkelling** is possible at low tide around the nearby reefs. There's also an uninhabited island nearby which local fishermen will take you to for more snorkelling and a taste of the desert island experience.

Practicalities

The heart of the park, on **Msimbati Peninsula**, is roughly an hour's drive from Mtwara. From Mtwara's Uhuru Torch roundabout head south for 900m

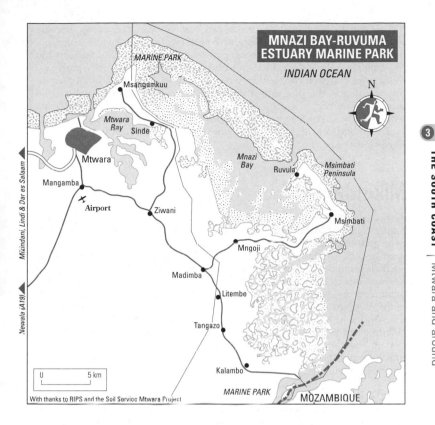

INDIAN OCEAN

N

MARINE PARK

Msangamkuu

*Mtwara
Bay* Sinde

Mtwara

*Mnazi
Bay* Ruvula

*Msimbati
Peninsula*

Mangamba

Airport Ziwani

Msimbati

Mngoji

Madimba

Litembe

Tangazo

Kalambo

MARINE PARK

MOZAMBIQUE

0 5 km

With thanks to RIPS and the Soil Service Mtwara Project

and then turn left. After 3.7km, turn left again off the tarmac on to the wide
murram road that heads to Kalambo. The road takes you past the sizeable village
of **Ziwani**, 8km from the junction and beautifully located in lush and shady
coconut and mango plantations. Watch out for a dangerously slippery descent
3km further on. The turn-off for Msimbati is at **Madimba**, 17.5km from the
junction; the road from here is deep sand.

By **public transport**, catch a daladala direct to Msimbati village, which lies
around 2km from Msimbati beach. To get to Ruvula, at the tip of the peninsula, you can either walk the remaining 8km along a sandy track, or wait for a
lift – you stand a better chance at weekends, when the Indian and European
communities decamp en masse to the Msimbati beach and Ruvula.
Alternatively, you could ask around at the *Finn Club* or the *Kwa Limo Motel* in
Mtwara beforehand, or at *Ten Degrees South Lodge* in Mikindani, which arranges
trips to Ruvula most weekends.

There are no park fees or any tourist infrastructure as yet. At present, the best
source of **information** is the manager of *Ten Degrees South Lodge*, who is a
marine biologist and PADI dive instructor. For information in Mtwara, contact one of the three official bodies managing the park: the Environment
Department on the first floor of the Regional Administration Building on
Tanu Road; or either the Fisheries Department or the Mangrove Management
Project in the Saba Saba Grounds along Zambia Road.

There's no accommodation in the park, though you can **camp on the beach** at Msimbati, which is a delight. You can buy fish and shellfish from local fishermen (including oysters, lobster, prawns and barracuda), and villagers can rustle up chickens and snacks for a barbecue. There are no security problems, though this may well change if or when hotel developers move in. At present, the only step in this direction is the combined eco-lodge, diving school and marine studies centre which is currently being constructed at Ruvula facing west over Mnazi Bay. There's already a small dorm for scientists, and ecological walks and bird-watching trips are planned. For more information, contact *Ten Degrees South Lodge*.

Mikindani

The contrast between the sprawling modern town of Mtwara and the tranquil fishing village of **MIKINDANI**, 11km back along the Lindi road, could hardly be greater – or more welcome. Beautifully set inside a sheltered, mangrove-lined bay, the village is home to some 12,000 people who rely on the ocean for their livelihood, catching fish and collecting cockles from the bay. Yet, as in so many other coastal villages, today's peaceful and languid atmosphere belies a turbulent and brutal past, when the town grew wealthy and powerful as one of the coast's major seaports for the ivory and slave caravans from the region of Lake Nyasa. Mikindani's many stone buildings, most of them in ruins, offer an eloquent and picturesque reminder of more prosperous times past, while its beautiful beaches, a wide choice of excursions and one of southern Tanzania's most beautiful hotels make it a superb destination for a few days of getting away from it all.

Some history

Mikindani's sheltered location offered an ideal base for early traders sailing up and down the coast, and the town – or rather Pemba village, on the spur of land enclosing the bay's western entrance – was swiftly incorporated into the Indian Ocean trading network, as proven by some of Tanzania's earliest signs of Arab habitation. The arrival of **Islam** stimulated trade, and by the end of the fifteenth century – when Mikindani proper replaced Pemba as the main port – the town was trading inland as far as present-day Malawi, Zambia, Angola and Congo.

Decline set in with the arrival of the **Portuguese** in the sixteenth century and their disruption of the old trade links, but the town's fortunes picked up again in the middle of the following century when the Portuguese were ejected and the coastal slave trade fell under Omani and Zanzibari control. Mikindani's real boom began during the reign of **Sultan Seyyid Barghash**, whose rule saw the consolidation of the town's importance and the construction of several fine buildings, notably the Friday mosque. The legacy of the slave trade is reflected, too, in the village's tribal make-up, which includes the descendants of Yao, Makua and Mwera slaves, as well as Ngoni who first came as caravan porters working for the Arabs, and Makonde, some of whom had been slave traders themselves.

German rule was marked by the introduction of cash crops such as sisal, rubber, coconut and oil seed, though this failed to reverse the decline in the town's fortunes that had followed the abolition of the slave trade. Things changed little under **British rule**, and by the 1950s Mikindani Bay had outlived its usefulness as a harbour as it was too shallow for the vessels of the time. Mikindani's decline accelerated when the Mtwara to Nachingwea railway, built in 1949 for the Groundnut Scheme, was ripped up in 1962 following the scheme's spectacular collapse. Many of the colonial plantations subsequently fell to waste, and the town reverted to its original status as a humble fishing village.

Arrival, information and accommodation

Frequent **daladalas** run **from Mtwara** to Mikindani throughout the day (Tsh200). Alternatively, all daladalas and buses **from Lindi** to Mtwara pass though (Tsh2000, or Tsh1300 from Mingoyo). Heading on from Mikindani, there are also a handful of daily buses **from Masasi** (Tsh2500).

The beautifully restored *Old Boma at Mikindani* hotel has a **tourist information centre** where they can fill you in about Mikindani and Mtwara, and also have details about hiking routes on the Makonde Plateau (p.231) and less common attractions in the region, such as the Tendaguru Hills (see p.217). Trade Aid, the NGO that runs the hotel, is actively involved in preserving the town's historical buildings, and hopes to kickstart the local economy by attracting tourists.

Accommodation

There are only three **hotels** in Mikindani, none of them cheap. If you're on a shoestring budget, the town is best visited as a day-trip from Mtwara. Camping on the beach is not recommended, since it's in full view of everyone, while the bay acts as the local latrine.

Makonde Beach Resort (also known as *Litingi's*) 1.2km off the main road 3.5km south of Mikindani ☎023/233 3635, ℱ023/233 3067. A newish if rather tatty option, with very slow construction work currently under way on a new bar and restaurant. The bedrooms are in round brick *bandas* in an unattractive and heavily fortified compound, though the rooms themselves are reasonable, with large double beds and nets, hot water, satellite TV, telephones and room service (more expensive ones have a/c). There's no beach (it's all mangroves), and the nearest one is 1km away, though a swimming pool is planned. Breakfast included. ❹

The Old Boma at Mikindani ☎023/233 3885, ⓦwww.mikindani.com (bookings also through Safari Scene in Dar; see p.125). Set inside the restored German Boma, this is southern Tanzania's best hotel by a long shot, with bags of atmosphere and outstanding accommodation, plus a wide range of activities and excursions (see p.228). The high-ceilinged rooms have large timber beds and are individually decorated with local handicrafts. There's no a/c, but the thick walls and sea breeze keep things cool. It's worth spending a little more for one of the corner rooms with balconies; the best is at the front under the parapet. All profits go into community development projects. Credit cards accepted by prior arrangement. ❻–❼

Ten Degrees South Lodge On the bay by the roadside ☎023/233 4053, ℮tendegreesouth@twiga.com. Good-value option, in a cool old house with thick walls. The four rooms boast solid Zanzibari beds with box nets and clean cotton sheets; some also have private bathrooms. The place is run by a British marine biologist (mind the jars full of octopus gonads on the verandah) who doubles as a PADI diving instructor ($300 for Open Water certification). ❸

The Town

Mikindani is small enough to get around easily on foot, and the plentiful trees provide enough shade. If you want a guide, contact the folks at *The Old Boma at Mikindani* (see above). As you're wandering along the narrow winding streets, look for the attractive first-floor wooden balconies, called *barazas*, and the elaborately carved wooden doorways, both typical features of Swahili coastal settlements. Most of the stone buildings, many of them in ruins, date from the

Ten Degrees South Lodge is the best place for water sports, offering a full range of **snorkelling and scuba-diving** trips (and lessons) in and around the **Mnazi Bay–Ruvuma Estuary Marine Park** (see p.224). They can also arrange Land Rover safaris into **Mozambique** (get your visa in Dar), and are currently building a dive school and marine education centre at Ruvula on **Msimbati Peninsula** (see p.224). Day- and overnight trips to the marine park can also be arranged by *The Old Boma at Mikindani* and are good value at $25 per person including the cook and driver.

For landlubbers, a whole range of **walks and bicycle excursions** are offered by *The Old Boma at Mikindani*, ranging from guided walks around town ($5 per person) to longer hikes and bicycle rides in the vicinity. A **guide** is recommended for most of these; charges vary between $5 and $15 per group. Easy **half-day trips** include the baobab-bedecked **Tingi Peninsula** (4km; 1.5hr on foot, 30min by bicycle), which protects the east side of the bay, and **Pemba Village** (7km) on the west side.

slaving era and are constructed of coral rock (ragstone) embedded in lime mortar. Much of the original lime stucco facing and cream or white limewash has disappeared, but where patches of limewash remain, the buildings make singularly photogenic subjects.

Friday Mosque

Notable among the buildings dating from the reign of Sultan Barghash is the **Friday Mosque** in the centre of town. Its beautiful carved door was the work of an Ndonde slave called Gulum Dosa (the Ndonde are closely related to the Makonde), who belonged to an Indian customs officer in the Arab government. The three **stone graves** outside the mosque are believed to date from the fifteenth century, and face north towards Mecca. They are marked by baobab trees, which has led some to believe that the graves belong to sultans. Although there's no direct proof of this, a local legend says that when a sultan died, two baobab saplings would be planted at either end of his grave so that they would eventually unite to form a single tree.

Livingstone House and the Slave Market

At bottom of the hill leading to the Boma, the nearly derelict **Livingstone House** has been ear-marked for renovation by Trade Aid and the Tanzania Gatsby Trust. The building – a rather bland three-storey construction with little decoration – was erected by the British colonial government in 1952 in memory of the famous missionary and explorer, and supposedly occupies the site of Livingstone's camp in 1866 at the start of his fifth and final expedition to the Great Lakes, which became famous for his encounter with Stanley (see p.530). The actual site of Livingstone's camp, however, is much more likely to have been in Pemba village, as he describes the location as a "point of land on the north side of Pemba (*alias* Pimlea) Bay."

When the Germans arrived, twenty years after Livingstone, slaves were still by far the town's most valuable asset, and it took them some time to eliminate the trade. Indeed, according to some accounts, it was the Germans themselves who built Mikindani's **Slave Market**. Facing the waterfront and Livingstone House across a small square, the building is said to date from the end of the nineteenth century, when the Germans were already in control. Some confusion remains about whether the building itself was used as a slave market, or if it was simply built on the site of an older one. The thick walls, some of them as deep as 60cm, seem to point to the former, which would show that slavery was at least tolerated during the early years of German occupation. Sadly, the building's recent renovation has completely destroyed the charm of the previously ruined building – its wonderful pastel-shaded arches and vaults now hidden by internal walls which have been built to house artists' workshops and galleries, and the stone platform that served as stalls during the building's use as a fish market in the 1950s has been demolished. The colour scheme, with lots of gaudy pink, doesn't help much either. The seven **artists' workshops** (roughly 10am–6pm) themselves though are well worth a visit, with some nice Tingatinga paintings and examples of Makonde woodcarvings on sale.

The German Boma and Bismarck Hill

A rather more sensitive example of restoration is the **German Boma**, which has been beautifully spruced up and converted into southern Tanzania's most luxurious and atmospheric hotel (see p.227). Built in 1895 as the seat of the German colonial administration, the limewashed building is the town's most distinctive and attractive landmark, combining German, Arab and Swahili architectural elements. The newly planted gardens surrounding the Boma are attractive, too, and shouldn't take too much longer to mature – in the meantime, the older frangipani and flame trees provide welcome splashes of colour and shade. Visitors are welcome to look around, as indeed you probably will anyway, seeing as the town's tourist information centre is located here. On entering, have a look at the stunning door carvings, the work of Gulum Dosa, who also carved the mosque's doorway. Inside there's a cool courtyard, with rooms arranged around it on two floors. One corner of the building has a three-storey tower with crenellated battlements, uncannily resembling an Andalucian minaret. There's an excellent view of the town from the tower, accessed by two flights of exceedingly steep steps.

Strangely enough, given their bloody colonization of Tanganyika, the Germans permitted the establishment of a separate tribal court in the Boma's grounds, which was presided over by a local chief from the raised platform at the back. The building still exists, albeit in greatly altered form, and now serves as the hotel's outdoor bar and restaurant.

Just behind the Boma above the coconut groves stands **Bismarck Hill**, named after the first chancellor of unified Germany – it's well worth making the thirty-minute climb up to the top, not only for its sweeping views but also for a curious piece of history. The hill is popularly known as Baobab Hill, on account of the lone baobab (*mbuyu*) which stands at its summit. These trees are traditionally thought to be inhabited by benevolent spirits, and so were considered safe places to bury things, like money, which gave rise to the common belief that the Germans buried treasure near baobabs when they left. Usually it's locals who excavate the land in the hope of finding valuables, but in this case the great big hole on top of the hill was made by a deranged European, who sadly failed to find anything.

Local beaches

The only real drawback to Mikindani from a tourist point of view is the lack of a central beach. Although the sandy shore on the other side of the road looks tempting, locals might well find sight of pink *wazungu* stripping off for a dip in what is effectively their toilet rather amusing, to say the least. Cleaner, and more private, is **Naumbu Beach** beyond Pemba village, some 7km from Mikindani (roughly thirty minutes by bike or ninety minutes on foot). To get there, head up the road towards Lindi and bear right before the bridge and past the boatyard. The track follows the old railway embankment skirting the electric fence of Mikindani Estate on the west side of the bay (watch out for snakes). If you stay on the track closest to the bay you'll eventually come to Pemba, which has the remains of an old Arab mosque (possibly from the ninth century), and some graves. The beach is on the ocean side of the village – ask for directions. For a more romantic way of getting there, ask at the Boma for help in arranging a lift with a local *ngalawa* outrigger. The price seems to depend on how well you talk Kiswahili, and ranges from Tsh2000 to Tsh10,000.

An alternative to Naumbu is **Tingi Beach**, near the *Makonde Beach Resort*. The walk from Mikindani takes sixty to ninety minutes: head down the road to Mtwara and turn left after the first salt pan some 3km down the road. Note the white pyres on your left before the salt pan, which you'll also see near the resort. These are for firing coral heads to produce lime for making mortar and paint, a practice that is sadly depleting the area's diminishing mangrove forests, which are harvested as fuelwood. From the salt pan follow the footpath either along the coast (low tide only) or veer right to join up with the access road for the resort, then head towards the baobab trees. Swimming is only possible at high tide unless you're happy wading out across the shallows for several hundred metres. If you're driving you can leave your car at the resort, whose *askari* will probably want a tip.

Eating and drinking

Although limited to the three hotels, Mikindani's culinary offerings are definitely a cut above most other places in southern Tanzania, and worth splashing out on. Nightlife varies according to the whims of local expats.

Makonde Beach Resort 1.2km off the main road 3.5km south of Mikindani. The menu here is huge, and especially good for Indian or seafood (best ordered in advance), with most mains costing Tsh3500–6000. The bar is dead midweek but gets lively – and occasionally wild – on Saturdays (except during Ramadan), when the Indian and expat communities get it together for a weekly disco, with all the lights and mirrorballs you could hope for.

Old Boma at Mikindani Inside the restored German Boma. Pricier than *Ten Degrees South* and with smaller portions, but usually good (the shark tail vindaloo is a slightly chewy novelty), and unbeatably fresh salads from their own market garden. Lunches cost Tsh3000–6000 for two courses, while three-course dinners go for around Tsh8000. There's no menu as such – the choice depends on what's available that day. The swimming pool is open to non-residents so long as you take a meal, and there's a pleasant bar in the reconstructed tribal courthouse.

Ten Degrees South Lodge On the bay by the roadside. The outdoor bar here, complete with satellite TV, is the best in town, attracting a regular clientele from both the local and expatriate communities and usually staying open until the last punter drops. The food can also be good, especially seafood, though the meat dishes are more average; the Goan prawn curry is excellent, and lobster and calamari are available should you fancy a splurge. Don't miss the evening barbecue (Tsh4000) on Saturdays.

The Makonde Plateau

The area west of the southern coastal strip is covered by the **MAKONDE PLATEAU**, a river-gouged massif rising 900m above sea level which is home to Africa's most famous woodcarvers, the **Makonde**. The plateau itself is a strikingly beautiful, if largely unvisited, area, ideally suited for hiking if you have time and patience to sort out the practical details. The plateau's reliance on **cashew nuts** as a cash crop is the key to its economy, but despite the boom-and-bust character of the international market (currently in deep recession), there's a visible sense of prosperity in some places. Tandahimba District, between Mtwara and Newala, has one of the highest per capita incomes in the country, and although day-to-day poverty is as prevalent here as it is elsewhere, you can't help noticing the well-constructed houses (whether of mud and tin or cement and bricks) and numerous schools scattered about the neat and tidy villages.

The primary attraction for visitors is the fact that life on the plateau has hardly been changed by the outside world. Although Christian missionaries have made their presence felt in many ways, the Makonde themselves have remained aloof to the developments that have overtaken the rest of independent Tanzania, and – for the patient traveller willing to learn – provide a superb opportunity to explore the traditional customs that are being swept aside elsewhere.

Getting to the plateau isn't too difficult, with the plateau's main towns, **Newala**, **Masasi** and **Ndanda**, being connected by several daily **buses** and pick-ups to the coastal towns of Lindi and Mtwara, running via Mingoyo. The stretch from Mtwara to Mingoyo is all tarmac except for a short section over the Lukuledi River between Mtama and Nanganga, which periodically gets washed away. If you're driving during the rains, avoid the direct road between Mtwara and Newala via Nanyamba: the deeply rutted fifteen-kilometre section through dense *miombo* woodland that starts some 30km from Mtwara turns (literally) into a river after heavy downpours, making getting stuck in metre-deep water-filled potholes a real possibility. The longer way round, using the dirt road which cuts straight across the plateau from Mtama to Newala, is in much better condition and is generally passable all year round. Lastly, if you're continuing west towards Tunduru, Songea and Mbeya (all covered in Chapter 10), be prepared for an exceedingly rough ride (and lengthy delays during the rains). In the dry season, the bone-shaking trail tests any vehicle to the limit; if you're driving yourself, a degree of mechanical competence is recommended. There are no buses west of Masasi, so if you don't have your own vehicle you'll probably end up paying for a lift in the back of a lorry. Some people find that standing makes the trip marginally more comfortable, so long as you keep your knees slightly bent to absorb the shocks.

Newala

The town of **NEWALA**, on the southwestern rim of the Makonde Plateau, is the best base for exploring the region, and makes a pleasant stopover in any case along the rough road from Mtwara to Masasi. Its climate, although considered glacial by locals, is just about right for visiting *wazungu*, and there's plenty of accommodation, while its transport connections – although not extensive – are handy for getting off the beaten track.

One of Tanzania's largest and most heterogenous tribal groups, the **Makonde** are world-famous for their intricate **woodcarvings**. The birth of the tradition is entwined with the mythical origin of the Makonde themselves:

In the beginning, there was a male creature who lived alone in the bush, unbathed and unshorn. The creature lived alone for a long time, but one day felt very lonely. Taking a piece of wood from a tree, he carved a female figure and placed it upright in the sun by his dwelling. Night fell. When the sun rose in the morning, the figure miraculously came to life as a beautiful woman, who of course became his wife.

They conceived a child, but it died three days later. "Let us move from the river to a higher place where the reeds grow," suggested the woman. This they did, and again she conceived, but again the child survived only three days.

"Let us move higher still, to where the thick bush grows," the woman said. And again they moved, and a third time a child was conceived, this one surviving to become the first true ancestor of the Makonde.

The myth alludes to the Makonde's movement away from low-lying and frequently flooded areas of northern Mozambique, as a result of which they became isolated from other tribes and developed an exceptionally strong sense of identity. They remain one of very few Bantu-speaking people in East Africa still to reckon descent matrilineally, and motherhood is considered a quasi-sacred state of being. Indeed, such is the female domination of Makonde society that men travelling alone still carry a carved female figure to give them protection.

Nowadays, Makonde carvings are much more abstract, in keeping with the tastes of tourists and collectors. Their best-known works are the "tree of life" or "people pole" carvings in the **Ujamaa** style; intricately carved columns of interlocking human figures representing both unity and continuity. *Ujamaa* has many meanings – brotherhood, co-operation, family and togetherness – and was a by-word in post-Independence Tanzanian politics. The central figure is invariably a mother surrounded by clinging children, supporting (both literally and symbolically) later generations. Lively and full of movement, rhythm and balance, these are the works that justly brought the Makonde their fame. Lesser-known styles include the naturalistic **Binadamu** style, which represents traditional modes of life: old men smoking pipes, women fetching water, and so on. The latest style to develop, **Shetani** ("spirits"), is much more abstract, its models being folkloric spirits presented in distorted, often fantastically grotesque forms.

For all the pre-eminence of figures in modern carvings, the most traditional form of Makonde carving is that of **masks**, representing spirits or ancestors and commonly used in dances for initiation ceremonies and harvest celebrations. There are three main kinds: face masks, body masks (which cover the dancer's torso) and helmet masks (*mapiko*), worn over the head like helmets and notable for their strong features. The masks are made in a secret bush location known as *mpolo*, which women are forbidden to approach. When not in use, the masks are taken back to the *mpolo*. *Mapiko* is also the name of a dance and the terrifying force which animates the dancers who perform it. *Mapiko* dances, together with *sindimba* dances (in which the dancers perform on stilts), still take place every year when a new generation is initiated into adulthood.

Finally, when buying Makonde carvings you should be aware that the fine-grained **African blackwood** ("Mozambique ebony"), the most widely used wood for carvings, has become endangered. Please buy pieces worked in other kinds of wood, and encourage others to do likewise. The future of the African blackwood is literally in your hands.

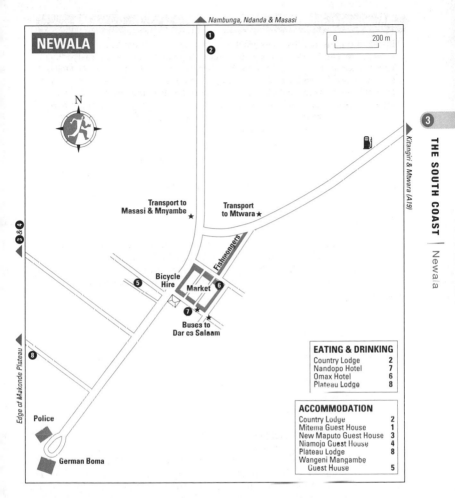

NEWALA

Nambunga, Ndanda & Masasi

N

0   200 m

Kitangiri & Mtwara (A19)

Transport to
Masasi & Mnyambe ★

Transport
to Mtwara ★

Fishmongers

Edge of Makonde Plateau

Bicycle
Hire   Market ⑥

⑤

⑦ ★

Buses to
Dar es Salaam

Police

German Boma

EATING & DRINKING

Country Lodge	2
Nandopo Hotel	7
Omax Hotel	6
Plateau Lodge	8

ACCOMMODATION

Country Lodge	2
Mitema Guest House	1
New Maputo Guest House	3
Niamojo Guest House	4
Plateau Lodge	8
Wangeni Mangambe Guest House	5

Newala's main street, lined with tall shady trees planted by the Germans at the end of the nineteenth century, runs 1km southwest from the post office to the police station and the **German Boma**, with its strange sloping black walls, perched right on the edge of the plateau. It may be possible to visit the Boma, but bear in mind that it's currently occupied by the police, so keep your camera out of sight. Other attractions, such as **Shimu ya Mungu** ("Hole of God"), where the plateau plunges into a deep chasm, and viewpoints on the plateau edge are best visited by bicycle with a local guide. Both the *Plateau Lodge* and *Country Lodge* can arrange for someone to accompany you (a tip would be appreciated), and you can hire bicycles at the stand facing the side of the post office at the edge of the market – it shouldn't cost more than Tsh1500 a day. A half-day trip you could do without your own transport is to **Nambunga viewpoint** along the road to Masasi, some 10km from town. Catch a daladala towards Nangomba or Masasi and ask to be dropped at Nambunga village. From here, walk along the left fork for a few hundred

Moving on from Newala

Buses **to Dar** (usually 5–7 weekly in the dry season) depart from beside the market between 6am and 8am. Get there no later than 5.30am to be sure of a seat, or buy your ticket the day before from the offices near the *Nandopo Hotel*. **Mtwara** is served by one or two buses a day, and by more frequent pick-ups and lorries; the first vehicle leaves around 4am, and the last around midday, but there's next to nothing on Sundays. Heading on **to Masasi**, you'll find buses (roughly hourly) and pick-ups until mid-afternoon. To reach the centre of the Makonde Plateau, your best bet is to take a Land Rover **to Kitangari** (hourly).

metres until the road begins its descent from the Makonde Plateau, giving a fantastic view over almost 100km, including the Ruvuma River to the southwest (the beige band of sand on your left) and the isolated peaks around Masasi in the distance.

Practicalities

There are several transport stands in Newala, each serving different destinations. Coming **from Mtwara**, you'll be dropped off at a junction on a road full of fishmongers. Coming **from Masasi**, you're dropped at the junction of the Masasi and Mtwara roads. Long-distance buses **from Dar es Salaam** stop at the market, right in the centre.

There are several cheap **guest houses** in the market area, though the better ones – with the exception of the *Country Lodge* – lie off the tree-lined road that leads to the Boma. Newala has water problems, and most of its supply is trucked in, so don't drink it (and don't expect hotel showers to work). The best choice by far is the *Country Lodge* (also known as *Sollo's*), 1.3km north of the post office along the road to Masasi (☎023/241 0355 or 241 0275, ⓕ023/241 0377; ❷–❸). Most of the rooms have bathrooms, and all come with large beds with adequately sized nets, plus a sofa, chair and table, and the luxury of cotton sheets. The owner also has somewhat outlandish plans to build a swimming pool. Another good choice, if much more basic, is the friendly *Plateau Lodge* ☎023/241 0442 (❷–❸), signposted 350m off the road between the post office and the Boma, with four rooms (one with private bathroom), in what's basically a family house. Cheaper options (all ❶) include the *Wangeni Mangambe Guest House* and *Niamoja Guest House*, both signposted off the road to the Boma. Marginally cheaper, but still acceptable, are the *Mitema Guest House*, near the *Country Lodge* (☎023/241 0459), which has safe parking and a bar, and the *New Maputo Guest House*, near the *Niamoja*.

The best of the **restaurants** is at the *Country Lodge*, but skip their pricey basics and go for the specialities instead: the deep-fried kingfish (Tsh3000) is good, as are the garlic prawns (Tsh3500), but give them at least an hour to get things together. Cheaper but perfectly decent places include *Omax Hotel* and *Nandopo Hotel*, both on the edge of the market, and the *Plateau Lodge* which serves filling meals for around Tsh1000 (order 2hr ahead). Most of Newala's **bars** are around the corner from the post office facing the market, and range from the tawdry and dodgy to peaceful haunts popular with old men. Rather posher is the *Country Lodge*'s bar, which also has a television.

Masasi and around

The busy market town of **MASASI** lies at the western end of the 125km tarmac strip from Mingoyo. Why the authorities bothered to build an all-weather road here and nowhere else in the south is thanks to Masasi's importance as the country's major trading centre for **cashew nuts**, without which the town would undoubtedly have been little different from the small villages around it (which, incidentally, include President Benjamin Mkapa's birthplace, **Lupaso**). The cashew-nut trade peaks between October and February (the two harvests are usually in October and December, depending on the weather), when the town's bars fill up with bored traders, many of them Asian or Arabian, all of them happy to make a night of it with a passing *mzungu*. If you're heading further west, you'll probably have to spend a night here in any case, as what transport there is leaves early in the morning.

Masasi's main tribe is the **Makua**, who were also the first of the present-day tribes to arrive, coming from northern Mozambique perhaps as early as the fifteenth century. They called their new home *Machashi*, a word meaning the head of the wild millet plant, which here was said to be large and heavy with grain. The traditional culture of the Makua has sadly all but disappeared, thanks to their relatively early contact with Christianity. If you're interested in finding out more, see *Excerpts of Makua Traditions* by Father Kazimierz Kubat and Brother Edwin Mpokasaye: Ⓦ www.sds-ch.ch/centre/artyk/articel/makua.htm.

The first missionary to arrive was Bishop Edward Steere, who came from Zanzibar in 1876 with high hopes of abolishing the slave trade. Although there was no slavery in Masasi, the town lay along the slave route from Lake Nyasa to the coast. Then, between 1926 and 1944, the equally remarkable Anglican Bishop of Masasi, W. G. Lucas, made his mark, as it were, by pioneering a Christian version of the *jando* initiation ceremony for boys. The combination of traditional circumcision and Christian confirmation flew in the face of more orthodox missionary beliefs, and the new rite was even accused by some of being "little better than an orgy". But his show of respect for local traditions – which he rather unfortunately once described as "a wonderful opportunity . . . to the Christian priest of getting into real personal touch with his boys" – won over the Makua.

Arrival and accommodation

Masasi is widely spread out and lacks an obvious focus – the most notable feature is the tarmac road, which runs east–west through the town for several kilometres and which is where you'll find most of Masasi's bars and hotels. **Buses and daladalas** from Lindi and Mtwara terminate at the stand at the east end of town near the post office. The stand doubles as a market, as does the one for vehicles to and from Songea and Tunduru, 1.6km along the tarmac at the west end of town opposite the junction for Nachingwea. **Leaving Masasi**, buses and daladalas leave in the morning, the last at around 10am, so it's best to arrange tickets the day before. If you're heading west, ask around at the Songea–Tunduru stand about lorries or Land Rover pick-ups. If you're **driving**, there's a good mechanic near the Songea–Tunduru stand; ask for the Longino Garage. There are two filling stations, one near the Lindi and Mtwara daladala stand, the other a few kilometres along the Lindi road.

Masasi has dozens of **guest houses**, mainly catering for the cashew-nut trade. The bulk of these lie around the two bus stands and along the strip of tarmac between them. The best is the *Sayari Guest House* (Ⓣ 023/251 0095;

❶–❷) at the east end of town, past the Mkuti filling station on the Lindi road. Frequently full, this has a choice of rooms with and without bathrooms, plus an excellent bar. Also good is the *Holiday Lodge* (☎023/251 0108; **❷**, including breakfast), at the west end of the tarmac near the Nachingwea junction and bus stand, which has seven small but perfectly acceptable rooms with bathroom, plus a bar at the back serving food. Another reasonable choice is the *Saiduna Guest House* next to the *Masasi Club* (☎023/251 0175; **❶**, including breakfast).

The Town

The Makua were not the first inhabitants of the region, as is shown by the prehistoric **rock paintings** which dot the isolated *inselbergs* surrounding the town, and which are not featured in any Makua tradition. The paintings are generally done in red ochre, and feature axes and geometric symbols. There are two sites close to town, the nearest on the other side of the hill behind Mkomnindo Hospital – you should ask for someone to guide you. The other site is on top of Mtandi Hill behind the Anglican church some 4km back towards Lindi; ask at the church. Before visiting either of these sites, please read the box on rock art etiquette on p.258.

Apart from the paintings, there's little else in Masasi to delay you, though you could check out either of two **Makonde woodcarvers' co-operatives**, 200m and 300m down the Nachingwea road.

Eating and drinking

Masasi's restaurants are primarily bars which also happen to serve food, mainly the ubiquitous *ugali*, *nyama choma* and sometimes fried fish. You won't find much to write home about, but the local **relish** sold in the markets is well worth searching out: ask for *kiungo cha embe* if you like mangoes, or *kiungo cha ndimo* for the version made with lemons.

For **restaurants**, try the *Masasi Club* or the relaxed and dirt-cheap *Mahenge Transit Cassino & Bravo Bar* near the *Mahenge Guest House*, with its famously awful service, but don't use the toilets, at least not before you've eaten. It has a large patio in front with plenty of seats and tables. For breakfast, try *uji*, a porridge made from millet flour.

You're spoilt for choice when it comes to **drinking**. The *Mahenge Transit Cassino & Bravo Bar* has a great atmosphere, helped along by a generator which ensures a non-stop supply of eminently danceable Congolese music. The *Masasi Club* opposite is a friendly and more intimate venue, with the bonus of video shows in the back room: the quality is eye-melting and the sound is terrible, but it's great fun all the same. The *Sayari Guest House*'s bar is another good place, with a decent restaurant and upbeat music. If you're feeling brave, search out the local brew (*pombe*), made from the distilled fermented juice of the cashew fruit.

Msanjesi and Lukwika-Lumesule Game Reserves

Apart from the rock paintings at Chiwata, the region's main attractions are the rarely visited Msanjesi and Lukwika–Lumesule game reserves, which occupy part of the migratory corridor connecting the Selous Game Reserve with Niassa Game Reserve in Mozambique. The closer of the two is the **Msanjesi Game Reserve**, 45km northwest of Masasi, but more interesting – both in terms of scenery and wildlife – is the **Lukwika–Lumesule Game Reserve**, 110km from Masasi along the Ruvuma River. The perennial waters of the river attract lions, leopards, hippos, crocodiles, antelopes and numerous bird species, as well as elephants, who migrate across the river from Mozambique. **Camping** is possible, but there's no other accommodation.

To get to and around either reserve you'll need your own **transport**, though you could try for a lift (for a fee) from the project manager at the Office of Natural Resources near the District Commissioner's headquarters at the west end of Masasi (Ⓣ023/251 0364). You'll need to drop in anyway to sort out the paperwork, as you may need a **permit**. Officially there are no fees to pay, but with the Wildlife Department being the shambles it is, you never know – at the time of writing, you were only expected to pay a tip to the obligatory ranger who will accompany you in the reserves (pick them up at the gate). Bear in mind that the reserves are currently still used for hunting, which sits uncomfortably with the photographic tourism the government apparently wants to develop.

Travel details

Buses and daladalas

Early morning, around 6am, is the best time to catch buses. Asterisks denote routes that are open in the dry season only; during the rains (usually Nov or Dec, and most of March–May) these routes are often closed for days, weeks or even months at a time. Buses that do attempt these routes in the rains are subject to lengthy delays, often meaning days.

Kilwa Kivinje to: Nangurukuru (hourly; 30min).
Kilwa Masoko to: Dar (1–2 daily*; 14–18hr); Nangurukuru (every 30min; 30min); for southbound buses, wait at Nangurukuru.
Lindi to: Dar (2–3 daily*; 22–28hr); Masasi (3–5 daily; 2hr 30min), Mikindani (hourly; 1hr 30min); Mingoyo (hourly; 30min); Mtwara (hourly; 2hr); Nangurukuru (1 daily*; 7–9hr).
Masasi to: Dar (1–2 daily*; 25–31hr); Lindi (3–5 daily; 2hr 30min); Mikindani (3–4 daily; 3hr 30min); Mtwara (4–5 daily; 6hr); Nachingwea (1–2 daily*; 1hr 30min); Newala (hourly; 3hr); Tunduru (1 daily*; 8–12hr).
Mikindani to: Lindi (hourly; 1hr 30min); Masasi (3–4 daily; 3hr 30min); Mtwara (hourly; 20min).
Mtwara to: Dar (2–3 daily*; 24–30hr); Kalambo for Mozambique (hourly*; 1hr); Lindi (hourly; 2hr); Masasi (4–5 daily; 6hr); Mikindani (hourly; 20min); Newala (1–2 daily; 5–6hr).
Nangurukuru to: Kilwa Kivinje (hourly; 30min); Kilwa Masoko (every 30min; 30min).
Newala to: Dar (5–7 weekly*; 26–30hr); Kitangari (hourly; 1hr 30min–2hr); Masasi (hourly; 3hr); Mtwara (1–2 daily; 5–6hr).

Ferries

The *MV Safari* and *MV Aziza* both run once weekly between Dar and Mtwara, taking around 22hr. For more details see p.220. There are no ferries to Kilwa, Lindi or Mafia.

Dhows

Commercial dhows sail irregularly between Kisiju on the mainland and Mafia Island, and along the mainland coast between Songo Songo, Kilwa Kivinje, Lindi, Mtwara and Mozambique. For more detailed information see the transport sections under Mafia Island (p.188), Kilwa Kivinje (p.210), Lindi (p.213) and Mtwara (p.223), as well as the section on travelling by dhow in Basics (p.37).

Flights

(ATC = Air Tanzania; EA = Eagle Air; PA = Precisionair.)
Kilwa to: Dar (EA: Wed, Fri, Sat & Sun, cancellations likely; 1hr 40min); Lindi (EA: Mon; 30min).
Lindi to: Dar (EA: Mon, Wed & Sun; ATC: Sat; upwards of 2hr 10min); Kilwa (EA: Fri); Mtwara (EA: Sat; 20min); Nachingwea (EA: Wed & Sun; 35min).
Mafia Island to: Dar via Zanzibar (PA: daily except Tues & Thurs; 45min); Dar direct (EA: currently suspended; 30min).
Mtwara to: Dar (EA: Mon, Thurs, Sat & Sun; ATC: Tues, Fri & Sun; 80min).
Nachingwea to: Dar (EA: Wed & Sun; 70–80min).

Central Tanzania

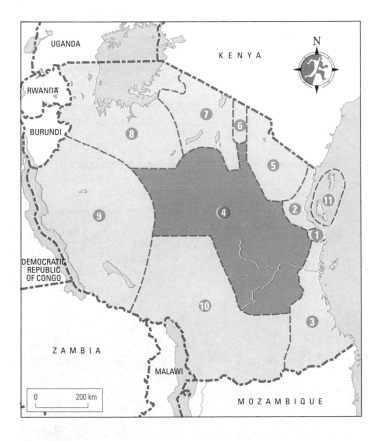

CHAPTER 4

Highlights

✳ **Irangi Hills** Scattered around the hills northeast of Kondoa is one of Africa's most extensive prehistoric rock art complexes, the oldest paintings dated to 18,000 years ago. See p.255

✳ **Uluguru Mountains** Accessed from Morogoro, these offer rewarding hikes through primeval rainforest and encounters with the Luguru tribe. See p.275

✳ **Udzungwa Mountains** Extremely rich rainforest habitat with several walking trails, especially good for spotting primates. See p.298

✳ **Kilombero River** Way off the beaten track, the river's swampy floodplains are paradise for bird-watchers, and contain several unique species. See p.304

✳ **Mikumi National Park** Easily reached from Dar es Salaam, this contains a high concentration of plains game, including lions and elephants. See p.280

✳ **Selous Game Reserve** Africa's biggest wildlife sanctuary, brought alive by the Rufiji River. Best seen on foot accompanied by an armed ranger. See p.288

Central Tanzania

D ry, dusty and only sparsely vegetated by *miombo* woodland, **Central Tanzania** is an amorphous region without distinct geographical or cultural boundaries. The presence of sleeping sickness, spread by the tsetse fly, has meant that the area's main settlements are located at its fringes: Morogoro and Uluguru in the east, Unyamwezi and Tabora to the west (covered in chapter 9) and Iringa in the south (covered in chapter 10). The exception, right in the middle of this apparently desolate land, is the planned city of **Dodoma**, which has served as Tanzania's political and administrative capital since 1973. Although the butt of many a joke, the city is pleasant enough, boasts a lively nightlife and provides a good stopover for those travelling by train between the lakes and the coast. And in the dry season, at least, Dodoma is an ideal springboard for exploring the area to the north, whose attractions include the ground-breaking cultural tourism programme in **Babati**, hikes up the 3418m **Mount Hanang**, the prehistoric rock paintings of the **Irangi Hills** near Kondoa, and a beautiful stretch of road between Babati and the attractive district capital of **Singida**.

The lively and bustling commercial and industrial town of **Morogoro**, 279km east of Dodoma along a good tarmac road, owes its existence to its fertile hinterland and to the fact that it straddles both the railway and the Tanzam Highway from Dar es Salaam to Zambia and Malawi. A few kilometres to the east, the rain-giving **Uluguru Mountains** have recently been opened up to hikers and offer outstanding scenery along with hundreds of rare plant and animal species.

For the majority of visitors, however, central Tanzania means one of two things: **Mikumi National Park** or the neighbouring **Selous Game Reserve**, which contain pretty much all the wildlife of the Northern Circuit but minus the crowds, although both are becoming more popular. For serious hikers, **Udzungwa Mountains National Park**, to the west of Selous, offers unrivalled opportunities to get out into the wild, along with the refreshingly different – if nerve-racking – experience of coming face-to-face with local wildlife, mainly monkeys and, if you're especially (un)lucky, buffalo and elephant. For those really wanting to get off the beaten track, the road south of here to **Ifakara** brings you towards the swampy **Kilombero floodplain**, one of the country's least travelled areas, and accessible only by boat.

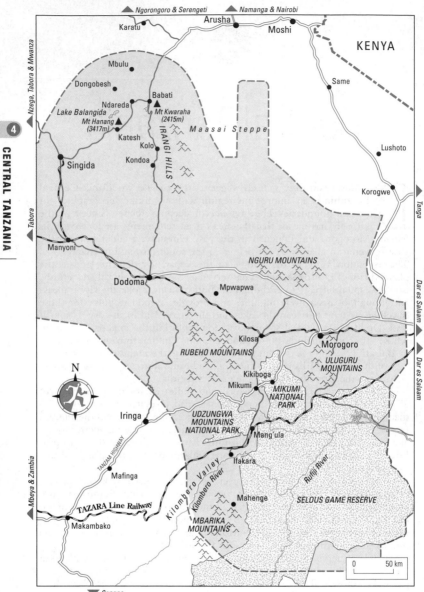

Dodoma and northwards

Situated among a desolate scatter of weathered granite outcrops, eroded gullies and sand-filled rivers, **DODOMA** is a surprisingly remote choice for a national capital, reminiscent of the similarly artificial planned capital cities of Brasília (Brazil) and Abuja (Nigeria), whose blueprints adorn the walls of the Capital Development Authority's mapping office. Unfortunately, Dodoma's unpromising location and lack of history mean that it's never really going to appeal much to visitors. In the hottest months (June–Oct), the desert-like climate sees temperatures rising to over 35∞C at midday before plummeting to 10∞C at night. There are no mountains or waterfalls nearby, nor historic buildings or bustling local districts to explore. Indeed, few Tanzanians have a good word to say about the place that was declared capital by President Nyerere in 1973

The Dodoma region: the destruction of a fragile environment

Passing through in the 1870s, the explorer Henry Morton Stanley was enchanted by Ugogo, the old name for what comprises most of the present-day **Dodoma region**. In the whole of Africa, he wrote, "there is not another place whose environment has attracted me as much as this". Mr Stanley, one presumes, would have been somewhat surprised to see the changes that have occurred over the 130 years since he was here. A large part of the region is a savanna plateau which receives little rain (around 570mm a year), most of which falls in heavy buroto in December and March or April, leaving the rest of the year hot, dry, windy and dusty. As a result, the region has long been prone to drought and famine, a natural cycle whose challenges the region's dominant tribe, the **Gogo**, mastered by developing a cyclical system of communal grazing that ensured than no one piece of land was ever exhausted.

The region's present problems can be traced back to the arrival of the Europeans, who made every effort to discourage the Gogo's nomadic lifestyle, which they considered backward (not unlike the present government's attitude to the Maasai). Land was confiscated, reducing the grazing ranges of the Gogo's cattle and encouraging the Gogo to settle and practise slash-and-burn agriculture instead, whose destructive long-term environmental consequences can now be seen in the dust that billows through Dodoma for much of the year, and in the eroded run-off gullies and sand-filled rivers that scar the landscape. By clearing the land of permanent bush or tree cover, the soil in such a harsh climate quickly loses its consistency and is more easily dried out by the sun – after which the wind blows away the topsoil and the rain carries yet more of it away. And so, as cultivators clear another patch of land to replace the one that has blown to dust, the cycle repeats itself.

Politics have also had an impact. Nyerere's idealistic **Ujamaa** policy (see p.718) had an equally catastrophic impact on this intrinsically fragile environment. Human and animal population density increased by fifty percent, placing unsustainable pressure on local resources. Livestock trampling on overused pasture and, especially, around waterpoints hindered the regeneration of vegetation, which in turn lessened the soil's ability to absorb rainwater. This led to lowering of local groundwater tables, a situation which wasn't helped by the creation of new farms on confiscated land.

With a population of over 1.3 million, the Gogo of today can hardly turn back the clock to revert to their previous way of life. One solution now being developed by the forestry department is to introduce sustainable modes of agriculture and plant varieties that won't leave the soil uncovered. But this will take time – and time, unfortunately, has all but run out.

more for its central geographical position than for anything else. For some, Dodoma is nothing more than a white elephant, a colossal waste of money that could have been better spent on less grandiose projects elsewhere. The local MP, however, would beg to differ: "There is fresh air here and serenity. Dar es Salaam is too noisy for government thinkers. They need a quiet and peaceful place like Dodoma."

To be fair, Dodoma is gradually outgrowing the rigidness of its original blueprint. Large sections of the city that had been planned for government offices or open spaces are already occupied by a maze of dusty roads packed with bars, food joints and shops. If you make the effort to explore some of these areas and the city's live-music venues you'll experience a welcoming and vibrant side to the life of Dodoma that no amount of town planning could ever have achieved.

Some history

Dodoma began life in the first half of the nineteenth century as a small Gogo settlement of traditional *tembe* houses no different from the ones you can still see today along the road to Kondoa. The settlement gradually grew in importance when the ivory and slave caravans from the lakes in the west began passing through the area, from which the Gogo exacted tribute ("a tusk, a gun or a man," it is said) in return for maintaining the water wells on which the caravans depended. Come **colonization**, the settlement was sufficiently developed for the Germans to consider making it the colony's capital. Thanks to World War I, however, the proposal came to nought, although much of the town's modern importance stems from this period – in 1910 the Central Line railway from Dar es Salaam reached Dodoma, bringing with it colonists and many of the missionaries whose churches now dot the city. During and after the war Dodoma was hit by two famines which killed 30,000 people, while an outbreak of rinderpest badly affected Gogo cattle herds. The British administration that replaced German rule was less taken by Dodoma, much preferring Dar es Salaam and Arusha. In the 1960s, Dodoma's importance decreased still further with the completion of the Chinese-built Tanzam Highway from Dar es Salaam to Morogoro and Iringa, which bypassed the city.

Dodoma's slow renaissance began in October 1973 when it was selected as the new **capital** of Tanzania. Although the decision was made partly through a desire to develop agriculture in the very centre of the country, the move is better understood through Nyerere's ideal of **"Villagization"** (see p.718), which

---

Dodoma: origins of a name

The origin of the city's name, which is a corruption of the Kigogo word *idodomia* or *yadodomela*, meaning "sinking" or "sunk", is worth relating. The prosaic (and most likely) explanation is that the name was a metaphor for the fate of invaders unable to escape the bows and spears of the brave Gogo defenders. The more colourful version refers to an elephant that came to drink in the Kikuyu River near Dodoma. Arriving at the river, the elephant became stuck and began to sink, hence the name (and the inevitable "white elephant" tag that newspaper columnists gleefully attach to the city). An alternative and no less amusing tale tells of a time when Gogo warriors secretly stole a herd of cattle from the Hehe, their neighbours to the south. The Gogo feasted on the cattle, leaving only their tails, which they then stuck into the ground. When the Hehe came looking for their herd, the Gogo pointed to the tails and said, "Look, your cattle have sunk into the mud."

aimed – and indeed succeeded – in creating a nation devoid of tribal or ethnic rivalry, albeit at the expense of destroying the country's economic viability. As the capital, Dodoma was to be the centrepiece of an ideology in which all tribes lived together in a shared sense of *Ujamaa* – togetherness, or brotherhood. However, the cost of physically moving the capital was exorbitant. Originally planned for completion during the 1980s, the final transfer of the ministries and state organs from Dar is now scheduled for 2005, although few believe that this will actually happen. Tanzania's National Assembly (the Bunge) has been in Dodoma since 1996, but the government ministries which wield the real power have been loath to leave the relative comforts of Dar es Salaam, and at the time of writing only three ministries remained in Dodoma, the rest having moved stealthily back to Dar.

Arrival

Dodoma is most easily reached by road from Dar es Salaam, a six-hour drive (469km on good tarmac); it's also a major stop on the Central Line railway between Dar and Kigoma and Mwanza. More difficult to negotiate are the unsurfaced roads north and west, especially the B129 to Manyoni and the A104 to Arusha (at least 14hr), which can become impassable for several days at a time during the rains. The southward continuation of the A104 to Iringa is somewhat better, although most drivers still find it quicker to take the longer route via Morogoro.

Dodoma's **bus stand**, from where all services (except Scandinavian Express buses and those coming from Arusha and Kondoa) arrive, is surrounded by shacks on the east side of the city in a plot once earmarked for the National Library, there are taxis inside the enclosure. Buses to and from **Kondoa and Arusha** arrive at Lindi Avenue close to Kuu Street. **Scandinavian Express** buses pull in at their own terminal on Dar es Salaam Avenue, 500m southeast of the bus stand.

Dodoma's **train station** is a ten-minute walk south of Zuzu roundabout. Trains from Dar (every Tues, Wed, Thurs, Fri and Sun) pull in at around 7.35am; coming from Mwanza or Kigoma, you'll arrive at 6.10pm. The **airport** is 3km north of the centre, and arrivals are greeted by taxis. Alternatively, daladalas to Jamatini Stand on Dar es Salaam Avenue in the centre can be caught along Arusha Road, 1.5km west of the airport.

City transport

Daladalas, locally nicknamed "Express", leave from the orderly Jamatini Stand, just east of Zuzu roundabout on Dar es Salaam Avenue, and cover the whole city (Tsh150 for most journeys). **Taxis** congregate inside the bus stand, outside the market and beside the BP petrol station near the Kondoa–Arusha bus stand; alternatively, call Mwani Taxi Services on ☏026/232 1360. Trips within the city cost Tsh1000–1500.

Accommodation

There are several basic guest houses around the bus station, none of which is particularly enticing. The main concentration of better budget and mid-range choices is in **Area "C"**, north of the airstrip. Single rooms can usually be shared by couples, though church-run places may refuse to give you a twin-bed room if you're not married. Dodoma's **water** supply is unreliable and in the past has been tainted by pesticides, so it's best to use bottled water.

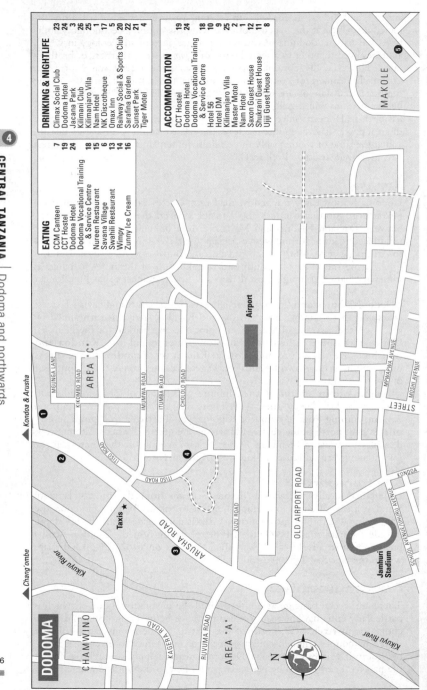

DODOMA

▲ Kondoa & Arusha

▲ Chang'ombe

▼ Singida

Kikuyu River

CHAMWINO

KAGERA ROAD

RUVUMA ROAD

AREA "A"

Kikuyu River

ITISO ROAD

MGUNGA LANE

KIKOMBO ROAD

AREA "C"

IMUMWA ROAD

ITUMBA ROAD

CHOLOLO ROAD

Taxis ★

ARUSHA ROAD

ZUZU ROAD

Airport

OLD AIRPORT ROAD

KONDOA

Jamhuri Stadium

SCHOOL AVENUE

CHIHURU AVENUE

MPWAPWA AVENUE

MOSHI AVENUE

STREET

MAKOLE

N

EATING

CCM Canteen	7
CCT Hostel	19
Dodoma Hotel	24
Dodoma Vocational Training & Service Centre	18
Nureen Restaurant	15
Savana Village	6
Swahili Restaurant	13
Wimpy	14
Zunny Ice Cream	16

DRINKING & NIGHTLIFE

Climax Social Club	23
Dodoma Hotel	24
Jacana Park	3
Kilimani Club	26
Kilimanjaro Villa	25
Nam Hotel	1
NK Discotheque	17
Omax Inn	5
Railway Social & Sports Club	20
Sarafina Garden	22
Sunset Park	21
Tiger Motel	4

ACCOMMODATION

CCT Hostel	19
Dodoma Hotel	24
Dodoma Vocational Training & Service Centre	18
Hotel 56	9
Hotel DM	10
Kilimanjaro Villa	25
Master Motel	2
Nam Hotel	1
Saxon Guest House	12
Shukrani Guest House	11
Uiiji Guest House	8

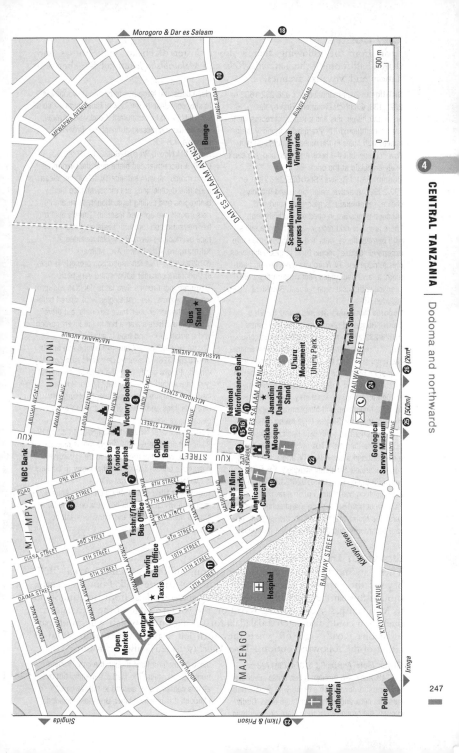

▲ *Morogoro & Dar es Salaam* ⑱

Bunge

BUNGE ROAD

Tanganyika Vineyards

Scandinavian Express Terminal

CENTRAL TANZANIA | Dodoma and northwards

4

0   500 m

DAR ES SALAAM AVENUE

MPWAPWA AVENUE

⑩

Morogoro & Dar es Salaam

Bus Stand ★

UHINDINI

MASHARIKI AVENUE

MASHARIKI AVENUE

ARUSHA AVENUE

MWANZA AVENUE

TABORA AVENUE

MBEYA AVENUE

LINDI AVENUE

MTENDENI STREET

MARKET STREET

CEMDI AVENUE

Victory Bookshop ⑧

National
Microfinance Bank

⑰

⑬

15 16

Uhuru Monument

Uhuru Park

⑳

㉑

Train Station

KUU

NBC Bank

Buses to
Kondoa
& Arusha ★

⑥

ONE WAY

2ND STREET

3RD STREET

4TH STREET

5TH STREET

CRDB Bank ⑦

KUU STREET

⑭

Jamatikhana Jamatini
Mosque Daladala
Stand

⑭

㉒

RAILWAY STREET

㉔

Geological
Survey Museum

KIKUYU AVENUE

㉕ (500m) ▼

㉖ (2km) ▼

MJI MPYA
ROAD

DIASA STREET

HABIBI ROAD

MADARA AVENUE

TEMBO AVENUE

6TH STREET

7TH STREET

8TH STREET

Tashrif/Takrin
Bus Office

Yasha's Mini
Supermarket

Anglican
Church

⑲

㉓

ZUZU ROUNDABOUT

DAR ES SALAAM AVENUE

DAIMA STREET

MWANZA AVENUE

9TH STREET

10TH STREET

11TH STREET

12TH STREET

⑫

⑪

Tawfiq
Bus Office

Taxis ★

Hospital ✚

Kikuyu River

RAILWAY STREET

PANDO AVENUE

IRINGO AVENUE

Open
Market

Central
Market

⑨

NDUYU ROAD

MAJENGO

Catholic
Cathedral ✝

KIKUYU AVENUE

Police

247

▼ Iringa

▼ (1km) & Prison   ㉓ ▼

▼ Singida

City centre

Apart from the following, there's also a cluster of cheap guest houses with shared bathrooms – the *Tanzania*, *Keko* and *Makaribisho Johari* (all ❶) – between Tabora and Mwanza avenues.

CCT Hostel Zuzu roundabout ☎026/232 1682 or 232 1136, ⓔcct-ctc@maf.org. Run by the Anglican Church, this has a variety of rooms with shared bathrooms. They're mostly shoddily maintained, with holes in the mosquito nets and window screens, but the beds are clean and you can't really complain at the price. ❶

Dodoma Hotel Railway St ☎026/232 2991 or 232 2992. Attractive, calm, clean and friendly choice, set around a large grassy courtyard, although things are in need of refurbishment. There are sixty-odd rooms – mostly large twins with parquet floors, nets and telephone; the more expensive "deluxe" rooms have large double beds, plus a fridge and TV. All rooms have private bathroom: a few have running hot water; others are supplied with buckets on request. Breakfast included. ❹

Dodoma Vocational Training and Service Centre Bunge Rd, 2km east of the city centre ☎026/232 2181, ⓔdodomarvtsc@twiga.com. Part of a regional training centre for chefs, waiters and hotel staff, and the teachers obviously know their stuff: rooms are clean and well kept, there's reliable hot water and the service is excellent, all making for a very pleasant stay. The 39 rooms all have TV, desk lamp and telephone; cheaper ones share bathrooms. Singles have round mosquito nets while doubles (with twin beds that can be pushed together) have box nets. There's a good restaurant and a bar with a TV, and a swimming pool is planned. Breakfast included. ❷–❸

Hotel 56 Bunge Rd ☎ & ⓕ026/232 2476. A large but uninviting two-storey option near the Parliament building, with dark and echoey corridors. The rooms are reasonable, though, with private bathrooms (and hot water in the mornings),

clean beds and large box nets, and they manage to stay cool despite the lack of fans; there's also a bar with TV and a restaurant. Good value overall, despite the depressing atmosphere. Breakfast included. ❶–❷

Hotel DM Ndovu Rd ☎026/232 1001, ⓕ232 0416. A recommended place near the market with good rooms, all with satellite TV, telephone, clean beds (the double beds are massive), nice tiled bathrooms and ceiling fans, though there are no nets (rooms are sprayed instead). There's also a bar-restaurant on top, with seats on a breezy terrace overlooking town. Breakfast included. ❸

Kilimanjaro Villa Biringi Ave, Mlimani ☎026/43258. This little suburban property is one of Dodoma's cheaper options and very basic. There are eight rooms (two large doubles with private bathrooms; the rest singles with shared bathrooms): the better ones have box nets, but there are no fans. There's also a bar in the lovely garden and a small shop, and food is available. ❶

Saxon Guest House Corner of Tembo Ave and 9th St ☎026/43269. A simple, clean and safe option – though it looks grotty from the outside, it's perfectly decent within, and very friendly too. Rooms (shared bathroom only) have plenty of furniture, box nets, fans and views of the street through chickenwire screens. ❶

Shukrani Guest House 12th St ☎026/232 1895. Basic but acceptable, with single rooms only, all with nets, while the marginally more expensive ones have private bathrooms (hot water in buckets is available in the evenings). ❶

Ujiji Guest House Lindi Ave (no phone). Another spartan if OK choice, with box nets on all beds, shared bucket showers and squat loos, but no food. ❶

North of the centre

There are further accommodation options in the residential **Area "C"**, beyond the airport north of the city, a thirty-minute walk from the centre, though this can be wearying in the midday sun. Daladalas from Jamatini Stand to Mnadani pass along Arusha Road on the western edge of the area; alternatively you could also catch a daladala for Chang'ombe, which will go up part of Arusha Road – get off when they turn left, leaving you within 500m of either of the following options. *Tiger Motel* (see p.251) also has rooms.

Master Motel Arusha Rd ☎0741/361723 or 318749. Accessed through a bar, these seventeen tatty and run-down rooms come with private bath, fans and nets, and some have huge beds. Oddly enough, the ground-floor rooms are breezier than

those on the first floor, though the latter benefit from big balconies. The staff are friendly, but overall this comes a poor second to the *Nam Hotel*, although it is much cheaper. Breakfast included. ❷–❸

Nam Hotel Arusha Rd ☏ & ⓕ 026/235 2255. Dodoma's leading tourist hotel, this well-kept, three-storey affair has thirty rooms, all with telephones, nets, carpet and bathrooms with cold running water (some also have satellite TV for the same price). Families might consider the huge suites. Prices drop by 25 percent when parliament is in recess. There are also two bars (one on the roof) and a restaurant, and breakfast is included. ④

The City

The town centre is a dusty and not terribly exciting grid of streets (which at least has the advantage of reducing your chances of getting lost). There are no problems safety-wise wandering around by day, though you'll encounter many more beggars and street children here than elsewhere. Caution (or a taxi) is advisable at night. The busiest commercial area lies west of **Kuu Street**, from where numbered streets radiate like a fan. The western edge of this area is bounded by the stagnant Kikuyu River, either side of which is the lively **Central Market**, renowned throughout Tanzania for its ability to provide fruit and vegetables even out of season – mysteriously so, given the desolation of Dodoma Region. The heart of the market consists of two modern buildings on either side of river (they're connected by footbridge). It's a good place to sample bitter-sweet baobab pods (*ubuyu*), which can either be sucked like sweets or pulped to make a very refreshing juice packed with vitamin C.

Heading south from here (or south along Kuu Street) brings you to **Zuzu Roundabout**, named after a defunct ceramics factory. This area is dominated by the brick **Jamatikhana Mosque**, with its strangely church-like clock tower, and the domed **Anglican Church** opposite. The most impressive of Dodoma's churches, however, is the **Catholic Cathedral**, 2km west along Railway Street. Rebuilt in 2001 in fantastic Byzantine style, the brickwork facade comes complete with mosaic frescoes heavy on the gold, and a pair of ornately carved Swahili-style doors. Beyond the cathedral, and before you get to the *Climax Social Club*, is **Mirembe Hospital for the Insane**, Tanzania's largest such establishment and, some might say, rather conveniently close to the corridors of power. The hospital's name has become something of a by-word in Tanzania in much the same way as Bedlam Asylum was in Victorian Britain. A few hundred metres further west, a narrow track leads to the heavily guarded gate of Isanga Magereza **prison**, whose shop sells sisal (*katani*) items produced by the inmates.

Back in the centre, just south of the Jamatikhana Mosque, Dodoma's main secular attraction (albeit only of specialist interest) is the **Geological Survey Museum** (Mon–Fri 8am–3.30pm) in the Ministry of Energy and Minerals on Kikuyu Avenue south of the railway station – look for the sign saying *Wizara ya Nishati na Madin*. The Tsh500 admission, paid at the "Sample Reception", gets you into a hall filled with display cases containing gemstones and minerals, the more valuable of which (gold, platinum, ruby, etc) are notably absent but for their labels and the patches of glue that once held them in place. Still, there's enough remaining to keep you interested for half an hour or so, including some enormous fossilized ammonites, flaky sheets of mica that resemble plastic (and are associated with emerald deposits), and a large wall map of Tanzania's minerals with blinking lights controlled from a massive Doctor Who-style dial that amazingly still works.

Heading east from Zuzu roundabout along Dar es Salaam Avenue brings you to the Jamatini daladala stand and the dusty **Uhuru Park**. Formerly occupied by the bus station, it now serves as an unofficial football ground. The Uhuru Monument here is an abstract representation of Mount Kilimanjaro topped by a representation of the Uhuru (Freedom) Torch that was planted on top of the mountain at Independence, together with a spear, a shield and a machine-gun. Some 1.5km further east (take a taxi) is the **Bunge**, Tanzania's modern parliament building. There's a visitors' gallery here from where you can watch parliamentary debates – not that you'll understand much, as proceedings are conducted in Kiswahili.

To the south of the Bunge on the circular Bunge Road are the headquarters of **Tanganyika Vineyards**, purveyors of what is widely considered some of the world's worst plonk. Grape cultivation was started here by Italian missionaries about a century ago; the grapes are harvested twice a year: during August to September and February to March. The quality problem appears to stem from blending the two harvests, as the February–March harvest is made during the rainy season, which makes the grapes bitter. They also make a sweet wine that enjoys a good reputation, though sadly the entire production is destined for church use in Holy Communion (though you might be able to talk them into selling you a bottle or two). The management are happy to show you around the factory, but they ask that visitors come after 4pm (Mon–Fri) and contact them in advance (PO Box 1565 ☏026/232 4430 or 0744/267811, Ⓔtangerm@africaonline.co.tz). If you still hanker after a glass of wine, a more palatable local alternative is the Bihawana Red, made at Bihawana Mission along the Iringa Road – bottles sell for Tsh1500 at Yashna's Mini Supermarket.

Eating

There are a few basic **restaurants** and **cafés** in the town centre. In addition, most hotels have their own restaurants.

CCM Canteen Behind the CCM building at the corner with Madaraka Ave. A large and lively courtyard, especially at lunchtimes, when the food is freshest and includes some of the best *nyama choma* and definitely the most scrumptious *ndizi* (grilled banana) in town. It's also cheap, charging Tsh500 for half a kilo of meat, and Tsh200 for *ndizi*. Good music, too.

CCT Hostel Kuu St. Meals are limited to one meat and one fish dish daily (Tsh1750) – nothing special, but filling.

Dodoma Hotel Railway St. Good and reasonably priced three-course meals for around Tsh4800, and plain steak and chips for Tsh3500.

Dodoma Vocational Training and Service Centre Bunge Rd, 2km east of the city centre ☏026/232 2181. Part of a training school, the chef here is the instructor and the rest of the staff his students: they're doing good work, as both the food and service are excellent. There's a wide choice of tasty dishes (though nothing vegetarian) as well as pastries and, if you order a day in advance, a selection of set menus. Mains cost Tsh3000–3500; starters around Tsh900. The bar outside also has *nyama choma* between 7pm and 11pm.

Nureen Restaurant Dar es Salaam Ave. A rather down-at-heel Indian place, but they sometimes do curries, which can be very good (if they just have snacks, forget it). Good *mishkaki* is sold on the street outside, and there's a good unnamed bar next door. Open lunchtimes only.

Savana Village 2nd St. Attractive Tanzanian restaurant with a cosy wooden interior, though food is only available if you order a couple of hours ahead.

Swahili Restaurant Market St. An excellent establishment with a wide selection of snacks and full meals, including some Lebanese and Middle Eastern dishes – the garlic and chili chicken is top-notch.

Wimpy Zuzu roundabout. A cheap and popular meeting place with outdoor seating serving fast-food snacks like samosas, fried chicken, chips and *kababu*, plus coffee, tea and sodas. Full meals are served at lunchtimes, but get there early as they often run out.

Zunny Ice Cream Dar es Salaam Ave. Good ice cream, plus a range of light snacks, and some seating in a small garden.

Drinking and nightlife

Dodoma has a good number of attractive outdoor **beer gardens**, all dishing up excellent *nyama choma*, grilled bananas, chicken and the rest. One or two places also have live music: the big **local bands** are Saki Stars and newcomers One to Nine. Sadly, **traditional Gogo music** (*ngoma ya kigogo*; see box on p.252) is difficult to find – ask for Peter Masima's Chimwaga Cultural Troupe. The "thumb pianos" (*mbiras*) that are so characteristic of Gogo music can be bought at a stall outside *Dodoma Hotel*.

Climax Social Club 3–4km west of the centre near the prison ☏026/239 0252. Until Independence, this was Dodoma's main colonial hang-out, and it still has the city's only swimming pool, as well as a bar and restaurant. Temporary membership costs Tsh1500 per day.

Dodoma Hotel Railway St. This has a calm and pleasant bar by day, and live music from the resident Diamond Star Band on Wednesday and Friday evenings (8pm–midnight; Tsh1000 if you're not staying at the hotel).

Jacana Park Arusha Rd, Area "C". A great outdoor place under a lovely stand of shady trees. The Super Melody Band play here from 9pm to around 2am on Fridays to Sundays, while the Papaupanga Cultural Troupe ("Swordfish") kick off Sundays at around 2–3pm with a mix of traditional *ngomas* from various tribes and acrobats (*sarakasi*), providing one of the nicest Sunday afternoons you could hope to spend. Food is available, including *supu ya mbuzi* (a stew of various bits of goat in a hot chili broth), beef, chicken and *chipsi mayai*. Daladalas from Jamatini to Chang'ombe or Mnadani pass by.

Kilimani Club 2km south of the railway station. A broad, unmarked red building on the edge of Dodoma, this is a dopey bar by day but has live music on Sundays, with the Diamond Star Band playing from 8pm (Tsh1000). Standard bar food available in the evenings.

Kilimanjaro Villa Biringi Ave, Mlimani. A small bar in a shady garden; food also available.

Nam Hotel Arusha Rd, Area "C". Two bars; the best one is on the roof and has great views of the city and the hills to the north.

NK Discotheque Corner Dar es Salaam Ave and Mtendeni St. Occupying a former cinema, this is Dodoma's only central disco and deservedly popular. They sometimes have live music, and it's worth asking if they'll be hosting any Kiswahili rap (usually Saturdays), which is much more mellow and musically experimental than its Stateside equivalent. Wed, Fri & Sat 9pm until late, Sun from 3.30pm; entry around Tsh1000.

Omax Inn Makole area, east of the centre. Popular local club offering free live music from the excellent Saki Stars (8pm–2.30am Wed, Fri, Sat and sometimes Sun). Food is available until midnight. Walking around here is not advised though; a taxi from town costs Tsh1500.

Railway Social and Sports Club East side of Uhuru Park, off Dar es Salaam Ave. A pleasant and quiet place, somewhat in the shadow of the much busier (and shadier) *Sunset Park* next door, with a TV and good traditional Tanzanian food.

Sarafina Garden Kuu St. Friendly outdoor place; but take care you don't come a cropper on the bizarre wooden flooring.

Sunset Park East side of Uhuru Park. An oasis of shady trees and shrubs with plenty of secluded seating, this outdoor place is very popular with workers at the end of their shifts (and yes, there *is* a sunset). Good music, *nyama* and snacks too.

Tiger Motel Itiso Rd, Area "C". A refreshingly African place that functions mainly as a bar, playing lively Congolese and Tanzanian tunes throughout the day. There's a TV in the courtyard, and food is available in a dark restaurant, but their discos had ceased at time of writing (though they may well return in the near future). They also have overpriced rooms if you need to crash after a heavy night.

Listings

Bookshops The only bookshop that stocks anything other than religious tracts is Victory Bookshop on Lindi Ave, although the choice is extremely limited. It's more useful for stationery.

Car rental There's no official car-rental company in Dodoma, though most taxi drivers are happy to negotiate for a day's drive.

Car repairs Land Rover CMC, on Railway St, 500m west of Zuzu roundabout.

Cinema Paradise Theatre, Kuu St, is a real old fleapit that screens (via a video projector) Kung Fu and US B-movies (Mon, Tues & Fri at 7pm), and Indian flicks (Wed & Thurs at 7pm, Sun at 2.30pm & 7.30pm).

The music of the Gogo

Mention **the Gogo** anywhere in Tanzania and you're almost certain to hear enthusiastic praise for their skills as musicians. With its polyrhythmic singing, insistent virtual bass line of *mbira* thumb pianos interwoven with the plaintive voices of one-stringed *zeze* fiddles, the traditional music of the Gogo, called **sawosi** in Kigogo (*ngoma ya kigogo* in Kiswahili), is some of the most beautiful, haunting and subtly rhythmical music you're ever likely to hear. *Sawosi* is a perfect blend of collective virtuosity, balancing mostly female choruses with a multipart rhythm played on *mbiras*, rectangular or rhomboidal wooden sound boxes fitted with metal forks (nowadays, more often than not, the metal shafts from screwdrivers). The combined effect is utterly hypnotic, displaying a mastery of multipart polyphony, complex polyrhythms and micropolyphony comparable to that of Pygmy communities in the Central African Republic, Congo, Cameroon, Gabon and elsewhere.

Highly **recommended listening** are the two tapes of Gogo recordings sold at Radio Tanzania in Dar es Salaam (see p.109). There are also a couple of Gogo pieces included on Rough Guides' Music of East Africa CD, including a marvellous recital of a lullaby composed for the birth of newly independent Tanzania. Outside Tanzania, look out also for the following CDs: *Nyati group: L'Élégance de Dodoma – Tanzanie* (MPJ 111021); *Wagogo & Kuria Chants* (Inedit W260041); and *The Art Of Hukwe Ubi Zawose* (JVC VIGC-5011). If you have time and a real interest in Gogo culture and music, the best time to seek out *sawosi* in its traditional setting is during the harvest and circumcision season from June to August, especially July, which includes the *cidwanga* dance, conducted by elder healers, in which ancestors are remembered and praised.

Embassies Despite being the country's capital, the nearest embassies and high commissions are in Dar (see p.115).

Hospitals The main government-run place is Dodoma General Hospital (℡026/232 1851), though either the private Aga Khan Health Centre on 6th St (℡026/232 2455) or Mackay House Health Clinic (℡026/232 1777) are better; the latter also has a good dental clinic.

Internet There's currently only one internet café in Dodoma, at the *CCT Hostel* (Mon–Fri 8am–8pm, Sat 10am–6pm, Sun noon–6pm; Tsh2000 per hour).

Library Dodoma Library, Dar es Salaam Ave, one block east of Zuzu roundabout (Mon–Fri 9am–6pm, Sat 9am–2pm; Tsh500 daily membership).

Money The best of the banks are NBC on Kuu St and the National Microfinance Bank on Dar es Salaam Ave. CRDB, Kuu St, is mind-numbingly inefficient for travellers' cheques and takes well over an hour. All three need to see purchase receipts. The town's only forex is the DCT Bureau de Change, next to the CRDB, which gives reasonable rates for cash but Tanzania's worst rates for travellers' cheques, a full 25 percent below those in the banks. Western Union money transfers can be received at the post office.

Pharmacy Central Tanganyika Chemist, Dar es Salaam Ave, west of Zuzu roundabout (℡026/232 4506).

Police The central police station is on Kikuyu Ave.

Post office Railway St, just west of the railway station; it's also the office for the EMS courier service.

Supermarket Yashna's Mini Supermarket, 6th St, near Zuzu roundabout (Mon–Sat 8.30am–6.30pm, or until 8.30pm when parliament is in session, Sun 8.30am–12.30pm), has a small selection of imported foods like Ceres juices, wines and preserves.

Sports *Climax Club* (see p.251) has the only pool in town at present, and also has a squash court, volleyball, pool table and table tennis. Daily membership costs Tsh1500.

Telephones TTCL (daily 7.30am–8pm), next to the post office on Railway St, has operator-assisted phones and cardphones.

Moving on from Dodoma

By bus

Buses **to Dar es Salaam** and **Morogoro** leave every thirty minutes or hourly from 6.30am (Champion) to around noon (JVC). The safest company is Scandinavian Express, whose services leave at 9.30am and 11.15am from its own terminal 500m southeast of the bus station at the big roundabout on Dar es Salaam Avenue. **Iringa** is covered by King Cross Bus and Urafiki (both around 7.30am). Urafiki continues on to **Mbeya** three times a week (5am). There's a daily bus to **Singida** (11.30am), continuing to Shinyanga and Mwanza, which is run on alternate days by SAS Bus and Takrim/Tashriff. **Bukoba** (also 11.30am) via Biharamulo is covered by SAS, Takrim and Tawfiq. There are no buses to Tabora or Kigoma. Takrim/Tashriff and Tawfiq also have ticket offices along Mwangaza Avenue; both companies are notoriously reckless on tarmac, but should be safe enough – given the awful roads – for destinations in the northwest. The ticket offices are on the east side of the bus station.

Buses to and from **Kondoa and Arusha** leave from Lindi Avenue close to Kuu Street. Arusha via Kondoa is covered by Mtei Express every two days, though you could catch a bus to Kondoa and change there (you may have to spend a night in Kondoa in the rainy season). All buses along these routes leave Dodoma in the morning. The longer but quicker way to Arusha is the 6.30am Urafiki International Coach via Morogoro.

By train

From Dodoma, trains head **to Mwanza** (8.10am on Mon, Wed, Thurs & Sat; 24hr) and **Kigoma** (8.10am on Mon, Wed, Fri & Sat; 23hr). Both trains pass through Tabora, from where there are connections to **Mpanda** (Mon, Wed & Fri nights). Trains for **Dar** leave daily (except Tues & Thurs) at 6.40pm, and there are also services along the northern branch line to **Singida** (10am on Wed, Fri and Sun; 11hr 25min), but check the time in advance as it's liable to change.

The **ticket office** (Mon–Fri 8am–noon & 2–4pm, Sat 8am–10.30am, and 2hr before departures) encourages tourists to take a bunk in second or first class, though if you're travelling to Tabora you'll arrive before sunset, so third class is an acceptable and much cheaper alternative (Tsh5500 compared to Tsh14,000 in second or Tsh18,200 in first).

By air

Eagle Air has two flights a week **to Bukoba** via Mwanza, and one **to Dar**. Air Tanzania has two weekly flights to Kigoma and Dar es Salaam. Dar es Salaam flights are often fully booked when parliament is in session, so reserve ahead.

Kondoa

Situated 158km north of Dodoma, the small and dusty town of **KONDOA** is a handy base for visiting the ancient and beautiful **prehistoric rock paintings** in the Irangi Hills (see p.257), one of the finest such collections in the world. Kondoa itself has no real tourist attractions, although the weird sight of gigantic baobabs growing in the town centre is memorable enough, and the people are exceptionally welcoming. Few speak English, but no matter – everyone is eager to help out, and even the taxi drivers and hotel touts at the bus stand are uncommonly apologetic in their advances. The town's **markets** are also fun: the main one is adjacent to the west side of the bus stand, and there's also a tiny produce market a few blocks to the east of the bus stand next to a church, whose aged vendors are wholly charming and well worth the extra few shillings they'll winkle out of you.

The town's inhabitants are mainly Rangi, though there are also Gogo and Sandawe, the last of whom were hunter-gatherers until a few decades ago. Most of the town's population is Muslim: if you're awake at 5.30am, listen out for the hauntingly ethereal chanting of *dhikiri* – recitations of the 99 names of Allah, which provide a soothing contrast to the more guttural calls of the muezzins which mark the passage of time during the day. Perhaps because of its common religion, the town has a strong if easy-going sense of identity, something strengthened by the feeling that the government has ignored the region for too long – in spite of years of promises, the roads remain some of the country's worst, and at the time of writing road bridges that had been washed away in El Niño four years earlier had yet to be replaced. Unsurprisingly, the region is a stronghold of the opposition Civic United Front (CUF).

Arrival and accommodation

Kondoa lies 3km west of the A104 Arusha–Dodoma road. Whichever direction you're travelling in you'll probably have to spend a night here, as most buses terminate in Kondoa. Access is no problem in the dry season, but it's a different story in the rains, when journey times can double and the road from Dodoma especially can become completely blocked, usually around Mtungutu. The road from Arusha fares better and remains passable in all but the heaviest downpours, though there are a number of slippery hills where black cotton soil brings many a truck to grief. The entire road is supposed to be asphalted by mid-2004, but at the time of writing only a few scattered parts of the highway had been widened and graded, so the already much-delayed tarmac ribbon may well take until the end of 2005 to complete, if indeed the project ever really starts in earnest.

Buses arrive at the bus stand at the west end of town one block south of the main road into town. Mtei Express is the main operator **from Arusha**, running every other day (6am from Arusha, arriving in Kondoa around 2pm) and continuing on to Dodoma, weather permitting. Tashriff also run from Arusha but have a reputation for dangerous driving along this route. Alternatively, catch an early bus to Babati, from where you can get an onward connection to Kondoa. A few daladalas also run between Kondoa and Arusha. Coming **from Dodoma**, there's a steady stream of buses and daladalas in either direction until around midday.

Kondoa is small enough to get your bearings quickly: the "main road" referred to in our directions is the one leading west into town from the Arusha-Dodoma highway. If you want to change **travellers' cheques**, the National Microfinance Bank is at the east end of town, though you'll need a proof of purchase and a good deal of patience. The **post office** is close to the bank, and also has phones.

Accommodation

Kondoa has over a dozen cheap and basic guest houses plus a couple of places geared more towards tourists and businessmen, most of them signposted off the main road and the bus stand. The best is the friendly and welcoming *New Planet Guest House* (T Kondoa 180; ❶–❷), 200m west of the bus stand along the continuation of the main road, with a choice of spotless rooms, all with large and comfortable beds and some with private bathroom. There are rooms of a similar standard, complete with spacious box nets, at the *Sunset Beach Guest House* (T Kondoa 152; ❶), an 800-metre hike west along the road to Singida and Kwa Mtoro, which runs parallel to the main road from the south side of the bus station – follow the signposts. It also has a choice of rooms with or without private bathroom, a TV in reception and does food to order (but no alcohol). Of the cheaper options (all ❶), the more salubrious are the *Kijengi Guest House and Tea House* (no phone), 200m along the Singida road, and the *New Al-Noor Guest House* (PO Box 16, ☎ Kondoa 169), next to the *New Planet*. If you're really strapped for cash, try any of the even cheaper guest houses around the bus stand or along the main road, or – for something different – the far from splendid *New Splendid Guest House* (☎ Kondoa 41), signposted 300m north of the main road near the bus stand, whose bar has the (dis)advantage of a cheerfully noisy musical ambience until well into the night.

Eating and drinking

There's not much in the way of **restaurants**, the exception being the *New Planet Guest House*, which offers a wide choice of tasty Tanzanian and continental dishes. A full meal with a soda or two costs under Tsh2500. As usual, most of the bars (see below) can also rustle up meals, mainly chips, chip omelettes and – if you're lucky – grilled meat. There are also some foodstalls around the bus stand. Fresh **coffee**, served in small Turkish-style porcelain cups, is sold from a stall on the west side of the bus stand.

For **drinking**, a popular local place is the 24-hour bar attached to the *New Splendid Guest House*, which plays good African music and has satellite TV. If you find this too tawdry, try the pleasant *Just Imagine Bar* opposite (which also has rooms), or the *Metro Garden Bar*, with its pleasant shaded garden on the main road at the junction with the street leading to the *New Splendid*. The restaurant at the *New Planet Guest House* also sells beer, but the atmosphere's more anodyne. Entertainment is limited to the loud **videos** which are screened daily in the darkened front room of *Ashura's Hotel* facing the bus stand.

Moving on from Kondoa

Leaving Kondoa, get up early, as most buses leave at 6am, and buy your ticket a day or two in advance to be sure of a seat. A number of companies run daily buses from Kondoa **to Dar es Salaam** (Tsh10,000) via Dodoma and Morogoro (Tsh8000). If you're headed **to Singida**, it's quickest to go to Babati or Dodoma and change there, as although the direct route to Singida via Kwa Mtoro is served by occasional pick-ups, there's a lively risk of being stranded if the vehicle doesn't go all the way. If you're contemplating the wild run east across the Maasai Steppe **to Korogwe**, you'll need to take the Mwambao Bus to Handeni (it currently leaves at noon on Fridays), from where there are plenty of connecting daladalas to Korogwe. For transport into the **Irangi Hills**, see p.256.

The Irangi Hills

The relatively isolated **IRANGI HILLS**, located between the Babati–Kondoa road and the low-lying Maasai Steppe to the east, are an exceptionally beautiful and rewarding area for off-the-beaten-track hiking, and also contain one of the world's finest concentrations of **prehistoric rock paintings**. The local **Rangi** tribe (also called Langi) are also an extraordinarily friendly and welcoming people, and wherever you go you'll be greeted with broad smiles and effusive greetings and handshakes, as well as the amusing sight of gleeful kids going berserk as you pass by. Indeed, after a few days of seeing and hearing children squealing and giggling in delight, you'll start to wonder just what it is that's so funny about a red-faced *wazungu* . . .

Nowadays primarily an agricultural people, the Rangi's cattle-herding past is reflected in the saying "it is better to hit a person than his cattle", so if you're driving, take extra care. Originally plains-dwelling, the Rangi moved up into the hills a couple of centuries ago to avoid the inexorable advance of the warlike Maasai. The subsequently defensive nature of Rangi society was characterized by their houses, unusual in that they were very low and built into wide natural hollows, rendering villages almost invisible to the Maasai on the surrounding steppe. Nowadays, with no more need to hide from their former enemies, Rangi villages are notable for their intricate brickwork, sometimes decorated with geometrical relief patterns similar to styles used in parts of the Sahara. The Rangi's expertise in creating earthenware objects is even more artfully shown in their beautiful **black cooking pots**, which can be bought for a few hundred shillings at any of the region's markets (there's one every day somewhere in the hills – just ask around). You'll see them perched on people's houses – the only place where they can be dried after washing without being smashed by the above-mentioned hyperactive children. In short, if you have a sense of adventure, don't mind roughing it for a while, and feel comfortable arranging accommodation with local families, the rewards of any trip here will more than outweigh the hassle of finding accommodation and getting around.

Practicalities

The gateway to both the Irangi Hills and the Kondoa-Irangi rock paintings is **KOLO VILLAGE**, 27km north of Kondoa along the Arusha road and 82km south of Babati. Coming from the north by **public transport**, there are several daily buses and daladalas from Babati, the last of which leaves around 10am. From Arusha, an early bus to Babati should get you there in time to catch the last of these to Kolo. Alternatively, catch the Mtei Express from Arusha to Dodoma (6am every other day), which passes through Kolo at around 3pm. Coming from Kondoa, catch any early morning bus or daladala for Arusha or Babati, or wait for the midday Rombo Bus which continues on to Pahi, deep in the Irangi Hills, returning the next day at 4am. Cheaper but less dependable is the midday Land Rover pick-up from Kondoa, which returns from Kolo at 6am. From Dodoma, catch either the Subra Coach or Rombo Bus at 6am. Note that the road between Kolo and Kondoa consists in parts of very loose sand or black cotton soil, and the partly washed away bridge just south of Kolo has yet to be replaced, so this route may well be closed during and just after heavy rains.

Unless you feel comfortable arranging lodging with local families (a few thousand shillings would be greatly appreciated; ask around local shopkeepers), the only **accommodation** in the Irangi Hills is the *Silence Guest House* in Kolo village, which the curator at the Antiquities Department can show you. There's no electricity and no fixed price, but it shouldn't cost more than Tsh5000 a double, and they can also arrange simple but tasty meals. The only alternative is to pitch a tent at the riverside **campsite** 4km along the track to the "Kolo B" rock paintings. However, there are no facilities whatsoever, no water for much of the year when the river runs dry, and locals advise that you use the site only if you're in a large group (three or four tents at least), as there have been instances of robbery in the past.

There are no restaurants as such in the Irangi Hills, though each village has a handful of *mgahawa* joints – small *hotelis* serving up tea, coffee and simple dishes like rice with beans. The weekly cycle of local **produce markets** is good for roasted maize cobs, freshly grilled beef and goat meat, as well as dried fish, sugar cane, live chickens and ducks, sandals made from car tyres, all manner of clothing and, of course, the beautiful Rangi cooking pots.

The Kondoa-Irangi rock paintings

The area between Singida and the Irangi Hills contains one of the world's finest groups of **prehistoric rock paintings**, with an estimated 1600 individual paintings at almost 200 different sites, the most accessible of which are in the Irangi Hills north of Kondoa. The most recent date from just a century or two ago, but the oldest are estimated to be between 19,000 and 30,000 years old (though wilder estimates date them as far back as 50,000 BC), making them among the world's most ancient examples of human artistic expression.

In the African context, the paintings – together with other sites in Singida and Bukoba districts – form part of a wider chain of stylistically similar sites ranging from the Ethiopian Highlands to the famous San (Bushmen) paintings of the Kalahari in Namibia and South Africa. There are also intriguing similarities with the world's most extensive rock art area in and around the Tassili n'Ajjer Plateau of the Algerian Sahara, notably the curious "round-head" style used in depicting human figures which also occurs here. Some of the paintings are believed to have been the work of the ancestors of the present-day Sandawe and Hadzabe, both of whom have preserved ritual traditions involving rock painting. The **Sandawe**, who live to the west of Kolo and Bahati, were hunter-gatherers until a few decades ago, while the **Hadzabe**, around Lake Eyasi to the north, still adhere to their ancient hunter-gathering way of life, albeit against increasingly unfavourable odds (see p.445). It's no coincidence that the Sandawe and Hadzabe are also the only Tanzanian tribes speaking languages characterized by clicks. The parallel with the San of the Kalahari – who speak a similar click language (called Khoisan), and who are themselves responsible for an astonishing array of rock art – is irresistible, and suggests that a unified group of hunter-gatherer cultures covered much of southern and eastern Africa until they were dispersed, annihilated or assimilated by the Bantu speaking tribes who arrived two to three thousand years ago.

Most of the paintings are located in rock shelters – either vertical rock faces with overhangs, or angled surfaces that resemble cave entrances – both of which have served to protect the paintings from millennia of rain, wind and sun. All the sites give striking views of the surrounding hills and over the Maasai Steppe to the east. The paintings vary greatly in terms of style, subject, size and colour: the most common consist of depictions of animals and humans done in red or orange ochre (iron oxide bound with animal fat). Particularly remarkable are the fine elongated **human figures**, often with large heads or hairstyles, unusual in that their hands generally only have three fingers, the middle one being much longer than the other two. The figures are depicted in a variety of postures and activities, some standing, others dancing, playing flutes, hunting and – in an exceptional painting at Kolo B1, dubbed "The Abduction", showing a central female figure flanked by two pairs of male figures. The men on the right are wearing masks (the head of one clearly resembles a giraffe's) and are attempting to drag her off, while two unmasked men on the left attempt to hold her back – the meaning of all this can only be guessed at. Animals are generally portrayed realistically, often with an amazing sense of movement, and include elephant, kudu, impala, zebra and, especially, giraffe, which occur in around seventy percent of central Tanzania's sites and which give their name to the so-called **giraffe phase**, tentatively dated to 28,000–7000 BC. The later **bubalus phase** (roughly 7000–4000 BC), generally done in black (charcoal, ground bones, smoke or burnt fat), depicts buffalo, elephant and rhinoceros. Of these, the highly stylized herds of elephants at Pahi are uncannily similar to engravings found in Ethiopia. The more recent paintings of the **dirty-white phase** (kaolin, animal droppings or zinc oxide) generally feature more abstract and geometric forms such as concentric circles and symbols that in places resemble letters, eyes or anthropomorphs.

As to the meaning of the paintings, no one really knows. Some believe they held a magico-religious purpose, whether shamanistic or as sympathetic magic, where the intent was to bring to life the spirit of an animal by painting it. This was either to enable a successful hunt, or was symptomatic of a more complex belief system which summoned the spirits of certain sacred animals, especially eland, to bring rain or fertility. The latter is evidenced by the practice of San shamans "becoming" elands when in a state of hallucinogenic trance. Another theory states that rock shelters – as well as baobab trees – are Sandawe metaphors for the "aboriginal womb" of creation. Indeed, the Sandawe have a dance called *iyari* which is performed when twins are born, and part of the ritual surrounding the dance involves rock painting. Other theories, nowadays pretty much discredited, go for the simple "art for art's sake". Either way, the rock art of Kondoa gives a vivid and fascinating insight into not just Tanzania's but humankind's earliest recorded history and way of thinking. For **further information**, seek out a copy of Fidel Masao's excellent monograph, *The*

Rock art etiquette

Many of the rock paintings have deteriorated at an alarming rate over the last few decades thanks to **vandalism** – whether deliberate or unintentional – by unsupervised and irresponsible visitors. Most obvious are the modern graffiti left by both Tanzanian and foreign tourists, which at two sites has defaced almost fifty percent of paintings that had hitherto survived thousands of years. Other panels have been disfigured by misguided "cleaning" efforts that have removed much of the original paint pigments, while others have been damaged by efforts to enhance the colours and contrast of the paintings for photography by wetting the panels with water, Coca-cola and even urine. In order to protect the paintings, it is now a legal requirement that you take a **guide** from the Department of Antiquities in Kolo. These guides can show you most of the rock art sites and can also be able to point out many details in the paintings that you might easily miss otherwise. Please adhere to the following rules when visiting the sites:

Do not touch the paintings or the rock face around them. Oil and acid from your hands destroy the pigments, and any form of direct physical contact damages the paintings by dislodging loose flecks of paint.

Do not wet the paintings under any circumstance. This fades and dissolves the pigments and very quickly renders the paintings almost invisible, as has happened at a number of sites.

Respect local communities and their feelings. Many of the sites are located in traditional Rangi hunting grounds, where excess noise and off-track bush walking by tourists and researchers has in the past disturbed wildlife (one site has been partially disfigured with anti-*wazungu* graffiti because of this). Some sites may also have a sacred importance to locals.

Rock Art of Kondoa and Singida, available at the National Museum in Dar es Salaam, or the expensive but extraordinarily beautiful *African Rock Art: Paintings and Engravings on Stone*, by David Coulson and Alec Campbell (Harry N. Abrams Publishers, New York, 2001; Ⓦ www.abramsbooks.com), which includes Kondoa-Irangi as part of its East Africa chapter.

Practicalities

Visitors intending to visit the rock paintings need a **permit and a guide** from the Department of Antiquities' office on the main road in Kolo. The permit costs Tsh3000 and covers as many sites as you have time for. The congenial guide-cum-curator is not paid a fortune, so a decent tip is in order. Visits to some of the rock paintings are also offered by some mid- and upper-range safari operators from Arusha, usually combined with a safari in Tarangire, but at over $1000 per person it's much cheaper to do it yourself.

The fourteen officially recognized sites, each with an average of three painted shelters located within a hundred metres or so of each other, were first studied by the archeologist Mary Leakey in the 1950s, after which she had them fenced with chicken wire to deter vandalism. Inevitably, the locals found better use for the fences, with the result that only one site still has its fence, but someone has stolen the door – rendering the whole thing rather pointless. The most accessible of the sites is **"Kolo B"**, a six-kilometre hike from Kolo village, which has three collections of paintings under rock overhangs on the side of a hill with spectacular 180-degree views of the surrounding countryside. Note that if you're driving to Kolo B, you'll need 4WD, as there are a few very tricky sections over loose scree. Access to other sites is only really possible with your own transport, as the paintings are spread out over a 35-kilometre radius to which there is little or no public transport, and certainly no accommodation. The sites are best viewed either in the morning or late evening, depending on their orientation, when the low sunlight enhances the paintings and lends a rich orange cast to the rock, making for some wonderfully vivid photographs.

Babati and around

The fast-growing town of **BABATI**, 105km north of Kondoa, is a great place to hunker down for a few days, and enjoys a pretty location flanked by the 2415-metre Mount Kwaraa to the east and the freshwater Lake Babati to its south. Although there aren't really any sights in the town itself, it's a friendly and lively base for visiting a number of attractions in the area, including the solitary volcanic peak of **Mount Hanang**, as well as trips to the local Barbaig and Sandawe communities, which can be arranged through Babati's **cultural tourism programme**.

Babati's *raison d'être* is its position at the junction of the roads from Arusha, Dodoma and Singida. Give their historically atrocious condition, Babati has long been a stopover for travellers, so much so that it's now a thriving market centre, with a population of over 20,000. The land around Babati is also fertile, a far cry from the rebarbative semi-desert to the north, and the area is a major producer of maize, which finds ready markets in Arusha, Dodoma and even Mwanza.

The town's major cultural event is the grand **monthly market** (*mnara*), held on the seventeenth of each month 4km south of town on a hillside next to the

Babati cultural tourism programme

The reason for the small but steady trickle of tourists who come to Babati these days is its **cultural tourism programme**, one of nineteen in Tanzania (see p.405), and amongst the best. The programme's co-ordinator, Joas Kahembe, was organizing small-scale ecological and cultural trips long before anyone else in Tanzania and, although he's not originally from Babati, is probably the best source of information about the town and surrounding region. The programme's office is located next to *Kahembe's Guest House* (℡027/253 1088 or 253 1377, ℮fidebabati@hotmail.com).

The programme offers a wide variety of flexible itineraries, ranging from a half-day visit to Managhat Village, home of the Gorowa tribe (including a visit to a "killer bee-keeping project"); a one-day walk around Lake Babati; climbs up Mount Hanang; walking trips (3–5 days) to a Barbaig community in the Mang'ati Plains; encounters with the Sandawe; and exhaustive bumper itineraries of up to sixteen days covering pretty much everything in the region. Local culture features heavily in all the tours, which include enlightening meetings with respected village elders. Particularly recommended, if you have the time, is their fourteen-day "Educational Tour", which features both the rock paintings at Kolo and a little visited site near Bukoba in the far northwest of Tanzania.

The basic costs are Tsh8000 for the guide (per group per day), plus a Tsh3500 co-ordination fee and a Tsh1500 village fee per person. Additional costs, all very reasonable, include breakfast (Tsh1500), other meals (Tsh2500), accommodation (Tsh3000), bicycles (Tsh3000), canoe (Tsh3000 for two people) and Tsh4000 per group for a visit to a local village. Longer speciality tours, including Mount Hanang climbs and Barbaig walks, cost $30–40 per person per day depending on group size. Local transport (extra) is used wherever possible. A portion of the fees is used to improve primary school facilities in two local villages.

Kondoa road. The event attracts almost half of Babati's 20,000 inhabitants, plus many other people from outlying districts, for whom the market is an ideal excuse to bunk off work and indulge themselves with grilled beef, fresh sugar cane and local brews at inflated prices (many are the tall stories of hung-over revellers waking up in the early hours the next day to see packs of hyenas scavenging around the remains). The cattle auction is perhaps the day's highlight, and draws Maasai and Barbaig from all around the region. All in all, a great day out.

Practicalities

Babati lies 68km beyond the end of the tarmac from Arusha, to which it's connected by several daily buses. There are also daily buses from Singida, 178km to the southwest along a particularly beautiful road (see p.263) flanking the Rift Valley's Malbadow Escarpment. The **bus stand** is just off the main road in the centre of town, next to the *Paa Paa Motel*.

Accommodation

The two **hotels** reviewed below are Babati's best. If you're really on a shoestring, even cheaper choices include the *Greenview*, at the west end of the bus stand; *New Dar Star*, next to the *Paa Paa Motel*; and the *Moonlight*, 200m along the street opposite the Aggarwal Star petrol station. **Camping** is possible at Joas Kahembe's farm 2km east of town; ask at *Kahembe's Guest House*.

Kahembe's Guest House 100m along the street heading west off the main road between Aggarwal Star and Total petrol stations at the north end of town, five minutes from the bus stand ℡027/253 1088 or 253 1377, ℮fidebabati@hotmail.com. Run by the co-ordinator of Babati's cultural tourism programme, the affable Joas Kahembe (see above), this has small and relatively clean rooms with shared bathrooms and mosquito nets in a quiet location. There's no restaurant and it's overpriced compared to the *Paa Paa Motel*, but Joas himself is an inexhaustible source of information about the region. **②**

Paa Paa Motel By the bus stand ℡027/253 1111. The best accommodation in town, this safe choice has both singles (with private bath but no hot water) and doubles with shared facilities. Rooms have electricity, clean sheets, mosquito nets and fans, and there's also a small and usually empty restaurant, a bar and a courtyard providing safe parking. **❶**

Eating, drinking and entertainment

Babati's line-up of **restaurants** contains one culinary gem in the form of the unassuming *Paradise Hoteli*, one block south of *Kahembe's Guest House* and one block west of the Total filling station, which serves up some of the tastiest and most tender fish in Tanzania, served with heaps of *ugali* and beans (all under Tsh1000), though you'll have to order a few hours in advance. *Paa Paa Motel* does great *nyama choma*.

There are loads of **bars** to choose from. Ever popular, both by day and at night, when the satellite TV provides the main draw for locals, is the one attached to *Paa Paa Motel*, which has tables in front of the bus stand. *New Dar Stars Bar*, next to *Paa Paa*, is also recommended. Also pleasant, especially for a drink during the day, is *Maasai Bar* on the other side of *Paa Paa*, though it can get rowdy at night.

As for **entertainment**, your only options are either the many bars or the town's handful of **video parlours** (though these are gradually disappearing, as TVs are introduced into the town's bars), where you'll see rows of enraptured locals watching anything from Kiswahili soap operas to UK Premier League football matches. Of the video parlours, the one inside the CCM Building, on the main road to the south, has an ever-changing choice of mostly second-rate movies, with screenings most days.

Moving on from Babati

Heading south towards Kondoa and Dodoma is no problem in the dry season, with at least two **buses** a day, but the stretch to Kondoa can get tricky in the rains (usually mid-March to May, and sometimes Nov or Dec), and the southward continuation to Dodoma is often closed. The best company for all routes is Mtei Express: the buses may be old and not overly reliable, but the company has a safer reputation than Takrim and some others. Most buses leave around 6–7am, although late risers shouldn't have too much difficulty getting a seat on one of the through buses from Arusha to Singida, Dodoma or Mwanza, which pass by between 10.30am and 1pm. The first bus to Arusha leaves at 4am, the last at around 2pm.

If you're driving your own **car**, make sure your vehicle is in good condition before proceeding west or south of Babati, as the roads are a trial. Be sure also to leave plenty of extra time so you don't get caught out after dark – the road to Singida has been the scene of a number of car-jackings and hold-ups at night.

Around Babati

A pleasant way to spend a day is to visit **Lake Babati**, an easy stroll one to two kilometres south of town: walk down the Kondoa road, and take the track to your right that starts at an old mango tree facing the District Court. The lake – one of the few freshwater bodies of water in the Rift Valley – is a paradise for **birds**: over three hundred species have been recorded so far, including flamingos. June to August is the best time for bird-watching, when many migrants arrive in time for the maize, millet and sunflower harvests.

Given the lack of a known outlet, the lake's level varies wildly according to the rains: at the time of writing it was at its lowest for years, while only three years before, during the 1997–98 El Niño rains, it rose so high that it flooded the Kondoa road in two places, providing a boon for fishermen who made a tidy profit ferrying people across. Parts of the town itself were also flooded, and locals joke that all they had to do for their dinner was reach out of a window to grab a fish. The event prompted an NGO to build an overflow pipeline from the lake to a river at lower altitude, which should prevent such flooding in future. The lake is said to be free of bilharzia, and locals are happy swimming in it. However, be aware that there are also hippos here, which can be unpredictable and therefore dangerous.

Although you don't really need a guide – you can follow the water's edge for most of the way, though a couple of swampy areas force you briefly back to the road – it's nonetheless worth taking one via the cultural tourism programme (see box on p.260), as it's the best way of getting to meet local people. The programme recommends a full day, giving enough time for spotting hippo in the morning or late afternoon, a wobbly excursion by dugout canoe, lunch, chats with local fishermen, boatmen and cattle herders, and a visit to a school to see what part of the programme's profits are being used for.

Mount Kwaraa

The flat-topped mountain rising 3km east of Babati is **Mount Kwaraa**, its 2415-metre peak swathed in heavy forest and usually also in mist, so don't

---

The Barbaig

The unremittingly dry expanse of savanna that stretches south of Mount Hanang, the **Mang'ati Plains**, is at first sight a deeply inhospitable place. Yet the plains are home to some 200,000 **Barbaig** (or Barabaig), a semi-nomadic, cattle-herding tribe distantly related to the Maasai. The key to their existence in such a barren land lies on the other side of Mount Hanang in the shape of **Lake Balangida**, a large freshwater expanse at the foot of the Malbadow Escarpment. The lake is fed by the mountain, which ensures that even when the lake is dry (an increasingly common occurrence), the deep wells that have been dug around its periphery still contain enough water for the Barbaig's herds.

Tall, handsome and proud, the Barbaig are at first glance very similar to the Maasai. They dress alike, and are also herders, in whose culture cattle occupy a pivotal place. Like the Maasai, their society is organized into age-sets and a clan system (*doshinga*) which governs rights over pasture and water sources. But for all their similarities, there's no love lost between the two peoples. The Maasai have two names for the Barbaig. One is *Mbulu*, by which many other tribes south of the Maasai are also known, and which means "unintelligent people". The other, reserved for the Barbaig alone, is *il-Mang'ati*, meaning "the enemy", a simple tag which, coming from East Africa's most feared and warlike people, is almost akin to a compliment. The name Barbaig itself comes from *bar* (to beat) and *baig* (sticks), alluding to a unique dance that is still held today, in which fights are mimicked using sticks for weapons.

The Barbaig are one of nineteen tribes that originally made up a broader cluster of people called **Datooga**. Like the Maasai and Kalenjin of Kenya, the Datooga are linguistically classed as Nilotic, meaning that they share a common origin, presumed to be in the Nile Valley of Sudan. A fascinating relic from this time, which could also explain the extreme ritual importance of cattle in all Nilotic societies, is the Barbaig word for God, *Aseeta*, which is related to the Kalenjin word *Asiis*, which also means sun. Both words have their root in the name of the ancient Egyptian goddess **Isis**, who wore a solar disc and the horns of a cow and was the focus of a cattle and fer-

expect panoramic views if you climb it. What you *will* see is some fascinating and virtually untouched forest. The mountain is used by migratory herds of elephant and buffalo: you almost certainly won't see them, but the presence of fresh dung and crushed undergrowth is enough to give most spines a tingle. The lower slopes, up to around 1750m, are mainly scrub, with dry montane forest and stunted woodland dominating the higher sections, which is part of the protected **Ufiome Forest Reserve**. The mountain can apparently be climbed in one day, but two days is preferable as you'd have much more time to explore the vegetation.

People are free to climb below the forest line, but for higher hikes you'll need a permit and a guide from the Forest Office in Babati (currently Mr Lwiza; his office is in the Municipal Council buildings on Kondoa Road). Alternatively, contact the cultural tourism programme (see box p.260), who can arrange everything for you. If you have the energy, **Bambaay Hill** – part of Mount Kwaraa – can also be climbed, though this is better done over a two-day trip, which would also give you time to visit the Gorowa village of Managhat.

The road to Singida

The road between Babati and Singida – the **B143** – is one of Tanzania's most beautiful, running for much of its 178 kilometres along the southern flank of

tility cult throughout much of antiquity. According to Roman mythology – which adopted many Egyptian cults – the beautiful Isis, whom the Romans called Io, was kidnapped by an amorous Jupiter, but her mother, Juno, gave chase. Rather than give her back, Jupiter rather unfairly turned his love into a cow. Not content with this punishment, he called down a bumble bee from the heavens and commanded it to sting the cow. Not terribly enchanted with this treatment, the miserable Io fled to Egypt, where she cried so much that her tears formed the Nile.

The Datooga's southward **migration** is believed to have started around 3000 years ago, possibly prompted by the massive climate changes that coincided with the expansion of the Sahara Desert. Around 1500, the Datooga arrived at Mount Elgon on the Kenya–Uganda border, where they stayed until the eighteenth century, when they migrated south once more into Tanzania. The Datooga first settled at Ngorongoro before being pushed further south by the Maasai, after which they separated into various tribes, many of which have now been assimilated by others. Lamentably, the Barbaig's southward migration continues even today. Loss of their ranges to commercial ranches, flower farms and seed-bean plantations, and encroachment by Maasai (who have themselves been pushed south in recent decades by the creation of the Serengeti and Tarangire national parks) mean that the Barbaig are among Tanzania's poorest people. Child mortality rates are high, as is the incidence of cattle disease. The fact that none of this used to be the case supports the Barbaig claim that nothing other than the loss of their traditional land has caused these problems, but unfortunately the scattered nature of Barbaig society means that they have largely been absent from politics, and have consequently been marginalized. Unfortunately, their latest efforts to regain access to their land via a series of legal actions in the courts have become snagged on the absurd grounds that they lack legally recognized title to the land.

For more information on the pressures facing Barbaig culture, see *Passions Lost* by Charles Lane (Initiatives Publishers, Nairobi, 1996).

the Rift Valley's Malbadow Escarpment and past the lone volcanic peak of Mount Hanang. Starting from Babati, the road crosses the floodplain of Lake Babati, then twists up into the hills amidst beautiful and ever-changing scenery before levelling out in a broad valley, with Mount Hanang to the south and the long barrier of the Malbadow Escarpment to the west. **Ndareda**, 26km from Babati, is where the road forks. A right turn takes you along a minor road (difficult or impassable in the rains) to the lively market town of **Dongobesh** and on to **Mbulu**, from where there's an even less-travelled but stunningly beautiful route north to **Karatu**, near the eastern entrance of Ngorongoro Conservation Area (upwards of 4hr from Ndareda). The route makes a fascinating diversion from the Northern Safari circus, but you'll need your own 4WD and, ideally, an experienced driver. This is the land of the **Iraqw**, a Cushitic tribe which is culturally more akin to Ethiopians and northern Kenyans than to the Bantu-speakers who dominate Tanzania; for more about them, see p.446.

Mount Hanang

Taking the left fork at Ndareda, the B143 Babati–Singida road veers south towards Tanzania's fourth highest mountain, **Mount Hanang**, roughly 60km southwest of Babati, and considered by many to be one of the most beautiful peaks in the country. Rising up from the Mang'ati Plains to three summits, the highest at 3418m, Hanang is sacred to the Gorowa (also called the Fiome) and Barbaig tribes, since its streams feed **Lake Balangida**, one of the Rift Valley's most important watering points. Hanang's height means that water vapour from clouds condenses on it, making it the region's primary source of water, and the high water table around it supports a surprisingly rich groundwater forest on the mountain's lower slopes. Higher up, the groundwater forest gives way to montane and upper montane forest, with trees up to 20m tall on the wetter southern, eastern and northern slopes, and dry montane forest on the western slopes. Above 2100m the forest gives way to grassland, thicket and bushland, while above 2700m moorland dominates.

Despite recent problems with illegal logging, much of Hanang's forest has survived intact, apparently thanks to the Gorowa's belief in underground earth spirits called *Netlangw*. The *Netlangw* are said to live under large trees where springs emerge, which makes Mount Hanang's girdling groundwater forest of prime importance. The *Netlangw* are guardians of the water; if they are offended, say by the clearing of trees, they move away, taking the water with them. The logic is clear and unassailable: destroy trees and you destroy your water supply.

Katesh

The main base for climbing Mount Hanang, especially if you're using the shorter but steeper ascent, is **KATESH** to the south. The town is liveliest on the tenth and eleventh of each month during the **mnara market**, held 2km south of town along the Singida road. The market's popularity explains Katesh's profusion of **guest houses** (all ❶): from east to west, these include the *Colt* (probably the best, with rooms with private bath), *Matunda*, *Tip-Top* (by the bus stand), *Hanang View*, *Computer Hotel* and *Plaza Bar*. The **bus stand** is about half-way along the road through town, and is nothing more than a tree with the Mtei Express timetable nailed to its trunk. The ride from Babati takes about ninety minutes, and there are at least three buses a day from Arusha (6am, 7.30am & 10pm) – basically, any service that goes to Singida or Mwanza.

Climbing Mount Hanang

The easiest way to arrange a **climb up Mount Hanang** is to contact the cultural tourism programme in Babati (see box p.260), which runs an excellent four-day trip, combining an ascent of the mountain with a visit to a Barbaig community. They charge $40 a day per person for a couple, which might be bargainable to $30 for larger groups. A guide is essential for the climb: you should be able to find someone in Katesh willing to show you up, but be aware that without a good knowledge of Kiswahili both the arrangements and the climb might prove to be more of a trial than you bargained for, and there's no guarantee that your guide will know the route any better than you do; all in all, it's much safer to arrange the trip in Babati. For general advice, read the section on Kilimanjaro on p.324. Take enough water, as there's none near the summit, and don't underestimate the mountain; it gets pretty cold at 3417m so you should be suitably equipped, though altitude sickness isn't a major worry – you might get a headache, but nothing more serious. The Forestry Department charges a $4 entry fee per person per day for walking and camping in Hanang Forest Reserve, which covers the entire mountain.

There are several routes up the mountain. The shortest and most popular is the **Katesh route**, which starts at Katesh village and goes up the southwestern ridge (5–6hr up, 3–4hr down). This normally takes two days, but can be done in one if the physical challenge is more important than enjoyment. The summit is reached on the first day, with an overnight camp at 3000m. The descent is sometimes via Ngendabi village (no accommodation). The main alternative to the Katesh route is the **Giting route**, which starts from Giting village on the northeast side of the mountain; this should be arranged in Babati, from where there's a daily bus to Giting. Accommodation along this route has been planned for years, taking advantage of the beautiful view of Lake Balangida; enquire in Babati whether this has finally happened. A longer alternative is the **Gendabi route** (3 days), which starts 16km (3hr) from Katesh. Accommodation in Gendabi is offered by teachers from the secondary school. Serious climbers might also consider tackling the mountain via the **southeastern ridge**.

There's a small **daily market** on the east side of the road between the *Hanang View Guest House* and *Computer Hotel*. The National Microfinance Bank, past the police station on the left on the way out south, may be able to **change money**, but you shouldn't bank on it, as it were.

Singida

The little-visited town of **SINGIDA** enjoys one of the most alluring locations in Tanzania, in a boulder-strewn and kopje-studded landscape flanked by two freshwater lakes, **Singidani** to the north and **Kindai** to the south. The mood is light and friendly, even if the traffic police are the exception that proves the rule – if you're driving, make sure your papers are in order. Coming from Babati, the road enters town through a natural "gate" made from two boulders on either side of the road, one emblazoned with a huge painted advert for Salama condoms. Lying as it does on the Tanzanian route between Arusha and Mwanza (the alternative, along much better roads, is via Kenya), Singida acts as the main overnight stopover for trucks and buses, and as such has dozens of surprisingly good hotels to choose from, as well as a motley assortment of bars. Apart from the lakes, Singida's "sights" are limited to the granite outcrops in and around the town, a nature reserve, and a small regional museum which, unfortunately, is usually closed. That said, the friendliness of town itself is really the main draw, making it as good a place as any for a few days of lazy relaxation.

Arrival and accommodation

Singida serves as a major overnight stop for **buses** plying between the Lake Victoria region and Arusha, Dodoma and Dar es Salaam, and also sits at the end of a branch of the Central Line railway that heads north from Manyoni. The road from Manyoni is often blocked by lorries bogged down in mud, the road being more or less ignored by the government because of the railway running parallel to it, so it's best not to approach from the south by bus. The **train station** is 2km along Karume Road. The train (third class only) currently leaves Dodoma at 10am on Wednesday, Friday and Sunday (but check the time beforehand), and heads back from Singida on Monday, Thursday and Saturday at 7am. The NBC and CRDB **banks** are both on Shinyanga Road close to Kawawa Road; as ever, NBC is the more efficient of the two. The **post office** is on Shinyanga Road; the **TTCL** office is opposite, though quicker service can be had at Kasi International Communications near the bus stand, or at a couple of "attended call" places within the stand itself.

Singida has literally dozens of budget **hotels**, most of them pretty good, plus a couple of mid-range options. In most places, single rooms can be taken by couples. Make sure your bed has a mosquito net – there are zillions of the critters. The following are the pick of the bunch.

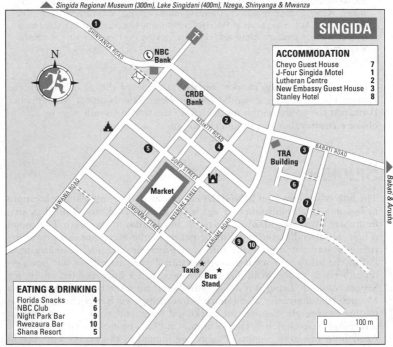

Singida Regional Museum (300m), Lake Singidani (400m), Nzega, Shinyanga & Mwanza

SINGIDA

N

NBC Bank

CRDB Bank

MSIKITI ROAD

SHINYANGA ROAD

SOKO STREET

KAWAWA ROAD

LUMUMBA STREET

NYERERE STREET

Market

TRA Building

BABATI ROAD

KARUME ROAD

Babati & Arusha

Taxis
Bus Stand

ACCOMMODATION

Cheyo Guest House	7
J-Four Singida Motel	1
Lutheran Centre	2
New Embassy Guest House	3
Stanley Hotel	8

EATING & DRINKING

Florida Snacks	4
NBC Club	6
Night Park Bar	9
Rwezaura Bar	10
Shana Resort	5

0   100 m

Train Station (2km)

Cheyo Guest House Off Babati Rd, beside the *Stanley Hotel*, entrance at the back ☎026/250 2258. A highly recommended budget option, and a bargain given that everything works: the rooms (all doubles) are clean and equipped with nets, and the shared bathrooms have powerful showers. There's also a bar with outdoor seating. **❶**

J-Four Singida Motel Shinyanga Rd, just past the hospital ☎026/250 2193, close to Singidani Lake, this is often empty but still recommended and good value. It's set in a large garden with plenty of tables under parasols, children's swings and (apparently) a mongoose colony. All rooms have private bathrooms with reliable hot water, table fans and box nets. There's also a big bar with a TV and good food, and breakfast is included. **❸**

Lutheran Centre Shinyanga Rd (no phone). A friendly place with good twin-bed rooms (all with nets) opening onto a courtyard – the more expensive ones have private bathroom and Western-style toilet, and there's also a good restaurant. **❶**

New Embassy Guest House Babati Rd ☎026/250 2123. Decent rooms with shared bathrooms. **❶**

Stanloy Hotcl Off Dabati Rd ①026/250 2351, ⓕ026/250 2285. The most popular option in town (its entrance marked by enormous animal sculptures), offering cheap rooms with shared facilities and more expensive ones (a tad overpriced) with private bathrooms and local TV. The toilets are squat-style and clean, and there's hot water, a restaurant and safe parking. **❶–❸**

The town and around

Singida's main attraction is its location, bordered by **Lake Singidani** to the north and **Lake Kindai** to the south, and set amidst a scatter of weathered granite bounders and outcrops (kopjes). On the west side of town, 100m from Lake Singidani, the **Singida Regional Museum** (Makumbusho ya Mkoa; ☎026/250 2449; Mon–Fri 9am–6pm in theory if not necessarily in practice) might be worth a visit, although the place is usually locked and the curator out of town. It's in the unmarked building on your right some 200m beyond the *J-Four Singida Motel*, its grounds surrounded by a fence. If there's no one around, ask at the District Council offices nearby. There's also a privately run **nature sanctuary** nearby: contact Mr Hilary Mlumba (☎026/250 2040) – his office is in the stationery shop next to the Lutheran Centre.

Eating, drinking and entertainment

Singida is best known in Tanzania for its **chickens**, which are sold as far away as Dar (hence the sorry spectacle of fowl stuffed into wicker baskets at the bus

Moving on from Singida

You're strongly advised to book bus tickets 24 hours before departure. If you're heading out in the morning, most long-distance buses arrive in town the evening before (around 8pm), so it should be possible to sleep on the bus rather than spend another night in a hotel if you're really strapped for cash. Of the **bus companies**, Mtei Express is the safest operator for **Arusha** (daily at 7am, 7.30am & 9am) and **Mwanza** (daily at 6am & 3pm). NBS Coach also runs to Arusha (Wed, Thurs & Sat) and Mwanza (Mon), stopping overnight in Igunga, and is the main company for **Tabora** (4pm on Wed & Sat, arriving the next day around noon). Super covers the Mwanza–Dar route (heading west on Mon, Tues, Fri & Sun; east on Tues, Thurs and Sat). Tashriff runs daily to Arusha and Dar, while Tawfiq goes from Dar to Biharamulo and Bukoba via Nzega (daily except Fri and Sun), but both have reputations for dangerous driving.

Drivers heading west towards Nzega are recommended to take an armed escort for the first 100km to Shelui, although there have been no incidents for several years and the police aren't too insistent. The escort is officially free, but a hefty tip is expected by some of the guards; you can pick them up at the roadblock just out of town.

stand). The town's other speciality is its especially fine **honey** (*asali*), which is sold in the market. The bus stand has lots of places for filling up on fried chicken and fish, chips, grilled bananas and goat-meat skewers. The main **restaurants**, all doubling as bars, are along the road just north of the bus stand. Other choices include *Florida Snacks* at the corner of Nyerere Rd and Msikiti Road, and *Shana Resort*, on Soko Street, which has a good range of dishes and is an excellent place for breakfast, with lots of snacks and freshly pressed mango juice.

The most popular **bars** in the evenings are the *Rwezaura Bar* and *Night Park Bar* at the entrance to the bus stand, the latter with a TV screening CNN news, football or whatever takes the fancy of the person with the remote. The *NBC Club*, close to the *Stanley Hotel*, is also worth a try. **Videos** are shown in a blacked-out room at Lemmy Video Show on Soko Street; entrance costs a few hundred shillings.

Morogoro and the Uluguru Mountains

The town of **Morogoro**, 190km west of Dar es Salaam along good tarmac, is little visited by tourists, who – if they stop at all on the way down to Mbeya in southern Tanzania – generally prefer Iringa (see p.565), 309km southwest. The **Uluguru Mountains** to the east and south of Morogoro, however, provide several excellent reasons to stop. Part of the Eastern Arc chain that includes the Usambaras in northern Tanzania, the rainforests of the **Ulugurus** are similarly blessed with natural beauty, hundreds of rare plant and animal species and a wealth of cultural interest – not to mention a recently established cultural tourism programme based in Morogoro.

Morogoro

The first thing that strikes you as you approach **MOROGORO** is its strikingly beautiful location, nestled at the foot of the rugged Uluguru Mountains. In the morning, as the sun rises above the mist and bathes the town in warm tones of orange and gold, even the bus station is momentarily imbued with a certain charm. Although seemingly nothing remains of **Simbamwenni**, the town's nineteenth-century precursor (see opposite), the legacy of that century's Muslim-dominated caravan trade lives on. In the town centre, the passage of time is marked by the five daily calls to prayer from the mosques, and Morogoro is one of very few places on the mainland where you'll see women wearing the black *buibui* veils which are so common in Zanzibar. The cultural mix is completed by a thriving Indian community, a welter of earnest-looking Europeans and Americans working as missionaries and developmental advisers and a few Maasai warriors, with their braided hairstyles, hunkered down in the town's bars in their traditional red *shuka* cloths, spears to hand.

The town has an instantly likeable and bustling feel, though its lack of obvious attractions means that it receives few visitors. Not that Morogoro is a backwater. The town's transport connections – it straddles the tarmac Tanzam Highway from Dar es Salaam to Mbeya and onwards into Zambia, and also lies on the Central Line railway – have ensured its prosperity. Morogoro is also Tanzania's second-largest producer of rice and supplies the country with sizeable amounts of sugar cane, coffee, cotton, sunflower oil, millet and maize, *Arabica* coffee, introduced to Tanzania by Jesuit priests operating from Morogoro in the 1890s, and sisal, brought to the area early in the twentieth century by Greek planters, whose estates still dominate the plains to the north and northeast. The town's population is growing fast, having doubled in the last decade to around 240,000, and the local mayor has high hopes that Morogoro is set to rival Dar es Salaam in economic importance.

Some history

Morogoro's existence stems from its location on a major crossroads whose importance dates from before the arrival of the Arabs right through to the present day. Legend has it that in the nineteenth century, a Luguru chief named **Kisabengo** led a group of fugitive slaves to a spot near modern-day Morogoro, where he founded a settlement modestly called **Simbamwenni**, the "Lion King". The story may well have been somewhat embellished, if only for the simple fact that matrilineal Luguru society would never have had a male chief. Whatever his status, Kisabengo's domain, although small, did include part of the major caravan route from the coast to the Great Lakes region, and so Simbamwenni inevitably became an important base for traders. Kisabengo, it is said, also welcomed Christian missionaries on their first forays into the interior, some of whom later settled in Morogoro on land donated by the chief. When Stanley passed through in 1871, en route to his historic encounter with Livingstone (see p.530), he described Simbamwenni as a sizeable fortress with square towers set in each corner beside a large river, though as Simbamwenni seems to have disappeared entirely, it's not clear whether Morogoro occupies the same site, or if Simbamwenni was located some distance away.

The present-day site of Morogoro was certainly known to the **Germans**, who used it as an infamous "hanging ground" during their military conquest of Tanganyika and subsequent repression of the Abushiri and Maji Maji rebellions, at which local people were forced to watch the executions. The site of the hanging ground is now perhaps fittingly occupied by the ruthless anti-riot Field Force Unit (FFU), the police headquarters and a remand prison. Morogoro was captured by the **British** on August 26, 1916, when the remnant of the German forces escaped southwards, though not before the German commander Paul von Lettow Vorbeck had taken the time to arrange a surprise for General Smuts and his army, leaving a mechanical piano playing "Deutschland über Alles" in the *Bahnhof Hotel* (now the *Savoy*), while his soldiers deposited some rather more earthy "presents" on the chairs and tables before beating a retreat.

After Independence, Morogoro became famous, in South Africa at least, as a major base for the **African National Congress** (ANC), whose fighters were trained in the Uluguru Mountains. It was at the ANC's 1969 Morogoro Conference, also attended by representatives from Mozambique's FRELIMO, Angola's MPLA, SWAPO of Namibia and ZAPU from Zimbabwe, that Oliver Tambo announced the beginning of the ANC's armed struggle against

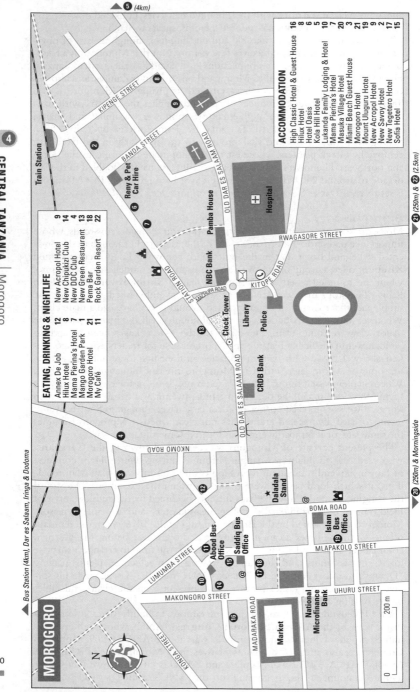

MOROGORO

ACCOMMODATION

High Classic Hotel & Guest House	16
Hilux Hotel	8
Hotel Oasis	6
Kola Hill Hotel	5
Lukanda Family Lodging & Hotel	10
Mama Pierina's Hotel	7
Masuka Village Hotel	20
Miami Beach Guest House	3
Morogoro Hotel	21
Mount Uluguru Hotel	19
New Acropol Hotel	9
New Savoy Hotel	2
New Tegetero Hotel	17
Sofia Hotel	15

EATING, DRINKING & NIGHTLIFE

Annex De Job	12	New Acropol Hotel	9
Hilux Hotel	8	New Chipukizi Club	14
Mama Pierina's Hotel	7	New DDC Club	4
Mango Garden Park	1	New Green Restaurant	13
Morogoro Hotel	21	Pema Bar	18
My Café	11	Rock Garden Resort	22

Train Station

▲ ⑤ (4km)

KIPENGE STREET

BANDA STREET

Remy & Pet
Car Hire

Pamba House

OLD DAR ES SALAAM ROAD

Hospital

NBC Bank

RWAGASORE STREET

STATION ROAD

MADCHPA ROAD

Clock Tower

KITOPE ROAD

Library

Police

CRDB Bank

OLD DAR ES SALAAM ROAD

▲ Bus Station (4km), Dar es Salaam, Iringa & Dodoma

NKOMO ROAD

LUMUMBA STREET

Abood Bus
Office

Saddiq Bus
Office

Daladala
Stand

BOMA ROAD

Islam
Bus
Office

MLAPAKOLO STREET

MAKONGORO STREET

MADARAKA ROAD

UHURU STREET

National
Microfinance
Bank

Market

KONGA STREET

N

▲ (250m) & Morningside ⑳

▲ (250m) & (2.5km) ㉑ & ㉒

0   200 m

apartheid. Following Portugal's relinquishment of her colonies in 1975, the ANC's **Morogoro Declaration** of the same year urged "a massive and concentrated onslaught on the Pretoria regime", expressing its "firm resolve to pursue the armed struggle until final victory".

Arrival

Morogoro lies on the **Central Line** railway between Dar es Salaam, Tabora, Kigoma and Mwanza. The station is 2km northeast of the centre along Station Road; there are several hotels nearby. Morogoro's **bus station** is unhelpfully located 4km out of town at the Kisamvu "keep lefti", the roundabout at the junction of the roads to Dar, Mbeya and Dodoma. A taxi into town costs Tsh1500, whilst a Hiace (pronounced "ice") minibus daladala charges Tsh150. Passengers arriving in Morogoro are greeted by a welter of pushy touts, hustlers and taxi drivers frantically trying to grab your attention and your bags; you can reduce the hassle by retrieving your stuff from the luggage hold before arriving – indeed some bus drivers stop just outside Morogoro to do just this. To escape the chaos, walk towards the rows of soda and food joints at the roadside – few hustlers will follow, as they'll miss potential pickings from other passengers.

Accommodation

Morogoro has a good selection of **mid-range accommodation**, some of which is even luxurious. **Budget** accommodation is more limited and basic, and for a half-decent room you're looking at Tsh6000 and upwards. You'll find most of these places north and south of Madaraka Road between the daladala stand and the market, and between Lumumba Street and Nkomo Road. Single rooms in the cheaper hotels can be shared by couples if the beds are big enough. **Water** is a problem in many of the cheapies. Although work is currently underway to rehabilitate the town's typhoid-prone water and sewerage system (you should already have been inoculated), you should be extremely wary of drinking tap water: use iodine or chlorine tablets and if you have a sensitive stomach take the usual precautions. **Camping** is possible at the *Morogoro Hotel* (no fixed price), a pleasant site in full view of the Uluguru Mountains, and at the *Kola Hill Hotel*, 4km to the east (Tsh4000 per person).

Budget

High Classic Hotel & Guest House Off Makongoro St ☎ 0741/322795. One of the cheapest choices in town, with decent rooms (shared bathrooms only) and a good restaurant which is popular with locals for its TV. ❶

Lukanda Family Lodging & Hotel Off Makongoro St ☎ 023/260 3870. A basic and clean family-run place with a choice of twins with shared bathrooms or doubles with big beds and private bathrooms. All rooms have fans, but some lack nets. ❶

Mama Pierina's Hotel Station Rd, next to *Hotel Oasis* (no phone). A quiet and friendly place offering twins with fans, nets and private bathrooms with good showers. There's a garden at the back and a restaurant and bar with cold beers and sodas. ❷

Masuka Village Hotel Boma Rd ☎ 0744/280223. A restful place set in large grounds with plenty of vegetation, though it appears to see little trade. Accommodation is in large rondavels, each with six rooms around a small courtyard, all with private bathroom, fans and small mosquito nets. It's getting a little tatty, but is still good value for couples. There's also a bar, and breakfast is included. ❷

Miami Beach Guest House Off Nkomo Rd ☎ 023/4375. One of a dozen lookalike choices in this neighbourhood, and ideal for sampling the bustling nightlife hereabouts. The rooms are all doubles with private bath. ❶

New Savoy Hotel Station Rd (no phone). This may have been good once, and certainly the owners – the Morogoro Institute of Hotel Catering – have delusions of grandeur, but the reality is somewhat different, with eight large but stuffy rooms with private bathrooms and saggy beds – some lack nets, while all lack fans (though some have a/c), and the bathtubs are wishful thinking given the unreliable water supply. Rates vary from room to room and seem to have little to do with quality, so look at a selection before choosing. The bar is popular with locals. Breakfast included. ②–③

New Tegetero Hotel Madaraka St ☎023/260 0195. A reasonable central choice: the rooms with private bathroom look out over the road (and also have a communal balcony); those with shared bathrooms face the *Pema Bar* at the back – needless to say, all are extremely noisy. The water supply is capricious, but the beds are clean and there are nets and fans in all rooms, plus a basic restaurant downstairs. ②

Sofia Hotel John Mahenge St ☎0741/334421. A good central choice with a range of spotless rooms (all with fans and mosquito nets) to suit most pockets. The cheaper rooms have twin beds and shared bathrooms; the more expensive have private bathrooms and TVs. There's also one double room with a huge bed, a/c, fridge, telephone and balcony. There's a bar and small restaurant on the ground floor, and breakfast is included. ②–④

Moderate

Hilux Hotel Old Dar es Salaam Rd ☎023/3946, ☞023/3956. A good-value, modern mid-range choice, if not particulary inspiring; the better rooms are at the back, all with a/c, TV, wall-to-wall carpet, phones, nets, good furniture and a private balcony – the bathrooms are spotless and the toilets even have seats. The fractionally cheaper rooms in the older wing lack TVs, and the cheapest ones have fans instead of a/c. There's a restaurant and two bars, the nicer one at the back under a *makuti* thatch structure with a pool table. No single rates. A full English breakfast is included. ④

Hotel Oasis Station Rd ☎023/4178, ✉oasis@raha.com. A new but overpriced business-class choice with 37 rooms, it compares badly with the cheaper *Hilux*, and despite a/c in some of the rooms, there's a pervasively musty smell. Apart from this, the rooms are comfortable, with mosquito nets, ceiling fan, fridge, TV, telephone and tiled bathrooms, though the beds in the single rooms are tiny. Amenities include a bar and restaurant, internet access and safe parking, and breakfast is included. ④

Kola Hill Hotel 4km along Old Dar es Salaam Rd ☎023/260 3707, ☞023/260 4394. In a quiet rural location close to the Ulugurus, the thirty rooms here (all twins or doubles) are in closely spaced granite bungalows, all with box nets, phones, clean toilets with seats and paper, and bathtubs with hot water. Most rooms have fans (more expensive ones also have a/c and local TV), there's a bar and restaurant, and the hotel can arrange hikes to Morningside (p.277). To get here by public transport, catch one of the daladalas to Bigwa from the stand at the corner of Boma Rd and Old Dar es Salaam Rd (daily until around 8.30pm). Breakfast included. ③–④

Morogoro Hotel Rwagasore St ☎023/3270 or 3271, ☞023/4001. The town's largest hotel and the most appealing architecturally, with a cluster of buildings presumably designed to look like traditional Luguru homesteads, but which actually bear an uncanny resemblance to flying saucers. The bedrooms are in segments of the smaller saucers, all clean with huge beds, fans, round mosquito nets and antique telephones. The more expensive "superior" rooms are newly refurbished and have a/c, and there are also some family suites ($70–80). Facilities include tennis courts, an eighteen-hole golf course ($10 for nine holes), a swimming pool which may yet one day see water, a restaurant (meals around Tsh3700), two bars, and discos (every Fri and Sat). Good value for money, and breakfast is included. ④

Mount Uluguru Hotel Mlapakolo Rd ☎023/260 3489. This five-storey hotel is the best in the town centre. The nicest rooms are at the top facing the mountains; all come with twin beds (which can be joined together for couples), fans, big mosquito nets, phones, wall-to-wall carpets, fridges, clean toilets and showers, and an either/or choice of local TV or a/c (same price). Suites cost double but can sleep up to four. The large downstairs bar has tables outside under parasols, and the restaurant does good cheap food, including *nyama choma*. No single rates. Full English breakfast included. ③–④

New Acropol Hotel Old Dar es Salaam Rd ☎023/3403, ☞023/3952. A very plush and sophisticated establishment run by a Greek-Canadian couple with just four rooms (so book ahead), all with private bathroom, a/c, fan, TV, fridge and a very big bed. There's also an attractive and well-stocked bar and a surprisingly posh silver-service restaurant, as well as safe parking. Full English breakfast included. ⑤

The Town

Aside from its proximity to the Uluguru Mountains (see p.275), there's not much reason to linger in Morogoro, although the bustling pace of life here makes a refreshing change after the somnolent towns that dominate the rest of central Tanzania. The best free entertainment is at the main **market** along Madaraka Road, which sees hundreds of vendors coming from the mountains each day to sell whatever they have: tomatoes, snow peas, delicious sweet tangerines, bananas, papayas and coconuts, as well as delicately woven baskets, woodcarvings and coconut-wood chairs.

With more time to kill, the **Rock Garden Resort**, 3km along Rwagasore Street (9am to around midnight; Tsh2000) is a suitably tranquil place to while away an afternoon, with its small streams, pathways and a small café at the entrance. It's pretty run-down nowadays but remains popular with romantic locals. You could also get here by bicycle, which can be rented outside the market. **Mindu Reservoir**, off the Iringa road, is another good destination if you've got a bike. For something completely different, a local school for disabled children offers **drum and dance lessons**; ask at the Wildlife Conservation Society of Tanzania's office in Pamba House on Old Dar es Salaam Road (see p.276).

Eating, drinking and nightlife

Almost uniquely in Tanzania, Morogoro keeps on bustling well into the night, with dozens of bars and cheap restaurants to keep you happy. The cheapest eats are at the various **street foodstalls** in the centre, especially at the corner of Madaraka Road and John Mahenge Street, which really get going towards dusk, when the air fills with plumes of aromatic smoke spiralling from dozens of charcoal stoves: grilled goat meat, roast bananas and maize cobs, chips and eggs are the staples, and a full meal won't cost over Tsh1000. Look out also for one of the many **coconut vendors**, who chop open the fresh nuts for you to drink the juice, and then scoop out the soft rubbery flesh using a piece of the shell. Of the cheap **restaurants** around the daladala stand, *Murad* is probably the best. The following are the best of the more conventional set-ups, but don't expect too much: epicurean delights have yet to make much of an impact.

Hilux Hotel Old Dar es Salaam Rd. This has a small selection of Chinese, Indian, seafood and continental dishes (around Tsh4000), plus all the usual Tanzanian favourites (chips, fried chicken, more chips).

Mama Pierina's Hotel Station Rd, next to the *Hotel Oasis*. The wide menu here is designed to appeal to travellers, but the place can be pretty empty at times. The pizzas are fairly dire, but the rest, including the steaks and pasta, are fine. Starters are overpriced at around Tsh3000, mains are better value at Tsh3000–5000.

My Café Lumumba St. Famous locally for being decorated entirely with Manchester United stickers and posters (and not a Coke or Fanta logo in sight). The food is limited to chicken and chips, but it's reasonably tasty and very cheap.

New Acropol Hotel Old Dar es Salaam Rd. Probably the best restaurant in Morogoro, with a sophisticated ambience, starched linen and silver service – and it's good value too. The menu covers most bases including lasagne, seafood and pork (all around Tsh5000), along with some cheaper snacks. They also do an excellent cup of coffee.

New Chipukizi Club Opposite the *Lukanda Hotel*. Good, cheap and filling meals throughout the day, including *supu* – a meaty broth – for breakfast.

New Green Restaurant Station Rd. Always busy, which is a good sign, with a wide selection of Indian dishes plus pork and seafood dishes. Full meals cost Tsh2500 and up, and there's also satellite TV. Closed Sun evening

Drinking and nightlife

As is so often the case in Tanzania, predominantly Muslim towns are, rather perversely, good for **bars**, and Morogoro is no exception; the following is a selection of some of the best. Walking around at night is generally considered safe, perhaps because there are plenty of people about, but it's still best to leave valuables at your hotel and take only the money you'll need.

Sadly, the **live music** for which the town was once famous has all but disappeared. Morogoro Jazz Band and Super Volcano, two of Tanzania's most popular dance bands in the 1970s and early 1980s, are long gone, and there's little to replace them, though any mention of music legends Mbaraka Mwinshehe Mwaruka, Juma Kilaza or Kulwa Sakum is guaranteed to raise a smile. Still, it should be worth enquiring about Dar es Salaam-based rap artist Boy 'G' from the Dog Posse crew, who occasionally returns home for a performance. Meanwhile, your best chance for catching live music is on Saturday at the *Morogoro Hotel*. You could also ask at *Mango Garden Park* (see below) or at the Vijana Social Hall, on the road to Sua, which hosts occasional events.

Annex De Job Between Lumumba St and Nkomo Rd. A local place with a pleasant rooftop terrace, related to the unexceptional *De Job* bar on Makongoro St. Both places also do fried food.

Mango Garden Park Off Nkomo Rd. An archetypal *nyama choma* beer garden, this also has discos on Sundays (8pm–4am; Tsh1000).

Morogoro Hotel Rwagasore St. This has two bars, the better of which occupies the terrace of the main hotel building and is busy throughout the week, with discos on Fridays and Saturdays (10.30pm–3.30am; Tsh1500).

New Acropol Hotel Old Dar es Salaam Rd. An attractive, upmarket bar that comes complete with dartboard, pool table and satellite TV in a side room. Good for a quiet drink.

New Chipukizi Club Makongoro St opposite the *Lukanda*. One of the largest and busiest local places, open all day and often far into the night, with a wide range of beers, good cheap food and a TV that alternates between Channel O (music), CNN, the Discovery Channel and pirated videos of US movies screened in the afternoon with Arabic subtitles.

New DDC Club Nkomo Rd. A big social hall with a shady garden attached. The big days here are Saturday and Sunday when you might catch an *ngoma* group playing traditional music.

Pema Bar Madaraka Rd, entrance beside *New Tegetero Hotel*. Excellent town-centre drinking hole, always lively, with lots of music, and a popular place to unwind in after work. The music gets particularly loud from Thursdays to Sundays. when the evenings often turn into discos (free admission).

Rock Garden Resort 3km south of town along Rwagasore St. The bar here has discos on Saturday and Sunday, but check whether they're still on before forking out Tsh2000 for the taxi ride. Food available.

Listings

Banks and exchange CRDB and NBC banks are both on Old Dar es Salaam Rd. The cumbersome CRDB charges $10 commission, the much more efficient NBC a mere 0.5 percent. The National Microfinance Bank on Uhuru Rd near the market has similar rates but is often busy. There are no forex bureaux.

Car rental Taxi drivers are happy to negotiate deals for day-trips, though if you'e planning one of the wilder trips into the Ulugurus, you'll need a 4WD with an experienced driver: ask around at the daladala stand. Otherwise try Reny & Pet Car Hire on Station Rd (PO Box 5449; ☎0741/630265), who charge Tsh16,000 a day plus Tsh300 per kilometre for a saloon car.

Football Matches are played at Jamhuri Stadium by top local team, Moro United.

Hospital The regional hospital is on Old Dar es Salaam Rd; the entrance is on Rwagasore St (☎023/232 3045).

Internet There are only two internet cafés at present (both daily 8.30am–10pm; Tsh1000 per hour): Internet Café is opposite the *New Tegetero Hotel*, the other – with no name, but under the same management – is on Boma Rd. Both get busy, so you'll usually have to book ahead for your slot.

Language courses Kiswahili lessons and courses are offered by Wageni Morogoro (☎023/260 0899) and the Institute of Adult Education – Expatriate Centre (☎023/260 2988), who also have accommodation for students on their one-month courses. Details of both can be had from the Wildlife Conservation Society of Tanzania office in Pamba House see p.276.

Post office The post office is on Old Dar es Salaam Rd. There's a DHL office on Boma Rd ☎023/260 4528, ⓦwww.dhl.com.

Supermarkets Morogoro's supermarkets are just west of the daladala stand. Try Pira's Cash & Carry or Mutaleeb's (which stays open to around 10pm), both on Lumumba St, or any of the ones on the north side of Madaraka Rd.

Telephones The TTCL office is at the side of the post office, entrance on Kitope St (Mon–Sat 7.30am–10pm, Sun 8am–8pm). It has cardphones outside and an operator-assisted service inside.

Moving on from Morogoro

Trains to Dar es Salaam leave (inconveniently) at 2.15am (Mon, Tues, Thurs, Sat & Sun). Heading west, trains leave at a quarter past midnight (Mon, Wed, Thurs & Sat for Mwanza; Mon, Wed, Fri & Sat for Kigoma). All **buses** leave from Kisamvu round-about, 4km from town. Some companies have central booking offices: Abood can be found at the top of John Mahenge Street; Hood are at Madaraka Road next to the *New Tegetero Hotel*; Islam are at Boma Road, opposite the mosque; and Saddiq are at the corner Madaraka Road and John Mahenge Road. The biggest companies are Hood and Abood, but both have reputations for perilous driving and are best avoided (Abood is owned by a rally-driving business tycoon, which explains a lot). Unfortunately the competition is little better, and reliable companies like Scandinavian Express and Fresh ya Shamba only rarely have spare seats (and neither allows standing passengers).

The good news is that there's lots of transport in all directions, with several buses hourly (6am–4pm) to **Dar**, and services roughly every hour to **Iringa and Mbeya**, along with less frequent buses to **Dodoma and Arusha**, and daily runs to **Ifakara** (on Islam Bus), so your best bet is just to get yourself down to Kisamvu roundabout early in the morning (6am latest), where you can choose your vehicle: check tyres for wear the driver's eyes for the effects of drugs and don't let yourself be harried onto one bus or another, as there are usually plenty to choose from. Unusually for Tanzania, the smaller vehicles are safer. **Daladalas** run to Dar from the old bus station, now the daladala stand, in the city centre at the corner of Boma Road and Old Dar es Salaam Road, but there's no guarantee of safety with these.

The Uluguru Mountains

South and east of Morogoro rise the spectacular **Uluguru Mountains** (from the local word *guru*, meaning mountain). Rising to around 2650m, the mountains contain some of the most luxuriant – but now sadly threatened – indigenous rainforest in the country. Spanning some 100km from north to south, and 20km from east to west, the range forms part of the ancient **Eastern Arc mountain chain** (see box on p.343) that stretches from the Taita Hills in Kenya to the Mufindi Highlands south of Iringa.

The great age of the mountains and of the forests that cover them (some of which are estimated to be 25 million years old), together with the region's high rainfall, wide range of altitudes and a climate which has remained remarkably stable over the ages, have all favoured the development of some of the world's richest and most species-diverse **rainforests**, which contain eleven endemic reptilian and amphibian species and over 100 endemic plants, including African violets, busy lizzies and begonias. Mammals include yellow baboons, blue monkeys, black-and-white colobus monkeys, wild pigs and duiker antelopes. But where Uluguru really comes into its own is its **birdlife**, which includes fifteen rare or unique species. Notable among these are the Usambara eagle owl, which was found here in 1993 – only its third known habitat – and the endemic Uluguru bush-shrike (*Malaconotus alius*), which is now critically endangered thanks to the ongoing loss of forest canopy on the lower slopes. Other birds worth looking out for include Loveridge's sunbird, Fulleborn's black boubou (both of which inhabit the forest around Lupanga Peak, the one closest to Morogoro), and the more common and more easily seen (or heard) Livingstone's turaco and silvery-cheeked hornbill.

At Independence, most of the mountains were still covered with forest, but one glance at the Ulugurus from Morogoro today tells of the enormous destruction that has occurred since then, either deliberately – through timber extraction or land clearance for cultivation – or accidentally by fire (whose depressing plumes are still a daily feature of the skyline). Yet things appear to be changing for the better. After having been closed for many years due to the presence of ANC training camps, the Ulugurus have recently been opened to tourism through the establishment of the ambitious **Uluguru Biodiversity Conservation Project** (Ⓦ www.africanconservation.com/uluguru), which aims to reverse the environmental degradation of Uluguru's forests. One of its projects is a **cultural tourism programme**, which uses natural attractions to provide an alternative source of income to local villages without affecting forest resources. For the visitor, this means an exciting range of walks and hikes that combine obvious natural attractions (forests, streams, waterfalls and beautiful views) with equally fascinating encounters with the Luguru, all at very affordable prices. It's still far too early to count successes, but the fact that the programme was embraced by a number of villages long before the first tourists arrived bodes well.

Practicalities

All trips to the Ulugurus should be arranged through the **Uluguru Biodiversity Conservation Project**, which is located in Morogoro at the offices of the Wildlife Conservation Society of Tanzania (WCST), 1st floor, Pamba House, Old Dar es Salaam Rd (PO Box 312, Morogoro; ☎023/23122, Ⓔ uluguru@morogoro.net); the project can also be contacted via WCST's headquarters in Dar on Garden Avenue (PO Box 70919, Dar es Salaam) ☎022/211 2518, Ⓔ wcst@africaonline.co.tz). In time, the newly formed **Mountain Conservation Society of Tanzania** will take over the running of the Uluguru Biodiversity Conservation Project, and it plans to open a tourist information office in Morogoro.

The **best time to visit** is during the dry season (July–Sept), as some of the hikes may not be possible during the rains. The main rains fall between February and June, with the lighter short rains coming between October and January. All routes are steep in places, so you should come with good walking boots or at least worn-in shoes with good tread, especially when wet. It's best to start off early on all treks, and you should also take water (at least a litre), some food, a light raincoat, suncream and a light fleece from June to September – temperatures can be surprisingly low, even if the weather is clear and bright. The project office can put you in touch with one of the **guides** – they're still a little raw around the edges, but things should improve over time. Exact **costs** have yet to be worked out, but certainly won't be more than Tsh10,000 per person per day – charges include a Tsh2000 "development fee" which goes into a fund for community-based projects. Overnight **accommodation** for longer trips costs around Tsh2000 per person; although there are a handful of guest houses in the mountains, a tent would certainly enhance your options. At present, fees are paid directly to the guide and the villagers. You'll need a **permit** to enter forested areas on higher slopes, which are part of protected forest reserves. The permit costs Tsh4000 per person per day and can be bought at the Regional Catchment Forest Project Office, 1km north of Morogoro: it's on your left immediately after the railway crossing along the road to Dar es Salaam and Iringa. A permit isn't necessary if you stay under the tree line.

The following sections cover a selection of the more feasible **day-trips**. Other possibilities, for which detailed information and advice should be sought from the project office in Morogoro (or from Ⓦ http://africanconservation .com/uluguru/ziparticles/touristinformation.zip), include a challenging four-day hike to the range's highest point, **Kimhandu Peak**; an equally adventurous hike around the **Lukwangule Plateau** from Nyandira village; and a hike up to the 2150m **Lupanga Peak**, which is the closest peak to Morogoro and can be scaled and descended in about six hours. It's a tough walk, though, and gets dangerously slippery in the rains, so you should take a guide. Forest permits are needed for all these climbs.

Ruvuma and Morningside

The half-abandoned colonial settlement of **MORNINGSIDE**, a two-to-three-hour walk due south of Morogoro, is now the site of a dilapidated weekend retreat dating from German times. It makes a very pleasant target for a day's walk from Morogoro. The views – over the Ulugurus and Morogoro – are well worth the effort of climbing the steep path, and the cool mountain air makes a bracing change from the sweltering heat of Morogoro. However, if it's forest you're after, choose another destination, as the forest reserve above Morningside is out of bounds thanks to the presence of a communications mast on Bondwe peak. Leave early (about 7am) as the lower part of the walk, which goes through open farmland, can get very hot. The walk starts along Boma Road – there's a shop halfway up which should have sodas, and there's also a waterfall en route. If you're feeling lazy, you could rent a taxi for part of the ascent, which gets you to **RUVUMA**, three-quarters of the way, beyond which the path is too steep for vehicles (Ruvuma may in the future have accommodation and tourist activities as part of the cultural tourism programme – ask at the Uluguru Biodiversity Conservation Project office in Morogoro; see opposite). Other than the views and cool climate, **Morningside** itself doesn't really have much more to offer. The old German building, which functioned as a hotel until the 1970s, is dilapidated but still used during occasional field trips by the Sokoine University of Agriculture. Energetic folk can continue up a steep track or along the winding road to the forest boundary, marked by an enormous eucalyptus tree planted in the 1960s – the hike from Morningside takes an hour at most.

Taking a **guide** in Morogoro to reach Morningside (Tsh2000–5500 per person depending on group size) is recommended, both to help you actually find Morningside (which can be obscured by cloud between November and June), and if you want to spend any time in Ruvuma, which is very much still a traditional village.

Nugutu village

An hour's walk or fifteen minutes' drive from Morogoro (Tsh2000 by taxi), the small and traditional village of **NUGUTU** is an excellent place to learn about the traditional culture of the **Luguru** (see box on p.278), especially since the village forms part of the Uluguru Biodiversity Conservation Project. The village's women's group has organized a number of activities for tourists, including an excellent Luguru-style lunch (featuring *pombe* beer), as well as the chance to see locals weaving and dyeing the mats and baskets which form the village's main source of income. The twine is made from the fronds of the *mkindu* tree (phoenix palm), collected in the forest or bought in Morogoro. One mat takes about two months to make, as they only have evenings in which to work on them – daylight is spent in the fields. The women are also talented musicians and for a small additional fee will introduce you to the delights of traditional Luguru music and dance (*ngoma*). Female visitors can be taught about *ngomas* reserved exclusively for women; and there's also a men's *ngoma* group which can be hired for performances. The village's other attractions include seeing how bricks are made, and visiting a men's co-operative where chairs are fashioned from bits of coconut trees.

Visitors are required to hire a **guide** at the project office in Morogoro, which will also contact the village to let them know you're coming. The trip, which is normally combined with a visit to Madola (see opposite), costs Tsh6500–9500 depending on group size; the development fee is being saved to build a dispensary. There's no accommodation.

The Luguru

For over three centuries the Uluguru Mountains have been home to the **Luguru** tribe, whose name literally means "people of the mountain". Although most of the 1.2 million Luguru now live in the lowlands in and around Morogoro and elsewhere, some 100,000 still inhabit the lower slopes of the mountains, using skilful agricultural practices like self-composting ladder terraces to make the most of the fertile soil and abundant rainfall. Apart from traditional staples like rice, maize, sorghum, vegetables and plantain, cash crops – especially coffee and fruits – are also grown to be sold to the burgeoning populations of Morogoro and Dar es Salaam.

Despite the growing influence of Islam and Christianity, Luguru society remains strongly **matrilineal**. Land is the property of women, passing from mother to daughter, either in their own name or in that of one of fifty clans to which all Luguru belong, which in turn are subdivided into around 800 **lineages**. Although a man may inherit land from his mother, it reverts to his sister's children on his death, even if he has children of his own; if a man needs more land, it can only be borrowed, not bought. Naturally, possession of land gives women an uncommon independence from their husbands, and divorce is common, after which the husband is sent away with nothing more than the clothes on his back. Not surprisingly, baby girls are much preferred to baby boys.

The structure of Luguru society also does away with the need for a centralized political system, as most matters can be dealt with at the lineage level. Matters affecting several lineages are heard by a highly respected council of elders who, of course, are elected by women. The feminine touch is also apparent in the traditional – but now increasingly rare – system of **"joking relationships"** (*utani* or *ugongo*) between villages, which avoided conflict between potential rivals through an institutionalized form of friendship, neighbourliness and good humour – villages in an *utani* relationship were expected to share food with each other in times of hardship. (Joking relationships still characterize relations between many of Tanzania's tribes even today). Things are changing, however: land scarcity is slowly altering the allocation of land and its inheritance, while the traditional emphasis on female sexuality and the encouragement of extramarital affairs has brought with it the devastating spectre of AIDS.

For more information on Luguru society, including lots of detail on the ceremonies that mark the lives of women from initiation to marriage, pregnancy, birth and motherhood, see Salha Hamdani's excellent *Female Adolescent Rites and the Reproductive Health of Young Women in Morogoro* at ⓦwww.hsph.harvard.edu/takemi/RP100.pdf. Also recommended – even if you manage to hear *ngoma* at Nugutu – are the two tapes of traditional music for sale at Radio Tanzania in Dar es Salaam (see p.109), in which remarkable instrumental skills are blended with voices to mesmerizing effect.

Madola

Nugutu, which is as far as you can go by vehicle, is usually combined with a visit to **MADOLA**, a ninety-minute hike further up the mountain (or 2hr 30min from Morogoro) – Madola is usually visited in the morning, before the sun gets too hot, with lunch in Nugutu. A guide is essential, as the track is steep and difficult to follow in places. You're rewarded with beautiful views, patches of forest between the fruit orchards and vegetable plots, and a small waterfall.

Madola is even tinier than Nugutu, with only six houses at the last count. The village specializes in woodwork, including dolls, figurines and combs, but is mainly known for its female **traditional healer** – a vocation for which the Luguru have long been famous throughout Tanzania – who uses her unusual talents of premonition and clairvoyance to heal sicknesses. Her "supernatural" powers (though they're considered perfectly natural by the Luguru) were first revealed to her in a series of dreams when she was six years old, the age at which she first started healing, and she still uses her dreams to determinine appropriate diagnoses and remedies; the treatment itself involves both medicinal plants and rituals, and is said to be particularly effective in cases of insanity – though happy to receive visitors, there's no guarantee that she'll be in the mood to talk with you.

Bunduki and around

The area east of **BUNDUKI** village, a challenging two-and-a-half-hour drive south of Morogoro (turn left at Kipera and left again at Mgeta, which is where the Luguru first settled), offers some excellent **hiking** possibilities, including one of the mountains' largest waterfalls and a walk to the **Lukwangule Plateau**, which separates the northern from the southern Uluguru Mountains. You can hire a **guide** informally in Bunduki, but you'll need to know Kiswahili; it's easier to arrange things in Morogoro. The best **accommodation** in Bunduki is at the house of the local priest, 2km before the entrance to Bunduki Forest Reserve: contact Reverend Gabriel Sengo at Bunduki Mission (PO Box 640, Morogoro). Alternatively, there's a small "guest house" (❶) inside the reserve, though it lacks beds (bring a sleeping bag or roll-up mattress). You can also camp here, while locals are happy to rustle up food and you can swim in the river nearby.

Bunduki Forest Reserve is partly natural forest, partly plantation, and is home to Mrs Moreau's warbler, amongst other rare bird species. No permit is needed for walking along the road, but you'll need one if you go higher up towards the ridge, from where there are superb views eastward towards Dar es Salaam. Just over an hour's walk from the mission are the **Hululu Falls** (no permit needed), where water cascades over a forty-metre drop in a cloud of spray. The site is sacred to local people, who use it for ceremonies, so you'll have to go with a local or a guide.

Mikumi and Selous

The **Mikumi–Selous ecosystem** covers a large part of central and southern Tanzania, stretching from the **Rubeho Mountains** and **Mikumi National Park** in the north to the vast wilderness of the **Selous Game Reserve** in the south, which stretches to within 150km of the Mozambique border, whose Niassa Game Reserve was formerly also part of this ecosystem. The extraordinary richness of wildlife encountered in this area is explained by the dry **miombo woodland** which covers almost three-quarters of it. *Miombo* woodland is dominated by trees of the *Brachystegia* genera, whose main characteristic is that they are deciduous, unlike the acacia which dominates Tanzania's arid, semi-arid and floodplain habitats. The leaves that are shed every year form the basis of a surprisingly complex food chain which creates an ideal habitat for dozens of species of mammal, including rhino and elephant. Unfortunately, *miombo* woodlands are also the favoured habitat for **tsetse flies** which, as is well known, carry sleeping sickness (*trypanosomiasis*). Wild animals possess an acquired resistance to the disease, but domestic livestock do not and so, in consequence, much of the Mikumi–Selous ecosystem survived intact until the twentieth century, when the devastating attentions of man – in the form of trophy hunters and poachers – resulted in the near extinction of both elephants and rhino. Thankfully, things have now improved, and elephants are frequently seen in both Mikumi and Selous. The ecosystem's rhinos, however, are still severely endangered, and are believed to be extinct in Mikumi, while their population in Selous barely numbers 150 – their exact location is a closely guarded secret.

The *miombo* woodlands are at their most beautiful in October and November, before the short rains start, when they put out new leaves in all shades of red, copper, gold and orange, as well as green. Mikumi National Park can easily be visited from Dar es Salaam, either driving yourself or on an organized safari. Selous is a different kettle of fish, with notoriously bad access roads, though this doesn't appear to bother the authorities too much, given that they're bent on promoting "high-income low-volume" tourism. Nonetheless, visiting Selous on a budget is possible, and can even be done by public transport – read on.

Mikumi National Park

Sitting astride the A7 Tanzam Highway 286km west of Dar es Salaam, the 3230-square-kilometre **MIKUMI NATIONAL PARK** – Tanzania's fourth-largest – is becoming increasingly popular with both foreign and Tanzanian tourists. Framed by the Uluguru Mountains to the northeast, the Udzungwa Mountains to the southwest and the Selous Game Reserve to the south, the park itself consists mainly of *miombo* woodland, and although the scenery gets a little tedious after a while, sightings of **plains game** like impala, buffalo and crocodile, giraffe and small migratory herds of zebra and wildebeest are common enough, especially in the swamps and grasslands of the Mkata floodplain in the centre. The absence of gazelles is curious – it seems that their ecological niche is occupied by impala. **Elephants** are common throughout the park; the best time to see them is in December and January, when the resident

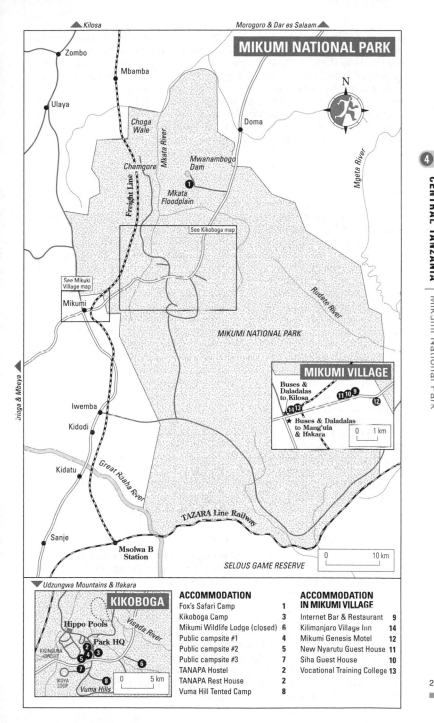

MIKUMI NATIONAL PARK

Kilosa

Morogoro & Dar es Salaam

Zombo

Mbamba

Ulaya

Choga
Wale

Doma

N

Chamgore

Mwanambogo
Dam

①

Freight Line

Mkata
Floodplain

See Kikoboga map

See Mikuki
Village map

Mikumi

MIKUMI NATIONAL PARK

Rudere River

Mgeta River

MIKUMI VILLAGE

Buses &
Daladalas
to Kilosa

⑪⑩⑨

⑫

⑭⑬

★ Buses &
Daladalas
to Mang'ula
& Ifakara

0   1 km

Iwemba

Kidodi

Kidatu

Great Ruaha River

iringa & Mbeya

Sanje

Msolwa B
Station

TAZARA Line Railway

0   10 km

SELOUS GAME RESERVE

Udzungwa Mountains & Ifakara

KIKOBOGA

Hippo Pools

Visada River

Park HQ

KISINGURA
CIRCUIT

② ③
⑤④①
⑦

⑥

IKOYA
LOOP

⑧

Vuma Hills

0   5 km

ACCOMMODATION

Fox's Safari Camp   1
Kikoboga Camp   3
Mikumi Wildlife Lodge (closed)   6
Public campsite #1   4
Public campsite #2   5
Public campsite #3   7
TANAPA Hostel   2
TANAPA Rest House   2
Vuma Hill Tented Camp   8

**ACCOMMODATION
IN MIKUMI VILLAGE**

Internet Bar & Restaurant   9
Kilimanjaro Village Inn   14
Mikumi Genesis Motel   12
New Nyarutu Guest House   11
Siha Guest House   10
Vocational Training College   13

population is boosted by migrants from Selous and a handful that have survived massive poaching in the Rubeho Mountains. **Predators** are much more elusive thanks to the woodland and grassland vegetation, though most guides will be able to locate a lion or two. Leopards are more difficult to see (your best chance is in trees along watercourses), while black-backed jackals can sometimes be seen in the evening, and the African civet is an intermittent nocturnal visitor at some of the lodges – though you'll be extremely lucky to see some African hunting dogs, one of Africa's rarest mammals. Mikumi's **birdlife** is profuse, with over four hundred species recorded to date, many of them Eurasian migrants present between October and April, including red-billed oxpeckers, marabou storks and the attractive turquoise and blue lilac-breasted roller, which often perches on dead branches. Other commonly seen birds include black-bellied bustard, cattle egret, francolin, guinea fowl, hammerkop, hornbill, malachite kingfisher and saddle-billed stork.

For those on a tight budget, **buses** between Morogoro and Iringa (or Dar es Salaam and Mbeya) pass straight through the park (a 50km stretch), giving you the chance of spotting a good selection of wildlife, including elephants, which invariably elicit much amazement and excitement among the passengers. Taking photographs from buses is difficult, given that the drivers only stop when large and potentially vehicle-wrecking wildlife wanders across the road. Somewhat ironically, Mikumi owes its protection to the construction of the Tanzam Highway, which began in 1951 and was completed in 1954. The immediate effect of the road was a massive increase in hunting along its verges, as a result of which Mikumi was accorded national park status in 1964. The highway was asphalted in 1972. In spite of an 80kph speed limit and dozens of speed bumps, most bus drivers treat the stretch of highway through the park as little more than a race track. Smaller creatures like mongooses and wild dogs obviously aren't worth wearing out brake pads for, as you can tell from the assortment of flattened roadkills by the wayside.

Mikumi can be visited all year round, but many of the park roads become treacherously slippery or completely impassable during the long rains (March or April to the end of May) and at times during the short rains (Nov–Dec). You'll find the greatest concentration of wildlife between December and March, but animals are most easily seen from mid-August to the end of October, when the last of the surface water from the long rains has dried up, causing animals to congregate around the river and the waterholes, including those near the *Kikoboga Camp* and *Mikumi Wildlife Lodge* (currently closed). For up-to-date information about the state of the roads, enquire at the park headquarters.

Arrival and information

Mikumi is about four hours by road from Dar es Salaam, two and a half from Iringa (along a gorgeous road that threads through the Ruaha Gorge) and six from Mbeya. There are frequent buses in either direction throughout the day, but as ever it's worth getting an early-morning bus to be sure of a seat. The dismal little roadstead village of **Mikumi**, which straggles along several kilometres of the Tanzam Highway just west of the park, is useful for cheap overnight stays and for catching public transport onwards to the Udzungwa Mountains National Park, Morogoro or Iringa. **Buses and daladalas** stop at the stand at the junction of the B127 to Ifakara with the Tanzam Highway. The luxurious alternative is to fly from Dar (all-inclusive packages starts at around $700 for two nights). Mikumi's **airstrip** is at Kikoboga near the park headquarters at Kikoboga; landing can be tricky in the rains.

The park itself can only be visited by 4WD, and so most people come on **organized safaris**; see "Safaris from Dar" (p.123) for a list of reliable companies. Forget the one-day safaris sometimes touted in Dar: with a minimum of eight hours spent on the road, you'll invariably feel short-changed. A "two-day" camping safari – which in practice means one overnight plus a couple of game drives, one in the evening, the other the next morning – starts at around $200 per person, while the same with accommodation in one of the lodges or tented camps goes for upwards of $330 (with the emphasis heavily on "upwards"). A possibly cheaper alternative in the future will be to visit with the **Uluguru Biodiversity Conservation Project** in Morogoro (see p.276), who are considering including Mikumi as part of their superb cultural tourism programme – these trips will probably include visits to Maasai settlements on the northern fringes of the park.

If there are at least two of you, a much cheaper alternative to an organized safari is to **rent a car** (ideally with a driver, unless someone in your party is experienced in off-road driving) and make your own way through the park. Vehicles can be rented in Dar es Salaam (see p.121) and at the *Mikumi Genesis Motel* in Mikumi village (roughly $100 per day including driver). There's also a 4WD available to rent at the park headquarters if you book ahead through the park warden. Taking the services of one of the **official guides** at the park gate is highly recommended, as they have an incredible eye for spotting things like a leopard's tail hanging from a tree half a kilometre away ($10 for a few hours, plus $15 if they stay with you overnight). **Mechanics** are available (though at well over the going rate) at the park headquarters; there's no petrol, so fill up in Mikumi village or Morogoro.

Information

The **park headquarters** are at Kikoboga, in the middle of the park, just off the highway. **Enquiries and reservations** for the TANAPA guest house, the special campsite or the park's 4WD should be addressed to: Park Warden in Charge, Mikumi National Park, PO Box 62 Mikumi; alternatively, contact the TANAPA headquarters in Arusha (see p.394). While the highway remains open throughout the night, driving in the park itself is only permitted between 6am and 7pm; the speed limit is 50kph. Entrance costs $15 per person per day plus Tsh5000 for a vehicle. There are no entry charges if you're just passing along the highway. The park headquarters sells a map and an excellent **guidebook** ($10), which you can also find at the lodge gift shops, at bookshops in Dar es Salaam and Arusha at the Ngorongoro Conservation information office in Arusha and at the TANAPA headquarters, also in Arusha.

Accommodation

Most visitors only spend 24 hours in Mikumi, so the choice of **accommodation** isn't that important, given that you'll probably be spending most of your time on game drives. Nonetheless, for an extended stay, *Kikoboga Camp* is recommended for its proximity to the wildlife, much of which can be seen from the bedrooms. Travellers on a budget have a choice between camping (see p.285), a guest house run by the park and a selection of cheap hotels outside the park in Mikumi village. The solution is to enter the park early in the morning and spend the whole day on a game drive. The following hotels serve **lunch** ($10–20) to day guests: *Fox's Safari Camp*, *Kikoboga* and *Vuma Hill Tented Camp*. The latter will also let you use their swimming pool.

Mikumi village

Mikumi village has plenty of basic guest houses, most of them pretty tawdry affairs with attached bars, restaurants and prostitutes servicing the needs of truckers and safari drivers, though luckily there are a handful of more appetizing options. The best is the *Mikumi Genesis Motel*, 4km east of the B127 junction (☎023/262 0461; ❹, including breakfast), which exploits its popularity with tourists by charging monopoly rates for both its rooms and meals (Tsh5500 and up). The rooms themselves are pleasant, with big beds and nets, and clean bathrooms, and the bar is a good place to meet up with other visitors if you want to share the cost of driving to the park (the hotel can also arrange car rental); there's also a snake park ($5). If you're in Mikumi only to get to Udzungwa, be prepared for a brisk hour's walk from the village to the bus stop at the junction of the B127 to Ifakara.

Slightly closer to the junction (3km) are a trio of much cheaper places: the *Internet Bar & Restaurant* is the best, with reasonably priced rooms without bath (and overpriced ones with bath; ☎023/262 0419; ❶–❷). The others here, with a much more disreputable feel, are the *Siha* (☎023/262 0465; ❶), which also has a bar outside, and the *New Nyarutu* next door (☎023/262 0475; ❶). About 1km from the junction are the more attractive *Kilimanjaro Village Inn* and the adjacent *Vocational Training College* (☎023/262 0429; ❷). There are also a couple of very basic places (❶) at the junction itself.

In the park

There's a good spread of accommodation **in the park** itself, most within a few kilometres of the park headquarters. The tented camps can be awkward about children under twelve, so prior arrangement is needed. Park fees aren't included in room rates, nor are game drives unless you're flying in, and even then you should double-check in advance. With the exception of *Fox's Safari Camp*, be prepared to have the wilderness illusion broken by glimpses of speeding buses and trucks on the highway that bisects the park.

Fox's Safari Camp Mkata floodplain, 25km north of the park headquarters (ⓦwww.tanzaniasafaris. info; reserve through Foxtreks in Dar; see p.125). Mikumi's newest and classiest option, this luxury tented camp is set on a rocky kopje in a prime game-viewing area with 360º views from its restaurant and bar. Accommodation is in eight en-suite tents, with solar-heated water, flush toilets and electricity, all with sweeping views over the Mkata floodplain. Optional activities include game drives, two-night fly-camping expeditions ($390 per person), guided walks ($20) and excursions to the Udzungwa Mountains. An additional $105 per person gets you two game drives a day, park fees and airstrip transfer. Full-board ❽

Kikoboga Camp Kikoboga, 400m from the park gate (reserve through *Oyster Bay Hotel* in Dar, see p.89). Located on a grassy plain, this is the best place for spotting wildlife from the comfort of an armchair, as several nearby waterholes (and sometimes also the swimming pool) attract a large variety of wildlife including elephant, buffalo, wildebeest and impala. Accommodation is in thir-

teen spacious African-style *bandas* (some of which can sleep up to six people). Facilities include a sundeck, a look-out tower with 360º views and a thatched bar. Dinner is taken around a campfire or in the dining area which overlooks a floodlit water-hole. The downside to all this is that traffic from the highway can sometimes be heard, and you'll need your own vehicle (there are no game drives). Rates work out remarkably cheap (down to $65 per person) if several people share a *banda*. Full-board ❾

TANAPA Hostel At the park headquarters, Kikoboga (reserve through the park warden or TANAPA in Arusha, see p.394). This is primarily intended for large school groups, but may be open to individuals when not in use. There are sixty bunkbeds and two single rooms, shared bathrooms and kitchen facilities. $20 per person.

TANAPA Rest House At the park headquarters, Kikoboga (reservations through the park warden or TANAPA in Arusha, see p.394). The park's cheapest accommodation, with two double rooms, shared toilets, a kitchen and sitting room. The park staff's social hall is in the same complex if you fancy a bite or a drink. Book well ahead. ➎

Vuma Hill Tented Camp 4km south of the park headquarters (✆www.mikumi.info; reserve through Foxtreks in Dar, see p.125). Run by a welcoming French family (and suitable for kids), with good food and service and a relaxed atmosphere. Accommodation is in a scatter of sixteen luxury tents, each sleeping two, set on a low exposed hill with sweeping views of the Mkata floodplain (and the highway, for that matter). The tents are spacious and comfortable, and come with attached bathrooms and large verandahs overlooking the grasslands. Facilities include a small swimming pool and sundeck overlooked by the bar and restaurant, plus an interesting library and gift shop. There are also game drives ($30 for a half day) and guided walks ($20). Full-board ➒

Camping

The cheapest **campsite** is outside the park at the *Mikumi Genesis Motel* (✆023/262 0461; Tsh2000 per person), 4km east of the B127 junction at the edge of Mikumi village. Inside the park (park entry fees apply) you've a choice of three **public campsites**. Campsite 1, near the park gate at Kikoboga, is the best equipped, with tap water, a pit latrine, bathroom, fireplace and wood for fuel. Campsite 2, along the Kisingura Circuit nearby, is under an old baobab and has a toilet but no water. Campsite 3 is in the south of the park under a large fig tree, and also has a toilet but no water. All three sites cost $20 per person, paid at the gate. As ever, be extremely wary of the resident yellow baboons: don't eat in their presence and keep your food in sealed containers.

The park

Mikumi boasts an impressive 200km of driveable tracks, though most become impassable during the rains. The main wildlife viewing area is the hot and low-lying **Mkata floodplain**, in the centre of the park north of the highway, which offers more or less guaranteed sightings of elephant, buffalo, herds of eland and a host of other plains game, good odds on spotting lion (sometimes in the branches of a tree) and occasionally delights in the form of a leopard (also in trees) or a pack of African hunting dogs. The floodplain's **northern section** consists of low ridges of relatively impervious "hardpan" soil separated by narrower depressions of easily waterlogged black cotton soil (*mbuga*), which turn to swamp during the rains. In the dry season, when the swamps recede, hippo and waterbirds congregate around permanent waterholes. The **southern part** of the floodplain, which includes Kikoboga, is drier and has some slow-flowing streams. The swamp edges are characterized by baobabs (see p.426) and rows of borassus palms, known in the local Kivindunda language as *mikumi*, from which the park gets its name. The *mikumi* grow up to twenty metres high and are easily distinguished from the often crooked *Hyphaene* palms by the strangely graceful swellings halfway up their trunks. The floodplain can be covered in two circuits: the **Kisingura Circuit**, which covers Kikoboga and the Hippo Pools (see p.286) near the park headquarters; and **Chamgore, Choga Wale and Mwanambogo Dam** to the north (see p.286), which can only be done in the dry season. Around the swamps is a large expanse of grassland bordered to the west and east by acacia and tamarind scrub, which in turn gives way to the *miombo* so characteristic of Selous. The grassland can be seen on the road to Chamgore and along the short **Ikoya Loop** south of the highway (see p.288), whilst *miombo* woodland is at its grandest in the park's **Southern Extension** (see p.288), close to the Selous Game Reserve.

Early morning and late afternoon is the best time for wildlife spotting, as most animals take cover in the midday heat. With the exception of official picnic sites and the Hippo Pools at Kikoboga, visitors must stay in their vehicles at all times. The numbered junctions in some of the descriptions below correspond to those in the TANAPA guidebook and map.

Kikoboga and the Kisingura Circuit

Kikoboga area is where most of the hotels are located, and there's a reason: occupying the southern end of the Mkata floodplain, this is one of the best areas for spotting wildlife, and access is guaranteed all year round. Of several routes around Kikoboga, the **Kisingura Circuit** (1–2hr), near the public campsites, is recommended for an early-morning game drive, ideally before breakfast. The Kikoboga area is especially good for elephants in December and January after the short rains, since the creatures are partial to swamp grass and completely bonkers about the fruit of the amarula tree, which grows along the fringes of the floodplain. The fruit, which resembles a small green or yellow plum, is eaten by the thousands and the pachyderms will shake the tree to get them to fall. The impressive side-effects of excessive ingestion of amarula, which is a strong laxative, can be found scattered throughout Kikoboga. Other mammals you're likely to see around the floodplain include herds of eland and Liechtenstein's hartebeest (usually close to the river where it crosses the highway). The antelopes are the main prey of the endangered African hunting dogs, which are occasionally seen here in small packs. At the northern end of the circuit, 5km northwest of the park gate, are the **Hippo Pools** where, apart from hippos, you're likely to see families of yellow baboons, open-billed storks and cattle egrets.

Chamgore, Choga Wale and Mwanambogo Dam

The following circuit takes you to the north of the park, but can only be visited in the dry season. Before attempting any of the various parts of the circuit, get up-to-date information on route markers and track conditions from the park headquarters. A ranger is obligatory if you want to ride to Choga Wale, and is recommended for trips to Chamgore and Mwanambogo Dam.

The road to the **Chamgore** ("Place of the Python") area starts from the Hippo Pools, and heads up north between the Mkata River to the east and the freight railway line to the west. The route covers a variety of habitats, from tsetse fly-infested *Combretum* woodland and swamps to a couple of waterholes. **Mkata waterhole** is signposted off junction 32, and **Chamgore waterhole** is 1km to the north (dry season only). Birds here include saddle-billed storks either alone or in pairs, frog-eaters, hammerkops and malachite kingfishers; bohor reedbuck are also sometimes seen. From here there's a seldom-used track onwards to **Choga Wale**, for which you'll need a ranger, and which can be impassable in the rains. This passes junctions 38 and 39 before reaching Choga Wale's glade of *Hyphaene* palms, pink jacarandas (the bark of which is used to protect against witchcraft), acacias and strangling fig trees; there's also a picnic site.

There's also a dry-season track from Chamgore over the Mkata River (near marker 32) to a dam at **Mwanambogo**, which attracts a wealth of wildlife and birdlife in the dry season. Non-venomous pythons can sometimes be seen here, either at the water's edge or coiled up in a tree, but take care – the python dispenses with poison because it doesn't need it: a single strike from this six-metre predator can knock down animals as large as impalas, whom it then asphyxiates by constriction.

△ Baboons and safari jeep

From Mwanambogo, you can get back to Kikoboga by heading south along the eastern fringes of the Mkata floodplain, ending up at marker 2 just north of the park headquarters. This track is probably the best place to see Mikumi's celebrated **sunsets**, when the sun dips towards the Rubeho Mountains, lighting up the floodplain in between. However, the track is liable to be impassable about halfway along during the rains should a tributary of the Mkata River be in spate.

Ikoya Loop
The **Ikoya Loop**, a few kilometres south of the highway west of the *Vuma Hill Tented Camp*, is a short clockwise drive that shouldn't take more than an hour. The route starts at junction 71, from where it rises gently through open bush and red-oat grassland before crossing several seasonal watercourse ravines (*korongo*; so forget about Ikoya in the rains). The Ikoya Loop proper starts after the third *korongo*, at marker 73. A right turn at marker 74 takes you parallel to the **Mkata River** – marked by a strip of woodland – which is a good place for spotting giraffe and lion. Further on, **Ikoya waterhole** attracts hippo and other animals in the dry season. The best time to visit is between June and November, when the rains are at an end and the fragrant *cassia* thickets are covered in yellow flowers.

The Southern Extension
The area south of Ikoya and the highway, which extends to the boundary with the Selous Game Reserve (marked by the Tazara railway), was added to the national park in 1975, but is seldom visited. Much of the area, including the ridges of the flanking hills, is dominated by *miombo* woodland, home to sable antelope, greater kudu, Liechtenstein's hartebeest and the black-and-white colobus monkey, as well as clouds of tsetse flies. If you're extremely lucky, you might also catch sight of some African hunting dogs. Another rare animal that made its home here, the black rhino, is believed to have been hunted to extinction in Mikumi in the 1970s. Specific places to head for include some **hot springs** and a large forest of **mikumi palms**. There are few roads as yet, and these are liable to become impassable during the rains, so check with the park headquarters before heading off. Hiring an official ranger for this sector is recommended – in fact the authorities may insist on it, given that none of the roads is marked. Incidentally, the much talked-about road that is supposed to link Mikumi with Selous is nowhere near completion, although you may be able to get through in dry weather; clear things first with the park headquarters.

Selous Game Reserve

Weighing in as Africa's biggest wildlife sanctuary, the 44,800-square-kilometre **SELOUS GAME RESERVE** – covering six percent of Tanzania's total landmass, or the equivalent of Ireland or Switzerland – is the highlight of Tanzania's Southern Safari Circuit. Together with the adjoining Mikumi National Park and a number of smaller reserves, Selous' rich and diverse ecosystem is home to an estimated 750,000 mammals, including the world's largest populations of elephant, African hunting dog, crocodile, buffalo and hippopotamus. Not surprisingly, the reserve is listed as a World Heritage Site by UNESCO.

The figures are impressive but are also misleading. The reserve does indeed contain more elephants than any other on earth, but given its size that's hardly surprising. Another superlative that no brochure will tell you about is that

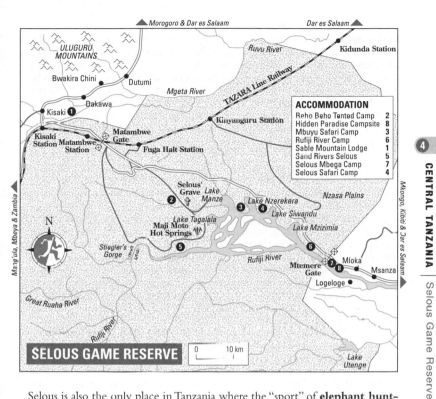

ULUGURU MOUNTAINS

Ruvu River   Kidunda Station

Bwakira Chini   Dutumi

Mgeta River

Dakawa

TAZARA Line Railway

Kisaki ❶

Kinyanguru Station

ACCOMMODATION

Beho Beho Tented Camp	2
Hidden Paradise Campsite	8
Mbuyu Safari Camp	3
Rufiji River Camp	6
Sable Mountain Lodge	1
Sand Rivers Selous	5
Selous Mbega Camp	7
Selous Safari Camp	4

Kisaki Station   Matambwe Station   Matambwe Gate   Fuga Halt Station

Selous' Grave   Lake Manze

❷

Lake Nzerekera

❸ ❹

Lake Siwandu

Nzasa Plains

Lake Tagalala

Maji Moto Hot Springs

Lake Mzizimia

Stiegler's Gorge

❺

Rufiji River

❻

Mtemere Gate

❼

❽ Mloka

Msanza

Logeloge ●

N

Great Ruaha River

Rufiji River

SELOUS GAME RESERVE   0   10 km

Lake Utenge

Selous is also the only place in Tanzania where the "sport" of **elephant hunting** is still permitted, even if only twenty kills are made with the fifty-odd licenses granted annually. In fact, trophy hunting is permitted in all but three of the reserve's 45 "management blocks", while tourists are limited to a small sector north of the Rufiji River, the rationale being that eighty percent of the reserve's income derives from hunting.

To be fair, the sector reserved for "photographic safaris" is by far the most attractive, its habitats ranging from grassy plains and rolling *miombo* woodland to dense patches of groundwater forest and, of course, the Rufiji River itself. It's in Selous that the river – Tanzania's largest – is at its most magnificent, its labyrinthine network of lagoons, channels, islets and swamps cloaked in extensive riverine forest, all of which attracts a mind-boggling number of bird species: over 440 have been recorded so far. And then, of course, there are the tourist lodges and tented camps, most of which are as luxurious and as exclusive as their brochures claim. Such exclusivity comes at a price, and you won't find a single room inside the reserve for under $470 (although special offers over several days can sometimes reduce the cost slightly). Should the prices scare you off, or the all-white, neo-colonial atmosphere prick your conscience, don't despair: there *are* cheap ways of getting to see Selous, and given the fact that **walking safaris** are possible if you're accompanied by a ranger, the overall cost can – surprisingly – actually be much less than in other Tanzanian parks.

The success of a safari in Selous depends on **when you visit**. The best time is from July to October, after the long rains, when the temperature is lower, the air less humid and the grass low. Depending on the weather, June and November can be fine too, though June also sees controlled fires by the reserve authorities to clear undergrowth in a bid to minimize wildfire towards the end of the dry season, with the result that some areas are bare and others are full of smoke. The short rains (usually Nov–Jan), make road conditions difficult to predict, though they're seldom cut for more than a day or two. January and February can also be good months, when the short rains leave the landscape covered in fresh vegetation. Selous should definitely be avoided at the height of the long rains (April–May), when in any case the lodges and tented camps are closed.

In the right season, however, Selous' wildlife is stupendous. **Plains game** is abundant, especially elephant, wildebeest, Burchell's zebra and Maasai giraffe, which can be seen in the wooded grassland north of the Rufiji. Antelopes also abound, with sizeable populations of impala, waterbuck, Roosevelt sable, Liechtenstein's hartebeest and greater kudu, though the latter are difficult to spot, as they prefer dense bush. Smaller and less glamorous nocturnal mammals like lesser bushbabies and small spotted genet are often see around the camps at night, while various species of mongoose – banded, dwarf and slender – can be seen scampering across the tracks. The forests backing the waterways are good places to spot **primates**, including vervets, large troops of olive and yellow baboons, and black-and-white colobus monkeys, as well as less frequently seen blue monkeys and samangos. Rare animals include Sharpe's grysbok, a tiny population of red colobus monkeys in the far northwest near the railway and approximately 150 black rhino whose population came perilously close to extinction in the 1980s; their exact location is kept a closely guarded secret. Of the **predators**, lions, often in large prides, are the most visible; leopards, despite their considerable population, are more elusive thanks to their preferred forest habitat. Cheetah and spotted hyena are also occasionally seen, but the real highlight is the African hunting dog, amongst the rarest of Africa's predators, which has found one of its last refuges in Selous.

Despite all this, Selous' wildlife can actually be rather elusive, especially if you come at the wrong time of year, which is part of the reason why tour operators recommend a three-night stay. Even at the best of times, though, don't expect to tick off species as you might do at Ngorongoro: much of Selous is hidden, and that, ultimately, is what gives it its romance.

Arrival and information

The easiest way to reach Selous is **by plane**, and given the sort of clientele that can afford the reserve's hiked-up accommodation rates, this is also the most popular mode of transport. The next easiest way in is **by train**, though you'll need to be picked up from the station by whoever you're staying with. The cheaper safari operators send in their clients **by road**. Going under your own steam, you have a choice of **bus** or **driving** yourself, both of which are deeply uncomfortable and perhaps a tad too nerve-racking for most, though they're both ultimately rewarding experiences.

By car

Driving yourself is by far the most adventurous way into Selous, given the atrocious state of the roads, although things have improved a bit over the last two years. A 4WD in excellent condition and with high clearance is essential (other vehicles aren't admitted into the reserve – not that you'd get far in a normal car). There are no garage facilities in the reserve, and the nearest petrol stations are at Morogoro and Kibiti, so fill up while you can. The reserve gates are open 6am to 6pm; driving is not allowed inside the reserve after 6.30pm.

Hunting, shooting and conservation

The history of the Selous Game Reserve is scarred with conflict. Its troubles began right at the start, when several hunting reserves were formed under German colonial rule after an epidemic of sleeping sickness gave them the excuse they needed to shift local populations elsewhere. According to the popular story, the reserves were given as a wedding anniversary present from the German Kaiser Wilhelm II to his wife in 1907, and so became known as Shamba la Bibi – the Lady's Farm. The reserve acquired its present name after **Captain Frederick Courteney Selous**, a British explorer and hunter, was shot dead near the Beho Beho River by the Germans in January 1917 while scouting for the 25th Royal Fusiliers. His grave, covered by a simple stone slab, can still be visited. Selous spent much of his life shooting his way through a depressing array of central and southern African wildlife. Although his behaviour would be harshly judged by present-day standards, his contemporaries appear to have considered him a quasi-heroic character. One account described how, when his horse became exhausted, he would leap from the saddle wearing (curiously enough) only a shirt and sandals, in which he would pursue his quarry on foot before, "closing in on the animals at full tilt, load his gun from a powder bag, slither to a stop and fire at point-blank range". Selous is thought to have killed over a thousand elephants in the reserve that now bears his name – all the more ironic given the decimation of the reserve's elephant population in the latter half of the twentieth century by poachers.

At the time that Selous was bagging mountains of ivory, elephants were being hunted at the rate of several tens of thousands a year, which – even by contemporary standards – was too much. In 1922, with Tanganyika firmly under British mandate, the various reserves established by the Germans were combined and expanded, and the remaining Africans who were unfortunate enough to still live inside the new reserve's boundaries were forcibly relocated. The reserve was expanded to its present size in the 1960s, when hunting tracks were also constructed. Intended to facilitate the gentlemanly sport of elephant hunting, the tracks were used in the 1980s by **elephant and rhino poachers** armed with automatic rifles who, in the eight years between 1981 and 1989, managed to obliterate over 75,000 elephants (three quarters of the population) and all but 100 of the reserve's black rhino, whose population had started the decade at around 3000.

Thankfully, the **Selous Conservation Programme** – a joint venture by the Tanzanian and German governments which kicked off with some urgency in 1988 – has managed to reduce poaching, and the elephant population is recovering well (55,600 were counted in a 1998 aerial survey). Many challenges remain, however, the overriding one being how to involve local communities on the reserve's fringes in the activities and profits of the reserve. Mistrust between the authorities and locals has long been a problem: to put it simply, the locals are at a loss to understand why a handful of rich *wazungu* (roughly 200 annually) are allowed to hunt in the reserve for pleasure while locals – whose land the reserve once was – are forbidden to hunt even for food.

Thankfully, the reserve authorities seem finally to have understood that the only way to significantly reduce poaching and the conflict with local people is to involve them in – and allow them to gain from – the conservation process. Consequently, a **Community Wildlife Management Programme** has been established whereby villagers agree to create Wildlife Management Areas on part of their land and to provide and equip village scouts to patrol the areas, in return for a sustainable hunting quota which can either be used by the villagers or sold to commercial or sport hunters, the profits being shared between the villages and the reserve. The new system has already proved its worth: over fifty villages now participate, though with the worrying side-effect that crop damage by wildlife is on the increase. But it's a start, at least, and the important thing is that for the first time in decades, relations between the reserve and locals can now be described as constructive, a far cry from the days when a farmer trapping animals that destroyed his crops was persecuted as a poacher by rangers.

There are **two routes** to the reserve: the track to Matambwe Gate in the far northwest of the reserve (285km from Dar, 155km from Morogoro), accessed from the Tanzam Highway near Morogoro, is the more spectacular but difficult of the two, passing along the eastern flank of the Uluguru Mountains before dropping down into a flat and often treacherously muddy plain. The easier route is to Mtemere Gate in the northeast (247km from Dar), accessed via Kibiti south of Dar (see below), which follows the north bank of the Rufiji.

For **Matambwe Gate**, the first part is easy, involving a straight 160km drive along good tarmac from Dar es Salaam to Mikese village, 30km short of Morogoro. From Mikese a minor road heads south along the eastern flank of the Ulugurus past lively villages and patches of forest. The rocky and sometimes steep surface means that the first 80km or so are usually passable, albeit very slowly. This section has recently been graded and takes about two and a half to three hours, but be aware that should the road deteriorate into its previous condition, the trip is more likely to take four to five hours. If the mountain scenery grabs your attention (as it should) and you have camping equipment, there's the gorgeously sited, community-run *Jukumu Campsite* near Mvuha village at Mambarawe Ridge, 55km before Kisaki, which has sweeping views over northern Selous and friendly locals. There are two creeks with waterfalls nearby where you can swim, and plenty of dense forest to explore. Water is available from a pump, and there are toilets, showers and firewood for sale.

Leaving the Uluguru foothills, the road descends towards the swampy north bank of the Mgeta River, which even in the dry season is hard going and needs 4WD. In the rains the road is impassable, while getting through the churned-up mud just after a shower requires a healthy dose of good luck as well as help from local villagers to drag you out of the quagmire. These 45km are some of the worst in Tanzania – allow at least ninety minutes in dry weather and anything from four hours to several days in the rains. Things improve once you get between Kisaki village and Kisaki train station, where the road crosses the Rudete and Msoro rivers before following the railway to the gate. Once at the gate, don't forget that there's at least another 70km to the tented camps unless you're staying at *Sable Mountain Lodge*, which is 10km away.

The easier access is from the east via Kibiti, Mkongo and Mloka to **Mtemere Gate**, which should take six to eight hours from Dar in decent conditions. The 138km stretch to Kibiti is officially tarmac, but at the time of writing the last 80km or so were badly broken up and so very slow going. At Kibiti (see p.185) take the right fork signposted to Utete along a rough but passable road and turn right at Mkongo (also called Kirimani) after 32km. The remaining 77km via Mloka follow the north bank of the Rufiji River and become impassable in the rains.

By bus

Probably to the chagrin of the reserve authorities (who are anxious to keep Selous the preserve of the monied elite), getting to Selous **by bus** is still possible, or at least as far as **Mloka**, about 10km short of Mtemere Gate. A daily bus to Mloka leaves Dar's Temeke bus stand at the unearthly time of 4am and arrives around 2pm. Alternatively, catch any bus from Dar's Ubungo bus terminal to Kibiti, Ikwiriri, Lindi, Masasi, Mtwara or Newala, and get off in **Kibiti**, where you'll have to spend the night (see p.185) before catching an irregular local pick-up or the bus from Temeke on to Mloka the next day. There's a dirt-cheap and extremely basic guest house (❶) in Mloka. From here, you can either walk 7km to the *Hidden Paradise Campsite*, which offers cheap game drives, boat safaris and bush walks, or try to hitch a lift to the park gate, where you can hire a ranger for a bush walk. Heading back to Dar, the bus leaves Mloka between 4.30am and 7am, depending on how quickly it fills up.

By train
A comfortable and reliable approach, if you're staying in a tented camp or lodge, is **by train** along the TAZARA railway **from Dar**, which currently heads off on Monday and Friday at 9.46am and on Tuesday (express service) at 1.43pm (times and days are liable to change). The journey takes four to five and a half hours to Fuga, Kisaki or Kinyanguru stations (which one you get off at depends on where you're staying). First or second class is recommended if you don't want to share your body space with suitcases, sacks of pineapples, chickens, children or other people's legs. All this has to be arranged in advance with a tented camp or lodge so that they can pick you up, a service that might add $50 to your bill. There are no vehicles for rent at any of the stations or at Matambwe Gate. Schedules for the return journey are so unreliable and changeable that it's pointless to mention them – check with a reliable travel agent or with *A Tent With a View Safaris* in Dar (see p.124). The same comment applies to trains to and **from Mbeya**, which take between fourteen and eighteen hours.

By air
There are **airstrips** at the *Beho Beho Tented Camp*, Matambwe (for *Sable Mountain Lodge*), Mbuyu (for *Mbuyu Safari Camp*), Mtemere (for *Rufiji River Camp*), Kibambawe (for *Sand Rivers Selous*) and Siwandu (for *Selous Safari Camp*). Daily **scheduled flights** from Dar and Zanzibar are operated by the reliable Coastal Travels (see p.124 in Dar, p.643 in Zanzibar), who continue on to Ruaha National Park on Monday, Thursday and Saturday. The short hop (45–60min) costs $120 one-way from Dar or $130 from Zanzibar; it's another $270 from Selous on to Ruaha. The only hitches in the procedure are when airstrips get overrun with wildlife, necessitating a couple of nifty fly-overs.

Information
The **reserve headquarters** and chief warden can be found at Matambwe Gate, but given communication difficulties enquiries should be addressed via the Selous Conservation Programme in Dar (PO Box 1519, Dar es Salaam ☏022/286 6065, ✉selousgamereserve@cats-net.com or scp@africaonline.co.tz) on Nyerere Road (Pugu Road) at the junction with the road to Chang'ombe. The best **guidebook** is the *Selous Travel Guide* by Dr Rolf D. Baldus and Dr Ludwig Siege, which might be available at the park gates ($10) and is sold in all the tented camps. The book can also be ordered though East African Movies (✉eam@raha.com), and parts of it are published on the internet at ⓦwww.wildlife-programme.gtz.de/wildlife/tourism_selous.html. **Entrance fees** are $25 per person for 24 hours and $30 for a vehicle pass.

Organized safaris
A minimum three-night stay is recommended for Selous. Reliable **safari operators** based in Dar are reviewed on p.124, and several operators also offer fly-in safaris from Zanzibar (see p.646). Some of the lodges and tented camps also have special package deals: *Rufiji River Camp* has a three-night fly-in excursion from Dar twice a month ($820 per person); *Sable Mountain Lodge*,

outside Matambwe Gate, asks $120–170 a day for all-inclusive packages; *Beho Beho Tented Camp* occasionally lays on a special train service from Dar for its clients; *Hidden Paradise Campsite*, just outside Mtemere Gate, offers two-night packages for $250–320 per person depending on group size, including road transport from Dar, full board, game drives and boat trips; and *Selous Mbega Camp*, also outside the reserve, does a three-night package for $475 including two days in the reserve, plus a six-night deal including several days of walking and fly-camping for $1680.

As to standard **budget safari companies**, you might find it difficult convincing any of them to take you into Selous, an indication that even they don't trust their vehicles (there are no garages or repair facilities in the reserve, so a major breakdown translates into a fiasco for all concerned). If you do find a company willing to take you, you should at the very least check the vehicle yourself or with someone mechanically competent before parting with any money (see p.33 for more advice). One or two safari companies in Dar (see p.124) also offer Selous as part of an extended **Southern Tanzania safari**, usually starting with Mikumi before continuing on through Selous to Kilwa on the coast and down to Mikindani and Mtwara.

Accommodation

Accommodation **inside the reserve** comprises a mixture of tented camps and "camps" with rooms in stone cottages, with prices starting at $470 for a double. Thankfully, a couple of public **campsites** have recently opened and there's also talk of the authorities opening some cheap *banda*-style accommodation – contact the reserve office in Dar es Salaam (see p.293) for the latest information. There's also a small but growing number of much cheaper places just **outside the reserve** gates, some of which also allow camping.

Inside the reserve

Selous's accommodation is grossly overpriced, and to be honest there's not a huge difference between the various establishments other than size, whether they have a swimming pool and whether accommodation is in tents or *bandas*. Where accommodation is in **tents**, these are large green or khaki canvas affairs, often topped with thatched roofs and pitched on wood or stone platforms. They're big enough to stand in and usually contain two beds and an assortment of more or less rustic furniture. All have attached bathrooms with shower, Western-style flush toilet and handbasin. Rooms in **bandas** (cottages) are little different but for their stone walls, though some guests may feel safer in these if wild animals drop by.

Standard rates are for full board, and are claimed to include two activities a day, usually a game drive and either a boat safari or a bush walk. However, there have been cases where clients have been charged extra for activities on the second or third day, so check in advance. Check also whether park fees and transfers from the airstrip or train station are included – another grey area that catches people unawares. All places are closed in April and May.

Beho Beho Tented Camp Reserve through *Oyster Bay Hotel* in Dar (see p.89). Unlike the other camps, which are located close to the Rufiji River, this is set on a hilltop near the Maji Moto hot springs and Lake Tagalala, with sweeping views over the plains below. Accommodation is in ten spacious whitewashed stone *bandas* with thatched roofs, each with a large bedroom and sitting area with attached open-air bathrooms (cold water only) and verandah. There's also a swimming pool. $500 per double.

Mbuyu Safari Camp Reserve through Southern Tanganyika Game Safaris & Tours, Dar es Salaam ☎0742/782421, ⓦ www.tanzania-safari.org.

Occupying a sweeping bend in the Rufiji River close to Lake Manze, this is a relatively large camp with twenty closely spaced tents (holding 40 beds) under thatched roofs, with attached bathrooms and solar-powered light. Part of the attraction is the lack of fences, which on occasion leads to hair-raising face-to-face encounters with elephants and hippos. While not as luxurious or as stylish as the other camps, *Mbuyu* does have an excellent reputation for its guides, and the accent is firmly on wildlife (be prepared to rise early for activities). The name of the camp comes from the ancient baobab tree (*mbuyu*) around which the camp is built. Rates include airstrip transfer and park fees. Full-board ❾ ($500)

Rufiji River Camp Reserve through Hippo Tours in Dar es Salaam (see p.125). A relatively large camp, attractively set on a high bank overlooking the Rufiji River and the plain beyond. Italian-run, unpretentious and relaxed, like the *Mbuyu* this enjoys an excellent reputation for its guides, especially for forest walks. Other activities include river and lake safaris by motorboat and all-day game drives. The twenty tents (40 beds; though only two with double beds), decorated in rustic style, are tucked away into secluded corners of the riverside forest, each with a shady verandah and cold showers. Rates include airstrip transfer, some activities, and park fees. Full-board ❾ ($470)

Sand Rivers Selous Reserve through Nomad Safaris ☎ 022/286 1297, ⊛ www.sandrivers.com. Overlooking a wide bend in the Rufiji River not far from the Maji Moto hot springs, this sells itself as Selous' most exclusive camp, presumably referring

to the price. To be fair, there are only eight thatch-roofed cottages (16 beds), secluded from each other and with views over the forest and river. The rooms are large and have stone floors and big double beds. The enormous main building containing the bar, restaurant and lounge area is stylish, with plenty of comfortable colonial-style furniture and cushions to recline on, and standards throughout are high. There's also a small swimming pool on the riverbank near a baobab tree with views of the plains beyond. Activities include motorboat rides to Stiegler's Gorge, excellent guided walks and Land Rover safaris. Full-board ❾ ($850)

Selous Safari Camp Reserve through The Selous Safari Company ☎ 022/213 4802, ⊛ www.selous.com. Set in *miombo* woodland on the shore of Lake Nzerekera, this enjoys excellent game viewing even within the camp, which is often frequented by a herd of impala, and has a solid reputation for good game guides. The attention to detail is unsurpassed; the downside is the expense and the fact that it's sometimes used by large tour groups. Accommodation is in twelve secluded tents mounted on platforms and dressed in rustic style, each with solar-powered light, a lake-facing verandah and a bathroom featuring an open-air shower (hot and cold water). The thatched roof of the main building, also on stilts, rises above the trees and contains the dining room and a comfortable lounge. Other facilities include a *dungu* game-viewing hide and a shaded swimming pool. Rates include park fees. Full-board ❾ ($720)

Outside the reserve

Accommodation **outside the reserve** is a good deal cheaper, and you can also save on entry fees if you take advantage of guided walks and game drives that stay outside its boundaries.

Hidden Paradise Campsite 7km west of Mloka village, 4km outside Mtemere Gate (reserve through Family Travel & Tour Services in Dar; see p.125). Covering an open twenty-acre plot close to the Rufiji River, this is the cheapest half-decent place outside the reserve. There are no rooms; a tent pitch costs $15 per person including breakfast, or $20 if you use the campsite's own safari-style tents ($30 full-board). Facilities include bathrooms, toilets, the use of a kitchen and a restaurant that hosts occasional performances of traditional music. Activities include half-day game drives and boat safaris for $30 per person and bush walks for $15.

Sable Mountain Lodge 10km from Kisaki village outside Matambwe Gate (reserve through Safari Scene in Dar; see p.125). Occupying two peaks of

the Beho Beho Mountains above thick bush, this has nine simple but stylish stone *bandas*, each with solar lighting, thatched roofs, and verandahs with views to the distant Uluguru Mountains (though only two have double beds). Attractions include a treehouse near a waterhole for game viewing, a "snug" for star-gazing, a good bar, restaurant and an evening campfire. Game drives cost $30 per person (minimum 2) and can be combined with bush walks along game trails and dry water beds. A walk (2–3hr) costs $15 per person, as does a night game drive. All trips are accompanied by a ranger ($10 per group). Overall a much more intimate and cheaper alternative to places inside the reserve. Rates include train or airstrip transfer. Full-board ❽

Selous Mbega Camp 9km west of Mloka village, 1.5km outside Mtemere Gate ☎ 022/265 0250, ⓔ zapoco@afsat.com. This is more expensive than *Hidden Paradise* but enjoys a better location, on the banks of the Rufiji River and surrounded by cool forest, which sometimes has colobus monkeys. Accommodation is in six en-suite tents with river-facing verandahs, and the restaurant is also under canvas. Activities include game drives and boat trips ($35 per person) and guided walks ($15); prices exclude entrance park fees. Full-board ❽

Camping inside the reserve

Apart from the mobile fly-camps offered by most of the upmarket tented camps (see above), **camping** inside the reserve is only allowed at Beho Beho bridge and Lake Tagalala, and costs $20 per person plus $20 for the obligatory armed ranger. Payment is made at the reserve gate. There's no fuelwood so bring a kerosene or gas stove for cooking. Small campfires are allowed, for which dead wood must be used. The sites have long-drop toilets and water, though this needs to be purified for drinking or cooking.

In a different league are the combined **fly-camp excursions** offered by all of the upmarket places (with the exception of the *Beho Beho Tented Camp*), which involve guided walks through bush and forest, sometimes over several days, accompanied by armed rangers and a white-hunter-type chap as your guide, plus sometimes a Maasai to give some local colour. Vehicle access is sometimes also possible. The camps themselves are set up ahead of your arrival by a remarkable invisible retinue of staff and are equipped with basic creature comforts like hot bucket showers hung from trees, long-drop toilets or portable chemical loos, and enjoyable luxuries like evening banquets around the campfire. Guests sleep on camp beds in small domed tents. Group sizes vary between two and ten; the often hair-raising proximity of wildlife means that children are not allowed.

The reserve

The special thing about Selous is that you don't have to be in a vehicle to see wildlife, as both bush walks and boat trips are offered by the hotels.

Bush walks

The reserve's **bush walks**, which can be arranged at the reserve gates or through any hotel, are an ideal way to get a feel for Selous. Hiring the obligatory guide at the gate costs $10 for a few hours, and an armed ranger – recommended and sometimes insisted on – an additional $20. Most hotels charge around $20–30 per person. The walks usually involve a two-hour wander through forest and savanna, during which you'll have plenty of time to observe monkeys, and perhaps experience a heart-stopping encounter with elephants or lions. Bush walks are also good for spotting details that you would otherwise miss, like the sticky black secretions that dikdiks deposit on the top of grass stems to mark their territorial latrines, or the tracks and spoors left by the animals whose strange noises kept you awake the night before.

Boat safaris

Boat safaris are a great way of spotting the abundant wildlife of the labyrinthine channels, lagoons and islets of the Rufiji River. The trips are invariably offered as a half-day excursion by the lodges and by some of the hotels outside the reserve, and cost around $30 per person for a half day, (excluding entry fees). **Lake Tagalala**, actually a lagoon, is the main destination and is where most of the lodges keep their boats. The lake apparently contains the densest population of crocodiles on earth, presumably fed by the profusion of wildlife that comes here to drink, and there are also plenty of hippos, though you shouldn't get too close though as they will charge a boat if they feel threatened. Another good destination is **Stiegler's Gorge**, where the Great Ruaha River flows into the Rufiji. The gorge takes its name from a hunter who was killed there by an elephant in 1907 and offers a fair chance of spotting leopard.

Birdlife is plentiful throughout the wetlands: on the lagoons, look out for African skimmers, pink-backed and great white pelicans, duck and Egyptian geese, giant kingfishers and white-fronted plovers, while the shallows and sandbanks are ideal habitats for waders like herons and storks as well as kingfishers, African skimmers (again) and white-fronted bee-eaters. The groves of *mikumi* borassus palms that line the shore in many parts are also rich in birdlife, including morning warblers, palmnut vultures, red-necked falcons, nesting African fish eagles, yellow-billed storks, ibises and palm swifts. **Mammals** that can be seen from a boat are usually drinking from the river: regular visitors include waterbuck, reedbuck, bushbuck, sable antelope and elephant. Behind them in the riverine forest (best visited on foot) you might also catch glimpses of black and-white colobus monkeys, or hear the crashing of branches as they flee your approach.

Game drives

Traditional **game drives** generally involve around four hours of bumping and sliding around in a Land Rover or Land Cruiser. Despite the discomfort, these trips have the obvious advantage of being able to get you from place to place in rapid time, and so turn up a greater diversity of animals than walks or boat trips. If you're driving yourself, hiring an official guide at the gate is highly recommended and may in any case be insisted on. It's impossible to recommend any one circuit or area for wildlife viewing as so much depends on the rains and the state of the roads. The best way is simply to ask your guide what's available and to decide from there. There are, however, a couple of places that you could include in your itinerary. These include the sulphurous **Maji Moto hot springs** on the eastern slope of Kipala Hill near Lake Tagalala, which are cool enough in places for swimming in (the springs can also be visited by boat), and the **grave of Frederick Courteney Selous** at Beho Beho. Also at Beho Beho, is the **grave of Alexander Keith Johnston**, leader of a British expedition to find a trade route to the Great Lakes, who died here of dysentery in June 1879. His gravestone, erected in 1890, reportedly took a hundred men one year to carry from the coast, though its current location is unknown. Given its size, however, the stone is unlikely to have got far, and it's probably just a matter of time until someone stumbles across it.

The Udzungwa Mountains and the Kilombero River

Turning south off the Tanzam Highway at Mikumi village you leave safari land behind and, after 40km or so, when the road crosses the Great Ruaha River, you leave the tarmac too. The dirt road continues south, wending its bumpy and dusty way between the flat green expanse of the sugar cane plantations and rice paddies of the Msolwa Valley to the east and the increasingly green and heavily forested **Udzungwa Mountains** to the west. Now a national park, the Udzungwas offer some of the most glorious hiking in the country, as well as the chance of coming face to face with some of its inhabitants, including the rare Iringa red colobus monkey and the Sanje crested mangabey. Further south along the track, **Ifakara** is a small but busy market town at the northern end of the vast and almost completely unvisited **Kibasira Swamp**, fed by the Kilombero River. There are no roads in the swamp, which can only be accessed by boat. A trip here, assuming you have the time to get everything together – supplies, boat, fishing and camping gear and a reliable guide – is one of the most exciting, adventurous and potentially dangerous journeys in Tanzania.

Udzungwa Mountains National Park

Tanzania's newest terrestrial wildlife park, the 1900-square-kilometre **UDZUNGWA MOUNTAINS NATIONAL PARK** was formed in 1992 by combining several forest reserves that had been established in the 1950s. Its streams and rivers form part of the Kilombero and Great Ruaha catchments, the lifeblood of the Selous. On the eastern side of the mountains in the Kilombero Valley, the waters are essential for the area's rapidly developing agriculture, especially the sugar cane which you can see along much of the road from Mikumi. By protecting the forest, the source of these waters has also been protected.

Of equal value is Udzungwa's incredible biodiversity. The mountains are part of the **Eastern African Arc** (see box on p.343), a chain of ancient mountains which runs from the Taita Hills in Kenya through the Pare and Usambara ranges in Tanzania to the Ulugurus near Morogoro and finally to Udzungwa. The great age and isolation of these mountains has enabled many species to evolve here in isolation, but whereas the forests of some Eastern Arc ranges have suffered major environmental damage over the last 150 years, Udzungwa has survived in pristine condition thanks to the unusually steep terrain which limits cultivation to patches of lowland foothills. Local legends and taboos have also contributed to Udzungwa's conservation, as large swathes of forest were left untouched on account of a belief that they were the abode of ancestors or spirits (a belief that seems especially common in places with long-established primate populations).

The park covers a wide range of altitudes, from 200m to over 2500m above sea level, and is claimed to be the only place in East Africa with unbroken forest canopy over this entire elevation, ranging from *miombo* woodlands, bamboo forest and lowland forest (the latter's canopy in places reaching heights of 50m), to distinct zones of moist montane forest and highland grassland. The upper montane forest on the eastern scarp is particularly rich in species diversity.

Given its exceptionally well-preserved forest cover, Udzungwa's **wildlife** is rich, if characteristically elusive. The park contains Tanzania's largest variety of **primates**, with its ten species (one more than the Mahale Mountains) including four which are found nowhere else: the Sanje crested mangabey, the Iringa (or Uhehe) red colobus monkey, the Matundu galago and a subspecies of the Amani mountain dwarf galago (bushbaby). Other primates found here include the thick-tailed galago, blue monkeys and black-and-white colobus. The primates are concentrated in the east of the park, which is good news for hikers as this is where the main walking trails are located. Other commonly seen **mammals** include buffalo (keep your distance), although the elephants who apparently routinely trek up and down the mountain at night are elusive, generally given away only by their droppings. Rarer animals include the red-legged sun squirrel, red duiker, Abbot's duiker (also called blue duiker), Livingstone's suni, bushpig, bushbuck and the comical chequered elephant shrew, so called because of its unusual trunk-like snout. **Birdlife** includes the rufous-winged sunbird and Udzungwa partridge, both rare endemics.

Other endemic wildlife includes three reptile species (a gecko, a skink and a chameleon), millipedes, a tree frog and over seventy different species of spiders. For the visitor, all this makes for a superbly refreshing – if exhausting – chance to hike in an unspoiled mountain wilderness of rainforest, rivers and waterfalls.

Arrival and information

Access to the park is via **Mang'ula village** on the B127, 60km south of Mikumi village, 47km north of Ifakara and just a kilometre outside the park entrance. The road is tarmac between Mikumi and Kidatu on the Great Ruaha River; the remaining 24km is decent *murram*. **From Mikumi**, catch one of the pick-ups or DCM minibuses to Ifakara, which leave from the junction 2km west of Mikumi village. The first of these leave Mikumi at around 10am, but are usually packed and badly driven, and their conductors aren't averse to overcharging *wazungu* either (the fare should be Tsh1500–2000). Much safer, if you can find room, is to catch one of the two daily buses **from Dar es Salaam** to Ifakara, which leave Dar at 8am (run by Baraka) and around 11am (Zanil/Tahezin), passing through Mikumi at around 1pm and 4.30pm respectively. **Leaving Mang'ula**, both companies pass through Mang'ula at around 11am for Dar es Salaam, as does the Reward One minibus for Morogoro. If you're heading on from Mang'ula to Ifakara, the Baraka bus passes through at around 2pm and the Zanil/Tahezim bus at 5.30pm. There are also DCM minibuses between Mang'ula and Ifakara (roughly hourly from 8am to 4pm).

Two weekly **trains** on the TAZARA line between Dar es Salaam and Mbeya stop at Mang'ula station, 1km from the *Udzungwa Mountains View Hotel* along unsignposted roads through Mang'ula village. On arrival, it should be quicker to walk north along the rails and ask directions to the *Hotel Twiga* rather than follow the circuitous route along the main road. Note that the weekly international service to and from Zambia doesn't stop here but at Ifakara (see p.302), though you can arrange in advance with the park to pick you up. Unfortunately, the TAZARA's sense of timing is notoriously fickle: delays of half a day or more are not uncommon, and they don't make things any easier by changing their timetables on an almost monthly basis (indeed, most locals believe that they don't even have a timetable), so check times before setting out.

Information

The **park headquarters** are at the park gate, 200m from the junction for the *Hotel Twiga* in Mang'ula (daily 8am–6pm; PO Box 99, Mang'ula; ☎023/262 0224, ✆udzungwa@twiga.com); they sell a colourful and informative guidebook to the park ($10) It's also worth checking out ⓦwww.habari.co.tz/tanapa/udzpakg.html and ⓦwww.easternarc.org/html/umfm.html. Strictly speaking, the **entrance fee** ($15 per person per day) is for a single entry only, but in practice the wardens don't mind visitors spending the night outside the park and returning the next morning. Most of the hiking trails (see opposite) require an official guide ($10 per day) and/or an armed ranger if the route is potentially dangerous ($25 per day); you can also arrange a meeting with a **traditional healer** (Tsh5000 per group). If you're coming by car a negotiable Tsh2000 is charged for someone to keep an eye on it while you're hiking. There's a similar arrangement at Sanje Ranger Post, 9km from Mang'ula, where several hikes start.

Accommodation, eating and drinking

Apart from camping (see below) there's no accommodation inside the park itself. There are a couple of decent **hotels** just outside the park, a short walk north of Mang'ula village. The best value is *Hotel Twiga* (☎023/262 0239 or 0744/694430; ❶–❷), with simple but perfectly good rooms with large mosquito nets and small balconies, some with bathrooms and even TVs – it's signposted 1km from the crossroads on the main road that also leads to the park headquarters; buses stop at the junction. The alternative is the overpriced *Udzungwa Mountains View Hotel*, 600m along the road to Ifakara from the same junction (☎023/262 0620; ❹, including breakfast); all rooms have private bathroom, two beds (a large double and a single, both with box nets) and a choice of fans or a/c. There are also two cheap **guest houses** (both ❶) in Mang'ula village itself close to the train station and about 1km from the main road: ask for the *New Ndowe Guest House* or the *Usangi Guest House*.

There are three numbered **campsites** within the park, each costing $20 per person per night, plus park entry fees. Campsite 1 is 700m inside the gate towards Prince Bernhard Falls. Campsite 2 is the best placed, some 2km from the gate in a beautiful patch of forest near a bubbling brook and some rock pools which you can swim in. Facilities at both sites are limited to pit latrines. Campsite 3 is better equipped, with proper toilets and showers, but its location only metres inside the park right next to the road makes it vastly overpriced given that the campsite at the *Udzungwa Mountains View Hotel*, 100m further along the road, charges just Tsh2000 per person.

Eating and drinking options are pretty limited. The *Hotel Twiga* serves up reliably good meals (with excellent bread) for around Tsh2500, while *Udzungwa Mountains View Hotel* charges Tsh4500 and upwards, but has the attraction of game meat (buffalo, impala or hartebeest). Both hotels can provide lunch boxes for longer hikes, and also have bars with satellite TV. For your own supplies, there's a reasonable shop at the road junction 200m from the park headquarters, and supplies can also be found in Mang'ula village, 1km south of the *Udzungwa Mountains View Hotel*. Lastly, if you have your own wheels, pay a visit to the women's group restaurant in Kisawasawa, 10km south of Mang'ula, which dishes up good local food; it's signposted 150m to the left on the main road.

Hiking in the reserve

Several unobtrusive **hiking trails** have been made in the reserve, ranging from an easy hour's walk to a serious three-day hike up the park's second-highest peak, and several more are planned to include cultural sites like ruins, caves and sacred groves. It's also possible to arrange your own itinerary for longer hikes – ask at the park headquarters. All the walks can be extremely steep in places, and on most treks a ranger or a guide is obligatory; they can be hired at the park headquarters. The guides speak English, as does one of the rangers. For information on hiking in the western flank of the Udzungwas, see p.572.

Equipment you should take includes good walking shoes; a light waterproof jacket if you're walking the three-day Mwanihana Trail or in the rains; a water bottle and sterilizing tablets or iodine (there's plenty of water along all the trails); and camping equipment if you're overnighting. A gas or kerosene cooking stove is also helpful. Although having your own vehicle is recommended by the park (most trails start some distance from the gate), it's not essential as there's public transport along the flanking B127 for much of the day. The *Hotel Twiga* can arrange car rental on an informal basis, and the park charges Tsh10,000 per group for a car to the Sanje Ranger Post in Sanje village, 9km north of Mang'ula, where several trails start. The park can also find you a **porter**; suggested fees are Tsh5000 for a 16-20kg load on the Sanje Falls Circuit, Tsh8000 for the hike up Mwanihana Peak and Tsh10,000 for the difficult ascent to Luhomero Peak.

The trails

Currently the only trail from the park headquarters, the **Prince Bernhard Trail** (1km; 40min; no guide needed) goes to the small Prince Bernhard Falls, named after the Dutch prince who, as president of the WWF, opened the park in October 1992. There's another waterfall en route. Habituated baboons are frequently seen (hide all food and take care); primates are more difficult to spot, as are red duiker. Another short trail, the **Sonjo Trail** (2.5km; 2hr; guide needed) starts 5km north of Mang'ula at Sonjo, passing through *miombo* woodland to two waterfalls. Primates and birds are the main animal attractions here.

The most popular route, however, is the **Sanje Falls Circuit** (5km; 4hr; guide needed), which starts from the Sanje Ranger Post. The trail heads through various forest zones to the Sanje Falls, a sequence of three waterfalls which drop over 170m. The first two provide a deeply refreshing experience, surrounded with mist spray, and have splashpools you can swim in. The third and longest fall is difficult to see as you emerge from the dense forest, as you're right on top of it, though the hollows and undulating channels gouged into the rock by water erosion are interesting. You can see the fall clearly on the way down to Sanje village, or from the bus from Mikumi for that matter. Primates are frequently spotted along the circuit, and there's plenty of birdlife and butterflies.

The **Campsite 3 Circuit** (13km; 10hr; ranger or guide needed) is the best trail for wildlife (or at least their dung), giving the chance to see bushbuck and duiker in addition to the ever-present primates, birds and butterflies. You'll need an armed ranger if there have been recent sightings of dangerous animals. The trail starts at Campsite 3, 100m before the *Udzungwa Mountains View Hotel* in Mang'ula, and ends up on the road 3km north of Mang'ula before Sonjo.

The **Mwanihana Trail** (38km; 3 days; armed ranger needed) starts at Sonjo, 5km north of Mang'ula, and is the highlight of many a visit to Tanzania, taking you to Udzungwa's second-highest peak, Mwanihana (2111m). Be warned, however, that the walk is exhausting and you need to be pretty sure-footed. The trail follows a river for the most part, its narrow and steep valley necessitating at least fifteen crossings; in the dry season this just means wading across, but in the rains you'll be struggling through torrents while hanging on grimly to a guide rope, so unless you're covered by ample life insurance this trek should be avoided during the long rains from March to May. At other times you have the pleasure of passing through every one of the park's forest zones, before emerging onto the grassy plateau by the peak. The park blurb promises a herd of buffalo, duiker and elephant, but you'd be lucky to see any of these. Much more likely are glimpses of various primates disappearing in a crackle of branches in the forest canopy, and there are also lots of butterflies and birds.

A hike up to the park's highest point, **Luhomero Peak** (2576m; 6 days; armed ranger needed), is a serious undertaking, and one that is rarely attempted. The walk isn't officially recognized, and the trail is poorly marked and difficult to follow at the best of times – and simply doesn't yet exist in places. The trail starts on the western side of the mountains from Udweka, so you'll need transport to get there. Another unofficial trail that should be possible if you have transport, the **Ruipa River** walk (variable distance; armed ranger needed) starts at Ruipa Ranger Post some 105km southwest of the park headquarters, access to which requires 4WD. The trail follows the Ruipa River and is good for seeing buffaloes, roan antelopes, klipspringers (around the rocks), dikdiks and diminutive suni antelopes. Elephants can also be spotted on this route, but don't count on it.

Ifakara

Just under 50km south of Mang'ula, beyond the point where the last of Udzungwa's foothills give way to the vast Kilombero floodplain, which stretches away to the steamy horizon, is the market town of **IFAKARA**. This is generally as far south as travellers go, and even then only a few dozen make it this far each year, though there's plenty to make the journey worthwhile: amazing birdlife attracted by the swampy floodplain; the possibility of arranging boat rides in quest of crocs and hippos along the Kilombero River; the even less visited town of Mahenge which lies another six hours further south; and (let's be honest) the joy of getting away from other *wazungu* – although you will have to share the town with the steady stream of researchers who have chosen Ifakara (whose hot and humid climate is notorious for malaria) as their field base in anti-malarial research work. It's courtesy of one such project, working to popularize Zuia Mbu brand insecticide-treated mosquito nets, that you'll see street-name signs throughout town, quite a rarity elsewhere.

The Town

The nucleus of colonial buildings from both the German and British eras is at the south end of Kilosa Road. Especially beautiful is the quasi-baroque former **Governor's Residence** just off the Uhuru Monument roundabout, a palatial structure built around a large courtyard that is now occupied by the Ifakara Rice Mill. A couple of cement lions guard the gate, in addition to a couple of cops – ask their permission before taking photos. The **market** is a solidly rural affair, also attracting Maasai from the south side of the Kilombero River complete with their inseparable cattle. Local specialities to look for are woven bamboo *tenga* baskets. Other **handicrafts**, including cotton items, can be bought at the Ifakara Women's Weaving Association (IWWA) shop at the south end of Kilosa Road.

Practicalities

Ifakara is most easily reached by **bus**, although there are also three **trains** a week along the TAZARA railway from Dar to Mbeya, one of which continues on to New Mposhi Kapiri in Zambia. The timetable, especially northbound, is deeply unpredictable. The **bus stand** is on Zuia Mbu Road beside the market. For **money**, the National Microfinance Bank on Benki Road, is efficient, has good rates and changes travellers' cheques (purchase receipt not always required). The **post office** is off the south end of Kilosa Road; turn left at the Uhuru Monument. The **TTCL office** is next to the post office at the southern end of Kilosa Road. There are attended-call offices between Kilosa and Uhuru roads just south of the market (Vatete ATCO) and just up the road opposite the bank (Bahati Tele Services).

There's plenty of **accommodation**, though it's all pretty basic. There are dozens of hotels to choose from, and all have mosquito nets. Single rooms can usually be shared by couples if the bed is big enough, though you'll only save a few hundred shillings. The best (❶–❷) are the *Bambo Guest House*, at the south end of Uhuru Road, and the *Goa II Guest House*, also on Uhuru Road, both of which have reasonable rooms with private bathroom. More or less opposite, *Goa I Guest House* is more basic, with shared bathrooms only and an erratic electricity supply; the *Kayuga Guest House* on the same street is similar. *Mahamba Guest House*, on Zuia Mbu Road facing the bus stand, is more run-down, with tattered mosquito nets, but does at least have working fans.

Like its accommodation, Ifakara's **eating and drinking** choices are basic but perfectly adequate, as well as cheap. The best of the lot is the *Zanzibar Restaurant*, on Kilosa Road facing the market, which could almost be described as posh. Also good is *Paradise Restaurant* on the same road, which also has good music. A good cheap place is *Al-Jazira Restaurant* on Kilosa Road, with a decent choice of Tanzanian food from grills and stews to fish (and good juices), but avoid the stuff in the glass cabinets; they also show videos. There's a good unnamed bar and restaurant on the street corner facing the bank on Benki Road, which is also popular, especially when Premier League football matches are on the telly. Less appetizing, but with some shaded seats outside, is the *Shengena Garden Bar* near the post office. If you're feeling strong, ask around whether anyone has any *ulanzi* (bamboo wine).

Moving on from Ifakara

Bus companies with offices in town are Baraka Bus, facing the market on Kilosa Road; Takrim, at the corner of Uhuru Road and Zuia Mbu Road (who have a reputation for dangerous driving); and Zanil, at the south end of Kilosa Road. All run to **Dar via Mikumi village** (3hr); it's possible to flag down buses **heading south** from Mikumi village. Dar is served by two or three buses a day, including Baraka and Zanil/Tahezin, both leaving around 9am. There are also a number of slightly smaller DCM minibuses, whose drivers' skills vary from the simply suicidal to uncommonly considerate – it's pot luck. The last of these heads back northwards off between 3 and 4pm, but may only go as far as Morogoro. The only bus **to Mahenge** is the 3pm Baraka bus (year round except from March to May or during exceptionally heavy rains).

The Kilombero Floodplain and Mahenge

Five kilometres south of Ifakara is the narrowest point in the broad **Kilombero floodplain**, a labyrinth of interconnecting waterways through which only experienced local boatmen can find their way, created by the Kilombero River as it descends from the Southern Highlands. Bordered by the Udzungwa Mountains to the west and the Mbarika Mountains to the east, the floodplain's central portion encloses the **Kibasira Swamp**. Although access to the floodplain is still very much the stuff of expeditions (there are no roads or tracks, only waterways, though the TAZARA railway skirts the western fringes), you can get a taste of the place by heading south from Ifakara along the broad road to Mahenge to the river. Bicycles (around Tsh2000 per day) are ideal for this, as public transport is extremely limited; there are several rental stands near the market and at a number of stands at the corner of Benki and Mangwale roads. You could easily spend a day here at the river wandering through the riverside fish market, watching the passengers, goats and the Maasai with their cattle coming and going. A **vehicle ferry** runs over the river to the settlement of **Kivukoni** on the south bank: services are suspended when the river is in spate (usually March–May, but sometimes starting as early as Nov), and may have been further affected by the disaster here in April 2002, when the ferry capsized, killing nine people.

Dugout canoes venture across the river throughout the year, and their owners are the people to talk to should you fancy spending a few hours – or a few days, for that matter – in search of crocodiles, hippos and the river's plentiful **birdlife**, including the African fishing owl, African pitta, African fish eagle and the endemic Kilombero weaver. A word of warning, though: dugouts are an intrinsically dangerous way to travel, given their instability, strong currents and the caprices of local wildlife, so any journey here is made at your own risk.

Should you feel a sudden urge to delve further into this area, **MAHENGE** town is connected by bus to Ifakara once a day (except during the long rains): Baraka Bus leaves Ifakara at 3pm, and heads back from Mahenge at 6am. Mahenge came briefly into the international spotlight in 2001 when a US expedition uncovered a 46-million-year-old fossilized bat, claimed to be the only known mammal from this period in Africa.

Travel details

Buses and daladalas

Asterisks denote routes that are open in the dry season only; during the rains (usually Nov or Dec and most of March–May) these routes are often closed for days, weeks or even months at a time. Buses that do attempt these routes in the rains are subject to lengthy delays, often meaning days. Journeys over 14hr are likely to involve an overnight stop.

Babati to: Arusha (4 daily; 4–5hr); Katesh (1 daily; 90min); Kondoa (2–3 daily*; 3–5hr); Mwanza (2 daily*; 28hr); Singida (2–3 daily; 4–5hr); Tabora (2 weekly*; 24hr).

Dodoma to: Dar (hourly until around noon; 6–8hr); Iringa (2 daily; 5hr); Kondoa (5 daily*; 4–5hr); Mbeya (3 weekly*; 11hr); Morogoro (1–2 hourly until around noon; 3hr); Mwanza (1 daily*; 28–30hr); Shinyanga (1 daily*; 25–27hr); Singida (1–2 daily*; 6–7hr).

Ifakara to: Dar (2 daily; 9hr); Mahenge (1 daily*; 6hr); Mang'ula (2 daily plus hourly daladalas; 1hr 30min); Mikumi (2 daily plus hourly daladalas; 3hr); Morogoro (3 daily; 6hr).

Kondoa to: Arusha (1–3 daily*; 8–9hr); Babati (2–3 daily*; 3–5hr depending on stops); Dar (3 daily*; 11hr); Dodoma (5 daily*; 4–5hr); Kolo (2–4 daily*; 1hr); Morogoro (3 daily*; 7–8hr); Pahi (1 daily*; 2hr).

Mang'ula to: Dar (2 daily plus occasional dal-adalas; 6hr); Ifakara (2 daily plus hourly daladalas; 1hr 30min); Mikumi (2 daily plus hourly daladalas; 1hr 30min–2hr 30min); Morogoro (2 daily plus occasional daladalas; 4hr 30min).

Mikumi to: Dar (hourly to 4pm; 5hr); Ifakara (2 daily plus hourly daladalas; 3–4hr); Iringa (hourly; 3hr); Mang'ula (2 daily plus hourly daladalas; 1hr 30min–2hr 30min); Mbeya (hourly; 8–9hr); Morogoro (hourly; 2–3hr).

Morogoro to: Arusha (daily; 8–10hr); Dar (2–3 hourly until 4pm; 2hr 45min); Dodoma (1–2 hourly until noon; 3hr); Ifakara (2 daily plus occasional daladalas; 6hr); Iringa (hourly; 6hr); Mang'ula (2 daily plus occasional daladalas; 4hr 30min); Mbeya (hourly; 11–12hr); Mikumi (hourly; 2–3hr).

Singida to: Arusha (3–4 daily; 8–9hr); Babati (3–4 daily; 4–5hr); Biharamulo (5 weekly*; 10–12hr); Bukoba (5 weekly*; 14hr); Dar (1–2 daily*, 13–16hr); Dodoma (1–2 daily*; 6–7hr); Morogoro (1–2 daily*; 9–10hr); Mwanza (2 daily*; 12–14hr); Nzega (daily*; 4hr); Tabora (2 weekly*; 20hr).

Flights

Flights are operated by Air Tanzania and Eagle Air.
Dodoma to: Bukoba via Mwanza (2 weekly; 2hr 45min); Dar (4 weekly; 90min); Kigoma (2 weekly; 2hr); Mwanza (2 weekly; 90min).

Selous Game Reserve to: Dar (1 daily; 45min); Ruaha National Park (3 weekly; 2hr 30min); Zanzibar (1 daily; 75min).

Train

The Central Line connects Dodoma and Singida with Dar, Kigoma and Mwanza. The TAZARA line runs from Dar along the edge of Selous and Udzungwa and south into Zambia.

Dodoma to: Dar (5 weekly; 14hr 10min); Kigoma (4 weekly; 23hr 10min); Manyoni (3 weekly; 5hr 15min); Morogoro (5 weekly; 5hr); Mwanza (4 weekly; 23hr 25min); Singida (3 weekly; 11hr 25min); Tabora (5 weekly; 10hr 15min).

Ifakara to: Dar (3 weekly; 9–10hr); Mbeya (3 weekly; 12–14hr); New Kapiri Mposhi, Zambia (1 weekly; 31hr).

Mang'ula to: Dar (2 weekly; 7hr).

Morogoro to: Dar (5 weekly; 6hr 35min); Dodoma (5 weekly; 7hr 20min); Kigoma (4 weekly; 31hr); Mwanza (4 weekly; 31hr); Tabora (5 weekly; 18hr).

Selous (various stations) to: Dar (2–3 weekly; 4hr–5hr 30min); Mbeya (2–3 weekly; 14–18hr).

Singida to: Dodoma (3 weekly; 11hr 25min); Manyoni (3 weekly; 5hr 15min).

5

The northern highlands

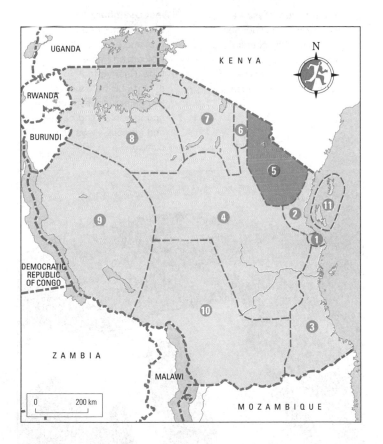

CHAPTER 5

Highlights

* **Mount Kilimanjaro**
  Africa's highest mountain, its perennial snow cap makes a beautiful sight from any angle. It can be climbed – by the hardy – over five or six days. See p.324

* **Amani Nature Reserve**
  Dubbed "the Galapagos of Africa", this contains one of the oldest and most biodiverse rainforests on earth, much of which can be seen on foot. See p.361

* **Pare Mountains** Part of the ancient Eastern African Arc mountain chain, this contains patches of rich rainforest, highland meadows, and the Pare tribe, renowned for their healers and witches. See p.342

* **West Usambara** Also part of the Eastern African Arc, and home to the welcoming Sambaa tribe. Best visited through Lushoto's excellent cultural tourism programme, blending nature and glorious views with culture. See p.350

The northern highlands

The lush and fertile **northern highlands** are one of the most scenically dramatic areas in Tanzania, running inland from the coast through a series of mountain chains which culminate in the towering massif of **Mount Kilimanjaro**, Africa's highest peak. The region's attractions are manifold, ranging from the arduous trek to the summit of Kilimanjaro itself to the less strenuous attractions of the cultural tourism programmes based in the **Usambara** and **Pare mountains**, whose great age and climatic stability has resulted in the development of a unique and extraordinarily rich plant and animal life. The jewel is the **Amani Nature Reserve** in the Eastern Usambaras, which protects some fantastic montane rainforest.

The region's main centre is **Moshi**, best known to visitors as the base for climbing Kilimanjaro, of which – cloud-cover permitting – it has fantastic views. The nicest town in the highlands, however, is **Lushoto**, capital of the Western Usambaras, whose friendly inhabitants, cool climate, spectacular vistas and well-established cultural tourism programme entices many visitors to stay longer than planned. Indeed the same could be said of the entire northern highlands – take your time; it's a vividly beautiful and hugely rewarding region to explore.

Kilimanjaro Region

At almost six thousand metres, the massive volcanic hulk of **Mount Kilimanjaro** is Africa's highest mountain, and dominates much of the region named after it, spiritually as well as physically and economically. Although some 20,000 tourists are drawn to "Kili" every year by the challenge of trekking to the summit, only a few spend more than a couple of days in the towns at its base, of which the bustling and friendly **Moshi** is by far the biggest. This is a

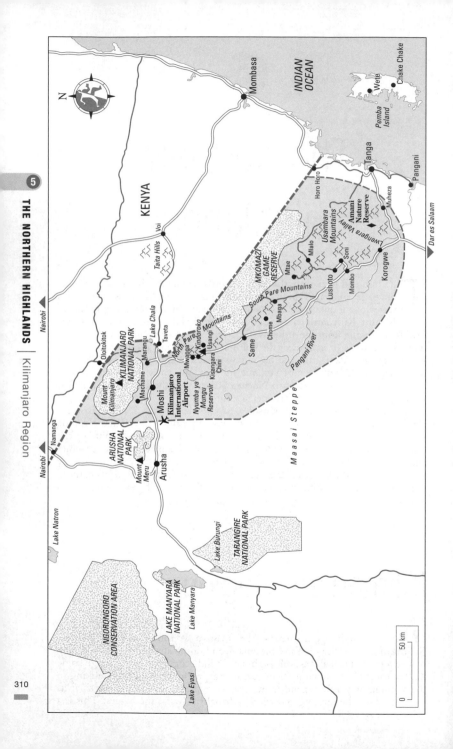

shame, as there's much more to the region than the challenge of conquering Kilimanjaro, and plenty to see and do on the mountain's lower slopes, notably in the band of tropical rainforest that skirts much of its base. Efforts have also recently been made to spread the economic benefits of tourism, with the result that community-based cultural tourism programmes have been set up in **Marangu** and **Machame**, the villages at the start of Kilimanjaro's most popular hiking routes. The programmes include a variety of half- and full-day hikes to rainforests, waterfalls, hot-water springs, farms and places with spiritual or historical significance. Similar trips can also be made from Moshi itself, although little is properly organized as yet.

Moshi

An hour's drive east of Arusha is the busy commercial town of **MOSHI**, capital of the Kilimanjaro region and beautifully located near the foot of the mountain. The views from here are unforgettable, especially when the shrouding blanket of cloud that usually clings to Kilimanjaro by day dissipates – with luck – just before sunset to give unforgettable glimpses of Kibo and Mawenzi peaks: a subtly dramatic and ever-changing scene accompanied by the tweeting of thousands of starlings wheeling overhead. The mountain's influence on the town is pervasive. Perennial meltwater streams permit year-round agriculture, especially of coffee (the basis of the town's relative wealth), while the mountain is even alluded to in the town's name: *moshi* in Kiswahili means smoke, presumably either from Kilimanjaro's last, minor eruption in the 1700s, or because of the smoke-like cloud that often covers the mountain. The town itself is refreshingly open and spacious, with broad, tree-lined avenues and leafy suburbs, and despite a population of over 200,000, it feels decidedly more laid back than Arusha. There's a wealth of good hotels to suit all pockets, too, and a couple of excellent restaurants, making the town both an ideal base for the climb up Kilimanjaro and an attractive destination in its own right.

For all that, Moshi's low altitude – 810m above sea level – means that it can get uncomfortably hot and sticky at times, a sweltering contrast to Kilimanjaro's ice caps looming high above. The hottest and most humid month is December, just after the short rains. November and January can be similar, as is the period from March to early June, during and shortly after the long rains. The coldest month is July, when the 17°C average can feel positively arctic if you've been in the country for more than a few days, but the clear skies at this time also offer the best odds on seeing – or climbing – Kilimanjaro with minimal cloud-cover.

Arrival, city transport and information

Getting to Moshi is simple, whether you're coming by road or flying to Kilimanjaro International Airport. International **flights** land at Kilimanjaro International Airport (KIA), 34km west of Moshi off the road to Arusha. See p.371 for more details about arriving there. A shuttle bus to Moshi connects with KLM flights ($10 one-way); Air Tanzania's shuttle bus is free. Either will drop you at your hotel so long as it's central.

Most **buses and daladalas** stop at the combined bus and daladala stand south of the clock tower between Market Street and Mawenzi Road. Coming from Arusha, you may be dropped just outside the stand along Kaunda Road, next to BP. To find your bearings, look for the large mosque or the Hindu

The Chagga

Now numbering over a million, the **Chagga** occupy the southern and eastern slopes of Kilimanjaro and are among East Africa's wealthiest and most highly educated people. Their wealth – and that of Moshi – stems from the fortunate conjunction of favourable climatic conditions with their own agricultural ingenuity. Watered by year-round snow and ice melt, the volcanic soils of Kilimanjaro's lower slopes are extremely fertile and are exploited by the Chagga using a sophisticated system of intensive irrigation methods and continuous fertilization with animal manure which permits year-round cultivation and supports one of Tanzania's highest human population densities. *Arabica* coffee has been the Chagga's primary cash crop since colonial times, although maize and bananas remain staple foods. The cultivation of bananas is traditionally a man's work, as is that of eleusine seed (*ulezi*), which is boiled and mixed with mashed plantain to brew a local beer (*mbege* or *mbega*) that is still used in traditional ceremonies and as a form of payment to elders in their role as arbiters in conflicts.

In the past, the potential for such conflicts was great: even today there are some four hundred different Chagga clans – indeed it's barely a century since the Chagga finally coalesced into a distinct and unified tribe. Most are related to the Kamba of Kenya, who migrated northwards from Kilimanjaro a few centuries ago during a great drought. Other clans descend from the Taita, another Kenyan tribe, and others from the pastoral Maasai, whose influence is visible in the importance attached to cattle as bridewealth payments and in the grouping of men into age-sets analogous to the Maasai system. Today, the Chagga wield considerable political and financial clout, both because of their long contact with European models of education and Christianity, both of which dominate modern-day political and economic life, and because of their involvement in the coffee business, which remains the region's economic mainstay in spite of volatile world prices. Indeed, the Chagga are the one tribe you're almost guaranteed to meet in even the most obscure corners of Tanzania, working as traders, merchants, officials, teachers and doctors.

temple, both on Mawenzi Road. The situation will probably be chaotic wherever you're dropped, as flycatchers touting for hotels and safari and hiking companies are quick to spot newly arrived tourists. So long as you stay calm and keep an eye on your bags, there's nothing to worry about, and in fact the flycatchers can be useful in locating a hotel (for a small fee, of course). Passengers on buses from Nairobi can be dropped at any central hotel: Davanu finish outside Kahawa House facing the clock tower, and Riverside services terminate at the THB Building on Boma Road.

There are no passenger **trains** to Moshi, incidentally, no matter what your map says, although the train on the Kenyan side from Taveta (see p.324) to Voi, operates four times weekly. There's talk of restarting passenger services if or when the railways get privatized, but don't hold your breath.

Town transport

Moshi's compact centre is easy to negotiate on foot and, unless you're carrying visibly tempting valuables, **safety** isn't much of an issue either. The exceptions are Kuheshimo area, about a kilometre south of the central market, and the bus and daladala stand, which has pickpockets and bag-snatchers. The cheapest way to the suburbs is by daladala, locally nicknamed **vifordi**, alluding to the town's first-ever vehicle, a Model-T Ford. Most leave from the main bus and daladala stand (for services to the south and west of town), or from along Market Street or Mawenzi Road on either side of it (for the north and east); journeys cost Tsh150. Daladalas heading along the Dar–Arusha highway can also be caught on Kibo Road.

Taxis park outside the larger hotels, at major road junctions, at the western side of the bus and daladala stand on Market Street and on the west side of the market, also on Market Street. A journey within town costs Tsh1000–1500; longer rides to the outskirts shouldn't be more than Tsh3000.

Information

Moshi lacks a **tourist office**, so don't be misled by safari companies displaying "tourism information" signboards; it's just a ruse to get you inside. The best source of information is the *Moshi Guide* (Tsh2500), which contains listings of pretty much everything you'll need. It's available at *The Coffee Shop* on Hill Street (and also at Kase Bookshop on Boma Road in Arusha). There are **notice boards** in *The Coffee Shop*'s restaurant and the lobby of the *Lutheran Uhuru Hostel*, but be warned that not all the safari and hiking companies featured on them are reputable or licensed.

Accommodation

Hotels in the **town centre** are plentiful and generally good value, both for budget and mid-range travellers (if possible, get a room with a view of Kilimanjaro – cloud-cover permitting – though quite a few hotels now have "summit bars" on their roofs, offering similarly expansive views). There are also some mid-range options and a handful of luxury lodges out of town in the **suburbs** and beyond. Mosquitoes are prevalent throughout town; most hotels have mosquito nets, but some rely on air-conditioning or bug spray to keep them out. Wherever you stay, protect yourself in the evenings, as malaria is present.

Some hotels permit **camping** in their grounds. The cheapest and most characterful is the *Golden Shower* restaurant and bar (see p.318), 2km east of town (☎027/275 1990, ✉images@africaonline.co.tz; $3 per person including hot showers), which also plays host to occasional overland trucks. Equally cheap but more peaceful is the beautiful *Green Hostels* ($3 per person). The *Kilimanjaro Tourist Inn* is similar ($5 per person) and has the advantage of a bar and restaurant. The *Lutheran Uhuru Hostel* and *Keys Hotel* also allow camping; there's no fixed price so you'll have to haggle.

Town centre
Budget

Buffalo Hotel New St ☎027/275 0270, ✉twigacom2001@yahoo.com. A modern, well-run and very good-value three-storey hotel. The large bedrooms come with fan, box nets, phone, hot shower and Western-style toilet, and the better rooms have balconies facing Kilimanjaro. There's also a good restaurant. Breakfast included. ❷

Coffee Tree Hotel Off Old Moshi Rd ☎027/275 5040. Popular with budget travellers, this outwardly charmless four-storey block is central Moshi's largest hotel, and perfectly good if you don't mind linoleum floors, saggy beds and the occasional cold shower. Rooms (with or without private bathroom) are huge and breezy, though most lack fans and the nets can be too small; some have views of Kilimanjaro. There's a lovely bar and restaurant on the top floor. ❷

Green Hostels Nkomo Ave ☎ & ℱ027/275 3198. At the end of a posh residential cul-de-sac near the *YMCA*, this friendly family-run place has ten rooms set in very peaceful grounds. The three rooms with private bathrooms and bathtubs are reasonably good value, even though there's not always hot water; rooms with shared bathrooms are much less enticing. Food and drinks available and breakfast included. ❸

Kindoroko Hotel Mawenzi Rd ☎027/275 4054, ⊛www.africaonline.co.tz/kindorokohotel. A spotless four-storey hotel with spectacular views of Kilimanjaro from the rooftop restaurant and bar. Most doubles are decently sized, and all have satellite TV, phone, fan and net. Singles are more variable, so see a selection. There's another adequate if uninspired restaurant downstairs and an excellent bar with a pool table, a curio shop, internet café and

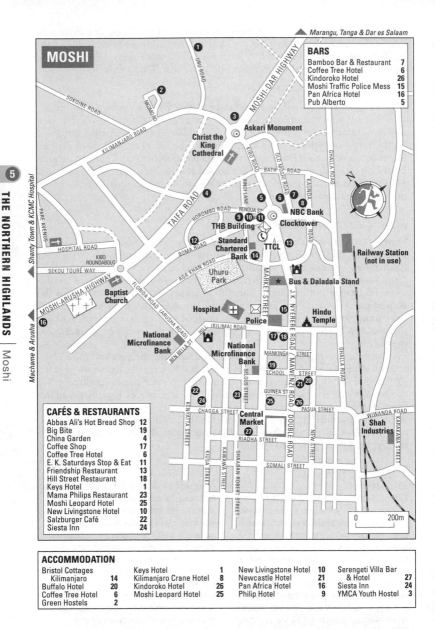

MOSHI

BARS
Bamboo Bar & Restaurant	7
Coffee Tree Hotel	6
Kindoroko Hotel	26
Moshi Traffic Police Mess	15
Pan Africa Hotel	16
Pub Alberto	5

CAFÉS & RESTAURANTS
Abbas Ali's Hot Bread Shop	12
Big Bite	19
China Garden	4
Coffee Shop	17
Coffee Tree Hotel	6
E. K. Saturdays Stop & Eat	11
Friendship Restaurant	13
Hill Street Restaurant	18
Keys Hotel	1
Mama Philips Restaurant	23
Moshi Leopard Hotel	25
New Livingstone Hotel	10
Salzburger Café	22
Siesta Inn	24

ACCOMMODATION
Bristol Cottages		Keys Hotel	1	New Livingstone Hotel	10	Serengeti Villa Bar
Kilimanjaro	14	Kilimanjaro Crane Hotel	8	Newcastle Hotel	21	& Hotel	27
Buffalo Hotel	20	Kindoroko Hotel	26	Pan Africa Hotel	16	Siesta Inn	24
Coffee Tree Hotel	6	Moshi Leopard Hotel	25	Philip Hotel	9	YMCA Youth Hostel	3
Green Hostels	2					

safe parking. Excellent value overall, especially for singles. Breakfast included. ❸

Newcastle Hotel Mawenzi Rd ☏027/275 3203, ℻027/275 1382. This four-storey building has seen better days, but is still very good value, with a choice of huge (if rather dark) rooms with or

without private bathroom. There's a good bar and restaurant on the first floor and another under a strange pagoda-style structure on the roof. Breakfast included. ❷

Pan Africa Hotel Moshi–Arusha highway, 600m west of Kibo roundabout (no phone). Large and slightly run down, but decent value nonetheless. Rooms have bathrooms and a choice of TV or fridge, and there's also a restaurant and bar, the latter with weekly discos and bands (see p.318). ❷

Serengeti Villa Bar & Hotel Riadha St (no phone). One of the cheapest choices in town, this cheerful local bar and flophouse has a choice of basic rooms with or without private bathroom. ❶

Siesta Inn Kiusa St ☎027/275 0158. A very calm, friendly and attractive place with a shady garden and a good restaurant and bar. There are ten large twin-bed rooms, some with private bathroom, but all are slightly musty and have saggy beds. Still, the Western-style toilets are clean, there are fans, and breakfast is included. ❷

Mid-range

Bristol Cottages Kilimanjaro Corner of Rindi Lane and Aga Khan Rd ☎027/275 3745, Ⓔbristolcottages@eoltz.com. A peaceful and homely choice, suitable for families, with eight large and spotless twin-bed rooms in cottages set in a small, neat garden, all with comfortable beds, a/c, TV, hot showers and Western-style toilets, but no mosquito nets (rooms are sprayed instead). There's also a coffee house, restaurant and safe parking. Breakfast included. ❺

Keys Hotel Uru Rd ☎027/275 2250 or 275 1875, Ⓦwww.keys-hotel.com. A long-established and friendly hotel in the style of an English inn. The fifteen cool, high-ceilinged rooms in the main building come with pine furniture, TV, phone, fan and (not always reliable) hot showers; there are also fifteen less attractive African-style cottages at the back (same price). All rooms have bathrooms, and more expensive ones have a/c. Facilities include a sauna, a small and rather grotty swimming pool, plus a bar and excellent restaurant. Overpriced for singles, but a good choice for couples. They also have an annexe 3km east of town with four-bedroomed houses sleeping six ($100 per day). Credit cards accepted. Breakfast included. ❺

Kilimanjaro Crane Hotel Kaunda Rd ☎027/275 1114, Ⓔkilicrane@eoltz.com. A large new business-class hotel – and perfectly decent, if

unexciting. All rooms have bathroom, phone, TV, fan and smallish nets. Doubles and suites have massive beds, others have balconies, and more expensive ones have a/c. Facilities include a rooftop bar, two restaurants, a gift shop, a swimming pool (though it often lacks water) and safe parking. Breakfast included. ❺

Moshi Leopard Hotel Market St ☎027/275 0884, Ⓔleopardhotel@eoltz.com. A large, modern and calm three-storey choice offering good-value twins and doubles, all with clean tiled bathrooms, fridge, TV, phone, fan, but no nets (rooms are sprayed instead). All have balconies, but these mainly face neighbouring buildings. There's also a good restaurant, a bar and safe parking. Breakfast included. ❺

New Livingstone Hotel Corner of Rindi Lane and Rengua St ☎ & Ⓕ027/275 5212. A large and cool hotel with Art Deco touches: it could do with some renovation, but prices are reasonable. There's a choice of singles or twins with shared bathrooms and doubles with bathtubs; rooms facing the road have views of Kilimanjaro. It also has a cavernous ground-floor bar, with some seats in a courtyard outside, which is nice for an afternoon drink. Breakfast included. ❸–❹

Philip Hotel Corner of Rindi Lane and Rengua St ☎027/275 4746, Ⓦwww.africaonline.co.tz/philip. Similar to the *New Livingstone* opposite but in much better condition, though doubles are all twin-bed. Most rooms have private balconies, TV, phone and clean tiled bathrooms, but there are no nets (rooms are sprayed) The restaurant and bar are expensive and dull, so eat elsewhere. Breakfast included. ❹

YMCA Youth Hostel Junction of Taifa Rd and Kilimanjaro Rd ☎027/275 1754, Ⓕ027/275 1734. A breezy and welcoming place popular with backpackers. Most rooms (singles or doubles) share bathrooms, but are clean and bright and have mosquito nets, fans and good beds. The main draw is the excellent swimming pool (with views of Kilimanjaro) and the fact that flycatchers are excluded. There's also a poolside snack bar, a good restaurant and a curio shop. Breakfast included. ❸–❹

Outside the centre

Unless you're in training for a Kili climb, you'll need to take a daladala or taxi to reach the following.

Impala Hotel Kilimanjaro Lema Rd, Shanty Town, 4.5km north of town ☎027/275 3443, Ⓦwww.impalahotel.com. Moshi's newest and most upmarket place, with very stylish architecture, a calm atmosphere and international standards for accommodation, food and service.

The eleven superb bedrooms, some with a/c, others with huge double beds, have wooden parquet, lots of reproduction furniture, and TVs in the "executive suites". There's a large swimming pool beside the bar and restaurant. To get here, catch a daladala for Kibosho. Breakfast included. ❻

Mountain Inn Lodge Moshi–Dar highway, 6km east of town ☏ 027/275 5622 or 0741/520030, ⓦ www.kilimanjaro-shah.com. Located in a beautiful garden amidst maize and banana plantations and with over thirty rather basic rooms, each with private bathroom and hot water (but avoid the "deluxe" rooms, which are little different other than having a fan). There's the bonus of a swimming pool, sauna and a good restaurant, as well as two bars, though hawkers and touts can be a pain. To get here, catch a daladala for Marangu. Breakfast included. ➍–➎

The Town

If you can cope with the persistent if generally friendly attentions of the local flycatchers, especially around the clock tower and along Mawenzi Road, Moshi is a relaxing place to wander around, although there are few actual "sights", since most of the town's buildings date from the 1930s onwards. The liveliest place is the bustling **central market**, south of Chagga Street (Mon–Sat 8am–4.30pm, Sun 8am–noon), which sells a garish variety of imported plastic and aluminium goods, as well as locally produced coffee, cardamom, spices, fruits and vegetables. Also keep an eye out for the traditional **herbalists** in and around the market (usually old men sitting beside vast quantities of glass jars containing multicoloured powders). There are more medicine men on Market Street next to *Big Bite* restaurant, plus some **jua kali** (literally "sharp sun") craftsmen on Guinea Road, who specialize in turning old tin cans into superb oil lamps, coffee pots, kettles and pans.

Moshi's only monuments of note are the structures dominating a trio of roundabouts. The centre of town is marked by the **clock tower** at the roundabout at north end of Market Street and Mawenzi Road; a signpost a few metres away gives the distances to dozens of places in Tanzania and East Africa. A few hundred metres to the north, the **Askari Monument** rises from the roundabout at the junction with the Arusha–Dar highway. The statue of the soldier with his rifle at the ready commemorates African members of the British Carrier Corps who lost their lives in the two world wars. On the south side of the roundabout is the Catholic **Christ the King Cathedral**, famed for its colourful Sunday Masses (6.25am, 8.30am, 10.30am & 4.30pm); the best is the 10.30am service, which attracts mostly children and their mothers and features plenty of traditional Chagga singing – worth catching even if you're not religious.

Kibo roundabout, 1km along the Arusha road from here, is marked by a stylized representation of the **Uhuru Torch**. The original was placed on Kilimanjaro's summit on the day of Tanzania's independence from Britain in December 1961 to – in the words of President Nyerere – "shine beyond our borders, giving hope where there is despair, love where there is hate, and dignity where before there was only humiliation." At the time, Kenya – whose border skirts the north and east side of the mountain – was still under colonial rule, having only recently emerged from the bloody Mau Mau Rebellion. If you have time, the short walk from here to **Arusha Road Cemetery** is worth the effort, as part of it contains the graves of British and Tanzanian soldiers who fought in World War I. It's just to the east of *Pan Africa Hotel*, and can also be reached along a path at the north end of Florida Road.

If you're really into markets, there are two more that are worth exploring: **Mbuyuni market**, four blocks south of central market (daily; don't take valuables), and **Kiboriloni market** (Tues, Wed, Fri & Sat; mornings best), 5km along the Moshi–Dar highway, which is known as far as Arusha for its cheap second-hand clothes, as well as hardware and food. There are frequent daladalas from the main daladala stand and from along Kibo Road.

Eating

Moshi has a wide choice of **restaurants**, one or two of which are quite outstanding. Local **specialities** include *uji*, a porridge made from finger millet which is traditionally eaten for breakfast, and a thick mash of bananas called *mtori* that is usually served with meat. More ubiquitous, especially in bars, are *nyama choma*, *ndizi* and *chipsi mayai*: the busier the bar, the better the food. **Street food**, mainly roasted maize cobs, is found throughout town. Ambulant **coffee sellers** in and around the central market dish up small porcelain cupfuls of the scalding brew for a mere Tsh20.

For your own **provisions**, fresh fruit and vegetables are best at the market, though women sell produce at various points along Mawenzi Road. Packaged and imported items are sold at groceries along Old Moshi Road and in several **supermarkets**: Carina Supermarket on Kibo Road near *Pub Alberto*; MDC Supermarket, at the corner of Kawawa Street and Florida Road; and Glory Mini Supermarket, on Kiusa Street at the west end of Riadha Street.

Abbas Ali's Hot Bread Shop Boma Rd. Popular for snacks and light lunches, with good samosas, sandwiches, cakes, cappuccino, ice cream and waffles. There are also seats in a pleasant garden. Closed Sun.

Big Bite Market St. Good cheap snacks (samosas, rice cakes, kebabs and bhajis) and icy passion juice. Good for a quick, unfussy meal.

China Garden Regional CCM Building, Taifa Rd. Despite the plastic beer ad tablecloths, this does authentic Chinese and Thai cuisine (albeit heavy on the MSG); there are also nicer tables in wooden shelters in the garden. A full meal with starter costs Tsh6000–8000 – the prawns are good, as is the hot lemongrass and prawn Thai soup.

Club Gentlemen Moshi–Arusha highway, 2km west of Kibo roundabout. Run by the folks from the *Salzburger Steak House* and with a similar menu (steaks, chicken, fish, curries), plus a popular bar and supremely succulent roast meats and bananas from the grill outside. Most dishes cost Tsh1000–3000.

Coffee Shop Hill St. A superb place with a warmly decorated dining room, a garden at the back with tables, and a wide range of delicious snacks, including soups, pies, mouthwatering cakes, samosas, ice cream and some of Tanzania's best coffee. Closed Sun.

Coffee Tree Hotel Entrance off Old Moshi Rd. The food here is perfectly acceptable, but the main attraction is the great view of both Moshi and Kilimanjaro from its breezy top-floor restaurant and bar.

E. K. Saturdays Stop and Eat Clock tower. A large and cheap self-service restaurant (there's also a bar) overlooking the clock tower roundabout; nothing much over Tsh1500. Closes at 6pm.

El Rancho 200m off Lema Rd, Shanty Town, 5km from town ☎027/275 5115. Superb if expensive north Indian food (and a wide selection of continental dishes too) in an affluent suburb, popular with European and Indian families at weekends. A full à la carte splurge with a drink or two costs around Tsh10,000; the famous Sunday eat-all-you-can lunchtime buffet goes for Tsh6500, and they also have an excellent wine list and selection of cocktails. There are also barbecues in the evenings (no beef or pork), plus a pool table, mini-golf and table football to keep the kids busy. Closed Mon.

Friendship Restaurant Mawenzi Rd. Very popular with locals throughout the day, dishing up good cheap food and drinks, including *nyama choma*.

Hill Street Restaurant Hill St. An unfailingly welcoming place serving up snacks and dirt cheap Tanzanian and Indian meals (well under Tsh1000), including aromatic *pilau*, plus bean stews, greens and fried fish. They also have seats outside. Daytime only; closed Sun.

Impala Hotel Kilimanjaro Lema Rd, Shanty Town, 4.5km north of town. Fine if expensive fare in Moshi's foremost hotel (around $15 for a full meal), plus optional use of the swimming pool (Tsh3000 extra).

Keys Hotel Uru Rd. A reasonably classy place with good service, and one of the few restaurants to feature *mtori* banana soup (Tsh1000). They also offer a daily Tanzanian dish (Tsh3000–3500) and have a wide menu of mainly French-influenced cuisine for upwards of Tsh2500.

Lutheran Uhuru Hostel Sekou Touré Way, 3km northwest of town. The restaurant here consistently gets good reports, especially for its grilled chicken and Vienna steaks. They also do local Chagga dishes (under Tsh1500) and are quite happy to satisfy the quirky needs of exhausted climbers. Closes at 8pm.

Mama Clementina's 500m south of the Moshi–Arusha highway, 2.5km west of Kibo roundabout; the turn-off is just after *Club Gentlemen* ☎ 027/275 4707. This women's vocational training centre makes some great food, with an à la carte menu daily. There's also a three-course Mexican set menu on Thursday (Tsh4500), Italian on Friday (Tsh3000) and a barbecue on Saturday (Tsh6000–7500). Eat inside or on a terrace.

Mama Philips Restaurant Selous St. Chow down on great *nyama choma* in this smoky, local *makuti*-thatched bar.

Moshi Leopard Hotel Market St. This probably has the cleanest and most modern kitchen in town (it's open plan), and is good value too, with most mains costing around Tsh2500 and tasty curried prawns for Tsh4000. They also do grilled goat and chicken, and occasional buffets.

New Livingstone Hotel Corner of Rindi Lane and Rengua St. Eat indoors or, better, in the courtyard under a thatched parasol, where the smell from the meat and bananas over the coals is difficult to resist. Most meals cost under Tsh4000, with *nyama choma* going for Tsh1000, and a set "Tanzanian lunch" for Tsh1800.

Salzburger Café Kenyatta St. Pleasingly bizarre, decorated like an Austrian bar and with lots of memorabilia from the local Volkswagen Members Club. The menu is extensive and extremely cheap (everything – including steaks – under Tsh2000), and the food is good, although not everything is always available. African dishes feature at lunchtimes (around Tsh1000), including *maini* (ox liver) in a sweet and sour sauce.

Siesta Inn Kiusa St. The restaurant in the garden at the back dishes up some great food, including delicious curried tilapia with fried bananas (under Tsh2000).

Drinking and nightlife

Whilst Moshi at night is not as lively as Arusha, there's plenty to keep you busy, and a couple of places host live bands. There are lots of friendly local **bars** throughout the town, few of which see many *wazungu*. Walking around the centre at night is generally safe, although if you're going more than a few blocks, it's probably wiser to catch a cab. Several **hotels** – including *Coffee Tree Hotel*, *Kindoroko Hotel* and *Newcastle Hotel* – have "summit bars" with views of Kili.

Bamboo Bar & Restaurant Old Moshi Rd. This calm and very welcoming bar is popular with elderly office workers and government staff; the *nyama choma* and *ndizi* is some of Moshi's best, and there's also a pool table and TV.

Coffee Tree Hotel Old Moshi Rd. A great top-floor bar, with nightly discos (except Mon & Thurs).

Golden Shower, 2km along the Moshi–Dar Highway. This unfortunately named place makes for a good night out, especially its popular weekend discos, which are notable for their "no photography" rule – intended to protect philanderers. Food available. Catch a daladala to KDC or Kiboriloni; the last leaves town around 7.30pm, so it's a taxi back after then.

Kindoroko Hotel Mawenzi Rd. The rooftop "Summit Bar" is for hotel residents and tourists only; the distinctly more earthy bar on the ground floor is where you can meet flycatchers and tour operators in a more relaxed atmosphere than at

the bus and daladala stands, and also has a pool table and internet café.

Moshi Traffic Police Mess Mawenzi Rd. A large and friendly place with both food and drinks, generally open 24 hours a day. There's also satellite TV and a live band on Saturday from around 4pm to midnight (free admission).

Pan Africa Hotel Moshi–Arusha Highway, 600m west of Kibo roundabout. There's a bar and *nyama choma* grill in the garden at the side, but most people come for the Friday disco (which is strangely popular with old men), and the live band on Saturday nights (free entry).

Pub Alberto Kibo Rd. Moshi's brashest nightclub, with all the loud music, lasers and spinning mirrored globes you might want, and plenty of prostitutes, though the music's pretty run-of-the-mill. There are also snacks and a pool table. Closed Mon.

Listings

Airlines Precisionair, next to Coffee Tree Arcade on Old Moshi Rd (℡027/275 3498); ATC, Rengua St just up from clock tower (℡027/275 5205). Also see travel agents on p.320.

Banks and exchange Foreign exchange bureaux charge no commission – reliable ones include Executive, THB Building, Boma Rd, and Trust, corner of Mawenzi Rd and Chagga St. Banks, by contrast, levy hefty commissions. Visa and Mastercard credit cards can be used for cash advances at Standard Chartered Bank's 24-hour ATM, next to *Bristol Cottages* on Rindi Lane.

Books Moshi Bookshop, at the corner of Kibo Rd and Rindi Lane; there's also a bookstore at the Lutheran Centre on Market St. Both major on stodgy Christian texts, with little of interest to visitors except for some illustrated children's books which make great presents. For Western novels, try the second-hand book stall at the corner of Mawenzi Rd and Mankinga St.

Car rental Mauly Tours & Safaris (p.334) offer car rental with driver for a $130 a day including 100km free mileage. Davanu Shuttle, Kahawa House, by the clock tower, also rent out vehicles (℡027/275 3416 or 275 3749, ✉davanu17@habari.co.tz), as do Riverside Shuttle, THB Building, Boma Rd (℡027/275 0093 or 0742/400031, ✉riverside_shuttle@hotmail.com).

Car repairs There are car-repair workshops along Rath Rd between Kaunda Rd and Old Moshi Rd. If you're driving a Volkswagen, ask at *Salzburger Café* (see opposite). For Land Rovers, the CMC agent is Chuni's Garage on Boma Rd. *Golden Shower* (see opposite) also has competent mechanics.

Crafts and souvenirs Souvenir shops are scarce compared to Arusha, although many hotels have their own curio shops. The best place in the centre is Our Heritage at *The Coffee Shop* on Hill Street, which has a range of carvings, batiks and "I climbed Kilimanjaro" T-shirts, plus cloth dolls from the Baptist Shangalia Women's Group. They also stock locally made curios fashioned out of cow horn, leather and pressed flowers manufactured at Shah Industries on Karakana St, whose workshop – occupying an old flour and animal feed mill – employs around forty people, some of them disabled. The factory is happy giving free guided tours around the workshops and gardens, and also has a shop.

Flying lessons Contact Kilimanjaro Aero Club, Moshi Airport ℡027/275 0193, ✉kac@eoltz.com.

Hospitals The best is Kilimanjaro Christian Medical Centre (KCMC), 6km north of town past Shanty Town (℡027/275 4377), though you need to be referred there by a doctor. Daladalas to KCMC leave from Market St or Kibo Rd.

Immigration The Immigration Office is in Kibo House by the clock tower (℡027/275 2284; Mon–Fri 7.30am–3pm), but they won't extend visas – you'll have to cross into Kenya for a few hours, then return and buy a new three-month visa at the border. Taveta (see p.324) is the closest crossing. You could spend a few days there exploring Lake Chala and the Taita Hills. Alternatively, catch a regular bus or a shuttle bus to Nairobi, getting off on the Kenyan side of the border at Namanga.

Internet and email access There are several internet cafés (Tsh1500–2000 per hour). The most reliable are Easycom in Kahawa House (Mon–Fri 7.40am–8.30pm, Sat–Sun 8am–8.30pm); Twiga Communications and IBC on Old Moshi Rd (both daily 8am–10pm); Duma on Hill St next to *Hill Street Restaurant* (daily 9am–9pm); and *Kindoroko Hotel*'s ground-floor bar (daily 8am–11pm).

Library Moshi Regional Library, Kibo Rd (Mon–Fri 9am–6pm). Daily membership costs Tsh500.

Newspapers and magazines Newspaper hawkers hang around the bus and daladala stand; they sometimes have old copies of US or UK news papers and magazines.

Pharmacies The dispensary at Sima Hospital, Kenyatta St, is open 24hr (℡027/275 1272) and does blood tests for malaria. Other reasonably well-stocked pharmacies include Moshi Pharmacy, Boma Rd, between the THB Building and Rindi Lane; AB Pharmaceuticals, between Twiga and IBC internet cafés on Old Moshi Rd; TM Pharmaceuticals, Mawenzi Rd (℡027/275 5032); and Kilimani Pharmaceutical, Hill St by Mawenzi Hospital (℡027/275 5110).

Photography The main labs are Burhani Photographic Services and Moshi Colour Lab, both on Hill St (also called Kilima St).

Police Market St (℡027/275 5055).

Post and couriers The main post office is opposite the clock tower. There's a branch in a converted shipping crate on Market St facing the police station. International courier companies include EMS at the post office and DHL at Kahawa House, by the clock tower.

Swimming pools The *YMCA*'s 25-metre pool is the best and the cheapest (Tsh2000). Other hotels which allow day guests to use their pools are the *Kilimanjaro Crane Hotel* (Tsh3000); *Impala Hotel Kilimanjaro* (Tsh3000 for a large pool in very formal surroundings); *Keys Hotel* (Tsh3000; small pool, but there's a sauna for an extra Tsh3000 for half an hour); and *Mountain Inn* (Tsh3000).

Telephones TTCL Building, next to the main post office on Market St.

Travel agents Emslies, Old Moshi Rd (☏027/275 1742 or 275 2701, ✉emslies.sales@eoltz.com)

sells domestic and international airline tickets and arranges other ticketing, notably to Zanzibar. Worldlink Travel, Boma Rd, is similar (☏027/275 4338 or 0741/653254, ✉world@raha.com).

Moving on from Moshi

By bus

The **bus stand**, between Market Street and Mawenzi Road, has parking bays clearly marked with their destinations. The new terminal building should eventually contain ticket offices for most companies, although at present the more reliable ones still have offices elsewhere (see below). The open area on the north side of the building is used by Coaster minibuses (basically large daladalas) which serve Arusha, Machame, Marangu and Usa River. The larger stand on the south side is used by daladalas to and from the south and east (including Tanga, Mombo and Lushoto), and by all buses regardless of their destination. When **buying tickets**, check the price before or you risk being overcharged.

The tarmac **highway to Arusha** is extremely perilous, and the antics of the average driver are enough to kick in visions of your life in flashback; the Coaster minibuses, especially, crash with alarming – and fatal – frequency. Note that a popular Coaster scam involves having a sane and respectable-looking gentleman occupying the driver's seat whilst the vehicle is at the bus stand, only for him to be replaced by a red-eyed teenage lunatic at the exit…

Whilst the Moshi–Arusha highway is Tanzania's most dangerous, you should also be on your guard on the run to Dar. Your safest bet is to travel only with one of the following reliable bus companies (and certainly don't go in a minibus). These are: Fresh ya Shamba, at the Caltex garage on Market Street (☏027/275 1762 or 0741/531925); Royal Coach, whose office and terminal is on Railway Street (☏027/275 0940); and Scandinavian, which stops by its office at the Gapco filling station on Market Street, facing the bus stand. Dar Express and Air Mtae have mixed reputations, and both have had fatal crashes in the recent past. **Companies to avoid completely**, even if this means having to do a journey in two legs rather than one, include Hood, Abood and Tawfiq.

Getting **to Nairobi** is easy, with two companies operating daily shuttle buses via Arusha. Davanu Shuttle ($35) leave Moshi at 11am from outside their office in Kahawa House, facing the clock tower. Riverside Shuttle operate from the THB Building on Boma Road ($25). Either can pick you up at your hotel if you pre-book. Kenyan visas, currently $50, are easily bought at the Namanga border point (p.408).

By air

The easiest way to **Kilimanjaro International Airport**, if you're flying with Air Tanzania or KLM, is on a shuttle bus run by the airlines. KLM's bus leaves Moshi at 6pm from the THB Building on Boma Road ($10). Air Tanzania's bus leaves from their office on Rengua Street and is free. A taxi to the airport costs around $20–40 depending on your bargaining skills. If you've got more time than money, you could catch a vehicle towards Arusha and get off at the signposted junction on the highway 30km west of Moshi, from where it's a six-kilometre walk or hitch.

Around Moshi

With the exception of Makuru Coffee Farm (see opposite), you won't find any organized **day-trips** around Moshi, although a number of flycatchers and hiking companies are happy to act as guides to various nearby sights – costs

Coffee

Kilimanjaro Region produces high-quality **Arabica coffee**, characterized by its mild flavour and delicate aroma. Most of the coffee farms are smallholdings whose production is collected and marketed by the Kilimanjaro Native Coffee Union, which provides a guaranteed minimum income to farmers at times when world coffee prices slump, something that has begun to happen with alarming frequency.

Coffee bushes flower during the short rains (Oct–Nov), when they become covered in white blossom and give off a pervasive, jasmine-like scent. The best time to visit if you're interested in seeing how coffee is processed is between July and September, when the berries are harvested. Following harvesting, the beans' sweet pulpy outer layer is mechanically removed, after which they are fermented in water and then dried in sunlight on long tables. After a few days, the outer casing (the "parchment") becomes brittle, and is easily removed at the coffee mill, after which the beans are graded for sale according to size and weight.

The best way to experience the coffee-making process is on one of the twice-weekly **walks** to Makuru Coffee Farm (Wed 2pm & Fri 10am; 2hr) arranged by the *Coffee Shop* (see p.317), where you see the whole process of coffee production. The walk costs Tsh12,500 per person in a party of six, or Tsh19,000 per person in a couple.

average $25–40 per person per day depending on group size, mode of transport and bargaining skills. *Buffalo Hotel* and Duma Internet Café on Hill Street are useful for finding reliable guides; most hiking companies (see p.334) can also fix you up. For transport, **bicycles** can be rented informally at most hotels; the cost should be Tsh2000 a day, though Tsh5000 is commonly quoted as a first price for tourists.

Possible day-trips include hikes in **Kilimanjaro Forest Reserve** at Kibosho (15km north of town) or **Rau Forest** (10km northeast), and trips to hot springs, waterfalls, and to see crocodiles (take care). You'll need a guide for any of these options. **Bird-watchers** should contact Moshi Birding Society (⊕027/275 0936), who organize outings on the second Saturday of each month.

Marangu

The base for most climbs up Kili along the Marangu route (see p.333) is **MARANGU** village, an hour's drive northeast of Moshi by road. Marangu actually consists of two villages, both situated on the tarmac road leading to the park gate: **Marangu-Arisi** is the section closest to the park gate, whilst **Marangu-Mtoni** (where daladalas drop you) is at the crossroads to Mamba and Rombo, 5.6km short of the gate.

There's more to Marangu than just a base for climbing the mountain, however. The scenery around the village is superb, especially close to the park gate, where you get unobstructed views of the Pare Mountains, Kenya's Taita-Taveta plains and Lake Jipe, and Nyumba ya Mungu reservoir, as well as Kilimanjaro. Marangu's hotels can also arrange a number of guided walks in the area as part of a community-based **cultural tourism programme**.

Practicalities

Frequent **daladalas** from Moshi (roughly 8am–6pm; 45min) run along the 30km of tarmac to Marangu-Mtoni. If you don't fancy the 5.6-kilometre walk uphill from Marangu-Mtoni to the park gate, there are occasional daladalas from Marangu-Mtoni to the gate from around 9am. **Camping** is possible at the *Bismark Hut Lodge* (officially $10 per person, though easily bargainable to $5 or less), *Coffee Tree Campsite* ($8, including hot showers and a sauna), and *Kibo Hotel* ($6 person, including use of kitchen and pool). The following hotels all have **luggage stores** for climbers.

Babylon Lodge 1km east of Marangu-Mtoni off the Rombo road ☎027/275 6597, ⓔbabylon@africaonline.co.tz. Fifteen good en-suite twins and doubles in modern buildings scattered across a slope – they're functional rather than special. There's also a restaurant and bar. safe parking, and free guides to waterfalls. Breakfast included. ❻

Hotel Capricorn 2.7km from the park gate ☎027/275 1309 or 0744/282001, ⓦwww.africaonline.co.tz/capricornhotel. A large, attractive and (currently) very good-value mid-range option dominated by a vast conical roof and surrounded by lush gardens. There are 24 good en-suite rooms in two-storey blocks, and facilities include a good restaurant (around $5 a meal), bar, gift shop, TV lounge and hiking company. Recommended so long as the planned takeover by the South African Protea Hotels chain (ⓦwww.pro-teahotels.com) doesn't result in prices shooting up. Breakfast included. ❼

Coffee Tree Campsite, 2km from the park gate (reserve through Alpine Trekking & Safari, see p.335). The closest accommodation to the park gate, with five rooms in a thatched chalet that's ideal for self-caterers. There's also a sauna, which is paradise after a climb. ❹

Kibo Hotel, 1.4km west of Marangu-Mtoni ☎ & ⓕ027/275 1308, ⓦwww.kibohotel.com. A rambling old hotel from German times with tons of charm, set in beautiful and slightly wild gardens. There are plenty of verandahs, nooks and crannies throughout, and the entire place is adorned with old prints, maps and antiques. The wonderful pub-like bar is covered with dozens of flags from climbing expeditions, and the lounge has a huge

central fireplace. Bedrooms are in two wings: the most atmospheric (nos. 1–7) are in the main building, many with bathtubs; the first-floor ones have balconies with great views. Facilities include a small swimming pool, and meals (Tsh5400–7200) are available. Breakfast included. ❻

KINAPA Hostels The national park has two hostels just inside the park boundary (so park fees apply). The first is 100m east of the reception area (currently closed); the second is in the reception area itself and has 24 beds above a cooking area. $10 per person.

Marangu Hotel 2km south of Marangu-Mtoni ☎027/275 6594, ⓦwww.maranguhotel.com. This frequently recommended option was originally a coffee farm started by Czech immigrants in 1907, and became a guest house in the 1930s. Extensive modernization means it lacks much of the *Kibo Hotel*'s charm, but standards are high, with 25 rooms (mostly twins and en suite) in bungalows scattered around spacious gardens with views of Kili. Facilities include a good bar and restaurant (meals $8–10), swimming pool, croquet lawn, gift shop and safe parking. Their hiking operation has an excellent reputation. Half-board ❼

Nakara Hotel 2km from the park gate next to *Coffee Tree Campsite* ☎027/275 6571 or 0744/277300, ⓦwww.nakaratz.com. A modern three-storey affair with sixteen clean and comfortable rooms, all with phone, bathtub (and hot water) and two beds that can be pushed together. Facilities are limited to a restaurant (meals $10–15) and a well-stocked bar with comfy leather sofas and TV. Nonetheless, it's overpriced compared to other options. Breakfast included. ❼

Walks around Marangu

Marangu can be an exceedingly hassly place to walk around, with most young men assuming you're only there to hire guides and porters for climbing the mountain; their persistent attention quickly becomes tedious. Luckily, Marangu's **cultural tourism programme** circumvents much of the hassle, and of course opens the door to a side of local life you wouldn't otherwise see. The tours on offer are all easy half-day walks (which can also be combined into a one- or two-day trips) and include excursions inside the park to and from **Mandara Hut**, including Maundi Crater and a waterfall; **Mamba village**, 3km towards Rombo, for a visit to traditional blacksmiths and a woodcarving school; a 120-year-old Catholic mission church at **Kilema village**, whose relics include what is purported to be a piece of Christ's own cross, and in whose grounds Kilimanjaro's first coffee tree was planted; and a hike up

Ngangu Hill for a great view and a cave containing the remains of a former chief. Seven **waterfalls** around Marangu can also be visited, and swimming is possible in some. The closest are **Kinukamori Falls**, 1km north of Marangu-Mtoni, and **Nduru Waterfalls**, 2km west of Marangu-Mtoni past *Kibo Hotel*. You can also visit these on your own, as they are signposted, but you'll probably be followed by a gaggle of wannabe guides.

The programme doesn't have a main office, so trips have to be booked through any of the hotels reviewed above. The main gripe about the programme is that prices vary enormously, depending on your bargaining skills and where you book, so some tourists end up feeling ripped off. The cheapest rates at present are through the *Coffee Tree Campsite*, who charge $2 per person per hour, and *Kibo Hotel*, who charge $5 for a few hours, excluding meals. Most places seem to charge around $25 a day, and more upmarket hotels, like the *Capricorn*, ask $50. In addition to the fee, you're expected to pay a "village development fee" (minimum Tsh1000) which goes into a fund for improving local primary schools. Avoid **bogus guides** – and there are plenty – by booking through one of the hotels. Don't trust their ID cards; the worst conmen simply print their own.

Machame

MACHAME, the village at the start of Kilimanjaro's second most popular climbing route (see p.338), is set in a beautiful area of valleys, river and fertile farmland on the southwestern side of the mountain, with good views of the summit. Most visitors only pass through en route to climbing the mountain, so the village's income from tourism has long been limited to wages paid to local porters and guides, though this may all change following the establishment of the **cultural tourism programme** (see below), which offers a variety of guided walks in the vicinity and gives you the chance to meet local villagers.

Getting to Machame by public transport is easy: daladalas to the village run every hour from Moshi's main bus stand, taking about an hour. Alternatively, catch a daladala or bus towards Arusha and get off at the signposted junction 12km west, where daladalas connect with Machame – 18km to the north – every ten minutes or so. The park gate is some 4km beyond the village. **Accommodation** is currently limited to the upmarket *Protea Hotel Aishi* (T027/275 6948, W www.proteahotels.com; ❸), with thirty newly renovated rooms in a large, neo-colonial-style complex with swimming pool and a health club; alternatively, the cultural tourism programme can arrange **home stays** for around Tsh3000 per person.

Walks around Machame

The **cultural tourism programme** (T027/275 7033) is based at Kyalia, near Foo village at the end of the tarmac, about 1km beyond Machame. Costs should be no more than $25 a day, all included. Make sure you arrange things through the office itself and not through someone on the street. There are several tours, including the **Sienye-Ngira tour** (4–6hr), which involves a fascinating hike through Sienye rainforest to Masama village southwest of Machame. The walk can be extended over two days to include **Ng'uni**, upstream from Masama, which has great views over the plains and where you can learn about constructing traditional *mbii* houses.

A good longer trip is the **Lyamungo tour** (2–3 days) to the coffee-producing village of Lyamungo, southwest of Machame, passing through Muwe and Nkuu villages and the Weruweru River. The trip includes hikes through rainforest, visits to the Lyamungo Coffee Research Institute and Narumu Women Pottery Centre, and overnight stays with local families.

The Kenyan border at Taveta

It's possible to cross into Kenya at **Taveta**, 34km due east of Moshi. Daladalas run roughly every hour from Moshi to the border. The drawback is that you'll face an hour's walk on the Kenyan side if you can't find one of the enterprising locals running bicycle taxis from the border into town (30–40 Kenyan shillings; roughly Tsh300–400). There's a bank and plenty of decent accommodation in Taveta, which also provides access to **Lake Chala**, set in a stunningly picturesque volcanic crater on the eastern flank of Kilimanjaro. Onward travel in Kenya includes early-morning buses and matatus (daladalas) to Voi and Mombasa, or the train to Voi (2.20pm on Tues, Wed, Fri and Sat).

Mount Kilimanjaro

> As wide as all the world, great, high, and unbelievably
> white in the sun, was the square top of Kilimanjaro.
>
> Hemingway, *The Snows of Kilimanjaro*

The ice-capped, dormant volcano that is **MOUNT KILIMANJARO**, has exerted an irresistible fascination since it was "discovered" by Europeans in the mid-nineteenth century. Rising almost five kilometres from the surrounding plains to a peak of 5891m, Kilimanjaro – a national park, and a World Heritage Site since 1989 – is Africa's highest mountain, the world's tallest free-standing massif and one of the world's largest volcanoes, covering some 3885 square kilometres. It is also an exceptionally beautiful mountain, both from afar and close up, and it fills up brochures as easily as it fills up the horizon.

The mountain that the Chagga call Kilemakyaro, the Mountain of God, was formed during the most recent faulting of the Great Rift Valley two to three million years ago, an event that also produced Mount Meru and Mount Kenya. Kilimanjaro has three main peaks, together with parasitic volcanic cones and craters dotted around its sides. The youngest and highest peak is the distinctive snow-capped dome of **Kibo**, actually a large crater, which was formed around 100,000 years ago during the last period of major volcanic activity. Kibo's highest point is **Uhuru Peak** on the crater's southwestern rim, whose official height of 5895m was downsized to 5891.6m in 2000 after a topographical satellite survey. Eleven kilometres to the east of Kibo (to which it's connected by a broad lava saddle) is the jagged **Mawenzi Peak** (5149m), all that remains of a volcanic cone that lost its eastern rim in a gigantic explosion. The oldest peak is **Shira**, on the west side of the mountain, which has mostly collapsed, leaving a spectacular lava plug.

For many visitors, the prospect of scaling the mountain is as exciting as it is daunting. The fact that no technical climbing skills are required to reach the summit means that Kilimanjaro has acquired something of an easy reputation – a dangerous misconception, and one which you should ignore. The high altitude and the possibility of a quick ascent mean that a dozen people, on average, lose their lives every year, usually as victims of **acute mountain sickness** (see box on p.332). In addition, almost everybody gets afflicted with screaming headaches and utter exhaustion on summit day, meaning that of the 20,000 people who attempt the climb every year, less than a third make it all the way to Uhuru Peak. Having said this, if you take your time and stay attentive to your body's needs, there's no reason why you shouldn't be able to make it to the top, while the mountain also offers plenty of less strenuous alternatives for those for whom the prospect of summiting smacks of a mite too much masochism: a walk on the lower slopes, through rainforest and on to the edge of sub-alpine moorland, makes no extreme fitness demands and can be done in a day.

Some history

Contrary to the assumption of Eurocentric historians, Kilimanjaro has been known to non-Africans since at least the sixth century, when Chinese mariners reported a "great mountain" inland. The mountain may even have been known in Ptolemy's time, although the snowy "mountains of the moon" referred to in his *Geography* are more likely to have been the Ruwenzori Mountains on the border of Congo and Uganda.

The Europeans remained ignorant of Kilimanjaro until 1848, when the German missionary **Johannes Rebmann**, having given up trying to convert coastal tribes to Christianity, headed inland to try his luck elsewhere. His report of a snow-capped mountain three degrees south of the equator was met with scorn and ridicule back home, and it wasn't until 1861, when Kilimanjaro was scaled to a height of around 4300 metres by Dr Otto Kersten and Baron Karl Klaus von der Decken, that his report was accepted by the likes of the Royal Geographical Society. The first Europeans to reach the summit were the German geographer Hans Meyer and Austrian mountaineer Ludwig Purtscheller, who reached Kibo in 1889. Mawenzi was climbed in 1912.

The origin of the **mountain's name** is confusing. To some explorers, it meant "that which cannot be conquered" or "that which renders a journey impossible". To others it was the "mountain of greatness", the "spotted mountain", the "white mountain" or the "mountain of caravans". The first part of the name is actually quite simple, as in both Kiswahili and Kichagga, *mlima* means mountain, while *kilima* is a hill. The use of the diminutive could be affectionate, though Kichagga place names are often preceded with *ki*, as are names around Mount Kenya – whose dominant Kikuyu and Kamba tribes are related to the Chagga. The second half of the name remains vague, however: *njaro* may be related to a Kichagga word for caravan, a throw-back to the slave and ivory trade, but an alternative and more likely meaning stems from the Maasai word *ngare*, meaning river – Kilimanjaro, of course, is the source of life for several rivers.

The Chagga have a wonderful tale about the origin of Kilimanjaro's main peaks, **Kibo and Mawenzi**, who, they say, were sisters. Kibo was the wiser of the two, and was careful to store away food for times of hardship. Her sister, Mawenzi, however, had no such cares for the future, and fell into the habit of asking Kibo for help whenever times were bad. Eventually, Kibo became angry with her sister's begging, and hit her on the head with a spoon. Hence Mawenzi's ragged and broken appearance. Another Chagga legend, apparently related to the distant tales of King Solomon, speaks of a great treasure on the mountain, one protected by powerful spirits who punished those foolhardy enough to dare climb it – extreme cold, exhaustion and altitude sickness are the very real modern forms of those spirits. This legend encouraged a curious expedition to the mountain by the Ethiopian **King Menelik II** in 1896, who is said to have been seeking the mortal remains of his thirteenth-century namesake, King Menelik I, the son of Solomon and the Queen of Sheba. According to legend, King Menelik I was wearing King Solomon's regalia when he froze to death on the mountain.

Meltdown: the end of Kilimanjaro's ice cap?

Incredible though it might seem, Kibo's emblematic white cap may soon be no more. Kilimanjaro is heating up, and its ice cap and glaciers are retreating at an alarming rate. Less than a century ago, the ice cap covered twelve square kilometres. By 2000, it had shrunk to just over two square kilometres, having diminished by a full third over the previous decade. A recent study has predicted that the ice cap will disappear completely in 2014.

The primary cause is global warming, although the destruction of forest cover on the lower slopes of the mountain through logging and uncontrolled fires are also to blame: forests trap heat from the sun, so less forest means warmer air, which means more rapid melting. This is particularly bad news for the millions of people living around the mountain and in the Pangani River basin, which is fed with snowmelt and rainwater run-off from Kilimanjaro.

Practicalities

Kilimanjaro National Park covers the entire mountain above the tree line (approximately 2750m), together with six forest corridors running down to around 2000m. The two most popular routes up the mountain start at the villages of **Marangu** (p.321) and **Machame** (p.323) respectively; reliable hiking companies based in Marangu are reviewed on p.335. The **national park headquarters** is at Marangu gate (daily 8am–6pm; ☏027/275 3195, ✉kinapa @habari.co.tz); they're not much help with questions, but do sell maps and books. There's also a park office at the start of the Machame route. The most up-to-date **guidebook** to Kilimanjaro is the one published by TANAPA ($10), which you can buy at the park gates or in Arusha's bookshops. Also recommended are the *Kilimanjaro New Millennium Guide* by Thomas Alexander (Tsh4000), which covers the Marangu and Machame routes (also available at Moshi's *Coffee Shop*); Cameron Burns' detailed *Kilimanjaro & Mount Kenya: A Climbing and Trekking Guide* (Mountaineers Books); and *Trekking in East Africa* by David Else (Lonely Planet). There's also lots of information on the **internet**, including dozens of journey accounts. A good place to start is the Kilimanjaro Summit Log at ⓦwww.peakware.com/wsl/logs/kilimanjaro.htm, which contains hundreds of detailed tips and comments from climbers.

Given that you'll be accompanied by a guide, **maps** aren't essential, but taking one is recommended for plotting your route, putting names to geological features and gauging distances and elevations – a guide's conception of "not far" can be radically different from your own. The best is the *Tourist Map of Kilimanjaro* published by the government's Surveys and Mapping Division (Tsh7000), which has an excellent general contoured map, although the plan of the summit is less clear; the 1:80,000 *Kilimanjaro Map and Guide* by Andrew Wielschowski is also good. The most attractive map is the colour 1:62,500 *Kilimanjaro* map from International Travel Maps' *Mountains of the World* series, which has full contours (but no heights other than peaks). The photocopied map sold at Marangu gate (Tsh500) is useless.

Costs

Kilimanjaro cannot be climbed on the cheap. If you go in a group with a hiking company (see box on p.334 for recommendations) you won't get much change from $600 for a budget trip, or $850 for a mid-range one. Given that you're spending this much already, don't scrimp by going with a dodgy company: it's not worth saving $100 if you're going to end up with inexperienced guides or dud equipment. Costs include **park fees** ($30 per person per day, plus $40 for a night's camping, or $50 for hut space on the Marangu route), which means that daily fees add upto $70–80. You'll also have to pay a one-off $20 rescue fee. **Additional costs** to be shared by the group are the obligatory guide (negotiable, but no more than $20 a day), porters, who often double as cooks (generally one per climber plus one for the guide; no more than $10 a day each), plus food, and equipment rental if you haven't arrived with heaps of stuff.

To these costs, you should add **gratuities**. Leaving unneeded equipment with the guide and porters after the climb is welcome, but no substitute for a cash tip. How much to tip is a perennial headache, not helped by the sour mood of some climbers who fail to reach the top or by the constant and not-so-subtle hints from the guide and porters that can plague some trips. The best way to deal with this hassle is to say that they'll get paid when you get down, but don't tie the promise of tips with a successful summit attempt: you'll be encouraging the guide to take risks with the group, and in any case success or otherwise rarely has much to do with the guide and porters, and almost everything to do with your body and attitude. As a rough idea, $40 for the guide and $20 for each porter from the group is about right, though if your group size is large (say over four people), it would be fair to double those figures. Of course, tipping is a personal matter: if Kilimanjaro is something you've dreamt of for ages, and everything went beautifully, well . . . stories of $1000 tips are common enough to encourage dozens of men waiting for work outside the park entrances to chase their own dreams. On the other hand, if the guide and porters were terrible, don't tip at all – but do explain to them why.

When to go

The most popular climbing **season** is December to February, when the weather is generally clear. July to September is also good, especially September, which is the driest month of the year, but also very cold; August can be overcast. Kilimanjaro can be climbed during the wet seasons, but the lower slopes will be exceedingly muddy and there's no guarantee of clear skies higher up; the long rains fall from March to May, and the short rains from early November to mid-December, and sometimes October. The southeastern slopes receive most rain, meaning that the Machame and Shira routes are generally drier than the Marangu route. It can snow on or near the summit all year round, though chances are highest during and shortly after the rainy seasons. If you have the luxury of a long stay in Tanzania, try to coincide with a full moon on summit day – it avoids the need for flashlights, and lends an eerie beauty to the scene.

Guides and porters

Climbers must be accompanied by at least one officially licensed **guide**. The names of accredited guides are kept on a list at the park desk where you pay the fees (if you're going through a hiking company, guides and porters are provided). There are dozens of guides (and even more porters) waiting for work outside the park gates – ensure that whoever you employ is experienced, especially on routes other than the Marangu. Getting a cheap deal is tempting, but there's no guarantee of experience. The guide should also possess a permit from KINAPA, the national park authority. Don't necessarily trust ID cards (unofficial guides simply print their own) and refrain from paying until you've checked out the guide's credentials at the gate. Despite these caveats, most of the guides are superb: many have climbed the mountain innumerable times,

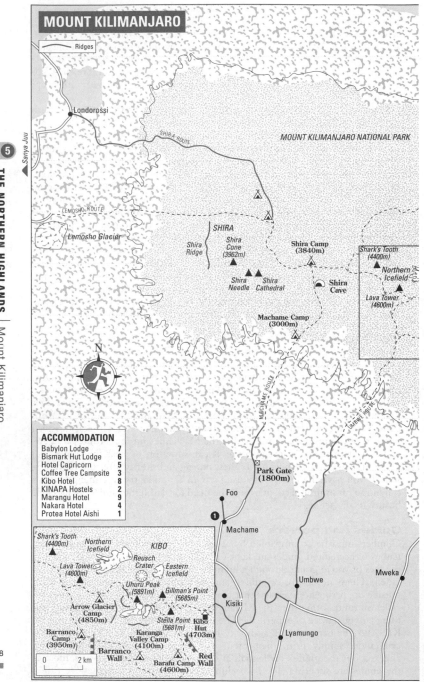

MOUNT KILIMANJARO

Ridges

Sanya Juu

Londorossi

MOUNT KILIMANJARO NATIONAL PARK

SHIRA-4 ROUTE

LEMOSHO ROUTE

Lemosho Glacier

SHIRA

Shira Ridge

Shira Cone (3962m)

Shira Needle

Shira Cathedral

Shira Camp (3840m)

Shira Cave

Shark's Tooth (4400m)

Northern Icefield

Lava Tower (4600m)

Machame Camp (3000m)

MACHAME ROUTE

UMBWE ROUTE

N

ACCOMMODATION

Babylon Lodge	7
Bismark Hut Lodge	6
Hotel Capricorn	5
Coffee Tree Campsite	3
Kibo Hotel	8
KINAPA Hostels	2
Marangu Hotel	9
Nakara Hotel	4
Protea Hotel Aishi	1

Park Gate (1800m)

Foo

Machame

Umbwe

Mweka

Kisiki

Lyamungo

KIBO

Shark's Tooth (4400m)

Northern Icefield

Lava Tower (4600m)

Reusch Crater

Eastern Icefield

Uhuru Peak (5891m)

Gillman's Point (5685m)

Arrow Glacier Camp (4850m)

Stella Point (5681m)

Kibo Hut (4703m)

Barranco Camp (3950m)

Karanga Valley Camp (4100m)

Barranco Wall

Red Wall

Barafu Camp (4600m)

0   2 km

Moshi–Dar Highway

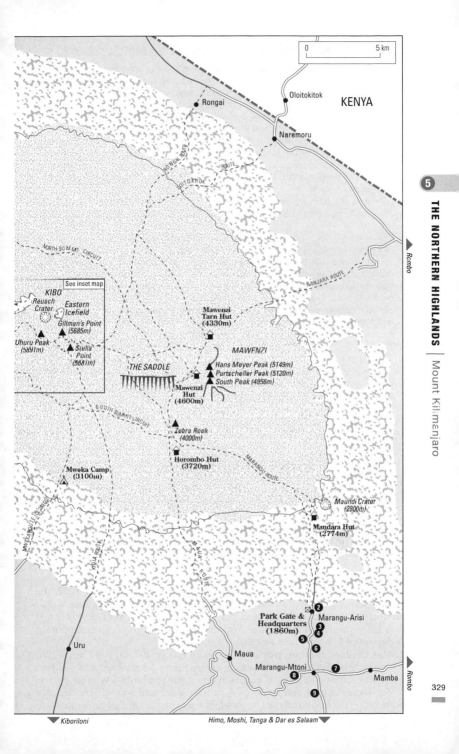

0   5 km

KENYA

Oloitokitok

Rongai

Naremoru

▶ Rombo

NORTH SUMMIT CIRCUIT

RONGAI ROUTE

LOITOKITOK ROUTE

NANJARA ROUTE

See inset map

KIBO

Reusch
Crater

Eastern
Icefield

Gillman's Point
(5685m)

Uhuru Peak
(5891m)

Stella
Point
(5681m)

THE SADDLE

Mawenzi
Tarn Hut
(4330m)

MAWENZI

Hans Meyer Peak (5149m)
Purtscheller Peak (5120m)
South Peak (4956m)

Mawenzi
Hut
(4600m)

SOUTH SUMMIT CIRCUIT

Zebra Rock
(4000m)

Horombo Hut
(3720m)

MARANGU ROUTE

Mweka Camp
(3100m)

Maundi Crater
(2800m)

MWEKA ROUTE

KIDIA ROUTE

MAUA ROUTE

Mandara Hut
(2774m)

Uru

Maua

Park Gate &
Headquarters
(1860m)

Marangu-Arisi

❷
❸
❺ ❹
❻

Marangu-Mtoni

❼

❽

Mamba

❾

▶ Rombo

329

▼ Kiboriloni

Himo, Moshi, Tanga & Dar es Salaam ▼

If you're going through a company, you don't have to come with mountains of gear: a good pair of boots and lots of warm clothes suffice. It's wise not to rely on hiring equipment locally. Although there's a lot of adequate stuff, it's difficult to find really good-quality gear. This applies especially to boots, sleeping bags and clothes. You don't need cooking equipment, as porters bring their own. If you don't want to lug around heaps of stuff for the rest of your travels, there's a ready market for used equipment in Marangu, Moshi and Arusha. In Arusha, you can rent basic gear at *Pizzarusha* or buy it at Widget (see p.390). In Moshi, *Keys Hotel* has a good selection. The park headquarters at Marangu sells sleeping bags and spare trousers, and the kiosk of the Kilimanjaro Guides Cooperative Society in the car park there also rents stuff.

Most of the following items are essential. Optional items include a compact umbrella, binoculars and a reflective metallic "space blanket" for emergencies.

Clothing

The important thing is to wear layers – several levels of clothing worn on top of one another provide better insulation than fewer but bulkier items. As you won't have much chance to dry things out (open fires are no longer permitted), waterproofs are vital, as is keeping spare clothes dry. Don't wear cotton next to your skin or you'll get soaked with sweat, leaving you cold and miserable. Too-tight clothing will hamper your circulation, also making you cold. Normal clothes to pack include shorts and T-shirts for the lower slopes, a couple of woolly jumpers and two pairs of comfortable trousers. A towel and scarf are also handy. Essential specialist clothing is:

Footwear Sturdy, well-broken-in and waterproof hiking boots are vital for the upper sections of the trek. Comfortable shoes with good grip are sufficient on lower slopes (in fact, some porters manage amazingly well with flip-flops). Wear two pairs of socks: light ones next to the skin, and a thick pair of wool or synthetic ones. Use thermal socks at higher altitudes.

Headwear A brimmed sun hat to avoid sunburn, and a fetching balaclava – a godsend on summit day.

Sunglasses Essential to avoid snow-blindness; ensure they're screened against UV radiation.

Thermal underwear Long-johns and hiking socks; polypropylene works well but avoid cotton.

Fleece A warm fleece jacket is essential, and a fleece sweater wouldn't go amiss either. You could take two sets – one for hiking, the other for sleeping in.

Waterproofs Jacket and trousers or gaiters. Should be lightweight and made of a windproof, breathable material like Goretex.

Gloves or mittens Ideally down-lined. Mittens are warmer; you can also buy Goretex outer mittens for breathable waterproofing.

and they're usually fluent in English. One last piece of advice: in 2002, the authorities were talking of introducing a **permit system** to regulate visitor numbers. If this gets implemented, you may have to book your permit a few days beforehand, so don't turn up expecting to be able to climb immediately. A deposit of $30 was also mooted.

Most climbers also hire **porters**; the guide can do this on your behalf, but settle the price beforehand. Although unscrupulous hiking companies expect porters to carry up to 50kg of gear, don't let them: just hire a few more porters to distribute the load, and try to carry at least some stuff yourself. Incidentally, porters don't actually scale the summit, but stay at the last hut or campsite to

Equipment

Backpack The porters carry your main pack but tend to dash off ahead, so bring a small daypack to carry stuff you'll need by day, like water bottles, snacks, toiletries, camera, waterproofs and gloves. Don't pack too much weight, and ensure the straps don't dig into your shoulders.

Sleeping bag An insulated synthetic sleeping bag ("–10", "five-seasons" or "zero-rated") is essential: you might experience night-time temperatures of –25ºC at the top. Insulating mats are usually provided by the tour operator.

Tent Essential on all but the Marangu route (where camping is banned). Your operator should provide one. If you bring your own, make sure it's light and insulated – the collapsible dome variety is ideal.

Torch With spare batteries (wrap them up well to stop the cold killing them).

Walking stick or trekking pole Saves your knees on the descent.

Water bottles Enough for three litres, and a way of insulating them. A thermos flask for soup or something hot is a boon at the top.

Miscellanous

Camera and film Take lots of film (a mixture of 100 and 200 ASA) and spare batteries. Keep your camera dry: on lower slopes, mist and rain drenches everything, so wrap it in something soft and insulating and stash it away in a sealable plastic bag. In sub-zero temperatures, batteries die and delicate shutter mechanisms jam with frozen condensation, so don't put cameras unprotected in your pocket as body heat condenses vapour. A small tripod is helpful in low light or if you're shivering.

Money Small notes and coins for buying drinks and snacks along the Marangu route.

Plastic bags Bring more than you think you'll need to keep things dry, and to carry down rubbish.

Toilet paper A roll of toilet paper is useful – but put used paper in a bag to dispose of at the next long-drop.

Snacks Sugary, high-energy snacks are always useful: chocolate, nuts, sweets and energy drinks.

Medicine bag

Apart from your standard medicine bag (see p.26), and optional high-altitude medication (see below), you should take plasters, bandages and gauze, sweets (to keep your throat moist), eye drops, lip salve, and suncream (minimum factor 25) – the sun is deceptively strong, and you can be burned even through cloud. You could also take a rehydration mix, consisting of one part salt to eight parts sugar, to mix with water; the solution tastes horrible but will keep you hydrated and doesn't freeze as readily as pure water.

pick you up on the way down. Most porters double as cooks, and rustle up some surprisingly delicious nosh.

Preparation and pacing

It cannot be said enough that the more days you have on the mountain, the higher are your chances of success – and the more time you'll have to enjoy the scenery. Small group sizes are also better, as the guide can be more attentive to your needs. A positive **mental attitude** is the key to success: climbing Kilimanjaro is difficult and usually painful, so brace yourself for a big effort and don't be overly confident – the bigger they come, the harder they fall. Being

Air gets thinner the higher you go; on the summit of Kili, a lungful contains only half the oxygen you would inhale at sea level. Given enough time, the human body can adapt to an oxygen-scarce environment by producing more red blood cells. But, without weeks to acclimatize, almost everyone climbing Kili will experience the effects of high altitude, known as **altitude (or mountain) sickness**: these include shortness of breath, lightheadedness, headaches, nausea, insomnia and, naturally enough, exhaustion. The symptoms appear towards the end of the second or third day. Normal altitude sickness isn't much to worry about, although vomiting should be treated seriously (staying hydrated is absolutely essential at high altitude).

Much more serious is **acute mountain sickness (AMS)**, the chronic form of altitude sickness. Symptoms of AMS include most of the above, plus one or more of the following: severe headache; shortness of breath at rest; flu-like symptoms; persistent dry cough; blood-tinged saliva or urine; unsteadiness or drowsiness; lack of mental clarity or hallucinations; and chest congestion. In these cases, **descend immediately** to a lower altitude. Be aware that mental fuzziness may convince the victim that he or she is fit to continue – they're not. A porter will usually accompany the victim, so the whole party won't have to turn back. Ignoring the symptoms of AMS can be fatal: complications like pulmonary oedema and cerebral oedema claim the lives of about a dozen climbers each year. Predicting who will get sick is impossible: AMS affects young and old alike, fit and not-so-fit, so don't deny the signs if you start feeling them, and heed your guide's advice.

Some **drugs** are claimed to eliminate such problems. However, opinion is sharply divided over their pros and cons, so consult a doctor before taking anything. The controversy is fiercest over the most commonly taken drug, **Diamox** (acetazolamide; available on prescription only), since no one seems to know whether it treats the cause of AMS or just masks the symptoms, which in the latter case could hide vital warning signs (like splitting headaches) that herald potentially life-threatening conditions. The British Medical Association suggests you start taking it three days before reaching high altitude (approximately 4000m), which means on the morning of the first day. The drug has two well-known short-term **side effects**: your fingers tingle, and the drug is an extremely efficient diuretic, so you'll be urinating every few hours both day and night – drink lots of water to compensate. Some (unconfirmed) reports suggest that in rare cases the tingling or numbness in fingers may persist for several years. Nonetheless, most climbers do tend to have an easier time of things when on Diamox. As an alternative, some climbers swear by **gingko biloba** (120mg taken twice a day, starting a few days before the climb). Don't take it if you bleed easily. Another alternative is a regimen of **aspirin and codeine** tablets, though this seems only to mask the symptoms, and so could be dangerous.

Given the confusion over medication, **prevention** is a better approach: let your body acclimatize naturally by taking an extra day or two when climbing the mountain (at least six days, whichever route you're taking, ideally seven); stay hydrated; climb slowly; and if you ascend a lot in one day, camp at a lower altitude, if possible. Lastly, don't go higher than the tree line (2700m) if you're suffering from fever, nose bleed, cold or influenza, sore throat or a respiratory infection.

adequately equipped and in good **physical condition** also helps your attitude. You don't have to be an athlete, but cut down on alcohol and cigarettes a few weeks before the climb, go cycling to tune up your lungs, and walk or jog to get your legs in shape. If you have the time and money, a climb up Mount Meru (see p.399) is recommended to help your body acclimatize. On the mountain itself, **take care of your body's needs**. Your appetite may vanish at high altitude, so make the effort to eat properly. You should also drink enough to keep your urine clear (generally 4–5 litres of water a day), taken in sips throughout the hike. Also, try to sleep properly, though this can be difficult at high altitude. For the night of the summit attempt, bring lots of energy foods and water.

The other key to success is to **take your time** – start early at a deliberately slow pace and take frequent rests and you'll find the ascent much less painful than if you charge up. On summit day, go very slowly (not that you'll feel like running), take five-minute rests every half-hour, drink plenty of fluids and breathe through a balaclava or scarf to minimize heat and fluid loss. When short of breath, inhale and exhale deeply and rapidly four or five times. Near the top, stay focused: don't be put off by grumbling climbers descending after failed attempts, and remember that the pleasure lies in the journey, not necessarily in reaching the destination. Also, be aware of your limitations, and listen to your guide – if he suggests you go no further, don't – he knows what he's talking about. Lastly, when **descending**, take it slow – the greatest risk of injury is on the way down, so use a walking stick or ski pole, and resist the temptation to slide down the scree.

The routes

There are three main routes up Kilimanjaro. The **Marangu (or "Tourist") route**, approaching from the southeast, is the most popular. Though usually offered as a five-day trek (three days up, two down), an extra day considerably increases your chances of reaching the top. The second most popular is the **Machame route** from the southwest, which requires at least six days, with seven being recommended. The Marangu requires minimal equipment, has accommodation in huts, and is the quickest and steepest way up – though it consequently has a higher incidence of altitude sickness. The Machame route is slower and more sedate (though it has some trying hands-and-feet scrambles), has campsites instead of huts, and enjoys more varied scenery, as you descend via another route (either the Marangu or the Kidia, which has replaced the closed Mweka route). You'll see plenty of fellow climbers on either route. The third main route is the distinctly less-travelled **Shira route** to the west, which is mainly used by more upmarket companies. It requires a minimum of five days, with six or seven being recommended, depending on how far you drive up (the track is passable to vehicles up to around 3600m). Routes for which special permission is required are the completely unspoiled **Rongai route** from the northeast (ascent only; descend via the Marangu or Kidia routes); the **Njara route**, which approaches from the east up to Mawenzi Peak; the short, scenic but very difficult and rarely attempted **Umbwe route** from the south; and the **Lemosho route** in the west, which joins the Shira route.

Overnights on the Marangu route are in a chain of relatively comfortable cabins; all other routes require camping, usually at recognized campsites equipped with long-drops and nothing much else. The "uniport" huts along these routes are for guides, porters and rangers only.

The Marangu route

Eighty percent of climbers ascend Kili along the **Marangu route**, a short, beautiful but steep trail that's anything but easy, especially if done over only five day – which probably explains why fewer than one in five climbers on this route reaches Uhuru Peak. Extending the trek over six days, as described below, is much preferable and greatly increases your chances of reaching the top. Depending on the season (see p.327), the Marangu route can be cloudy and

Kilimanjaro hiking companies

Most hiking companies which organize trips up Kili are based in Moshi or Marangu, but of the fifty-odd outfits which existed at the time of writing, barely a third were **officially licensed**. You can find the list of licensed operators at the park offices in Marangu and Machame, but make sure you go unaccompanied or your escort may sway the official's impartiality.

The following companies are among the more reputable, and at the time of writing were all members of the self-regulating Union of Kilimanjaro Tour Operators (UKTO), whose members are pretty reliable; you can check out the membership list at MEM Tours & Safari in Moshi (see below). Be wary of companies not reviewed below, including those with offices in popular hotels, as appearances are not everything. In addition, don't necessarily believe recommendations you might read on the internet: several companies are adept at plugging themselves. And if a flycatcher claims to work for one of the following, ensure that you end up at the correct address – there have been several cases of disreputable outfits "borrowing" the names of other companies to snare clients. Note that whilst most of Arusha's safari companies (see p.395) offer Kilimanjaro climbs, the majority are run through operators in Moshi or Marangu, so check which one they're using. An excellent exception is Nature Discovery (see p.396), who run a superb seven-day trip up the Lemosho route for $900–1200.

Companies in Moshi

Ahsante Tours & Safaris New St ☏027/275 0479, ⓦwww.ahsante.com. Helpful and friendly company that generally comes in for praise, and appears to deal well with complaints. Prices are cheaper than most, with a six-day Marangu climb going for upwards of $600, and a six-day Machame hike for around $580.

Keys Hotel Uru Rd ☏027/275 2250, ⓦwww.keys-hotel.com. Keys has enjoyed a solid reputation for years, though you'll pay for their experience and thorough preparation, with hikes costing $150–200 more than the competition (which also includes two nights at their hotel, but excludes equipment). An excellent choice if you want to be certain of a professionally run trip.

Mauly Tours & Safaris Next to Kahawa House, Mawenzi Rd

☏027/275 0730, ⓦwww.glcom .com/mauly. An Indian-run company whose formerly excellent reputation has been getting tarnished of late. Quality very much depends on the guide; the best is Frederick. The price appears to depend on their perception of your ability to pay, so beware.

MEM Tours & Safari (Moshi Expedition and Mountaineering) Granado Hotel Building, Chagga St ☏027/275 0669 or 0741/214967, ⓦwww.memtours.com. A professional, conscientious and keenly priced company happy to tailor itineraries to suit your needs. A five-day Marangu climb goes for roughly $600, and a six-day Machame hike for $580. They also offer good-value wildlife safaris.

Samjoe Tours & Safaris (also called W. J. Travel) Coffee Tree Arcade,

muddy, and is often very busy. The route's popularity means that the path is badly eroded and trampled in many places, and the lower slopes turn into a mudfest in the rains. At times there's also a lot of garbage left by dumb climbers (hence the trail's nickname, the "Coca Cola Route"), and graffiti adorn the three **accommodation huts**: Mandara, Horombo and Kibo. These are equipped with mattresses, twelve-volt solar lighting, kitchens, toilets and a rescue team. Snacks and drinks, including beer, are available at all the huts – but wait until you descend to indulge in the beer. Bunks can be reserved through the park headquarters at Marangu gate (see p.326); TANAPA headquarters in

access from Kibo Rd or Old Moshi Rd ☎027/275 1484 or 0744/269880, ℮samjoetours@yahoo.com. A small, cheap, long-established and frequently recommended company. A five-day Marangu hikes costs $580; a six-day Machame is $640. The quality of your trip will depend on the guide.

Zara International Next to the *New Livingstone Hotel*, Rindi Lane ☎027/275 0011, ⓦwww.kilimanjaro.co.tz. A large operation that has been recommended for many years, despite the odd dud trip. Five-day treks cost upwards of $650.

Companies in Marangu

Most of the following can also arrange climbs up the Machame route; the mark-up shouldn't be more than $100 per group for the hour's Land Rover ride to Machame. Apart from these companies, there are a handful of unlicensed ones which come in for both glowing and scathing feedback – you've been warned. Note that whilst the prices mentioned below include park fees, you'll usually be quoted rates excluding them – so don't get too excited if you're offered a hike for $300.

Alpine Trekking & Safari Just outside the park gate, Marangu-Mtoni ☎027/275 6604 or 0744/372134, ℮alpinetrekking@kilionline.com. Reliable and friendly, offering the usual Marangu and Machame climbs ($660 and $840 respectively), and a couple of less common routes: a six-day Umbwe climb goes for around $1000, and a six-day hike up the Rongai route for $950. They also run day-trips to Mandara Hut ($55 per person including park fees).

Hotel Capricorn 2.7km from the park gate ☎027/275 1309 or 0744/282001, ⓦwww.africaonline.co.tz/capricornhotel. Upmarket and frequently recommended, with hikes going for $800–1200 depending on the route and group size. Apart from Marangu and Machame, they're also knowledgeable about the Shira, Umbwe and Lemosho routes; an eight-day trip on any of these costs $1600.

Kibo Hotel 1.4km west of Marangu-Mtoni ☎027/275 1308, ⓦwww.kibohotel.com. One of the best

mid-range companies for the Marangu route so long as you're adequately equipped (hiring stuff here is expensive), offering a five-day climb for around $700. They also do other routes, including the Rongai, for which a five-day trip goes for around $660 per person plus $200–300 per group for road transport.

Marangu Hotel 2km south of Marangu-Mtoni ☎027/275 6594, ⓦwww.maranguhotel.com. A long-established company with excellent guides and a reputation for thorough preparation, offering a choice of "fully equipped" climbs, where all you need to bring is warm clothes and (preferably) a good pair of boots, and "hardway" climbs, where you bring everything you'll need (tent, equipment and food) and the hotel arranges guides, porters and accommodation. A fully equipped five-day Marangu hike costs around $800; a six-day Machame will set you back $900–1000.

Arusha do *not* handle bookings for this. Although numbers are officially limited to sixty climbers a day, the procedure isn't perfect so you may find yourself sharing a bunk. Camping isn't allowed.

Day 1: Marangu Gate to Mandara Hut

The Marangu route starts at **Marangu Gate** (1860m), 5.6km north of the village, where you pay the park fees and hire a guide and porters if you're not on an organized climb. You can also buy last-minute supplies like energy food here. Start as early as possible to give yourself plenty of time to enjoy the tangle of rainforest and to increase the odds of avoiding showers, which tend to fall in the afternoon. The entire day's walk (8km; count on around 3hr) becomes very slippery and muddy in the rains, so take care. You'll may well get soaked along this section, even if it's not raining, as the cloying mist effectively drenches everything.

Immediately after the gate, the broad track plunges into dense forest. If time isn't a concern, the narrower signposted track to the left is a preferable but slightly longer alternative to the main track, as it follows a small stream and gives a better view of the forest, as well as being less busy. The track adds about an hour to the day's hike. Both tracks merge into a narrow and much-eroded trail after some 5km. **Mandara Hut** (2774m) is 3km further on. If you arrive early and feel up to it, there's a pleasant walk from Mandara Hut to the rim of **Maundi Crater** (2800m) 1.5km northeast, the remnant of a volcanic vent from where there are glorious views. The crater can also be fitted into the next day's walk.

Mandara Hut, just inside the upper boundary of the forest, comprises a complex of comfortable wooden cabins sleeping sixty people, most containing two rooms with four bunks apiece. The exception is a large two-storey house which has a large dormitory on top and the communal dining area downstairs. Eat well, as you might lose your appetite higher up.

Day 2: Mandara Hut to Horombo Hut

After an early breakfast (try for 6.30am), the trail emerges from the rainforest and veers northwest. If the sky is clear, there's a great view of the craggy Mawenzi Peak to the north and of the plains to the south from here. The trail heads up through alpine meadows and crosses a stream to emerge onto grassland, which eventually thins into surreal moorland scattered with bushes and short trees. If it's cloudy, don't fret – the vision of the plants emerging from the mist in a cocoon of silence can be magical, and you stand a reasonable chance of clear skies in the afternoon. As you approach Horombo Hut, 15km from Mandara, across a series of moorland ravines, ragged stands of giant groundsels and giant lobelia take over, lending an equally strange and unearthly quality to the scene, often complemented by magnificent sunsets from Horombo – hopefully not too clouded by the effects of altitude, which most people begin to feel on this day. **Horombo Hut** (3720m), in a rocky valley, comprises a collection of huts similar to Mandara and sleeps 120 people. There are some old-fashioned long-drops down the slope, and newer toilets flushed with piped from a stream behind the huts. It gets cold very quickly after sunset, so wrap up well. Count on five to seven hours for the day's walk.

Day 3: Horombo Hut

Most people begin to feel the effects of altitude on the walk up to Horombo Hut, so a **rest day** at Horombo is advisable even if you're in good physical shape: no great hardship given the stunning location. You can help yourself acclimatize more easily if you spend at least a couple of hours walking to a higher altitude: most people head for **Zebra Rock** (4000m), named after its peculiar weathering pattern. If you're feeling particularly fit, you could try a day-trip to **Mawenzi Hut** (4600m), at the foot of Mawenzi Peak.

Day 4: Horombo Hut to Kibo Hut

The next stage, 13km up to Kibo Hut, can be tough if your body hasn't fully acclimatized, so keep an eye out for symptoms of acute mountain sickness beyond simple headaches, and leave Horombo early, as you'll have little time to sleep in the evening before the wake-up call for the summit attempt. The whole stage takes about five to seven hours.

Just beyond Horombo, two trails diverge, both heading up to the **Saddle** – the broad lava-stone ridge between Mawenzi and Kibo peaks. The right-hand trail, which is very rocky and eroded, veers north, and is the quicker, albeit the more difficult, of the two routes (2–3hr compared to 3–4). From the Saddle, a track heading east takes you to the 4600-metre mark on **Mawenzi**, which is as far up that peak as you can get without technical gear. Ignore this track and carry straight on instead – Kibo Hut is three to four hours away across an otherworldly alpine desert of reddish gravel and boulders. The alternative route from Horombo to the Saddle takes upwards of four hours, but leaves you little under two kilometres from Kibo Hut. Both routes have a number of steep uphill and downhill sections.

Kibo Hut (4703m) is a stone construction with a dining room and bunks for sixty people. There are long-drops outside the huts – take care at night. There's no water, so fill up near Horombo, either at one of the tarns on the eastern route, or at "Last Water" stream on the western route. Assuming you're up for the ascent the same night, try to catch some sleep in the afternoon and evening as the next stage, starting around midnight, is by far the hardest.

Days 5 and 6: Horombo to the summit and back down

The summit push on **day 6** is the steepest and most strenuous part of the hike, taking around five to six hours up to Gillman's Point (and an extra ninety minutes to Uhuru Peak), followed by a nine- or ten-hour descent. After a generally fitful sleep due to the cold and the altitude, hikers set off between 11pm and 1am for the final ascent (the earlier you set off the better, as the icy path around the summit can become treacherously slippery after sunrise). Temperatures are well below zero, and visibility is difficult, especially if there's no moon or if flashlights conk out. The trail leads past **Hans Meyer Cave** – handy for a sheltered rest – before turning into a painful series of single-file zigzags up loose scree. At the top of the zigzags, a short rocky scramble gets you over **Johannes' Notch** and to within staggering distance of Gillman's Point. The thin air forces frequent stops, and means that the hike to Gillman's Point takes at least five or six hours. Most climbers get light-headed and nauseous along this stretch, and headaches afflict pretty much everyone.

Gillman's Point (5685m), on the crater rim, is where many people call an end to their attempt, to be consoled with the stupendous view and the sun rising from behind Mawenzi Peak. If you're up to it (fewer than one in five climbers on the Marangu route are), an even more exhausting ninety-minute clockwise walk around the crater rim past **Stella Point** – where the Machame route joins up – and Hans Meyer Point brings you to the roof of Africa, **Uhuru Peak** (5891m). Those ninety minutes (or two hours if you're really whacked) may not sound like much, but will likely be the hardest, most painful and – with luck – most rewarding ninety minutes of your life. Sunrise here above a sea of clouds is unforgettable (though the majority of climbers arrive about an hour after sunrise), as is the feeling of elation, even if, right then, your only desire is to get down as quickly as possible. There's a summit log you can sign, and remember to take a photograph with that famously battered yellow sign – the pounding headache that you will more than likely be feeling means that many people forget.

It's possible to **hike into the crater** if this is arranged in advance with your guide (at extra cost). Measuring 2km in diameter and 300m deep, the crater contains another, smaller crater named after Dr Richard Reusch, who in 1926 discovered the frozen leopard later made famous by Hemingway. In the centre of this is an ash pit, and there are some small but active steam fumaroles on its northern and eastern rim. Incidentally, it's not a good idea to spend a night on the summit (**Furtwangler Camp**, 5600m) unless you're taking at least ten days for the hike, as you'll need to be totally acclimatized to avoid coming down with altitude sickness.

Most folks only spend a few minutes at the bitterly cold summit before **heading back down**. Try to avoid the temptation of "skiing" down the scree – it makes things even more difficult for climbers after you, and of course you risk a painful tumble. Most climbers get back to Kibo Hut around 10am, take a rest, and then retrace their steps back to Horombo, for their last night on the mountain before continuing down to the gate.

The **final day** should be bliss, but by now your knees may be complaining – take it easy, and use a walking stick. Mandara Hut is usually reached by lunchtime, and the park gate in the afternoon. Don't forget your certificate at the gate.

The Machame route

Nicknamed the "Whiskey Route", presumably because of its intoxicating views, the long, winding and dramatic **Machame route** is the next most popular way up after the Marangu route, and increasingly so: encounters with eland and

---

Kilimanjaro's high-altitude flora and fauna

Kilimanjaro in covered by a series of distinctive habitat zones, determined by altitude. Above about 1800m, farmland ceases and forests take over. Up to around 2000m, much of the forest is secondary growth, but beyond here is dense primary **cloudforest**, containing over 1800 species of flowering plants. The forest is dominated in its lower reaches by ferns, podocarpus and camphor trees, and is home to three primate species: blue monkey, western black-and-white colobus, and bushbaby (galago). Leopards also live here (though you're most unlikely to see one), preying on mountain reedbuck and members of the world's largest population of Abbot's duiker. Curiously, the belt of giant bamboo that characterizes Mount Meru and Mount Kenya is absent on Kilimanjaro.

Rainfall is less heavy at higher altitudes, so from around 2400m the forest becomes less dense. The tree line (2800–3000m) is start of the peculiar **afro-alpine moorland** (also called upland grassland), the land of the giants – giant heather, giant groundsel (or tree senecio) and giant lobelia. The cabbages on stumps and the larger candelabra-like "trees" are two forms of the **giant groundsel**, an intermediate stage of which has a sheaf of yellow flowers. The giant groundsel favours damp and sheltered locations such as stream beds; they're slow growers but, for such weedy-looking vegetables, they may be extraordinarily old – up to two hundred years. Higher up, in the alpine bogs, you'll see groundsel together with another strange plant, the tall and fluffy **giant lobelia** – the animal-like furriness insulates the delicate flowers. A number of **mammals** habitually pass into the moorland zone from the forests: grey duiker and eland are most commonly seen; bushbuck, red duiker and buffalo are rarer. There are few birds: the most common is the white-necked raven, often seen at campsites.

Above 4600m is the barren **alpine desert** zone. The sub-zero conditions here mean that few plants other than mosses and lichens are able to survive, although the daisy-like *Helichrysum newii* has been seen on Kibo's summit caldera at 5760m close to a fumarole. Even stranger was the mysterious **leopard** whose frozen body was found close to the summit in 1926 and which featured in Hemingway's *The Snows of Kilimanjaro*. No one knows what it was doing so far up the mountain.

other wildlife are no longer so common, and you'll see dozens of other climbers along the way – the official daily limit of sixty climbers a day is apparently not enforced. Six days is usual for the ascent along this route, but seven is recommended. The walk is more difficult than the Marangu, but the advantage is that, being longer, acclimatization is easier and so the success rate is higher. There are several routes to the summit from the **Shira Plateau**, and two choices of descent: either the Marangu route or the new **Kidia route**, so all in all you get to see a lot of the mountain. The Machame route can also be combined with lesser-known ascents such as the **Umbwe** or **Shira routes**. Accommodation is in tents at several recognized campsites. These are usually called "huts" on maps, but the metal "uniport" huts are for guides and porters only.

Day 1: Machame Gate to Machame Camp
As with the Marangu route, start early to fully enjoy the day. Count on an hour to complete formalities at the **gate** (1800m), and a couple of hours more if you're walking the 5km from Machame village to the gate (which you may have to do in the rains, when the steep road can become impassable to vehicles). Leave the gate no later than 11am; the day's walk takes five to seven hours.

From the gate, the trail heads up to the west of Makoa stream into dense, steamy and ever-changing **rainforest** alive with birdsong (look out for wild orchids). The trail narrows after thirty minutes to follow parts of a rocky ridge, where the vegetation becomes thicker, characterized by giant heather, and Spanish mosses hanging from the trees. The trail is steep, muddy and very slippery in places, especially beyond the two or three-hour mark. As you approach Machame Camp, the vegetation thins out and the path emerges onto alpine moorland. **Machame Camp** (3000m) occupies a clearing on the ridge. There are long-drop toilets, water from a nearby stream and great views of the Western Breach.

Day 2: Machame Camp to Shira Camp
So long as you're in good shape, this is a very pleasant and easy day's hike (around 5hr) that brings you out of the forest (and usually above the clouds, though it can still be misty) and onto the drier and rockier **Shira Plateau**. From Machame Camp, the trail continues northeast along a steep and rocky ridge (which needs some scrambling) scattered with giant heather, and passes several clearings with great views of mounts Meru and Longido in the west. The top of the ridge – after three hours or so – ends in a small cliff up which a rudimentary staircase has been built. Lunch is taken on top. From here, the incline lessens and the trail veers northwards across several ravines through land studded with giant lobelia and giant groundsels. This leads on past **Shira Cave** (actually more of a rock shelter), before reaching the exposed **Shira Camp** (3840m) on the edge of the Shira Plateau, an immense, gently sloping expanse of desolate moorland marked by **Shira Cone** – the remnants of Kilimanjaro's oldest crater. There's a good view of the Western Breach from the camp, and awe-inspiring sunsets over Mount Meru. Night-time temperatures usually stay a few degrees above freezing, but the wind chill makes it feel much colder – wrap up. The first symptoms of altitude sickness begin to appear here.

Day 3: Shira Plateau
The Shira Plateau is a great place to spend an extra **rest day** acclimatizing. The main attraction is **Shira Cone** at the west end of the plateau, which rises about

200m above the plateau to 3962m, and has two impressive pinnacles on its southern rim – volcanic plugs named Shira Needles and Shira Cathedral. Eland are sometimes seen on the lower reaches of the Plateau. Ask your guide if the **frozen buffalo** carcass that was found between the plateau and the Western Breach a few years back is still there; like the frozen leopard, no one knows what the buffalo was doing so far up the mountain.

If you're feeling OK, however, you may prefer to acclimatize later on, especially as the next day's hike – to Barranco Camp – is good for one day's acclimatization; rising to around 4400m before dropping back down to 3950m.

Day 4: Shira Camp to Barranco Camp
There are **two routes** to the summit from Shira Camp: either via Barranco Camp and Barafu Camp to Stella Point, or straight up the Western Breach. The former, described below, is by far the easier. For a description of the Western Breach route, see opposite.

The boulder-strewn trail to Barranco Camp (Umbwe Hut on some maps) takes five to seven hours and is extremely beautiful in a lunar kind of way. The walk starts with a gentle incline east towards Kibo. At the top of a ridge marked by a rock called the **Shark's Tooth** (4400m) – where vegetation is limited to lichens and mosses – the trail veers south to traverse a series of shallow up-and-down valleys at the base of the Western Breach and the 4600m **Lava Tower**, gradually descending to **Barranco Camp** (3950m). Set in alpine tundra, the camp has a great view of the icy Western Breach as well as the Barranco Wall – which you'll be climbing the next day, and which appears intimidatingly vertical from here. If you're going to suffer badly from altitude sickness, it really kicks in at Barranco, so be reasonable with your expectations. Porters prefer to camp in a rock shelter at the foot of the wall, about thirty minutes' walk away.

Day 5: Barranco Camp to Barafu Camp
Although we've given a one-day route description from Barranco to Barafu Camp, this section is best done in two four-hour segments, with an overnight half-way in the Karanga Valley. This is especially recommended if you didn't spend a day acclimatizing at Shira. Some people attempt the walk from Shira to the Karanga Valley in a day (around 9hr), but this is exhausting and not recommended.

Although steep, only few stretches of **Barranco Wall** require hands-and-feet climbing, and the zigzagging path is for the most part clearly marked. The path is narrow, which means the "experienced" climbers can get huffy about the slow pace – ignore them, and take your time. The wall normally takes ninety minutes to scale. At the top, there's a great view of the Heim, Kersten and Decken glaciers. The path follows a spectacular traverse east along the base of Kibo. The top of the icy **Karanga Valley** (4100m) is usually reached by midday, giving you a lazy afternoon to rest and sleep before heading off the next day to Barafu.

Continuing on from Karanga Valley, the track continues its eastward traverse, after about two hours reaching the crossroad with the Mweka route. Turn left for Barafu Camp – an exhausting ninety-minute climb up a steep and rocky lava ridge. It often snows, and in the rainy seasons this area can be blanketed. **Barafu Camp** (4600m) is on the ridge close to the southern edge of the Saddle, and has a great view of Mawenzi Peak. The downside is the often filthy state of the campsite – take your trash down with you. The long-drops here are close to the ridge edge – take care at night, as several climbers have fallen to their deaths from here. Go to sleep no later than sunset.

Days 6 and 7: Barafu to the summit and back down

Day 6 – summit day – is the most exhausting, and involves at least seventeen hours of hiking from Barafu Camp to the summit (6–8hr) and down to Horombo Hut on the Marangu route, or to High Camp on the Kidia route (the replacement for the Mweka route). The "day" starts before midnight, when you're woken for breakfast, and most climbers set off between midnight and 1am. The trail follows an increasingly steep valley on the edge of scree fields before passing between the Rebmann and Ratzel glaciers to emerge at **Stella Point** (5681m) on the southern rim of Kibo; the last few hundred metres are the hardest section on the climb. **Uhuru Peak** (5891m) is about an hour further along an ice-covered trail; see day 5 of the Marangu route (p.335) for a description. The trail for the most part is steep and extremely loose scree, which makes for painfully slow progress.

Heading **back down**, most people reach Barafu Camp around 9–11am, where an hour's rest is followed by a long hike down. The **Mweka route**, which was the usual route down until August 2001, is closed for environmental recovery (a large part had become a muddy quagmire). Its replacement, the **Kidia route** (also known as the Old Moshi route) is not as steep. It runs east of the Mweka route, and emerges at Kiboriloni, 5km northeast of Moshi. You should reach High Camp before nightfall.

Whichever route you're following, **day 7** is generally just a few hours of relatively easy – if sometimes very muddy – downhill walking. Take it easy.

The Western Breach route

For experienced climbers taking the Machame or Shira routes, a challenging alternative to the ascent from Barafu Camp is the approach over the **Western Breach**, a steep slope flanked by glaciers that was created when the western rim of Kibo exploded. The Western Breach is sometimes touted as a short-cut to the top (theoretically feasible in five days), but don't believe the hype, which is highly irresponsible. Nicknamed "the Torture Route", the Western Breach ascent is very steep and potentially dangerous – landslides and rock falls claim victims most years, and although much of the permanent snow and ice that formerly made the route a technical climb has melted, you still risk encountering snow and ice, especially between December and February, so at the very least you'll need to pack ice picks, crampons and ropes. Another danger is that turning back on the last part is impossible without proper climbing equipment, so if you feel anything more than just a headache, turn back well before. Also be aware that the trail is unmarked and easy to lose, and most guides don't know the route well; go with a reputable hiking company.

The route starts at the **Arrow Glacier** at the foot of the Western Breach. The last **camps** for the summit attempt are either at the base of the spectacularly located **Lava Tower** (4600m), four hours from Shira Camp, or the equally dramatic **Arrow Glacier Camp** (4850m), next to an area of boulders and snow fields. It takes at least six hours to the crater rim from Arrow Glacier, and around nine hours from the Lava Tower.

The Shira route

The extremely photogenic **Shira route** (also called the Londorossi route) approaches the mountain from the west through forest used as a migration route by elephants (hence the more open canopy than in the south), and joins the Machame route at the Shira Plateau, at the end of the second day's hike. The route is actually driveable to around 3600m, leaving you with an easy half-day walk to Shira Camp (see p.339). If you do drive, spend at least two nights on the Shira Plateau to acclimatize before climbing further. The route is favoured by some upmarket companies, and the chances are you'll be the only group on any one day. Walking the whole distance, it takes at least six days to the summit.

The Pare Mountains and Mkomazi Game Reserve

Southeast of Kilimanjaro rise the much older but equally beautiful **Pare Mountains**, a green, fertile and infrequently visited region divided into two distinct ranges – north and south. The practical business of getting around is not as difficult as it was, thanks to the establishment of three **cultural tourism programmes**, two in the north at Usangi and Kisangara, another at Mbaga in the south. Each programme offers a range of affordable activities based around guided walks in the mountains and their forests, and encounters with the rural culture of the **Pare** tribe, who have been living in the mountains for the last six hundred years.

The Pare are northeastern Tanzania's most traditional tribe. In the same way that the geologically separate Eastern Arc forests have developed an especially rich flora and fauna, so the isolation of the Pare from other tribes has resulted in their strong and distinctive culture and sense of identity. Whereas traditional knowledge of plants and their uses is fast disappearing elsewhere, the Pare have kept much of their knowledge intact, and are famed throughout northern Tanzania for the power of their healers, and sometimes also feared for witchcraft – witches, called *ndewa* in Kipare, are invariably associated with botanical knowledge garnered over many centuries. It's thanks to the continuity of Pare culture that many of the mountains' indigenous forests have been preserved, despite high human population densities, since the Pare consider the forests sacred places, guarded by the spirits of their ancestors. Add to all this the fact that the Pare, like their Sambaa cousins to the south (see box on p.350), are an unfailingly welcoming bunch, and you have an immensely rewarding place to visit.

In the plains between the mountains and the Kenyan border lies the **Mkomazi Game Reserve**, which became the scene of controversy following the forcible expulsion of Maasai cattle herders in the 1990s. It contains a rhino sanctuary, but otherwise probably isn't worth the effort if the Northern Safari Circuit figures in your plans.

North Pare

The **North Pare Mountains** are best visited through the cultural tourism programme at **Usangi**. Another programme, at **Kisangara** on the Dar–Arusha highway, also offers walks into the mountains, but is better for trips to Nyumba ya Mungu reservoir (see p.344) in the plains to the west.

The Eastern Arc Mountains

The Pare Mountains are part of the **Eastern Arc Mountains**, an isolated range of ancient massifs that stretch from the Taita Hills in southeastern Kenya into Tanzania, where the range includes the Pare Mountains, East and West Usambara (p.360 and p.350 respectively), the Ulugurus near Morogoro (p.275) and the Udzungwa Mountains (p.298). Despite the proximity of the northern part of the Eastern Arc to the volcanic massifs of Mount Meru and Kilimanjaro, the steep crystalline ridges and peaks of the Eastern Arc are a much older and geologically separate formation. The current ranges began to take shape some 100 million years ago, and attained their present form at the start of the Miocene Epoch, 25 million years ago.

The great age of the Eastern Arc Mountains, along with the physical isolation of the various ranges from one another, is one reason for their exceptional **biodiversity**. Another is the region's remarkable climatological stability over the last forty million years, thanks to the proximity of the Indian Ocean, whose monsoon system dictates weather patterns over much of the Eastern Arc, producing ample mist and rainfall from moisture-laden clouds coming in from the ocean, Together, these factors have fostered the evolution of the mountains' tremendously rich ecological systems, notably their forests, which contain literally thousands of plant and animal species found nowhere else on earth – not for nothing is the Eastern Arc often referred to as the "Galapagos of Africa".

Usangi

The base for the North Pare Mountains cultural tourism programme is **Usangi village**, 25km east of the Dar–Arusha highway in a beautiful location surrounded by no fewer than eleven peaks. Try to visit on a Monday or Thursday, when the village's **market** is held. The cultural tourism programme offers a range of trips; profits are currently used to promote energy-efficient stoves, reducing both the pressure on forests and the workload of women who collect wood.

Transport from Arusha or Moshi is on the Sahara Beach bus, which goes direct to Usangi early each morning. Coming from Dar es Salaam, catch a bus for Moshi or Arusha and get off in the district capital, Mwanga, 50km southeast of Moshi, from where a handful of daily buses grind uphill along a good sandy road to Usangi (90min). At Usangi, get off at Lomwe Secondary School and ask for the project co-ordinators, Mr Kangero or Mr Mashauri (T Usangi 7). If you get stranded in Mwanga, the school for deaf children has a good little guest house (ask for Peter Elisha; T027/275 7727; ❷).

In Usangi, several families – most of them connected to the school – offer **accommodation** through the cultural tourism programme. The school itself also has a guest house, sleeping six people, and there's also a guest house in the village near the mosque. **Meals** are provided by the Usangi Women's Group.

Guided walks and tours

A guided half-day walk takes in farms on the lower slopes of the Pare Mountains before climbing to **Mangatu moorland** (1600m), near the sacred forest of the Mbale clan, with superb views of Kilimanjaro and Lake Jipe on the Kenyan border. A full-day trek can be arranged up North Pare's highest peak, **Mount Kindoroko** (2113m), 9km south of Usangi, which gives grand views of Kilimanjaro, Mount Meru, Lake Jipe and Nyumba ya Mungu reservoir. The walk goes through the surrounding rainforest, home to blue monkeys and birds, and you can also visit a women's pottery co-operative and a traditional healer. Another day-trip goes up **Mount Kamwala**, whose forests are sacred. Walks over several days can also be arranged; Ugweno village, near **Lake Jipe** on the Kenyan border, is a handy base and has accommodation at the local school. You can also camp in the mountains; bring your own gear.

If you're not up to long hikes, there are several things to do in and around Usangi, including visits to a brick-making co-operative, other artisans producing pottery, clothes and traditional beer, and – if you're lucky – a local wedding, to which you'll probably be invited. **Costs**, including food, guide and all fees, average Tsh4500 per person in a couple for half a day, Tsh7000 for a full day, and Tsh13,000 if you stay overnight.

Kisangara

The easiest of Pare's cultural tourism programmes to visit is at **Kisangara Chini**, 12km south of Mwanga on the Dar–Arusha highway in the shadow of Mount Kindoroko, North Pare's highest peak. Profits from the programme equip a local primary school. All **buses** running between Dar and Moshi or Arusha pass through Kisangara, but don't leave too late as you won't find much setting off after midday. The **cultural tourism programme** is thirty minutes' walk east of the village; follow the signposts for "Hasha Project", the local NGO running the project (T Mwanga 8; or c/o Litetema office T027/275 5600, F027/275 5612; you can also book things through TACTO in Arusha – see p.405). The centre has **accommodation** in various cottages (with bathrooms), and can help out with camping. There are also two simple guest houses in the village (both ❶): *Enimasha House*, and the grottier *Paris Hotel*. The tourism centre can arrange food, and there are basic restaurants in the village by the main road.

Guided walks and tours

The tourism programme's **guides** are former secondary-school pupils, and carry ID cards. The main walk in the mountains is a hike up **Mount Kindoroko** (also offered by Usangi's cultural tourism programme, see p.341), combined with visits to sites of ritual importance. The programme can also arrange a day-trip to **Nyumba ya Mungu** ("House of God") reservoir in the plains to the west for bird-spotting, fishing excursions by canoe and encounters with local fishermen, some of whom emigrated here from Lake Victoria. Closer to Kisangara, various **half-day walks** combine visits to carpentry workshops, brick and sisal factories, a traditional brewery producing beer from sugar cane, and Lembeni Herbal Hospital. Especially entertaining is the full-day **spice tour** through herb and spice gardens, which includes a suitably spiced lunch and dances performed by the women's group. Kisangara's **market days** are Thursday and Sunday. **Costs** are very reasonable: a guide costs Tsh6000 a day for groups of up to five, to which you should add Tsh1500 per person for the development fee, Tsh1500–2500 for a meal and Tsh2000 for a night's accommodation.

South Pare: Same and Mbaga

The district capital of the Pare region, **SAME** (pronounced *sah-mê*), straddles the Arusha–Dar highway at the foot of the South Pare Mountains. Same's main attraction is its **Sunday market**, which draws farmers from all over the mountains. A local speciality is honey (*asali*); the normal variety, called *msiku*, is from

△ Trekking to Kibo

tended hives hung from trees; the sweeter and superior variety (the bee stings are also said to be more painful) is called *mpako*, and comes from wild bee hives in the ground. Another item worth seeking out is the local **scorpion and snakebite cure**, called *nkulo*, which looks to be a mineralized form of charcoal, sold in powdered or stick form, that literally sucks venom out of wounds.

Practicalities

Buses to Same leave from Arusha, Moshi and Dar every half-hour or so until around midday; avoid arriving on Sunday, when there's no onward public transport to Mbaga in the mountains. **Leaving Same**, buses for Dar pass through town every half-hour from 7am to around 3pm; later buses from Nairobi and Kampala also pass through, but there's no guarantee of a seat. Buses to Moshi and Arusha pass through between 6am and 3pm. Forget the afternoon bus from Mbeya operated by Hood; their drivers are insane. *Sasakazi Restaurant* (☏027/275 8176), facing the bus stand, is the place for **information** about the cultural tourism programme. The restaurant can also arrange short walks around Same for Tsh1000 a person.

There's lots of **accommodation**. The most comfortable is *Elephant Motel*, 1.4km south of the bus stand on the Dar highway (☏027/275 8193; ❷ including breakfast), which is getting a little tired but has large and clean rooms, all with showers and big enough nets. There's also a bar and TV, good filling meals (under Tsh2000), and camping ($3 per person). The best of the cheapies is the *Tumaini Guest House* (☏027/275 8052; ❶), whose clean and fresh-smelling rooms (with or without bathroom) all have box nets, fan, table and chair – it's 500m north of the bus stand but difficult to find, so ask someone at the *Sasakazi Restaurant* to take you. Also good is the *Amani Lutheran Centre* (☏027/275 8107; ❶), between the bus stand and the market on the road heading uphill from the *Sasakazi Restaurant*, which has twelve clean en-suite rooms with round nets but no fans, a pious Christian atmosphere and safe parking. Also with safe parking is the *Kambeni Guest House* (☏027/275 8186; ❶), down the side street opposite the *Amani Lutheran Centre* This is actually two hotels: "Number 1" is dingy, so go for "Number 2", which has cleaner and brighter rooms, all with box nets (no fans), and one room with private bathroom.

The best **restaurant** is the *Sasakazi* (closed Sat), whose pleasant shaded outdoor terrace facing the bus stand is a perfect place to watch the world go by. The food is excellent, with a full English breakfast going for Tsh1000, and most other meals no more than Tsh1500-2000, including *sembe* (a local variant of *ugali* made from shelled maize) and *mchanganyiko*, which is a combination of more or less everything. For **drinks**, a friendly place is the strangely named *Honey Port Bar* opposite *Sasakazi*. If you need to **change money**, the National Microfinance Bank will oblige.

Mbaga

The winding road uphill from Same takes you past the entrance to Mkomazi Game Reserve (see p.348) and on to **MBAGA**, a former missionary station set in a lush area of terraced cultivation. Mbaga is now home to Pare's biggest **cultural tourism programme**, offering a wide variety of walks to various attractions and small villages little changed from centuries ago, and giving you a chance to experience local Pare life and culture at first hand. Profits from the project have already paid for the construction of a pre-school building. A good time to come is Wednesday, coinciding with the weekly **market**.

Practicalities

The drive up from Same takes ninety minutes by private car (you'll need a 4WD in the rains) or two hours by public transport. A small bus runs from Same no later than 2pm, returning from Mbaga at 5am, while a handful of Land Rovers and pick-ups also cover the route, though they can't be relied on. There's no public transport on Sunday. In Mbaga, vehicles stop outside the market facing the *Hill-Top Tona Lodge*, the base for the **cultural tourism programme** (c/o *Sasakazi Restaurant* in Same, ☎027/275 8176; bookings also through TACTO in Arusha, see p.405). At the start of the twentieth century the lodge's main building was the residence of a German missionary named Jakob Dannholz, who wrote what is still the best work on Pare culture (*Im Banne des Geisterglaubens*, 1916) – you can buy a copy of the English translation at the lodge.

Accommodation at the lodge (❸ including breakfast) consists of modest brick cottages a few minutes from the main building, with several rooms in each, electricity and a bathroom with running water. There are also four rooms in Dannholz Cottage. **Camping** costs Tsh2500 (bring your own tent). **Meals** are available if ordered early; try the *makande*, a light stew of maize and beans cooked with milk and vegetables. There's more basic accommodation (and food) at *Sunrise Lodge*, 5km beyond Mbaga along the road to Gonja, and a guest house in Gonja itself.

Guided walks and tours

The cultural tourism programme offers a range of walks from easy half-day hikes to treks of three days or more (the following is just a selection); they can also arrange a day's safari in Mkomazi Game Reserve (p.348). Walks begin at the *Hill-Top Tona Lodge*. One fascinating (and rather disturbing) half-day walk goes to the **Mghimbi Caves** and **Malameni Rock**. The caves provided shelter from slave raiders in the 1860s, whilst the rock, further up, was the site of child sacrifices until the practice was ended in the 1930s. The rock can be climbed, but you need to be instructed on the appropriate behaviour by an elder first – your guide can arrange this. Other good half-day destinations are the mountain-top **Red Reservoir**, near the Tona Moorlands, which is frequently covered with water plants, making it good for bird-watching, and **Mpepera View Point**, whose hill-top location gives views – on clear days – of Kilimanjaro and Mkomazi Game Reserve. A recommended full-day trip is to the tiny and beautiful agricultural village of **Ikongwe**, which is said to have been a gift from God. Overnight stays in the village can be arranged with local families, and the trip can be combined with Mpepera View Point. The most adventurous option is the three-day hike to **Shengena Peak** (2463m), the highest point in the Pare Mountains, and the species-rich **Shengena** and **Chome rainforests**, including overnights with a local family at Chome village (see below) and under canvas at the forest edge before a 4am start to catch sunrise from the peak.

Costs are Tsh6000 for a guide for up to three people, Tsh2000 per person for the village development fee, and extras like meals (Tsh2500), porter (Tsh2000) and a visit to a healer (Tsh1000). A full-day programme, including a night at the *Hill-Top Tona Lodge*, costs $25 per person. If music appeals, Tona Traditional Dancing Troupe can be hired for Tsh5000 plus tips.

Chome village

Chome village, hidden in a lush green valley at the western base of Shengena Peak, is one of Pare's gems: a small, traditional and immensely friendly place, despite having suffered the mysterious abduction of dozens of villagers in 1929 – no one knows where they ended up. The village can be visited as part of Mbaga's cultural tourism programme (it's a day's walk along narrow footpaths), or through *Kisaka Villa Inn* in Chome itself (☎027/275 6722 or 0744/288858, ⓦhttp://x-borderbiodiversity.tripod.com/kisaka.htm; ❸ for en-suite double with breakfast), a large and modern two-storey alpine-style building. There's no public transport along the 35km from Same, but a vehicle can be arranged through the *Sasakazi Restaurant*: you may well have to push it part of the way as the road is very steep.

Apart from the hike up **Shengena Peak**, local attractions – most of which can be walked in a few hours – include the Namoche Valley (scene of a victorious battle against the Maasai), warriors' graves, German ruins, local farms, waterfalls and viewpoints, and the **Kings' Stone**. This huge rocky outcrop about two hours from Chome was used for human sacrifices: victims were thrown off the top, whilst deformed or otherwise ill-starred babies were simply left there, along with many prayers, for God to take them back to the spirit world. It's a very steep and slippery climb through thick bush.

Mkomazi Game Reserve

Much of the grey-green bushland beyond the Pare and Usambara mountains is covered by **Mkomazi Game Reserve**, a wild and scenic stretch of baobab-studded savanna adjoining Kenya's Tsavo West National Park. The reserve provides an ideal habitat for a wide range of wildlife, including over 400 types of bird and dozens of species of large mammal. Of these, antelopes, lesser kudu, dikdik, gazelle and impala are frequently seen, whilst migratory herds of elephant, buffalo, oryx and zebra are also common. There are good odds on spotting lions, though the reserve's other predators – including leopards, cheetahs, and spotted and striped hyenas – are more elusive. A rarity is the gerenuk, an agile antelope that gets up on its hind legs to browse trees. Mkomazi's other two rare species, the African hunting dog and black rhino, are currently being bred in semi-captivity after having been hunted to extinction in the reserve.

Mkomazi is seldom visited by tourists and is – it must be said – a deeply controversial place. The controversy stems from the forcible **eviction of Maasai pastoralists** in 1988 on the grounds that their presence was destroying the reserve's fauna and flora. At the time, two decades of rampant poaching across Africa had pushed elephant and rhino populations to the brink of extinction. In Mkomazi, the entire stock of at least 150 black rhinos had been wiped out, and by 1988 there were only eleven elephants remaining. Given these desperate circumstances, extreme measures were called for, helped along by prevailing environmental wisdom that favoured the total exclusion of humans from wildlife parks and reserves (with the exception of researchers and tourists, of course). The Maasai were therefore evicted from the reserve, even though they had no tradition of hunting elephant or rhino, and the link between them and the depletion of wildlife in the reserve has never been proven.

The years since the expulsion of the Maasai have seen the gradual regeneration of Mkomazi's wildlife and ecology – a clear vindication for the policy of exclusion, or so it would seem. The truth, however, is much messier. Although internationally applauded by environmentalists, the eviction was condemned by human-rights groups for its forceful – and indeed illegal – nature. In any case, Mkomazi forms part of a much larger ecosystem that includes Kenya's Tsavo complex, to which many species – including elephants – migrate annually. It's possible, therefore, that some of Mkomazi's elephants may have been killed there, rather than in Tanzania, especially given the degree of poaching which Tsavo suffered until the Kenya Wildlife Service was reorganized on military lines and adopted an aggressive shoot-to-kill policy against suspected poachers. The 1989 international moratorium on the ivory trade also had a remarkable effect in reducing the number of elephant corpses logged in Tsavo, and so the argument that the expulsion of Mkomazi's Maasai revived elephant populations is open to doubt, at least.

Whatever the truth, the fact is that the majority of Mkomazi's former Maasai inhabitants now live in much more crowded areas just outside the reserve, which are insufficient to meet their needs in the dry season – indeed, fines paid by cattle herders caught inside Mkomazi's boundaries (whose pastures are greener than those outside the reserve) are apparently the reserve's single biggest source of income. Although efforts have been made to involve Maasai in an outreach programme (which, to be fair, is a huge task, involving at least 41 villages), Mkomazi's Maasai remain both powerless and voiceless over the running of the reserve which occupies their traditional lands.

For more on the environment-versus-pastoralism conflict, see the box "Ngorongoro's ecology" on p.449.

Practicalities

Mkomazi is not set up for tourism, although it's still possible to visit, which is best done as a day-trip from the South Pare Mountains. There are two main **gates**: the easiest to reach is Zange Gate, 7km east of Same along the road to Mbaga, which is where the reserve headquarters are located. The other is Njiro Gate, 19km beyond Zange Gate on the same road. **Transport** into the reserve can be arranged in Same through *Sasakazi Restaurant* (p.346) or via *Hill-Top Tona Lodge* in Mbaga (p.347). The cost, including a vehicle and driver, varies from $50 to $80 depending on the distance covered, plus $15 per person for the entry fee. Armed **ranger-guides** can be hired at the gates for walks inside the reserve; advance booking is recommended (write to the reserve headquarters at PO Box 41, Same, or phone ✆ Same 54). Accommodation is limited to one public **campsite**: Ibaya Camp, 15km from Zange Gate, though it has no facilities at all. Luxury walking and camping trips to the reserve are offered by the East African Safari & Touring Company in Arusha (p.397).

The **best time** to see wildlife is during the long rains (end of March to end of May), when around a thousand elephants, as well as other species, migrate down from Tsavo, although unfortunately the reserve's roads are liable to be impassable at this time. Dindira Dam is currently waterless, so the best places for spotting wildlife are Mbula and Kavateta waterholes. The **Mkomazi Rhino Project**, which currently houses eight translocated rhino in a heavily guarded enclosure at Kisima, 76km from Zange Gate, can only be visited by prior arrangement: for more information, see ⓦ www.mkomazi.com.

The Usambara Mountains

Southeast of the Pare Mountains rise the granite **USAMBARA MOUN-TAINS**, known as *Shambalai* by the local Sambaa tribe. Like the Pare Mountains, the Usambaras are part of the Eastern Arc chain (see p.343) and, again like Pare, form two distinct ranges – east and west – divided by the

Lwengera valley. The attractive town of **Lushoto** is the main settlement in **West Usambara** and the base for the region's outstanding cultural tourism programme – the perfect way to explore one of Tanzania's friendliest and most scenic areas. In the **East Usambaras,** the **Amani Nature Reserve** comprises one of the most diverse ecosystems on earth: a glorious area of thick rainforest clinging to steep slopes.

West Usambara

Around halfway along the Arusha–Dar highway, the spectacularly craggy western rim of the **West Usambara Mountains** rises with startling abruptness from the east side of the road to over one thousand metres above the plains.

The Sambaa and the Lion King

One reason for the survival of traditional **Sambaa culture** is that the steep Usambara Mountains were much more easily defended than the plains surrounding them – access was difficult until the construction of roads in the twentieth century. In addition, unlike most of northern Tanzania's tribes, who were originally – or still are – cattle herders, the Sambaa have always been cultivators (one possible derivation of their name is from *shamba*, a farm), resulting in settled communities and favouring intricate systems of leadership, and the Sambaa were no exception.

From around 1700 onwards, the Sambaa coalesced to form a kingdom under a chief called **Mbega** (or Mbegha), born to a Zigua chief in Ngulu, down in the plains. However, he was cheated of his rightful inheritance and forced to leave his birthplace, after which he wandered for many years, gaining fame as a skilled and generous hunter. Mbega finally settled in Kilindi in the plains, from where his reputation spread. At the time, the Sambaa were experiencing problems with an infestation of wild pigs, who were uprooting their crops, so they went to the famous hunter to ask his assistance. Mbega treated them with uncommon courtesy, and accepted the task of ridding Usambara of the problematic swine. Mbega set about his work, all the while distributing gifts of meat to the local people. Word of his skill, wisdom and fairness spread swiftly, and soon Mbega also became sought after for his skills in settling disputes. So much so that the people of Vuga, near Soni in West Usambara, asked him and his family (clan) to become their leader.

During his reign, which was characterized by intelligence and consideration, Mbega united the various rival Sambaa clans into one kingdom, the **Kilindi dynasty**. Mbega himself became known as Simbawene, **the Lion King**. The Kilindi dynasty reached its height at the start of the nineteenth century, when the Sambaa ruled not only over Usambara, but also over the Pare Mountains and much of the plains to the south and east. By the 1840s, however, the Zigua tribe of the plains was becoming dominant, thanks to their involvement in the **slave trade**, which gave them easy access to firearms, and by the time the Germans arrived in the 1880s, the Sambaa's military weakness was such that they capitulated to colonial rule without a fight.

The Kilindi dynasty ruled until 1962, when the Tanzanian Government abolished tribal chiefdoms. Nonetheless, the lineal descendants of Mbega are still known by his title of Lion King. The last, **Kimweri Mputa Magogo** (Mputa II) took office in 1947 and died in 1999. Although few people speak openly about his successor, there is little doubt that the new Lion King is already known by his subjects. Although the political power of the Sambaa is long gone, the effects of the Kilindi dynasty's domination are still evident – not so much outside Usambara, but in the way the Sambaa consider themselves: with great pride and humility, in the manner of Mbega. Wherever you go, you'll be made to feel very much at home.

Often shrouded in mist, these unexpected green mountains contain some of Tanzania's most spectacular hiking terrain, and are also as friendly and as welcoming a place as you're ever likely to find.

The practical nitty-gritty of getting around the mountains is a breeze, following the establishment of the **West Usambara Cultural Tourism Programme**, based in the region's main town, **Lushoto**, which offers a wealth of trips accompanied by qualified local guides, from half-day walks to longer treks over several days traversing the mountains from Lushoto to Mtae, whose vertiginous views are something you're unlikely to forget. Blend in low costs and a rich and colourful history and you have what should, by rights, become one of Tanzania's leading tourist destinations, on a par with Kilimanjaro, Serengeti and Zanzibar.

Mombo

The easiest way to reach Lushoto is on one of the direct early-morning buses from Arusha, Moshi or Tanga. If you can't do this, access to Lushoto is easiest via the hot and humid town of **MOMBO** at the foot of the mountains, 216km southeast of Moshi on the Arusha–Dar highway. **Daladalas** to Lushoto (90min) run every half-hour or so, leaving from the bottom of the road to Lushoto, 100m from the Arusha–Dar highway. In the unlikely event of getting stuck, there are some basic **hotels**, of which *Madaa Guest House* (no phone; ❶), 40m along the road to Lushoto, is probably the best. There are a few other choices on the highway towards Arusha, but these are more useful for **food and drink**. Another good place for eating is *New Liverpool Hill Breeze*, 1km north of town towards Moshi, where a lot of long-distance buses take a break: the food, especially grilled *mishkaki* meat skewers, is superb, as is the selection of Usambara fruit sold from the kiosks in the parking lot. The *New Liverpool Hill Breeze* is also a good place for finding safe and comfortable transport to Arusha or Dar – buses from better companies like Scandinavian stop here, but not always in Mombo itself.

A word of caution: **don't hire a guide in Mombo** or on the daladala to Lushoto, no matter how genuine they appear to be. None is officially authorized, and although one or two might be reasonable, most are just in it for a quick buck, and there have also been reports of robberies. Wait until you get to the tourist office in Lushoto, and hire a guide there.

Soni

The road up into the mountains from Mombo follows the vertiginous gorge of the **Bangala River** which, if you can stop worrying about the unfenced chasm to your left, is an absolutely spectacular ride that takes you from the flat and dry expanse of the Maasai Steppe into an utterly different world: green, lush and heavily forested, with towering mountain peaks glimpsed over waterfalls and some precariously balanced ridgetop villages and farmhouses. The first major place you hit is **SONI**, a bustling village just above the **Soni Falls**, where the Mkuzu River becomes the Bangala, which is famed for its twice-weekly **market** (Tues & Fri) at which the entire array of West Usambara produce can be found. The plums, passion fruit, mountain papaya (sweeter and more delicate than the lowland variety), coconuts and pineapples are especially good. The prices, for tourists, aren't always as good as they should be, but you can't really complain given the quality – and the taste. Soni is part of the **cultural tourism programme** based in Lushoto; see p.356 for more details.

Accommodation is available at the *New Soni Falls Hotel*, which has twin rooms with bathroom (**❷**). Another good place, which is also great for arranging **hiking**, is *Maweni Motel*, a few kilometres east of Soni (PO Box 6, Soni; **ⓔ** elct_ned@tanga.net), which is run by Juma Kahema – an experienced guide, and one of only a few who really know the five-day trail to Amani in East Usambara (see p.364).

Lushoto

Past Soni, the scenery becomes even more spectacular as you wind further up into the mountains and through a land of forest and steep cultivated slopes to reach **LUSHOTO**, half an hour beyond Soni and 34km from Mombo. Despite being the biggest town in the Usambaras, with population of over 100,000, the district capital is an intimate, friendly and instantly likeable kind of place, and enjoys an especially beautiful setting among high forested peaks. And for the visitor, there's the double bonus of good cheap accommodation and an excellent cultural tourism programme.

The first European to reach Lushoto was the missionary **Johann Ludwig Krapf**, who in 1849 was given a warm welcome by King Kimweri I. European interest remained marginal until 1886, when arch-colonist Karl Peters – nicknamed "the man with bloodstained hands" by locals and described as "a model colonial administrator" by Adolf Hitler – entered the Usambaras and "persuaded" the local chief to sign away his domain for a pittance. The subsequent German advance was made easier in that, in the latter half of the nineteenth century, Usambara was racked by chaos: the **slave trade** had begun to turn its sights to the mountains, and at the same time the Kilindi dynasty was caught up in a civil war against the Bondei tribe, who wanted independence.

Lushoto's altitude (1500m) ensures a cool and temperate climate all year round, and made it a favoured mountain retreat for German colonial administrators, who called the town **Wilhelmstal** (after the German Kaiser). For a time, it even served as the unofficial "summer capital" of German East Africa – a welcome change from the sweltering heat and humidity of Dar es Salaam.

Arrival

Lushoto is served by direct early-morning **buses** from Arusha, Moshi and Tanga, and by direct **daladalas** from Tanga. If you miss these, catch a bus to Dar or Tanga from Arusha or Moshi (or to Arusha and Moshi from Dar or Tanga), and get off in Mombo (p.351), from where there are frequent daladalas throughout the day to Lushoto. The **bus stand** is in the centre of town next to the market. The first place to head for is the **Tourist Information Centre** (**☏**027/264 0159, **ⓔ**usambaras2000@yahoo.co.uk or elct_ned@tanga.net; daily 8am–6pm), behind the National Microfinance Bank and signposted from the bus stand. Try not to be waylaid by guides pretending to be "official" along the way – the tourist office is clearly marked. Operated by the Friends of Usambara Society, the staff are friendly and helpful, and provide up-to-date information and impartial advice on accommodation, nightlife, transport and practicalities, as well as the various locally run **cultural tourism programme** tours (see p.356), which are organized from here. They should also have a copy of *Usambara View* to consult, an excellent annual guidebook to the area, packed with useful information and well-written articles.

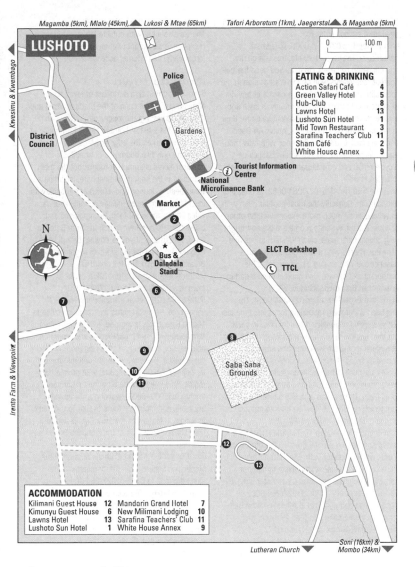

Magamba (5km), Mlalo (45km), ▲ Lukosi & Mtae (65km)   Tafori Arboretum (1km), Jaegerstal ▲ & Magamba (5km)

LUSHOTO

0   100 m

Krvesimu & Kwembago

Police

District
Council

Gardens

Tourist Information
Centre

National
Microfinance Bank

Market

ELCT Bookshop

TTCL

N

Bus &
Daladala
Stand

Irente Farm & Viewpoint

Saba Saba
Grounds

EATING & DRINKING

Action Safari Café	4
Green Valley Hotel	5
Hub-Club	8
Lawns Hotel	13
Lushoto Sun Hotel	1
Mid Town Restaurant	3
Sarafina Teachers' Club	11
Sham Café	2
White House Annex	9

ACCOMMODATION

Kilimani Guest House	12	Mandarin Grand Hotel	7
Kimunyu Guest House	6	New Milimani Lodging	10
Lawns Hotel	13	Sarafina Teachers' Club	11
Lushoto Sun Hotel	1	White House Annex	9

Soni (16km) &
Lutheran Church ▼   Mombo (34km) ▼

Accommodation

Lushoto has a good spread of budget and mid-range **hotels**, and there are a couple of charmingly rustic farmhouses further out (though you'll really need your own wheels for these). **Camping** is allowed at *Lawns Hotel* in town (Tsh3000 per person), and also outside town at *Grant's Lodge* and *Müller's Mountain Lodge*.

In town

Kilimani Guest House (no phone). A quiet place with twelve rooms (shared bathrooms only) flanking a courtyard containing a somnolent bar. Food is

available, including breakfast (Tsh1000). ❶

Kimunyu Guest House (no phone). The best of several hotels on the road looping above the Saba Saba Grounds, with a friendly welcome and simple but clean rooms with shared bathrooms (the better ones have big box nets). **❶**

Lawns Hotel ☎027/264 0005, ✉lawns@ habari.co.tz. Over a century old, this is a quirky and charming place – so long as you heed the belligerent "complaints won't be tolerated" sign in the reception. The bedrooms have a choice of private or shared bathrooms but vary greatly in style and quality: the better ones are excellent value for their creaking floorboards, fireplaces, heavy Art Deco beds and cast-iron baths; the ones with tatty modern furniture are overpriced. Amenities include bicycle rental and a restaurant and bar. Breakfast included. **❸–❹**

Lushoto Sun Hotel ☎027/264 0082, ✉bhazali@ hotmail.com. Currently the most popular hotel with travellers, albeit much more expensive than other options. The ten en-suite rooms are big and bright, with double beds, nets, clean Western toilets and showers. There's also a twin-bed room, and a cheaper one with shared bathroom (**❷**). The restaurant and bar are also good, and safe parking is available. Breakfast included. **❸**

Mandarin Grand Hotel ☎027/264 0014. This has been undergoing rebuilding for at least the last ten years, and resembles a building site in parts, but the view over Lushoto is the saving grace. The seventeen rooms are well kept and spacious; you've a choice of overpriced singles sharing bathrooms, or much better-value en-suite doubles and twins, some with bathtubs *and* enough hot water to fill them. There's also a sleepy bar and a restaurant which requires at least an hour to produce anything. Breakfast included. **❸**

New Milimani Lodging ☎027/264 0151. Very cheap and clean if slightly tired, with a choice of rooms with or without bath – the former have large double beds, mosquito nets and cement baths (but no plugs and erratic hot water only). **❶**

Sarafina Teachers' Club ☎027/264 0087. Cheap, clean and good-value rooms (shared bathrooms only) in a calm and friendly place. **❶**

White House Annex ☎027/264 0177, ✉whitehouse@raha.com. One of the best cheap options, this popular and friendly family-run place has seven rooms, five with private bathroom. There's also a bar with outside tables, TV in the reception, a restaurant with an excellent reputation (order early) and internet access. **❶–❷**

Outside town

Grant's Lodge 14km northeast of town at Migambo by the junction of the roads to Mlalo and Kifungilo ⊕www.grantslodge.com; reserve on ☎ & ℱ027/264 2491. A homely 1950s farmhouse in a 35-acre farm on the edge of Magamba Forest. There are only five bedrooms (four suitable for families), some sharing bathrooms, but the main attraction is the country atmosphere, including a wood-beamed lounge and a lawn at the back with lots of birds. Amenities include a Finnish sauna, a video library, excellent food, hiking guides and babysitters. To get there, catch the 2pm Satellite Bus from Lushoto; if you're driving, turn right at Magamba and follow the signs to Migambo. Breakfast included. **❻**, full board **❼**

Müller's Mountain Lodge 12km northeast of town near Mkuzi Forest ☎027/264 0204, ℱ027/264 0205, ✉mullersmountainlodge@ yahoo.com. Set in orchards and farmland close to Mkuzu Forest, this is a grand, two-storey 1930s farmhouse with steep gable roofs and a comfortable interior, including a cosy living room with a big fireplace. There are seven bedrooms; the better ones (Tsh4000 extra) come with private bathrooms. Amenities include a bar and restaurant (meals Tsh5000–6000), walking trails (guides available) and mountain tours by car. To get there, turn right at Magamba towards *Grant's* and turn right again after 5:3km at the signpost. Breakfast included. **❹**

Saint Eugene's Hostel Catholic Mission of the Montessori Sisters, Ubiri (thirty minutes' walk along the road to Soni) ☎027/264 0055, ℱ027/264 0267. Fourteen clean and comfortable en-suite rooms in a modern Swedish-style building, each with a balcony. There's a warm welcome, and great food. A good if pricey choice. Breakfast included. **❹**

The Town

Apart from its views and the cultural tourism programme (see p.356), Lushoto's main attraction is its colourful **market**, which is liveliest on Thursday and Sunday, when farmers descend from all around. Sunday is especially good for buying **traditional pottery** – either plain, or decorated with geometric incisions inspired by plants. **Fruit** is another Usambara speciality, especially apples and pears around Easter time, peaches and plums from December to February, and berries all year round, but best from October to January. Look out for traditional medicinal herbs and bark (*madawa asili*), honey (*asali*) and *viungo vya* *chai*, which is powdered ginger (*tangawizi*) mixed with other spices for adding to tea – a small jar costs Tsh500. The best bargains can be found late evening when vendors want to go home.

In addition, many buildings survive from the period of German rule, including a bizarre construction at the top end of town whose belfry is topped by an onion-shaped steeple made from iron sheeting. Also dating from colonial times is **Tafori Arboretum**, 1km north of town, which contains botanical gardens and houses thousands of pressed plants collected from all over the country. To see the collection, ask at the arboretum for Mr Msangi or Mr Mabula.

Eating, drinking and nightlife

The fare in local **restaurants** isn't up to much, although if you have time try to get someone to cook up *bada*, a Sambaa speciality consisting of a thick, greenish-brown porridge of pounded maize flour and dried fermented cassava mixed with hot water and oil and served in aromatic banana leaves. It's exceedingly tasty, and is eaten like *ugali* by being dipped in sauces. *Bada* is usually served with chicken or meat, fried bananas or potatoes. Lushoto is also a delight if you're **self-catering**. Your first stop for putting together a picnic should be the market (see above) for fruit and vegetables – amazingly cheap, even by Tanzanian standards. Irente Farm (p.357) is a good place to stock up on homemade jams, preserves and cheeses, as is the Catholic Mission of the Montessori Sisters in Ubiri (see opposite), who also brew and sell the surprisingly palatable Dochi banana wine. If you're still thirsty, the Benedictine Fathers, in Sakharani near Soni, make Tanzania's best grape wine under the Sakharani label, as well as macadamia nuts and oil.

Action Safari Café This sees plenty of tourists, and is consequently slightly more expensive than other places, but still perfectly good, offering a mixture of local dishes and tourist favourites like spaghetti.

Lawns Hotel A tasty three-course lunch or dinner in a quirky dining room decorated with commemorative plates from around the globe goes for Tsh5500 (Tsh4500 for vegetarian; free if you bring a plate to add to the collection), plus snacks and light meals for under Tsh1500.

Lushoto Sun Hotel Good cheap food (under Tsh1500), including steak, which you can eat at the streetside terrace-bar.

Mid Town Restaurant. Cheap local eats: *nyama choma*, fried chicken and chip omelettes.

Sham Café A great little place for cheap and unfussy meals, and they're happy to rustle up something special if you contact them beforehand. They also provide hot milk – a favourite with locals and gorgeous on a cold day.

White House Annex One of the best places for eating out in Lushoto, there's an extensive menu covering most bases and, if you order early, they'll come up with pretty much anything you might want. Full meals for under Tsh5000.

Drinking and nightlife

The following are the best of the town's numerous **bars**. Many sell the favourite local hooch, *boha*, a sugar-cane wine popular with both men and women – especially the latter during musical festivities such as Holy Communion, when the night resounds to drum beats and songs.

Green Valley Hotel This restaurant nowadays mainly sees service as a friendly and laid-back drinking place, popular with both sexes as well as the odd *mzungu*.

Hub-Club Functions as a bar by day, screens films on Wednesday and Friday at 7.30pm, and has a lively disco on Saturday nights with a big range of musical styles.

Lawns Hotel Contains Lushoto's nicest bar, very cosy and pub-like, and equipped with satellite TV. The Cypriot owner offers a free drink for unusual foreign coins to add to the zillions glued to the counter.

Sarafina Teachers' Club A pleasant and laid-back place open till past midnight; also does good *nyama choma*.

Listings

Banks National Microfinance Bank, at the corner near the Tourist Information Centre, changes cash and travellers' cheques without fuss, and doesn't normally need to see a purchase receipt.
Bicycles Mountain bikes from *Lawns Hotel* cost Tsh500 per hour or Tsh3000 a day.
Bookshop ELCT Bookshop, has some English-language books and also sells stationery. It's next to the telephone office on the main road.

Car rental Ask at *Lawns Hotel*, People's Communication Centre at the Saba Saba Grounds, or the Tourist Information Centre.
Hospital The district hospital is about 1.5km back along the road to Soni.
Internet and email access There are three places with internet access: *White House Annex* (daily 8am–midnight; Tsh3000 per hour), ELCT-NED Computer Centre on the main road (Mon–Fri 9am–6pm; Tsh4000 per hour), and People's Communication Centre at the Saba Saba Grounds.

Moving on from Lushoto

Lushoto has daily **bus** services to Arusha, Dar and Tanga, as well as Mtae (see p.358). To **Arusha**, Fasaha VIP heads off around 7.30am – get there early as the exact time depends on when it arrives from Mtae. There's also a minibus with less regular times. There are at least two daily buses to **Dar**, both rickety; the last leaves around 10am. For **Muheza and Tanga**, Umba River Tours and Sai Baba are the main bus companies; the Nevada minibus, which heads off at 6am, is quicker (and potentially more dangerous). Alternatively, catch a daladala down to Mombo (every 30min), and change there for another one to Tanga.

West Usambara Cultural Tourism Programme

Over the past decade, Lushoto has become home to one of Tanzania's foremost cultural tourism programmes, and deservedly so. Set up by local farmers with assistance from German and Dutch NGOs, the **West Usambara Cultural Tourism Programme** offers almost a dozen different guided tours around West Usambara, ranging from three-hour strolls to challenging five-day hikes through some of Tanzania's most inspiring landscapes. The most popular "modules" are described below. Several can be combined into tours lasting several days.

Although you're not obliged to take a **guide**, most of them know the trails backwards, and of course your payments help local people directly. All speak at least reasonable English and all are of course fluent in Kiswahili and Kisambaa, which makes for intimate and enjoyable encounters with local people. **Payments** are made at the Tourist Information Centre; ensure that you're issued a receipt. Day walks are a bargain at Tsh10,000 for the first person plus Tsh2000 for additional visitors up to a maximum of five people (larger groups are assigned additional guides). Longer treks over several days cost a little more, around Tsh17,000 per person per day including accommodation. Please do not dole out pens, sweets, money or anything else to local kids – you'll be encouraging a begging culture which is currently almost absent. Lastly, a **word of warning**: there have been a number of unpleasant incidents involving unofficial guides, ranging from shoddy service to knifepoint muggings. Authorized guides have photo ID cards, but these aren't infallible as some con-merchants make their own. The only sure way is to hire a guide at the Tourist Information Centre in Lushoto, not in hotels, on buses or anywhere else.

Bangala River, Growing Rock and Mazumbai Forest

There are a couple of good half-day tours around Soni, taking about six hours each. The refreshing **Bangala River Tour** starts at Mbuzi ("Goat") village between Lushoto and Soni, and follows the river downstream to the Soni Falls (you may be obliged to wade across). The **Growing Rock**, near Magila village, tells the story of soil erosion – the rock (and the story) seems to grow taller every year, though in fact it's the soil around the base that is disappearing. The tour includes Mount Kwamongo (good views and butterflies) and Shashui and Kwemula villages. The **Mazumbai Forest** trip is more challenging, taking at least four days (Tsh25,000 per person plus Tsh4000 forest fee) through a variety of terrain to Mazumbai rainforest – a great place for birds.

Irente Viewpoint, Irente Farm and Orphanage

The walk to and from **Irente Viewpoint** (5–6hr) is the most popular short trek from Lushoto, and relatively easy; take a guide, though, as muggers have been known to prey on lone tourists. The viewpoint, perched on the southwestern edge of the Usambaras, is reached after a two-hour walk through farms and small villages and offers a truly breathtaking panorama over the Maasai Steppe almost a kilometre below. The isolated range facing you with the knuckle-like outline is Mount Mafi. If you'd like **to stay**, *Irente Viewpoint Campsite* (T & F 027/264 4693) has camping space (Tsh2500 per person), two *bandas* and two permanent tents (2) right on the cliff edge, hot showers and a small bar (but no food).

On the return leg, most people stop by the Lutheran-run **Irente Farm** (T 027/264 0089, E irente@elct.org), an ideal picnic break with plenty of seating in colourful shaded gardens. The farm shop sells organic produce, cheese (German-style quark curd, a kind of Camembert and one like Tilziter), pickles and preserves, macadamia nuts, *Arabica* coffee and various flavoured teas from the Lutindi Mental Hospital near Korogwe at the base of the mountains. Staying overnight, you can either **camp** (Tsh1000 per pitch, including shower and toilet, plus Tsh1000 for a watchman), or use their en-suite double room (2). Breakfast costs Tsh1500 and they do a good picnic lunch – a bargain at Tsh1000 (minimum three people).

Adjacent to the farm is **Irente Children's Home**, also run by the church, around which the matron will be happy to accompany you. Poverty and AIDS are the main problems affecting the age-old stability of the extended family; in some cases the latter has wiped out entire generations. The home houses over twenty orphans, disabled children and children of parents with psychiatric disorders, and also trains older girls – who look after the little 'uns – in prenursing care and basic schooling. The home has had no regular funding since 1996; **accommodation** for tourists is in the pipeline – ask at the Tourist Information Centre or ring ahead (T 027/264 0086).

Magamba Rainforest

The physically demanding but extremely rewarding walk through **Magamba Rainforest** north of Lushoto gives you the chance of spotting black-and-white colobus monkeys, exotic birds like the paradise flycatcher, plenty of butterflies and weird fungi. The name of the forest means fish or snake scales in Kiswahili, referring to the bark of the trees which had to be stripped away before the wood could be used. Most visitors come on a round trip from Lushoto (5–6hr), though the forest can easily be combined with a trip to Irente Viewpoint.

The tour begins with a stiff uphill hike along tracks to the east of the Lushoto–Magamba road, passing through the former colonial settlement of

Jaegerstal and a camphorwood forest. Just north of **Magamba village** (there's a small café here, and fruit and vegetable hawkers), a track heads west into the forest. Emerging onto a forestry road, you have the choice of delving back into the forest for a quick descent towards Kwembago (see below) or continuing uphill along the road to a ridge offering expansive views over Lushoto, the Maasai Steppe, and an area of low bushland to the northwest studded with dead trees destroyed in a devastating 1996 fire.

From the ridge, the track continues south to a **rest house** on top of Kiguu Hakwewa hill, whose name translates as "unclimbed by short leg", meaning steep. There are 360-degree views and a toilet, while a bar and restaurant are planned. If you (literally) stomp around here, you'll notice that the hill appears to be hollow, as indeed it is: it was excavated during World War I for use as a bunker by German residents. The bunker is said to contain almost one hundred rooms: you're free to explore them, although you'll need a torch, and watch out for snakes. The entrance is a hundred metres downhill on the southeastern flank.

From the hill, a steep and rocky path heads down through farmland to the royal village of **Kwembago**, which was one of the seats of the Kilindi dynasty and which has a good view over Lushoto.

Mlalo

The walk from Lushoto to **MLALO** and back takes three or four days (with some sections covered by bus), but is best combined with a visit to Mtae (see below) to make a six- or seven-day round trip. The walk includes Magamba Rainforest (see p.357), followed by a bus ride direct to Mlalo, or to Malindi, from where you walk. There's simple **accommodation** in several villages along the way, and also at the *Silver Dollar Guest House* (❶) in Mlalo, which has clean rooms with shared bathrooms, and a good restaurant.

Mlalo is a good base for a day or two. **Mtumbi Hill** – Usambara's highest – can be climbed from here, and there are several good markets in the area. **Kileti village** (also called Kwemieeti) is the main attraction, being one of the best places for meeting female potters. The Sambaa liken the art of pottery to the creation of life in a mother's womb, so it's no surprise that pottery is traditionally a woman's occupation, with knowledge and rituals connected with the craft being passed from mother to daughter. Although men are allowed to collect clay, they are excluded from the pot-making process itself – it's believed that their presence may anger spirits, who might crack the pots during firing or, still worse, cause sterility.

Mtae and around

The **road to Mtae**, on the far northwestern rim of the Usambaras, is the most popular long excursion from Lushoto, taking three to five days depending on how much you "cheat" by catching the bus. Although the trip can be done without a guide, you'll miss much of the local context and contacts that make this walk special. The views are spectacular, especially as you approach Mtae, and the villages between are as fascinating and pretty as they are friendly, offering plenty of opportunities for getting to meet locals.

Passing by Magamba rainforest (see p.357) and **Shume rainforest** (where you might glimpse black-and-white colobus monkeys, even from the bus), **LUKOSI** is the first stop, an attractive agricultural village set in a high valley with a couple of basic **guest houses** (❶) should you want to stay. The forest has been cleared around the village, but comes back to flank the road between

Lukosi and **Shume-Viti**, an equally attractive, if dusty, village in a wide valley entirely covered with small plots which reminds some people of Europe. The village is the first place you'll see the unusual two-storey houses with intricately carved wooden balconies, accessed via outside staircases, which are a feature of all the villages north of here, including **Shume-Manolo**, **Shume-Kibaoni**, **Rangwi** and **Sunga**, all of which can be reached on foot. Also distinctive are the whitewashed houses with facades and interiors painted with decorative geometric designs reminiscent of Ndebele house paintings in South Africa or Ethiopian religious art – perhaps no coincidence, as some oral histories place the origins of the Sambaa in Ethiopia.

The village of **MTAE** itself, situated on the northwesternmost edge of the Usambara Mountains, is a delightful place that regales the eyes with views that you'll remember for the rest of your life. The location is everything: isolated on a spur that juts out from the mass of West Usambara, and flanked by tiny hamlets with rust-red roofs perched along nearby ridges and peaks. At some places you have a plunging 270-degree view over the plains almost a kilometre below, giving the impression that you're hovering above them, and with clear skies, especially in the evenings, you can see the Taita Hills in Kenya to the north and the Pare Mountains and sometimes Kilimanjaro to the southwest – before the sun disappears in a kaleidoscope of colours and smoke from kitchens drifts into the air. During and just after the rains you might wake to the extraordinary sight of being above a blanket of clouds that stretches all the way over Mkomazi to the north and the Pare Mountains in the west. At any time of year, you'll wake to the drifting sound of cock crows and lowing cattle, followed by goats and children, while on Sundays the bells ring out from the nineteenth-century Lutheran church, complete with the church's boisterous (if not always tuneful) brass band.

Practicalities

Mtae is best visited as part of Lushoto's cultural tourism programme (see p.356), with whom you can walk all or part of the way. **Public transport** is limited to one or two buses daily. The ride up from Lushoto, along a narrow dirt road, often with sheer drops on one side, is one of the bumpiest (if most scenic) in Tanzania, but isn't advisable in the rainy seasons. The most reliable bus is Fasaha VIP, which leaves Lushoto at 2pm (3–4hr), passing via Magamba, Lukosi, Shume-Viti, Shume-Manolo and Shume-Kibaoni. Arrive early to be sure of a seat. There's often an additional service coming from Dar or Tanga that leaves Lushoto at the same time or a little earlier. The Fasaha VIP bus **back from Mtae** leaves at the unearthly time of 3am or 4am (double-check the day before), with the other bus – if there is one – leaving when full, which can be anything between 4.30am and 6am. If you miss these, you'll have to spend another night in Mtae – no great hardship. Ask the driver or conductor to wake you up, but take care with the fare, as some conductors aren't averse to overcharging.

The goat and the leopard

Mtae's motto is *Kesi ya mbuzi hakimu ni chui haki hakuna*, which means, "In the case of the goat with the leopard as judge, there is no justice." The saying is illustrated by paintings hung up in some of the town's bars, and depicts a courtroom presided over by a leopard. The plaintiff is a lion, the defendant a goat. The saying alludes to colonial times, when there was little chance of justice for an African from a German judge when the plaintiff was a German farmer.

The best **restaurant** is attached to *Mwivano Guest House #1*. For **drinking**, *Mtitu wa Ndei* bar is next to the *Pendo Guest House*. If you need medical attention, try the dispensary in the Lutheran mission. Mtae's high altitude, exposed location and strong winds make it chilly at night, so bring a sweater, and wear suncream – the suns burns more quickly at this altitude. **Accommodation** is limited to the following.

Kuna Maneno Guest House ☎027/264 0200. Currently being renovated, this is the only establishment in the village with electricity, though powered by a none-too-reliable generator. There are nine rooms (eight doubles and one twin; shared bathrooms only) and reliable piped water, plus a large but usually empty bar. ❶

Lutheran Mission c/o ELCT in Lushoto ☎027/264 0102. This has nine recently converted rooms in a wing adjacent to the church, all of them spacious and with high ceilings and creaking floorboards. Food is available if ordered in the morning for the evening. ❷

Mount Usambara Guest House (no phone). Eight rooms with shared facilities (and hot water in buckets), of which two have fantastic views westwards over Lake Kalimawe and the Pare Mountains beyond. ❶

Mwivano Guest House ☎027/264 0198. This is actually two hotels on the main road. Number 1 has nine cell-like singles with clean shared showers and toilets, next to a restaurant. Number 2, 200m back on the left, is more attractive, and has double rooms with shared bathrooms and stunning views through chicken-wire mesh windows over Mkomazi Game Reserve. ❶

Pendo Guest House ☎027/264 0198. Mtae's least attractive choice, with five dingy and dirty-looking singles and one twin-bed room. ❶

Mtae Mtii

A leisurely and recommended four-hour walk goes from Mtae to the small village of **MTAE MTII**, the traditional seat of the Kilindi dynasty in northwest Usambara until the chiefdoms were abolished in 1962 (the main seat was Vuga near Soni). Mtae Mtii was also the site of a semi-mythical nineteenth-century battle between the Sambaa and the Maasai, who lived in the plains below. The story goes that the Maasai believed that the king of Usambara had the power to bring rain to the plains, so one day they went to ask him for rain. He refused, and the Maasai resolved to fight. Although the Maasai were better equipped, the Sambaa vanquished their attackers by rolling boulders down the steep inclines, killing most of them. As spoils, the Sambaa seized the Maasai cattle (the Sambaa had previously never owned cattle), which locals say are the ancestors of the cows you'll see grazing contentedly in the mountains today.

The last king of Mtae Mtii died in the late 1990s. His **compound** can be visited as part of the cultural tourism programme and has a fantastic location on a crag overlooking the Mkomazi plains. Next to the surprisingly humble (and now abandoned) hut where the king lived is an enclosure made from branches, bushes and some recently planted seedlings.

East Usambara

Some forty kilometres inland, the mountains of **EAST USAMBARA** rise abruptly from the coastal lowlands, their steep escarpments levelling off at about a kilometre above sea level onto a deeply furrowed plateau. The range is separated both physically and biologically from West Usambara by the four-kilometre-wide Lwengera valley. With the exception of the dry lowlands to the north, the climate is warm and humid, influenced by the proximity of the Indian Ocean. Rainfall averages 2000mm a year which, together with the deeply weathered red loam soils, has created ideal conditions for the evolution of an astonishingly rich and complex tropical rainforest ecosystem.

The figures speak for themselves: East Usambara's rainforests contain well over 2000 vascular plant species, over a quarter of which are found nowhere else in the world, as are sixteen of East Usambara's 230 different tree species. The proportion of unique species amongst animals is even more astounding, ranging from ten to sixty percent depending on the family and genera. Other inhabitants of East Usambara include over thirty species of snakes and chameleons, amongst them the terrestrial pygmy leaf chameleon, the larger arboreal three-horned chameleon and a remarkable species of toad, *Nectophrynoides tornieri*, which gives birth to live offspring instead of eggs. There are also over 200 species of butterfly and close to 350 types of bird. The most famous of Usambara's endemics, however, is the **African violet**. Their botanical name, *Saintpaulia*, comes from Baron Walter von Saint Paul Illaire, the Tanga district commissioner of German East Africa, who in 1892 shipped a consignment of the small blue flowers to Berlin, thereby starting a horticultural craze which continues to this day.

The most accessible part of the East Usambaras is the **Amani Nature Reserve**, a fantastic area of mountainous rainforest reached from the Dar–Tanga highway, where you'll find hiking trails, guides and reasonably priced accommodation.

Amani Nature Reserve

Established in 1997, the mountainous **Amani Nature Reserve** (Amani means "peace" in Kiswahili) is one of Tanzania's most attractive and under-visited destinations, offering beautiful scenery, weird and wonderful flora and fauna, a constant chorus of cicadas and tree frogs (joined by the screeching of bushbabies at night), one of Africa's largest botanical gardens and enough hiking trails through primeval rainforest to keep you in raptures (or blister packs) for weeks. Even if your interest in things botanical is limited to the greens on your plate, the sight of the towering East African camphor trees festooned with vines, lianas or strangling fig trees that flank much of the drive up to the reserve is the stuff of dreams.

Bird-watchers will also be in dreamland, despite difficult viewing conditions (the forest canopy conceals birds well), with 335 species having been recorded, including the endangered Amani sunbird, the long-billed apalis and the banded green sunbird which, although rare outside East Usambara, can sometimes be seen at Amani in flocks of up to sixty. Other rare species include the Usambara red-headed bluebill, long-billed tailorbird, Sokoke scops owl (named after Arabuko-Sokoke forest in Kenya), Usambara eagle owl, Tanzanian weaver and the green-headed oriole.

There are few large **mammals** in the forest, which makes sighting them all the more rewarding, though all you're likely to see of the shy black-and-white colobus monkey is a flash of black and white in the canopy as it retreats into deeper forest. Other primates include yellow baboons and blue monkeys, both of which are pests for farmers – it's said that if you throw stones at blue monkeys to chase them off crops, they just pick them up and hurl them back, often with better accuracy. The Tanganyika mountain squirrel is the most common of the three squirrel species; if you're really lucky, the rufous elephant shrew may put in a fleeting appearance on the forest paths.

Practicalities

Amani is reached via **MUHEZA**, a bustling small town at the junction of the A14 highway and the road to Pangani, 45km southwest from Tanga. **Sigi Gate**, where you pay your entrance fees, is on the reserve's eastern edge, 26km west of Muheza along a graded all-weather murram road. The next 9km to Amani

Conserving Amani

Up until the end of the nineteenth century, East Usambara was extensively covered with forest, with a small human population. The advent of colonialism had far-reaching consequences for natural habitats in Tanzania. The main factor was the **expulsion of local people** from land that colonists wanted to use for commercial ranches and plantations. The Usambaras were an obvious destination for people displaced in the northeast of Tanzania, and very soon the forests began to shrink. The figures are sobering: from an estimated 100,000 hectares of prime forest cover in 1900, East Usambara now contains only 33,000 hectares, of which only a tenth remains relatively intact and undisturbed.

The single most damaging force to hit East Usambara's forests, however, was the large-scale **timber logging** which took place between the late 1950s and the 1980s. The now infamous Sikh Saw Mills was established in Tanga for processing East Usambara timber into plywood and sawnwood, and in the 1970s expanded its operations with funding from the Finnish government's development agency. It was only in 1986 that the Finns abruptly realized how grossly they had underestimated the damage that their rough logging methods were causing. Commercial logging was terminated, and the Finns promptly performed a perfect volte-face to espouse the cause of conservation, to the tune of $6.1 million between 1991 and 1998, in funding the delete **East Usambara Catchment Forest Project**.

The nature reserve, the first of its kind in Tanzania, was created as part of the project, both to protect one of East Africa's finest surviving rainforests and to safeguard Tanga's water supply against the effects of unchecked forest clearance and unsustainable farming methods. To the lasting credit of the reserve's new management, the renamed **East Usambara Conservation Area Programme** has not only managed to stem the destruction of the forest but has also embarked on ambitious reforestation and educational outreach programmes in sustainable agriculture for local farmers. In 2001, they achieved the long-delayed protection of Derema Forest Reserve, adjacent to Amani, and now plan to link a series of existing and planned forest reserves north to south across East Usambara to create a "biological corridor" for plants and animals.

---

village, much of it hairpins, is much rougher, and becomes treacherously slippery in the rains (especially in Nov and April), when it may require 4WD.

Muheza is served by frequent daladalas from Lushoto, Mombo and Tanga, and by buses connecting Tanga with Dar and Arusha. **Buses** and **daladalas** drop you on the main road or at the bus stand. To reach the transport stand for Amani from the main road, walk up into town following the large sign for Amani Nature Reserve and passing the bus stand on your left. Some 200m beyond the bus stand, the road forks: bear right and then take the first right. The unmarked stand for Amani is about 50m along on the left before the railway crossing, opposite the encouragingly named Death Row Electronics shop. All transport to Amani – pick-ups, Land Rovers and lorries – leaves Muheza between 1pm and 4pm, so aim to get there by midday. If you're feeling energetic, you could catch a vehicle to **Kisiwani village**, 3km short of Sigi Gate, leaving you a very pleasant three-kilometre uphill walk through forest. If you arrive at Muheza in the morning, you shouldn't have too much trouble hitching (payment will be requested), but if you arrive after 4pm you'll probably have to spend the night there. The town's best **accommodation** is the *Ambassador Guest House* (**2**), 300m along the Tanga road by the Oryx Filling Station. The *Ambassador Hotel* next door serves good **food**, as does the *Step Inn Hotel*, also on main road next to the bus stand. If you've a few hours to kill, Muheza's busy **market** is worth poking around, and is a good place to stock up on honey (*asali*), a speciality from Amani that is especially delectable after the rains. Heading **back to Muheza** from Amani, most transport leaves Amani village between 6am and 7am, passing Sigi Gate about half an hour later. After then you'll have to hitch.

Entry fees and information

Entry fees are paid at the reserve's **information centre** at Sigi Gate: fees are $5 per person (no time limit), plus $2 vehicle entry and $4 for a photo permit. A guide (optional) costs $10 a day, and camping is $5 per person. Payment in shillings is accepted at the current exchange rate. The centre also provides informative leaflets and maps, and sells the detailed *Guide to Trails and Drive Routes in Amani Nature Reserve*; they may also have vehicles for hire at the gate and can advise about campsites and arrange guided walks. A small shop sells attractive painted cards and the lavishly illustrated *Trees of Amani Nature Reserve*, which details hundreds of Amani's tree species together with a general introduction about the reserve and its ecosystem. But the centre's main draw is its thoughtfully presented displays about local flora, birdlife, chameleons, butterflies and moths, amphibians, plant ecology and biodiversity and, of course, African violets, as well as a few rooms of Sambaa and Bondei artefacts. For booking accommodation and further information, contact the chief conservator at the **reserve headquarters** in Amani village: PO Box 1, Amani ☎027/264 3453 or 264 6907, ⓦ www.usambara.com; the headquarters should also have stocks of books and leaflets for sale.

Accommodation in the reserve

The reserve has three **rest houses**. At Sigi Gate, the modern and comfortable *Sigi Rest House* (reservations through the chief conservator, see above; ❸) has nine large, triple-bed rooms with electricity, mosquito nets, hot showers and the use of a kitchen. A small bar and restaurant sells cold sodas and beers, and rustles up great meals if ordered in advance. There are two more rest houses in Amani village, 9km from Sigi Gate. The *Amani Conservation Centre Rest House* is similar to *Sigi Rest House* (same contacts and prices) and receives occasional visits from a troop of blue monkeys. The *Amani Malaria Research Centre Rest House* (☎027/264 0311; full board ❺) is in a medical research complex established by the Germans in 1893. It has eight beds, a cosy lounge with a huge fireplace, and food is available. For **drinks**, try the *Welfare Club* nearby.

Camping ($5) is possible at the rest houses, and in over half a dozen campsites along various hiking trails in the vicinity of Amani village; contact the reserve headquarters in Amani or the information centre at Sigi Gate. All have water and toilets, at least in theory.

The Sigi–Tengeni Railway

The information centre at Sigi occupies the beautifully restored wooden German **Station Master's House**, which was the terminus of the short-lived **Sigi–Tengeni Railway**. Built between 1904 and 1910 by the Sigi Export Gesellschaft, the narrow 75cm-gauge railway opened up 12,000 hectares of forest to timber exploitation. The railway fell into disuse after World War I, and an accident in 1929 forced its closure. In 1931 the road from Muheza to Sigi was opened, and the railway was finally dismantled. Apart from the Station Master's House, which later saw use as a primary school, all that remains is a diminutive freight carriage and a square block in front of the house, which housed the station bell. There's also a giant cogwheel from a demolished sawmill.

Walking trails and driving routes

There are nine walking trails and three driving routes in the reserve, some starting from Sigi Gate, some from Amani village, and others from elsewhere. The **driving routes** are intended for visitors with their own transport, although several of these trails are accessible by bus or pick-up so long as you don't mind camping (vehicles heading into the reserve generally leave Sigi Gate or, better, Amani village in the afternoon, only returning the next morning). **Information** on the various trails is given in leaflets available at the information centre at Sigi Gate and at the reserve headquarters in Amani village, as well as in the *Guide to Trails and Drive Routes in Amani Nature Reserve*. None of the trails is marked, so it's easy to get lost. If you have plenty of time, this isn't a problem, but consider taking a guide, as they're also pretty clued up on botany and ecology.

The **walking trails** – none longer than a day – go through rainforest, botanical gardens, tea plantations (and a tea factory), viewpoints on a ridge overlooking West Usambara across the Lwengera valley, historical and cultural sites like sacred caves and the remains of a fortified Iron Age settlement, waterfalls, villages and farms. The rainforest is best seen along the **Amani-Sigi Mountain Trail** (3–5hr starting at Sigi Gate), a fairly tough and steep round trip climbing 450m through primary and secondary lowland and submontane forest to the top of a ridge. The area has particularly tall trees (many over 60m); on the lower stretches, look out for bright orange land crabs, which you might see hiding under fallen leaves.

Another good trail, especially for getting between Sigi Gate and Amani village, goes through **Amani Botanical Garden**, one of Africa's largest. Founded in 1902, the garden contains around 300 tree species (both indigenous and exotic), a large expanse of original forest, a spice garden and a palmetum, whose indigenous cycads – an ancient and primitive species of palm – hint at the great age of East Usambara's forests. The garden's original function was to study the flora and fauna of German East Africa. "Any such activities that have no effect in improvement of standards to the east African culture should not be conducted," emphasized Graf von Götzen, the governor of German East Africa, in 1904. Sadly, the fruits of this research (4000 books and 300 journals) were transferred to Berlin and destroyed in a 1943 bombardment.

Two more adventurous options not covered by the leaflets (and for which you definitely need a guide) are a full-day hike up **Lutindi Peak** (1360m), which has jaw-dropping views over the Lwengera valley, and a five-day hike to **Soni** in West Usambara: at the time of writing, the only guide who knew this route well was Juma Kahema, the owner of the *Maweni Motel* near Soni (p.352) (PO Box 6, Soni; ✆elct_ned@tanga.net); the route is therefore best attempted from west to east.

Travel details

Passenger trains no longer run to Moshi or Taveta. For information on internal flights from Kilimanjaro International Airport, see the travel details for Chapter 6 (p.411). There are no scheduled flights from Moshi airport.

Buses and daladalas

Lushoto to: Arusha (1–2 daily; 6–7hr); Dar (4 daily; 7hr); Mombo (every 30min until 5pm; 1hr); Moshi (3–4 daily; 4–5hr); Mtae (1–2 daily; 3–4hr); Muheza (every 2hr until mid–afternoon; 2hr); Tanga (every 2hr to mid–afternoon; 3hr).

Moshi to: Arusha (3 hourly; 1hr 30 min); Dar (hourly until 2pm; 8–9hr); Iringa (1–3 daily; 9–10hr); Kisangara (2 hourly; 1hr); Lushoto (3–4 daily; 4–5hr); Machame (hourly; 1hr); Marangu (hourly; 45min); Mbeya (1–3 daily; 15hr); Morogoro (3–4 daily; 6–7hr); Muheza (3–4 in the morning; 4hr); Mwanga (1–2 hourly; 1hr); Nairobi (3–4 daily; 6–8hr); Same (1–2 hourly; 2hr); Shinyanga (1 weekly; over 24hr); Tanga (3–4 in the morning; 5–6hr); Taveta (hourly; 45min); Usangi (1 daily; 4–5hr).

Muheza to: Amani (irregular transport 1–4pm; 1hr); Arusha (3–4 in the morning; 5hr 30min); Dar (3 daily; 4–5hr); Lushoto (every 2hr until mid–afternoon; 2hr); Mombo (hourly; 1hr); Morogoro (every 2hr until 1pm; 4–5hr); Moshi (3–4 in the morning; 4hr); Pangani (2 daily except in the rains; 2–3hr); Tanga (every 30min; 45min).

6

Arusha and around

CHAPTER 6 Highlights

✳ **Cultural tourism** Arusha is the base for many of Tanzania's groundbreaking community-run cultural tourism programmes, offering intimate encounters with local tribes, and dozens of walks to local attractions. See p.405

✳ **Arusha Declaration Museum** Small but well-arranged collections covering most aspects of Tanzania's history, prehistory and culture. See p.381

✳ **Longido** A cultural tourism programme run by Maasai, who offer a challenging climb up Mount Longido. See p.408

✳ **Mount Meru** Tanzania's second-highest peak can be climbed in three days, and offers stunning scenery all the way. See p.399

✳ **Safaris** With over 200 companies vying for your business, choose carefully; there are a lot of predators around. See p.393

✳ **Tingatinga paintings** Vivid, bright colours and humorous designs are often used to depict *sheitani* spirit myths in these paintings, available in many souvenir shops in town. See p.387

6

Arusha and around

eading west from Moshi, the last major town before the rolling savanna of the Rift Valley kicks in is **Arusha**, Tanzania's safari capital and third-largest city. The town receives around 400,000 visitors each year, and although most of these use Arusha only as a base from which to explore the nearby parks, the town's lively shops and markets, vibrant nightlife, innumerable bars and some excellent restaurants provide plenty of interest to reward a longer stay.

Overlooking Arusha is the magnificent **Mount Meru**, a dormant volcanic cone which, at 4566m, is Tanzania's second-highest mountain; the three- or four-day hike to the top passes through some exceptionally beautiful (and bizarre) scenery. Another climbable mountain close by is the mist shrouded **Mount Longido**, close to the Kenyan border. This can be visited via the region's outstanding **cultural tourism programme**, which also offers trips in a range of other locations, giving visitors the opportunity of combining encounters with local people like the Maasai with hikes to unspoilt forests, rivers and waterfalls.

Arusha

Nestled among the lush foothills of Mount Meru, the booming town of **ARUSHA** is northern Tanzania's major commercial centre and the country's undisputed safari capital. In clear weather, the sight of Mount Meru's near-perfect cone rising majestically to the north provides the town's abiding memory, while the exceptionally rich volcanic soils on and around Meru's slopes account for the modern town's prosperity – every inch of the area seems to be taken up by *shambas* and settlements, producing half of the country's wheat and substantial amounts of coffee, flowers, seed-beans and pyrethrum for export, along with bananas, maize, millet and vegetables for domestic use. The rainforests on higher ground are the traditional land of the **Meru and Arusha tribes**. The former are related to disappeared hunter-gatherer communities; the latter are agricultural cousins of the Maasai who dominate the savanna around Arusha.

Despite a burgeoning population of over 350,000 people, which is increasing by seven percent annually largely thanks to immigration from outlying areas, Arusha has a remarkably laid-back, small-town atmosphere, an impression accentuated by the unexpected sight of small fields of maize and vegetables running straight through the centre of town along the banks of the Naura, Goliondoi and Themi rivers. Even so, Arusha, like Dar, is a cosmopolitan and

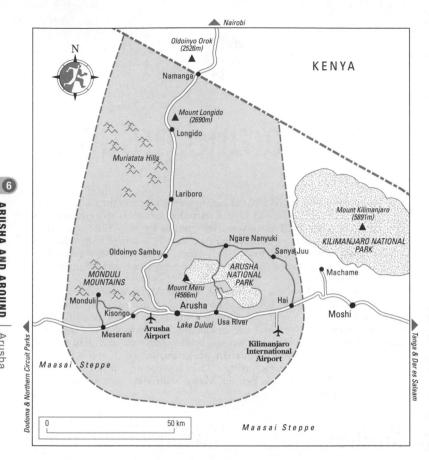

diverse place. The presence of tourists and expatriates keeps Western culture prominent, while around the market Asian and Muslim businessmen dressed in loose white or pale blue cotton garments mingle with Nike-capped youths and streetboys, and on the balconies above you might see African women in brightly patterned kangas talking to Asian neighbours dressed in lurid sarees.

And, of course, there are the **Maasai**: the men in traditional red tartan *shukas* (tartan replaced leather towards the end of the nineteenth century), the women with shorn heads wearing huge disc-like necklaces sewn with hundreds of tiny beads and bangles. Some look bewildered in the metropolitan setting, but most are as nonchalant and at ease with themselves as they are in the savanna – contrary to their popular image as stubborn traditionalists, the Maasai are an extremely adaptable people. And then there's you, the tourist, being followed by trains of young men brandishing reams of batiks, stacks of newspapers or crumpled brochures from disreputable safari companies. If you can weather the attentions of the flycatchers for the first few days, Arusha is one of the most vibrant, infuriating but ultimately enjoyable towns in Tanzania.

Arusha's altitude, at around 1500m, ensures a temperate **climate** for most of the year; the cold season (mid-April to mid-Aug) requires nothing thicker than a sweater for the average *wazungu*, though nights can be truly chilly in July. It gets hot as hell in November before the short rains start.

Some history

Arusha is, unsurprisingly, home to the Arusha people and the related Meru. The **Meru** seem to be the original inhabitants of the foothills of the mountain that bears their name, whereas the **Arusha** (also called Arusa or Arusi) are said to have migrated here about two centuries ago from Arusha Chini, south of Moshi. The reason for the migration remains obscure: one theory holds that they were taken or captured by Maasai to dig wells and build irrigation furrows, and later intermarried (the Maasai have always been happy incorporating conquered tribes into Maasaidom). Their Maasai heritage is evidenced by the language of the Arusha – Kirusha – which is a dialect of Maa, and in the fact that the Arusha practise horticulture rather than agriculture, dispensing with ploughs – a remnant of the Maasai taboo against breaking soil. Cattle are sacred, and so too is the soil that nurtures the grass that feeds them.

The town of Arusha came into existence in the 1880s during **German colonial rule**. In 1886, a military garrison was established, and the settlement that grew up around it became the main market centre for the surrounding European-owned plantations. Later, it became a stopover for vehicles travelling down from Nairobi and the Ngong Hills in Kenya on what became known as the **Great North Road** (now the Tanzam Highway), which continued south into Zambia. Arusha's increasing importance was confirmed when it was made capital of Tanganyika's Northern Province. A 1929 brochure for the province, published to coincide with the opening of the railway from Moshi, enticed prospective settlers with the offer to recreate a little piece of England, and went on to explain: "Looking back . . . to that period immediately after the war, Arusha was scarce a hamlet . . . Those who see it to-day, with its railway just completed, its up-to-date hotel and its stores, see but the half completed dream of the early settlers. *Floreat Arusha!*"

In some respects, the dream remained half-complete. The planned extension of the railway to Mwanza never happened, but Arusha's importance as a commercial and agricultural centre continued. Even so, the population remained surprisingly small, with the 1952 census putting it at just under 8000, of which less than half were Africans. After **independence**, the pace of development increased dramatically, and by 1980, the population had rocketed to 100,000. The present population numbers well over 350,000, the majority of them migrants seeking waged employment.

Arrival and information

Arusha is well connected to the rest of Tanzania (and with Nairobi in Kenya) by both road and air. The railway from Moshi and Dar marked on most maps no longer has passenger services.

By air

International flights touch down at **Kilimanjaro International Airport (KIA)**, 48km east of Arusha off the road to Moshi. Passport formalities are efficient, and you can buy your visa at the immigration office if you haven't already got one. There are **foreign exchange bureaux** at passport control and in the arrivals hall, offering reasonable rates for travellers' cheques, though rates for cash are about twenty percent lower than at the forexes in town. The airport has a number of gift shops, a restaurant and bar, a post office and a pharmacy, though the signposted "tourist office" is just a desk in the departure hall and is rarely staffed.

Transport from the airport to either Moshi or Arusha can be expensive, as there are no local bus services (the closest are 6km away on the main highway). Taxis charge a set rate of $50 to either town, and bargaining is difficult because they have a monopoly. If you've arrived with KLM/Kenya Airways or Air Tanzania (ATC), who shares routes with Precisionair, it's much cheaper to use their **shuttle buses** to Moshi and Arusha which coincide with their flights. KLM's shuttle costs Tsh8000 ($10). ATC's bus is free for their customers, though you may have to pay a bargainable tip of around Tsh2000 (the equivalent of a taxi fare in town) if you want to be taken directly to your hotel. If you've come on another airline, you might be able to get on a KLM or ATC shuttle bus for $10. Incidentally, look out for the nearby trees hung with fish on Tuesday and Thursday afternoons – enterprising flight crews from Mwanza on Lake Victoria have taken to importing fresh fish to sell to airport staff, who dry them from the trees.

Arriving from elsewhere in Tanzania, most flights land at the small **Arusha airport**, 7km along the Dodoma road. Precisionair has a shuttle bus coinciding with its flights (Tsh1000). Alternatively, a taxi into town from here costs Tsh5000, or you could walk the 1.5km to the main road and catch a daladala (every 15–30min) for Tsh150 from there.

By road

The **bus station** between Zaramo Street and Makua Street is being rebuilt, so most buses currently arrive and leave from Kilombero Market, on Sokoine Road, west of town. If you're worried about security, get a cab. There are plenty of taxi touts but don't be rushed. Companies that use their own bus stands (thus minimizing hassle) are Scandinavian Express, on Kituoni Street just south of the old bus stand; Akamba Bus, beside the *Eland Motel* on the Nairobi–Moshi highway; and Royal Coach at the *Golden Rose Hotel* on Colonel Middleton Road.

Details of **onward bus connections** from Arusha are given on p.392.

Town transport

Daladalas (nicknamed *Vifordi*) cover much of the town's outskirts; most trips cost Tsh150, though destinations further out cost a few hundred shillings more; destinations are painted on the front of the vehicles. The main daladala stand is north of Makongoro Road and the (currently closed) bus terminal. The stand's triangular layout can be bewildering, and isn't helped by the maze of alleys surrounding it, but there's less hassle here than at the bus stand, as few tourists come this way. Services **heading east** to Kikatiti, Ngulelo, Usa River and Moshi are best caught at Sanawari junction (the intersection of Simeon Road and the Nairobi–Moshi highway). Services **heading west** along the Nairobi–Moshi highway are best caught along Colonel Middleton Road. Daladalas to Kijenge, Njiro and the TANAPA headquarters can be boarded along Sokoine Road.

Taxis can be rented during the day outside the *New Arusha Hotel* facing the clock tower, outside the AICC, along Sokoine Road, along the eastern stretch of Makongoro Road, along Joel Maeda Street and at most other main road intersections in town. Chances are that the a taxi driver will find you first anyway. A ride within town as far as the Nairobi–Moshi highway costs Tsh1500–2000; short journeys of only a few blocks are Tsh1000. At night (when it makes sense to take a taxi), cabs congregate outside popular bars and clubs and along Boma Road and Joel Maeda Street in the centre.

Given the volume of tourists, many of them first timers in Africa, who pass through Arusha each year, don't be surprised if some people treat you as little more than an easy source of income. That said, so long as you use common sense, there's little to worry about, certainly when compared to the endearments that travellers receive in Nairobi. The warnings and advice below (and in Basics on p.63) may appear daunting, but there's no reason to be overly paranoid; after a few days, you'll probably be wondering what all the fuss was about.

The main hassle is from **flycatchers**, mostly young men who try to sell suspiciously cheap safaris to new arrivals. Remember that any company using flycatchers certainly isn't reputable, and probably isn't licensed either. Although some people find it almost impossible to shake them off, most flycatchers are a nuisance rather than a threat. The easiest way to shake them off is to tell them that you've already either been on safari or have booked one – to make it convincing, mention a reputable company, the parks you've seen or will see, and how much you paid (see p.395). You'll also find flycatchers in the town centre. Apart from safaris, they also offer to change money, sell batiks and foreign newspapers, and entice the unwary with marijuana (*bhang*). The batiks and newspapers are fair game if you're happy bargaining, but you need your head examining if you try to buy dope on the street or fall for the money-changers, who are guaranteed to rip you off, or worse.

As to **theft and robbery**, you'd be extremely unlucky to have any problems by day, though keep a close eye over your bags and pockets in the bus and daladala stands and around markets. After dark, however, taking a taxi is strongly advised. If you ignore this advice, there are a number of **areas to avoid at night**. These include bridges, which attract thieves as they give the victim little room to escape: especially notorious are the ones over the Themi River along the Nairobi Moshi highway, and along Old Moshi Road just east of the clock tower. Indeed, the entirety of **Old Moshi Road** should be avoided at night. North of town, **Sanawari** is the roughest district, though serious incidents are rare; taking the footpath from Sanawari and *Novotel* to the AICC along the Themi River, however, would be asking for trouble. In the town centre, **Sokoine Road** – especially the junction with Factory Road known as France Corner (or Friends Corner), the area fronting Lepers' Gardens, and the western stretch towards Kilombero Market – is known for opportunistic bag-snatchers and pickpockets, and walking there at night is the height of folly. If you're driving, roll up your windows.

Lastly, although **taxis** are usually safe (ignoring their parlous and often comical state of disrepair), avoid taking a cab if there's already a passenger inside – although most are just friends of the driver, cases of robbery have been known.

Bicycles can be rented at the stalls on the east side of the Central Market and also outside *Barracuda Bar* on Makongoro Road. They cost around Tsh2000 a day (or Tsh500 an hour).

Tourist information

The helpful **Tanzania Tourist Board office** is on Boma Road (Mon–Fri 8.30am–4pm, Sat 8.30am–1pm; ℡027/250 3842, ℮ttb-info@habari.co.tz). They have a list of licensed safari operators, plus a blacklist of really bad ones, though the latter is only sporadically updated. They also stock information about the various **cultural tourism programme** tours both in Arusha Region and nationwide (see box on p.405 for more details), many of which can be booked here. **National parks information** can be obtained at the Ngorongoro Conservation Area Tourist Office on Boma Road and at the national parks headquarters (TANAPA) outside town; see p.394 for details.

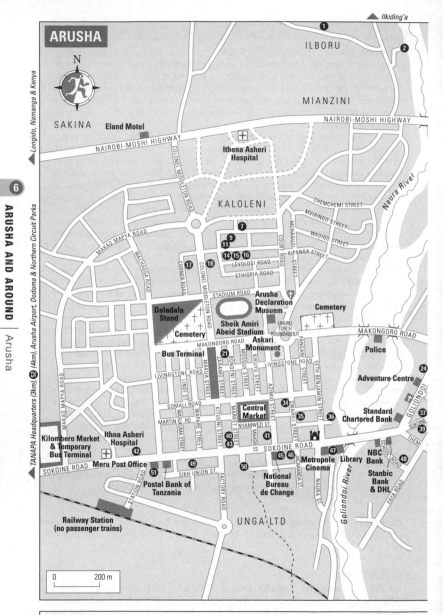

ARUSHA

N

▲ *Ilkiding'a*

① ②

ILBORU

MIANZINI

SAKINA   Eland Motel

NAIROBI-MOSHI HIGHWAY

NAIROBI-MOSHI HIGHWAY

Ithena Asheri Hospital

KALOLENI

CHEMCHEMI STREET

MVIRINGO STREET

WADIGO STREET

⑦
⑨
⑪
⑭ ⑮ ⑯
⑰ ⑱

LEVOLOSI ROAD

ETHIOPIA ROAD

STADIUM ROAD

Arusha Declaration Musuem

Cemetery

Daladala Stand

Cemetery

Sheik Amiri Abeid Stadium

UHURU TORCH ROUNDABOUT

Askari Monument

MAKONGORO ROAD

Bus Terminal

MAKONGORO ROAD

㉑

LIVINGSTONE ROAD

LIVINGSTONE ROAD

Police

Adventure Centre

㉔

Standard Chartered Bank

㉞

Central Market

㉟ ㊱

Kilombero Market & Temporary Bus Terminal

Ittha Asheri Hospital

㊷

SOKOINE ROAD

Meru Post Office

㊺ ㊻

㊹

㊾

⑤⓪

National Bureau de Change

Metropole Cinema

Library

NBC Bank

Stanbic Bank & DHL

㊶
㊸

㊼

SOKOINE ROAD

㊾

⑤①

Postal Bank of Tanzania

Railway Station (no passenger trains)

UNGA LTD

0   200 m

ACCOMMODATION

Arusha by Night	35	Ilboru Safari Lodge	1	Meru House Inn	42	Pallson's Guest
Arusha Coffee Lodge	52	Impala Hotel	57	Mezza Luna	54	Hotel	40
Arusha Naaz Hotel	37	Karama Lodge	65	Moivaro Coffee		Ruby Guest House	41
Arusha Resort Centre	48	Klub Afriko	12	Plantation Lodge	13	Seven Eleven	21
Arusha Vision Campsite	27	L'Oasis Lodge	3	Monje's Guest House	16	William's Inn	17
Centre House	33	Maasai Safari Centre	2	New Arusha Hotel	38	YMCA	25
Equator Hotel	30	Masai Camp	64	New Safari Hotel	26		
Golden Rose Hotel	18	Mashele Guest House	7	Novotel Mount Meru	8		
Hanang Guest House	15			Outpost Guest House	62		

EATING

Amar Cuisine	50
Arusha Naaz Hotel	37
Bamboo Café	32
Big Bite	34
Bindya Restaurant	49
Chick-King	28
Cosy Café	24
Dragon Pearl	60
Greek Club	56

Longido, Namanga & Kenya

TANAPA Headquarters (3km), ① (4km), Arusha Airport, Dodoma & Northern Circuit Parks

Naura River

Goliondoi River

COLONEL MIDDLETON ROAD

MAKAO MAPYA ROAD

WACHAGGA ROAD

CORNER ROAD

COLONEL MIDDLETON ROAD

COURT ROAD

MICHAGUZI STREET

KIPANGA STREET

PANGANI STREET

SETH BENJAMIN STREET

AZIMIO ROAD

SWAHILI STREET

MAANGA ST

MUDANGA ST

NAURA ST

GOLIONDOI

SOKOINE

THEMI

SCHOOL ROAD

FATA ROAD

ZARAMO STREET

BONDENI STREET

MOSQUE STREET

KIKUYU STREET

MARKET STREET

KITUONI STREET

NYAMWEZI ST

LINDI S

WAPARE STREET

SOMALI ROAD

MARTIN RD

WAJUNIMA STREET

SIKH UNION ST.

STATION ROAD

FACTORY ROAD

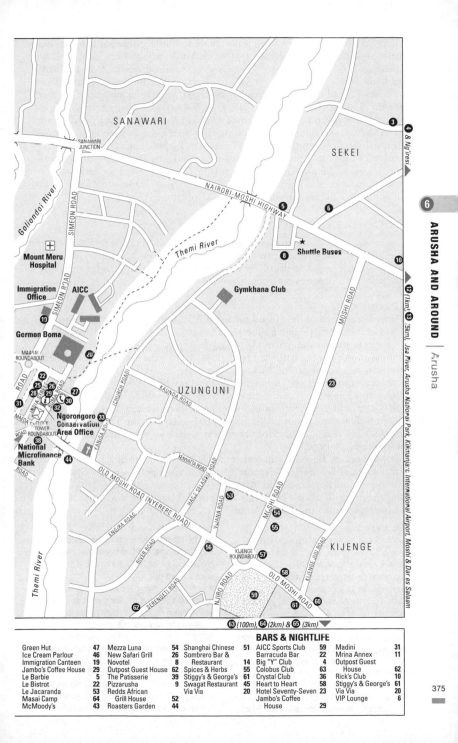

Green Hut	47	Mezza Luna	54	Shanghai Chinese	51	**BARS & NIGHTLIFE**	
Ice Cream Parlour	46	New Safari Grill	26	Sombrero Bar &			
Immigration Canteen	19	Novotel	8	Restaurant	14	AICC Sports Club	59	Madini	31
Jambo's Coffee House	29	Outpost Guest House	62	Spices & Herbs	55	Barracuda Bar	22	Mrina Annex	11
Le Barbie	5	The Patisserie	39	Stiggy's & George's	61	Big "Y" Club	4	Outpost Guest	
Le Bistrot	22	Pizzarusha	9	Swagat Restaurant	45	Colobus Club	63	House	62
Le Jacaranda	53	Redds African		Via Via	20	Crystal Club	36	Stiggy's & George's	61
Masai Camp	64	Grill House	52			Heart to Heart	58	Via Via	20
McMoody's	43	Roasters Garden	44			Hotel Seventy-Seven	23	VIP Lounge	6
						Jambo's Coffee			
						House	29		

BARS & NIGHTLIFE

AICC Sports Club	59	Madini	31
Barracuda Bar	22	Mrina Annex	11
Big "Y" Club	4	Outpost Guest	
Colobus Club	63	House	62
Crystal Club	36	Stiggy's & George's	61
Heart to Heart	58	Via Via	20
Hotel Seventy-Seven	23	VIP Lounge	6
Jambo's Coffee			
House	29		

TANAPA also publish a beautifully illustrated little **guidebook** to Arusha, including Arusha National Park ($10 from Arusha's bookshops, *Jambo's Coffee House* and the Ngorongoro Conservation Area office on Boma Road). Additional local information can be found in the often humorous *Arusha Times* (published Sat; also at Ⓦ www.arushatimes.co.tz) and the annual *Little Big Town* booklet (Tsh500 from *Bamboo Café*, Kase Bookstore and the tourist office). Similar but free (and copying parts of *Little Big Town*) is *Arusha Eye*. A visually appealing and accurate **map** is Giovanni Tombazzi's *Arusha Town & Surrounding Area* colour map, available at *Café Bamboo* (Tsh3000). The main travellers' **notice boards** are outside *Macs Patisserie* on Sokoine Road and in the corridor leading to *Jambo's Coffee House* on Boma Road. Houses for rent and cars for sale are advertised on the board inside the alleyway leading to *Meat King* on Goliondoi Road, and outside *Bamboo Café* on Boma Road.

Accommodation

Arusha has lots of **accommodation**, ranging from dirt-cheap town-centre guest houses with shared squat loos and bucket showers to mid-priced hotels and top-dollar neo-colonial places in the town's leafy suburbs and surrounding plantations. **Campsites** are detailed on p.379.

Town centre

The main concentration of **budget accommodation** is in Kaloleni district, north of the daladala stand; it's pretty safe, in spite of its dilapidated appearance. The streets around the (currently closed) bus stand and market are also lively and have some decent **mid-range** options. More sedate is the grid of tarmac streets in the eastern part of the town centre, where you'll find more mid-range and a few **upmarket** establishments. This is also where most of the safari companies and souvenir shops are based. The tranquil wooded residential suburb east of here and the Themi River – Uzunguni – was built by British and Greek colonists. The area's disadvantage is that the bridge over the Themi River near the clock tower is notorious for muggers after dark, so you'll need to splash out on cab fares after 6pm.

Power cuts are frequent (the better hotels have generators). This means that water supplies are also erratic: part of the town's supply depends on electric pump-powered boreholes, and many hotels use pumps to fill their tanks. Hotels near the bus and daladala stands are noisy by day, but night noise isn't usually a problem, as Arusha shuts up at around 9pm.

Budget

Arusha by Night Swahili St, reception on the second floor (no phone). Would be the best of the lot were it not for its perennially unreliable electric supply and the lack of nets. Nonetheless, it's very good value for its large and bright en-suite twins (bring a plug for the bathtubs in case you strike lucky with hot water). ❶

Arusha Vision Campsite Boma Rd (no phone). Mainly a campsite (see p.379), this also has some extremely cheap bunk beds in three dorms. Very basic, but you can't really complain at the price. ❶

Centre House (Catholic Hostel) Catholic School, Kanisa Rd ☎ 027/250 2313, Ⓔ angelo.arusha@habari.co.tz. An uninspiring but safe and perfectly acceptable option, and good value for singles (though it's expensive for couples, and the 10pm curfew hampers night owls). Rooms share bathrooms, and food is available if pre-ordered (meals Tsh3000). Take a cab after 6pm. Breakfast included. ❸

Hanang Guest House Kaloleni (no phone). A very basic, somnolent and not overly welcoming cheapie, though the rooms – all sharing bathrooms – are adequate and have nets. ❶

Mashele Guest House Kaloleni (no phone). Despite its popularity with travellers, this is one to avoid given the lax security and the fact that the place is infested with flycatchers. ❷

Meru House Inn Sokoine Rd ☎ 027/250 7803 or 0744/288740, Ⓦ www.victoriatz.com. Popular with backpackers, and deservedly so, with comfortable and well-maintained rooms on three floors (singles or twins) with nets and constant hot showers; some also have streetside balconies, while the most expensive have private bathrooms. There's a pleasant courtyard café-bar with satellite TV and good food. The downside is that the resident safari company – the usually reliable Victoria Expeditions (see p.396) – are pushy in plugging their tours. ❷–❸

Monjes Guest House Levolosi Rd ☏027/3060. An adequate flop-house if you're stuck for a night, with no flycatchers and piping hot showers whenever there's electricity. The rooms themselves, sharing bathrooms and long-drops, are rather dismal and can have grubby sheets, but are acceptable at this level. ❶

Ruby Guest House Azimio St (no phone). Very basic, but friendly and safe, and clean enough. Some rooms have cold showers and squat toilets (only the shared bathrooms have hot water); most beds have nets, and there are also some large twin-bed doubles. ❶

Seven Eleven Zaramo St ☏027/250 1261 or 027/6131. Facing the currently closed bus stand, and handy for early-morning departures, with a wide selection of good-value rooms, more expensive ones with large double beds, all with tiled bathrooms and hot water. ❷–❸

Williams Inn Corner Rd ☏027/250 3578. If you can deal with the totally turbid service and atmosphere, this is pretty decent at the price, with good en-suite rooms, and breakfast included. ❸

YMCA India St ☏027/6907. Not as pious as you might expect (alcohol is served in the ground-floor bar), and the friendly atmosphere makes it popular with backpackers – and with flycatchers too. There are seven rooms, all with nets and shared bathrooms (erratic water), and there's also a cheap restaurant (meals Tsh1000–1500) and roof terrace. Overall a pretty decent option, if a little overpriced. Breakfast included. ❸

Mid-range

All the following include breakfast in their rates except the *Arusha Naaz.*

Arusha Naaz Hotel Sokoine Rd ☏027/250 2087, ✉arushanaaz@yahoo.com. A good if somewhat dreary choice, with 21 clean en-suite rooms (including doubles and triples), all with nets, fans, Western-style toilets and hot showers. There's also a good cheap restaurant and internet café. ❹

Arusha Resort Centre Corner of Faya Rd and School Rd ☏027/250 8326, ℻027/250 8233. With its Colditz-style security (including barking dogs at night) and sludge-brown accommodation blocks, this places scores *nul points* for atmos-

phere. That aside, however, it's a perfectly reasonable mid-range option, with clean rooms equipped with Western-style toilets, showers and phones (doubles also have balconies). Much better value, however, are the spacious apartments, which come with fully equipped kitchens. There's a TV lounge, bar and restaurant, and safe parking. Credit cards accepted. ❺

Golden Rose Hotel Colonel Middleton Rd ☏027/250 7959, ⊛www.goldenrose.20m.com. A decent mid-range option, with forty spacious en-suite twins and doubles, all with nets and phones, though they can get musty in the rains. There's a restaurant, a bar with satellite TV, internet café and safe parking. Credit cards accepted. ❺

Le Jacaranda Vijana Rd, Kijenge ☏027/6529, ⊛www.chez.com/jacaranda. Run by a welcoming Breton woman, this atmospheric colonial-era house has seven rooms (two with private bathroom), though they lack nets and could all do with some refurbishment. The best room is on the first floor with a large balcony. There's also a good restaurant, bar and mini-golf. Take a taxi after 6pm. ❺

Mezza Luna Moshi Rd, Kijenge ☏ & ℻027/254 4381. Eleven clean and attractively decorated rooms, all with good bathrooms, nets, and some with beds large enough to swing a family of cats – they're better than those at *Spices & Herbs* next door, but overpriced, nonetheless. Take a taxi after 6pm. ❺

Outpost Guest House Serengeti Rd, off Old Moshi Rd ☏027/254 8405, ✉arushaoutpost@yahoo.com. Excellent-value mid-range option (and an especially good choice for families) occupying a converted colonial-era house set in rich gardens, with fourteen rooms in the main building and in various *bandas* in the gardens. The cheaper rooms share bathrooms; others have a choice of bathtubs or showers. There's also a good bar and restaurant (see the reviews on p.386 and 384); the only minor gripe is that they don't keep out flycatchers, not that it's overrun. ❹

Pallsons Hotel Market St ☏027/3790 or 027/254 8602, ✉pallsons@habari.co.tz. A decent if unexciting modern place with 28 en-suite rooms, all with fans, clean bathrooms and hot water; some have TVs. There's also a bar, and a restaurant specializing in Indian food. ❺

Expensive

The following places all include breakfast in their rates.

Equator Hotel Boma Rd ☏027/250 8409, ✉nah@tz2000.com. Run by the *New Arusha*

Hotel, this has several very large and airy tiled rooms (doubles or twins), each with a private balcony overlooking mature gardens, plus spotless bathrooms with bathtubs, TV and phone. There's also a bar and restaurant, a *nyama choma* bar in the gardens, and a gift shop. Good value. ⑤

Impala Hotel Kijenge roundabout ☎027/250 2398, ⓦwww.impalahotel.com. Arusha's second-biggest hotel, with 153 en-suite rooms (doubles or twins), many in a nine-storey block fitted with panoramic lifts running up the outside. Some rooms have TV, while others offer great views of Mount Meru; all have nets and phone. The downside is street noise (get a room higher up). Amenities include three restaurants, two bars, swimming pool, foreign exchange, 24hr internet café and a safari outfit (the reliable and licensed Classic Tours). Prices drop forty percent in low season. Credit cards accepted. ⑦

New Arusha Hotel Facing the clock tower ☎027/250 3244, ⓔnah@ark.eoltz.com. Established in the 1920s, this rambling place is one of Arusha's biggest and oldest hotels. It's currently closed for extensive renovations (due to reopen in 2003), but if the work is as thorough as it was for the *Equator* (which is under the same management) it should be an excellent choice. Amenities include a swimming pool, pleasant, shaded gardens, a bar and restaurant and foreign exchange (cash only). Credit cards accepted. ⑥

New Safari Hotel Boma Rd ☎027/250 3261. A colonial survivor (Hemingway stayed here in 1933) which remains popular with large tour groups. The two three-storey accommodation blocks (no lifts) were undergoing extensive renovation at the time of writing: all have twin beds, nets, large windows, bathrooms and telephones (TVs cost extra). There's a restaurant but no bar. ⑤

Novotel Mount Meru Nairobi–Moshi Highway, 1km east of Sanawari junction ☎027/250 2711, ⓔmtmeruho@africaonline.co.tz. Arusha's main package-tour hotel, with 192 bright and airy rooms, half of which have views of the mountain. Staff aren't particularly forthcoming, however, and it can feel like a tourist ghetto. On the plus side, there are TVs in all rooms, a swimming pool, bar and restaurant, massage, gift shops, foreign exchange, and traditional dancing on Friday and Saturday nights. Credit cards accepted. ⑧

Out of town

The advantage of staying outside town is the more peaceful and rural atmosphere. The drawback is the cost of taxi fares (Tsh5000 and upwards). See also the accommodation options for Lake Duluti (p.406) and Usa River (p.407).

Arusha Coffee Lodge Burka Coffee Estate, 6.5km along the road to Dodoma, near Arusha airport ☎027/254 4521, ⓦwww.arushacoffeelodge.com. Arusha's newest and classiest option, set at the edge of a working coffee estate, with 25 luxurious rooms decorated in rustic style. Those in the converted stables are good value, but the standard ones – two to a cottage spread out in the gardens – are overpriced. Meals are taken at *Redds African Grill House* (see p.385). There's also a bar and swimming pool, and guided walks around the estate. Stable rooms ⑦ , standard ⑨

Ilboru Safari Lodge Off the Nairobi–Moshi highway, Ilboru (450m west from Sanawari junction, then 700m north) ☎027/7834, ⓦwww.habari.co.tz/ilborulodge. A peaceful retreat set in spacious gardens. The ten round bungalows each contain two neat, en-suite rooms (double or twin), and there are three more cottages and two rooms in a new wing by the huge swimming pool. Other amenities include a bar with satellite TV and a good restaurant (mains Tsh4500, set menu Tsh13,000). ⑥

Karama Lodge 3km northeast of Kijenge, off Old Moshi Rd, Suye Hill ☎027/250 0359, ⓦwww.karama-lodge.com. One of Arusha's newest lodges, this cosy and quiet establishment has twelve rooms in individual log cabins on stilts, all en-suite and with large balconies for views of Mount Meru, a distant Kilimanjaro and the Maasai steppe. There are similar views from the bar and restaurant, and plenty of wildlife wandering in from the surrounding forest, including bushbabies, dikdik, genet and mongoose. Breakfast included. ⑦

Klub Afriko Off the Nairobi–Moshi highway, Kimandolu (3km east from Sanawari junction, then signposted south) ☎027/250 9205, ⓦwww.klubafriko.com. Within walking distance of the town centre by day (take a taxi at night), this is a hospitable and well-maintained place, with accommodation in six comfortable thatched bungalows (sleeping 15 in all). There's good food and two bars, and their safari company has a solid reputation for tailor-made tours. ⑥

L'Oasis Lodge Off the Nairobi–Moshi highway, Sekei (signposted 800m north from *Novotel*) ☎027/250 7089, ⓦwww.loasislodge.com. Set in a populous area of small farms and mud houses, this has twenty cosy en-suite doubles – choose from those in the main building or in large, African-style *bandas* in the lush gardens. Their much cheaper "Backpackers Paradise" annexe (**④**) has twelve rooms sharing bathrooms. The open-air restaurant specializes in Thai and Indonesian food, and there's also a bar and internet café. **⑥**

Maasai Safari Centre Off the Nairobi–Moshi highway, Ilboru (450m west from Sanawari junction, then 500m off to the north) ☏027/254 8535. Six cottages containing rooms with double bed, shower, toilet and small verandah – the banana-leaf thatch ceilings add an attractive rustic touch. The gardens contain many weird and wonderful plants, and there's also a bar (but no restaurant, though food can be arranged). **⑤**

Moivaro Coffee Plantation Lodge Off the Nairobi–Moshi highway, Moivaro (5.2km east from Sanawari junction, then 1.8km off to the right) ☏027/255 3242, ✐www.moivaro.com. A recommended getaway set in a coffee plantation and enjoying a solid reputation. Accommodation in 26 rural-style cottages, with a choice of twins or doubles, all with box nets (no fans), good bathrooms, phone, small verandahs and fireplace. Amenities include room service, a swimming pool with a lovely view of Mount Meru, bar and restaurant, 2km jogging circuit, children's playground and gift shop. **⑦**

Camping

The following are the best **campsites**; the *Meserani Snake Park*, 30km west of town at Meserani (see p.409), is also recommended. Other places that allow camping are the *Hotel Tanzanite* (p.407; $5), *Le Jacaranda* (p.377; $5), and the *Maasai Safari Centre* (see above; $10).

Arusha Vision Campsite Boma Rd (no phone). Nestled above the Themi River (actually more of a stream), this is a surprisingly central oasis, though the location leaves niggling worries about safety – although there hasn't been an incident for several years, the fence surrounding the site isn't much of a deterrent, and you'll get hassled by flycatchers. There's a bar and restaurant, along with laundry and (sometimes) hot water. Tsh2000 per person.

Masai Camp Old Moshi Rd, 2km east of Kijenge ☏027/255 8299, ✐www.tropicaltrails.com. Set in tropical gardens, this is popular with overlanders and has an excellent restaurant and bar (the latter with pool tables and satellite TV), and a great children's play area; it's also the base for Tropical Trails safaris. Forget the handful of rooms (**③**), which are very basic, and don't come here if dogs turn you off – there are plenty; $4 per person (reductions for stays of over four nights).

The Town

Arusha has two distinct centres: the old **colonial quarter** between Goliondoi and Boma roads in the east, which contains most of the shops and offices you might need; and the larger and earthier grid of streets around the **central market and bus stand** to the west. Further east, beyond the Themi River, is

Guided walks in Arusha

Several safari companies offer **guided walks** around town, averaging $30–40 for the guide (up to five people), but excluding lunch. Cheaper – and with a very good reputation – are the walks and bicycle trips offered by *Jambo's Coffee House* on Boma Road (☏0744/305430, ✉jambocoffee@habari.co.tz), and by *Via Via* in the grounds of the German Boma (☏0744/384992, ✉arusha.tanzania@viaviacafe.com). These take in most of the central sights, plus a range of more intimate experiences in the suburbs, including local weekly markets, church gospel music on Sunday mornings, flower and spice gardens, and even a tour around a banana wine factory. *Jambo's* charge Tsh10,000 for the first person for a full day, plus Tsh6000 for additional visitors (up to five); half-day trips cost Tsh7000 for the first person and Tsh4000 for additional people. *Via Via* are cheaper for groups, charging around Tsh10,000 per day, plus Tsh3000–5000 per person. One of *Via Via*'s more unusual offerings is an evening spin around local bars in places like Sanawari, Sekei and Sakina, though you may have to carry your guide back home. They also do a Tanzanian cooking course.

Uzunguni ("the place of Europeans"), a spread-out area of trees and heavily guarded houses where the local elite live, along with a good many expats.

To the north and south of these three areas are the populous **residential suburbs** – areas like Sanawari, Sekei and Sakina to the north, and Kijenge to the east – which are where the majority of the town's inhabitants live. With their earthen roads, wood-and-thatch houses, goats and chickens in the street, impromptu markets, local bars and children who are both delighted and scared stiff by your presence, these typically African areas provide a hugely welcome contrast to the largely European and Asian feel of the centre.

The clock tower and the German Boma

The **clock tower**, at the bottom of Boma Road, is Arusha's best-known landmark and a good place to get your bearings from, though it's also where most of the town's flycatchers, second-hand newspaper vendors and "batik boys" hang out. A small plaque at the base of the clock tower states that Arusha is the half-way point between Cape Town and Cairo, though this is something of a fib – if you draw a line between the two cities, you end up somewhere in swamps of the Congo River basin. The story seems to have come from the megalomaniacal ambitions of the British arch-colonialist Cecil Rhodes, who dreamt of seeing the entirety of eastern Africa, from Egypt to South Africa, painted red on the map. Had his vision of a projected "Cape to Cairo" railway ever come to fruition, Arusha may well have been the mid-point.

Heading up Boma Road past the tourist office brings you to a squat white wall and a number of equally defensive-looking whitewashed buildings. This is the **German Boma**, built in 1886 as a military and administrative headquarters during the German colonization of Tanganyika. The building to your left houses the neglected **National Natural History Museum** (daily 9am–5pm; Tsh1000; Ⓦ www.habari.co.tz/museum), a dusty hotchpotch of flaky exhibits which mostly illustrate the evolution of mankind (hominid skulls, stone tools, and a cast of the 3.6-million-year-old footprints found at Laetoli in Ngorongoro – see p.455); the questionable highlight is an amusing diorama of a cave painter looking distinctly shifty as he daubs the wall.

The museum occasionally hosts **cultural events** such as art exhibitions; the best place to enquire about these is at *Via Via* (see box on p.379) in the museum grounds (it's on the grassy slope to the east of the fortified quadrangle), who also have their own – and more reliable – programme of performances and exhibitions. Both the museum and *Via Via* are also accessible in daytime from the road leading to the AICC car park – there's a gate at the end on the right.

The AICC and west

Immediately behind the German Boma are the three office blocks of the **Arusha International Conference Centre (AICC)**, built in the 1960s to serve as the headquarters of the original, ill-fated East African Community (which was resurrected in 2001). The triangular design of three wings (named Kilimanjaro, Serengeti and Ngorongoro) represent Tanzania, Uganda and Kenya. The original community collapsed in the 1970s following ideological differences between Nyerere's socialist Tanzania and Kenyatta's capitalist Kenya, and sour relations with Uganda's brutal dictator, Idi Amin.

The complex currently houses offices (including a good many safari operators, not all of them up to scratch), and the **International Criminal Tribunal for Rwanda** (Ⓦ www.ictr.org), set up by the UN in November 1994 following the horrific hundred-day genocide in Rwanda that same year which claimed the lives of over 800,000 people. The tribunal delivered its first genocide verdict in September 1998, when former Rwandan Prime Minister Jean Kambanda was found guilty, but has been dogged by controversy for much of its life. By 2000, only forty arrests had been secured, and in 2001 a number of Rwandan defence lawyers were suspended on the grounds that they were genocide suspects themselves. But the main gripe is the UN's characteristically lavish bureaucracy: by December 2001, only nine judgements had been made, at an estimated cost of $800 million dollars. The notice board outside the Press & Public Affairs Unit on the ground floor of the Kilimanjaro Wing has a weekly timetable of **court hearings** (if any); they're usually open to the public (free).

Just southwest of the AICC. the so-called **Maasai Roundabout** at the junction of Simeon and Makongoro roads is graced by a colourful set of statues depicting a rural family. The story behind the statues is an amusing one. In 2000 the roundabout became the object of a local controversy when a nearby bar (the *Barracuda*, see p.385), erected a giant beer bottle on it and had the cheek to rename the section of Makongoro Road to the east after itself. Neither the bottle nor the road sign survived long (they were mysteriously attacked one night), so the council – presumably to forestall any further attempts at expropriation – commissioned the statues you see now, only to come under a hail of criticism itself for having depicted the male – evidently Maasai, judging by his dress – carrying a heavy bunch of bananas on his head. As everyone knows, the only thing that Maasai men carry on their shoulders is a spear or walking stick, and bananas don't even feature in their diet, either.

Heading west, Makongoro Road crosses the Goliondoi and Nauru rivers before reaching, after 1km, a far more imposing roundabout monument – the concrete-arched **Freedom Torch** – symbolizing the torch that was set atop Kilimanjaro on the eve of Tanzania's independence (see p.316). Sadly, the eternal flame in the centre went out ages ago, but the relief panels in the sides of the monument have recently been repainted in colourful detail. Southwest of the roundabout, a small patch of grass is home to the **Askari Monument** – a clumsy, red-painted statue of a burly soldier who has lost half of the machine gun he's brandishing over his head. The prosaic inscription reads, "We have completed the task you assigned us", commemorating Tanzania's victory over Idi Amin's forces in the Kagera War of 1978–79 (see p.719).

The Arusha Declaration Museum

Much more eloquent than either monument in telling Tanzania's recent history is the **Arusha Declaration Museum**, on the northwest side of the roundabout (daily 9.30am–5.30pm; Tsh1000). This packs in a wealth of carefully explained archeological, historical and ethnographic material, and needs at least an hour, preferably two, to see properly. The smaller sections near the entrance feature the material culture of local tribes, a few stuffed animals, stone tools and animals, including hominid skulls from Olduvai in Ngorongoro (see p.453). The bulk of the exhibits, however, are taken up by Tanzania's history from just before colonial times to the period of *Ujamaa*, President Nyerere's experiment in self-reliant rural socialism; these include rare documentary photographs that serve as an unusually enlightening tool for understanding Tanzania, its people and their history. The section begins with the arrival of the Germans and their suppression of the Abushiri War and Maji Maji Uprising, followed by the impact of World War I in Tanganyika. The most striking exhibit however is a photograph of a dead African wearing just a single sandal and a hat, lying on the ground with twisted sheets of corrugated metal in the background.

Notwithstanding the fragmentary nature of the section leading to Tanzania's independence, you can't fail to be moved by the inevitable climax, typified by a wonderful photograph of a grinning Nyerere amidst a jubilant crowd. The ceremonial **Torch of Unity** in the corner was used by President Julius Nyerere after independence, and recalls the original Uhuru Torch (now in Dar's National Museum) that was planted on top of Kilimanjaro on December 9, 1961. The display goes on to document **Ujamaa** (see p.718), which started with Nyerere's "Arusha Declaration" on February 5, 1967. The declaration (under the original title of "On the Policy of Self-Reliance in Tanzania") was drawn up and passed in the museum building, which at the time served as a community centre and popular bar. The declaration stressed the importance of hard work and longer working hours as the key to Tanzania's future economic success, rather than dependence on foreign aid, loans and industrialization, which had by then trapped most other African nations in a vicious cycle of dependency and crippling interest repayments to the Western world.

The reality, however, proved to be an economic disaster. In forcibly moving people from outlying villages into communal "*Ujamaa* villages", the policy laid waste to large areas of formerly productive land – indeed the communal system proved a more fertile soil for corruption than for agricultural production. Yet the same communal villages, populated by a mixture of many different tribes, had an unexpected and priceless side effect, creating the strong and peaceful sense of Tanzanian identity which has allowed the country to remain wholly unaffected by ethnic or religious conflict, and whose people, uniquely in Africa, take pride both in their tribal and national identity.

The **museum shop** has a limited selection of postcards and books published by the national museums of Tanzania, including otherwise difficult-to-find compilations of articles from the academic journal *Tanzania Notes & Records* (formerly *Tanganyika Notes & Records*).

The central market

The city's enjoyable **central market** (Mon–Sat 7am–6pm, Sun 7am–2pm) is five minutes' walk southwest from the Arusha Declaration Museum between Somali Road and Market, Nyamwezi and Azimio streets, and in the thick of the Muslim district. Don't be intimidated by the swarming mass of people (but do beware of pickpockets) – the market and the streets to the west of it offer a dazzling variety of produce, from fruit and vegetables, meat and fish (fresh or sun-dried) to herbs, spices, traditional medicine, cooking implements, colourful kangas and clothing, all displayed with geometric perfection. Kids sell plastic bags for a few shillings, but better would be to search out one of the traditional grass baskets. A couple of other unusual things worth seeking out are pale pink baobab seeds (used to make juice, or just sucked like sweets), and fresh tamarind – also good for juices, and great for cooking with.

Eating

After years of *ugali* and chips with everything, Arusha's **restaurants** have finally got their gastronomic acts together, and the visitor can now choose between a wide selection of top-notch restaurants. Arusha is famed for its **beef** (*ng'ombe*), both grilled (*ng'ombe choma*) and dished up in a variety of stews, notably *trupa* (or *trooper*), which is a mix of bananas, beef (or chicken), seasonal vegetables and potatoes – it sounds weird but is rather tasty. Another local speciality is a thick banana mash called *mashalali*. For your **own supplies**, check out the central market (see above) or the supermarkets and groceries listed on p.392.

There's also plenty of **street food** to be found around town. Roasted maize cobs, fried cassava and sometimes stir-fries can be bought from the women at the corner of Sokoine Road and Seth Benjamin Street, and at various other street corners throughout town. Up in Kaloleni, excellent charcoal grilled meat skewers (*mishkaki*), chips, omelettes and salad can be had at the corner opposite *Mashele Guest House*. None of this should cost you more than Tsh500. You'll find more *mishkaki* places along Swahili Street one block south of *Big Bite*. There's a good hot-dog stand in the passage to the right of the Adventure Centre on Goliondoi Road. Don't miss the **fruit** sold by ladies all over town – the yellow passion fruit, especially, is a delight – but make sure they don't overcharge you. As well as the restaurants below, don't forget the **bars** listed on p.385, all of which rustle up cheap and filling meals, mainly based on meat, eggs and chips.

In the centre

Arusha Naaz Hotel Sokoine Rd. Good, cheap if unexciting restaurant, with most meals around Tsh2000. They also have snacks, and put on a nightly barbecue.

Bamboo Café Boma Rd. A decidedly upmarket travellers' café, and very pleasant and comfortable too, with helpful and friendly staff. There's nothing much Tanzanian (though the *chai tangawizi* – ginger tea – is good if they have it), so you may have to settle for pizza, lasagne or spaghetti, plus home-made cakes, ice cream, fresh juices, milkshakes, fresh salads and good if expensive breakfasts. Closed Sun.

Chick-King India St. Good cheap eats, and popular with office staff at lunchtimes. Dishes include ox-liver and *ugali*, roast beef, chicken and chips, and *mtori* – a banana stew. There's another branch on the ground floor of the AICC's Serengeti Wing. Daytimes only.

Cosy Café Goliondoi Rd. Very cheap snacks and meals (nothing over Tsh1000), the latter Tanzanian rather than European. Snacks include hot-cross buns, kebabs, samosas, *kitumbua* (rice bread) and passion-fruit juice. The meat dishes are good, but avoid the fish and chicken. Daytimes only; closed Sun.

HSS Fresh Snacks Shop Ground floor, Ngorongoro Wing, AICC. A handy and cheap place for pies and burgers, cakes, chocolate brownies, sodas and bread.

Immigration Canteen Simeon Rd. Self-service Tanzanian food, popular with office staff; full meals for Tsh1000. Lunchtimes only; closed Sun.

Jambo's Coffee House Boma Rd. A long-standing Arusha institution. The small café at the front is *the* place for coffee, whilst the gorgeously decorated courtyard at the back under a vaulted *makuti* roof combines a bar and restaurant, and becomes especially atmospheric at night. The food, a mixture of Tanzanian and European, is variable – sometimes excellent, sometimes average – but well priced at around Tsh2000–3000. Open until 8pm or later; closed Sun.

Le Bistrot Corner India St and Makongoro Rd. A quiet and cosy two-level place, with a mainly *wazungu* clientele, offering all the usual tourist fare (spaghetti, quiche, moussaka) for around Tsh2500–3500, and starters – including brilliant salads – for under Tsh1000. Daytimes only; closed Sun.

New Safari Grill Boma Rd, in the *New Safari Hotel*. Reasonable prices and food, if not over-generous portions, catering mainly to a dwindling tourist clientele. The atmosphere's as flat as a pancake, but it's handy on Sundays, when most other central places are shut. Of the few local dishes on offer, the *ugali nyama kwa mchicha* (ugali with stewed beef and spinach) is good.

The Patisserie Sokoine Rd. Patisserie-cum-internet café popular with tourists and Indians. The light meals and snacks are reasonably priced (the chicken is excellent), and they also do cappuccino, espresso, fresh juices, cakes and fresh (and not-so-fresh) bread. Daytimes only; closed Sun in low season.

Roasters Garden Old Moshi Rd. In nicely overgrown gardens by the Themi River, this is good for *nyama choma* with a few beers, but check the price beforehand. It also does a cheap African lunch buffet and Western dishes.

Via Via In the grounds of the German Boma. This friendly Belgian-run restaurant-cum-bar, popular with travellers and locals alike, is a real delight, with great music, a relaxed bar, a small but growing library of Tanzania-related material, a lovely garden, live traditional music most weekends (usually Saturday night), and great food. The menu is a cosmopolitan mix of European, African and Asian dishes (the tilapia is especially tasty), and they also do great sandwiches, freshly pressed juices, milk shakes and good coffee. Closed Mon.

West of the centre

Amar Cuisine Sokoine Rd. A stylish Indian restaurant with tasty vegetarian and non-vegetarian dishes, specializing in tandoori. Mains costs around Tsh5000.

Big Bite Corner of Swahili St and Somali Rd. One

of the best Indian restaurants in East Africa, and reasonably priced for that (full meals upwards of Tsh7000). The naff name and the grimy street outside belie the quite exquisite Mughlai and tandoori cooking served within, the latter from a traditional clay oven. The chicken in spinach puree is unbelievably succulent, and even simple side dishes like buttered naan bread are saturated with subtle flavours. There's also a wide vegetarian choice and, as the name suggests, the portions are indeed big. Ask for the day's specials. Closed Tues.

Bindya Restaurant Sokoine Rd. A strange place that functions mainly as a bar, but with surprisingly good and cheap food available upstairs if you pre-order. Birianis are a speciality.

Greek Club Old Moshi Rd, before Kijenge roundabout on the right. Established in the 1930s by Greek planters, this social club remains popular with expats and well-to-do-locals, especially at weekends, when it puts on barbecues and serves up great Greek salads. They also do Italian food, including pizza.

Green Hut Sokoine Rd. The best fast-food place in Arusha, and deservedly popular, with good hamburgers, even better samosas, *kebabu*, juices and very cheap full meals (around Tsh1200). A great place for breakfast; also does takeaways.

Ice Cream Parlour Sokoine Rd. Fast-food emporium dishing up ice cream, popcorn and snacks; the hot snacks look and taste better earlier in the day. Daytimes only; closed Fri morning.

McMoody's Corner of Sokoine Rd and Makua St. Junk-food joint whose decor will be appreciated by homesick Yanks, as will the food, which includes pizza, hamburgers, ice cream, fish fingers, milkshakes and some Chinese. Closed Mon.

Shanghai Chinese Sokoine Rd. An attractive and genuinely Chinese restaurant, though at the price (full meals average Tsh10,000) you might as well be back home.

Swagat Restaurant Sokoine Rd. Authentic and delicious Indian and tandoori dishes, plus friendly staff. Full meals cost in the region of Tsh5000–7000. Closed Sun.

East of the centre

Dragon Pearl Old Moshi Rd, Kijenge. A very good if pricey Chinese (try the chicken wings), related to the *Shanghai* on Sokoine Rd, with full meals from upwards of Tsh10,000.

Le Jacaranda Vijana Rd. Set on a breezy first-floor terrace of the guest house, this is a pleasant – if perhaps slightly overpriced – venue for a changing menu of mainly French dishes. Snacks like Breton crepes start at Tsh1000, and full meals

go for around Tsh8000. There's also a bar and a mini-golf course.

Masai Camp Old Moshi Rd, 2km east of Kijenge. Excellent and very reasonably priced food majoring on Tex-Mex dishes (very tasty chicken enchilada), plus a good choice of pizzas (all day Sun, otherwise evenings only), pasta and burgers, and lots of other choice.

Mezza Luna Moshi Rd. Expensive but generally excellent Italian restaurant, with large gardens, plenty of privacy and a pretentious art gallery. The food (mains upwards of Tsh5000) consistently receives rave reports, and the lobster is a bargain at Tsh12,000. They also have a good selection of Italian and South African wines.

Outpost Guest House Serengeti Rd, off Old Moshi Rd. Part of the family-run hotel, this serves snacks and light meals throughout the day, and a famous all-you-can-eat evening buffet (7–9.30pm) for Tsh5500. Take a taxi at night.

Spices & Herbs Ethiopian Restaurant Moshi Rd. Excellent vegetarian and carnivorous food, with a quiet and dignified atmosphere, in spite of the flamingos and storks with clipped wings in the caged garden pond. Tsh5500 gets you a selection of most dishes for two people, all served on *njera* – a huge soft pancake. Meat dishes start at Tsh3750, and there's a surprisingly extensive menu of Western food if you don't like spices (Ethiopian food is *hot*).

Stiggy's & George's Old Moshi Rd, Kijenge. A well-regarded place popular with expats and specializing in Thai and South Seas seafood. There's also a pool table and bar (see p.386).

Kaloleni and the Nairobi–Moshi highway

Le Barbie Nairobi–Moshi highway, opposite *Novotel*. Set under a massive vaulted *makuti* roof, the rustic atmosphere here belies the slick service and mostly chargrilled cooking that's far from bland. Try the red snapper or barbecued pork ribs, or any of the daily specials – there are also some vegetarian options. Starters start at Tsh1800, and mains cost Tsh4000. There's also a bar, which has some wines, and an internet café.

Novotel Nairobi–Moshi highway. Expensive meals ($17) aimed at the package-tour tourist market, and the quality isn't always what it should be. Still, they have a couple of alternating theme nights on Saturdays from 7pm: either a "Jungle Night Dinner" by the pool ($10, including game meat), or a seafood buffet indoors ($15, including lobster, prawns and, apparently, fish flown in from Mafia Island), all accompanied by traditional music and the cheesy Sunset Survivors band.

Pizzarusha Opposite *Mashele Guest House*, Kaloleni. "The best damn pizza in Africa" it says over the door, and despite the exaggeration this place is already a firm favourite with travellers, not least for its early breakfasts, rustic decor and candlelit dinners. Apart from Italian favourites, the menu also features curries and other dishes, all at around Tsh3500 with drinks, plus sandwiches from Tsh1000.

Sombrero Bar & Restaurant Behind the *Golden Rose Hotel*. This claims to be the birthplace of *trupa* (a filling stew of beef, bananas and vegetables), and is one of the best places to try the dish (available daily 1–9pm); there's standard bar food at other times.

Outside town

Redds African Grill House *Arusha Coffee Lodge*, Burka Coffee Estate, 6.5km along the Dodoma road ☎027/254 4521. Upmarket, touristy place with an extensive (but confusing) menu; the best bet is the rotisserie grill, which is an empty plate that waiters fill up with meat until you're full (there are also veggie burgers and a vegetarian menu). It's busiest on Sundays, when there's a live band and DVD movies. Saturday evenings feature seafood flown in from Zanzibar. Expect to pay at least Tsh12,000, plus (expensive) drinks.

Bars and nightlife

Arusha's ever-changing drinking and nightlife scene makes tracking down what's really hot an (enjoyable) challenge. Your best starting point is *Via Via* in the grounds of the German Boma, who can point you in the right direction, and who also offer an innovative guided nightlife tour in the populous outskirts (Tsh5000 excluding drinks and taxi rides). For something equally different, sample the **traditional dancing** at *Novotel* on Friday and Saturday nights (performances start at 9pm in the bar; admission free), though they're far from authentic. More genuine is the traditional music at *Via Via* on Sunday afternoons. Arusha's **rap and hip-hop** scene is difficult to track down; again, *Via Via* is the place to ask, while the *Big "Y"* and *Crystal Club* are the most likely venues. Crews to look out for include Flavour Dogz, Hardcore Unity and X Plastaz, whose music includes experimental fusions with Maasai vocal rhythms.

The main area for **nightlife** is along the Nairobi–Moshi highway, which has a slew of bars from Sakina in the west to Sekei in the east. Places go in and out of fashion frequently, so if one of the following has fallen out of favour, you shouldn't have problems finding somewhere better nearby.

Worth trying at least once is **Meru banana wine**, which you'll find at *Via Via* and in some of the more local bars, as well as in supermarkets. The wine – which does indeed have a slight taste of banana – comes in two varieties: one clear and light in colour, the other darker and cloudier. Both are made by Banana Investments, signposted off Old Moshi Road 2km east of Kijenge roundabout, who are happy giving guided tours and tastings so long as you buy a bottle or five. You can find locally brewed versions in villages closer to Mount Meru.

AICC Sports Club (New AICC Club) Old Moshi Rd, 150m east of Kijenge roundabout. A great place on a Sunday afternoon, when it's especially popular with families enjoying the Sound of Serengeti band (not as cheesy as their name suggests, and with the superb Congolese frontman Boniface). Food includes *nyama choma* and roast gizzards (*filigisi*).

Barracuda Bar Makongoro Rd. This has declined in popularity over the last few years, but remains a favourite among local drinkers attracted by good *nyama choma* and grilled bananas. It's liveliest on Friday afternoon.

Big "Y" Club Off the Nairobi–Moshi highway, Sekei (turn left at the signpost east of *Novotel* and walk uphill for 800m). A large, two-storey ship-like structure in the thick of a lively local area. There's excellent *nyama choma*, some of the best *trupa* stew in town, pool tables, plus discos from Saturday afternoon until late and a live band on Sundays from 9pm.

Colobus Club Old Moshi Rd, 500m east of Kijenge roundabout. The Friday and Saturday discos (from 10pm until late; Tsh3000) are Arusha's most popular: brash, lively and extremely loud, heavy on techno and Western pop (there are actually two venues, both with state-of-the-art light shows, so you can always jump ship if the music in one doesn't appeal). There's also an internet café, and a restaurant with well-priced meals and snacks.

Crystal Club Seth Benjamin St. A large old club near the central market that still pulls in the punters, with lots of dancing, a young and easy-going crowd, and some superb Swahili rap music after midnight (and sometimes also on Sunday afternoons). Catch a cab home. Wed & Fri–Sun only; entrance Tsh1500–3000.

Greek Club Old Moshi Rd, before Kijenge roundabout on the right. Currently one of the most popular expat joints, and good food too (see p.384).

Heart to Heart Old Moshi Rd, 100m beyond Kijenge roundabout on the left. One of Arusha's most popular discos, packed out with locals, Asians, *wazungu* and tarts (though sadly the Russian gogo dancers went home a few years back).

Hotel Seventy-Seven (Hotel Saba Saba) Moshi Rd. If it hasn't yet been knocked down to make way for a planned upmarket hotel, the legendary nightly discos here – although quieter than they once were – are worth the taxi fare (Tsh2000), featuring almost entirely African music and an African crowd. The Sound of Serengeti band performs on Saturdays, and Friday is also busy. Closed Mon.

Jambo's Coffee House Boma Rd. A stylish and abidingly popular central bar and restaurant (see p.383). Closed Sun.

Madini Goliondoi Rd. Busy in the afternoons, especially for its pool table, and with a cosy little patio at the back which serves good *nyama choma*.

Mrina Annex Kaloleni. This local dive seems never to close, and hosts a weird (but friendly) crowd well past midnight. The *trupa* is good.

Outpost Guest House Serengeti Rd, off Old Moshi Rd. A quiet (indeed often empty) and relaxing bar, with satellite TV and a lush garden.

Police Mess School Rd, off Sokoine Rd. Forget the

indoor bar and head to the beer garden beside it, a lovely relaxed place serving up superb *nyama choma*.

Rick's Club 50m north of the Nairobi–Moshi highway, 2km east of Sanawari junction. A large *makuti*-thatched venue which hosts the New Olduvai Band (Wed, Thurs, Sat & Sun from 9pm; Tsh2000), unless there's a big-name group visiting from Dar es Salaam. Friday features discos, and Sunday afternoon has family-oriented events like acrobats and traditional dance. There's also food until 11.30pm.

Seven Up Bar Nairobi–Moshi highway, 1.2km west of Colonel Middleton Rd, Sakina. One of the best of the highway's bars, with great food (nothing much over Tsh1500), fast service and a more mentally stable clientele than in some neighbouring joints.

Stiggy's & George's Old Moshi Rd, on the right beyond *Heart to Heart*. One of the main expat meeting places, both for its restaurant (see p.384), and its bar and beer garden. There's satellite TV, a pool table and occasional live music on Friday. Closed Mon.

Triple-A Nairobi–Moshi highway, Sakina. One of Arusha's favourite discos, and more mellow than either *Colobus Club* or *Heart to Heart*, with a much more African feel, too. Discos are held most nights, but the club is best known for its live bands.

Via Via In the grounds of the German Boma, top end of Boma Rd. One of the nicest and friendliest bars in town, with great music (including a stack of traditional *ngoma*), good food (see p.383), and a grassy lawn to chill out on. Closed Mon.

Village Square Nairobi-Moshi highway, Sakina. A great local place, with an eminently danceable live band on Saturday night to around 2pm.

VIP Lounge Off the Nairobi–Moshi highway, Sekei (turn left at the signpost for *Big "Y" Club* east of *Novotel* – it's 100m along on the left). Ever popular with locals, this is a fine place to hang out for an evening, with good music, gorgeously succulent *nyama choma* and chicken, and cheap booze.

Shopping and souvenirs

Arusha has a vast range of **souvenirs** to choose from, bringing together arts and crafts from all over the country, as well as from Kenya (especially luridly coloured soapstone carvings) and reproduction tribal masks from central and western Africa. Typical items include Makonde woodcarvings (see p.232), bright Tingatinga paintings (see box opposite), batiks, musical instruments (the metal-tongued *mbira* "thumb pianos" of the Gogo, from around Dodoma, are great fun, as are the slender *zeze* fiddles), Maasai bead jewellery and a whole lot more. Music cassettes also make excellent souvenirs: there are several ambulant vendors around town with trolleys packed with tapes. The most popular musical genre is Christian *kwaya* – either spiritually uplifting or cheesily irritating

Tingatinga paintings

Arusha is a great place to buy **Tingatinga paintings** – vibrantly colourful tableaux of cartoon-like animals and figures daubed in bicycle paint and sold virtually everywhere. The style takes its name from the artist **Eduardo Saidi Tingatinga**, who was born sometime in the 1930s in Mindu village in southern Tanzania to a rural Makonde family, and moved to Dar es Salaam when he was sixteen. He worked on building sites, and in his spare time made paintings and signboards for shops. In the mid-1960s, he began selling his paintings from Morogoro Stores in Dar es Salaam. His Makonde heritage is echoed in his use of *sheitani* ("spirit") imagery – often amusingly grotesque beings. Tingatinga died in 1972, when he was shot by police who mistook him for a criminal.

Modern Tingatinga paintings are usually more geared to tourists, depicting safari animals, baobab trees, Kilimanjaro and rural scenes. This is not to dismiss them – they make singularly cheerful and attractive souvenirs. Prices are generally very cheap, and a large A3-sized painting shouldn't cost more than Tsh5000–10,000, depending on your bargaining skills.

depending on your mood. You can also find the full range of the latest dance hits from Tanzania and the Democratic Republic of Congo.

The main concentration of **souvenir shops** is the eastern part of the centre between Goliondoi Road and Boma Road, especially Joel Maeda Street and all along the unnamed alley (more of a rat-run) running between, and parallel to, Goliondoi Road and India Street. The alley can be intimidating if you're not in the mood for bargaining, with dozens of stalls and over-eager salesmen, complete with the "but how am I going to feed my family" line of patter, so you might like to pay a first visit with no money to get a feel for it. **Prices** are rarely, if ever, fixed, and depend entirely on your bargaining skills. Starting prices vary wildly: sometimes not much more than the real price, at other times ten times as much. Luckily, getting a decent final price isn't too difficult thanks to the welter of competing shops and stalls (you can play them off against each other). However, there's always a mark-up for tourists, so the main rule is to aim for a price you're be happy with. Anything under that, and you've got yourself a bargain. For more advice on shopping and bargaining, see p.62.

The following is an entirely unrepresentative selection of souvenir shops, as these (with the exception of the Maasai market) are among the few which have marked prices – handy for getting an idea for how much stuff should cost.

Cultural Heritage 5km along Sokoine Rd on the left; catch a daladala from the main stand to Majengo. Huddled inside its electric fence, this is Arusha's largest – and most expensive – tourist emporium, with stacks of stuff at prices that leave you reeling. Usually visited by safari groups. Closed Sun pm.

Jambo's Coffee House Boma Rd. The bar-restaurant area at the back has a series of month-long art exhibitions, with most pieces for sale, and there's also a small bookshop and gift shop.

KAM Real Arts Centre Boma Rd, next to *Jambo's Coffee House*. Mainly Tingatinga paintings, banana-fibre collages and locally made batiks, some tailored into clothes. Prices vary between Tsh600 and Tsh30,000, depending on size. You can also visit the workshop in the German Boma – ask the attendant there to show you – the crafts-

men and -women are happy to give hands-on lessons for around Tsh5000. Closed Sun.

Lookmanji Curio Shop Joel Maeda St. One of the best selections in town, especially for carvings. They also stock carvings from the Kamba tribe of Kenya, who make good figurines. Other stuff includes masks from Congo and Mali, and – occasionally – a circumcision mask from the Luguru tribe of Morogoro. Prices are keen. Closed Sun pm.

Maasai market Corner of Joel Maeda St and Boma Rd by the clock tower. An impromptu pavement market where Maasai women make and sell beadwork necklaces and bracelets. Closed Sun.

Via Via In the grounds of the German Boma. Sells great life-size wooden busts from the sculpture school and carvers' co-operative in Bagamoyo (see p.149), and have good contacts with local artists. Closed Mon.

Northern Tanzania – specifically the graphite Mererani Hills between Arusha and Moshi, and an as-yet undeclared location in the Pare Mountains – is the only place on earth known to contain **tanzanite**, a precious transparent gemstone first discovered in 1967. In its natural form, the stone is an irregular brownish lump, but when heated to 400–500°C it acquires a characteristic colour and brilliance, predominantly blue, although with other shades, ranging from violet to a dullish olive green. Determining the real colour isn't too easy, however, as the stone is trichroic, meaning it shows three different colours when viewed from different angles: blue, purple or red. The facets are not natural, but made by gemologists.

Arusha is the main marketing (and smuggling) centre for tanzanite, and for other local gemstones – ruby, green garnet (locally called tsavorite), green tourmaline, emerald and sapphire. After initial interest in the 1970s, the international market for tanzanite has almost vanished, not helped by unfounded allegations in the US that the trade was a major source of revenue for al-Qaeda. These claims apart, you should think twice about the consequences of the tanzanite trade before buying. The Mererani Hills are an environmental mess as a result of tanzanite mining, while local miners have gradually been pushed out of the most productive areas by large-scale operations, including a couple of multinational enterprises whose heavy-handed tactics in dealing with "scavengers" – as they refer to artesanal miners – are reported with depressing frequency in the press. The mines themselves are primitive by international standards, and have a lamentable safety record: in 1998 over 50 miners drowned in a flood after heavy rain, and in June 2002, 42 more suffocated when a fresh air pump failed. So badly managed is the industry that in 1998, Kenya – which doesn't even produce tanzanite, and whose supplies come entirely from smuggling – exported more of the gemstone than Tanzania.

There's no official **grading system** for tanzanite, although unofficially stones are classified into five main grades – AAA, AA, A, B and C (with AAA being finest). As a rough guide, the price depends on colour (deep and radiant is most expensive), size and grade – minor flaws like faults or inclusions will halve the value, at least. A-grade stones cost $250–500 per carat, B-grade $150–200, and C-grade $100–150. The bigger the stone, however, the higher the per carat price (a really large stone, say ten carats, would cost well over $500 per carat). If you want to buy tanzanite, be aware that you're likely to get ripped off unless you're clued up on gemstones. The many shades of tanzanite makes scamming easy; a common trick is to pass off iolite (which costs $10 per carat) as tanzanite, and there are all sorts of cheaper stones that could pass for the rare "green" variety of tanzanite (which costs upwards of $500 per carat).

Arts and traditional music

After lying dormant for decades, Arusha's **arts and culture** scene has finally woken up with a small but satisfying jolt. The main venue for performances and art exhibitions is *Via Via* in the grounds of the German Boma, which has an outdoor stage facing the Themi River (seating is in a grassy "amphitheatre" studded with cement busts). They currently stage performances of **traditional music** most weekends (usually Saturday night) and, together with *Jambo's Coffee House*, mount an annual weekend "Art in the Street" festival along Boma Road in August. *Via Via* is also a good place to enquire about art exhibitions: they regularly host exhibitions from various sculpture schools and associations from Bagamoyo (see p.148), and also put on occasional displays in one of the Boma buildings. *Jambo's Coffee House* is also a good place to ask about forthcoming events.

△ Yuccas and Mount Meru

Listings

Air ambulance Flying Doctors (AMREF):
℡027/254 8578; emergency numbers in Kenya
(as dialled from Tanzania): ℡005/233 6886,
005/260 2462 or 005/250 1280.

Air charters Flights to the national parks are usually combined with mid-range or upmarket safaris.
Especially recommended are Coastal Travels, ATC
House, Boma Rd ℡027/250 0087,
ⓦwww.coastal.cc. Other charter companies
include Air Excel, Njiro Rd ℡027/254 8429,
ⓔreservations@airexcelonline.com; Fleet Air,
Sokoine Rd ℡027/254 8126, ⓔfleetair@africaon-
line.co.tz; Northern Air Charter, Goliondoi Rd
℡027/254 8060, ⓔnorthernair@habari.co.tz;
Precisionair, Ground floor, Ngorongoro Wing, AICC
℡027/6903, ⓦwww.precisionairtz.com; Regional
Air, CMC Building, Sokoine Rd ℡027/250 2541,
ⓔregional@africaonline.co.tz.

Airlines Air Tanzania Corporation, Boma Rd
℡027/3201, ⓔmdir@airtanzania.com; Coastal
Travels, ATC House, Boma Rd ℡027/250 0087,
ⓦwww.coastal.cc; Eagle Air, Easy Travel & Tours,
2nd floor, Clock Tower Centre, Joel Maeda St
℡027/250 3929, ⓦwww.easytravel.co.tz;
Ethiopian Airlines, Boma Rd ℡027/250 6167,
ⓔtsm-a@ethair.co.tz; Gulf Air, Old Moshi Rd
℡027/254 4154; KLM, next to the *New Safari
Hotel*, Boma Rd ℡027/254 8062,
ⓔklm.arusha@ark.eoltz.com; Precisionair, Ground
floor, Ngorongoro Wing, AICC ℡027/250 6903,
ⓦwww.precisionairtz.com; Regional Air, CMC
Building, Sokoine Rd ℡027/250 2541,
ⓔregional@africaonline.co.tz; ZanAir, Arusha airport ℡027/250 9498, ⓦwww.zanair.com. Tickets
for other airlines can be booked through travel
agents – see below.

American Express c/o Rickshaw Travels on
Sokoine Rd facing Wapare St.

Banks and exchange There are banks and foreign exchange bureaux throughout town. Bank
rates are around ten percent better than forexes,
but the commission can be painful and transactions can take over an hour. The best are the
National Microfinance Bank, facing the clock
tower; NBC, at the corner of Sokoine Rd and
School St; and the National Bureau de Change,
further along Sokoine Rd. Standard Chartered in
Sykes Building on Goliondoi Rd charges a reckless
$20 commission on cheques, but has a 24hr Visa
card ATM (though it doesn't always work). There's
another machine inside the *Impala Hotel*. Forex
bureaux are much quicker and less hassle than
banks, and don't normally require purchase
receipts for travellers' cheques. The most helpful is

Exchange Centre on Joel Maeda St (Mon–Fri
8am–4.30pm, Sat 8am–1pm), who are happy
dishing out small-denomination notes; also good is
Equator Exchange next to the *New Safari Hotel* on
Boma Rd. On Sundays, Northern Bureau de
Change on Joel Maeda St is handy (Mon–Sat
8.30am–5.30pm, Sun 8.30am–4pm). Other forex
offices (usually open until 5pm) are less reliable,
and sometimes refuse travellers' cheques – you'll
find them along Goliondoi Rd, India St and Boma
Rd, and at the eastern ends of Sokoine and
Makongoro roads. The *Impala Hotel* arranges cash
advances on credit cards at exorbitant fees.
Visa/MasterCard holders are better off at the
Barclays Merchant Services representative (TMCS
Co Ltd) at the *Arusha Resort Hotel*.

Books and maps Arusha's best bookshops are
Kimahama, on Colonel Middleton Rd, and
Bookpoint, on Swahili St, both with good selections
of coffee-table books, maps and some Tanzanian
novels in English. Also worth rummaging through
are either of Kase Bookshop's branches (on Boma
Rd and Joel Maeda St). The Clock Tower Book
Centre by the clock tower is little more than a cub-
byhole but has a wide range of glossy coffee-table
tomes, English bestsellers, wildlife videos and
maps and guidebooks.

Camping equipment Widget Safari & Camping
Equipment, by the clock tower on the north side of
Joel Maeda St on the first floor (Mon–Fri
8.30am–5pm, Sat 8.30am–1pm; ℡027/250 1522)
sells sleeping bags, made-to-order tents and
handy combined mattress and mosquito nets. They
also have walking sticks, headlights, stoves and
warm jackets. Tents, sleeping bags and hiking
boots can also be rented from *Pizzarusha*
restaurant in Kaloleni.

Car rental Fortes Safaris, Goliondoi Rd ℡027/250
8096, ⓔarushafortes@habari.co.tz. A self-drive
TDI Land Rover with pop-up roof costs $110 per
day; add $40 per day for driver and fuel. Serena
Car Hire, India St ℡027/250 6593,
ⓔserenacarhire@africaonline.co.tz. Reliable vehicles and good drivers; a 4WD with driver starts at
$120 per day. Shidolya Tours & Safaris, Room
238–239, Ngorongoro Wing, AICC ℡027/254
8506, ⓦwww.shidolya.net. A 4WD with driver and
unlimited mileage goes for around $120 per day.
Rates are bargainable for long trips. No self-drive.
Sunny Safaris, Colonel Middleton Rd, opposite the
Golden Rose Hotel ℡027/250 7145, ⓦwww.sun-
nysafaris.com. A 4WD costs $135 per day includ-
ing driver and fuel for the Northern Circuit, or
$0.60 per kilometre elsewhere. No self-drive.

Dentists The best dentist is at the Old Arusha Clinic, Old Moshi Rd ☎ 027/2134.

Diplomatic representation UK, c/o Kudu Safaris (p.395); US, c/o Gary Balfour ☎ 027/250 8627.

Football Matches are generally held on alternate Saturdays at Sheik Amiri Abeid Stadium. You can buy tickets at the gate on Makongoro Rd by Colonel Middleton Rd.

Hospitals Ambulances can be called on ☎ 99928. The main hospitals are the AICC Hospital, Old Moshi Rd ☎ 027/250 2329; the Ithna Asheri Hospital (consultations on Sokoine Rd ☎ 027/6206); Mount Meru Hospital, Simeon Rd ☎ 027/250 3351; and Selian Lutheran Hospital, Ngara Mtoni ☎ 027/3726. For minor ailments and blood tests, visit Trinity Medical Diagnostic Clinic, Enqira Rd, off Old Moshi Rd (☎ 027/254 4392, ✉ kfg@habari.co.tz), which has a solid reputation and does twenty-minute tests for malaria and amoebic dysentery. Dr Urasa at the Old Arusha Clinic, off Old Moshi Rd (☎ 027/2134), also has a good reputation. For alternative medicine, try Urafiki Hospital on Swahili St near the market (☎ 027/254 4318), which practises both Chinese and Western medicine; The Natural Therapy Centre, 1st floor, Jumbo House, Maasai St, facing the central market (☎ 0741/652175), offers natural remedies for a variety of ailments; Dr Shastri, on Kituoni St (☎ 027/250 6157), deals in Indian herbal medicine; or try the self-proclaimed traditional herbalist at the southeastern corner of the (closed) bus stand on Somali Rd.

Immigration The Immigration Office on Simeon Rd near Makongoro Rd (Mon–Fri 7.30am–3pm; ☎ 027/3569), won't extend visas unless you're happy paying $400 for a two-month special permit (which can be extended for another two months for free). The workaround is to cross into Kenya at Namanga before your visa expires, stay for a few hours or overnight, then return to buy a new three-month visa at the border (payable in dollars).

Internet and email access There are loads of internet cafés. Connections are generally fast and reliable, and prices ever cheaper, currently averaging Tsh1000 per hour. Cheapest is the Arusha Regional Library on Sokoine Rd (Mon–Fri 9am–6pm, Sat 9am–2pm; Tsh500 per hour), though there's also a daily membership fee of Tsh500. Cyberspot, Jacaranda St (Mon–Sat 9am–11pm, Sun 10am–8pm; Tsh1000 per hour) is one of the best commercial options, with good machines, a cool a/c interior and juices and sodas. Similar rates are offered by Silver Touch at the corner of Makongoro Rd and Azimio St (daily 9.30am–9.30pm); Arusha Art on India St; *Arusha Naaz Hotel*, Sokoine Rd (daily 7am–11pm); Ram

Internet Café, Old Moshi Rd next to the *Impala Hotel* (Mon–Fri & Sun 8am–9pm); and Cyberboma by the clock tower (Mon–Sat 9am–6pm). *The Patisserie* on Sokoine Rd has only four computers, often booked by overlanders, but a wide range of snacks, meals and drinks (Mon–Sat 7am–6pm).

Language schools Ask at *Via Via* about private language tuition – they know good teachers.

Library The well-stocked Arusha Regional Library is on Sokoine Rd (Mon–Fri 9am–6pm, Sat 9am–2pm; Tsh500 daily membership).

Newspapers & magazines Newspaper hawkers are concentrated along Boma Rd and will pester you with old copies of *USA Today*, *Newsweek* and *The Guardian*. The best stands, with a wide selection of Tanzanian and Kenyan dailies, weeklies and sometimes magazines, are at the east end of Joel Maeda St by the clock tower outside the supermarket, and on Goliondoi Rd near Makongoro Rd.

Opticians Sunbeam Optical Centre, Sokoine Rd, next to Benson Shop ☎ 027/7757.

Pharmacies Hoots the Chemist, Azimio St (open 24hr) ☎ 027/3124; Chemo Pharmacy, CCM Building, Makongoro Rd ☎ 027/2751; Khanbhai Pharmacy, Metropole Cinema, Sokoine Rd ☎ 027/3316; Al-Hakimi Pharmacy, Sokoine Rd ☎ 0744/311100; Moona's Pharmacy, Sokoine Rd ☎ 0741/510590; Acacia Pharmacy, south end of Colonel Middleton Rd ☎ 027/250 3240; Mak-Medics, Seth Benjamin St facing the mosque ☎ 027/254 8640.

Photography Film stocks are usually fresh. Passport photos, film developing, battery and film sales and camera repairs (no guarantee of success) are available at Astah (nicknamed "Fuji Shop"), by the clock tower on Sokoine Rd, who charge Tsh6000 for 1hr processing. Slide film can be bought and developed at Burhani Photographic Services ("Kodak Shop") next to the *Impala Hotel* on Old Moshi Rd; it's well equipped and sells batteries and professional slide film; they also offer slide processing, though it's expensive (Tsh5000 plus Tsh100 per mount) and they can be sloppy cutting film. Kwik, on Naura St off Sokoine Rd, is also well equipped, offering 1hr processing.

Police The central police station is on Makongoro Rd ☎ 027/3641 or 0741/123929.

Post, couriers and freight The main post office is on Boma Rd by the clock tower (Mon–Fri 8am–12.30pm & 2–4.30pm, Sat 9am–noon), and also has a stationery shop and philatelic bureau. For sending international parcels, you'll need to visit Monday to Friday 8.30am to 10am, when the customs official is on duty. There are two branch offices along Sokoine Rd, a third in the AICC complex and a fourth at the bus station. If you want to

Arusha is northern Tanzania's main transport hub, with several daily **bus connections** to all major towns in northern and eastern Tanzania, including Babati, Dar es Salaam, Lushoto, Morogoro, Moshi, Namanga, Singida and Tanga. In the dry season, there are also buses to Dodoma and Kondoa, but the abysmal state of the roads in central and northwestern Tanzania means that most buses to Mwanza, Musoma and Bukoba go through Kenya, where the route is all tarmac (so you'll need to add $50 for a Kenyan visa to the cost of your bus ticket). **Domestic flights** take off from Arusha airport, 7km west of town, and from Kilimanjaro International Airport, 50km to the east, off the highway to Moshi.

By road

Road conditions to Dar es Salaam, Tanga and Nairobi are good (tarmac), though the stretch up to Namanga on the Kenya border is prone to flooding during heavy rains. Conditions on routes heading west vary with the season, as the tarmac only goes as far as Tarangire National Park before the road splits: northwest towards the Northern Circuit parks, southwest towards Dodoma. The road to Dodoma, via Babati and Kondoa, has been widened and graded in preparation for tarmac, but the planned completion date of 2004 is widely regarded as a joke, given that the project has been stalled and abandoned so many times in the past. For now, the section beyond Babati is extremely tricky, if not totally impassable, during the rains.

The main hazard on tarmac is **reckless driving**, especially between Arusha and Moshi. If you're driving yourself, be on your guard when the road swoops down towards bridges at Wami, Kikafu and Karanga, as fatal high-speed crashes and collisions at these places are depressingly common. The route is safest in the morning when drivers are less tired and you can catch buses run by one of the **safer companies**: these include Fresh ya Shamba (for most destinations) at Kilombero Market (☏0744/295960); Akamba (for Dar and Nairobi) beside the *Eland Motel* on the Nairobi–Moshi highway (☏027/250 9491); Royal Coach (for Dar) at the *Golden Rose Hotel* on Colonel Middleton Road (☏0741/651168); and Scandinavian Express on Kituoni Street south of the (currently closed) bus stand (☏027/250 0153), which charges a premium for its tout-free bus station in Dar, comfortable modern buses fitted with speed-limiters and relatively sane drivers; they run to Dar, with next-day

send things quickly and reliably, use one of the following couriers: DHL, Sokoine Rd next to Stanbic Bank ☏027/254 4113 (plus another branch on the ground floor of the AICC Kilimanjaro Wing ☏027/7509); EMS, at both the clock tower and AICC post offices; FedEx, Wachagga Rd ☏027/3845; Skynet, Room 680, Serengeti Wing, AICC ☏027/250 0116; TNT, Sokoine Rd ☏027/254 8043.

Sports and health clubs AICC Sports Club, Old Moshi Rd, has squash, tennis, darts and volleyball, though it's more popular for its bar and *nyama choma* joint. The nine-hole Arusha Golf Course, south of the *Novotel*, is part of the irksomely snobbish Gymkhana Club, but membership policy is extremely strict so you're unlikely to be admitted unless a member signs you in. The annual Mount Meru International Marathon takes place in July or August, attracting over 1500 runners; you can register at the Sheik Amri Abeid Stadium or contact

Hoopoe Adventure Tours (see p.397). *Stiggy's & George's* on Old Moshi Rd is the venue for the Hash House Harriers' weekly runs (Friday 5.30pm; usually 5km, with or without beers to start with). For the less energetic, the mini-golf at *Le Jacaranda* (Tsh500) comes complete with all the miniature bridges and concrete spirals you could wish for.

Supermarkets and groceries Modern, Sokoine Rd, just west of the corner with Goliondoi Rd; Kibo, Sokoine Rd near Sikh Union St; Karim's, Jacaranda St; Makwani, Swahili St; Kijenge Self-Service Supermarket, Old Moshi Rd next to *Spices & Herbs*. Good fruit and vegetables can be bought here, at *Mambo Italiano* restaurant and, of course, at the central market. Meat King, in the passageway beside the Adventure Centre on Goliondoi Rd, is a favourite with expats, despite its famously grumpy owners, stocking imported beef, cheese, smoked hams, sausages and salami.

connections to Iringa, Mbeya, Kyela and Songea. Companies with particularly **dangerous reputations** include Air Msae, Hood, Tawfiq, Takrim and Coaster Bus. Dar Express comes in for more praise than criticism, though the latter is generally scathing. Especially terrible are the larger daladala "coasters" that run throughout the day to Moshi – avoid these if you possibly can. **Bus tickets** for most other companies can be bought at the stands in the bus station. It's best to buy tickets the day before, or to leave very early: most buses have left by mid-morning.

Although a handful of standard buses go daily to **Nairobi**, it's quicker and less hassle (but more expensive) go on one of the daily **shuttle buses**, which leave from *Novotel's* parking lot (although they can pick you up at your hotel if you buy the ticket in advance, and will drop you at your chosen hotel in Nairobi). There are eight buses, with (rather bizarrely) four leaving all together at 8am and another four at 2pm; officially they cost $20, but this can be bargained down to around Tsh10,000. Kenyan visas are issued without fuss at the Namanga border ($50 for most nationalities). The relevant companies are: Davanu Shuttle, with offices at *Novotel* and at the Adventure Centre on Goliondoi Rd; FS Shuttle Services; Riverside Shuttle, ACU Building, Sokoine Rd; and Pallson's, whose office is at *Pallson's Hotel*.

By air

For a list of destinations and flight frequencies, see Travel details on p.411. Airline offices are listed on p.390. A $6 **departure tax** is levied on internal flights ($20 on international flights), if not already included in the ticket. **Arusha Airport** is 7km along the road to Dodoma. To get there, catch a daladala to Monduli and drop off at the airport sliproad, leaving you with a 1.5km walk. A taxi from town shouldn't cost more than Tsh5000. The easiest way to reach **Kilimanjaro International Airport**, 60km east of town, is to catch one of the airline shuttle buses. Both leave from *Novotel's* parking lot, but may be able to pick you up in town if you arrange things beforehand. See p.372 for fares. Note that the airport closes after to the last flight and only reopens at 6am, so you won't be allowed to spend the night there. Taxis to the airport are expensive: you'll do well to get the fare down much under Tsh25,000 ($25). Alternatively, you could get a daladala to Moshi and get off at the junction on the Arusha–Moshi highway, from where it's a six-kilometre walk.

Swimming pools The outdoor pool at the *New Arusha Hotel* (daily 10am–5pm) costs Tsh2000 for non-guests and is the only central option. The pool at *Ilboru Safari Lodge* is Arusha's biggest, and is set in lovely gardens. Access to the *Novotel's* pool (daily 10am–6pm) is a mean Tsh4000.

Telephone The cheapest place to phone or fax is the TTCL on Boma Rd (Mon–Sat 7.30am–10pm, Sun 8am–8pm), which has card-operated phones outside and an operator-assisted service inside. Be very careful with the phone services offered by some foreign exchange bureaux, which can be exorbitant.

Travel agents Reliable agents, all of which can arrange rail, bus and plane tickets, car rental,

safaris and trekking, include Easy Travel & Tours, 2nd floor, Clock Tower Centre, Joel Maeda St ☎027/250 3929, ⓦ www.easytravel.co.tz; Emslies, Goliondoi Rd ☎027/254 8048, ⓔ emslies.ark@ark.eoltz.com; Kearsley Travel and Tours, Sokoine Rd, near Roy Safaris (☎027/254 8044) ⓦ www.kearsley.net; and Let's Go, Adventure Centre, Goliondoi Rd ☎027/7111, ⓔ letsgotravel@habari.co.tz, who can also get you five to ten percent discounts on upmarket accommodation.

Western Union Western Union money transfers can be received at the clock tower post office or at the Postal Bank of Tanzania, next to Meru post Office on Sokoine Rd.

Safaris from Arusha

Arusha is the **safari capital** of Tanzania, and the best place for arranging safaris to the "Northern Circuit" (covered in Chapter 7). There are more than three hundred companies in town, including an awful lot of dodgy outfits. If you want more flexibility, hiring a your own vehicle (preferably with a driver, though most companies insist on this anyway) is a great alternative to an organized safari, and can actually work out cheaper if you can fill all the seats (five in a 4WD, nine or more in a minibus). See the "Safaris" section on p.55 for more details on choosing a safari.

No matter what your budget is, the longer the trip, the better it's likely to be. Although some operators offer **one-day trips** to Manyara or Ngorongoro, travel to and from Arusha will take up half the day, giving only few hours for spotting wildlife (the exceptions are Arusha and Tarangire national parks, both of which are within a couple of hours' drive of Arusha). The same applies to **two-day trips**, which usually only give you time for two game drives: one in the afternoon when you arrive, the other the next morning before heading back to Arusha. Over **three days**, trips become much more rewarding and flexible: a good combination would be Ngorongoro and either Lake Manyara or Tarangire. The former is good for birdlife, the latter for elephants. Over **four days**, the Serengeti is a possibility, though five or six days are recommended to avoid rushing.

Other trips offered by many operators include canoeing, cycling and rock-climbing near Lake Manyara, guided walks in and around Ngorongoro and Tarangire, hikes up Mount Meru or Kilimanjaro (though these are cheaper if arranged in Moshi or Marangu), visits to local cultural tourism programmes, and − particularly recommended − a **Crater Highlands trek**. Although the exact route and length varies (usually five days), these always start in Ngorongoro, and head northeast past Empakai and Olmoti craters before descending the Rift Valley escarpment towards Ol Doinyo Lengai − Tanzania's only active volcano − which you can climb, before continuing on through an arid wasteland to the desolate Lake Natron. Most of the trek is on foot, camping in the wild at night. You're accompanied by a guide and Maasai warriors; gear is carried by donkeys or on a vehicle.

Information

The headquarters of the **Tanzania National Parks Authority (TANA-PA)** are unhelpfully located 5km along the Dodoma road (Mon−Fri 8am−4pm; PO Box 3134 ☎027/250 3471, ✆tanapa@habari.co.tz). A taxi costs around Tsh3000; cheaper is to catch a daladala towards Monduli and ask to be dropped at TANAPA, a few hundred metres beyond the souvenir centre. The booking office here deals with reservations and pre-payments for "special campsites" (essential for Tarangire, Lake Manyara and Serengeti) and bedspace on Mount Meru. Travel agents can also handle bookings for a fee. For information about Ngorongoro, the **Ngorongoro Conservation Authority Office** is a few doors down from the tourist office on Boma Road (Mon−Fri 8am−5pm, Sat 8am−1pm; PO Box 776 ☎027/254 4625, ✆027/250 3339). Like the tourist office, they maintain a list of generally reliable tour operators.

TANAPA publish a series of **guidebooks** (covering Kilimanjaro, Ngorongoro, Serengeti, Ruaha, Udzungwa and Arusha) as well as excellent **maps** of Lake Manyara and Ngorongoro. Also available in town is a series of very attractive national park maps by Giovanni Tombazzi, each of which contains two versions: one for the dry season, the other for the rains. The road details are out of date on several, but they're still helpful − and make pretty souvenirs.

Arranging your own safari

Arranging your own safari is an attractive alternative, giving you much more flexibility. Car rental starts at around $110 per day; some reliable companies are reviewed on pp.396–8 (see also the list of air charter operators on p.390 if time is more of a concern than cost). For off-the-beaten-track safaris, the **Professional Tour Guide School** in Sanawari, just off the Nairobi–Moshi highway, is happy to provide students as guides for a maximum of two weeks. The fee is a negotiable daily allowance; a written recommendation from you is appreciated if the student deserves one. Contact the Principal, Vedasto Izoba, PO Box 12582, Arusha ⊕027/250 9845, ⊛http://protschool.tripod.com. Two former students who come highly recommended as personal guides are Hyasintha Lucas (PO Box 12582, Arusha, ⊕0744/843154, ⊜hyasithalucas@hotmail.com) and Joseph John Nyabasi (PO Box 7204, Arusha ⊕0741/355862, ⊜nyabasi@yahoo.com), who is extremely knowledgeable about northern Tanzania's tribes. Both charge around $20 a day plus living costs. For details of hiring **camping equipment**, and also for details of car rental, see p.390.

Safari operators

First, read the section on safaris in Basics on p.55. The importance of taking your time to choose a reliable and trustworthy operator cannot be stressed highly enough, and on no account buy a safari that has been touted by fly-catchers. **Prices** depend on both type of accommodation and group size. When calculating the cost, don't forget **gratuities**, which are always expected (some companies pay their staff so badly that tips account for most of their staff's income). There's no hard-and-fast rule about this, and tipping is entirely a personal matter: $40 from the group to both the driver and the guide (if there's a separate one), plus $20 to the cook, seems about right, though if your group size is large (say over four people), it would be fair to double those figures. On the other hand, if the driving was dangerous and the service awful, tip less or don't tip at all – but do explain why. Lack of wildlife is no reason to tip less, however – animals don't keep to schedules.

The companies below have been carefully selected: all come in for far more praise than criticism – nonetheless, common sense and a healthy dose of cynicism is helpful. Of course, fellow travellers are among the best sources of up-do-date advice, but be aware that even bad companies can come up with the occasional good safari, so don't trust everything you hear. *Via Via, Bamboo Café, Jambo's Coffee House* and *The Patisserie* are all good places to meet up with travellers.

Budget

Whilst not particularly cheap, **budget camping safaris** are the most affordable way to visit the parks, with nights spent in basic tents in even more basic campsites (the companies provide mats and sleeping bags), either inside or outside the parks, simple but filling food, and – hopefully – a vehicle that won't break down. Although some cheaper companies use minibuses, 4WDs are preferable; check that all the seats have clear window views, however. Group participation – sharing simple chores like clearing up after meals – is the norm. Prices start at around $90 per person per day including everything except drinks and gratuities. Although many outfits offer safaris for less than $85 per person per day, these bargain-basement tours inevitably have to cut corners, with poorly maintained vehicles, bad food, irresponsible drivers and so on, and certainly aren't worth the small saving.

The following companies are recommended for their own safaris, though all companies (even mid-range ones) farm out customers to other operators if they can't fill enough seats to make a trip profitable. You should be informed of this at the very least, and be given a chance to back out – keep your options open by paying only on the day of departure. If you're short of time, arrive in Arusha before Friday, as the better companies tend to close on Saturday afternoon and all day Sunday.

IntoAfrica *Manor Hotel*, Nairobi–Moshi highway, Sakina (PO Box 12923) ☎027/250 2139, ⓦwww.intoafrica.co.uk. A conscientious Tanzanian–British operation with the emphasis on fair-trade and community involvement, meaning that many trips include modules from local cultural tourism programmes. They also offer hikes up Kili and Mount Meru, but their main business is a seven-day "Tanzania Explorer" ($1080 per person), which includes two days of cultural activities.

Nature Discovery North of the Nairobi–Moshi highway, 5km west of Sanawari junction, Sakina (PO Box 10574) ☎027/254 4063, ⓦwww.nature-discovery.com. An efficient, conscientious and keenly priced French–Tanzanian outfit offering camping and lodge safaris (from $80 and $130 per day respectively; transport by 4WD), plus a number of interesting off-the-beaten-track options including the Crater Highlands, Ol Doinyo Lengai and Mount Gelai (by Lake Natron), donkey trekking from Longido, birding and walks along the eastern side of Lake Eyasi. Trips outside the parks are remarkably cheap, with donkey treks going for just $50–70 per day all inclusive. Mountain climbing is another speciality – they're fully licensed and enjoy an outstanding reputation for Kilimanjaro climbs.

Nyika Treks & Safaris *Arusha Resort Centre*, corner of Faya Rd and School Rd (PO Box 13077) ☎027/250 1956, ⓦwww.nyikatreks.com. One of the best budget to mid-range companies, with a reputation for good, basic safaris and honest service. If you want to see a bit of everything, their five-night combo featuring Arusha, Tarangire, Manyara, Serengeti and Ngorongoro is very good value at $540 per person in a group of five; other safaris use the cultural tourism programme at Mto wa Mbu. They also offer a Crater Highlands trek and culturally oriented trips to the Pare and Usambara Mountains. Prices for standard camping safaris start at $95 per day; lodge safaris cost from $140.

Safari Makers India St, above *Mirapot Restaurant* (PO Box 12902) ☎0744/300817, ⓦwww.safarimakers.com. A US–Tanzanian outfit with good vehicles and a wide choice of itineraries, from standard camping safaris ($85–135 per day) to extended lodge-based itineraries including the Southern Circuit parks. Their hikes range from a day's walk in Ngorongoro or a couple of days with the Hadzabe at Lake Eyasi to up to ten days in the

Crater Highlands. Many options can be combined with local cultural tourism programmes.

Shidolya Tours & Safaris Room 238–239, Ngorongoro Wing, AICC (PO Box 1436) ☎027/254 8506, ⓦwww.shidolya.net. A long-established company offering a comprehensive range of tours to suit all pockets. Budget camping safaris start around $135 per day, lodge safaris upwards of $150, and luxury tented safaris from $200–300. Transport is by Land Rover or Land Cruiser, and cultural tourism programme modules, trips to the Hadzabe and Crater Highlands treks can be appended. They also have licensed guides and porters for Mount Meru and Kilimanjaro (upwards of $650), and offer horse riding at the foot of Kili.

Sunny Safaris Colonel Middleton Rd, opposite the *Golden Rose Hotel* (PO Box 7267) ☎027/250 8184, ⓦwww.sunnysafaris.com. A long-established outfit specializing in lodge safaris as well as camping, with transport in 4WDs with roof hatches and guaranteed window seats. Budget camping trips average $85–130 per day, and safaris with overnights in special campsites go for $130–200 – much the same price as for lodge safaris. Their Crater Highlands trek (five days minimum) costs $140 per person per day in a couple, and a six-day Kilimanjaro climb is $700.

Swala Safaris Off Njiro Rd, Njiro (PO Box 207) ☎027/250 8424, ⓦwww.safaris-tz.com. A very competitively priced operation that could easily pass as mid-range. Their safaris – including a number of walking options outside the parks – tend to use cheaper (but no less atmospheric) tented camps, including their own *Migunga Forest Camp* (Mto wa Mbu), *Lake Natron Camp*, and *Ikoma Bush Camp* (just outside Serengeti). Unusual offerings include a trip to the Kondoa–Irangi rock paintings, wildlife walks around Tarangire and Crater Highlands treks with a climb up Ol Doinyo Lengai. Prices start at $110–120 per day.

Victoria Expeditions *Meru House Inn*, Sokoine Rd (PO Box 14875) ☎0744/288740, ⓦwww.victoria-tz.com. Experienced Tanzanian-owned company: their camping safaris (transport by 4WD) go for $85–100 per day, while lodge safaris cost $165–335 depending on the lodge and group size. They also do an excellent seven-day Crater Highlands trek from Ngorongoro to Lake Natron ($140–160 per day) and offer Kilimanjaro climbs for around $700.

Mid-range

There are plenty of **mid-range operators** offering comfortable safaris for upwards of $120–150 per person per day, with accommodation in lodges, permanent tented camps or in large "Meru" tents pitched on public campsites; the tents are fitted with camp-beds, linen and sometimes showers and toilets. Take care with transport, however – some big companies ferry their clients around in convoys of minibuses, which definitely detracts from the charm: at this price, you should really be getting 4WD Land Rovers or Land Cruisers and guaranteed window seats.

Prices for lodge safaris depend on the standard of **lodge** used: the cheapest are the formerly government-run TAHI lodges. Next up is the small chain operated by Sopa, followed by the luxurious Serena chain. More expensive still are a handful of privately run lodges and tented camps; most are reviewed in Chapter 7. Safari prices fall during the long rains (usually April–June, sometimes from as early as Feb), when lodge prices fall dramatically.

Dorobo Tours & Safaris 10km west of town: 6km along the Dodoma road, then 3km south (PO Box 2534) ☏027/250 9685, ✉dorobo@ habari.co.tz. A small, exclusive, socially responsible and very personable outfit run by three American brothers. Their tailor-made trips ($175–350 per day) feature an enjoyable and instructive blend of culture and wildlife and cover largely untravelled locations, excelling in rugged treks outside the national parks. If you have enough time and money, a two- or three-week trip is recommended to really get under the skin of rural Tanzania.

East African Safari & Touring Company Adventure Centre, Goliondoi Rd (PO Box 1215) ☏027/7111, ⚲www.eastafricansafari.info. A pleasingly offbeat operator with an excellent reputation for trips to suit all pockets, specializing in off-the-beaten-track destinations like Tarangire Conservation Area, northwestern Ngorongoro, Selous, Lake Natron, Mkomazi and the west and northwest of Tanzania. More unusual offerings include birding, an orchid tour, mountain biking and a six-night trip combining Tarangire with the Kondoa–Irangi rock paintings. Costs range from $100 to $180 per day for camping safaris, $185–230 for lodge safaris, and $420 for luxury camping safaris.

Farasi Safaris India St (PO Box 49) ☏027/250 0695, ☏027/250 8547, ⚲www.farasisafaris.com. A respected horseback safari company, with stables at Manyara, offering full- and half-day rides accompanied by knowledgeable wildlife guides. A half-day's ride costs $95, a full day $135 including lunch; longer trips are also possible. Transport from Arusha costs $110 per vehicle (seating six passengers).

Flycatcher Safaris Serengeti Rd (PO Box 172) ☏027/6963, ⚲www.flycat.com (in German). A Swiss–Tanzanian operation enjoying a good repu-

tation, despite its unfortunate moniker. They specialize in long luxury safaris (10 days plus), mostly flying, with the emphasis on the Tanzanian northwest (they have luxury tented camps at Katavi and Mahale, and are knowledgeable about Gombe and Rubondo Island). They also run driving trips through Ruaha and Selous from June to October. Upwards of $200 per day for normal trips, or $300–500 for flying safaris.

Fortes Safaris Goliondoi Rd (PO Box 1364) ☏027/250 8096, ✉arushafortes@habari.co.tz. Another long-established company with a good reputation, and the advantage of an office in Mwanza, meaning that safaris don't have to be round-trips, but can run clean through the parks from either end without retracing your steps. Most overnights are in lodges or tented camps. From $150–200 per person per day.

Hoopoe Adventure Tours India St (PO Box 2047) ☏027/7011, ⚲www.hoopoe.com. A major and much-praised mid-range operator offering mainly lodge safaris and – through their subsidiary, Tropical Trekking – a range of hiking and mountaineering expeditions pretty much all over the country. They also run the *Tamarind Camp* near Tarangire, *Kirurumu Tented Lodge* at Manyara and camps at Loliondo (near Serengeti) and west of Kilimanjaro.

Kudu Safaris Njiro (PO Box 1404) ☏027/254 8193, ✉kudu@habari.co.tz. Another large, mid-range operator offering a range of safaris, with ground transport in Land Cruisers. Seats on set departures for lodge safaris cost $180–230 per day in peak season; flying safaris with overnights in luxury tented camps are around $250–300 in low season rising to $420–470 in peak (excluding flights).

Predators Safari Club 2nd floor, *Golden Rose Hotel*, Colonel Middleton Rd (PO Box 2302) ☏027/250 6471, ⚲www.predators-safari.com. A well-organized and very reasonably priced outfit covering most options. Their longer trips are especially good, including a bumper nine-day Northern circuit itinerary (from $1400), with accommodation in moderate lodges or mobile camps, and a five-day Crater Highlands trek ($380–550 per person).

Roy Safaris Sokoine Rd, next to Stanbic Bank, and also at the *YMCA* building, India St (PO Box 50) ℡027/250 2115, ⓦwww.roysafaris.com. A long-established outfit that claims to specialize in virtually everything. Feedback ranges from average to excellent – a lot depends on the driver. Popular with those without much time is the three-night Olmoti Crater and Empakaai Crater trek in Ngorongoro. Camping safaris cost around $200 per night.

Scan Tan Tours Room 306, Serengeti Wing, AICC (PO Box 2611) ℡027/254 8170, ⓦwww.scantantours.com. Reliable safaris with standard camping trips from $140 per day, and lodge safaris from $150. They also offer cultural trips to a number of tribes, including the Maasai, Arusha and Iraqw.

Serengeti Select Safaris Haile Selassie Rd (PO Box 2703) ℡027/254 4222, ⓦwww.serengetisafaris.com. Specialists in mid-range lodge safaris, all tailor-made, and usually including nights at *Tarangire Safari Lodge*. Costs average $220 per day in a group of four.

Takims Holidays Tours & Safaris 4th floor, Ngorongoro Wing, AICC (PO Box 6023) ℡027/254 8026, ⓦwww.takimsholidays.com. A long-established Indian-run outfit which receives consistently good reports. They offer a range of lodge-based trips, with optional cultural tourism modules. Transport is mainly by minibus. Costs for lodge safaris start at $150 per day, depending on the lodges used. Southern Circuit trips are run by their office in Dar es Salaam.

Tanzannature Tours & Safaris *Pallson's Hotel*, Market St (PO Box 13317) ℡027/6502, ⓦhttp://users.belgacom.net/tanzannature. Cover most bases, from $100 per day camping trips to $400 luxury lodge safaris. Most of their trips are tailor-made.

Tropical Trails (Wilderness Trails) *Masai Camp*, Old Moshi Rd (PO Box 223) ℡027/250 0358, ⓦwww.tropicaltrails.com. A highly respected outfit offering personalized safaris, either by vehicle or on foot outside the parks (anything up to two weeks), with knowledgeable guides and reliable vehicles. Their camping safaris cost from $100 to $155 per day; lodge and tented-camp safaris are tailor-made, so prices vary, but expect to pay upwards of $160 per day. They also offer Crater Highlands hikes, cultural treks in the Rift Valley with Maasai guides, and a range of specialist activities arranged through other companies. They're also experts for Kili climbs, for which they have their own licensed guides.

Upmarket

At the bank–breaking level, you'll usually be accompanied by a "white hunter" chap as your guide – and although you'll be largely removed from Africans and the "real" Africa (excepting a few token Maasai warriors as picturesque guards), the quality of the guiding and service is invariably superb. Accommodation is in luxury tented camps or mobile luxury camps, catered by a retinue of staff who will set up everything before your arrival each evening.

Abercrombie & Kent Plot 11/1, Njiro Hill (PO Box 348) ℡027/6788, ⓦwww.abercrombiekent.com. A large and long-established operator catering mainly to the US market, with accommodation in lodges and luxury tented camps. They have good vehicles and back-up, but group sizes can be large on the more popular options. From $200 per day.

Coastal Travels ATC House, Boma Rd ℡027/250 0087, ⓦwww.coastal.cc. Primarily an aviation company, Coastal also offer entirely tailor-made flying safaris, specializing in lesser-known destinations like Rubondo Island National Park, which can be combined with Serengeti. They also do last-minute holiday deals to Pemba and Zanzibar – handy if you're short of time.

Gibb's Farm Safaris Based at Gibb's Farm in Karatu; Arusha office on Haile Selassie Rd (PO Box 6084) ℡027/253 4302, ⓦwww.gibbsfarm safaris.com. Attention to detail and personal service is the hallmark here – as it should be, given that their luxury camping safaris average $300–550 per day (including flights; a little less for lodge safaris). Most options are tailor-made and feature a mobile camp, and they have plenty of experience with elderly clients. They also offer flying safaris to the southern parks.

Greystoke Safaris Usa River (PO Box 1404) ℡027/254 8050, ℻027/255 3819. Specialize in flying safaris to the far west, where they have quirky luxury tented camps at Mahale Mountains and Katavi national parks, both within reach of Gombe. Prices start at $400 per day.

Around Arusha

For all the hundreds of thousands of tourists passing through Arusha each year en route to the Northern Circuit parks and reserves, only a tiny proportion see much more of the region surrounding the town than the stretch of highway running in from the airport. Yet there are lots of things to keep you occupied. **Arusha National Park** – which encloses Tanzania's second-highest mountain, **Mount Meru** – is an obvious and attractive destination, while the moutain's lower slopes are now home to several **cultural tourism programmes** which provide an intimate glimpse into rural life among the Maasai, Meru and Arusha tribes, and serve as an ideal complement to a wildlife safari. There are similar programmes at **Longido**, close to the Kenyan border, and at **Monduli** off the road towards the national parks.

Arusha National Park

In spite of its proximity to Arusha town, **ARUSHA NATIONAL PARK** is little visited, thanks to the siren lure of more famous destinations nearby, like Serengeti, Ngorongoro and Kilimanjaro – which is good news for visitors who do make it here, who can enjoys the park's stunning volcanic scenery, expansive views (especially of its giant neighbour, Kilimanjaro), hauntingly beautiful rainforest and plentiful wildlife in relative solitude.

Dominating the park is the volcanic cone of **Mount Meru** (4566m), the country's second-highest mountain. While Meru appears as an almost perfect cone when viewed from Arusha, from the east it shows the effects of the cataclysmic volcanic event which a quarter of a million years ago blew away the entire eastern side and top of the mountain – which was once taller than

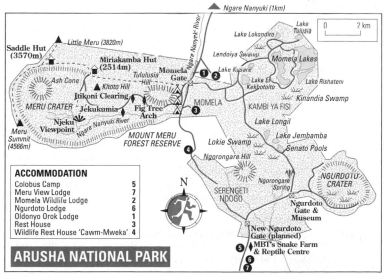

Ngare Nanyuki (1km)

ACCOMMODATION

Colobus Camp	5
Meru View Lodge	7
Momela Wildlife Lodge	2
Ngurdoto Lodge	6
Oldonyo Orok Lodge	1
Rest House	3
Wildlife Rest House 'Cawm-Mweka'	4

ARUSHA NATIONAL PARK

Arusha-Moshi Highway & Usa River (7km)

Kilimanjaro – in a series of gigantic explosions which hurled boulders over 70km to the east and unleashed a devastating flood of water, rocks, mud, ash and lava. Although the volcano is now classed as dormant, earth tremors still occur, and a series of minor eruptions were recorded in colonial times, the most recent in 1910.

The national park and its fringing forest reserve encloses much of the mountain, including the 3.5km-wide **Meru Crater** on the summit (often snow-capped in Dec and Jan) and the entire shattered eastern slope, as well as the mountain's eastern foothills, where you'll find **Ngurdoto Crater**, an unbroken 3km-wide caldera whose wildlife has earned it the nickname "Little Ngorongoro", and the shallow, alkaline **Momela Lakes**, known for their birdlife, especially flamingos. **Wildlife** you're likely to see includes buffalos (especially in forest glades), elephants (who are responsible for creating the glades), hippos, giraffes, warthogs, antelopes, zebras, black-and-white colobus and blue monkeys. Leopards and hyenas are present but rarely seen (there are no lions), while there are also some extremely rare black rhinos, though the park authorities are understandably loath to make too much noise about them, given the ever-present risk from poachers. There are also over 400 species of bird, and butterfly fanatics are in for a treat, too.

Arrival and information

Access is easiest from the south via Usa River (see p.407). The park has two gates: **Momela Gate**, 24km north of Usa River, which houses the park headquarters and is the starting point for hikes up Mount Meru; and **Ngurdoto Gate** to the south. At present, Ngurdoto Gate only gives access to Ngurdoto Crater and Momela Lakes, but work is in progress to move the gate 3km south, thereby making it the main park entrance when approaching from the south.

Most visitors come to the park on **organized safaris** from Arusha – a list of reliable safari companies is given on pp.396–8. A typical day-trip includes a three- or four-hour walk in the morning followed by a game drive in the afternoon. Visiting the park **independently** is a feasible and much cheaper alternative, given that hiking is possible throughout the park so long as you're accompanied by an official ranger or guide, who can be hired at the gate. To reach the park by **public transport**, catch the daily bus from Arusha towards Ngare Nanyuki, via Usa River, which is run by Urio Bus Service; it leaves Arusha at 1pm, and passes back by Momela Gate at around 7am in the morning. Alternatively, catch a daladala to Usa River, from where Land Rovers and trucks run every hour or two up to Ngare Nanyuki, again passing Momela Gate. If you're **hiring a car** to visit the park, a two-wheel-drive vehicle is sufficient for most roads in the east of the park during the dry season, but 4WD is nonetheless advisable, and essential during or shortly after the rains.

The **best time to visit** depends on what you want to do. Mount Meru can be climbed throughout the year, but is best avoided during the long rains (March–May), when you can get very wet, cold and muddy. Skies are clearest in September (when the mountain is bitterly cold), and again from December to February (when the temperature is marginally more clement). Birdwatching is best between May and October, when migrants visit.

Information and fees

The **park headquarters** are at Momela Gate, 24km north of Usa River (daily 6.30am–6.30pm; Ⓔanapa@habari.co.tz); this is where rangers, guides and porters can be found. **Park entry fees** are paid here or at Ngurdoto Gate.

Entrance costs $25 per person per day, plus Tsh5000 for a vehicle entry permit. **Camping** or a bunk in one of the two **mountain huts** on the path up Mount Meru cost $20 per person. Climbers need to be accompanied by a ranger-guide ($15 per day per group), and pay a one-off $20 rescue fee if going beyond Miriakamba Hut, meaning that fees for a three-day ascent and descent of the mountain work out at $180, excluding transport, food or porters. **Porter fees** are negotiable: Tsh2500–3500 per day is the norm, but there's no harm paying more (say Tsh5000–8000), given the derisory nature of this sum.

A **ranger** is also obligatory for walks in the eastern section of the park, though strangely enough the cost ($20 per group) is more than for climbing, and there may be an unofficial time limit of three or four hours, after which hefty "tips" are expected. If you're driving yourself, the services of an **official guide** ($10 per day) are optional. Although the mountain huts are rarely full, the park advises climbers to **pre-book accommodation**: you can do this at the gate or at TANAPA's headquarters in Arusha (p.394), where you can also book a ranger.

The beautifully illustrated *Arusha* **guidebook** ($10), published in 2001 by TANAPA, contains lots of information about the park and the town, and is especially recommended if butterflies are your thing – it's available from Arusha's bookshops, *Jambo's Coffee House* or the Ngorongoro Conservation Authority office on Boma Rd. The only decent **map** is Giovanni Tombazzi's painted version (see p.394).

Ngurdoto Crater and Momela Lakes

The highlights of the **eastern section** of the park, covering the forested foothills of Mount Meru, are the Momela Lakes and Ngurdoto Crater. Both can be visited on an organized day-trip from Arusha, which combines a walk in the morning (3–4hr) with a game drive in the afternoon. If you're visiting independently by public transport, you'll have to walk: the Momela Lakes are accessed from Momela Gate (2–3hr each way), where you'll have to hire a guide, while Ngurdoto Crater is accessible from Ngurdoto Gate (2km to the crater rim, and a further 3km to Buffalo Point). At the time of writing, however, there were no guides at Ngurdoto Gate, so visitors had to go to Momela Gate to hire one, then return to Ngurdoto Gate to begin the walk. This faintly absurd situation should be rectified when Ngurdoto Gate is moved south and becomes the park's main southern entrance.

The **Momela Lakes** in the northeast of the park comprise seven shallow, alkaline lakes formed from the volcanic debris created when Mount Meru blew its top 250,000 years ago. The alkalinity is ideal for various forms of algae, which account for the lakes' opaque shades of emerald and turquoise and provide an ideal habitat for filter-feeders like flamingos. Other birds include pelicans and ducks, and a host of migrants, especially between May and October. Glimpses of black-and-white colobus monkeys are virtually guaranteed in the forests around the lakes, and you may also catch sight of blue monkeys, bushbucks, buffalos, hippos, giraffes and zebras.

Three more lakes and Lokie Swamp flank the driveable road south from Momela Lakes to **Ngurdoto Crater**, an unbroken, 3km-wide, 400m-deep volcanic caldera (inevitably dubbed "Little Ngorongoro") produced when two volcanic cones merged and finally collapsed – you can walk along the crater's western and southern rims. Like Ngorongoro, Ngurdoto plays host to a rich variety of wildlife, including buffalos, elephants, baboons and occasionally rhinos. To protect this little Eden, especially the highly endangered rhinos (which were hunted to the point of extinction in the 1980s), visitors aren't allowed to descend to the crater floor. Instead, you can view the crater's denizens from a series of viewpoints on the south side of the rim, which also gives good views of Kilimanjaro, weather permitting.

Two kilometres west of the crater, at least for now, is **Ngurdoto Gate** and **Ngurdoto Gate Museum** (free), which has modest displays of butterflies, moths, insects, birds and – more worryingly – snares used by poachers. The most startling exhibit is a rhinoceros skull with a wire snare embedded several centimetres into it; the rhino survived several years before the wire finally killed it. It's not clear whether the museum will be shifted with the gate, when the latter is moved 3km to the south. Back on the main Usa River–Momela road, 1km south of the park boundary (and 7.5km north of Usa River), **MBT's Snake Farm & Reptile Centre** (daily 8am–5pm; Tsh2400), opposite *Colobus Camp*, is worth a visit if you're in the area. Its main purpose is breeding snakes and reptiles for export, and there's an extensive collection of scaly critters on display, including chameleons.

Heading back towards Momela, keep an eye out for wildlife in the diminutive patch of grassland to the right. Dubbed **Serengeti Ndogo** ("Little Serengeti"), it contains a variety of plains game, including a population of zebra introduced following the collapse of an export scheme.

Mount Meru

MOUNT MERU is sometimes treated as an acclimatization trip before an attempt on Kilimanjaro, but although the summit is over a kilometre lower, the climb can be just as rewarding, with spectacular scenery and dense forest. The mountain's **vegetational zones** are similar to Kilimanjaro's, though the high-altitude glaciers and ice fields are absent. Evergreen forest begins at around 1800m, moist, cool and thick at first, then thinning as you rise. The higher forest, including giant bamboo thickets (up to 12m tall), offers an ideal habitat for small duiker antelopes and primates, notably blue monkeys and black-and-white colobus monkeys, which are often seen by climbers. The forest disappears at around 2900m, giving way to floral meadows where you might spot buffalo, giraffe or warthog, followed by a zone of giant lobelia and groundsel, and finally – above the last of the trees at 3400m – bleak alpine desert where the only sounds, apart from your breathing, are the wind and the cries of white-necked ravens.

The ascent

The ascent starts at Momela Gate (1500m), where rangers (obligatory), guides and porters can be hired – for details of park **fees** and other costs, see p.401. The trek is usually done over three days (two up, one down), but an extra day will help you acclimatize, and in any case the views are something to be savoured. Climbs of Mount Meru are usually done through a safari company, though if you're suitably equipped (see "What to take" on p.330), you can save a modest amount of money by arranging things yourself. **Altitude sickness** (see p.332) isn't as much of a problem on Mount Meru as on Kilimanjaro, but symptoms should nonetheless be treated seriously. If you come down with the mild form of altitude sickness, Little Meru Peak, also on the crater rim but 750m lower than Meru Summit, is an easier target than Meru Summit itself. Be aware of an **apparent scam**, reported by some climbers. This involves rangers who don't wish to ascend all the way setting too fast a pace in order to deliberately tire out their charges, who are consequently only too happy to turn back if given the chance.

Day one (4–5hr) goes from Momela Gate to **Miriakamba Hut** (2514m). There are two routes, the steeper and more direct one heads up due west (and is mainly used by walkers when descending); the longer and more picturesque route follows a driveable trail to the south which begins by hugging the boulder-strewn **Ngare Nanyuki** (Red River); look for tawny eagles in the yellow-bark acacia trees here. The trees were called "fever trees" by early explorers, as they were believed to cause malaria – in fact, it's the swampy ground they favour that attracts the mosquitoes which carry the disease. The trail curves around **Tululusia Hill** (Sentinel Hill), in the lee of which stands an enormous strangling fig tree whose aerial roots have formed a natural arch; there's a waterfall on the Tululusia River near the tree. A kilometre beyond the tree is **Itikoni** clearing, a popular grazing area for buffalos, and 1km further on is Jekukumia, where a small diversion takes you to the confluence of Ngare Nanyuki and **Jekukumia** rivers. At around 2000m both routes enter the rainforest, characterized by the African olive (rare elsewhere thanks to its useful timber). Bushbuck may be seen here. Buffalo and elephant droppings mean you should be careful when walking around Miriakamba Hut at night

Day two heads on up to the **Saddle Hut** (3570m) below the northern rim of the summit crater (2–3hr). If you have time and energy, a short detour to **Little Meru Peak** (3820m) is possible (5–6hr from Miriakamba Hut), though the symptoms of altitude sickness kick in on this day, so spending an extra day at Saddle Hut to climb Little Meru is recommended. **Day three** (or day four if you spent an extra day at Saddle Hut) starts no later than 2am for the 4–5hr ascent to **Meru Summit** (4566m), following a very narrow ridge along the western rim of the crater, to arrive in time for sunrise over Kilimanjaro. Lunch is taken on the way down at Saddle Hut, and the park gate is reached by late afternoon. Alternatively, you could take it easy and spend an extra night at Miriakamba Hut, some four to five hours' walk from the summit.

Accommodation

The only accommodation within the park are a park-run **rest house**, three **campsites** a kilometre or two southwest from Momela Gate and the two **mountain huts** on the route up Mount Meru (see above). All these options cost $20 per person, plus park entry fees; bed space can be reserved through TANAPA in Arusha (p.394). Apart from the rest houses (there's another in the forest reserve south of the park), you don't have to pay park fees to stay at the following places.

Colobus Camp 7.3km north of Usa River on the left (bookings through Shidolya Tours & Safaris, p.394). A brand-new complex with a gigantic *makuti*-thatched bar and restaurant. There are three stone *bandas* (with another 17 planned) and a campsite. ❺

Meru View Lodge 6.5km north of Usa River on the right ☏027/255 3876. Run by an elderly German couple, this quiet and charming option is set in sunny and colourful gardens containing a number of aviaries. There are seven, clean simple but comfortable rooms in individual cottages, five en suite, and all with big double beds. Food and drinks are available, and hikes in the park can be arranged. Breakfast included. ❺

Momela Wildlife Lodge (Momela Lodge) 2km north of Momela Gate (no phone; bookings on ☏027/250 6423, ⓦ www.safariestal.com). The biggest and least intimate option, with 55 faded rooms in a series of not very beautiful wooden thatch-roofed *bandas* supposedly styled after an African village. Still, there's hot water and good views of Mount Meru, while for film buffs, this is where the cheesy John Wayne movie *Hatari* was shot – quite literally, as the bow-legged strongman bagged an elephant on celluloid. There's a bar and lounge with a fireplace, a restaurant ($10 a meal) and a big swimming pool for guests only. Free early-morning bird walks are offered. Breakfast included. ❻

Ngurdoto Lodge 7km north of Usa River, just beyond *Meru View Lodge* ℡0744/476677, ✉ngurdoto-lodge@habari.co.tz. An expensive upmarket choice with a classy two-storey main building styled after a colonial farmhouse, though unfortunately the five thatched guest cottages in the gardens are very average in comparison (each has two single beds, which can be joined). On the positive side, the bathrooms are good, the main building is a real delight, and its verandah has a fantastic view of Kilimanjaro, as does the small swimming pool. Breakfast included. ❽, half-board ❾

Oldonyo Orok Lodge 1km north of Momella Gate (reservations required; contact *Serengeti Select Safaris*, p.398). Another exclusive choice, even more expensive than *Ngurdoto*, but equally formal. There are twelve en-suite rooms: six in the main "Centre House", the others in a less attractive new wing. The glimpses of the unlovely *Momela Wildlife Lodge* nearby are compensated for by local

wildlife: giraffes frequently come right up to the lodge, bushbabies and genets are seen at night, and the calls of spotted hyenas are suitably spine-tingling. Breakfast included. ❾

Rest House 1.3km south of Momela Gate; turn east at the signpost for "Halali" (reservations through TANAPA in Arusha; pay at the park gate). Perfectly decent bunks and bathrooms, though park fees apply. $20 per person.

Wildlife Rest House "Cawm-Mweka" 6km south of Momela Gate in the Mount Meru Forest Reserve (reservations through Mweka College of African Wildlife Management, PO Box 3031, Moshi ℡ Kibosho 18). In a grassy forest clearing beside the roadside, this has just two beds, solar electricity, a toilet and bucket shower. Rates are $10 per person ($5 for camping), and $5 for an obligatory ranger-guide (not much English spoken) if you want to walk in the surrounding forest; you'll also have to pay forest reserve fees of $15 for each 24hr period.

Cultural tourism programmes around Mount Meru

Although Arusha National Park covers only the eastern flank and the summit of Mount Meru, the southern and northern slopes can also be visited through a number of **cultural tourism programmes**, combining beautiful views, encounters with rural communities and hiking.

Ilkiding'a

Seven kilometres northwest of Arusha on the southern slopes of Mount Meru is **ILKIDING'A** village. The **cultural tourism programme** here offers half- to three-day guided tours, including walks through farms, visits to a healer and local craftsmen, and hikes along the thickly vegetated Njeche Canyon, which has some caves to explore, and up Leleto Hill. The three-day hike (or one day by mountain bike) also features forest reserves and local markets, with nights spent camping or with local families. **To get there**, turn north at the signpost for the *Ilboru Safari Lodge* on the Nairobi–Moshi highway (Mianzini junction) and follow the signs. If you don't have your own transport you can hire a taxi at the junction or walk (2hr). Alternatively, you can arrange to be picked up in the morning by a guide in Arusha and spend the day walking to Ilkiding'a and back (at least 8hr). Bookings and guides can be arranged through the tourist office in Arusha, or directly on ℡0741/520264 or ✉enmasarie@yahoo.com. **Costs** depend on group size, ranging from Tsh6500–12,000 per person for half a day up to Tsh16,000–21,500 for a full day and night.

Mkuru

On the north side of Mount Meru, some 70km from Arusha, the Maasai settlement of **MKURU** is famed for its camels, which were introduced in the

Tanzania's pioneering **cultural tourism programme** was set up in 1995 by the Netherlands Development Organisation (SNV) following a request from Maasai in Longido for assistance in establishing a form of community-based tourism that would benefit them, rather than just the big boys in Arusha. The idea was to provide visitors with a parallel experience to standard wildlife safaris, while allowing local communities to enjoy the benefits of participation in the tourist trade.

The programme has grown in leaps and bounds since: it currently receives almost 10,000 visitors annually and offers dozens of community-based experiences in almost twenty locations (mainly in northern Tanzania) which give visitors the opportunity of getting to know local people, their cultures, ways of life, history and environment in a friendly, intimate and invariably memorable way. The villagers, in turn, benefit directly from tourists in form of services bought (local guides, food, accommodation, entrance fees), and through a modest "development fee" which goes into a community fund for local projects. Costs are extremely reasonable: a typical trip average $10–20 for a full day, a little more if you stay overnight.

The various programmes (called "modules") range from two hours to several days. There are several modules within reach of Arusha: Ilkiding'a (p.404), Longido (p.408), Mkuru (p.404), Monduli Juu (p.410), Mulala (below), and Ng'iresi (p.406). The various modules can be visited under your own steam or through a safari company, often as an option tacked on to a standard wildlife safari. The programme is co-ordinated by TACTO (Tanzania Association of Cultural Tourism Organizers), based in Arusha at the tourist's board office on Boma Road (PO Box 2348, Arusha ℡027/250 3842, Ⓦwww.tourismtanzania.org. Many of the trips can be booked through them, at the tourist office on Boma Road in Arusha, or sometimes directly with the local project itself – details, where applicable, are given in the guide. A quick word of warning: ensure that your guide carries photo ID, as the project's success has inevitably attracted the attention of a motley crew of scammers and dupers.

early 1990s, as they fare better in semi-arid conditions than cattle. Like Ilkiding'a, Mkuru has its own **cultural tourism programme** whose trips include camel rides (from a few hours to a week-long expedition to Ol Doinyo Lengai and Lake Natron), encounters with Maasai, bird-watching walks in acacia woodland guided by warriors and a short but stiff climb up Mount Ol Doinyo Landaree (3hr 30min return trip). At least one overnight is needed, preferably several nights; accommodation is in three two-bed cottages at the camp (bring your own bedding, food and drink).

Most visitors come as part of a regular safari to Arusha National Park, but there's **public transport** most of the way: catch a daladala to Usa River and change there for one to Ngare Nanyuki, 30km north of Usa River and 5km beyond the park's northern boundary. From here, walk the remaining 5km (signposted). Arrive the day before to give yourself time to arrange things. **Costs** depend on group size, ranging from Tsh13,000 to 16,000 for a full day plus Tsh2000 for accommodation. A two-night camel trek to Mount Longido costs Tsh41,000–50,000 per person.

Mulala

On the southeastern slopes of Mount Meru, 30km from Arusha, is the beautifully located Meru village of **MULALA**. The **cultural tourism programme** here is run by the Agape Women's Group, who will show you their cheese dairy (which supplies a good many tourist hotels), bakery, stores and farms. There are also a few short (2–3hr) walks around the village, including Masisha

River (for thick tropical vegetation and monkeys), and Ziwa la Mzungu – White Man's Lake – where legend recounts that a European disappeared while fishing, after frightening demonic sounds came from lake. The various walks can be combined into a full day, or – better – spread over two days if you have a tent. To get to Mulala by **public transport**, catch a daladala towards Usa River and get off 1km before at the signboard for the *Dik Dik Hotel*. From here, catch a pick-up or Land Rover for the nine kilometres to the Ngani (pronounced *njani*) Cooperative Society. Ask for Mama Anna Palangyo, whose house is nearby. **Costs** depend on group size, from Tsh6000–10,000 per person for a half-day to Tsh14,500–18,500 for a full day and night.

Ng'iresi

Seven kilometres north of Arusha on the verdant southern slopes of Mount Meru, **NG'IRESI** village – a microcosm of the Arusha tribe – is in transition: from cattle-herding and life in Maasai-style *bomas* (cattle corrals) to agriculture and permanent stone buildings. Several easy tours for visitors are offered as part of the **cultural tourism programme**, from half-day walks to two-day camping trips, and include visits to farms, an encounter with a local healer, hikes through Olgilai Forest Reserve, Songata and Navaru waterfalls, hilltop viewpoints and visits to development projects. **To get there**, walk 5km up the road that goes past the *VIP Lounge* and *Big "Y" Club* from the so-called Kwangulelo junction on the Nairobi–Moshi highway, or arrange **transport** from TACTO at the tourist office on Boma Rd (Tsh7500 for a vehicle each way). **Costs**, excluding transport, depend on group size, from Tsh7000–11,000 per person for half a day to Tsh17,000–21,000 for a full day plus overnight stay.

East of Arusha

The fertile lands either side of the highway **east of Arusha** were among the first in northern Tanzania to be colonized by Europeans, who grew tobacco here to barter with Maasai for livestock. Coffee later took over, and remains the area's major crop. The region offers unobstructed views over Mount Meru to the north – a feature much touted by the area's mid-range and upmarket hotels – though apart from the views, rural atmosphere and proximity to Arusha National Park, there are only two rather minor attractions: **Lake Duluti** and a small game sanctuary at **Usa River**.

Lake Duluti

Twelve kilometres east of Arusha and just south of the Moshi highway, **Lake Duluti** is a small crater lake which was formed at the same time as Mount Meru; the lake, and a small section of fringing forest, are now part of a 46-acre forest reserve. Like the forest at Lake Manyara, Lake Duluti's forest is swampy, being fed more by groundwater than rainfall. A signposted path has been cleared around the lake, but is difficult to follow. The lake is a popular destination at weekends for picnics, and easily reached by **daladala**: catch one towards Maji ya Chai, Tengeru or Usa River, and get off at Tengeru village. From here, walk south past a busy local market area (especially lively on Weds and Sun) and veer left on the road that follows the eastern side of the lake (follow the signs for the lakeshore *Serena Mountain Village Lodge*; about 2km from the highway). The lake can be reached though the grounds of the lodge or along public footpaths: one starts just before the lodge, another about five minutes' walk beyond. **Guided visits** to the lake can be arranged with *Jambo's Coffee House* and *Via Via* in Arusha.

Accommodation is limited to the lakeshore *Serena Mountain Village Lodge* (bookings through Serena Lodges, 6th floor, Ngorongoro Wing, AICC ⓣ027/250 8175, ⓦwww.serenahotels.com; ❽ including breakfast), a homely retreat of thatched *bandas* covered in creepers set 300m back from the lake in tropical gardens, complete with babbling brook. The better rooms have lake views, and some have funny sunken baths. It's a good place for lunch ($15), and there's also a bar.

Usa River

Apart from **USA RIVER** village's proximity to Mount Meru (the settlement straddles the road junction to the park), its only real attraction is a modest **game sanctuary** at the *Mount Meru Game Lodge* (daily 7am–5pm; Tsh600), which started off as a zoo for ill or orphaned animals, and also has a pond with flamingos, pelicans and herons and gardens grazed by eland and zebra – a good place for a lazy Sunday afternoon with the kids. Other than this, the main reason to stay at Usa River is to enjoy the peaceful (if somewhat neo-colonial) atmosphere of its hotels.

Daladalas to Katiti, Maji ya Chai and Moshi pass by regularly throughout the day; access after dark is by taxi (anything up to Tsh15,000). There are a handful of basic **guest houses** in Usa River itself (❶), plus various mid- to upmarket **hotels**. The nicest of the lot is *Rivertrees*, 22km from Arusha and 300m south of the highway (ⓣ027/255 3893, ⓔrivertrees@africaonline.co.tz; ❼ including breakfast). Part of a flower and vegetable farm, it's the cosy and homely European farmhouse atmosphere that makes this special, and the gorgeous garden flanking Usa River is good for birdlife. The rooms are all are en suite, and there's also excellent food (meals $16–20), while trips on foot or horseback around the estate and to nearby villages can be arranged. Another colonial-era farmhouse is the *Ngare Sero Mountain Lodge*, 1.5km north of the highway at the sign for "Leganga" (ⓣ027/255 3638, ⓔngare-sero-lodge@habari.co.tz; full board ❾), but the eleven bedrooms, although attractive and well kept inside, are arranged in an uninspiring terrace row facing scrubby gardens and are massively overpriced, as is the food ($28 a meal). More reasonable is *Mount Meru Game Lodge* on the north side of the highway opposite (ⓣ027/250 8346, ⓦwww.sanctuarylodges.com; ❽ including breakfast), an ageing but comfortable choice somewhere in style between colonial hunting lodge and traditional African. It has sixteen large, wood-panelled en-suite rooms in wooden bungalows, plus a bar and restaurant and – the main draw – a 22-acre wildlife sanctuary (see above). More humdrum but much cheaper is the *Hotel Tanzanite*, signposted 700m north of the highway (ⓣ0741/610254; ❺ including breakfast), a 1960s hulk with attractive gardens, a bar and restaurant (meals $8) and a swimming pool (Tsh2000 for day guests).

The road to Kenya

The bus ride from **Arusha to Kenya** is a delight, especially early in the morning when the mist shrouding Mount Meru begins to dissipate. The rolling hills and acacia-studded plains beyond can be fantastically green after the rains, but the lush appearance is illusory: like the area to the west of Arusha, the plains north of Mount Meru suffer from massive erosion as a result of overgrazing by Maasai cattle herds, itself a consequence of their expulsion from traditional pastures following the establishment of the region's wildlife parks and commercial ranches.

Longido

Located 80km north of Arusha along the Nairobi highway in the heart of Maasai land, **LONGIDO** is the most distant but most accessible – and popular – of the **cultural tourism programmes** around Arusha. The village's name comes from **Mount Longido**, the mountain that looms over it to the east, rising abruptly from the surrounding plains. The mountain's height of 2690m makes for a dramatic change of vegetation, winding up through dense cloudforest before following a series of buffalo trails across drier montane forest and scrub. The climb is possible in a day (8–9hr return trip), but two days, with overnight camping at Kimokouwa (bring your own tent), is recommended. With clear skies, the views from the summit are stunning; good weather is most likely from May to October. **Other walks** are possible in the plains around the mountain, including a half-day hike to Maasai *bomas* at Ol Tepesi, and a day-trip to Kimokouwa's "Valley of Wells" (the wells lead to an underground river used by Maasai herders), both of which offer the chance of sighting gerenuk (common in southern Kenya but rare in Tanzania), lesser kudu and klipspringer, giraffe, zebra, gazelle and buffalo. The guides are all young Maasai warriors, and most speak reasonable English.

The best **day to visit** is Wednesday, to coincide with the weekly cattle market, where you can also buy *kiloriti*, a root taken as an infusion for its stimulating properties – it may have something to do with the astonishing ability of the Maasai, and other pastoral tribes, to cover enormous distances on foot, seemingly without fatigue. **Buses** from the main bus stand in Arusha leave every hour or so, taking ninety minutes. The **cultural tourism programme** office is signposted a short distance from the highway in Longido. There's a basic and clean **guest house** (❶) in the village, and three **campsites** connected to the tourism programme. **Food** is available from local *hotelis* and the FARAJA Women's Group. **Costs** depend on group size, from Tsh9600–16,000 for a half day to Tsh18,000–24,500 for a full day plus overnight stay. The cost for climbs up Mount Longido varies but shouldn't be much more. Book at the tourist office in Arusha (see p.373), or ring the project co-ordinator in Longido on ☎027/253 9209.

Namanga

Passing Mount Longido, the road veers northeast towards **Ol Doinyo Orok** (2526m), a mountain which is sacred to the Maasai. At its base, 110km north of Arusha, is the bustling settlement of **NAMANGA**, which straddles the border with Kenya. **Buses and daladalas** to Namanga run once or twice an hour throughout the day from both Nairobi and Arusha; the trip from Arusha takes ninety minutes to two hours. Locals pass between Kenya and Tanzania with impunity, but travellers wishing to **cross the border** have to complete formalities, a simple procedure, though one which can take up to half an hour on each side if several buses pull in at the same time. **Visas** (currently $50 for Kenya) are priced and usually paid for in dollars (cash); some travellers report being able to pay the equivalent in sterling, but don't rely on it. If you need to **change money**, there's a branch of KCB bank on the Kenyan side, and NBC on the Tanzanian side within the customs area. The exchange rate between the two countries is fairly stable: 100 Kenyan shillings should get you about

Tsh1000, but don't be suckered into changing money on the street (or in to accepting offers of dodgy safaris from flycatchers). Incidentally, if someone feeds you the line that you need to have some Tanzanian shillings to enter Tanzania, ignore it – it's just a ruse leading into the money-changing scam.

The Kenyan side of the border is famed for its admirably tenacious Maasai women, who sell trinkets and pose for photos. The Tanzanian side is marginally calmer if you can avoid the red-eyed daladala touts, but watch your luggage on both sides – there are rather too many drugged-up lads hanging about. If you want or need to spend the night at Namanga, there's a slew of cheap **guest houses** (all ❶) on either side, the better ones in Tanzania. For something more comfortable, Kenya is better: try *Namanga River Lodge*, a colonial oddity composed of wooden cabins set amid pretty gardens (❹), or the better-value *Namanga Safari Lodge* next door (❷), which also allows camping.

West of Arusha

Heading **west from Arusha** along the Dodoma road towards the wildlife parks and central Tanzania, the landscape changes with startling abruptness from Mount Meru's lushly forested foothills into a broad and largely featureless expanse of savanna. Although it turns green in the rains, for much of the year it's an unremittingly dry and unforgiving area, where the disastrous effects of overgrazing are depressingly apparent. With little plant cover left, the soil no longer absorbs rainwater as it should, and the resulting floods have gouged deep, lunar gullies across the land. Often taken as an indictment of the Maasai obsession with cattle, the massive erosion is actually more the result of the eviction of Maasai herders from their traditional ranges further west, which has created unnaturally high population densities elsewhere.

Kisongo and Meserani

KISONGO village, 16km from Arusha, is the first settlement of any size along the highway west, and hosts a lively cattle market on Wednesdays attended by herders from all over the area. To catch the best of it, you'll have to stay over the night before: there are cheap and basic **rooms** (❶) at *Sinya Bar* and *2000 Millennium Bar*, on the left of the main road at the west end of the village; both places also have food and drink. The Kisongo Maasai Gallery and Cultural Centre, 800m east of the village, is one of several souvenir emporiums along the road to the parks: you'll have to bargain hard, and bear in mind that if you're on safari, your driver will be paid a 20–30 percent kickback on anything you buy. Credit cards are accepted, but whether you can trust them with your card details is another matter. **Daladalas** from Arusha to Monduli also pass through.

Past Kisongo, the landscape becomes increasingly bleak, especially in October before the onset of the short rains, when the flat brown plains and distant inselbergs are edged by mirages under a leaden sky and danced over by spiralling dust devils. The next major settlement is **MESERANI**, 30km from Arusha, which holds livestock auctions on Tuesdays and Fridays. There are several cheap and basic **guest houses** with bars and restaurants: try the *Vulilia*, *Engigwana* or *Parselian*, but don't expect anything more than a grubby bed under a roof (all ❶). Much better, if you have a tent, is **Meserani Snake Park** (☎027/253 8282, @snakepark@habari.co.tz). Started by an Australian family in 1993, the park was almost wholly desert when they arrived, but the judicious planting of drought-resident indigenous trees has now (almost) created an oasis. **Camping** costs Tsh2000–3000 per person including hot showers and admission to the snake park. There's good, touristy grub and one of East Africa's funkiest bars (cold beers, cool cocktails, warm atmosphere), which becomes something of a riot whenever overland truck groups are in residence. The interesting **snake park** itself (Tsh3000) contains a variety of snakes and other reptiles, including lizards, chameleons and crocodiles. Most of the snakes were collected from local farms and villages. In return for not killing them, locals benefit from free antivenin. Highlights include black and red spitting cobras, and several black mambas, which are actually green: their full name is black-mouthed mamba, not that you'd have much time to savour the sight. There's also a crocodile pool, the fence serving mainly to keep out drunken overlanders.

Outside the snake park are a dozen thickly thatched houses built by Maasai, who sell **handicrafts**; there's little hassle, so take your time. If you don't find something to your liking, there's more choice at Tingatinga Art Gallery in the centre, and Oldonyo Orok Arts and Gallery at the north end of Meserani – both significantly cheaper than the place in Kisongo. The Maasai outside the snake park can also arrange **camel rides** (Tsh1000 for a short jaunt, Tsh5000 for a few hours), and guided walks through the village are also possible. To get to Meserani from Arusha, catch a **daladala** from Sokoine Road to the stand beyond TANAPA and the change to one for Monduli; alternatively, catch a direct bus towards Monduli (several daily; 1hr).

Monduli

The **Monduli Mountains**, north of Meserani, act as condensers for rainfall, and so are of obvious importance to the Maasai, providing year-round water and pasture. The area's main town is **MONDULI CHINI** (Lower Monduli; usually just called Monduli), 12km north of Meserani and the highway, at the foot of the mountains. Monduli's **cultural tourism programme** is based at **MONDULI JUU** (Upper Monduli), 10km further into the mountains. Monduli Juu is actually a cluster of four small Maasai villages: Emairete, Enguiki, Eluwai and Mfereji. Emairete is the main one, and occupies a crater that was once considered sacred. If you can, it's worth coinciding with Emairete's weekly market on Saturday.

The cultural tourism programme's various **tours** range from half a day to four days or more – all feature visits to local *bomas* (semi-permanent settlements formed around protective cattle corrals). The half- and full-day walks include a hike up Kona Saba escarpment for great views, a clamber up through rainforest to Kilete Peak, a trip to a herbal doctor and a visit to a small jewellery "factory". With more time, the two-day Olkarya tour (bring a tent) includes an *orpul* "meat feast" (a feasting and socializing camp traditionally reserved for Maasai warriors and their friends) and a visit to Olkarya, where warriors collect the red ochre with which they adorn themselves. The trip can be extended to three days, with a beautiful walk in the O'Liyamei Valley, and over four or five days with hikes up mounts Komoloniki or Tarosero.

Olarash village, a ten-minute walk from Monduli Chini, is home to another cultural project, **Aang Serian** ("House of Peace" in the Maasai language, Maa), founded in 1999 with the aim of preserving the indigenous cultures of northern Tanzania (especially music and oral traditions) at a time when westernization risks sweeping away many of the old beliefs and values. The project has already organized several arts festivals in Arusha, as well as producing CDs, tapes and books, and initiating a fair-trade programme with the UK. You can buy their publications (mostly about Maasai) and recordings from *Jambo's Coffee*

House and *Via Via* in Arusha, and online at ⓦ www.aangserian.co.uk. They also arrange a series of **tours** from their base at Monduli Chini, including a traditional medicine tour, indigenous knowledge tour, night-time visits to Maasai *esoto* (a traditional forum for young people to meet) and short ethno-botanical walks. Costs are no more than $40 per day; though more expensive than the cultural tourism programme, the guides (all locals) are excellent, and of course the money goes to a good cause. For more information about the trips and accommodation at their *Peace Village*, contact the project at PO Box 2113, Arusha ⓣ0744/318548, or visit ⓦ www.aangserian.org.uk.

Apart from Aang Serian's *Peace Village*, **accommodation** is at any of four family-run campsites; the best is the *Esserian Maasai Camp*, which has running water (the others have long-drops and firewood but nothing else). All tours start at Naramatu Maasai Jewel Market in Emairete. **Access** is easiest by 4WD, although it's possible to catch a daladala or bus to Monduli Chini and walk from there (10km). Ask for Mama Esther in Monduli Chini, who works with the tourism programme and may be able to fix you up with a bicycle or a lift. Costs (yet to be fixed at the time of writing) are likely to be around Tsh7000–11,000 per person for half a day, rising to Tsh17,000–21,000 for an overnight stay. Tours can be booked at the tourist office in Arusha (p.373), or directly on ⓣ0741/510170 or via ⓔ ctpmonduli@yahoo.com.

Travel details

Full details on moving on from Arusha are given in the box on p.392. Bus routes marked with an asterisk below are liable to delays or cancellations for several weeks at a time during the rains.

Bus

Arusha to: Babati (4 daily; 4–5hr); Dar (10 daily; 9–11hr); Dodoma (1–2 daily*; 12–15hr); Iringa (1 daily; 12hr); Kondoa (1–3 daily*; 8–9hr); Lushoto (1–2 daily; 6–7hr); Mbeya (1 daily; 15hr); Morogoro (1–3 daily; 8–10hr); Moshi (every 20min; 1hr 20min); Mwanza via Nairobi (3–4 daily; 15–20hr); Mwanza via Singida (4 weekly*; 24–35hr); Nairobi by normal bus (3 daily 4–6hr); Nairobi by shuttle bus (6–8 daily; 3–5hr); Singida (3–4 daily; 8–9hr); Tabora (2 weekly*; 28hr); Tanga (3–4 in the morning; 6hr).

Flights

Airline codes used below are: AE (Air Excel), ATC (Air Tanzania), CT (Coastal Travels), EA (Eagle Air), PA (Precisionair), RA (Regional Air) and ZA (ZanAir).
Arusha Airport to: Bukoba via Mwanza (PA: 2 weekly; 2hr); Dar direct (CT, EA: 1–2 daily; 90min); Dar via Zanzibar (PA: 1 daily; 2hr 30min); Kilimanjaro (PA; 4 weekly; 20min); Lake Manyara (RA, AE: 2 daily; 25min–1hr); Musoma (EA: 2 weekly; 1hr); Mwanza (PA; 2 weekly; 1hr); Serengeti (PA, AE: 2 daily; 1hr–2hr 50min); Shinyanga (PA: 1 weekly; 1hr); Zanzibar direct (CT, PA, ZA, EA: 3–4 daily; 90min); Zanzibar via Dar (CT: 1 daily; 2hr 10min).
Kilimanjaro International Airport to: Bukoba via Mwanza (PA: 1 weekly; 2hr 35min); Dar (ATC/PA, EA: 6 daily; 1hr 10min–1hr 30min); Dar via Zanzibar (EA: 4 weekly; 2hr 20min); Musoma (EA: 2 weekly; 1hr 10min); Mwanza (ATC/PA, EA: 6 weekly; 1hr 10min–2hr); Zanzibar (EA: 4 weekly; 1hr 30min).

The Northern Safari Circuit

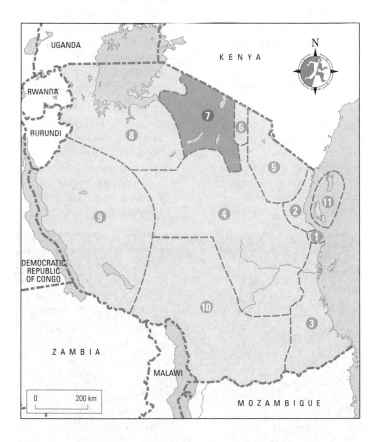

CHAPTER 7 Highlights

✳ **Ngorongoro Crater** When a volcano collapsed 2.5 million years ago, it left a huge crater, which now contains the world's biggest concentration of predators. See p.451

✳ **The Serengeti** The name says it all. When the migration of 2.5 million wild animals is at home, the Serengeti Plains contain the world's largest number of mammals. See p.456

✳ **Olduvai Gorge** The archeological site that revealed the cranium of 1.75 million-year-old "Nutcracker Man", and many other hominid fossils and stone tools. See p.453

✳ **Ol Doinyo Lengai** The Maasai's "Mountain of God", this near-perfect cone is East Africa's only active volcano, and can be climbed in a day. See p.440

✳ **Lake Natron** A gigantic sump of soda and salt, much of it caked with crystals, and home to the world's largest breeding colony of flamingos. See p.441

✳ **The Maasai** East Africa's emblematic tribe, and one of the more traditional. Aside from their imposing appearance, their singing is among the continent's most beautiful. See p.434

The Northern Safari Circuit

ead west out of Arusha, and the land quickly turns to dry and dusty savanna, marking the start of traditional Maasai pasture land, and the journey to paradise for hundreds of thousands of safari-goers each year – eighty percent of Tanzania's visitors. The pride of the country's blossoming tourist industry is a quartet of wildlife areas between Arusha and Lake Victoria, collectively known as the **Northern Safari Circuit**.

The most famous of its destinations, known worldwide through countless wildlife documentaries, is **Serengeti National Park**. Its eastern half comprises the Serengeti Plains, which in the popular imagination are *the* archetypal African grassland. If you time your visit right, they also offer one of the most spectacular wildlife spectacles on earth: a massive annual **migration** of over 2.5 million wildebeest, zebra and other animals, from the Serengeti Plains north into Kenya's Maasai Mara Game Reserve, then back down into the hills of western Serengeti, following the life-giving rains. Even if you can't coincide with the migration, there's abundant wildlife, and the plains are as good a place as any for seeing lions, often in large prides, and packs of hyenas.

The northern circuit's other undeniable jewel is the **Ngorongoro Conservation Area**, the centrepiece of which is an enormous volcanic caldera – one of the world's largest – whose base, comprising grassland, swamp, forest and a shallow lake, contains an incredible density of plains game, and a full complement of predators. Ngorongoro is also one of few Tanzanian wildlife areas to allow human presence beyond tourism: the undulating grasslands around the crater are the land of the cattle-herding **Maasai**, whose redrobed, spear-carrying warriors are likely to leave an indelible impression. To cynics, Ngorongoro's popularity makes it resemble little more than a zoo at times, with the uneasy cultural voyeurism of Maasai *bomas* (villages) set up expressly for tourists, and the presence of dozens of other safari vehicles each looking for that perfect photo opportunity. But overall, Ngorongoro is the highlight of many a trip, and its popularity is a small price to pay for the virtually guaranteed sight of lion, buffalo, leopard, cheetah and highly endangered rhino.

East of the Serengeti and Ngorongoro, in the **Great Rift Valley**, are two more national parks, less well known, but each with its own appeal. **Lake Manyara**, at the foot of the Great Rift Valley's western escarpment, is one of

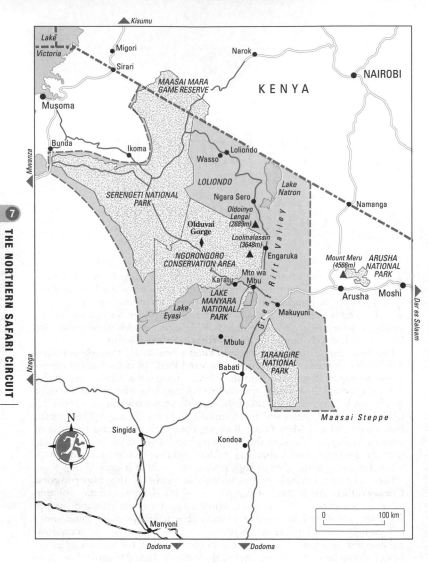

the smallest of Tanzania's national parks, despite which its wide variety of habitats attracts a disproportionately dense wildlife population. The bushy terrain, while not as immediately gratifying as the wide-open spaces of Serengeti and Ngorongoro, can still make for sudden, heart-stopping encounters with animals. The lake itself is a popular feeding ground for large flocks of flamingos, and has a series of picturesque hot-water springs on its shore. Southeast of the lake, only two hours by road from Arusha, is **Tarangire National Park**, a likeably scruffy place, whose millenarian baobab trees dwarf even the park's substantial elephant population; in the dry season, this is probably the best place in all of Africa to see pachyderms. Adjoining the park's northeastern boundary is **Tarangire Conservation Area**, a vast conjunction of community-managed wildlife areas, where the main attractions are guided bush walks, night game drives illuminated by spotlights and some consummately romantic accommodation.

But the northern circuit isn't just about wildlife. Two **cultural tourism programmes**, one at Mto wa Mbu near Lake Manyara, the other at Engaruka, a remote Maasai settlement, offer intimate and enlightening encounters with local communities, and there are also a number of archeological sites worth visiting. Engaruka contains the ruins of seven villages and a vast irrigation network, while the Serengeti's weathered granite outcrops, called kopjes, have **rock paintings** of shields and animals daubed by Maasai warriors a century or two ago, and an enigmatic **rock gong**, part of a huge boulder that was once used as a musical instrument.

Fans of really wild places also have a couple of other destinations to head to. **Lake Natron**, in the desolate north of the country, is an enormous soda sump, much of its surface covered by a thick crust of pinkish-white soda crystals. At its southern end rises the perfectly conical and supremely photogenic **Ol Doinyo Lengai**, the Maasai's "Mountain of God", which is East Africa's only active volcano. It can be climbed in a day, or as part of a longer hike from Ngorongoro's **Crater Highlands** to Lake Natron.

Access to the northern safari circuit is usually from Arusha, though you can also get there from Mwanza. The road from Arusha is asphalt to Tarangire, and an on-going Japanese-funded construction project should see tarmac all the way to Ngorongoro by mid-2005. Almost everyone comes on an **organized safari**. Recommended companies are listed on p.396 (Arusha), p.124 (Dar es Salaam) and p.484 (Mwanza). Most of Moshi's Kilimanjaro climbing specialists (see p.334) also offer wildlife safaris, albeit at a slight mark up. It is possible to visit the parks under your own steam, the easiest way being to **rent a vehicle** (preferably with an experienced driver worked into the bargain) – the price is competitive if you fill all the seats. Access to the parks by **public transport** is hit-and-miss and limits you to seeing wildlife on foot – something that was only recently permitted – so long as you're accompanied by an armed ranger. However, the parks have yet to work out the practicalities fully, so you should not rely on this.

Guidebooks and **maps** are sold at the park gates and lodges, but are not always in stock: buy them beforehand in Arusha. For practical advice on arranging safaris and avoiding dodgy companies, and for information on what to expect, see pp.55–61.

The Great Rift Valley

The **Great Rift Valley**, which furrows its way clean across Tanzania from north to south, is part of an enormous plate tectonic fault that began to tear apart the earth's crust twenty to thirty million years ago. This geological wonderland runs from Lebanon's Bekaa valley to the mouth of the Zambezi River in Mozambique, passing through a network of cracks across Kenya and Tanzania – a distance of 6600km.

The gigantic fracture is at its most dramatic in East Africa, where the valley reaches up to 70km in width, and whose floor, in places, has sunk more than a kilometre beneath the surrounding plains. There are actually two distinct valleys in Tanzania: the western branch, which includes depressions occupied by Lake Tanganyika (see p.519) and Lake Nyasa (see p.595); and the eastern branch, dubbed the Great Rift Valley, which is at its most spectacular west of Arusha, where it's marked by a long and almost unbroken ridge. In places, the exact limits of the fault are blurred by associated volcanic activity: Mounts Kilimanjaro, Meru and Hanang are products of these cataclysms, as is Ol Doinyo Lengai (see p.440).

Three major lakes fill depressions within the Great Rift Valley: Natron, Manyara and Eyasi. The southernmost is **Lake Eyasi**, at the base of the Ngorongoro Highlands, and the surrounding woodland is home to one of Africa's last hunter-gathering tribes, the **Hadzabe**, whose future looks as bleak as the lake itself. Increasing encroachment on their territory, the conversion of scrubland around their habitat into farmland and ranches, and insensitive tourism hyped around "Stone Age" images, may soon consign their way of life to oblivion – keep away.

Less morally challenging is **Lake Manyara**, at the foot of the highest and most spectacular section of the escarpment, whose northern extent is protected as a national park. The lake's water, though alkaline, is fresh enough for animals, including dense populations of plains game and large flocks of flamingos. **Mto wa Mbu**, the village serving as the base for visits here, has a popular cultural tourism programme that provides a good way of getting to know some of the dozens of tribes that have settled here, attracted – as with the wildlife – by the year-round water supply. There's another cultural tourism programme at **Engaruka** to the north, an excellent place for getting to know Maasai in a genuine context. The village lies within walking distance of one of Africa's most enigmatic archeological sites: the ruins of a city about which little is known other than that it was founded around six hundred years ago and abandoned in the eighteenth century.

North of Engaruka is the bleak and windswept terrain around **Lake Natron**, a vast and largely lifeless soda lake that will appeal to desert aficionados. At the lake's southern end rises **Ol Doinyo Lengai** ("The Mountain of God"), one of the few volcanoes in the world to spew out sodium carbonate (soda), with the result that the water is exceedingly alkaline – so that a thick, pinkish-white crust forms on its surface in the dry season. The unremittingly dry and desolate nature of the lake and its shore excludes most forms of life, the major exception being **flamingos**, who thrive on the soda-loving diatom algae, and who have made the lake their most important breeding ground on earth. At times, literally millions of birds paint the horizon with a shimmering line of pink; Lake Natron was recently declared an Important Wetland Area under the international Ramsar Convention.

Safari operators usually offer trips to Lake Manyara as an either/or choice with **Tarangire National Park**, southeast of the lake. But the two parks actually complement each other, both for wildlife and visually. Tarangire is the more open of the two, with lots of (partly seasonal) plains game and an immense variety of birds (over 550 species at the last count), and it is indisputably one of the best places in Africa to see elephants, especially in the dry season when animal densities in the park are second only to those of the Serengeti-Ngorongoro.

Tarangire National Park

Occupying 2600 square kilometres of wilderness in the Rift Valley southeast of Lake Manyara is **Tarangire National Park**, uncrowded and unspoiled, and possessing a wild and unkempt beauty. Together with the adjacent **Tarangire Conservation Area**, it plays host to an annual wildlife migration, which makes for fantastic game viewing in the dry season.

Although not as well known as the other Northern Circuit parks, Tarangire contains pretty much every animal species you're likely to see on safari, with the exception of rhino, which were wiped out here by poachers in the 1980s. Its major attractions are the **elephants**, of which the park has plenty even when the migration is outside the park (head counts of several hundred a day are not unusual), and **baobabs**, weird and hugely impressive trees that can live for several thousand years, providing wonderful silhouettes for sunset photographs.

Tarangire's wildlife importance stems from the **Tarangire River**, which loops through the park in an anticlockwise direction, emptying into the shallow and alkaline **Lake Burunge** just outside the park's western boundary. The river rarely dries up completely, and even in the driest of summers always has some water pools nearby. This is the catalyst for an annual **wildlife migration** (see box on p.420), which means that the park is best visited in the dry season (July to October or November), when the park's concentration of wildlife is second only to the Serengeti–Ngorongoro ecosystem.

Don't fret if you can't coincide with the migration: many animals, including some elephants, stay in Tarangire all year round, as do significant numbers of buffaloes, giraffes, zebras, ostriches and warthogs, and a full range of **antelopes**. Also

Bird-watching in Tarangire

With its wide variety of habitats and food sources, bird-watching in and around Tarangire is a major draw, with over 550 species recorded to date, the highest count of any Tanzanian park, and about a third of all Tanzania's species. In the swampy floodplains in the south and east, Tarangire also contains some of earth's most important breeding grounds for **Eurasian migrants**. Wherever you are, you'll rarely be left in silence: birdsong starts well before dawn, and continues deep into the night.

It's impossible to give a full list of what's around, but, to give an idea, the woodlands are particularly good for hoopoes and hornbills, brown parrots, and the white-bellied go-away-bird (named after its curious call), and for game birds like helmeted guinea fowl, yellow-necked spurfowl and crested francolin. Other commonly sighted birds include yellow-collared lovebirds and lilac-breasted rollers, barbets and mousebirds, swifts, striped swallows and starlings, bee-eaters, hammerkops, owls, plovers and cordon bleus. There are also four bustard species, including the kori, the world's heaviest flying bird, which is usually seen on the ground. High above, especially close to hills, soar bateleur eagles, their name – meaning "tumbler" in French – aptly describing their acrobatic skills. Over fifty more species of raptors (birds of prey) have been recorded, from steppe eagles (migrants from Russia) and giants like lappet-faced vultures, to the tiny pygmy falcon.

The **best months** for bird-watching are September or October to April or May, when the migrants are present, though access – especially to the swamp areas – can become impossible at the height of the long rains in March to May. A recommended **safari company** offering specialist birding safaris is The East African Safari & Touring Company in Arusha (p.397), whose trips are based at *Naitolia* or *Boundary Hill Lodge* in Tarangire Conservation Area, and cost $120–180 per person per day.

Tarangire's wildlife migration

Albeit nowhere near as grand as Serengeti's world-famous migration, Tarangire is the centre of an annual **migratory cycle** that includes up to 3000 elephants, 25,000 wildebeest and 30,000 zebras, plus large numbers of gazelles and antelopes, including the fringe-eared oryx, which is rare elsewhere. The migration follows a pulse-like motion, expanding outwards from Tarangire National Park and to a lesser extent from Lake Manyara National Park during the rains, and contracting during the long dry spell that equates to the European summer. The reason for the migration is not yet fully understood (given that Tarangire has both water and food all year round), but research suggests that minerals play a part; the park lacks phosphorus, which is essential for lactating elephants, and so perhaps explains at least their part in the migration.

In the dry season, from July to late October or even early November, animals concentrate along the Tarangire River and its waterholes, before the onset of the short rains prompts wildebeest and zebra to head off north towards Lake Manyara, and east into the Simanjiro Plains of the Maasai Steppe. Over the following months, the short rains give way to a short dry spell and the wildebeest and zebra give birth to their calves, before the arrival of the long rains, bringing with them large herds of other animals. By April or May, when the long rains are at their height, the migration is also at its peak, with animals scattered over an area ten times larger than Tarangire, some even reaching Kenya's Amboseli National Park, 250km northeast on the northern side of Kilimanjaro.

When the rains come to an end, usually in early June when the plains dry up quickly and lose their colour, eland and oryx turn back towards Tarangire, followed by elephants, and then, by July, zebra and wildebeest. In August, with the weather now hot and dry, the bulk of the migrants are back in Tarangire, where they will stay a few months before the whole cycle begins anew.

present are **predators**; lions can usually be viewed lazing around by the river and, with luck, you might also catch sight of a leopard (best seen in the Conservation Area, where night game drives by spotlight are allowed). Cheetahs exist but are rare, as the long grass doesn't favour their hunting technique, and you'd also be lucky to see hyenas, whether spotted or striped.

Arrival

Tarangire National Park's **entrance gate** is at the park's northwestern extremity, 111km west of Arusha. The first 104km from Arusha to Kigongoni village is along fast tarmac; the park gate is 7km south of here along an all-weather gravel road and is open from 6.30am–6.30pm (driving is not allowed in the park between 7pm and 6am). Special permission is required to enter or leave through other gates (marked on our map as ranger posts); the most useful of these is Boundary Hill in the northeast, which gives access to Tarangire Conservation Area.

Walking in the park is permitted, so long as you're accompanied by an armed ranger hired at the park headquarters, but at present is limited to the far south, so forget about turning up without a vehicle expecting to be able to walk around from the main gate. The situation may well change, however: contact TANAPA (see p.394) or the East African Safari & Touring Company (see p.397), both in Arusha.

All of Arusha's **safaris operators** (see p.395) cover Tarangire, usually tacked on to a trip to Ngorongoro and/or Serengeti. Day trips are possible, but bear in mind that you'll be spending at least two hours on the road from Arusha in

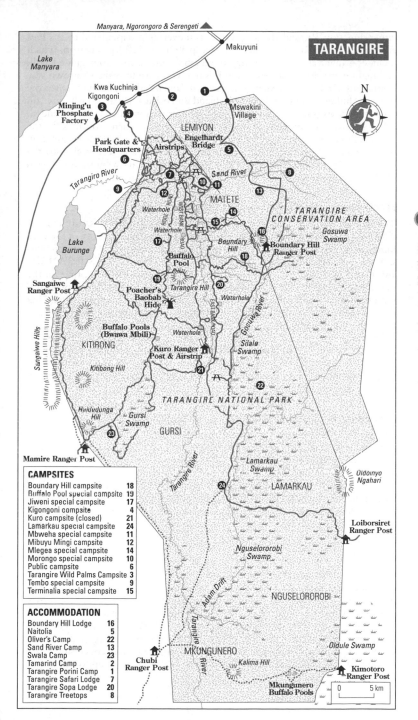

Manyara, Ngorongoro & Serengeti

Makuyuni

TARANGIRE

Lake Manyara

Kwa Kuchinja
Kigongoni

Minjing'u
Phosphate
Factory

Mswakini
Village

LEMIYON

Park Gate &
Headquarters

Airstrips

Engelhardt
Bridge

Tarangiro River

Sand River

MATETE

TARANGIRE
CONSERVATION AREA

Waterhole

Gosuwa
Swamp

Boundary Hill
Ranger Post

Boundary
Hill

Waterhole

Lake
Burunge

Sangaiwe
Ranger Post

Buffalo
Pool

Poacher's
Baobab
Hide

Tarangire Hill

Waterhole

Buffalo Pools
(Bwawa Mbili)

Waterhole

Silale
Swamp

KITIBONG

Kitibong Hill

Kuro Ranger
Post & Airstrip

TARANGIRE NATIONAL PARK

Hinledunga
Hill

Gursi
Swamp

GURSI

Mamire Ranger Post

Lamarkau
Swamp

Oldoinyo
Ngahari

LAMARKAU

Loiborsiret
Ranger Post

CAMPSITES

Boundary Hill campsite	18
Buffalo Pool special campsite	19
Jiweni special campsite	17
Kigongoni campsite	4
Kuro campsite (closed)	21
Lamarkau special campsite	24
Mbweha special campsite	11
Mibuyu Mingi campsite	12
Mlegea special campsite	14
Morongo special campsite	10
Public campsite	6
Tarangire Wild Palms Campsite	3
Tembo special campsite	9
Terminalia special campsite	15

ACCOMMODATION

Boundary Hill Lodge	16
Naitolia	5
Oliver's Camp	22
Sand River Camp	13
Swala Camp	23
Tamarind Camp	2
Tarangire Porini Camp	1
Tarangire Safari Lodge	7
Tarangire Sopa Lodge	20
Tarangire Treetops	8

Nguselororobi
Swamp

Chubi
Ranger Post

MKUNGUNERO

Adam Drift

Tarangire River

Kalima Hill

Oldule Swamp

Kimotoro
Ranger Post

NGUSELORORLOBI

Mkungunero
Buffalo Pools

0   5 km

either direction. Particularly good value is an overnight trip offered by the East African Safari & Touring Company (see p.397) for $120 per person, which includes a night at *Naitolia* in the conservation area, a five-hour guided walk and night game drive; the minor catch is that you have to make your own way from Arusha to and from Makuyuni (several daily daladalas and buses cover the route, including Mtei Coach and Highland Video Bus), where they'll pick you up. A similar trip over two nights costs $330 per person, and can be extended.

To get to **Tarangire Conservation Area**, turn south off the Arusha–Dodoma highway 3km west of Makuyuni, the village at the junction of the road to Manyara, Ngorongoro and Serengeti. The dirt track into the Conservation Area is passable by 2WD as far as *Naitolia*; in the rains, you'll need 4WD to get in deeper.

Information and entrance fees

The best source of information is one of TANAPA's **guidebooks** to the park, which can bought in Arusha's bookshops, at the park gate or in any of the park lodges and tented camps. The old black-and-white version ($5) is comprehensive but out of date for roads; the new full-colour version costs $10. TANAPA and Harms-Verlag were preparing a new **map** at the time of writing. In the meantime, the only one is Giovanni Tombazzi's hand-painted version ($10), with two plans for the dry and rainy seasons. It makes a beautiful souvenir, but the road network north of the Tarangire River has completely changed since the 1997–98 El Niño rains.

Entrance fees, paid at the gate, are $25 per person per day plus Tsh5000 for a vehicle. An optional **wildlife guide**, handy if you're self-driving, can be hired at the gate: $10 a day on weekdays, $15 at weekends. **Armed rangers**, for wildlife walks, cost $20 for 24 hours; tips are appreciated. The park headquarters are 1km inside the gate.

Accommodation, eating and drinking

The park and its environs have **accommodation** for most tastes and pockets, though budget travellers are best off bringing a tent: twelve campsites lie within the park, with several more near the highway to the north, where there are also basic guest houses (❶).

As far as **eating** is concerned, apart from picnics and some basic *hotelis* and bars in the villages along the highway, a few lodges and tented camps are happy to serve lunch to day guests, and also have bars: *Tarangire Porini Camp* ($12); *Tarangire Sopa Lodge* ($25; use of swimming pool Tsh3000 extra); *Tarangire Safari Lodge* ($15-18; use of swimming pool is Tsh1250); and *Tarangire Treetops* ($15 including use of pool; reservations required).

Lodges and tented camps

The **national park** contains two lodges and two luxury tented camps. The best upmarket accommodation however is a trio of tented camps in **Tarangire Conservation Area** (see box on p.424), hugging the park's northeastern boundary, namely *Boundary Hill Lodge*, *Naitolia* and *Tarangire Treetops*. The conservation area also has a cheaper option (*Tarangire Porini Camp*), which allows camping, and there's another modest tented camp in a private concession north of the park (*Tamarind Camp*). **Room rates** are discounted by up to half in low season (April–June).

Boundary Hill Lodge Tarangire Conservation Area, 47km from the highway ⓦwww.tarangireconservation.com (bookings through The East African Safari & Touring Company in Arusha, p.397). Close to Boundary Hill Ranger Post, this is a truly eco-friendly lodge – relying on rainwater, solar panels and wind turbines – with Lolkisale village having a fifty percent stake in the venture. The eight spacious, en-suite rooms ($440 per night per two people) are built of natural materials, and have verandah views of Gosuwa Swamp, as does the dining and bar area. All-inclusive ❾

Naitolia Tarangire Conservation Area, 18km from the highway ⓦwww.tarangireconservation.com (bookings through The East African Safari & Touring Company in Arusha, p.397). Located in baobab- and acacia-studded woodland, this is a small, informal place with friendly staff. Accommodation is in five secluded tents or an achingly romantic treehouse. All have flush loos and bucket showers – if elephants haven't drunk the water – but no electricity. Included in the cost ($350 per night) are game drives (also at night with spotlights), visits to Maasai *bomas* and sundowners on Sunset Hill. All inclusive ❾

Oliver's Camp Tarangire National Park, east of Silale Swamp ⓦwww.oliverscamp.com (bookings through ☏0744/465473. Nestled around a hillside with good views of the nearby swamps, this is a painfully expensive (full-board $400, all-inclusive $750), known however for its experienced wildlife guides - especially if birds are your thing; the location is a twitcher's paradise. Accommodation is in comfortable tents, all en-suite. ❾

Swala Camp Tarangire National Park, 67km from the gate, next to Gursi Swamp ⓦwww.sanctuarylodges.com (bookings through Sanctuary Lodges, Njiro Hill, Arusha, ☏027/250 8346). Sheltered in a grove of acacias well away from the crowds, and popular with the said *swala* (impala), this is a shockingly expensive luxury camp (full-board $660, all-inclusive $770) with en-suite tents, each fitted with a wealth of period furniture. The dining room and library are in similar style. Bush walks and game drives in open-topped vehicles are on offer. Closed April–May. ❾

Tamarind Camp Outside the park in the north: 14km west of Makuyuni, then 4km south ⓦwww.hoopoe.com/ktl/tamarind.htm (bookings through Hoopoe Adventure Tours in Arusha, p.397). Not the most appealing of sites, as the long grass and trees preclude good views, and the tents resemble a military camp, but no matter; elephants are frequent visitors throughout the year, and the place has a friendly and very wild feel. Accommodation is in ten large canvas tents, each

en-suite (chemical toilets and bucket shower) and with a shady verandah. Included are ethnobotanical walks guided by Maasai. Visits to Maasai *bomas*, fly-camping and game drives, also at night (through prior arrangement), are optional extras. Half-board ❼, full-board ❽

Tarangire Porini Camp Tarangire Conservation Area, 9km from the highway (bookings through ☏0742/401282, ✉tporini@habari.co.tz). The cheapest of the tented camps, this has a wonderfully peaceful hillside location with sweeping views over northern Tarangire. There's no fence, meaning that wildlife can pass through. Accommodation is in eight en-suite tents under thatched roofs, each with two beds and breathtaking views. There's also a campsite 800m uphill, with toilets and showers but not much shade (Tsh3000 per person). Drinks and food are available, and wildlife walks guided by Maasai are on offer, with lunch taken in the bush. The 9km from the highway, past Maasai villages, are walkable if you take care with wild animals. Breakfast included. ❺

Tarangire Safari Lodge Tarangire National Park, 10km from the gate, overlooking the Tarangire River ⓦwww.tarangiresafarilodge.com (bookings through Serengeti Select Safaris in Arusha, p.398). This 86-bed lodge is the only one in northern Tarangire, and consequently busy, but its popularity with package tourists also does away with privacy. Still, the rooms are fine (though don't have nets) and have bathrooms with hyper-efficient solar panels for hot water and a verandah overlooking the lawn, popular with dikdiks at night. The shoddy service doesn't matter, given the extraordinary location. There's also a bar, gift shop and a big swimming pool also open at night. Half-board ❽

Tarangire Sopa Lodge Tarangire National Park, 32km from the gate, south of Matete ⓦwww.sopalodges.com (bookings through Sopa Lodges, Savannah Rd, Arusha ☏027/250 6886). A large and functional rather than beautiful 150-bed lodge on a wooded hillside east of the Tarangire River. There's not a lot of wildlife interest, but the views are good, and the bedrooms (some designed for disabled people) are spacious and comfortable if a little dark. There's a small pool, large bar, restaurant and gift shop. Half-board ❽, full-board ❾

Tarangire Treetops Tarangire Conservation Area, 37km from the highway ⓦwww.tarangiretreetops.com (bookings through Halcyon Africa, ☏027/254 4521). This luxury retreat offers Tanzania's most atmospheric accommodation, with twenty quirky treehouse tents. Each has two beds, stone bathrooms, electricity and sweeping 270° views from the balcony. In similar style are the dining room and bar, close to a small swimming pool and a waterhole frequented by elephants. Optional extras are short ethnobotanical and wildlife walks, mountain biking (also with a guide), night game drives (daytime drives cost extra), and bush dinners. Highly recommended if money is no object ($440 per two people). Full-board ⑨

Tarangire Conservation Area

In recent years, a very positive development has been the creation of **Tarangire Conservation Area** outside the park's northeastern boundary. Formerly a series of "hunting blocks", local communities were given back control of their land in 2000, and they have subsequently banned hunting safari companies in favour of photographic tourism from a number of lodges and tented camps (see p.423), from which they derive an income. Environmentally, the move is also welcome, as it protects one of the main migratory corridors outside the park.

The area has similar habitats to the park's, except that it lacks the perennial flow of the Tarangire River. Instead, a number a seasonal rivers ("sand rivers") flow during the rains, and turn into a series of water pools during the dry season. The **best times to visit** coincide with the migration: usually late December to February as it moves out of the park, and from mid-May to the end of June as it comes back.

Apart from elephants, which inhabit the area all year round, you'll find much of the park's wildlife here, too, including impala, Thomson's gazelle, oryx and dikdik, ostrich, giraffe and wildebeest. All the lodges and camps offer **guided bush walks**, a great way of getting a feel for the wild. Another special way of seeing the place is on a **night game drive**, which is not permitted inside the park. This gives you the chance of seeing otherwise elusive animals like leopards and fringe-eared oryx.

Campsites

The park's **public campsite** ($20 per person) lies 4km south of the main gate, and is well signposted. There's plenty of shade, few tsetse flies, flush toilets and cold showers. Deeper in the park are eleven **special campsites** ($40 per person), which should be booked and paid for in advance at TANAPA headquarters in Arusha (see p.394), though you may strike lucky if you just turn up. None has facilities of any kind, and are often unnervingly close to wildlife; hiring an armed ranger may be necessary for staying at some of them. Firewood collection is forbidden, so bring gas cans, or buy charcoal at Kigongoni or Kwa Kuchinja before entering the park.

There are also a few **privately run campsites** outside the park, handy for a cheap overnight (all Tsh3000 per person). The most picturesque is *Tarangire Porini Camp* (see p.423). Well placed for those trying to hitch around the park is *Kigongoni Campsite*, 1km south of Kigongoni towards the park gate, which is used by safari drivers. It occupies a shadeless and dusty plot but is adequate: there are hot showers in the morning and evening, a bar and restaurant and a kitchen, and it also has some tents for hire (an extra Tsh3000 per person). Further from the park is *Tarangire Wild Palms Campsite*, 3km west of Kigongoni beyond the end of the tarmac, then 1km along a dirt track to the right in a scrubby area with fan palms, shady trees and a nearby phosphate factory. The attraction is its proximity to Lake Manyara (a 30min walk). There are squat toilets and showers, a bar with cool drinks, but no food or cooking facilities.

The park

Tarangire contains a range of different habitats, from grassland and woods in the north, to low hills, scrub and swampland further south. Cutting through these habitats is an evergreen corridor, the **Tarangire River**, which empties into Lake Burunge in the west. The river is the key to life here, and its northern extent – close to the park gate and *Tarangire Safari Lodge* – is the most popular area for game drives. In the dry season, when the bulk of the migration congregates around the river and its water pools, the area is phenomenal for game viewing. Fauna on the gently inclined grassland and woodland either side of the river is thinner, but the chance of spotting rarer animals like klipspringers and Bohor reedbuck, and rich birdlife, makes up for this, and the **baobab forests** in both areas are a big attraction.

With an extra day or two, you can venture farther afield. The shallow and saline **Lake Burunge** is an attractive destination, and usually has flocks of pink flamingos. South of here is **Gursi Swamp**, one of many marshes dominating the park's southern half and a paradise for birds. The **far south** is extremely remote and rarely visited; you need a permit from park headquarters to go beyond Kuro Ranger Post, in the centre of the park, and access by vehicle is only guaranteed in dry weather.

Walking in the park has recently been allowed, but practicalities are still at an early stage: walks are offered as part of the package for guests of the two expensive tented camps in the south (*Oliver's* and *Swala*), but for less bulging wallets, it's a matter of arranging things with the tourist warden at the park headquarters near the main gate, who can provide an armed ranger to accompany you ($20 for 24hr, plus tip). Wildlife walks are also offered by the lodges and tented camps in Tarangire Conservation Area east of the park, who can lay on night game drives illuminated by spotlight; see the box opposite.

Lemiyon and Matete

The park's northern section, between the main gate, the Tarangire River, and the eastern boundary, consists of **Lemiyon** and **Matete areas**. Their proximity to the park gate makes them easily visitable – and there's an extensive network of roads and tracks throughout the area – and together they contain a broad range of habitats, from grassland plains (where fringe-eared oryx can be seen), umbrella and flat-topped acacia woodland (great for birds) and more open woodland to the east that is dominated by **baobab trees** (see box on p.426). The **acacia woodland** is always good for wildlife viewing, providing year-round shelter and food, and there's abundant birdlife. Vervet monkeys and olive baboons are common in both areas, especially around picnic sites where they scavenge for food – be wary of baboons, which can be dangerous, especially if you have food in view.

The Tarangire River

The park's peerless attraction is the **Tarangire River**, which forms Lemiyon's southern boundary and Matete's western boundary. Although good for wildlife all year round, the river is at its most special in the dry season, when the migration concentrates around it and its water pools. The section where the river flows from east to west has sandy cliffs along much of its northern bank, and there are several **viewpoints** and a picnic site to the east of *Tarangire Safari Lodge* – bring some binoculars.

This east–west section of the river can be crossed at two points: across a concrete **causeway** in the west (dry season only) towards Lake Burunge (see p.427), and over **Engelhardt Bridge** close to *Tarangire Safari Lodge*, which offers access to two south-running routes: Ridge Road down to Gursi Swamp, and West Bank Road which hugs the river. Following the east bank is another road, accessed from Matete, which heads down to Silale Swamp. Either of these riverside drives is ideal for getting close to wildlife. In the dry season, a number of **water pools** attract large numbers of thirsty zebra, wildebeest, elephant

Baobab trees

The one thing that never fails to amaze visitors to Tarangire is its giant **baobab** trees. Known in Kiswahili as *mbuyu*, and to botanists as *Adansonia digitata*, the baobab is one of Africa's most striking natural features. With its massive, smooth silver-grey trunk and thick, crooked branches, it's the grotesque and otherworldly appearance of the trees that impresses more than anything. The **trunk's circumference** grows to ten metres after only a century, and by the time the tree reaches old age, it may be several times more. Most live to at least 600 years, but exact dating is difficult as the tree leaves no rings in its often hollow trunks. Carbon radio-dating however suggests that the **oldest** can reach three thousand years or even more.

Needless to say, the baobab is supremely adapted to its **habitat**, usually semi-arid terrain, its range stretching right across Africa and eastwards to Australia, where it's known as the bottle tree. One of the secrets to its longevity is its fibrous wood, which is extremely porous and rots easily, often leaving a huge cavity in the trunk that fills with water during the rains. The immense water-carrying capacity of the trunks – anything from 300 to 1000 litres – enables the tree to survive long spells of drought. For this reason alone, the baobab has long been useful to humans, and the Kamba tribe of Kenya, who migrated north from Kilimanjaro five centuries ago, say in their legends that they moved in search of the life-giving baobabs, and the Ukambani Hills, where they settled, are full of them.

The tree's shape has given rise to several **legends**. Some say that baobabs used to be in the habit of walking around the countryside on their roots, until one day God got tired of their endless peregrinations and resolved to keep them forever rooted to the soil, replanting them upside-down. On the Tanzanian coast, a pair of baobab saplings were traditionally planted at either end of the grave of an important person, which in time grew together to form one tree, enclosing the tomb within their roots. Baobabs were also, therefore, a propitious place to bury treasure, as the spirits of the ancestors would ensure their safe-keeping.

The baobab has myriad other more **practical** uses. The gourd-like seed pods, which grow up to 25cm long, form handy water containers and bailers for boats, and the seeds and fruit pulp ("monkey bread") are rich in protein and vitamin C, and are apparently effective against dysentery and circulatory disease, and a source of "cream of tartar". When soaked in water, the seeds make an invigorating drink (you can buy baobab seeds at Arusha's market); when roasted and ground, they taste similar to coffee. Young leaves are edible when boiled, and also have medicinal uses, and the bark, when pounded, yields a fibre suitable for making rope, paper and cloth, while glue can be made from the pollen. It's not just humans who benefit from the baobab. Wild bees use the hollow trunks for hives, hornbills nest in their boughs, and elephants like to sharpen their tusks by rubbing them against the trees. In exceptionally dry seasons, they gouge deeper into the trunk to get at the water stored in the fibrous interior: the scars left by these activities are clear wherever you go in Tarangire.

(who are responsible for creating a good many pools themselves by digging up the dry riverbed with their tusks), giraffe, eland, gazelle, impala, warthogs and buffalo. Olive baboons are resident, and lions too are often found nearby. The bush on either side is ideal for hartebeest, lesser kudu and leopard, which usually rest up in the branches by day, their presence given away by little more than the flick of a tail. This part of the river, before it veers west, can be crossed along various dry-season causeways and small bridges.

There's a pleasant **picnic site** by the river south of Matete, about 6km north of the turning for *Tarangire Sopa Lodge*. The site, by a huge mango tree, gives a good view of the river, which at this point provides a popular mud wallow for elephants.

Lake Burunge

The Tarangire River empties into **Lake Burunge**, a shallow soda lake just outside the park's western boundary, which is home to flocks of flamingos from July to November. The lake is surprisingly large, and makes a pretty picture with the Great Rift Valley's western escarpment in the background. There's no outlet, so salts and other minerals washed in by the river have turned the lake inhospitably saline, although during the rains the water is fresh enough to serve as a watering point for animals, including elephants and lions (look for their tracks in the mud). The lake's shallowness (barely two metres) means that its extent fluctuates widely. It tends to dry up completely at the end of the dry season, leaving only a shimmer of encrusted salt on its surface.

The road from the north – the last 3km of which are impassable in the rains – crosses the Tarangire River south of the park gate and isn't the most spectacular game-viewing area. You may catch glimpses of lesser kudu or eland, steinbok in undergrowth, and small herds of shy and rare fringe-eared oryx. Closer to the lake are plains of tussock grass and clumps of fan palms, hemmed in by acacia woodland and scattered baobabs, and weird candelabra "trees" (euphorbia) – imposing, cactus-like plants. Their sap is extremely corrosive, so the trees are usually left alone by wildlife: the exception were the rhinos, which sadly were poached to extinction in the park in the 1980s.

The plains are best for wildlife at either end of the migration (see box on p.420), when they fill up with large herds of wildebeest and zebra. But the main species to leave a mark, literally, are **tsetse flies**, clouds of them, especially in the vicinity of wildebeest (see Contexts, p.723).

There are two **onward options** from the lake: east along one of two roads crossing woodland to join the Ridge Road; or south along the park boundary and past the Sangaiwe Hills to Mamire Ranger Post and Gursi Swamp (p.428).

Ridge Road

A right fork just south of Engelhardt Bridge marks the start of **Ridge Road**, a superb forty-kilometre drive south through acacia woodland to Gursi Swamp, which in places offers beautiful vistas over much of the park and further afield. While wildlife is not as dense as around the river, there's still a pretty decent selection, with mostly solitary elephants, giraffe, eland, warthog and buffalo. They're best seen at two sets of signposted **buffalo pools** along the way.

The other main attraction here is **Poacher's Hide**, its name possibly explaining the unusual jumpiness of the area's elephants. The hide is an enormous old baobab tree out of whose hollow trunk a small door has been carved, to resemble the dwellings of elves and sprites in children's books. The artificial doorway has led to lots of speculation about the original use of the hide: it seems likely that hunter-gatherers, possibly ancestors of Lake Eyasi's Hadzabe tribe (see box on p.445), or the Sandawe further south, used it as a shelter or for keeping honey-bee hives. The hide was certainly used by poachers in the 1970s and 1980s, hence its name – thick grass around the site, and a boulder that could be rolled across the entrance, completed the disguise. The hide is now used by animals: hyena cubs, bats and bat-eared foxes have all been seen inside – take care.

The swamps

In the dry season, access to the **swamps** of central and southern Tarangire is possible. The swamps, which feed the Tarangire River, are among the richest areas in Tanzania for **birdlife**, especially water birds from November to May. During the dry season as the swamps begin to dry, the receding waterholes and remaining patches of marshland also offer superb game viewing, including large buffalo herds (up to a thousand strong) and elephants in search of mud baths. The most easily visitable are Gursi Swamp, at the end of Ridge Road close to *Swala Camp*, and Silale Swamp at the end of the East Bank Road on the park's eastern border.

A game track runs all the way around **Gursi Swamp**, much of the grassland on its periphery studded with tall termite mounds. Bushy-tailed ground squirrels are common, as are giraffes in the woodland. African hunting dogs, although extremely rare in the park, have also been reported around the swamp in the recent past. **Silale Swamp**, which should be accessible all year round, is perhaps even better for birdlife, and lions, preying on herds of zebra and wildebeest, are often seen on the western side in October. The fringing woods are said to contain huge tree-climbing pythons.

At its southern end, Silale merges into the enormous **Lamarkau Swamp** (whose name comes from *armarkau*, Maasai for "hippo"), which itself merges into **Nguselororobi Swamp** (Maasai for "cold plains"). Both areas, together with Ngahari Swamp and Oldule Swamp in the park's southeastern extremity, are exceedingly remote and largely unknown. You'll need a permit and accompanying guide or ranger from the park headquarters to proceed beyond Silale Swamp.

Lake Manyara and Mto wa Mbu

One of Tanzania's most dramatically located wildlife areas is **Lake Manyara National Park**, which occupies the northwestern section of a shallow soda lake at the foot of the Great Rift Valley's dizzying western escarpment. Despite being one of the smallest parks, the varied shoreline habitats contain a wide variety of animals, including one of Africa's largest concentrations of **elephants**, and the continent's densest biomass (the average weight of plants and animals per square metre). The park has been a UNESCO World Biosphere Reserve since 1981.

Much of the land is covered by groundwater forest or thick bush, which, though it makes **spotting wildlife** a matter of luck, allows an intimate and heart-stopping sense of being in the wild when the animals suddenly appear as you turn a corner. Algae in the lake itself attract large flocks of flamingos, and a series of water springs along the shoreline – heated by geothermal activity associated with the Rift Valley's on-going expansion – is another picturesque attraction. Although the park is usually tacked onto the end of a safari, after Ngorongoro or Serengeti, the grandiose nature of those places means that Manyara is best visited at the start of a trip, before you become too jaded with wildlife. A day-trip is sufficient to see most of the park's sights.

Lake Manyara is accessed through the small town of **Mto wa Mbu**, 2km east of the park gate. The verdant, oasis-like area around town, whose name means River of Mosquitoes, was a thinly populated patch of scrubland until the 1950s, when the colonial government began an ambitious irrigation project, aimed at controlling Lake Manyara's cyclical floods and for turning swampland into farmland. The project was a big success, and attracted farmers from the surrounding region. Then, in the 1960s, Mto wa Mbu was declared a collective "*Ujamaa* village" as part of Tanzania's ultimately disastrous experiment in "African socialism" (see p.718), into which thousands of people were sometimes forcibly resettled from outlying rural areas. In Mto wa Mbu, the main effect of the *Ujamaa* period is its extraordinary **ethnic mixture**: the population represents almost fifty tribes, including Hehe from Iringa, Gogo, Gorowa, Mbugwe, Nyamwezi and Rangi from central Tanzania, Barbaig and Hadzabe from close by, Ha from Kigoma on the shore of Lake Tanganyika (who introduced oil palms) and the Arusha, Chagga, Iraqw and Meru from the north and northeast. Some of these tribes can be visited as part of a **cultural tourism programme**; also recommended, as much for culture as for colour, are several **markets**: a daily one in town, and weekly and monthly affairs on the road back towards Makuyuni.

Arrival and information

Lake Manyara is usually visited as part of an organized safari, either at the start or at the end of a trip. The park gate is 2km west of Mto wa Mbu, 115km west of Arusha. As you approach Mto wa Mbu from Makuyuni, 37km southeast, you pass several Maasai *bomas* set up for tourists, which charge a per vehicle entry fee (usually around Tsh10,000) giving the occupants the right to take photos. Several **buses** to Mto wa Mbu leave Arusha's main bus terminal throughout the day, returning the following morning. The journey takes about three hours by bus, or two hours in a private vehicle. There's also a daily bus from Babati. The lodges on the escarpment (see p.430) can arrange road transport from Arusha for their guests; about $50 a person. Farasi Safaris (see p.436), which operates horse-riding trips around Manyara, charges $110 for a vehicle seating up to six people. If you've come on public transport and need a vehicle for visiting the park, any of the main tourist hotels can help out, or contact the cultural tourism programme (see p.432).

The **national park** is open all year round, but is best avoided in the long rains, especially April and May, when road access can be limited to the far north. 4WD is recommended although 2WD will get you to most places in the dry season. The **best time to visit** for big mammals is June or July to September or October, and again in January and February. For birds, November to May is best. **Park entry fees**, paid at the gate (6.30am–6.30pm), are $25 per person per day and Tsh5000 per vehicle. An official **guide** (optional) costs $10–20. The best source of information is the TANAPA **guidebook** to Manyara, available in Arusha ($10). There's an accurate **map** published by Harms-Verlag in association with TANAPA ($5), not that you really need one for getting around, and a more attractive hand-painted one by Giovanni Tombazzi ($10).

Accommodation

Accommodation is in three distinct geographical areas, the choice depending on your budget. The cheapest rooms, and a number of campsites, are in **Mto wa Mbu**, just outside the park. In **the park** itself are three special campsites which are actually nothing special, plus three beautifully sited public campsites and a small complex of *bandas* by the park gate, which are exempt from park entry fees. Three upmarket choices – not the best that Tanzania has to offer – overlook the lake from the **Great Rift Valley escarpment** west of Mto wa Mbu, and there's a fourth upmarket place to the north.

In Mto wa Mbu

Mto wa Mbu has dozens of cheap local **guest houses**, especially south of the market, and a few not-so-cheap places aimed at backpackers and overlanders. Most have restaurants and bars. Given the town's use as an overnight safari stop, **room rates** are often inflated (upwards of $20 a double), but there are still a few perfectly decent basic hotels with rooms under $5.

Adventure Migungani Lodge 1.5km east of the centre, then 200m off the main road ☏ 027/253 9178. In a large garden with some fever trees but little shade, this has four large, clean but over-priced en-suite rooms with nets and Western toilets. Better value are beds in the lodge's own tents, each with attached bathroom. Camping is allowed (no fixed price), and food can be arranged. Bargaining is possible. **❹**

Holiday Fig Resort In the centre, 200m off the main road just beyond *Red Banana Café* ☏ 027/253 9102. Lots of good, large rooms in this peaceful and relaxed place, all with nets, fans, clean sheets, hot water mornings and evenings, and electricity. The big draw is the swimming pool (Tsh2000 for day guests). Camping is $5 per person, and includes use of the pool. There's also a quiet "bar" (no alcohol) with TV, and a restaurant. Breakfast included. **❹**

International Mashanga Guest House In the centre, one block south of the market (no phone). A good choice for cheap, no-frills accommodation, all rooms with nets and fans, some with attached bathrooms. Little English is spoken but they're a friendly bunch. Safe parking. **❶**

Jambo Campsite and Lodge 1.2km east of the centre on the main road ☏ 027/253 9170. A big favourite with overland trucks, the fourteen rooms here, only one of which is en-suite, are depress-ingly cramped and dirty, and contain nothing other than beds and mosquito nets. Camping is cheap at Tsh2500 per person, however, though the site gets flooded in the rains. Food is available, and there's a gift shop. **❷**

Lodge (formerly *Camp Vision*) Just beyond the *International Mashanga* ☏ 027/253 9159. A friend-ly place that's more inspiring than its name sug-gests, with basic but good-value twin-bed rooms with fans, nets and shared bathrooms arranged around a courtyard with a big shady tree. They also have an annexe with en-suite rooms for Tsh1000 more. Safe parking. **❶**

Lodge & Car Parking In the centre on the main road near the post office (no phone). This even more invitingly named hotel is also pretty decent, quiet, and has clean, basic rooms, all with nets, fans and shared bathrooms. Safe parking. **❶**

Migunga Forest Camp 2km east of the centre, then 2km south of the main road (bookings through Swala Safaris in Arusha, p.396). The best and priciest of the lot, with 27 beds in seven tents and three bungalows (more planned), all with bal-conies facing a central lawn. All rooms have nets, attached bathrooms and solar-powered light. There's a pleasant open-sided bar and dining room, seating in the garden, a gift shop, and activ-ities including wildlife safaris, nature walks (included in the price) and two-day Crater Highlands treks (see p.452). Rates are negotiable. Half-board **❼**, full-board **❽**

Twiga Campsite and Lodge 1km east of the centre ☏ 027/253 9101. The best of the moderate-ly priced places, this also has a campsite popular with overlanders ($5 per person), and ten good en-suite twin-bed rooms with hot water mornings and evenings. There's a bar and restaurant and a lounge with satellite TV and "wild video shows", which means wildlife documentaries, and tradi-tional dance whenever it's busy. Rates are bar-gainable. Breakfast included. **❹**

The escarpment

For upmarket accommodation, head to the top of the Great Rift Valley's **west-ern escarpment**. It's a stunningly beautiful drive, where every hairpin gives you an increasingly breathtaking view of Lake Manyara and the green expanse of vegetation around its shore. There's a **viewpoint** on top, complete with ubiquitous curio shops, and also a new **campsite** called the *Panorama*.

None of the tourist-class establishments (three on the escarpment, one on a ridge north of Mto wa Mbu) has much in the way of wildlife except for birds, but the views can be great – make sure your room has one, as not all do. Nonetheless, at the price (upwards of $180 for a double room on half-board), there are much better pampered retreats elsewhere.

Manyara village, or **Kibaoni** (Kiswahili for "signboards"), is the first settle-ment once on top, where the hotels, restaurants and bars are used by safari driv-ers after dropping off their charges. Some of the accommodation is tawdry in the extreme, but as a refuge from the rose-tinted excesses of safariland, this is a great place. Heaps of fresh *nyama choma*, chicken and *ugali*, is served up in a wel-ter of ramshackle structures, and the bars, despite their prostitutes, are great for lively conversation. A recommended place to stay, if you can ignore the mural of a scantily clad woman, is *Mavanja Guest House* (no phone; **❶**).

E Unoto Retreat 10km north of Mto wa Mbu, accessed off the road to Lake Natron starting 3km east of town ☏ 027/254 8542 or 0744/360908, ⓦ www.maasaivillage.com. New luxury lodge aiming at upmarket package tour clientele, this has 25 individual bungalows – some with disabled access – on a ridge overlooking the small Lake Miwaleni, styled after Maasai homesteads. Personal butlers cater to your every need; there's a swimming pool, bar and restaurant; guides on hand for bird-watching, and bicycle trips. Half-board/full-board ❾

Kirurumu Tented Lodge 6km northeast of Kibaoni (bookings via Hoopoe Adventure Tours in Arusha, p.397). On the escarpment ridge with twenty large tents spread out over a wide area, most, unfortunately, lacking views of the lake or valley. Service is formal but friendly and efficient, and it's good value compared to the rest. Most of the tents, all en-suite and with shady verandahs and electricity, have two beds: couples should book the "honeymoon" tents instead. Facilities include a good restaurant (fruit and vegetables from their organic garden), bar, a swimming pool, vehicles for game drives ($25 a person for half a day plus park fees) and ethnobotanical walks accompanied by Maasai warriors. Half-board/full-board ❽

Lake Manyara Hotel 3km southeast of Kibaoni ☏ 027/253 9131, ℻ 027/254 8502 (office at *Novotel Mount Meru Hotel* in Arusha, p.378). A 1970s concrete hulk with 100 rooms, complete with a giant chess set in the bar. The only real attraction is the spectacular location, with magnificent views over the lake (also from most bedroom balconies). Otherwise the rooms urgently need attention. There's a swimming pool (Tsh2000 for day guests), a bar with TV, restaurant, gift shops and foreign exchange. Half-board ❽, full-board ❾

Lake Manyara Serena Safari Lodge 2km east of Kibaoni (bookings through Serena Lodges, AICC Ngorongoro Wing, Arusha ☏ 027/250 8175, ⓦ www.serenahotels.com). The poshest of the lot, with 67 rooms in two-storey "rondavels", though only a few have lake views. The swimming pool does, however. There are a couple of bars, a restaurant, gift shop and gardens planted with mostly indigenous species, many of them labelled (there's an accompanying leaflet). The downside is the formal service and impatient room staff. Full-board ❾

Accommodation in and around the park

Accommodation in **the park** is limited to three special campsites (see below) and an obscenely overpriced tented camp that has not been reviewed. Much better are the campsites and *bandas* just outside the park gate.

TANAPA Bandas Park gate (bookings through TANAPA in Arusha, p.394). Just outside the park's entrance (no park fees apply) is a complex of ten basic brick *bandas* (cottages), which, although somewhat basic for the price, are nonetheless comfortable, and have hot showers, Western toilets and electricity but no nets. There's no food, so bring your own; firewood is supplied free of charge, and there's a kitchen and dining room. $20 per person.

TANAPA Public Campsites Park gate (bookings not required; pay at the park gate). The three park-run public campsites, just outside the park (no

other park fees apply), occupy lovely forest clearings, each with toilets and cold showers. Although camping in Mto wa Mbu is much cheaper, the beauty and intimacy of these sites can't be matched. $20 per person.

TANAPA Special Campsites Lake Manyara National Park (bookings through TANAPA in Arusha, p.394). There are three special campsites in the park itself that need to be booked in advance, two near the Bagayo River, one at Endabash further south, but there's really nothing special about any of them, and no facilities whatsoever. $40 per person.

Eating and drinking

There are lots of basic **restaurants** (*hotelis*) in Mto wa Mbu, especially south of the market, most doubling as bars. One of the best, despite appearances (and horrid guest rooms), is *Rembo Guest House and Bar*, a block south of the market, which has excellent and filling food for around Tsh700. Most of the hotels reviewed above also have restaurants. The cheapest is *Holiday Fig Resort* (all meals Tsh3500). Slightly more expensive (Tsh5000–6000), but sometimes limited to the chickens running around their grounds, are *Jambo Campsite and Lodge* and *Twiga Campsite and Lodge*. More expensive are *Migunga Forest Camp*

($10), *Lake Manyara Hotel* ($15), *Kirurumu Tented Lodge* ($17) and *E Unoto Retreat* (upwards of $25).

For **drinks**, locals frequent the bars south of the market. A good place, popular with both locals and tourists, is *Red Banana Café* on the main road, which also happens to be the base of Mto wa Mbu's cultural tourism programme (see below).

Mto wa Mbu

Apart from its proximity to Lake Manyara, **Mto wa Mbu** has two big attractions: a cultural tourism programme, which provides a great way of getting to know some of the town's fifty-odd tribes, and markets, including a weekly animal auction on Thursdays and a big bash on the second of each month.

Mto wa Mbu cultural tourism programme

Mto wa Mbu's ethnic diversity is best seen as part of a **cultural tourism programme** (☏027/253 9101), one of over a dozen in northern Tanzania (see p.405). Mto wa Mbu's programme has two offices, at *Red Banana Café* and *Twiga Campsite and Lodge*. They can fix you up with an accredited English-speaking **guide**, all former pupils of Manyara Secondary School. To avoid the attentions of hustlers and a growing number of conmen, do not hire guides elsewhere, and make sure you get a receipt.

The various **guided tours**, each usually just a few hours, are also offered as optional extras for standard wildlife safaris from Arusha. While the tours are not as immediately exciting as those of similar cultural tourism projects elsewhere, they are particularly good for getting to know a wide variety of **tribes**, as all include visits to farms, local artisans and small-scale development projects. There are three main half-day tours, which can be combined into a full-day excursion. Starting at the market, the **farming tour** covers a number of farms (*shambas*) north of town, where you'll meet farmers from various tribes. "Papyrus lake", 5km north and known locally as **Lake Miwaleni**, is at the foot of the Rift Valley and, along with a nearby waterfall, is accessible by trails following small streams. Another waterfall, called Njoro, and hot-water springs can be visited as part of a short trek up **Balaa Hill** (30min up), which has a good view over town. Other options, including treks over several days, can also be arranged.

Group **costs** for up to five people, excluding food and drink, are Tsh5000 for a guide for half a day, or Tsh10,000 for a full day, plus Tsh10,000 to "contact persons", meaning the people you visit. There's also Tsh3500 per person to pay, for the village development fee and administration fee. **Bicycle rental** is Tsh4000 a day, and a canoe costs Tsh2000 for a few hours.

Markets

Given Mto wa Mbu's ethnic diversity, it's no surprise that the town's **markets** are among the liveliest and most colourful in the country. The main **permanent market** is in the town centre, a confusion of shops and stalls where you'll find pretty much everything that's produced locally, including many of the town's estimated eighty varieties of **bananas**. One corner of the market, the so-called **Maasai Central Market**, is a tourist trap with all the usual trinkets like Maasai beadwork jewellery and tartan *shuka* cloth, but an enjoyable one at that. Much more authentic is the Thursday **animal auction** held at the roadside 7km east of Mto wa Mbu, and a monthly market on the same site held on the second of each month, which attracts buyers and herders from as far away as the Zanaki tribe of Mara Region. Some of these herders continue to Arusha and a handful even make it to Dar es Salaam – an epic journey of at least 900km.

Lake Manyara National Park

Set against the impressive backdrop of the Great Rift Valley's western escarpment, Lake Manyara – or more specifically, its north and western shoreline – is a rare flash of green in an otherwise unremittingly dry land. Much of it is protected as **Lake Manyara National Park**, a 360-square-kilometre area of which two-thirds is water. The entrance gate is in the north, 2km west of Mto wa Mbu. From here a small network of tracks covers most of the vegetational zones in the northern section, and a single track (with some short game-viewing loops) heads south along the narrow strip of land between the lake and the escarpment. For its small size, the park contains a wide range of **habitats**: evergreen groundwater forest in the north fed by springs; a swampy fan delta crowning the top of the lake, acacia woodland at the foot of the scarp scattered with baobab trees; a small grassy plain; and, of course, the lake itself. Together, they provide a oasis for wildlife, and the presence of year-round water also makes the lake part of the same migratory system of which Tarangire is the heart (see box on p.420).

Manyara is perhaps most memorable for its **elephants**, whose population in the 1960s was estimated at 640. Heavy poaching for ivory in the intervening decades massacred over eighty percent of them, but with poaching now under control if not entirely eradicated, the elephants are making a gradual comeback, and now number around 160 individuals. Other impressive denizens include **buffalo**, sometimes in large herds, who feed on sedge by the lakeshore, and **hippo**, seen in water pools in the northern fan delta. **Antelopes** include impala, bushbuck and waterbuck, and agile klipspringers on the rocky escarpment wall. Other plains game are zebra, giraffe, mongoose and warthog, together with their predators: leopards and, famously, **tree-climbing lions**, which are sometimes seen – your best bet for this is between June and August – resting up in the boughs of acacia trees south of the groundwater forest. The reason for their arboreal prowess is a mystery, though there's no shortage of possible explanations, the most plausible of which is their attempt to avoid the unwelcome attention of tsetse flies. The phenomenon isn't unique to Manyara – lions have also been seen up in trees at Tarangire, Serengeti, Ngorongoro and Selous.

Primates are represented by numerous baboon troops, and blue and vervet monkeys in the forests. The latter are preyed on by crested hawk eagles, one of Manyara's over 380 **bird species**. Birdlife is at its most spectacular in and around the lake, especially in the form of pelicans and the great flocks of flamingos.

For all these riches, all is not well. Massive **human population** increase in and around Mto wa Mbu, together with the clearance of swamps, woodlands and forest for arable land, hunting and poaching, and pollution of the lake, has taken a terrible toll, and prompted the local **extinction** of at least nine mammal species: lesser kudu in 1957, hunting dogs in 1960 (though a migratory pack was seen in the late 1990s), cheetah in 1980, mountain reedbuck and hartebeest in 1982, eland and oribi the following year, black rhino in 1985 and the common reedbuck in 1991. On-going plans to incorporate the adjacent Marang Forest Reserve in the southwest into the national park may improve matters a little, but the basic problem is pressure from Mto wa Mbu's human inhabitants.

The Maasai

Exotic, noble, aristocratic, freedom-loving, independent, savage, impressive, arrogant and aloof…you'll find these adjectives scattered all over travel brochures whenever they talk of the **Maasai**, one of East Africa's most emblematic tribes.

Meeting a Maasai warrior, with his red robe, spear and braided ochre-smeared hair, is one of the high points of many a safari holiday. Depending on the tour company, **visits** cost anything from a few dollars to $50 to spend half an hour in a "genuine" Maasai village (*boma*) in Ngorongoro or along the road coming from Arusha. The money buys the right to take photographs and perhaps witness a dance or two, though you may also be mercilessly pestered by old ladies selling beaded jewellery and other trinkets. Depending on your sensibilities, the experience can either be an enlightening and exciting glimpse into the "real" Africa, or a rather disturbing and even depressing encounter with a people seemingly obliged to sell their culture in order to survive.

In the popular imagination, the Maasai – along with South Africa's Zulu – are the archetypal Africans, and as a result a disproportionate amount of attention, and nonsense, has been lavished on them, ever since the explorer Joseph Thomson published his best-selling book *Through Maasailand* in 1885. In those days, the Maasai were seen as perfect "noble savages", but their story is much more complex.

What we know of their distant **history** is little more than conjecture proposed by romantically minded Western scholars. Some say that they are one of the lost tribes of Israel. Others that they came from North Africa. Still others believe that they are the living remnants of Egyptian civilization, primarily, it seems, on account of their warriors' braided hairstyles. Linguistically, the Maasai are the southernmost of the Nilotic-speaking peoples, a loosely related group that came from the north, presumably from the Nile Valley in Sudan. It's thought that they left this area sometime between the fourteenth and sixteenth centuries, migrating southwards with their cattle herds along the fertile grasslands of the Rift Valley. The Maasai eventually entered Kenya to the west of Lake Turkana, and quickly spread south into northern Tanzania, whose seasonal grasslands were ideal for their cattle. They reached their present extent around the eighteenth century, at which time they were the most powerful and feared tribe in East Africa. Their tight social organization, offensive warfare and deadly cattle raids, and mobility as semi-nomadic cattle herders, ensured that they could go where they pleased, and could take what they wanted. Their military prowess and regimentation meant that they were rarely defeated. As a result, their history before the arrival of the British was one of ceaseless expansion at the expense of other people.

Their combined Kenyan and Tanzanian territory in the seventeenth century has been estimated at 200,000 square kilometres. But all this is just one side of the story. The other is told by their territory today, which is less than a quarter of what it was before the Europeans arrived. The Maasai have been progressively confined to smaller and smaller areas of land. The British took much of it away to serve as farm- and ranchland for settlers, and in recent decades the land expropriations have continued, this time to form the wildlife parks of Serengeti, Tarangire, Mkomazi (see p.348), and part of Ngorongoro, to which the Serengeti Maasai were relocated when they were evicted. Politically and economically, the Maasai remain marginalized from the Tanzanian mainstream, having stubbornly refused to abandon their pastoralist

The groundwater forest

Walking west out of Mto wa Mbu, and over its eponymous river, the abruptness with which thick green forest appears to your left is quite startling. This is part of Manyara's evergreen **groundwater forest**, a soothingly cool, refreshing and very special habitat that dominates the northern section of the park

way of life, or their traditions, despite repeated attempts by both colonial and post-independence governments to cajole or force them to settle. Many men persevere with the status of **warriorhood**, though modern Tanzania makes few concessions to it. Arrested for hunting lions, and prevented from building *manyattas* for the *eunoto* transition in which they pass into elderhood, the warriors (*morani*) have kept most of the superficial marks of the warrior without being able to live the life. The ensemble of a red or purple cloth *shuka* tied over one shoulder, together with spear, sword, club and braided hair, is still widely seen; and after circumcision, in their early days as warriors, you can meet young men out in the bush, hunting for birds to add to their elaborate, taxidermic headdresses.

But the Maasai **lifestyle** is changing: education, MPs and elections, new laws and new projects, jobs and cash are all having mixed results. The traditional Maasai staple of curdled milk and cow's blood is rapidly being replaced by cornmeal *ugali*. Many Maasai have taken work in the lodges and tented camps while others end up as security guards in Arusha and Dar es Salaam, and a main source of income for those who remain is provided by the **tourist industry**, which gives the Maasai a major spot in its repertoire. Maasai dancing is *the* entertainment, while necklaces, gourds, spears, shields, *rungus* (knobkerries), busts and even life-sized wooden warriors (to be shipped home in a packing case) are the stock-in-trade of the curio and souvenir shops.

For the Maasai themselves, the rewards are fairly scant. **Cattle** are still at the heart of their society but they are assailed on all sides by a climate of opposition to the old lifestyle. Sporadically urged to grow crops, go to school, build permanent houses and generally settle down, they face an additional dilemma in squaring these edicts with the fickle demands of the tourist industry for traditional authenticity. Few make much of a living selling souvenirs, but enterprising *morani* can do well by just posing for photos, and even better if they hawk themselves on the coast; one or two can even be seen in Zanzibar.

For the majority, who still live semi-nomadic lives among a growing tangle of constraints, **the future** would seem to hold little promise, although a promising recent development has been the creation of various community-run conservation areas outside the parks and reserves, which generate income from annual land rents paid by tourist lodges and tented camps, and, often enough, a percentage of profits or overnight receipts. That stubborn cultural independence may yet insulate the Maasai against the social upheavals that have changed the cultures of their neighbours beyond recognition.

Unless you're really short on time, a much more satisfying and less voyeuristic way of meeting Maasai than in the *bomas* of Ngorongoro is via Tanzania's community-run cultural tourism programmes (see p.405), some of which are run by Masai. These are at Engaruka (see p.437) in the Rift Valley, and at Longido (see p.408), Mkuru (see p.404) and Monduli (see p.410) close to Arusha. In addition, the cheaper Crater Highlands treks (see p.452) from Ngorongoro to Lake Natron are usually guided by Maasai, and may include overnights in genuine, non-touristic bomas. For **more information**, see Ⓦwww.bluegecko.org/kenya/tribes/maasai, a comprehensive resource about Maasai culture, including Maasai music and some of the most hypnotic singing you're likely to hear.

next to the escarpment. Although it looks and feels like rainforest, Manyara's average annual rainfall of 760mm would be nowhere near sufficient to sustain trees of this size on its own. Instead, groundwater forest, as the name suggests, is fed by water from mineral springs which seeps through the ground's porous volcanic soil.

Apart from the **hikes** and **canoeing** offered by Mto wa Mbu's cultural tourism programme (see p.432), the easing up of park regulations means that a number of hands-on activities are now possible. The folks to contact are Serena Active at *Lake Manyara Serena Safari Lodge* (℮lakemanyara@serena.co.tz), who offer a range of professionally run "soft adventures" including abseiling, mountain biking, canoeing and hiking. Best value is their abseil down the escarpment, followed by a rope climb back up ($55). Canoeing is expensive at $60 for three hours, excluding park fees, though an exciting prospect would be to take a combined canoeing and hiking trip over several days, including a potentially hair-raising walk along the lakeshore. Mountain **bike trips** are $35 an hour or $55 for three hours; the cost includes a vehicle ride back up the escarpment. You can hire bikes in Mto wa Mbu for a fraction of the price. For something completely different, Farasi Safaris next to *Kirurumu Tented Lodge* (office in Arusha, see p.397) are Tanzania's **horse-riding** specialists, offering a range of options from an hour's trot ($30) to day trips with lunch in the bush ($135) and longer, tailor-made rides over several days.

Lastly, a recent rule change has given the go-ahead for **night game drives** inside the park, though this is likely only to apply to pre-arranged safaris: contact a safari company in Arusha, or one of the lodges and tented camps on the escarpment.

The tall mahogany, croton and sausage trees, tamarind, wild date palms and strangling fig trees, are home to a variety of wildlife, including blue monkeys, vervet monkeys and baboons (all of whom are fond of crashing around in the branches, especially at the park gate's picnic site), and there's plenty of **birdlife** too, though seeing anything more than a flitting form disappearing into the foliage is a challenge. More easily seen are ground birds, including two species of guinea fowl, and the large silvery-cheeked hornbill, which lives in the canopy but is often seen on the ground. Forest plants which benefit from the shade of the trees include orchids. **Elephants** are occasional visitors, and partial to using larger trees as back-scrubbers, much to the anguish of the park authorities who have tried to deter them by wrapping some trees with prickly corsets of chicken wire.

The fan delta and hippo pools

About 4km southwest of the park gate along the main track is a signposted left turn towards a loop road around **Mahali pa Nyati** – the Place of Buffaloes – which, as you might expect, is a good place for spotting those rather cantankerous and temperamental beasts, who are invariably accompanied by oxpeckers and buff-backed herons, feeding on insects disturbed by the passing of their hosts. South of the buffalo circuit is another loop (flooded at the time of writing), which leads to the mouth of Mto wa Mbu River, and a series of **hippo pools**. This naturally swampy area is part of a **fan delta**, formed by river-borne sediment. The shallow lakeshore is especially favoured by **water birds**, including pelicans, storks, herons, ibis, jacanas, egrets, plovers and lots of ducks and geese. But the undoubted avian stars are the vast flocks of pink **flamingos**, attracted by the profusion of algae in the lake's shallow, alkaline waters.

The acacia woodland, Msasa and Ndala rivers

To the south and east of the groundwater forest is more open **woodland**, dominated by umbrella acacia and dotted here and there by ancient baobab trees. It's a good habitat for all sorts of big game, especially elephant, giraffe and buffalo, and is good for spotting **birdlife**, too, including various species of plover and kingfishers, larks and wagtails.

South of the groundwater forest, the park's main track crosses a series of small rivers, sometimes by bridge, other times by causeway which can become impassable if the rains hit hard. The main watercourse in the park's northern section is the **Msasa River**, whose bridge was washed away in 1998 and at the time of writing had yet to be replaced. The area near the former bridge is good for seeing solitary old male buffaloes, and if you're going to see lions in trees, it'll be here. There's a signposted **picnic site** under a big tree with benches, tables, a lake view and often uncomfortably close sightings of buffalo. There are two more picnic sites near the **Ndala River**, 9km south of the Msasa River, one of which has good lake views. The presence of buffalo, often in large herds, means tsetse flies start to be a nuisance south of the Msasa River.

The hot-water springs

Flamingos can also be seen on the western shore, close to a series of pungently sulphurous **hot-water springs**, of which there are two main groups. The smaller but most accessible are **Maji Moto Ndogo**, 22km south of the park gate, which keep to a very pleasant 33°C and get covered whenever the lake level is high. Some 17.5km further south, past the patch of grassland formed by the modest delta of the Endabash River, are the bigger and more scalding **Maji Moto Kubwa** springs, whose temperature averages 76°C – hot enough to give you a nasty burn and to melt the soles of your shoes if you wander too close. They're at their most impressive when the lake level is low, and then especially in the rains (higher water pressure), when the water erupts in a series of highly pressurized flumes. Even when the lake level is high, however, there are some small springs closer to the road, which are remarkable for the beautiful colours and patterns formed by the heat- and sulphur-loving algal blooms, lichens and assorted slime moulds growing in and around the shallow pools.

Engaruka

The most enigmatic of northern Tanzania's attractions is a complex of stone ruins at **ENGARUKA**, at the foot of the Great Rift Valley's western escarpment. Standing in the shadow of the forested eastern rim of Ngorongoro's Crater Highlands, the ruins comprise at least seven villages and an astoundingly complex irrigation system of stone-walled canals, furrows and dams. Being in a naturally dry and stony environment, where natural vegetation is limited to thornbush and spiny acacias, the most amazing thing about the site is that it existed at all.

First recorded in 1883 by the German naturalist, **Dr Gustav Fischer**, the ruins extend over 9km of the escarpment base and cover 20 square kilometres. Various dating methods indicate that the site was founded early in the fifteenth century, but was mysteriously abandoned between 1700 and 1750. The question of who was responsible for creating what must have been an extraordinary sight amidst this dry and desolate wasteland, and which at its height supported a population of over 5000 people, continues to leave archeologists largely baffled.

Most of Engaruka's present-day occupants are Maasai, but the absence of any Maasai tradition mentioning Engaruka indicates that the settlement had already been abandoned when they arrived, at most two centuries ago, and consequently little is known of Engaruka's original inhabitants. Research, however, shows that they were most likely the ancestors of the **Iraqw** tribe (see box on p.446), who now live around and to the south of Karatu, and whose techniques of intensive, self-contained agriculture are uncannily similar to the remains of systems found at Engaruka. Iraqw oral history also recounts their last major migration, some 200 to 300 years ago, which followed a battle with Barbaig cattle herders (who, until the arrival of the Maasai, occupied the highlands above Engaruka). This fits in perfectly with the presumed date of Engaruka's desertion. Another present-day tribe that has been linked to Engaruka is the numerically small **Sonjo**, who presently live 100km north of Engaruka and to the west of Lake Natron (see p.469). Their last migration also coincides with Engaruka's dates, and their traditional method of building houses on raised stone platforms is identical to remains found at Engaruka.

Apart from the Iraqw's story of the Barbaig war, a likely factor contributing to Engaruka's desertion was environmental. Engaruka's very success at irrigation in such a dry land may have proved counter-productive, when the demands of a vastly increased human population became too much for the area's limited water supplies. There's also evidence that the flow of the Engaruka River, and of other streams descending from the Ngorongoro highlands, began to diminish 300 to 400 years ago, perhaps due to the presence of pastoralists like the Barbaig, and then the Maasai, for whom forest clearance to make way for cattle pasture was and remains a way of life. Other suggested causes include outbreaks of diseases or other natural disasters.

Despite – or perhaps because of – its uncertainties, Engaruka provides a fascinating and thought-provoking glimpse into the history of pre-colonial Tanzania, and a reminder that we still remain ignorant about much of the continent's history.

Arrival

Getting to Engaruka can be a big hassle, and you can forget it in the rains, when the road in all directions is impassable. Unless you're coming from the Serengeti's Klein's Gate across Loliondo (see p.468), the only access is from the road junction 3km east of Mto wa Mbu (see p.428), leaving you with a wild 64-kilometre ride. The first section, to **Selela village**, is decently graded, but beyond there you need a measure of luck to stay on track, as well as experience of 4WD in rough and sandy conditions, as the road disappears into a number of poorly defined trails. If you're driving yourself, bear in mind that the road to Engaruka initially veers away from the escarpment to avoid gullies and hills. The ride from Mto wa Mbu takes two to four hours depending on the state of the road and how often you get lost.

Public transport is more reliable, but has no fixed timetable. This means enquiring in Mto wa Mbu at least the evening before you intend to travel, for information on the handful of Land Rover pick-ups that cover the route every day or two. Most of these head off in the afternoon, returning in the morning.

Accommodation and eating

There are actually two Engarukas in addition to the ruins – a dusty spread of huts at Engaruka Chini along the road from Mto wa Mbu to Lake Natron, and the bustling Maasai market centre of Engaruka Juu, 3km west of here towards the escarpment, which is much livelier and greener, its fields watered by the permanent Engaruka River.

Engaruka Chini, at the junction of the main road and the one heading to Engaruka Juu, has one shop (Engaruka Shop and Garden) selling beer, soda, water, diesel and petrol, and *Saimon Kamakia Campsite* (Tsh2500 per person), which is almost derelict and lacks shade or any facilities but for long-drop loos. It's much better to stay at **Engaruka Juu**, which has two choices: rooms at the basic *Mlezi Guest House* (●), 2km west of Engaruka Chini, or camping at *Jerusalem Campsite* (Tsh2000 per person), 6km west of Engaruka Chini and close to the escarpment, in the grounds of Engaruka Primary School. Despite being signposted, the campsite is awkward to find: turn left just beyond *Mlezi Guest House*, cross the river immediately, and take the right fork on the opposite bank; the campsite is 4km on along a rough track. The site itself is pleasantly shaded, thanks to the proximity of the Engaruka River. You're best bringing your own food, though a local women's group can rustle up meals given enough time – it should cost Tsh2500 per person.

The site

Old Engaruka can only be visited on foot; *Jerusalem Campsite*, which provides guides and now has two helpful and informative **site custodians** provided by the Antiquities Department, is the departure point.

Several paths from the campsite go to the ruins; the best follows the Engaruka River's south bank, rising quickly towards the escarpment and the closest remains, 1km away. The site's extent and lack of obvious landmarks makes it impossible to give directions beyond here, but you can find a representative selection of the main structures throughout the area, notably the extensive network of stone-walled irrigation and drainage ditches, and small dams. When visiting the ruins, take care not to dislodge any stones, and avoid climbing cairns, stone circles, walls or other structures.

Two curious features characteristic of Engaruka are cairns and stone circles. The **cairns**, particularly well preserved in the west where they measure up to five metres long and two metres high, appear to be little other than places where rocks and stones cleared from fields were gathered, although their carefully arranged square or angular faces suggest something rather more useful, or spiritual, than just a heap of stones. A human skeleton was found under one cairn, but other than that, excavations have yielded few other clues as to their real purpose. More readily explained are the large **stone circles**, especially on the south side of the river, which measure up to ten metres in diameter and functioned as cattle pens – manure was used to fertilize the fields (a trick also used by the Iraqw).

Look out also for clusters of **raised stone platforms** on ground unsuitable for irrigation, which mark the sites of Engaruka's seven villages. The platforms served as bases for houses, in the same way that the Sonjo tribe still build their homes. Excavations in these areas have revealed an iron-working forge and remains of meerschaum pipes, thought to have been used for smoking **cannabis** (*bhangi*); cannabis remains an important part of many northern Tanzanian cultures, including that of the Hadzabe (see box on p.445) and Kuria (see p.496).

For **more information**, John Sutton's exhaustive and scholarly work about Engaruka is available at *Jerusalem Campsite*, at Kase bookshop in Arusha (see p.390), and at A Novel Idea bookshop in Dar (see p.113).

⑦ Ol Doinyo Lengai

Located at the south end of Lake Natron is East Africa's only active volcano, **OL DOINYO LENGAI**, whose name – in Maasai – means the "Mountain of God". Despite its active status, very little is known about the mountain, other than that it tends to erupt explosively every twenty to forty years, and manages smaller **eruptions** every decade or so (the last major explosive eruption was in 1966, followed by minor ones in 1983 and 1993). If history is a guide, this means that a major explosive eruption is due any time now.

For geologists, the special thing about Ol Doinyo Lengai is that it is one of few volcanoes worldwide to emit sodium carbonate and potassium, whose run-off accounts for the extremely alkaline and corrosive swill of neighbouring Lake Natron (see opposite).

For photographers, Ol Doinyo Lengai's perfectly conical shape is a delight, especially if you can get Maasai cattle herders in the foreground. Climbers, too, are in for a treat, despite the volcano's summit (2889m) being but a pimple compared to the majesty of its giant but dormant brothers to the east, Meru and Kilimanjaro. Admittedly, the treat of climbing the mountain (which can be done without any special equipment) is distinctly masochistic, because of both the heat of the baking sun and the mountain's notoriously prickly vegetation. But as a reward for your travails, there's the weird, wonderful and quite positively perilous sight of **magma flows** bubbling at 510°C on top. There are two summit craters: the southern one is extinct and almost filled to the brim with ash, but the northern one, whose depth reaches over 200 metres, remains active and should be treated with extreme caution – one visitor a few years back lost a leg when foolishly testing the temperature of one of the magma flows by jumping over it.

Practicalities

Climbing must be done with a guide who knows the mountain and its capriciousness. There are two ways of going about it: the easiest is simply to tackle the mountain as part of an extended "Crater Highlands" trek (see box on p.452) from Ngorongoro to Lake Natron. Many of Arusha's safari operators (see p.395) now offer this as a regular trip, but do check that they have both their own experienced guides, and that – if you need it – there's adequate back-up (vehicles rather than donkeys, and HF radio for emergencies). For more modest budgets, it's perfectly feasible to arrange things at *Lake Natron Camp* or *Saimon Kamakia's Campsite* in Ngara Sero (see p.442). The cost for the day's hike, including the guide, is about $30 per group plus $10 per climber, though there's talk of bumping up the group fee to $45.

The climb starts about 10km south of Ngara Sero, and takes at least seven hours: four hours up and three back down. If you don't have a vehicle and don't fancy walking from Ngara Sero to the start of the trail, you'll have to wait until a vehicle is available. The ride shouldn't cost more than a few thousand shillings. The ascent is steep and mostly on loose and uncompacted soil, and there's no shade, so set off before dawn to arrive at the summit by mid-morning.

With your own vehicle, you could try searching out one of several **volcanic cones** and craters on the eastern side of the mountain, the biggest of which is called *Shimo la Mungu* (God's Hole).

Lake Natron

To desert rats, the land around **LAKE NATRON** – a vast, shallow soda lake bordering Kenya in Tanzania's far north – is something of a dream: hellishly hot, dry, desolate and bizarrely beautiful, especially with the grandiose peak of Ol Doinyo Lengai rising at its southern end. This volcano is the cause of the lake's extreme alkalinity, which forms a pinkish-white crust of soda crystals across much of its surface, cracked into a polygonal patchwork.

Measuring 56km by 24km, the lake, like its smaller cousin Lake Magadi in Kenya, lacks any outlet, and receives only 400mm of rain a year, part of it falling as "phantom rain", meaning that the raindrops evaporate before hitting the surface. The amount lost by **evaporation** is eight times that; the shortfall is made up by volcanic springs and temporary streams, whose waters leach through Ol Doinyo Lengai's caustic lava flows before reaching the lake. The concentration of salt, sodium carbonate (soda) and magnesite in the lake water is highly corrosive and the surrounding land isn't much more hospitable.

Not surprisingly, the lake isn't the most conducive to life, the big exception being a flourishing population of sometimes several hundred thousand **lesser flamingos**, who feed on the lake's microscopic diatom algae, and who have made the lake the most important flamingo breeding ground on earth.

Security around Lake Natron and Loliondo

The wild and remote territory all around Lake Natron, eastern Loliondo, and south between the lake and Engaruka, is known for **bandits**, many of them Somali, who in the past attacked travellers, herders and villagers. The problem peaked in the 1990s, and although no incidents have been reported since 2000, most safari companies give the area a wide berth.

At the time this book was researched, the police and army presence had been greatly beefed up, and a successful manhunt in September 2000 by Tanzanian and Kenyan armed forces netted three bandits. Nonetheless, the area is difficult to control, and so any form of travel here remains potentially dangerous.

Whether you're coming on an organized safari or are driving yourself, check and double-check the latest situation with as many people as possible (police, safari companies and drivers). When driving, beware of stopping for anyone except soldiers and police; stories circulate of bandits dressed up as Maasai disguising their AK-47s as millet stalks. If you do get **held up**, common sense is to give in to their demands, and never, ever try to resist. Lastly, remember that it's not just you taking the risk, but your driver too, so make sure you're clear about where you want to go before finalizing car hire.

Arrival

The only settlement of any size is **Ngara Sero** (or Engare Sero; also called Natron Village), near the lake's southwestern shore, 56km north of Engaruka and 120km from Mto wa Mbu. The name means "water forest", referring to the woods flanking a small river that flows south of town.

The easiest way to get here is on an **organized safari**. Companies running trips through this area (all in Arusha, see pp.396–397) include: Hoopoe Adventure Tours, who have a seasonal camp in Loliondo; The East African Safari & Touring Company, who have a seasonal camp near Ngara Sero; Swala Safaris (The Safari Company), who own *Lake Natron Camp*; and Dorobo Tours & Safaris, who offer walking and camping trips to Loliondo. The lake also features on a growing number of **Crater Highlands treks** from Ngorongoro; see box on p.452.

The next easiest way to Lake Natron is to rent a vehicle with a driver in Arusha or Mto wa Mbu, as there's **no public transport** north of Engaruka. Theoretically, the drive from Mto wa Mbu should only take a few hours, but the road is in a terrible state (impassable in the rains) and is difficult to follow, so count on a full day. Locals either walk or wait around, sometimes for a day or three, for a lift on one of the very few private vehicles that make it up here, usually carrying supplies for Ngara Sero's shops. Alternatively, if you're planning on staying at *Lake Natron Camp*, contact them in advance; they charge $45 per person for the ride up from Mto wa Mbu.

Ngorongoro District Council has set up a **toll gate** 3km south of Ngara Sero, which charges tourists $15 each for entering the area; this covers Ngara Sero, the lake and Nguruman Escarpment, and Ol Doinyo Lengai. New arrivals must **sign in** at the police station at the north end of town.

For information about the rough route to Lake Natron **from Loliondo**, see p.468.

Practicalities

Ngara Sero contains a handful of poorly stocked **stores** (the best of which is Coca Cola Maasai Shop), a **bar** (the *Lake Side*) – and that's about it. There's no petrol or diesel, and the place has all the charm of a frontier outpost, which of course it is. Apart from a seasonal tented camp set up by Arusha's The East African Safari & Touring Company (see p.397), **accommodation** is limited to two places.

Lake Natron Camp 2.5km south of Ngara Sero, 1km north of the toll gate (bookings through Swala Safaris, ☎ & ⊕ 027/250 8424, ⊛ www.swalasafaris.com). Set in a bone-meltingly hot and dusty grove of trees 4km from the lake, this has the lakeside's only guest rooms. The five dilapidated en-suite tents are massively overpriced, but then there's no competition. Much better is to pitch your own tent ($10–20 per person). There's a bar and good simple food, but the main reason for staying here is to organize excursions, including hikes up Ol Doinyo Lengai, and visits to Maasai *bomas* (Tsh2000 per person). Half-board ❻, full-board ❼

Saimon Kamakia's Campsite In a ravine next to the river; turn left at the toll gate, then right as you approach the escarpment (PO Box 345 Ngara Sero; ☎ 027/6349). Despite being less shady than *Lake Natron Camp*, this has a much nicer and marginally cooler location, and there are rock pools in the adjacent river where you can cool down. Still known after the original owner, it's now run by a friendly Maasai who plans to build some rooms. At present it's camping only; $5 per person. Cool drinks and meals ($5) are available, and there's a full range of guided walks.

Around Ngara Sero

Ngara Sero itself has little to detain you, but is the only base for visiting a number of attractions. The most obvious, of course, is the **lakeshore**, currently 4km away across scorching grey sand (the level varies). As you approach the edge, soda and salt crystals appear, concealing a foul-smelling slurry of mud, which can burn your skin. To reach the **hot-water springs** on the eastern shore calls for 4WD and a driver experienced on loose sand. Take care not to drive too close to the shore, where you're likely to get bogged down. The soda flats in the southeastern corner are used by **flamingos** to mate and nest between August and October; the nests, which you can see from a distance, are made from mud and resemble miniature volcanoes. Other **wildlife** you might see on the way, especially close to the springs, includes zebra, wildebeest, gazelle, ostrich and golden jackal, and more rarely fringe-eared oryx, lesser kudu and gerenuk.

The **Nguruman Escarpment**, within walking distance of Ngara Sero, contains a number of attractions, including a volcanic implosion crater, ravines containing nesting sites for Ruppell's griffon vultures, and several waterfalls. The most picturesque of these is along **Ngara Sero Gorge**, 1km upstream from *Saimon Kamakia's Campsite*. Swimming is possible, though women are expected to cover up while bathing – shorts and a T-shirt. Walks further up the escarpment can be arranged at either camp, who can also fix up a visit to a Maasai *boma*.

Ngorongoro and around

One of Tanzania's best-known wildlife areas is **Ngorongoro Conservation Area**, which, together with the adjoining Serengeti National Park (see p.456), forms an immensely rich ecosystem. Ngorongoro's highlight is an enormous volcanic crater, which provides one of Africa's most stunning backdrops for viewing a glut of wildlife, especially lion, elephant and some highly endangered black rhino. There's plenty of upmarket **accommodation** inside the conservation area, some more affordable campsites and a good range of hotels in **Karatu town**, outside Ngorongoro's eastern gate.

Karatu

The dusty town of **KARATU** is the main supply base for Ngorongoro Conservation Area (see p.447), and capital of a densely populated district – not surprisingly, given that cultivators were evicted from Ngorongoro in the 1950s. The town, which is periodically swept by red twisters, has little of interest, but is a handy base for visiting Ngorongoro, whose Lodoare Gate is 18km away.

Given the steady stream of safari vehicles passing through town, tourists are generally seen as a source of money, and local children are unusually insistent in their demands for not just pens and shillings, but dollars. Still, you'll have to

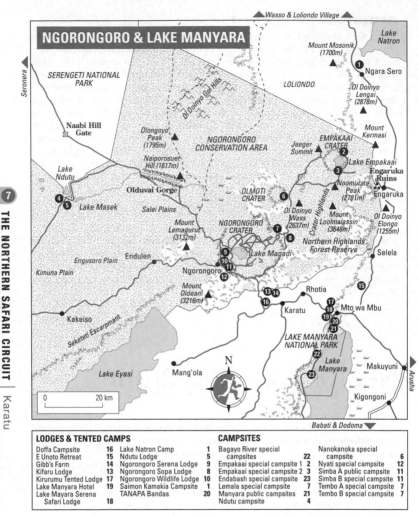

NGORONGORO & LAKE MANYARA

Wasso & Loliondo Village ▲▲

Lake Natron

Seronera ◄

SERENGETI NATIONAL PARK

Mount Mosonik (1700m) ▲ ● 1 Ngara Sero

LOLIONDO

Ol Doinyo Gai Hills

Naabi Hill ⊠ Gate

Olongoyo Peak (1795m) ▲

NGORONGORO CONSERVATION AREA

Mount Kermasi ▲

Ol Doinyo Lengai (2878m) ▲

Jaeger Summit

EMPAKAAI CRATER ● 2

Lake Empakaai

Engaruka Ruins

Naiporosuet Hill (1617m) ▲

● 3

Noomurata Peak (2781m) ▲

Engaruka ▲

Lake Ndutu

Olduvai Gorge

OLMOTI CRATER

● 6

Crater Highlands

Mount Loolmalassin (3648m) ▲

Ol Doinyo Elongo (1255m) ▲

● 4 ● 5 Lake Masek

Salei Plains

Ol Doinyo Wass (2637m) ▲ ● 7

● 8

Selela

Mount Lemagurut (3132m) ▲

NGORONGORO CRATER

Lake Magadi

Northern Highlands Forest Reserve

Engusoro Plain

Endulen

● 9 ● 10 ● 11

Ngorongoro ● 12

● 15

Kimuna Plain

Mount Oldeani (3216m) ▲

● 13 ● 14

Rhotia

● 17

Kakeiso

● 16

Karatu

● 18 Mto wa Mbu

● 19

● 20

● 21

Seketeti Escarpment

LAKE MANYARA NATIONAL PARK

● 22

Arusha ►

Lake Eyasi

Mang'ola

N

Lake Manyara

● 23

Makuyuni

Kigongoni

0   20 km

Babati & Dodoma ▼

LODGES & TENTED CAMPS

Doffa Campsite	16
E Unoto Retreat	15
Gibb's Farm	14
Kifaru Lodge	13
Kirurumu Tented Lodge	17
Lake Manyara Hotel	19
Lake Mayara Serena Safari Lodge	18
Lake Natron Camp	1
Ndutu Lodge	15
Ngorongoro Serena Lodge	9
Ngorongoro Sopa Lodge	8
Ngorongoro Wildlife Lodge	10
Saimon Kamakia Campsite	1
TANAPA Bandas	20

CAMPSITES

Bagayo River special campsites	22
Empakaai special campsite 1	2
Empakaai special campsite 2	3
Endabash special campsite	23
Lemala special campsite	7
Manyara public campsites	21
Ndutu campsite	4
Nanokanoka special campsite	6
Nyati special campsite	12
Simba A public campsite	11
Simba B public campsite	11
Tembo A special campsite	7
Tembo B special campsite	7

stay overnight if you're on a low budget and don't have a tent. Car rental, for visiting Ngorongoro, is available at most of the hotels reviewed below, and – assuming you can fill the vehicle (usually five seats) – works out cheaper than arranging a trip in Arusha.

The best day to visit is on the seventh of each month, for a big market and livestock auction (*mnada*), which attracts thousands of Maasai and Barbaig cattle herders, and Iraqw farmers.

Practicalities

You can **change money** at the National Microfinance Bank on the main road close to the Caltex petrol station. For **medicine**, head to Karatu Dispensary and Human Diagnostic Centre: from the bank, go down the side street on the

Lake Eyasi and the Hadzabe

Occupying a shallow trough in the shadow of Ngorongoro's Mount Oldeani is **Lake Eyasi**, another of the Rift Valley's soda lakes. In the dry woodland around its edges live the **Hadzabe** tribe. Numbering between 500 and 2500, depending on how "purely" you count, the Hadzabe are Tanzania's last hunter-gatherers, a status they shared with the Sandawe further south until the latter were forced to settle forty years ago. Sadly, the Hadzabe appear to be heading the same way: much of their land has been taken by commercial plantations and ranches, which also form effective barriers to the seasonal wildlife migrations on which the hunting part of the Hadzabe lifestyle depends, whilst the unwelcome attentions of outsiders is rapidly destroying their culture.

Being absolutely destitute in monetary terms, the Hadzabe are in no position to resist the more pernicious elements of modernity, with its trade, evangelical missionaries, enforced schooling, the cash economy, AIDS and indeed tourists, the majority of whom consider the Hadzabe to be little more than primitive curiosities. The supposedly backward and primeval form of Hadzabe society has also attracted a welter of researchers, whose dubious activities range from the "discovery" that grandmothers are useful for feeding their grandchildren, to thinly veiled attempts by multinational pharmaceutical companies to patent their DNA.

In 2000, a news report stated that the Hadzabe were preparing to leave their land and way of life for the brave new world of Arusha. Though at that time the story turned out to be a hoax, sadly, within five to ten years, it may become a reality. Short of convincing the Tanzanian government to protect Hadzabe land and its wildlife routes (most unlikely given the government's previous attempts to forcibly "civilize" the Hadzabe), the best thing that you can do to help preserve their culture is to leave them well alone.

---

opposite side of the main road and take the first left. There are lots of cheap and basic **restaurants and bars** throughout town; particularly good for a drink with *nyama choma* are *Elephant Bar* in the centre and *Sunset View Garden* near the *Safari Junction*, which does indeed have its eponymous panorama. Many of Karatu's **hotels**, see below, also provide food and drink. Apart from a handful of really basic places (all ①), room rates are higher than elsewhere, but are still considerably cheaper than places inside Ngorongoro. Karatu's altitude means it has no malaria, but it does have mosquitoes; get a room with a mosquito net.

Doffa Campsite 8km west of town, 500m beyond the Mang'ola junction (no phone). A simple campsite and bar. Tsh3000 per person.

Gibb's Farm 5km northeast of town; turn off a few hundred metres east of the bank ☎027/253 4040, ⑩www.gibbs.net. A formal atmosphere, but this is the nicest place around Ngorongoro. A working farm, surrounded by dry forest and coffee plantations, the eight best rooms are in an old 1930s farmhouse, while seven more rooms occupy a row of garden bungalows. Included in the price are guided walks, and the food is superb ($16.50 for a meal and walk). Upmarket safaris are offered by Gibb's Farm Safaris (p.398). Full-board ⑧

Karatu Lutheran Hostel At the west end of town, 100m to the right ☎027/253 4230. A good peaceful choice with large, clean en-suite rooms in a curved brick building. All have nets, screened windows, hot water and electricity. There are also two suites (④). Breakfast included ③

Kifaru Lodge 2.2km west of town, then 6km north along a track (bookings via Tanzania Photographic Tours & Safaris, Sokoine Rd near Stanbic Bank in Arusha ☎027/250 8790, ⑥tzphotosafaris@habari.co.tz). Second-best to *Gibb's* thanks to its elevated price and less shaded setting, although the ten rooms are extremely attractive, especially in the Coffee House (with balcony views over the estate) and in the main house (an unerring imitation of an old farmhouse). Facilities include a small swimming pool, tennis courts, restaurant ($12 lunch, $17 dinner) and walks around the estate, where you might see blue monkeys. Closed April–mid May. Breakfast included ⑧, full-board ⑨

Kudu Campsite & Lodge At the west end of town; turn left for *Safari Junction* ☎027/253

4055, ℗ 027/253 4268. Set in characterful gardens, this has four large, en-suite bungalows, each nicely decorated and with running water and electricity, but overpriced nonetheless. There are also two rooms in the main building sharing bathrooms (no fans or nets). Camping is allowed; $5 per person. There's a curio shop, bar and restaurant (£10 a meal). Breakfast included. ⑥

The Iraqw

Karatu's main tribes are the cattle-herding Barbaig (see p.262) and the agricultural Iraqw. The history of the 200,000-strong **Iraqw**, who occupy much of the area between Karatu and Mbulu town in the south, is a fascinating enigma, though the theory that they originally came from Mesopotamia (Iraq, no less) is too simplistic to be likely. Nonetheless, the Iraqw language is related to the "southern Cushitic" tongues spoken in Ethiopia and northern Kenya, meaning that at some point in their history they migrated southwards along the Rift Valley, something you can also tell by their facial features, which are finer than those of their neighbours and similar to those of Ethiopians.

Exactly when the Iraqw arrived in Tanzania is not known, but a number of clues offered by their agricultural practices – the use of sophisticated terracing to limit soil erosion, complex irrigation techniques, crop rotation and the use of manure from stall-fed cattle – provide uncanny parallels to the ruined irrigation channels, terraces and cattle pens of Engaruka (see p.437), at the foot of the Rift Valley escarpment.

Iraqw **oral legend** makes no mention of a place called Engaruka, but that's hardly surprising given that Engaruka is a Maasai word. Instead, legends talk of a place called **Ma'angwatay**, which may have been Engaruka. At the time, the Iraqw lived under a chief called **Haymu Tipe**. In what is suggestive of a power struggle or civil war, the legend says that Haymu Tipe's only son, Gemakw, was kidnapped by a group of young Iraqw warriors and hidden in the forest. Finally locating him, Haymu Tipe was given a curious ultimatum: unless he brought to the warriors an enemy to fight, his son would be killed. So Haymu Tipe asked the cattle-herding Barbaig, who at the time occupied the Ngorongoro highlands, to come to fight, which they did. Many people were killed, and it seems that the Iraqw lost the battle, as Haymu Tipe, his family and his remaining men fled to a place called Guser-Twalay, where Gemakw – who had been released as agreed – became ill and died. Haymu Tipe and his men continued on to a place called Qawirang in a forest west of Lake Manyara, where they settled. The legend then becomes confusing, but it appears that Qawirang is the same as the most recent Iraqw "homeland", the **Irqwar Da'aw valley**, 70km south of Karatu, where the Iraqw settled at least 200 years ago, shortly after Engaruka was abandoned. Subsequently, population pressure in Irqwar Da'aw led to further migrations; the first Iraqw to settle in Karatu arrived in the 1930s. For more about Iraqw **history**, see Bjørn-Erik Hanssen's "Three stories from the mythology of the Iraqw people" at ⊛www.leopardmannen.no/hanssen/tanz-eng.htm.

But the best place to learn more about the Iraqw is **Sandemu Iraqw Art and Culture Promoters Centre** at Njia Panda village, 9km west of Karatu (turn left at the junction for Mang'ola and it's 1km further on). This recently established community-based initiative aims to promote and preserve Iraqw culture. The centre is built in the form of a traditionally fortified house, nestling so snugly into the hillside that it only needs a front wall (a construction that is remarkably similar to the former fortified houses of the Rangi; see p.256). Historically, fortification and camouflage was essential to avoid the warlike attention of the Maasai and Barbaig. The centre also contains an underground bunker with escape tunnels, which contain a display of weapons, tools, grinding stones and furniture. The centre supports its work by selling crafts: mats, baskets, traditional clothes and jewellery, clay pots, gourds and calabashes. Camping should be possible (but enquire beforehand in Karatu), and there's also *Doffa Campsite* (see p.445), 500m west of the junction to Mang'ola. Given enough time, the centre can arrange performances of traditional music.

Ngorongoro Safari Resort On the main road behind Caltex ☎ 027/253 4290. A campsite dedicated almost entirely to overland trucks, as belied by their supermarket, which stocks everything from Red Bull and Marmite to Pringles and champagne. There's also a gift shop, bar and a surprisingly swish restaurant, either a la carte ($4–6) for tourist favourites like pasta, pizzas and steaks, or set menus at $9–10. Camping $3 per person.

Safari Junction Camp By the communications tower at the west end of town (no phone). Set in a pleasant flower garden, this hot and dusty collection of brick and wood buildings has clearly seen better days, and isn't great value either. There's a choice of en-suite rooms with nets and Western toilets, or beds in a dorm. Better value is camping at $5 per person, and there are tents for hire ($10 extra). Meals cost $5–6. Breakfast included ❹

Tanzania Tree Planting Project Rest House 1.5km east of town: turn south (right) just after the Agip petrol station, and right again at the fork 250m along ☎ 027/253 4249. Overlooking some fields, this has two singles and one double sharing bathrooms (no nets), a large sitting room and a kitchen, making it ideal for self-catering. ❷

Ngorongoro Conservation Area

"The eighth wonder of the world" is the clarion call of the brochures, and for once, they're not far wrong. The spectacular geography of the 8288-square-kilometre **NGORONGORO CONSERVATION AREA** occupies the volcanic highlands between the Great Rift Valley's western escarpment and the Serengeti Plains. It's the product of the volcanic upheavals that accompanied the formation of the Rift Valley, and its varied habitats virtually guarantee sightings of "the big five" – elephant, lion, leopard, rhino and buffalo. For animals, the place is a haven, while for tourists, it's something close to heaven.

Coming from the east, the magic begins the instant you pass through Lodoare Gate. The road begins to climb up through the tall and liana-festooned Oldeani Forest, giving way to an unforgettable view of **Ngorongoro Crater**: a fluid and ever-changing patchwork of green and yellow hues streaked with shadows and mist, in the centre of which Lake Magadi reflects the silvery sky, while on the western horizon, there's the seemingly endless shimmer of the Serengeti Plains. The nineteen-kilometre-wide crater is Ngorongoro's incomparable highlight, a vast, unbroken caldera left behind when an enormous volcano collapsed. Its grasslands, swamps, glades, lakes and forests contain vast numbers of herbivores, together with Africa's highest density of predators. **Game viewing**, needless to say, is phenomenal, as is the abundance of photo opportunities, the crater's deep, blueish-purple sides providing a spectacular backdrop to any shot. The crater also contains a few highly endangered **black rhino**, which despite their disastrously reduced population (now under ten), are easily seen. **Birdlife** is pretty decent, too, and includes ostriches, Verreaux's eagles, Egyptian vultures, kori bustards and lesser flamingos, the latter feeding on soda lakes occupying Ngorongoro and Empakaai craters, and at Lake Ndutu on the border with Serengeti.

Although the crater is often all that tourists see of Ngorongoro, there's much more besides. In the west, the rolling hills give way to the expansive grassland of the **Salei Plains**, which receive a good part of the Serengeti's annual wildlife migration between December and April (see box on p.457). Both hyena and cheetah are frequently seen here, though in the dry season, the plains resemble a desert. Right on the edge of the plains is a remarkable geological fissure, **Olduvai Gorge**, famous among paleontologists as the site of important hominid finds dating back millions of years. To the northeast, close to the edge of the Great Rift Valley's escarpment, are two smaller craters, **Olmoti and Empakaai**, which are also rich in wildlife yet see very few visitors. The craters, which form part of the so-called **Crater Highlands**, can be visited on foot if accompanied by an armed ranger – an exciting if hair-raising prospect. For those with more time, and a sturdy pair of legs, it's also possible to walk across the highlands from Ngorongoro to Lake Natron via Ol Doinyo Lengai volcano, a journey that can take anything from two to seven days (see p.452).

Another attraction, especially for visitors with limited time, is the chance to meet the red-robed **Maasai** for whom the conservation area provides year-round pasture. Package tours are catered for by **cultural bomas**; "traditional" Maasai villages set up expressly for tourists. The experience can feel uncomfortably staged and voyeuristic at times, but for many it's the only time they'll be able to meet one of Africa's traditional tribes. With more time, much better would be a Crater Highlands walk, which passes clean through Maasai territory, or a visit to one of Tanzania's cultural tourism programmes; see p.405.

Given these manifold attractions, Ngorongoro is Tanzania's most visited wildlife area, attracting over 300,000 tourists annually, and this, in fact, is the main drawback. To some, large numbers of visitors make Ngorongoro resemble a zoo, and spoils the experience of being in a true wilderness. Nonetheless, for all the tourists and the hype, Ngorongoro – designated a World Heritage Site in 1979 – is still a place that enchants, and few people leave disappointed.

Arrival and entry fees

Pretty much every tour operator in Tanzania offers **safaris** to Ngorongoro. The widest choice and keenest prices are from Arusha (see p.395 for a list of recommended companies), though safaris are also possible from Moshi (p.334) and Mwanza (p.484). If you're adept at bargaining, it's cheaper to arrange **car rental** in Karatu (p.443) than buying a safari or organizing a vehicle in Arusha. *Kudu Campsite & Lodge* and the various petrol stations there are good places to ask; under $100 for half a day's car rental including the driver is reasonable, or $120 for a full day, excluding entry fees. Self-drive is possible, as everything is well signposted, but you won't be allowed into the crater without an officially licensed guide or driver-guide; they can be hired at the park gate for $20 a day. Armed rangers, obligatory for walks, cost the same.

It's not possible to get around the conservation area by **public transport**, but there is a daily bus run by the Ngorongoro Conservation Area Authority from Arusha to their headquarters close to the crater, where you can hire a vehicle and a guide; enquire at the conservation area's tourist office on Boma Road in Arusha.

Entry fees, paid at Lodoare Gate if you're coming from the east, or at Naabi Hill Gate coming from Serengeti, are $30 per person per day, plus Tsh1500 for a vehicle permit. There's also a $15 per person **crater fee** if – as is likely – you'll be descending to the floor of Ngorongoro Crater.

Regulations are similar to those in the national parks, namely that off-road driving is forbidden, as is collecting plants (other than dead wood if you're camping). You should also remain inside your vehicle except at designated picnic sites, campsites, viewpoints or Olduvai Gorge, or if you're accompanied by an armed ranger.

Information

There are **tourist information centres** at Lodoare Gate and at Olduvai Museum. The conservation area **headquarters**, useful mainly for research queries, are at Ngorongoro village, southwest of the crater (☎027/253 7046, ⓦwww.ngorongoro-crater-africa.org). They also have an office in Karatu, on

Ngorongoro's ecology: a precarious balance

Ngorongoro is a wilderness, but one that has also for long been inhabited by humans, originally by hunter-gatherers collectively known as **Dorobo**, and later by cattle herders, including the ancestors of the Barbaig (see p.262) and then the Maasai (see box on p.434). As with the Serengeti, humans were and are very much part of Ngorongoro's delicate **ecological balance**, a balance however that has become increasingly precarious since the end of the nineteenth century, when the Europeans began to colonize East Africa.

The first *mzungu* to set eyes on Ngorongoro and its famous crater was the German explorer, **Dr Oscar Baumann**, who in March 1892 reported a magnificent abundance of game, and promptly went on to bag three rhinos. So began a long history of European involvement, first for hunting, then for conservation, and which, for all their efforts and theories, has witnessed a massive decline in animal numbers.

Originally heavily exploiting the area for hunting, the British administration quickly realized that their activities in Ngorongoro were having a detrimental effect on its wildlife, and so, in 1921, Ngorongoro was made a **Game Reserve**. Seven years later, locals were prohibited from hunting and cultivating in the crater, although – hypocritically – Europeans continued do as they wished until the end of the 1930s, when trophy hunting was finally banned. In 1951, Ngorongoro became part of Serengeti National Park, and in 1958 the Maasai – under formidable pressure – formally renounced their claim to Serengeti. The following year, they were evicted and moved into Ngorongoro, which was declared a **multiple land use area**. This special status still allows Maasai to settle and graze their cattle in coexistence with wildlife, but this admirable idea, however, conceals a more disturbing reality.

Although the **law** states that In cases of human–wildlife conflict in Ngorongoro, Maasai rights are to take precedence, this has rarely been the case, and relations between the authorities and the Maasai have become extremely bitter of late. Settlement in the crater itself was banned in 1974, and cultivation, which the Maasai were increasingly having to adopt, was prohibited throughout Ngorongoro in 1975, and only periodically allowed since. Livestock, too, has been excluded from the crater since the early 1990s, denying the Maasai a critical dry-season pasture for their cattle, and the last decade has been peppered with deeply troubling allegations. For more details see @http://elj.warwick.ac.uk/global/issue/2000-1/lissu.html.

The underlying problem is that the Maasai presence is barely tolerated by Ngorongoro's authorities, who have progressively made it harder for them to scrape a living from their diminishing resources. Having lost water and pasture rights to the crater (and eighty percent of the land they controlled until a century ago), and been forbidden from hunting or cultivating, an estimated forty percent of Ngorongoro's Maasai are considered destitute, owning less than two livestock units per household. Some conservationists see **tourism** as the solution, but to date, the Maasai have seen little of Ngorongoro's gate receipts beyond the construction of a few wells, dams and dispensaries.

Ngorongoro's problems aren't just with the Maasai, however. The changing ecological balance caused by the ban on subsistence hunting and the exclusion of cattle from large areas has favoured increased wildebeest and buffalo populations with the unfortunate knock-on effect of an increased incidence of **malignant catarrh fever**, which is fatal to cattle. Diseases affecting wildlife have also become more common, disastrously so in 2000 and 2001, when an outbreak of an unidentified illness claimed the lives of over six hundred animals. The changing ecological balance may also have been responsible for swarms of aggressive blood-sucking flies, *Stomoxys calcitrans*, which in March 2001 killed at least six lions and injured 62 more.

It can only be hoped that Ngorongoro's authorities can find the wisdom to settle their differences with the Maasai once and for all. As has recently been shown in several other protected areas in Tanzania, the key to successful wildlife conservation lies in fully involving local communities, both in the running, and in the profits, of wildlife areas.

the same road as *Elephant Bar* and *Milano Bar* that runs parallel to and north of the main road, and in Arusha on Boma Road. The latter has brochures and also sells books, maps and videos covering not only Ngorongoro but most of Tanzania's national parks.

The most detailed and accurate **map** is the 1999 edition by Harms-Verlag. Not as detailed but more visually attractive is the painted dry-season/wet-season map by Giovanni Tombazzi. Maps and guidebooks are usually available in Arusha, at the conservation area's gates, at Olduvai Museum and at the lodges.

Recommended reading is either of two guidebooks published by the Ngorongoro Conservation Unit. The older one ($5), by Jeannette Hanby and David Bygott, is out of date (1989), but contains a wealth of information about the region, its history, geology and inhabitants (animal and people) and remains useful. The new one is similar in scope and in full colour ($10), and is accompanied by a number of other booklets covering Ngorongoro's geology, birdlife, wildlife, tree and plants, and prehistory.

Accommodation

The only regular **accommodation** inside Ngorongoro is a number of expensive **lodges**, all but one of which are on the crater rim. Environmentally and ethically, none of the crater-rim lodges enjoys an unblemished reputation, and anyway, much cheaper – and superior in many ways, especially for the feeling of being in the wild – is **camping**, which costs $20 or $40 per person depending on the site; see opposite. There are more campsites, and also much cheaper hotels, outside the conservation area in Karatu; see p.445.

Lodges

Ndutu Lodge Next to Lake Ndutu on the border with Serengeti (office at 50 Haile Selassie Rd, Arusha ☏027/250 6702, ⓦ www.ndutu.com). A welcoming and friendly place run by the same people as *Gibb's Farm* in Karatu, this has 32 comfortable bungalows, the best at the front facing the lake. With no fences, wildlife can come and go – best from February to June. There's an open-sided bar, a lounge and dining room (meals $19), and evening meals can be taken around a campfire within earshot of roaring lions. Breakfast included ➐, full-board ➑

Ngorongoro Serena Lodge On the crater rim (book through Serena Lodges, AICC Ngorongoro, Arusha ☏027/250 8175, ⓦ www.serenahotels.com). The usual standards of creature comforts from this chain making a very stylish yet impersonal place. Most if not all of its 75 rooms overlook the crater from their verandahs. There are various bars and lounges, a restaurant and a terrace with views. Full-board. ➒

Ngorongoro Sopa Lodge On the crater rim (book through Sopa Lodges, Savannah Rd, Arusha ☏027/250 6886, ⓦ www.sopalodges.com). The only hotel on the eastern rim, this is perfect for sunsets, but also the largest and least personal of the lodges, with 90 mostly twin-bed rooms. The external architecture is an eyesore, but the views are fantastic, whether from public areas, the balconies of most of the rooms or the swimming pool. The food isn't up to much though. Full-board ➑

Ngorongoro Wildlife Lodge On the crater rim (book through *Novotel Mount Meru Hotel* in Arusha, p.378). Another architectural mess, this one – nicknamed the "ski lodge" – is government-owned and has been slated for privatization for years, which should finally lift its drooping standards and very average food, although the staff are friendly. For the time being it's the cheapest of the lot, especially if booked through a safari company, and the views are superb, whether from the 75 bedrooms (just four with balconies), or from the lounge. Half-board ➑

Camping

Campers can choose between one public campsite, which is always open and doesn't require reservations, and several "special campsites" which are often block-booked by safari companies months if not years in advance.

The **public campsite** ($20 per person, paid at the gate) is *Simba A* on the southwestern rim of Ngorongoro Crater, which has toilets and showers, but gets packed, noisy and often filthy in high season. Nonetheless, the views of the crater are jaw-dropping, and the Woodstock/Glastonbury feel appeals to many, despite the discomforts.

The **special campsites** ($40 per person), where you're guaranteed to be the only campers, are usually in very scenic locations but have no facilities at all. The only one to be avoided is *Nyati*, near Ngorongoro Crater, which lacks any kind of views. The rest, all recommended if you can find them free for a night, are: *Simba B*, which has similar views to *Simba A* 1km away, but without the crowds; *Nanokanoka*, close to Olmoti Crater and Nanokanoka village, which means you can wander in for a chat with local Maasai; two sites next to Empakaai Crater, perfect for descending into it the next day; and three sites on the wooded northeastern rim of Ngorongoro Crater, *Tembo A*, *Tembo B* and *Lemala*, all of which occasionally see elephants. There are also seven special campsites around Lake Ndutu in the west.

Ngorongoro Crater

Some 2.5 million years ago, the reservoir of magma under an enormous volcano towering over the western flank of the Great Rift Valley emptied itself in an enormous explosion, leaving a vacuum which caused the mountain to implode under its own weight. In its wake, where its heart had been, it left an enormous 600-metre deep crater (caldera), its nineteen-kilometre diameter now making it the world's largest unbroken and unflooded caldera. This is **Ngorongoro Crater**, one of Tanzania's undisputed wonders, covering approximately 300 square kilometres and providing a natural amphitheatre for the wildlife spectacle on its floor. The crater contains 25,000 to 30,000 large mammals, which from the rim resemble a strew of pulsating specks arranged in fluid formations, while above the crater, eagles, buzzards, hawks and vultures circle.

The main feature of the crater floor is the shallow and alkaline **Lake Magadi**, whose extent varies widely according to the rains. Thousands of flamingos can usually be seen feeding on the lake. On the western shore is an enigmatic scattering of stone **burial mounds**, believed to have been left by the Datooga, ancestors of Barbaig cattle herders who occupied the crater until they were pushed out by the Maasai. At the lake's southern edge is **Lerai Forest**, a large patch of acacia woodland that takes its Maasai name from the dominant yellow-barked acacia (or fever trees). The forest is a good place for seeing waterbuck and flitting sunbirds. Swamp, thorn scrub and grassland fill the rest of the crater, and provide the bulk of the game viewing.

The majority of the animals are **herbivores**, supported by year-round supplies of water and fodder, and include vast herds of wildebeest (up to 14,000), zebra, buffalo, Grant's and Thomson's gazelle, eland, hartebeest and mountain reedbuck, warthog and hippo, and two of Africa's giants: elephants, of which a handful of bulls are always present, and a small population of **black rhino**. Once common across all of eastern and southern Africa, rhino poaching in the 1970s and 1980s took a terrible toll on this magnificent creature, decimating the population from 108 in the 1960s to only 14 in 1995. Although poaching is now under control (if not completely eradicated), the rhino suffered a major blow in 2000–2001, when a mysterious disease killed five of the remaining beasts, pushing the population to under ten.

Apart from rhino, the big draw is the transfixing sight of Africa's densest population of **predators** in action. Lions are very common and easily seen (best in the dry season), as are hyenas and jackals. Cheetahs are also sometimes present, while leopards require some patience to spot, as they rest up in trees or thick bush by day.

There are three **access roads**. The eastern Lemala route, from *Lemala* and *Tembo* campsites, can be driven in either direction. In the south, the steeper Lerai route from Lerai Forest on the crater floor is for ascent only, while the Seneto route in the west is only for descent. A **crater fee** of $15 per person applies in addition to standard entry fees, and you'll need to hire an official guide if you're driving yourself (this doesn't apply if your driver is licensed by the authorities, or if you're on an organized safari). Only 4WD vehicles are allowed in the crater, and in theory you need to carry a heavy-duty jack, chains or a tow rope, a shovel or hoe, and an axe or *panga*. The speed limit is 25kph,

The Crater Highlands

The **Crater Highlands** is the informal term for the mountainous eastern part of Ngorongoro that forms the lush forested ridge of the Great Rift Valley's western escarpment, and which the Maasai call Ol Doinyo Ildatwa. The area includes Ngorongoro Crater, the 3216-metre Mount Oldeani to its south, the isolated Gol Mountains in the north, Olmoti and Empakaai craters in the northeast, Mount Loolmalassin (the range's highest point at 3648m) and Ol Doinyo Lengai, East Africa's only active volcano (see p.440), which rises in a perfect cone just outside the conservation area's northeastern corner.

Since the rules regarding walking in the conservation area were relaxed a few years back, one of Ngorongoro's major attractions has become a **Crater Highlands trek**, which can be as short a day, and as long as a week, giving you ample time to get to Lake Natron (see p.441), perhaps including a climb up Ol Doinyo Lengai along the way. The exact distance, and number of days required, depends on where you start, and how much time (and money) you want to spend. For example, a two-day (44km) trek to Lake Natron starts at Empakaai Crater, while a seven-day trip gives you plenty of flexibility, allowing you to amble at your leisure from the rim of Ngorongoro Crater, and overnight at Maasai *bomas*.

Costs vary according to the level of service and back-up: count on between $100–250 a day. Upmarket operators offer something close to bush luxury, where a full camp attended by plenty of staff is set up ahead of your arrival, including mess tents, furniture, chemical loos and ingenious bucket showers. On these trips you'll generally be guided by a white-hunter kind of chap, with a Maasai warrior escort serving mainly to provide local colour. Much cheaper, more adventurous and definitely more "authentic" are humbler trips where the gear (dome tents, usually) – and you if you're tired – is carried by donkey. These trips are often guided by Maasai, who make up for their sometimes limited knowledge of English with tremendous practical botanical know-how and an uncanny ability to spot all sorts of wildlife.

For **one-day trips**, contact the conservation area headquarters (see p.448), who can fix you up with an armed ranger, or Serena Active (@ ngorongoro@serena.co.tz), based at *Ngorongoro Serena Lodge* (see p.450). The latter offer two-hour nature walks around the lodge ($10), a three-hour drive, hike and picnic to Mount Oldeani's foothills ($40) or a full day's hike to Oldeani summit for $60, all prices including the ranger. Particularly recommended **safari companies** offering Crater Highlands treks are Swala Safaris, Victoria Expeditions and The East African Safari & Touring Company (all in Arusha; pp.396–397), and MEM Tours & Safari in Moshi (p.334).

and you must be out by 6pm, so start ascending no later than 5.30pm. Visitors must stay in their vehicle except at two **picnic sites**: one next to Lerai Forest at the foot of the Lerai ascent route, the other at Ngoitokitok Springs in the east next to a small lake. A day is enough to see most of the crater's denizens.

Olmoti and Empakaai Craters

North of Ngorongoro Crater are two smaller craters, Olmoti and Empakaai. The rims of either can be reached by vehicle, but are best seen on foot, ideally prearranged as part of a Crater Highlands trek (see box opposite). Though ranger posts are close to both craters, if you're intending to walk it's best to organize in advance with the conservation area headquarters (see p.448) for a ranger to accompany you.

The shallow and grassy **Olmoti Crater**, accessed from Nanokanoka village (there's a special campsite there), contains several antelope species, and there are waterfalls nearby on the Munge River, which starts life inside the crater. Accompanied by an armed ranger (the post is in the village), the crater rim and its fringing forest can be explored on foot, taking anything from two to seven hours.

Northeast of here is the six-kilometre-wide **Empakaai Crater**, much of which is filled with a beautiful, forest-fringed soda lake. This is better for wildlife than Olmoti, and resident species include bushbuck, reedbuck and waterbuck, buffalo, monkeys and an abundance of birds, including flamingos. You can walk along the rim (again, if accompanied by an armed ranger – the post is about 5km southeast) and into the crater itself (at least 7hr). There are two special campsites on the rim.

Olduvai Gorge

Gouged into the edge of the Salei Plains is **Olduvai Gorge**, a steep-sided, 48-kilometre-long ravine whose depth reaches 150m in places. Furrowed out of the volcanic land by the capricious Olduvai (or Oldupai) River, the rock strata on either side of the gorge have exposed the fossilized remains of animals and over fifty hominids dating back almost two million years, and – when taken together with finds from Lake Turkana in northern Kenya, Ethiopia and elsewhere in Africa – comprise an archeological trove of inestimable importance for understanding the origins of humankind.

The fossils were first noted in 1911 by **Professor Kattwinkel**, a German butterfly collector, who stumbled across them quite by chance, and took the fossilized remains of a three-toed horse back to Berlin's Museum für Naturkunde. Two decades later, his findings aroused the curiosity of a Kenyan-born British anthropologist, **Louis Leakey**, whose name now features in almost any discussion on human prehistory. In 1931, inspired by nothing more than a gut feeling that Africa was the "cradle of mankind" rather than Asia, as was then thought, Leakey began excavating at Olduvai Gorge.

For almost thirty years, Louis and his wife, Mary, found only stone tools, the oldest belonging to the so-called **Oldowan industry** (1.2 to 1.8 million years ago). Spurred on by the belief that the remains of the hominids that had created the tools could not be far behind, they persevered, and their patience was finally rewarded in 1959 by the discovery of two large human-like teeth and a piece of skull. Further digging provided over 400 additional fragments, which were painstakingly reassembled to form the 1.75 million year-old skull of *Australopithecus boisei* ("southern ape"), nicknamed **Nutcracker Man** on account of his powerful jaws. The tool-maker had been found, and the discovery – at the time, the oldest known – provoked a sea-change in paleontological circles, especially as the skull's size and dentition displayed uncanny similarities with modern man. The unavoidable conclusion was that the Leakeys had unearthed a direct ancestor of modern man, and in fact that the much vaunted "missing link" had been found.

The theory was accepted until disproved by much older finds from Ethiopia and Laetoli, south of Olduvai (see box opposite), and since then poor old Nutcracker Man has been consigned to history as an evolutionary dead end. His importance remains, however, in showing that hominid evolution was not a simple linear progression. The find also spurred on a flurry of **further excavations** at Olduvai, which showed conclusively that two other hominid species, almost certainly our ancestors, lived contemporaneously with *Australopithecus boisei* – *Homo habilis* ("handy man") and *Homo erectus* ("upright man").

Over the years, various claims have been made for one place or another being the "cradle of mankind", but it's way too early to say this with any certainty (indeed, a recent find of seven-million-year-old hominid fossils in Chad makes the East African fossils look positively juvenile), and of course fossil beds are usually revealed by geological chance, which in East Africa was the Rift Valley. What is certain, however, is that the incredible journey into our prehistory first began to make sense at Olduvai, and it's a journey that, if it can be traced at all, should happily continue to baffle humankind for many years to come.

Practicalities

Olduvai Gorge can be seen on foot or by vehicle, and even if old bones and stones don't appeal, the gorge itself is a pleasant diversion off the road to Serengeti, and there's also a range of fast-moving black sand dunes to explore. The entrance to the gorge, next to a small but fascinating museum that documents the finds, lies about 30km west of Ngorongoro Crater, and 7km north of the road to Serengeti. The Tsh2000 **entrance fee** also gives access to the museum, but to enter the gorge you'll need to hire one of the **official guides**, who tout their services at the picnic site beside the museum. Unfortunately, there are no fixed prices for their services, and the **cost** depends entirely on their perception of your ability to pay, meaning $2 to $25 per person; haggling is necessary, but something like $10 per group is reasonable. That said, the guides do know their stuff – they reel off entertaining lectures and can put a context to even the most mundane-looking of rocks or fossil fragments. The average tour lasts thirty minutes to two hours if you're in a car. If you want to walk, your guide will expect a hefty additional "tip". Count on at least an extra hour for looking around the museum, more if you want to read and understand everything.

Olduvai Museum

Despite its modest size, **Olduvai Museum** (daily 8am–4.30pm; ☎027/253 7037) at the gorge entrance packs in a bewildering amount of information, too much in fact for non-experts to digest comfortably in a single visit, though the museum shop usually has copies of a guidebook covering Ngorongoro's prehistory. The three rooms are full of bones, tools and skilful reproductions of skulls (the original Nutcracker Man is at Dar es Salaam's National Museum; see p.94), all well documented as long as you turn a blind eye to the uncomfortably hagiographic praise for the Leakey family. Should museum-fatigue strike you down, there's a shady picnic area outside, with soft drinks, beers and sweets for sale, and a *nyama choma* (grilled meat) "bar" is planned.

The gorge

As you head into the gorge, its stratified nature is immediately apparent, with the oldest layers of stone, volcanic deposits and sediments at the bottom. Each of the clearly defined strata ("**beds**") contains a rich record of fossils and tools, and their neat layers have made dating the finds easy.

The oldest and lowest stratum is the sixty-metre-thick **Bed I** (2.1 to 1.7 million years old), where the fossilized remains of both *Homo erectus* and *Australopithecus boisei* (Nutcracker Man) were found, proving that two species coexisted at the same time. The spot where Nutcracker Man was found is now marked by an unsightly concrete block. Bed I also contained stone tools, remains of animals (especially antelopes) whose bones have been split and broken and a circular shelter made from lava-stone.

Hot on the heels of Nutcracker Man came a series of hominid finds in the 1960s in **Bed II** (1.7 to 1.2 million years old) that were markedly different from *Australopithecus*. The new species, small and compact, and with a dentition approaching that of modern man, was named *Homo habilis* ("handy man"), and is believed to be one of our ancestors. The upper strata of Bed II also yielded a partial skull of *Homo erectus* (dubbed OH 9), a more recent ancestor, together with more advanced stone tools, and the bones of giant tusked pigs the size of hippos. But the strange thing about Bed II is that the more primitive *Australopithecus boisei* is also found throughout, showing that *Australopithecus* coexisted with both *Homo* species for a considerable time before becoming extinct.

Moving up, the narrower and more recent **Bed III** (1.2 million to 850,000 years old) revealed more remains of *Homo erectus*, but not many: an unusually hot climate at the time is the suggested cause for the sparsity of human remains. **Bed IV**, whose top level dates back 600,000 years, revealed more finds of *Homo erectus*, and plenty of stone tools: cleavers, knives and scrapers, and throwing stones.

Overlying these beds are several more recent ones. The **Masek Beds** (600,000–400,000 years old) record a time of explosive volcanic activity, and

Laetoli

For all Olduvai Gorge's paleontological wonders, perhaps Tanzania's most astonishing prehistoric find occurred at a place called **Laetoli** (or Garusi), 40km south of Olduvai, which gave up its first fossils in 1938. The most spectacular discoveries came in the 1970s, first of which were thirteen jaw fragments dated at 3.6 million years, unearthed by Mary Leakey. They belonged to a species called *Australopithecus afarensis*, taking its Latin name from the first finds of the species in Ethiopia's Afar desert, which in 1974 introduced the world to "Lucy" – a half-complete female skeleton which circumstantial evidence suggested had been bipedal, and which was dubbed Dinqenesh ("you are amazing") by Ethiopians.

In 1979, Laetoli offered up something equally amazing: a trail of **fossilized footprints** that had been left in wet volcanic ash by two adults and a child. The discovery was dated to around 3.75 million years ago, and attracted worldwide attention as it provided incontestable proof that hominids were walking (and running) upright way before anyone had imagined. Further research suggested that *Australopithecus afarensis* stood fully erect, was about 100–150cm tall, and weighed up to 50kg. The skull, although only fractionally larger than that of modern chimpanzees, had dentition similar to modern humans.

Access to Laetoli is not possible, and the footsteps have been covered up again, but plaster casts are on display at Olduvai Museum, at both museums in Arusha, at the National Museum in Dar and in Nairobi's National Museum.

revealed only tools, and the later **Ndutu Beds** (up to 32,000 years old) are similarly poor. The most recent are the **NaisIusiu Beds** (to 15,000 years old), which came up with more tools and a skeleton of *Homo sapiens* – modern man – who appeared on earth around 50,000 years ago.

The Shifting Sands

Providing an appropriate metaphor for Olduvai's immense sweep though time are the **Shifting Sands**, roughly 15km northwest of the museum and beyond the northern edge of the gorge, which are a range of elegant black sand dunes forever being pushed eastward by the wind (an estimated 17 metres a year). Taking a guide is obligatory as you have to pass through the gorge to get there, and the authorities also discourage folk from clambering over the dunes, which destroys their fragile plant cover and hastens their onward advance.

The Serengeti and around

As one of the world's most famous wildlife areas, the **SERENGETI** needs little introduction. Bordering Ngorongoro in the east, Kenya's Maasai Mara Game Reserve in the north, and reaching to within eight kilometres of Lake Victoria in the west, the Serengeti is also Tanzania's largest national park, and any safari here promises wildlife galore, especially when the **annual migration** of plains game – mainly wildebeest and zebra and their natural predators – is in residence. The migration, which swings up to Maasai Mara, also passes through **Loliondo**, a remote and little-visited wilderness sandwiched between Serengeti, Ngorongoro, Lake Natron and the Kenyan border. Loliondo has a couple of upmarket tented camps, offering much of Serengeti's wildlife in exclusive wilderness concessions, and if you're coming by rented car, a rough road through the area from Serengeti gives an alternative – and highly adventurous – way of getting back towards Arusha via Lake Natron.

Serengeti National Park

As Tanzania's oldest and largest national park, and one of the world's best-known wildlife sanctuaries, the 14,763-square-kilometre **SERENGETI NATIONAL PARK** is one of the jewels in Tanzania's wildlife crown. Protected since 1929, at a time when white trophy hunters were wreaking havoc on wildlife populations, and declared a national park in 1951, the Serengeti is also – together with Ngorongoro – a UNESCO World Heritage Site and International Biosphere Reserve. And with good reason. The Serengeti lies at the heart of the world's largest and most impressive **wildlife migration** (see box opposite), at the peak of which the national park contains the highest concentration of mammals on earth.

Serengeti takes its name from the flat **grassland plains** that cover the eastern section of the park next to Ngorongoro, which the Maasai called *siringet*,

The Great Migration

The Serengeti owes its hallowed place in our imagination to the annual 800-kilometre **migration** of over 2.5 million animals, the largest mammalian migration on earth. A continuous, milling and unsettled mass, including 1.7 million wildebeest and close to a million other animals, the migration offers visitors one of nature's most staggering displays, one in which the ever-vigilant predators – lions, cheetahs, African hunting dogs and spotted hyenas – play a vital part. The river crossings are the biggest obstacle, namely the Grumeti in Serengeti, and the Mara along the border with Kenya in the north, and both can be the scene of true carnage as the panicked herds struggle across the raging flows in a writhing mass of bodies while the weak and injured are picked off by crocodiles and lions.

The migration's ceaseless movement is prompted by a seasonal search for fresh water and pasture dictated by the rains. It moves in a roughly clockwise direction, concentrating in the national park from **April to June**, towards the end of the long rains, before leaving behind the withering plains of the Serengeti by journeying northward towards the fresh moisture and grass of Kenya's Maasai Mara Game Reserve, which the migration reaches in August. By **September** and **October**, the bulk of the migration is concentrated in Maasai Mara. By **late October** and **early November**, the Mara's grasslands are approaching exhaustion, so the migration turns back towards northern and eastern Serengeti, following the fresh grass brought by the short rains. In this period, the migration is widely spread out, and a large part of it circles through Loliondo and into Ngorongoro, beyond the Serengeti's eastern border. From **December to March**, the migration settles in the Serengeti Plains and western Ngorongoro, where it remains until the onset of the long rains. The wildebeest take advantage of this temporary pause to give birth (especially from late January to mid-March), accounting for half a million calves annually. The timing of this mass birthing provides security in numbers: predators will eat their fill, but within a few months, the surviving calves are much stronger and able to outrun their pursuers; nonetheless, the hazards of the migration are such that only one in three calves makes it back the following year. By April, the migration is once more concentrated inside Serengeti, and the whole cycle starts again.

The exact time and location of the migration varies annually, depending on the rains and other factors, so coinciding with it cannot be guaranteed; in 2000 for example, prolonged drought shifted the whole cycle forward by two months, flat-footing thousands of safari-goers. Nonetheless, as a general rule, the **best months** for seeing the migration in the Serengeti are from December to July, especially February and March in the plains when the wildebeest herds are dotted with newborn, and April to June when animal concentrations are at their highest. June is also the best time for catching the migration's perilous crossing of the Grumeti River, while the spectacular Mara River crossing, best seen from Kenya but also in northern Serengeti, is at its most awesome (and gruesome) in July and August.

meaning "endless plain". Along with the Kalahari, these plains are the archetypal African savanna of the Western imagination, and the highlight of many a visit, certainly when the migration is in full swing. Even outside the migration, there's plenty of wildlife to see, including large clans of hyenas and thriving lion prides, and a series of weathered granite outcrops called **kopjes** (pronounced kop-yees; from the Afrikaans for "little head"), one of which contains rock paintings, while another has a mysterious "rock gong". Of course, there's more to Serengeti than the plains, which cover only one third of the park. In the hilly centre, around **Seronera** – where a good deal of the park's accommodation is located, as well as an excellent visitors' centre – a series of lightly wooded valleys provide excellent year-round game viewing, while in the **north**, along a forty-kilometre-wide corridor that connects with Kenya's Maasai Mara Game

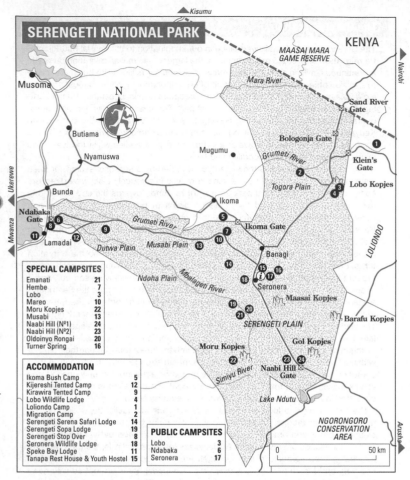

SPECIAL CAMPSITES

Emanati	21
Hembe	7
Lobo	3
Mareo	10
Moru Kopjes	22
Musabi	13
Naabi Hill (Nº1)	24
Naabi Hill (Nº2)	23
Oldoinyo Rongai	20
Turner Spring	16

ACCOMMODATION

Ikoma Bush Camp	5
Kijereshi Tented Camp	12
Kirawira Tented Camp	9
Lobo Wildlife Lodge	4
Loliondo Camp	1
Migration Camp	2
Serengeti Serena Safari Lodge	14
Serengeti Sopa Lodge	19
Serengeti Stop Over	8
Seronera Wildlife Lodge	18
Speke Bay Lodge	11
Tanapa Rest House & Youth Hostel	15

PUBLIC CAMPSITES

Lobo	3
Ndabaka	6
Seronera	17

Reserve, rolling hills and thorny acacia woodland dominate. To the west, another corridor runs along the **Grumeti River** to within 8km of Lake Victoria; the river's flanking evergreen forests are another special habitat, providing a home for primates as well as lurking leopards, and the small lakes, swamps and waterholes of the river are perfect for water birds as well as for crocodiles preying on thirsty wildlife, a sight that is as enthralling as it is gruesome when the migration passes through the area.

Wildlife, of course, is why people come to Serengeti, and the figures are flabbergasting. Of the five million animals to be found during the migration (double the resident population) there are wildebeest, who numbered 1.7 million at the last count, gazelle, both Grant's and Thomson's, who are estimated at around half a million, and some 300,000 zebra. But even when the migration is up in Maasai Mara, or spread out across Ngorongoro and Loliondo, the park contains substantial populations of **plains game**, including buffalo, giraffe and warthog, and a wide range of antelopes, including dikdik, bushbuck, waterbuck and mountain reedbuck, eland and impala, and the rarer oryx and topi. Some

1500 elephants, too, are present, though they are largely migratory and can easily be missed.

But all this is to forget perhaps the most memorable of Serengeti's animals, its **predators**, who thrive off the regal banquet on offer. Indeed, apart from Ngorongoro, Serengeti is probably the best place in Tanzania to see predators in action. Foremost are nearly eight thousand much-maligned spotted hyenas, who live in clans of up to eighty individuals. Also very visible are the park's three thousand or so lions, whose males have characteristic black manes. Other predators include cheetahs, which have been the subject of on-going research since 1975, leopards and bat-eared foxes. Scavengers, apart from hyenas (who also hunt) include both golden and side-striped jackals and vultures. There are six species of the latter, a fraction of Serengeti's 520 **bird species** (including Eurasian winter migrants) – the country's second-highest count after Tarangire National Park. Keen birders can expect to see several hundred species in a two- or three-day safari, including many of the park's 34 raptors (birds of prey).

The **best time to visit** depends on a combination of weather and the extent of the migration. All things considered, June is probably optimum. The Serengeti is at its busiest in the European holiday months, meaning December to February and, to a lesser extent, July and August. Still, it's a big park, so you won't get anything like the congestion that beleaguers Ngorongoro. The driest months are June to October and mid-December to January or early February. The scattered **short rains** fall between November and December, while the **long rains** are from February or March to the end of May. The wildlife migration passes through Serengeti between December and July; see box on p.457 for more information.

Arrival

Serengeti's eastern entrance, shared with Ngorongoro Conservation Area, is **Naabi Hill Gate**, 17km inside Serengeti, 45km southeast of Seronera Visitor Centre and approximately 300km from Arusha. The western entrance, 145km from Seronera, is **Ndabaka Gate**, next to the Mwanza to Musoma highway. Two other, less used, gates are **Ikoma Gate** north of Seronera (see pp.498–499 for a description of the road from Bunda), and **Klein's Gate** in the northeast, which gives access to Loliondo and the wild road to Lake Natron (see p.468). **Park entry fees**, paid at the gates, are $30 per person per day, plus $5 for a vehicle permit.

Apart from the irregular City Mist bus which runs weekly between Arusha and Musoma (see box on p.495), and a handful of unpredictable Land Rover pick-ups from Mwanza, there's no **public transport** through the park or to its eastern gate, and no vehicles for hire at Ndabaka Gate in the west, either. **Hitch-hiking** is almost impossible, and you'll have to pay for the ride and park entry fees in any case. Still, if you want to try, the only practical place to angle for lifts is Ndabaka Gate. There's a public campsite here ($20 per person), cheap accommodation at *Serengeti Stop Over* (see p.463) 2km towards Mwanza, and basic rooms at Lamadi village, 4km further on.

All this means that most visitors come either in a rented car (4WD), on an organized safari (recommended **safari companies** are reviewed on p.395 for Arusha, p.334 for Moshi and p.484 for Mwanza). Upmarket safari companies, and many of the park's lodges, specialize in **flying safaris**, using charter flights or one of the daily scheduled hops from Arusha to the airstrips at Seronera, Lobo, Grumeti or southern Serengeti; see travel details, p.470.

Renting a 4WD vehicle, in either Arusha, Karatu or Mwanza, gives you more flexibility than a standard safari, and works out pretty cheap if you can

Crossing the Kenyan border

Strictly speaking, the border crossing between the Serengeti and Kenya's Maasai Mara Game Reserve, north of Bologonja Gate, is closed to tourists, but in practice a handful of travellers do pass this way every year via the so-called **Sand River Crossing**, especially to catch the migration as it heads north. The route needs to be done in a private car, however, as safari vehicles and hire cars are not allowed through. Check out the latest situation with the **immigration office** at Seronera Visitor Centre beforehand. Even with official Tanzanian blessing, you may still be left open to potential hassle and bribe-paying on the Kenya side: up to $50 *chai* seems to be usual.

Heading into Kenya, complete exit formalities at the immigration office at Seronera Visitor Centre. In Kenya, the nearest immigration office is in Narok. **Arriving in Tanzania**, immigration formalities are dealt with at Bologonja Gate, 108km north of Seronera, though they may direct you on to the immigration office at Seronera. Park entry fees can be paid at *Lobo Wildlife Lodge*. The nearest **official border crossings** are between Migori and Tarime in the west (see p.496), and through Namanga (see p.408) in the east.

fill all five or six seats. **Self-drive** is possible, although in theory this restricts your movements to the main roads through the park, so it's better to rent a vehicle with a driver (who usually doubles as a wildlife guide), or to hire an official guide at the park gate ($10–15 per day), pretty essential in any case given that Serengeti's roads aren't particularly well signposted. Fill up on **petrol** wherever you can, as supplies are limited and expensive. The cheapest petrol is at Seronera village in the centre. Much more expensive, and sometimes reluctant to sell it except in emergencies, are the garages at *Lobo Wildlife Lodge, Migration Camp, Serengeti Serena Safari Lodge* and *Serengeti Sopa Lodge*.

Information

The park's **administrative headquarters** are just outside Ikoma Gate and of little use to tourists, but the park still maintains offices behind the excellent **Seronera Visitor Centre** (see p.466). There's also tourist information at **Naabi Hill Gate**, which has a viewpoint over the plains, and an informative park office at *Lobo Wildlife Lodge*.

Maps, leaflets and guidebooks can be bought at the park gates (if they're not out of stock), in Arusha (cheaper), or in the park's lodges. The best **guidebook** is the full-colour pocket-size edition published in 2000 by TANAPA. Given that driving off the main routes is only allowed with a professional guide or driver-guide, finding a decent **map** isn't that important. Still, the publication of a long-promised map by Harms-Verlag, in association with TANAPA and the Frankfurt Zoological Society, is imminent, and should be accurate. For Seronera, the park publishes an A4 leaflet containing a detailed map showing all the routes and road junction markers. There are lots of **internet sites** dedicated to Serengeti; the official one is Ⓦ www.tanapa.com.

Accommodation

There's plenty of accommodation both inside and outside the park, and a couple of park-run hostels at Seronera mean that, unlike Ngorongoro, you don't have to be loaded to sleep under a roof within the park. But the most atmospheric (and nerve-jangling) way of spending a night is to camp; see p.462.

Balloon safaris

From the ground, the wildebeest migration is a compelling phenomenon, bewildering and strangely disturbing, as you witness individual struggles and events. From the air, in a **hot-air balloon**, it resembles an ant's nest. At around $400 for the sixty-to ninety-minute flight plus champagne breakfast, **balloon safaris** are the ultimate in bush chic. The inflation and lift-off at dawn from the launch site near *Seronera Wildlife Lodge* is a spectacular sight, and the landing is often interesting, to say the least, as the basket may be dragged along before finally coming to rest.

You don't need to stay at the lodge to fly; they'll pick up from any of the central lodges or campsites before dawn. There are only two balloons, one for 12 people, the other for 16, so book in advance, whether through a lodge or safari company, or directly with Serengeti Balloon Safaris in Arusha at the Adventure Centre on Goliondoi Road (☏027/250 8578, ⊛www.balloonsafaris.com).

Inside the park

Wildlife and scenery vary greatly from one lodge and tented camp to the other, but don't believe the hype about the **migration** passing right under your nose. We've given a rough indication of the best months for each of the following places, but as you'll have a vehicle in any case, you can always catch up with the herds elsewhere. Room rates can drop by half in low season, which varies according to the lodge's location on the migratory route.

The two places run by the park authorities (TANAPA) lack any kind of "in the wild" feeling, but benefit from the proximity of Seronera village, which has three *hotelis* dishing up cheap meals, some local bars and shops selling everything from chocolate to champagne.

Kirawira Tented Camp Kirawira Hills, 100km west of Seronera (Serena Lodges, AICC Ngorongoro Wing, 6th floor, ☏027/250 8175, ⊛www.serenahotels.com). On a hilltop overlooking the savanna in the western corridor, this place will pamper you silly with its valets, solar-heated showers, luxurious double tents, "plunge pool" and refined cuisine. Overpriced at $560, but ideally placed for catching the migration between May to July, especially in June. Full-board ➒

Lobo Wildlife Lodge Lobo Kopjes, 76km north of Seronera ☏ & ℗028/262 1505 (office at *Novotel Mount Meru Hotel* in Arusha, p.378). This is one of northern Tanzania's nicest lodges, built around the top of a kopje, and with awesome views, especially eastwards where the land drops away to a vast game-filled plain, which receives a small part of the migration between July and September, and the southbound movement in November and December. Each of the 75 rooms has views, cranky telephones and wooden floorboards. The restaurant and bar incorporate part of the kopje's boulders in their walls, and there's a swimming pool on the panoramic terrace. Service and meals are a bit sloppy, and plenty of steps make this unsuitable for disabled people. Full-board ➑

Migration Camp Ndassiata Hills, 80km north of Seronera (Halcyon Africa, ☏027/254 4521, ⊛www.serengetimigrationcamp.com). Built into a

kopje overlooking the Grumeti River, this is a good location for wildlife and has a friendly atmosphere. There are 21 tents, an open-sided bar which is great for sunsets and a small swimming pool. The African-style meals are good, with dinner usually served around a campfire. A small floodlit waterhole attracts resident wildlife, and the migration normally passes by between June and August, returning south in late October and November. Like *Lobo*, the rocky location doesn't favoured disabled people. Full-board ➒

Serengeti Serena Safari Lodge Mbingwe Hill, 24km northwest of Seronera ☏028/262 1507 (Serena Lodges, AICC Ngorongoro Wing, 6th floor, ☏027/250 8175, ⊛www.serenahotels.com). An architecturally inventive lodge with 23 two-storey rondavels, topped with spiky thatch roofs. Natural materials and local decor feature throughout, and the lodge is unobtrusively hidden behind acacia trees. The best rooms for views are on the upper floors of the rondavels lower down the hill. Service is attentive, there's a kidney-shaped swimming pool with a telescope, two rooms for disabled guests, and bush dinners cost an extra $30 per person. The migration passes through between April and May, and straggles on to July. Full-board ➒

Serengeti Sopa Lodge Nyarboro Hills, 46km southwest of Seronera (Sopa Lodges, Savannah

Rd, Arusha ☏027/250 6886, ⊚www. sopalodges.com). Occupying a ridge, this is sadly an architectural blot, but things perk up considerably inside. The public areas are airy and pleasant, while the 79 rooms are large and comfortable, and have balconies with sweeping views over acacia-studded hills and plains. Service is friendly and efficient, the food is good, and there's a swimming pool on a panoramic terrace. February to June are the main migration times, especially April. Full-board ❾

Seronera Wildlife Lodge Seronera ☏028/262 1508 (office at *Novotel Mount Meru Hotel* in Arusha, p.378). This breezy government-run place, like *Lobo*, has aged well and still looks good, though the 75 rooms are a little basic. The best, and with better views, are at the back. The bar,

restaurant and terrace have beautiful views over the Seronera Valley, and there are plans for a swimming pool. The migration is in Seronera between April and July. Half-board/full-board ❽

TANAPA Rest House 1km from Seronera village and the Visitor Centre (booking unnecessary; pay at the park gate). This park-run place has three en-suite rooms each with two beds, but it's over-priced given that an extra $10 will buy you a night at the far more attractive *Ikoma Bush Camp* (see below), or in a special campsite for that matter. ❺

TANAPA Youth Hostel (Simba Hostel) 1km from Seronera village and the Visitor Centre (enquire at the park gate, where you pay). This is the cheapest place inside the park, and has rooms with eight bunk beds each. It's closed to tourists when occupied by school groups, however. ❹

Camping

Apart from the TANAPA youth hostel and rest house, **camping** is the only cheap way to stay in Serengeti, at $20 a person for a pitch in a public campsite, and $40 in a special campsite. Outside the park, camping is possible at *Kijereshi Tented Camp*, *Serengeti Stop Over* and *Speke Bay Lodge*, all off the Mwanza to Musoma highway; they charge $5 per person.

The park's **public campsites** – one at Ndabaka Gate, another at Lobo in the north and the others in a tight cluster a few kilometres northeast of Seronera Visitor Centre – have water, toilets and showers (which don't always work). The **special campsites** are spread all over the park, have no facilities whatsoever, and need to be booked months if not years ahead through TANAPA in Arusha (see p.000), who can give details on locations. However, you may strike lucky if you enquire at the park gate on arrival.

Neither style of campsite is fenced, so wildlife comes and goes. As a result, Seronera's public campsites have become notorious for nocturnal visits by **lions**. Needless to say, take extreme care. The lions are generally just curious, so the rule is to stay calm and remain inside your tent. Similarly, take care with **baboons**, who are well used to people and quite capable of mauling you: don't tempt or tease them, and keep food in air-tight containers.

Collecting **firewood** in the park is currently prohibited; stock up on fuel before entering. If you're staying at Seronera, you're permitted to drive along the shortest route to *Seronera Wildlife Lodge* in the evening for dinner, so long as you're back by 10pm (driving elsewhere is forbidden after 7pm).

Outside the park

Staying outside the park will save you a day's entry fees if you're on your way in or out. Particularly recommended is *Ikoma Bush Camp* (full-board ❽) just outside Ikoma Gate, which is reviewed opposite. For hotels in Bunda town along the Mwanza to Musoma highway, see p.498.

Dorobo Safaris (Arusha, see p.397). This socially responsible safari operator sets up a temporary camp in Loliondo, northeast of the Serengeti, as part of its adventurous cultural and walking trips. Local communities take a share of the profits, and are involved throughout.

Kijereshi Tented Camp Accessed from the Western Corridor or from the Mwanza to Musoma highway; turn right 2km north of Lamadi and follow the signs for 18km (book through *Tilapia Hotel* in Mwanza, p.480). This place is nicely located for seeing the resident wildlife of the Western Corridor, and for catching the migration as it crosses the

Grumeti River, and is one of the cheapest options outside Serengeti. There are various rooms, most in tents, and although a bit small are adequate. Facilities include a swimming pool, games room, curio shop, restaurant, a good bar, vehicle mechanics and fuel. Full-board ⑤

Loliondo Camp Loliondo, 1hr drive east from Klein's Gate ⓦ www.hoopoe.com/ktl/loliondo.htm (Hoopoe Adventure Tours, Arusha; p.397). A semi-permanent camp benefiting from an exclusive 200-square-kilometre concession, providing year-round game viewing, especially good in August and November when the migration passes through. At other times, a nearby waterhole draws wildlife. Accommodation is in large furnished tents with attached bathrooms (hot showers). Service is good, as is the food, and dinner is taken by candlelight, or around a campfire. There's a range of activities and the local community, Oloipiri village, takes a share of the camp's profits. Full board including game drives and activities $770. ⑨

Serengeti Stop Over On the highway 2km south of Ndabaka Gate ☎ 028/262 1531, ⓔ serengetiso@yahoo.com. A pleasant if largely shadeless place within walking distance of the park gate and Lake Victoria (no swimming due to bilharzia). Accommodation is in a series of small, clean *bandas*, each with two beds, big nets and bathrooms (good showers). Expensive but good food is available, and there's also a beer garden. Breakfast included ④

Speke Bay Lodge 13km south of Ndabaka Gate; the turning is 6km south of Lamadi ☎ 028/262 1236, ⓦ www.spekebay.com. On the lakeshore (no swimming due to bilharzia), this occupies a lovely, lightly wooded plot with lots of birdlife, and great sunsets over the lake. Accommodation is either in a series of stuffy tents lacking bathrooms and views, or in eight attractive bungalows on the shore. There's a bar and restaurant, plus lake excursions, mountain biking and canoe rental. Breakfast included: tents ④, bungalows ⑥

Eating and drinking

Unless you're on a package tour, **picnic lunches** are the norm. All lodges can provide guests with "lunch boxes", either as part of a full-board package, or for an extra $10–15. For the same price, though, you're better off splashing out on a proper meal at one of the lodges that welcome guests for lunch. **All-you-can-eat buffets** are the usual fare, especially in high season. Cheap local meals (no more than Tsh2000) are dished up at three *hotelis* in Seronera village.

Ikoma Bush Camp 3km outside Ikoma Gate (p.499). In a wonderfully open location, lunch or dinner are a snip at Tsh3000, and there's an excellent wildlife library.

Lobo Wildlife Lodge The $12 lunch includes use of the swimming pool, which is Tsh1000 otherwise. The views are spectacular.

Migration Camp Lunch is great value at $10 (and you can use the pool), or just drop in for a drink at this superbly sited camp.

Serengeti Serena Safari Lodge $24 gets you pampered by the waiters, but wildlife interest is limited and the pool is for overnight guests.

Serengeti Sopa Lodge Good but overpriced, though the $25 does include use of the pool (otherwise Tsh3000), and there are good views, plus a telescope for game viewing.

Seronera Wildlife Lodge Centrally located and an obvious choice for resting between game drives. Lunch or dinner costs $15.

In the national park

The park is divided into four – the Serengeti Plains and their kopjes, Seronera in the centre, the Western Corridor and the north – each warranting at least half a day, meaning that two or three days in the Serengeti is the ideal minimum to see a bit of everything. Coming from the east, the road from Ngorongoro Crater to central Serengeti is one long game drive in itself, passing through the heart of the **Serengeti Plains**. Scattered around the plains are a number of weathered granite outcrops called kopjes, which are miniature ecosystems, providing some shade, and limited water supplies in pools left in the rock after the rains. **Moru Kopjes** are the most visited.

The park's centrepiece is the **Seronera Valley**, which contains a complex network of game-viewing tracks, and is where most of the public campsites, a couple of lodges, the rest house, youth hostel and the Seronera Visitor Centre are located. To the west is the **Western Corridor**, a wedge of land along the Grumeti River that reaches to within 8km of Lake Victoria. To **the north** is another corridor, covering part of the migration as it heads both up and down from Kenya's Maasai Mara.

Before starting a game drive, check the latest rules regarding **off-road driving** with the park authorities, which is allowed only in certain areas (mainly the western edge of the plains). The rule when off the main roads is never to follow tracks left by other vehicles, as this hastens soil erosion. However, at the time of writing all off-road driving had been banned for environmental reasons following a two-year drought. **Restricted areas** which you always need special permission to visit include Gol Kopjes in the east, which is a vital habitat for cheetah (whose hunting patterns are easily disturbed by safari vehicles), and sometimes Moru Kopjes; the permit for the latter costs $10.

The Serengeti Plains

The cornerstone of Serengeti's ecosystem is the undulating semi-arid **Serengeti Plains**. For a bird's-eye view, walk up the kopje behind **Naabi Hill Gate**, whose viewpoint and picnic site are ideal for observing the **migration** (see box on p.457) between January and April, especially February and March, when literally hundreds of thousands of wildebeest, zebra and gazelle munch their way across the grasslands below. The popularity of the plains with wildlife appears to owe something to the alkaline nature of the soil, whose volcanic ash was laid down during the eruptions of Ngorongoro's Crater Highlands, and is therefore rich in **minerals** – something accentuated by the annual cycle of rain and evaporation, which sucks minerals to the surface. The main ones are calcium, potassium carbonate and sodium carbonate, which recent studies have shown are an essential component of many animal's diets, especially when lactating (and which explains why eighty percent of Serengeti's wildebeest give birth on these plains).

Even when the migration moves out of the area, and the plains turn into a dry and dusty expanse of beige, there's still plenty of resident **wildlife** around, including lion prides, unusually large clans of hyenas (up to eighty strong), plus hartebeest, topi, warthog and ostrich. **Birdlife** is richest during the rains, through you'll see secretary birds and kori bustards throughout the year. Another bird worth looking for is the **black-throated honey-guide**, which has a remarkable symbiotic relationship with the ratel (honey badger). The honey-guide, as its name suggests, leads the ratel to wild bee hives in trees, which the ratel – seemingly immune to the stings – pulls down and breaks open. The ratel eats the honey, and the honey-guide treats itself to beeswax.

Moru Kopjes

The flat plains are broken in several places by isolated and much-eroded granite "islands" called **kopjes**. Also known as inselbergs ("island hills"), the kopjes were created millions of years ago when volcanic bubbles broached the surface and solidified, and were subsequently eroded by rains and floods, carving out the singularly beautiful and sensuous forms you see today. Rainwater run-off from the kopjes and permanent water pools caught in rocky clefts make them particularly good for spotting wildlife in the dry season, when **lions** like to lie in wait for other animals coming to feed or drink – take care when walking around the kopjes for this reason.

Humans, too, have long been attracted to kopjes, both hunter-gatherers like the Dorobo, who were evicted in 1955, and seasonal "migrants" like Maasai

△ Zebras at pool, Serengeti National Park

cattle herders. The latter, evicted in 1959, left their mark – literally – in a rock shelter on one of the **Moru Kopjes** 32km south of Seronera. Here, a natural rock shelter is daubed with **rock paintings**. The artists were unmistakably Maasai, as the many depictions of shields, daubed in red, white and black, bear markings identical to those of ceremonial shields still used today. The shields are accompanied by drawings of elephants, and less distinct animal and human forms. Believed to have been made just over a century ago, the paintings are curious in that the Maasai have no tradition of rock painting elsewhere, and so their purpose, if any, is unknown. They may have been created by warriors at temporary camps, or at *orpul* meat-feasts, something also suggested by the soot-covered ceiling. Whatever their meaning or age, the paintings should be treated with the same respect as their millenarian cousins near Kolo in the Iringi Hills (see box on p.257).

One kilometre away is another, even more enigmatic kopje containing **rock gongs**, which are an ensemble of three loose boulders balanced on a kopje. One in particular – a large lemon-shaped wedge – bears dozens of circular depressions, created by people repeatedly striking the rock with stones to produce weirdly reverbative and metallic sounds (the sound differs depending where you strike the rock). Although rock gongs are nowadays played only by tourists, the wedge-shaped one was certainly used as a instrument way before the Maasai arrived a couple of centuries ago, as they lack any musical tradition involving percussive instruments. Similar gong rocks have been found across the Mwanza Region to the west, which was never inhabited by Maasai. However, as little is known of the traditions of the Dorobo hunter-gatherers who used to live here (and were later partly assimilated by the Maasai), the exact age and purpose of the gongs remains a mystery. Incidentally, time spent poking around the boulders may turn up a surprise – in 1992, a species of **tree frog** hitherto unknown to science was discovered in one of the rock gong's depressions.

Seronera

The central part of Serengeti is **Seronera**, which comprises the wooded valleys and savanna of the Grumeti River's main tributaries. There are a large number of driveable circuits in the area, which your driver or guide should certainly know well, and the wildlife is representative of most of Serengeti's species. For many, the highlight is Seronera's famous black-maned **lions**, the cause of sleepless nights at the campsites. **Leopards**, too, abound, though you'll need a dash of luck, as they chill out by day in the leafy branches of yellow-barked acacias close to the rivers. The migration usually moves up to Seronera from the plains in April, before continuing on north and west.

A great place to head for, after an early morning game drive, is **Seronera Visitor Centre** (daily 8am–4.30pm; ⓣ & ⓕ028/262 1515), close to Seronera village, the public campsites and *Seronera Wildlife Lodge*. This brilliantly designed centre is a real pleasure, combining permanent exhibits, displays and wildlife video screenings at lunchtime (if the generator's working), with a humorous **information trail** up and around a nearby kopje. There's also a picnic site where semi-tame rock hyraxes and birds, including hoopoes and adorable Fischer's lovebirds, eye up your lunch, and a shop with drinks and snacks. The centre's gift shop should have a booklet containing the information presented on the trail, and also a leaflet with a map and detailed descriptions of the various game drives around Seronera. The staff can usually fill you in on recent predator sightings, and road conditions, while for more detailed queries, a number of park wardens are also based here.

A quick run-down of the **main trails** follows. Most have numbered road junctions corresponding to those on the leaflet. The **Seronera River Circuit** (junctions 1–26) starts at Seronera Hippo Pool and follows the river, and, as well as lions, leopards, crocodiles and waterbuck, offers sightings of hippos, giraffes, vervet monkeys, baboons and many birds. The circuit can be combined with the **Kopjes Circuit** (junctions 52–62; enter at junction 18 on the east bank of the Seronera River), which goes anti-clockwise around Maasai, Loliondo and Boma Kopjes. Climbing on the rocks is forbidden. **The Hills Circuit** (junctions 27–29) cuts through grassland to the wooden foothills of the Makori and Makoma Hills west of the Seronera Valley, and is good for hyena, zebra, ostrich, warthog, gazelle, topi and hartebeest. A drive along this circuit is best combined with the **Songore River Circuit** (junctions 30–34), which loops into the plains south of the Seronera River. Thomson and Grant's gazelle, topi, hartebeest and ostrich are frequent, as are cheetah during the dry season. Lastly, the **Wandamu River Circuit** (junctions 40–49) covers similar habitats to the Seronera River Circuit, and hugs the banks of the Wandamu River, especially popular with buffaloes.

The Western Corridor

The **Western Corridor** is the unlovely name given to a forty-kilometre-wide strip of land that goes west from Seronera to within 8km of Lake Victoria. The forests and swamps of the **Grumeti River** mark the northern boundary, while to the south is an area of grassland flanked by low wooden hills. The area receives the annual migration between May and July, after which time the bulk of the herds heads on north over the Grumeti River towards Maasai Mara. This is the best time to visit the area, especially if the river is in flood, when the crossing is extremely perilous. At first hesitant, the herds surge headlong with a lemming-like instinct into the raging waters, while crocodiles and lions lie in wait for those injured in the effort, too weak for the strong currents or who get stuck in the muddy quagmire at the river's edges. You can find the crossings just by looking for vultures circling overhead.

A small part of the migration, however, forgoes the pleasures of the river crossing to stay behind in the grasslands in the western part of the corridor, which also contains substantial populations of **non-migratory animals**, including some wildebeest and zebra, and smaller populations of giraffe and buffalo, hartebeest, waterbuck, eland, topi, impala and Thompson's gazelle. Hippo are present in large numbers, and in the dry season can always be seen at **Retima Hippo Pool**, 20km north of Seronera. Given the abundance of food, predators flourish, too, **leopards** in the lush tangled forests and thickets beside the river, and **crocodiles** – especially around Kirawira in the west – for whom the migration's river crossing provides a Bacchanalian feast. A speciality of the forest is a population of **black-and-white colobus monkeys**, though you'll need time and patience to track them down. The forests are also rich in **birdlife**, especially during the European winter. With luck, a rare species you might see is the olive-green bulbul.

Northern Serengeti

The patches of acacia woodland at Seronera begin to dominate the rolling hills of northern Serengeti. The area contains at least 28 acacia species, each adapted to a particular ecological niche, and the change in species is often startlingly abrupt, with one completely replacing another within a distance of sometimes only a few dozen metres. The undulating nature of the landscape makes it easy to spot animals from a distance and, further north, especially around

Lobo Kopjes, higher ground provides fantastic views of the migration in the grasslands to the east (the best months are July to September when it heads north, and November to December when it turns back). Elephant, buffalo, zebra, gazelle and warthog can be seen all year. There's a game-drive circuit to the east of *Lobo Wildlife Lodge*, whose waterholes attracts a variety of wildlife, although the natural spring mentioned on older maps has now been capped by a pump.

Loliondo

Located outside the Serengeti's northeastern boundary, and hemmed in by Ngorongoro, Lake Natron and the Kenyan border, is **Loliondo**, a wild and little-visited region. Nowadays offered by a handful of safari companies as a venue for off-the-beaten-track wildlife trips, Loliondo will also appeal to lovers of wild and desolate landscapes, especially if you've rented a vehicle – the drive across Loliondo, from Serengeti's Klein's Gate to Lake Natron (see below), is spectacular and, in places, hair-raising (especially the hairpins down Nguruman Escarpment in the east). It's also potentially dangerous, thanks to past incidents involving **armed bandits** – read the warning on p.441.

Yet for all its aridity and wild frontier feeling, Loliondo is also a subtle land, even in the dry season, when – if you look carefully – even the leafless trees and bushes are full of colour, from the blue or yellow bark of some acacias, through violet and rusty orange bushes, and the mauve and green of thorn trees.

The area is especially good for **wildlife** in November and December when a good part of the annual migration heads back down from Maasai Mara. In consequence, Loliondo has long been favoured by **trophy hunters**, most notoriously over the last decade by a brigadier of the Dubai army, whose activities – including the alleged use of machine-guns – have prompted much controversy. Hopefully, a recent change in the law giving back control of "Game Controlled Areas" to local communities will favour the shooting of wildlife through cameras instead. Recommended **safari companies** operating walking and camping trips in Loliondo are Dorobo Safaris, Hoopoe Adventure Tours, The East African Safari & Touring Company and Swala Safaris, all in Arusha (see pp.397–398).

Klein's Gate to Wasso

With the exception of an irregular **weekly bus** connecting Loliondo village with Karatu, there's no public transport to or in Loliondo, so other than buying a safari, you'll need your own car, an experienced local driver and plenty of petrol and water. A decent map would be helpful, too, not that you'll find one: all currently available Tanzania road maps are completely wrong on Loliondo, but the following route directions are accurate. Note that the western section of the route, between Klein's Gate and Wasso, goes across patches of **black cotton soil**, which can make it impassable in the rains, while the zigzagging road down the Nguruman Escarpment in the east sometimes loses sections of the road.

Leaving Klein's Gate, the road heads southeast towards Wasso, 70km away, passing through impressively craggy hills, heavily wooded except for clearings made by Maasai for their cattle and limited agriculture. The road is easy to follow for the most part, although there are some confusing forks: just keep asking for Wasso. Along the way you pass many Maasai who, unlike their cousins in Ngorongoro, are not accustomed to tourists, so make a point of always obtaining (or paying for) permission before taking photos.

Wasso, 70km along (about two hours from Klein's Gate), is the first major settlement. A government building on the left with a flag, and a transmitter on the right, marks the entrance. There's a small river crossing beyond here, then a junction. Bear left for Loliondo village, or turn right into Wasso itself and the road to Lake Natron and Ngorongoro Conservation Area. Wasso has a hospital but no accommodation.

Loliondo village

Before the tarmac ribbon from Kenya to Tanzania that goes through Namanga was built, Loliondo was a major stop on the Great North Road from Nairobi to Arusha, which went on, ultimately, to Cape Town in South Africa. The sight of **Loliondo village**, about 6km northeast of Wasso, is probably the biggest surprise you'll have in the region. Amidst such desolate terrain, the village is a cool oasis of lush vegetation, and its high altitude gives it a pleasantly breezy and cool climate, which can be quite nippy at night. A handful of Europeans settled here early on, and the village still has an old colonial feeling to it, both in the style of its buildings, and the wide main road which some thoughtful soul long ago planted with beautiful purple-flowered jacaranda trees. There's a post office, a branch of the National Microfinance Bank, petrol and a **campsite**: ask for *Saimon Kamakia's Oloolera Holiday Campsite* (PO Box 34 Loliondo; Tsh3000 per person).

If the description appeals but you don't have your own wheels, a weird-looking **bus** connects Loliondo to Karatu (see p.443) every week, and in future may continue on to Arusha.

Wasso to Sonjo

Entering Wasso from the west (Serengeti), turn right after the river crossing, where a decently graded road heads south. If you're on the right road, you'll pass the entrance to Wasso airfield on your right after 2km. Bear left at any road fork, and continue for another 13km (15km from Wasso), where the road forks again. The right fork heads on down to Ngorongoro Conservation Area, while the left one continues south/southeast for 8km before turning east into a valley. Follow this until the road goes south again (there's a beautiful viewpoint near the top).

Sonjo village, a large cluster of round thatched huts in the lee of an escarpment, is 5km south of the viewpoint, and the main settlement of the agricultural **Sonjo tribe**. The Sonjo, who supplement their subsistence agriculture by hunting, may be one of the peoples responsible for constructing the now-ruined villages and intricate irrigation complex at Engaruka, 100km to the south (see p.437), and have similar stone bases for building houses on. They settled in their present location at least 300 years ago, but their more distant origins remain unknown, and academics can't agree on whether their language – quite distinct from Maasai – is Bantu or Cushitic, though it's probably a bit of both. There's no accommodation, and you should certainly not take pictures without permission.

Sonjo to Lake Natron

From the north side of Sonjo village, the road veers east once more, starting a long, straight and very dusty drive due east to the edge of the Nguruman Escarpment. The low craggy mountain that gradually appears to the southeast is **Mount Mosonik**, rising on the southwestern side of Lake Natron. Beyond its peaks is the distinctive pyramidal mass of Ol Doinyo Lengai (see p.440). The road is extremely sandy in places, and 4WD is helpful even in dry weather. Along the way, there are fantastic candelabra euphorbia trees to admire, as well as bizarre giant aloe, which resemble palm trees with upturned fronds. With luck, you'll also see ostrich.

At the edge of the escarpment, the road – now a narrow rocky trail barely wider than a Land Rover – twists down a frightening stretch known as **Seventeen Corners**. Some sections get washed away in the rains, so check on the road's condition at the army post before Sonjo (or at Ngara Sero if you're coming from the lake). Once down, the road heads south across a weird and extremely beautiful moonscape pitted with craters and gullies, before skirting the lake to arrive at Ngara Sero (see p.442), an hour's drive from Seventeen Corners. The route from Mto wa Mbu to Lake Natron is covered on pp.437–441.

Travel details

Bus

Mto wa Mbu to: Arusha (2–4 daily; 3hr).
Karatu to: Arusha (2–3 daily; 4hr); Babati (1 daily; 5hr); Loliondo village (1 weekly; 10hr).
Kigongoni to: Arusha (4 daily; 2hr); Babati (4 daily; 2–3hr); Singida (3–4 daily; 6–7hr).

Flights

Charter flights to the Northern Circuit parks are operated by Air Excel, Coastal Travels, Northern Air, Precisionair and others; see p.390 (Arusha) for their contacts. Air Excel (AE), Coastal Travels (CT) and Precisionair (PA) also operate scheduled flights:

Grumeti (Serengeti) to: Arusha (CT: 2 weekly; 2hr); Mwanza (CT: 2 weekly; 40min).
Lake Manyara to: Arusha (AE: daily; 20min); Arusha via Seronera (PA: daily; 1hr 55min); Seronera (PA, AE: 2 daily; 40min–1hr 35min); South Serengeti (AE: daily; 25min).
Lobo (Serengeti) to: Mwanza (CT: weekly; 1hr 10min).
Seronera (Serengeti) to: Arusha (AE, PA, CT: 2–3 daily; 1hr 10min); Mwanza (CT: 3 weekly; 40min).
South Serengeti to: Arusha (AE: daily; 2hr 15min); Manyara (AE: daily; 1hr 40min); Seronera (AE: daily; 55min).

8

Lake Victoria and northwestern Tanzania

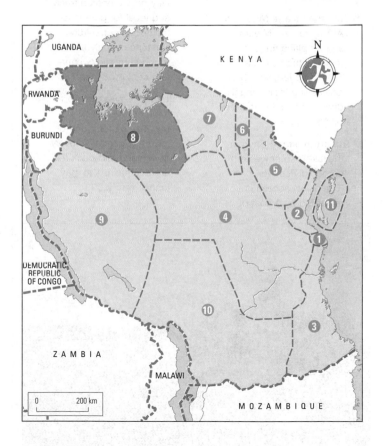

CHAPTER 8

Highlights

✳ **Lake Victoria** The world's second-largest fresh-water lake is also the fabled source of the Nile, an enigma that baffled Europeans until Speke stumbled upon it in 1858. See p.473

✳ **Sukuma Village Museum** At Bujora near Mwanza, a great place for getting to know the Sukuma, Tanzania's largest tribe, and seeing their annual dance competitions. See p.486

✳ **Rubondo Island** Snug in the lake's southwestern corner, difficult (or expensive) access is rewarded by a host of endangered animals and breeding bird colonies. See p.507

✳ **Ukerewe and Ukara** Long-inhabited and heavily agricultural, these lake islands are way off the beaten track, and ideal for getting a feel for an agricultural existence largely un-touched by the twenty-first century. See p.488

✳ **Bukoba** A pleasant port town connected to Mwanza by ferry and by road to Uganda. A lovely beach and laid-back feel are the reasons to stay longer. See p.500

8

Lake Victoria and northwestern Tanzania

Tanzania's northwest is dominated by **LAKE VICTORIA** (Lake Nyanza), which fills a shallow depression between the Western and Eastern Rift Valleys. Covering an area of 69,484 square kilometres, and with a shoreline of 3220km, the lake is Africa's largest, and the world's second-largest freshwater lake; it's also the primary source of the River Nile, providing it with a steady, year-round flow. The lake region is densely inhabited by farmers and cattle herders, and also by people living in the major cities on its shores: Mwanza, Musoma and Bukoba in Tanzania, Kampala and Jinja in Uganda, and Kisumu in Kenya. Sadly, the pressure of overpopulation has been too much for the lake to withstand. Over the last few decades, three hundred of its five hundred native fish species have become extinct, while commercial fish stocks have also plummeted – see the box on p.475.

The three main towns on the Tanzanian side – **Mwanza**, **Bukoba** and **Musoma** – are all worth visiting, and there are also several islands in the lake which can be explored, notably **Ukerewe** and **Ukara** between Mwanza and Musoma, and **Rubondo Island** in the lake's southwest corner, whose diverse birdlife – along with subsequently introduced species like elephants, chimpanzees and sitatunga antelopes – is protected by national park status.

The main hassle for visitors is **getting around**, at least by land: most roads are in awful shape, and are likely to be closed in the rains. If you're driving, you'll need plenty of spare petrol, food and water, a tent and ample mechanical expertise. You should also ensure that your vehicle and its papers are all shipshape: police throughout the region are known for their corruption, and you'll quickly get fed up with the daily routine of roadblocks and bribes. Buses are prohibited from travelling between 10pm and 4am because of the risk of accidents and armed bandits, part of the reason why it's quicker to get to Tanzania's northwest from Kenya or Uganda, where there are no restrictions on night transport and the roads are all sealed tarmac.

Lake Victoria itself also presents a couple of potential **health hazards**. Bilharzia-carrying snails flourish in the reeds around the lake's fringes, and although you'll see local kids and fishermen in the water, the danger of contracting the disease is all too real. Take care if you're going boating on the lake, and treat local advice on swimming with a measure of suspicion. The steamy shore is also a fertile breeding ground for malarial mosquitoes.

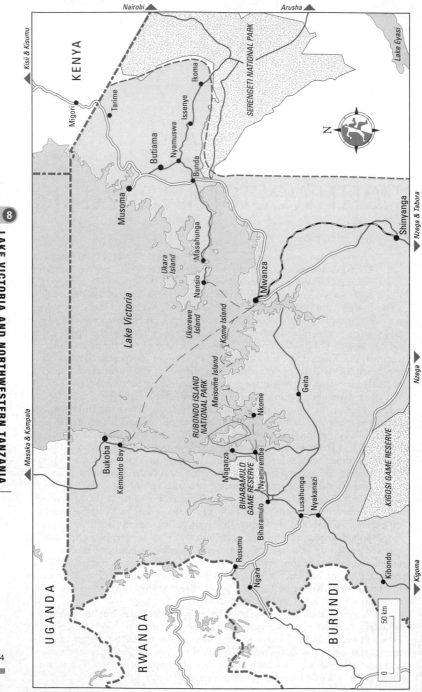

Lake Victoria: the collapse of an ecosystem

Just over a century ago, Lake Victoria contained one of the richest freshwater ecosystems on earth, with an estimated five hundred fish species, including many brilliantly coloured cichlids. Today, only two hundred remain, the rest having vanished in the biggest mass extinction of vertebrates since the demise of the dinosaurs, while the lake itself is being systematically polluted, starved of oxygen and invaded by infestations of water hyacinth – all of which offers a bleak prospect for the thirty million people who depend for survival upon the lake.

The alarming collapse of Lake Victoria's ecosystem can be traced back to the arrival of the railways in colonial times and the subsequent development of lakeside cities – Mwanza in Tanzania, Kisumu in Kenya, Kampala in Uganda – which began to place unsustainable pressure on the lake's resources. The Europeans also started commercial fishing, which rapidly depleted traditional fish stocks, until by the 1950s, catches of the two main edible species of tilapia fish had fallen to uneconomic levels. In a bid to find an alternative, moves were made to introduce non-native **Nile perch** (*mbuta*) into the lake, whose size (up to 250kg) and carnivorous habits, it was hoped, would convert smaller and commercially worthless cichlid species into profitable dinner-table protein. The proposal was fiercely opposed by scientists, who correctly predicted ecological disaster. Nonetheless, Nile perch found their way into the lake, having either been surreptitiously introduced, or having swum in along the Victoria Nile from Lake Kyoga in central Uganda. From a commercial point of view, the arrival of Nile perch in the lake was an enormous success, and catches spiralled, fuelling a lucrative export trade to Europe and Asia. Ecologically, however, the Nile perch was an unmitigated disaster: by the 1970s, Lake Victoria's cichlid populations, which had previously constituted eighty percent of the lake's fish, had fallen to under five percent (they're now estimated at just one percent): the Nile perch were quite literally eating their way through the lake's native species.

Sadly, the Nile perch are only part of the problem. **Pollution** on a massive scale is the major cause of the lake's oxygen depletion, and another legacy of colonial rule. Both the British and Germans were keen to use the lake's fertile hinterland for commercial plantations, and set about clearing vast area of forests and other natural vegetation. With no permanent cover, soil erosion became an acute problem, as shown today in the sludge-brown colour of many of the region's rivers. In addition, the drainage of lakeside swamps (which are natural filters of silt and sediment) removed the barrier between the lake and rain-carried chemical residues from farms (especially pesticides and fertilizers) and mines, whose slurry is poisoned by mercury and other heavy metals. Add to this vast quantities of untreated effluent from the lakeside cities (Mwanza alone discharges an estimated 65 million litres of sewage into the lake every day) and you have some idea of the scale of the problem.

The result – unnaturally high levels of nutrients in the lake water, especially nitrates – has caused the proliferation of algae near the lake surface and the acidification of the water, which in turn has provided an ideal habitat for another unwanted species, **water hyacinth**. This pernicious (albeit beautiful) floating weed is native to South America, and was introduced to Africa as an ornamental pond species. It found its way into the lake sometime after 1989, having been washed into rivers by floods. It grows in a thickly tangled mat by the shore, often in rafts several kilometres wide. Apart from hindering shipping, the blanket of weed cuts off sunlight to the water beneath, creating stagnant areas of lake and leading directly to an increased incidence of diseases like cholera, malaria and bilharzia. The weeds also deplete oxygen levels, which has much the same effect on cichlid populations as the jaws of the Nile perch.

Now, the vicious cycle of destruction appears to have turned full circle. In 2001, stocks of Nile perch themselves collapsed for want of food – a singular irony for a lake that, at its height, produced half a million tons of fish a year.

Mwanza Region

Mwanza Region, on the south side of Lake Victoria, is dominated by the port city of **Mwanza**, Tanzania's second-largest city. Despite Mwanza's size and economic importance, it − and the surrounding area − remain very poor, not helped by the collapse of Lake Victoria's ecosystem (see box on p.475) and the diminishing rainfall it has experienced in recent decades. The region, much of it undulating plain scattered with large granite outcrops called *kopjes*, is home to the **Sukuma** − Tanzania's largest tribe − who are cattle herders by tradition, although many are now subsistence farmers. Mwanza is a handy base for a number of nearby attractions, including the **Sukuma Village Museum** and the islands of **Ukerewe** and **Ukara**, and also serves as a potential base for visiting Serengeti National Park, whose western border is barely 5km from the lakeshore.

The road north into Kenya is mostly good tarmac and is passable in all weather. Other roads − especially south and west − are in a dire state, and can become impassable in the rains. Still, onward travel is assured by a ferry connection across the lake to Bukoba, and by the northern branch of the Central Line railway, which provides all-weather access to Tabora, Morogoro, Dar es Salaam and Kigoma.

Mwanza

Located on Mwanza Gulf on the southeast shore of Lake Victoria, the scruffy and weatherbeaten city of **MWANZA** is Tanzania's second-largest city, and the country's busiest port on the lake, handling most of Tanzania's trade with Uganda. The city was founded in 1892 as a cotton-trading centre, and although cotton has declined in importance as a result of low world prices and erratic rains, fishing, trade and some light industry have stepped in to fill the economic gap. Its inhabitants, many of them economic migrants, now number over a million, seventy percent of whom live in crowded, unplanned and insalubrious slums on and around the hills on the city's outskirts. The pace of population growth has now far outstripped the development of the city's infrastructure, much of which − water and sewerage, solid waste disposal, electricity and roads − is in a pitiful state, where it exists at all. Catastrophic flooding in the long rains is becoming an annual occurrence, and cuts in the infamously unreliable electricity supply routinely plunge whole districts into darkness for days. The roads are also in a complete mess, with more potholes than asphalt.

Despite all this, Mwanza is a friendly and lively place, and its location − snug among rolling lakeside hills, and with great views − is handsome indeed. It also has good transport connections: by **train** to Dar, Tabora and Kigoma; by **ferry** to Bukoba; by **plane** to most other Tanzanian towns and cities; and by **road** to Kenya and − in the dry season at least − to most places in northwestern Tanzania.

Arrival

Mwanza is the terminus of the **Central Railway Line**'s northern branch, served by four trains weekly from Dar (a fascinating if exhausting 36hr ride) via Morogoro, Tabora and Shinyanga. The station (☎028/42202) is on Station Road, 500m south of the centre, and within walking distance of most hotels, although you could always catch one of the cabs which congregate at the entrance whenever a train is due.

All buses terminate at Mwanza's **bus stand** in the centre of town, apart from Scandinavian Express services, which stop at their office at the south end of Rwagasore Road. There's another major bus stand at **Buzuruga**, 5km east of the city along the Musoma road, where services coming from the north call in. Buzuruga is slated to replace the central bus stand; if this happens during the lifetime of this edition, there should be plenty of daladalas running from there into the centre.

If you have your own vehicle and are arriving from the west, you'll have to catch one of the **ferries across Mwanza Gulf**. You have a choice of two ports. The easiest is the northern crossing from **Kamanga** to the harbour in the city centre (Mon–Sat until 6pm, Sun until 5pm; Tsh3000 for a car with driver, plus Tsh500 for each passenger; 1hr). The disadvantage is that not all ferries on this crossing take vehicles and, if they do, your vehicle may have to be hoisted aboard by crane. There's a less nerve-wracking roll-on roll-off ferry from **Busisi to Kigongo** further to the south (daily until 9pm; same prices as other ferry), although this option leaves you with a thirty-kilometre drive into the city once you're across the creek. If you arrive at night, vehicles are supposed to travel in convoy, with armed policemen at the front and rear.

Ferries from Bukoba and Ukerewe dock at the ferry port in the city centre. Despite the welter of people and hawkers that greet ferry passengers, there's not much hassle, but keep an eye on your bags. **Mwanza Airport** lies 8km northeast of the centre along a road so terrible that at the time of research there were no daladalas, and only a few taxi drivers were happy to make the trip (and were charging Tsh10,000 to compensate for the vehicle-trashing state of the road against a normal fare of Tsh5000). If you've pre-booked a safari or upmarket accommodation, the company or hotel should be able to pick you up, either for free or for a nominal charge (Worldlink Safaris & Tours were asking Tsh2000 for their "shuttle bus"; non-clients may be able to hitch a ride on this for little more).

The city centre is small enough to walk around. **Taxis** can be found at the bus and train stations, outside the *New Mwanza Hotel* and at Fourways Junction (the Kenyatta Road and Station Road intersection); a ride from the bus stand to Capri Point costs around Tsh3000.

For information about **moving on from Mwanza**, see p.485.

Accommodation

There's lots of centrally located **accommodation** in all price ranges, and most hotels will let couples share a single room. Water and electricity cuts are frequent, though the better hotels, including the *Aspen, Christmas Tree, New Park* and *Tilapia*, have generators.

Budget

Busigasolwe Guest House Lumumba Rd (no phone). One of several basic places on this road, and adequate so long as you can get clean sheets. There's a choice of singles or doubles, some en suite (though there are water problems, and no toilet seats), plus a bar and restaurant at the back. ❶–❷

Coconut Hotel Liberty St ☎028/42373. A modern and clean choice overlooking the dirty Mirongo River. All rooms are en suite with TV, fan, carpet and reliable hot water. There's a surprisingly posh bar and restaurant on top. Breakfast included. ❷–❸

Deluxe Hotel Corner Uhuru St and Kishamapanda Rd ☎028/40644. A rambling place that's getting a

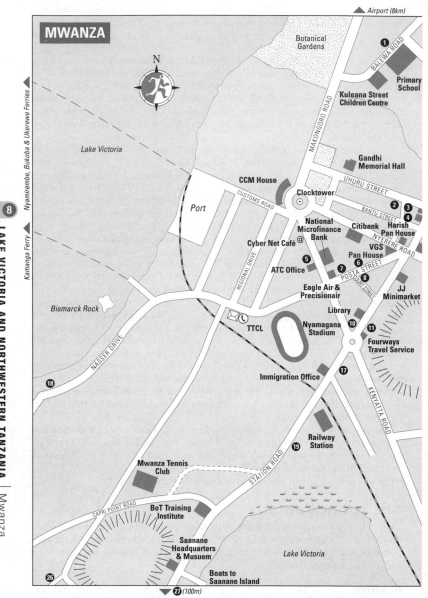

MWANZA

Airport (8km)

Botanical Gardens

Nyamirembe, Bukoba & Ukerewe Ferries

Kamanga Ferry

Lake Victoria

BALEWA ROAD

MAKONGORO ROAD

Primary School

Kuleana Street Children Centre

Gandhi Memorial Hall

UHURU STREET

CCM House

CUSTOMS ROAD

Clocktower

BANTU STREET

Port

REGIONAL DRIVE

National Microfinance Bank

Citibank

Harish Pan House

Cyber Net Café @

NYERERE ROAD

VGS

ATC Office

Pan House

POSTA STREET

SOUTH STREET

Bismarck Rock

NASSER DRIVE

Eagle Air & Precisionair

JJ Minimarket

Library

TTCL

Nyamagana Stadium

Fourways Travel Service

KENYATTA ROAD

Immigration Office

Railway Station

STATION ROAD

Mwanza Tennis Club

CAPRI POINT ROAD

BoT Training Institute

Saanane Headquarters & Musuem

Lake Victoria

Boats to Saanane Island

(100m)

bit run down, though its en-suite rooms remain good value at the price. There's also a bar, and breakfast is included.

Kishamapanda & Geita Guest House Corner Uhuru St and Kishamapanda St ☎028/41254. Two basic hotels sharing the same entrance. The *Geita*

is the building immediately behind the reception and should be avoided. The much preferable *Kishamapanda* is to the left; rooms are airier and come with nets (some also have fans and private bathrooms: ask to see a selection as rooms vary greatly), and there's also a bar and restaurant,

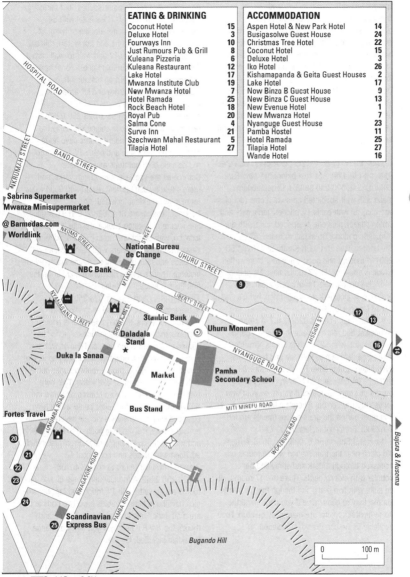

EATING & DRINKING	
Coconut Hotel	15
Deluxe Hotel	3
Fourways Inn	10
Just Rumours Pub & Grill	8
Kuleana Pizzeria	6
Kuleana Restaurant	12
Lake Hotel	17
Mwanza Institute Club	19
New Mwanza Hotel	7
Hotel Ramada	25
Rock Beach Hotel	18
Royal Pub	20
Salma Cone	4
Surve Inn	21
Szechwan Mahal Restaurant	5
Tilapia Hotel	27

ACCOMMODATION	
Aspen Hotel & New Park Hotel	14
Busigasolwe Guest House	24
Christmas Tree Hotel	22
Coconut Hotel	15
Deluxe Hotel	3
Iko Hotel	26
Kishamapanda & Geita Guest Houses	2
Lake Hotel	17
New Binza B Guest House	9
New Binza C Guest House	13
New Evenue Hotel	1
New Mwanza Hotel	7
Nyanguge Guest House	23
Pamba Hostel	11
Hotel Ramada	25
Tilapia Hotel	27
Wande Hotel	16

Bujica & Musoma

Map labels: HOSPITAL ROAD, NKRUMAH STREET, BANDA STREET, Sabrina Supermarket, Mwanza Minisupermarket, @ Barmedas.com, Worldlink, NKUMO STREET, MTAKULA STREET, National Bureau de Change, UHURU STREET, NBC Bank, LIBERTY STREET, NYAMAGANA STREET, SHERIFF DEWJI ST, Stanbic Bank, @, Daladala Stand, Uhuru Monument, MISSION ST, Duka la Sanaa, MITUMBA ROAD, NYANGUGE ROAD, Fortes Travel, Market, Pamba Secondary School, MITI MIREFU ROAD, Bus Stand, WURZBURG ROAD, RWAGASORE ROAD, PAMBA ROAD, Scandinavian Express Bus, Bugando Hill, 0 100 m

Busisi Ferry & Shinyanga

though the latter is best avoided, since the kitchen's none too clean.

New Binza C Guest House Uhuru St (no phone). Good, cheap, basic and clean rooms (shared bathrooms only) in the thick of a busy local area, with lots of cheap restaurants and foodstalls nearby. If

it's full, the similar *New Binza B* is on the same road closer to the centre.

New Evenue Hotel Balewa St ☎0741/233646. A calm, family-run place north of the centre, with the boon of cotton sheets. Most rooms have two beds and share bathrooms. The main drawback is the

lack of fans, while some rooms lack nets (they're sprayed instead). Breakfast included. ❷ – ❸
Nyanguge Guest House Lumumba Rd ☎ 0744/310820. Probably the best on this road, with simple but decent rooms on four floors – the better and brighter ones are on top – with large nets and two beds. All but one share bathrooms (bucket showers). ❶
Pamba Hostel Station Rd, by Fourways roundabout (no phone). Run by the Nyanza Cooperative Union, this is a good, calm budget choice, with decent shared showers, clean sheets and nets, but rarely any electricity. ❶

Mid-range and expensive

Aspen Hotel Uhuru St, just before the *New Park Hotel* ☎ & ℗ 028/250 0988. A large, modern place with well-appointed en-suite rooms (doubles or twins), all with cable TV, phones, fans, nets and cotton sheets, plus one overpriced suite with a/c (❺). Safe parking. Breakfast included. ❸ – ❹
Christmas Tree Hotel Off Karuta St ☎ 028/250 2001. A modern and good-value four-storey affair which is often full. All 27 rooms have TV, phone and a big double bed. There's also a bar, and breakfast is included. No single rates, but it's well priced for couples. ❸
Iko Hotel Capri Point ☎ 028/42467. A pleasantly somnolent and relaxed place in the posh Capri Point district, with 52 en-suite rooms, including some gigantic doubles with a/c and fridge; the even bigger suites have TV, a/c and bathtubs. It's getting a bit tatty, and so is overpriced, but it's good if you need space, or if you're on your own (prices are per person). There's a basic restaurant and quiet bar on the ground floor (meals around Tsh2500). Breakfast included. ❹ – ❺
Lake Hotel Station Rd ☎ 028/250 0658. A funny old place near the train station whose rooms are accessed through a dark and sprawling bar popular with elderly gents. There are 47 rooms, all en suite with two beds, and though they're pretty simple, they're good value if you don't mind the noise (upstairs rooms are marginally quieter). Food available in the bar. Breakfast included. ❸

New Mwanza Hotel Posta Rd ☎ 028/250 1070, ✉ nmh@raha.com. A rather soulless but perfectly adequate "international" class hotel with 54 recently refurbished rooms (double or twin), all with bathrooms (bathtubs and hot water), minibar, telephone, a/c, satellite TV and wall-to-wall carpet. Facilities include a swimming pool, room service, coffee shop and bar (but no restaurant), beauty parlour, health club, casino and lift access. Breakfast included. ❺
New Park Hotel Uhuru St ☎ 028/250 0265. A recommended mid-range choice similar to the *Aspen* nearby. The standard rooms have huge beds, big box nets, fan and cable TV; the "large" rooms have both bathtubs and showers. Bathrooms are spotless, everything works, and there's also a posh bar and restaurant. Good value for money. Breakfast included. ❸
Ramada Rwagasore St ☎ 028/250 1691. A good and secure mid-range choice, despite the noisy location, with bright and breezy rooms, some with views over the bay, others with balconies, all with big beds and fans but no nets (rooms are sprayed instead). There's a nice restaurant and bar on the first floor. Breakfast included. ❸
Tilapia Hotel Capri Point ☎ 028/250 0517, ✉ tilapia@mbio.net. Plugged as the "best in Mwanza" for years, this bayside place is popular with expatriates and package tourists (hence the upmarket hookers in the bar), and comes with plenty of mod cons. All rooms have cable TV, phone, big bed(s), fan and fridge; more expensive ones come with a/c and (sometimes) lake views. The more atmospheric rooms are on a houseboat called the *African Queen*, while the suites come with a fully equipped kitchen. Amenities include several restaurants and bars, a swimming pool, curio shop, safaris and yacht cruises. No single rates. Breakfast included. Rooms ❻, suites and houseboat ❼
Wande Hotel Off Uhuru St ☎ 028/40708, ℗ 028/250 2242. A friendly mid-range choice. All rooms are en suite with TV, fridge and fan; the singles have huge beds, doubles have two beds and are a bit dark. Food and drink is available, and there's the *Hai Bar* nearby if you fancy a change. Breakfast included. ❸ – ❹

The city and around

Mwanza's lakeshore location is its main attraction, and is best savoured from along Nasser Drive, which runs southwest from the ferry port. Some 100m along Nasser Drive is **Bismarck Rock**, a weathered granite *kopje* just off shore which provides Mwanza's main photo–opportunity. Although local kids are fond of swimming around it, it's not recommended due the city's lack of sewage treatment (sadly, the same applies to all the beaches close by).

John Hanning Speke and the search for the source of the Nile

Lake Victoria remained virtually unknown outside Africa until well into the second half of the nineteenth century, when it suddenly became the centre of attention in the midst of the scramble to pinpoint the **source of the Nile**, a riddle that had bamboozled geographers since the days of Herodotus. No one was more obsessed with solving this geographical puzzle than the English adventurer **John Hanning Speke**. Speke had been told of Lake Victoria's existence by an Arab slave trader, and as soon as he set eyes on it in August 1858, he was convinced that the long search for the source of the Nile was over – though true to Victorian custom, he ignored the local names for the lake (Ukerewe and Nyanza) and renamed it in honour of his own dour sovereign.

To verify his theory, Speke returned to Lake Victoria in October 1861, accompanied by the Scottish explorer **James Augustus Grant** and, after circling half the lake in a clockwise direction, sailed down the River Nile in 1863 all the way to Cairo. "The Nile is settled," he wrote in a telegram from Khartoum to the Royal Geographic Society, much to the chagrin of Richard Burton, who had accompanied Speke on his 1858 expedition but had been prevented by illness from revisiting the lake. Many people remained sceptical of Speke's claim, however, while Burton himself continued stubbornly to insist that Lake Tanganyika was the true source of the Nile. In the end, it took a daring circumnavigation of Lake Victoria, led by Stanley in 1875, to prove Speke right. Sadly, Speke didn't live to enjoy this triumph, having died in a hunting accident in 1864.

Back in the city centre, the main landmark is the **clock tower** on the roundabout at the west end of Nyerere Road. A plaque here reads "On 3rd August 1858 from Isamilo Hill one mile from this point Speke first saw the main waters of Lake Victoria which he afterwards proved to be the source of the Nile" – see box above. Next to the clock tower is a small **memorial** commemorating Africans and Europeans from Mwanza who died in the two world wars (the British served as soldiers, the Africans were conscripted as porters). About 400m north of here off Makongoro Road are Mwanza's lakeside **Botanical Gardens**, which make a pleasant target for a short walk, despite being neglected. That's pretty much it on the west side of the city. In the east is the distinctly livelier quarter around the **market** and bus stand. Close to the market, next to the daladala stand, is **Duka la Sanaa** (Mon–Sat 8.30am–5pm), a shop that sells handicrafts, many of them made by the Mwanza Women Development Association. There's some especially good bright and chunky jewellery, plus pottery from the Gita and Sukuma tribes.

A popular day-trip among locals is to the ninety-acre **Saa Nane Island Game Reserve**, in the bay between Capri Point and the rest of the city. The island is attractive, and the big rocks that stud it make for popular picnic spots, but the "game reserve" itself – established in 1964 as a quarantine station during the creation of Rubondo Island National Park (see p.507) – encapsulates all that's most dismal and depressing about zoos. The first elephant was shot when it refused to return to its pen at night; the hippos died of poisoning after the water in their pool became toxic; and the original wildebeest was killed by an enraged male zebra. Luckier were the crocodiles and pythons, who managed to escape, and the present zebra and wildebeest, who at least aren't penned into cages. Less fortunate is the thoroughly depressed chimpanzee, which has endured decades of taunts from visitors from behind the bars of his cage. **Access** is by boat from the jetty at the south end of Station Road on Capri Point daily at 11am, 1pm, 3pm and 5pm; the Tsh900 return fare includes entry to the reserve.

Saa Nane Museum, close to the jetty on Capri Point (no fixed hours; usually open daily to around 5pm; free), fares little better, but does at least dispense with live animals and contains enough whacky oddities to make the walk here worthwhile. Aside from various decaying trophies and manky stuffed animals, questionable highlights (collected by a foot fetishist, it seems) include a hippo's foot, a chair fashioned from an elephant's foot and table lamps made from ostrich and eland legs.

Eating, drinking and nightlife

Uhuru Street is a good place for **street food** at night, with numerous stalls dishing up grilled meat (goat is best), fish and bananas cooked on smoky charcoal *jikos*. For a taste of *paan* (see p.92), try either *VGS Pan House* or *Harish Pan House*, both at the junction of Nyerere Road and Posta Street.

Coconut Hotel Liberty St. Reasonably priced food with most meals around Tsh1500, but eat in the upstairs bar if you can rather than in the small and stuffy dining room downstairs.

Deluxe Hotel Kishamapanda St. Popular with locals at lunchtimes, this has the usual range of Tanzanian favourites plus an excellent bean *matoke* (a stew made primarily from bananas). Around Tsh1000 a plate.

Kuleana Pizzeria Posta St. Run by the Kuleana Centre for Children's Rights, this cheerfully decorated and highly recommended place is as popular with locals as it is with travellers. The food – strictly vegetarian – is invariably delicious: large pizzas go for around Tsh3500, and there are also good sandwiches and a range of snacks including cakes, biscuits and fresh bread (great for breakfast with honey). There's also a TV and notice board.

Kuleana Restaurant Uhuru St. This is very much a local *hoteli*, serving up cheap eats like *pilau*, bananas, rice or *ugali* with fish, chicken, meat or beans. Perfectly adequate if you're staying up this end of town.

Hotel Ramada Rwagasore Rd. A pleasant first-floor restaurant and bar, with most dishes costing around Tsh2500. The bar is open daily until midnight, and has satellite TV.

Rock Beach Hotel Nasser Drive. The only completed part of an abandoned project to build a posh resort-style hotel on the lakeshore (the gaping hulk of the accommodation block looms over the site). Despite this, it's Mwanza's most attractive eating venue, with neatly thatched conical roofs huddled beside a huge lakeside terrace offering unmatched views. The long menu wanders all over, from seafood and curries to lamb with mint sauce. Most mains cost Tsh4000.

Salma Cone Bantu St. Mainly ice creams and juices.

Surve Inn Lumumba Rd. A good, calm and clean *hoteli* which is especially good for breakfast, with decent *supu*, tea, samosas and even espresso.

Szechwan Mahal Restaurant Kenyatta Rd. Good North Indian cuisine, much of it cooked in a clay *tandoor* oven. It's expensive (mains cost around Tsh5000), but recommended if your tastebuds need reviving. Evenings only.

Tilapia Hotel Capri Point. The hotel houses various expensive restaurants serving up continental, Indian and Thai cuisine (mains Tsh5000–7000), plus Japanese *teppanyaki* (where you cook your own meal at your table) and full English breakfasts. It has tables by the lakeside, and others on breezy terraces.

Drinking and nightlife

Coconut Hotel Liberty St. Great open-sided rooftop bar on two levels.

Fourways Inn Fourways roundabout, junction of Kenyatta Rd and Station Rd. A pleasant and peaceful place for a drink or quick meal, with plenty of tables under mature trees on the street corner.

Just Rumours Pub & Grill Corner of Posta St and Court St. The only posh drinking hole in the centre, looking something like a wine bar (lots of mirrors, glass and polished wood), and with Castle lager on tap. There are (free) discos on Fri and Sat nights.

Lake Hotel Station Rd. A large, dark and popular old-timers' bar, fitted with satellite TV. There's also a reasonable restaurant (meals around Tsh2500), but eat in the bar rather than in the glum, striplight-lit dining room.

Mwanza Institute Club Station Rd. Another pleasant and unhustly place, with seats in a shady garden at the back.

New Mwanza Hotel Posta St. The most reliable place for live music, with Jambo Stars playing

△ Sailboats, Lake Victoria

every Saturday from 9pm (admission Tsh3000). There's also a casino upstairs.

Rock Beach Hotel Nasser Drive. A very plush bar with glorious lake views, pool tables and discos on Fridays and Saturdays from 8pm (Tsh3000 entry).

Royal Pub Off Karuta St. Popular throughout the day and well into the night, and also good for a nourishing breakfast of chapati and *supu*.

Tilapia Hotel Capri Point. The well-stocked bar here has a great view over the bay to Bugando Hill and Saa Nane Island and is the main weekend hang-out for the well-to-do. Sports are screened on satellite TV.

Safari companies

Mwanza is sometimes, perhaps rather desperately, touted as an alternative base to Arusha for Northern Circuit safaris, since it's better placed for visits to Serengeti and has good connections to the as yet little-visited bird haven of Rubondo Island National Park. Costs, however, are often much higher than in Arusha – unless you can fill up a vehicle (five or six people in a Land Rover or Land Cruiser), "budget" safaris weigh in at over $150 per person per day. Still, if you've just arrived from Uganda or Rwanda, starting a trip in Mwanza makes sense, as you'll have the chance of doing a safari en route to Arusha without having to retrace your steps.

Dolphin Tours & Safaris Posta St, opposite the *New Mwanza Hotel* ☎028/250 0096, ⊛www.dolphintours.net. A new and very competitive company: 4WD hire costs upwards of $105 a day, or a bargain $90 a day with unlimited mileage for trips of over four weeks. As with the other companies, you'll need to add accommodation and park fees to the cost. They can also arrange air charters.

Fortes Safaris Lumumba Rd, near Karuta St ☎028/250 0561, ℮fortes@twiga.com. A long-established and reliable company offering both tailor-made safaris (upwards of $200 per person per day) and car hire: Land Rover TDIs with pop-up roofs cost $110 per day self-drive, or $150 with driver.

Fourways Travel Service Station Rd, at the roundabout with Kenyatta Rd ☎028/40653, ℮fourways.mza@mwanza-online.com. A long-established and knowledgeable Indian-run opera-tion, though costs vary according to your perceived ability to pay. Prices for a vehicle are around $200 per day for Serengeti, $300 for Ngorongoro, plus park fees and accommodation.

Worldlink Travel & Tours Corner of Nyerere Rd and Nkrumah St (there's another branch at Mwanza Airport) ☎028/250 0214, ℮worldlink.mwz@africaonline.co.tz. A large and efficient company charging much the same as Fourways, though they're cheaper for longer trips (a four-day trip to Arusha averages $750 for the vehicle, plus fees and overnights). They can also arrange trips to Uganda and Rwanda, and offer luxurious weekend retreats at "Wag Hill", an exclusive set-up on Mwanza Gulf specializing in lake fishing, which costs around $150 per person a day (full board), including transport from Mwanza.

Listings

Air charter Auric Air Services, see Dolphin Tours & Safaris, above; Coastal Travels ⊛www.coastal.cc; Renair, Mwanza airport ☎028/256 2069, ⊛www.renair.com.

Airlines ATC, Kenyatta Rd ☎028/256 1846; Eagle Air, *New Mwanza Hotel* building, corner of Posta St and Kenyatta Rd ☎028/250 0828, ℮028/250 0867; Precisionair, *New Mwanza Hotel* building, corner of Posta St and Kenyatta Rd ☎028/256 0027, ⊛www.precisionairtz.com. Fourways (see above) and Worldlink (see above) also handle airline ticketing.

Banks and exchange Cash can be changed at any bank in town. Travellers' cheques can be a pain, however. The best choice is the National Bureau de Change, Nkomo St. Other places that might accept cheques include NBC, next door, and National Microfinance Bank on Kenyatta Rd. Neither Stanbic (Uhuru roundabout) or Standard Chartered (CCM Building by the clock tower roundabout) change travellers' cheques, although Standard Chartered has a 24hr Visa card ATM which may on occasion deliver the goods. There are no forex bureaux, although the *New Mwanza Hotel* may help you out in an emergency.

Car hire See "Safari companies", above.

Hospitals The main hospital is the state-run Bugando Hospital (☎028/40610) on the east side of Bugando Hill, accessed off Würzburg Rd, itself off Nyanguge Rd. For alternative cures, try

8

Your options for **moving on by road** are determined by the seasons: in the rains, many bus services to the south and west are delayed or cancelled, and so journeys that normally take, say, ten hours, can drag on for two whole days. That said, the road north to Musoma and beyond to Kenya (and from there back into Tanzania via Nairobi to Arusha) is good tarmac and open all year round. Most buses heading to eastern Tanzania from Mwanza take this route (18–24hr to Arusha), but unless you've got multiple entry visas for both Kenya and Tanzania, it's an expensive business, with Kenyan visas currently costing $50 for most nationalities, and $20–40 for Tanzania.

There are two alternative ways of getting **to Arusha**: the main one (dry season only) passes through Shinyanga, Nzega and Singida, and takes upwards of thirty hours depending on the state of the road. The other is to head through Serengeti and Ngorongoro. Buses have been banned from this route following one too many roadkills, but there is still at least one Land Rover that covers the journey once weekly; ask around at the bus stand. The drawback is that, in addition to the fare, you'll have to pay park entry fees ($30 for Serengeti, $25 for Ngorongoro). The journey shouldn't take more than 24 hours.

Heading **west** by road, most people catch the ferry from the city centre to **Kamanga** (Mon–Sat at 8.30am, 10.30am, 12.30pm, 4pm & 6pm, fewer on Sun), from where there are irregular pick-ups and daladalas heading on to **Geita** and **Biharamulo**. This isn't recommended, however, unless you're unencumbered by too much baggage, as passengers compete in a sprint to the vehicles on disembarking from the ferry – there are rarely enough seats to go around. If you miss it, or don't fancy having to stand, you'll have to wait for a vehicle meeting the next ferry. A more comfortable and sedate way westwards is by **lake ferry**. The MV Victoria sails three times a week to **Bukoba** (currently 10pm Tues, Thurs & Sun), stopping en route at **Kemondo**, 21km south of Bukoba. The fare to Bukoba, including a $5 port tax, is approximately $18 in first class (two bunks to a cabin), $16 in second (four bunks to a cabin) and $12–13 in either second-class seating or in third-class. Cabins are recommended if you want to arrive refreshed. There are also daily ferries to **Ukerewe Island**, and an island-hopping weekly sailing by the MV Serengeti that goes as far as **Nyamirombe**, close to Biharamulo and Rubondo Island (11am Weds; Tsh3300 plus $5 tax).

If you're heading to anywhere else in Tanzania, it's much easier to take the **train**, which goes four-times weekly direct to **Tabora**, from where there are connections to Kigoma, Mpanda, Morogoro and Dar (currently 6pm Tues, Thurs, Fri and Sun). Mwanza–Dar currently costs Tsh44,600 in first class, Tsh32,600 in second and Tsh12,300 in third. Mwanza–Tabora costs Tsh17,600/13,600/5400. For first class, buy your ticket a few days before if possible to be sure of a compartment; second-class tickets can usually be bought on the day of departure, but reserving a day or two ahead is recommended.

Flying isn't as expensive as you might fear, with few domestic flights costing more than $200. There are scheduled domestic services to Arusha, Bukoba, Dar, Dodoma, Kilimanjaro, Shinyanga, Tabora and Zanzibar, plus international flights to Nairobi (Air Tanzania; 3 weekly) and Johannesburg (Charlan Air – tickets through Fourways Travel Service, see opposite; 1 weekly). For more information, see "Travel details" on p.512.

Matunge Herbalist Hospital at the end of Uhuru St beyond New Binza C Guest House (℡0741/325590).

Immigration Station Rd, just before the train station ℡028/250 0585.

Internet and email access Internet access costs around Tsh1000 per hour. Most reliably is Barmedas.com, Nkrumah St. Cyber Net Café, Kenyatta Rd, usu-ally has a waiting list, but has sodas and some snacks. Alternatively, try Satyam Communication, Nyerere Rd facing Rwagasore Rd, or Links Training Centre, on the first floor of the office building in the car park of the New Mwanza Hotel.

Library Mwanza Regional Library, Station Rd (Mon–Fri 9am–6pm, Sat 9am–2pm; Tsh500 daily membership).

Mechanics There are lots of car workshops along Pamba Rd, and spares at the Land Rover garage at Fourways roundabout, between Station Rd and Kenyatta Rd.

Pharmacies CD Medipharma, Uhuru St, and FDS Pharmacy, *New Mwanza Hotel* building, corner Posta St and Kenyatta Rd, are reliable and reasonably well stocked.

Police The main police station is on Kenyatta Rd near the ferry-port gate.

Post and couriers The main post office is on Posta St. There's another on Pamba Rd near the bus stand. DHL can be contacted on ☏0742/781057. Skynet (☏028/250 2405) is based at the *New Mwanza Hotel*.

Supermarkets Mwanza's supermarkets are expensive. Imalaseko, CCM Building by the clock-tower, has the best selection. Others include Mwanza Mini Supermarket and Sabrina Supermarket almost next to each other on Nkrumah St, and JJ Minimarket on Station Rd.

Swimming pools The *New Mwanza Hotel* charges day-guests Tsh2500 to use its pool. *Tilapia Hotel* doesn't have a fixed rate; you should be able to use it for free if you buy a meal.

Around Mwanza: Sukuma Village Museum

An excellent day-trip from Mwanza is to the **Sukuma Village Museum** at Bujora, 15km east of the city just off the road to Musoma, which covers in

Sukuma dance societies

The **Sukuma** are Tanzania largest tribe, numbering well over five million, yet despite their size – and the proximity of Mwanza's urban sprawl – many of their traditions (*utamaduni*) have remained intact, having adapted to modern socio-economic realities. Particularly exuberant examples of this synthesis of old and new are the annual Sukuma **dance competitions**, held in June and July (and sometimes also in August) after the harvest that follows the long rains. The two oldest dance societies (*wigashe*), both of which perform annually at Bujora, are the **Bagika** and **Bagalu**, founded in the mid-nineteenth century by rival healers, **Ngika** and **Gumha**. As Ngika and Gumha could not agree about which of them had the most powerful medicine (*dawa*), a dance contest was organized to decide the issue.

The format, which remains unchanged, is for two competing dance societies to perform at the same time, with the crowd being free to move between the two. The better the medicine, the bigger the crowd. Obviously, good preparation is the key to success, and nothing is more important than **good luck medicine** (*samba*). This is dispensed by each dance society's healer (*nfumu*), and is intended to make the dancers, especially the dance leader (*mlingi*), appealing to the crowd. The *samba* can be applied in many ways: buried or placed on the dance ground, worn in amulets, applied to the body in a lotion, rubbed into skin cuts or inhaled through smoke. Given that crowd size is the key to success, each passing year sees new and innovative dance routines, tricks and costumes: in 1995, one group won by using a toy plastic monkey given by a Japanese traveller. Others used articulated wooden puppets as props, others stilts or fire breathing, while all dancers possess the most outrageous gymnastic agility. Although dance moves and lyrics change annually, there are some enduring favourites, notably the *Bugobugobo* **snake dance**, a speciality of the Ngika Society, hugely theatrical affairs starring live pythons.

The dance contests are best experienced at Bujora (see opposite), whose two-week dance festival – following the Christian festival of Corpus Christi (usually early or mid-June) – is one of the biggest, and, for tourists, the most accessible. Alternatively, the Sukuma Village Museum at Bujora can arrange dances at any time of year, though a day's notice is appreciated. Tapes of **traditional Sukuma music** (*ngoma*) can be found in Mwanza if you're particularly determined, and more easily at Radio Tanzania in Dar es Salaam (see p.109). For more on the Sukuma dance societies, and some fantastic pictures, see the museum's website at ⓦ http://photo.net/sukuma.

great detail the culture and traditions of the **Sukuma**, Tanzania's largest tribe (see box opposite). The museum is in the compound of the **Bujora Catholic Mission**, founded in 1952 by a Canadian missionary, Father David Clement. Clement's open-minded approach saw Sukuma music, dance and history introduced into the mission's religious services, and is also reflected in the mission's **church**. Modelled on Sukuma lines, it has a round peaked roof resembling a traditional Sukuma house, and is decorated inside with traditional Sukuma symbols of chiefly power: the altar is in the shape of a royal throne, and the tabernacle resembles a chief's house (*ikulu*), complete with a shield and crossed spears on the door.

The **museum** entrance is marked by a monument depicting a painted royal drum placed on a bas-relief map of Tanzania. The exhibits, which cover every aspect of Sukuma life from the humdrum to the ritual, sacred and chiefly, are contained in a number of startlingly designed and colourfully painted pavilions. A reconstruction of a traditional family house and compound incorporates material artefacts from daily life; the thatched dwelling of the blacksmith (*malongo*) contains the tools of his trade, as does the replica of a traditional doctor's house (*iduku*). Sukuma history is presented in the "Royal Pavilion", designed in the form of a royal throne and containing a mass of genealogy, as well as royal drums, fly whisks, headdresses and other objects donated by the descendants of local chiefs. The liveliest area, however, is the Dance Society Pavilion, which has a wealth of information on the competing Bagika and Bagalu dance societies.

Practicalities

Buses and daladalas run approximately every half-hour from Mwanza to Kisesa, 14km along the Musoma road. The museum is 1km north of here – it's not currently signposted, so you'll have to ask directions. **Accommodation** is available at the Bujora Cultural Center next to the museum, either in small rooms or in one of three replica blacksmith houses (❷–❸); there's also a large campsite. Performances of **traditional dances** can be arranged at a day's notice. For more about the museum and its activities, including hands-on lessons in traditional arts, see the museum's excellent website at Ⓦ http://photo.net/sukuma, which features hundreds of jaw-droppingly gorgeous photographs and reams of text. If you're around in early or mid-June, try to coincide with **Corpus Christi** (the exact date varies), known in Kisukuma as *Bulabo*, during which the Eucharist is carried from Bujora to the Kisesa Red Cross Stadium, an event which marks the beginning of a two-week dance festival – see box opposite.

The MV Bukoba disaster

Eleven kilometres along the Musoma road from Mwanza, just before Kisesa, is a small gate on the left surmounted by a scale model of a ferry, the **MV Bukoba**. Grossly overloaded and badly maintained, it capsized near Mwanza on May 21, 1996. Most of the passengers were trapped inside the hull as the ship keeled over. Some were rescued through a hole burned into the hull by rescue workers, but a second hole proved catastrophic: air trapped in the hull escaped, the vessel lost its buoyancy and disappeared beneath the calm surface of the lake. The graveyard behind the gate contains the remains of some of the victims; the exact number of fatalities was never established, but was somewhere in the region of 550 to 800.

Ukerewe and Ukara Islands

Lake Victoria's largest island is **Ukerewe Island**, due north of Mwanza and separated from it by Speke Gulf. Nicknamed "U.K." by locals, this densely populated island of low wooded hills, craggy granite outcrops, boulders and small-scale subsistence farms is the district capital of an archipelago comprising 26 other islands and islets, including **Ukara Island** (see p.491). Despite its proximity to Mwanza, Musoma and the tourist traffic in the Serengeti, these islands are among the least-known areas in Tanzania. Don't come expecting anything really exceptional – there are few sights apart from the views – but do expect to encounter a kind of rural arcadia that has remained virtually unchanged from before colonial times. The isolation, in fact, is a good part of the attraction, though it makes travelling here – and around the islands – something of an adventure.

There are two ways of reaching the island, either via the land route from Bunda described below, or on one of the three ferries which connect Mwanza with Ukerewe's main town, **Nansio**; tickets on all services cost Tsh2000–3000. The newest and most reliable is the **MV Nansio** (Mon–Sat; 3hr 30min), which leaves Mwanza at 2.30pm and Nansio at 8am. Cars can be carried for Tsh18,000 and food is available. The smaller **MV Airbus** (Mon–Sat; 3hr–3hr 30min) leaves Mwanza at 2pm and Nansio at 8am. Older but faster is the **MV Butiama** (daily; 2hr 30min), which leaves Mwanza at 8am Monday to Friday and at 9am on Saturday and Sunday, and heads back from Nansio at 1pm (all days). The *MV Butiama's* schedules are prone to change, and there's talk of replacing it with the *MV Clarias* when the latter's repairs are complete, so check in advance.

Bunda to Nansio

The unsurfaced 83-kilometre road from Bunda (see p.498) to the ferry at **Masahunga** passes through attractive countryside scattered with the small homesteads of the Luo tribe, between which marshy areas attract a wealth of **birdlife**, including grey herons, egrets, marabou storks, vultures, fish eagles (the big birds with white heads perched in trees) and weavers (the little yellow ones who weave intricate, sock-like nests). The trip is a two-hour drive in good weather if you have your own vehicle, or three to four hours by **bus**. Two companies – Bunda Bus Service and Trans Africa – cover the route daily, continuing on to Nansio after the ferry crossing; Bunda Bus is the more reliable, leaving Bunda every day at 10.30am to arrive in Nansio around 3.30pm.

The **ferry** from Masahunga on the mainland to **Rugezi** on Ukerewe takes thirty minutes and can carry up to six cars (Tsh3000 for a car with driver, Tsh200 for each passenger or pedestrian). The ferry leaves from Masahunga at 9.30am, 11.30am, 1.30pm, 3.30pm and 6pm, and from Rugezi at 8.30am, 10.30am, 12.30pm, 2.30pm and 5pm. The ferry is met in Rugezi by daladalas going to Nansio. Should you get stranded in Masahunga, there are a couple of hotels (both ❶): the *Bwanza* is very basic; much better is *Deo Guest House*, on the left before the jetty. For food, try the *Tata Taigo Café*, on the right just before the colourful fishing canoes beside the jetty, which serves great *maini rosti* (liver stewed with tomatoes, green peppers and onions).

The island

The island's capital, **NANSIO**, is one of Tanzania's doziest towns – even the market is a low-key affair. Travellers here are rare, and people are quite visibly startled to see *wazungu*. You can **change money** at the National Microfinance Bank between the bus stand and the market. **Internet access** is available on a slow dial-up at the *Gallu Beach Hotel*.

Public transport on the island is very thin, so **hiring a bicycle** (or bringing your own) is the best way around: ask at Nansio's market or at the *Gallu Beach Hotel*, which can also arrange **excursions** by car (around Tsh30,000). The hotel also sells photocopied maps of the island (Tsh1000), essential if you're planning on exploring the island on your own.

Bukindo palace

The closest "attraction" to Nansio is the semi-ruined **Bukindo Palace**, 8km to the north (and 2km north of Bukindo village). It's a few hundred metres to the right of the road in a stand of trees, but isn't signposted so you'll have to ask directions: ask for Kasale Victor Mazura Rukumbuzya, the grandson of the last king of Ukerewe, who owns the place.

Built in 1928, apparently by an Italian architect named Tonerro, the palace is a grand, colonial-style two-storey construction, surrounded on both levels by a wide balcony. It served as the palace of **Chief Gabriel Ruhumbika** (died 1938) and then of his son, **Chief Rukumbuzya**, who was the last king of Ukerewe. After his death in 1981, the palace was abandoned by the family, most of whom emigrated to North America. The gardens, which contain two of the biggest mango trees you're likely to see, have become gloriously overgrown, but the building itself is beginning to collapse. There's talk of renovation, but for the time being it's just a pretty ruin buzzing to the sound of cicadas. Some of the ground-floor rooms are used by a local family: they'll appreciate a tip to show you around, not that there's much to see. To get there, catch a **pick-up** from Nansio to Bugolora, which run at irregular intervals throughout the day.

Handebezyo Museum

Ten kilometres west of Nansio, **Handebezyo Museum** is not so much a museum as a glorified picnic site, but an entertaining excuse for a day-trip nonetheless. The site, to which you'll be accompanied by dozens of hyperactive children, is perched on top of one of several low granite hills in the centre of the island, distinguished by the rather charming christening of its "peaks" after 1960s African leaders: Nyerere, Karume, Kaunda, Kenyatta and Kawawa. Concrete steps have been built all the way to the top, giving sweeping views over much of the island and the lake: the hill was used to scout for enemies in pre-colonial times.

Access is easiest via **Mahande**, about 10km northwest of Nansio. If you're driving, head 2km along the road towards Bukindo then turn left at the school. At Mahande, ignore the main road running north–south but continue due west along a less-used road. This crosses a river planted with rice paddies (look for herons, open-billed storks and egrets) before curving right to join another north-south road. Turn right (north): the site is signposted on the left after 1km. By **public transport**, catch the first daladala from Nansio to Rubya (currently 11.30am) and get off at Mahande, leaving you with a pleasant 3km walk. Ensure you get back to Mahande before 4pm to catch the last daladala on the Rubya–Nansio route, but double-check all times before setting off to avoid getting stranded.

Beaches

Bilharzia is a problem around Ukerewe, though no one seems to know – or want to say – exactly where. The most accessible beaches, such as the one beside the *Gallu Beach Hotel*, may or may not be infected, so swimming is at your own risk. The only beach that is definitely free of bilharzia is beyond **Rubya Forest** in the far west. Two daladalas cover this route, but at the time of writing only one was running, leaving Nansio at 11.30am, 3pm and 5pm. If you're not planning on camping overnight at the beach, the 11.30am run is your only option, giving you around three hours by the lake before the last daladala returns from Rubya (around 4pm); again, double-check times with daladala drivers in Nansio before setting off. If you do camp overnight, the first daladala back to Nansio leaves at 6am. The journey takes just under an hour in good weather.

Accommodation

The only **accommodation** on Ukerewe Island is at Nansio.

Gallu Beach Hotel 600m west of the ferry jetty on a headland facing Nansio Bay ℡028/251 5094, ✉gbh@africaonline.co.tz. Nansio's best, this breezy place is set by the lakeside with wide lawns, an attractive view and a bar and restaurant. The rooms (with or without bathroom) are spacious, though single rooms can only be used by one person. There are also some expensive suites. Electricity (from a generator) runs from 7pm to 10pm. There's no running water, and the management insists on waking you at 6am to ask whether you want a hot shower. Breakfast included. Rooms ②, suites ❸

Island Guest Inn Posta St, facing the Uhuru Monument (no phone). The cheapest rooms in town, some en suite, and all clean, well-kept and with friendly management. They're often full, so arrive early. ❶

Kazoba Lodging & Boarding Posta St, near the *Island Guest Inn* ℡028/251 5146. Quiet and peaceful (indeed almost dull), with basic rooms (some en suite) with nets. Avoid the stuffy singles with no external windows. ❶

Pamba Hostel Facing the bank by the bus stand ℡028/251 5019. An unappetizing, albeit cheap, option now used mainly for amorous encounters. The tatty rooms aren't totally clean, and there's no running water, but at least most have nets and fans, and some of the doubles have bathrooms. There's electricity from 7pm to midnight, plus a restaurant and two bars. ❶

Saganya Guest House Between *Pamba Hostel* and the main road in from Rugezi. Closed at the time of writing, this appears to be much quieter and much more salubrious than the *Pamba*. ❶

Eating and drinking

The following are virtually the only places on the island where you can buy cooked **food**. The best is the *Gallu Beach Hotel*, which serves up good meals from Tsh2000. Less enticing is the *Pamba Hostel*, which nowadays functions mainly as a bar, although the food – if ordered early enough – can be good. There are a couple of *mishkaki* (grilled meat) stalls along the main road between the ferry jetty and *Gallu Beach Hotel*, and a couple of basic cafés at the west end of town. And that's it.

For **drinking**, the *Gallu Beach Hotel* is the most civilized place, with tables under parasols in the garden by the lake. There are more good lake views, but no food, at *Picnic Villa* (also known as *Sunset Beach*), 50m from the ferry jetty,

---

Moving on from Nansio

Leaving Nansio, the Trans Africa **bus** departs around 7am to catch the 8.30am ferry, followed by Bunda Bus Service at around 9am to catch the 10.30am ferry. If you miss these, get a **daladala** from Nansio to Rugezi before 3.30pm to arrive in time for the last ferry (but don't bank on transport on the other side). A local departure tax is levied at Rugezi: Tsh50 per person and Tsh200 for a vehicle and driver.

which has some tables in a small lakeside garden, and is useful for finding your feet if you've just arrived by ferry or are waiting for the *MV Butiama* in the afternoon. The downstairs bar at the *Pamba Hostel* looks pretty rough; nicer is its rooftop bar which catches the evening sun. Apart from these places, boozers have wide choice of "groceries" to choose from: semi-legal joints hidden behind net curtains which cater for the more alcoholically challenged members of Nansio's society.

Ukara Island

Even further off the beaten track is **Ukara Island**, an hour's boat ride north of Ukerewe, which is home to the Kara tribe. Like Ukerewe, it's heavily populated and has few attractions you can pin down, other than the isolated rural

---

The journey of Lukanga Mukara

The Journey of Lukanga Mukara into the innermost of Germany is the title of a bitingly satirical book by the German explorer and pacifist, **Hans Paasche** (1881–1920), who was posted to Tanganyika between 1905 and 1906 during the brutal repression of the Maji Maji Uprising. The book, published in instalments in 1912 and 1913, seems to have been Paasche's way of expunging the guilt he felt about his role in the conflict. In it, an imaginary character from Ukara Island, one **Lukanga Mukara**, recounts his often hilarious impressions of the Fatherland in a series of letters to his chief back home. The following extract, concerning the nature of German women, gives a flavour of his style.

Here it becomes difficult for me to follow things to the heart of the matter. Only this one thing I already know for sure: the women of the Wasungu are artificially deformed and their crippled bodies are dressed in furs, woven material skins and feathers of wild creatures, so that a new figure is created which has nothing in common with the natural, beautiful woman-sculpture as we know it with the Watinku. Nude girls and women are nowhere to be seen, not on the streets, nor at the harvest work. Also, they do not all bathe, and those who do bathe, wear suits and it is not allowed to take a close look at them. Only in the evenings when the Wasungu eat and dance together, the girls are as good as nude and only a part of their body is covered with clothing. They do not dare to come completely without clothes because their body consists of two parts which are only loosely connected and are held together with a stiff outer construction. This construction, they cover up in the evening with a little clothing. But of course, not more than absolutely necessary. If the women did not have this construction they could not walk upright and would collapse. This construction is most likely to be an ancient invention of the men. They forced it onto the women in order to remain superior to them in health and stamina, in spite of their own laziness and bad habits. This frame is designed in such a way that the women cannot breathe, so that a part of the lung rots and dies. They lack the deep breath. Consequently, the women cannot run or move. So the flesh under the frame withers away and the body becomes grossly fat on the upper and lower parts, which is something the Wasungu find beautiful.

Paasche was arrested for treason in 1917, having resigned his commission in the navy, and was locked away as insane in the Berlin Sanatorium. He was released during the chaos of the November Revolution of 1918, but was shot dead in mysterious circumstances in May 1920 after having been anonymously denounced as "a known pacifist and antimilitarist". There's an English translation of Paasche's book on the internet at Ⓦ www.cs.ucl.ac.uk/staff/a.steed/lukanga.html, from where this extract is taken.

---

ambience and a clutch of distant legends. The most vivid of these concerns the **Dancing Stone of Butimba**, on the western shore, which is a boulder balanced on top of another boulder. You'll need a bicycle (hire one in Nansio) and a guide who knows the place; the *Gallu Beach Hotel* in Nansio can arrange one, or ask the boatman when you're coming across to find someone when you arrive. A fee or tip of at least Tsh3000 would be in order, and they'll need their own bike. You may also need to locate the stone's "guardian", who lives thirty minutes' walk inland from the stone, and demands payment (up to Tsh6000 per group) in order to make the rock "dance", even though traditionally the rock only dances when people sing. All very mysterious.

Access to Ukara Island is by boat from **Bugolora** (on the north side of Ukerewe Island) to **Bwisya** on Ukara. One DCM minibus and two Hiace daladalas run daily from Nansio to Bugolora, the first leaving around 7am, the last heading back to Nansio at 4pm. There's nothing organized about the boats from Bugolora, but if you arrive before 11am, chances are that you'll be able to get a ride on a boat with local passengers (no more than Tsh1000 per person). If you miss this, however, or if the passenger boat isn't running that day, the price for hiring an entire boat will depend entirely on your bargaining skills. Coming back from Ukara, there's usually a passenger boat just after sunrise. If you want to stay, or you get stuck (as is likely), there are a couple of basic **guest houses** (**①**) at Bwisya where the boat lands, and a beautiful beach to boot. The boats cannot take cars; bicycles are much more appropriate.

Mara Region

The eastern shore of the Tanzanian portion of Lake Victoria is part of **Mara Region**, named after the **Mara River**, which rises to the north of Kenya's Maasai Mara Game Reserve. The river is famed as the scene of the carnage that results every year when massive herds of wildebeest and zebra attempt to cross the raging river on their great migration (see p.457), providing a feast for countless crocodiles, lions and other carnivores. By the time the river approaches the lake, however, it has become one of the most sedate and beautiful of East Africa's rivers. While there's not currently an awful lot actually to do in the region (a cultural tourism programme or two certainly wouldn't go amiss), the region's natural beauty makes any journey here a pleasure in itself.

Musoma

Mwanza's expansion has been at the expense of **MUSOMA**, a small port town located on a peninsula that juts out into Mara Bay, 120km south of Kenya. What the town lacks in terms of cosmopolitan delights it makes up with its instantly likeable, laid-back charm, its gorgeous setting and a fresh climate which is quite different from the strength-sapping humidity of Mwanza. There aren't any sights as such, though a walk to the end of the peninsula is always fun, both for the views and for the local **birdlife**, especially the waders and raptors which can be found around the papyrus beds that fringe the beaches. There are also couple of small **markets**: one by the lakeshore to the east of town close to where fishing boats are repaired, the other a more generic affair next to the bus stand in the centre.

Unfortunately, **swimming** – although popular with local children – doesn't appear to be terribly safe, despite local assurances to the contrary. The papyrus and reed beds at the waterline offer an ideal habitat for bilharzia-infected blood flukes, and the water itself gets murky during and shortly after the rains, so take local advice with a pinch of salt.

Arrival and accommodation

The **bus stand**, just off Kusaga Street in the centre, is an orderly affair, with the ticket offices arranged on its northern side. There are frequent services from Mwanza (at least every hour), and a handful each day from Arusha via Kenya (the safest company is Scandinavian). The only company running from Arusha to Musoma through Tanzania (via Singida, Shinyanga and Mwanza) is Mtei Express (but see also the box on crossing the Serengeti by bus, p 495). **Taxis** wait at the west side of bus stand – helpful if you're staying north of town along the peninsula.

Planes land at **Musoma Airport**, 500m west of town at the end of Kusaga Street. There are currently only two flights a week (Wed & Sun), from Dar via Kilimanjaro or Arusha, then back again. They're operated by Eagle Air (☏028/262 2585), at the corner of Mukendo Road and Mwigobero Street. Passenger **ferries** from Musoma were discontinued years ago when the road from Kenya to Mwanza was tarmacked. There's a slender chance that the Kenyan ferries may resume if, or when, the Kenyans manage to eradicate the pernicious water hyacinth weed from their ports. For what it's worth, the ferry port is 2km southeast of town.

Moving on from Musoma, there's transport all day to Mwanza from 6am, and frequent daladalas to Tarime and on to Sirare on the Kenyan border, where you can catch a Kenyan matatu (daladala) to Migori or Kisii. There are also DCM minibus daladalas (roughly every two hours) to Butiama. Bunda Bus Service runs daily to Shinyanga via Mwanza at 7am.

There are two **banks** on Mukendo Road, CRDB and NBC – the latter has lower commission and more efficient service. The TTCL office is at the post office. The bus station also has telephone offices, and there are cardphones at the *Afrilux* and *Orange Tree* hotels.

Accommodation

Musoma's best **accommodation** is a couple of places by the beach north of town: nothing fancy, but the locations may entice you to stay longer. **Camping** is possible either on the narrow sandy beach at the *New Tembo Beach Hotel* ($5 per person) or in the garden at *Silver Sands Inn* (no fixed price).

Afrilux Hotel Town centre, close to the fish market ☏028/262 0031. The town centre's best hotel, a four-storey affair with en-suite rooms (singles, which can be shared by couples, or twins), most with cable TV, and good views of Mara Bay from the upper floors. There's also a bar and restaurant, room service, safe parking and a pissed-off vervet monkey holed up in a cage. Breakfast included. ❸ **Musambwa Annex** Uhuru Rd ☏0741/429983. A calm, friendly and good-value place with nine en-

suite rooms, seven of them singles that can be shared by couples. The bathrooms and Western-style toilets are well kept, there's reliable electricity, and food is planned. Breakfast included. ❶ **New 5 Emu 2001 Guest House** Kawawa St (no phone). Silly name but good cheap rooms, mostly en suite. ❶ **New Tembo Beach Hotel** 2km north of town, 800m beyond the turning to *Silver Sands* ☏028/262 2887. Near the tip of the peninsula,

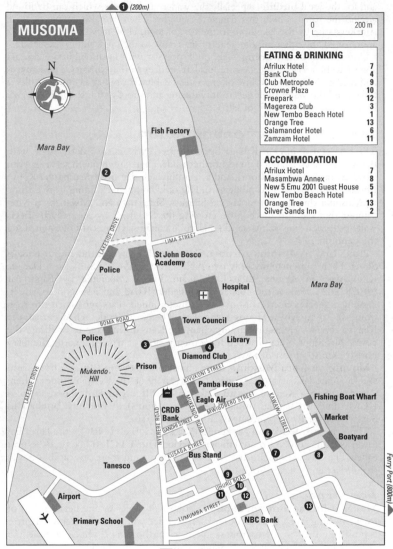

MUSOMA

0	200 m

EATING & DRINKING

Afrilux Hotel	7
Bank Club	4
Club Metropole	9
Crowne Plaza	10
Freepark	12
Magereza Club	3
New Tembo Beach Hotel	1
Orange Tree	13
Salamander Hotel	6
Zamzam Hotel	11

ACCOMMODATION

Afrilux Hotel	7
Masambwa Annex	8
New 5 Emu 2001 Guest House	5
New Tembo Beach Hotel	1
Orange Tree	13
Silver Sands Inn	2

this occupies a superb location over the lake, though the beach is better for waterbirds than for swimming. There are eleven rooms (three en suite): the "suites" are a bit scruffy; the cheaper ordinary rooms, with clean twin beds, fans and nets, are better. Breakfast included. Rooms ②, suites ③

Orange Tree Kawawa St ☎028/262 2353. This was Musoma's main hotel before the *Afrilux*, to

which it now comes second-best, and the rooms, while clean, are overpriced, especially if they collar you with their non-resident dollar rates. Rooms include singles and twins, with or without private bathroom. There's also an attractive bar (with discos three nights a week) and food. Breakfast included. Residents ②, non-residents ③–④.

Silver Sands Inn 1km north of town, off Lakeside Drive ☎028/262 2740. The location is the thing here, with lovely views west over Mara Bay and a visibly cleaner beach than at the *New Tembo*, which is popular with local kids. The rooms are simple but, if you choose carefully, perfectly ade-quate; all are en suite, with big beds and nets, and reliable water and electricity. A limited selection of beers and sodas is available, but no food. ➊

Eating, drinking and nightlife

There's not a big choice for **food**, but what there is is good. The best located is the *New Tembo Beach Hotel*, 2km north of town, which is good value for Tanzanian food, less so for more touristic fare; they also do *nyama choma* and sandwiches. In the town centre, the best local place is the *Salamander Hotel*, which dishes up combo-plates of tasty African food, whether fresh fish, meat, chicken or liver, all for around Tsh600. Another good little place is the *Zamzam Hotel* on Mukendo Road, which is ideal for breakfast and cheap meals at lunch and dinner. Posher and more expensive is the *Afrilux Hotel*, with a huge menu (including Indian dishes).

Most of the town's **bars** also serve food, and are the best places for *nyama choma*. The liveliest and most atmospheric bars, especially at night, are the *Freepark* and *Crowne Plaza*, facing each other down a little cul-de-sac off Mukendo Road, which in addition to a wide range of drinks and brilliant bar food (succulent *nyama choma* and grilled bananas), have plenty of outdoor tables – a great place to meet people. Other notable places include *Magereza (Prison) Club*, just after the prison off Mukendo Road, a friendly place frequented by prison wardens and with good food and music; and the *Orange Tree* hotel, whose bar hosts discos on Wednesday, Friday and Sunday nights (Tsh1000–1500). The *New Tembo Beach Hotel* has outdoor seating and a comfy lounge with TV, while *Diamond Club Camp Noren* and *Bank Club*, next to each other on the road opposite the prison, become lively at weekends (they may be closed midweek by day). The only real **nightclub** is *Club Metropole* on Mukendo Road, which gets busy on Friday and Saturday nights.

By bus across the Serengeti

Although bus services have officially been banned from crossing Serengeti National Park after one too many giraffes were killed by speeding coaches (thus effectively blocking the quickest overland route from Lake Victoria to Arusha), there's one exception, called **City Mist**, which is by far the quickest way to Arusha (although it's not actually clear why this bus is still allowed to run, meaning that it might well be cancelled in future). This shuttles between Musoma and Arusha once a week (Tsh22,000), currently leaving Musoma every Sunday at 5am and returning from Arusha on Thursday at the same time. The journey should take around twelve hours, but the bus is notorious for breakdowns. The fare includes park fees for Tanzanians but, as a tourist, you'll technically be breaking the law if you try to avoid paying the full whack ($30 for Serengeti and $25 for Ngorongoro) when you arrive at the gates, even though you'll only be passing through. If the bus gets stuck for more than a day, you'll have to pay additional park fees.

North to Kenya: Tarime

Heading north from Musoma, the landscape becomes hillier and very beautiful as the road drops down into the valley of the Mara River, which begins in

Kenya's famous Maasai Mara Game Reserve. Much of the valley here is occupied by the **Masura Swamp**, consisting of extensive papyrus beds through which the river meanders. The river marks the southern border of Tarime District, an area of rolling hills scattered with small homesteads and plenty of granite crags, outcrops and boulders, the latter sometimes balanced one on top of each other. The drive itself is the main reason to come to the friendly hilltop agricultural town of **TARIME**, 24km south of the Kenyan border, which is the main market town for the **Kuria tribe**. Although there are absolutely no "sights" as such, the main attraction are the Kuria themselves, who – despite modern attire – have kept much of their traditional culture intact; see box below.

Tarime lies 4km to the east of the highway into Kenya. **Daladalas** run roughly every hour to Musoma and Sirare, on the Kenyan border, pulling in at the bus stand one block south of the market. There are some **guest houses** around the market, but better are the handful of places back along the road towards the highway (Nyerere Road). The best is the friendly *AMA Hotel*, 300m from the bus stand (☏028/269 0371; ❷), with eight en-suite doubles, all with TV, fan and net, plus a garden bar and a good restaurant (meals around Tsh1500). A little cheaper is the *CMG Motel*, 450m from the bus stand and then 500m along Ngombe Road (☏028/269 0149; ❶–❷), with large and bright en-suite rooms, each with two beds, running hot water in the morning (and in buckets in the evening) and a nice garden. The cheapest but tattiest is *Queens Inn & Guest House*, 350m from the bus stand (☏028/269 0730; ❶), which has a choice of shared or en-suite single or twin-bed rooms, but no running water, nets or fans (rooms are sprayed instead); there's also a small bar with a TV.

Both *AMA* and *CMG* do **food**. Alternatively, try the *Sunshine Hotel & Restaurant*, on the east side of bus stand. To **change money**, the National Microfinance Bank is on south side of bus stand – be patient.

The Kuria

Straddling the border with Kenya, the **Kuria tribe** are among the first Bantu-speaking peoples to have settled in East Africa, possibly as long as two thousand years ago. Although traditionally cattle herders, larger and more powerful groups – such as the Luo on the lakeshore, and the Maasai in the plains – have restricted the Kuria to the hill country just east of **Lake Victoria** and forced them to adopt a settled, agricultural way of life. Nonetheless, cattle remain ritually important, especially in marriage negotiations, where hefty dowries, paid for in cattle, remain the norm. Rainfall is generally favourable, allowing the cultivation of cash crops such as coffee, sugar cane, tobacco and maize. Another cash crop is **marijuana** (*bhang*), which serves the same purpose as locally brewed beer elsewhere, being taken communally by elders when discussing tribal affairs. Disputes over control of the marijuana-producing areas, however, have been the main cause of recent and bloody conflicts between rival clans, which have claimed dozens of lives.

Music and dance accompany almost every traditional ceremony and rite of passage for the Kuria, especially weddings and circumcisions, and also serve as entertainment in their own right. The music itself is characterized by one of Africa's largest lyres, the *litungu*, which gives a distinctly metallic timbre, the strings' deep and resonant buzzing providing a hypnotic impetus. For more information about Kuria music and culture, see ⓦwww.bluegecko.org/kenya/tribes/kuria, which includes music from the Kuria, as well as the Luo and Maasai, and has full-length sound clips.

South of Musoma

The hilly country inland from the lake between Musoma and Tarime to the north and Serengeti's "Western Corridor" to the south is home to several small tribes, most of them agricultural. One of these tribes (the Zanaki) provided Tanzania's first president, **Julius Nyerere**, who was born – and is now buried – in the town of **Butiama**, where there's a museum dedicated to his memory. East of here is an infrequently travelled dirt road offering access to Serengeti's remote **Ikoma Gate**. There's also an excellent upmarket tented camp just outside the park at **Ikoma**, offering a range of entertaining wildlife walks and excursions to local attractions.

Butiama

Apart from Musoma, Mara Region's other major town is **BUTIAMA**, about 45km southeast of Musoma, which would be an unremarkable place were it not the birthplace of Tanzania's revered founder, **Julius Kambarage Nyerere** (see box below), whose life is commemorated by the **Mwalimu Julius K. Nyerere Memorial Museum** (daily 9.30am–6pm; $3), which opened in July 1999, a few months before his death. The guided tour (included in the entry fee, though a tip is always welcome) starts with a short talk about the president's life before you're taken around the exhibits. These are a mixture of personal items like clothing, shoes, his favourite (and very battered) radio, presents from official tours and archival material documenting his presidency, including plenty of photos, an *Ujamaa*-style Makonde carving (see p.232) depicting the

---

Julius Nyerere

Tanzania's first and much-loved president, **Julius Kambarage Nyerere**, was born to a chief of the small Zanaki tribe in Mwitongo village, near Butiama, in 1922, when Tanganyika was under British rule. Nyerere was educated at Tabora Secondary School in central Tanzania and at Makerere College in Uganda before going on to study history and economics at Edinburgh. He returned to Tanganyika in 1952, where he became the leader of the pro-independence **Tanganyika African National Union** (TANU). As leader of TANU, Nyerere preached a creed of non-violence and succeeded in securing Tanzania's peaceful transition to independence in 1961 (in sharp contrast to neighbouring Kenya, whose road to independence was long and bloody), following which he was elected Tanganyika's first president. Known to Tanzanians as **Mwalimu** (the Teacher) and **Baba ya Taifa** (the Father of the Nation), his unpretentious, softly spoken and light-hearted style (his wonderful smile features in pretty much every photo ever taken of him) perfectly complemented his political vision of tolerance, courtesy, modesty and non-violence, words that could equally be applied to the nation as whole.

Nyerere's legacy, however, is mixed. His decade-long experiment in self-reliant socialism, **Ujamaa** (see p.718), ended in economic disaster, while his insistence that Zanzibar remain part of the 1964 Act of Union that created Tanzania is seen by many, especially in Zanzibar, as a mistake. Nonetheless, the one unassailable achievement over his 24-year tenure as president was his role as a nation builder. From 128 different tribes, he forged a cohesive state completely free of the divisive tribalism that has plunged many other African countries into chaos.

Nyerere died of leukaemia at St Thomas' Hospital, London, on October 14, 1999, and is buried in the family graveyard close to the museum in Butiama. He ranks with Nelson Mandela as one of the twentieth century's great African statesmen.

founding members of TANU who had spearheaded the drive to independence and an oddly beautiful set of carved plaques commemorating the 1978–79 Kagera War with Idi Amin's Uganda. You should also be able to visit his **grave**, close to the museum, which was being enclosed within a permanent building at the time of writing.

Access by **public transport** is easiest from Musoma, from where daladalas run every hour or two; the visit can be done as a half-day trip. If you're driving from Musoma, head along the tarmac road towards Mwanza. Ignore the first signposted junction to Butiama (which leads you along 17km of bad road) and take the second instead, leaving you with only 11km of rough road. The museum itself is signposted at several places along the highway, but these disappear in Butiama itself, so you'll have to ask: it's at Mwitongo, about 1km west of the centre along a tree-lined avenue that passes a transmitter mast. Hang around, or ask at the army base just before the museum, and the curator will come to let you in. There's no accommodation in Butiama.

Bunda

The small and bustling town of **BUNDA**, on the Mwanza–Musoma highway 30km north of Serengeti National Park's Ndabaka Gate, owes its importance to a couple of unsurfaced side roads which originate here: one heading west to Masahunga and the ferry to **Ukerewe Island** (see p.488); the other running east around the northern boundary of **Serengeti** to the park's Ikoma Gate, 125km east of Bunda.

There are plenty of **buses and daladalas** connecting Bunda to Mwanza and Musoma. Bunda Bus Service is probably the safest operator (they also have a daily run down to Shinyanga which passes through Bunda around 9am). Their office is 70m from the bus stand, on the left along the road to Ukerewe. Heading into Kenya or on to Arusha, flag down the daily Scandinavian Express bus from Mwanza, which passes by no later than 8am. Avoid Zuberi and Tawfiq buses, whose drivers are reckless. For details on getting to Ukerewe, see p.488. The route to Ikoma Gate is covered below.

There's no shortage of good, cheap **accommodation**, with plenty of choices lining the Mwanza–Musoma road. The best hotel, however, is the friendly *Bhukenye Bar & Guest House* (no phone; ❶), to the west of the highway: take the side road by the post office (look for the transmitter) and then the third right (signposted). Some rooms have bathrooms (bucket showers and spotlessly clean squat toilets), and there's a friendly bar at the front which also serves roast meat, chips and omelettes. Also good, but much pricier, is the new *CN Hotel* on the highway at the north end of town (☎028/262 1298; ❷–❸), which has en-suite rooms with fans, nets and clean Western-style bathrooms. The town's only real **restaurant** is the *A&B Restaurant*, behind *Hotel Inchage Galaxy* and the National Microfinance Bank, 50m east of the Mwanza–Musoma road. It has a big choice of Tanzanian food (superb *pilau*, good liver stew and delicious stewed fish), and nothing costs over Tsh1000. There's a good **bar** at the *Hotel Inchage Galaxy*.

Nyamuswa and Issenye

The *murram* road east from Bunda to Serengeti's Ikoma Gate (the turn-off isn't signposted, so you'll have to ask) passes through a rural area full of small villages, cassava fields, mango trees and banana plantations – rainfall, as you can tell, is uncommonly reliable in this corner of the country. **NYAMUSWA**, 24km from Bunda at the junction of a minor road to Butiama, is the first set-

tlement of any size. There are basic **rooms** at *Wakuru Guest Bar & Hotel* (T
Issenye 26), 50m from the junction by a huge amarula tree under which the
village's elderly *wazee* like to while away the day.

The next major town is **ISSENYE**, the end-point for most of the pick-ups
from Bunda. There's **accommodation** in several cheap guest houses on the
main road and at the *Issenye Serengeti View Campsite*, situated in the grounds of
the Anglican Issenye Secondary School, signposted 2.5km south of the main
road. You can either camp here or stay in the school's bizarrely misnamed *Savoy
Game Lodge*, which comprises two very basic rooms with nets and shared bathroom. Costs aren't fixed and are treated as donations: Tsh3000–5000 per person is about right. The school is a good base for **hiking**, and the headmaster is
happy to fix you up with a suitable pupil as guide. They can also arrange **traditional dance** (*ngoma*) concerts for around Tsh20,000.

The only regular transport along the road from Bunda is the daily **bus** to
Mugumu, beyond Ikoma, which leaves Bunda at around 11am. In the other
direction, it passes through Issenye at 7.30am. Land Rover **pick-ups** also cover
the route from Bunda to Issenye: these leave Bunda after midday, and head back
to town the next morning around 6–7am.

Ikoma

Forty kilometres further along the road from Issenye, and roughly 110km east
of Bunda, is **IKOMA**, named after the local tribe. It's not a village as such,
but rather a collection of small settlements which form part of the four hun-
dred-square-kilometre Ikoma Wildlife Management Area, one of several
buffer zones around the Serengeti. **Public transport** from Bunda is on the
daily bus for Mugumu, which leaves Bunda at around 11am and passes
through Ikoma on the way back at around 6am. **Accommodation** is available at the *Ikoma Bush Camp*, 3km outside the park's Ikoma Gate (no phone;
book through Swala Safaris in Arusha, p.396; full board ●), which is in a
great location on the edge of a major wildlife migration route (Nov–Jan and
May–July) If you miss the migration, there are resident herds of impala and
topi, distant lions and lots of birdlife to keep you occupied. The camp has sixteen large and comfortable en-suite tents, a relaxed, peaceful and friendly
atmosphere and good food. The camp also offers a number of **excursions**
(also available to non-guests) on foot or by vehicle outside the park. Prices
are very reasonable: a three-hour bush walk costs $10; a half-day game drive
is $30; and a full day inside Serengeti is $70 (all prices are per person). If you
stay overnight, an unusual option is a **night drive** ($20), which offers the
chance to see genet, civet and serval cats, lesser bushbabies, white-tailed mongooses, African and spring hares and, if you're really lucky, aardvarks, porcupines and hyenas.

Apart from wildlife, other attractions include the ruins of **Ikoma Fort**, situated on top of the most easterly of the Nyabuta Hills. The fort was built by the
Germans in 1900 and controlled by them until 1917, when it was shelled and
taken by a Kenyan detachment of the King's African Rifles; it's currently slated for restoration. The nearby **Ikoma Refuge** comprises a series of stone-
walled corrals where the Ikoma and their cattle used to hide from advancing
Maasai. With more time, you could also visit **Nyagoti gold mine** (a 64km
round-trip from Ikoma); officially abandoned, the mine is still worked by locals
using traditional methods – they'll happily sell you nuggets, should they have
found any.

Kagera Region

The thickly forested hills, raincloud-filled skies and vibrant red laterite soil of **Kagera Region** in Tanzania's far northwest provide a very welcome and truly tropical contrast to the unremitting scrub of central Tanzania. However, mention of the region sends a shiver down many a spine: bordering Rwanda and Burundi, Kagera is synonymous with armed incursions and attacks by rebels from those countries interminable conflicts (although Rwanda is mostly peaceful at present, rebel activity in the border region persists). While this restricts your land movements to the main north–south highway from Biharamulo up to the Ugandan border, it certainly shouldn't put you off visiting the region: the landscape is very beautiful, the lakeshore a delight and the harbour town of **Bukoba** – connected to Mwanza by passenger steamer – is an attractive and lively stop-over for travellers to Uganda, and also has some nice beaches. With more time and money there's also the little-visited **Rubondo Island National Park** in the lake's southwest corner to explore, especially if birds are your thing. The park's isolation, and hence inaccessibility to poachers, has also made it a preferred place for relocating species endangered elsewhere, including chimpanzees, black rhinos and even elephants.

Bukoba

Tanzania's only major town on Lake Victoria's western shore is **BUKOBA**, a bustling, upbeat and friendly place, even if it's become infamous for the lazy service offered in its hotels and restaurants. Given the impossibility of venturing far off the main road into Uganda (none of the region's game reserves is safe), most tourists who come here are generally passing to or from Uganda. Its gorgeous lakeshore location, backed by boulder-strewn and thickly vegetated hills, and plentiful birdlife in the surrounding swamps, make it a pleasantly relaxing place to spend a few days before – if you're heading north – facing the rigours of the muddy road to Uganda.

Arrival and accommodation

The **bus stand** is at the west end of town off Kawawa Street; taxis congregate at the roundabout at the south end of the stand. The **airport** is near the lakeshore to the east at the end of Aerodrome Road; there are rarely any taxis here, but the walk into town is very pleasant. The **ferry port** lies 2.5km southeast of town. There's a bar and canteen at the port, but beware of pickpockets and thieves. A taxi into town from here costs Tsh2000–3000; a cheaper and funnier way in, so long as you don't have mountains of luggage, is to catch a bicycle taxi for a few hundred shillings. For details of **onward transport** from Bukoba, see p.505.

The main concentration of budget **guest houses** is on Miembeni Street about 600m east of the bus stand. Mid-range places are situated closer to the lake, and two are right on the shore. **Camping** is possible at the *Lake View Hotel* (Tsh3000 per person).

Haya proverbs

As with all Tanzania's tribes, the telling of **proverbs** amongst the Haya is a sophisticated and ancient art, and a favourite means of passing on nuggets of knowledge to children. The following selection of Haya proverbs is taken from Ⓦ www.afriprov.org and the book *500 Haya Proverbs* by Hellen Byera Nestor (available in Bukoba's bookshops).

Akanyonyi kataharara tikamanya ruhanga rweza buroi
– A bird that does not fly does not know the valley where millet grows best

Atakwendera bana abeta ruuto
– One who does not like your children calls them "mouths to feed"

Bagaya akatoju kaija kabachumbagiza
– A small fire destroys a big forest

Mukama wa akaze takachwa
– Habits are easily entered but difficult to stop

Ntuma nkutume mukazi alikwonkya
– A small child bothers its parents; when big, the parents bother him

Obukuru bushemeza ekitoke
– Old age sweetens the banana but not the human

Obworo ntara kotarashaine yakulya
– Poverty is a lion; if you do not fight you get eaten

Okuha kuheleka okwima kuzika
– To give is to save, not to give is to bury

Omwana atagenda ati maw'Achumba
– A child that does not travel praises its mother's cooking

Ashidu Guest House & Café Miembeni Rd (no phono). Very basic and cheap rooms (shared bathrooms only) furnished with just a bed, net and small table; the only single lacks an external window. Food available. ①

Bukoba Kolping Guest House Miembeni Rd, opposite the *Wawala Kolping* ☏ 028/222 1461. A secure if dull and not overly welcoming choice, with eight good en-suite doubles, each with tiled bathroom, cable TV, fan and telephone. The rooms have two beds, which can be put together. Soft drinks and food are available to order, and breakfast is included. ③

Edan Hotel Uganda Rd ☏ 028/222 0626, Ⓔ edanhotel@africaonline.co.tz. A two-storey business-style option with a range of good-value rooms, all but one with private bathroom. All have TV, hot water and phone, and some also have balconies or fridges. The suite-like doubles come with large beds, box nets, settee and TV. Breakfast included. ③–④

ELCT Nyumba ya Vijana Uganda Rd ☏ 028/222 0069, Ⓔ elct_nwd@twiga.com. This Lutheran youth hostel has little going for it other than dirt-cheap rates. The small, clean, cell-like rooms, all sharing bathrooms, have either two or four unduly narrow beds (the latter rooms function as dorms; Tsh1500–2000 per person). Food available to order. No smoking ①

ELCT Vocational Training Centre Aerodrome Rd ☏ 028/222 3121, Ⓔ elct-ctc@africaonline.co.tz. Also run by the Lutheran Church, this enjoys large and beautiful grounds with plenty of birds, lawns and mature trees. There are 22 rooms ranging from doubles with shared bathrooms, en-suite twins (the better ones with TVs and box nets) and suites. All are clean and have phones. Safe parking. Breakfast included. ③–⑤

Kahawa Guest House Miembeni Rd ☏ 0741/450025. Not the best on this road but acceptable, with clean twin-bed rooms, most sharing dilapidated bathroom. ①–②

Kanoni Lodge Off Uganda Rd ☏ 0741/431775. An odd place among fields with friendly but disorganized management. The cheap rooms (with or without bathroom) in the old part are

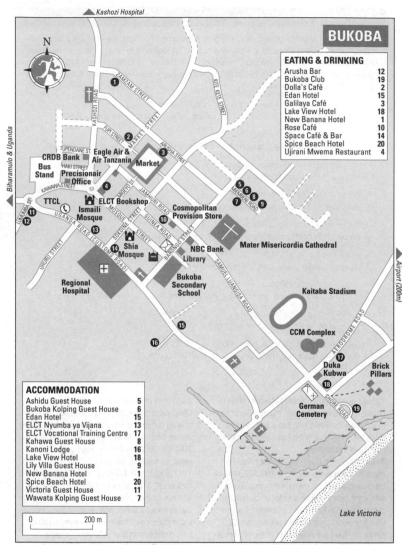

BUKOBA

EATING & DRINKING

Arusha Bar	12
Bukoba Club	19
Dolla's Café	2
Edan Hotel	15
Galilaya Café	3
Lake View Hotel	18
New Banana Hotel	1
Rose Café	10
Space Café & Bar	14
Spice Beach Hotel	20
Ujirani Mwema Restaurant	4

Kashozi Hospital

Biharamulo & Uganda

Airport (200m)

TTCL
Ismaili Mosque
ELCT Bookshop
Cosmopolitan Provision Store
Shia Mosque
NBC Bank
Library
Mater Misericordia Cathedral
Regional Hospital
Bukoba Secondary School
Kaitaba Stadium
CCM Complex
Duka Kubwa
Brick Pillars
German Cemetery
CRDB Bank
Eagle Air & Air Tanzania
Bus Stand
Precisionair Office
Market

Lake Victoria

ACCOMMODATION

Ashidu Guest House	5
Bukoba Kolping Guest House	6
Edan Hotel	15
ELCT Nyumba ya Vijana	13
ELCT Vocational Training Centre	17
Kahawa Guest House	8
Kanoni Lodge	16
Lake View Hotel	18
Lily Villa Guest House	9
New Banana Hotel	1
Spice Beach Hotel	20
Victoria Guest House	11
Wawata Kolping Guest House	7

0   200 m

20 (200m) & Ferry Port (1km)

good value if a bit dingy. The new two-storey wing is totally different, with excellent suites. Even so, a little more money will get you much better accommodation at the *Edan Hotel*. ①–③

Lake View Hotel Shore Rd ☎028/222 1845. A colonial survivor set in gardens by the lakeshore – like many hotels around Lake Victoria it claims a connection with the film *African Queen*, apparently being where Humphrey Bogart and Katherine Hepburn stayed during the shooting. There's a

choice of huge rooms (with or without bathroom) fitted with twin beds, box nets, phone and wash-basin; the best have lake views. ③

Lily Villa Guest House Miembeni Rd (no phone). Cheap and welcoming place. The rooms (all with twin beds) share clean bathrooms with surprisingly powerful showers. Check the mosquito nets, though – some are too small for the beds. ①

New Banana Hotel Zamzam St ☎028/222 0861. The Maasai *askaris* at the entrance announce this place's tourist pretensions, as do the rooms, all of which are en suite with well-kept Western-style toilets (most also have TVs); the doubles have huge beds with box nets and phone, and there are also some suites, as well as a restaurant, bar and secure parking. Breakfast included. ❸

Spice Beach Motel On the beach 2km south of the centre ☎028/222 0142. This recommended option occupies a neat cluster of old German buildings near a patch of *kopjes* and boulders in an attractive and breezy lakeside location facing Mumblii Island. The six en-suite doubles are big and bright, with twin beds, box nets, cable TV, clean showers and Western-style toilets. There's

also a great beachside bar, and food is available. Breakfast included. ❸–❹

Victoria Guest House Corner Lumumba Rd and Kawawa St ☎028/222 3100. Basic, but no complaints at the price, with six musty, twin-bed rooms (all sharing bathrooms) with saggy beds, nets and tables. ❶

Wawata Kolping Guest House Miembeni Rd ☎028/222 1289. Run by the Catholic Church, and with a fittingly calm and meditative atmosphere. There's one en-suite double room (❶), and a single-sex dorm with six beds and a shared bathroom, which you can either rent in its entirety (Tsh9000) or by the bed (Tsh1500). Breakfast and lunch available.

The Town

One of the things you'll notice in Bukoba is the presence of lots of earnest-looking *wazungu* working for aid agencies and Christian NGOs, many concerned with dealing with AIDS – a particularly acute problem on this side of the lake thanks to the presence of the road into Uganda and the traditionally open sexual mores of Haya women. Few of the expatriates seem to mix with locals, however, and the overall feeling is that a lot of the money could be better spent elsewhere. The present-day aid workers are merely the latest in a long line of *wazungu* – the influence of their predecessors, the European missionaries, is visible throughout town in the form of several very large churches. The biggest and most grandiose is the Catholic **Mater Misericordiae Cathedral** at the corner of Barongo Street and Samuel Luangisa Road, which recently acquired an enormous, architecturally adventurous and presumably very expensive concrete spire. It's not just Christians vying in terms of ostentatious presence: the **Ismaili Mosque** at the west end of Mosque Street boasts an impressive clock tower, while the **Shia Mosque** on same street occupies a grand old colonial building.

Daily life centres around the bus stand and the lively and colourful **market** to its east, right in the middle of town. It's a good place to buy *Robusta* coffee, the region's major cash crop, and also to admire the many shapes and colours of bananas (*ndizi*), which form local inhabitants' staple food – some are used for steaming, others for stewing, grilling or roasting, and some just for eating raw (the small finger-sized ones, and the big red ones, are usually the best).

About twenty minutes' walk east of the market area, along Uganda or Samuel Luangisa roads, is the **lakeshore**, the southern part backed by pretty freshwater swamps full of papyrus and reed beds which are a good place to see water birds. There's also a narrow but attractive stretch of beach between the swamp and the lake – *Spice Beach Motel*, at its south end, is a wonderful base, and has a bar and food. According to locals, **swimming** is safe and bilharzia is said to be absent, though you might like to treat this assertion with a pinch of salt, since the swamps behind the beach could be a possible breeding ground for the parasite-carrying flukes. There are no reports of crocodiles, but be aware that the Ugandan section of the lake saw a spate of crocodile attacks during 2001–2002, and also note that there are hippos in the waters around the rocky **Mumbili Island**, facing the beach. The island can be visited by boat: either ask around at the fishing port just north of the ferry port or at the *Spice Beach Motel* or *Lake View Hotel*.

There's an untended and overgrown **German cemetery** on Shore Road opposite the *Lake View Hotel*, and another reminder of colonial rule at the corner of Shore Road and Aerodrome Road in the form of **Duka Kubwa** ("Big Shop"). Now abandoned and close to ruin, it served as the town's first general store in German times. Also ruined are the three **brick pillars** behind the nearby *Bukoba Club*, which are said to have been built during the 1978–79 Kagera War with Uganda for use as look-out posts (the soldiers simply stood on top), although no one seems quite certain that this is what they were really intended for – it seems odd, in any case, to have built look-out posts, as the hills behind Bukoba would surely have given better views.

Eating, drinking and nightlife

Restaurants in Bukoba close when their supply of food for the evening is finished, meaning that whatever's on offer is cooked in a great big pot, and when it's empty, that's your lot. This means you should either find a place early, or risk encountering locked doors and an empty stomach. The local speciality is **matoke**, a thick stew of bananas which, when well made, is similar to a sticky potato stew.

Dolla's Café Market St. This has a limited menu of Tanzanian dishes, even fewer of which are actually available, but what there is is good. Full meals, like *pilau* or meat with *ugali* or rice, cost Tsh800–1500. Closed Sat evenings.

Galilaya Café Arusha St. A small and unassuming place that serves some of the best food in town – it's also pretty much the only cheap place guaranteed to be open at night. Stuff yourself silly with a gorgeously aromatic *pilau*, or steamed or broiled fish, all for under Tsh1000. They also have fresh milk (hot or cold) and juices.

New Banana Hotel Zamzam St. This has a big menu of both Tanzanian and European dishes and is handy for breakfast, though not everything is always available. Mains around Tsh2000–2500.

Rose Café Jamhuri Rd. A long-standing favourite, with good breakfasts and snacks, and simple but filling full meals, including *matoke* and – a sop to tourists – hamburgers. Daytime only; closed Sun.

Spice Beach Motel On the beach 2km south of the centre. A brilliant location and very good food, served under parasols facing the beach (there's no dining room as such). *Nyama choma* is available all day, but you'll have to wait for stuff off the menu: mains cost Tsh2500.

Ujirani Mwema Restaurant Market St. The large dining room here is popular for quick bites or a cup of tea or coffee, though arriving at a time when they have full meals is pot luck. Erratic hours; closed Sat evenings.

Drinking and nightlife

The unfinished (and now abandoned) CCM complex along Samuel Luangisa Road is the unlikely venue for **visiting bands**; check posters around town for details of upcoming events. It's also worth asking about performances by Bukoba's big star, **Saida Karoli** (of Saida Group), whose song *Maria Salome* was one of Tanzania's biggest hits in 2001, despite being sung in the local language, Kihaya.

Arusha Bar Lumumba Rd. A busy local bar, even by day.

Bukoba Club Off Shore Rd. This former colonial social club is now mainly a bar, charming in a dusty and tattered way, with seats inside and out in the garden (but cover your limbs with clothes or repellent, as there are zillions of mosquitoes). There's also a snooker table, dartboard, table tennis and lawn tennis. Food is limited to *nyama choma* (sometimes) and chip omelettes.

Edan Hotel Uganda Rd. This has a good bar open until midnight – nothing special, but it does the trick – and discos are planned.

Lake View Hotel Shore Rd. The lake view from the terrace or the tables on the lawn is the main draw in this calm and dignified place. Food is available, but isn't up to much.

Space Café & Bar Corner of Uganda Rd and Sokoine St. One of the better places in the centre, with lots of space and seats in or out, a TV and *nyama choma*.

Given the usually parlous state of the road around the lake on the Tanzanian side (especially to the east of Biharamulo), most travellers take the *MV Victoria* **ferry**, which sails between Bukoba and Mwanza, calling en route at the small port of Kemondo, 21km south of Bukoba. The ferry currently leaves Bukoba after sunset on Monday, Wednesday and either Friday or Saturday, arriving in Mwanza the next morning. The fare, including $5 port tax, is approximately $18 in first class (two bunks to a cabin), $16 in second (four bunks to a cabin) and $12–13 in either second-class seating or third class. Cabins are recommended if you want to arrive refreshed; book these a day or two before.

Bus services from Bukoba are sketchy and usually deeply uncomfortable experiences, but if you're up for a lash or two of masochism, there are daily buses – at least in the dry season – all the way to Dar es Salaam, passing through Biharamulo, Nzega, Singida (where the bus stops for the night), Dodoma and Morogoro. Two operators currently do this route: Takrim, whose office is on the north side of the stand (departures at 6am on Tues & Sat), and Tawfiq (Tues, Thurs, Sat and Sun at 6am), though they have a reputation for dangerous driving. A more comfortable alternative, though it will cost you a fortune in visa fees, is to catch Tawfiq's 7am bus on Tuesday or Saturday through Uganda and Kenya to Arusha or Dar. The road beyond Biharamulo to Kigoma is one of Tanzania's worst, so bus frequencies and schedules change frequently: Takrim currently operate two buses a week, on Wednesday and Friday at 7am (Tsh10,000). There are no direct buses to Mwanza: change in Biharamulo or, much better, catch the ferry.

Airlines operating from Bukoba are Eagle Air, whose office is at the corner of Market Street and Jamhuri Road, and Precisionair, on Karume Street nearby. Eagle Air have eleven flights weekly to Mwanza, two of which carry on to Tabora. Precisionair have ten flights weekly to Mwanza, two or three of which continue to Arusha, Dar es Salaam, Shinyanga or Zanzibar.

Tanzania's only overland crossing into Uganda is at **Mutukala**, 80km northwest of Bukoba. Several uncomfortably packed daladalas and pick-ups run hourly from Bukoba to the border. The road isn't in too good a shape, so the ride can take up to four hours. **Immigration** can be awkward if the official decides to be, well, officious, so ideally get a visa beforehand in Dar. There are money-changers at the border: the rate should be around 2000 Ugandan shillings to Tsh1000. There's plenty of onward transport in Uganda to Masaka and Kampala. There are no ferries to Uganda.

Spice Beach hotel On the beach 2km south of the centre. Excellent restaurant (see opposite) in a superb location; the bar is open until midnight.

Listings

Banks and exchange NBC, at the corner of Barongo St and Jamhuri Rd, is helpful, efficient and doesn't always require travellers' cheque receipts. There's also a CRDB on Kashozi Rd.
Bookshop The ELCT Bookshop at the corner of Mosque St and Market St has some interesting books about the local Haya tribe, as well as beads, necklaces, basketry and carvings for sale.
Car repairs The best place is the ELCT Garage along Mosque St.

Hospital Hospitali ya Mkoa, Uganda Rd, is reasonably well equipped. Alternatively, try Kashozi Hospital along Kashozi Rd.
Library Barongo St (Mon–Fri 9am–6pm, Sat 9am–2pm; Tsh500 daily membership).
Post office Corner of Mosque St and Barongo St.
Telephones TTCL is on Uganda Rd near the bus station. There are cardphones outside *Dolla's Café* on Kashozi Rd.

Biharamulo

The small town of **BIHARAMULO** is a handy overnight stop, especially if you're heading west into Rwanda or east to the fishing village of Nyamirembe, where you can arrange a local boat to take you to Rubondo Island (see p.507). Set on a high ridge, Biharamulo itself is a small, lively and very friendly little town, and has some good basic hotels, and one or two restaurants. Sadly, the three **game reserves** immediately north of Biharamulo – Kimisi, Burigi and Biharamulo – have had their wildlife populations and forests decimated over the last three decades, first during the Kagera War with Idi Amin's Uganda, and then as a result of the conflicts in Burundi and Rwanda; the presence of refugee camps on both sides of the border has placed a destructive burden on bush meat and firewood. All three reserves are effectively out of bounds at present, while locals live in fear of attack by armed rebels and bandits from both countries; as a result, road travellers are accompanied by armed escorts along several stretches.

There are a couple of things to see. The **market** is halfway up the hill – the easiest way to find it is to head up the main road to the bank, turn left along Makongoro Road just before it, and then turn left between Rugaga and Songoro (Kenyatta) Street. At the top of the hill, close to the police station, is the **German Boma**, about 1km from the bus stand. This has been extensively restored and is apparently inhabited by a lone *mzungu* working for an NGO. Visits should be possible if you can track him down.

Practicalities

The **bus stand** is in the clearing at the bottom of town; bus company ticket offices are scattered around its edges. There are daily buses from Bukoba and Mwanza. Neither journey should take more than a day, but the roads get muddy and slippery in parts during the rains, especially if they haven't recently been graded, so expect delays. Some buses coming from Mwanza continue on to Kigoma – days and time change frequently, but are approximately once every day or two in the dry season only: Lake Transport is the most reliable company on this route. If you have time and don't mind roughing it a bit, you can also get to Mwanza from Nyamirembe (see p.507), 43km east of Biharamulo, which is the terminus for the island-hopping *MV Serengeti* **ferry**.

If you're **driving north**, pick up an armed guard at the junction for Mwanza a few kilometres outside town, who will accompany you as far as Muleba, 108km to the north. **Heading south**, there's a good unsurfaced road as far as Lusahunga (31km) at the junction of the tarmac road into Rwanda (the Burundi border is only open to locals and aid workers). Armed escorts join you here for the Rwanda border. Heading south towards Kigoma, you'll have to pick up an armed escort at **Nyakanazi**, at the junction with the tarmac road that goes most of the way to Shinyanga. Although the armed escorts are officially free, the guards usually expect payment, anything from Tsh2000 to Tsh10,000. Incidentally, it's not obligatory to take an escort, but skimping on this would be extremely foolish: the border region is volatile, and incidents do happen.

There are three main **hotels**. Hot water is provided on request in buckets; the water is extremely silty, so don't drink it. The best place is *Robert Hotel*, facing the bus stand on the main road into town (❷), which has en-suite rooms with big double beds, nets, Western-style bathrooms and a generator (Biharamulo has no regular electricity supply). The two other options, both very cheap and with shared bathrooms and kerosene lamps, are *Sunset Inn* next door (**❶**), and the friendly and clean *Victoria Guest House* (**❶**) on Ndara Road off Mwinyi Street, two blocks uphill from the bus stand (and not to be confused with the other *Victoria* at the bus stand itself, also known as *Nusura Hotel*).

Both *Sunset Inn* and *Robert Hotel* are good for **food**, the latter with a jungly garden where you can chow down on outstandingly good roast goat meat. Meals at either place cost no more than Tsh1500, and both also do breakfast – try the *supu* broth. Street food is limited to roast maize cobs, which are sold at the bus station until around 10pm. The best **bar** is at *Robert Hotel*. The National Microfinance Bank, at the top of the town 800m from the bus stand, changes **money**. There are **telephones** at TTCL by the post office: turn left along Makongoro Road just before reaching the bank.

Nyamirembe

If the journey by road from Biharamulo to Mwanza turns you off (and it may well be impassable in the rains, in any case), an alternative approach is via the fishing village of **NYAMIREMBE**, 43km east of Biharamulo, which is the last port of call for the *MV Serengeti* ferry from Mwanza. The ferry's schedule changes with annoying frequency: for what it's worth, at the time of writing it arrived in Nyamirembe on Thursday evening, and turned back the next morning (officially at 8am), docking at Nkome, Kanyara and three ports on Kome Island – Ntima, Lugata and Mchangani – before arriving in Mwanza that night. The journey takes ten to twelve hours and costs Tsh3300 (third class only), plus $5 port tax when leaving Mwanza.

You'll have to spend the night at Nyamirembe to catch the ferry, however, as daladalas from Biharamulo don't coincide with the boat (they leave at 11am, 12.30pm and 4pm; 90min). **Accommodation** at Nyamirembe is limited to the basic *Maendeleo Guest House* (**❶**), 1km from the shore and the ferry jetty at the junction with the minor road to Maganza. The shore is a nice place to while away the time, with lots of birds (look for marabou storks, egrets and jacanas), although the water's edge is a bit reedy, so bilharzia may be present. The last building on your left before the lake contains a small **dairy** which makes delicious cheese (Tsh2500 a kilo).

Rubondo Island National Park

Nestled snugly into the lake's southwestern corner, **RUBONDO ISLAND NATIONAL PARK** is one of Tanzania's least-visited and best-preserved wildlife areas. The park covers 457 square kilometres, of which little more than half is land, and includes eleven minor islets in addition to Rubondo Island itself. Most of the main island is scattered with the granite outcrops so characteristic of the Lake Victoria region and covered by moist evergreen forest (great for spotting butterflies). The rest is grassland, open *miombo* woodland, sandy beaches and papyrus swamps. The variety of habitats favours high species diversity in both plants and animals, something that is especially evident in **birdlife** – close to four hundred species have been recorded so far. Among the more easily identifiable species are hammerkops, cormorants, Goliath herons, saddle-billed storks, egrets and sacred ibises, kingfishers, geese, darters, bee-eaters, flycatchers, parrots, cuckoos, sunbirds and birds of prey, including martial eagles and the world's highest density of African fish eagles. A particular highlight is an unnamed islet to the east of Rubondo Island, which serves as a breeding ground for tens of thousands of birds.

In addition to the park's birdlife, a number of endangered animal species have been introduced, since the island's isolation from the mainland makes it inherently safer from the predations of poachers. While attempts to introduce black rhinos and roan antelopes haven't – at least yet – met with much success, the introduced populations of elephants, chimpanzees, black-and-white colobus monkeys, suni antelopes and African grey parrots are flourishing and – with the exception of the elephants – can be seen with relative ease. The forest-dwelling **chimpanzees** descend from a population of seventeen individuals who were introduced in the late 1960s, having been rescued from smugglers. Most had been kept in cramped cages, some for as long as nine years. It speaks for the adaptability of chimps (like humans) that these ragged survivors apparently had few problems in establishing themselves on Rubondo, and their population now numbers around 35. The chimps are habituated – meaning that they're used to humans – and so can be visited (but see the box on chimp etiquette on p.535).

Of the native species, the undoubted stars (together with the birds) are the amphibious **sitatunga antelopes**, an unusual species with splayed and elongated hooves, though unless you catch a glimpse of one straying into the forest, you probably won't see them in all their glory, as they spend much of their lives partly submerged in the marshes and reedbeds along the shore. Other frequently seen native mammals include vervet monkeys, bushbucks, large numbers of hippos and crocodiles and a number of small predators including genets, spotted-neck otters and marsh mongooses. There are no large predators.

The **best time to visit** depends on how important clear skies are to you: the best weather is in the dry season from June to the end of October, but butterflies and flowers – most spectacularly forest orchids, fireball lilies and red coral trees – are at their showiest in the rains (Nov–March), at which time migratory birds also arrive at the island.

Arrival

Access to Rubondo is either awkward and hit-and-miss, or easy and expensive. The latter means **flying** to the island by light aircraft, which is how most of Rubondo's visitors come (most are guests of the upmarket *Rubondo Island Camp*). If you're not staying at the camp, things get trickier. **Scheduled flights** (likely to change) are currently operated by Northern Air Charter from Arusha via Manyara, Serengeti and Mwanza (Tues & Sat), and by Coastal Travels, who follow a similar route (Tues & Fri). See "Air charters" on p.390 for details of both companies; the fare from Mwanza to Rubondo is around $70 one way. Alternatively, enquire in Mwanza about **charter flights**, which start at around $550 for a five-seater plane.

The awkward way – actually the easiest of several awkward ways – is to catch the weekly *MV Serengeti* from Mwanza to **Nkome**, the last port before Nyamirembe (see p.507), and from there take a boat run by the park authorities to Rubondo (you could also catch the ferry in Nyamirembe in the opposite direction). The ferry schedule changes with annoying frequency (not that it ever leaves on time), so double-check everything in Mwanza beforehand. At the time of writing, it sailed from Mwanza at 11am on Wednesday, arriving sometime on Thursday morning, then returning from Nkome in the early afternoon on Friday. The journey takes ten to twelve hours and costs Tsh3300 (third class only) plus $5 port tax when leaving Mwanza. There's no fixed price for the boat ride from Nkome to Rubondo, but it shouldn't be over $50 one way. Alternatively, if you arrange things in advance with TANAPA in Arusha (see p.394), the park staff could pick you up by boat from **Maganza**, about 25km north of Nyamirembe – all three daily daladalas to Nyamirembe continue there. Lastly, you could charter a boat in Mwanza; prices start from around $200.

Practicalities

Visitors are dropped off at the **park headquarters** in Kageya, halfway up the island. **Entry fees**, paid here, are $15 a day. You have three choices for **accommodation**: a campsite, simple park-run accommodation in *bandas* and a luxury tented camp. The campsite ($20 per person) is close to the park headquarters, and offers unnervingly close contact with grazing hippos at night (never position yourself between them and water, which panics them and usually prompts an attack). The park-run accommodation ($20–30 per person) is in *bandas*; there are only six beds so you're advised to book ahead at the TANAPA headquarters in Arusha (see p.394). Bring enough food and drink for the duration whether you're camping or staying in the *bandas*. The upmarket option is *Rubondo Island Camp*, overlooking the lake (reservations via Flycatcher Safaris in Arusha, p.397; full-board ❾), which has ten large, twin-bed tents under thatched roofs between forest and shore, each with attached bathroom, electricity and lake views from a terrace. There's a bar and swimming pool, and bathing in the lake is also possible.

There are no vehicles, so **getting around** the park is either on foot or by boat. **Guides** are obligatory ($10–20 per walk per group). There are several walking trails from the park headquarters, including forest and crocodile and sitatunga habitats. **Boats** for excursions (no more than $50 for half a day) can be hired at *Rubondo Island Camp* or the park headquarters.

South of Lake Victoria

Situated in the plains between Tabora and Mwanza south of Lake Victoria are the towns of **Nzega** and **Shinyanga**. Neither is worth visiting in its own right, but if you're coming by road from the south or the east, or from the west along the tarmac from Nyakanazi close to the Burundi border, an overnight stop at one of these towns is pretty much inevitable.

Shinyanga

The land south of Mwanza, scattered with weirdly eroded boulders, is fertile and well watered, with pastures grazed by the long-horn Ankole cattle of Sukuma herders, along with a mixture of subsistence farms and large commercial plantations; the main crops are cotton and rice, the latter grown in extensive paddies. Some 160km south of Mwanza is **SHINYANGA**. Sadly, you'll be

Witchcraft: fear and loathing in Shinyanga

Greed and a traditional fear of witchcraft among the dominant Sukuma tribe are a deadly combination: fifty witchcraft-related murders were reported in Shinyanga region in 1998 alone. The victims are usually elderly widows or spinsters, singled out on account of their red eyes – caused by years of huddling over smoky fires. Sadly, the traditional fear of witchcraft is not the only motive behind the killing of old women. Pressure on land means that there is also a financial motive, whilst the presence of diamonds in the region offers another reason: human sacrifice is believed by some to bring good fortune, whilst others are tempted to hasten an elderly relative's demise in order to begin prospecting on their land. The police are at a loss as to how to deal with the problem. At best, they can only arrest suspected witches and lock them up, away from the reach of mob justice.

hard pressed to find a duller place in Tanzania: there's no sense of community, nothing to see and little to do, virtually zero nightlife, and a severe shortage of eating places and bars. The things that Shinyanga does have in plenty are modern churches, abandoned factories, corrupt traffic police and dodgy Lebanese diamond dealers trading in stones mined at Mwadui, 35km north of town (site of the huge, open-cast Williamson Diamond Mine, operated by De Beers, which turned up a 241-carat diamond in 1956). According to the Tanzanian press, at least, Shinyanga also has more than its fair proportion of **witches** – see box above.

Practicalities

Most visitors are connected to the diamond trade, and so fly in. The **airstrip** is north of town. Precisionair, whose office is in the CCM NPF Building near the market next to CRDB bank, has six flights a week from Mwanza and Dar, and three weekly from Kilimanjaro and Nairobi. Eagle Air, which has offices on the main road near the market, and facing the CCM NPF Building, has twice-weekly flights from Dar, which head back via Mwanza. The **bus stand** is also north of town. There are daily services from Mwanza, Musoma and Nzega, and buses running to Mwanza from Arusha or Kigoma also pass through. In the dry season, the exceedingly battered West Star bus runs once a week to and from Moshi. If you're heading to Mwanza or Tabora, it's much more comfortable to catch the **train**, which passes through four times a week. The train station is at the south end of town – follow the tracks.

The town's best **hotel** is the *Shinyanga Motel* (☏028/276 2369, ☏028/276 2518; ③–④), facing the railway station beside the post office, a modern three-storey affair with large en-suite rooms, all with big nets, TV, fan, telephone and private balcony; an extra Tsh5000 gets you air-conditioning, but forget the laughably overpriced suites (⑤). The *Ashiyana Hotel* (☏026/276 3996; ①), 200m south of *Shinyanga Motel* facing the rail tracks, is cheap, friendly and very tatty. The rooms, all twin-bed, are OK for the price and have nets and fans. If you're desperate there's also the *Butiama Hotel* (☏028/276 2479; ①–②), at the south end of town behind the *Shinyanga Motel*, though it's run-down and decrepit, service comes with a scowl, the guard dogs get vocal at night . . . the list goes on.

The town's top place for **food** is the unfortunately named *Shitta Café*, a great little family-run place on a street corner one block from the CCM NPF Building (ask for the Shitta Hair Salon, which is next door). They do great breakfasts (superb roast liver, chapati and spiced tea), plus more predictable chicken-and-chips-style fare for lunch and dinner. If you order in advance, you can ask for pretty much anything. The *Butiama Hotel* has more expensive food (Tsh3000 and up), but the bar's good, and they have discos at weekends and occasional live acts like rappers. *Ashiyana Hotel* has a rooftop bar that also does food, and there are more bars in the Ngokolo area, 3km north of town. The best place for **changing money** is the National Microfinance Bank near the market, though you may have to queue for ages; CRDB is as hopeless as ever, and NBC – on the road by the railway – cheats shamelessly on commission.

Nzega

There's little reason to dally in the poor, dusty and fly-ridden town of **NZEGA**, 79km south of Shinyanga, though you may have to spend a night here if you're travelling by bus. Nzega occupies a major crossing on the roads between Singida, Arusha, Shinyanga, Mwanza, Biharamulo, Kigoma, Bukoba and Tabora, meaning that there's daily transport in most directions, at least in the dry season. In the rains, the road to Tabora becomes impassable, and the others can get tricky, though you'd be unlucky to be delayed for too long unless a bridge is washed out.

Coming from Singida, the dirt road is extremely dull, passing through a dusty and scrubby plain on the edge of the Central Plateau. The only place of note is where the road winds down the short but steep **Sekenke Hill**. The hill is notorious for accidents, as testified by the wrecks of vehicles that tumbled off the road into the numerous *korongos* (gullies) on either side. At the bottom of the hill, trucks queue up with their engines off to cool down before the laborious crawl to the top. Sekenke is also famous for its **gold**, known since at least colonial times (the Germans used Sekenke gold to mint the Tabora sovereign, prized among coin collectors). The mines closed in the 1940s, but were reopened in 1998 under the name Golden Pride, becoming Tanzania's first large-scale gold mine.

Practicalities

The **bus stand** is in the centre of town, about 1km south of the Shinyanga–Singida road. Most buses leave early (no later than 6am), though you may find a seat on a later bus coming from somewhere else. There are daily buses to Mwanza via Shinyanga, to Dar via Singida and Dodoma in the dry season, and on most days to Arusha via Singida. If you're driving to Singida, you'll need to pick up an armed guard at the roadblock outside town (free in theory, though a tip is expected in practice). For Tabora (dry season only), NBS Coach services leave daily at 7am and 8am, and there are also some extremely packed pick-ups later on. Some buses between Mwanza and Kigoma also pass through Nzega. For the brave, an exhausting and deeply uncomfortable possibility is Sabena Bus's twice-weekly ride to Mbeya in southern Tanzania, which starts at Mwanza and passes through Nzega on Wednesday and Saturday – the journey takes at least 24 hours.

There's plenty of cheap **accommodation**, the best on the Singida road 1km northeast of the bus stand: from the stand, turn left at the big sign for "Toilet Services", then right at the end after the bank. The *Nzega Motel*, opposite the Oryx petrol station (T026/269 2534; ●), has good rooms with shared bathrooms and some en-suite singles, all with mosquito nets. There's also a cool restaurant (nothing over Tsh1500), a bar and cardphone. Fifty metres from here is *Fourways Executive Hotel* (℡026/269 2577; ❶), a down-at-heel place with a deserted bar and restaurant. The en-suite rooms are good value if you choose carefully (check sheets and nets). Nzega has water problems, so shower while the going's good.

The National Microfinance Bank, northeast of town just off the Singida–Shinyanga road, can **change money**. The **post office** and TTCL **telephone office** are a short distance northwest at the roundabout between the roads to Singida, Shinyanga and Tabora.

Travel details

Bus, daladala and pick-up

The following journey times are absolute minimums; breakdowns, washed-out roads and bridges and prolonged stops play havoc with timetables. Routes that are especially prone to long delays and cancellations during the rainy seasons are marked with asterisks.

Biharamulo to: Bukoba (2–3 daily*; 4–6hr); Dar (4–6 weekly*; 30–35hr); Kigoma (3–4 weekly*; 13hr); Maganza (3 daily; 4hr); Mwanza (2–3 daily*; 11–12hr); Nyamirembe (3 daily; 1hr 30min); Nzega (4–6 weekly*; 7hr); Singida (4 weekly*; 14hr).

Bukoba to: Arusha via Uganda and Kenya (2 weekly*; 26–30hr); Biharamulo (2–3 daily*; 4–6hr); Dar via Tanzania (4–6 weekly*; 40–50hr); Dar via Uganda and Kenya (2 weekly; 34–40hr); Nzega (4 weekly*; 11–13hr); Singida (4 weekly*; 18–20hr); Uganda border (hourly; 3–4hr).

Musoma to: Arusha via Kenya (2 daily; 15–20hr); Butiama (every 2hr; 1hr 30min); Mwanza (hourly; 3–4hr); Shinyanga (daily; 10–11hr); Sirare (hourly; 2hr); Tarime (hourly; 2hr).

Mwanza to: Arusha via Kenya (3–4 daily; 18–24hr); Arusha via Tanzania (4 weekly*; 24–35hr); Biharamulo (3–4 daily*; 10–12hr); Bunda (hourly; 2hr); Dar via Kenya (3–4 daily; 27–34hr); Dar via Tanzania (daily*; 34–45hr); Dodoma (1 daily*; 22–25hr); Geita (4–5 daily; 4hr); Kigoma (5 weekly*; 14–18hr); Mbeya (2 weekly*; 2 days, overnight in Tabora); Mombasa (1 daily; 20–22hr); Morogoro (4–5 daily*; 22–27hr); Moshi via Kenya (2–3 daily; 20–26hr); Moshi via Tanzania (4 weekly*; 26–37hr); Musoma (hourly; 3–4hr); Nairobi (3–4 daily; 12–15hr); Ngara (1–2 daily*; 12–14hr); Nzega (3–4 daily; 10–12hr); Shinyanga (5 daily; 5hr); Singida (2 daily*; 20–22hr); Sirare (hourly; 5–6hr); Tabora (2 weekly*; 13–15hr); Tanga via Kenya (1 daily; 25–30hr).

Nzega to: Arusha (1 daily*; 15–17hr); Dar (2–3 daily*; 24–35hr); Dodoma (2–3 daily*; 12–17hr); Kigoma (3–4 weekly*; 20hr); Mbeya (2 weekly*; 2 days); Mwanza (3–4 daily; 10–12hr); Shinyanga (every 2hr; 2–3hr); Tabora (4 weekly* and daily pick-ups; 3hr).

Plane

Airline abbreviations used below are: ATC (Air Tanzania), CT (Coastal Travels), EA (Eagle Air), NA (Northern Air Charter), and PA (Precisionair). Where more than one company covers a route, the one with more flights is mentioned first. The domestic departure tax ($6) is not always included in the ticket price.

Bukoba to: Arusha (PA: 4 weekly; 2hr); Dar (PA: 3 weekly; 5hr); Mwanza (PA, EA: 3 daily; 45min); Shinyanga (PA: 2 weekly; 1hr 30min); Tabora (EA: 2 weekly; 2hr 25min); Zanzibar (PA: 3 weekly; 6hr).

Musoma to: Dar (EA: 2 weekly; 4hr 10min); Kilimanjaro (EA: 2 weekly; 2hr 30min); Mwanza (EA: 2 weekly; 20min).

Mwanza to: Arusha (PA: 3 weekly; 1hr–1hr 30min); Bukoba (PA, EA: 3 daily; 45min); Dar (ATC, PA, EA: 2 daily; 2hr 30min–3hr 30min); Dodoma (EA: 2 weekly; 90min); Kilimanjaro (ATC, EA: 1 daily; 70min–2hr); Nairobi (ATC: 3 weekly; 1hr 30min); Rubondo Island (CT, NA: 2–4 weekly; 40min); Shinyanga (PA/ATC: 2 weekly; 30min); Tabora (EA: 2 weekly; 70min); Zanzibar (PA: 2 weekly; 3hr).

Rubondo Island to: Arusha (CT, NA: 2–4 weekly; 4hr); Geita (CT, NA: 2–4 weekly; 30min); Mwanza (CT, NA: 2–4 weekly; 40min); Serengeti (CT, NA: 2–4 weekly; 2hr 40min).

Shinyanga to: Arusha (PA: 1 weekly; 1hr); Bukoba (PA: 3 weekly; 1hr 30min); Dar (PA/ATC, EA: 6 weekly; 3hr–3hr 30min); Kilimanjaro (PA: 1 weekly; 1hr 30min); Mwanza (PA, EA: 6 weekly; 30min).

Train

Mwanza to: Dar (4 weekly; 35–36hr); Dodoma (4 weekly; 24hr); Morogoro (4 weekly; 18hr); Mwanza (4 weekly; 4–5hr); Tabora (4 weekly; 10hr).
Shinyanga to: (4 weekly; 31–32hr); Dodoma (4 weekly; 20hr); Morogoro (4 weekly; 14hr); Mwanza (4 weekly; 4–5hr); Tabora (4 weekly; 6hr).

Ferry

Ferries between Mwanza and Bukoba (*MV Victoria*) and Mwanza and Nyamirembe (*MV Serengeto*) suffer from frequent delays and timetable changes; the times given below are the minimum any journey will take.
Bukoba to: Mwanza (3 weekly; 11hr).
Mwanza to: Bukoba (3 weekly; 11hr); Nkoma (1 weekly; 10hr); Nyamirembe (1 weekly; 12hr); Ukerewe Island (3 daily; 2hr 30min–3hr 30min).
Nkoma to: Mwanza (1 weekly; 10hr).
Nyamirembe to: Mwanza (1 weekly; 12hr).
Ukerewe (Nansio) to: Mwanza (3 daily; 2hr 30min–3hr 30min).

LAKE VICTORIA AND NORTHWESTERN TANZANIA | Travel details

9

Lake Tanganyika
and western Tanzania

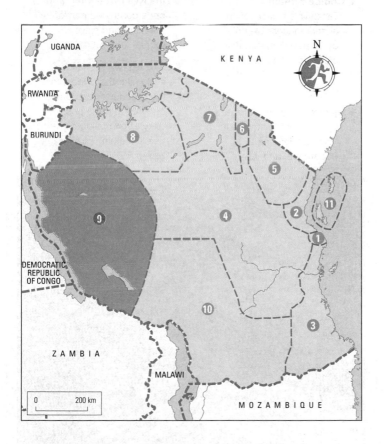

CHAPTER 9

Highlights

✳ **MV Liemba** Lake Tanganyika, the world's second deepest, is best savoured from the venerable *MV Liemba*, an old German troopship. **See p.523**

✳ **Gombe Stream** Tanzania's tiniest national park, accessible only by boat, Gombe's chimpanzees have been studied since 1961. **See p.529**

✳ **Ujiji** Now a fishing village, Ujiji was at the start of a 1200km slave route to Bagamoyo, and where Stanley gave the world those immortal words, "Dr Livingstone, I presume?" **See p.528**

✳ **Tabora** The only big town on the Central Plateau, and the historical seat of the Nyamwezi tribe, who once controlled part of the ivory and slave routes. **See p.541**

✳ **Lake Rukwa** A shallow soda lake that's ideal for wild scenery, traditional cultures and the possibility of glimpsing oddities like albino giraffe. **See p.557**

Lake Tanganyika
and western Tanzania

Westtern **Tanzania** is as fascinating and rewarding to explore as it can be frustrating to get around, especially during the rains, when most roads become impassable. The region is dominated by **Lake Tanganyika**, which separates the semi-arid *miombo* woodland of Tanzania's Central Plateau from the lush forests of Central Africa. The lake also marks the border with Burundi, Congo and Zambia, and as such is a veritable crossroads of cultures. This mixture is best seen in the region's largest town, **Kigoma**, on the northeast shore of the lake, though for tourists, Kigoma's main attraction is its proximity to **Ujiji**, the former slave-trading centre where Stanley met Livingstone and uttered those famous words, "Dr Livingstone, I presume?". Kigoma is also the starting point for ferry connections to Zambia and Burundi, and the most convenient base for visiting **Gombe** and **Mahale national parks**, both of which contain large populations of chimpanzees.

Heading away from the lake to the east, the railway follows the line of the old caravan routes across the Central Plateau almost exactly, bringing you to the large and bustling town of **Tabora**. Occupying the historically strategic junction of the trade routes from Lake Tanganyika and Lake Victoria, Tabora controlled much of the slave trade in the latter half of the nineteenth century, though like Kigoma it owes its modern importance to the railway. The region to the **south of Kigoma and Tabora** is seldom visited, mainly because of the difficulty of getting around, although a branch line of the Central Railway Line runs to Mpanda, just beyond which is **Katavi National Park**, a small version of Selous Game Reserve, dominated by tsetse fly-infested *miombo* woodland and rich in wildlife. Further south, **Lake Rukwa** and the **Mbizi Mountains** are completely off-the-beaten track destinations for adventurous travellers, both reached from the area's only significant town, **Sumbawanga**.

Getting around

Travel in western Tanzania is for the most part a wild and adventurous affair. Language is limited to Kiswahili and local tongues, though if you really get stuck some bus drivers and hotel managers can usually muster a few words in English. **Road conditions** throughout the region are dreadful. In the **dry season** you can get through to anywhere if you don't mind a dusty and very bumpy ride; during the **short rains** (Oct–Dec) you can still get to most places

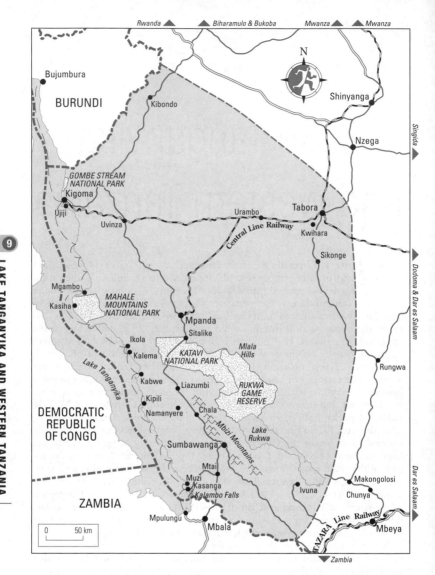

Bujumbura

BURUNDI

Kibondo

Shinyanga

Nzega

GOMBE STREAM
NATIONAL PARK
Kigoma

Ujiji

Uvinza

Urambo

Tabora

Central Line Railway

Kwihara

Sikonge

Singida

Mgambo

MAHALE
MOUNTAINS
NATIONAL PARK

Kasiha

Mpanda

Sitalike

Ikola

Kalema

KATAVI
NATIONAL PARK

Mlala
Hills

Lake Tanganyika

Kabwe

Liazumbi

RUKWA
GAME
RESERVE

Rungwa

Dodoma & Dar es Salaam

Kipili

Namanyere

Chala

DEMOCRATIC
REPUBLIC
OF CONGO

Sumbawanga

Mbizi Mountains

Lake
Rukwa

Mtai

Muzi

Kasanga

Kalambo Falls

Ivuna

Makongolosi

Chunya

Dar es Salaam

ZAMBIA

Mpulungu

Mbala

TAZARA Line Railway

Mbeya

0   50 km

9

but may be delayed waiting for the road to dry out; in the **long rains** (March–May), however, you can forget about roads, as most routes are closed for weeks on end. The only half-decent stretches are between Tabora and Mwanza, and south from Mpanda to Sumbawanga, but even these are likely to become impassable if not properly maintained. Wherever you're driving, always seek local advice about the state of the road before heading off, as well as security: there's a slight but ever-present risk of attack from armed bandits masquerading as refugees, especially around Kigoma and northwards, making the road from Kigoma to Biharamulo (see p.506) Tanzania's most dangerous. If things are considered risky, you'll invariably be offered armed escorts at road-blocks when leaving towns.

Security concerns also mean that **buses** are forbidden to travel between 10pm and 4am, so long-distance services have to spend the night somewhere. Most passengers sleep on the bus, though as a tourist you'll have to keep an extra close eye on your bags. Less fraying on the nerves would be to break your journey for a day or two at the overnight stop, which for east–west travellers is usually Singida (see p.265) – a lovely destination in its own right. Luckily, the **Central Line Railway**, which connects Dar es Salaam with Tabora, Mpanda, Uvinza and Kigoma, runs throughout the year and is one of Africa's classic journeys.

Lake Tanganyika

Occupying the southern end of the Western Rift Valley, and bordered by Tanzania, Burundi, Congo and Zambia, **LAKE TANGANYIKA** attracts a string of superlatives. Measuring 677km from north to south, it is the **world's longest freshwater lake**, fed by the Malagarasi and Kalambo rivers on the Tanzanian side, and by the turbulent Ruzizi River, which drains Lake Kivu and defines the border between Rwanda, Burundi and Congo. The lake's maximum recorded depth of 1436m (the lake bottom at its deepest lies 358m below sea level) also makes Tanganyika the **world's second deepest lake** after Siberia's Lake Baikal (though the lake's life forms live only in the top two hundred metres, as there is little or no oxygen further down). Covering some 32,900 square kilometres, Lake Tanganyika is also **Africa's second largest permanent lake** (Lake Victoria is the biggest) and, last but not least, is also one of the world's **oldest lakes**, having been formed around twenty million years ago during the tectonic upheavals that created the East African Rift Valley. Its great age, size, freshness, ecological isolation and geological and climatological stability have fostered the evolution of a remarkably diverse local flora and fauna. Animals include various species of crabs, molluscs and crustaceans, the usual hippos and crocodiles, and over 250 fish, including more than 200 **cich-lids**, small and often brightly coloured (yellow, blue and green predominate) creatures, most of which are unique to the lake.

The main settlement on the Tanzanian shore is the lively harbour town of **Kigoma**, at the end of the Central Railway Line from Dar es Salaam, which has weekly ferries north into Burundi and south to Zambia via a string of little Tanzanian fishing villages, some of which have road access inland towards Mpanda and Sumbawanga (for details, see p.526). Ten kilometres south of Kigoma is the old Arab slave-trading town of **Ujiji**, the place where the immortal words "Dr Livingstone, I presume?" were uttered by Henry Morton Stanley. Accessible by boat from either Kigoma or Ujiji are the **Gombe Stream National Park** and the **Mahale Mountains National Park**, both of which are famous for their chimpanzees, a few troops of which can be visited.

The MV Liemba

A much-loved feature of Lake Tanganyika is the **MV Liemba**, which has been ferrying passengers and cargo up and down the lake once a week for much of the last eighty years. Originally christened the *Graf von Götzen* (after a former governor of German East Africia), the 1300-tonne steamship was constructed in Germany in 1913 and then transported by train from Dar es Salaam to Kigoma in the early stages of World War I, where she was reassembled for use as an armed troop transport. In June 1916 the ship was bombed by Belgian aircraft but escaped with light damage. However, when the British took control of the Central Line Railway the following month, the Germans scuttled the ship at the mouth of the Malagarasi River south of Kigoma rather than have her fall into enemy hands. The *Graf von Götzen* remained submerged for eight years until, following an unsuccessful effort by the Belgians in 1921, the British finally salvaged the vessel in March 1924 and renamed her the *MV Liemba*, after the lake's original name.

Any journey on the *MV Liemba* is a memorable one: both for the gorgeous views of sunsets and the shore, and for a glimpse of the frenetic activity that erupts in the port villages along the way whenever the ferry arrives. Details of **sailing times**, fares and onward road transport are given in the "Moving on from Kigoma" box on p.526.

Kigoma

Tucked into the southeastern corner of Kigoma Bay at the end of the Central Railway line, the bustling harbour town of **KIGOMA** is Lake Tanganyika's busiest port and handles most of Burundi's foreign trade, as well as serving as the main arrival point for refugees fleeing Central Africa's interminable conflicts. Head out of town and you're bound to come across a UNHCR facility of some kind, whether a long-term refugee camp or a heavily guarded "reception centre". In town you'll hear plenty of French, the lingua franca of Burundi, Rwanda and Congo, and many business signs include French translations in addition to Kiswahili and English. The refugee presence also means that people are well used to seeing *wazungu*, the majority of whom work for one of the plethora of international aid organizations based here.

The town itself is very attractive, its lush tropical vegetation providing a welcome contrast to the monotonous *miombo* woodland which covers much of central Tanzania. For tourists, the town serves as the base for the **Gombe Stream** and **Mahale Mountains** national parks, and for day-trips to **Ujiji**, scene of Stanley's famous meeting with Livingstone. There's also a wide selection of accommodation and a few beautiful beaches if you want to escape the strength-sapping heat and humidity.

The road network south of town is virtually non-existent, but the historic steamship **MV Liemba** provides a weekly service southwards into Zambia, calling at a succession of minor ports on the Tanzanian side, some of which have road connections inland to Mpanda or Sumbawanga, from where there's more reliable transport to Mbeya and beyond – see the box on p.526 for full details.

Some history

Western Tanzania was a major source for the Arab slave trade in the nineteenth century. Slaves were captured as far west as the Congo Basin, from where they were transported across Lake Tanganyika to a number of transit centres on the Tanzanian shore, of which **Ujiji** was the most infamous. For much of this time,

Kigoma was a small fishing village, and it wasn't until towards the end of the nineteenth century that its importance grew, just as Ujiji's began to wane. The slave trade was at an end, and Germany controlled much of what is now Tanzania, Rwanda and Burundi. Kigoma's sheltered location inside Kigoma Bay gave it the edge over Ujiji, and the site was consequently developed into the regional headquarters. The town really took off in February 1914, when the 1254-kilometre **Central Railway** from Dar es Salaam finally reached the lake, nine years after construction had begun, establishing a reliable and rapid connection between the Indian Ocean and Lake Tanganyika which has ensured the town's livelihood to this day. The Germans, however, had little time to enjoy the fruits of their labour: World War I soon followed, and in 1916 they were ejected by troops from Belgian Congo.

The indigenous population of Kigoma (and Kasulu and Kibondo districts to the north) is the **Ha tribe**, who number nearly a million. They call their country Buha, which before the arrival of the Germans contained six independent chiefdoms organized into elaborate hierarchies of subchiefs and headmen similar to that of the Nyamwezi (see p.542). Oral traditions state that the Ha have always lived in Buha, so it's likely that their ancestors were among the first Bantu groups to arrive in eastern Africa from Central Africa, some two thousand years ago. Over the last three centuries the Ha have developed close ties with the **Tutsi** of Burundi. Through intermarriage and commerce, the two tribes have come to share a good part of their language, and the Ha in the grasslands south of Kigoma – where tsetse flies are not so much of a problem – have adopted the Tutsi cattle-herding culture. Although primarily still an agricultural people, their long-horn cattle play a vital social role as tokens of inter-family bonds and friendship, especially in marriage, when cattle are exchanged as bridewealth.

Arrival and information

The easiest way to reach Kigoma is by **train** from Dar es Salaam or Tabora. Trains pull in early in the morning; taxis wait outside the station. The **bus station** is 4km uphill at Mwanga near a big market; daladalas charge Tsh150 into the centre, and taxis cost Tsh1500. Kigoma **airport** is 5km east of town. Precisionair, in conjunction with Air Tanzania, have three weekly flights to Kigoma from Dar es Salaam (Tues, Thurs & Sun). A taxi to or from the airport costs Tsh3000. For getting around, **taxis** can be hired at the daladala stand in the town centre, next to the central market, and along Lumumba Street; alternatively, Mwani Taxi Services (8am–6/8pm; ☎028/280 3617) are located on Mwanga Road on the northeast side of the central market. Short journeys cost Tsh1000–1500.

Precisionair (☎028/280 4720), on Mlole Road facing the market, can provide limited information about boat charters to Gombe Stream or Mahale Mountains national parks. For more comprehensive information about the national parks, you'll have to visit the new **TANAPA information centre**, which should be up and running by the time this book is published, though unhelpfully it's at Kibirizi, 3km north of town just past a small oil terminal (Tsh1500 by taxi, Tsh150 by daladala from the central market). Another source of practical (and scientific) information, especially about Mahale Mountains, is the **Mahale Mountains Wildlife Research Centre** (PO Box 1053, ☎028/280 2072), 1.2km along Bangwe Road in the building opposite the TANESCO power station.

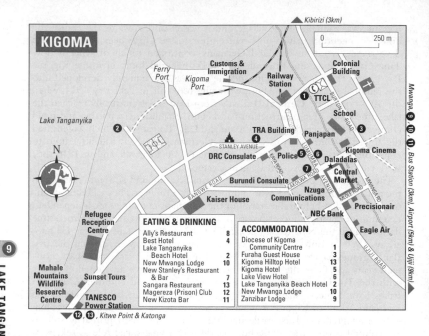

KIGOMA

Kibirizi (3km)

0 ——— 250 m

Ferry Port
Kigoma Port
Customs & Immigration
Railway Station
Colonial Building
TTCL
School
Panjapan
Kigoma Cinema
Lake Tanganyika
TRA Building
DRC Consulate
Police
Daladalas
Central Market
Burundi Consulate
Nzuga Communications
Kaiser House
NBC Bank
Precisionair
Refugee Reception Centre
Eagle Air
STANLEY AVENUE
BANGWE ROAD
KAKOLWA ROAD
LUMUMBA AVENUE
MIDDLE ROAD
MWANGA RD
UJIJI ROAD
BURTON ROAD
KAWE ROAD

Mahale Mountains Wildlife Research Centre
Sunset Tours
TANESCO Power Station

Mwanga, ❾, ❿, ⓫, Bus Station (3km), Airport (5km) & Ujiji (3km)

EATING & DRINKING
Ally's Restaurant	8
Best Hotel	4
Lake Tanganyika Beach Hotel	2
New Mwanga Lodge	10
New Stanley's Restaurant & Bar	7
Sangara Restaurant	13
Magereza (Prison) Club	12
New Kizota Bar	11

ACCOMMODATION
Diocese of Kigoma Community Centre	1
Furaha Guest House	3
Kigoma Hilltop Hotel	13
Kigoma Hotel	5
Lake View Hotel	6
Lake Tanganyika Beach Hotel	2
New Mwanga Lodge	10
Zanzibar Lodge	9

❶❷, ⓬, ⓭, Kitwe Point & Katonga

Accommodation

Kigoma's **town centre** guest houses are extremely basic and not terribly salubrious, and are only recommended if you're on a tight budget or want the convenience of staying near the railway station or port. More attractive options include a couple of good-value **lakeside** options to the southwest and a few places in **Mwanga**, occupying a ridge a few kilometres east of town along the road to Ujiji – this is far and away Kigoma's liveliest area, boasting an excellent market and several video lounges screening second-rate pirated films. Kigoma's cheaper hotels have water problems, so shower when you get the chance. The town also suffers regular power cuts, sometimes lasting over a day, but most hotels have back-up generators.

Diocese of Kigoma Community Centre Kiezya Rd, close to the railway station ☎ 028/280 2520. A friendly and quiet choice with 22 basic and very cheap rooms sharing bathrooms (with rather dingy showers and toilets, though they do have running water). Singles are like cells, doubles fare little better. The beds are droopy but have mosquito nets, and all rooms have a sink. ❶

Furaha Guest House Burton Rd ☎ 028/280 3665. A dirt-cheap place with eight rooms, some with private bathroom. The beds are a bit saggy, but have mosquito nets and fans, and are fine at the price. ❶

Kigoma Hilltop Hotel 4km west of town on a raised headland by the lakeshore; Tsh2000 by taxi ☎ 028/280 4435, ⊛ www.kigoma.com. The poshest place in Kigoma by miles, but the electric fence, armed guards and wildlife trophies gracing

the lobby hardly make for a happy first impression. There are thirty rooms in chalets strung out across the headland, giving spectacular views over the lake. All rooms have a/c, satellite TV, fridge and a balcony; more expensive ones have lounges. Facilities include two restaurants, swimming pool, sandy beach, tennis court and gym, and (at extra cost) jetskiing, waterskiing, parasailing, snorkelling and diving. The hotel also organizes day-trips around Kigoma and Ujiji, and safaris to Gombe and Mahale. Breakfast included. ❺–❼

Kigoma Hotel Lumumba Ave (no phone). This very run-down but cheap establishment covers all bases, with a noisy *makuti*-thatched bar at the front, a hot and unattractive restaurant at the back, and some large rooms off at the side, most of which lack nets. Bucket showers only. ❶

Lake Tanganyika Beach Hotel West of the ferry port off Stanley Ave; there's a signboard on Bangwe Rd ☎028/280 2694. An extremely tatty but thoroughly charming option, with a fantastic lakeshore location, though only a few rooms have lake views, and even these are through a wire mesh. All rooms have nets and private bathrooms (with, supposedly, 24hr hot water), while the lack of fans in some rooms shouldn't be a problem given the lake breezes. The hotel bar and restaurant are popular with *wazungu*, and the management can help hire local boats for Gombe or Mahale at much more reasonable rates than the *Kigoma Hilltop Hotel*. Breakfast included. ❸

Lake View Hotel Lumumba St (no phone). Closed for major renovations at the time of writing, this used to be the best of Kigoma's central budget hotels – clean, comfortable and with functional showers – and should reopen by mid-2002. There's no lake view, however.

New Mwanga Lodge On the main road in Mwanga ☎028/280 4643. A perfectly decent hotel with a good restaurant attached. All rooms have nets, standing fans and bathrooms boasting relatively clean raised squat loos and showers (which don't always work, however). ❶

Zanzibar Lodge On the main road in Mwanga ☎028/280 3306. Run by the same people as the *New Mwanga* (a fact given away by the same silver-painted pebbles in the plant pots), this is the best of Kigoma's budget places, with nice clean rooms (more expensive ones with private bathrooms), nets and standing fans, and some of the top-floor singles with shared bathrooms give glimpses of the lake. There's also a restaurant, but no alcohol is served. ❶–❷

The Town

Kigoma's most impressive building is the **railway station**, built by the Germans shortly after the Central Railway arrived in 1914; it boasts a colonnaded first-floor balustrade with horseshoe arches, though the whole effect is rendered a little queer by a brand new shiny corrugated metal roof. According to some sources, **Kaiser House**, 700m southwest along Bangwe Road, is connected to the station by a tunnel, which seems likely given that it was constructed just after the outset of World War I. It's now a government residence where the president stays when in town, and comes complete with painted red "carpet" up the staircase (no photography).

Heading along Lumumba Avenue from the station you'll pass the **central market** on your left before the road climbs up towards Mwanga. About 2km along on the right is the **Church Missionary Society graveyard**. It's not signposted: look for the CCM building on the right with the "Pride Tanzania" sign; the graveyard is behind it. This contains three notable nineteenth-century graves. The Reverend J. B. Thompson (died September 1878) and Reverend A. W. Dodgshun (died April 1879) were ministers from the London Missionary Society, under whose auspices Livingstone had worked in Africa – the two were on an expedition to establish a string of missions along Lake Tanganyika when they succumbed to illness. The third grave contains the remains of an eccentric French clergyman named Michel Alexandre de Baize (Abbé de Baize), who reached Ujiji in 1878 with two suits of armour, a portable organ and twenty-four umbrellas, before passing away there in December 1879. The London Missionary Society abandoned their stations in Ujiji and Kigoma in 1884 and the graveyard is now very neglected.

Carrying on up the hill to Mwanga brings you to **Mwanga Market**, 4km from town at the junction of the roads to Kasulu and Ujiji. Aside from normal produce (the pineapples are especially delicious), the market offers an eye-opening insight into the infamous corruption that afflicts many United Nations agencies. Military-style "Compact Food Rations", presumably diverted en route to Kigoma Region's refugee camps, are sold openly at stalls sheltered from the sun by plastic hessian sheeting stamped with the initials of the UNHCR, beside which you might find piles of rice and flour sacks bearing legends from a variety of aid agencies.

The lakeshore

Lake Tanganyika's surface water is a very pleasant 23°C, and according to locals **swimming** near Kigoma is safe so long as there's no reedy vegetation nearby (in which case there might be a risk of bilharzia). There are no reports of crocodiles in the area, either – presumably there are too many boats for their liking. For the sceptical, the *Kigoma Hilltop Hotel* charges Tsh2000 for the use of its pool. The *Lake Tanganyika Beach Hotel* (see p.523) is *the* place for a dip in the lake, or just to spend a blissfully lazy afternoon doing nothing more energetic than watching crows and distant dhows while sipping a beer. Entrance to the hotel and its beach is free so long as you buy some food or a drink.

There are two private beaches 7km south of town near Kitwe Point. The best is the small **Jacobsen's Beach** (Tsh2000), which has coarse red sand and a few parasols in a secluded cove, but no facilities. Just to the south, in a less sheltered location, and with pebbles instead of sand, **Zungu Beach** (Tsh500) has three parasols, a couple of shelters and some warm sodas and cans of Castle lager for sale, but no food. Tsetse flies can be a pain but don't carry sleeping sickness. To get to either beach, take a taxi (Tsh3000–4000) or catch a daladala to Katonga village from outside the TRA Building – these will leave you at the junction for the track leading to the shore (there's a green sign to Zungu Beach), a sweltering three-kilometre walk over the hills to either beach. The intermittent signposts aren't much help: for Zungu, turn left at the first fork after about 2km and bear right at the next junction; for Jacobsen's, just keep right at every fork. Incidentally, the Jane Goodall Institute's **animal orphanage** on Kitwe Point is now closed to the public (and no longer signposted), apparently because the chimps went bananas and took to chucking rocks at tourists. The institute's presence is marked instead by recent plantations of slow-growing hardwood saplings, part of the TACARE project aimed at reducing the currently unsustainable pressure on timber in protected areas such as Gombe (see Ⓦ www.janegoodall.org for more information).

KIBIRIZI, 3km north of town, is the best place to see how **dagaa** – the lake's main commercial catch – is dried. This diminutive fish, which measures between 2cm and 10cm, is related to the herring and may originally have entered the lake via the River Congo. *Dagaa* live in immense shoals near the surface, and are caught at night using pressure lamps mounted on wooden boats to attract the fish. At a given moment, the fishermen beat on the sides of the boat to panic the fish into tight shoals, which are then scooped up in nets. The flotilla leaves Kibirizi late in the afternoon in pairs, the lead boat towing the other to conserve fuel, and you can see their lights bobbing up and down from the coast at night; the season peaks in the second half of September. The fish are spread out the following morning to dry. A recent innovation is the use of suspended wire mesh for drying, which is cleaner and quicker than beach-drying and extends the shelf-life of the fish, attracting premiums in the market. To get to Kibirizi, follow the railway tracks or catch a daladala from the central market. A taxi costs Tsh2500–3000.

Eating and drinking

The local delicacies are **migebuka**, which looks like a thin mackerel and tastes similar, and of course **dagaa**, which is best roasted in palm oil (*mawese*, which gives it a nutty taste) and served with dark *ugali* made from cassava. **Street food**, especially fried cassava, roasted maize cobs and seasonal fruit, is best along Lumumba Street between the daladala stand and the train station. There are also plenty of dirt-cheap grilled meat and *chipsi mayai* places around the daladala stand, especially on Mwanga Road. Mwanga itself, a few kilometres uphill along the Ujiji road, is especially good in the evenings, with dozens of stands serving up fried *dagaa* and tasty *mishkaki* goat-meat skewers. There are lots of cheap *hotelis* facing the square in front of the railway station.

Ally's Restaurant Lumumba St. A friendly place in the town centre. Some of the pre-cooked snacks are a bit grim (especially the egg chops and "pizzas", which are actually greasy stuffed chapatis), but the aromatic cinnamon-laced tea is wonderful, and full meals (Tsh1000–2500), including birianis if ordered in advance, are good.

Lake Tanganyika Beach Hotel West of the ferry port off Stanley Ave; there's a signboard on Bangwe Rd. Offers a wide selection of Tanzanian, Chinese and Indian dishes as well as continental, costing Tsh2500–4000 for main courses. The service has been achingly slow for years, and doesn't look like changing, but who cares – the lake view shouldn't be rushed!

New Kizota Bar 100m on the right beyond Kasulu junction, Mwanga, 4km from town. This serves up Kigoma's best *nyama choma* and fried bananas

(*ndizi*), so arrive early if you want a table to yourself.

New Mwanga Lodge Mwanga (p.523). The *migebuka* fish here is usually good, as is their *dagaa*, and it's very cheap, costing under Tsh1000 for a meal. No alcohol.

New Stanley's Restaurant & Bar Kakolwa St. The ground-floor restaurant here is the most elegant-looking place in town, but the food is distinctly average, and the chicken just plain awful.

Sangara Restaurant at the *Kigoma Hilltop Hotel* (see p.522). Expensive continental and Indian style meals served up in an anodyne atmosphere, though this is more than compensated for by the superb views over the lake. There's also an ice-cream parlour. No alcohol, but they don't mind if you bring your own.

Bars and nightlife

Unsurprisingly, Congolese music reigns supreme, with long-established *Ndombolo* and *Mayemu* stars Koffi Olomide, Le General Detao *et al.* strutting their stuff from radios and tape players in the streets and in a number of bars which sometimes double as discos. **Home-grown bands** perform several times a week – as well as consulting the listings below, it's worth double-checking with locals before making plans, as venues and days change frequently.

Best Hotel Stanley Ave. If you're waiting for a train or ferry, this quiet place is handy but otherwise unexceptional, though there's a pleasant small garden at the back.

Lake Tanganyika Beach Hotel West of the ferry port off Stanley Ave; there's a signboard on Bangwe Rd. Idyllically located on the breezy lakeshore with seats under thatched parasols supported by iron rails stamped "1899", this is the best bar in town. It sometimes hosts live music on Sundays, including hip-hop (3–8pm; Tsh500), and has a popular disco on Saturday (10pm–3am; Tsh1500). On other days, the bar closes around 11pm.

Magereza (Prison) Club 2km along Bangwe Rd, just before the prison on the right. Another popular place on the beach – its weekend discos give the prisoners next door something to dance to.

New Kizota Bar 100m off the Ujiji road on the right, past Kasulu junction, Mwanga. One of Kigoma's liveliest bars, especially in the evenings, thanks to its outstandingly good *nyama choma*.

New Stanley's Restaurant & Bar Kakolwa St. The restaurant here serves drinks all day, but most people head to the raised disco behind for the "Bahama Disco Sound", sometimes featuring live bands, on Wednesday and Friday nights from 9pm, and on Sundays from 3pm.

Listings

Airlines Air Tanzania Corporation (ATC), TRA Building at the north end of Lumumba St ☎028/280 2508; Eagle Air, Lumumba St ☎028/280 4488; Precisionair, Mlole Rd, facing the central market ☎028/280 4720 (or ☎028/280 3166 at the airport).

Cinemas Kigoma Cinema, tottering on its last legs, is just north of the market.

Consulates Burundi, Kakolwa St ☎028/280 2499; Congo, corner of Bangwe Rd and Kaya Rd ☎028/280 2401.

By train

Trains to Dar via Tabora and Dodoma (change in Tabora for Mwanza or Mpanda) depart at 6pm on Tuesday, Thursday, Saturday and Sunday. The ticket office is open from 8am to noon and 2 to 6pm on these days, and until 4.30pm on others; see p.559 for journey times. **Flights** from Kigoma to Dar leave on Wednesday (via Tabora), Friday and Sunday. Eagle Air's schedule has been unreliable of late.

By road

The only practical **road** out of Kigoma is north, either to Bukoba via Biharamulo or to Mwanza via Shinyanga, both of which are tough rides in the dry season and can become impassable during the rains. The three main bus companies are all based in Mwanga: Adventure Bus (formerly Saratoga Line) and Zainab's Bus, who both have offices at the bus stand, and Lake Transport, who are based at *Mukatanga Guest House* along the Ujiji road. Book all tickets at least a day in advance, ideally earlier. The following schedules are liable to change and are intended only to show what's feasible.

Heading north, **Mwanza** is covered by a handful of buses weekly during reasonable weather: Zainab's Bus (via Biharamulo) on Tues and Fri (5am) and Sat (7.30am), Adventure Bus (via Biharamulo) on Tues (5am) and Lake Transport (via Shinyanga) on Fri (5am). Much of the journey is exceedingly uncomfortable, though a new 260km strip of tarmac to Shinyanga has reduced journey times to around fourteen hours in good conditions. In bad conditions, expect the trip to take upwards of 36hr, including an overnight at Nzega. There are no direct buses to **Bukoba**: catch one of the Mwanza buses run by Zainab's or Adventure Bus and get off in Biharamulo. Alternatively, catch one of the daily buses or pick-ups to **Kibondo**, 250km northeast of Kigoma, and change there (you might have to stay overnight though). Forget about getting to **Mpanda** by road unless you've got a 4WD in bone-dry weather, as there's no public transport and you may have to wait a week or more in Uvinza for a lift on a truck. The land border with **Burundi** is – when open – for local traffic only. If you have no pressing business steer well clear.

By boat

Local open-topped **lake taxis** (nicknamed *kigoma-kigoma*) leave from Ujiji for ports to the south, and from Kibirizi, 3km north of Kigoma, for ports to the north. There are no lake taxis from Kigoma itself. Their unpleasant reputation is due not so much to the risk of sinking, nor because they can be massively uncomfortable and offer no shade, water or toilets, but because they sometimes carry "dangerous passengers", meaning anything from mild drunks to the armed bandits who, in January 2001, shot dead two passengers and drowned twenty others between Kigoma and Mgambo by throwing them overboard.

Much safer and more comfortable are the two weekly **passenger steamers** run by the Marine Services Company (☎028/280 3950), which leave from the ferry port southwest of the commercial harbour. The **MV Liemba** sails every Wednesday at 4pm for Mpulungu in Zambia, if all goes well arriving around 10am on Friday, returning at 4pm on Sunday. It stops more or less everywhere, offering a number of feasible if rough-going overland connections in the dry season to Mpanda, Katavi National Park and Sumbawanga – see below for full details. The *MV Liemba* is also helpful for getting to Mahale Mountains National Park, as it stops at Mgambo (also called Lagosa), 15km north of the park – see p.536 for more information. In theory, the Yugoslav-built **MV Mwongozo** plies between Kigoma, Bujumbura in Burundi and Kalemie in Congo, though at the time of writing the service had been suspended due to conflict in both countries. Both ships have restaurants and sell drinks.

Fares for non-Tanzanians are quoted in dollars (they can sometimes be paid for in shillings, but don't count on it). First-class cabins on both boats are small but have two bunks, a window and fan. Second-class (in cabins with 4–6 berths) get hot and stuffy – given the meagre difference in price, go for first-class. Third-class is seating only. Fares (1st/2nd/3rd class) are: Mgambo $25/$20/$15; Kalema $30/$27/$22; Mpulungu (Zambia) $55/$45/$40; and Bujumbura $30/$25/$20. In theory this includes the $5 harbour tax. Tanzanian **immigration and customs formalities** for Zambia should ideally be cleared in Kigoma (p.525), although there's an immigration post at Kasanga, the last stop before entering Zambian waters. There's no Zambian consul in Kigoma (the nearest is in Dar es Salaam), but visas are usually given without fuss at Kasanga. Should the ferry to Burundi and Congo resume, visit their respective consuls in Kigoma first.

The following are the most feasible onward road connections from lakeside towns served by the *MV Liemba*. None of these routes is recommended (or sometimes even passable) in the rains; during these periods, the most feasible way of getting from Kigoma to southern Tanzania is to catch a train to Tabora, then another to Mpanda (p.548), and to make your way down by road from there.

Kalema or Ikola to Mpanda

The *MV Liemba* usually docks at **Ikola** on Thursday morning, and then sails on another 10km to the port of **Kalema**. If you're not planning to spend a night on the lakeshore, get off at Ikola, from where there's connecting road transport to Mpanda (at least 5hr). If the lake appeals, however, continue to **Kalema** (or Karema), where the Catholic Mission has a **rest house**. Kalema was a regular staging post during the slave trade, connecting Congo with the Tanganyikan route to the Indian Ocean. It was occupied by Belgian slavers in 1879 but, with the slave trade by then effectively at an end, it was left to the White Fathers, who arrived in 1885. Their church was erected five years later and the fortified mission house – which still stands – was completed in 1893. There are regular Land Rover pick-ups to Mpanda from Kalema (upwards of 6hr), leaving most days around noon, especially when the *MV Liemba* calls.

Kabwe to Liazumbi, Mpanda and Sumbawanga

The *MV Liemba* arrives in **Kabwe** around Thursday lunchtime. There's a **guest house** here and dry-season transport to the tiny settlement of **Liazumbi**, some 60km southeast on the main B8 highway between Mpanda and Sumbawanga. However, chances are that you'll get stuck for the night in Liazumbi, so it's better to spend a night or two in Kabwe, leaving to coincide with one of the buses which run three times weekly between Mpanda and Sumbawanga. For Sumbawanga, the bus passes through Liazumbi between 1.30pm and 4pm on Tuesday, Thursday and Saturday. Heading to Mpanda, it passes through on Monday, Wednesday and Friday at around 4pm. If you miss the bus or arrive earlier, there might still be a pick-up or two passing in either direction, but they're usually packed, so expect a cramped, dusty and bumpy ride. There are plenty of food and *chai* stalls in Liazumbi, but no hotels.

Kasanga to Sumbawanga

Kasanga, formerly Bismarck Fort (the ruins are just outside the village), is the last Tanzanian port before Zambia, and is where customs and immigration are dealt with if you haven't already done so in Kigoma. With time, the Kalambo Falls are an attractive target from here – see p.558. The *MV Liemba* usually arrives here between midnight and dawn on Friday. For accommodation (all ❶), there's the *Mwenya Guest House* in Kasanga and the *Muzi Guest House* (no nets but plenty of mosquitoes), 5km north in the tranquil fishing village of Muzi (an hour's walk, or squeeze into a local boat for Tsh1000). There are daily Land Rovers and pick-ups to **Sumbawanga** (4–5hr in the dry season, 9hr in the rains; Tsh5000), leaving around 6–7am. Returning from Sumbawanga, the pick-ups head off around 9am.

Hospitals Both Kigoma's hospitals are in Mwanga. The best is the mission-run Baptist Hospital (☏ 028/280 2241) about 1km from Kasulu junction: turn left at the junction then first right. The alternative is Maweni Hospital (☏ 028/280 2671), on the Ujiji road beyond Kasulu junction and Mwanga Market.

Immigration Exit formalities are done on the ferry, though it's worth clearing things beforehand to be on the safe side. The easiest place to do this is at the shack-like customs post just inside the entrance to Kigoma Port, accessed from the road down to the lake on the south side of the railway station building. If you have problems, the main immigration office is on the Ujiji road in Mwanga, 100m beyond Maweni Hospital on the left.

Internet access There are no internet cafés in Kigoma as yet, although the *Kigoma Hilltop Hotel* can send emails in an emergency.

Money NBC Bank, corner of Lumumba St and Mlole Rd by the market, changes cash and travellers' cheques (receipt required). The only forex bureau, which should certainly be quicker than the bank but was closed at the time of writing, is Panjatan Bureau de Change on Lumumba St.

Police Bangwe Rd, near the TRA building, and in the train station.

Post office The post office is on Kiezya Rd. You can also send faxes here, and there's an office for EMS express mail.

Safari operators There are two operators in Kigoma: *Kigoma Hilltop Hotel* (p.522), which has some reasonably priced packages to Gombe and Mahale but is otherwise expensive; and Sunset Tours ☏ 026/280 2586, ☏ 026/280 3707), in the unmarked building with the blue wire gate immediately before AngloGold Mining on the right side of Bangwe Rd, about 100m before the TANESCO generator. They offer cheaper trips to the parks, and also rent boats, but it's advisable to ring them in advance as there's rarely anyone there.

Telephone The TTCL office is next door to the post office (Mon–Fri 7.45am–12.45pm & 2–6pm, Sat 9am–1pm). Much more efficient, and offering almost identical rates for local and international calls (though national long-distance calls are more expensive), is Nguza Communications at the corner of Lumumba St and Kakolwa Rd (daily 8am–7pm). Calls are charged for a minimum of three minutes.

Ujiji

The pleasantly relaxed atmosphere of **UJIJI**, 10km southeast of Kigoma, belies a terrible past when, as the main Arab trading post on Lake Tanganyika, it was the place from where tens of thousands of shackled slaves began their gruelling 1200-kilometre march towards the Indian Ocean. The journey from Ujiji to Bagamoyo, Saadani or Pangani took anything from three to six months, and many died along the way, either perishing from exhaustion or being shot when they became too ill to move or tried to escape – it's thought that in the fifty years during which the Omani Arabs controlled the route, over a million Africans (mostly from east Congo) were enslaved, though the true figure may have been much higher, as estimates are based on those who survived the arduous journey to the coast. Now little more than a suburb of Kigoma, Ujiji has few visible reminders of its infamous past other than its distinctive Swahili-styled houses (more typical of the Indian Ocean coast) and a profusion of mango trees, said to have grown from stones discarded by slaves.

Ujiji was also the scene of Henry Morton Stanley's legendary meeting with David Livingstone, which is commemorated by a memorial and small museum. The alleged site of the famous meeting between the two explorers is marked by the **Livingstone Memorial** (ask for "Livingstone"), halfway along Livingstone Street some 500m before the harbour; coming into town along Kigoma Road, the junction for Livingstone Street is on the right before the *Matunda Guest House*. A plaque beside two mango trees said to have been grafted from the tree under which the duo met allegedly marks the spot. Ironically enough, the original tree died after World War I when Belgian authorities laid out a concrete platform around the trunk as a memorial, promptly starving it

Ujiji and the search for the sources of the Nile

From the 1850s onwards, European explorers venturing into the interior also used the slave routes, and – so long as they were armed with letters of recommendation from the sultan in Zanzibar – generally had little to fear. The first to visit Ujiji and set eyes on Lake Tanganyika were **Richard Burton** and **John Hanning Speke**, who arrived in February 1858 during their search for the source of the Nile. This was a riddle that had puzzled geographers and travellers since ancient times, when Herodotus, the "Father of History", wrongly stated that West Africa's Niger River was a branch of the Nile. Pliny the Elder compounded the confusion with his belief that the Nile had its head in a "mountain of lower Mauretania, not far from the [Atlantic] Ocean", whilst early Arabs geographers didn't help matters by calling the Niger *al-Nil al-Kebir*, meaning the Great Nile. British interest in the source of the Nile was fuelled by the desire to consolidate their grip over Egypt by controlling the source of its principal river. The impetuous Burton believed instinctively that Lake Tanganyika was the source, but Speke argued – correctly, as it turned out – that the lake lay too low, and went on alone to find Lake Victoria, the true source, later the same year.

of moisture. It was cut down in 1930. The small **museum** (Tsh1500) contains amusing local paintings depicting the famous encounter, some equally offbeat papier mâché figurines, and nothing much else.

Frequent **daladalas** run to Ujiji from the east side of the market in Kigoma, dropping you along Kigoma Road, from where it's a ten-minute walk to the Livingstone Monument. A taxi from Kigoma costs Tsh2500, or Tsh3000 direct to the monument. If you want to stay, try one of cheap and basic **guest houses** (●) on Kigoma Road as it heads into town.

Gombe Stream National Park

Just 16km north of Kigoma, **GOMBE STREAM** is the smallest but one of the most inspiring of Tanzania's national parks – and also the most expensive. Its 52 square kilometres cover a narrow strip of hilly country rising from Lake Tanganyika to the eastern ridge of the Western Rift Valley escarpment and cut by thirteen steep-sided river valleys running east to west. The variation in altitude and the variety of habitats make the park one of the country's most rewarding places for observing wildlife and flora, but you can forget about the "Big Five" – the Gombe ecosystem is a far more subtle affair. Lake Tanganyika and the unremitting *miombo* woodland which stretches to the east have acted as a natural barrier for the last twenty million years, and as a result Gombe contains several plant and animal species common in West Africa but unknown further east.

Gombe's diminutive size and the dense human population that surrounds it on three sides make it highly vulnerable to environmental degradation, a fact that was recognized early on under British rule, when Gombe's buffalo herds became extinct. Gombe was gazetted as a national reserve in 1943 and its human inhabitants evicted; it became a national park in 1968. The evergreen riverine forests are especially diverse, and are the abode of the park's famous wild **chimpanzees** which have, since 1960, been the subject of what is now the world's longest-running survey of a wild animal species; one troop has been habituated to humans and can be visited. Other **primates** include the olive baboon, along with less common red colobus, redtail and blue monkeys. The

Livingstone...

Born on March 19, 1813, near Glasgow in Scotland, the introspective **David Livingstone** turned to a religious life at a young age, joining the London Missionary Society, under whose auspices he travelled to Cape Town in 1841, where he married a missionary's daughter and set to work as a preacher and doctor. On his early expeditions he crossed the Kalahari Desert and "discovered" Lake Nyasa, but his most famous discovery, in November 1855, was that of Mosi oa Tunya – the "Smoke that Thunders" – which he dutifully rechristened the **Victoria Falls**. His fourth major expedition (1858–64) covered the area between the Lower Zambezi and Lake Nyasa.

After a brief sojourn in Britain, he returned to Africa in 1866, having been commissioned by the Royal Geographical Society to explore the country between Lake Nyasa and Lake Tanganyika and to solve the riddle of the source of the Nile. So began the five-year odyssey that was to end with the famous **encounter with Stanley**. At the time of the meeting, Livingstone was suffering from dysentery, fever and foot ulcers, but within two weeks had sufficiently recovered to explore the northern shores of Lake Tanganyika with Stanley, before returning to Kazeh near Tabora (p.546), where Stanley headed back to the coast and worldwide acclaim.

Livingstone stayed behind awaiting supplies, and then set off on his fifth and final expedition in August 1872, during which he again fell ill with dysentery and died at **Chitambo** village close to Lake Bangweulu (in present-day Zambia) in May 1873. His heart and viscera were removed by his African companions Susi and Chuma and were buried in a tin under a tree at the spot where he died. Susi and Chuma embalmed and dried the missionary's body, then wrapped it in calico and encased it in a bark cylinder, which in turn was sewn into a large piece of sailcloth, and was tarred shut. Thus wrapped, they attached the bundle to a pole and carried the body back to Bagamoyo – an epic eleven-month journey. From Bagamoyo the body was transferred to Zanzibar for shipment to London. Livingstone was buried as a national hero at Westminster Abbey on April 18, 1874, with Kirk and Stanley among the pallbearers.

...and Stanley

Twenty-eight years younger than Livingstone, **Henry Morton Stanley** was born John Rowland at Denbigh, Wales, on January 29, 1841. His childhood included nine years in a workhouse, before – at the age of 17 – he took work on a ship from Liverpool to New Orleans where his new employer – a cotton merchant – gave him his new name of Henry Stanley (Morton was added later). Always the self-assured self-publicist, eleven years on saw him working as the *New York Herald*'s scoop

---

redtail and blue monkeys are unusual in that, despite their striking physical differences, they have only recently diverged as separate species, and hybrids occur, usually with the redtail's white nose and the blue monkey's dark tail and larger size. Other **mammals** include grey duiker antelope, bushbuck and marsh mongoose, as well as the chequered elephant shrew, which eats insects and can be seen patrolling the forest floor – it's named on account of its comical trunk-like snout and long legs. Over 230 species of **birds** have been recorded, along with over 250 species of butterflies.

There are no **roads** in the park, a definite plus, as visitors get to see the place on foot, accompanied by an official guide.

Arrival, information and accommodation

Gombe can only be reached by boat. **Water taxis** leave daily (except Sun) from Kibirizi beach, 3km north of Kigoma, to the park headquarters at

journalist when he was commissioned by the paper's eccentric manager, James Gordon Bennett (he of "Gordon Bennett!" fame), to first cover the inauguration of the Suez Canal and then to find Livingstone, who had been "missing" for five years.

Arriving in Zanzibar, he borrowed a top hat from the American consul and paid a visit to Sultan Barghash, who issued him with letters of recommendation, the nineteenth-century version of a passport plus perks. In keeping with Stanley's larger-than-life character, the expedition set off with 192 men and six tonnes of stores, including glass beads, reams of American cloth, coral and china for trading, as well as two silver goblets and a bottle of champagne for the day he met Livingstone.

Exactly 236 days later, 76 pounds lighter and having buried eighteen porters and guards, his two European companions, both his horses, all 27 donkeys and his watchdog, Stanley arrived in Ujiji, having heard in Tabora that an elderly white man was there. The date was November 10, 1871. "I would have run to him," wrote Stanley, "only I was a coward in the presence of such a mob – would have embraced him, only, he being an Englishman, I did not know how he would receive me, so I did what cowardice and false pride suggested was the best thing – walked deliberately to him, took off my hat, and said, 'Dr Livingstone, I presume?'"

The studied nonchalance of those now legendary words was well in keeping with Stanley's character. Following his successful encounter with Livingstone, Stanley abandoned journalism and dedicated himself to exploring Africa, which he subsequently recounted in a series of derring-do books bragging about his adventures. Receiving a commission to find the southernmost source of the Nile, Stanley returned to Zanzibar in September 1874, this time for an epic 999-day journey across the breadth of Africa following the Lualaba and Congo rivers to the Atlantic, which he reached on 12 August 1877. His third and fourth trips, from 1879 to 1884, were commissioned by King Leopold II of Belgium to lay the foundations of the **Congo Free State** (subsequently the Belgian Congo) by establishing settlements, constructing roads and negotiating land deals with local leaders, effectively robbing them of their territory. The 450 treaties which Stanley agreed during these expeditions effectively laid the ground for one of the most glaring examples of European misrule ever witnessed. The Congo Free State, despite its name, was little more than a gigantic slave colony, in which order – and production quotas – were maintained by means of officially sanctioned torture, summary executions, assassinations, the taking of hostages and myriad other abuses.

Stanley – an "ugly little man with a strong American twang", as Queen Victoria privately described him – was knighted in 1899, and died in London on May 10, 1904.

KASAKELA. There's no fixed schedule, though most tend to leave between 8 and 11am, so get there early. The 24-kilometre trip takes two to three hours depending on how many times the boat stops en route, and costs upwards of Tsh2000. The taxis can be crowded and offer only limited (if any) shelter from the sun. The return leg is not guaranteed, though park staff can help you find a boat; 5–6pm appears to be the best time.

Quicker and more comfortable, but much more expensive unless you're in a large party, is to **charter a boat** in Kigoma. The *Lake Tanganyika Beach Hotel* (see p.523) can find you one for $80–100 return (for 10–12 people), plus an extra $10–15 if you stay overnight in the park. Much more pricey is the speedboat run by the *Kigoma Hilltop Hotel* (see p.522), which takes just 25 minutes but costs a mean $250 for a day return (up to 8 passengers), or $35 per person if they have a spare seat. The *MV Mwongozo* steamer from Kigoma to Burundi no longer stops at Kasakela (and the service is, in any case, currently suspended). **Organized safaris** are run by Sunset Tours (see p.528) and the *Kigoma*

Chimpanzees are our closest living relatives: they share 95 percent of our genome, and of course – unless you're a Creationist – we share common ancestors. Like us, chimpanzees are intelligent social creatures who feel and share emotions, and who are able to adapt to different environments and foods, pass on knowledge, and make and use simple tools. They also hunt in a human way, use plants medicinally, raid each other's communities and sometimes descend into a state of war. We owe much of our knowledge of chimpanzees to two ongoing research projects in Tanzania, one at Gombe, the other at Mahale (p.538), both of which started in the early 1960s. **Dr Jane Goodall** arrived at Gombe to begin her study of chimpanzees in June 1960, having been encouraged by the Kenyan paleontologist Louis Leakey, who believed that by observing the behaviour of great apes we could reconstruct something of the early life of mankind. Goodall remained in Gombe until 1975, though her study – now under the auspices of the Jane Goodall Institute (Ⓦ www.janegoodall.org) – continues, having entered its fifth decade.

The study's first surprising finding was the discovery that chimpanzees were capable of making and using simple **tools**. This is best seen in November at the start of the rains, when they go "fishing" for termites by inserting sticks into termite mounds, and then withdraw the probe to lick it clean of insects. Another example of a tool, which also demonstrates chimpanzees' knowledge and use of **medicinal plants**, is their use of *Aspilia mossambicensis* – a local medicinal plant – to clean their intestines of worms. The leaves contain an antibiotic and worm-killer, and are eaten in the morning before moving on to other foods. The method of eating the leaves is as important as their chemical content: using their lips, the chimps carefully remove one of the rough and hairy leaves from the plant and pull it into their mouths using their tongue. This causes the leaves to fold up like an accordion, which are then swallowed without chewing, thereby not only killing but physically removing worms.

Altogether, Gombe's chimps have been observed to eat 147 different plants, but contrary to what had previously been thought both the Mahale and Gombe studies

Hilltop Hotel. Depending on group size, a three-day trip costs around $400–500 per person all inclusive; the *Kigoma Hilltop Hotel's* trips also include a visit to Ujiji.

Information and park fees

The **park headquarters** (PO Box 185, Kigoma; no phone) is on the shore at Kasakela where the boats tie up. Visits are limited to four groups a day (maximum six people each including the guide). The shore and campsite are outside the park boundary, so you shouldn't have to pay park fees if you have to wait for a slot. **Entrance fees** are $100 per person per day, plus $10 per group for the obligatory guide. Children under 7 are not allowed. If the cost is prohibitive and you really want to see chimps, head to Mahale Mountains or Rubondo national parks instead. The best source of **information** is the excellent guidebook published by TANAPA which you can buy in Arusha (p.394). It contains masses of information on the park's wildlife and the chimpanzees, and also covers the Mahale Mountains National Park (p.536). The **best time to visit** depends on your interest. Photography is best in the dry season (July to mid-Oct and mid-Dec to January), but the chimps are easier to see in the rains (roughly Feb to June and mid-Oct to mid-Dec), when the vegetation on the higher slopes is at its greenest and most beautiful. There are occasional windy thunderstorms during April and May and from August to September.

revealed that chimpanzees are omnivorous rather than vegetarian. Indeed, their success rate at **hunting** – primarily of red colobus monkeys, young bushpigs and bushbuck – is far higher than that of some specialized predators such as lions. The secret of their success is co-operative hunting, as several chimps can block any possible escape routes; it has been estimated that chimps may be responsible for killing fifteen percent of the red colobus population every year.

Goodall's study also found that most of the dominant **"alpha" males** in the studied community were not necessarily big or physically strong, but gained their status through persistent or inventive macho displays of power. In one case, the alpha male used empty fuel-cans to terrify his peers; in another, two brothers – one of whom had lost an arm through polio – worked as a team to intimidate their competitors; others use family connections to gain influence. All in all, uncomfortably human. The parallels became even more unsettling when the study revealed that chimps also engaged in **warfare**, which had all the depressing hallmarks of our own conflicts. There are presently three communities: Mitumba, Kasakela and Kalande, whose borders are patrolled every few days by male groups. On occasion these groups invade neighbouring territories, attacking and sometimes killing any strangers encountered, with the exception of young females without young who are taken into the community. In a series of raids between 1974 and 1977, the males of the Kasakela community exterminated those of the Kahama community, with whom they had formerly been allied. The males also attacked strange females, and in three cases the stranger's child was killed and later eaten. **Cannibalism**, which was first seen in Mahale, was also observed in a Kasakela female and her daughter, who calmly went around killing and eating the newborn infants of other females belonging to their own community.

For more **information** about Gombe's chimpanzees, see the Jane Goodall Institute's website @www.janegoodall.org, or seek out Goodall's books: *In the Shadow of Man* (1971), *The Chimpanzees of Gombe: Patterns of Behaviour* (1986) and *Through a Window: My Thirty Years with the Chimpanzees of Gombe* (1991).

Special **equipment** to bring includes dull-coloured clothes, a pair of shoes which have a good grip in wet conditions, rain gear, a torch for walks along the beach at night and bottled water if you're planning long hikes. Binoculars are pretty much de rigueur, and take plenty of fast film to handle the subdued forest light (400–800 ASA at least) – flash photography is not permitted. For swimming, a face mask and snorkel are an advantage. If you plan to cook, take a kerosene or gas stove, as firewood or charcoal isn't always available. Fish can be bought from fishermen on the beach, but bring all other food, and conceal it in a sealed container to avoid unpleasantness with baboons.

Accommodation

Accommodation is at the basic **park hostel** at Kasakela ($30 per person), which has room for twenty people. It has bed sheets, mosquito nets, a communal verandah, dining area and library, but you'll need to be self-sufficient in food (there are plans to move the hostel to a more comfortable building at the head of Mitumba Valley). **Camping** is usually permitted on the beach ($20 per person), but you'll need permission from the park warden. Wherever you stay, **beware of baboons**, which can be extremely dangerous if teased or tempted. The golden rules for avoiding hassle are: keep all food (and valuables) out of sight; keep tents and rooms closed; never eat outdoors; and never stare at a baboon (if threatened, look away, turn your back, and move away slowly).

Should a baboon snatch something from you, don't resist but alert the park staff instead, who'll try to get it back.

The lakeshore

The shoreline lies outside the national park, so you can walk along the beach without a guide. The temporary camps along the beach are occupied by *dagaa* fisherman, who spend around ten days here every month in the dry seasons around full moon when the catches are best. The fishermen and their camps are regulated by the park authorities to protect natural resources, and to shield the chimpanzees from infectious diseases. The mango trees and oil palms in the bays are human introductions, the latter a familiar sight in West Africa, but unknown elsewhere in Tanzania.

In parts the forest reaches down to the beach, but there's little other permanent vegetation along the shore. As a result, hippos and crocodiles are rare if not completely absent; seek advice from the park staff before **swimming**. Bilharzia is also believed to be absent. If you've given the all-clear, head to the river mouths or the rocky shore just north of Mitumba beach, where a mask and snorkel will reveal many beautifully coloured cichlids. In deeper water you may see the harmless Lake Tanganyika jellyfish, a tiny (2cm diameter) semi-transparent pulsating disc. Many beach strollers here are spooked by the sight of harmless **Nile monitor lizards**, which look like little crocodiles, but these skittish fellows are just as easily spooked as you and dash off into the water when approached. Gombe's most common primate, the stocky and thick-furred **olive baboon**, is generally the only mammal seen by day on the shore, where they scavenge for fish and occasionally swim and play in the water. Baboons have been studied at Gombe since 1967 and are used to human beings, so they can be dangerous – keep your distance.

The lack of mud flats, weeds or perches means there's little **birdlife**, though the reeds at the mouths of streams are good habitats. Pied kingfishers, African pied wagtails and common sandpipers are most frequently seen, the giant kingfisher less so, while fish eagles are comparatively rare. Palm-nut vultures can sometimes be seen over the lake angling for fish. Winter migrants include white-winged black terns, hobbies and the lesser black-backed gull.

Night walks are an exciting novelty around full moon (or if you have a torch), giving glimpses of nocturnal animals such as genet, white-tailed mongoose, the slow-moving giant rat (up to 90cm long, including the tail), porcupine and bushbuck. You might also hear the loud cracking of palm nuts, a favourite with the hairy bushpig and also popular with palm civets.

Evergreen riverine forest

Of Gombe's various habitats, the narrow **evergreen riverine forests** are the undoubted highlight, especially in the north. These originally formed part of the great forests of Central and West Africa, but became isolated by climatic change during the last eight thousand years, and more recently from each other by human activity. The nearest is straight up the valley from Kasakela: a high, tangled canopy of trees and vines, the cool obscurity below illuminated here and there by narrow shafts of sunlight where you'll see butterflies and flowers amidst the shrubs and ferns. As you walk along, crushed undergrowth marks the hasty retreats beaten by chimpanzees, red colobus, redtail or blue monkeys. Your guide should know where chimpanzees were last seen.

There are two main **walking trails** through Gombe's riverine forest. The easiest heads from Kasakela to the **chimpanzee feeding station** fifteen

Despite living in a national park, Gombe's chimpanzee population has dwindled from 150 in the 1960s to 110 today, thanks to poaching and outbreaks of human-transmitted diseases. The following rules are designed to protect both you and the chimps.

Do not visit chimpanzees if you are ill: chimpanzees are susceptible to many of our diseases without necessarily possessing our immunity: an epidemic of infectious pneumonia killed almost a third of Gombe's main study community in the 1980s.

Keep your distance: never approach closer than 5m, or 8m if a chimp is being observed by a researcher. If approached by a chimp, move away quietly or, if you can't, ignore it.

No food: visitors are not allowed to eat or display food in front of chimpanzees, nor to feed them.

Sit while observing chimps: standing upright can intimidate.

Stay with your group: do not spread out, as surrounding chimpanzees disturbs them.

Respect chimp feelings: don't follow chimps who appear to be shy or are avoiding you, and talk quietly.

Photography: be patient and don't try to attract the chimps' attention. Flash photography is not allowed.

Safety: chimpanzees are much stronger than us and can attack humans. Never come between a mother and her child. Should a chimp charge you, stand up, move quickly to a tree and hold on tightly to signal that you're not a threat. Do not scream or run away.

minutes up the Kakombe valley. The station consists of two huts and a small clearing. Individual visiting chimps are given a few bananas at intervals of seven to ten days, so the feeding station is a good place to begin your search for them. The trail continues up through the forest to the twenty-metre **Kakombe waterfall** – this only takes another fifteen minutes, but can easily be spun out to an hour. The other trail winds up the **Mitumba valley**, some forty minutes walk from Kasakela.

Forest **birdlife** is melodious but difficult to see, usually no more than a brief flash of colour disappearing into the undergrowth or up into the canopy. The more easily seen birds are crimson-winged turacos: the mainly green Livingstone's; and Ross's, the latter with a blue body, yellow face and red crest. Both have raucous calls. Of the four species of fruit-eating barbets, the only one you're likely to see is the tiny yellow-rumped tinkerbird, which has black and white facial stripes, a yellow rump and a monotonous "tink, tink, tink" call. More pleasant to the ear are the flute-like calls of the tropical boubou, a black-and-white shrike that duets in dense foliage. The African broadbill gives itself away by periodically flying up from its perch to do a somersault, emitting a small screech. The ground-feeding Peter's twinspot is an attractive finch with a red face and a white-spotted black belly. Winter migrants include various species of cuckoo, Eurasian swifts, bee-eaters and rollers, and four species of flycatcher. With a good deal of luck, you might also spot the pennant-winged nightjar, or one of two species of warbler (icterine and willow).

Dry woodland and upper ridges

The drier valleys and higher slopes, especially in the south of the park, are neither as rich nor as interesting as the forest, and the semi-deciduous woodland and thorn scrub that covers them can look rather bleak in the dry season, the result of fires which formerly devastated large areas. Firebreaks have now been made by the park authorities by lighting controlled fires at the start of the dry season, at which time damage to young trees is minimal because the still green grass burns at lower temperatures than when completely dry. In the wet season it's a different world, with the vivid green grass being scattered with pink gladioli and giant heather. The poor soil and lack of year-round food supports few mammals, however, the exceptions being olive baboons, vervet monkeys and bushbuck. Even so, a hike to the top of the escarpment (over 700m above the lake) rewards the effort with sweeping views over the park, a luxuriant contrast to the dry and crowded farmland to the east. On ridges, you might also see **crowned eagles** circling over the forests in search of imprudent monkeys. There are several routes to the top, all of them steep; leave early in the morning, and don't expect to be back until around nightfall.

Mahale Mountains National Park

Located 120km south of Kigoma on a wide peninsula jutting out into Lake Tanganyika, **MAHALE MOUNTAINS NATIONAL PARK** is one of the country's least visited (and indeed least accessible) parks. Covering 1613 square kilometres, the park is around thirty times bigger than Gombe and contains an extraordinarily rich range of habitats, dominated by the **Mahale Mountains**, a rugged chain that cuts across the middle of the park, rising to 2462m at the summit of Mount Nkungwe.

Like Gombe, the park's ecology is characterized by a curious mixture of habitats and species typical of both the East and West African bio-geographical zones, and includes forest, mountain, savanna, *miombo* woodland and lake environments. As might to be expected from such a range of habitats, Mahale is exceptionally rich in **birdlife**, and also has lots of **butterflies**, including over thirty species of fast-flying charaxes that feed on animal dung. **Mammals** include elephant, buffalo, lion and leopard, giraffe, kudu and eland, as well as rarer species such as roan and sable antelope and the brush-tailed porcupine, but it's for the nine species of **primates** that Mahale has gained international renown. Like Gombe, the park is home to a large number of **chimpanzees**, some of which can be visited, and there are also populations of both red and black-and-white colobus monkeys.

Walking is the only way around, a sometimes heart-stopping but always memorable experience.

Arrival, information and accommodation

Unless you have the money to **charter a plane** (see the "Listings" sections in Arusha and Dar es Salaam, p.390 and p.114), the only access to Mahale is by **boat from Kigoma** (3hr by speedboat; upwards of 9hr otherwise). The *MV Liemba*, sailing every Wednesday from Kigoma to Zambia, calls at **MGAMBO** (also called Lugaso), 15km outside the park's northern boundary, some 130km south of Kigoma ($25 first class, $20 second class, $15 third class). The ferry arrives around 11pm, so radio-call the park authorities from Sunset Tours

Mahale's first conservationists: the Batongwe and Holoholo

The Mahale Mountains are the traditional home of the **Batongwe** and **Holoholo** (also known as Horohoro or Kalanga) tribes – the Batongwe are the larger of the two, with an estimated population (in 1987) of 22,000, while the Holoholo number some 12,500. Following the establishment of the Mahale Mountains Wildlife Research Centre in 1979, however, all human habitation was demolished to make way for the new national park (which was created in 1985), despite the fact that the Batongwe and Holoholo's lifestyle was highly adapted to the local environment. The Batongwe lived in compact communities of around forty people and practised a sustainable form of shifting cultivation over a cycle of thirty to fifty years, giving ample time for forest regeneration. They practised little or no commercial hunting, and what fishing they did was with nets whose mesh size was no smaller than 12cm, while some parts of the land – especially rivers, waterfalls, large trees, and the entirety of Sinsiba Forest and the forest fringing the summit of Mount Nkungwe – were considered the sacred abodes of guardian spirits, and so were left completely untouched. As such, it is deeply ironic that the first real conservators of the Mahale Mountains, the Batongwe and Holoholo, who lived in a near-perfect symbiosis with their environment, have now been completely excluded from their ancestral land.

(p.528) or the Mahale Mountains Wildlife Research Centre (p.521), both in Kigoma, so they can pick you up. **Returning to Kigoma**, the *MV Liemba* leaves Mgambo on Sunday afternoon. Alternatively, the military vessel *MV Burombora* (which has the reputation of being the safest vessel on the lake) sails to Mgambo from Kibirizi (see p.524), 3km north of Kigoma on Monday and Friday at 5pm, charging an extremely reasonable Tsh3500. Again, you should radio-call the park in advance to get them to pick you up from Mgambo.

A distinctly more romantic-sounding (if actually much less comfortable) approach is to hire a **local boat** from Kibirizi or Ujiji (16–24hr); bring plenty of food and expect a sleepless night. The cost is around Tsh3000 for locals, probably more for tourists, depending on your bargaining skills. The *Kigoma Hilltop Hotel's* **speedboat** is much quicker (3hr) but ludicrously overpriced at $1000 for up to eight people. You could also check with the TANAPA office in Kibirizi (p.524) or the Mahale Mountains Wildlife Research Centre in Kigoma (p.521) whether they have a trip heading down to Mahale, as they may have a spare seat.

If you arrive in Mgambo without having contacted the park authorities, you'll need to hire a local boat for the trip (2–3hr) to the park headquarters at **Kasiha**. In the past some visitors have tried to walk from Mgambo into the park but, although this is physically possible, you risk running into serious problems with the park authorities, who will automatically assume that you're trying to avoid park fees; there's also the chance you'll be attacked by wild animals. Lastly, you could try getting a seat on Greystoke Safaris' Fokker **aircraft**, which flies almost daily from Kigoma to restock their camp.

The other way of visiting the park is to go on an **organized safari**. The *Kigoma Hilltop Hotel* runs a number of trips to Mahale, with a five-day excursion costing $900–1200 per person depending on group size, and a bumper eight-day trip combining Gombe and Mahale for $1500–1850. Sunset Tours, also in Kigoma (p.528), should be cheaper – if you can actually find anyone there. Fly-in safaris are offered by Flycatcher Safaris and Greystoke Safaris, who use their own semi-permanent camps in the park, whilst the East African Safari and Touring Company is recommended for offbeat tailor-made trips. All three companies are based in Arusha and reviewed on pp.397–398.

Information and park fees

You can get **information** about the park at the TANAPA headquarters in Kibirizi (see p.524) and at the Mahale Mountains Wildlife Research Centre in Kigoma (p.521). There are no roads in the park, so game-viewing is done on foot in the company of an armed ranger. **Park fees** are currently $50 per person per day, while the obligatory guide/armed ranger costs $20 per walk, more if you're fly-camping and he stays overnight. The park is **best visited** during the dry season (May to mid-Oct), though the short rains pose no logistical problems other than the luxury camps being closed (usually mid-Oct to mid-Dec, and also during the long rains from mid-Feb to May).

Accommodation

Basic **rooms** are available at the park-run *Kasiha Guest House* near the park headquarters ($30 per person), but **camping** is the most atmospheric way of staying over. The main campsite is close by at Kasiha village ($20 per person); facilities are limited to long-drops and water. Camping in the bush is possible elsewhere, but has to be arranged with the park headquarters. Bring enough food for the duration.

In addition, there are a series of more or less permanent **luxury tented camps** on the beach. The cheapest is the *Nkungwe Luxury Tented Camp* (reservations through *Kigoma Hilltop Hotel*, p.522; full board ⑨), 2km south of the park headquarters, with six lake-facing tents, each with attached toilet and bathroom. The other two camps are more expensive: *Mahale Mountains Tented Camp* (reservations via Greystoke Safaris in Arusha, p.398; open May–October only; $450 per person), with six tents and plans to build a forest treehouse; and the camp run by Flycatcher Safaris in Arusha (p.397; ⑨). All three are closed in the rains (usually mid-Oct to mid-Dec and mid-Feb to May).

Mahale's chimpanzees

Like Gombe, the Mahale Mountains are one of the last strongholds for **wild chimpanzees**. Although their population is estimated at 700 to 1000 individuals in between fifteen and twenty communities (with many more outside the park), the chimps can be difficult to see, so be patient. **Visits** are limited in length to one hour, and group sizes to ten people, five being preferable. Read the box on "Chimpanzee etiquette" on p.535; the minimum distance between you and Mahale's chimps should be 10m.

Wildlife research in the Mahale Mountains has been dominated by Japan's Kyoto University since 1961, when primate expert Junichiro Itani and his colleagues began exploring the shoreline south of Kigoma. In 1965, the first permanent research camp was established at Kansyana, from where the habituation of two troops of chimpanzees began. The Japanese primatologists' work has focused on two communities in the northwest of the park in the Kasoge area. Areas of research include their use of medicinal plants, predatory behaviour, infanticide and cannibalism, temporary adoption of infants and "dialects" in their gestural language (there's an excellent essay on chimpanzee communication at ⓦ http://emuseum.mnsu.edu/cultural/language/chimpanzee.html.

Mahale's chimps have been separated from Gombe's for quite some time, as their social behaviour, use of tools and diet differ markedly – Gombe's chimps eat termites by probing the mounds with sticks, for example, but do not eat tree ants, whereas Mahale's chimps catch tree ants in the same way but leave the termites alone. For more **information** about chimp research at Mahale, see ⓦ http://jinrui.zool. kyoto-u.ac.jp/ChimpHome/mahaleE.html (keep the mixed case or it won't work), or TANAPA's Gombe guidebook, which contains a detailed section on Mahale.

△ Waterfall, Gombe Stream N.P.

Walks in the park

Mahale offers a wide range of **walks**. You must be accompanied by an armed guard, who will be able to advise you about recent sightings of chimps and leopards. The **lakeshore**, with its reeds, swamps and grassland is good for birds, including the nesting speckled mousebirds in the stands of oil palms around Kasiha. Large game is rare on the shore, although antelopes come here to drink and African hunting dogs are also seen from time to time. Mahale's richest habitat, however, is the lowland **gallery forests**, in the northwest of the park, where the mountains rise from close to the shoreline, ascending to around 1300m. Apart from the famous chimpanzees (p.538) and the leopards, the forest – like Gombe's – contains several animal and plant species more typical of West than East Africa, including the brush-tailed porcupine, the red-legged sun squirrel, the giant forest squirrel and the bushy-tailed mongoose. Forest birds to look out for are the crested guinea fowl and Ross's turaco – the latter is evasive, despite its vivid coloration, as it spends all its time in the forest canopy.

The misty **mountains** themselves are also home to a small population of black-and-white colobus monkeys. Their range is restricted to the belt of bamboo and montane forest above 2000m on Mount Nkungwe. Above 2300m the forests give way to grassland. One-day hikes up and down **Mount Nkungwe** are possible, but must be arranged in advance; longer trips can be arranged to explore the drier **eastern slopes** of the mountains, which are covered by *miombo* woodland, acacia, and "terminalia" savanna (characterized by termite mounds). Plains game is abundant, including elephant, giraffe, zebra, buffalo and warthog, together with rarer roan antelopes and their predators: lion, spotted hyena and the endangered African hunting dog.

Unyamwezi

Occupying much of the tsetse fly-infested *miombo* woodland of the Central Plateau, the **Unyamwezi** region formerly straddled two of East Africa's most lucrative and heavily travelled nineteenth-century ivory and slave caravan routes: from Ujiji on Lake Tanganyika, which was the main transit port for slaves from the Congo Basin, and from Lake Victoria in the north. These routes converged on **Kazeh**, 15km southwest of Tabora, which at its height in the 1860s saw an estimated half a million porters and uncounted slaves pass through each year.

Kazeh has now all but disappeared, its site being occupied by the dusty little village of **Kwihara**. Later in the nineteenth century, the focus of trade shifted to Arab-controlled **Tabora**, a bustling town of 200,000 people which is now the regional capital. Tabora has retained its importance as a trading centre thanks to the **Central Line Railway**, which follows the route of the old caravan trails almost exactly and provides easy access westwards to Kigoma on Lake Tanganyika, and north to Mwanza on Lake Victoria. The legacy of the slave and ivory caravans lingers on in the form of Islam, which is becoming the region's dominant religion, and in the name of the region's major tribe, the million-

It was only in the nineteenth century that the Nyamwezi coalesced into a unified state, **Unyamyembe**, largely built on wealth accrued from the ivory trade, much of which was controlled by the Nyamwezi themselves. The appearance of wealthy Nyamwezi traders in the coastal ports soon aroused the avarice of the Zanzibari sultanate, which from the 1850s onwards launched increasingly confident incursions along Nyamwezi caravan routes, dealing not only in ivory but increasingly in slaves. As a result, the balance of power between hundreds of central Tanzanian clans and tribes broke down, and a new generation of leaders with little respect for the established way of things rose to prominence.

One of these was **Chief Mirambo-ya-Banhu**, who by 1871 had managed, mainly through conquest, to establish a rival state to Unyamyembe called **Unyamwezi**, which at its zenith between 1876 and 1881 extended as far as northwest Tanzania and Congo. Mirambo controlled the entire western caravan route from Tabora to Ujiji, including the valuable salt workings and Malagarasi river crossing at Uvinza, as well as another caravan route heading up the western shore of Lake Victoria towards Uganda's powerful Bunganda empire, whose hegemony he briefly threatened – not without reason did European historians begin to dub him "the Bonaparte of Central Africa". Like Bonaparte, Mirambo's rule was very much a product of his character, "Throughout all my travels in Africa I have not yet met such disinterested kindness as I have received from the great bandit Mirambo", effused Stanley in 1876. "He is tall, large chested and a very fine specimen of a well-made man [and] as quiet as a lamb in conversation, rather harmless looking than otherwise, but in war the skulls which line the road to his gates reveal too terribly the ardour which animates him."

Mirambo's success was manifold. Geographically, his empire effectively blocked the Arab trade routes to Lake Tanganyika. Militarily, the vast wealth that the Nyamwezi had gained from the ivory and slave trade enabled the purchase of firearms from Zanzibar and the hiring of *ruga-ruga* mercenaries from the Ngoni tribe, who had conquered their way up from southern Africa over the previous two centuries. To consolidate his power, Mirambo reappointed governors of captured territories as agents and consuls, and even made an alliance with Sultan Barghash of Zanzibar, who had been trying to extend his own influence into the interior.

The fact that the empire was held together largely by the force of Mirambo's personality meant, however, that it quickly disintegrated following his death in December 1884, paving the way for the arrival of the Germans a few years later. Nowadays, Mirambo is considered as something of a national hero, not so much for his empire-building skills as for the fact that he managed to trump the Arabs over so many years.

strong **Nyamwezi**, which means "of the moon" in Kiswahili – an appellation used by the coastal Swahili and Arabs to describe a number of tribes to the west, where the moon sets.

Tabora

Whereas Kazeh (see opposite) has all but disappeared, its hot and dusty neighbour **TABORA** has continued to prosper as a major trading centre thanks to its position on the Central Railway line. Like the old slaving routes, the railway branches at Tabora, the northern line heading to Mwanza on Lake Victoria, the western one going on to Kigoma on Lake Tanganyika. Except for a handful of German buildings, there's not all that much to see in town, but it's a friendly place, and the shady, tree-lined streets provide an attractive and soothing break from the blistering *miombo* woodland that stretches for hundreds of kilometres around, making it a good place to break the exhausting (35–40hr) train journey from Dar es Salaam to Kigoma or Mwanza. There's also a pleasant side trip to the **Livingstone Museum** (Tembe la Livingstone), 15km southwest of town at Kwihara (see p.547), the modern incarnation of Kazeh.

Tabora's **climate** is hot all year round, with temperatures peaking at an average of 32°C in September and October before the arrival of the short rains. Still, it's perfectly bearable if you've arrived from the sweltering humidity of Kigoma or the coast. The long rains – scattered heavy showers rather than continuous downpours – generally fall from February to May.

Some history

The history of Tabora and its forerunner Kazeh is very much the history of the **Nyamwezi people** who by the mid-1700s had come to dominate the ivory trade of central Tanzania. A century later, with the Omani-dominated slave trade eclipsing ivory, Nyamwezi traders and porters were commonly seen on the coast, having followed the trading routes that they had developed, while the Nyamwezi themselves also organized slave hunts. By the 1850s, under the rule of chiefs Swetu I and Saidi Fundikira I, both Tabora and Kazeh were well established, and over the following decade an estimated half-million porters passed through the twin towns every year. The towns – and the Nyamwezi – grew rich on taxes levied on caravans, as well as from the profits of caravans operated by the Nyamwezi themselves, whilst their increasing power was typified by the establishment of a short-lived but extremely powerful new state established by Chief Mirambo (see box on p.541) that successfully challenged Arab hegemony over the slaving routes in the 1870s.

During the **German conquest** of Tanganyika, an outpost and then a fort (the still existing Boma) were raised in Tabora, surviving an armed rebellion in 1891 led by Chief Isike "Mwana Kiyungi" of Unyamyembe – defeated the following January, Isike chose to blow himself up in the armoury of his fort rather than surrender. The German victory made a considerable impression on lesser chiefs, some of whom took to sending envoys to Tabora for help in local conflicts. In signing treaties with the Germans, they effectively handed over their land to the colonists, and with the Nyamwezi "pacified", the Germans set about developing Tabora itself. The **Mittelland Bahn** (Central Railway) from Dar es Salaam reached Tabora in 1912, and two years later was extended to Kigoma. For the Germans, however, their efforts to open up the territory were in vain: in September 1916 they were ejected from Tabora after a fierce ten-day battle against Belgian troops from Congo under the command of Colonel Tombeur. The British took control of Tabora after the war, and in 1928 gave the go-ahead for the extension of the railway from Tabora to Mwanza, thereby assuring the continued prosperity of both towns.

Arrival

The **train station** is at the east end of Station Road, 1.5km from the bus stand and 400m from the *Tabora Hotel* – taxis converge on the train station whenever a train is due, charging Tsh1000–1500 for the trip into town. Trains from Dar and Dodoma arrive between 6.30pm and 8pm, connecting with services for Kigoma and Mwanza on the days when they're running. Coming from Mwanza or Kigoma, you'll arrive just after sunrise. If you're changing trains here, you'll have to spend the day in Tabora, and possibly a night if there's no

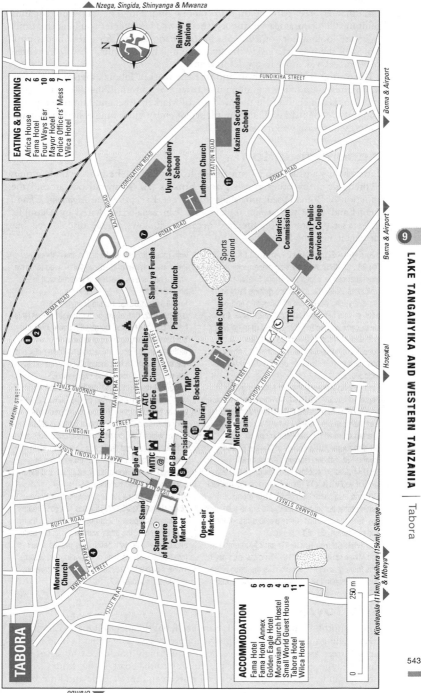

TABORA

▲ *Nzega, Singida, Shinyanga & Mwanza*

▼ *Urambo*

▼ *Kipalapala (11km), Kwihara (15km), Sikonge & Mbeya*

▼ *Boma & Airport*

▼ *Boma & Airport*

▼ *Hospital*

EATING & DRINKING

Africa House	2
Fama Hotel	6
Four Ways Ear	10
Mayor Hotel	8
Police Officers' Mess	7
Wilca Hotel	1

ACCOMMODATION

Fama Hotel	6
Fama Hotel Annex	3
Golden Eagle Hotel	9
Moravian Church Hostel	4
Small World Guest House	5
Tabora Hotel	11
Wilca Hotel	1

Railway Station

Kazima Secondary School

Uyui Secondary School

Lutheran Church

District Commission

Tanzanian Public Services College

Shule ya Furaha

Pentecostal Church

Sports Ground

Catholic Church

Diamond Talkies Cinema

TMP Bookshop

Library

National Microfinance Bank

TTCL

Moravian Church

Statue of Nyerere

Covered Market

Open-air Market

Bus Stand

Eagle Air

MITIC

NBC Bank

Precisionair

Precisionair

ATC Office

FUNDIKIRA STREET

BOMA ROAD

STATION ROAD

CORONATION ROAD

KAZIMA ROAD

BOMA ROAD

BOMA ROAD

MANYEMA STREET

KAMBINI STREET

SONGOBO STREET

GUNGONI STREET

BALEWA STREET

LUMUMBA STREET

MARKET (SOKONI) STREET

USAGALI STREET

RUFITA ROAD

MWANZA KAPEMBE STREET

TUTU ROAD

JAMHURI STREET

CHOPJ-TSHUTI STREET

TIELEMA STREET

NDAMBO STREET

0   250 m

train that day (see "Moving on from Tabora" on p.546). The train from Mpanda pulls in at 2.45am, at least in theory; the *Tabora Hotel* will let you in at this time. If you're looking for somewhere cheaper, hang around for a few hours until sunrise – there's a café inside the station, while the 24-hour *Police Officers' Mess* on Boma Road also sells food and drinks.

Buses stop at the bus station opposite the market. Tabora's **airport** lies a few kilometres south of town – a taxi into town costs around Tsh4000. In the town itself, **taxis** can be found at the junction of Market Street and Lumumba Street, and outside the market. There are plenty of cheap guest houses here, and many more within easy walking distance.

Accommodation

Listed below are all Tabora's mid-range **hotels** and the best of the budget ones – there are many other cheap **guest houses** (all ❶) spread out around the junction of Boma Road and Manyema Street. Excepting the *Moravian Church Hostel* and *Shule ya Furaha*, single rooms can usually be shared by a couple. Tabora's tap water is, on the rare occasions it flows, highly discoloured but drinkable if properly purified.

Fama Hotel Signposted off Lumumba St ☎026/260 4657. A lovely little place tucked away in a quiet corner with a few shady Indian almond (*mkungu*) trees. The rooms are getting tatty and not everything works, but all have fans and box nets, private bathrooms with Western-style toilets, clean beds with cotton sheets, and running water. The "single" rooms have huge beds and can be occupied by couples. The restaurant is Tabora's best, and there's also safe parking. Breakfast included. ❷

Fama Hotel Annex Corner of Manyema St and Boma Rd ☎026/260 6294. Nowhere near as nice as the *Fama Hotel* itself, but it's friendly and costs less than half the price for a large if somewhat spartan room with private bathroom. ❶

Golden Eagle Hotel Corner of Market St and Jamhuri St, entrance through the car park ☎0744/389250. Another good-value place, especially if you want a TV (though cheaper rooms lack TVs, and also share bathrooms). The rooms are getting tatty, but all have fans, and some also have box nets and bathtubs. There's also a first-floor bar and restaurant. ❶–❷

Moravian Church Hostel Corner of Kapembe St and Mwanza St ☎026/4710, ✉mcwt@maf.org.tz. This friendly and pleasant place is the best-value budget option in town, with clean and cool rooms

with mosquito nets and washbasins – though there are only ten of them, so you'll need to arrive early. Food is also available if ordered well in advance. ❶

Small World Guest House Manyema St ☎026/5992. One of the better budget places, this has a choice of clean rooms with squat loos and bucket showers, or cheaper ones with shared bathrooms. The beds are large and have nets, and there's a TV in the bar, though food is limited to the usual *chipsi mayai* and *mishkaki*. ❶

Tabora Hotel Station Rd, 400m from the station ☎026/6670 ext 2378. Run by the railway authority, this has 31 high-ceilinged rooms in a faded but very charming German colonial building, all but five of which have bathtubs (the other rooms are singles with shared facilities). There's running water in theory, but hot water only comes in buckets. There's also a bar, restaurant and safe parking. Breakfast included. ❸

Wilca Hotel Boma Rd, just beyond the *Africa House* bar ☎026/5397. This has ten good rooms in a calm and peaceful atmosphere, two of them with twin beds, the other with large double beds and box nets, all with bathrooms (minus a few toilet seats), ceiling fans and running hot water. There's also a bar, restaurant, and safe parking. Breakfast included. ❷

The Town

There's nothing much to see in Tabora itself, but the plentiful mango and flame trees shading many of its streets provide a pretty spectacle when in bloom – the mango trees are believed to have been unwittingly introduced by slaves who discarded the stones during their painful trek to the coast. Relics from German times include the **railway station**, with its steep central gable and lime-green roof, and the imposingly robust **German Boma** (or fort), at the south end of Boma Road overlooking a small valley to the east. It's now occupied by the military, so a visit (or photography) is sadly out of the question.

The lively **central market** is also worth a wander, especially in its crowded western extension, with distinct areas set aside for anything from bicycle parts and tyre recyclers to a huge section dedicated to the diminutive dried *dagaa* fish which is brought in by rail from Kigoma. For kangas (the colourful wraps worn by Tanzanian women), try any of the shops on Balewa Street off Market Street. Just to the north of the market, in a small enclosure off Ujiji Road on the left, is a statue of **Julius Nyerere**, who was educated at Tabora Secondary School in the 1940s.

Eating and drinking

If you thought Dodoma was a gastronomic wilderness, then Tabora is a real desert. Apart from local bars and those attached to guest houses, all serving pretty standard grilled meat skewers, chip omelettes and chicken, **eating out** is limited to the places reviewed below. **Nightlife** is pretty quiet as well, although it's always worth hunting out performances of the famous and eminently danceable Tabora Sound Band (formerly Tabora Jazz). You can buy the entire nine-volume collection of their hits, plus a heap of other hard-to-find recordings, from the stall 100m from the railway station along Stesheni Road on the left. A *kanda* (tape) costs Tsh1000. Apart from *Africa House*, reviewed below, two other places that occasionally host visiting big-name bands are the Secretarial College, near the police station, and the Tanzania Public Service College at the end of Jamhuri Street (tickets cost around Tsh3000).

Africa House Boma Rd. A dozy bar for most of the week (it sometimes closes mid-afternoon), things gets busy on Saturdays with live music (Tsh1000), usually from the Tabora Sound Band, though they also occasionally host big names from Dar es Salaam. Food consists of the usual grills and chip omelettes.

Fama Hotel Signposted off Lumumba St. The pleasantly calm bar here (even the TV volume is kept down) also serves up some superb food for under Tsh2500 – their *maini* (ox liver), in particular, is delicious.

Four Ways Bar Jamhuri St. A long, dusty garden which hosts live music some Saturdays (from 8pm), usually the Tabora Sound Band when they get displaced from Africa House by touring groups. Grilled meats, chips and eggs are available throughout the day.

Mayor Hotel Usagalla St, facing the covered market. This makes a pleasant change from the usual fare so long as you don't look too closely at what's crawling around on the counter. The food is self-service Indian-Tanzanian (you can fill up for Tsh1000) and includes snacks like soft ice cream, fruit juices and weirdly tasty vanilla-laced tea (flavoured with last week's ice cream?). Despite the dubious hygiene, it's popular for breakfast and gets packed at lunchtimes.

Wilca Hotel Boma Rd. A very calm place with a wide choice of well-prepared food, all for under Tsh2500 – the roast chicken is especially good, and there are also a few cheap vegetarian dishes and pizzas. There's also a pool table and shaded seating under trees.

Listings

Airlines Eagle Air, opposite the bus stand; Precisionair, Old Bhakhresa Building, Market St ✆026/260 4818 or 0744/496766 (there's also another branch on Lumumba St); Air Tanzania Corporation, Lumumba St ✆026/260 4401, has a route-sharing agreement with Precisionair, so you can buy tickets at either office.

Bookshops and newspapers There's nothing much in the way of Western novels or tomes on Tanzanian culture, and indeed English-language Tanzanian newspapers generally arrive two or three days late; if you're looking for children's books to give as presents, try the TMP Bookshop on Lumumba St.

Cinema The main cinema is Diamond Talkies on Lumumba St, which shows videos using a projector (6.30pm; Tsh300). The day's fare is announced on a board outside, including such kung-fu classics as *Incredible Shaolin Thunderkick*. They also screen live satellite transmissions of UK football matches.

Football Local matches are played at the small stadium at the corner of Boma Rd and Kazima Rd most Saturdays. Entrance is a few hundred shillings.

Hospital The government-run district hospital is on Kitete St west of the Boma ☎026/5269.

Internet There is, amazingly, an internet café in Tabora: MITEC (daily 8am–6pm; Tsh6000/hr), at the west end of Lumumba St on the right (first floor), but they use a land line, so it's agonizingly slow.

Library The municipal library is on Lumumba St (Mon–Fri 9am–6pm, Sat 9am–2pm; daily membership Tsh500) and is well stocked with English-language works on Tanzania and Africa.

Money NBC Bank, at the corner of Market St and Lumumba St, is the most efficient, taking around thirty minutes to process travellers' cheques, less for cash.

Pharmacy There's a reasonably well-stocked pharmacy next door to Air Tanzania on Lumumba St.

Police Jamhuri St, near the junction with School St.

Moving on from Tabora

Onward **bus** connections from Tabora are extremely sketchy, and there are no buses at all to Dodoma or Kigoma, which are covered by train – be aware that all the following schedules and companies are liable to change. **Heading south** you have two choices (though neither operates during the rains, when the road south of Tabora becomes impassable): Shakila run to Inyonga, sometimes further, whilst the route to Mbeya via Rungwa is covered by Sabema on Sunday and Thursday, and by Supersonic Coach on Wednesdays. There are also daily buses (Sabema and Shakila) to Sikonge, if you want to try your luck with onward connections on other days. **Heading west**, there are daily Sabema buses to Urambo (around noon), but nothing further west. Road conditions are better **heading north**, and only rarely get cut completely. There are two weekly buses to Mwanza via Shinyanga, run by Shakila (Sun) and Naaman's Coach (Mon). NBS Coach runs to Arusha at 7am on Wednesday and Saturday via Singida and Babati. Supersonic Coach run to Nzega, Kahama and Shinyanga on Tuesday, Thursday and Saturday. Alternatively, you could catch one of the daily **Land Rovers** to Nzega, where you can change for Bukoba, Mwanza, Shinyanga and, sometimes, Dodoma. The Land Rovers leave from Ujiji Road between the bus stand and the market.

By **train** (ticket office open daily 8am–noon & 2–4.30pm, and for two hours before departures), onward destinations include Shinyanga and Mwanza (Mon, Wed, Thurs & Sat at 9.30pm), Dodoma, Morogoro and Dar es Salaam (Mon, Wed, Fri, Sat & Sun at 7.25am), Kigoma (Mon, Wed, Fri & Sat at 8.10pm) and Mpanda (Mon, Wed & Fri at 9pm). The timetables posted up outside the ticket office are ancient history, by the way. By **plane**, Precisionair/Air Tanzania have three weekly flights to Dar es Salaam (Wed, Fri & Sun) and two to Zanzibar via Kigoma (Fri & Sun). Eagle Air have two flights a week to Dar, Kagera and Mwanza, and weekly connections to Bukoba and Dodoma. Airline offices are listed on p.545.

Kwihara

Fifteen kilometres southwest of Tabora is **KWIHARA**, known to nineteenth-century explorers as **Kazeh**. Until the German development of Tabora, Kazeh was by far the more important of the two towns, serving as a major caravanserai along the slave route from Ujiji to the coast. Speke and Burton passed through in 1857, and visited the town again in June 1858, having "discovered" Lake

Tanganyika. Burton, who had fallen ill, stayed behind while Speke went on to find Lake Victoria and the source of the Nile, to Burton's lasting chagrin. Three years later, Speke returned with Grant en route to sailing down the Nile to Khartoum, thus proving beyond doubt that Lake Victoria was indeed the source of the Nile. But the most famous of Kazeh's visitors were undoubtedly Stanley and Livingstone, who arrived here in 1872 following their legendary meeting in Ujiji (see p.528). Stanley was most impressed by Kazeh: "On my honour, it was a most comfortable place, this, in Central Africa."

It seems incredible that all that remains of this famous town is a handful of crumbling earth houses, a few mango trees and coconut palms introduced by the Arabs, and a quirky **museum** dedicated to Livingstone. Despite all this, the place's historical importance, as well as the rural scenery scattered with flat granite outcrops, repays the hassle of reaching it.

The Livingstone Museum

The **Livingstone Museum** (Tembe la Livingstone; no set times; Tsh1500), which boasts a beautiful Swahili-style carved doorframe, is a 1957 reconstruction of the fortified house (*tembe*) that the good doctor stayed in after having met Stanley at Ujiji. The pair arrived in Kazeh on February 18, 1872, and while Stanley went back to the coast, Livingstone stayed on awaiting supplies. He left Kazeh on August 25 for what proved to be his final journey, dying eight months later at Chitambo, near Lake Bangweulu in present-day Zambia (for more on Livingstone, see p.530).

The curator will show you a box containing a lock of hair from the famous missionary, and a piece of the mango tree from Ujiji under which, allegedly, Stanley met Livingstone. There's a room containing photostats of pages from Livingstone's journals, reproductions of hand-drawn and later maps, and copies of contemporary US newspapers ("Livingstone Safe" ran the headline on the same day that "Imperial Courtesies between the Courts of Rome and Berlin" and the calming of Vesuvius's latest eruption were reported). The other rooms are empty but bear labels: "Donkeys", "Kitchen", "Askaris", "Bombay". The latter refers to one of Livingstone's African servants, one of six former slaves who had been rescued by the Royal Navy in the 1850s. The six were taken to Nasik Mission in India, 187km from Bombay, where they received a thoroughly British education, including a grounding in the fine art of cricket. The group returned to Africa at Freretown near Mombasa, where they were recruited to take the stores and medical supplies to Livingstone, who was waiting in Kazeh. It is not clear exactly who "Bombay" was, though it's likely to have been Mathew Wellington (original name Chengwimbe, nicknamed Susi), a member of the Yao tribe from southwestern Tanzania and Malawi, who was later given the task of preserving Livingstone's body with brandy and salt before accompanying it back to Zanzibar – an eleven-month journey – from where it was shipped to London for burial at Westminster Abbey.

A lesser mortal whose corpse evidently didn't warrant such exalted treatment was **John William Shaw**, who fell ill and died here in 1871 whilst accompanying Stanley on his quest for Livingstone, and whose grave lies a hundred metres from the museum under a coconut tree. During their search for Livingstone, Stanley and Shaw travelled for a time with an Arab army, thinking it would offer safe passage further west, though unfortunately for them it was routed by Chief Mirambo at Wilyankuru. In typically obtuse form, Stanley blamed Shaw for the defeat, calling him "base and mean" in his memoirs, though the phrase is surely more applicable to the racist and murderous Stanley himself.

Practicalities

There's no accommodation in Kwihara, so it can only be visited as a day-trip from Tabora, though this can be awkward, as there are no daladalas. The easiest way to get here is by taxi (Tsh7000–8000), though the last 4km will be a struggle in the rains. Alternatively, if you don't mind walking you could catch a bus bound for Sikonge, Sumbawanga or Mbeya, and ask to be dropped off at **Kipalapala village**, 11km south of Tabora, from where Kwihara is a very pleasant (if largely shadeless) four-kilometre hike though villages and farmland; at Kipalapala, turn right at the sign for Kwihara School (there's also a small sign for Tembe la Livingstone, though it's easily missed). Heading back to Tabora, there's no guarantee of public transport from Kipalapala, so you might have to hitch. The museum is the large red building on the left just after Kwihara village – the children will alert the curator for you.

Rukwa Region

South of the Central Railway Line between Lake Tanganyika and the western arm of the Great Rift Valley, **Rukwa Region** offers a refreshing change of scenery from dusty *miombo* woodland to the north. The *miombo* continues to **Katavi National Park** but gives way to open rolling hills as you approach the fresh and relaxing town of **Sumbawanga**, only a few hours from the Zambian border. To the east of Sumbawanga, the **Mbizi Mountains**, still virtually unknown to the outside world, provide a picturesque backdrop. Further east, a shallow depression holds **Lake Rukwa**, a desolate, hot, humid but enchanting destination for those who really want to get away from it all – assuming you can get there at all. Details of travel by boat around the southern part of **Lake Tanganyika** are covered in the box on pp.526–527.

Mpanda

Sprawling over several kilometres at the end of the Central Railway's southern branch, the dusty town of **MPANDA** serves as a transit point for travellers heading between Sumbawanga and Mbeya in the south and Tabora in the north. For the trickle of tourists who make it here, the town also acts as a springboard for visits to **Katavi National Park**, 35km south (see p.551).

As might be expected from its strategic location, Mpanda served as a collective village during the failed *Ujamaa* experiment of 1967–77 (see p.718), into which numerous small agricultural tribes such as the Konongo, Bende, Pimbwe and Rwira were forcibly relocated, followed in 1979 by people evicted when Katavi National Park was created. Given the vastly increased population and the district's low rainfall and poor soil, the environmental outcome has been predictably destructive. The continued use of unsustainable slash-and-burn agriculture has removed all tree and shrub cover in many areas, causing flooding and massive soil erosion during the rains. This in turn has led to the silting up and disappearance of Lake Chada in Katavi National Park, and billowing clouds of dust in the dry season, which account for the unusually high rate of eye disease among Mpanda's inhabitants. Things haven't been helped by an influx of cattle herders from Shinyanga over the last thirty years, who have placed even greater pressure on the region's meagre natural resources. For all their woes, the people are an exceptionally friendly and welcoming lot, and deserve much better than they've got.

Arrival

Most people arrive on the **train from Tabora**; this theoretically pulls in at 10.30am, but is often delayed by an hour or two. Make sure you get up at sunrise to catch the evocative sight of the subtly coloured and misty deciduous woodland west of Ugalla River Game Reserve, and the tiny settlements of bark gum tappers and honey collectors by the rail tracks. The railway station is at the west end of town. To get to the centre, follow the stream of passengers back along the rail tracks and turn left onto the first road. *Super City Hotel* is 100m ahead, and the roundabout referred to in our reviews is 50m further on.

Arriving **by road** you're most likely coming from the south, as the roads north and east (towards Uvinza and Inyonga respectively) are in a dire state and become impassable during the rains, and the road from Inyonga on to Sikonge is feared for its occasional bandit attacks. Mpanda lacks a bus station. Buses, trucks and pick-ups arrive at the **bus stand** outside *Super City Hotel*, apart from some pick-ups coming from the south, which stop at the Tawaqal petrol station on the west side of town. To get to the main guest houses from here, turn right and walk 200m up the avenue, then take the second left. Continue straight for 800m and you'll arrive at the roundabout beside the *Super City Hotel*. For details on getting to Mpanda from the **Lake Tanganyika port** of Kalema, see the box on p.527.

For money, the National Microfinance Bank takes forever but does eventually change **travellers' cheques**; it's about 1.5km from the market on the northeastern fringes of town. The **post office** is close to the main market in the centre of town. The **TTCL** phone office is close to the police station at the northwestern edge of town; alternatively, there's a cardphone at *Super City Hotel*. If you're ill, Mpanda Hospital is pretty basic, but the only choice for severe problems.

Accommodation

There are plenty of perfectly decent cheap **hotels** scattered around town, of which the following are the best. Running water is erratic, so you'll probably have the pleasure of bucket showers (again).

Super City Family Guest House Mjimwema area, 400m northeast of the *Vatican Guest House* (no phone). A brand-new place run by a charming and very helpful man who is also happy to show guests around town. The fifteen spotless rooms all have ceiling fans, nets, showers and Western-style toilets; there's also a small bar, and food is available. ❶

Super City Hotel By the transport stand ☎025/282 0160. A longstanding favourite, this two-storey hotel (another level is half-built) has rooms with fans, nets and either private and shared bathrooms – the toilets lack seats, but there's running water most of the time. There's also a good bar in front, although service is somnolent. ❶

Vatican Guest House Immediately behind *Super City Hotel* ☎025/282 0065. A friendly, family-run budget option with large clean rooms, some with private bath, and all with ceiling fans and nets. Go down the alley on the right side of *Super City Hotel*, or walk around the parking lot by the roundabout. ❶

Eating, drinking and nightlife

Mpanda's most atmospheric **restaurant** is the *Garden Club*, close to the *Paradise Discotheque* (see below). The nameless restaurant next to *Super City Hotel* serves up tasty if somewhat dentally challenging grilled chicken, together with *ugali*, beans or rice, all for under Tsh1500. The little brick café facing it is handy for an early breakfast and does a lovely cup of tea; cups of *uji* finger-millet porridge are served up by women outside. For your own supplies, head to one of the town's **markets**, both of which are extraordinarily cheap. The larger one (ask for the *sokoni kuu* – large market) is in the Majengo area: walk northeast from the roundabout and follow the road around to the left after 700m, then take the first right and turn left after the Free Pentecostal Church: the market is behind the buildings on your right. There's a smaller market on the north side of town off the avenue between Tawaqal petrol station to the south and TTCL and the police station to the northeast.

Mpanda's **bars and nightlife** revolve around four very different places. You can break into a sweat at the *Paradise Discotheque*, southwest of the large market (open Fri & Sat nights, and on Sun from mid-afternoon). Unfortunately, walking back isn't advisable after midnight and there are next to no taxis, so take a reliable local with you if you want to stay out late. The *Super City Hotel*'s bar, with seats under thatched parasols, is the most dignified place for a drink, and also has a TV, but the barmaids have a propensity to overcharge if you don't keep count. Equally pleasant is the *Garden Club*, close to the *Paradise Discotheque*, which has a shady garden and also does food. At the other end of the scale, *Soweto Bar (Kalambo Falls Club)* promises an adventurous night elbow-to-elbow with local men inebriated on local hooch; again, a reliable local companion is helpful to avoid drunken hassle. To get there, walk northeast from the roundabout by *Super City Hotel*, and turn right just before the road bends left.

Moving on from Mpanda

Moving on from Mpanda, the **train** heads back to Tabora at 1pm on Tuesday, Thursday and Saturday. Heading to Kigoma by train, get off at Tabora rather than Kalilua, where the lines meet, as you'll arrive at the latter at midnight and the onward connection leaves at 11pm the next night (or two nights later if you take the Saturday train); much better to kick around in Tabora.

Buses, trucks and pick-ups leave from the stand outside *Super City Hotel*. The only **buses** leave between 11am and 1pm on Tuesday, Thursday and Saturday, with Amour Video Coach going to Mamba in the north of the Mbizi Mountains, and Sumry Bus going to Sumbawanga. They meet the train at the station, but you can board them before at the stand. A handful of **pick-ups** also go to Sumbawanga: the first leaves around 7–8am, charging Tsh10,000 to Sumbawanga or Tsh2000 to Sitalike at the entrance to Katavi National Park. You'd be unlucky to stumble on a day when nothing's going at all. The drive south to Sumbawanga goes via Katavi National Park and takes five hours in a private car or pick-up, six or seven hours by bus. The road has recently been upgraded to all-weather murram, but be warned that if it's not properly maintained it will give way to a quagmire of black cotton soil. Excepting one or two lorries a month, there's no road transport to Uvinza or Kigoma; catch the train via Tabora instead.

Katavi National Park

Some 35km south of Mpanda and 143km north of Sumbawanga, **KATAVI NATIONAL PARK** is best known for its floodplains, which in the dry season support large concentrations of plains game and one of Africa's most extensive buffalo populations, estimated at the last count to number around 60,000. As well as the plains, the park's **habitats** also include *miombo* and acacia woodland in the northwest; the palm-fringed Lake Katavi; rivers inhabited by hippo and crocodile; and the Mulele escarpment in the east, known for its pretty waterfalls, which forms a natural barrier between the park and the adjacent Rukwa Game Reserve. **Wildlife** you're likely to see includes elephant (there are well over four thousand), giraffe, zebra and lion (though, as ever, leopards keep themselves well hidden), gazelle, large herds of roan and sable antelopes, topi, eland and – in reed beds near the swamps – the southern reedbuck. Birders are in for a treat, too, with over four hundred recorded species. But the main attraction for many is simply the park's remoteness, and the fact that – given that it attracts a mere 1200 visitors each year – you're pretty much guaranteed to have the place to yourself.

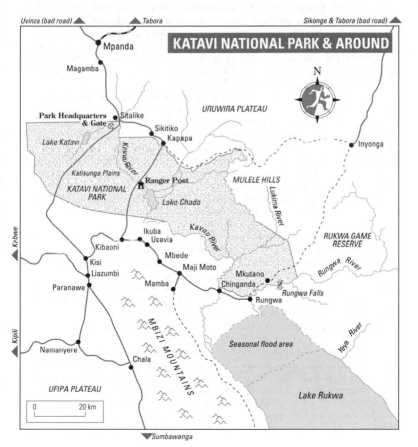

Katavi National Park was gazetted in 1974 and extended eastwards to the boundary of Rukwa Game Reserve in 1997 – it now covers an area of 4471 square kilometres, making it Tanzania's fourth-largest protected wildlife area. Given its poor soil and the presence of tsetse flies, the area has always been sparsely inhabited, although it attracted small numbers of hunters in the days before the park's creation, after which all human settlement was prohibited. Some of those who were evicted now live in **SITALIKE**, on the park's northern boundary. Like Mpanda, Sitalike is a former *Ujamaa* village but is a good deal poorer, its inhabitants relying on subsistence farming, along with fishing whenever the Katuma River is in spate. The injustice of excluding locals from parks and restricting their activities in game reserves whilst accommodating a handful of tourists is rendered starkly apparent by the adjacent Rukwa Game Reserve, whose regulations permit trophy hunting by tourists while forbidding hunting for food by locals.

Arrival, information and accommodation

Uniquely for a national park, Katavi is most easily reached by public transport. Coming **from the north**, catch the train from Tabora to Mpanda (p.546), from where there are daily road connections to Sitalike, just 1km north of the park headquarters; for details of bus companies and pick-ups, see "Moving on from Mpanda" on p.550. You might also get a lift from one of the vehicles used by the tented camp or park staff; they usually park next to the *City Guest House* in Mpanda. The ride takes under an hour, costs Tsh2000 and passes through desolate terrain whose few villages are notable for some beautifully decorated houses painted with geometric and floral motifs.

From Sumbwanga, catch a bus or pick-up towards Mpanda (see p.556 for more details) and get off in Sitalike. Incidentally, the fifty-kilometre stretch of road which bisects the park is open 24 hours and doesn't require the payment of park fees if you're just passing through.

Leaving Katavi, buses to Mpanda pass Sitalike around 7pm on Monday, Wednesday and Friday. To Sumbawanga, they pass on Tuesday, Thursday and Saturday between noon and 2pm. On other days, lifts in passing trucks and pick-ups are best caught at the road barrier at the north end of Sitalike. The village has a few sparsely stocked shops, lots of little bars and soda joints and a couple of basic restaurants, but no accommodation and precious little else.

Information and park fees

The **park headquarters** is a few hundred metres south of Sitalike: follow the road out of the village, cross the bridge which marks the park's northern boundary (look for the hippo wallowing in the Katavi River below), and turn right after 100m, where you'll pass a number of metal huts; the park headquarters is in a cluster of brick buildings just beyond here. The **entrance fee** is $15 per person per 24-hour period. The permit for a Tanzanian-registered vehicle is due to increase to Tsh5000 (currently Tsh1000), or $30 if foreign-registered.

Although hiring a **guide** is not compulsory, it's advisable given the lack of proper roads, signs or maps – they cost $10 during normal working hours, plus $15 overtime outside these hours (for example if your guide stays overnight when you're camping). A new TANAPA **guidebook** was planned for 2000 but hadn't appeared by mid-2002; if and when it sees the light, chances are you'll only be able to buy a copy in Arusha. In the absence of printed information, the principal park warden is happy to answer your questions. There are no park maps other than four adjoining sheets from the government's Surveys and Mapping Division in Dar (see p.116), which are way out of date – there's a copy on the wall of the principal park warden's office. The **best time to visit** is during the dry season (May–Oct, especially from July, and less so from mid-Dec to Feb). At other times the park is liable to be inaccessible due to the rains, and much of the plains game migrates beyond the park boundaries or into hillier and less accessible terrain.

Accommodation

There's basic **accommodation** ($30 per person) at the park-run *Chief Nsalamba Rest House*, less than 1km south from the park headquarters off the main road. The rest house is named after a traditional leader of the Konongo tribe, who later became an MP and finally one of Katavi's wardens. Book well ahead as it only has three rooms (this is most conveniently done at TANAPA's headquarters in Arusha, see p.394). You'll have to say whether you're bringing your own food or want park staff to arrange meals or cooking equipment. There's no problem walking from the rest house to the village along the main road.

A highly recommended alternative is **camping** ($20 per person), which enables you to do walks over several days, though you'll need your own tent, equipment, food and water – there are no formal campsites, but the rangers can indicate good spots. Katavi's two **luxury tented camps** are obscenely expensive (over $400 per person). If you can't find a more useful way of spending your money, contact Greystoke Safaris (p.398) for information on *Katavi Tented Camp* on the northwestern side of the Chada floodplain, or Flycatcher Safaris (p.397), whose site is close to the park headquarters.

The park

Walking in Katavi is possible as long as you're accompanied by an armed ranger ($20 per walk, more if you camp overnight; they also double as guides). There are no set routes or itineraries, so arrange things with the ranger. You should plan for at least two days, camping overnight, to really get anywhere. A good place to head to is the viewpoint over Lake Katavi and its floodplain, a forty-kilometre round trip from Sitalike. If you're strapped for time, it's possible to do a day's walk from the gate along the Katavi River and back through *miombo* woodland. If you've come by public transport and don't want to walk, the authorities might oblige with a lift or a spare vehicle, though there's nothing formal about this, so you certainly shouldn't count on it, and payment will of course be expected.

The dusty *miombo* and acacia **woodland** that skirts much of the B8 highway through the park is a favoured haunt for giraffe, antelope and elephant. The park's main attraction is its **seasonally flooded grassland**, occupying the area around Lake Katavi (20km southwest of Sitalike), the Katisunga Plains in the centre flanking the Kavuu River, and much of the eastern extension. In the dry season, the grasslands support vast herds of buffalo and plains game, and when still flooded attract waterbirds in their thousands (though driving around the grasslands in the rains is treacherous if not impossible). If you're exceptionally lucky, you may see the shy and rare puku antelope (*kobus vardoni*), about which very little is as yet known – it's also found in Mahale, the Kilombero Valley and in isolated pockets across southern Africa. The **thickets and short grasses** around the edges of the floodplains are inhabited by leopard, lion and elephant, and by various antelope species: roan and sable, southern reedbuck, eland and topi. The leopards are, as ever, difficult to spot, but your guide or ranger should be able to point out most of the antelopes.

Lake Chada, which sits at the confluence of the Kavuu and Nsaginia rivers in the centre of the park, is nowadays only a seasonal floodplain. The once permanent lake's disappearance is due to river-borne silt deposits from the arid badlands between Mpanda and the park, and provides a vivid example of the environmentally damaging consequences of concentrating human settlement in marginally productive areas, the result both of Nyerere's failed *Ujamaa* programme and of evicting people from the park. The palm-fringed **Lake Katavi**, 20km southwest of Sitalike, has so far avoided Lake Chada's fate, and remains an excellent place to see buffalo, elephant and antelopes as well as crocodile, hippo and large flocks of pelicans; an observation hut overlooks the lake and its grasslands.

With your own transport, you could visit the permanent streams and small cascades of the **Mulele Hills** (also spelled Mlala) at the eastern boundary of the park, while in the far southeast you might head to the **Ndido Falls** on the Rungwa River. If you get this far down, instead of retracing your steps you could follow the dirt road outside the park west from Rungwa village to Kibaoni, where a right turn takes you back into the park. Roughly 40km west of Rungwa you'll pass through the village of **Maji Moto** ("hot water"), just before which there are – no surprise – hot-water springs.

Sumbawanga

The capital of Rukwa region is **SUMBAWANGA**, a pleasantly unimposing sort of place set in the lee of the Mbizi Mountains, whose breezes lend the town a refreshing climate – chilly at night, and just right by day. As a bonus for travellers emerging battered and bruised from a bumpy journey, there's no hassle either. The town's main attraction is the cosy **central market** off Mpanda Road – just the place for cheap seasonal fruit and vegetables, *dagaa* fish from Lake Tanganyika and the traditional assortment of imported plastic and

The Fipa

Numbering over 200,000, the **Fipa** (also called the Ichifipa or Fiba) are the largest tribe in Rukwa Region. The majority are farmers who practise an inventive method of cultivation called *ntumba*. In preparation for the short rains, small mounds 40–60cm high are made from soil and grass, with vegetables sown on top. Following the rains and the harvest, the now highly composted mounds (mixed with the leaves and stems of the vegetables) are levelled and the main crop – finger millet (*ulezi*) or maize – is planted for the long rains. The method minimizes soil erosion, retains moisture long after the rains are gone, ensures the continued fertility of the soil season after season, and dispenses both with fertilizers and the destructive slash-and-burn techniques that have laid waste to much of Mpanda district to the north.

The Fipa's knowledge of soil is also shown by the many brick kilns on the outskirts of town, and by their skill in iron-smelting and iron-working, which they and several other tribes have possessed for at least two millennia. Knowledge of iron-working in Africa is often associated with witchcraft, and the Fipa are no exception, with Sumbawanga being especially famous for it. This is mirrored by the town's name, which appears to be a combination of *sumba*, meaning to light or to kindle, and *mwanga*, which is an enlightened person as well as a witchdoctor. The name may also be a corruption of *simbamwanga*, meaning the "lion witchdoctor".

9

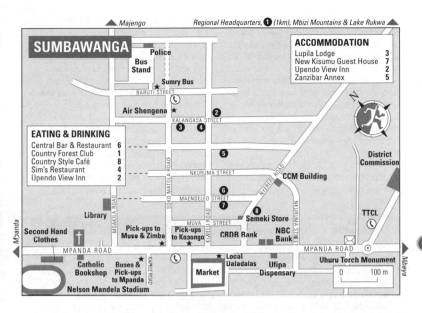

SUMBAWANGA   Police
Bus
Stand
Sumry Bus

BARUTI STREET

Air Shengena ★   ❷

KALANGAJA STREET

❸ ❹

ACCOMMODATION
Lupila Lodge   3
New Kisumu Guest House   7
Upendo View Inn   2
Zanzibar Annex   5

EATING & DRINKING
Central Bar & Restaurant   6
Country Forest Club   1
Country Style Café   8
Sim's Restaurant   4
Upendo View Inn   2

❺

NKURUMA STREET

CCM Building

District Commission

MAENDELEO STREET
❻
❼

Library

Second Hand
Clothes

Pick-ups to
Muse & Zimba

MPANDA ROAD

MUVA STREET

Pick-ups
to Kaoonga

CRDB Bank

❽
Semeki Store

NBC
Bank

TTCL

MPANDA ROAD

Mpanda

Catholic
Bookshop

Buses &
Pick-ups
to Mpanda

Nelson Mandela Stadium

Market

Local
Daladalas
Ufipa
Dispensary

Uhuru Torch Monument

0   100 m

Mbeya

aluminium household goods from China and Taiwan. For cheap second-hand clothes and sandals made on the spot from recycled truck tyres, have a browse through the stalls outside Nelson Mandela Stadium on the way out of town on Mpanda Road. There's really nothing else to see in town, however, so unless you've got the patience and the stamina to arrange a hike in the **Mbizi Mountains** (p.556) or down to **Lake Rukwa** (see p.557), most people just stay a night before heading on towards Mpanda, Katavi National Park, Mbeya or – in the dry season – Kasanga on the shore of Lake Tanganyika.

Practicalities

The **guest houses** immediately adjacent to the bus stand are pretty grim; the ones a few minutes' walk away in the grid of streets to the south are much better.

Lupila Lodge Kalangasa St ☎025/280 2418. Simple but well-kept rooms, some with private bath, all with nets. ❶
New Kisumu Guest House Maendeleo St ☎025/280 2927. A decent budget option similar to the *Lupila* – it's well kept, and some rooms have private bathrooms. ❶
Upendo View Inn Corner Kiwelu Rd and Kalangasa St ☎025/280 2242, ℗025/280 2502. The town's best hotel, with large clean twins (no

single rates) with private bathrooms, reliable running water, Western-style toilets and even toilet paper. There's also a restaurant and bar, but the adjacent nightclub is exceedingly noisy. ❷
Zanzibar Annex Off Kiwelu Rd ☎025/280 0010. An excellent choice should the *Upendo* be full, with a choice of rooms with or without private bathroom (the latter are much cheaper). Beds have nets, bathrooms have running water and clean, tiled squat loos. ❶

Eating and drinking

The main concentration of **restaurants** is on Maendeleo Street, where the competition keeps standards fairly high. For your own supplies, Semeki Store, at the corner of Nyerere Road and Muva Street, has a reasonable selection of imported produce including tasty South African Ceres juices.

Central Bar & Restaurant Maendeleo St. Friendly local restaurant which is good for cheap breakfasts (with great savory *supus*; take your pick of goat, chicken or liver) and lunches (under Tsh700), while the attached bar is great for an afternoon drink, its TV tuned to Discovery Channel and CNN during the day to keep locals riveted to the screen.

Country Forest Club 2km along Nyerere Rd. Before the *Upendo View Inn* opened its bar, this was Sumbawanga's main nightspot, but even then only at weekends – midweek, it's drowsy and empty.

Country Style Café Nyerere Rd. A neat little café and restaurant with a wide range of snacks and affordable meals.

Sim's Restaurant Corner Kiwelu Rd and Kalangasa St. Long-established place serving up delicious and filling meals for under Tsh1000, with a choice of meat stew, roast chicken, fish or liver with *ugali* or rice, plus beans and greens. No alcohol.

Upendo View Inn Kalangasa St. This is the most kicking nightspot in town, especially on Wednesday, Friday and Saturday. Entertainment features live music from the Rukwa International Band, plus a "*wazee* disco"(*wazee* are old men), with Tanzanian golden oldies (possibly Fri), some *ngoma kiasili* (traditional music) and a children's disco (Sun 2–7pm) followed by one for adults. There's good and reasonably priced food too.

Moving on from Sumbawanga

Despite the welter of (boarded-up) bus company offices in and around the now defunct bus stand, only two companies currently operate from Sumbawanga. These are Air Shengena, whose services leave from their office on Soko Matola Road, and Sumry Bus, whose services depart from their office on Baruti Street. **Mpanda** is served by Sumry Bus on Monday, Wednesday and Friday at 1pm, arriving in time to catch the train to Tabora the following day. Pick-ups to Mpanda can be caught most days at the petrol station on the corner of Mpanda Road and Kapele Road. For **Mbeya via Tunduma**, Sumry leaves daily at 6.30am, and Air Shengena at 5am. Air Shengena also runs an exhausting service to **Dar es Salaam** and **Tanga** on Sundays at 5am (roughly 24hr).

There are also daily **pick-ups** from Mpanda Road. Those to **Muse** (1hr), on the eastern flank of the Mbizi Mountains north of Sumbawanga, leave between 11am and 12am; the pick-up to **Zimba**, near the shore of Lake Rukwa, heads off around 11am; in the dry season, there's at least one vehicle heading to **Kasanga** on Lake Tanganyika at 9am (sometimes later). There's no regular transport to Mbala in **Zambia**, so it's a matter of asking around at the petrol station at the corner of Mpanda Road and Kapele Road for a truck.

Around Sumbawanga: the Mbizi Mountains

Sumbawanga is the base for hikes in the **Mbizi Mountains**, which are almost completely unknown outside Sumbawanga – and indeed to a good many people in Sumbawanga as well. You'll need to be completely self-sufficient and have a tent, as the only **guest houses** are at Zimba, a former German camp (now run by the Catholic Mission) an hour's drive from Sumbawanga on the eastern slopes of the range overlooking Lake Rukwa, and 100km to the north at Mamba, which lies 10km south of the hot-water springs at Maji Moto (see p.554). When camping, make sure you get permission from locals before you pitch your tent. A good source of **information** before leaving is the District Commissioner's Office in Sumbawanga (100m beyond the TTCL), or the Regional Block, 1km along Nyerere Road.

The easiest way to reach the mountains is to take one of the **pick-ups** to Zimba which leave daily from the petrol station at the corner of Mpanda and Kapele roads between 10am and noon, returning to Sumbawanga around 4pm. From Zimba, you could explore the western shore of Lake Rukwa (see opposite) before heading northwest along a little-used road to Muse (40km). Pick-ups back to Sumbawanga from Muse leave around 4pm. If you want to go directly to Muse, pick-ups depart from Sumbawanga at the same place and time as those for Zimba. For something even more adventurous, the 60–70km trek northwest towards **MAMBA** takes you along the eastern ridge of the mountains via the villages of Nkwilo, Mfinga, Finga and Kilida. Amour Video Coach runs from Mamba to Mpanda, 120km north, on Monday, Wednesday and Friday, arriving in time to catch the train to Tabora the following day. Coming in the opposite direction, buses leave Mpanda around noon on Tuesday, Thursday and Saturday, arriving in Mamba before nightfall.

Lake Rukwa

Occupying the lowest part of the Rukwa Rift Valley (also called the Rukwa Trough), **Lake Rukwa** follows the same northwest–southeast faultline as Lake Nyasa to the south. The water is extremely alkaline, and there are salt pans at **Ivuna**, 15km from the lake's southern shore, fed by hot brine springs. Excavations have established that Iron Age people lived on the lakeshore from as early as the thirteenth century, working the salt, cultivating cereals, keeping cattle, goats, chickens and dogs, and hunting zebra and warthog for food. The trade in Ivuna's salt was sufficiently important to have made the southern shores of Rukwa figure as a stopover on a slaving caravan route to Bagamoyo during the nineteenth century.

Crocodile, hippopotamus and fish abound, of which tilapia provide the basis for a flourishing fishing industry that exports its dried catch as far away as Zambia's Copperbelt. Despite the fishery the lake could hardly be more different from its western neighbour, Lake Tanganyika: the latter's enormous depth contrasts with Rukwa's average of a mere 3m, while given the lack of an outlet and the unreliability of the streams feeding it, the lake's size is prone to wild variations – at times it actually splits into two lakes separated by a narrow belt of swamp. During the 1820s and 1830s the lake almost dried up, and when the explorer John Hanning Speke passed by in 1859 he saw only an impassable swamp. The lake's chronic siltation over recent decades, hastened by deforestation in its catchment area, appears to have bucked the trend by permanently flooding large expanses of formerly seasonal floodplain, an effect that has grown worse since the exceptionally heavy 1998 El Niño rains. The **Uwanda Game Reserve**, established in 1971 and still marked on maps, has for all practical purposes ceased to exist, as over half of it now lies permanently under water.

Rukwa's main natural attraction is its **birdlife**, with over four hundred species recorded, many of them waterfowl. The disappearance of much of the floodplain and grassland ecosystem has greatly reduced the numbers of **plains game** that once frequented the area, especially after the short rains from November onwards. Still, you might still see zebra and buffalo, and perhaps – at least according to rumour – an albino giraffe or spotted zebra, but rarer species such as topi and puku antelopes may prove to be elusive.

Practicalities

Lake Rukwa can be accessed either from the northwest or the southeast, but whichever route you choose, take everything you'll need with you, and be prepared for the lake's unpleasantly hot and muggy atmosphere. The easiest of the two routes is from **Sumbawanga** in the northwest, which has daily pick-ups to Zimba (see opposite), about 5km from the lakeshore. Access along the southeast route from Mbeya is much more difficult and really only feasible with your own 4WD, and even then only in the dry season. If you want to chance it by public transport, there are daily vehicles from Mbeya to Chunya (p.590), but only infrequent vehicles further west. Makongolosi, 37km beyond Chunya and 40km short of the lake, is generally the furthest you can get, though you may strike lucky with a mission vehicle for the next 22km to Saza. Without your own wheels you'll have to walk from there, unless you can manage to hire a bicycle. If you're driving, note that the road west of Saza becomes exceedingly muddy in the rains.

There are no restrictions on **camping** at the lakeshore (or as near as you can get without becoming stuck in a swamp), but you should seek permission from any locals you can find and keep an eye out for crocodiles and hippos. Swimming is not advisable for this reason, especially on the southeast shore, where the crocs are known to be particularly dangerous.

Kalambo Falls

Sitting square on the border with Zambia, and only a few kilometres east of Lake Tanganyika, the breathtaking 215-metre **Kalambo Falls** are the second-highest uninterrupted falls in Africa, their waters plunging into the canyon of the river that forms the border with Zambia. Aside from the falls' natural beauty, they're also a breeding ground for the giant marabou stork, and several sites in the vicinity have great archeological importance: 300,000-year-old Stone Age tools have been uncovered, as well as the world's oldest evidence for the use of wood in construction, dating back 60,000 years. Excavations of early Iron Age villages and campsites have revealed a wealth of earthenware pottery – mainly globular pots and shallow bowls – the earliest of which have been dated to around 350 AD.

Access to the falls, which lie 130km southwest of Sumbawanga, is awkward without your own vehicle. The best way to visit is to overnight at Muzi on the lakeshore, which you can reach by ferry from Kigoma (see p.527). Catch a pick-up at around 6am the next day to Kalambo village, 5km north of the falls, from where you'll have to walk. If you're coming from Sumbawanga, catch a pick-up towards Muzi or Kasanga but get off in Kawala, from where it's an exhausting fifteen-kilometre walk to the falls through Kalambo village. A tent would be useful as there's no accommodation in either Kalambo or Kawala, nor any regular transport back to Sumbawanga after 9am, though a few pick-ups run from Kawala to Muzi until late afternoon. Seek local advice about **crocodiles** if you want to swim.

Travel details

Buses and pick-ups

The pick-ups listed below are usually trucks or 4WD vehicles that leave when full; details are given in the arrival sections throughout this chapter. An asterisk denotes that transport may not run in the rains – again, read the arrival sections of the relevant town for more details. Journey times are for the dry season, though bearing in mind the vagaries of local transport and roads, journey times may in practice be considerably longer than those given below.

Kigoma to: Biharamulo (4 weekly*; 7–9hr); Kibondo (1–3 daily*; 4–6hr); Mwanza (5 weekly*; 14–18hr); Shinyanga (weekly*; 10–12hr); Ujiji (2–4 hourly*; 20min).

Mpanda to: Kalema (pick-ups*; 6hr); Mamba (3 weekly; 3–5hr); Sumbawanga (3 weekly and daily pick-ups; 5hr).

Sumbawanga to: Dar es Salaam (weekly; 2 days); Kasanga (daily pick-ups*; 5–9hr); Mbeya (2 daily; 6–7hr); Mpanda (3 weekly and daily pick-ups; 5hr); Muse (daily pick-ups; 2hr); Tanga (weekly; 2 days); Tunduma (2 daily; 5hr); Zimba (daily pick-ups; 1hr).

Tabora to: Arusha (2 weekly*; 28hr); Babati (2 weekly*; 24hr); Chunya (3 weekly*; 22hr+); Makongolosi (3 weekly*; 21hr+); Mbeya (3 weekly*; 24hr+); Mwanza (2 weekly*; 10–12hr); Nzega (4 weekly* and daily pick-ups; 3hr); Shinyanga (4 weekly*; 6–8hr); Singida (2 weekly*; 8hr).

Trains

See p.35 for general information on Tanzania's train network. Times and days are given in the relevant arrival sections.

Kigoma to: Dar (4 weekly; 39hr 50min); Dodoma (4 weekly; 25hr 10min); Morogoro (4 weekly; 32hr 35min); Tabora (4 weekly; 11hr 30min).

Mpanda to: Kaliua (3 weekly; 10hr 50min); Katumba (3 weekly; 2hr 15min); Tabora (3 weekly; 13hr 45min).

Tabora to: Dar (5 weekly; 24hr 25min); Dodoma (5 woekly; 10hr 45min); Kaliua (3 wcckly; 2hr 44min); Katumba (3 weekly; 11hr 48min); Kigoma (4 weekly; 11hr 15min); Morogoro (5 weekly; 18hr 10min); Mpanda (3 weekly; 13hr 30min); Mwanza (4 weekly; 10hr 5min).

Ferries and lake taxis (Lake Tanganyika)

There are two weekly steamers on Lake Tanganyika, the *MV Mwongozo* which goes from Kigoma to Bujumbura (Burundi), and the *MV Liemba* which sails from Kigoma to Mpulungu in Zambia via a chain of minor Tanzanian ports. See the boxes on "Moving on from Kigoma" (p.526) and the *MV Liemba* (p.520) for more details. There's also a military vessel, the *MV Burombora*, which takes passengers, sailing from Kigoma to Mahale Mountains National Park (see p.536). Local taxi boats link the various Tanzanian ports, but can be exceedingly uncomfortable and dangerous at times.

Flights

EA indicates Eagle Air; PA is Precisionair, who have a route-sharing agreement with Air Tanzania. Tickets can be bought from either company but Precisionair are more reliable.

Kigoma to: Dar es Salaam (PA; 3 weekly; 3hr).

Tabora to: Bukoba via Mwanza (EA; weekly; 2hr 25min); Dar via Kigoma (PA; 2 weekly; 2hr 45min); Dar direct (PA & EA; 2 weekly; 2hr); Dodoma via Mwanza (EA, weekly, 3hr 10min); Kagera (EA; 2 weekly; 1hr 10min); Kigoma (PA; 2 weekly; 1hr); Mwanza (EA; 2 weekly; 70min); Zanzibar via Kigoma & Dar (PA; 2 weekly; 3hr 15min).

LAKE TANGANYIKA AND WESTERN TANZANIA | Travel details

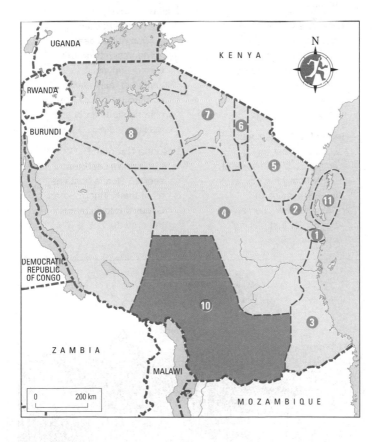

Southern Tanzania

✳ **The Southern Highlands** From Mbeya or Tukuyu, guided walks and day-trips are possible to waterfalls, volcanic crater lakes, a lava-stone bridge, a meteorite, and up the forested peaks of several mountains. **See p.580**

✳ **Lake Nyasa** The most beautiful of the Rift Valley lakes, best seen from the weekly ferry, which gives access to Mbamba Bay and Malawi. **See p.595**

✳ **Mbamba Bay** Tanzania's southernmost town, actually a big, dusty and fantastically friendly village. The miles of dreamlike beaches are perfect for just chilling out. **See p.602**

✳ **Kalenga** The historical seat of the Hehe, who under Chief Mkwawa fought the Germans for almost a decade. A museum tended by his descendants contains his skull. **See p.570**

✳ **Isimila** Quietly spectacular series of eroded gullies near Iringa, resembling the Grand Canyon in miniature, and site of numerous finds of pre-historic stone tools and fossils. **See p.570**

✳ **Ruaha National Park** "Tanzania's best-kept secret", Ruaha contains all of the Northern Safari Circuit's wildlife minus the crowds. **See p.574**

Southern Tanzania

M uch of **southern Tanzania**, from the volcanic Southern Highlands to scenic Lake Nyasa, is mountainous and wildly beautiful terrain, although the majority of visitors pass through quickly en route to Malawi or Zambia – a shame, as there's lots to see and do, and access to the region's various attractions is now relatively easy thanks to the establishment of tourism programmes in Iringa, Mbeya and elsewhere. Most people approach southern Tanzania along the Tanzam Highway. The first major town after Morogoro is the lively and charming centre of **Iringa**, 500km southwest of Dar es Salaam, which makes an excellent base for exploring the numerous cultural and natural attractions nearby, including the forests of the **western Udzungwa Mountains**. Iringa is also the main base for visits to **Ruaha National Park**, the equal of the Northern Circuit parks in terms of animal numbers, but with only a fraction of the crowds.

Southern Tanzania's other big town is **Mbeya**, set on a plateau amidst the verdant **Southern Highlands**. The highlands were created during the volcanic upheavals that formed the Rift Valley, and there are crater lakes aplenty, along with hot springs and patches of ancient rainforest. South of Mbeya, near the foot of the dormant Mount Rungwe volcano, is the small agricultural town of **Tukuyu**, a good alternative base for exploring the highlands, despite having the distinction of being Tanzania's wettest place. South of Tukuyu lies **Lake Nyasa**, a stunning Rift Valley lake that forms the border with Malawi and Mozambique, flanked to its east by the soaring Livingstone Mountains. There are a couple of beautiful beaches to visit, at **Matema** in the north, and **Mbamba Bay** in the far south. From Mbamba Bay, a road heads east to **Songea**, a large and exceedingly remote town close to the Mozambique border.

There are three main **overland routes into southern Tanzania**: the fast Tanzam Highway, which starts in Dar es Salaam and goes all the way to Zambia (a branch also heads into Malawi); the TAZARA railway, which follows much the same route; and the more adventurous approach from western Tanzania (covered in Chapter 9), either along Lake Tanganyika by ferry, or by road through Katavi National Park, which routes join at Sumbawanga and then continue down to Mbeya. Even more adventurous is the approach from the Indian Ocean, along a rarely travelled and extremely rough dry-season road to Songea via Masasi and Tunduru.

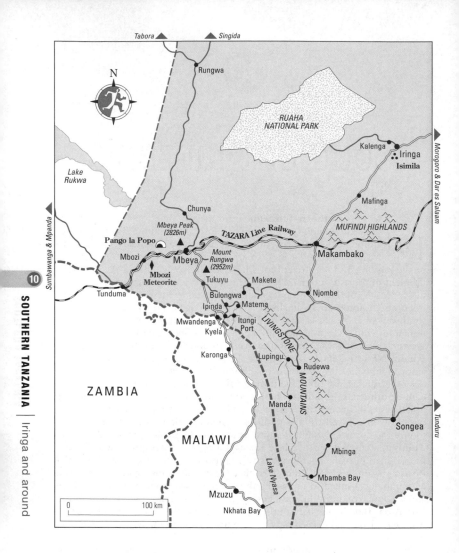

Iringa and around

The only major settlement between Morogoro and Mbeya is the pleasingly
relaxed town of **Iringa**, set amidst a region of appealingly bare and jagged hills,
scattered with weathered granite boulders and covered here and there with
deep green patches of ancient forest – wild country that's ideal for hiking.
There are plenty of worthwhile destinations here, from the beautiful forests of

the **western Udzungwa Mountains** and **Mufindi Highlands** to sites of historical importance related to the Hehe Chief Mkwawa's long and, for a several years, successful stand against the Germans at the end of the nineteenth century.

For most visitors, however, Iringa is only a stop en route to **Ruaha National Park**, a few hours west by road. Tanzania's second-largest national park, Ruaha's amazing variety and quantity of animals is quite the equal of the Northern Circuit parks, but without the crowds.

Iringa

Gloriously perched on top of an escarpment overlooking the valley of the Little Ruaha River, and backed by a range of undulating hills and cracked boulders, **IRINGA** is one of Tanzania's most attractive towns. It's also an unusually friendly and welcoming place, despite the rareness of tourists and the fact that not many people speak English, while *wazungu* used to northern climes will appreciate the cool climate afforded by the relatively high altitude (1600m – it gets positively chilly in June and July). Apart from the surrounding views, the town's main attraction is unquestionably its market, one of the country's liveliest and most atmospheric. Iringa is also a handy base for visiting a number of attractions in the surrounding region, many of which can be done as day-trips – see p.570.

Arrival and accommodation

Iringa lies 2km north of the Tanzam Highway, 309km southwest of Morogoro, and 362km northeast of Mbeya. There are three weekly Precisionair **flights** from Arusha via Moshi and Dar to the airstrip at Nduli, about 10km north of town. The **bus stand** is in the centre of town, 500m west of the new **tourist information centre** at the Natural Resources Office on the corner of Mkoa Street and Dodoma Road (usually Mon–Fri 8am–5pm), which should have maps and information on hotels, safari operators, transport and the various hikes in the region (see p.570).

Accommodation

There's plenty of good budget and mid-range accommodation, plus a couple of attractive rural places out of town popular with overland truck parties – both the latter also have **campsites** as does the *Huruma Baptist Conference Centre*.

Town centre

Dr Amon J. Nsekela Bankers Academy Uhuru Ave ☎026/270 2431, ℱ026/270 2563. Part of a defunct college now offering reasonable-value ensuite rooms (couples are welcome to share single rooms) plus some suites, which have bigger beds and also fridges. Check the mosquito nets: some are missing, others are too small to fit the beds. Safe parking. Breakfast included. ②–③

Embalasasa Hotel Uhuru Ave ☎026/270 1938, ℱ026/270 2948. One of the town's better options, with en-suite rooms, all with huge beds and box nets, plus some suites, and a bar and restaurant downstairs. ③–④

Huruma Baptist Conference Centre 2.5km north of town along Uvinza St; turn left after 2km, opposite Mkwawa Secondary School ☎026/270 0184, ℮hbcc@maf.org.tz. A comfortable place set in expansive gardens (a swimming pool is due for completion by 2003). There are lots of clean and well-kept rooms, with constant hot water, ranging from dorms (Tsh4100 per person) to en-suite twins and huge four-bed apartments with kitchens. There's also a good cheap restaurant, and safaris to Ruaha National Park and Mikumi (see p.576) can be organized here. Daladalas from the bus stand run from 6.30am until 7pm. No smoking. Breakfast included. ②–④

IRINGA

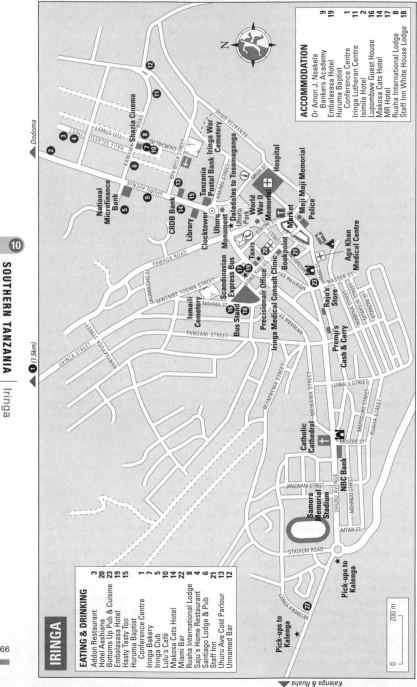

EATING & DRINKING

Addon Restaurant	3
Hotel Aashiana	20
Bottoms Up Pub & Cuisine	23
Embalasasa Hotel	19
Hasty Tasty Too	15
Huruma Baptist	
Conference Centre	1
Iringa Bakery	7
Iringa Club	5
Lulu's Café	10
Makosa Cats Hotel	14
Miami Bar	22
Ruaha International Lodge	8
Saju's Home Restaurant	4
Santiago Lodge & Pub	6
Staff Inn	21
Uhuru Ave Cold Parlour	13
Unnamed Bar	12

ACCOMMODATION

Dr Amon J. Nsekela	9
Bankers Academy	19
Embalasasa Hotel	1
Huruma Baptist	
Conference Centre	11
Iringa Lutheran Centre	2
Isimila Hotel	16
Lupombwe Guest House	14
Makosa Cats Hotel	17
MR Hotel	8
Ruaha International Lodge	18
Staff Inn White House Lodge	

Iringa Lutheran Centre Kawawa Rd ☎026/270
1990. The town's best cheapie, this is a quiet and
adequate if extremely dull option, and there's a
10pm curfew – though it's not a problem getting
past the *askari* later. "It is forbidden to use loin
cloths to dust the body" is one of their more
obscure rules. Single rooms are very small; doubles (some en suite) fare better, but bed sheets are
invariably too small. Soft drinks are available, but
no food. Safe parking. ❶

Isimila Hotel Uhuru Ave ☎026/270 2605.
Friendly and calm place with 48 en-suite rooms in
several big blocks, surrounded by cypress and
bottlebrush trees. Despite being a bit damp and
forlorn, it's still comfortable and is well-priced.
There's also a stuffy restaurant, bar and safe
parking. Breakfast included. ❸

Lupombwe Guest House Mahiwa St (no phone).
Simple and basic, but conveniently close to the
bus stand if you're leaving early the next day. ❶

Makosa Cats Hotel Uhuru Ave ☎026/270 1560.
Named after the original owner, who had an insa-
tiable love for felines, this attractively quirky option
has seven en-suite rooms in an enchanting "Alice
in Wonderland"-style garden. Two of the rooms are
small and unexceptional, the rest are huge and
have bathtubs and Western toilets. There's also a
bar and restaurant at the front, and a large swimming pool under construction. Safe parking.
Breakfast included. ❷

MR Hotel Mkwawa Rd ☎026/270 2006,
ⓦwww.mrhotel.co.tz. The town's main mid-range
choice, aimed squarely at the business market,
with seventeen bright and spotless rooms on three
floors; the higher the room, the less noise from the
bus stand. All come with TV, phone, balcony and
hot water, and facilities include a restaurant (no
alcohol), internet café and safe parking. Breakfast
included. ❹

Ruaha International Lodge Corner of Kawawa
Rd and Churchill Rd (no phone). A pretty basic
place that mainly fills up with couples after its
weekend discos. The best rooms share bathrooms
(the en-suite rooms can get smelly, and there's no
hot water in any case); look at several before
choosing, as they vary greatly in cleanliness and
repair – those in the south wing are marginally
quieter. Safe parking. ❶

Staff Inn White House Lodge Mahiwa St
☎026/270 0161. A reasonable budget choice,
albeit more expensive than the competition, with
loads of clean and mostly en-suite rooms. Singles
are tatty; much better are the doubles with box
nets, phones, Western toilets and bathtubs. ❷

Out of town

Kisolanza Farm Lodge 59km southwest of Iringa
towards Mbeya (no phone) ⓔkisolanza@
cats-net.com. This is a major stopover for overland
trucks heading south into Zambia, but this
shouldn't put you off: apart from camping ($3 per
person), there are attractive twin-bed chalets sharing bathrooms (with reliable hot showers), and
much more expensive en-suite cottages with log
fires. There's also a bar and a farm shop that sells
lovely fresh bread. Reservations by email are
essential for rooms. Chalets ❸, en-suite cottages
(half board) ❼

Little Ruaha Riverside Campsite 14km east of
town (12.5km towards Morogoro then 1.5km
south) ☎026/272 5280, ⓔmasumbo@
masumbo.co.tz. Set beside the Little Ruaha River,
this lovely hideaway, offers both a campsite (with
four-person tents for Tsh2000) and a chalet with
kitchen for up to three adults and two children
(Tsh10,000). The main attraction is the welter of
activities, including several kilometres of walking
trails, swimming in the river, tours to Wangama
and Lundamatwe villages, mountain-biking, horse-
riding and visits to Lugalo, Isimila and Kalenga.
Walking and birding safaris in the western
Udzungwa Mountains (see p.572) can also be
organized by prior arrangement, as can safaris into
Ruaha National Park.

The Town

Iringa's main attraction is its **market**, on the south side of town between
Jamhuri and Jamat streets. Built in 1940, it's a colourful and vibrant shambles,
and is the closest you'll get to an Arab souk outside Zanzibar's Stone Town. You
could spend hours rummaging around here amongst the many oddities on
offer, including beautifully woven (and sometimes aromatic) baskets made from
reeds or sisal, pumice stones, bath sponges and loufas imported from the coast,
and even cow bells. There's also a riotous selection of kanga wraps, traditional
medicines, *kibatari* oil lamps, pungent dried fish from Mtera Dam, gold jewellery and pottery from all over, including – if you're lucky – examples of the
gorgeous cream-and-red ware from the Kisi tribe of Lake Nyasa (see p.599).

The historic streets of the compact **German quarter** around and to the **west of the market** are also worth exploring, since these are where most of the town's surviving colonial buildings are located – look for the tall, Bavarian-style building with the clock tower on Jamat Street, originally the town hall, now the Ismaili mosque.

On the south side of the market in front of the police station (no photography) is the **Maji Maji memorial**, erected by the Germans after the uprising, which commemorates African *askaris* (soldiers) who died while in their service. Another poignant memorial is **Iringa war cemetery**, 600m northeast of here at the junction of Dodoma Road and Ben Bella Street, which contains both British and German graves from World War I, as well as those of locals and European settlers who fought in World War II – the neatly arrayed headstones reveal that most died when in their early twenties. The cemetery gate is not always open; it's a matter of pot luck.

One more attraction, an hour's walk away, is **Gangilonga Rock** – a large, orange-streaked boulder nestling in a vale between two peaks south of town, where Chief Mkwawa (see p.571) is said to have come to meditate. In Kihehe, the rock's name means "talking stone", alluding to a legend that the rock gave advice when asked – perhaps inspired by the whistling sound which cracks in the boulder emit when the wind blows in the right direction. Either way, it's a nice walk, and rewards you with a panoramic view of Iringa. Giving directions is difficult without a local to guide you, though you can see the rock to your right as you walk along the north of Uhuru Avenue, past the grain silos. It's best visited in the afternoon to catch sunset.

Eating

For your own **supplies**, Iringa Bakery on Churchill Road has good bread and does cakes to order. For imported packaged stuff, try Premji's or Raju's supermarkets on Jamhuri Street, though both are pricey.

Addon Restaurant Haile Selassie St. Specializes in Indian, Chinese and vegetarian dishes (whatever's cooking, rather than what's on the menu; mains around Tsh3500). The Indian dishes are the real thing and quite delicious; the Chinese food is also good but isn't authentic. There are seats under parasols at the back, and fresh juices and alcohol are available.

Embalasasa Hotel Uhuru Ave. The rather glum dining room here has a wide menu, although little of it is ever available. Still, the food is generally good, and the fish (around Tsh2000) can be excellent. There's also a bar with a TV.

Hasty Tasty Too Uhuru Ave ☎026/270 2061. This is something of an Iringan institution, both for its meals and snacks and also as a place where locals meet friends and catch up on the latest news. Breakfasts are uncommonly good, full meals are tasty, and they also have treats like chocolates, jam, cakes, and fresh coffee and juices. The friendly owner is knowledgeable about all things Iringan, and can set up safaris or car hire for Ruaha. Closed Sun afternoon and evening.

Hotel Aashiana Akiba House, Soko Kuu St. This cheerful option dishes up shakes and cheap snacks, as well as decent full meals like curries, Chinese dishes and pizza. Daily until 8.30pm.

Huruma Baptist Conference Centre 2.5km north of town. The restaurant here is bit of a hike if you're not staying overnight, but perhaps the prospect of pork or tortilla will tempt you. There's a big menu averaging Tsh2500 for mains, though you'll have to arrive early and be patient for their Indian, Chinese and Mexican dishes.

Lulu's Café Churchill Rd. Like *Hasty Tasty Too*, this is a favourite with travellers and expats alike, though it's more expensive and not as welcoming or cosy. Breakfasts are good (including sausages, baked beans and fresh juices), as are snacks – toasted sandwiches, burgers and ice cream. The menu (mains Tsh3000–4000) features Euro-Asian cooking with a touch of Greek, but the quality is hit and miss.

Makosa Cats Hotel Uhuru Ave. The staff here are slooow, as is the food (around Tsh1500) in coming, but when it does it's often very good. There are some reports of overcharging, so check your bill.

Saju's Home Restaurant Haile Selasie St. An attractive and peaceful split-level place doing standard Tanzanian dishes like *ugali*, rice or chips with fish, beef, chicken or vegetables (Tsh800–1500), plus lots of snacks, TV and alcohol.

Staff Inn Between Miomboni St and Jamhuri St. Although pretty empty these days, the food remains good, albeit a little pricier than other places – the liver stew is excellent. There's also a TV.

Uhuru Avenue Cold Parlour Corner of Ben Bella St and Uhuru Ave. No-frills fixes for ice-cream junkies.

Drinking and nightlife

There are lots of local "groceries" serving beers throughout town, none of which is particularly enticing. More attractive are the following.

Bottoms Up Pub & Cuisine Miomboni St. The town's only upmarket bar, with a dartboard and TV, plus a good restaurant. Closed Mon.

Iringa Club Off Uhuru Ave. Ignore the "members only" sign – someone forgot to take it down – this is a genteel local place happy to serve everyone.

Makosa Cats Hotel Uhuru Ave. Forget the dismal bar at the front and walk through to the wonderful garden at the back, whose tables – under shady magnolia trees, yellow-bark fever trees and bougainvillaea bushes – are a blissful setting for a quiet afternoon drink.

Miami Bar Kalenga Rd. A lively, friendly and often packed local bar, with – weirdly – an excellent selection of Scotch whiskies. A taxi from the town centre costs Tsh1000.

Ruaha International Lodge Corner of Kawawa Rd and Churchill Rd. This normally sedate bar and restaurant hosts loud discos on Friday and Saturday.

Santiago Lodge & Pub Kawawa Rd. A quiet and dark place for a drink, assuming you succeed in waking up the staff. (The "lodge" part died years ago, incidentally.)

Unnamed bar Corner of Kawawa Rd and Dodoma Rd. A nice local place, especially by day, with seating around big trees in the back garden. Bar food available, too.

Listings

Banks and exchange NBC Bank, Uhuru Ave, is more efficient than CRDB, also on Uhuru Ave east of the clock tower.

Cinema Shazia Cinema, Kawawa Rd, is the only surviving cinema, mainly showing Bollywood epics and gung-ho Hollywood action movies. Screenings are at 7pm Monday to Saturday, plus a 3pm matinee on Saturday. Beware the double bills on Tuesday and Thursday: the second movie is soft porn.

Hospital The town's best hospital is the Aga Khan Medical Centre on Jamat St near the market ☎ 027/2700581. Iringa Medical Consult Clinic, Akiba House, Soko Kuu St ☎ 026/270 2819 (daily 8am–8pm), does blood tests and handles minor ailments.

Internet The only decent options at present are the Cyber Internet Centre, under *Bottom's Up* on Miomboni St, and the *MR Hotel*.

Kiswahili lessons Huruma Baptist Conference Centre offers two- to four-month courses, starting

Moving on from Iringa

The Tanzam Highway is good tarmac and terrifyingly fast in places. The unsurfaced road to Dodoma, in contrast, is always in bad shape, despite periodic regrading. The condition of other regional routes, such as the road to Ruaha National Park, varies according to the severity of the last rains and how quickly repairs are completed. Nonetheless, they're rarely impassable.

Long-distance buses leave from the bus stand in the centre of town. There are frequent services in either direction along the Tanzam Highway, northeast to **Morogoro** and **Dar**, and southwest to **Mbeya**. There are also frequent minibuses to Mbeya, Songea and Kyela; these depart either from the bus stand or from the round-about at the west end of Uhuru Avenue, but their safety reputation isn't great. Several bus companies also run daily to **Kyela** and **Songea**; the safest is Scandinavian Express, whose office is on Soko Kuu Street near the bus stand. Unfortunately the only daily bus to **Moshi** and **Arusha** is run by the notoriously reckless Hood; much safer is to catch a Scandinavian Express bus to Dar and head on to Arusha the next day. **Dodoma** is served by at least two daily buses.

on the 15th of Jan, Feb, Mar, Aug, Sept, Oct and Nov. The cost is $450 per month including tuition and full board. For something less intensive, contact the affable Mrs John though the Iringa Bakery (or ☎0744/373211), who charges Tsh3000 per hour.

Library Iringa Regional Library, Uhuru Ave by the clock tower (Mon–Fri 9.30am–6pm, Sat 8.30am–2pm; Tsh500 daily membership).

Newspapers There's a good stand on Uhuru Ave just west of the clock tower, and another the east end of Miomboni St.

Pharmacy Acacia Pharmacy, Uhuru Ave ☎026/270 2335 (Mon–Sat 8am–8pm, Sun 8am–2pm).

Post office Just west of the clock tower roundabout.

Telephones TTCL is next to the post office (Mon–Sat 7.30am–10pm, Sun 8am–8pm).

Around Iringa

There are loads of things to see and do around Iringa, including hikes through rainforests rich in birdlife, the Stone Age site of **Isimila**, and the historic villages of **Kalenga** and **Tosamaganga**, which played a pivotal role in Chief Mkwawa's confrontations with the Germans. For all the following options, the best starting point is the **tourist information centre** at the Natural Resources Office in Iringa, at the corner of Mkoa Street and Dodoma Road (usually Mon–Fri 8am–5pm; PO Box 148, Iringa ☎026/270 2246, ⓔmemairinga@twiga.com), who are developing low-impact tourism in the region. Although it's still early days, they have all the information you'll need, and may be able to fix you up with a guide.

Kalenga and Tosamaganga

An easy half-day trip from Iringa is to **KALENGA** village, 15km west of town along the road to Ruaha National Park. Kalenga was the headquarters of **Chief Mkwawa** (see opposite) until he was driven out by the Germans in 1894, and there's a small museum here tended by the great warrior's descendants, as well as the remains of the fortifications which he began in 1887. The history of Mkwawa's struggles with the Germans is recorded in Kalenga's **Mkwawa Memorial Museum** (daily; Tsh1500), signposted 1.5km from the village. The museum contains an assortment of clubs, spears and shields, plus the shotgun with which Mkwawa committed suicide. The chief exhibit, though, is Mkwawa's skull, which was returned to the Hehe in 1954 after a 56-year exile in Germany. Outside the museum are some **tombs** of Mkwawa's descendants, including his son, Chief Sapi Mkwawa, and his grandson, Chief Adam Sapi Mkwawa. Some 500m away is another tomb, recently restored, containing the body of **Erich Maas**, a German commando who attempted to infiltrate the fort and capture Mkwawa alive; the unfortunate Maas was discovered by Mkwawa himself, at whose hands he met his death.

A daily bus from Iringa run by Kiponza Transport passes by in the early afternoon, but most people catch one of the frequent pick-ups or daladalas (6am–6pm; every 30min) from the roundabout at the west end of Uhuru Avenue, at the junction with Kalenga Road and the road to Mbeya. If you like the area, Kalenga can be combined with a visit to the Catholic mission at **Tosamaganga**, a pleasant six-kilometre walk southwest, from where there's frequent transport back to Iringa (6am–6pm). There's no accommodation in Kalenga or Tosamaganga.

Isimila

Just over 20km southwest of Iringa, just off the Tanzam Highway, is **ISIMILA**, one of the richest Stone Age sites in Africa: since 1958, excavations here have uncovered thousands of stone tools dating from the so-called Acheulian period,

Chief Mkwawa of the Hehe

The Tanzanian interior in the latter half of the nineteenth century was in a state of chaotic flux. Incursions by Arab slave traders from the coast had disrupted the balance of power between clans and tribes, while the invasion of the militaristic Ngoni in the south proved another source of chaos, and the trigger for several mass migrations. This uncertain climate provided ideal soil on which opportunistic leaders such as Chief Mirambo of the Nyamwezi (see p.541) could create their own personal kingdoms.

Another leader who emerged triumphantly from this confusion was the son of a Hehe chief named Mtwa Mkwawa Mwamnyika ("Conqueror of Many Lands"), better known as **Chief Mkwawa**. Born near Kalenga in 1855, Mkwawa's ambitious character was well suited to his times. By 1889, he had become undisputed leader of the Hehe, whom he made the region's dominant tribe by uniting, though force or diplomacy, more than one hundred clans and smaller tribes. It was not just numbers, but regimented military organization that formed the basis of Hehe power, and that gave Mkwawa the ability to stem the hitherto inexorable southward advance of the Maasai. Mkwawa also began to threaten Arab control over the lucrative slave and ivory-carrying caravan routes that passed through his territory, though the decline in Arab power meant that it was not against the sultans of Zanzibar that the showdown came, but against the war machine of colonial Germany.

At first, Mkwawa tried to secure treaties with the Germans, but when they refused, the Hehe turned their arms against the arrogant newcomers. On August 17, 1891, a year after the Germans had placed a garrison in Iringa, Mkwawa's troops surrounded and ambushed a German expeditionary force led by Lieutenant Emil von Zelewski in the Lugalo Hills east of Iringa, killing nearly five hundred soldiers and capturing a vast quantity of firearms and munitions. Only two German officers and fifteen men escaped.

Mkwawa was no fool, however, and anticipated German revenge by building a thirteen-kilometre, four-metre high wall around his palace and military base at Kalenga. The Germans took their time to reorganize, and it wasn't until October 1894 that they made their move, establishing themselves on a hill overlooking Kalenga, now the site of Tosamaganga village, and beginning a two-day bombardment of Kalenga (the name *tosamaganga* means to "throw stones"). On October 30, 1894, the Germans under Tom von Prince stormed and took Kalenga with relative ease. The extent of Mkwawa's wealth can be gauged by the fact that it took four hundred porters to carry all his ivory away. The Germans also found 30,000 pounds of gunpowder, which they used to level the town. For Mkwawa, the loss of Kalenga was a double tragedy, since his mother — who had been told that her son had been captured – committed suicide.

In fact, Mkwawa escaped into the forests west of Kalenga, from where he waged a four-year **guerrilla war** against the Germans. He was finally cornered in 1898, having been betrayed by informants attracted by a 5000-rupee reward. Rather than surrender, he shot his bodyguard, and then himself. The Germans, arriving on the scene shortly after, placed another shot into Mkwawa's head, just to be sure, then severed it to serve as proof that their adversary was dead. The chief's headless body was buried by his family at Mlambalasi, 12km south of the road to Ruaha National Park, while his **skull** was sent on to Berlin and then on to the Bremen Anthropological Museum. There it remained until 1954, when it was finally returned to the Hehe – it's now the star exhibit of Kalenga's Mkwawa Memorial Museum.

Mkwawa's death marked the end of two decades of resistance to German rule across Tanganyika, and the end of the Hehe empire, but the ensuing peace was short-lived. Seven years on, the Maji Maji Uprising erupted, which took the Germans over two years to crush.

For more on Chief Mkwawa and Hehe history, see Ⓦ www.mkwawa.com.

some 60,000 years ago. Even if archeology isn't your thing, the scenery – small but spectacular canyons studded with bizarrely eroded pink and orange sandstone needles – makes the trip worthwhile, as do the rock hyrax, small and furry creatures (they look a bit like guinea-pigs) whose unlikely claim to fame is that they're the closest living relatives of elephants. Look out also for swifts and sand martins.

Erosional forces associated with the Isimila River created the strange natural sandstone sculptures you see today, and were also responsible for uncovering the stone tools. At the time the tools were made, part of the site was occupied by a small and shallow lake, which attracted both men and animals. The tools, made from a variety of locally available stones, cover much of the area, but are most easily seen in one of the five excavation sites – you're allowed to handle them, but not remove them. Pear-shaped hand-axes and cleavers are most common; there are also cutters, hammers, picks and scrapers, and spherical balls whose use has never been fully explained. The **fossil remains** of various animals discovered at the site hint at an environment not too different from today: elephants and antelopes, and various extinct mammals, including a giant hog, a short-necked giraffe and a weird species of hippo, which appears to have been even more boggle-eyed than the modern form.

The site is 21km southwest of Iringa off the Tanzam Highway. The curator's hut is signposted 1km southeast of the road, and sits at the edge of a low escarpment overlooking the eroded gully where the stone tools were found. There's a small **museum** beside the hut, which also sells a short but informative guidebook. **Admission** to the site and museum costs Tsh1500 (a tip is also appreciated), which gets you an entertaining two-hour tour of the gully, including two of the five excavated sites, each containing hundreds of stone tools scattered among unworked stones.

Udekwa and western Udzungwa

East of Iringa, the forested western foothills of the **Udzungwa Mountains** have recently been opened up to small-scale tourism by the establishment of several walking trails. The foothills are especially rich in endemic and near-endemic birds (over three hundred species), including the Udzungwa partridge, rufous-winged sunbird, dappled mountain robin, spot-throat, Nduk eagle owl, and Iringa akalat. The best time for birding is September to early December. Apart from the birds, the forests are an attraction in their own right, as are the expansive views from their various peaks and ridges. For more on **Udzungwa Mountains National Park**, which covers the central and eastern section of the range, see p.298.

Access is through **UDEKWA** village, about three hours' drive (in dry weather) east of Iringa. From Iringa, follow the Tanzam Highway for 45km to **Ilulu** (or Ilula) village, northeast of town. Shortly after here, there's a right turn onto the unsurfaced road to Udekwa (at least 2hr) – there should be pick-ups at the junction covering this stretch. If you're driving, ask for directions whenever you can as there are no signposts. With your own wheels, a day-trip from Iringa is feasible, but it would be much better to spend a few days in the area, for which you'll need a tent; you can hire one at *Little Ruaha Riverside Campsite* (see p.567), who are very clued-up and also provide excellent guides who are completely bananas about birds. Costs aren't yet fixed, but shouldn't be more than $30 a day, including guide, permits and porters. It can get chilly at night, so bring warm clothes, and rain gear. Most of the foothills are protected as forest reserves: you'll need a **permit** to enter (Tsh5000 a day from the Natural Resources Office in Iringa). Show the permit to the village government officer near the school in Udekwa. You'll also need a guide, and (optionally) porters if you're hiking for more than a day; the government officer can select reliable locals for this purpose.

There's no regular accommodation in Udekwa, though there are three **campsites** in the area. The easiest to reach is *Chui Campsite*, 7km into the forest reserve, which serves as the main base for hikers. *Luala Valley Campsite* is set on a grassy glade in the forest on Ndundulu ridge (5–6hr walk from *Chui Campsite*). From *Luala*, you can birdwatch along forest trails northeast towards Mount Luhombero, Udzungwa's highest point. It's a good place to find the Udzungwa partridge and rufous-winged sunbird. The third campsite is *Mufu Camp*, a six-hour walk from Chui along a steep trail. The camp is right in the forest, and has wealth of birdlife around it.

For more information, contact the tourist information centre in Iringa or the *Little Ruaha Riverside Campsite*.

The Mufindi Highlands

The tea estates and forests of the **Mufindi Highlands**, 100km south of Iringa, have recently been made accessible to tourists by the opening of *Fox's Southern Highland Fishing Lodge* (see below), which can arrange all the practicalities for you. If your budget won't stretch to this, the tourist information centre in Iringa (see p.570) is a good source of information on local guest houses and guides, and may be offering its own guided visits to Mufindi in the near future.

The highlands are exceptionally scenic: the bright green of the tea estates, scattered lakes, rainforests – and, of course, the views from the peaks and ridges. The forests are especially rich in **birdlife**, with rare species including blue swallows, the Uhehe fiscal, short-tailed pipit, the mountain marsh whydah and Iringa akalat. At the top of the forest, an escarpment gives dramatic views to the south and east over the Kilombero Valley. Add in the altitude (around 2000m), and you have a refreshing and mosquito-free getaway.

Access is via **MAFINGA** (John's Corner), 90km southwest of Iringa along the Tanzam Highway; all buses heading to Mbeya or Songea pass by. If you're driving and just fancy a pleasant side trip for the day, the road from Mafinga eventually loops around at Kibao (Kibaoni), coming back to the tarmac highway at Nyororo (James' Corner), an eighty-kilometre round trip. **Accommodation** is available at *Fox's Southern Highland Fishing Lodge* (also called *Mufindi Highland Lodge* or *Fox Farm*; bookings through Foxtreks in Dar, see p.125; full-board ❼), 40km south of Mafinga. Located in a 1500-acre estate, the main building is a rustic two-storey granite-and-timber affair containing a bar, dining room, TV lounge, snooker room and a large verandah with great views of the surrounding forests. The bedrooms are in eight en-suite log cabins; room rates include guided forest walks, birding, mountain-biking, horse-riding, boating, a cultural tour to local villages and fishing for rainbow trout, and as such represent excellent value for money. Two nights at least are recommended. The easiest way to get there is to arrange beforehand for the lodge to pick you up either from Mafinga ($50 per vehicle) or from Sawala ($25 per vehicle), 25km south of Mafinga, to which it's connected by frequent daladalas; there's also a daily bus from Iringa and Makambako train station. If you're driving, turn off the highway at Mafinga and head south into the hills until Sawala, then turn right along the road to Lupeme Tea Estate and follow the signs for 15km.

Ruaha National Park

Straddling the Rift Valley west of Iringa, and covering almost thirteen thousand square kilometres, **RUAHA NATIONAL PARK** is one of Tanzania's largest and most remote wildlife areas, well deserving its moniker of "Tanzania's best-kept secret". The park's comparative inaccessibility means that it receives an average of just six thousand visitors a year, although a growing number of luxury tented camps and lodges, plans to extend the park's road network and on-going efforts to open up the "Southern Circuit" to tourism may soon put an end to that.

The **Great Ruaha River**, which runs along much of the southeastern boundary, is the park's lifeblood, attracting great numbers of wildlife in the dry season, when all else around is parched and yellow. Since 1993, however, the river has dried up completely in the dry seasons, each time for longer periods, thanks to unsustainable water use for rice paddies in the Usangu Flats north of Mbeya. In response to this worrying state of affairs, the Friends of Ruaha Society is spearheading a project to reduce water wastage in Usangu, and is quietly confident that Ruaha's year-round flow can be restored by 2010: for more information on the Society's "Save our Rivers Appeal", see Ⓦ www.friendsofruaha.org. In the meantime, the animals are still around, albeit in reduced numbers.

Although most visitors are confined to the southeastern section of the park around the Great Ruaha River Valley, which is separated from the rest of the park by the dramatic Ruaha Escarpment, the area is representative of all of Ruaha's rich habitats, including *miombo* woodland plateau broken by isolated hills in the west, undulating plains, acacia and baobab bushland, palm-fringed

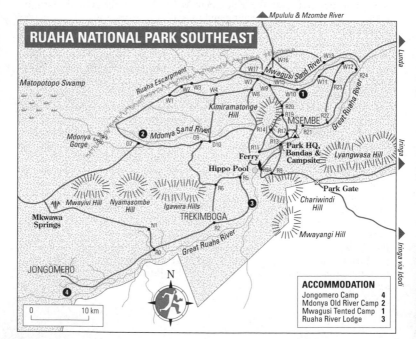

RUAHA NATIONAL PARK SOUTHEAST

ACCOMMODATION
Jongomero Camp	4
Mdonya Old River Camp	2
Mwagusi Tented Camp	1
Ruaha River Lodge	3

0   10 km

swamps, grassland, evergreen forest around the rivers, seasonal sand rivers whose water pools are magnets for wildlife in the dry season and, of course, the Great Ruaha River itself.

Straddling a **transitional zone** between eastern and southern African plant and animal species, the park contains over 1650 plant species, most of them flowering. This rich floral diversity is reflected in a wealth of **wildlife**. Ruaha contains pretty much every species you're likely to see on the Northern Circuit, with the exception of **black rhinos**, whose population and whereabouts are a well-guarded secret, understandably so given the predations wrought by poachers in the 1970s and 1980s; also targeted by poachers were the park's **elephants**, though their present population of around 15,000 is the largest and densest of any Tanzanian park. Ruaha is also noted for its **antelopes**, being one of only few places where you can see both greater and lesser kudu, and the elusive sable and roan antelopes, the latter sometimes in groups of up to twenty. Other denizens include zebra, the shy bushbuck, Grant's gazelle, eland, giraffe, impala, reedbuck, Defassa waterbuck, Liechtenstein's hartebeest, klipspringer, Kirk's dikdik, mongooses (slender, banded and dwarf) and large herds of buffalo near water. With so much potential food around, it's no surprise to find **predators** out in force, including lions, leopards, cheetahs, jackals, crocodiles and several packs of highly endangered African hunting dogs; the park is also the southernmost range of the striped hyena. **Nocturnal animals**, which may be glimpsed in the early morning or late evenings, include the aardwolf, ratel, lesser galago (bushbaby), porcupine and bats.

Ruaha's **birdlife** is equally rich and colourful, with over 480 species recorded to date. The best time for **migrants** is from mid November to March, when two special species to look out for are the rare sooty falcon, which breeds in the Sahara and the Middle East, and Eleonora's falcon, which breeds further north in the Mediterranean. **Birds of prey** include the African hawk, Pel's fishing owl and the bateleur, martial, long-crested and snake eagles. Other resident species to look for are the rare ashy starling and the almost tailless Bochm's spinetail.

The **best time to visit** for mammals is the dry season (July–Nov and, to a lesser extent, June), when animals concentrate around the Great Ruaha River and the receding waterholes of the park's seasonal "sand rivers". Although animal concentration at this time is high, much of Ruaha can be unremittingly dry, and July and August are also the peak tourist months (not that Ruaha receives anything like the attention of Ngorongoro or Serengeti). Avoid the park in the rains from March and May, when a good many tracks are cut.

Visiting the park

The park is 115km west of Iringa along a graded all-weather road (a 3-4hr drive). Park **fees**, paid at the gate, are currently $15 per person per day, plus Tsh5000 per vehicle; an optional guide costs $10–15 per day, and an armed ranger – obligatory if you want to walk – is $20 for a few hours. The best sources of **information** are either of TANAPA's guidebooks to the park, which can be bought at the park gate, at the lodges or in bookshops in Arusha or Dar. The older 64-page monochrome booklet (Tsh5000) describes the game drives in scientific detail, while the new full-colour edition ($10) makes an attractive souvenir. For queries about road conditions and other matters, drop by the **park headquarters** in Msembe area, 18km beyond the entrance gate near the north bank of the Great Ruaha River. There are two ways to

Msembe from the park gate: a hand-pulled ferry over the Great Ruaha River at junction R9A, and a new bridge to the east (turn right at junction R9 or RA).

Organized safaris

Most visitors fly into Ruaha on an **all-inclusive safari packages**. These can be arranged through Ruaha's lodges and tented camps (see below), or a safari company: see p.123 and p.395 for recommended operators in Dar and Arusha. Safaris from Dar are cheaper, as the city's closer to the park, although the Arusha-based Dorobo Safaris (see p.397) are particularly recommended for combined driving and walking trips in the park between June and October.

Several operators also offer **road safaris**, usually including Mikumi National Park and sometimes also Selous Game Reserve, though to make visiting Ruaha worthwhile, you'll need at least six-or seven days for the lot, especially as much of your first and last day will be spent whizzing along the Tanzam Highway (it's roughly 12hr from Dar to Ruaha). You can avoid this problem by arranging things in Iringa.

Getting there from Iringa

The best way of reaching the park from Iringa is to **hire a 4WD**, though as prices are per vehicle, this is only worthwhile if you can fill all five seats. The best place for arranging this is the *Little Ruaha Riverside Campsite*, 14km from Iringa (see p.567). who charge $110 per day for the use of an a/c Toyota Land Cruiser with driver. Much more expensive, although rates should be bargain-able, is the *Huruma Baptist Conference Centre* (see p.565), which has a well-maintained fleet of vehicles. *MR Hotel* and *Hasty Tasty Too* can also arrange trips, and may be cheaper. Alternatively, the tented camps and lodges in the park can arrange **vehicle transfer** from Iringa to the park gate (around $180 per vehicle), where they'll pick you up. There's no **petrol** in the park, although the lodges and park headquarters can help out in an emergency.

Public transport to the park is problematic, as the closest you can get by bus is **Tungamalenga**, 20km away (Kiponza Transport from Iringa, daily at 1pm; also pick-ups from the junction of Uhuru Avenue and Kalenga Road). However, a recent change in park regulations means that walking in the park is now allowed as long as you hire a ranger at the gate, so a cheap trip is still on the cards if you don't mind walking or trying to hitch to the gate from Tungamalenga. There's a campsite with bungalows (❷) at Tungamalenga. Check all this with the tourist information centre in Iringa, however, as the rule change regarding walking hadn't been implemented at the time of writing.

Getting there by plane

The park has two **airstrips**, both in Msembe area. Coastal Travels (see p.643) have scheduled flights on Monday, Thursday and Saturday mornings from Zanzibar (2hr 5min) via Dar and Selous. The plane returns around midday on the same day, skipping Selous; the cost is around $300 each way ($270 from Selous). You'll need to pre-arrange transport to pick you up at the airstrip, which either means booking accommodation or arranging vehicle hire from the park authorities (through TANAPA headquarters in Arusha, p.394) well in advance.

Accommodation

Ruaha has three luxury tented camps and one lodge, all of them neo-colonial in feel and searingly expensive. None is fenced, however, which provides an exciting chance of seeing (or hearing) wildlife pass through at night. Luckily for more modestly heeled travellers, the park authorities maintain some more sanely priced accommodation in the form of *bandas* near the park headquarters. All accommodation is best reserved in advance.

Apart from the *bandas*, the only other budget option is **camping**. The main park-run campsite is on the Great Ruaha River near the park headquarters at Msembe ($20 per person, paid at the gate). The site has pit latrines but nothing else, though you can use the showers at the *bandas* nearby. There are also a number of **special campsites** scattered around ($40 per person) – the locations change every five years; those at Mbagi and, especially, Mdonya are recommended, but you'll have to reserve these well in advance as they tend to be block-booked by safari companies.

At a different level, both *Mwagusi Safari Lodge* and *Ruaha River Lodge* offer luxury **fly-camping excursions** at a cool $390 per person per night (minimum two nights), though this does include everything from personal butlers and guided walks to champagne breakfasts in the bush.

Jongomero Camp 63km southwest of the park headquarters, ⓦ www.selous.com (bookings through the Selous Safari Company in Dar, p.125). A shockingly expensive camp set in glorious isolation in a grove of acacias on the north bank of the Jongomero River. There are eight comfortable en-suite tents, each with a verandah for wildlife spotting and a dining room under canvas. Game drives are included in the price. All-inclusive ❾ ($590).

Mdonya Old River Camp 40km west of the park headquarters ⓦ www.coastal.cc/coastal_ruaha.htm (bookings through Coastal Travels in Dar, p.124). A recently opened camp next to Mdonya Sand River, set under large sycamore figs and acacia. Like *Jongomero Camp*, it has eight en-suite tents, each with two beds and a verandah. Game drives are available, and residents get a fifty percent discount on Coastal Travels flights into Ruaha. ❾ (Full-board $250, all-inclusive $400).

Msembe Bandas Near the park headquarters in Msembe (bookings through TANAPA in Arusha, see p.394; pay at the park gate). The park maintains several basic *bandas*, sleeping between two and five people each. Sheets, blankets and firewood are provided, and there's also a kitchen, dining area, toilets and showers. Bring your own food and drink. The roofs are corrugated metal, so are suffocatingly hot by day. There's also a park-run hostel nearby, theoretically for large groups only,

which has mattresses and a kitchen. $30 per person.

Mwagusi Safari Lodge 27km north of the park headquarters ⓦ www.ruaha.org (bookings through Safari Scene in Dar, p.125). The Mwagusi Sand River, on whose banks this lodge is located, is prime game-viewing territory thanks to the presence of its year-round waterholes. Accommodation is in eight large and comfortable tents (twin or double), with private verandahs giving views of the river plus attached bathrooms with hot showers. The emphasis lies squarely on wildlife: game drives are in open-topped 4WDs and they also offer walking safaris. Closed Jan–June. All-inclusive ❾ ($560).

Ruaha River Lodge 18km southwest of the park headquarters ⓦ www.tanzaniasafaris.info (bookings through Foxtreks in Dar, p.125). Built on and around a granite outcrop overlooking rapids on the Great Ruaha River popular with hippos and crocs, this is the cheapest of the lodges, and another fine place for spotting wildlife (from armchairs on the private verandahs outside guest rooms, in fact). The spacious cottages come with private verandahs and attached bathroom. Facilities include two bars (with glorious views), lounges, evening campfires, a library and dining rooms. Game drives are in open-topped 4WDs, and guided bush walks are also available. Full-board ❽; all-inclusive ❾ ($420).

The Park

The park's 400km of tracks mainly cover the southeastern sector around the Great Ruaha River, within reach of the lodges. Access to the *miombo* woodlands in the west is difficult and time-consuming, but there are plans to expand the road network to 1500km. Unless they've been trashed by elephants looking for back scrubbers, road junctions are marked by numbered signposts, which correspond to the ones marked in the park's guidebooks. The guidebooks are essential for exploring more than the Msembe area around the park headquarters, and a guide – if you've hired a car – is also recommended for spotting animals. Always enquire beforehand as to which roads are open, as some are impassable during and shortly after rain. **Driving** is only allowed between 6am and 7pm, and remember that off-road driving is illegal as well as environmentally destructive.

If you're short on time, the tracks along the Great Ruaha River downstream from Msembe are always good for a broad range of wildlife. With more time, the roads along the Mwagusi and Mdonya sand rivers are rewarding, as is the long drive southwest to the Jongomero River. Early morning and late afternoon are the best times for spotting wildlife, as many species take shelter at midday.

The park's pristine condition owes a lot to the humble if deeply irritating **tsetse fly**, which transmits sleeping sickness. The disease doesn't affect wildlife but does bring down domestic animals and humans, so herders have traditionally avoided the area. Don't worry about contracting the disease yourself – infections are extremely rare, and the main tsetse-infested area is in the *miombo* woodland northwest of the main tourist area. The only sure way to avoid getting bitten is to cover up with *thick* clothes, or – if you're driving – roll up the windows. Some people also say that blue or green attracts the flies.

Lastly, a word of warning about Ruaha's **elephants**. The inaccessibility of huge swathes of the park, especially in the rains makes it ideal territory for ivory poachers, an ongoing problem, albeit nowhere near as bad as it was in the 1980s. However, the massacres of that decade have made older elephants nervous and sometimes aggressive when humans are present, particularly when they're with calves. Treat any elephant you encounter with uncommon courtesy and caution, and back off if they show signs of irritation.

Msembe

The most accessible game drive, certainly if you're staying at the *bandas* or the campsite near the park headquarters, is the web of tracks in and around Msembe area. The dominant tree species here is the tall **acacia albida**, which has bright orange sickle-shaped seed pods. These trees play an important ecological role in providing shade in the dry season, thereby limiting the evaporation of moisture from soil, and binding the riverbank with their roots. Elephant poaching in the 1980s, however, had a unfortunate side effect on this area. The presence of the national park headquarters meant that elephants learned that Msembe area was their only safe haven, and so congregated here, unwittingly damaging the acacia groves. Things haven't been helped much either by the drying up of the Great Ruaha River in the dry seasons since 1993, which has vastly increased pressure on the areas surrounding the few remaining waterholes.

Highlights of this area include the **Hippo Pool** close to junction R8, which also has crocs; the drive west from Msembe to junction B7 for views of the river and escarpment; and the circuit around **Kimiramatonge Hill** to the north, where you might see klipspringers.

Great Ruaha River and Mwagusi Sand River

A excellent circular drive heads northeast from Msembe. The first section, from junction R21 to R24, takes you along the north bank of the **Great Ruaha River** to its confluence with the Mwagusi Sand River, passing tamarind and palm woodland, patches of thorn scrub and grassy plains scattered with candelabra trees. There are lots of animals all year round, including elephants, most of the park's ungulates, and lions and leopards. Hippos and crocs also make inevitable appearances, but you'll need luck to see sable antelopes, cheetahs or hunting dogs. There's a **picnic site** in a grove of fig acacia trees by junction R24.

From here, head back west to the Msembe area by following the south bank of the **Mwagusi Sand River**. Like many of the park's rivers (and now, sadly, also the Great Ruaha), the Mwagusi only sees water in the rains, when floods wash down vast quantities of silt and soil. When the rains end, the waters recede beneath the riverbed, eventually leaving only small pools on the surface These are the main attractions of the sand rivers, as the pools provide valuable year-round sources of water. Elephants are frequent visitors, as are predators – who are easily camouflaged in the flanking vegetation.

Ruaha Escarpment and Mdonya Sand River

In dry weather, a recommended circuit for seeing a variety of habitats (and which can be tacked onto the circuit described above) covers the foot of the Ruaha Escarpment and Mdonya Sand River. The first part of the drive, west from junction W8, hugs the base of the **Ruaha Escarpment**. After some 10km you reach **Mwayemebe Spring**, whose salty residue makes it a popular salt lick for elephant and buffalo. In the surrounding swamp, you might spot the rare Bohor reedbuck. The road continues along the escarpment base to the Nyakatoa and Mdonya sand rivers, just below **Mdonya Gorge**.

To return to Msembe, turn southeast and follow the southern bank of the Mdonya Sand River, passing tamarind woodland and evergreen riverine forest (with good birdlife). Keep an eye out for eland and black-backed jackals. The longer way back from Mdonya Gorge is from junction D7 to Mkwawa Springs in the west, then downstream along the Great Ruaha River. This route is closed in the rains, but should be passable at least from May to December – check at the park headquarters beforehand.

Msembe to Jongomoro

A good long drive, even at midday (animals come to the river to drink), follows the north bank of the Great Ruaha upstream from Msembe to Mhawa, then past **Trekimboga** ("the cooking of meat" in Kihehe) Nine kilometres beyond the *Ruaha River Lodge* is junction R2: a right turn here offers a scenic drive to the Mdonya Sand River (junction D9) or a loop back to junction R5 near Trekimboga. Carrying straight on instead for another 36km through acacia and commiphora woodland gets you to **Jongomero**, where the Jongomero River joins the Great Ruaha. This riverside trees are a good place to nose around for leopards.

The road to Mpululu

This route starts at the Mwagusi Sand River (junctions W14, W15 or W17) and heads up 95km northwest to the Mzombe River. Crossing the Mwagusi Sand River is impossible in the rains, but should be feasible at other times – again, check with the park headquarters. Up the escarpment, the road passes through undulating woodland where you should see small groups of elephants, and perhaps also sable antelope or Liechtenstein's hartebeest. There are some walking trails at Mpululu by the Mzombe River, which marks the border with Rungwa Game Reserve and is dry from July to September (hippos congregate in pools), but you'll need to be accompanied by a park ranger or guide to attempt them.

The southern highlands

North of Lake Nyasa, the fertile **SOUTHERN HIGHLANDS** extend from around Mbeya in the west to the Kipengere Range, close to Njombe, in the east. Despite the region's high population density and reliance on cash crops like coffee, cocoa and bananas, many of the highlands' **forests** have survived, providing one of the region's highlights, along with other natural attractions including impressive waterfalls, crater lakes and hot-water springs. Given the mountainous terrain (and often stunning views), the highlands are ideally suited for hiking.

The prosperous town of **Mbeya**, which lies on both the Tanzam Highway and the TAZARA Railway, makes a good base for exploration, and is also an important gateway to both Malawi and Zambia. Another good base as is the agricultural town of **Tukuyu**, in the foothills of Mount Rungwe volcano. All of these sites, and much more besides, are beautifully covered on the website of the Southern Highlands Conservation Programme, Ⓦ www.southernhigh-landstz.org.

Mbeya and around

Some 140km north of Lake Nyasa, the regional capital of **MBEYA** nestles on a small highland plateau between the Mbeya Range and Panda Hills. Founded in 1927 as a supply town during the gold rush at Lupa, Mbeya's importance was assured by its position on the **Great North Road** (now the Tanzam Highway), which is still the major overland route from eastern to southern Africa, covering over five thousand kilometres from Nairobi to Cape Town. The town's importance increased still further during the 1960s with the construction of the TAZARA railway from Dar to Zambia, which passes just south of the town. Zambia is also easily reached by good road, as is Malawi. Mbeya is now the biggest town in southern Tanzania, with a population of over 400,000, yet it remains an easy-going and laid-back sort of place, at least once you've extricated yourself from the hustlers at the bus stand or train station. Although there's nothing much to see in the town itself, the local **cultural tourism programme** offers a wide range of hikes and excursions in the vicinity – including walks up the nearby Loleza and Mbeya peaks, trips to hot-water springs, waterfalls and (more unusually) to a giant meteorite – making a stay of a few days well worthwhile.

Except for the rare days when dust storms cloud the horizon and billow up through town from the east, Mbeya has a refreshing **climate** and can be very pretty when the many jacaranda and bottle brush trees are in blossom.

Arrival

The **bus station** is on Mbalizi Road, a few hundred metres south of the centre, and within walking distance of most hotels. The **train station** is 5km south of the centre on the Tanzam Highway towards Tunduma and Zambia. A taxi into town shouldn't cost more than Tsh2500; **daladalas** arrive at the stand on School Street at the top end of Jacaranda Road. Beware of pickpockets and bag-snatchers on daladalas and at the station. **Taxis** can be caught on Mbalizi

Safety

Mbeya is amazingly laid-back for a town of its size, but first impressions are often quite the opposite. Whether you arrive by bus or train, you'll be greeted by self-appointed **guides and hustlers** eager to escort you and your baggage to a hotel. Although some of the guides are genuine, several travellers have been robbed by such types, so stay cool, and keep an eye on your bags and valuables while you get your bearings. At the **bus stand**, you can shake the hustlers by heading to the *New Millennium Inn*, which faces the stand on Mbalizi Road, where at least you'll have the chance to collect your thoughts. If you do need a guide (necessary only for hikes around Mbeya) make sure you arrange things at the **cultural tourism programme** (Sisi kwa Sisi) at the corner of Mbalizi Road and School Street (see p.586). Lots of other operators sell themselves as "cultural tourism programmes", and while some might be okay, it's well to be cautious.

In the **town centre**, the only areas to avoid when walking with luggage or valuables are the side streets behind the bus stand, and along Jacaranda Road leading to the *Moravian Church Hostel*, which is a popular haunt for muggers preying on new arrivals. Although there have been no incidents reported of late, it's advisable to catch a cab for the short journey to the hostel, especially early in the morning, late evening or at night.

Road just south of the centre, either at the bus stand or at the BP petrol station.

For details about **moving on from Mbeya**, see p.585 and p.587.

MBEYA

EATING & DRINKING

Babukubwa Bakeries	8
Eddy's Coffee Bar & Snacks	6
Holiday Lodge	12
Karembu House	2
Mbeya Peak Hotel	5
Mambeu Restaurant	4
Mount Livingstone Hotel	14
Nkwenzulu Motel No.3	15
PM's Corner Restaurant	7
Sombrero Hotel	1

ACCOMMODATION

Holiday Lodge	12	Mount Livingstone Hotel	14
Katumba Guest House	9	New Millennium Inn	16
Mbeya Green View Inn		Newton's Hotel	10
& Campsite	11	Rift Valley Hotel	13
Mbeya Peak Hotel	5	Sombrero Hotel	1
Moravian Church Hostel	17	Warsame Guest House	3

Tamzam Highway (2km) & Train Station   Tamzam Highway (2km) & Airport (2.5km)

Accommodation

In spite of the altitude, Mbeya has plenty of mosquitoes, so ensure that mosquito nets fit the beds and that window screens, if any, are intact (or use bug spray or smoke coils). It's possible **to camp** at the *Mbeya Green View Inn & Campsite* and *Karibuni Center Hotel*.

Holiday Lodge Jamatikhana Rd ⓣ025/250 2821. A really friendly place with big, bright rooms in a two-storey block – the cheapest share bathrooms, others have showers, while the most expensive also have TVs. There's a restaurant but no bar. ❶–❸

Katumba Guest House Circle Rd ⓣ025/250 2947. Very basic, dirt cheap and welcoming, with shared bathrooms and no hassle. ❶

Karibuni Center Hotel Off the Tanzam Highway, 4km from town ⓣ & ⓕ025/250 3035, ⓦwww.twiga.ch/TZ/karibunicenter.htm. Run by the Swiss Mbalizi Evangelistic Church, this has en-suite rooms with hot showers, safe parking and a decent restaurant. From Mbalizi Rd, catch a dala-dala through Mafiati to Mbalizi and get off at the second stop. ❷

Mbeya Green View Inn & Campsite Off Chunya Rd, 1km east of town ⓣ0744/381153. An appealing place built in vaguely Scandinavian style with plenty of pinewood furniture, offering four doubles with shared bathrooms and three bright en-suite rooms upstairs with bathtubs and hot water. Food, sodas and beers are available, and there's an attractive rooftop verandah and a communal kitchen. ❷–❸

Mbeya Peak Hotel Acacia St ⓣ025/250 3473. Good-value mid-range place, with Western toilets, showers and telephones in its standard rooms (for Tsh3000 more you get cable TV). The suites, at twice the price, are too expensive. Breakfast included. ❸

Moravian Church Hostel Jacaranda Rd ⓣ025/250 3263. The main backpackers' choice for decades, with small but decent rooms, clean communal showers and squat loos. The downside is the lack of single rooms, the fact that nets don't fit the beds and the need for a taxi at night. Food is occasionally available, but don't rely on it. ❶

Mount Livingstone Hotel Off Jamatikhana Rd ⓣ0741/350484, ⓔmtlivingstone@hotmail.com.

Mbeya's leading tourist-class hotel, with 47 mostly twin-bed rooms equipped with carpet, shower and Western toilet, though it's overpriced given the lack of TV and phone – and you'll have to ask for a mosquito net. There's also a bar and restaurant, gift shop, internet and safe parking, plus noisy Friday and Saturday discos. Breakfast included. ❹

New Millennium Inn Mbalizi Rd ⓣ025/250 0599. The best budget choice by miles, with good clean rooms (singles only, though they can be shared by couples) with or without bath. All have the unusual luxury of a radio, while the more expensive ones have cable TV. ❶–❷

Newton's Hotel Off Chunya Rd ⓣ025/250 0455. Small double rooms in chalets in an attractive if cramped garden – each chalet has its own lounge, toilet and kitchen. Closed at the time of writing, but may reopen soon. ❸

Rift Valley Hotel Corner of Jamatikhana Rd and Karume Ave ⓣ025/250 4351, ⓕ025/250 4429. If you don't mind the slightly tatty feel and saggy beds, this large four-storey business-class hotel is a reasonable choice, with clean en-suite rooms with nets, phones and Western toilets – some also have balconies. The "executive doubles" have satellite TV, and there are also some suites, as well as two bars and a restaurant. Breakfast included. ❸

Sombrero Hotel Post St ⓣ025/250 3636. The town centre's newest and biggest hotel, with twenty small rooms and two suites, all with hot showers, Western toilets, wall-to-wall carpet, TV, phone and piped music, but no nets (as yet). There are two restaurants, and a bar on the rooftop. ❹

Warsame Guest House Sisimba St ⓣ0744/311086. If you're OK with the sometimes less than spotless shared bathrooms and unreliable hot water, this is a good budget choice, with large rooms and good beds, but no mosquito nets (the windows are screened). ❶

The Town

The abiding memory of Mbeya is of its views, especially of the 2656-metre **Loleza Peak** that looms over town from the north, topped by an array of antennae and transmitters. From some places in town, the sharper outline of **Mbeya Peak** (2834m) can be seen protruding behind it. Both can be climbed; see p.587 for details. As most of the town's population live in crowded, slumlike suburbs some kilometres out, the town centre itself is eerily quiet at times. The town's main focus is, of course, the **market**, which although modest in size is always interesting. The northwest corner has vendors selling medicinal herbs, beans, bark and assorted powders, and there are usually also some beautiful cream-and-ochre Kisi pots from Ikombe near Matema on Lake Nyasa. North of here, at the top end of Mbalizi Road by Uhuru roundabout, is a poignant riddle. Although the town's official history states that it was founded in 1927, this is contradicted by local stories concerning the **"hanging tree"** over the river by the junction, which it's believed was used by the Germans during the 1905–07 Maji Maji Uprising to execute opponents of their oppressive rule. The tree in question does indeed have a strange metal winch with a hook attached to its largest branch, but the slender wire that ties it to the tree seems too thin to have supported the weight of condemned people. More certain is the sacrifice made by local people during World War II while fighting for the British: the names of the dead are commemorated on a small **memorial plaque** by the roadside just along Karume Avenue.

Eating

Eating out in Mbeya is pretty much limited to the following.

Babukubwa Bakeries Lupa Way. Only does snacks, but delicious at that, especially the samosas and the meat *chops* (balls of minced meat fried in a thick and creamy coating of mashed potato), all served with assorted relishes. (There's no bread, incidentally, despite the name.) Open until 8pm.

Eddy's Coffee Bar & Snacks Sisimba St. Popular with locals and tourists alike, this is the nicest central place for a meal or a drink, with *supu* for breakfast, full meals for lunch and dinner, a *nyama choma* barbecue in the garden at the side with seating in round huts and a leafy verandah up front. Closed Sun.

Holiday Lodge Jamatikhana Rd. This has a small menu with just nine dishes – reasonable, if nothing special, with everything under Tsh2000. No alcohol.

Mambeu Restaurant Corner of Mbalizi Rd and Sisimba St. This local eating place does good tripe *supu* for breakfast (if you like that kind of thing), or a more palatable *mtori* banana soup, as well as

very cheap lunches and dinners (Tsh500–900) – the liver is particularly good.

Mbeya Peak Hotel Acacia St. Delicious *nyama choma* and grilled bananas served in garden *bandas*.

Mount Livingstone Hotel Off Jamatikhana Rd. The massive à la carte menu has almost a hundred dishes from all over the world, from Chinese and Italian to Bourguignonne fondues, kedgeree chicken and seafood paellas. It's expensive for Mbeya (mains from Tsh3700), but gets consistently good reviews.

PM's Corner Restaurant Corner Mbalizi Rd and Sisimba St. Always popular, this glorified café serves up tea, succulent *mishkaki*, chicken and chips, and rice and *ugali* (full meals under Tsh1500). No alcohol or smoking. Open until 8pm.

Sombrero Restaurant Post St. One of the town's best restaurants, with good pasta, curries (the kidney stew is an especial wow), fresh juices, milkshakes and friendly service. Meals around Tsh2000–2700.

Bars and nightlife

The majority of Mbeyans live out in the crowded suburbs, so there are few bars in the centre. Mbeya is considered Tanzania's second city after Dar on the **rap scene**; local names to look out for include Doctor Wise, who mixes rap and ragga, and Mbeya-raised Bantu Pound Gangstarz; although they're now based in Dar, group member Soggy Doggy occasionally performs in Mbeya. Live performances are sometimes hosted at *Nkwenzulu Motel No.3* and at NBC Investment House on Karume Avenue (generally Fridays from 7.30pm) – the latter also hosts beauty contests and other one-off events at weekends. Ask around, or check out the posters that adorn much of town.

△ Ruaha river ferry

Karembu House 3rd St. A great local bar, always busy, with a TV for European football and a popular dartboard. Take a taxi at night.

Mbeya Peak Hotel Acacia St. The garden bar here, with its shaded *bandas*, is a nicely relaxing place for a daytime drink, and also does meals, including good *nyama choma*.

Mount Livingstone Hotel Off Jamatikhana Rd. This has an indoor bar and a couple of tables in a garden outside, both of which are pretty dead except on Friday and Saturday nights, when there are ever-popular discos (10pm to late; Tsh1000).

Nkwenzulu Motel No.3 Mbalizi Rd, opposite the bus stand. The busiest bar near the bus stand, complete with loose women, grumpy barmaids.

Moving on from Mbeya

Mbeya has good transport connections, with the **Tanzam Highway** running northeast to Iringa, Morogoro and Dar, and west to Tunduma on the Zambian border. There's also good tarmac to Kyela in the south, close to the Malawian border at the Songwe River, and southeast to Songea via Njombe. Kyela gives access to the ferry on Lake Nyasa, providing an idyllic alternative route into Malawi, or, for that matter, to Tanzania's southernmost town, Mbamba Bay, from where there's onward road transport to Songea.

For details of bus routes on to **Zambia** and **Malawi** from Mbeya, see p.587.

By bus

For long-distance journeys, buy your ticket the morning of the day before you plan to travel to be sure of a seat. Some bus companies will try to charge you the "government rate" (currently Tsh13,500 to Dar instead of Tsh12,000). The journey to **Dar** (11–12hr) passes through Iringa, Mikumi and Morogoro. There are at least ten daily buses, most leaving Mbeya between 5am and 6.45am. Later buses coming from Kyela are usually packed. The road is perilously fast in places, so choose a reliable operator: Scandinavian Express (6.30am & 7am) and Fresh ya Shamba (5.30am) have good reputations. For **Dodoma**, Urafiki International Coach run on Monday, Wednesday and Friday at 5.30am. The rough and wild road to **Tabora** via Chunya, Rungwa and Sikonge is travelled by Sabena Video Coach (5am) on Sunday and Monday, taking at least 24 hours. **Chunya** is also connected to Mbeya by pick-ups from the Chunya road junction opposite the *Rift Valley Hotel*; the first leave around 7am, but arrive early to be sure of a ride. Hood run to **Arusha** via Morogoro daily at 5am but have a dangerous reputation; it's safer to catch a Scandinavian Express service to Morogoro or Dar – stay overnight and head on the next morning.

Going south, **Tukuyu** and **Kyela** are connected to Mbeya by DCM minibuses and daladalas roughly hourly from around 6am until late afternoon. Less frequent minibuses run to **Songea** and **Mbinga**. Songea is also served by Raha Transport (daily at 5.30am), which continues on to **Tunduru**. Avoid the perilous Super Feo. **Sumbawanga** is covered daily by Sumry and Air Shengena (5–6am).

By train

Mbeya is the last Tanzanian stop on the TAZARA railway before it enters Zambia. The **train station** is 5km south of the centre on the Tanzam Highway towards Tunduma and Zambia (the ticket office is open Mon–Fri 7.30am–12.30pm & 2–4pm, Sat 8am–12.30pm, Sun 7.30–11am); there's also a ticket office (Mon–Fri 8am–3pm) in town on Maktaba Street behind the post office. A taxi from town shouldn't cost more than Tsh2500; daladalas to the station leave from School Street at the top end of Jacaranda Road. Timetables change with annoying frequency. At the time of writing, ordinary trains currently leave for **Dar** on Tuesday and Saturday at 3.20pm; the "express" service leaves on Wednesday at 3.42pm, though the latter, especially, is subject to massive delays, as it comes in from Zambia. The train to **Zambia** leaves on Wednesday at 10.45am. The fare to Dar is Tsh9800–24,200, depending on the class and whether it's an ordinary or express service.

and grim toilets, but it remains popular for its discos (Fri & Sat from 9pm; Tsh1500), and hosts special events from time to time.

Sombrero Hotel Post St. The rooftop "summit" bar has superb views over town and the Mbeya Range.

Listings

Banks and exchange The best bank for changing cash or cheques is Stanbic on Karume Ave, with exceptionally friendly and efficient service (generally under 10min), good rates and only Tsh6000 commission on any transaction under $800. The NBC in NBC Investment House on Karume Ave is also good. The other banks – CRDB on Karume Ave, and National Microfinance Bank, corner Mbalizi Rd and Highland St – are much slower. Faster service but worse rates for cash are available at Ndingo's Bureau de Change off Lupa Way (Mon–Fri 8.30am–5pm, Sat 8.30am–4pm), which is awaiting a licence to process travellers' cheques.

Bookshops Mbeya Book Shop next to the Anglican church on Karume Ave, Tanzania Elimu Supplies on Lupa Way and Volile Investment on South St all have a few books in English; Elimu and Volile also have copies of Sister Mirambo's introduction to Sukuma culture, recommended reading if you're heading up to Mwanza.

Car repairs CMC Land Rover on Karume Ave have skilled mechanics and genuine spare parts, and also-deal with Nissan, Volvo and Volkswagen. Spare parts can also be found at Mbeya Spares and Hardware, South St.

Football Mbeya's local team, Prison, play at Sokoine Stadium, as do the far more popular second-division Tukuyu Stars, much to the chagrin of their home fans in Tukuyu, who face a 140km round-trip to support their side.

Hospitals The Aga Khan Health Centre, corner North St and Post St, should be the first port of call. The main hospital is on Hospital Hill north of town.

Immigration Behind the District Commissioner's Office off Karume Ave, though they're not much help, and you'll need to leave the country to get a new three-month tourist visa.

Internet and email access Nane Information Centre, Mbalizi Rd (daily 8am–10pm), and Mbeya Internet Centre, Lupa Way (daily 8am–9pm), charge Tsh1000 per hour and have fast connections; alternatively, try Plaza Internet Café on Lupa Way, or the *Mount Livingstone Hotel*.

Library Maktaba St (Mon–Fri 9am–6pm, Sat 9am–1pm; Tsh500 daily membership).

Pharmacy Zary Pharmacy, Lupa Way (Mon–Sat 8am–8pm, Sun 10am–2pm).

Photography Saifee Color Lab, Mbalizi Rd, is the Agfa outfit; Burhani Photographic Services, West St, is the Kodak agent and has modern equipment.

Police Independence Ave.

Post and couriers The post office is on the corner of Lupa Way and Post St. DHL can be contacted on ☎025/250 2088.

Supermarkets Ramji's, corner Lupa Way and Post St (Mon–Sat 9am–8pm, Sun 10am–2pm), has a good range of imported packaged stuff, and sometimes foreign newspapers. Also good is Nelly's, South St (Mon–Fri 9am–2pm & 3–5.30pm, Sat 9am–3pm, Sun 11am–2pm), and Babukubwa Bakeries, Lupa Way.

Telephone TTCL, corner Maktaba St and Post St next to the post office (daily 7.45am–8pm), has both operator-assisted phones and call boxes outside. Nane Communications Centre (see Internet and email access, above) has software for web phonecalls.

Around Mbeya

Mbeya Region's attractions can be visited as part of the local **cultural tourism programme** run by Sisi kwa Sisi Youth Group, whose office is at the corner of Mbalizi Road and School Street (daily 8am–6pm, closed for lunch; ☎0744/463471, ✉sisikwasisi@hotmail.com). Be extremely wary of other operators and guides; some have no experience while others are just out to rob you – if someone tells you that they're with Sisi kwa Sisi, believe them only when you get to the office.

The project offers a wide range of hikes, although many will be cheaper if arranged in Tukuyu (these trips are covered on p.593). Some trips include a Tsh1000 per person village development fee, which has so far paid for a small dispensary and books for a primary school. Also worth enquiring about are the

The Zambia border

For **Lusaka**, Sayuni Traveller's Coach leaves Mbeya at 4pm on Monday, Tuesday, Thursday, Friday and Sunday, and Masia Tours Line departs on Tuesday and Friday. Masia also runs daily to the border at **Tunduma**, as do plenty of minibuses. The road from Mbeya to the border is reasonable tarmac. All visitors to Zambia need a **visa**; these can be bought at the border. Costs vary according to nationality: they're currently $25–30 for most travellers, except for UK nationals, who pay twice that, though it may be possible to get a free one-week tourist visa. The visa situation is fluid, so bring enough dollars in cash to cover things. If you're travelling by road, be prepared for hassle and pick-pockets at **Tunduma** on the border, 114km southwest of Mbeya. The money-changers on both sides are notorious con-artists (read the warning on p.67; the rate in mid-2002 was approximately 1000 Zambian Kwacha to 240 Tanzanian shillings). If you're arriving in Tanzania, you can **change money** safely at the National Microfinance Bank at the start of the road to Mbeya on the left, though it'll take an hour or more to process travellers' cheques and you'll need the purchase receipt. If you *must* change money on the street, keep it small – $20 (approximately Tsh20,000) is more than enough to see you to Sumbawanga or Mbeya and to pay for a meal and night in a hotel. Other than changing money, there's no reason to stay in Tunduma and, given the attention of the pushy hawkers, you'll probably be glad to jump on the next bus out anyway.

The Malawi border

The nicest way to reach **Malawi** from southern Tanzania is by ferry from Itungi Port to Nkhata Bay (see p.601). A more humdrum but quicker approach is by road from Mbeya. There are daily daladalas direct from Mbeya to the border post ("Bodaboda") at **Mwandenga** on the Songea River. If you miss these, catch a bus or daladala towards Kyela and get off at the junction at **Ibanda**, 11km before Kyela, from where bicycle taxis (*pikipikis*) cover the remaining 7km. There's a bus direct from Mbeya to **Lilongwe** at 2pm on Tuesday run by Takabari/Taqwa, which arrives the following morning, passing through Chitambo and Mzuzu.

At present, **visas** are not required for US or EU citizens, though corrupt immigration officials on both sides can be a nuisance; be patient and polite and – so long as you haven't overstayed your visa – you'll eventually get through unscathed. As ever, give money-changers and other scammers a wide berth; if you really need to change money, it might be useful to know that the exchange rate in mid-2002 was approximately 100 Malawian kwacha to 1500 Tanzanian shillings. There's a simple guest house (❶) and onward transport on the Malawian side. Keep your eye on your luggage both in the daladala and on the border, as thefts have been reported.

weekend trips to Lake Nyasa planned by the *Sombrero Hotel* (ask for Mr Sombrero). For information on **Lake Rukwa**, see p.557.

Loleza and Mbeya Peaks

Dominating the skyline north of Mbeya are the highest points in the Mbeya Range, Loleza and Mbeya peaks, both of which can be climbed. Directly above town is the 2656-metre **Loleza Peak** (also called Kaluwe), which is covered in beautiful flowers in the rainy season. Security concerns mean that taking a guide is advisable (Tsh8000 per person from Sisi kwa Sisi, see opposite). The walk starts from Hospital Hill off Independence Avenue and follows a forested ridge that slopes up towards the peak, a steep, three-hour climb. It's not possible to reach the very summit, which is occupied by transmitters.

The Kipengere Range

The **Kipengere Range**, which straddles much of the region between Mbeya and Njombe, contains areas of immense botanical importance, notably the remote grasslands of the **Kitulo Plateau**, known locally as Bustani ya Mungu (God's Garden). Much of the plateau lies above 2600m and contains great numbers of endemic wildflowers, including 45 species of terrestrial **orchids**, 31 of which are unique to the Kipengeres. In the rainy seasons, the plateau erupts in a glorious show of colour which, apart from its intrinsic beauty, also attracts breeding colonies of rare birds, including the pallid harrier, Njombe cisticola and Kipengere seed-eater.

In February 2002, the Tanzanian government announced its decision to protect the northern half of the Kitulo Plateau (approximately 135 square kilometres) by establishing a new **national park** – the first protected area in sub-Saharan Africa to be created primarily on account of the significance of its flora. Although at present the park exists only on paper, it should be up and running during the lifetime of this guidebook. For more information, contact TANAPA in Arusha (see p.394), or the Wildlife Conservation Society's **Southern Highlands Conservation Programme**, who can be reached through Sisi kwa Sisi in Mbeya (see p.586), or directly at PO Box 1475, Mbeya, ☏025/250 3541, ⓦwww.southernhighlandstz.org.

Slightly higher (2834m) is **Mbeya Peak**, to the west of Loleza Peak. There are two routes to the summit, both of which require a guide (Sisi kwa Sisi charge around Tsh15,000 per person). The quickest and easiest is from the north, starting at the end of a driveable track that begins in **Mbowo** village, 13km along the Chunya road; a taxi to the top of the track costs at least Tsh7000. From the end of the track, the path to the summit takes around two hours, passing through eucalyptus forest. The summit is marked by a wooden cross, and gives excellent views of the Rift Valley. The walk is also good for flowers in the rains and for rare butterflies at other times. The alternative route, best done over two days (you'll either need to camp or spend the night at *Utengule Country Hotel*; see opposite), is more strenuous but more rewarding, involving steep and difficult scree in parts. The route starts at a coffee farm 20km northwest of Mbeya; there's public transport as far as **Mbalizi** on the Tunduma Highway, leaving you with a nine-kilometre walk past Utengule (see below); to the start of the trail; from there it's a six-hour climb to the summit. The traverse along the seven-kilometre ridge joining Loleza and Mbeya peaks is possible but rarely attemped.

Utengule

For those with transport (or a bicycle), a pleasant alternative to Mbeya as a base for visiting the Southern Highlands is **Utengule**, a village and district roughly 20km northwest of town at the western edge of the Mbeya Range. The area's history is worth relating. In the 1870s, the **Sangu tribe** were forced out of the Usangu Flats to the north of here by the territorial expansion of the Hehe (see p.571). Under **Chief Tovelamahamba Merere**, the Sangu settled at Utengule, whose name meant "the place of peace". Located on a ridge overlooking the plains, it must have been appropriately named, as there were very few other safe havens in southern Tanzania at the time, what with Chief Mkwawa's Hehe warriors roaming to the north and east, and the even more militaristic Ngoni to the west and south. Nonetheless, peace didn't come easily: the remains of a defensive structure called **Merere's Wall** can still be seen at Utengule, and it was from here that the Sangu launched attacks against the Germans during the Maji Maji Uprising. At the end of the uprising, the

German administration considered it better to allow the troublesome Sangu back into the Usangu Flats, and so further away from the main colonial base at Mbeya.

It's also worth seeking out one of the several **pitagos** – ritual sites next to ravines from where the Sangu threw their dead (and, sometimes, the living, if they had been convicted of certain crimes, including philandering). The exceptions were chiefs, who were treated to lavish burials which reportedly included the interment of retainers or slaves. The explorer Captain James Elton, visiting in the 1870s, described the scene at the base of one *pitago*: "... now over a heap of skeletons, scattered leather aprons and beads, hovered flocks of vultures and gigantic storks ... gorged with their loathsome feast". The *pitago* sites are still considered with apprehension by locals, although the practice itself survives only in words: the polite way of referring to burial in the Sangu language is *kitaga umunu* – which means "to throw away a person". For more information, see *Throwing Away the Dead* by Martin Walsh at Ⓦwww.museums.or.ke/mvita/walsh.html.

Unless you arrange a day-trip with Sisi kwa Sisi in Mbeya (see p.586), the only practical way to get to know Utengule is to **stay overnight** at the upmarket *Utengule Country Hotel*, 3km from Utengule village (Ⓣ025/256 0100, Ⓦwww.utengule.com; ❻); turn right at Mbalizi, 11km along the highway to Tunduma, and follow the signposts. The hotel is set in lovely gardens on a 500-acre coffee estate and offers a wide choice of colourfully decorated rooms and bungalows, some with views over the Rift Valley. There's also a restaurant and bar, and guided walks and excursions are available to Kimani Falls and Pango la Popo. If you're staying overnight, the hotel arranges free transfers from Mbeya.

Pango la Popo

The easiest and cheapest trip from Mbeya is a combined visit to **Pango la Popo** (the "cave of bats") and the nearby **hot-water springs** (*maji ya moto*), roughly 40km west of Mbeya Access is easiest by taxi, costing upwards of Tsh8000 return if arranged for you by Sisi kwa Sisi in Mbeya (see p.586). If you're driving, head along the road to Tunduma for about 25km until Songwe, where there's a dust-belching cement factory. The cave is 14km north of here.

Mbozi Meteorite

Weighing in at a cool twelve tons, the irregularly shaped **Mbozi Meteorite** – which lies on the southwestern slope of Marengi Hill, 70km west of Mbeya off the road to Tunduma – is the world's eighth largest known. The meteorite is a fragment of interplanetary matter that was large enough to avoid being completely burned up when entering earth's atmosphere, and small enough to avoid exploding; of the estimated five hundred meteorites that fall to earth each year, only thirty percent strike land, and less than ten are reported and recorded. Mbozi has been known for centuries by locals, who call it Kimwondo, but the absence of legends recounting its sudden and undoubtedly fiery arrival indicate that it fell to earth long before the present inhabitants arrived, a thousand years ago. The meteorite was officially discovered in 1930. At the time only the top was visible. To reveal the whole meteorite, the hillside around it was dug away, leaving only a pillar of soil under the meteorite, which was then reinforced with concrete to serve as a plinth. The irregular notches on the pointed end of the meteorite were caused by souvenir hunters hacking out chunks – no easy task given the strength of the nickel-iron of which it's made. Most meteorites consist of silicates or stony-irons, so Mbozi is uncommon in that it's composed mainly of iron (90.45 percent) and nickel (8.69 percent), with negligible amounts of copper, sulphur and phosphorus.

The turn-off from the highway is signposted 4.5km before Mbozi village; catch one of the frequent minibuses plying between Mbeya and Tunduma. Bicycles can be hired at the junction (Tsh1000–2000) to cover the remaining 13km. The cultural tourism programme combines the meteorite with visits to coffee farms (five hours in all), but at Tsh30,000 per person it's much cheaper to visit on your own. Entrance is free, but the guardian would appreciate your buying a copy of Hamo Sassoon's brief but informative *Guide to the Mbozi Meteorite*. If you want to stay overnight, you'll have to arrange things with the cultural tourism programme, who have a **campsite** 7km from the site in a large plot donated by the government to enable unemployed youths to start profitable agricultural projects.

Ngosi Crater Lake

Some 35km southeast of Mbeya in the Poroto Mountains, **Ngosi Crater Lake** (marked as Poroto Crater Lake on some maps) is the most popular destination for day-trippers from both Mbeya and Tukuyu. In the local language, Kisafwa, Ngosi means "very big", referring to the lake rather than the conical mountain that contains it. The two-kilometre lake occupies the crater floor 200m beneath the highest point of the 2620-metre Mount Ngosi. Although the lakeshore is tricky to reach (it's 200m down in the crater along a steep and potentially dangerous footpath), the walk there is really the attraction, winding uphill through tropical rainforest, stands of giant bamboo and wild banana plants. Among the forest denizens are black-and-white colobus monkeys and many colourful birds. Local legend speaks of the lake's magical powers, and of a **lake monster** that has the ability to change the colour of the water from time to time (a hint that underwater volcanic activity may still be occurring). Though quaint, tales of the lake monster should urge caution, as such stories usually have some basis in real-life perils such as man-eating crocodiles or unpredictable currents – note that locals themselves don't swim in the lake.

The lake is most easily visited with a guide from Mbeya or Tukuyu, although it's quite feasible to visit on your own. Coming from either place, catch a bus or daladala to Mchangani (nicknamed "Mbeya Moja"), where there's a signposted turn-off. From here it's 6km west along a rough road (4WD only) to the bottom of the mountain, and then another hour's quite strenuous climb on foot up the southeastern slope to the crater rim. You could walk all the way from Mchangani (2–3hr each way). A **guide** is recommended for the last bit up the forest on Ngosi Hill, as the path isn't marked: guides offer their services at Mchangani. From Mbeya, the cost is Tsh10,000 per person if you can find a few other tourists to share the cost. Hiring a car in Tukuyu for the round-trip costs around Tsh25,000. There's a **ticket office** in Mchangani at the start of the road to the lake which collects Tsh1000 per visitor, and a **campsite** at Ngosi; it's free if you've paid the entrance fee, though you'll have to stump up the cost of a night watchman if the locals advise it (no more than Tsh2000).

Chunya

Some seventy kilometres north of Mbeya, the town of **CHUNYA** was at the centre of a **gold rush** in the 1920s and 1930s. When the mines were exhausted, the town enjoyed a short-lived tobacco boom before world prices collapsed. The mines resumed operation in the 1990s under South African ownership, though small-scale traditional gold-seekers are excluded, and locals are now pretty much restricted to panning in the rivers. There's not really much reason to come to Chunya unless you're attempting the tricky eastern access route to Lake Rukwa or the even trickier road up to Tabora. There are plenty of **guest houses** in the centre by the bus stand, catering mainly for miners, but the mood isn't as gruff or macho as you might fear. If you're driving, don't miss the **World's End Viewpoint** (2640m) just off the road 21km from Mbeya, whose sign claims it to be the "highest point of all main road in Tanzania" and which gives fantastic views over the marshy Usangu Flats, the main source of the Great Ruaha River.

Tukuyu and around

The ride south from Mbeya to Lake Nyasa is one of Tanzania's most scenic, wending up through the lush volcanic foothills of Mount Rungwe before descending into the tropical humidity and forests of Lake Nyasa's northern shore. Close to the highest point of the road, 71km southeast of Mbeya, is the overwhelmingly rural town of **TUKUYU**. Founded about a century ago by the Germans as a replacement for the mosquito-ridden lakeshore town of Matema (Langenburg), Neu Langenburg – as they called Tukuyu – became a local administrative headquarters. The **German Boma**, whose surviving ramparts have been incorporated into today's municipal buildings, date from this time. Tukuyu could scarcely be more different from prosperous Mbeya to the north. There's none of the cosmopolitan feeling of Mbeya, and the atmosphere is decidedly small town (or big village). Yet Tukuyu is certainly an attractive and refreshing place to stay, with wonderful views over the lushly vegetated hillocks and valleys far below, many of them extensively cultivated with tea, banana groves and sweet potatoes.

The main reason for coming here is to visit the various natural attractions surrounding the town (many can also be visited through the cultural tourism programme in Mbeya, see p.586, but are more expensive from there). Foremost among the local sights are the dormant volcanic mass of **Mount Rungwe** (which can be climbed), various associated crater lakes in the Poroto Mountains to the west, waterfalls and a natural lava-stone bridge over a river.

The best months to visit are September and October, as for much of the rest of the year it rains... and rains – with annual precipitation of almost three metres, Tukuyu is the wettest places in the country.

Age villages of the Nyakyusa

The **Nyakyusa** are the dominant ethnic group between Tukuyu and Lake Nyasa, numbering well over a million in Tanzania, and around 400,000 in Malawi, where they're called Ngonde (or Nkonde). A unique but now extinct feature of traditional Nyakyusa society was their **age villages**, brand-new villages established by boys between the ages of 11 and 13, to which they would later bring wives and start families of their own. The villages died upon the death of their last founding member, after which the land was reallocated by the district chief. Age villages served both to preserve the privileges and land of the older generation, and also to spread population pressure on the land more evenly, thereby avoiding unsustainable agricultural use. However, with each generation, the available land was repeatedly divided amongst the sons of each chief, until the system finally collapsed when the land plots became too small to subdivide (a problem that also affects the Chagga around Kilimanjaro). Nowadays the pressure on land is so acute that few if any new age villages are founded.

Arrival and accommodation

Frequent **daladalas** between Mbeya and Kyela pass through Tukuyu. The **bus stand** is on the west side of the highway. A word on **safety**: there have been instances of tourists being robbed by newly made "friends" in Tukuyu, often in their bedrooms: don't let strangers into your room, and insist on carrying your own bags from the bus stand.

There are few mosquitoes in town and malaria is absent, which is just as well as none of the **hotels** have mosquito nets. The three places reviewed below are all east of the Mbeya–Kyela highway: from the bus stand, turn left (north) along the tarmac so that the market is on your left, and take the first right after 100m or so: the directions given below ("from the highway") are from this junction. The best of the hotels is *Langboss Lodge* (℡025/255 2080; ❶–❷), 1.5km east from the highway: keep walking past the NBC bank, straight across the round-about, and turn right after a clothes market and school, keeping the school's playing field to your right. The better rooms here are large en-suite doubles; the singles share rather grim toilets and showers, and all the rooms are getting scruffy; there's also a bar and restaurant. Rather more humble, but clean and usually calm, is the *Laxmi Guest House*, just off the roundabout 500m east from the highway (℡025/255 2226; ❶), with a choice of singles and doubles with or without bathroom, plus a bar and restaurant. For really cheap rooms (❶), try the *Mount Rungwe Guest House*, 100m from the highway on the left. Lastly, check out the new (and as yet nameless) hotel facing the roundabout 500m east of the highway, which was almost complete at the time of visiting, and promises to be the town's most attractive option.

Eating and drinking

Tukuyu's **restaurants** invariably double as bars and are mostly pretty tawdry affairs in which some knowledge of Kiswahili is helpful to overcome small-town reticence. The most pleasant is the busy and cheerful *Laxmi Garden Centre Bar & Restaurant*, just past the post office (turn left opposite the petrol station about 250m east of the highway), which is good for roast meat in the garden at the back and even has fresh pork (*kiti moto*, meaning "hot chair"). Another good choice is the *Langboss Lodge*, which lacks a garden and isn't as character-ful, but dispenses with *Laxmi*'s prostitutes. Both have TVs. The food at *Langboss* is perfectly decent, with meals costing under Tsh2000, but the service is achingly slow (give them at least an hour). Other joints you could try include *Topcut Garden & Bar*, behind the football ground opposite the bus stand, which has a few *bandas* in the garden and serves the usual grills, rubbery chicken, fish, chips and somewhat better liver. For **breakfast**, try the *supu* at *Laxmi's* or *Topcut*. The best place for a **drink** is *Laxmi's*, which is especially lively at

---

Moving on from Tukuyu

Leaving Tukuyu, the first vehicles to Mbeya and Kyela leave at 6am, the last at around 7pm. The route from Tukuyu to Matema is covered in the box on p.597; pick-ups in this direction, usually two a day (though there are days when nothing runs), leave from the roundabout beside the NBC bank, about 500m east of the Mbeya–Kyela highway and the bus stand; the first heads off between 8am and 9am, the second at midday. If there's nothing there, enquire at the petrol station next to the bank, or at the Lutheran Church offices next door, who might have a vehicle heading south. The best day for catching a lift is Friday, which is market day in Ipinda.

weekends (open until midnight) and hosts occasional live music promotions. The *Langboss*'s bar is calmer, and its TV makes it a popular venue for watching European football matches.

Around Tukuyu

There are lots of things to see around Tukuyu, most of them – including crater lakes, a natural lava-stone bridge and waterfalls – associated with **Mount Rungwe**'s more excitable volcanic past. Its last eruption was about two centuries ago, but **earthquakes** are still a common occurrence, frequently making thousands of people homeless. All the sights can be visited through Mbeya's cultural tourism programme (see p.586), but it's usually cheaper to arrange things in Tukuyu. There's nothing particularly organized, though: *Langboss Lodge* (see opposite) is the best place to hire a reliable guide (about Tsh10,000 per group per day, excluding transport). It should be possible to work things out for longer trips (maximum Tsh20,000 per day excluding food and accommodation), which would make walking down to Matema (70km over three days, at least) a possibility.

Tourism is in its infancy here, so people aren't used to seeing *wazungu* poking around: be tactful and cheerful, polite to suspicious officials, and always ask permission before pitching a tent – it's not only good manners, but may also get you invited to a local home – always a memorable experience.

Mount Rungwe

With a full day, preferably two, a climb to the 2960-metre summit of **Mount Rungwe**, a dormant volcano, is an enticing prospect, passing through wild and varied scenery. Formed 2.5 million years ago, the volcano – which comprises at least ten craters and domes – dominates the skyline for miles around. Its forested flanks, protected as the **Rungwe Forest Reserve**, are an important wildlife habitat, whose denizens include a unique subspecies of black-and-white colobus monkey and the threatened Abbot's duiker. You'll need a guide: ask at *Langboss Lodge* in Tukuyu, or at the cultural tourism programme in Mbeya. Locals in Rungwe village are also knowledgeable about the route, but speak little or no English. There are two main approaches to the summit, both passing through several habitat zones, from montane forest at 1500m, through upper montane forest and grassland, to higher-altitude bushland and heath. The summit itself gives breathtaking views of the Nyasa Trough to the south and the Kitulo Plateau (see box, p.588) to the east.

The easiest route to climb, but the more difficult to access without your own vehicle, is **from the northeast**, starting on the track that runs between Isongole and Ndala, passing by Shiwaga Crater. The longer route, more heavily forested and therefore more scenic, is **from the west**, starting at Rungwe village, 7km off the Mbeya highway. To get to the trail head from Tukuyu, catch the 7am **daladala** to Kikota, a ninety-minute walk from Rungwe Secondary School, which is another hour from the base of climb; alternatively, rent a **taxi** from Tukuyu to the school (around Tsh15,000 each way; you'll have to make it worth the driver's while to wait for you, or arrange for him to pick you up the next day). The climb itself takes at least four to five hours up to the southern rim of the summit crater, and around two and a half hours back down. The last daladala back to town from Kikota leaves no later than 7.30pm – if you get stranded, Rungwe Secondary School has beds in a **hostel** (Tsh2000 per person), and there's also a **campsite** run by the Moravian Mission. If you're coming from Mbeya, leave no later than 7am, and allow at least twelve hours for the round trip. The **best time to visit** is September or October, when there's less chance of rain.

Masoko Crater Lake

An attractive product of Mount Rungwe's volcanic rumblings is **Masoko Crater Lake**, 15km southeast of Tukuyu along the unsurfaced road to Ipinda and Matema. It's easy to find, being right next to the road (on the right coming from Tukuyu). Like Ngosi Crater Lake near Mbeya, Masoko also has a legend, this one more explicable: the stone building on the crater rim housed the German Fifth Field Garrison before and during World War I, and was afterwards occupied by British troops, who later turned it into a courthouse (*mahakama*). In common with legends all over Tanganyika, locals believe that before the Germans were routed by the British, they buried treasure here – or, more precisely, dumped it in the lake – a theory borne out by the old German coins which are periodically washed up on the shore (locals offer them for sale at around Tsh600 each) and which encourage intrepid locals to dive in to search for treasure.

Access to the lake is relatively easy: catch the first of the two crowded daily pick-ups (8–9am) which head from Tukuyu to Ipinda and get off when you see the lake on your right. There's no entrance fee or facilities of any kind. There should be a pick-up or two in the opposite direction in the afternoon: check in Tukuyu before leaving – there's more transport on Friday and Saturday, the market days in Ipinda and Ntaba respectively. From Mbeya, the only practical way of visiting the lake as a day-trip is by private car: the cultural tourism programme offer day-trips combining Masoko Crater Lake with Kisiba Crater Lake (94km from Mbeya) for Tsh20,000–40,000 per person, depending on group size.

Kaporogwe Falls

The 25-metre **Kaporogwe Falls** (also called Kala Falls) on the Kala River, a tributary of the Kiwira River, 25km south of Tukuyu are a good target for a day-trip. Apart from swimming, you can walk between the tumbling torrent and the cave behind it, home to a concrete wall where Germans are said to have hidden during World War I. Finds of **stone tools** above the waterfall – scrapers, knives, picks and core axes from the so-called "Kiwira Industry" – indicate that the place was intensively occupied during the Stone Age. It was later abandoned, possibly when it became covered by pumice and volcanic debris from one of Mount Rungwe's eruptions.

Transport from Tukuyu is most convenient by private vehicle – or by bicycle if you can face the uphill ride back into town. With a tent, you could also walk there: the turning for the falls is at **Ushirika**, 10km south of Tukuyu along the highway to Kyela (there are frequent daladalas in either direction), which leaves you with a 12–15km hike each way (the falls are west of the road). You'll have problems hiring a car in Tukuyu at short notice, but bicycles are no problem; you should be able to arrange something at your hotel (from Tsh1500 a day). Alternatively, the cultural tourism programme in Mbeya (see p.586) arrange trips to the falls (5hr return; Tsh30,000 per person), which also includes a visit to tea, banana or coffee plantations. A Tsh500 **entrance fee** is collected in the car park near the falls on behalf of the local village.

The Kiwira River

The **Kiwira River**, about 20km north of Tukuyu, has three distinct attractions: God's Bridge and the Kijungu Pot Falls, which can be visited together as a day-trip, and the Marasusa Falls, which have to be visited separately. **God's Bridge** (Daraja la Mungu) is a natural lava-stone archway over the Kiwira River that was formed a few hundred years ago during one of Mount Rungwe's eruptions and acquired its unusual shape when river water cooled a lip of lava before it could collapse. Three kilometres away, on the same river, are the **Kijungu Falls**. Their name, meaning "cooking pot" in the Kinyakyusa language, alludes to the impressive pothole into which the river falls and disappears, flowing underground before reappearing further down. The sites are about 20km west of from Tukuyu, and can be be visited eiher with a guide from *Langboss Lodge* in Tukyu or with the cultural tourism programme in Mbeya.

To reach God's Bridge and the Kijungu Falls by public transport, catch a daladala from Tukuyu or Mbeya to **Kyimo**, leaving you with an eleven-kilometre walk or bicycle ride west from the highway (Kyimo's villagers rent out bikes for around Tsh1000). There's a basic guest house in Kyimo, should you miss the last daladala back. A taxi from Tukuyu costs around Tsh12,000. There's no entrance fee, but you'll need your passport because the sites are on military prison land: register first at the gate by the prison near God's Bridge, where you'll be assigned a prison guard to escort you to the river (a tip is appreciated). Mbeya's cultural tourism programme offers the trip (roughly 8hr) for Tsh15,000 per person.

Further upstream on the Kiwira River are the impressively thunderous **Marasusa Falls**. From either Tukuyu or Mbeya, catch a daladala to **Kiwira** (or Kiwila) village, 20km north of Tukuyu, from where it's a forty-minute walk to the Kiwira River. Mbeya's cultural tourism programme also offers the tour (6hr; Tsh12,000 per person). The last daladala back to Tukuyu passes through Kiwira at 6pm. If you miss it or want to stay overnight, *Mapembero Guest House* is the best of several here (all ❶).

Lake Nyasa and eastwards

Straddling the border between Tanzania, Malawi and Mozambique, the 31,000-square-kilometre **LAKE NYASA** (also called Lake Malawi) is East Africa's third largest lake, and one of its most beautiful. The first European to hear about the lake was the Portuguese explorer Gaspar Bocarro in 1616, but it took until the 1770s for the first non-Africans to reach it, when Arab slavers began following a caravan route developed by the Yao tribe, making Nyasa a major source of slaves for the Omani empire.

Geologically, the lake is similar to Lake Tanganyika, having been formed in the same period of Rift Valley faulting some twenty million years ago. Like Lake Tanganyika, Nyasa is long and narrow, measuring 584km from north to south, but only 80km at its widest. A maximum depth of almost 700m was recorded at the northern end near the Tanzanian shore, where the jagged and largely unexplored **Livingstone Mountains** rise precipitously to over 2500m, providing an unforgettable backdrop, especially if you take the lake ferry from Itungi Port to Mbamba Bay or Malawi – one of Africa's great journeys.

Snorkellers are in for a treat, as most of the lake's four hundred colourful cichlid species favour the clear waters just off the rocky northeastern shoreline, easily reached by dugout or motorboat from the village of **Matema**, which also has one of Tanzania's most alluring beaches. Equally relaxing is the diminutive and exceptionally friendly town of **Mbamba Bay**, near the Mozambique border. Unfortunately there's a price to pay for paradise in the form of plagues of mosquitoes, which are especially ravenous in the first few hours after sunset. **Cerebral malaria** is a big problem around the lake, so make sure you're adequately protected (see p.23).

East of the lake, the small agricultural settlement of **Njombe** makes for a pleasant if nondescript stop, although for keen hikers it marks the beginning of an adventurous route over the Livingstone Mountains to Lake Nyasa. South from here is the remote town of **Songea** – a surprisingly populous place given its distance from anywhere else, and one of the focal points of the 1905–07 Maji Maji Uprising. From here, rough roads continue west to Mbamba Bay on the lake and east to Lindi and Mtwara on the Indian Ocean.

The **best time to visit** the lake region is from September to November, when the weather is hot and dry, and from June to August, which is cooler and sometimes windy, and has fewer mosquitoes. At other times it can get unbearably humid.

For details of **ferry services** on Lake Nyasa, see p.601.

> ### The Nyasa ecosystem
>
> Although eclipsed in absolute size and depth by Lake Tanganyika, Nyasa (meaning "great water" in the language of the Yao) trumps its big brother in terms of **biological diversity**. Whilst Tanganyika boasts a hugely impressive two hundred cichlid species, Lake Nyasa contains over four hundred, an astonishing figure, representing no less than one-third of the world's known species, most of which exist only here. However, commercial **overfishing** has wrought havoc on the lake's ecology in recent decades. Catches of the freshwater *dagaa* sardine have declined drastically, and stocks of catfish, carp and the large Malawi bass have also fallen, giving rise to fears of environmental disaster if strict quotas aren't imposed. An additional worry is the development of a large gold mine near Manda – no guesses as to what the toxic effluent might do to the lake's already precarious ecology if not adequately treated.

Matema and around

Tucked into the northeastern corner of Lake Nyasa between the Lufilyo River floodplain and the peaks of the Livingstone Mountains, the fishing village of **MATEMA** enjoys both an inspiring location and a magnificent beach. There's superb snorkelling on the rocky shoreline just to its east, and for the energetic a waterfall in the mountains can be explored, as can the thick forest and *shambas* (farms) at their base. In short, it's a perfect place in which to unwind.

The village served for a brief time as the regional headquarters under **German colonial rule** before the mosquitoes forced them out. Matema's oldest building is the **Lutheran mission house**, which looks somewhat like a Bavarian barn. Another reminder of colonial rule is the bay on which the village sits, named after the nineteenth-century explorer Hermann von Wissmann, whose two successful crossings of Africa spurred on his country's colonization of East Africa. Later, in his capacity as imperial commissioner of

German East Africa, Wissmann brutally fought and won the Abushiri War (1889–91). Matema is now inhabited mainly by members of the Nyakyusa tribe – see p.591.

Arrival and accommodation

Ferries no longer call at Matema and, given the cramped conditions on local road transport (whether from Tukuyu or Kyela), getting to Matema can be a deeply uncomfortable experience. An alternative and highly adventurous approach would be to hike over the Livingstone Mountains from the east: the nearest villages are Makete and Bulongwa, both connected to Njombe by bus; see the box on p.605 for more details.

There are two ways to get to Matema **from Tukuyu**. The easier way, in the dry season only, is to catch an early-morning daladala or bus to Kyela, and change to a pick-up there: with luck, you'll get one all the way to Matema, but you're more likely to be dumped in Ipinda, 30km north of Matema (see below), where you'll have to change again. The whole journey from Kyela should take about two hours, though three or four times that isn't unknown if the road or the vehicle is bad.

The alternative approach from Tukuyu, especially recommended for its scenery, is to catch an early morning **pick-up or truck** direct to Ipinda, which passes by Masoko Crater Lake. The pick-ups (usually 2 daily, though there are days when nothing runs) leave from the roundabout beside the NBC bank, about 500m east of the Mbeya–Kyela highway and the bus stand; the first heads off between 8am and 9am, the second at midday. If there's nothing going, ask at the petrol station next to the bank or at the Lutheran Church offices next door, who might have a vehicle heading down. The best day for lifts is Friday, which is market day in Ipinda. The journey normally takes two and a half hours, but can be longer in the rains. With luck, you might find a vehicle going all the way from Tukuyu to Matema.

Chances are that you'll have to change transport in the hot and dusty town of **IPINDA**, 30km north of Matema, from where a handful of vehicles head down to Matema daily, generally leaving after midday. The ride is very crowded and uncomfortable, especially if you find yourself in the back of a Mitsubishi truck. The Land Rovers and Toyotas fare better, though breakdowns are common; 4WD might be necessary in the rains. Should you get stuck in Ipinda, there are two basic **guest houses**: the *Kamwene* and the more rudimentary *Gerias* (both ❶), plus lots of grocery stores, *chai* stalls and eating houses, the best of which is the *Burudan Hotel*.

Leaving Matema, get to the Ipinda junction by the hospital before 6am to catch the first pick-ups to Ipinda and Kyela. For Tukuyu you'll probably have to change vehicles in Ipinda. If you're heading to Itungi Port for the Lake Nyasa ferry, you could hire a **dugout canoe** for the 16km ride (at least Tsh5000–6000), but unless you're sure of the ferry's day of departure and time (see p.601) you risk getting stranded at Itungi Port. *Matema Eco-Tourism Resort* has a **Land Rover** for hire, charging Tsh300 per kilometre if over 100km a day, or Tsh20,000 to Ipinda and Tsh40,000 to Kyela.

Matema lacks electricity, restaurants, telephones and a bank, so bring enough **money** for your stay. Should you need it, the mission-run **hospital** at the Ipinda junction enjoys a good reputation. For **food** supplies, there are some *dukas* at the Ipinda road junction, or check out the market (see p.598).

Accommodation

Matema's only **accommodation** is in two modest church-run places a couple of kilometres west of Matema village at Matema Beach. Both are good value, given their locations. **Camping** is possible at either place: (around Tsh2500 per person).

Lutheran Beach Resort 600m west of Ipinda junction in the mission school's compound (c/o Tukuyu's Lutheran Mission ☎ 025/255 2130). Idyllically located in the grounds of the historic mission: though the rooms and *bandas* (some en suite) are getting run-down, they remain comfortable, and the best ones are set directly on the beach. There's a small provision shop, meals and soft drinks are available, and a generator provides electricity until 10pm. Rates are cheaper if three or four people share a room. Spartan breakfast included. ❷

Matema Eco-Tourism Resort 2km west of Ipinda junction (bookings through *Karibuni Center Hotel* in Mbeya, p.582). A new place with nicer rooms than the *Lutheran Beach Resort* – all spotless, with large box nets and Western loos – but the beach has been cleared so there's no shade. Accommodation is in four beach-front buildings sleeping three or five people; rates are per building (Tsh15,000 for a three-bed house; Tsh25,000 for a five-bed house), so things are cheaper if you can fill all the beds. There's also a communal kitchen, and barbecue facilities and cheap meals are also available.

The village and around

There are a number of possible hikes and day-trips from Matema should you feel the need to rouse yourself from your arcadian reverie, including one to **Ikombe village**, famous for its potters. With time, you could also walk back along the Ipinda road, which passes through thick vegetation with a wealth of birdlife. Some of the vegetation is wild (look for the vervet monkeys in the tall and bushy palms), but much is planted with banana and papaya plants, mango trees, stands of giant bamboo and sugar cane. Many of the houses in the clearings are built in traditional Nyakyusa fashion, using straight bamboo stalks lashed together for walls, and reeds for their pointed roofs. Look out too for the curious cylindrical toadstool-like granaries made from woven reeds topped by broad straw thatch roofs.

Matema's diminutive **market**, in the area known as Lyulilo, is 2.5km east of the *Lutheran Beach Resort* across a river ford. If you're feeling especially lazy, a dugout ride costs around Tsh1000 (you'll see men carving out trunks to make the boats en route). The market itself has only the barest necessities, though the clearing at the end by the beach usually has piles of Kisi pots (see p.599) awaiting transport, which you should be able to buy. There are also a couple of people selling skewers of grilled goat meat, fish and bananas, but other than that there's little else to it other than the fun of either amusing or inadvertently terrifying the local kids, some of whom have the enormous distended bellies which are symptomatic of protein deficiency – curiously so, given the lake's abundance of fish.

The coarse grey sand of **Matema Beach** itself starts at Ipinda junction beside the hospital a little over 2km west of the market. The water is free of bilharzia, and the crocodiles, which elsewhere have a habit of lunching on locals, are thankfully absent. The walk to the mouth of the **Lufilyo River**, 4km west of the hotels along the beach via a small lagoon, is recommended. Both banks are thickly vegetated, which makes walking difficult, and there are crocodiles here – as the fishermen will tell you – so beware (there are also apparently hippos upstream). If you're too lazy for the return trip, you can catch a ride in a canoe for Tsh1500 per person.

Matema lies tantalizingly close to the northernmost spur of the **Livingstone Mountains**, which run most of the way along the Tanzanian shore of the lake. The mountains' thick forests and steep slopes are sparsely inhabited, and the entire range is little explored. For a taste, there's a **waterfall** a couple of hours' walk from Matema, for which you'll need a guide: *Matema Eco-Tourism Resort* should be able to sort you out (no fixed prices). For advice on hiking further afield, and road transport on the eastern side of the mountains from Njombe, see p.605.

Ikombe village

IKOMBE village, a few kilometres south of Matema on a small peninsula on the lake's east shore, is populated by the **Kisi tribe**, whose women have long been famous for their skills as potters – you can find Kisi pots in the markets at Matema, Ipinda, Kyela, Tukuyu, Mbeya and sometimes even in Iringa and Dar. Unlike other Tanzanian potters, the Kisi women use wheels – actually thick, ash-sprinkled plates – which help create the finished pots' characteristically rounded forms. As the pot grows, one hand is used to support it and, at the same time, rotate the wheel. When the pot is ready, it's smoothed with pebbles or maize cobs and rubbed with a greyish clay which gives a creamy colour after firing. After a few days of drying, the pots are decorated with red ochre and sometimes incised with motifs. The final firing is done in a shallow depression in the ground lined with dry banana leaves. The resulting pottery is non-porous, making it ideal for both cooking and storing cool liquids.

The **best time to visit** is on Friday to coincide with the weekly market.

Access to Ikombe is by dugout canoe from Matema, which takes just over an hour and costs Tsh2000–2500. Alternatively, the *Matema Eco-Tourism Resort* has a **motorboat** which costs Tsh10,000 per hour (maximum six people). There's no accommodation and only a handful of basic *dukas*, so bring everything you'll need.

For **full-day trips** on the lake, negotiate a discount for the motorboat, or hire a **dugout canoe**. However, past incidents of theft and other hassle mean you should consult either of the resorts before hiring a boat. **Snorkelling** (you'll need your own gear) is best off the rocky eastern shore, where you'll see several of the lake's many cichlid species in the crystalline water. There are also some shoreline **caves** nearby. Access depends on the lake level – the best time is towards the end of the dry season (Oct & Nov), when the water is lower.

Kyela

The hot, loud, dusty and mosquito-infested town of **KYELA** is no one's favourite place, with the possible exception of cyclists, for whom the 55-kilometre descent from Tukuyu is something close to heaven. For non-Africans, the town also has the dubious honour of being one of only very few places in Tanzania where the insistent shouts of "*mzungu*" (or the more economical "hey!" or "you!"), coupled with "give me money" repeated *ad nauseam*, make visitors feel like little more than zoological curiosities. Not surprisingly, most travellers just pass through, at most spending a night on their way to or from the Lake Nyasa ferry at Itungi Port, the Malawian border or the beach at Matema, 46km to the east. Having said that, the general *wazungu*-baiting is at least partly offset by the soothing choruses of "good morning, teacher!" and "*shikamoo*" from the town's children – or at least the ones who aren't totally petrified by your mere appearance – so turn a deaf ear and take it all in good spirit, and you'll hopefully find that Kyela provides a bearable, if not wholly enjoyable, experience.

Arrival and accommodation

Kyela's **bus stand** is normally only used to deposit passengers, as buses generally leave from outside the ticket offices on Itungi Road next to *Gwakisa Guest House*. **Leaving Kyela**, there are daily services to Dar es Salaam via Mbeya, Iringa and Morogoro. The first leaves at 6am (Hood), followed by Scandinavian Express (6.15am) and Zainab's (6.45am) – Scandinavian has the safest reputation; Hood the worst. Ipinda and Matema are served by irregular pick-ups that cruise around town in the morning looking for passengers. Ask the touts on Mwakalinga Road next to the market, who will point you in the right direction. Route details and information on getting to Matema are given on p.597. There are pick-ups and daladalas throughout the day to Tukuyu, Mbeya and the Malawi border (see p.587).

The National Microfinance Bank, Msitikini Road, changes cash and travellers' cheques. The **post office** is between Posta and Mwakalinga roads. You can **phone** from one of three call centres on Itungi Road – TTCL, EMT Telephone House and Mnasi Attended Call at the *Makete Half London Guest House* – as well as from Kyela Communication Centre next to *Steak Inn*.

Accommodation

Kyela has loads of **accommodation**, much of quite reasonable. Inspect several rooms or hotels before choosing, though: if a bed lacks an adequately sized mosquito net, forget it: this is malaria country, and the alternative of a window screen and ceiling fan isn't totally effective. In Kyela a double room means it has two beds, so "singles" can be shared by a couple if the bed's big enough.

Gwakisa Guest House Corner of Itungi Rd and CCM Rd ☎025/254 0078. The rooms here are large and have ceiling fans, the shared toilets and showers are clean and there's also a laundry area. The only drawback is the lack of mosquito nets. ❶

Makete Half London Guest House Corner of Itungi Rd and CCM Rd ☎025/254 0459. Only six rooms (all "singles"), with private bathrooms (clean squat loo and shower), mosquito net, fan, carpet, table and chair. ❶

New Bitutuka Guest House Bitutuka Rd (no phone). The rooms here (with or without private bathroom) are glum but hygenic, with clean squat loos and showers. Some rooms have nets, and all have fans. There's also a bar. ❶–❷

Pattaya Centre Guest House Itungi Rd ☎025/254 0015. Probably the best central choice, and so a little pricier than the others, with good clean en-suite rooms and a separate bar and lounge next door. ❷

Side Villa Hotel Mwafongo Rd, 100m west of the road in from Mbeya ☎025/254 0348. This part of town is surprisingly rural, and so quieter and calmer than elsewhere. The hotel is a welcoming family-run affair, and all rooms are en suite with Western-style toilet, double bed, mosquito net and ceiling fan. It can be loud in the evenings thanks to the adjacent bar: get a room at the back on the right. ❶

Twetange Guest House Bitutuka Rd ☎025/254 0121. Friendly, very cheap and reasonably well kept, with shared bathrooms and nets in most rooms. The annexe just up the road has a bar. ❶

Eating and drinking

Kyela's best **food** is served by the *mama ntilies* at the stalls off Posta Road between the bus stand and the market, who are also refreshingly friendly and polite compared to their *mzungu*-yelling male counterparts. Meals are basic but can be delicious, featuring fresh fish, fried cassava, bananas, grilled goat meat and boiled cakes, all going for a few hundred shillings. Breakfasts are good too, whether you go for *supu*, fried cassava with chilli sauce, or porridge. Of the proper restaurants, the best are the *Mummy Classic Restaurant* on Itungi Road, with good and very filling lunches and dinners (around Tsh1000) and CNN on the telly, and *New Karuma Restaurant*, facing the southeast side of the

Lake Nyasa ferries

There are only two ferries currently operating on the Tanzanian side of Lake Nyasa: the *MV Songea*, weekly from Itungi Port to Mbamba Bay, then across Nkhata Bay in Malawi; and the Malawian vessel *MV Ilala*, whose only Tanzanian port of call is Mbamba Bay. The main Tanzanian harbour is **Itungi Port** (also called Ziwani), 15km east of Kyela at the estuary of the Kiwira River. The road from Kyela is in a dreadful state, and the port itself only has a handful of buildings and a pontoon jetty where motorboats take passengers to the ferries moored offshore (the port itself has silted up). **Access** from Kyela is by pick-up or daladala, taking about an hour in normal conditions. They circle around Kyela in the morning angling for passengers, but get up early in case your vehicle takes ages to fill up. You can also board them on Mwakalinga Road facing the market. The touts are pests, so go for the vehicle that seems most likely to leave – minibuses are preferable to the deeply uncomfortable open-backed pick-ups. For an alternative approach, you could hire a dugout in Matema to get to Itungi Port.

At the time of writing, the **MV Songea** left Itungi Port at 1pm on Thursday, calling at a string of minor ports before docking at Mbamba Bay around Friday lunchtime. From Mbamba Bay, it continues to Nkhata Bay in Malawi, before turning around to arrive back in Itungi Port on Monday (the smaller **MV Iringa**, which used to cover the same route, is currently awaiting spares and only has third-class seating). The *MV Songea* has first-class cabins on top, each with two bunks and a table, and numbered third-class seating below. If you opt for third class, get your ticket as soon as the ticket office opens (three hours before departure) or you'll be stuck in the steamy windowless confines of the dungeonlike lower deck. First class to Mbamba Bay costs Tsh15,000, third class Tsh5250 (there's no second class). Cheap meals (around Tsh600) and drinking water are available. For up-to-date **ferry schedules**, ask the daladala and pick-up drivers in Kyela who cover the run to the Malawi border, as they're the same ones who connect with the ferry. Alternatively, enquire at the Fisheries Research Department in Kyela at the east end of Msitikini Road, who should know the score.

The ferry stops at a number of villages and small towns along the way, including **Lupingu** (6–7hr from Itungi Port; road access to Lupingu is also possible from Njombe – see p.605), **Manda** (13hr), **Lundu**, **Nindai**, **Mango** and **Liuli**, the latter with some impressive boulder outcrops: the large one furthest from the shore just to the south – in appearance vaguely like a sphinx – inspired the Germans to call the place Sphinxhafen. At Lupingu, the boat is greeted with a wonderfully surreal spectacle of the women and kids who have perfected the art of selling meals (fish and cassava) to hungry passengers by using plastic jugs strapped to long poles to reach up to the deck while wading up to their necks in the water. The ferry reaches Mbamba Bay about 24 hours after leaving Itungi Port and, after unloading and reloading, continues across the lake to Nkhata Bay in Malawi.

market, which does good cheap fish with *ugali*, rice or chips, and other dishes (well under Tsh1000). The poshest place is the *Steak Inn Hotel & Bar*, on the same street as the *New Karuma*, though the service can be somewhat abrupt.

Kyela has scores of **bars** to choose from, mostly pretty tawdry dives where manhood – and occasionally womanhood – seems to be measured by the quantity imbibed. There are no taxis in town, so if you want a night out, drink close to your hotel to avoid the potentially hazardous walk back – an ability to humour the town's dipsomaniacs would also be an asset. The following are the more salubrious places.

New Bitutuka Guest House Bitutuka Rd. The bar here is open till late and is one of the more dignified drinking holes, even if the barmaids are unusually sulky. The downside is the risky walk back into town at night if you're staying elsewhere.

Pattaya Centre Itungi Rd. The bar and lounge next door to the guest house is popular yet calm, and its TV is a good place for European football.

Side Villa Hotel Mwafongo Rd. This has two bars, both of which are perfectly decent in the evenings, and there's also food, though it's usually limited to chicken and chips.

Twetange Annex Bitutuka Rd. The bar here is popular with government functionaries.

Mbamba Bay

The hot and dusty town of **MBAMBA BAY** is the last port on the Tanzanian side of the lake, and the nation's southernmost town, although that word is a tad generous for a small and dusty place lacking running water, electricity or a bank, and which until recently had its road to the rest of the world cut off annually during the rains. Although Mbamba Bay serves as a border town of sorts for travellers arriving from or going to Malawi, only few people disembark here, finding Itungi Port – which lies less than an hour from a good tarmac road – a more practical place from which to continue on into Tanzania.

The feeling of laid-back isolation, though, is all part of Mbamba Bay's charm, and there are miles of sandy beaches to loll about on to either side of town, especially to the south – the enormous **Mohalo Beach** begins about 5km south of town. You'll see drying racks for *dagaa* sardines everywhere, plenty of shady mango and coconut trees, and even a few baobabs, but there's one thing that really makes Mbamba Bay special: the people. Even the children, instead of running away in terror like some do in Kyela and Matema, become delighted whenever they elicit a "*marahaba*" from *wazungu* in reply to their chirpy "*shikamoo*" (Mbamba Bay is one of few places where the kids aren't limited to "Good morning, teacher"). In short, there are few more welcoming and relaxing places in which to savour that one long moment that starts at sunrise and ends just after sunset.

Practicalities

The **MV Songea** ferry arrives next to Mbamba Bay's ruined jetty about 24 hours after leaving Itungi Port (curently early Fri afternoon). The ferries are met by two or three Land Rover **pick-ups** headed to Mbinga and Songea (Tsh5000), but there's no reason to rush, and the daily 5am **bus** is in any case more comfortable. Services are run by Madamba Video Transport and Kisuma Pai Bus on alternate days: buy your ticket the day before; the bus drivers are happy to wake you if you're staying in the centre.

Getting to Mbamba Bay **by land** means coming from Songea. The whole road between Songea and Mbamba Bay was being widened and graded at the time of writing, which should make the journey a far more pleasant ride than it was. However, given the mountainous terrain, the road is still liable to be cut off in heavy rains. From Songea's bus stand, catch the daily bus to Mbamba Bay (departure times vary; check the day before), or get on one of the regular minibuses to **MBINGA**, a wealthy coffee-growing centre 66km short of Mbamba Bay, where you might have to spend the night before heading on down through the forests and farms of the Matengo Highlands to the lakeshore. There are several basic guest houses around Mbinga's bus stand, but the best accommodation is at the *Mbicu Lodge* (☎025/254 0168; ❷), 1.5km towards Songea, which has en-suite doubles and a bar and restaurant.

Leaving Mbamba Bay by ferry, the *MV Songea* continues on to Nkhata Bay in Malawi after offloading and loading, which can take well into Friday. Also sailing to Nkhata Bay is the Malawian vessel **MV Ilala** (✆ ilala@malawi.net), which sets off from Mbamba Bay at 4.30am on Tuesday (times liable to change). The *MV Ilala* continues south along a chain of ports in Malawi, but in Matema you can only buy a ticket as far as Nkhata Bay, as you'll need to deal with customs and immigration there. Heading back to Itungi Port, the *MV Songea* calls at Mbamba Bay on Sunday morning.

If you need to **change money** (dollar banknotes only), money-changers hang around to meet the ferry; otherwise, track down one of the bus owners. The nearest bank is at Mbinga.

Accommodation, eating and drinking

There's a cluster of very cheap **lodgings** signposted a few hundred metres from the beach near the bus stand, the best of which is the *Tumaini Hotel*, also called *Satelite Hotel* (☎ Mbamba Bay 24; ❶), a friendly place with good clean rooms with big mosquito nets, but rather basic shared toilets and bucket showers. Other choices include the *Nyasa View Lodge*, about a kilometre inland (☎ Mbamba Bay 15; ❶); the *New Bay Annex Guest House*, 50m south of the roundabout (no phone; ❶), with good simple rooms; and the welcoming *Mabuyu Guest House*, 200m east of the roundabout (no phone; ❶), though its rooms are very grotty. Much better than any of these, but awkwardly placed if you're catching the early bus, is the *Neema Beach Garden Guest House*, 2km south of the centre at the foot of the boulder-strewn headland (☎ Mbamba Bay 3; ❷), with six good en-suite rooms with mosquito nets, and the advantage of being right on the beach. To get there walk south along the Mbinga Road (it starts on the right just before the bus stand if you're looking from the shore), turn right after 1km just after the bridge, and follow the track for another 1km.

Restaurants are limited to the *Neema*, which offers salads, chicken, fish and rice if ordered in advance, and a small unnamed *mgahawa* tea room on the corner of the street leading to *Tumaini Hotel*, which serves delicious and very filling meals for around Tsh600 (usually fish with *ugali* or rice). The only real **bars** are a small packed room on your left just before the bus stand if you're coming from the beach, and the *Neema*, which also has **discos** on Saturday and Sunday. There's no problem walking back to the centre at night, but you'll need a torch if there's no moon.

Njombe

Straddling a ridge at the eastern end of the Kipengere Range, midway between Mbeya and Songea, is the agricultural centre of **NJOMBE** – one of Tanzania's highest, coolest and breeziest towns. The fresh climate and expansive views are the main attractions, making Njombe a suitably refreshing and likeable sort of place to break a journey at, something you'll have to do if you're attempting the wild overland route from Njombe to Lake Nyasa via the Livingstone Mountains. If you've a few hours to spare in Njombe itself, there are some patches of rainforest and a couple of waterfalls within walking distance.

Arrival and accommodation

Orientation in Njombe is relatively simple, as the Mbeya–Songea highway runs north to south through town. The **bus stand** is on the west side of the highway at the south end of town, near the Catholic cathedral. It's a schizophrenic sort of place: in the afternoon there's virtually no hassle, but on leaving in the morning the pushy touts can be a right pain. Njombe's **banks** are relatively efficient: the NBC is at the north end of town at the corner of the highway and Bank St; the National Microfinance Bank is on the highway halfway between the NBC and the bus stand. The **post office** is behind the cathedral on the south edge of town; the **TTCL** office is next door and has operator-assisted phones inside and card-operated phone booths outside. There's also a cardphone at *Chani Hotel*, which sells the cards. There are "attended-call" offices on the south side of bus stand, at Mnasi Attended Call next to *Edina Hotel*, which charge little more than TTCL.

Many **hotels** lack nets, but given Njombe's altitude it's not a problem as there are few if any mosquitoes – certainly outside the rains – and malaria is absent. "Single" rooms in all the following can be shared by a couple.

Annex New Sangamela Guest House UWT St, two streets north of the bus stand on the west side of the highway ☏026/278 2083. Adequate if gloomy, with "single" rooms only (some en suite), all with big beds. There's hot water early in the morning and evenings, and a good bar next door. ❶

Chani Hotel 1.5km north of the bus stand off Usunguni Rd: walk up the highway, turn left at *Edina Hotel*, and right after *Mpoki Hotel 1994* ☏026/278 2357. In the lower part of town, this posh hotel caters to earnest missionary types. The twelve comfortable rooms have wall-to-wall carpet, big beds and spotless Western-style toilets and showers. There's a good restaurant with an attached lounge and satellite TV, plus a garden bar and safe parking. Breakfast included. ❷–❸

Mbalacha Guest House 800m north of the bus stand: turn right at *Edina Hotel* and it's on the next corner ☏026/278 2164. A friendly place with extremely spartan rooms, but at least the sheets are clean. ❶

Mpoki Hotel 1994 1.2km north of the bus stand on Usunguni Rd: turn left at *Edina Hotel* ☏026/278 2349. Good en-suite rooms off dark corridors, especially good value for singles. Doubles have

lounges complete with three-piece suites and telephone. Some beds have box nets. There's also safe parking, and breakfast is included. ❷

New Magazeti Highland Green Inn 800m north of the bus stand on Usunguni Rd: turn left at *Edina Hotel* ☏026/278 2913. The somnolent atmosphere conceals some cheerful rooms decorated with wood carvings and Tingatinga paintings; some are en suite (with so-so squat toilets and showers). There's also a quiet restaurant, and an even quieter bar where the locals apparently like staring at the wall for hours on end (perhaps someone stole the TV). ❶

Ufunguo Guest House 600m north of the bus stand: turn left at the Total filling station ☏026/278 2290. Other than the brothels by the bus stand, this is the cheapest in town, and although very basic is acceptable if you're used to such places. ❶

Wasia Hotel & Guest House Mbeyela St, one block east of the highway opposite the bus stand ☏026/278 2817. The best budget option, with excellent en-suite rooms complete with piping hot water, desk and chair. The staff are friendly and efficient, and excellent breakfasts are available (Tsh1200). ❶

The town and around

Apart from the views of nearby forests and more distant hills, there's little to keep you in Njombe for long unless stores stocking farm supplies are your thing. Still, the **market**, one street west of the highway at the end of both Mlowezi Street and UWT Street, is a good place to buy naturally dyed **woven baskets** made from a reedlike grass called *milulu*; the baskets are at their freshest and most aromatic after the long rains. On Sundays, the imposing **Catholic Cathedral of St Joseph** at the south end of town next to the bus stand celebrates Mass (7am, 9am, 10.45am & 3pm) in effervescent musical style.

There are two easily accessible stands of **rainforest** just outside town: one occupies a small hill less than a kilometre east of the cathedral; the other, occupying several vales and low hills, starts one kilometre northwest of *Chani Hotel*, from where there's a footpath into the forest. There are also a couple of **water-**

falls near town: one is right next to the Mbeya highway 800m north of the NBC bank; the other is a couple of kilometres south of town, next to the Songea road.

Eating and drinking

There's little choice when it comes to **eating out**. With its linen tablecloths and silver service, *Chani Hotel* is the town's best restaurant, and very reasonably priced too, with mains for around Tsh1800. Also good is the cosy restaurant at *Wasia Hotel & Guest House*, which serves reliably good food (including vegetable stews and massive breakfasts; nothing over Tsh1500); there's no bar, but they can find a few bottles of beer to accompany a meal. More modest choices include *Happy Restaurant* (facing the post office at the south end of town beyond the cathedral, one block west of the highway), which is popular with middle-aged ladies at lunchtime; *Kidugala Restaurant* on Bank Street at the north end of town (turn east from the highway at the NBC bank), which also has a bar with tables on a streetside verandah; and the similar *Desdelia Bar & Restaurant* on Usunguni Road, which gets lively at times.

For **drinking**, *Annex New Sangamela Guest House*, *Kidagala Restaurant* and the *Desdelia* are all good, as is *Edina Hotel* at the north end of town on the highway, which has a streetside verandah that catches the afternoon sun. The most

Moving on from Njombe

Leaving Njombe, there are hourly minibuses throughout the day to **Songea**, **Mbeya** and **Iringa**, and several an hour to **Makambako** on the Tanzam Highway (45min), which has onward connections to Mbeya and Iringa. Two bus companies have offices in town. Makete Transport run daily to Dar at 6am, arriving around 9pm – buy your ticket the day before. Mwafrika Bus run to Iringa at 8am, and cover a couple of other adventurous routes (see below). Buses to Songea from Mbeya and Dar es Salaam pass through Njombe in mid-afternoon but are often full, so don't rely on them; the safest buses are those run by Scandinavian, and the most dangerous by Super Feo. Note also that the roads around Njombe can get dangerously foggy in the morning – good reason to leave later, as few bus drivers reduce their speed to compensate.

Overland to Lake Nyasa

Mwafrika Bus covers a couple of decidedly off-the-beaten-track routes, both of which could get you to the rarely visited eastern shore of Lake Nyasa. The easiest of the two is the 9am bus to **Rudewa** (Ludewa), just over 10km southeast of **Lupingu** on Lake Nyasa where, if you time it right, you could catch the *MV Songea* ferry to Mbamba Bay or Malawi – double-check ferry times with the bus company in Njombe. There are also daily **daladalas** from Njombe to Rudewa. From Rudewa, a pair of Land Rover pick-ups cover the remaining distance to Lupingu, arriving in time for the ferry. There are a couple of basic guest houses in Rudewa, should you get stuck.

A more adventurous possibility would be to catch a Mwafrika bus along the southern flank of the Kipengere Range to **Makete or Bulongwa** (9.30am except Thurs), which lie tantalizingly close to Matema Beach (see p.596) on the northeastern shore of Lake Nyasa. You'll have to hire a reliable local to guide you across the Livingstone Mountains or follow the open ground near the Lufilyo River to the lakeshore (the river itself has crocs and hippos); the relevant topographical sheets, available at the Surveys & Mapping Department in Dar es Salaam (see p.116), are 259/1 and 259/2. The trip shouldn't be taken lightly: you'll need to be completely self-sufficient (including a tent), and seek local advice about routes wherever you can.

pleasant surroundings for a drink should be in the *Chani Hotel*'s garden bar, which was being constructed at the time of research. In the meantime, Njombe's **nightlife** is limited to the distinctly downmarket *Turbo Club* in a building off the small enclosure opposite the sorry-looking Uhuru obelisk next to the market, which has discos on Friday and Saturday nights, though some of the lads can be vaguely aggressive. The club screens football matches during the day.

Songea

If you can ignore the often reckless driving, the long, swooping descent from Njombe to **SONGEA** is gloriously exhilarating, passing through majestic granite scenery reminiscent of the Scottish Highlands, complete with rushing mountain streams, misty moorlands and incredibly long views over the hills. Songea itself, 237km south of Njombe, is a large and bustling town, despite its remoteness, although the only reason to come here is if you're either travelling on to Mbamba Bay on Lake Nyasa (see p.602) or attempting the adventurous overland route eastwards to the Indian Ocean (see p.608).

The Ngoni invasions

Songea is the main town of the **Ngoni** tribe, who occupy much of southwestern Tanzania (they are also found in Malawi, and in scattered groups as far north as Lake Victoria). Although now numerous, the Ngoni are relatively recent immigrants, having arrived only in the 1840s, at the end of a remarkable twenty-year migration from southern Africa.

The Ngoni originated in KwaZulu-Natal, 3500km south of Songea in South Africa. At the beginning of the nineteenth century, the rise of the militaristic **Zulu empire** under King Shaka began to make its presence felt, until by the 1830s many of southern Africa's people were on the move, either fleeing the Zulu armies or the famine and drought that accompanied the conflict. Twelve major migrations out of South Africa occurred during this period, half of which resulted in the creation of new kingdoms elsewhere: the Basotho in Lesotho; Ndebele in Zimbabwe; Gaza in Mozambique; Kololo in Zambia; and the Ngoni in Malawi and Tanzania.

The Ngoni were led by **Zwangendaba**, a former Zulu commander who had fallen out of favour. Copying the regimented military organization and strategies of the Zulu, in 1822 Zwangendaba and the Ngoni crossed into southern Mozambique, and subsequently followed the course of the Zambezi River into Zimbabwe, where, in 1834, they destroyed the 300-year-old Changamire empire of the Shona people. The following year, the Ngoni crossed the Zambezi and headed into Malawi, and by 1840 they had reached the Ufipa Plateau in southwestern Tanzania.

On Zwangendaba's death in 1845, the Ngoni split into several groups and continued their odyssey of conquest and migration: one group, known as the **Tuta**, headed north and settled between Lake Tanganyika and Unyamwezi, where they were welcomed by Chief Mirambo (see p.541), who took advantage of their military skills by hiring them as mercenaries for his own expansionist plans. Other groups went southwest to Malawi and eastern Zambia, while others headed east to set up independent states at Songea and Njombe in Tanzania, displacing the indigenous Ndendeule and Matengo tribes respectively, all the while waging war against other tribes, and amongst themselves. The ensuing chaos that enveloped southern Tanzania greatly eased the German conquest of the country fifty years later – although the Germans themselves would later meet with serious opposition from the Ngoni during the 1905–07 Maji Maji Uprising.

Arrival and accommodation

Songea's **bus stand** is at the west end of town on Sokoine Road. **Taxis** can be found here and at the southeastern corner of the market. For **changing money**, the NBC bank, corner of Jamhuri and Karume roads, is helpful and averagely efficient; CRDB, Njombe Road, is slower. There are two **post offices**: the main one is at the eastern end of Sokoine Road, the other also on Sokoine Road between the bus stand and the market. The **TTCL** office is next to the main post office; handier and only fractionally more expensive are the "attended-call" offices in the bus stand and at the *Songea De Luxe Hotel*.

There are dozens of cheap **guest houses** scattered about town, most of them very basic and uninviting. Songea experiences frequent and prolonged **power cuts**, which also affect the pumped water supply of many hotels.

Golani Bar & Guest House At the bus stand ☎025/260 2023. The best of an otherwise grotty set of hotels by the bus stand, offering reasonably priced rooms with shared bathrooms and a good bar up front screening CNN et al. They also do meals. ❶

New Star Guest House & Bar One block south of the market (no phone). Clean and friendly, with slightly shabby rooms sharing bathrooms, all with nets, some with fans. There's a small verandah at the front with a couple of tables for drinks, and a restaurant inside. The annexe, diagonally opposite, is not as good. ❶

OK Hotel 92 Two blocks south of the market ☎025/260 2640. This has been the travellers' favourite for years, but is shoddily maintained: the plumbing needs repairing, as do the holier-than-thou mosquito nets. On the positive side the beds are comfortable, and cheap if uninspiring food is available. Safe parking. ❷

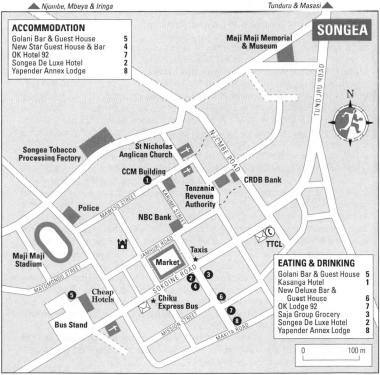

ACCOMMODATION

Golani Bar & Guest House	5
New Star Guest House & Bar	4
OK Hotel 92	7
Songea De Luxe Hotel	2
Yapender Annex Lodge	8

Njombe, Mbeya & Iringa

Tunduru & Masasi

SONGEA

Maji Maji Memorial & Museum

Songea Tobacco Processing Factory

St Nicholas Anglican Church

CCM Building ❶

Tanzania Revenue Authority

CRDB Bank

NJOMBE ROAD

TUNDURU ROAD

Police

MAWESO STREET

KARUME STREET

NBC Bank

JAMHURI ROAD

TTCL

Maji Maji Stadium

MATOMONDO STREET

Taxis

Market ★

Cheap Hotels ❺

SOKOINE ROAD

Chiku Express Bus ★

Bus Stand

MISSION STREET

MAKITA ROAD

EATING & DRINKING

Golani Bar & Guest House	5
Kasanga Hotel	1
New Deluxe Bar & Guest House	6
OK Lodge 92	7
Saja Group Grocery	3
Songea De Luxe Hotel	2
Yapender Annex Lodge	8

0   100 m

Mbinga & Mbamba Bay

Songea De Luxe Hotel Sokoine Rd ☎025/260 2378. The glum and basic rooms in this two-storey building need an overhaul, but they're cheap and the beds have nets. There's a bar next door. ❶

Yapender Annex Lodge Two blocks south of the market (no phone). The large and clean en-suite doubles are the best in town, and consequently often full, so arrive early. There's a restaurant, a calm bar with tables in a garden and safe parking. The related *Yapender Lodge* on the same street is nowhere near as nice, but also quiet. ❷

Moving on from Songea

Leaving Songea, there are several **buses** a day to **Dar es Salaam**, passing via **Njombe**, **Iringa** and **Morogoro**, plus frequent minibuses to Njombe, Iringa and Mbeya. The safest company is Scandinavian Express. Chiku Express, whose booking office is 150m east of the bus stand on Sokoine Road, also has new buses and appears to be a decent alternative. **Mbamba Bay** is served by one bus a day, alternating between Madamba Video Transport and Kisuma Pai Bus. If you miss these, there are plenty of buses and minibuses leaving roughly hourly to Mbinga (see p.602), where you can stay the night before heading on. For Tunduru and beyond, see below. There's no direct (or at least legal) overland route into Mozambique from Songea: the easiest way in is via Lake Nyasa: from Mbamba Bay to Nkhata Bay in Malawi, then back across the lake via the Malawian islands of Chisumulu and Likoma to Nkhotakota. The only official land border crossing between Tanzania and Mozambique is south of Mtwara on the coast; see p.223.

From Songea to the coast

An adventurous and infrequently travelled route from Songea is the rough road east to **Mtwara** or **Lindi** on the Indian Ocean, a distance of almost 700km. With plenty of luck (including good weather and no mechanical problems), the whole journey takes three days, but if you're travelling in or just after the short rains (approximately Nov to early Dec), count on four or five days at least. The section from Songea to **Masasi** (see p.235) via Tunduru is impassable in the long rains (roughly March–May). The journey is done in three legs: from Songea to Tunduru, on to Masasi, and then on to Lindi or Mtwara. Be prepared for an exceedingly rough ride; if you're driving, a degree of mechanical competence is recommended, as the bone-shaking road tests any vehicle to the limit. The 273km to Tunduru are the worst in terms of road condition, but are covered by buses (run by Baba Transport and Rishma's Twiga Express) whenever the road is passable.

In unusually good conditions, the first day's journey takes as little as six hours, but a full day is more usual. The gemstone mining town of **Tunduru**, where you'll have to spend the night, is best known for its **man-eating lions** (avoid camping wild in the region). The gruesome attacks, which have been occurring on and off for almost two decades, have been given a surreal slant by superstitious locals. One belief is that witches – especially in neighbouring Mozambique – are able to invoke evil in the form of lions. The tale goes that a man had a quarrel with a neighbour, and so consulted a witch in Mozambique, who gave him a rope that could be turned into a lion to attack his neighbour if he followed strict instructions. The man created the lion, but forgot the instructions and was himself eaten by the lion, who thereby acquired a taste for humans. A more prosaic explanation is that lions turned into man-eaters during the carnage of Mozambique's civil war. There's lots of cheap and unspectacular **accommodation** in Tunduru, but make sure your bed has a mosquito net: *Naweka Guest House* (☎Tunduru 98; ❶–❷) is probably the best, and there are several cheaper places (❶) by the bus stand.

The road from Tunduru to Masasi (196km) is a little better, though buses aren't as frequent: you may find yourself having to pay for a lift in the back of a lorry. Masasi, and the final leg to the coast, is covered in Chapter 3 (p.235).

The Town

Songea's main attraction is the **Maji Maji Memorial and Museum** (daily 8am–7pm; donation expected), northeast of the centre. The memorial ground is a large square lawn flanked on three sides by the cement busts of twelve Ngoni chiefs who were captured and executed by the Germans during the Maji Maji Uprising. The centre of the ground is dominated by a bulky statue of a soldier with a machine-gun in his hand, while facing the ground in a pagoda is a large cement statue of Nyerere looking uncharacteristically solemn. Though crudely fashioned, the busts are rendered poignant by garlands hung around their necks. Three of the chiefs are depicted with turbans, a unwitting reminder of the Arab-dominated slave trade in which the Ngoni also participated. One of these is **Chief Songea Luwafu Mbano**, from whom the town takes its name. As the most famous of the Ngoni resistance leaders, the Germans honoured him with decapitation rather than hanging.

The curator speaks no English, but is happy to take you around. Inside are photographs and full-length paintings of the twelve chiefs, some of them pictured in the style of Ethiopian Christian icons. The upper floor contains three drums (two still playable), a couple of grinding stones, bellows used in ironworking, a beautiful tobacco horn (which might also have been used for storing marijuana, traditionally smoked by Ngoni elders), weapons and some surprisingly light hide shields. A mass grave from the uprising lies behind the building, marked by an obelisk and a low rectangular wall. Chief Songea's grave is 50m away.

Other than the museum, there's really only the **market** to keep you occupied. If you're looking for kanga or kitenge cotton wraps, rummage through the shops and stalls at the west end of Jamhuri Road.

Eating and drinking

Eating out is rare in Songea, and apart from the restaurants at *Golani Bar & Guest House*, *OK Lodge 92* and *Yapender Annex Lodge*, there's little other than the town's bars, which serve the usual chip omelettes and grilled meat. One exception is the friendly and unassuming *Kasanga Hotel* on Maweso Street, which dishes up good cheap meals and also sells beers and sodas.

The best **bars** are the *Golani Bar & Guest House* at the bus stand, and a cluster of places on the road heading south from *Songea De Luxe Hotel*, including the *Saja Group Grocery*, which attracts drunken but inoffensive white-collar types in the evenings, and the *New Deluxe Bar & Guest House*, which has plenty of comfortable seats and satellite TV screening CNN and European football.

Travel details

Buses, daladalas and pick-ups

Although Iringa, Njombe and Tukuyu lie on main routes, most buses passing through are already full, so we've only mentioned frequencies for buses starting their journeys in those towns. Routes liable to long delays or cancellation in the rains are marked with asterisks.

Iringa to: Arusha (1 daily; 12hr); Dar (7 daily; 8–9hr); Dodoma (2 daily; 5hr); Kalenga (hourly daladalas; 20min); Mbeya (hourly; 3hr 30min–4hr); Morogoro (2 hourly; 3–4hr); Moshi (1 daily: 11hr); Songea (hourly daladalas; 8hr).

Kyela to: Dar (4 daily; 13hr); Ipinda (2–3 pick-ups daily*; 1–1hr 30min); Iringa (4 daily; 6hr); Itungi Port (pick-ups on ferry days; 1hr); Malawi border (hourly pick-ups and daladalas; 30min); Matema

(2–3 pick-ups daily*; 2–3hr); Mbeya (4 daily plus hourly daladalas; 2hr 30min–3hr); Morogoro (4 daily; 10hr); Tukuyu (4 daily plus hourly daladalas; 1hr 30min).

Mbamba Bay to: Mbinga (1 daily plus occasional pick-ups*; 3hr 30min); Songea (1 daily plus occasional pick-ups*; 6hr).

Mbeya to: Arusha (1 daily; 15hr); Chunya (2 weekly plus daily pick-ups; 2hr); Dar (10 daily; 11–13hr); Dodoma (3 weekly; 11hr); Iringa (11 daily; 3hr 30min–4hr); Kyela (hourly pick-ups and daladalas; 2hr 30min–3hr); Lilongwe, Malawi (1 weekly; 18hr); Lusaka, Zambia (6 weekly; 20–22hr); Mikumi (hourly; 8–9hr); Morogoro (11 daily; 11–12hr); Njombe (hourly minibuses; 4hr); Rungwa (2 weekly*; 8–10hr); Songea (2 daily; 8–9hr); Sumbawanga (2 daily; 6–7hr); Tabora (2 weekly*; 24hr); Tukuyu (hourly minibuses; 1hr 30min); Tunduma (hourly pick-ups and daladalas; 1hr 30min–2hr); Tunduru (1 daily*; 14–21hr).

Njombe to: Dar (1 daily; 9hr); Iringa (1 daily plus hourly minibuses; 4hr); Mbeya (hourly minibuses; 4hr); Morogoro (1 daily; 7–8hr); Songea (hourly minibuses; 4hr).

Songea to: Dar (3–4 daily; 13hr); Iringa (3–4 daily plus hourly daladalas; 8hr); Mbamba Bay (1 daily plus occasional pick-ups*; 6hr); Mbeya (2 daily; 8–9hr); Mbinga (3 daily plus hourly daladalas and pick-ups*; 4hr 30min); Morogoro (3–4 daily; 10hr); Njombe (hourly 3–4 daily plus hourly minibuses; 4–5hr); Tunduru (2 daily*; 6–12hr).

Tukuyu to: Mbeya (hourly minibuses; 1hr–1hr 30min); Kyela (hourly daladalas; 1hr 30min); Ipinda (1–3 daily pick-ups*; 1hr 30min–2hr 30min); Matema (1 daily pick-up*; 4–8hr).

Trains

Mbeya to: Dar (3 weekly; 19hr 15min–22hr 30min); Ifakara (2–3 weekly; 11hr 40min–14hr 10min); Mang'ula (2 weekly; 12hr 20min–15hr); New Kapiri Mposhi, Zambia (3 weekly; 19hr 10min); Selous Game Reserve, various stations (2–3 weekly; 15hr–18hr 10min); Tunduma (3 weekly; 3hr).

Ferries

For more details, see p.601.

Itungi Port to: Mbamba Bay (*MV Songea* Thurs 1pm; 20–24hr); Nkhata Bay, Malawi (*MV Songea* Thurs 1pm; 30–34hr).

Mbamba Bay to: Itungi Port (*MV Songea* Sun; 20–24hr); Nkhata Bay, Malawi (*MV Songea* Fri afternoon or evening, *MV Ilala* Tues; 4–5hr).

Flights

(CT = Coastal Travels; PA = Precisionair).

Iringa to: Arusha via Dar and Moshi (PA: 3 weekly; 4hr 10min); Dar (PA: 3 weekly; 1hr 20min); Moshi via Dar (PA: 3 weekly; 3hr 25min).

Ruaha National Park to: Dar (CT: 3 weekly; 1hr 35min); Zanzibar (CT: 3 weekly; 2hr 5min).

Zanzibar

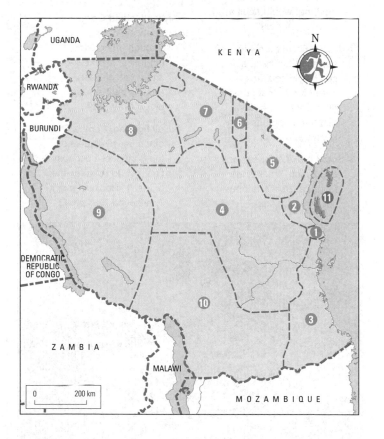

CHAPTER 11

Highlights

* **Stone Town** Africa meets the Orient in the most atmospheric town south of the Sahara. See p.615

* **Forodhani Gardens** Stone Town's nightly waterfront street food market, with a choice of food that would spoil a sultan. See p.637

* **Jozani Forest** Ideal for escaping the heat, a soothingly cool and shady forest that contains troops of endangered red colobus monkeys. See p.658

* **Spice tours** A must-do: see, touch, smell and taste Zanzibar's famous spices in the field, followed by a slap-up meal. See p.647

* **Nungwi** A former hippy beach now discovered by mainstream tourism, but still offering a lively and enjoyable beach holiday. See p.681

* **Misali Island** Gorgeous beaches, nature trails through mangroves, flying foxes, snorkelling and some of East Africa's best scuba-diving. See p.693

* **Bull fighting, Pemba** One of the few reminders of the Portuguese occupation, but don't worry, the bull isn't killed, just mightily annoyed. See p.699

Zanzibar

This is the finest place I have known in all of Africa...
An illusive place where nothing is as it seems. I am mesmerised...

David Livingstone, 1866

ying 35km off the coast of mainland Tanzania, the **Zanzibar archipelago** is one of Africa's best-known and most enticing destinations.
Comprising the islands of **Unguja** and **Pemba**, along with a number of
smaller isles and coral atolls, the very name evokes images of an exotic
paradise replete with coconut palms, multicoloured coral reefs and, of course,
miles and miles of white sands lapped by warm, translucent waters.

The image is not without justification, of course, but there's a whole lot more
to Zanzibar than beaches and tropical languor. Its history, for a start, has seen
more than its fair share of invasions, empires and intrigues, and Zanzibari culture reflects this mixture of influences, not just in the colourful architecture of
Stone Town and the ruined cities and palaces scattered across the islands, but in
a wealth of festivals ranging from Islamic celebrations to bull-fights.

If Zanzibar feels like a different country to mainland Tanzania, it's because it
is – or at least it was. Zanzibar was a separate country until 1964, when it united with mainland Tanganyika to form the present-day nation of Tanzania. The
awkward terms of this union, in which Zanzibar retains a good deal of autonomy (too much for the liking of mainlanders, too little for Zanzibaris), has
been a source of political unease and unrest ever since.

The archipelago's biggest and most important island is **Unguja**, 1651 square
kilometres of low-lying fossilized coral separated from the mainland by the
Zanzibar Channel. **Stone Town**, on the west coast of Unguja, is one of the
world's most alluring cities, centred on an Arabian-style labyrinth of crooked
narrow alleyways, packed to the rafters with nineteenth-century mansions,
palaces and bazaars. The town itself has enough of interest to merit several days
of aimless wandering, while it also provides a good base for visiting the rest of
the island.

The wetter western side of Unguja is where most of the island's famous **spice
plantations** are located, easily visited on an organized tour, as are a number of
other attractions including ruined Omani palaces, Persian baths, and a number
of uninhabited islands whose surrounding coral reefs are ideal for snorkelling.
Another viable day-trip is to **Jozani Forest**, Zanzibar's largest tract of indigenous evergreen forest, which shelters several endemic species of wildlife including the endangered red colobus monkey; it's usually combined with a boat
excursion off Kizimkazi on the south coast in search of the resident dolphins.

But Unguja's main attraction after Stone Town is its **beaches**. The most beautiful are on the east and northeast coasts and either side of Unguja's northern-

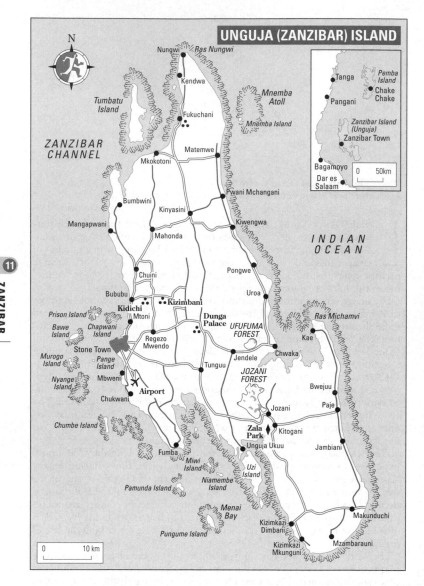

UNGUJA (ZANZIBAR) ISLAND

N

Nungwi • Ras Nungwi

Kendwa

Tumbatu
Island

Fukuchani

Mnemba
Atoll

Mnemba Island

ZANZIBAR
CHANNEL

Mkokotoni

Matemwe

Pwani Mchangani

Bumbwini

Kinyasini

Mangapwani

Mahonda

Kiwengwa

INDIAN
OCEAN

Chuini

Pongwe

Bububu

Kizimbani

Uroa

Prison Island

Kidichi

Mtoni

Dunga
Palace

UFUFUMA
FOREST

Ras Michamvi

Bawe
Island

Chapwani
Island

Regezo
Mwendo

Kae

Stone Town

Jendele

Chwaka

Murogo
Island

Pange
Island

Tunguu

JOZANI
FOREST

Nyange
Island

Mbweni

Airport

Bwejuu

Chukwani

Jozani

Paje

Chumbe Island

Zala
Park

Kitogani

Jambiani

Fumba

Unguja Ukuu

Miwi
Island

Uzi
Island

Pamunda Island

Niamembe
Island

Makunduchi

Menai
Bay

Kizimkazi
Dimbani

Mzambarauni

Pungume Island

Kizimkazi
Mkunguni

0   10 km

Inset:

Tanga

Pemba
Island

Chake
Chake

Pangani

Zanzibar Island
(Unguja)
Zanzibar Town

Bagamoyo

0   50km

Dar es
Salaam

most tip, Ras Nungwi. Although parts of the coast, notably the northeast, have
been swamped by monstrous package resorts, development remains for the
most part low-key, with a selection of beach accommodation ranging from
homely bungalow-style set-ups to plush five-star resorts. As well as standard
water sports, **scuba-diving** is offered by an increasing number of PADI-
accredited dive centres and schools.

Unguja's sister island of **Pemba**, 48km to the north, is quite a contrast. Few tourists come here and facilities are limited, while the beaches are less numerous and less accessible – though you're at least likely to have them to yourself. The island's main attraction is its fringing **coral reef**, offering exhilarating scuba-diving and snorkelling, whilst terrestrial attractions include the pristine Ngesi Forest and a host of medieval ruins dating from the height of the Swahili trading civilization.

Zanzibar's climate is typically **tropical**, making for hot and humid weather most of the year. There are two **rainy seasons**. The "long" *masika* rains (dubbed the "Green Season" by some hoteliers) run from March to May, and are especially heavy from April onwards, when some of the larger hotels close. The lighter "short" *mvuli* rains fall between October and early December. The end of both rainy seasons is heralded by blustery winds. The rest of the year is hot and dry, with temperatures gradually increasing from July until the onset of the short rains. **Ramadan** (see p.51 for dates) is not the best time to visit, as most restaurants are closed by day and the atmosphere, especially in Stone Town, is not at its brightest.

Zanzibar: one name, many uses

Technically, the name **Zanzibar** applies to the entire archipelago, although, rather confusingly, the island of **Unguja** is also known as **Zanzibar Island**. To add to the conundrum, the capital of Unguja, **Zanzibar Town**, is often referred to as **Stone Town** (as we have done) – although properly speaking this name refers only to the older sections of Zanzibar Town, rather than to the entire city.

Stone Town

Located on Unguja's west coast, **STONE TOWN** is the cultural and historical heart of Zanzibar, and probably the most fascinating and atmospheric African city south of the Sahara. Known locally as *Mji Mkongwe* (Old Town), Stone Town in many ways resembles the medinas of Arabia and North Africa, with its magical labyrinth of narrow, twisting streets, bustling bazaars and grand Arab mansions. In spite of the neglect which followed Tanzania's independence, the town's original **layout** and fabric remain virtually intact, making it easily the finest and most extensive example of the Swahili trading settlements that dot the islands and coastline of East Africa. Most of the town was built in the nineteenth century at the height of the monsoon-driven dhow trade, when Zanzibar was the most important commercial centre in the western Indian Ocean, acting as a conduit for all manner of goods shipped in from the mainland, most notoriously ivory and slaves. The pitiful cells under the last slave market can still be seen, as can two former palaces (now museums), an early eighteenth-century Omani fortress, two cathedrals and some Persian-style baths, along with a wealth of less important but no less impressive buildings.

Above all, Stone Town is a city of contrasts. The essence of the city is its cosmopolitanism, its ability to absorb and blend outside influences, and the fusion of cultures can be read in the faces of its inhabitants: African, Indian, Arabian,

European, and every possible combination in between. Nowadays, hydrofoils bob up and down beside the fishing dhows in the harbour, and there are internet cafés in glorious old mansions with crumbling facades. Women in black *buibui* veils chat on mobile phones, with kids dressed in baseball caps in tow; noisy scooters mingle with hand-carts, and hotels now flaunt satellite TV and air-conditioning as well as traditional *semadari* four-poster beds. Yet somehow everything, even the tourists, seems to fit.

Some history

In spite of its centuries-old aura, Stone Town is a relatively young place, most of its buildings dating only from the last 150 years or so. Although the **Portuguese** established a small trading post at Shangani promontory in 1503, Stone Town's history only really starts after their expulsion by the **Omani Arabs**. Fearing a counter-attack by the Portuguese, or from rival Mazrui Arabs based in Mombasa, the Omanis quickly constructed a fort, largely unaltered today, which was completed in 1701.

It wasn't until the start of the nineteenth century, however, that the town began to grow up around the fort. The first **stone buildings** were constructed during the reign of the Omani Sultan Seyyid Said, who in 1832 shifted his capital from Muscat to Stone Town. Helped by the establishment of clove plantations that had been introduced from Madagascar in 1818, Zanzibar quickly grew rich, and the town's mud houses were replaced with multi-storeyed constructions made of coral stone quarried from nearby islands. This period coincided with the rising importance of the **slave trade**, which at its height saw the transportation of 60,000 slaves annually from the mainland to Zanzibar, from where they found ready markets in Arabia, India and French Indian Ocean possessions. The sultan received a tax on every sale, and as the town expanded and his revenues multiplied, so did his palaces.

The building boom lasted almost sixty years and was responsible for most of what we see today. But behind the waterfront facade of palaces all was not so grand. David Livingstone, passing through in 1865–66 before starting his final journey, noted that the town "might be called 'Stinkibar' rather than Zanzibar" due to the stench from "two square miles of exposed sea-beach, which is the general depository of the filth of the town" – a far cry from the celebrated scent of cloves that sailors could allegedly smell from far out at sea. Similarly, the English physician Dr James Christie (who arrived in 1869 at the start of a devastating cholera epidemic that claimed 10,000 lives in Stone Town alone) described the town as "a closely-packed, reeking suffocation of dirt-caked stone and coral-lime houses, whose open drains, abundant night-soil and busy vermin help erase any image of oriental glamour".

The end of the epidemic, in 1870, coincided with the accession of **Sultan Barghash**, who must have felt particularly ill-starred when, only two years into his reign, a violent cyclone swept across the island devastating his fleet and decimating the clove plantations on which much of his revenue depended. The **slave trade**, too, was increasingly being hindered by British warships, and was banned in 1873, effectively marking the end of Zanzibar's economic independence. Nonetheless, Stone Town continued to grow and the sultan embarked on the construction of several monumental palaces and civic buildings.

When the **British Protectorate** over Zanzibar was imposed in 1890, the development of Stone Town was more or less complete, and an 1892 map of its labyrinthine street plan would still be useful today. The main changes were outside Stone Town: the reclamation of Darajani Creek to the east (which previously separated the Stone Town peninsula from the rest of Unguja), the conversion of the open area south of the town into the leafy European residential quarter of Vuga, and the filling out of the administrative district at Shangani. The waterfront gained an involuntary facelift after a **British bombardment** in 1896 to ensure that their choice of sultan took power. The bombardment, known as the shortest war in history (see p.715), lasted all of 45 minutes, destroyed two palaces and was sufficient to elicit the prompt surrender of the usurper. British influence in Stone Town itself, however, was negligible, although their gradual sanitization of the city meant that by the 1920s a more romantic vision of Zanzibar had begun to replace the images of filth, squalor and slavery that epitomized the nineteenth century.

The **1964 Revolution** (see p.717) was the single most important event in modern-day Stone Town's history. In one night of terror, some 12,000 Indians and Arabs were massacred by a ragtag army of revolutionaries, prompting the mass exodus of all but one percent of Stone Town's non-African population. The new government, steeped in the socialist ideology of the Eastern Bloc (witness the regimented housing blocks in Ng'ambo, built by East German Friendship Brigades), had neither the money nor the political inclination to concern itself with Stone Town's upkeep. Tenants of the palaces and merchants' houses that had been converted into low-cost state housing could not hope to keep the lavish buildings in any decent state of repair, and so the old town was left to crumble into the advanced state of decay and disrepair in which it languishes today.

The **economic liberalization** ushered in by President Mwinyi's election in 1985 finally brought hope to Stone Town. The Zanzibar Stone Town Conservation Unit was set up the same year, and by the early 1990s several restoration projects had got off the ground. In 1994, Stone Town was declared a Conservation Area, and it's hoped that the recent addition of Stone Town to UNESCO's World Heritage list will attract further funding to help restore the town to its original magnificence.

Arrival, city transport and information

Most people arrive in Stone Town **by plane** or **by ferry** from either Dar es Salaam or Pemba; for details of airlines and ferry companies, schedules and costs (as well as advice on how to attempt the crossing by dhow), see Travel details on p.705.

By air

Zanzibar International Airport – which goes by the delightful nickname of *Uwanja wa Ndege*, the Stadium of Birds – is 7km south of Stone Town. There are several exchange bureaux in the arrivals hall; rates are decent and they also change travellers' cheques. Daladalas on the "U" route start from the north end of the traffic island outside the airport and charge Tsh250 to Creek Road. A taxi shouldn't cost more than Tsh2000, though for that the driver will be expecting commission from the hotel; if you're pre-booked somewhere, the taxi may be Tsh1000–2000 more. However, international arrivals will often be charged five times that with little room for bargaining. Alternatively, upmarket hotels and tour operators can pick you up if you contact them in advance: the cost averages $12–20 for a car seating up to six.

By ferry

The **ferry port** is in the harbour at the north end of Stone Town. Passengers arriving from Dar es Salaam are expected to visit the immigration and customs offices before leaving the port, a somewhat farcical procedure given that Tanzanian visas are also valid for Zanzibar – see p.17 for more details. **Taxi drivers** hang around for new arrivals: using a cab to find a hotel on your first day is recommended if only to avoid the clouds of commission-hunting *papasi*. If you're **walking**, the easiest way to a hotel is to stay on one of the main roads flanking Stone Town for as long as possible before diving into the labyrinth.

By daladala

The main **daladala** terminus is in Darajani along Creek Road opposite the Central Market on the eastern boundary of Stone Town. There are few if any hustlers here (as few if any tourists travel by daladala), and the narrow alleyways of Stone Town are close by. Finding a taxi here is easy.

City transport

The best way of getting around Stone Town is **on foot**. Distances are relatively short, and in any case most of Stone Town's streets are too narrow for cars (though not for scooters – be prepared to leap out of the way). Still, if you're feeling lazy in the midday heat or need a ride back at night, there are plenty of **taxis** around. The main stands are at Darajani Market; the north end of Kenyatta Road; Vuga Road near the old Majestic Cinema; south end of Kaunda Road; Forodhani Gardens; and outside the port, as well as outside the busier night-time venues. Drivers are happy to escort you on foot to your hotel inside Stone Town for an additional tip. A ride across town currently costs Tsh1500 (Tsh2000–2500 at night).

All of Stone Town's **tour operators** (see p.646) offer half-day guided walks through the town – a good way to get your bearings – going to all the major sights, and costing $10–20 per person. Alternatively, your hotel should be able to fix you up with a reliable guide for much less.

Information

The Zanzibar Commission for Tourism maintains three **tourist information offices**, but only the one at the port (Mon–Fri 8am–4pm, Sat 9am–1pm) is of any real use. There's another office at the top of Creek Road, near Malawi Road (same hours; ☎024/223 8630, ✉ztc@zanzinet.com), which sell maps and does hotel bookings. The commission's headquarters in Livingstone House on Gulioni Road (Mon–Fri 8am–4pm; ☎024/223 3845, ⊛www.zanzibar-tourism.net) is unhelpful and unwelcoming, but is unfortunately the place to head for if you need some kind of official assistance.

Much more useful are a number of **private tour companies**, the most helpful of which is Suna Tours (daily 9am–6pm) at the south end of Forodhani Gardens. Sun 'n' Fun Safaris & Travel (see p.646) is also helpful but more pushy. A decent **map** of Stone Town (with a less useful one of Unguja on the reverse) can be bought for Tsh3000 in Stone Town's bookshops and at Tropical Tours & Safaris on Kenyatta Road in Shangani.

Printed practical information is limited to annual **listings brochures** issued by the Zanzibar Commission for Tourism, the *Zanzibar Travel Trade Manual* published by Gallery Publications, and the quarterly *Recommended in Zanzibar*, a free glossy listings booklet that includes some interesting articles as well as tide tables – helpful for timing trips to the beach; it's available at the tourist office in the port and various venues around town. *The Swahili Coast* contains colourful photos, articles, listings and write-ups of hotels. On the **internet**, Ⓦ www.allaboutzanzibar.com is an outstandingly comprehensive resource where you can also book hotels, taxis and excursions. For specialized queries contact the Stone Town Conservation & Development Authority between the House of Wonders and Palace Museum on Mizingani Road (☎024/223 0046, Ⓔ stonetown@zanzinet.com).

Accommodation

There's a huge range of **hotels** to choose from in and around Stone Town, fitting all tastes and pockets – though (as throughout Zanzibar) it's almost impossible to find a double room for much under $20. Only a few officially drop their rates in low season, but **bargaining** is possible – in fact expected – pretty much everywhere except the posher places. Street noise is not really a problem, though the proximity of mosques can be – but given that there are 51 mosques in Stone Town, there's not much you can do about this other than using ear-plugs and shifting rooms the next day. The advantage of staying in the labyrinth is that prices are cheaper and you'll be in the thick of things, and there's little difference in atmosphere or price between the various wards. Be aware that most hotels are at least five minutes from the nearest driveable road. Room rates usually include breakfast; exceptions are noted. Many rooms also come equipped with traditional Zanzibari *semadari* beds: indestructible four-poster affairs often inlaid with painted panels.

Inexpensive

Bandari Lodge 100m north of the port gate, Malindi ☎024/223 7969 or 0741/613101, Ⓔ next@zenjcom.com. One of Malindi's better budget choices, and especially cheap for singles. The nine high-ceilinged rooms are fresh and clean, and all come with private bathroom (except for one double), *semadari* beds and box nets. Guests have use of a kitchen. ➍

Blue Ocean Hotel East off Kenyatta Rd, Baghani ☎024/223 3566 or 0747/410210. Reasonable place with a mixed bag of rooms over three floors (eight doubles, one single and one triple), all with private bathrooms and fans (if little else). The best are on the third floor, and the street-facing rooms are larger and fresher. ➍

Flamingo Guest House Mkunazini St, Kibokoni ☎024/223 2850, Ⓔ flamingoguesthouse

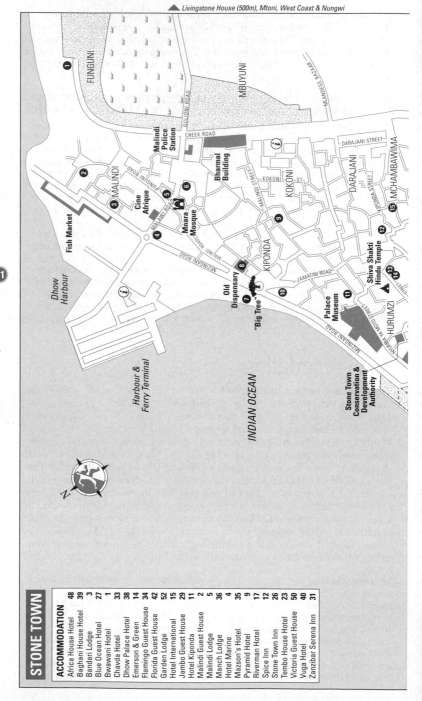

▲ Livingstone House (500m), Mtoni, West Coast & Nungwi

STONE TOWN

ACCOMMODATION

Africa House Hotel	48
Baghani House Hotel	39
Bandari Lodge	3
Blue Ocean Hotel	27
Bwawani Hotel	1
Chavda Hotel	33
Dhow Palace Hotel	38
Emerson & Green	14
Flamingo Guest House	34
Florida Guest House	42
Garden Lodge	52
Hotel International	15
Jambo Guest House	29
Hotel Kiponda	11
Malindi Guest House	2
Malindi Lodge	5
Manch Lodge	36
Hotel Marine	4
Mazson's Hotel	35
Pyramid Hotel	9
Riverman Hotel	17
Spice Inn	12
Stone Town Inn	26
Tembo House Hotel	23
Victoria Guest House	50
Vuga Hotel	40
Zanzibar Serena Inn	31

FUNGUNI

MBUYUNI

GULIONI ROAD

CREEK ROAD

MLANDEGE BAZAAR

Malindi
Police
Station

DARAJANI STREET

Bharmal
Building

DARAJANI

KOKONI - ST

MALINDI

MALINDI ROAD

FUNGUNI ROAD

Cine
Afrique

MNAWI ROAD

KOKONI

MCHAMBAWIMA

Mnara
Mosque

KIPONDA STREET

Fish Market

*Dhow
Harbour*

MZINGANI ROAD

MALINDI ROAD

KIPONDA

JAMATINI ROAD

Shiva Shakti
Hindu Temple

Old
Dispensary

"Big Tree"

HURUMZI

Palace
Museum

*Harbour &
Ferry Terminal*

INDIAN OCEAN

Stone Town
Conservation &
Development
Authority

MZINGANI ROAD

NYUMBA YA MOTO STREET

N

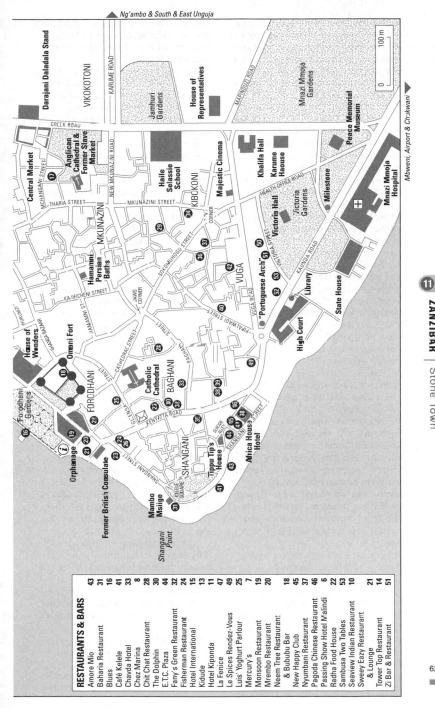

RESTAURANTS & BARS

Amore Mio	43
Baharia Restaurant	31
Blues	16
Café Kelele	41
Chavda Hotel	33
Chez Marina	8
Chit Chat Restaurant	28
The Dolphin	30
E.T.C. Plaza	44
Fany's Green Restaurant	32
Fisherman Restaurant	24
Hotel International	15
Kidude	13
Hotel Kiponda	11
La Fenice	47
Le Spices Rendez-Vous	49
Luis Yoghurt Parlour	25
Mercury's	7
Monsoon Restaurant	19
Mrembo Restaurant	20
Neem Tree Restaurant & Bububu Bar	18
New Happy Club	45
Nyumbani Restaurant	37
Pagoda Chinese Restaurant	46
Passing Show Hotel Malindi	6
Radha Food House	22
Sambusa Two Tables	53
Seaview Indian Restaurant	10
Sweey Eazy Restaurant & Lounge	21
Tower Top Restaurant	14
Zi Bar & Restaurant	51

Ng'ambo & South & East Unguja

Mbweni, Airport & Chukwani

@hotmail.com. One of the cheapest options, with six good if simple rooms around a small courtyard with a fountain. All rooms (single, double or triple) have box nets and fans, and some ($4 more) have private bathrooms with Western-style toilets. Breakfast is served on the roof, and the management can arrange tours. ❸

Florida Guest House Vuga Rd, Vuga ☎024/223 3136. Another good cheapie at the southern edge of Stone Town, with eight clean rooms, most with private bathrooms. There's also a suite for two or three people, with two beds, satellite TV, a fridge and a spotless modern bathroom. ❸

Garden Lodge South of Stone Town on Kaunda Rd ☎024/223 3298. The gloomy ground-floor rooms are far inferior to the slightly more expensive and cooler first-floor twins and doubles which have tiled floors, better bathrooms (hot showers) and balconies. All have fans and nets. There's a TV lounge, and tours are offered through Island Discovery (p.646). They're currently building an extra floor, however, so things might be noisy until construction is complete. ❹

Jambo Guest House Signposted west off Mkunazini St, Mkunazini ☎024/223 3779 or 0747/415948, ⓔjamboguest@hotmail.com. Popular with backpackers, with a friendly feel and cheap rates. The nine rooms (some triple, six with a/c) share bathrooms and there's also a dorm ($8–10 per person). The owners can arrange budget tours, bicycles and motorbikes. Cheap internet access is available for guests (Tsh500/hr) and there's satellite TV in the lounge. ❸–❹

Hotel Kiponda Behind the Palace Museum on Nyumba ya Moto St, Kiponda ☎024/223 3052, ⓔhotelkiponda@email.com. Fourteen rooms in a well-kept restored mansion. Rooms vary in size and price: the cheapest ones are little more than cells sharing bathrooms; the larger and more expensive ones have day-beds and private facilities. Most have box nets and the bathrooms have clean Western-style toilets complete with seats and paper. Tours can be arranged. Credit cards accepted. ❸–❺

Malindi Guest House 200m north of the port, Malindi ☎024/223 0165, ⓔmalindi@zanzinet.com. The best of Stone Town's budget guest houses. Recently refurbished, there's a friendly ambience and helpful service along with wonderful decor and faultless rooms, all with nets and fans and some en suite. The manager can help arrange reliable tours with no mark-up on prices. Highly recommended. ❹

Malindi Lodge Funguni Rd, Malindi ☎024/223 2359, ⓔsunsetbungalows@hotmail.com. An attractive option with nine good rooms, all with nets, a/c and shared bathrooms with Western-style toilets and reliable hot water. The hotel makes up for the lack of a rooftop terrace with a common balcony on both floors. ❹

Manch Lodge Between Vuga Rd and Sokomuhogo St, Vuga ☎024/223 1918, ⓕ223 7925. A large, good-value hotel, with twenty rooms including three with bathrooms and some with four beds, all with nets and fans. The tiled, Western-style toilets are clean, and there's a pleasant balcony with recliners on the first floor. ❹. If this is full, *Haven Guest House*, almost next door, is a reasonable place and similarly priced.

Pyramid Hotel West of Malindi St, Kokoni ☎024/223 3000, ⓔpyramidhotel@yahoo.com. A good-value backpacker's favourite. The eleven rooms (one with private bathroom) come with *semadari* beds, box nets, fans and high ceilings. There's also a TV lounge and laundry service, and an excellent Zanzibari breakfast is included. ❹

Riverman Hotel East of Tharia St, Mchambawima ☎024/223 3188, ⓔrivermanhotel@hotmail.com. The rooms (all with shared bathrooms) are stuffy, but this three-storey place just north of the Anglican Cathedral remains one of the best budget hotels in town thanks to its friendly staff and manager, who can arrange rail tickets and cheap tours at non-inflated prices. Free luggage storage and a safe for valuables. ❸–❹

Stone Town Inn Shangani St ☎0741/346933. An odd little place with nine widely differing rooms and prices, though all have *semadari* beds and box nets and there's hot water. It's worth bargaining over rooms with shared bathrooms, but the standard doubles with private bathroom are reasonably priced. ❹–❺

Victoria Guest House Victoria St, Vuga ☎024/223 2861, ⓕ223 3566. One of the oldest budget options, nicely kept and good value, with friendly and helpful staff. Rooms sharing bathrooms are fractionally cheaper. ❸

Vuga Hotel Pipalwadi St, Vuga ☎024/223 3613, ⓔvugahotel2001@yahoo.com. Appealing two-storey Swahili-style house, centred around a sunny courtyard, though the neighbourhood is less appealing. The ten rooms are generally good, though those without windows to the street can get stuffy. Depending on the room and your bargaining skills, this can be very good value. ❸–❹

Moderate

Africa House Hotel Suicide Alley, Shangani ☎024/223 0708, ⓕ223 1827. Recently renovated, the former English Club has twelve rooms in a glorious setting on the shore and grand architecture inside. The terrace bar remains an ever-popular venue for sun-downers. ⑥

Baghani House Hotel Signposted east off Kenyatta Rd, just after the *Dhow Palace Hotel*, Baghani ☎024/223 5654, ⓔ baghani@zanzinet.com. An attractive and recommended choice in a big old house handsomely furnished with antiques, masks and archive photographs. The hotel is popular with families (and often full in high season), and its eight clean, high-ceilinged rooms – singles or doubles – have private bathrooms, TV, fans and box nets. Credit cards accepted. ⑤

Bwawani Hotel North of Gulioni Rd between the ocean and a saltwater swamp, Funguni ☎ & ⓕ024/223 1184 or ☎0747/419765. This formerly government-run hotel is one of Zanzibar's largest and ugliest hotels. Luckily, outward appearance isn't everything, and most of the 108 large rooms have been renovated. Each has a private balcony, clean bathroom and tiled sitting area, and renovated rooms have a/c, telephone and TV – the better ones (same price) are at the back with ocean views. Facilities include the adjacent *Komba Discotheque*, internet access and a restaurant/bar. ⑤

Chavda Hotel Baghani St, Baghani ☎024/223 2115, ⓔ chavda@zanzinet.com. A lovely, well-maintained Arab mansion decorated with reproduction furniture and Chinese vases that were a common feature of nineteenth-century aristocratic houses. All rooms have private bathrooms (doubles have bathtubs) with *semadari* beds, safes and satellite TV. The more expensive twin-bed rooms have balconies. There's also a rooftop bar, a coffee shop and the *Kisimani Bar & Restaurant* in a ground-floor courtyard (closed Ramadan). Free airport pick-up. Credit cards accepted. ⑥

Dhow Palace Hotel Signposted east off Kenyatta Rd, Shangani ☎024/223 3012, ⓦ www.zanzibar.net/dhow. This beautifully restored nineteenth-century mansion is one of Stone Town's plusher offerings. Service is smart and efficient, and the sixteen spacious rooms are very good value, with bathrooms, a/c, telephone, minibar, big *semadari* four-posters with box nets, Persian rugs and a smattering of antiques. For $10 more you also get a balcony and satellite TV, and residents can use the pool at the *Tembo House Hotel*. The attractive rooftop restaurant has panoramic views and affordable a la carte, which works out cheaper than taking half- or full-board. No alcohol. Credit cards accepted. ⑥

Hotel International Just south of Kiponda St, Mchambawima ☎024/223 3182, ⓔ hotelinternational@hotmail.com. This four-storey former

palace, restored to resemble a giant cuckoo clock, is an attractive option. The twenty rooms are arranged around a big atrium and have bathrooms, box nets, TV and plenty of windows. Six rooms also have balconies (same price); triples cost $10 more. There are a few tables and chairs on a rooftop gazebo giving great views over the town, plus a restaurant at the front (see p.638). ⑥

Hotel Marine Corner of Mizingani and Malawi roads, facing the port entrance, Malindi ☎024/223 2088. The 23 en-suite rooms, arranged around an airy atrium dominated by a wooden staircase, have satellite TV, minibar, telephone, a/c, wall-to-wall carpet and small but mighty fans. Triples are also available. The management can arrange tours (at capricious prices) and somewhat doubtfully claims that the hotel's *Dandari Restaurant* (closed Ramadan) is open 24hr. Credit cards accepted. ⑤

Mazson's Hotel Kenyatta Rd, Shangani ☎024/223 3694 or 0741/340042, ⓔ mazsons@zenjcom.com. One of Stone Town's oldest buildings, though it could do with some sprucing up. The 35 rooms are comfortable in a functional way, and come with a/c, satellite TV, telephone, and wide balconies shared by several rooms at the front. There's also a restaurant but no bar. ⑥–⑦

Spice Inn Junction of Tharia St and Changa Bazaar, Mchambawima ☎0747/415048, ⓕ223 2174. An atmospheric and elegantly dilapidated Swahili townhouse with large rooms (some en suite, some with balconies) and apart from the noisy mosque opposite, it's as calm a place as you're likely to find. Recommended if atmosphere counts more than mod cons. ④–⑤

Expensive

The following all accept credit cards.

Emerson & Green Hurumzi St, Hurumzi ☎024/223 0171, ⓦ www.zanzibar.org/emegre. Set in Tharia Topan's magnificent and lovingly restored Hurumzi House (see p.634), this is without doubt Zanzibar's most atmospheric hotel, packed with antiques from carved Zanzibari doors to Omani bronzeware. Each of the ten spacious rooms has its own character, from the "Ballroom", dominated by a giant chandelier, to the "North Room", whose stone bathtub is half open to the sky. Apart from the rooms, the hotel is famous for its *Tower Top Restaurant* on the roof (p.640), and there's also the *Kidude Restaurant* (p.639) next door. If you have money for a splurge, this is definitely the place. ⑧

Tembo House Hotel Shangani St, Shangani ☎024/223 3005, ⓦ www.zanzibar.net/tembo. Consisting of a sympathetically refurbished nineteenth-century merchant's house, and a less impressive wing added in 1994, this hotel's main draws are its beachfront location and lovely swimming pool. Filled with oriental and Zanzibari antiques, the welcome is warm and the 32 rooms, decorated in Swahili style, are spacious and come with all mod cons, but get a room with an ocean view to justify the expense. ❽

Zanzibar Serena Inn Kelele Square, Shangani ☎ 024/223 3587, ⊛ www.serenahotels. com/main_za.html. Located at the westernmost tip of Stone Town, the *Serena* occupies the former Cable & Wireless Telegraph House and the adjacent Chinese Doctor's House (see p.630). Communal areas are palatial but have been overly restored and lack a feeling of authenticity, and though the rooms are similarly spacious, with ocean views and a/c, it's impossible to justify the price. Facilities include a waterfront restaurant and bar and a large outdoor swimming pool. ❽–❾

The Town

Stone Town divides into several distinct sections, centred on the grandiose **waterfront**, whose monumental buildings run south from the port to the Forodhani Gardens. To the south is **Shangani promontory**, the site of an early fishing village and later the city's principal European quarter. East of here is the leafy residential and administrative suburb of **Vuga**, founded by the Europeans. Heading inland from the waterfront brings you to the most atmospheric of the city's districts, **central Stone Town**, a bewildering, souk-like labyrinth of narrow streets and alleyways, flanked with crumbling mansions and mosques. On its east side, the labyrinth is bounded by Creek Road, beyond which is **Ng'ambo**, a packed and tumbledown area which is where the majority of Zanzibar Town's inhabitants now live.

The waterfront

Stone Town's **waterfront** is the town's showpiece, a glorious strip of monumental architecture through which the nineteenth-century sultanate expressed its wealth and power. The bulk of the buildings you see today were erected by Sultan Barghash (1870–88), whose reign coincided with the end of the slave trade and, not unrelatedly, the eventual loss of the Busaidi dynasty's independence two years after his death, when Zanzibar was declared a British Protectorate. The approach by ferry from Dar es Salaam gives you the best view over the waterfront panorama, starting with the port to the north, then south along Mizingani Road past the Palace Museum and the jewel-box House of Wonders to the squat bulk of the Omani Fort and the grassy Forodhani Gardens.

The **port** itself was built on land reclaimed by the British in 1925. The northern continuation of Mizingani Road, past Malawi Road in Malindi area, takes you to a streetside **fish market** which is every bit as pungent as you might fear. This area is dangerous after dark, however, so take care. The dhow harbour is accessed from within the port and is nowadays mainly used as a fishing wharf. There are only few of the large commercial *jahazi* dhows left nowadays; your best chance of seeing them is during the *kaskazi* monsoon season between December and March.

Although you'll see kids swimming off the **beach** in Stone Town, the water is very polluted; the nearest clean beaches are either north of Bububu (see p.654) or around one of the islands off Stone Town (see p.647).

The Old Dispensary and "Big Tree"

About 200m south of the port entrance, on your left at the junction with Malindi Road, is the **Old Dispensary** (also known as the Ithna'asheri Dispensary or Nasser Nurmahomed Charitable Dispensary), a grand four-storey building which, in spite of the disused customs sheds opposite robbing it of its waterfront location and views, is one of Stone Town's most beautiful landmarks. The sumptuousness of the dispensary's design and decoration is reminiscent of British colonial architecture in India – no coincidence, really, given that it was constructed by craftsmen brought in especially from India by the dispensary's founder, **Sir Tharia Topan**. An Ismaili businessman, Topan was one of the wealthiest men in Zanzibar at the end of the nineteenth century, much of his wealth having accrued from his multiple functions as head of customs, financial adviser to the sultan and banker for the most infamous of slave traders, Tippu Tip (see p.631). Perhaps to atone for his relationship with the latter, Topan's charity financed the building of the dispensary, as well as a non-denominational school, the first in Zanzibar. The **foundation stone** was laid with a golden trowel by Topan himself in 1887 to mark Queen Victoria's Golden Jubilee. Unfortunately, Topan died in India in 1891 without ever seeing the building complete.

In 1900, the building was bought for use as a charitable dispensary. The dispensary itself occupied the ground floor, while the first and second floors – whose galleries overlook a U-shaped courtyard – were converted into apartments for the use of the doctor and his family. Following the 1964 Revolution, the building was abandoned by its occupants and fell into a grave state of disrepair until, in 1990, the Aga Khan Trust for Culture leased the building from the government. Following an ambitious restoration programme, the dispensary formally reopened in 1996, beautifully and sensitively returned to its former glory in a new incarnation as the **Stone Town Cultural Centre** (T & F 024/223 3378, E stcc@zanzinet.com). It now houses the Stone Town Exhibition Centre, the *Chez Marina* restaurant and a number of offices. There's no entry charge, and visitors are encouraged to look around.

Some 100m beyond the Old Dispensary, opposite *Mercury's* restaurant, is the **"Big Tree"** – a gigantic Indian banyan which spreads its crown over the junction between Jamatini Road and Mizingani Road. The tree was planted by Sultan Khalifa bin Haroub in 1911 and has grown so large that it is now home to a family of vervet monkeys. The ample shade offered by its boughs and aerial roots has long been a favourite place for dhow builders. Although these are not so much in evidence today, it's still a good place to enquire about boat trips to the islands off Stone Town.

Palace Museum

Continuing along the seafront, beyond the Big Tree, the large, whitewashed, three-storey building facing the ocean is the **Palace Museum** (Mon–Fri 9am–6pm, Sat & Sun 8.30am–3pm; Ramadan daily 8am–2.30pm; Tsh3000 or $3). Apart from the distinctly Arabic-style architecture, the main draw is the chance to see inside the former sultan's palace, with the furniture and other possessions he left behind when his family fled the Revolution, including one of the world's most famous Formica wardrobes.

The present building, constructed in the late 1890s, is the second to have occupied the site. The **first palace**, the Beit al-Sahel (House of the Coast), was built between 1827 and 1834 by Sultan Seyyid Said as his official town residence, but was completely destroyed, along with the Beit al-Hukm (House of Government) behind it, by the British bombardment of 1896. The Beit al-

The doors of Zanzibar

The traditional modesty shown in Islamic architecture mattered little to Stone Town's richer inhabitants at the height of the city's growth in the middle of the nineteenth century. Social standing, largely determined by wealth, was far more important, and thus **doors and door frames** became the favoured means of expressing the opulence and grandeur of one's mansion. Unsurprisingly, Zanzibar's largest and heaviest door guards the entrance to Sultan Barghash's House of Wonders, whose interior contains another twelve spectacular examples.

Many of Stone Town's original doors are over 150 years old; the oldest dates from 1700 and now stands at the back of the Palace Museum, having been salvaged from Sultan Seyyid Said's ruined palace at Kidichi (see p.655). Their longevity – they've often outlasted the houses whose entrances they once formed – is the result of the hardwoods they're made of, which are resistant to termites, water and decay. Local tree species used included jackfruit or breadfruit, while teak and sesame were imported from as far away as India (the use of sesame perhaps lending sense to Ali Baba's "Open Sesame"). The studs are said to have been intended to repel marauding elephants, and there may be a grain of truth in the story, as the Arab chronicler al-Masudi, visiting in 916, reported that Zanzibar abounded in elephants. By the nineteenth century the studs symbolized the protection of a house. Further symbolic protection is given by the common chain or rope motif carved around the door frame to guard against bad luck and the evil eye.

Residential doors are the most elaborate. Divided into two panels, the male (*mlango mdume*) on the right and female (*mlango jika*) on the left, many also have a smaller door inset into the left-hand panel for the use of children. The oldest, in the **Persian or Omani style**, are characterized by carved rectangular frames, massive plain panels and rectangular lintels with floral and geometric patterns. Over time, the **frames and lintels** became more intricate and ornate, often with an Arabic arch or semicircular panel above. The arch usually contains a rectangular frieze with a date, the owner's monogram and inscriptions from the Koran. Both door leaves are studded with brass bosses. Decorative motifs include fish (a symbol of fertility), smoke (prayers rising to heaven) and lotus flowers, which represented fertility in ancient Egypt and peace in India. More common are doors in the plainer and smaller **Indian style**, many of them serving as entrances to shops. Their abundant floral motifs represent God's presence in the natural world: pineapples are a variation of the fish symbol, and palm leaves are another ancient symbol, inferring good health and plenty. A startling variant of the Indian style are Gujarati doors, invariably made of teak imported from Kutch, distinguished by their coffered panels, many studs and delicately carved frames.

For more on the subject, get a copy of *The Doors of Zanzibar*, by Uwe Rau and Mwalim A. Mwalim, available in Stone Town bookshops (see "Listings", p.643).

Sahel was used by Sultan Seyyid Majid for entertaining visitors with *taarab* music and concubines. When **David Livingstone** passed by in 1865, the traditionally hedonistic welcome was put aside and the doctor's conservative tastes catered to with fruit syrups and a band playing British tunes.

The new building, erected shortly after, served for a time – at the sultan's invitation – as the residence of General Lloyd Mathews, who had arrived in Zanzibar in 1877 at the age of 27 to organize and command a European-style army for Sultan Barghash. The palace subsequently became the sultanate's official residence in 1911, when Seyyid Ali abdicated in favour of Sultan Khalifa bin Haroub, and remained so until the Revolution, when the sultan escaped on his yacht to Dar es Salaam and thence into exile in England. After 1964, the building – renamed the Peoples' Palace – was used for government cabinet meetings and gatherings of the Revolutionary Council, during which time it was stripped of most of its internal fittings (which presumably now beautify the houses of former politicians). The palace was converted to its present use as a museum in 1994, but is still used for *Idd Barazas*, opulent banquets held at the end of Ramadan.

The bulk of the museum's collection comprises the furniture and fittings that survived the Revolution, a selection as eclectic as the tastes of the sultans who lived here. The **lower floors** are dominated by a wealth of ebony furniture, gilt Indian chairs, Chinese recliners, formal portraits and boxed international trade treaties and other documents, whilst the **top floor** gives way to the surprisingly proletarian taste of the last sultan, Jamshid bin Abdullah, including a Formica wardrobe captioned "A style much favoured in the Fifties". The real **highlight**, though, is the room recreated from the memoirs of Princess Salme (see p.653), a daughter of Sultan Seyyid Said, whose elopement in 1866 with a German merchant caused such a scandal that she was effectively ostracized by her family until the end of her life. Also interesting are a pair of rooms that belonged to two of Sultan Seyyid Khalifa's wives, one furnished in staid British Victorian style, the other with a more flamboyant Indian touch. Most exhibits are self-explanatory and well-labelled, although official guides offer their services at the entrance. Their English may not be all that good, but they know their stuff. The service is free, but a Tsh1000–2000 tip is expected.

The **graveyard** in the Palace's untended garden houses the mortal remains of Sultans Khaled, Barghash and Khalifa, as well as the unfinished tomb of Seyyid Said. The area is usually closed to visitors, though an extra tip might facilitate access.

The House of Wonders

The next major building along the waterfront is Zanzibar's most distinctive and emblematic landmark, the Beit al-Ajaib, or **House of Wonders**, which has recently been converted into the **National Museum** (Mon–Fri 9am–6pm, Sat & Sun 9am–3pm; Ramadan Mon–Fri 8am–2.30pm, closed Sat & Sun; Tsh2000 or $2). With its balconies, colonnaded facade and large clock tower, this ceremonial and administrative palace, completed in 1883, was the culmination of Sultan Barghash's extravagant building spree. Its statistics amply justify its name: it was the tallest building in East Africa at the time (and remains the tallest in Stone Town); it was the first to have running water and electric lighting (installed in 1906 as a sweetener by an American company in return for the contract to construct the Bububu railway); and it was also the first to have an electric lift (long since broken). However, a legend that thousands of slaves are buried under the House of Wonders' foundations to ensure their strength appears to be nonsense, given that the last slave market closed in 1873, and that by 1883 British influence in all official matters was pervasive.

The House of Wonders joined two other palaces in the sultanate's Stone Town complex, the Beit al-Sahel and the Beit al-Hukm, which were subsequently connected by elevated suspension bridges so that the sultan, his family and ministers would not have to mingle with the masses down below. The **entrance** to the building is guarded by two sixteenth-century bronze Portuguese cannons captured by the Persians at the siege of Hormuz in 1622 and brought to Zanzibar during the reign of Sultan Seyyid Said. One of them bears an embossed Portuguese coat of arms: an armillary sphere (a globe encircled with bands) that was introduced by Dom Manuel I (1495–1521). One of the cannons dates from his reign, the other from his son's, Dom João III (1521–57). Both guns also bear Persian inscriptions.

The cannons didn't much help the Portuguese at Hormuz, but they do appear to have worked magic in protecting the House of Wonders during the 45-minute **British bombardment** of the waterfront on August 27, 1896, when both the Beit al-Sahel and Beit al-Hukm were reduced to rubble, and a lighthouse that had been constructed in front of the House of Wonders was so badly damaged that it had to be pulled down. The House of Wonders itself escaped the bombardment virtually intact, and even the crystal chandeliers in its salon remained in place. The decision was made, nonetheless, to reconstruct the front facade, which was fitted with a new tower containing the old light-house clock – note that this **clock** tells the time according to the Swahili system: to get Western time, add or subtract six hours.

Stylistically, the building is something of a jumble, perhaps owing partly to the fact that a British marine engineer had a hand in its design. The cast-iron pillars that support the surrounding tiers of balconies are really far too thin for the building's grandiose proportions, centred around a huge roofed atrium. The rooms, all long and relatively narrow, are accessed from broad galleries indoors and from balconies outside. Their heavy ornamental doors are ostentatious statements of the wealth of the sultanate – most of it gleaned from the slave trade – and their gilded Qur'anic inscriptions have recently been restored.

The **museum** currently occupies the front room on the first floor, but is due to expand in the near future, when the remainder of the collection (including a bottle said to contain a genie) is transferred from the Peace Memorial Museum. Even with only one room, though, the museum is well worth a visit, and its exhibits are much more interesting than the Palace Museum's collection of furniture. The displays are well presented and informatively described in both Kiswahili and English, and cover most aspects of Zanzibari life. Making an odd contrast is the dusty collection of flat-tyred 1950s automobiles in the atrium below, which belonged to the Afro-Shiraz Party. Rumour has it that the locked rooms off the atrium contain stacks of uncounted ballot papers from past elections.

The Omani Fort

Just southwest of the House of Wonders, the **Omani Fort** (daily 9am–8pm or later; free entry except evenings when performances are held) comprises four heavy coral ragstone walls with squat cylindrical towers and castellated defences (take care when clambering up the battlements as the stonework is unsafe) and makes for a calm and hustler-free place to sit for an hour or two. The fort dates back to the years following the expulsion of the Portuguese by the **Omanis** in 1698. The victorious Omanis quickly set about defending their gains, completing the fort in 1701. Its **walls** incorporate the last remnants of 200 years of Portuguese presence on the island: the foundations of a chapel (erected 1598–1612) and an adjoining merchant's house which were incorporated into the wall of an early fortification which was, in turn, incorporated into the fort.

The garrison was modest, however, with only fifty soldiers billeted there in 1710, and the fort saw little action for much of the nineteenth century – Zanzibari control over the western Indian Ocean was so complete that the defence of Stone Town wasn't seen as a priority. During this time the fort served as a jail and the venue for public executions, which were held outside the east wall. In the **twentieth century** the fort saw a variety of different uses, first as a market, then as a customs house, and in the 1920s as a depot and shunting yard for the Bububu railway (p.655), which was routed directly into the courtyard through the main entrance. In 1949 the fortified entrance was removed and the courtyard found a new vocation as the Zanzibar Ladies' Tennis Club. After an inevitable period of neglect following the Revolution, the fort was restored in 1994 and now functions as the **Zanzibar Cultural Centre**, containing various craft shops, a small internet café, an open-air amphitheatre that hosts live music concerts several evenings a week, an expensive tour company, the *Neem Tree* restaurant (p.638) and the office for the Zanzibar International Film Festival (p.642).

Forodhani Gardens

The formal **Forodhani Gardens** were the original site of the two cannons now outside the House of Wonders, part of a battery of guns which gave their name (*mizingani* means cannons) to Mizingani Road. The name *forodhani* – meaning a ship's cargo or a reloading place – alludes to the slave trade, when slaves would be landed here before being taken to the market. The site was occupied by customs sheds until 1935, when the Jubilee Gardens were laid out in honour of King George V's Silver Jubilee. The following year, coinciding with the Silver Jubilee of Zanzibar's Sultan Khalifa bin Haroub, the central bandstand, fountain, seats and the small pier now occupied by *Blues* restaurant were added. The "ornamental arch" at the entrance to *Blues* is a bland concrete affair, erected in 1956 for the arrival of Princess Margaret – though, as it turned out, she eventually landed elsewhere.

The gardens are a pleasant, shady place to relax under the midday sun, and there are a handful of curio stalls and Maasai waiting to have their pictures taken (for a fee), but Forodhani really comes alive after sunset when it hosts the best **street food market** in East Africa (see p.637). If you're around in January, ask about the **dhow races**, usually involving *ngalawa* outriggers, which sail from Forodhani to Prison Island and back.

Shangani and Vuga

The westernmost point of Stone Town is **Ras Shangani**, a triangular promontory flanked by a narrow beach that was originally the site of a small fishing village, of which no trace remains. Shangani was also where, in the mid-nineteenth century, Sultan Seyyid Said gave Europeans land for building their embassies, consulates and religious missions. Towards the end of the century, when the Europeans became the dominant force on Zanzibar, the area naturally became the nucleus of their new administration, whilst the area to its south, Vuga, was developed into a residential and diplomatic district, its wide boulevards and open green spaces providing a soothing contrast to the claustrophobic hustle and bustle of Stone Town itself. Nowadays, Shangani is where you'll find most of Stone Town's upmarket hotels, restaurants, bars, and – of course – a good deal of *papasi* too.

The British Consulate and Old Post Office

From the southeastern corner of Forodhani Gardens a footbridge leads to the Zanzibar Orphanage. Passing through the tunnel under the Orphanage, the road continues straight on to the junction of Kenyatta Road and Shangani Street. The building facing you on your right is the **British Consulate** from 1841 to 1874, during which time it hosted various nineteenth-century explorers. The building is now home to the Zanzibar State Trading Corporation (ZSTC) and cannot be visited.

Taking a left up Kenyatta Road, the impressive colonnaded green and white building on your left beyond the junction with Gizenga Street is the **Old Post**

Farok Bulsara, better known as **Freddie Mercury**, the flamboyant lead singer of the glam-rock group Queen, was born in Stone Town on September 5, 1946, to a family of wealthy Parsees from India. At the age of nine, the young Farok left Zanzibar forever, first going to boarding school in India then travelling to London, where he studied graphics at Ealing College before joining Queen in 1970 and adopting his now famous stage name. Somewhat ironically, given that the Bulsaras fled Zanzibar in the aftermath of the bloody 1964 Revolution, Queen's song "Bohemian Rhapsody" – which contains the phrase "Bismillah [in the name of God], will you let him go?" – was embraced by Zanzibari secessionists campaigning for independence from the mainland.

Various houses around Shangani claim to be the former Bulsara family home; the most likely is the building occupied by *Camlur's Restaurant* on Kenyatta Road (the restaurant is currently closed, but the sign is still there). If you're really into tracing roots, *Mercury's Restaurant* on Mizingani Road is the best place to ask.

Office (or Shangani Post Office), which served as Zanzibar's main post office from its inauguration in 1906 until the end of sultanate – it's now a branch office. This is one of several buildings in and around Stone Town designed by **J. H. Sinclair**, who came to Zanzibar in the wake of the British bombardment of 1896 as a young administrator and gradually worked his way up the ranks to become British Resident between 1922 and 1924. His early work is characterized by an easy blend of Islamic forms and Classical detail, but over time his style – dubbed "Saracenic" – became increasingly detached from European tradition, so much so that his contemporaries joked about him having "gone native".

Kelele Square

Heading down Shangani Street from the British Consulate brings you to **Kelele Square**. Though it's now one of Stone Town's most peaceful areas, its name – which means "shouting", "noisy" or "tumultuous" – hints at its terrible past, when the square was used as Zanzibar's main **slave market**. At its height in the 1830s, an estimated 60,000 slaves passed through the market every year. The first building on your right is **Mambo Msiige**, meaning the "Inimitable Thing", its name apparently deriving from the extravagance of its construction, for which thousands of eggs were used to strengthen the mortar (the building's structure was also reinforced with the bodies of slaves, who were entombed alive in the walls during its construction – a common enough practice at the height of the slave trade). Mambo Msiige was erected between 1847 and 1850 by a prominent Arab merchant, and later served as the town's first post office and the headquarters of the Universities Mission to Central Africa (1864–74) – a sombre irony given that they had come to Africa to eradicate the slave trade. **Sir John Kirk**, an abolitionist luminary, lived in the house from 1874 to 1887 in his capacity as the British consul general and, at Kirk's invitation, the explorer **Henry Morton Stanley** spent time here: the room at the top, quite visibly not part of the original structure, is said to have been built especially for his use. After 1913 the building became a European hospital, and presently houses a number of government departments, though there are long-standing plans to convert it into a Museum of Exploration.

The **Zanzibar Serena Inn** next door occupies two recently restored buildings which reopened in 1997 as part of the Aga Khan's luxury *Serena* hotel chain. The main building (you can get inside as long as you don't look too scruffy) was the Cable & Wireless Building, which was connected via Bawe

Tippu Tip

Tippu Tip, the most infamous of East Africa's slave traders, was born in 1830 as Hamed bin Muhammed al-Murjebi in Tabora on the mainland to an Arab plantation owner and trader. He acquired his nickname from a bird with characteristic blinking eyes, as for much of his life he suffered from a pronounced facial twitch.

The second half of the **nineteenth century** was a time of great change in the interior of Africa. Old tribal alliances were breaking down and young upstarts were busy carving out their own chiefdoms. Tippu Tip was just such a man, and through a combination of ruthlessness and financial good sense, he swiftly became one of the richest and most influential slave traders in East Africa. By the late **1860s**, Tippu Tip was leading slave caravans of more than 4000 men, and over the years become kingmaker among many of the chiefdoms the caravan routes passed through, including Upper Congo, of which he was de facto ruler. Stanley, whom he accompanied down the Congo River in 1876, considered Tippu Tip "the most remarkable man ... among the Arabs, Waswahili and the half-castes in Africa".

By the end of the 1880s, however, European ascendancy in East Africa had put an end to the slave trade. With his trading options now limited, Tippu Tip decided to call it a day in 1890 and returned to Zanzibar, where he lived out his retirement as a wealthy and respected member of Swahili society, his pension assured by seven plantations and at least 10,000 slaves, until his death in 1905.

Island to Aden (Yemen) by telegraphic cable. The smaller adjacent building was built in 1918 and is popularly known as the Chinese Doctor's House.

Tippu Tip's House

The riches to be had from the slave trade are perhaps best understood (with a little imagination, admittedly) by visiting **Tippu Tip's House** along the poetically named Suicide Alley, south of Kelele Square. Although the home of the infamous slave trader (see box above) is now in an advanced state of decay, its door is one of Stone Town's most elaborate, and it also boasts a set of black and white marble steps. The house is currently occupied by various local families, evidently undaunted by the popular belief that the house is haunted by the spirits of slaves. A polite enquiry may elicit an invitation to have a look around; a tip (no pun intended) would be appreciated.

Africa House Hotel and the High Court

Continuing down Suicide Alley, past the infamous *New Happy Club* (see p.640), you come to a small square dominated by the **Africa House Hotel**, a grand old building with a heavy carved door studded with brass spikes. The building was erected in 1888 as the exclusive English Club (the oldest such establishment in East Africa), though in time membership was opened to Americans and other Europeans. It provided members with a taste of Old Albion: gin and tonics on the terrace, a library, wood-panelled committee rooms, billiard halls and powder rooms for the ladies. Social activities included cricket, golf, hockey and a New Year fancy dress ball, which attracted sizeable crowds of excited locals eager to witness this amusing manifestation of *wazungu* culture. After the 1964 Revolution, the building was predictably neglected, and has only recently been restored as a luxury hotel (see p.622). The club remains famous for its ocean-facing terrace bar; non-guests are welcome to have a look around, and a sunset drink on the outdoor terrace is one of the highlights of a stay in Stone Town.

Continuing southeast, Suicide Alley runs into Kenyatta Road (watch out for traffic here), which opens into a small roundabout at the junction with Vuga and Kaunda roads. The **High Court** (Korti Kuu) on the right (1904–8), is another of J. H. Sinclair's syncretic creations, and perhaps the most successful. The domed tower was apparently originally fitted with a golden ring so that the Archangel Gabriel could carry the structure up to heaven on the day of reckoning, although quite why heaven would need a courthouse remains a mystery. Another mystery is the forlorn Doric stone arch standing in the triangular garden opposite, which some claim to date from the Portuguese period, though no one knows for sure

Victoria Hall and Gardens and the State House

Some 100m further along Kaunda Road on the left are **Victoria Hall and Gardens**, once used by Sultan Barghash's harem, and presented to the town in 1887 on the occasion of Queen Victoria's Golden Jubilee. The hall itself, locked at the time of writing, was built over the harem baths and functioned as Zanzibar's Legislative Council Chamber from 1926 until the Revolution, and was restored in 1996 to house the all-too-necessary Zanzibar Sewerage and Sanitation Project. The gardens contain some graves of the Barwani family of Omani Arabs, and many exotic plant species like tea, cocoa and coffee. The south end of the hall and gardens is marked by an octagonal marble **milestone**, showing London as 8064 miles away – the distance by ship after the Suez Canal was opened in 1869.

Set back from Kaunda Road opposite the Victoria Gardens is the **State House**, another of Sinclair's works, which originally housed the British Resident. The building is now home to the President's Office and is out of bounds. Photography of any part of the building is forbidden.

Central Stone Town

Away from the waterfront, Stone Town is a labyrinth of narrow, twisting streets, dotted with faded mansions and mosques and criss-crossed by serpentine alleyways that unexpectedly open out onto semi-ruined squares alive with food vendors, hawkers and, at night, crowds of people enjoying coffee on the stone *barazas*. Getting lost is unavoidable – and part of the pleasure. If you really get stuck, any local will show you the way, or just keep walking along the busiest street and you'll emerge onto one of the main roads that bounds the old town. Safety is not a problem by day, though you should take care at night since parts of the town lack street lights; although still rare, muggings and other incidents involving tourists are becoming more frequent.

The slave market and Anglican Cathedral

On the eastern edge of Stone Town, the former **slave market** (daily 9am–6pm; Tsh800 including guided tour) and adjacent Anglican Cathedral Church of Christ provide a devastatingly poignant memorial to the horrors of the slave trade. Stone Town's original slave market was at Shangani, but it's here in Mkunazini, where the market relocated in the late 1860s, that the appalling cruelty of the trade hits home. The guided tour includes the tiny, dingy cells that housed the slaves until market day. Conditions were squalid in the extreme: up to 75 slaves were cramped into cells so small that most people couldn't stand upright. The only furnishings were a pit in the centre and a low platform around the sides. There were no windows: one of the cells is now lit by artificial light; the other has been left unlit save for two slits at one end that hardly make a dent in the gloom. The market – Africa's last – was finally closed in 1873 by a reluctant Sultan Barghash under pressure from the British, though slavery itself was only abolished in 1897, and domestic slavery continued in Zanzibar until 1917.

The juxtaposition of the slave quarters with the imposing Anglican **Cathedral Church of Christ** beside it might appear grimly ironic but, in the spirit of Christian evangelism, replacing the inhumanity of the slave trade with the salvation of God made perfect sense. Named after Canterbury Cathedral, the foundation stone was laid on Christmas Day 1873, the year the market closed. The project was funded by the Universities Mission in Central Africa from Oxford, and construction proceeded under the supervision of **Bishop Edward Steere**, third Anglican bishop of Zanzibar. Steere, who had been pivotal in securing the mission's support, appears to have been a tireless individual, his other achievements including the compilation of the first English-Kiswahili dictionary and the first Kiswahili translation of the Bible. Steere himself conducted the first service, on Christmas Day, 1877. The cathedral's design follows a basilican plan, blending the Perpendicular neo-Gothic form then popular in Victorian England with Arabic details. The unusual barrel-vaulted roof was completed in 1879, and the spire was added in 1890. The clock in the cathedral's steeple was donated by Sultan Barghash on condition that the spire's height did not exceed the House of Wonders, which remains Stone Town's tallest building. A stark and pensive modern sculpture in the cathedral courtyard shows five bleak figures, placed in a rectangular pit and shackled together with a chain brought from Bagamoyo, the most notorious of the mainland slave-trading ports.

The **interior** of the cathedral is full of reminders of the slave trade too. A red circle in the floor beside the altar marks the position of a post to which slaves were tied and whipped to show their strength and resilience before being sold, while behind the altar is the grave of Bishop Steere. The small crucifix on a pillar beside the chancel is said to have been fashioned from a branch of the tree under which David Livingstone's heart was buried. Livingstone is also remembered in a stained glass window, as are British sailors who died on anti-slaving patrols in the western Indian Ocean. The cathedral organ, made by Henry Willis & Co. of Ipswich, England, can be heard during Sunday services (weekly in Kiswahili, monthly in English), together with joyous gospel singing.

Hamamni Persian Baths

The contrast between the misery of the slave market and the slave-financed luxuries of the **Hamamni Persian Baths** (daily 10am–4pm or 5pm, ask for the caretaker across the road to let you in; Tsh1500 including a short guided tour – tip expected; guidebook Tsh2000), 250m to the west, can come as something of a shock. Commissioned in the early 1870s by Sultan Barghash, the Hamamni baths (from the Arabic word for baths, *hammam*) were designed in the Persian style by the architect Hadj Gulam Husein and opened to the public, with the proceeds going to a charitable trust managed by the sultan. The baths are quite small and their design is surprisingly plain; the only decoration of note is the red-brick pattern above the lime stucco rendering outside, topped by a crenellated parapet. The baths ceased functioning in the 1920s, and despite partial restoration in 1978, remain bone dry. The guided **tour** isn't up to much, and the caretaker none too forthcoming, but the baths are a good place to head for in the midday heat, the dry air, thick walls and stone floors providing a welcome respite from the swelter outside.

The Catholic Cathedral of Saint Joseph

The twin towers of the **Catholic Cathedral of Saint Joseph** can be seen from pretty much every rooftop balcony in Stone Town, but the cathedral isn't all that easy to locate on foot. The best way is to start on Kenyatta Road and head down Gizenga Street, where a right turn down Cathedral Street brings you to it. Although the site lacks the historical significance of the Anglican Cathedral, the Catholic Church was equally involved in the struggle against the slave trade, its main memorial being the Freedom Village for slaves in Bagamoyo (see p.145). The cathedral's foundation stone was laid in July 1896, and the first Mass was celebrated on Christmas Day, 1898, two years before completion. The design is loosely based on the Romano–Byzantine cathedral of Notre Dame de la Garde in Marseilles, while the interior is painted with badly deteriorated frescoes depicting scenes from the Old Testament. Masses are held regularly and are the best time to visit. The main entrance is usually closed at other times, though you may be able to get in through the small passageway leading through the convent at the back of Shangani post office.

Hurumzi House

Running a short distance west to east from behind the House of Wonders is **Hurumzi Street**, one of Stone Town's best places for rummaging around souvenir and antique shops. About halfway along on the right, an unassuming sign marks the entrance to **Hurumzi House**, now functioning as Stone Town's best hotel, *Emerson & Green* (see p.623). The house was constructed by the wealthy Ismaili businessman Tharia Topan (also responsible for the Old Dispensary, see p.625) to serve as both the customs house and his private residence. Topan's good relations with Sultan Barghash allowed him to make it the second highest building in Stone Town, after the House of Wonders. Its name comes from its use by the British in the 1880s and 1890s to buy the freedom of slaves; *hurumzi* means "free men" (literally "those shown mercy"). The conversion into the present hotel has been gloriously done, and it's well worth looking around even if you've no intention of staying here; the rooftop restaurant is also the best place to see the colourful tower of the Shiva Shakti Hindu Temple across the road.

A few metres west of Hurumzi House hang spiders' webs belonging to some of the biggest arachnids you're ever likely to see. That no one has brushed them away is explained by an Islamic tradition which recounts that the Prophet Muhammad once took refuge from his enemies in a cave and was saved by a spider that swiftly spun its web across the cave entrance; the Prophet's enemies saw the unbroken web and went on their way.

Mnara Mosque

Most of Stone Town's 51 **mosques** are surprisingly restrained and unobtrusive affairs, certainly compared to the ostentation of the waterfront palaces, but then few if any of the sultans were much given to religious contemplation. Indeed, you won't even notice the majority of the mosques unless you walk past their entrances and glimpse their simple prayer halls (strictly no photography). There are few embellishments, and only four have minarets, one of which is the Sunni community's curious **Mnara Mosque** (or Malindi Mosque), near the northern tip of Stone Town, its strange minaret (*mnara*) one of only three conical minarets in East Africa (the other two are on the Kenyan coast) and decorated with a double chevron pattern which is best seen from Malawi Road. The mosque is probably Stone Town's oldest, the minaret most likely pre-dating the first mention of the mosque in 1831, when it was rebuilt by Mohammad Abdul

Qadir al-Mansabi, whose remains are buried in front of the *mihrab* prayer niche. Non-Muslims aren't allowed inside.

Creek Road and eastwards

The whole area running up the east side of Stone Town along the fume-filled dual carriageway of **Creek Road** was, until the twentieth century, a saltwater creek. Its name, Darajani, came from the first bridge (*darajani*) to be erected across the creek in 1838 during the reign of Sultan Seyyid Said. The creek separated Stone Town from the mud-and-thatch district of Ng'ambo to the east, which remains much more African in feel than the oriental alleyways and grand buildings of Stone Town. Officially Creek Road is now Benjamin Mkapa Road, after the Tanzanian president, but his unpopularity in Zanzibar means it's still universally known by its old name.

The British reclaimed the southernmost portion of the creek in 1915 to make way for the English Club's playing fields, and this broad and grassy area is now municipal land, known as **Mnazi Mmoja** ("one coconut tree"), despite there being dozens of them. The derelict cricket pavilion still stands here, just, in the southeast corner. At the end of Ramadan, the park serves as the main focus for the Idd al-Fitr celebrations, attracting thousands of people over the four-day holiday. At other times it's used for football matches. It wasn't until 1957 that the rest of the creek – by then a filthy and foul-smelling swamp – was drained, leaving only a small reed-filled marsh between Gulioni Road and the *Bwawani Hotel*.

At the southern end of Creek Road stands the **Peace Memorial Museum** (Mon–Fri 8.30am–6pm, Sat & Sun 8.30am–3pm; Tsh2000), a squat but elegant octagonal building topped by a Byzantine-style dome. Known locally as Beit al-Amani – the House of Peace – the museum is the last of J. H. Sinclair's creations, and opened in 1925 on the anniversary of the 1918 armistice – hence its name. It's the most Islamic of his works, dubbed "Sinclair's mosque" by detractors, and the "House of Ghosts" by locals for whom the concept of a museum was a strange novelty. Formerly the National Museum, it's due at some point to house the collection of the defunct Natural History Museum nearby.

Central Market

Zanzibar's lively and colourful **Central Market**, also called Darajani Market, lies just outside Stone Town, about half-way up Creek Road. Liveliest in the morning from 9am onwards, the market and streets around it have pretty much everything you might need, from meat and fish, cacophonous bundles of trussed-up chickens and seasonal fruit and vegetables (and some exotics, like apples) to herbs and spices, radios, TVs and mobile telephones, bicycles, shoes and sandals, swaths of brightly patterned cloth and Teletubbies. The main building, a long tin-roofed affair flanking Creek Road, opened in 1904 as the **Seyyidieh Market** and is probably the second of J. H. Sinclair's constructions after the Bharmal Building. Actually little more than a glorified shed, it houses the meat and fish sections, the smell of which announces the market's presence from a fair distance.

More enjoyable for sensitive souls is the **fruit and vegetable area** in the enclosure behind the main building. Though the mythical scent of cloves and spices is absent (most are nowadays sold in sealed plastic bags), the fruit and vegetables are presented with care, arranged according to shape, with anything round – oranges, mangoes, passion fruit – usually in a unit of five called a *fumba* (meaning heap), while less spherical fruits come ready-wrapped in palm-frond baskets.

The Bharmal Building, Blue Mosque and Livingstone House

Constructed around 1900, the **Bharmal Building**, towards the top of Creek Road on the left is the earliest and most European of Sinclair's buildings (the comparison with his last work, the Peace Memorial Museum, which bears nary a wisp of his classical training, is startling). Stylistically somewhere between an Arab palace and English manor house, the Bharmal Building is not Sinclair's best creation, though the profusion of plaster mouldings hints at the Orientalist direction his work was to take, and one should bear in mind that when built it would have been facing the creek rather than a fume-filled highway. Previously the office of the British provincial commissioner, the building currently houses the offices of Zanzibar Municipal Council.

Reaching the north of Creek Road, a left turn takes you down Malawi Road to the roundabout by the port entrance, while a right skirts the reed-filled saltwater swamp between Gulioni Road and the *Bwawani Hotel* – the only remnant of Darajani Creek. Some 700m along Gulioni Road is a modern mosque built out over a small artificial lake, which goes by the name of the **Blue Mosque**. A left here, which leads to the service entrance of the *Bwawani Hotel*, takes you past tidal flats which are still used for **dhow building**. The occasional spice tour stops by here, but the area is largely ignored, and the workers should be happy to show you round if they're not too busy.

Back on Gulioni Road, the old two-storied house on the opposite side of the road, now almost surrounded by new apartment blocks, is **Livingstone House** (ostensibly Mon–Fri 8am–4pm, but don't bank on it). Built in 1860 by Sultan Majid, the building saw use as a rest house for various European explorers and missionaries, most famously Dr Livingstone, who spent time here in 1865–66. There's a small, one-room museum here, apparently containing papers and other articles that belonged to the good doctor, but you'd be a lucky soul indeed to gain admission even during the hours it claims to be open: the intransigent staff are resolutely unhelpful, amazingly so given that Livingstone House also functions as the headquarters of the Zanzibar Tourist Corporation.

Ng'ambo

Returning to Creek Road, then heading east along Karume Road brings you to the poorer but vastly more populous half of Zanzibar Town known as **Ng'ambo**. The name is a throwback to the days when Stone Town was still a peninsula, bounded to the east by Darajani Creek. As Stone Town filled up, its poorer inhabitants, most of them African, were forced to decamp to the main island opposite, which the Arab elite patronizingly referred to as *ng'ambo*, "the other side". The centrepiece of Ng'ambo is **Michenzani**, 600m along Karume Road. Its pretty name (the "mandarin-orange trees") spectacularly fails to disguise Tanzania's most ghastly and dismal experiment in socialist urban housing. Flanking each of the four roads radiating from a vast roundabout are the kind of grey, numbered and deeply neglected multi-storey blocks of flats one would expect to see in Stalinist Russia. No surprise, then, to learn that their design and construction were supervised by East German engineers in the late 1960s and early 1970s, during Tanzania's economically disastrous experiment with African socialism, *Ujamaa*. Nonetheless, the monstrous housing blocks – and the ramshackle slums around them – do provide an abrupt return to reality for those who have become jaded with the tourist trap some consider Zanzibar to have become.

Eating

Stone Town offers an embarrassment of choice when it comes to **eating out**, ranging from the glorious nightly food market in the Forodhani Gardens to dozens of sophisticated restaurants and even a restaurant on a converted dhow. Following the success of the *Tower Top* restaurant at *Emerson & Green*, many hotels have also installed **rooftop restaurants**, most with good views over the old town and the harbour. Equally romantic are a number of sophisticated waterfront establishments, though you'll invariably be paying a premium for the view. Menus generally feature traditional **Zanzibari cuisine**, combining subtle use of the island's spices and coconuts with seafood including prawns, crab, octopus and lobster, while more conservative tastes are catered for with pasta, pizzas and Indian and Chinese dishes.

Apart from the Forodhani Gardens, the market on **Creek Road** is a good place for street food, especially in the morning when a number of *mama lishas* (literally "feeding ladies") dish up cups of scalding *uji* porridge, and *supu*, a savoury stock containing pieces of meat, chicken, vegetables or fish. In the evenings, it's worth seeking out one of the **coffee barazas** inside the old town, where the coffee is roasted and brewed on the stone benches that line the streets; a cup of piping *Arabica* costs a negligible Tsh20–30. One of the liveliest *barazas* is in Sokomuhogo Square – popularly known as Jaws Corner, possibly after the film once shown on its TV – whose walls are adorned with the initials of the opposition CUF party. Some *barazas* also serve spiced tea called *zamzam*, named after a sacred well in Mecca.

Unfortunately, eating out during **Ramadan** can be quite expensive as the government bans restaurants not attached to hotels from opening during the day. There are some exceptions, however; the restaurants reviewed below are open during Ramadan unless otherwise stated.

Forodhani Gardens

For all its refined restaurants, the best place for eating out in Stone Town, indeed in the whole of Zanzibar, is the open-air street food market held in the waterfront **Forodhani Gardens** after sunset, which combines a magical twilight atmosphere with a variety and quality of food to put many a five-star hotel to shame. It's also one of the cheapest places to eat; for a couple of thousand shillings you can get well and truly stuffed.

Food is prepared by fifty or sixty *mama* and *baba lishas*, working on charcoal stoves (*jikos*) set up on trestle tables. The choice is regal, ranging from seafood caught that morning and sauced with local spices, to goat meat served with a superb homemade chilli sauce (*pilipili hoho*). The market is also a great place to try "Zanzibari pizzas" (*mantabali*), actually chapatis stuffed with egg, cheese or whatever takes the cook's fancy, and resembling fat spring rolls. Other **snacks** worth sampling include spiced *naan* bread and *andazi* doughnuts, grilled cassava (*muhogo*), fried potato and meat or vegetable balls (*katlesi* or *kachori*), samosas (*sambusa*) filled with meat or vegetables and salads. You can even get grilled bananas topped with melted chocolate. **Drinks** are abundant too, with sodas, freshly pressed seasonal juices, gently spiced *zamzam* tea, Turkish coffee, coconut milk (*dafu*) and tamarind juice (*mkwaju*) all available.

Restaurants

Stone Town has plenty of **inexpensive** restaurants aimed as much at locals as tourists. Unless you're splurging on lobster or prawns, a full meal with soft drinks shouldn't cost more than Tsh5000, and individual dishes average Tsh2500–3500. **Moderate** places are generally aimed at tourists, with main courses averaging Tsh4000–6000 and full meals going for Tsh5000–8000. Many sell alcohol. Stone Town's **expensive** restaurants match or surpass US and European prices, with mains costing upwards of Tsh6000, and full meals lightening your pocket by anything between Tsh10,000 and Tsh40,000. All these places sell alcohol.

Inexpensive

Café Kelele Shangani St, just south of Kelele Square, Shangani. One of few cheap local places outside the labyrinth, and easy to find, with simple and filling meals for around Tsh1000. Closed Ramadan.

Chit Chat Restaurant South of Cathedral St, Baghani. A friendly, family-run place specializing in Goan and Zanzibari dishes. The place is popular with locals as with tourists, and no wonder: the food is invariably of high quality (the garlic prawns are especially good) and prices are reasonable. Tues–Sun evenings only; closed Ramadan.

The Dolphin Half-way along Kenyatta Rd, Shangani. An attractive place adorned with turtle shells, a boriti mangrove pole ceiling and a noisy African grey parrot. The daily specials are tasty and good value at Tsh3200 for a starter and main course, though portions aren't overly generous. Finish your meal with a Turkish-style *shisha* water pipe (Tsh1000). No alcohol; open evenings only during Ramadan.

E.T.C. Plaza Corner of Suicide Alley and Shangani St, Shangani. Highly recommended bar and restaurant on three floors, with views over the ocean and good music on the breezy rooftop. The food is good too; try the excellent seafood.

Fany's Green Restaurant Kenyatta Rd, next to *The Dolphin*, Shangani. Pleasant, intimate bistro-style place with attentive service and very good food. Fresh salads, seasonal juices, seafood and pizzas; they also do a full English breakfast for Tsh3000. No alcohol; closed last two weeks of Ramadan.

Hotel International South of Kiponda St, Mchambawima. Incorporating *Zee Pizza*, this is a reliable choice (and one of the few places open at lunchtimes during Ramadan), with seats in the courtyard at the front of the hotel. Mains include pasta, chicken, fish and cheap pizzas.

Luis' Yoghurt Parlour Gizenga St, Baghani. A friendly little place with a local feel, although it caters mostly to tourists nowadays. Several menus of the day feature Zanzibari dishes (around Tsh4000), and a nice range of snacks including yoghurts (*lassi*), milk shakes, fresh juices and spiced tea. Mon–Sat lunchtimes only; closed Ramadan.

Mrembo Restaurant South end of Forodhani Gardens. This first-floor dining room has a massive choice of refreshingly different Zanzibari dishes (around Tsh2500) and continental dishes (Tsh4000). The *ugali wa muhogo* – a thick maize and cassava flour porridge – is more delicious than it sounds, and the whole lobster thermidor is a bargain at Tsh8000. No alcohol; closed Ramadan.

Neem Tree Restaurant Omani Fort, Mizingani Rd. Relaxed place for a meal, with mainly Zanzibari cooking. There's a good choice of vegetarian meals too, as well as snacks, yoghurt, coffee and alcohol from the attached *Bububu Bar* (closed Ramadan), which boasts a decent wine list. Closed Ramadan daytime.

Passing Show Hotel Malindi Malawi Rd, opposite *Mzuri Guest House*, Malindi. Good local food, filling stews, fried chicken and chips, fish in coconut sauce, and everything for under Tsh3000. Lunchtimes only; closed Ramadan.

Radha Food House One street east of Kenyatta Rd, next to the *Karibu Inn*, Forodhani. An exclusively vegetarian Indian restaurant famed for its *thali* (Tsh3500), and also offering tasty samosas, spring rolls, lentil or chickpea cakes and perfumed sweets for dessert. There's a small but well-stocked bar too. Recommended.

Zi Bar & Restaurant Vuga House, Victoria St, Vuga. Smart and surprisingly cheap place in a converted colonial-era house. Good range of tasty Swahili and Mediterranean food (including pizza, salads and pasta), and the well-stocked bar is good for a drink at any time of day. "African Night" is on Thursday, and there's a Saturday disco. Recommended. Closed Ramadan daytime.

Moderate

Amore Mio Shangani St near *Africa House*, Shangani. Right by the ocean, the owner immodestly but accurately describes his *gelato* as the best on the island (it can also be sampled at *Blues* and *Mercury's*). Ice creams cost Tsh2000–3500 and there's also good coffee and milk shakes, but proper meals are limited in choice, and pizzas are restricted to margheritas.

Chavda Hotel Baghani St, Baghani. The breezy rooftop here is occupied by a café, and the tempting menu covers a wide range from Zanzibari and seafood to Indian, Chinese and continental. Mains cost around Tsh4500–5500. Closed Ramadan during the day.

Kidude Next to *Emerson & Green*, Hurumzi St, Hurumzi. Named after Zanzibar's much-loved octogenarian *taarab* singer and suitably kitted out in traditional decor, this place is open for snacks, lunchtime light meals and a la carte in the evening. The Friday buffet (from 8pm) is a bargain at $8.

Hotel Kiponda & Restaurant Nyumba ya Moto St, behind the Palace Museum, Kiponda. Perched at the top of the hotel, with fine views and Swahili cuisine, the daily specials include chicken in tamarind and ginger, and are invariably enticing. Evening a la carte is also good. No alcohol; closed Sun and Ramadan during the day.

La Fenice Shangani St, one block north of *Africa House*, Shangani. Upmarket Italian restaurant with ocean and various pasta dishes, but small portions. They also do real coffee and milk shakes, and have a good wine list.

Mercury's North end of Mizingani Rd near the Big Tree. A stylish and informal venue right next to the ocean and named after the rock star, with a wide choice of both Zanzibari dishes and usual favourites, and a recommended seafood grill served with roast potatoes, salad and finishing with vanilla or chocolate cake for Tsh10,000. Live music some nights too. Closed daytime during Ramadan.

Monsoon Restaurant Forodhani Gardens ☎0747/411362. One of Zanzibar's most atmospheric restaurants: meals are served in a pillared dining room, with cushions on woven rugs replacing seats. The menu is short, concentrating on seafood, and prices are cheap for the setting. Reservations are advisable, especially Wed and Sat evenings when the atmosphere is completed with live *taarab* music.

Nyumbani Restaurant Off Sokomuhogo St, facing *Haven Guest House*, Vuga ☎0741/610910. A private home belonging to an artist and his wife that doubles as a restaurant in the evenings. The Tsh5000 set menu, all traditional Swahili, is guaranteed to fill you up and tickle your taste buds. Book ahead; deposit required. Recommended. Mon–Sat evenings only.

Pagoda Chinese Restaurant Suicide Alley, facing *Africa House*, Shangani. Family-run Chinese place with average food and moderate prices. They also do vegetarian dishes and more expensive seafood. No pork. Licensed.

Sambusa Two Tables Victoria St, just off Kaunda Rd, Vuga ☎024/223 1979. Highly recommended family-run place situated on the second-floor verandah of a private house. The traditional Zanzibari food just keeps on coming, and costs around Tsh6000. Phone or pass by beforehand to let them know you're coming. No alcohol; open evenings only; closed Ramadan.

Seaview Indian Restaurant North end of Mizingani Rd. It's the glorious view from the first-floor balcony – arrive early to get a table there – that makes this long-established place special, not the very slow service. There's a wide choice for breakfast, and snacks and *paan* throughout the day; main dishes, mostly Gujarati, go for around Tsh6000 excluding rice. Licensed.

Expensive

Baharia Restaurant *Zanzibar Serena Inn*, Kelele Square, Shangani ☎024/223 1015 or 0741/333170. Upmarket dining in elegant surroundings with fine, pricey food and service designed to pamper. The menu is features a cosmopolitan spread of dishes, and the Saturday Swahili buffet is recommended, as is the Tsh7000 Sunday brunch (10am–3pm). Book ahead or arrive early for tables with ocean views.

Blues Forodhani Gardens ☎0741/328509. Built on a wooden pier on the site of the former sultan's landing, this upmarket establishment has great ocean views and expensive food. Seafood is the speciality, with a "seafood fiesta" (for two) going for a cool Tsh39,000; there's also a good range of beers and fine wines. Credit cards accepted.

Chez Marina Stone Town Cultural Centre (Old Dispensary), Mizingani Rd; ☎0747/410244. Posh French seafood establishment with an indoor dining room and a lovely sunset terrace. The lunchtime set menu costs Tsh15,000, a la carte substantially more, and you could break the bank with their seafood platter (Tsh34,000). Closed Ramadan.

Dhow Restaurant Moored opposite the House of Wonders ☎0742/740336. An unusual and highly romantic place for dinner, where $25 gets you a sumptuous seafood buffet of Zanzibari specialities including grilled lobster and prawns, live Swahili jazz and a welcome drink on the upper deck. Reservations are essential: ring up, or book at the desk outside Coastal Travels in Kelele Square (noon–1pm) or outside *Blues* in Forodhani Gardens. Evenings only.

Fisherman Restaurant Shangani St, opposite *Tembo House Hotel*, Shangani. Run by a Frenchman, this long-established place majors in seafood prepared in a variety of styles, including Alsatian. It's a little pricey, but the food is always fresh and the welcome is warm and unpretentious. Apart from seafood, the a la carte menu also features pasta, meat and poultry.

Le Spices Rendez-Vous (New Maharaja Restaurant) Kenyatta Rd, Vuga ☎024/223 4241 or 0747/413062. Set in an attractive terracotta-tiled interior, this place is famed for its superb north Indian food as well as a good range of French a la carte. Pricey but big portions, and there's live entertainment Tuesday evenings. Closed Mon.

Sweet Eazy Restaurant & Lounge Kenyatta Rd, opposite the Old British Consulate, Forodhani. A moderately priced, highly recommended restaurant and bar, offering an immense choice of outstandingly good and totally authentic Thai and Japanese food, including cook-your-own *teppanyaki* (Tsh6000). Burgers and sandwiches are also available.

Tower Top Restaurant Emerson & Green, Hurumzi St, Hurumzi ☎024/223 0171. Atmospheric, pricey restaurant on the roof of the second highest building in Stone Town. The six-course menu, with something for everyone (including vegetarians) costs $25 Monday–Thursday and $30 Friday–Sunday, when live music completes the mood. Diners can stay all evening, with the expensive cocktails and liqueurs adding to the bill. Reservations necessary. Evenings only.

Drinking and nightlife

The increase in tourism to Zanzibar has brought with it a small but growing number of **bars and nightclubs**. Apart from *Africa House*, the longest established are a number of very local dives on the outskirts of Stone Town that cater primarily for mainland Tanzanians: recommended among these (take a taxi to find them) are *Kwa Kimti*, and *Sai Bar*. Places geared more towards tourists are reviewed below. Beers cost Tsh1200 and up at touristic places; local bars charge Tsh700–800.

Africa House Hotel Entrance at the junction of Suicide Alley and Kenyatta Rd, Shangani. For decades this has been the favoured haunt of expats, tourists and mainland Tanzanians alike, drawn to its terrace bar to watch the sun set over the ocean. Be careful in the surrounding area after dark though.

Blues Forodhani Gardens. Another place with great sunsets, but very touristy and completely devoid of locals – ideal if you're fed up being hassled by *papasi*.

Bottoms Up Between Changa Bazaar and Hurumzi St, Hurumzi. A famously eccentric local dive in the thick of the old town, with stone walls hideously painted in red with white outlines to resemble a brain.

Bububu Bar Omani Fort, Mizingani Rd. A peaceful place to while away an afternoon in the hassle-free confines of the old fort. Closed Ramadan.

Chavda Hotel Baghani St, Baghani. One of many breezy hotel rooftop bars, with traditional marble-topped tables, antique chairs and good views of the city and sunsets.

E.T.C. Plaza Corner of Suicide Alley and Shangani St, Shangani. One of the most appealing bars in the city (and with superb food; see p.638), with

three levels, the best on top with nice ocean views. The staff are friendly, there's good music (and impromptu jam sessions), and milk shakes and juices are also available along with the cocktails.

Garage Club Shangani St, Shangani. Stone Town's leading disco, with plenty of spinning globes, strobe lights and a lively mixture of music ranging from modern *taarab* to rave. Thurs–Sun from 9pm only.

Komba Discotheque Bwawani Hotel, Funguni. Times and days vary so check ahead on ☎024/223 1184; closed Ramadan. Stone Town's oldest disco and popular with locals, with a large swimming pool beside it. Cool Para, the pioneer of "Taa-Rap" (*taarab* and rap), is the resident DJ.

New Happy Club Suicide Alley. A very local dive that attracts a startling array of low-life. Good as an antidote to the excesses of tourism but otherwise probably best avoided (as should Suicide Alley at night unless you're in a large group).

Starehe Club Shangani St, Shangani. Formerly the European Yacht Club, this is now an unpretentious bar, with a terrace overlooking the beach and harbour, cheap beers, bar food and live bands on Sat nights. Closed Ramadan.

Sunrise Restaurant & Bar Kenyatta Rd, Shangani. Another cheap place with coolish beers and sodas and some tables in a courtyard at the back. Also does a well-priced mixture of local and international food.

Live music

The **live music scene**, although vibrant, can be difficult to find as a lot of bands only play for weddings and other social functions, with few venues for more public performances. Still, with a little patience and probably a lot of asking around, you should be able to track down a few events. The following information is intended as a guide only, as venues and acts change frequently. Apart from groups mentioned below, it's also worth seeking out performances by *Nadi Ikhwaan Safaa* (also called *Akhwan Safaa* and *Malindi Taarab*), one of Africa's oldest orchestras, and *Culture Music Club*, Zanzibar's best-loved *taarab* orchestra. For more about *taarab*, see p.754.

East African Melody Vuga Rd, next to the *Florida Guest House*. The headquarters of one of Zanzibar's most popular *taarab* outfits, who practise here and occasionally also put on concerts.
Haile Selassie School Creek Rd, opposite Jamhuri Gardens. Unlikely as it sounds, this school is a good place to see performances of *taarab*.
Khalifa Hall Ben Bella School, corner of Creek Rd and Vuga Rd. A good place to track down *taarab*.
Mercury's Mizingani Rd. This popular bar and restaurant puts on live music most nights of the week.
Omani Fort Mizingani Rd. The open-air amphitheatre here hosts "A Night at the Fort" (7–10pm) a few times a week according to the season. The entry fee depends on the event and whether you get resident rates, but shouldn't be more than $5, or $10 including a barbecue buffet at the *Neem Tree Restaurant*. A sign outside the fort announces the next performance.
Police Mess Off the road going to the airport. The *Police Band*, performing a lively brand of the jazz or dance music so popular in Dar es Salaam, perform here Friday and Saturday nights. Take a taxi.
Starehe Club Shangani St, Shangani. A local bar with a live band Sat from 0pm, usually reggae (Tsh1000 entry).
Sweet Eazy Restaurant & Lounge Kenyatta Rd, Forodhani. *Islanders Band* play here every Fri night from 10pm (free entry).

Film

Films can be seen at the art nouveau Cine Afrique on Malawi Road (daily 7.15pm & 9.15pm; Ramadan 3pm & 9pm daily), which mixes gung-ho American action trash with more wholesome Bollywood movies, and at the Majestic Cinema on Vuga Road (variable times). Equally recommended is an evening glued to a **television screen** in one of the old town's outdoor coffee *barazas*, which invariably feature pirated movies, more often than not bizarrely dubbed or subtitled into Chinese. The best *baraza* for this is Jaws Corner (Sokomuhogo Square) at the corner of Sokomuhogo, Cathedral and Baghani streets. TVs are usually set up about half-way along Baghani Street and along New Mkunazini Road just west of Mkunazini Street too; "TV Corner", at the bottom of Mkunazini Street near Vuga Road, is another likely spot.

Crafts and souvenirs

Stone Town is a veritable Aladdin's Cave for souvenirs, with hundreds of shops containing a huge variety of handicrafts, Arabian and Indian antiques and local products. Prices can be reasonable if you're into bargaining, and competition

The **Zanzibar International Film Festival** (ZIFF), also known as the Festival of the Dhow Countries, is already a firm fixture on the African cultural calendar, and provides as good a reason as any to try to get to Zanzibar in the first half of July. No longer restricted to cinema, the festival has been growing, and recent years have brought together over fifty groups of musicians from all over Africa, Arabia, the Near East and Indian Ocean, 25 films and several art exhibitions, together with film and video workshops, special activities for women and young people, award ceremonies and an innovative mobile wide-screen cinema that brought the magic of cinema to dozens of outlying villages on Unguja and Pemba. No mean feat considering the traditional foot-dragging, pocket-lining nature of Zanzibari bureaucracy. The main **venues** are the Forodhani Gardens, Omani Fort and Cine Afrique for film and dance, the House of Wonders for exhibitions and children's activities, and the Old Dispensary. The cost for non-Tanzanians is Tsh3000 per day or Tsh20,000 for access to all events. Check out the website for exact dates: ZIFF, PO Box 3032, Zanzibar ☏0741/411499, ⊛www.ziff.or.tz.

makes it easy to play one shop's prices off against another's. Local items to look out for include all manner of **jewellery**, modern and antique **silverwork**, and hefty brass-studded Zanzibari **chests**. More portable are phials of essential oil, henna, incense, soaps and even bubble bath. Also typically Zanzibari are woven **palm-leaf items** like mats (*mkeka*) and baskets (*mkoba*), the latter often containing a selection of spices. **Clothing** – and **fabrics** – are another speciality: these include colourful cotton *kangas* (see p.113) and more simple woven *kikois*, together with intricately embroidered *kofia* caps. It's illegal, both in Tanzania and internationally, to buy or export items made of **ivory**, **coral**, **turtle shell**, unlicensed **animal skins** and **furs**. Trade in several species of **seashell** is also illegal, and in any case their collection has dire consequences for the marine environment. Please don't buy any of these products.

The biggest concentration of souvenir and craft shops is along **Gizenga Street** (especially behind the Omani Fort and House of Wonders) and its continuation **Changa Bazaar**. **Hurumzi Street**, which runs parallel to Changa Bazaar, is also good and has several henna "tattoo" parlours and chest-makers. **Kiponda Street**, east of Changa Bazaar, has more antique shops and places specializing in silverwork, while **Tharia Street** and its continuation **Mkunazini Street** is where most of the gold jewellers are. Shops generally open Monday to Saturday 9am to noon and 2pm to 6pm, and Sun 9am to 1pm. The following is a tiny selection of the more unusual places.

Abeid Curio Shop Cathedral St, opposite the Catholic Cathedral. One of several antique shops between the Cathedral and Sokomuhogo St (Jaws Corner), good for antiques like Zanzibari chests, silverwork, clocks and British colonial kitsch.

Capital Art Studio Kenyatta Rd. Established in 1930, this sells a huge selection of archive black-and-white photos (both on display and in boxes you can rifle through), covering pretty much every aspect of Zanzibari life and history.

Duka la Uwazi Mizingani Rd. An open-air handicrafts market with a wide selection of products from local artists and women's groups, ranging from herbs, spices, teas and flavoured coffee to basketry, tapestries and money belts. There are some great (and good-value) original Tingatinga paintings by resident artists, and henna painting is also offered.

Forodhani Gardens Best in the evening when the food market is held and there are a dozen or so stalls selling mainly Makonde woodcarvings, together with cheap wooden and beaded jewellery in the style of the Maasai, who are among the stall-holders.

Kanga Bazaar Mchangani St, behind Central Market, off Creek Rd. The whole street here is stuffed with shops and stalls selling *kangas*, *kitenges* and *kikois*, in a glorious feast for the eyes.

Kibiriti Gallery Boutique Gizenga St. Hand-painted batiks – the stock is limited and expensive, but lovely.

Lookmanji Arts & Antiques Next to *Mrembo Restaurant* facing Forodhani Gardens. A large selection covering most bases, especially good for woodcarvings and batiks.

Memories of Zanzibar Kenyatta Rd, opposite Shangani Post Office. A huge souvenir shop with masses of choice and a good selection of books too.

Omani Fort Mizingani Rd. A very calm place to browse for an hour or two, with a handful of souvenir shops, a workshop making reproduction Zanzibari chests, a gold jeweller, and the exceptional Zanzibar Art Studio (closed Ramadan) in the northwest tower selling quality paintings and batiks.

Zanzibar Curio Shop Changa Bazaar. A glorified junk shop, packed to the rafters with fascinating stuff from old marine compasses and Omani astrolabes to gramophones and novelty tin models from British times. One of the best places to get an idea of the opulence and decadence enjoyed by Zanzibar's wealthy before the 1964 Revolution.

Zanzibar Gallery Kenyatta Rd. Zanzibar's best curio shop, selling everything from clothes to pickles. It's also the best bookshop on the isles, with a huge selection of Africana as well as novels and some gorgeous works on Zanzibar published by the gallery's owner and renowned photographer, Javed Jafferji.

Listings

Air charters The average price for a five-seater plane to Dar es Salaam is $290; to Mafia Island $720. Reliable companies include ZanAir, Malawi Rd ☎024/223 3670, airport ☎024/223 2993; and Zanzibar Aviation Services & Transport, airport ☎024/223 1336, ✉zat@raha.com.

Airlines (domestic) Air Tanzania Corporation (ATC), Majestic Cinema Building, Vuga Rd ☎024/223 0297 or 223 0213; Coastal Travels, Kelele Square, and at the airport ☎024/223 3112 or 0741/334582, ⊛www.coastal.cc; Precisionair, Mazsons Hotel ☎024/223 4521; ZanAir, Malawi Rd ☎024/223 3670, airport ☎024/223 2993.

Airlines (international) Air Tanzania Corporation, Majestic Cinema Building, Vuga Rd ☎024/223 0297 or 223 0213; Ethiopian Airlines, Maha Tours, Vuga Rd ☎024/223 0029; Gulf Air, off Mizingani Rd, opposite *Mercury's* ☎024/223 2824; Kenya Airways, Zanzibar Aviation & Travel (p.644). See also "Travel agents", most of whom deal with airlines.

Bicycle rental The main places for renting bikes are the shops and stands outside Central Market along Creek Rd; ask for Maharouky Bicycle Hire. Several tour companies and hotels can also fix you up, but watch out with the price: the standard rate is Tsh2000, though as a tourist you might have difficulty getting it much below Tsh4000 or $5. Start at Island Discovery Tours behind *Africa House*, or at the *Jambo Guest House*. You may be asked for a deposit, anything up to $50; get a receipt.

Books Zanzibar's best bookshop is Zanzibar Gallery (see above), and there's also a good if slightly more expensive choice at Memories of Zanzibar on the same road. Much more modest is Masomo Bookshop, behind Central Market which also has newspapers and some imported magazines.

Car rental A 4WD Suzuki Vitara is around $80 per day (unlimited mileage), and a 4WD Suzuki Samurai is $70. A normal saloon isn't generally more than $40 a day, and it's not much more expensive to rent a vehicle with driver. Reliable companies include Easy Travel and Tours, at *Hotel Marine* ☎024/223 5372 or 0744/260124; Island Discovery Tours, Shangani St, under *Africa House's* terrace-bar ☎024/223 3073; *Jambo Guest House* ☎024/223 3779; Ocean Tours, Kelele Square ☎024/223 8280; Tima Tours & Safaris, Mizangani Rd ☎024/223 1298 or 0741/238220; ZanTours, on the west side of the open ground south of Malawi Rd ☎024/223 3042; and Zenith Tours, behind the Omani Fort ☎024/223 2320.

Hospitals and medical centres The main hospital is the poorly equipped government-run Mnazi Mmoja Hospital, Kaunda Rd ☎024/223 1071. Much better are the Afya Medical Centre, between Kenyatta Rd and Baghani St ☎024/223 1228 (Tsh2000 fee); Dr Mariani at the Zanzibar Medical & Diagnostic Centre, Tiger House, behind the Majestic Cinema ☎0741/750040 ($30 consultation fee); and Zanzibar Medical Group, Kenyatta Rd near Vuga Rd ☎024/223 3134.

Internet There are lots of internet cafés around Stone Town, charging a standard Tsh1000 an hour. The exception is Macrosoft, Hurumzi St (Tsh500 an hour). Others include Azzurri, New Mkunazini Rd; Green Garden, just south of *Jambo Guest House*; Heeba Business Centre, Omani Fort; Rima

Enterprises, next to *Chick Wing*, just off Shangani St (which stays open later than the others); Seafront Internet Services, Mizingani Rd under the *Seaview Indian Restaurant*; Shangani Internet Café, Kenyatta Rd; Two Shot Internet, next to *Mrembo Restaurant* at the south end of Forodhani Gardens; www.zenjcom.com, Kenyatta Rd; and ZITeC, Tiger House, behind Majestic Cinema.

Language courses The Institute of Kiswahili and Foreign Languages, Vuga Rd, Vuga ☎024/223 0724 or 223 3337 is the main place for tuition, charging around $4 per hour. The usual course is a one-week course (20hr); cheaper deals available for longer courses, and there's the possibility of accommodation included into the bargain.

Library The library occupies the former *Zanzibar Gazette* office, Kaunda Rd next to the High Court (Mon–Fri 9am–6pm, Sat 9am–2pm).

Money The best rates, with minimal commission, are at the NBC bank at the top of Kenyatta Rd beside the tunnel. The other main bank is the People's Bank of Zanzibar, whose foreign exchange branch is opposite the main building on the south side of the Omani Fort (same hours). Rates at forex bureaux are not as good but service is much quicker: try Malindi Bureau de Change, Malawi Rd, Ramadhani Bureau de Change next door, or one of the forex bureaux at the north end of Kenyatta Rd near Shangani St. Credit cards (Mastercard, Visa, Delta and JCB) can be used for cash withdrawals at Coastal Travels next to the *Zanzibar Serena Inn* at Kelele Square; the maximum is $500 a week. Other places that do cash advances on Visa cards include Local Currency at the port gate and in the airport arrival lounge. Western Union Money Transfers can be picked up at Tanzania Postal Bank, Malawi Rd. Otherwise, most of the upmarket hotels have change facilities, but usually only for their guests, and with bad rates.

Motorbike rental Motorbikes and scooters (*pikipiki*) are not recommended for safety reasons.

Pharmacies Shamshu & Sons, behind Central Market ☎024/223 2641. Some pharmacies now sell generic drugs: ask around if the price for your medicine seems too expensive.

Photography There are no slide-film processing facilities on Zanzibar. For prints, Capital Art Studio, Kenyatta Rd processes and develops colour and black-and-white film (around Tsh5000 for developing and printing a roll of 36) and also sell film. Another good place is Majestic Quick Foto, Creek Rd opposite the BP filling station, which develops films while you wait.

Police Corner of Malawi Rd and Creek Rd in Malindi ☎024/223 0771.

Post, couriers and freight The main post office is on Karume Rd in Ng'ambo (daladala routes "A" and "M"). More practical for tourists is the Shangani office on Kenyatta Rd, which has a not entirely reliable poste restante service (make sure letters are addressed to "Shangani Post Office, Kenyatta St, Shangani"). Reliable international courier companies include DHL, Kelele Square ☎024/223 8281; EMS, Shangani Post Office, Kenyatta Rd ☎024/223 0889; Fedex, Mkunazini St opposite Cathedral Bookshop ☎024/223 6685; Skynet, inside the Omani Fort ☎0741/248860; and TNT, Kenyatta Rd ☎024/223 3592.

Supermarkets Stone Town's biggest supermarket is Shamshuddin Cash & Carry (daily 9am–6pm) at the former Empire Cinema off Creek Rd behind Central Market. Malkia Mini Supermarket, south end of the tunnel in Forodhani (daily 9am–12.30pm & 4–9pm) stays open during Ramadan. Alcohol is sold in various shops nearby.

Swimming pools *Bwawani Hotel* charges non-guests a very reasonable Tsh1000 to use their huge pool with swim-up bar and sun loungers. *Tembo House Hotel* charges $4. There's also a pool at the *Zanzibar Serena Inn*, but this is usually reserved for their guests.

Telephones Zantel, Kaunda Rd, next to the High Court (Mon–Fri 8am–5pm, Sat 8am–1pm), charges $2.40 a minute during the day and $1.92 in the evenings for international calls. The *Dolphin Restaurant* charges $2 a minute for international calls; Next Step Services on Hurumzi St is more expensive. The manually operated mahogany telephone booths at Shangani post office on Kenyatta Rd require some tedious form-filling (Mon–Sat 8am–8pm, Sun 9am–noon); more practical are the cardphones outside (buy cards inside the office; you need at least 100 units/Tsh4000 for an international call). Telephone calls via the internet can be made at Silu Telecom & Internet Café on Malawi Rd (daily to 8pm) and Shangani Internet Café on Kenyatta Rd; the line quality isn't up to much, but at half the price of normal calls, you can't complain.

Travel agents The following are all reputable and well-established companies: Coastal Travels, Kelele Square ☎022/211 7959; ZanTours, west side of the open ground off Malawi Rd, Malindi ☎024/223 3116 or 223 3042; Zanzibar Aviation & Travel, Vuga Rd ☎024/223 5775 or 223 8355, for airline ticketing only; and Zenith Tours & Travel, behind the Omani Fort ☎024/223 2320.

Around Stone Town

There's a wealth of possible **day-trips** from Stone Town, all of which can be arranged through the tour operators listed on p.646 – an option worth considering, as the mark-up isn't always that much more than the cost of arranging things yourself. A number of standard excursions are offered by pretty much every tour company and hustler in town, of which a half-day **spice tour** is virtually obligatory. This usually includes a visit to **Kidichi Persian Baths** and sometimes also **Mangapwani** or **Mtoni** (these can also be visited under your own steam). Other possibilities include a half-day **dolphin safari** to Kizimkazi, which can also be combined with a soothing walk through **Jozani Forest** (see p.658) with its colony of endangered red colobus monkeys.

Also recommended is a half- or full-day trip to **Prison Island**, during which you can snorkel and feed a colony of giant tortoises, and a visit to **Chumbe Island Coral Park**, which contains some of the world's most stunning snorkelling reefs in addition to virtually untouched coral rag forest and a gem of a lodge. Other islands that could conceivably be combined with a trip to Prison Island are **Chapwani**, which also has a lodge as well as a lovely beach, and **Bawe Island**, with another good beach and excellent snorkelling. Scuba-diving is possible around all the islands with the exception of Chumbe.

Apart from the islands off Stone Town, the best **beaches** are around Bububu and Fuji, roughly 8km north of town, and further north at Mangapwani. The nearest clean beach south of town is at Mbweni.

Organized tours

There are close to one hundred **tour operators** in and around Stone Town, most of them offering a standard choice of excursions at pretty standard prices: $10–15 per person for a half-day spice tour; $20–25 for a half-day dolphin safari ($30–35 for a full day with Jozani included); and $15–20 for Prison Island. Note that at these prices you'll be sharing your transport – usually a daladala or minibus – with up to eight other tourists. For private trips in an air-conditioned Land Rover or Land Cruiser expect to pay around three times as much. Unfortunately, a lot of tour companies are unreliable and quote ludicrously inflated "starting prices"; if this happens, look elsewhere. Similarly, ignore approaches by *papasi* and stick to the companies reviewed below who should be reliable – though, as ever, feedback from fellow travellers is the best source of up-to-date advice.

For a more flexible tour, you can **rent a car** (preferably with a driver; see "Listings", p.643 for a list of companies). Most hotels can fix you up with a reliable guide; make sure that they speak your language and have a valid ID card issued by the Commission for Tourism. A number of Zanzibari tour operators offer wildlife **safaris** on the Tanzanian mainland; these are invariably much cheaper if arranged in Dar es Salaam or Arusha, where you'll also have much more choice.

Tour companies

Apart from dedicated tour operators, most of Stone Town's budget **hotels** can also arrange trips and transfers, though it's worth being careful, since some deal with dodgy companies and are not averse to overcharging. Reliable exceptions include the *Jambo Guest House* and *Riverman Hotel*. **Prices** below are per person. Where two prices are given (e.g. $15/35), the first is for a person in a group of four people, the second in a couple. Discounts are available for larger groups. Most tour company offices are open Monday to Friday 7.30am to 4pm, Saturday 8.30am to 2pm and Sunday 8.30am to 10am. A couple of Stone Town's diving outfits also offer **snorkelling**. Bahari Divers and One Ocean (see p.648) charge $20 per person (minimum two) for a trip to two reefs, including Bawe Island, Prison Island and Panga sandbank.

Eco+Culture Tours Hurumzi St, opposite *Emerson & Green*, Hurumzi ☎024/223 6808, ⓦwww.eco-culture-zanzibar.org. This is a fund-raising arm of Eco+Culture/Zanzibar, an NGO promoting various projects including ecological and cultural tours. Their wide range of tours includes a spice tour with local medicine man "Mr Madawa" ($15/30 including a superb lunch), a city walk ($10/20 excluding the Palace Museum entrance fee), day-trips to Nungwi ($15/40 including lunch), Jambiani village ($18/45 including lunch) and Unguja Ukuu ($20/50). Recommended.

Fisherman Tours & Travels Vuga Rd, Vuga ☎024/223 8791, ⓦwww.fishermantours.com. Long-established outfit specializing in personalized tours: city tour ($25/37), spice tour ($22/38), Prison Island ($26/43), Jozani Forest ($35/50), dolphins ($46/80). They also offer combinations of these with small discounts. For a Land Cruiser add $4 per person; for lunch, add $12.

Island Discovery Tours Shangani St, under *Africa House*'s terrace bar, Shangani ☎024/223 3073, ⓔahmadahassan@hotmail.com. A cheap and cheerful outfit offering all the usual tours including a shared Jozani excursion with up to eight people for $18 (including entrance fee). Standards are average, however, and a lot depends on the knowledge and experience of the driver.

Kigaeni Travels Auction Mart Building, Darajani St, behind the market ☎024/223 7327, ⓔkigaeni@yahoo.com. Friendly and knowledgeable budget operator. A shared spice tour with lunch is $10 per person; Prison Island is a bargain at Tsh3000 per person sharing for the boat (Tsh15,000 for the entire boat), and city tours cost just $5 excluding entrance fees.

Madeira Tours & Safaris Baghani St, Baghani ☎024/223 0406, ⓔmadeira@zenjcom.com. An efficient operation offering the usual options: city tour ($25/35), spice tour ($25/35), half-day Prison Island ($20/30), Jozani ($35/50), dolphins ($50/65

excluding lunch) and a trip combining a spice farm visit, Mangapwani and Nungwi beach ($45/65). Prices include entrance fees.

Mitu's Spice Tours Off Malawi Rd, Malindi ☎024/223 4636. Self-proclaimed inventor of the spice-tour industry, former taxi driver Mr Mitu has now retired but his company continues to offer reliable and entertaining tours at a standard $8–10 per person in a large group.

Ocean Tours Kelele Square, opposite the *Zanzibar Serena Inn*, Shangani ☎024/223 8280, ⓔocean-tours@twiga.com. A reputable upmarket operation. Individual spice tours cost $25 per person excluding lunch; adding Mangapwani to the trip will relieve you of close to $100 per person. A combined Jozani and dolphin tour goes for $94. More reasonable is the Prison Island trip, at $22.

Sama Tours Gizenga St, behind the House of Wonders ☎024/223 3543, ⓦwww.samatours.com. A recommended outfit noted for the unhurried nature of its trips. The standard tours include a city tour ($15/20), spice tour ($20/35), Jozani ($20/25) and a full-day Prison Island ($15/25). Other trips include a full day on the east coast ($15/30), a three-hour dhow cruise ($20/30) and one-day cultural tours of Jambiani or Nungwi ($30/$55). A full-day combining dolphins with Jozani Forest goes for $40/70 including lunch and fees.

Sun 'n' Fun Safaris & Travel Mizingani Rd, 1st floor, next to *Seaview Indian Restaurant* ☎024/223 7381, ⓔzanzibarsun@hotmail.com. Under the same ownership as the restaurant, this offers a huge range of cheap and often recommended trips including a suspiciously economical $18 dolphin and snorkelling tour (check what is and isn't included).

Tima Tours & Safaris Mizangani Rd between the Old Dispensary and Palace Museum ☎024/223 1298, ⓦwww.zanzibar.net/timatours. A small and friendly company happy to tailor itineraries, with some tours better value than others: a seat on a

Spice tours are now Zanzibar's most popular excursion. All tours leave in the morning (the last at 9.30am) and return around 2pm unless the tour includes Mangapwani. The guides know their stuff, even on the cheaper tours, though make sure you have a responsible driver. The trips centre on a **guided walk** around a spice farm (shamba) where you're shown herbs and spices, fruits and other crops, and are given fascinating descriptions of their uses, with plenty of opportunities for smelling and tasting. Other things to look out for include the "lipstick tree", whose pods produce a vibrant red dye, the "iodine tree", whose clear sap is used as an antiseptic, and a "soap bush", whose berries lather like soap. **Lunch** is usually included in the price. Additional options can include a visit to Kidichi Persian Baths (p.655) and Mangapwani (p.655); some trips also include the Maruhubi ruins and Livingstone's House, neither of which are particularly exciting. The tours finish with a stop at one of the roadside kiosks selling packaged spices, essential oils and tourist trinkets.

shared spice tour costs a standard $10, Prison Island goes for $45 for two people, city tours are $25 per person in a couple, but the combined Jozani and dolphins trip is overpriced at $130 for a couple.

ZanTours On the west side of the open ground south of Malawi Rd, Malindi ☎024/223 3116, ⑩www.zantours.com. An expensive if thoroughly reliable company which offers a variety of unusual trips, including full days on Chumbe or Fumbe islands (around $100 per person), live-aboard diving, and flying safaris to Selous Game Reserve on

the mainland. Their standard trips include city tours and spice tours ($21 apiece), Prison Island ($27), and a combined dolphin safari and Jozani Forest excursion for $44–72 depending on group size.

Zenith Tours Behind the Omani Fort, Forodhani ☎024/223 2320, ⑩www.zenithtours.net. One of the most professional and reliable operators, who also act as airline agents. Apart from the usual tours, they also have frequent special offers (see their website) and all-in packages such as a twelve-day affair including Selous and Pemba.

Islands around Stone Town

There are a number of small islands within a few kilometres of Stone Town which provide ideal refuges from the frenetic atmosphere of the town – all can be visited as day trips. **Prison Island**, the main destination offered by tour operators, combines the attractions of snorkelling on a shallow reef with the chance to pet giant tortoises; there's also cheap accommodation available. The largest island, **Bawe Island**, is infrequently visited, but also has good snorkelling. There are also a couple of "private" islands: the incomparable **Chumbe Island** at the heart of Tanzania's first protected marine area – which boasts one of the world's most beautiful snorkelling reefs and a virtually untouched coral rag forest, home to the rare Ader's duiker and coconut crab – and **Chapwani Island**, with a small and intimate lodge, lovely beaches and some dikdik antelopes.

A pleasant way to spend a day is on the **MV Umande**, a traditional Arab dhow that leaves daily at 9.30am from the beach near the *Sweet Eazy Restaurant & Lounge* in Shangani. Reef snorkelling is followed by a seafood barbecue lunch on Bawe Island and a visit to Prison Island in the afternoon. The $45 price includes lunch, soft drinks and the Prison Island entrance fee. Advance reservations are required: book at Coastal Travels in Kelele Square next to the *Zanzibar Serena Inn* (☎024/223 3112 or 0741/334582, ⑩www.coastal.cc) or phone Hassan on ☎0747/410346.

Prison Island (Changuu Island)

A trip to **Prison Island**, 5km northwest of Stone Town, is a popular, enjoyable and cheap way of getting out of town. There's a beautiful beach, good snorkelling on the shallow fringing reef, some late-nineteenth-century ruins, patches of coral rag forest and, of course, the giant tortoises (*changuu*) from which the island gets its Kiswahili name.

The island's more sombre English name comes from a prison that never was: according to a popular but inaccurate story, the **prison** was built in 1893 by General William Lloyd Mathews – then first minister of Zanzibar – to house "violent and hard-core criminals from Tanganyika". The fact that Tanganyika was controlled by Germany at the time puts paid to that story, and in any case the "prison" only saw use as a yellow-fever quarantine camp. However, it was used as a kind of prison before Mathews' time, either as a slave transit camp or to house rebellious slaves. The crumbling cells and ruins of the hospital boiler house can still be seen, while the courtyard is nowadays inhabited by a colony of showy peacocks.

A narrow trail behind the ruins leads into a patch of forest, home to a herd of diminutive **suni antelope** – spotting them isn't usually difficult as long as you tread softly. The forest is also good for **birdlife**; look for the intricately woven nests of weavers hanging from the trees. The **tortoise sanctuary**, in the large fenced enclosure behind the restaurant, contains a colony of giant tortoises imported from Aldabra Atoll in the Seychelles in the late nineteenth century. Their average weight is 100kg, and many are believed to be over 100 years old. Tsh500 buys you a bowl of spinach (they tend to hiss at you if you pet them without feeding) and some quality bonding time with the venerable centenarians. Watch out for their sharp beaks though.

Practicalities

Prison Island can be visited as a half-day or full-day excursion, with **boats** from Stone Town leaving in the morning and early afternoon (30–45min) from the beach landing just past *Sweet Eazy* at the end of Kenyatta Road. The crossing takes thirty to forty-five minutes. All hotels and tour operators can arrange the trip, though you could also arrange things directly with the boatmen; the boat ride itself shouldn't cost more than Tsh3000–4000 for the return trip. More expensive are the smart modern boats, their sun screens usually adorned with

Diving off Stone Town

Visibility west of Stone Town is generally low (around 10m), but the sheltered coast is ideal for novices, and experts have a number of wrecks to explore. **Murogo Reef** has lots of marine life and some of Zanzibar's most beautiful coral gardens. With dramatic pinnacles, swim-throughs and gullies, it's rated highly. **Pange Sandbank**, east of Murogo, is a reasonable place for novices, and there's an unidentified wreck at 40m between the two. More wrecks lie off **Bawe Island**, which is also known for sand sharks and blue-spotted stingrays. The wreck of the **Great Northerner** (see opposite) lies at 14m off Fungu Reef.

   Bahari Divers (Forodhani ☎0772/750293, ⓦwww.zanzibar-diving.com) offer a range of PADI courses up to Divemaster, are knowledgeable about most sites off Stone Town, and offer night and wreck dives. **One Ocean** (Kenyatta Rd, next to *Sweet Eazy* ☎ & ℻024/223 8374, ⓦwww.zanzibaroneocean.com) are an experienced and highly rated outfit, offering wreck dives, the little-known Boribo Reef and tuition up to Instructor. They also have dive centres on the northeast coast (see p.680).

advertising, but apart from that there's little difference in the quality of service on offer. An entrance fee of $4 (or shilling equivalent; not included in the tour rates) is paid at a small shack near the landing. Snorkelling gear (around Tsh1000–2000) can be hired in Stone Town or on the island.

Accommodation is available at the *Changuu Island Guest House* (❸), a set of basic wooden bungalows set back from the beach and run by the Zanzibar Tourist Commission. You can book them at the Commission's offices on Creek Road and Livingstone House (see p.618). Most people bring picnic lunches, but **food** and **drinks** are available at the island's restaurant facing the beach where the boats arrive (meals from Tsh3000).

Bawe Island

Lying 6km west of Stone Town, **Bawe** is the largest of the islands near Stone Town and is popular with scuba-divers. Uninhabited for want of fresh water, the island acquired modest fame in the 1880s when it served as a base for East Africa's first underwater telegraphic cable. The cable ship, *The Great Northerner*, arrived in Zanzibar in 1882 and eventually laid 1950 nautical miles of cable between Aden (Yemen) and Mozambique via Zanzibar. The ship's wreck lies off Fungu Reef.

The easiest way of **getting to Bawe** is to combine the trip with a visit to Prison Island; most tour operators can arrange this. The more interesting way of getting here is to rent a boat at the dhow harbour (turn right 50m inside Stone Town's harbour entrance). The journey takes thirty to ninety minutes depending on the seaworthiness of your conveyance. There are no facilities whatsoever on Bawe, so if you plan on snorkelling, eating or drinking, bring everything you'll need with you from Stone Town.

Chumbe Island Coral Park

The small coral atoll of **Chumbe Island Coral Park**, 6km off Chukwani south of Stone Town, contains Tanzania's first marine protected area and one of the richest and finest coral gardens in the world, **Chumbe Reef Sanctuary**. Coral growth and diversity along the shallow reef is among the highest in East Africa, and marine life diversity is astonishing, with more than two hundred species of stone corals and around ninety percent of all East African fish species, over four hundred in all. Needless to say, snorkelling is superb, though scuba-diving within the park is prohibited.

It's not just marine life that makes Chumbe special. Most of the island is covered with pristine **coral rag forest** (also protected as a reserve), which contains a surprisingly rich variety of flora and fauna given the lack of permanent groundwater. The survival of the forest has been largely due to the absence of humans on the island, settlement having been limited to temporary fishermen's camps and the keeper of the lighthouse (which was built in 1904 and fitted with its present gaslight in 1926). The forest is one of the last natural habitats of the rare coconut crab and the endangered Ader's duiker, and can be explored via a number of **nature trails** that have been carefully laid without breaking the forest canopy.

Snorkelling and forest trails

The island and its reefs can be explored either in the company of one of the park's **ranger-guides**, a friendly and informative bunch of former fishermen, or on your own with the laminated route plans and leaflets available from the visitor's centre. For many, the shallow **coral gardens** are the main attraction.

With its modest sixteen-metre drop-off on its fringes, the reef contains most of Zanzibar's 200 coral species, and the cover is remarkably dense. Several snorkelling trails with "floating underwater information modules" have been established. Marine life includes parrotfish (the ones that peck at the coral), lobsters, giant groupers, Moorish idols, lion fish, angelfish, butterfly fish and triggerfish. Rarer are large blue-spotted stingrays, dolphins and a couple of bat-fish who like following snorkellers. Look out for Louise, the resident hawksbill turtle and Oscar, a large cave-dwelling potato grouper.

On land, it's possible to walk around the island at low tide, which is a good way of seeing mangroves, and you can also poke around intertidal rock pools for crabs, starfish and shellfish. Over on the bleak and rocky eastern side of the island, look out for petrified corals and fossilized giant clams, the latter esti-mated to be 15,000 years old. Several nature trails cut across the southern part of the coral rag forest, which covers ninety percent of the island and is home to a small and shy population of severely endangered **Ader's duiker** (*Cephalophus adersi*), reintroduced in December 1997 after being wiped out by hunters in the 1950s. The species exists only in Zanzibar and in Kenya's Arabuko-Sokoke Forest. Chumbe's other very special species is the coconut crab (see box opposite).

Practicalities

Visiting the island can be done as either as a day-trip or as a longer stay, with accommodation in the intimate and justifiably pricey lodge (all profits go to conservation or educational activities). Chumbe is reached by boat from the beach at *Protea Hotel Mbweni Ruins* (see p.652), 5km south of Stone Town. The boat leaves Mbweni daily at 10am and the nine-kilometre crossing takes thir-ty to forty minutes. The transfer is free for overnight guests; day-trippers pay $70, which includes entry fee, lunch and activities; note that day-trips may not be allowed if the lodge is full, so book a few days in advance. The park head-quarters and **visitors' centre** are housed in the lighthouse keeper's house, along with a restaurant with a beautiful sea-view terrace. For reservations and information, contact Chumbe Island Coral Park (T & F 024/223 1040 or T 0747/ 413582, W www.chumbeisland.com).

Accommodation at the *Chumbe Island Eco-Lodge* (full board ❾; closed mid-April to early June) is in seven romantic palm-thatched *bandas* overlooking the sea. All have twin or double beds, large living rooms, handmade furniture and hammocks, and the "ecotourism" tag is more than just an advertising gimmick – rainwater is filtered and stored under the floors and hot water and electrici-ty are provided by solar power. There are no TVs or phones and, apart from the activities on the island, entertainment is limited to watching the palm trees. Meals are a mixture of Zanzibari, Arabic, Indian and African cuisine, with good options for vegetarians too, and the price includes transfer from Mbweni, entry fees, soft drinks, walks and snorkelling. Rates are cheaper if booked though a reputable travel agent in Stone Town.

Chapwani Island (Grave Island)

Like Chumbe, **Chapwani Island** – 3km due north of Stone Town – is a pri-vate island; you're only allowed to land if you buy a meal or are spending a night in the lodge, both of which require reservations. The island is tiny, bare-ly measuring 600m long by 60m wide, with a beautiful sandy beach on one side and a series of coral inlets dotted with tidal swimming pools on the other. Though it lacks the quantity and quality of Chumbe's coral reefs and terrestrial

The coconut crab

The **coconut crab** (*Birgus latro*; also known as the robber crab) – nicknamed "the rhino of the invertebrates" – is the world's largest land crab, reaching 60–100cm in length and weighing 3–4kg. Originating in Polynesia, it made its way to the western Indian Ocean, carried either by ocean currents when in its plankton stage or by early sailors as food. The crabs are crimson or bluish black in colour, and the unusual name comes from their amazing ability to climb trees, a skill popularly believed to be used for wrenching off coconuts. True or not, they do climb trees and certainly feed on fallen coconuts, as well as on hermit crabs, to which they are related. The main differences between the two species, other than size and an aptitude for arboreal gymnastics, is that the coconut crab sheds its shell and is also nocturnal. By day, you might see them hiding in rocky crevices on the coral cliffs or burrowed in the roots of palm trees. By night they emerge to forage for fruit and coconuts, which can be stored in their burrows.

Coconut crabs have long been considered a delicacy throughout the Indian Ocean, and also an aphrodisiac, and so have been hunted to the point of extinction. On Zanzibar, the crabs were also used as bait in fish traps – their struggles attracted fish – though the crabs drowned after two days in water. Other factors contributing to their decline are unnatural predators such as rats (introduced when the lighthouse was built in 1904, but eradicated in 1997), pigs (introduced by the Portuguese) and monkeys. In Tanzania, the species is limited to Chumbe and only two other islands: Misali Island off Pemba (p.693) and Mbudya Island north of Dar es Salaam (see p.131).

flora and fauna, Chapwani still has plenty to make it an ideal hideaway, including dikdik antelopes, good snorkelling and a Christian cemetery established in 1879 from which the island draws its English name.

Chapwani Island Lodge (half board; low season **⑥**, high season **⑨**; **ⓦ** www. chapwaniisland.com) has ten simple but comfortable rooms in five *bandas* on the south side of the island, each with its own secluded area of beach and a sea-facing terrace. The bedrooms are large, and everything is cheerfully kitted out with African prints and antiques. The restaurant, on the beach, offers mainly Italian dishes and seafood, with a touch of oriental and African. Activities include snorkelling and boat excursions. Reservations can be made through Stone Town's travel agents (Safari Scene, see p.125, are the lodge's official agents) or direct on **ⓣ**024/223 3360 or 0744/570988, or in the UK on **ⓣ** & **ⓕ**01737/241 892.

Mbweni

Five kilometres south of Stone Town, **MBWENI** is a popular day-trip with locals and visitors alike, thanks to its botanical gardens and poignant ruins of a nineteenth-century mission and colony of freed slaves. In addition, the excellent restaurant at the *Protea Hotel Mbweni Ruins* offers reason enough to come here at lunchtime. The hotel is set in a magnificent **botanical garden** amidst the ruins of a nineteenth-century **Anglican mission**. Formerly a plantation, the seven-acre site was purchased in 1871 and used to house a colony of freed slaves. The ruins of a chapel and St Mary's School for Girls date from this time – the school was used by girls freed from captured slave dhows and by daughters of freed slaves. Caroline Thackeray, the school's first headmistress and cousin of novelist William Makepeace Thackeray, is buried in the graveyard of St John's church nearby. The church, in late English Gothic style, was built in 1882. In 1920 the school and buildings were sold to the Bank of India, under whose ownership they fell into ruin.

Aptly complementing the ruins are the glorious cascaded botanical gardens, recently spruced up, which were founded by Britain's first consul general, Sir John Kirk. A botanist by profession, Kirk was the main authority on East African flora, introducing many of the 650 species found in the garden, including sausage trees, Madagascan periwinkle, devil's backbone and over 200 palms. Many of the plants are labelled, and there's a nature trail which you can walk on your own (the hotel has bird, plant and butterfly lists) or accompanied by a guide from the hotel. For more information about the Mbweni mission, see Flo Liebst's book *Zanzibar, History of the Ruins at Mbweni*.

Practicalities

There's no problem walking or cycling the 5km from Stone Town, but it's far easier to catch the free **shuttle bus** to the *Protea Hotel Mbweni Ruins*, which runs five times a day from the Omani Fort. The first leaves at 9.30am, the last (for hotel guests) at 10.30pm. The pick-up point and schedule is liable to change so ring ahead (☏024/223 1832). Coming by public transport, catch a "U" route daladala from Creek Road and get off at Mazizini police station next to the signposted junction for Mbweni. Follow the Mbweni road and turn right again after 800m. The Mbweni ruins and *Protea Hotel Mbweni Ruins* are 900m along.

The only choice for accommodation is the *Protea Hotel Mbweni Ruins* (☏024/223 1832, ⓦwww.proteahotels.com; ❽), a peaceful and cosy **hotel** with thirteen rooms including a suite and three family rooms; all have air-conditioning and are furnished in traditional style with four-poster beds. The private beach isn't Zanzibar's best, as there are plenty of mangroves, but this at least attracts a rich variety of birdlife. Facilities include a swimming pool, beach bar, an excellent clifftop restaurant and a natural health centre. **Entertainment** features barbecues, torchlight dinners in the ruins or on a dhow and trips to Chumbe Island (see p.649).

North of Stone Town

Attractions north of Stone Town include a couple of ruined palaces at **Maruhubi** and **Mtoni** and the Persian baths at **Kidichi**, all of which can be visited as part of a spice tour (see box on p.647). Some tours also include **Mangapwani**, about 20km north of town, which apart from a lovely beach, has a natural cave and a manmade cavern that was used for holding slaves. All these places can be visited under your own steam. There's also a good beach near Bububu at **Fuji Beach**.

Maruhubi

Just off the road to Bububu, 3km north of Stone Town amidst mango and coconut trees, are the ruins of **Maruhubi Palace**, built by Sultan Barghash in 1882 to house his harem of 99 concubines and one wife. Dark legends tell of the former being killed if they did not satisfy the sultan, and of others being put to death after having fulfilled the desires of visiting dignitaries. The largely wooden palace, one of the most beautiful of its time (there's a photo in the

Princess Seyyida Salme was born on August 30, 1844 to Sultan Seyyid Said and a concubine named Jilfidan. Although Salme's early childhood, much of which was spent at Mtoni, was by her own account idyllic, her adult life was to be much more turbulent. Sultan Said died when Salme was 12, beginning a period of rivalry which ended with the creation of the separate sultanates of Zanzibar and Oman. In the former, Salme's brother **Barghash** unsuccessfully attempted to usurp the throne from his half-brother Majid. In 1859, Salme's mother died in a cholera epidemic, and Salme went to live with her half-sister, Khole, with whom she played a minor role in Barghash's second and equally doomed attempt to seize power. For her part in the plot, Salme spent several years in internal exile before making peace with Majid – something that permanently soured her relations with Barghash.

Salme returned to Stone Town in 1866, where she lived next door to, and started an affair with, her future husband, a German merchant named **Rudolph Heinrich Reute**. Heinrich's Christianity meant that problems were inevitable and when, in the same year, Salme became pregnant, Heinrich realized the danger and made arrangements to smuggle her out of Zanzibar aboard the German vessel *Mathilde*. Although this attempt at escape was foiled at the last moment, Salme, aided by Dr John Kirk and the wife of the acting British consul, suceeded in boarding *HMS Highflyer* on August 24 and fled to Aden.

Salme's child was born in December, and when Heinrich arrived on May 30, 1867, Salme converted to Christianity, being baptized as Emily, and married her lover – all on the same morning. In the afternoon, they set sail for Hamburg. Although their first child died young, Salme and Heinrich went on to have three more children before Heinrich was killed in a tram accident in 1870. Following the death of her husband, Salme spent much of her time campaigning for the restitution of the "rights" she had forfeited by converting to Christianity, but her family remained deaf to her entreaties. Finally, in 1885, the German government sent her to Zanzibar aboard the *Adler*, escorted by five warships, the idea being to use her as a pawn in obtaining Zanzibar as a German protectorate. The attempt backfired, and Sultan Barghash refused to see her. When Barghash died in March 1888, Salme hoped for a change of heart from his successor, Sultan Sayyid Khalifa bin Said, and once more returned to Zanzibar, only to be shunned again. She spent ten days on the island before leaving for the last time in October 1888. The rest of her life was one of restless travel; when she died from pneumonia in Germany in 1924, the dress she had worn during her elopement and a bag of sand taken from the beach at Mtoni were found among her possessions.

The Palace Museum in Stone Town has an entire room dedicated to the errant princess. For **further information**, contact the Princess Salme Institute, 38 King Street, Covent Garden, London WC2E 8J5 ℡ & ℻ 020/7240 0199.

House of Wonders), was gutted by fire in 1899 and the marble from its Persian-style bath house was subsequently stolen, leaving only the foundations of the bath house, an overgrown collection of coral stone pillars and a small aqueduct that carried water from a nearby spring. To get here, walk or catch a route "B" daladala. Access is free.

Mtoni Palace

About 1.5km beyond Maruhubi is the bustling village of **Mtoni** and the ruins of **Mtoni Palace**. Built by Sultan Seyyid Said between 1828 and 1832 as his first official residence, the palace at one time contained his three wives, 42 children and hundreds of concubines. The main building had two floors with elegant balconies, and other buildings included baths, a mosque and an unusual conical tower that served both as a meeting place and for meditation, while the gardens contained a menagerie of wildlife, including ostriches, flamingos and gazelles.

Like Maruhubi, much of Mtoni Palace was destroyed by fire in 1914, leaving only the mosque intact. The advent of World War I saw the mosque converted into a warehouse, and it was later destroyed when the present oil depot was constructed. Nowadays nothing more than a few walls and collapsing roofs remain, and the ruins would be unremarkable were it not for their association with **Princess Salme** (see box on p.653), daughter of one of Sultan Seyyid Said's concubines, whose elopement with a German merchant caused a scandal. In her autobiography, *Memoirs of an Arabian Princess*, she beautifully describes the opulence of palace life at Mtoni in the 1850s and 1860s, where she spent her early childhood.

Practicalities

The remains of the **palace** can be seen off the path that goes beside the oil depot to the beach; route "B" daladalas from Creek Road pass by the junction. **Accommodation** is offered by the *Mtoni Marine Centre* (☎024/225 0140 or 0741/323226, ⓦwww.zanzibar.cc; ❻–❼), a relaxing hotel set in palm-tree-studded lawns with good views over the ocean to Stone Town. There's a wide variety of accommodation, all with private bathroom, and facilities include the *Mcheza Bar* near the beach, with a good range of cocktails, snacks and full meals (Tsh2800–5000). More formal but also recommended is the *Mtoni Marine Restaurant*, which does a good seafood lunch for Tsh4000–6000 as well as à la carte. A *taarab* group performs on Tuesdays, coinciding with a beach barbecue (8.30–10pm; Tsh10,000), and there's also live African Jazz (Wed, Fri and Sat from 7.30pm) and a beach barbecue on Saturday (Tsh12,000). Room rates include trips to Prison Island.

Bububu and Fuji Beach

The first clean beach north of Stone Town is **Fuji Beach** at **BUBUBU**, a densely populated area 9km north of the city. There's a reasonable range of cheapish guest houses and one exceptionally atmospheric upmarket option, but if it's a beach holiday you're after you'd probably be better off heading to Unguja's north, northeast or east coasts, where the beaches are nicer and there's a wider range of accommodation.

Practicalities

Route "B" daladalas from Creek Road terminate at Bububu. **Fuji Beach** is 300m off the main road down a track that starts from Bububu police station, and takes its name from the *Fuji Beach Bar*, which was set up here a couple of decades ago by a Japanese expatriate. He's long gone, but the bar, which also serves cheap meals, still exists and remains popular with locals and day-trippers from Stone Town. Don't leave items unattended on the beach: there has cases of theft in the past.

There are two good **accommodation** options: the most atmospheric is *Salome's Garden* (reservations through ⓦwww.salomesgarden.com or travel agents in Stone Town – Safari Scene, p.125, are the official agents; ❼), a restored nineteenth-century country house just behind Fuji Beach. The building belonged to the sultanate and is claimed to have been inhabited by Princess Salme. The eighteen acres of orchards, gardens and ruins are enclosed by a tall wall, giving the place an Alice in Wonderland feel. Another good choice is

Zanzibar has the honour of having had the first railway in Africa when, in the 1880s, a two-foot-gauge track was laid from Stone Town to Sultan Barghash's summer palace at Chukwani, south of the city. The railway saw little use, however, and was pulled up after the sultan's death. Between 1905 and 1909, a second line – the Bububu Light Railway – was constructed by the American company Arnold Cheney & Co. It consisted of seven miles of three-foot gauge and connected Stone Town's Omani Fort with Sultan Seyyid Ali bin Hamoud's clove plantation at Bububu. The railway quickly became infamous, as a government official recounted in 1911: "The whole width [of the railway] is blacked, while the engines, which belch forth clouds of smoke and sparks into the front upper storey windows, cover the goods in the shops below, not to speak of the passengers, with large black smuts. Funeral processions are interrupted, old women are killed, houses and crops are set on fire . . . and no redress can be obtained." The advent of the motorcar scuppered plans for the railway's extension to Mkokotoni, and the track was finally abandoned in 1927.

Imani Beach Villa, virtually next door (T & F 024/225 0050, W www.imani.it; ⑥), an Italian-run mini-resort set in a garden with lots of whitewash and *makuti* thatch. The restaurant in the garden is good for seafood and Swahili dishes, and a full range of excursions is offered.

Kidichi Persian Baths

Usually included in a spice tour, the **Persian Baths** at **Kidichi**, 2.5km east of Bububu, have survived in remarkably good condition. They once formed part of a palace built by Sultan Seyyid Said around 1850 for the use of his second wife, a granddaughter of the Shah of Persia named Binte Irich Mirza. Their decoration, with ornamental stuccowork depicting flowers, birds, coconut palms and dates, was in keeping with the Persian style favoured at the time and probably done by Persian craftsmen, presumably Zoroastrians, as local Muslims would have been forbidden by the Qu'ran to depict representations of Allah's creations. The baths are open daily 8am–4pm; entrance costs Tsh500, though the guide will expect a tip. Take a route "B" daladala to Bububu, then walk the remaining 2.5km; the baths are on the right hand side of the road.

About 2.5km further east at **Kizimbani** are another set of baths, less elaborate and in a more ruinous state, also dating from Seyyid Said's reign. His estate at Kizimbani was where, in 1818, clove trees were first planted in Zanzibar; at its height the estate here was said to have contained 300,000 of them.

Mangapwani

Some 20km north of Stone Town is **Mangapwani** village, with a lovely stretch of clean beach and a couple of caves in the coral ragstone. The name means "Arab Shore", alluding to the manmade chamber used for hiding slaves after the trade with Oman was outlawed in 1845, and even more so after the rest of the slave trade was abolished in 1873. The dank and claustrophobic **slave chamber** is one of the most shocking of Zanzibar's sights and, like the cells under Stone Town's last slave market, conveys the full horror and misery of the East African trade. The cavern is a rectangular cell, hewn out of the soft coral rock, accessed along a deep and narrow passage and sealed by a heavy door, all of which served to hide slaves from the eyes of British anti-slavery patrols, and meant that no light penetrated inside.

Two kilometres south is a **coral cave**, this one natural and larger than the

△ Stone Town

slave chamber, and of interest due to its spiritual importance for locals. The pool of fresh water inside was accidentally discovered by a young slave boy when one of the goats he was herding disappeared. Like other caves in Zanzibar and along the coast, the cave has offerings to ancestors left inside to seek their intercession in mortal affairs.

Practicalities

Mangapwani can be visited as part of a spice tour if the entire group agrees, though operators can be reluctant given the bad state of the road and the extra distance involved: the **usual rate** for this is $15 per person on a shared trip, much more on a exclusive tour. It can also be incorporated in one of the north-coast day-trips offered by many tour operators, which includes a spice tour and Nungwi beach; the total cost averages $35.

To reach Mangapwani village by **public transport**, catch a #2 daladala from Creek Road in Stone Town towards Mangapwani or Bumbwini. Some daladalas turn left at the village and continue towards the coast, which is preferable if you don't fancy walking too much. If you're dropped on the main road between Chuini and Bumbwini, walk northwest through the village towards the coast; after 1.5km, just before the beach, the road veers north – the cave is 1km further on. To get to the coral cave from the main road, walk northwest through the village and turn left on to a narrow track after 600m; the cave is 1km further on. If the daladala terminates in Mangapwani, most drivers will be happy to continue on to one of the caves for a negotiable tip. Lastly, if you're taking lunch at the *Mangapwani Seafood Grill* you can catch their complimentary shuttle bus from Stone Town: it leaves from outside the *Zanzibar Serena Inn* at 8.30am and 11.30am, and returns at 4pm or 5pm. The restaurant itself is pricey but worth it, blending high style and service with a relaxed atmosphere. It's open daily for lunch, and for dinner by reservation through the *Zanzibar Serena Inn* (see p.624). There's no accommodation at Mangapwani.

South Unguja

For most visitors, Unguja's **south coast** means only one thing: dolphin tours. Visits to the resident pods off the fishing village of **Kizimkazi** are Zanzibar's most popular excursion after spice tours, and the opportunity of swimming with dolphins exerts an irresistible allure – although there are serious concerns about the impact of this popularity on the dolphins themselves. A fine alternative to Kizimkazi for spotting dolphins is a boat tour from **Unguja Ukuu**, which also contains some of the oldest ruins on Zanzibar. Another natural highlight is **Jozani Forest**, with frequently sightings of troops of red colobus monkeys and walks through the primeval forest. East of Kizimkazi lies **Makunduchi**, a sleepy fishing community that comes alive once a year for the vibrant Mwaka Kogwa festival.

Few people stay overnight on the south coast, though the number of hotels is increasing. There's **public transport** to all these places.

Jozani Forest and around

Lying 38km southeast of Stone Town and just north of the road to the east coast is the magnificent **Jozani Forest** (daily 7.30am–5pm; $8), the largest remaining patch of indigenous groundwater forest that once covered most of Unguja. The forest is now protected by the Jozani–Chwaka Bay Conservation Project, and part of your entrance fee goes directly to development projects and to compensate farmers for crops destroyed by the monkeys. Despite its tiny area (around ten square kilometres) the forest contains several different types of habitat including swamp forest, evergreen thickets, mangroves and salt-tolerant grassland, and is home to a variety of wildlife once common all over the island, including Sykes and red colobus monkeys, bushpigs, diminutive Ader's duiker and suni antelopes, elephant shrews, chameleons and lots of birdlife.

The forest has several **nature trails**, ranging from an easy hour's stroll to a half-day hike. Route descriptions are given in a series of leaflets but these are often out of print, so taking an official guide is recommended, and obligatory if you want to see monkeys inside the forest (those outside the gate can easily be spotted on your own). The guides are knowledgeable and helpful; there's no fee for their service but a tip is expected and invariably deserved. The **entrance gate** to the forest is 2km beyond Pete along the surfaced road to Paje. There's an information centre at the gate, as well as a café, snack bar and community-run gift shop. Jozani is usually visited as part of an organized day-trip to see Kizimkazi's dolphins (see p.646 for recommended companies), but the forest can also easily be visited by **public transport**: #9 daladalas from Stone Town pass by the gate throughout the day. Alternatively, taxi or car rental from Stone Town costs around $30 for half a day.

The best **time to visit** Jozani is early morning or late afternoon, when there are fewer visitors and the wildlife is at its most active. Evening light is superb for photographing the troop of red colobus monkeys near the gate.

Red colobus monkeys

Jozani is best known for its large and characterful population of **Kirk's red colobus monkeys** (*Procolobus kirkii*). The species is endemic to Unguja, as it has been isolated from other red colobus populations on the Tanzanian mainland for at least 10,000 years, during which time it has evolved different coat patterns, food habits and calls.

A decade or so ago, the monkeys were considered to be on the road to extinction, but the protection of the forest in the 1990s appears to have reversed the trend. Their current population is estimated at around 2500 in and around Jozani, accounting for one third of their total number. The local population is steadily increasing, perhaps not so much because of conservation but through the continued destruction of their natural habit elsewhere.

The monkeys are known locally as *kima punju*, poison monkeys, as it was believed that dogs who ate them would lose their fur, and trees and crops would die if the monkeys fed off them. Two troops of thirty to fifty individuals are frequently seen, one inside the forest (usually flashes of red accompanied by the crashing of branches) and another that frequents a patch of open woodland just outside the gate. The latter are habituated and completely unfazed by human presence, making them incredibly photogenic. However, for your own and their safety, do not approach them closer than three metres, avoid eye contact and noise, and do not feed or otherwise interact with the monkeys. Also, it's not advisable to visit Jozani if you're ill: monkeys are susceptible to infectious human diseases and have little resistance.

Pete–Jozani Mangrove Boardwalk and Zala Park

South of the forest entrance, on the other side of the road, the **Pete-Jozani Mangrove Boardwalk** loops through coral thicket vegetation, mangrove forest and across a creek in the north of Pete Inlet. The walk starts in a car park under a large tamarind tree 1km south of the forest gate and finishes nearby. An informative leaflet containing a sketch map is available for free from the forest entrance gate; the boardwalk entrance fee is covered by the ticket for Jozani. Typical thicket **fauna** includes snakes, lizards, mongooses, Ader's duikers and the nocturnal civet cat. Birdlife is also good, ranging from purple-banded and olive sunbirds to kingfishers and blue-cheeked bee-eaters.

As a complement to Jozani Forest, you could pay a visit to **Zala Park** (Zanzibar Land Animals Park; daily 8.30am–5.30pm; Tsh2500 including guided tour), 5.5km south of Jozani along the Kizimkazi road at Muungoni. Founded by a school teacher in 1994 for educational purposes, this is basically a small family-run zoo for reptiles and amphibians that gives you the chance to see chameleons and snakes at close quarters. Organized trips to Kizimkazi may stop by on the way back. You can also get here from Stone Town on a #10 daladala.

Kizimkazi

At the south end of Unguja, 53km from Stone Town, is the pretty fishing village of **KIZIMKAZI**, known by tourists for its **dolphin tours**. Little of its history is known other than that it's one of the oldest continuously inhabited settlements on Zanzibar, and that it probably served as Unguja's capital until the seventeenth century. The village actually comprises two places: **Kizimkazi Dimbani**, which contains East Africa's oldest mosque and is where most dolphin tours depart from; and **Kizimkazi Mkunguni** (sometimes called Kizimkazi Mtendeni), 3km to the south, which has a fledgling hotel strip. The **beaches** at both places are beautiful, and swimmers are likely to share the water with easily amused local children; be wary of stepping on sea urchins. Kizimkazi and Pungume Island also offer excellent but largely unexplored **diving**. Contact Rising Sun Dive Centre in Bwejuu (see p.669) or Mawimbi Watersports in Uroa (see p.680) for more information.

Kizimkazi Mkunguni has a couple of ancient **baobab trees**, the oldest and biggest of which, towering over the car park, is estimated to be over 600 years old and was used as a transmissions mast in World War II when communications gear was strapped to its crown.

Arrival and accommodation

Most tourists come to Kizimkazi as part of a dolphin tour (see p.646), but it's easy to get here by public transport: catch a #10 daladala from Stone Town. Few people stay **overnight**, but if you do you'll have the chance to get out on the water the next morning before the crowds arrive. Kizimkazi Dimbani is the more beautiful of the two villages, with a lovely sheltered bay in which dozens of outrigger canoes are moored, but there's only one accommodation option. More choice can be had at Kizimkazi Mkunguni, spread out along 1.5km of dirt track south of the village. All hotels can arrange dolphin and snorkelling trips.

Dolphin Shadow 500m south of the 600-year-old baobab at Kizimkazi Mkunguni (no sign and no phone), ✉ abubakarally@hotmail.com. Currently six cramped but clean rooms (more are being built) in a large plot facing the beach, all with box nets and Western-style bathrooms. If you can deal with the pushy manager and bargain down the prices, this place is good value for money. ❸

Funky Shamba 1.4m south of the baobab at Kizimkazi Mkunguni ☎ 0747/419008. A new place with a kind of rustic beachcomber chic, that was planning to open ten "bush *bandas*" by mid-2002, all with private bathrooms. Though new, the restaurant (see p.661) has already gained an excellent reputation. ❺

Kizidi Restaurant & Bungalows Kizimkazi Dimbani ☎ 024/223 0081, ✉ kizidi@hotmail.com. On the northern headland flanking the bay, this has glorious views from each of its five, large, clean rooms. There's also a good upmarket restaurant, a bar and a phone service. ❺

Kizimkazi Dolphin View Cottage 1.5km south of the baobab at Kizimkazi Mkunguni (no phone). A youthful place with several cottages on a cliff owned by the same people as *Paje Ndame* (see p.666). The double rooms are large and breezy, and those with sea views are more expensive. Single rooms can be shared by couples. The bar and restaurant attract busloads of visitors at mid-day. ❹

Dolphin tours

The waters off Kizimkazi are home to several pods of **bottlenose and humpback dolphins**, now officially protected by the 420-square-kilometre Menai Bay Conservation Area, established in 1997. The dolphins are, of course, the main reason tourists come here and, for many, the chance to swim with them is the experience of a lifetime; the odds of sighting dolphins on any given day are put at eighty percent (calm days are best, as rough seas force the dolphins into deeper water). Whether you want to "play and swim" – as the brochures and tour companies wax lyrically – is really up to your sensibilities: for some visitors, the experience comes depressingly close to Disneyland, with dozens of noisy boats crowding and hounding the dolphins on a daily basis, and tourists encouraged to leap into the water just as pods are passing by. The detrimental effects of this regular disturbance is the subject of on-going research, so think twice before taking part in the melee. If you do decide to go, try and adhere to the following **guidelines**: encourage your skipper not to chase the pods; if you enter the water, do so away from the dolphins and with as little disturbance as possible; when in the water, stay close to the boat; avoid sudden movements; allow the dolphins to come to you and do not under any pretext attempt to touch them.

Dolphin tour practicalities

Visitors coming on **prearranged tours** have nothing to pay in Kizimkazi itself other than lunch, if that's not already included. Some trips also include snorkelling on an extensive coral reef fringing Pungume Island, 13km offshore. Note that most of the boats are shared between companies no matter what you're paying; the only real differences with more expensive upmarket excursions is that group sizes are smaller, road transport is by Land Cruiser rather than minibus, and the boats are fibreglass rather than wood. If combined with Jozani Forest (see p.658), an extra $8 to cover the forest entry fee is charged; any extra payment over this is really just a gratuity.

Arranging dolphin trips in Kizimkazi works out a good deal cheaper than organized tours from Stone Town. Both *Cabs Restaurant* and *Kizidi Restaurant & Bungalows* charge $35 per boat (eight people); *Dolphin Shadow* asks $25–30, or $15 if you're in a couple, but bear in mind that these prices are well below the minimum set out by the authorities (see below). Snorkelling equipment costs an extra Tsh2000–4000 per person. Doing a deal with one of the touts by the big baobab tree in Kizimkazi Mkunguni may bring the price down a bit but there's no guarantee in terms of quality or reliability. Whatever deal you do, ensure the boat has adequate shade.

The official side of things is a quagmire of contradictions: a Tsh5000 conservation area entrance fee has been talked about for years, but at present only Tsh500 is levied, which is usually levied in the boat fare. According to officials the minimum for a boat (up to eight) is Tsh35,000, excluding snorkelling equipment, though at present not a single company or boatman in Kizimkazi charges that much. Should the powers that be get their act in order, you may have to pay the entrance fee at a roadblock or at their office next to *Jichane Restaurant* in Kizimkazi Mkunguni – make sure you get a receipt.

Eating and drinking

Kizimkazi's popularity with day-trippers means there's plenty of choice for **eating out**. With the exception of *Jichane Restaurant* the following places remain open during Ramadan.

Cabs Restaurant & Dolphin Safaris Kizimkazi Dimbani. An enticing menu, with seafood a speciality: try the seashell meat with potatoes, spices and ginger. Most fish dishes are good value at Tsh2400; other meals less so at around Tsh4000. Evening barbecues are held whenever there are enough punters.

Dolphin Shadow 500m south of the baobab at Kizimkazi Mkunguni (no sign). Small but decent menu, with fish dishes for Tsh2500–3000 and lobster for Tsh8000.

Funky Shamba 1.4m south of the baobab at Kizimkazi Mkunguni ☏0747/419008. A new place constructed with driftwood, other flotsam and assorted junk. The restaurant and bar have already garnered a reputation for good Swahili food, with meals for around Tsh9000 and up. Reservations advisable.

Jichane Restaurant Kizimkazi Mkunguni, near the big baobab. The only really local place in Kizimkazi, with basic meals for Tsh1000 (at least that's what locals pay). If you want something other than rice with fish or chicken – prawns or lobster, for example – ask what's available in the morning.

Kizidi Restaurant & Bungalows Kizimkazi Dimbani. More upmarket and expensive than *Cabs*, with a surprisingly sophisticated ambience. Mains cost upwards of Tsh5000 (lobster is Tsh10,000) and there are barbecues most nights.

Kizimkazi Dolphin View Cottage 1.5km south of the baobab at Kizimkazi Mkunguni. No fixed menu here, only what you arrange with the cook. Standard dishes (chicken or fish with chips or rice) cost Tsh2000; fancier things like prawns, octopus and spaghetti Tsh3000, and lobster are also available. Popular with day-trippers at lunchtime.

Dimbani Mosque

Apart from dolphins, Kizimkazi's other claim to fame is the **Dimbani Mosque**, founded in 1107, and thus East Africa's most ancient mosque and the oldest surviving building in Zanzibar. The mosque is on the main road 100m back from the bay at Kizimkazi Dimbani and is still in use, so admission is prohibited to non-Muslims during prayer times and to women at all times. Male visitors should ask permission before entering or taking photographs, and cover up bare limbs. The mosque is invariably included in organized dolphin tours.

From the outside, the mosque doesn't look too different from any other building in Dimbani and there's little other than a roadside plaque to indicate its importance. Most of the mosque was completely rebuilt in the eighteenth century on top of the original foundations, and the corrugated metal roof doesn't lend an impression of antiquity, but the atmosphere inside could hardly be more different. In the original north wall is an ornate *mihrab* prayer niche that indicates the direction to Mecca, while to its left a Kufic inscription carved in coral stone bears the date 500 AH (the Islamic Hegira calendar), equating to 1107 AD, and commemorates the building of the mosque by Sheikh Abu

Mussa al-Hassan bin Muhammad. The inscription to the right of the *mihrab* is in Arabic and mentions 1184 AH (1770 AD) as the year of rebuilding.

The **graves** outside the mosque, one with a headstone resembling a toadstool, another with a curious checkerboard engraving, include – in the words of the signpost – the "pious single-handed Sheikh Ali Omar, one-legged Sayyid Abdalla Said bin Sharif, Mwana bint Mmadi and her son Mfaume Ali Omar the Guard of the Town Drum". With luck, this drum – which would have been used on ceremonial occasions as a symbol of authority – should be on display in the House of Wonders in Stone Town in the near future.

Miza Miza Cave

Some trips to Kizimkazi also include a visit to **Miza Miza Cave** (or Kizimkazi Cavern). The cave contains a freshwater pool and a vaguely human-shaped stone, and has a taboo associated with it stating that one should not call out the name of a person inside the cave. The story goes that once upon a time a local chief had two wives who quarrelled incessantly. One day they both went to the cave to fetch water. The elder wife filled her calabash and emerged from the cave while the younger one, who was called Miza, was still inside. The elder wife called Miza by name, which echoed inside the cave, whereupon the unfortunate Miza was turned to stone.

Another legend connected to the cave recalls the founder of Kizimkazi, who twice called upon Allah to protect the town's inhabitants from invaders. The first time a swarm of bees saw them off; the second time, the population took refuge in the cave, whose entrance miraculously sealed itself up until the invaders had passed by.

Makunduchi

Despite its proximity to Kizimkazi and Jambiani, the nebulous settlement of **MAKUNDUCHI**, in the far southeast of Unguja, hardly receives any visitors, and though the beach is as beautiful as any other on the island, its last hotel closed several years ago. Most of the inhabitants survive on fishing and seaweed collecting, colourful piles of which you'll find laid out to dry all over the place. The settlement is for the most part modern, with a few large blocks of Soviet-style flats, a post office and bank (usually closed) and a police station. But despite the socialist veneer of modernity, Makunduchi remains a very traditional sort of place, something best seen during the exhilarating **Mwaka Kogwa festival** in July (see box opposite). The beach is at the end of the road at Kigaeni; snorkelling and fishing excursions can be arranged with local fishermen, but bring your own equipment as there's no guarantee of finding stuff in Makunduchi.

The 69km of road from Stone Town are covered by #10 daladalas throughout the day. There's no accommodation, but there are a couple of simple restaurants on the main road where the daladalas drop you, and a diminutive fish market 2km to the west.

Unguja Ukuu

Should Kizimkazi's tourist spectacle turn you off, a recommended alternative way of seeing dolphins – and virtually no other tourists – is via the excellent

Unguja Ukuu Boat Trip run by the NGO *Eco+Culture* (see p.646; you can also book through *Sama Tours*, p.646). The trip starts at Unguja Ukuu, a village 20km southeast of Stone Town, and heads off to the uninhabited islands of Miwi and Niamembe in Menai Bay, known for their unspoiled flora and fauna, delightful beaches, good snorkelling and dolphin-spotting opportunities. The cost ranges from $20 per person in a group of eight to $50 per person in a couple, and includes a seafood barbecue. An additional $16–40 per person, depending on group size, gets you a canoe excursion through mangroves and a visit to a cave.

The **ruins of Unguja Ukuu**, 1km beyond the modern village at the neck of Ras Kitoe peninsula, are known to archeologists as one of the oldest settlements on Zanzibar. Excavations have unearthed a gold dinar, dated 798 AD, that was minted during the reign of Haroun bin Rashid (anti-hero of the *Arabian Nights*), and sixth-century Sasanian pottery from pre-Islamic Persia. In later years, Unguja Ukuu – "Great Unguja" – served as the island's main port, and also as capital of Unguja under the Hadimu tribe. The rapacious Portuguese captain Ruy Lourenço Ravasco put an end to the town in 1503 by completely sacking it, after which the Hadimu moved their capital inland to Dunga (see p.673). There's little to see now except a few disintegrating walls.

East Unguja

Unguja's **east coast** is a major tourist destination, its magnificent white sandy **beaches** lined for the most part with swaying coconut palm and casuarina trees. Despite the attention of sun-worshippers, the east coast retains a much more local, isolated and meditative feel than the north coast – Unguja's other big beach draw – and with the exception of a handful of expensive resorts along Michamvi Peninsula, tourist development remains a low-key affair. There are no tall buildings, nor many walls to keep locals out, and in fact in most places you'll be sharing the beach with women collecting seaweed, spear-carrying fishermen and children who are invariably delighted to kick a football around with you.

The main beaches to head for are Paje, Bwejuu or Jambiani. **Paje** village boasts the most beautiful beach, and water deep enough to swim in at all tides, though the proximity of the village to the beach makes some people feel awkward about donning bathing shorts or bikinis, so be discreet. A few kilometres to the north of Paje, **Bwejuu** has a big choice of more upmarket accommodation and restaurants, some of them seriously good. The longest of the beaches is at **Jambiani**, which starts 5km south of Paje and whose sands roll on for another 5km. Small affordable hotels are scattered all along the strip and Jambiani is also home to a cultural village tour, a community-run initiative providing a welcome glimpse into the real life of local people.

It's also possible to arrange several **excursions** from the east coast similar to those offered in Stone Town (see p.645). Many hotels can help you sort out a vehicle or bicycle, and Stone Town's tour operators are happy to drive all the way to the east coast to fetch you – at a price. Spice tours are more expensive than those arranged in Stone Town, but the flip side is that trips to Jozani Forest are cheaper, and the cost of dolphin safaris off Kizimkazi shows no real difference (roughly $25–35 per person). In addition, the whole of the east coast is protected by a fringing **coral reef** and calm conditions in the shallow lagoon make for some superb snorkelling, which can be arranged almost everywhere and cost as little as $5–10 per person. For information on diving see p.669. Other water sports are offered by the big hotels on Michamvi Peninsula.

Paje

The fishing village of **PAJE**, 51km east of Stone Town, is the easiest place on the east coast to get to by public transport. The village is a nondescript shamble of houses, but is also one of the more characterful places, and the white sandy beach is gorgeous.

To reach Paje by public transport, take a **#9 daladala**, which leaves Stone Town at 9am, 11am, noon, 1pm, 1.30pm and at 2pm or 3pm. Timings are more fluid when leaving Paje; the first leaves around 6.30am, the last no later than 5.30pm. Alternatively, you could take one of the shared **"beach transfer" minibuses** from Stone Town, which are more comfortable than daladalas and will deposit you directly outside your hotel. Most tour operators and budget hotels in Stone Town (*Riverman Hotel* comes recommended) can fix you up with a seat. The ride costs Tsh2000–4000 depending on the season and who you talk to; more if you can't be bothered to bargain or if the minibus leaves almost empty. Note that the minibuses only cover Paje, Jambiani and Bwejuu on the east coast and Nungwi on the north coast. Be clear where you want to go; otherwise the driver will take you to a hotel that pays him the best commission. Upmarket hotels and travel agents run a similar service but milk their captive audience by charging $50–70 for a four-to-six-seat vehicle (and sometimes per person). Hiring a taxi works out cheaper (starting price $40–50) and gives you the chance of sharing the cost with other beach-goers.

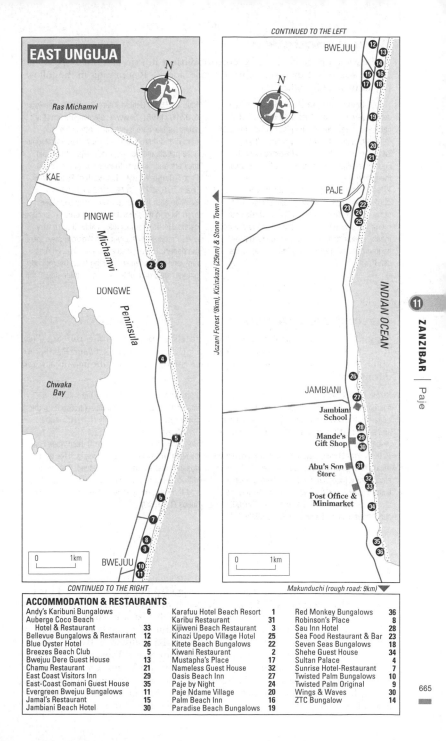

CONTINUED TO THE LEFT

EAST UNGUJA

N

Ras Michamvi

KAE

PINGWE

Michamvi

DONGWE

Peninsula

Chwaka
Bay

0   1km

BWEJUU

CONTINUED TO THE RIGHT

BWEJUU

N

Jozani Forest (8km), Kizinkazi (25km) & Stone Town

PAJE

INDIAN OCEAN

JAMBIANI

Jambiani
School

Mande's
Gift Shop

Abu's Son
Store

Post Office &
Minimarket

0   1km

Makunduchi (rough road: 9km)

11 ZANZIBAR | Paje

ACCOMMODATION & RESTAURANTS

Andy's Karibuni Bungalows	6	Karafuu Hotel Beach Resort	1	Red Monkey Bungalows	36
Auberge Coco Beach		Karibu Restaurant	31	Robinson's Place	8
Hotel & Restaurant	33	Kijiweni Beach Restaurant	3	Sau Inn Hotel	28
Bellevue Bungalows & Restaurant	12	Kinazi Upepo Village Hotel	25	Sea Food Restaurant & Bar	23
Blue Oyster Hotel	26	Kitete Beach Bungalows	22	Seven Seas Bungalows	18
Breezes Beach Club	5	Kiwani Restaurant	2	Shehe Guest House	34
Bwejuu Dere Guest House	13	Mustapha's Place	17	Sultan Palace	4
Chamu Restaurant	21	Nameless Guest House	32	Sunrise Hotel-Restaurant	7
East Coast Visitors Inn	29	Oasis Beach Inn	27	Twisted Palm Bungalows	10
East-Coast Gomani Guest House	35	Paje by Night	24	Twisted Palm Original	9
Evergreen Bwejuu Bungalows	11	Paje Ndame Village	20	Wings & Waves	30
Jamal's Restaurant	15	Palm Beach Inn	16	ZTC Bungalow	14
Jambiani Beach Hotel	30	Paradise Beach Bungalows	19		

Accommodation

There's not a huge choice of **accommodation** in Paje, and not all places are on the beach (see the map on p.665 for locations). Room rates in the following all include breakfast.

Kinazi Upepo Village Hotel Facing the beach next to *Hotel Paje by Night* ☎024/224 0151. A calm and breezy locally run place beside the palm-fringed beach, with five large rooms all with Zanzibari beds, showers and Western-style toilets. Food is available. Good value if you can bargain them down. ❹

Kitete Beach Bungalows On the beach ☎024/224 0226, ✉kitete@hotmail.com. This place has six clean rooms (all with private bathroom; three with kitchens), and reasonably priced meals, snorkelling trips and a cardphone (lads hang around with cards; pay them by the units used). ❹

Paje by Night Behind *Kitete Beach Bungalows* ☎0741/211981, ⊛www.pajebynight.com. The excellent bar here is the main attraction (see below) and there's also a good restaurant. Rooms have private bathrooms; rates depend how big they are and whether there's hot water. ❹–❺

Paje Ndame Village 2km north of Paje on the beach ☎024/224 0179, ✉rukiandame @yahoo.com. The rooms here have sea views even though they're set back in a grove of coconut palms. Horrible lampshades aside, they're very comfortable, with shower and Western-style toilet (no paper). There's also a bar and seafood restaurant, and expensive snorkelling trips. Overpriced, but you should be able to bargain them down. ❹

Eating and drinking

Most of Paje's **restaurants** are in the hotels – exceptions are the *Sea Food Restaurant & Bar* and a number of local places of which, *Chamu Restaurant*, 500m south of *Paje Ndame Village*, comes recommended (though it's closed during Ramadan).

Kitete Beach Bungalows Good home-cooked seafood and continental dishes eaten outside at tables with sea views. Choose from light lunches and snacks (Tsh1500) or a set three-course dinner (Tsh4000).

Paje by Night One of Zanzibar's best bars, with good music, strange herbal smells, a laid-back feel and a small library. Meals are good too, blending international cuisine like pizzas with Swahili fare, and there's always a vegetarian option. Lunch costs Tsh3000, and a three-course dinner goes for Tsh6500.

Paje Ndame Village Nothing but fish and seafood, but superb for all that. Choose from the small menu chalked up daily (Tsh2500–4000). There's also a bar.

Sea Food Restaurant & Bar Behind *Hotel Paje by Night*. A wooden shack which, despite its name, doesn't offer all that much seafood. Still, the fish with coconut rice and spinach is good (Tsh3500), and they also do spaghetti (Tsh3200) and lots of soups (Tsh1500).

Bwejuu

Three kilometres north of Paje along the graded but still bumpy road is the even smaller village of **BWEJUU**. The beach north of here is highly rated, as you can tell from the string of bungalow hotels that back it. The tide heads out a long way here, meaning that there's no swimming at low tide, though there are some excellent snorkelling spots within walking distance. Bwejuu is covered by at least three daily #9 **daladalas** from Stone Town (9am, 11am & 1.30pm), which all pass through Paje; make sure you're not on one going to Jambiani or you'll have to walk from Paje. The ride takes just over an hour. When leaving Bwejuu, the first daladala passes through at 6.30am, the last at around 5pm. For information on minibus transfers from Stone Town, see p.664.

Accommodation

There's a huge choice of **accommodation** – including one or two truly excellent choices – and most are reasonably priced. Breakfast is usually included in room rates. Camping, though technically illegal on Zanzibar, should be possible at *Andy's Karibuni Bungalows* or *Evergreen Bwejuu Bungalows*. There are no fixed prices, but a pitch shouldn't be more than $5 per person. Distances given below assume *Bwejuu Dere Guest House* to be the centre of the village. See map on p.665.

Andy's Karibuni Bungalows 3km north of the village ☎0747/414371 or 0742/740037, ⓔmakupenda@bluemall.ch. Run by a charming Hungarian woman, this simple, laid-back place on a sandy beachside plot has seven bungalows (all with showers and Western-style toilets) sleeping two to seven people each. The food, cooked to order, is exquisite. ❹

Bellevue Bungalows & Restaurant 500m north of the village ☎0744/328361 or 0747/423103, ⓔbellevue01@hotmail.com. A friendly, locally owned place on a hill on the land side of the road, with good views and the beach just a minute away. The four rooms in two bungalows (more planned) come with private bathrooms, big heavy beds and nets. There's good food, too, and a variety of activities on offer including sailing trips by *ngalawa*. ❹

Bwejuu Dere Guest House Village centre ☎024/224 0068. Three lacklustre but cheap guest houses in one, set back from the beach. Rooms are cleanish but small and only worth it if you're on a strict budget (hence its popularity with backpackers) ❸

Evergreen Bwejuu Bungalows 800m north of the village ☎0747/416932, ⓔzanzievergreen@yahoo.com. The beachfront plot is the best thing here, though the accommodation, in four bungalows with private bathrooms, is good value. Food available. ❹

Mustapha's Place Under 1km south of the village ☎024/224 0069, ⓦwww.fatflatfish.co.uk/mustaphas. A long-established and very welcoming place run by local rasta Mustapha and his family, on the land side of the road. Accommodation is in several coral-walled thatched-roof *bandas* set in beautiful gardens, and the bar is as good a place as any to learn African drumming. ❹–❺

Palm Beach Inn 400m south of the village ☎024/224 0221 or 0747/411155, ⓔmahfudh28@hotmail.com. An intimate clutter of buildings beside the beach, well run and with good service. Rooms have a/c, hot showers and *semadari* beds, and there's a large bar, expensive restaurant and inexpensive excursions. Big discounts in low season. ❺

Paradise Beach Bungalows 1.6km south of the village ☎024/223 1387, ⓔsaori@cats-net.com. Next to the beach in a grove of coconut palms, this is one of the nicest places on the east coast and is famed for its excellent food. The seven Swahili-styled bedrooms, all with showers and toilets, have sea views, and facilities include a bar, a good library and dhow trips (Tsh4000). Bicycles and snorkelling equipment are available. Recommended. ❹

Robinson's Place 1.3km north of the village ☎0747/413479 (evenings only), ⓔrobinsonsplace@hotmail.com. A small, whimsical and highly recommended place run by a Zanzibari–European couple. There are only four rooms (so book well ahead), all equally eclectic in design, though the best is at the top of a two-storey Robinson Crusoe-style house by the beach. Facilities are shared, but are very clean, while the lack of electricity is billed as an attraction (lighting is by kerosene lamps). Meals are limited to a sumptuous breakfast and dinner (guests only; around Tsh5000). ❻

Sunrise Hotel-Restaurant 2km north of the village ☎ & ⓕ0741/320206, ⓦwww.sunrise-zanzibar.com. A cheerfully offbeat choice with a friendly, unfussy atmosphere and a swimming pool. The restaurant is one of the best round here, while the accommodation is all self-contained, and good value, especially rooms in the bungalows facing the beautiful beach. The usual range of tours can be arranged. No single rates. ❻

Twisted Palm Bungalows 800m north of the village ☎0747/418213, ⓔerwinfink@gmx.net. A German-run place that pinched its name from the original *Twisted Palm* (see below), with nine self-contained bungalows and a restaurant and bar on an open-sided first-floor terrace. The diving school offers tuition, but wasn't registered with PADI at the time of writing. ❹

Twisted Palm Original 1.2km north of the village; no phone. Overlooking the beach, this enjoys a good reputation with backpackers, with good food and friendly management. The rooms are getting run down, however, and the plot is largely shadeless. ❹

ZTC Bungalow On the beach next to *Bwejuu Dere Guest House* (bookings through the Zanzibar Commission for Tourism; see p.618). This contains four of Zanzibar's cheapest hotel rooms located in a single building on the beach. The rooms are basic (toilet and bathroom are shared), though they do have electricity and nets, but there's no food or any other facilities. ❷–❸

Eating and drinking

Most of Bwejuu's **restaurants** are attached to hotels, and some are outstandingly good. For your own supplies, try Mbochwe Minimarket on the main road south of *Palm Beach Inn*.

Andy's Karibuni Bungalows Superb Hungarian cooking plus Zanzibari delights in a laid-back venue. The speciality is *lecso*, a Hungarian stew with onion, tomato, chili, garlic and spices. Full meals around Tsh5000.

Bellevue Bungalows & Restaurant Another good place for home cooking, with good seafood (full meals around Tsh5000) and freshly roasted coffee (natural, spiced or laced with ginger).

Bwejuu Dere Guest House A fairly average if cheap restaurant, plus a more attractive beer garden behind the main building with drinkers' favourites like grilled goat meat and bananas. Closed Ramadan.

Jamal's Restaurant Opposite the *Palm Beach Inn*. A not-so-cheap local place capitalizing on the tourist trade. Seafood dishes cost around Tsh3000, chicken up to Tsh4000, and they also do old favourites like spaghetti. Beer available. Closed daytime during Ramadan.

Mustapha's Place. A great option for drinks or meals, with lunch (Tsh3000) and candlelit dinners (Tsh4000) featuring fresh seafood (fantastic octopus). Mellow jam sessions some nights.

Palm Beach Inn This has a big, cluttered bar and pricey restaurant (over Tsh20,000 for a half lob-ster), though specialities like duck (Tsh7000) and dikdik steaks (Tsh5000) are more reasonable. Order at least two hours in advance.

Paradise Beach Bungalows An unusual and good mix of Swahili and Japanese cuisine, and excellent value at around Tsh3000 for lunch or Tsh4500 for a three-course dinner (the menu changes daily). The Japanese food is especially recommended, and there's also a small bar.

Seven Seas Bungalows This is Bwejuu's main local bar, where the cheerful proceedings are helped along by the manager's own predilection for the amber nectar. There's good food (Tsh2000–2500) and snacks, too, and they also have nine clean rooms (❹) if you can't find your way home.

Sunrise Hotel-Restaurant Quirky surroundings to suit an attractively quirky menu, covering seafood plus unusual treats like gazpacho and an acclaimed chocolate mousse. They also do sandwiches and have a nice wine list.

Twisted Palm Bungalows Mainly seafood and some unexciting continental dishes. Prices are a reasonable Tsh3000–4000 for mains or Tsh6000 for a beach barbecue. The bar is on the open-sided first floor of the main house.

Michamvi Peninsula

North of Bwejuu the road deteriorates as you head up **Michamvi Peninsula**, the last of the bungalows giving way to coral rag thickets, a scatter of tiny settlements and a handful of large, expensive holiday resorts dealing mainly with pre-booked package holidays. If you're happy to forgo local authenticity for pampered service and all mod cons, these hotels are worth considering. **Public transport** is scarce beyond Bwejuu, but there are at least two daily #9 daladalas going all the way to Michamvi, 13km from Bwejuu, that can drop you off at hotel entrances. Schedules are unpredictable, but at the time of writing one left Stone Town at 1.30pm, passing through Bwejuu about an hour later. The easiest method is to cycle; bikes can be rented at most of Bwejuu's hotels.

Accommodation

A couple of Italian all-inclusive places, *Pongwe Blue Marlin* and *Club Vacanza/Dongwe Village*, need to be prebooked in Europe and have not been reviewed. All the following are shown on the map on p.665.

Breezes Beach Club Dongwe ☎0741/326595, ⓦwww.breezes-zanzibar.com. Upmarket beach resort with tons of activities, high standards and a stylish and intimate ambience. Rooms are spacious, with all mod cons, and facilities include the Rising Sun Dive Centre (see box, below), a huge swimming pool, massage parlour, internet services and restaurants, plus African dance classes and evening entertainment. Credit cards accepted. Half-board low ❼, high ❽–❾

Karafuu Beach Resort Towards the end of the peninsula ☎0741/325157, ⓦwww.karafuu hotel.com. Occupying seven hectares of previously untouched coastal thicket, this Italian package resort boasts a wide range of expensive activities; rooms are very average for the price. Half-board low ❼–❽, high ❾

Sultan Palace North of *Club Vacanza* and its pier ☎024/224 0173, ⓦwww.sultanzanzibar.com. Overlooking a narrow beach, this is small for a "palace", but its standards of service and architecture are suitably sultanic and the fifteen idiosyncratically designed rooms are spacious and have everything you'd expect for the price (though only eight have sea views). Meals – mainly Swahili and Mediterranean – can be taken on the beach or one of the secluded terraces in the main building. Closed April and May. Full board only ❾

Eating and drinking

For upmarket dining try the hotels; much cheaper are a couple of idyllically located *hotelis* on the beach south of the *Karafuu Beach Resort*.

Kijiweni Beach Restaurant On a small, breezy coral outcrop facing *Kiwani Restaurant*, about 3m above sea level (at high tide you wade out to it), this has one of the nicest locations in Tanzania. Dishes are well priced: potato masala for Tsh2500, octopus or grilled fish for Tsh3000 and lobster for around Tsh10,000. Order at least two hours in advance. No alcohol; closed Ramadan lunchtimes.

Kiwani Restaurant 2km south of the *Karafuu Beach Resort*. Small but enticing menu (order a few hours ahead), mainly rice with fish (Tsh3500), prawns (Tsh6500) or lobster (Tsh8000). They don't usually have drinks, so bring your own. Closed Ramadan lunchtimes.

Diving off Unguja's east coast

The entire east coast is fringed by a long barrier reef: the shallow coral gardens inside the lagoon offer ideal conditions for novices, while deeper reefs outside the barrier attract more experienced divers (but can only be attempted in calm weather). The east coast is good for dolphins and turtles, the latter especially at **Turtle Garden** which also hosts giant eels, triggerfish and puffers. Other good reefs include **Stingray Alley** off Jambiani, where hundreds of blue-spotted stingrays have been reported, and the exquisite corals at **Unicorn Reef**. For trips, contact one of the following.

Paje East Coast Dive Centre, next to *Kitete Beach Bungalows*, Paje ☎024/224 0191 or 0741/607436, ⓔpajediving@zanzinet.com. No tuition and apparently lacking PADI accreditation – one for qualified divers only.

Profondo Blu, *Karafuu Beach Resort*, Pingwe. Proficient if overpriced, but with high standards and courses at all levels.

Rising Sun Dive Centre, *Breezes Beach Club*, Bwejuu ☎0742/750841, ⓦwww.risingsun-zanzibar.com. Highly experienced, well-equipped and with solid safety standards, offering one of Zanzibar's most exhaustive Open Water courses as well as tuition up to Divemaster. They also offer "exploration" and night dives.

Kae

The road west of the *Karafuu Beach Resort* becomes exceedingly rocky as it heads 2km towards the village of Pingwe, the entrance to which is marked by a grove of coconut palms. There's nothing to see in Pingwe, and the few tourists who come here generally continue to the beach and tiny settlement at **KAE**, one kilometre further on, which looks west over the bay towards Chwaka and Uroa, on the eastern shore of Chwaka Bay. There are some coconut palms here, a few huts and even fewer people, so it can be quite a trial finding someone to open one of the two **restaurants** at the end of the road. *Kae Restaurant*, in a palm- and banana-thatch hut, offers snorkelling and mangrove trips as well as local food, whilst *Makwega's Beach Restaurant* facing it also offers sailing. There's no accommodation, but **camping** may be tolerated – ask at *Makwega's*. Both places need at least an hour or two to prepare food, assuming that anyone's actually there.

The handful of travellers who do come here generally do so to catch a **boat to Chwaka**, avoiding a lengthy detour by road. The thirty-minute crossing is by local fishing boat, one or two of which venture across every day. Inevitably, anyone not totally fluent in Kiswahili pays far above local rates, and you'll have to bargain hard – anywhere close to Tsh3000 per person is a good price. Finding a boat is generally a matter of arriving early and asking around; the first generally pushes off around 7am, and returns before sunset. Forget the "ferry" marked on some maps: it doesn't exist.

Alternatively, you could try **renting** an entire boat (up to 20 passengers): this costs Tsh15,000–30,000, depending on your perceived wealth. **Transport** to Pingwe and Kae by daladala is possible, though timings are uncertain. There are usually a couple of #9 daladalas each day from Stone Town, one of which leaves the capital at 1.30pm (two others, which sometimes head up beyond Bwejuu, leave at 9am and 11am). The cost is Tsh700 though as a tourist you may be charged more. Heading back, vehicles leave at noon and 4pm, but don't bank on any of this – and be prepared for a long walk to a hotel if you get stranded.

Jambiani

The long stretch of beach at **JAMBIANI**, 5km south of Paje, possesses a wild, windy and fascinating beauty. The fringing reef lies several kilometres out and the intervening area is a mix of sandbanks, coral reefs and shallow water, which at low tide can turn up a surprising variety of marine life. The people of Jambiani have long been involved in **fishing**, and at times dozens of *ngalawa* fishing boats are moored together just off shore, while in the evenings there's the joyous spectacle of young boys racing after their handmade model dhows, painstakingly made from sandals or bits of wood with plastic bags for sails. It's the community feeling of Jambiani that makes it special, something worth exploring further through the highly recommended **local cultural tourism programme**, which offers visits to traditional herbalists, seaweed farms and a sacred local cave.

Walking north or south of Jambiani beach, you'll see strange rock mounds at the water line. Called *maviko ya makumbi*, these contain **coconut husks**, which are buried for three to six months for softening (salt water deters rot), then beaten to separate the fibre, which is used to make rope (*coir*). Another local produce is **seaweed** (*mwani*), one of Zanzibar's biggest foreign-exchange earners, with farms along the east coast. Seaweed farming was introduced to Jambiani over a decade ago as an income-generating project for local women, for whom it has brought a measure of financial independence in what is a very male-dominated society. The seaweed is "planted" by tying it to ropes that are then staked in rows in the shallow intertidal zone of the lagoons, before being harvested and dried for a week, when it turns beautiful shades of russet, purple, green, mustard and blue.

Arrival, information and accommodation

The tourist **minibuses** take about ninety minutes to cover the 56km from Stone Town; #9 **daladalas** take two to three hours, and leave Stone Town at 9am, noon, 1pm and at 2pm or 3pm. As always, double-check the destination when you board. The daladalas return to Stone Town at 6am, 7am, 10am and 3pm. The **post office/minimarket** (daily 6am–10pm) on the main road opposite *Karibu Restaurant* rents out bicycles, as does *Abu's Son Store*, also on the main road. For **changing money**, *East Coast Visitors Inn* should oblige; they can also change travellers' cheques, but it's best to change money in Stone Town in case the hotel lacks cash. **Internet access** is available at the *East Coast Visitors Inn* (Tsh1500 per 15min) and at Jambiani Secondary School, 1.5km south of the post office (Mon–Thurs 8am–1pm & 3–6pm, Fri 8am–noon & 3–6pm, Sat & Sun 2–5pm, Tsh1500 per 30min, which goes to the school).

When choosing a room, note that **hotels** on the northern part of the beach are pretty isolated from most of the bars and restaurants. All the following are shown on the map on p.665.

Auberge Coco Beach Hotel & Restaurant ℡024/224 0246 or 0747/414254, ℮cocobeach @zitec.org. A recommended place right on the beach, with eight fresh and comfortable rooms in individual thatched bungalows, all with sea views and private bathrooms. There's also an excellent restaurant. Credit cards accepted. No single rates. ④

Blue Oyster Hotel ℡ & ℱ024/224 0163, ⓦwww.zanzibar.de. An architecturally clumsy two-storey affair, but good value nonetheless, with friendly and efficient service and ten clean rooms, five with private bathroom. They can also arrange cheap and reliable excursions, and there's a restaurant and bar on the ocean-facing terrace. ④

East Coast Visitors Inn ℡024/224 0150, ℮eastcoastinn@allaboutzanzibar.com. An upmarket but very affordable set-up offering thirty self-contained rooms in beach bungalows and twelve cheaper rooms sharing bathrooms in a guest house set back from the beach. The rooms are well kept and there's a large open-sided restaurant and bar offering reasonable if unexciting food, internet access (Tsh1500 per 15min) and various activities. ④

Jambiani Beach Hotel ℡024/224 0155, ℱ024/223 4165. The main building on this sandy plot wouldn't win any design awards, and the ten

rooms are run down, though still acceptable, each with a private terrace and Western-style toilet. There's a restaurant and bike rental too. ④

Nameless Guest House (contact the *Auberge Coco Beach*) Jambiani's cheapest establishment by far with just three, basic but clean rooms and shared bathrooms. Their shop on the beach sells souvenirs including *kangas* and soapstone. ②

Oasis Beach Inn ℡024/224 0259, ℮kishukaissaman@yahoo.com. Jambiani's best-value hotel, with lovely beachfront views, a friendly welcome, a good selection of rooms and an equally good beach bar and restaurant. ②–③

Red Monkey Bungalows ℡024/224 0207. On a small breezy beach plot, this place has five doubles with private bathrooms in individual bungalows, and a standard restaurant (no alcohol). No single rates, though bargaining is possible. ④

Sau Inn Hotel ℡024/224 0169 or ℡ & ℱ0741/337440, ℮sau-inn@cats-net.com. This medium-sized resort is the only place with a swimming pool (Tsh4000 for day guests), and also the only place on the east coast where you're likely to get bothered by beach boys. The 27 rooms in thatched cottages have spotless bathrooms and most overlook the pool. Facilities include a bar and restaurant, and a telephone, fax and email service (but no internet). ⑥

Shehe Guest House ☎024/224 0149. This place has a great view from its first-floor bar and restaurant, and the rooms, in a row of cottages facing the ocean, are fine and have bathrooms. Good value if you can bargain the price down. ❹

Jambiani Cultural Village Tour

Zanzibar's first cultural tourism programme, the **Jambiani Cultural Village Tour**, was recently set up with the help of the NGO Eco+Culture. Part of a wider effort to establish small-scale community-run development projects, the village tour offers a highly recommended half-day diversion, exploring aspects of local life and culture, something that is lamentably lacking in so many other tourist areas in East Africa. Part of the $5 fee goes into a village development fund to finance primary healthcare, a children's nursery and various educational projects.

The **tour** itself is guided by the local co-ordinator, Kassim Mande, who fills you in on Jambiani's history before taking you round a subsistence farm; to a *mganga* (herbalist) to learn the medicinal uses of various herbs and plants; and on to a seaweed farm. There's also the option of visiting a sacred limestone cave (*kumbi*). The exact itinerary is flexible and is determined by your interests. The project's Jambiani **office** (open daily) is at Mande's Gift Shop, 100m north of the *Jambiani Beach Hotel* on the main road. The shop stocks a small selection of curios, including spices and essential oils. For further information and reservations for day-trips from Stone Town ($18–45 per person depending on group size), contact Eco+Culture Tours (see p.646).

⑪

Eating and drinking

There are a lot of **restaurants** to choose from, and not just in the hotels, so prices are keen by Zanzibari standards.

Auberge Coco Beach Hotel & Restaurant A calm and breezy bar-restaurant with a sophisticated menu and daily specials and snacks for under Tsh2000. The bar has a good range of spirits and liqueurs.

East-Coast Gomani Guest House A good range of cheap and filling dishes, with fish of the day for Tsh2500 and grilled lobster in lemon butter for Tsh8000. There's a nice view of the ocean. Order an hour in advance; no alcohol.

East Coast Visitors Inn Reasonable value if you choose carefully, with some mouthwatering dishes like banana fritters (Tsh1000), marinated prawns in coconut sauce and a large number of crab and jumbo prawn dishes for Tsh3000–4000. They also do milk shakes.

Karibu Restaurant 500m north of *Shehe Guest House*. Fast becoming a Jambiani institution, everything here is literally home-cooked (the restaurant is in a family home). The food – all local Swahili dishes – is good as well as cheap: drop by a good few hours before you dine to discuss what you'd like to eat.

Kimte Beach Inn This place has an unusual menu including roast dikdik and mocha cake in chocolate sauce, plus cheap snacks and alcohol.

Red Monkey Bungalows A pretty standard menu with most mains around Tsh4000 and daily specials for Tsh2500. Soups go for Tsh1200, and pizzas under Tsh3000. Alcohol available.

Sau Inn Hotel A breezy restaurant and bar with a sea view and a choice of seafood, continental or Zanzibari, ranging from Tsh4000–5000, and there are occasional "Swahili Night" buffets for Tsh8000.

Shehe Guest House The first-floor open-front bar enjoys a fantastic view over the beach and lagoon. The limited choice of dishes should be ordered well in advance, and range from average to excellent depending on who's cooking.

Wings & Waves *Jambiani Beach Hotel*. Unlike many extensive menus, most of the stuff on this one is actually available, so long as you give them at least an hour's notice. Aside from the usual favourites (fish, pizzas and lobster) choose from lesser-known dishes like dikdik in masala (Tsh3500) or coconut-crusted fish with mango "combat" (compote), also at Tsh3500.

Northeast Unguja

Following the abolition of the East African slave trade by a reluctant Sultan Barghash in 1873, a number of places along the remote **northeast coast** of Unguja – especially Chwaka Bay, Uroa and Pongwe – saw use as illegal slaving ports, continuing the trade with the Seychelles and French Indian Ocean possessions. Much of the coast retains an attractively isolated feel, in spite of the road connecting it with Stone Town, and for the most part sees few tourists.

As you approach from the west, the vegetation becomes scrubbier, with coconut palms, baobabs and thorny thickets replacing the lush spice plantations of the interior, before giving way to a broad swath of fine white sand backed by a line of waving palm trees and the turquoise expanse of the Indian Ocean. The main **beaches**, from south to north, are Chwaka, Uroa, Pongwe, Kiwengwa, Pwani Mchangani and Matemwe. The sheltered coves of Pongwe and the sprawling expanse of sand at Matemwe are especially beautiful, whilst for a really local feel, Chwaka, Uroa and Pwani Mchangani are recommended. The unfortunate exception is Kiwengwa, where a number of huge all-inclusive package resorts have blighted one of the most beautiful stretches of beach on Unguja. All these places have accommodation, and whilst the choice isn't huge, there's enough to suit all tastes and pockets. A host of **activities** are offered by most of the larger hotels, including reef walks, sailing and water sports, while **snorkelling** gear can be rented locally and is superb in the shallow intertidal waters. **Scuba-divers** will find their nirvana on the northeast coast, especially off Matemwe which has three dive centres and easy access to exhilarating diving reefs around Mnemba Atoll (see p.680)

Daladalas serve all these places, but for getting around there's nothing better than hiring a bicycle and heading off along the beach, which serves as a highway for locals. Bikes are also ideal for getting to the ruins of **Dunga Palace**, the last seat of the traditional rulers of Zanzibar.

Stone Town to Chwaka

There are a couple of places worth visiting along the road from Stone Town to Chwaka: the ruins of **Dunga Palace**, and the delightful **Ufufuma Forest**, which, like Jozani, gives visitors the chance of spotting red colobus monkeys.

Dunga Palace

Nineteen kilometres east of Stone Town (#6 and #14 daladalas) lie the ruins of **Dunga Palace**, a pleasant stop to or from the coast. Apart from its sense of history, the site offers views over much of the island, and the overgrown garden is an attraction in itself, with some beautiful Indian almond trees (*mkungu*). Unlike Unguja's other palaces, which were built by the Omani sultanate, Dunga was the last seat of the traditional rulers of Unguja, the **Wawinyi Wakuu**. Oral tradition links the Wawinyi Wakuu to Shirazi settlers from Persia who arrived over 1000 years ago and with whom Unguja's original inhabitants intermarried to create the Hadimu tribe. The ruling dynasty's family name of al-Alawi, however, suggests roots in the Filal district of Saudi Arabia, where Morocco's present-day royal family also originated.

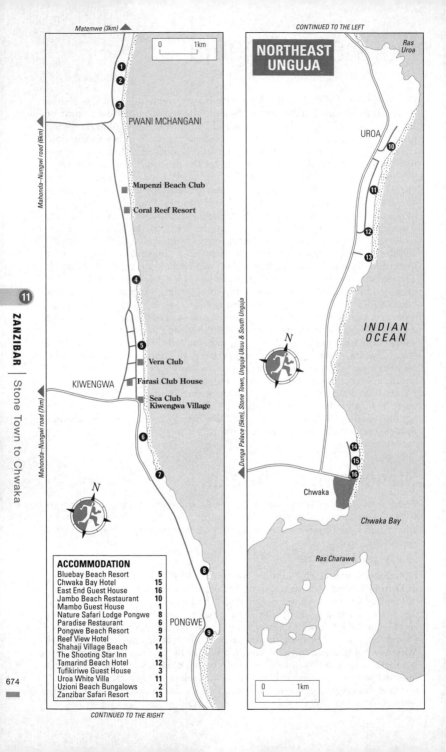

0   1km

PWANI MCHANGANI

Mapenzi Beach Club

Coral Reef Resort

Vera Club

Farasi Club House

Sea Club
Kiwengwa Village

KIWENGWA

ZANZIBAR | Stone Town to Chwaka

11

Mahonda–Nungwi road (8km)

Mahonda–Nungwi road (7km)

N

ACCOMMODATION
Bluebay Beach Resort	5
Chwaka Bay Hotel	15
East End Guest House	16
Jambo Beach Restaurant	10
Mambo Guest House	1
Nature Safari Lodge Pongwe	8
Paradise Restaurant	6
Pongwe Beach Resort	9
Reef View Hotel	7
Shahaji Village Beach	14
The Shooting Star Inn	4
Tamarind Beach Hotel	12
Tufikiriwe Guest House	3
Uroa White Villa	11
Uzioni Beach Bungalows	2
Zanzibar Safari Resort	13

PONGWE

674

Ras
Uroa

NORTHEAST UNGUJA

UROA

Dunga Palace (5km), Stone Town, Unguja Ukuu & South Unguja

N

INDIAN
OCEAN

Chwaka

Chwaka Bay

Ras Charawe

0   1km

The **palace** was built early in the nineteenth century by Hassan bin Ahmad al-Alawi, whose rule coincided with the gradual usurpation of his power by the Omani Sultan Seyyid Said in Stone Town, who demanded tribute from the Alawi in return for "protection". Nonetheless, Alawi retained the right to dispense justice over and collect taxes from his African subjects, and despite the curtailing of his powers, remained far from impoverished, as can be seen at Dunga. The **palace**, built around a central courtyard, originally had two storeys and a rooftop garden, and its windows were fitted with stained glass, now exhibited in the House of Wonders.

Excavations in the 1920s turned up drums and horns – traditional emblems of power along the Swahili coast. The excavations also revealed a well half filled with human skeletons, possibly the victims of an archaic belief that mixing blood with mortar would ensure the solidity of a building's foundations. Dunga's victims may have been killed when the palace was fortified under the rule of Muhammad bin Ahmad al-Alawi (1845–65). The Wawinyi Wakuu remained important enough to justify the clearing of the road from Stone Town to Dunga during the reign of Sultan Majid (1857-70) so that the Sultan's stagecoach – a gift from Queen Victoria to Sultan Seyyid Said – could pass through.

Muhammad bin Ahmad al-Alawi died in 1865 at the age of 80 and was succeeded by his son, Ahmad bin Muhammad al-Alawi. Ahmad was jailed by Sultan Barghash in 1871, allegedly for tyranny, and died of smallpox two years later without leaving an heir, marking the end of the Wawinyi Wakuu. The palace was demolished in 1910, and the ruins you see now – low walls, archways, stone staircases and some pillars – are mostly the product of a 1994 reconstruction.

Ufufuma Forest

Five kilometres west of Chwaka is the locally managed **Ufufuma Forest**, harbouring a small population of red colobus monkeys (see p.658), dikdiks, impala and a rich variety of birdlife. There are also a number of sacred caves that are used by locals – along with ancestral spirits, they're also home to colonies of bats. The forest is run by EPUJE (Environmental Protection of Ufufuma/Jendele), whom you should contact before coming to be sure of finding someone there. Write to PO Box 1861, Zanzibar, or contact Mustafa Makame (✆himanje@yahoo.com), Hussein Ame Njuma (☎0747/423255), or Sama Tours in Stone Town (see p.646). The $6 entry fee includes a guided walk, seasonal fruits and other refreshments.

The forests near Chwaka provided the last evidence for the existence of the **Zanzibar leopard** (*Panthera pardus adersi*). Once used by Zanzibari witchdoctors in ceremonies, this nocturnal animal was last seen in the 1970s, and since prints, droppings and a suspected den were discovered near Chwaka in 1994, no trace has been found, leading to the sad conclusion that the Zanzibar leopard is now extinct.

Chwaka

The largest settlement on the northeast coast is **CHWAKA**, a fishing village on the west shore of the wide mangrove-fringed Chwaka Bay. The village receives few visitors (there are only three hotels), which means that you're likely to be the only tourist here – and the centre of attention for dozens of excitable kids. Apart from men and women out on the shallow sandbanks and exposed reefs collecting shellfish and octopus, the beach is largely deserted. Although swimming is impossible at low tide, this is the best time to see the waders and other birds that feed on the plentiful shellfish hidden just beneath the sands. Sunrise over Michamvi Peninsula on the other side of the bay is always special, and there are few if any mosquitoes thanks to a sturdy sea breeze.

Apart from the beach and the bay, the open-air **market** at the end of the road on the shore is another attraction. A quiet place for much of the day, it becomes lively at high tide and in late afternoon, when the fishermen pull up in their *ngalawa* outriggers to sell the day's catch. To the north of the market, beside a compound of holiday homes, is a cluster of men weaving wicker lobster pots, while to the south of the market, 100m beyond an enormous baobab tree, wooden dhows continue to be made using traditional methods.

A worthwhile **excursion** from Chwaka is to the mangrove forests that line much of its bay, combined with a boat trip through the twisting maze of channels and a walk to inspect local wildlife, especially crabs. *Shahaji Village Beach* (see below) can arrange day-trips for around $30 including *ngalawa* outrigger for up to seven people; otherwise, hire a boat and guide at the fish market.

Practicalities

Chwaka lies 32km east of Stone Town along fast tarmac. **Daladalas** on routes #6 and #14 pass by Chwaka, leaving Zanzibar Town roughly every hour from 4am to 7pm; they depart from Mwembe Ladu and Amani Stadium respectively – to get to either from Stone Town's Creek Road terminus, catch a route "A" daladala. Check beforehand whether the vehicle actually goes into Chwaka as some only stop at the junction 1km west before heading north to Uroa or Pongwe. Details on boats across Chwaka Bay from Michamvi are given on p.670.

Chwaka has three **hotels**, including a modest beach resort. All three can arrange food. There are also a couple of basic *mgahawas* (tea houses serving simple meals) in the area behind the market; you'll need to ask directions as they lack signs.

Chwaka Bay Hotel 500m north of the market; fork left after 200m or follow the beach (reservations through *Tembo House Hotel* in Stone Town, p.623). Recently reopened, this large hotel is set on broad seaside plot with access to a lovely beach. The ten clean, self-contained rooms are on a raised area set well back from the beach. Facilities are limited to a bar, a cavernous restaurant and a new swimming pool. Excursions to Kizimkazi and Jozani Forest can be arranged. ❺

East End Guest House & Restaurant 300m north of the market next to the derelict *You Stay House* hotel (no sign) ☎0741/320267. A peaceful, basic place facing the bay with three rooms with private bathroom in two functional bungalows set back from the beach (no sea views), each with two beds, nets, reliable cold water and clean squat loos but no electricity. Food to order. ❸

Shahaji Village Beach & Restaurant Formerly *Raha Beach*, 500m beyond *Chwaka Bay Hotel*. Two rooms in two bungalows, with attached shower (cold water) and clean squat loos, but no electricity. The views across the bay from the terraces are the main draw. Food needs to be ordered well in advance and can be bland. Haggle to avoid the inflated starting prices. ❸

Uroa and Pongwe

About 9km north of Chwaka is the spread-out village of **UROA**. The welcoming cries of "Jambo" from excited toddlers are more appealing than the village itself, but the beach, albeit bleak and windswept at times, is certainly refreshing. Despite some modest hotel developments, life for the villagers continues as it always has, with fishing, seaweed collection and some cultivation comprising the main livelihoods. **Getting to** Uroa, take one of the hourly #6 or #14 daladalas from Zanzibar Town, which leave from Mwembe Ladu and Amani Stadium respectively; to get to either from Stone Town's Creek Road terminus, catch a route "A" daladala. Several **hotels** – all with restaurants – are spread along the coastline; see the map on p.674.

Jambo Beach Restaurant 500m north of Uroa village; follow the signs for *Jambopoa*. Highly recommended locally run place on a lovely stretch of beach. At the time of writing, two of a planned ten basic but beautiful beach bungalows had been built – all are made from natural materials like banana thatch and coir rope (shared bathrooms only). There's also a good restaurant, snorkelling equipment is available, and boat trips can be arranged. Evenings see occasional performances of traditional music. ❸

Tamarind Beach Hotel 1.5km south of Uroa village, follow the signs for *Uroa White Villa* ☎ 024/223 7154 or 0747/413709, ⓦwww.tamarind.nu. An informal and remarkably good-value resort-style hotel, with fourteen clean rooms (all with private bathroom) in attractive stone cottages, each with a small roof terrace. The gardens adjoin the beach, and there's a breezy bar and restaurant. Snorkelling trips available. ❹

Uroa White Villa In the centre close to Uroa Primary Health Care Unit; follow the signs ☎ 0741/326874, ⓔmwadini@zitec.org. A modern, German-run place on the beach with comfortable, spotless accommodation (mostly en suite). The licensed restaurant does good Swahili dishes (mains Tsh3600–6000) – the pilau with fresh tuna is especially tasty. Boat trips and snorkelling are available, and there are discounts on rooms if booked ahead. ❸–❻

Zanzibar Safari Resort 2.5km south of Uroa village ☎ 024/223 8553, ⓦwww.zanzibarsafari.co.tz. A friendly, well-run resort with a lovely stretch of beach and activities offered by Mawimbi Watersports (see p.680). The forty rooms have hot water and terraces, and the pool is open to non-guests (Tsh4000 a day). There are two bars and two restaurants, one with sweeping views of the ocean, the other specializing in grills; full meals average $10, and seafood barbecues are sometimes held on the beach. Low ❻, high ❽

Pongwe

The tiny fishing village of **PONGWE** lies at the end of the fifteen-kilometre stretch of road from Chwaka, and 46km from Stone Town. There's nothing much to it, but the beach – a series of small sheltered coves with unbelievably clear water and lots of swaying palm trees – is the stuff of dreams, and unlike the rest of the northeast coast is free of seaweed all year round and deep enough for swimming even at low tide. Some #6 **daladalas** from Mwembe Ladu in Zanzibar Town terminate here after passing through Chwaka and Uroa. More reliable is service #14, which leaves Zanzibar Town's Amani Stadium at 11am, 1pm and 5pm and returns from Pongwe at 6am, 9am and 2pm.

There are two **hotels** in Pongwe, one of them on a beach that's as close to paradise as you're likely to get in this life. Prices are negotiable.

Nature Safari Lodge Pongwe 17km from Chwaka junction ☎ & ⓕ024/223 0462. This is the less attractive and more somnolent of Pongwe's two options, its beach lacking palm trees (though still beautiful) and with slightly dilap-idated en-suite rooms. There's a small bar and overpriced restaurant (mains from Tsh3000). ❹

Pongwe Beach Resort 15km from Chwaka junction ☎ 0747/414134, ⓔfisherman@zanlink.com. If it's a perfect beach you're after, then this is the one. The hotel's not bad either, with ten spacious en-suite rooms. The cheaper beach *bandas* each have three beds and, apart from cement floors, are made entirely from natural materials. There's a bar and restaurant too with a daily menu (meals cost Tsh2500–4000). Highly recommended for its rooms and views, but overpriced for activities. **④–⑤**

Kiwengwa and Pwani Mchangani

As Zanzibar's main package holiday resort, **KIWENGWA** is dominated by enormous all-inclusive resorts catering almost entirely to the Italian package-tour market. The clientele cocooned inside the resorts has little chance to experience Zanzibar, and local sensibilities are too often ignored, while the destructive excesses of development are glaringly apparent – erosion during the rains and a dusty atmosphere in the dry season that have been caused by wholesale land clearance – and typify the environmental and ethical nightmare that awaits other parts of the coast should the Zanzibari government continue to prefer short-term gains from foreign investors to less profitable but sustainable long-term development with local participation. Residents have not remained indifferent to all this, however: two resorts were torched early in 2001 in the aftermath of the government's bloody crackdown on opposition supporters.

That said, there are a handful of other places more in tune with local life; these are reviewed below.

Practicalities

Kiwengwa is 40km northeast of Stone Town along a good road. Route #17 **daladalas** go to Kiwengwa village, the last leaving Stone Town at 4.30pm. If you're heading to *Bluebay Beach Resort* or *The Shooting Star Inn*, get off at *Sea Club Kiwengwa Village* from where you'll have to walk. Alternatively, daladala drivers should be happy to take you directly to the hotel for an extra Tsh2000 or so. *Shooting Star* arranges transfers from the airport or Stone Town for $40 per vehicle; *Blue Bay* charges $25 per person. If you're **driving from Pongwe**, note that the road to Kiwengwa is in a bad state and requires 4WD in some sections. Farasi Club House along the road to *Vera Club* offers **horse riding**. Contact them on ☏0747/413001.

The following are recommended **accommodation** options.

Bluebay Beach Resort ☏024/224 0240, ⓦwww.bluebayzanzibar.com. Similar in size to the all-inclusives, but this slick five-star resort has made efforts to minimize its environmental impact. There's a fine stretch of beach and a range of activities on offer, while accommodation is in 88 luxurious rooms. Water sports and diving are offered here by One Ocean dive centre (see p.000). Half-board low **⑧**, high **⑨**
Paradise Restaurant Behind the school in Kiwengwa village (no sign) ☏0747/415351. Three bungalows with two rooms each, on a scrubby patch of land next to a nice beach with coconut palm trees. The rooms are all doubles with private bathroom. Snorkelling and boat rides can be arranged and food is available (no alcohol). **④**
Reef View Hotel 1.5km south of Kiwengwa at Kumba Urembo ☏0747/413294,

ⓦwww.reefview.com. The southernmost of Kiwengwa's hotels with basic but very good-value accommodation in ten thatched *bandas* with shared bathrooms and sea views through the strange *mikadi* palm trees. Facilities include free canoes for the use of guests, a pleasant bar and a good restaurant: full lunches go for Tsh4000, and the evening buffet costs Tsh5000. **③–④**
The Shooting Star Inn 4km north of Kiwengwa ☏024/223 2926 or 0747/414166, ⓦwww.zanzibar.org/star. Kiwengwa's most romantic option, occupying a cliff top with lovely sea views (the beach is accessed down a steep flight of steps). There are three types of rooms, all attractively furnished and with private bathrooms, plus a free guided walk and an outstanding restaurant (with three daily specials) and well-stocked bar. **④–⑦**

Pwani Mchangani

Heading north from Kiwengwa, the strip of package hotels fizzles out a few kilometres south of **PWANI MCHANGANI** (also called Kwa Pangaa). Despite the proximity of the brash all-inclusives, Pwani Mchangani remains very much a traditional village, surviving on fishing, coconut cultivation and the farming of seaweed, which you'll see hung out to dry everywhere. The village sees few visitors and is ideal for getting away from the usual tourist circuit, though Italians have left their mark in the way local kids greet you: the habitual "Jambo!" is being replaced by "Jao!", their way of saying "Ciao!". The #18 **daladalas** from Stone Town to Matemwe run through Pwani Mchangani, as do #17 daladalas to Kiwengwa.

As well as the three **accommodation** options below (see map on p.674), there are also two all-inclusive package resorts south of Pwani Mchangani, *Coral Reef Resort* and *Mapenzi Beach Club*.

Mambo Guest House 1.5km north of the village ☎0741/223661. A cheap and friendly locally run place with basic but cheap rooms, each with a shower and squat toilet, all set well back from the beach. The restaurant does good, cheap food. ❸

Tufikiriwe Guest House In the centre of the village right by the beach (no phone). The cheapest place in Zanzibar, at an amazing $3 for a (not surprisingly) very basic room. ❶

Uzioni Beach Bungalows 1km north of the village ☎0747/417701, ✉uzioni@hotmail.com. The most upmarket of the lot, albeit overpriced, with five bungalows at the back of a sandy garden a minute or two from the beach. Each room has a shower with hot water and Western-style toilet, and the *Shukrana Restaurant* dishes up a range of local and continental food. Activities can be arranged. ❺

Matemwe

The beautiful palm-fringed beach either side of the fishing village of **MATEMWE**, 5km north of Pwani Mchangani, is the last of the northeast coast resorts, and one of the more intimate. **Accommodation** is not cheap, however, although the older establishments – *Matemwe Beach Village* and *Matemwe Bungalows* – are highly recommended for a splurge. Along with much of the east and northeast coast, **swimming** at low tide is awkward as it involves a long walk out over the reef, but no matter: low-tide walks across the lagoon to the barrier reef a kilometre offshore are part of the attraction. The hotels have kayaks and can organize sailing trips, though it's cheaper to arrange things yourself with locals. The main reason for coming here is for the superb **diving and snorkelling**, both in the lagoon and around Mnemba Atoll. All three hotels have dive centres.

Matemwe lies 50km from Stone Town with #18 **daladalas** running throughout the day from Creek Road along a tarmac road which ends at the shore. The rough and sandy road from Pwani Mchangani, 5km to the south, can be slow going, and there's no public transport along this stretch. Transfers in comfortable air-conditioned vehicles from Stone Town for overnight guests and scuba air-conditioned divers are run by *Matemwe Bungalows* (free) and *Matemwe Beach Village* ($5), and can be combined with a spice tour on the way.

There are only three **hotels** at present, though the latest – the large *Protea Hotel Zanzibar Beach Resort* – may be indicative of further large-scale development. Book ahead for *Matemwe Beach Village* or *Matemwe Bungalows*, both of which fill up quickly in season.

Matemwe Beach Village 1km north of the village ☎0742/417250, ✇www.matemwebeach.com. Highly recommended place, located amid palm trees on a large beachside plot. Accommodation is in seventeen spacious *makuti*-thatched bungalows with sea views from the verandahs. There's a good bar and restaurant (full meals around $10) and water sports are offered by One Ocean dive centre (see box, below). Low ⑤ , high ⑥

Matemwe Bungalows 3km north of the village ☎024/223 6535, ⓦwww.matemwe.com. An unpretentious place overlooking the beach and Mnemba Atoll. The fifteen rooms in thatched bungalows have verandahs with hammocks, and seafood is the speciality of the gloriously positioned restaurant. Non-guests are welcome for lunch but should book ahead. Biking and water sports are offered by Dhow Divers (see box, below). Closed April–May. Full board ⑦

Protea Hotel Zanzibar Beach Resort 2km south of the village ☎0747/417782, ⓦwww.proteaho-tels.com. Matemwe's newest and largest hotel lacks the intimacy and charm of the other two options, but does have a swimming pool and a wide range of activities and facilities including an internet café, a restaurant (meals average $15) and nightly entertainment. Accommodation is in smallish chalets or four villas (up to six people in each) with kitchens. All rooms have bathrooms, a/c and balconies, most with sea views. Half-board ⑧

Mnemba Atoll

Off the coast between Matemwe and Nungwi, **Mnemba Atoll** is a shallow expanse of coral reef with a tiny heart-shaped island on its western fringe. Contrary to Zanzibari law which states that beaches cannot be privately owned, landing on the island itself is not allowed unless you're super-rich and are staying at the obscenely priced *Mnemba Island Club* ($1200 a double). No matter – the atoll is a "must do" for many visitors, especially if snorkelling or scuba-diving appeals (see p.000). Day-trips can be arranged from both Matemwe and Nungwi (see p.000). The fairly standard price of $20–25 includes transport, lunch and snorkelling equipment.

North Unguja

Life for tourists on Unguja's **north coast** centres on the beach at **Nungwi**, at the northernmost tip of the island, a favourite with backpackers, combining beautiful beaches with Zanzibar's liveliest nightlife, some excellent restaurants, and snorkelling and scuba-diving. If the place feels too touristy, there's an equally beautiful stretch of beach a few kilometres to the south at **Kendwa**.

Nungwi

From humble beginnings as a little fishing and dhow-making centre known only to a handful of hippies, **NUNGWI** has become, in little more than a decade, Zanzibar's most popular beach resort. The place is positively infested with tourists, and much of the western flank of the cape has been overrun by a flurry of development, behind which the actual village is practically invisible. But things aren't as bad as they sound: the buildings are for the most part modest, locals remain unfazed by the invasion, and the atmosphere is remarkably easy-going, with little real hassle. As long as you're not pursuing the "real" Zanzibar, you're almost guaranteed to have a good time.

The **beach** is of course the main enticement; it's narrower on the western side and gradually gets wider as you round the cape to the east, while the sea is resplendent in all directions, especially when dhows drift into view. As along the east coast, the wide tidal range here, especially around the top and to the east of the cape, means that swimming at low tide requires a long walk across the sands to get to deep water. Apart from the beach, there's a natural tidal aquarium that is home to **marine turtles**, plus a number of other activities including sunset dhow cruises, scuba-diving (see p.684) and snorkelling. When swimming at Nungwi and Kendwa be wary of treading on **sea urchins** at low tide. If you are stung, remove all pieces of the spines and douse your foot with iodine.

Arrival and information

Nungwi is 59km from Stone Town and 8km beyond the end of the tarmac, and #16 **daladalas** run there throughout the day (roughly 2hr). Most tourists, however, come on **shared minibuses** (see p.664). These leave Stone Town at 8am and sometimes also at 3pm, dropping passengers off above the beach next to the *Kigoma Beach Hotel* near the south end of the western beach. A **taxi** from Stone Town costs $40–50; renting a daladala costs the same and works out cheaper if you're in a large group.

Organized trips to Nungwi are offered by a number of Stone Town tour operators (see p.646). The best is the "Nungwi Village Tour" run by *Eco+Culture Tours* (see p.646), which includes meetings with dhow builders and fishermen and visits to a fish market, Mnarani Aquarium and a local handicraft group who produce woven mats and baskets. It's expensive for a couple ($40 per person) but good value in a group of eight ($15 per person). There's an unofficial **information centre** at Zanzibar Sail, just south of *Amaan Bungalows* (℡0747/418378, ✉zanzibarsail@yahoo.de); their main business is scuba-diving using their yacht, *Wimbi Nyoto* (see p.685).

Accommodation

Nungwi has over a dozen **hotels**, mostly whitewashed bungalows with standard-issue *makuti*-thatched roofs, along with a handful of more characterful places. The cheaper options are on the **"Zanzibar Strip"** on the cape's western flank, which is good for sunsets, eating out and nightlife. The **eastern cape** enjoys good sunrises and has a handful of more upmarket places, including a big resort. It's generally quieter than the western cape but has little choice of restaurants and bars, and walking along the beach east of the lighthouse is unsafe at night. Note that the shoreline east of *Smiles Beach Hotel*, including the eastern cape, is covered in seaweed at times between November and January. The presence or absence of water sports doesn't really matter as you can arrange them virtually anywhere, which makes the mid- and upper-range hotels rather overpriced. Camping is technically illegal, though *Cholo's* lets people pitch tents in their grounds for $5 per person. All hotels include breakfast in their rates. See map below for locations.

Amaan Bungalows ☎ 024/224 0026 or 0741/327747, ⓦ www.amaanbungalows.com. A massive and not terribly charming place, with dozens of closely packed bungalows on the central beach area and a mix of rooms, some en suite, some with sea views. Staff aren't overly welcoming, and there's no restaurant or bar. ❸–❻

Baobab Beach Bungalows ☎ & ⓕ 024/223 0475 or ☎ 0747/416964, ⓦ www.baobabbeach bungalows.com. An unexciting mid-range place away from the crowds with twenty smallish rooms in thatched bungalows set back from the beach (no views), all with nets, fans and clean bathrooms. There's a bar and restaurant overlooking the sea. ❺

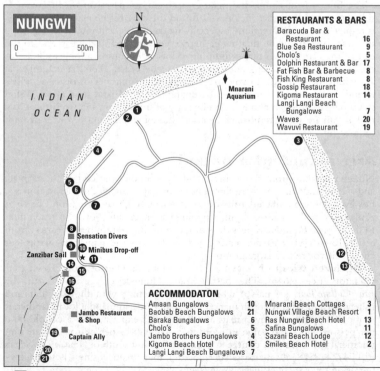

NUNGWI

N

0   500m

INDIAN
OCEAN

Mnarani
Aquarium

Sensation Divers

Minibus Drop-off

Zanzibar Sail

Jambo Restaurant
& Shop

Captain Ally

RESTAURANTS & BARS

Baracuda Bar & Restaurant	16
Blue Sea Restaurant	9
Cholo's	5
Dolphin Restaurant & Bar	17
Fat Fish Bar & Barbecue	8
Fish King Restaurant	8
Gossip Restaurant	18
Kigoma Restaurant	14
Langi Langi Beach Bungalows	7
Waves	20
Wavuvi Restaurant	19

ACCOMMODATON

Amaan Bungalows	10	Mnarani Beach Cottages	3
Baobab Beach Bungalows	21	Nungwi Village Beach Resort	1
Baraka Bungalows	6	Ras Nungwi Beach Hotel	13
Cholo's	5	Safina Bungalows	11
Jambo Brothers Bungalows	4	Sazani Beach Lodge	12
Kigoma Beach Hotel	15	Smiles Beach Hotel	2
Langi Langi Beach Bungalows	7		

▼ *Boats to Kendwa*

▼ *Matemwe, Mahonda & Stone Town*

Baraka Bungalows ☎024/224 0412, ⓔbarak-abungalows@hotmail.com. A friendly place with twelve rooms (some triples) in garden bungalows beside the beach. Single rooms share bathrooms, others are en suite, all have fans, *semadari* beds and nets. There's a restaurant but no bar. ❹–❺

Cholo's (no phone). Nungwi's most chilled-out set-up, right on the beach and run by a bunch of rastas. Accommodation is in small open-fronted *bandas* (security doesn't seem to be a problem) and there's a great "Mad Max"-style bar, with good food, a psychotic pet monkey and hammocks between the palm trees. The music goes on till late, so not ideal for early risers. ❸

Jambo Brothers Bungalows ☎024/224 0002. One of Nungwi's oldest hotels, with a friendly atmosphere and a lovely nearby beach. The ten rooms have hot showers and Western-style toilets and most have limited sea views. East African Diving & Watersport Centre is based here (see p.684). ❹

Kigoma Beach Hotel ☎0747/415496 or 415421, ⓔkigomabeach@hotmail.com. Next to where the minibuses drop you, this has eighteen clean rooms, most with tiled bathrooms, hot water and small balconies; some also have sea views. Overpriced in high season. ❹–❺

Langi Langi Beach Bungalows ☎024/224 0470, ⓔlangi_langi@hotmail.com. The "beach" bit is actually across a road and past some restaurants, but the fourteen rooms in semi-detached bungalows have clean modern bathrooms, a/c and balconies. Facilities include internet access, rooftop restaurant and snorkelling. ❻

Mnarani Beach Cottages ☎0741/334062, ⓦwww.mnaranibeach.com. There's a warm welcome at this relaxed mini-resort on the quieter eastern flank of the peninsula. The twelve smallish rooms all have private bathrooms and a/c, and a few have sea views too. The beach is wonderful,

and there's also a restaurant specializing in seafood. Snorkelling equipment is available and dhow trips can be arranged. Credit cards accepted. ❻

Nungwi Village Beach Resort ☎0741/606701, ⓦwww.nungwivillage.com. A range of rooms in a graceless collection of thatched buildings facing a broad, picturesque stretch of beach. There's also a good restaurant and bar. Water sports are offered by Dive Zanzibar (see p.684). Credit cards accepted. Low ❺–❻, high ❻–❼

Ras Nungwi Beach Hotel 1.7km from lighthouse ☎024/223 2512, ⓦwww.rasnungwi.com. Nungwi's most expensive accommodation, this large resort is set on a palm-dotted outcrop. Prices depend on room size, proximity to the beach and whether there's a/c. The hotel also boasts Nungwi's only swimming pool, as well as a beach bar and restaurant (occasional live music). Closed April–June. Full board ❽–❾

Safina Bungalows ☎0747/415726. Clean and comfortable rooms with spotless bathrooms, but no sea views. Hot showers cost extra. ❹

Sazani Beach Lodge ☎024/224 0014 or 0741/324744, ⓦwww.sazanibeach.supanet.com. A small, relaxed place on a lovely beach next to *Ras Nungwi Beach Hotel*. There are nine well-equipped rooms of various kinds, the cheapest (with the best views) are in *ambras* (round *bandas*) with shared bathrooms. Diving and watersports are offered through Divemaxx, and there's a good beachside bar and restaurant. Credit cards accepted. *Ambras* ❹, other rooms ❼

Smiles Beach Hotel ☎024/224 0472 or 0747/418293, ⓔsmiles@zanlink.com. An amusing foray into kitsch, with toytown houses and model lions and giraffes in the garden. The sixteen rooms (some triples) have a/c, sea views, phone, TV and spotless bathrooms. There's a restaurant by the ocean too. ❻

Mnarani Aquarium and the lighthouse

At the northernmost tip of Unguja, Ras Nungwi, stands **Mnarani Aquarium** (daily 9am–6pm; Tsh2000), a small natural tidal lake surrounded by porous coral ragstone that contains dozens of endangered hawksbill and green turtles (*ng'amba* and *kasakasa* respectively). The first were introduced in 1993, both for study and to provide a sanctuary for injured animals. New arrivals are bought from fishermen who occasionally catch them in their nets. Males are retained, whilst females are released when sexually mature. There's a walkway over the pond from where you can feed seaweed to the denizens; the murky water, whose level varies according to the tide, also contains grey mullet and trevally. The 1886 **lighthouse** (*mnara*), which looms over the aquarium and gives it its name, is sadly out of bounds.

Dhows

The art of sailing has been known to East Africans for at least two millennia, but it was the Arabs who introduced the lateen-rigged vessel that became the maritime emblem of East Africa: the **dhow**. The main dhow-building centre on Unguja was the north coast, though its teak (*mvulu*) forests are now sadly almost all gone. Also now vanishing are the **jahazi** dhows, the largest and grandest of East Africa's sailing ships, which reach up to fifteen metres in length. Their construction took up to half a year, and launches were accompanied by animal sacrifices and much celebration. Few *jahazis* are built today (having been superseded by freighters and tankers), but one or two examples can still be seen, including one at Nungwi that has been converted for sunset cruises (see p.685) and a couple in Stone Town: the *MV Umande* (see p.647) and the *Dhow Restaurant* (see p.639).

Still common, however, are the smaller **mashua** dhows that shuttle between Zanzibar and the mainland, and the delightful sail-powered **ngalawa** outriggers, whose design is said to have come from Indonesia. The lowliest of the lot are the paddle-powered **mtumbwi** canoes, traditionally dug out from a single trunk, but nowadays made from planks. Dhows were originally sewn or lashed together with coconut-fibre coir rope, and, apart from iron nails, modern **construction methods** and tools remain unchanged from those used a thousand years ago. You can watch the fascinating process at several places along the beach in Nungwi; the craftsmen are used to inquisitive tourists, but ask before taking photos.

Diving and snorkelling

Snorkelling isn't that good in Nungwi – currents can be strong, coral cover patchy and local reefs display a lot of damage from over-exploitation, dynamite fishing, drag nets and coral mining. Swimming out to the reef on the western shore is not recommended due to strong currents, but it's perfectly safe to go snorkelling off a boat from one of the companies below. Snorkelling is best at low tide when the current is weak and you're closer to the reef. Prices for snorkelling trips depend on the duration and location. Cheapest are those just offshore ($15), but a day-trip to Mnemba Atoll (see p.680) is highly recommended. Trips are offered by virtually everyone. Snorkelling equipment, if it's not already included in the price of a trip, can be bought at a nameless blue shack between the *Kigoma* and *Baracuda* restaurants, and lots of places rent equipment, the cheapest (at around $2 a day) being Captain Ally, next to *Wavuvi Restaurant* at the south end of the beach. Other places ask no more than $5 and include *Baraka Bungalows*, *Ras Nungwi Beach Hotel*, Sensation Divers and *Smiles Beach Hotel*.

For **diving**, Nungwi has some reasonable reefs, but the main attraction is Mnemba Atoll (see p.680). Of the local reefs, the best – for experienced divers only – is the spectacular **Leven Bank** in the Pemba Channel; strong currents usually make this a drift dive. Coral cover is sparse but completely unspoiled, and there's ample marine life. Other good locations include the shallow **Kichafi** reef, good for night dives; **Big Top** with gamefish; and **Mbwangawa**, good for novices, with occasional reef sharks. To organize a trip, contact one of the following operators.

Dive Zanzibar *Nungwi Village Beach Resort* Ⓦ www.divezanzibar.net. Offers PADI courses up to Divemaster.

Divemaxx *Sazani Beach Hotel* ☏ 024/224 0014, Ⓦ www.divemaxx.com. A long-established, responsible outfit, offering courses up to Divemaster.

East African Diving & Watersport Centre *Jambo Brothers Bungalows* ☏ 0747/420588, Ⓦ www.sansibar-tauchen.de. A cheap but reliable German-run company with courses up to Divemaster.

Ras Nungwi Diving *Ras Nungwi Beach Hotel.*
Experienced with novice divers, and, though
expensive, you pay for the high safety standards
and well-equipped boats.
Sensation Divers Facing *Amaan Bungalows*
℡0747/418453, ⓦwww.sensationdivers.com. Full
range of courses; also good for Leven Bank and
night dives.

Zanzibar Sail Next to *Kigoma Restaurant*
℡0747/418378, ⓦwww.zanzibarsail.com. A
German outfit offering live-aboard diving trips off
Unguja, Pemba and Mafia Island for around $170 a
day (full board).

Other water sports and cruises

Windsurfing is cheapest through Captain Ally (see opposite; $6 an hour). *Ras Nungwi Beach Hotel* and *Waves*, at the south end of the western cape, charge $10 an hour. *Ras Nungwi* also has kayaks ($25 for 3hr) and *Waves* rents sailing boats for $10 an hour. Motorized water sports are pricey: waterskiing and wakeboarding (being dragged on a surfboard across a speedboat's wake) are both $15 per fifteen minutes, and are offered by *Jumbo Brothers* and *Ras Nungwi Beach Hotel*.

Sunset cruises – the more romantic ones by dhow – are offered by a number of places including Mnarani Aquarium, *Nungwi Village Beach Resort*, *Ras Nungwi Beach Hotel* and Sensation Divers and generally cost $10 per person. The catamaran *Bahati* also does sunset cruises ($20 per person, minimum eight people) but is usually rented for trips over several days to **Pemba**, when its five double bedrooms cost $95 per person per day (minimum six people). The price includes snorkelling, meals, accommodation and trips on Pemba Island. Reservations can be made through Bushbuck Country Bumpkin (see "Car rental", p.686).

Eating and drinking

Nungwi's bars and restaurants, most on the west side of the peninsula, are one of its main attractions. The **restaurants** are similar both in their *makuti*-roofed appearance and choice of menu (pizzas, pasta, seafood with rice), so choose by location. The best are on the beach or on small rocky headlands. Most have daily specials chalked up on boards by the beach, and some do beach barbecues in the evening. Order early for things not on the menu (in the morning for dinner, for example), as the cook will have to tell the fishermen what to catch. Nungwi's **nightlife** is Zanzibar's liveliest, with plenty of bars to choose from and impromptu moonlit drumming sessions on the beach. The following are some of the best places.

Baracuda Bar & Restaurant A good place, close
to the minibus stop, with lots of seafood
(Tsh3000–4000), toasted sandwiches (Tsh2000)
and great stuffed Zanzibari pizzas (*mantabali*).
They also do cocktails.
Blue Sea Restaurant A smaller choice, and pricier than most, but with brilliant pizzas courtesy of
its wood-fired pizza oven and always popular in
the evenings. The sea view from the terrace is
superb; the most romantic tables, right by the
ocean, require reservations.
Cholo's Rasta heaven, and Nungwi's weirdest and
funkiest place. The bar, right on the beach, is constructed almost entirely from flotsam, and has reasonably priced beers, fresh juices and cocktails –

including a very good "Banana Blowjob". There's a
beach fire at night and a Tsh4000 barbecue buffet.
Dolphin Restaurant & Bar A great place for traditional Swahili food like banana curries, as well as
seafood and pizzas (Tsh2500–3000) and toasted
sandwiches (Tsh2500).
Fat Fish Bar & Barbecue One of several upmarket places: the main attraction here is the view
from the bar, which also has satellite TV. The small
menu changes daily; meals cost under Tsh4000,
and they also do snacks and occasional seafood
buffets for Tsh6000. Discos are held Tues, Fri, Sat
and Sun (except Ramadan; free entry), and there's
sometimes live music.

Fish King Restaurant Under the same roof as and virtually indistinguishable from *Fat Fish*, with satellite TV and the same views. The main difference is the cheaper menu, with good pizzas for Tsh2000–3500.

Gossip Restaurant Daytime fare here is the usual sandwiches, seafood and some vegetarian dishes (Tsh2000–3500). Come the evening they put on a sumptuous barbecue including lobster and crab. No alcohol.

Kigoma Restaurant In a good position on a small headland with great views west and south. There's no fixed menu; daily specials include fish, squid (Tsh3000), prawns (Tsh5000) and half-lobster (Tsh7000).

Langi Langi Beach Bungalows. The shaded rooftop restaurant here is nothing spectacular but it does do Indian and Chinese dishes should you need a change.

Waves A bar and restaurant on a raised wooden platform with good sea views in a breezy location. It serves both European and Zanzibari food, and there are some tables on the beach.

Wavuvi Restaurant Cheaper than most, with snacks, lobster (Tsh6500) and ice cream. There's also a bar.

Listings

Bicycles can be hired cheaply from locals. Renting from companies is expensive: Bushbuck Country Bumpkin in the square facing *Amaan Bungalows*, and *Nungwi Village Beach Resort* charge $10 a day; *Waves* is even pricier at $12 a day.

Car and motorbike rental Bushbuck Country Bumpkin in the square facing *Amaan Bungalows* (℡0747/418392, ✉bbcbtz@yahoo.com) rents AC Suzuki Escudo 4WDs for $50 a day self-drive excluding fuel, and motorbikes for $25–35 including 40km of fuel. Insurance arrangements are dodgy: it apparently covers major accidents but not "little things", so get a driver from them too (no more than $15).

Health The larger hotels have doctors on call. For anything complicated you'll have to get to Stone Town.

Internet Alzara Internet Café next to Bushbuck Country Bumpkin (daily 8am–10pm; Tsh1500 per 15min). *Langi Langi Beach Bungalows* also has internet access.

Money It's best to change money in Stone Town, as you'll get 7–12 percent less in Nungwi. If you're stuck, travellers' cheques can be changed at *Kigoma Hotel* and, at worse rates, at Alzara Internet Café. Rates are negotiable. Credit cards are accepted by the more expensive hotels.

Telephones There's no official telephone office, though the hotels will oblige for a substantial mark-up. *Jambo Restaurant & Shop*, south of *Gossip Restaurant*, charges Tsh3000 per min for international calls.

Kendwa

About 3.5km southwest of Nungwi lies **KENDWA**, a low-key and refreshingly untouristy place with a lovely beach and several hotels geared to budget travellers. This is the place to head if Nungwi feels too busy and brash, although things may not remain like this forever – Kendwa's full-moon beach parties have already gained a reputation and have even begun to attract international club DJs. **Kendwa beach** is wide and the sea here is deep enough close in for swimming. As yet, there are no noisy water sports, and nothing much to do except swim, snorkel and lounge around in a hammock.

Arrival

A free **boat transfer** operated by Kendwa's hotels leaves from the beach just south of Nungwi's *Kigoma Restaurant* daily at around 10.30am, coinciding with the arrival of tourist minibuses from Stone Town. On the return leg, the boat leaves Kendwa at around 9am. You're not obliged to take a room at the hotel that organizes the boat (they operate on a rota system), although most guests do. The boatman or the self-appointed guide will receive one night's commission from your hotel, amounting to Tsh1000–3000, so bear this in mind when bargaining room rates for several days. Private boats – just ask around in Nungwi – sometimes run to Kendwa (Tsh2000 per person), or you can also arrange something directly with a fisherman. When sea conditions are rough the boats may be delayed or not sail at all.

The alternative is walking 3.5km along the beach. This can only be done at low- and mid-tides unless you're happy clambering up loose coral ragstone covered with thick and spiky scrub. You should definitely not walk if you're carrying valuables or luggage, as muggers have preyed on tourists here in the past. If you're staying at *Kendwa Rocks*, they can arrange for a Land Rover to pick you up for free in Nungwi (or for a fee from Stone Town). If you're driving, or for some reason want to avoid Nungwi, the turn-offs to Kendwa are 3.5km and 4.5km south of Nungwi. Both have hotel signposts, and Kendwa is 1.5km along.

Accommodation, eating and drinking

There are only **four hotels** at present, with a fifth in the offing (*Venice Beach*). Room rates (including breakfast) can be bargained down, sometimes quite substantially, so have a look at several places before deciding. Camping may be possible at *Kendwa Rocks* but shouldn't be relied on. Each hotel has its own bar, restaurant and musical tastes; you're welcome at any of them. The venue for the full-moon beach parties changes monthly.

Kendwa's hotels can hook you up with local fishermen for **snorkelling** trips and **dhow cruises**. The cost averages Tsh4000 for a half day. **Water sports** can be arranged through Scuba Do, between *Sunset Bungalows* and *Kendwa Rocks*, though it hadn't received PADI certification at the time of writing.

Amaan Annex South of *Kendwa Rocks* (reservations through *Jambo Guest House* in Stone Town, see p.622). The most upscale of the lot and excellent value, with large bungalows set back from the beach. All rooms are self contained, some with hammocks on their verandahs, and there's a beach bar and restaurant with occasional live music. ❹

Kendwa Rocks South of *Sunset* ☎0747/415475, ✉bububu@zanzinet.com. Recommended as a quiet and affordable getaway with a range of accommodation and prices. The beach bar and restaurant are quieter than most. ❷–❹

Sunset Bungalows Just south of *White Sands* ☎0747/413818, ✉sunsetbungalows@

hotmail.com. Owned by Stone Town's *Malindi Lodge*, accommodation here is on the bluff well back from the beach, but there's a range of rooms from spacious *bandas* sharing bathrooms to better-equipped self-contained bungalows. The breezy *Bikini Beach Bar* is right on the beach and food is reliably good. ❷–❺

White Sands Beach Hotel North end of the beach ☎0747/415720 or 0747/411326. Mellow place, popular with rastas, and with fourteen self-contained rooms as well as six basic, windowless *bandas* on the beach. There's a bar and good food, and evening barbecues whenever there are enough people (Tsh5000). ❷–❺

Tumbatu Island

A few kilometres off the northwestern seaboard of Unguja is the dagger-shaped **Tumbatu Island**, whose inhabitants are famed for their pride, aloofness and lack of hospitality when dealing with visitors. Their claims to be direct descendants of ancient Persian kings and to speak the purest form of Kiswahili have some justification, since oral and written traditions trace the island's history back to at least 1204, when a flotilla led by a Persian prince arrived from Basra (now in Iraq). Around the same time, a group of mainland Africans led by a man named Chongo arrived and settled in the south of the island at Jongowe (formerly Chongowe). Stormy early relations between the two groups gradually disappeared through intermarriage, which has created the present-day Tumbatu people. For much of its history, Tumbatu functioned as an independent state, distinct from Unguja and the mainland. Indeed, Tumbatu ruled over Unguja for several centuries, and even now some consider that the larger island still belongs to Tumbatu. The island contains extensive ruins of a stone town that may have been Zanzibar's first capital.

Visitors with a genuine interest in the history and traditions of Tumbatu – and with more than a smattering of Kiswahili – will find the place fascinating, but the majority of tourists are definitely not made welcome. *White Sands Beach Hotel* in Kendwa can help arrange a day-trip ($20–30). In Nungwi, Captain Ally offers a day-trip with snorkelling for $150 for four people.

Pemba

The island of **PEMBA**, 48km northeast of Unguja and 56km off the Tanzanian mainland, is Zanzibar's forgotten half, and far removed from the commercialization of Unguja. Despite a wealth of attractions, including primeval forest, atmospheric ruins, deserted beaches, beautiful offshore islets and some of the best diving reefs in the Indian Ocean, there are rarely more than a few dozen tourists on the island at any one time. With its low hills gouged by gullies and snaking, mangrove-lined creeks, the island presents a lush and fertile contrast to much of Unguja and aptly fits the name given to it by the Arab geographer Yakut ibn Abdallah al-Rumi (1179–1229), who called it *Jazirat al-Khadhra*, the Green Island – though holiday brochures have now changed this to the Emerald Island.

Pemba has three main towns, all on the west coast: the capital **Chake Chake**, in the centre, which is where Pemba's airport is located; **Mkoani** in the south, which is the main port and where ferries land; and **Wete**, a dhow port in the north and the most attractive of the three. There's admittedly not an awful lot to do in any of them, but they do have most of Pemba's accommodation and are good bases for exploring further afield. Pemba is extraordinarily rich in **ruined cities**, especially in the centre and north, from the ninth-century Quanbalu to a scattering of medieval settlements dating from the height of the Swahili trading civilization, which together tell the story of much of the Swahili coast.

Pemba is one of Tanzania's poorest regions, largely due to the low prices the government monopoly pays for its cloves, the island's most important export. Poverty has led to political unrest and violence on the island, most recently in January 2001, but the improved situation since then means Pemba remains one of the most peaceful places for tourists in the whole of East Africa. Tourism is in its infancy here; there are few facilities outside the towns and **hotels** are expensive. Public **transport** is limited to surfaced and graded roads; beyond these, walking is your only option. Extensive coral cover and mangroves limit Pemba's sandy stretches, and accessing them can be an adventure – but that is part of what makes Pemba special.

Chake Chake

Pemba's capital and largest town, **CHAKE CHAKE** ("Chake" for short), lies
about half-way up the west coast at the end of a long and silty mangrove-lined
creek. The town is lively by Pemba's standards, and contains a small and busy

market along with a well-preserved **Arab quarter** that resembles a very miniature Stone Town. Chake's history dates back to at least the Portuguese occupation, as is evidenced by the style of the town's **fortress** – now a museum – which was largely rebuilt by the Omanis on the original Portuguese foundations. The main reason for coming to Chake though is for the **scuba-diving** and **snorkelling** off Misali Island (see p.693), an unspoilt gem of a place. Other excursions include the ruins at **Pujini** and the ancient city of **Quanbalu** on Ras Mkumbuu Peninsula.

Arrival, information and accommodation

Karume Airport lies 6km southeast of Chake Chake. There are no daladalas from the airport, but one or two private vehicles wait outside just in case. More reliable is a pre-arranged pick-up with *Swahili Divers* (see p.691), who charge $30 per vehicle. Otherwise, hitching with fellow passengers or walking are your only options. Arriving by daladala from Wete or Mkoani, you'll be dropped at the stand behind the market.

The **Commission for Tourism**, in the building facing *Chake Chake Hotel* (℡024/245 2124, ✉cnrpemba@zitec.org) doesn't normally deal directly with tourists, but can be helpful if you have specialized queries. The guestbook at *Swahili Divers* is a good source of **information**, as is the management, while an excellent, government-produced **map** covering Pemba and including lots of practical information can be bought at the Survey Department of the Commission for Lands & Environment (Ofisi ya Mazingira; Mon–Fri 7.30am–3.30pm; Tsh3500), 2km north of town in Machomane. *Swahili Divers* may also have copies for sale.

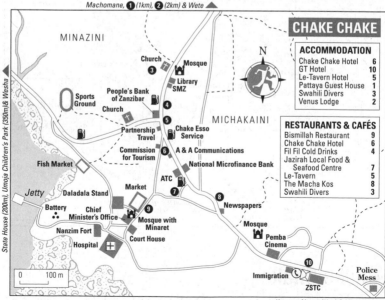

Accommodation

Bucket showers are the norm as Chake Chake's water supply, pumped up from boreholes, depends on the sorry antics of the electricity company. Room rates invariably include breakfast.

Chake Chake Hotel (aka *Government Hotel*) In the centre ☎024/245 2069. Seven twin-bed rooms, often full, all with fans and nets. There's also a bar, and an achingly slow restaurant. ❸

GT Hotel 1km along the Mkoani road on the left ☎024/245 2823 or 0741/660326. A huge place with dark but reasonable rooms, and a TV lounge. ❸

Le-Tavern Hotel Main road, 200m north of *Chake Chake Hotel* ☎024/245 2660. Recently renovated, and a good option; there's a mixture of rooms (with or without private bathroom), and the better ones have views over town. ❹

Pattaya Guest House Machomane; turn right at the junction 2km north of town and it's 100m on the left ☎024/245 2827. Good twin-bed rooms with fans and nets, all but one room sharing bathrooms. ❸

Swahili Divers (Old Mission Lodge) 300m north of *Chake Chake Hotel* ☎024/245 2786, ⓦ www.swahilidivers.com. Set in a restored Quaker Mission house, this is Chake's most atmospheric choice, with something to suit all pockets, including dorms. Facilities include a bar, massages, use of bicycles, a good library and great food, but the main attraction is their diving centre. Dorms ❸–❹, rooms ❺

Venus Lodge 3km towards Wete before Gombani Stadium ☎0744/312484. An average place, in an inconvenient location, but with the bonus of satellite TV in the lounge. Two of the seven rooms have bathrooms and *semadari* four-posters. Food takes at least an hour and a half to prepare. Couples can share single rooms. ❸

The Town

Chake Chake contains a strange but attractive fusion of buildings and is well worth a wander. The atmosphere is relaxed and friendly, and people are genuinely pleased – and curious – to see tourists poking around. Starting in the centre, head for the **market** (daily from 7am). Aside from a selection of herbs and spices, you can buy aromatic essential oils and tasty clove honey (*asali*). It isn't cheap, with small bottles starting at Tsh700, but worth it; you can also buy spices in a small kiosk on the left coming from *Swahili Divers* into the centre. For something different try *Nassab* next to *Macha Kos Restaurant*, who sells colourfully painted straw hats. Heading east from the market towards the dual carriageway is a gorgeous narrow souk-like street (home to the *Jazirah Restaurant*) stuffed with shops and shoppers.

At one corner of the market is an **old mosque** with a softly rounded minaret. Following the narrow road past the mosque brings you to the **Chief Minister's Office**, a bizarre, pale blue building dominated by a round tower studded with protruding hollow cylinders. Opposite is the glorious colonial-era **Omani Court House** with an impressive carved door and clock tower with a defunct clock.

Continuing along the same street and turning right at the junction brings you to the diminutive **Nanzim Fort**, with its commanding view over the creek. The current fort was built in the eighteenth century under Omani rule, but incorporates the foundations of a Portuguese fortress built in 1594. The square towers are an indication of the Portuguese influence, as Omanis generally preferred round towers. Much of the fort was demolished in the early 1900s to make way for the present hospital. The remains were used as a prison and then police barracks before falling into disrepair, but part of what's left has recently been converted into the **Zanzibar National Archives**, with its entrance through a battered but sturdy wooden door. The archives contain a small but charming **museum** (Mon–Fri 7.30am–2.30pm; Tsh700), at present consisting only of three display cases containing bits of pottery and old photographs depicting island life and medieval archeological sites. Downhill towards the creek on your right are the remains of the fort's battery, comprising some rubble and a couple of rusty cannons.

Eating and drinking

Chake's best and cheapest eats are at the **foodstalls** on the main road between *Swahili Divers* and *Chake Chake Hotel*. Busiest at night, this is where you can find everything from the usual *chipsi mayai* and goat-meat *mishkaki* (with spicy potato stew) to grilled octopus (*pweza*), bite-sized fishcakes, various juices (try tamarind, *mkwaju*), and grilled squid and fish. For sweets, there's *halawa*, a sticky boiled goo inherited from the Omanis. To finish off, track down one of the coffee vendors who serve scaldingly hot and bitter coffee in tiny Persian-style porcelain cups for Tsh20.

As for proper **restaurants**, the choice is more limited. *Swahili Divers* is the best, but order in the morning (full meals around Tsh6000). In the town centre, *Jazirah Local Food & Seafood Centre* has a reasonable reputation, but the place and its menu is uninspiring (rice with fish costs Tsh2500). Other places to try include *The Macha Kos* on the main road and *Bismillah Restaurant* opposite the market. As its name suggests, *Fil Fil Cold Drinks* on the main road near *Le-Tavern* is good for cool fresh juices and sodas. The food at *Chake Chake Hotel* requires at least half a day's notice, while its **bar** is one of only three in town, the others being *Swahili Divers* and the Police Mess, one kilometre along the Mkoani road.

Listings

Airline tickets Tickets for Coastal Travels can be bought at several places, including Intercommunication & Travel Agents next to Chake Esso Service, the ATC office opposite the National Microfinance Bank, Partnership Travel, and *Swahili Divers*. The latter two also issue tickets for ZanAir.

Cinema Pemba Cinema, despite its dilapidated appearance, is still open and provides a unique and highly recommended experience: weekday evenings feature Bollywood pics and weekends have third-rate American dross; a great night out for Tsh300.

Ferry tickets Ferry schedules are given on p.705. The one-stop shop is Partnership Travel on the main road near *Chake Chake Hotel*, who deal with all the ferries, though you may pay a small mark-up. To book direct: SMZ next to the library is the place for the *MV Mapinduzi* (they should also know about the *MV Maendeleo* should it restart its service); tickets for the *MV Barracuda* can be bought at the hardware shop just south of SMZ (℡0744/474603) and the next sailing day and time is chalked up outside; Modern Travelling Agency near Chake Esso Service handles bookings for the *MV Sepideh*.

Football The local team, Manchester, plays at the imposing Chinese-built Gombani Stadium 3km along the Wete road. There are no fixed match days; tickets cost a few hundred shillings.

Health There's a good private hospital at Machomane, 2km north of town: ask *Swahili Divers* for details. The government-run Chake Chake Hospital next to Nazim Fort (℡024/245 2311) is very run down.

Internet A&A Communications (daily 8am–8pm) charges Tsh1000 for a connection plus Tsh200 per min on a slow dial-up link. *Swahili Divers* may help out in an emergency.

Library The public library (Mon–Fri 8am–4pm, Sat 8am–2pm; Ramadan Mon–Fri 8am–2pm, Sat 8am–noon; free) has lots of English-language works on Zanzibar and Tanzania.

Money The People's Bank of Zanzibar changes travellers' cheques though it can take up to half a day; National Microfinance Bank might be better. Tanzania Postal Bank at the post office handles Western Union money transfers.

Telephones The main telephone office, operated by TTCL is at the post office. Marginally more expensive (Tsh2500 per min international) but more convenient are a couple of agents: Intercommunication & Travel Agents next to Chake Esso Service (open 24hr), and an unnamed office opposite *Chake Chake Hotel* (daily 7.30am–9pm). A&A Communications are expensive at Tsh5000 per min.

Around Chake Chake

Given Pemba's relatively small size, it's perfectly feasible to use Chake Chake as a base for visiting the north of the island (see pp.699–705); Chake's main tour operators offer such trips. Other than Misali Island (see below), the easiest **beaches** to get to are beyond Vitongoji on the east coast of the island. For information about **scuba-diving** off Pemba, see p.694.

Vitongoji

An ideal and easy half- or full-day trip by bicycle east of Chake is to the sandy coves beyond **VITONGOJI**, which offer excellent swimming at high tide and reef walking at low tide. Heading out from Chake Chake, take the road to Wete for 2km and turn right (southeast) at Machomane. At the end of the tarmac (1km from the junction) turn left. Vitongoji village is 5km further on. Follow the main track beyond Vitongoji to get to Liko la Ngezi beach, or branch left 2km beyond the village to reach Liko la Vumba and Makoba beaches. The alternative access is by #16 **daladala** from Chake Chake to Vitongoji, but this leaves you with 3km walk to the nearest beach.

Misali Island

The island of **Misali**, 17km off the coast west of Chake Chake, is one of Pemba's highlights, offering idyllic beaches, nature trails, the chance of spotting turtles and a colony of rare flying foxes, snorkelling and superb diving. The island is a fragment of coral rag rock that emerged from the ocean 15,000 years ago. It also has a touch of historical romance, as the legendary pirate **Captain Kidd** is said to have used the island as a hideaway, and to have buried booty here.

A more certain treasure is Misali's rich ecosystem, which boasts 42 types of coral, over 300 species of fish, a rare subspecies of vervet monkey, endangered colonies of flying foxes, nesting sites for green and hawksbill turtles, and a large if rarely seen population of nocturnal coconut crabs. In 1996, the island and its reefs became Pemba's first (and as yet only) **marine sanctuary**; in exchange for a portion of tourist revenues, local fishermen have agreed to abandon destructive fishing techniques, to respect no-go zones established for restocking and to protect the turtle nesting sites. The island is uninhabited except for the sanctuary's rangers and passing fishermen. The sanctity of the island, and its name, are explained by the legend of the prophet Hadhara (a name meaning knowledge or culture), who appeared before Misali's fishermen and asked them for a prayer mat (*msala* in Arabic). There was none, so Hadhara declared that since the island pointed towards Mecca, it would be his prayer mat.

A $5 **entrance fee** is payable on the island. There's also an anchoring charge: $30 for foreign boats, Tsh2000 for local. The latter fee is included in the price of day-trips organized through Partnership Travel and Swahili Divers. The island's **visitor centre** is on Baobab Beach where the boats pull up, and has good displays on ecology and wildlife plus information sheets that you can take with you while snorkelling or walking the trails. There's no accommodation on the island, camping is prohibited and so is alcohol.

Diving off Pemba

Almost entirely surrounded by coral reefs, Pemba is fast becoming known as one of world's the most exhilarating underwater destinations, ranking alongside the Red Sea and the Maldives. Surgeonfish, barracuda, kingfish, wahoo, tuna, giant trevally, giant groupers and Napoleon wrasse can be found, and diving companies can suggest the best places for dolphins and turtles. Visibility is generally excellent, averaging 20–40m and often increasing to 60–70m on incoming tides, even during the rains.

There are two indisputable **highlights**: dreamlike **Manta Point** – the tip of a 400m underwater mountain – with coral formations, a profusion of fish and, with a bit of luck, giant manta rays (best seen during their northward migration between December and March); and **Misali Island**, with steep drop-offs, exceptional visibility, pristine corals and the chance of spotting sharks and mantas. Currents can be strong, so Misali is usually for experienced divers only. Also recommended is **Emerald Reef**, which may lack the other sites' profusion of underwater life but enjoys great visibility; barracuda and sharks are sometimes seen. Another good spot is the shallow but steep **Kokota Reef**, ideal for night drift dives, whose highlight is the chance to spot Spanish dancers, a species of nudibranch which gets its name from its reddish colour, fringed "skirt" and graceful movements. Good dives can also be had at **Fundu Reef**, **Njao Gap** and either side of **Uvinje Gap**. Lastly, there are a couple of wrecks at **Panza Point** in the south, the more photogenic one – probably a 1950s steamer – breaking the surface at low tide.

Pemba has four shore-based PADI-accredited **diving centres**. The only **liveaboard** is *Pemba Afloat*, though *Swahili Divers* are planning to adapt a *jahazi* dhow ($100–200 a day including dives).

Dive 7–10 *Fundu Lagoon*, Wambaa Beach. Solid reputation, state-of-the-art equipment and good instructors offering PADI courses at all levels. The only drawback is that you'll have to stay at the expensive *Fundu Lagoon*.

Manta Reef Lodge Panga ya Watoro Beach, Kigomasha (see p.703). A good, cheap and reliable operation with a full range of PADI courses. The drawback for those on a tighter budget is that you have to stay at the lodge.

Pemba Afloat Based in the sixty-foot ketch *Karibu*, moored at Njao Gap near Wete; office in Wete ℡024/245 4352 or 0741/330904, ⌨www.pembaafloat. com. A great choice and

surprisingly cheap, costing $50 per person full-board, and each dive $35. They also have a sister ship, the *Sitra*.

Pemba Blue, *Jondeni Lodge*, Mkoani. No courses here so you'll need Open Water qualification. Misali Island is the main site, and they're also knowledgeable about southern sites like Panza Island and Emerald Reef.

Swahili Divers, *Old Mission Lodge*, Chake Chake. A conscientious, knowledgeable and highly recommended operation, offering courses up to Divemaster. They also offer overnight trips by dhow, camping on uninhabited islands, for $150 per person including two dives a day.

Snorkelling

The shallow reef around Misali is good for snorkelling, though the current can be trying for weaker swimmers and you should stay close to the shore as currents further out can be dangerously strong; ask the folks at the visitor centre for advice. For confident swimmers, a **submerged coral mountain** off the western shore is an extraordinary place; the mountain, one of four in the area, is 3–5m below sea level. You'll need a boat to get there. More accessible is the shallow reef flanking Baobab Beach, which starts a mere 10–40m from the shore. The shallower part features **conical sponges**, traditionally collected by fishermen for use as hats; further out, the reef is cut by sandy gullies and teems with life.

Nature trails

A series of nature trails have been established around the island; pick up one of the information sheets from the visitor centre. The **Mangrove Trail** can be done on foot at low tide or in combination with snorkelling. The **Intertidal Trail** (low tide only) starts at Turtle Beach on the west side of the island and includes a small isle connected by causeway that is popular with nesting seabirds. Mangroves and low-tide pools also feature. Another trail takes you past one of Misali's three **sacred caves**, believed by locals to be the abode of benevolent spirits. Each cave has a specially appointed traditional healer (witchdoctor), and people leave offerings to the spirits (or Allah) to seek intercession in worldly matters. The caves' sacred nature means that tourists should not enter, especially not if scantily dressed.

There's also a trail from Baobab Beach to Turtle Beach and to Mpapaini whose caves contain roosts of **Pemban flying foxes** (an endangered species of bat). Go with a guide to avoid disturbing them. If you can get to Misali very early in the morning (leave before sunrise), you stand a slim chance of spotting a rare and shy subspecies of **Pemba vervet monkey**; your best bet is on the western beaches where they hunt for ghost crabs.

Ras Mkumbuu and Quanbalu

The long and narrow peninsula north of Chake Chake Bay is **Ras Mkumbuu**, its name, meaning a belt or sash, aptly describing its shape. Close to Ngagu village at its far western tip are the remains of East Africa's oldest-known Muslim town, **Quanbalu**, which may have been founded as early as the eighth century. The town was mentioned by several early writers as one of two major trading centres on Pemba (the other being Matambwe Island, 30km north).

The Muslim rulers were descendants of religious refugees from the eighth century who achieved power through force, and the extent of Quanbalu's early prosperity and importance is testified by recent finds of Persian and Arab pottery, Madagascan soapstone bowls and a Chinese coin. The **ruins**, mostly from the thirteenth and fourteenth centuries but built on older foundations, include a large congregational mosque which was the largest in sub-Saharan Africa until the Great Mosque at Kilwa Kisiwani on the mainland pipped it in the fourteenth century. Quanbalu's mosque has an especially fine arched *mihrab*, as well as a minaret. Other remains include houses and at least fourteen tombs, some of them surmounted by chimney-like pillars and decorated with Chinese porcelain. Both the pillars and inclusion of chinaware are common throughout the Swahili coast. For reasons as yet unknown, the town fell into decline in the sixteenth century and was eventually abandoned.

There's no road along the peninsula, so Quanbalu can only be accessed by **boat** from Wete or Chake Chake to Ngagu village, from where you'll have to walk; a visit to the ruins could also be combined with Misali Island. *Swahili Divers* (see p.693) should be able to sort you out.

Pujini ruins

Some 10km southeast of Chake Chake, **Pujini ruins** provide an enjoyable if not overly spectacular half-day excursion. Pujini is the site of a citadel built during the heyday of the **Diba tribe**, who ruled eastern Pemba from the fifteenth to seventeenth centuries, and whose influence at one time spread as far as Pate in northern Kenya, Kilwa on the mainland and the Comoros Islands in the Indian Ocean. The Diba are believed to be descendants of Shirazi settlers from the Persian Gulf, possibly from Diba in the present-day UAE, and are said locally to have introduced coconut palms and the art of constructing dhows using ropes instead of nails.

Pujini was built by the tyrant Muhammad bin Abdulrahman, a merchant and pirate whose nickname, **Mkama Ndume**, means "grasper of men". The **ruins** (also known as Mkama Ndume) are defensively located on a hilltop with difficult sea access and are now mostly rubble, though the remains of walls, fortifications, a moat and a well can still be made out and the presence of several old tamarind and baobab trees, many with graffiti, makes the site singularly photogenic. The **mosque** is the best-preserved building, and draws worshippers from as far as Unguja. Also noteworthy is the **well**, now half-filled with rubble. Legend has it that Mkama Ndume had two wives who were jealous of each other, so to prevent them meeting at the well he had a dividing wall built inside it. One of the wives would use a bucket and rope whilst the other descended by a staircase – still partially visible – to reach the water. Another **staircase** leads up to what may have been battlements, while the ditch on the other side was possibly a moat.

The ruins aren't signposted and are difficult to find without a guide – just make sure that whoever accompanies you knows the place. **Renting a car** is the simplest but most expensive way to get there; half-day hire with a driver costs around $30 from Chake Chake. Alternatively, rent a **bicycle**. From Chake Chake head towards the airport along the road and turn right after 5km (1km before the airport). Pujini village lies 4km along a rough dirt road. **Guides** can be hired informally in Pujini, though few people speak English, and they'll need their own bicycle. The site lies a few kilometres southeast of the village in a grove of baobab and tamarind trees south of a football field.

Mkoani

MKOANI is where most visitors to Pemba arrive, as all ferries from Unguja and Dar es Salaam dock here. In spite of being Pemba's biggest port, the town itself is unexciting, though the fish and produce market on the beach south of the jetty is always worth a look. There's little choice of accommodation and few restaurants, though it does have one of Pemba's nicest budget guest houses, the *Jondeni*. Mkoani is also a handy base for visiting Kengeja, one of several places in Pemba that adopted **bull-fighting** from the Portuguese.

Practicalities

Ferries from Stone Town and Dar es Salaam dock at Mkoani port, 1km downhill from the centre along Uweleni Street (information on ferry schedules and companies is given on p.705). There's no bus station; you can catch a #3 daladala to Chake Chake along the main road. A shuttle bus to Wete is run by Raha Tours & Travel (Tsh1000) and coincides with the *MV Serengeti* and *MV Sepideh*; it leaves Wete at 6.30am and 10am respectively. *Swahili Divers* (see p.693) can arrange a pick-up from Mkoani to Chake Chake for $30 per vehicle. The offices for ferry **tickets** are by the port entrance, mostly in converted shipping crates. Companies represented are: Megaspeed Liners for the *MV Sepideh* (☏024/245 6100); Bachaa Travel & Touring, also for the *MV Sepideh*; Mkunazini Shipping Enterprises for the *MV Aziza*; and Azam Marine for the *MV Serengeti*. The offices are closed when no arrivals or departures are imminent.

Faizin Tours, in the weird gazebo in a small park off the Uweleni Street, functions as Mkoani's unofficial **tourist office**, not that they know all that much. More knowledgeable are the folks at *Jondeni Guest House*, who also have maps to consult. Mkoani's beach boys apparently work for *Mkoani Sun Set Lodge* and may greet you at the port: you'll get ripped off buying daladala tickets through them, and their line that *Jondeni Guest House* is closed is a complete lie. The People's Bank of Zanzibar (Tues & Thurs 8.30am–1.30pm) may be able to **change money**, but it would be unwise to rely on it; Chake Chake banks are more dependable. The **post office** is along the main road beside a huge transmitter; there's a smaller office, together with a cardphone, at the ferry port. If you get ill, the town's **hospital** (☏024/245 6075 or 245 6011) is probably Pemba's best.

Mkoani has only a few **restaurants**, and the choice of dishes is limited, to say the least. Still, if you order early most places should be able to rustle up something reasonable – the local gastronomic delight is octopus. The main restaurant is *Mkoani Sun Set Lodge*, which needs an hour's notice. Meals cost Tsh3000, and it's the only place that remains open for lunch during Ramadan. *Jondeni Guest House* also has a good reputation and a lovely location; meals cost Tsh4000. Other places to try include the *New Haroub Restaurant* and *Subet Restaurant*, facing each other on Uweleni St and *Salsad Café* at the port. The only place serving **alcohol** is the *Government Hotel*.

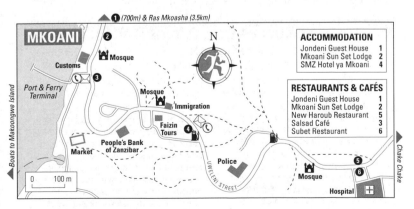

Accommodation

Mkoani has three cheap **hotels**. Breakfast is included in room rates.

Jondeni Guest House 1km north of the port ☎024/245 6042, ✉pembablue@hotmail.com. Along with *Swahili Divers* in Chake Chake, this is Pemba's best place for budget and mid-range travellers. Accommodation ranges from dorms ($8) to rooms with big *semadari* beds (three with private bathrooms). The guest house is also home to Pemba Blue Divers (see p.694), and there are lots of excursions on offer. ❹

Mkoani Sun Set Lodge 100m north of the port ☎024/245 6102. Six clean rooms, all with big *semadari* beds and box nets; the only rooms with private bathrooms are singles, though couples should be able to use them. The small restaurant has seats in a *banda* at the front. Rates can be bargained down in low season. ❸–❹

SMZ Hotel ya Mkoani (also known as *Government Hotel*) 1km uphill along Uweleni St ☎024/245 6271. Identical in every respect to the government hotels in Chake Chake and Wete, giving a weird sense of *déjà vu*. Rooms are tatty twin-beds (and no single rates, at least officially), but they do have private bathrooms, fans and nets. ❸

Around Mkoani

Mkoani is ideal for day-trips by boat, as there are several places within an hour's sail: **Makoongwe Island**, 3km offshore, has a roost of rare flying foxes, while minuscule **Kwata Islet**, 7km west of Mkoani, is practically all beach and has decent snorkelling and a patch of mangroves nearby. Land excursions are more difficult as transport can be prohibitively expensive once you get off the broken road to Chake Chake. That said, there's a lovely sandspit beach 4km north of town at **Ras Mkoasha**: to get there follow the road from the port towards *Jondeni Guest House* and keep on walking. The people you'll meet along the way are unfailing friendly, making the walk itself part of the pleasure.

Wambaa Beach

The sheltered western shore of **Wambaa Peninsula** north of Mkoani has several kilometres of dreamy white sand of the kind that upmarket lodge developers dream about, though at present there's only one such place. In addition, the untouched mangrove forests at either end are a bird-watcher's delight. There's **no public transport** to Wambaa, though you may get a lift from the occasional cars that runs up to *Fundu Lagoon*; the junction is 3km north of the

---

Tour operators in Mkoani

Ignore the *papasi* and, if you're thinking of renting a car or motorbike, do it in Chake Chake, where it's cheaper and there's more choice.

Faizin Tours In a small garden off Uweleni St, and also at *Mkoani Sun Set Lodge* ☎024/245 6102 or 0744/366489. Disorganized and not averse to using touts, the management does at least try to be helpful. They can arrange a number of trips, and although prices look shocking at first, things get cheaper in a group. Kwata Islet ($55 per group plus $5 per person); Ras Mkumbuu ($160 per group plus $5 per person); Misali

Island ($100 per group plus $10 per person). Prices include transport, lunch and any entry fees.

Jondeni Guest House A reliable operator and very good value for money: especially recommended are their combined Makoongwe Island and Kwata Islet boat trips ($20 per person including lunch), high-tide mangrove tours by dugout canoe for bird-watching and swimming, and *ngalawa* sailing (both $5 per person).

turning to Mtambile (#3 daladalas run past it). Much easier would be to rent a car for the day, but cheaper and more pleasurable is to arrange a trip **by boat** through *Jondeni Guest House*, which also gives you the chance to spot dolphins. You could conceivably also reach Wambaa by **bicycle**, though it's about 25km each way from Mkoani across a lot of hills and sandy tracks. The only regular **accommodation** (until the *Sahel Resort* run by *Jondeni Guest House* opens) is at the woefully expensive *Fundu Lagoon*, 2km north of the village (☎0741/326552, ⓦwww.fundulagoon.com; bookings also through Safari Scene in Dar, see p.125; ❾), which has twenty secluded "tented bungalows", all with sea views, plus lots of water sports and a diving centre. As camping is illegal in Zanzibar, your only other overnight option is to arrange something with a local family in Wambaa village.

Wete

The friendliest and most likeable of Pemba's main towns, **WETE** counts a dhow port and two markets among its attractions (the reason for its having two markets, incidentally, is to divide local fishermen from competitors from Tumbe in the northeast: the former occupy the central market; the latter the one near the government hotel; both are open 10–6pm). The **port** itself is at the bottom of a steep hill just past some government buildings, and still receives the occasional *jahazi* trading dhow. Other than arriving or attempting to leave Pemba by dhow (see p.706), the main reason for coming here is as a base for visits to Ngesi Forest, the beaches further north and a number of fascinating ruins to the northeast.

Arrival and information

There are **two roads** from Chake Chake to Wete: the old and more direct one (30km) to the west, whose surface is rapidly vanishing, and the fast new Pemba

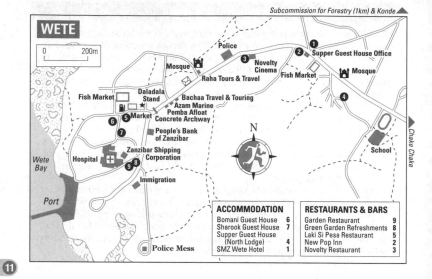

WETE

0   200m

Police

Mosque
Raha Tours & Travel

Novelty
Cinema
Fish Market

❶ Supper Guest House Office

❷

❸

Mosque

Fish Market
Daladala
Stand
Bachaa Travel & Touring
Azam Marine
Pemba Afloat
Concrete Archway

❻ **❺** Market
People's Bank
of Zanzibar

❹

N

School

Chake Chake

Wete
Bay
Hospital
Zanzibar Shipping
Corporation

❼

❾ **❽**
Immigration

Port
Police Mess

ACCOMMODATION		RESTAURANTS & BARS	
Bomani Guest House	6	Garden Restaurant	9
Sharook Guest House	7	Green Garden Refreshments	8
Supper Guest House		Laki Si Pesa Restaurant	5
(North Lodge)	4	New Pop Inn	2
SMZ Wete Hotel	1	Novelty Restaurant	3

North Feeder Road (35km), which starts 7km north of Chake Chake at Melitano junction. The drive takes about an hour. Wete's **daladala** stand is next to the market near the *Sharook Guest House*; you can also catch vehicles along the main road. The best source of **tourist information** is the *Sharook Guest House*, which also runs a variety of excursions in the area. Daily **permits** are demanded at police checkpoints along the road north of Wete, and sometimes between Wete and Chake Chake, as part of the government's attempt to stop clove smuggling. Permits can be bought from the first police roadblock you come to; though officially free, a little *chai* will save hassle.

Street foodstalls by the post office sell juice, octopus, *kababu*, fish and chapati, while several **restaurants** along the main road provide pretty good fare, including the cheap *Garden Restaurant*, *Green Garden Refreshments* for ice cream and cakes, *Laki Si Pesa Restaurant* for cheap *pilau*, and the dingy but excellent *New Pop Inn* for local dishes such as *supu ya kuku* (chicken broth). The recently renovated *Novelty Restaurant*, next to Novelty Cinema on the main road, should also be a good choice. **Drinkers** are catered for by the *Government Hotel* and Police Mess.

Accommodation

You should bargain at all of Wete's **accommodation** options to get reasonable room rates. Electricity and water supplies are erratic throughout town. All except *Bomani* include breakfast in the rates.

Bomani Guest House Between the market and *Sharook Guest House* ☏ 024/245 4384. A sleepy Muslim place with eight rooms (singles and doubles), seven of them sharing bathrooms. ❸–❹

Sharook Guest House In the centre ☏ & ☏ 024/245 4386. Run by a friendly local family, this is Wete's best hotel, offering a range of tours, and five clean rooms (shared showers). There's satellite TV in the entrance, and a good restaurant (order in advance). ❹

SMZ Wete Hotel (also known as *Government Hotel*) Junction of the Chake Chake and Konde roads ☏ 024/245 4301. The third of Pemba's identikit government-run hotels, this one still with some broken windows from a bomb blast following the 2000 elections. All rooms are doubles with private bathrooms; there's also a TV lounge, bar and restaurant. ❸

Supper Guest House (also known as *North Lodge*) Behind the Soviet-style apartment blocks west of the Chake Chake road ☎024/245 4193, ©abouy_aka@www.com. Five rooms, two with showers and squat loos, but mosquito nets are too small, and some rooms are stuffy (though a/c is planned). There's also a reasonable restaurant. ❸–❹

Listings

Airline tickets Bachaa Travel & Touring, 30m beyond the post office (☎024/245 4136), sells tickets for Coastal Travels (see p.705).
Car rental The only places are *Supper Guest House* and *Sharook Guest House*.
Cinema Novelty Cinema (daily 6.30pm and 9pm) screens Indian flicks during the week and cowboy-style American movies at weekends.
Ferry tickets Bachaa Travel & Touring (see "Airline tickets") is the agent for the *MV Sepideh*. The Azam Marine agent, for the *MV Serengeti*, is 30m further along on the same side. Zanzibar Shipping Corporation's office, for the *MV*

Mapinduzi, is next to the hospital. Raha Tours & Travel, east of the post office (☎024/245 4228), do bookings for the *MV Sepideh* and *MV Serengeti* and also operate the connecting shuttle buses to Mkoani (Tsh1000); the Sepideh shuttle leaves at 10am, the one for the Serengeti at 6.30am.
Health Wete Hospital ☎024/245 4001, between the centre and the port, is in reasonable shape. The best pharmacy is Clove Island Pharmacy opposite *Garden Restaurant*.
Post and telephones The post office is on the main road; there's a cardphone outside.

Around Wete

Northern Pemba contains a scattering of atmospheric medieval **ruins**, of which those at Hamisi near Chwaka are especially beguiling. There are plenty of **beaches**, too, but getting to them involves either a lot of effort or money. Easiest to reach is Vumawimbi on Kigomasha Peninsula, just north of Ngesi Forest, another worthwhile destination. As Wete is Pemba's main dhow harbour, there are lots of possible day-trips by **boat**, notably to the casuarina-covered Uvinje Island, Fundo Island, Misali Island (see p.693), and the ruins of Matambwe Mkuu (3hr sail). Scuba-diving is offered by Pemba Afloat (see p.694) off the *Karibu*, a 65-foot ketch.

Wete's two **tour operators** are at the *Sharook* and *Supper* guest houses. *Sharook* offer trips including Ngesi Forest for Tsh35,000 or a full day at Fundo Island for Tsh30,000, and a bargain Tsh20,000 per person for Matambwe Mkuu (minimum two people). They are also agents for Pemba Afloat scuba-divers. *Supper Guest House* do Ngesi Forest for Tsh30,000, while Misali is a very cheap Tsh9000 for the boat (no snorkelling equipment at present). A trip to Fundo Island by dhow with a night's camping is $55 per person plus meals, and they also have sunset cruises and good value spice tours (Tsh8000 per person including lunch).

Matambwe Mkuu

About 1km southwest from Wete harbour lies **Matambwe Mkuu** ("Great Peninsula"), actually a small island connected to the main island by a trail through mangroves at low tide. There's only a small fishing village here now, but the thirteenth-century Arab geographer Yakut mentioned Matambwe as Pemba's second-most important town after Quanbalu, and excavations here have unearthed gold coins from the ninth century (possibly minted at Cairo), and a hoard of over 2500 silver coins from the tenth and eleventh centuries. The foundations of a mosque date from the same period. Admittedly, the ruins are little more than rubble and it takes an especially vivid imagination to picture them in their prime, but there are good views over Wete, and the short crossing by dhow is fun.

Cloves

Pemba's low hills, fertile soil and tropical climate are ideal for growing **cloves** (*kara-fuu*). Cloves are the dried flower buds of the dark-leafed evergreen *Syzygium aromaticum*, a tall thick-trunked tree – the buds are picked from the tree and laid out to dry by the roadside. The pungent but pleasant **smell** derives from a high concentration of *eugenol*, an essential oil used medicinally as a local anaesthetic (especially toothaches), in perfumes and, of course, in cooking and mulled wine. Eighteenth-century French traders smuggled cloves from the Dutch East Indies to Madagascar, from where, in 1818, Sultan Seyyid Said transplanted several thousand saplings to Zanzibar, and by the 1850s Zanzibar had become the world's largest clove producer. Unguja's plantations exceeded Pemba's until 1872, when a hurricane destroyed two-thirds of Unguja's clove trees and the balance shifted. Nowadays, Pemba accounts for ninety percent of production from a combined total of three and a half million clove trees.

Recent times have been hard for Pemba's clove producers, due to the Zanzibar State Trading Corporation's monopoly. With the corporation paying well under open-market rates for cloves, a large proportion of each harvest is smuggled by dhow to Mombasa in Kenya, where producers receive up to three times as much (this smuggling is the reason for the many roadblocks north of Chake Chake). Unfortunately, the only visible signs of the government revenue from cloves are the seaside mansions built by local politicians and "big men", while the islanders themselves are left with a collapsing infrastructure.

Ngesi Forest

Until the introduction of clove cultivation, sixty percent of Pemba was covered by indigenous forest. Nowadays the only sizeable remnants are small patches at Ras Kiuyu and Msitu Mkuu in the northeast, and the fourteen-square-kilometre **Ngesi Forest** that straddles the neck of Kigomasha Peninsula in the northwest. Protected as a reserve since the 1950s, Ngesi (also written Ngezi) is a veritable ecological island, of which about a third is incredibly lush tropical forest characterized by unusually tall hardwood trees (notably the endangered *mvule* teak species, that grows to over 50m). Most of the trees are festooned with vines and creepers, and their canopies conceal a thick tangle of undergrowth as well as a few small ponds. Other habitats in the reserve include coastal evergreen thickets, mangroves, swamps and a central heathland, the latter dominated by a species of heather (*Philippia mafiensis*) unique to the islands of Pemba and Mafia.

The major attraction for naturalists is the chance of spotting the endemic Pemba **flying fox**, a large species of bat (*popo*) that feeds on figs, mangoes, papaya and tree blossoms, thereby playing an important pollinatory role. Other mammals include the marsh **mongoose** – Pemba's only indigenous carnivore – and the endemic Pemba **vervet monkey** (or green monkey, locally called *tumbili*). With luck, you might also see the diminutive Pemba **blue duiker** (*chesi*), feral pigs introduced by the Portuguese, and the Zanzibar **red colobus**, introduced in 1970 when fourteen monkeys were relocated from Jozani Forest on Unguja (see p.658). Unfortunately the experiment hasn't had much success so far, and only ten individuals were sighted at the last count. Another exotic species is the Javan **civet cat**, believed to have been brought to the island by traders from southeast Asia for musk production. The ancient Indian Ocean trading links are also evidenced by the presence of several plant and tree species native to Asia and Madagascar. The forest's **birdlife**, too, has more than enough to interest keen twitchers, including the threatened Russets scops owl, the Pemba white-eye, Pemba green pigeon and the violet-breasted sunbird.

Locals consider the forest sacred, and Ngesi contains at least six ritual areas called *mizimu* that are periodically swept clean for the benefit of the ancestral spirits who dwell there. Two of these, containing the tombs of *shariffs* (people claiming descent from the Prophet Muhammad), lie along the road that bisects the reserve.

Practicalities

Getting to Ngesi can be awkward. Daladalas (#35 from Chake Chake and #24 from Wete) stop in the scruffy market town of **Konde**, 4km short of the reserve; there's no accommodation either here or in the reserve itself (and camping isn't allowed). Luckily, daladala drivers are usually happy to earn a few thousand extra shillings by taking you right up to the gate. Alternatively, you could cycle from Wete (a 36km round-trip) or take an organized tour from Wete, Chake Chake or Mkoani.

The **reserve office** beside the gate (daily 7.30am–3.30pm) collects entry fees: these are Tsh2000 to drive or cycle through to the *Manta Reef Lodge* and the beaches, plus Tsh2000 for hiking. There are a few interesting leaflets posted on the walls inside but nothing to take away. For more information, contact the Conservation Section of the Subcommission for Forestry in Wete, 2km from the *Government Hotel* along the Konde road (☏024/245 4126). You might also find information at the Commission for Natural Resources in Chake Chake (☏024/245 2252), which is in the office of the Zanzibar Investment Promotion Agency (ZIPA); it's 1km along the Mkoani road on the right before the post office.

A two-kilometre **nature trail** has been set up near the gate. The trail is good for birds and passes by ponds, the remnants of a sawmill and endemic palm tree species. Other activities include scouting for night scops owl, mangrove walks, and a guided quest for the Pemba flying fox, for which two days' notice is required; contact the Wete forestry office. Hiring a **guide** at the gate is recommended, both for their knowledge and for security (there have been muggings in the forest). The service is theoretically free, but a reasonable tip is expected.

Kigomasha Peninsula

Passing through Ngesi Forest, the reserve ends almost as suddenly as it began, giving way to scrub, patches of cultivation, a neglected rubber plantation started by the Chinese, and a couple of fabulous and virtually deserted beaches on either side of Pemba's northernmost point, **Kigomasha Peninsula**. On the western side is a fabulous five-kilometre stretch of sand known as **Panga ya Watoro**, a curious name meaning "the knife of the refugees". To the east, **Vumawimbi** ("roaring surf") beach covers 4km of gently curving bay backed by Ngesi Forest. Vumawimbi has been earmarked for development but at present there are no facilities whatsoever, so bring everything you'll need.

Public transport stops at Konde, so access is limited to car hire or organized tours. Cycling isn't really a possibility unless the sixty-kilometre round-trip from Wete leaves you unfazed. Remember that camping on Pemba is illegal. The only accommodation is at *Manta Reef Lodge* at the north end of Panga ya Watoro beach (☏0741/320025, ⊛www.mantareef.com; full board ❽), with fifteen comfortable cottage-style cabins on stilts with sea views, and a PADI diving centre and school. The place sees little trade so the management put on frequent special offers, invariably including diving.

Tumbe

Heading east from Konde, a sandy track to your left after 6km leads to the sprawling village of **TUMBE**, known for its lively fish market and skilful dhow builders. Beyond the village, the road heads on to the beach, where Tumbe's fishermen land and auction their catch. The best times to visit are at low tide (especially in the afternoon) and early in the morning, when there's a lively assortment of traders from Wete and elsewhere.

As you approach the village, keep an eye out for a small black sign on the right reading "SMZ Historical Monument", indicating the remains of **old Tumbe** – Tumbe Mjini. The signpost itself leads precisely nowhere, but the elderly shopkeeper beside it can have someone guide you to the "site", almost all of which has been reclaimed for farmland. The only clue to past habitation initially seems to be a still-functioning mosque nearby, but closer inspection reveals a few clumps of lemon grass (*mchaichai*) scattered among the crops. These have been left untouched as planting lemongrass was the traditional – and very fragrant – way of marking the graves (*kaburi*) of ordinary people. The **graves** of more important folk are given away by pairs of massive baobab trees (see p.426). The only other trace of the old village are the carved wooden doors in the present village, which are visibly much, much older than the houses they guard.

Tumbe lacks **accommodation**, so has to be visited as a day-trip, either from Wete or Chake Chake. Tour operators include Tumbe in most northern itineraries. By **public transport**, things are easiest from Chake Chake: catch a #35 daladala and get off at the junction 1.5km beyond Chwaka. From Wete, catch a #24 daladala to Konde and change there for a #35, and get off at the same junction. The village is 1km walk from there, and the beach 1km beyond.

Hamisi ruins

Several medieval ruins lie between the road and the coast east of Tumbe, of which the sixteenth-century **Hamisi ruins** (also known as the Haruni or Chwaka ruins), close to the bay, are the most impressive and easiest to find. Tradition has it that the fortified town and palace were the seat of Harun bin Ali, son of the tyrant Muhammad bin Abdulrahman (see p.696). Tyranny seems to have been a family trait, as is shown by Harun's nickname, *Mvunja Pau*: *mvunja* means destroyer, and *pau* is the pole that takes the weight of a thatched roof.

Haruni is signposted on the main road about 2km east of the junction for Tumbe. From here, walk down the footpath from the sign into a depression with lush vegetation on your right. Turn right at the first fork so that you're walking parallel to the road, passing some temporary pools on your right which are used by locals to wash in. The track eventually veers left and up towards some tall coconut palms. Walk through the coconut palms into an area of cassava fields, from where the bay is visible. The first of the ruins – part of a palace – can be seen on the left. The track disappears a few hundred metres further on in another cassava field. The bulk of the ruins lie another 100m further on.

The first building you see is a small **mosque**, much of it reduced to blocks of collapsed masonry. The *mihrab* remains more or less intact, however, in spite of a tree root growing into it. The mosque was built for Harun's wife and gets its nickname of *Msikiti Chooko* ("Mosque of the Green Bean") from the ground beans that were blended with the mortar to strengthen it. Some 100m southeast of the mosque are the remains of a particularly large **tomb** surmounted by a ten-sided pillar bearing curious upside-down shieldlike indents on one side. On the other side of the pillar is an incised eight-petalled floral motif, oddly off-centre. The tomb is said to be that of Harun.

Fifty metres south of here is a large **Friday mosque** that appears to be raised by a metre or so above the ground, a false impression caused by the amount of rubble covering the original floor. The *mihrab* here is in almost perfect condition; the five circular depressions on either side of it originally held Chinese porcelain bowls, and people still leave offerings here, as shown by a broken incense burner and an old metal tin.

Travel details

Flights to Unguja (Stone Town)

Scheduled flights from Dar es Salaam to Stone Town are operated by Air Tanzania (@www.airtanzania.com), Coastal Travels (@www.coastal.cc), Eagle Air (@eagleair@africaonline.co.tz), Precisionair (@www.precisionairtz.com) and ZanAir (@www.zanair.com). Two new companies, Air Express and Tropical Air, were poised to start operations at the time of writing. Prices for plane tickets are the same whether you book via a travel agent or through the airline itself. A Tsh2000 departure tax for flights within Tanzania is payable in cash at the airport if not included in the ticket.

Air Tanzania: Dar (1–2 daily). Unreliable, with a reputation for delays and cancellations.

Coastal Travels: Arusha (daily); Dar (2–3 daily); Pemba (daily); Ruaha National Park (3 weekly); Selous Game Reserve (1–2 daily).

Eagle Air: Arusha (2 weekly); Dar (1 daily). Schedules prone to cancellations and last-minute changes.

Precisionair: Arusha (1 daily); Dar (1 daily); Mwanza (2 weekly). Connections via Dar to Bukoba, Kigoma, Kilimanjaro, Mafia Island, Shinyanga and Tabora.

ZanAir: Arusha (1 daily); Dar (3 daily); Pemba (1 daily); Selous Game Reserve (1 daily); Tanga (2 weekly). They're also planning to start direct flights between Zanzibar and Mafia Island.

Flights to Pemba (Chake Chake)

The main airlines flying to Pemba are Coastal Travels, who have daily flights to and from Dar, Stone Town and Tanga, and ZanAir, who fly to and from Dar and Stone Town (Mon–Sat), with connections to Arusha and Selous on Wednesday and Saturday, and direct flights to Tanga on Wednesday and Saturday. There are airline ticket offices at Chake Chake (p.692) and Wete (p.701). The twenty-minute hop from Stone Town is short but

glorious, giving spectacular views of coral reefs, mangroves, sandbanks and the heart-shaped Mnemba Island off Unguja's northeast coast. The fare is $70 from Stone Town and $90 from Dar.

Ferries between Dar and Unguja (Stone Town)

The majority of visitors get to Zanzibar on one of several daily passenger ferries which run between Dar es Salaam and Stone Town. There's invariably a boat every hour or two in either direction from around 7am to 4.30pm. Ferry companies in Dar are listed on p.120.

Azam Marine (Zanzibar ☎0741/334347, Dar ☎022/212 3324 or 0741/303308, @azam@cats-net.com). Dar to Stone Town. Operates several fast catamarans called *MV Sea Bus* (they are distinguished by numbers). Daily sailings at 4.15pm, often with early-morning departures too.

MV Sepideh (Megaspeed Liners; Zanzibar ☎024/223 2423 or 0741/326414). Dar to Stone Town, continuing on to Pemba.

MV Aziza (Mkunazini Shipping Enterprises). Once-weekly sailings from Dar to Pemba via Stone Town.

Sea Express (Zanzibar ☎024/223 3002 or 0744/278692, Dar ☎022/213 7049). Dar to Stone Town. Operates several boats, including the *MV Sea Star I*, *MV Sea Star II* and *MV Flying Horse*.

Ferries to and from Pemba (Mkoani)

There are daily ferries from Stone Town to Mkoani in Pemba, and five services weekly from Dar es Salaam via Stone Town. There's also a weekly cargo boat from Tanga – the *MV Baracuda* – which also takes passengers. For a list of ferry companies and their booking offices in Dar es Salaam, see p.120.

MV Aziza (Mkunazini Shipping Enterprises). Stone Town to Pemba (variable schedule, currently Wed & Fri; $25 including port tax).

MV Barracuda Tanga to Pemba (usually Mon night, arriving Tues morning; departing from Pemba Sun 11am; $15–25 including port tax; there's a shuttle bus from Chake Chake at 8am).
MV Mapinduzi (Zanzibar Shipping Corporation). Stone Town to Pemba (Fri 10pm; 7hr; no fixed tourist (dollar) rates at the time of writing; locals pay Tsh4500). Returns from Pemba on Sunday at 10am. Schedule is liable to change.
MV Sepideh (Megaspeed Liners). Dar to Pemba via Stone Town. The fastest of the lot (2hr 30min from Stone Town), and the only service which continues to and from Dar (departs Dar Mon, Wed, Fri and Sun mornings, and sails on from Stone Town early afternoon, returning from Pemba the same day; $40 from Stone Town, $75 from Dar, including port tax).
MV Serengeti (Azam Marine). Stone Town to Pemba (leaves Stone Town on Mon, Wed and Fri mornings, returning from Pemba on Tues, Thurs and Sat at 10am; 6hr; $20 including port tax).

⑪ Dhows to Zanzibar

The main ports for catching dhows to Zanzibar are Bagamoyo, Pangani and Tanga; finding something in Dar is virtually impossible, and Mombasa's port is awkward for tourists to enter. For more information on travelling to Zanzibar by dhow, see p.37.
Bagamoyo Ask at the *Bagamoyo Beach Resort*, who can usually find you room on a boat going to Kizimkazi. The forty-kilometre crossing takes around six hours.
Mombasa (Kenya) There's steady traffic between Mombasa and Wete in northern Pemba (minimum 5–6hr), but the harbour officials can be awkward, and it's difficult to get access to the port. Most dhows head to Pemba on Monday night, arriving Tuesday morning.
Pangani More laid back than Tanga and much easier to arrange a passage from, with little official hassle. The *Pangadeco Bar & Lodge* can organize things for you (Tsh8000–15,000). Most boats from here pull up at Nungwi or Mkokotoni in Unguja; get down to Stone Town to sort out paperwork within two days.
Tanga Tanga's harbour officials can be awkward, especially as there's a semi-official cargo boat – the *MV Baracuda* – that takes passengers to Mkoani (Pemba). The crossing by dhow from Tanga to Wete takes at least four hours. Most dhows

leave for Pemba on Monday night, arriving Tuesday morning.

Dhows from Zanzibar to the mainland

Kizimkazi (Unguja) Kizimkazi is the main place for dhows to Bagamoyo (and possibly Stone Town too), but don't be misled by *papasi*.
Nungwi (Unguja) Nungwi is where most dhows from Pangani arrive, but catching something back to the mainland is difficult – don't bank on finding a passage.
Stone Town Catching a dhow from Stone Town to Bagamoyo and Dar es Salaam is cumbersome but possible, and the small *MV Al Husein* has been known to take passengers to Mombasa (16hr). Malindi Sports Club, next to *Mzuri Guest House* on Malawi Road, is a good place to enquire; it's also worth asking the dhow builders under the "Big Tree" on Mkunazini Road. The dhow harbour is inside the main port complex; turn right fifty metres inside the gate.
Wete (Pemba) Wete is home to Pemba's major dhow harbour, and the place for arranging passage to Tanga (4–5hr+) or Mombasa (5–6hr+). Dhows tend to leave Wete on Sunday morning. Renting a dhow with outboard motor and sail (maximum 15 passengers) costs around $200 to Tanga or $250 to Mombasa. Passage for individuals on a cargo boat is also possible: tourists generally pay $15–20 to Tanga. You'll also have to pay harbour tax and visit immigration who – beyond their routine advice not to take dhows – will usually give you an exit stamp without much fuss. They may require you to sign a disclaimer, however. Dhow passages from Wete are best arranged through the *Sharook Guest House* (see p.700).

Daladalas

Public transport around Unguja and Pemba is by daladala, also known as *gari ya abiria* (passenger vehicle). The older vehicles are delightfully converted Bedford lorries with wooden bodies; newer and smaller ones are in a similar style but have wrought-iron sides and wooden roofs. They operate during daylight hours, usually 7.30am to 5pm. Short journeys cost Tsh150–250, longer ones up to Tsh1000. Useful routes have been mentioned throughout this chapter.

Contexts

Contexts

History

Tanzania's history is one of many themes, with the main distinction being between inland Tanganyika, and Zanzibar and the coast. Of the former, little is known beyond four or five centuries ago, other than some vague notions about mass migrations and what little can be deduced from archeological finds. The history of Zanzibar and the coast, however, can be traced with considerable accuracy over several thousand years, thanks to chronicles left by ancient Greeks, Romans and Egyptians, and later by Persians, Arabs and even Chinese. The coast's turbulent and often brutal history has been shaped both by its geographical position on the edge of Africa, and by the monsoon system of the western Indian Ocean, which brought it within reach of sailing ships from Arabia, India and the Far East.

The first historical link connecting Tanganyika with Zanzibar was the ivory and slave trade, which took its primary materials from the mainland but was dominated by Zanzibar. The second was the unification of Tanganyika and Zanzibar in 1964 to create the present **United Republic of Tanzania**. A marriage of convenience, some say, and indeed the united parties have shown little affection towards one another over their four-decade-old union. In spite of this, the United Republic continues to be held up as an example of mutual co-operation between different peoples and cultures, showing that ethnic conflict ignited by the artificial national boundaries imposed by the Europeans can be overcome.

Tanzania's first inhabitants

Mainland Tanzania has been inhabited since the dawn of humankind. Some 3.75 million years ago, a family of hominids with chimpanzee-like faces strode across an area of wet volcanic ash in **Laetoli** (see box on p.455) in Ngorongoro; at the time of their discovery in the 1970s, the fossilized footprints of these three *Australopithecus afarensis* provided the first absolute proof that our ancestors were walking upright way before anyone had imagined. Other fossils and stone tools found at Ngorongoro's **Olduvai Gorge** (see p.453) trace the evolution of man from those first faltering steps to the genesis of modern humans, some 50,000 years ago.

Tanzania's historical record – one of immense worldwide importance– starts around 30,000 years ago, in the form of **rock paintings**, especially in the Irangi Hills of north-central Tanzania (see p.257). Comprising one of the oldest and most extensive rock art complexes on earth, the thousands of paintings, many remarkably well preserved, depict a land of wild animals and everyday domestic life not too different from today.

The people who left those paintings were small groups of **hunter-gatherers**, living from game meat, honey, wild berries, fruits, nuts and roots, although some also practised limited agriculture, which is believed to have begun here as early as 3000 years ago. Most of these "aboriginal" hunter-gathering cultures have long since disappeared, having been either annihilated or assimilated by more powerful newcomers over the years. Two exceptions are the Hadzabe and Sandawe tribes of central Tanzania; the Sandawe abandoned their ancient way of life a few decades ago, but the Hadzabe persist, albeit under immense adverse pressure which will probably consign their way of life to oblivion within the next decade. Both tribes are unusual in that their languages are characterized by clicks, similar in sound to the Khoisan spoken by southern Africa's San (or "Bushmen"), who were also hunter-gatherers until recently and had a strong tradition of rock painting. The similarities point to the existence of widely dispersed if isolated hunter-gathering cultures across much of sub-Saharan Africa, before the arrival of the Bantu turned their world upside-down.

The Bantu

Cameroon is considered to be the cradle of the loosely connected ethno-linguistic group known as the **Bantu**. Nowadays spread over much of Africa south of the equatorial rainforest belt, the Bantu are primarily an agricultural people, and have been for thousands of years. Their success at agriculture in their original homeland led to an increased population and, ultimately, to over-population. So started the first of several waves of **Bantu migrations** in search of fresh land. The first to reach Tanzania arrived at least two thousand years ago, possibly much earlier, and the last settled just a few centuries ago. Over time the migrants split into a myriad of distinct tribes, each developing their own cultures, belief systems, languages and way of dressing. Elements common to most Bantu societies, apart from distant linguistic roots, are of course their agricultural way of life, the belief in a unique God, and a knowledge of **iron working**. Excavations in Ufipa in southwestern Tanzania, and in the land of the Haya west of Lake Victoria, have led to the astounding conclusion that, until the European method of mass-produced steel was perfected, Tanzania's deceptively simple furnaces produced the world's highest quality steel, fired at temperatures that were unthinkable in eighteenth-century Europe. Nowadays, Bantu-speaking tribes comprise all but a handful of Tanzania's 129 officially recognized ethnic groups.

Early coastal trade

Little is known about the coast's early history other than that its first inhabitants, African fishermen who also populated Zanzibar and the Mafia archipelago, arrived almost six thousand years ago. The first non-Africans to visit the coast, sometime before 2000 BC, were **Sumerian traders** from Mesopotamia, followed a millennium later by the **Phoenicians**, who used Zanzibar as a stopover en route to Sofala (Mozambique). Around this time, **Assyrian traders** were also active on the East African coast. The earliest coins found on Zanzibar are over two thousand years old, and come from Parthia, Sassania, ancient Greece and the Roman Empire. Egyptian coins and a dagger have also been found, as have Roman glass beads, all proving that trading connections between East Africa and the **Mediterranean** were strong. At that time it would appear that Zanzibar and the coast were controlled by Sabaeans from the kingdom of Sheba (modern Yemen), who brought weapons, wine and wheat to exchange for ivory and other East African goods.

The **monsoon weather system** of the western Indian Ocean meant that traders, coming by boat, were obliged to stay for part of the year in East Africa, before the monsoon changed direction and provided sufficient winds for the return journey. In due course, **trading towns** grew up along the East African coastline. The second-century *Periplus of the Erythraean Sea* mentions one such place called **Rhapta** (see p.170), which scholars have tentatively identified with Pangani or an as yet unknown location in the Rufiji delta. Also mentioned is the island of **Menouthias**, probably Pemba or Unguja.

In later centuries, the East African coastline became part of a vast trading network that included China, Malaysia and Indonesia. Malay and Indonesian influence lasted from the sixth century to at least the twelfth, and the **Indonesians** are believed to have introduced coconuts and bananas, and possibly the Polynesian-style outrigger canoes (*ngalawas*) still used today. Chinese presence is seen in numerous finds of coins and porcelain, and in written accounts.

Swahili civilization

The first outsiders to establish a permanent presence in East Africa were **Persian traders** who, by the end of the first millennium AD, ruled a series of settlements along the coast, from Somalia in the north to Mozambique in the south. According to legend, they arrived in 975 AD after the king of Shiraz dreamt that a giant iron rat destroyed the foundations of his palace. Taking it as a bad omen, the king set sail with his six sons in seven dhows. Separated in a storm, each son founded a city along the East African coast, including Kizimkazi in Zanzibar, and Kilwa on the mainland. Whatever the historical truth of the tale, Persian traders were already well acquainted with the East African coast – which they knew as Zang-I-Bar or the "sea of the blacks" – and the influx of a ruling class encouraged many to settle.

The Persians were not averse to intermarrying with indigenous inhabitants, and in so doing gave rise to the **Swahili civilization** (from the Arabic word *sahel*, meaning "coast") – a blend of African, Persian and Muslim elements that later also received sizeable Arab input. The birth of the Swahili civilization coincided with an upsurge in the Indian Ocean trading network. **Gold** and **ivory** were the main African exports, though slaves, tortoiseshell, leopardskin, rhinoceros horn, indigo and timber also found ready markets. The Swahili civilization reached its peak in the fourteenth and fifteenth centuries, when the coastal towns – especially Kilwa – controlled the flow of gold from mines near Sofala, that some scholars believe to have been the original "King Solomon's Mines".

The main legacy of Swahili civilization is its language, **Kiswahili**, which is essentially a Bantu tongue enriched with thousands of loan-words from Persian and Arabic, and nowadays also with Portuguese, Hindi, English and German. Kiswahili spread into the interior along trade routes over following centuries, and is now the official language of Tanzania and Kenya, and the lingua franca of eastern Africa.

The Portuguese period

The growth and prosperity of the Swahili came to an abrupt end in the early 1500s on the arrival of **the Portuguese**. The first to visit was Vasco da Gama in 1498, en route to discovering the ocean route to India, which would circumvent the need to trade across a series of Arab middlemen in the Middle East.

Although Portuguese involvement in East Africa was initially limited to its use as a staging post, the riches of the Swahili trade soon kindled a more avaricious interest. In 1503, part of Unguja Island was sacked by the Portuguese captain **Ruy Lourenço Ravasco**, who exacted annual tribute in gold from Unguja's traditional ruler, the Mwinyi Mkuu. **Kilwa Kisiwani** (see p.200) on the mainland – by then East Africa's most prosperous city – was sacked two years later, and within a decade the Portuguese had conquered most of the Swahili coast. However, the Portuguese presence disrupted the ancient western Indian Ocean trading network so badly that the entire coast fell into decline, and formerly prosperous cities were abandoned and crumbled into ruins.

The collapse of the old trade network deterred further Portuguese interest in East Africa other than maintaining a number of harbours to act as stepping stones along the route to India. This lack of attention, coupled with their increasingly stretched military resources, opened the way for a new power to take control of the old and abandoned trade routes – **Oman**. In 1606, Pemba was taken by Omanis based in Malindi, Kenya, and in 1622, the Portuguese suffered a monumental defeat at the **Battle of Hormuz**. The defeat signalled the *de facto* ascendance of Omani power in the region, although the Portuguese held onto Unguja until 1652, when the Omani sultanate sent a fleet at the request of the Mwinyi Mkuu. The modest Portuguese garrison at Stone Town was captured and burned, and the Europeans expelled. The last Portuguese stronghold in East Africa north of Mozambique, Mombasa's Fort Jesus, fell to the new rulers in 1698.

Omani domination and the slave trade

Having ejected the Portuguese, Oman was the western Indian Ocean's major trading and military power, and was swift to assert its control over East Africa. The only real threat to Omani sovereignty was from a rival Omani dynasty, the Mazrui family, based in Mombasa. The Mazruis seized Pemba in 1744, but were unsuccessful in their attempt to take Unguja eleven years later. In spite of the rivalry, Zanzibari trade flourished, and key to its wealth was the **slave trade**. The establishment of sugar and clove plantations in European Indian Ocean possessions boosted demand, and by 1776 – when the French joined the trade – some 3000 slaves were being traded annually at Zanzibar and Kilwa. The increased demand, as well as rocketing prices for ivory, also encouraged Oman to extend its control over the mainland trade routes.

Given its increasing economic independence, Zanzibar was becoming politically autonomous from Oman. The pivotal figure in Zanzibari history was **Sultan Seyyid bin Said** (ruled 1804–1856), who at the age of 15 assassinated his cousin to become the sole ruler of the Omani empire. Seyyid Said recognized the economic potential of Zanzibar and East Africa, and spent most of his reign developing and consolidating it, encouraging merchants to emigrate from Oman, and continuing incursions on the African mainland. In 1811 he opened Stone Town's notorious **slave market**, which during the following sixty years traded over a million lives. Shrewd diplomacy with the British – who were increasingly pushing for the abolition of the slave trade – allowed Seyyid Said to wrest Mombasa from the Mazrui family in 1827. With the entire East African coast now under his control, Seyyid Said took the unusual step of moving the Omani capital from Muscat to Zanzibar in 1841, and a short-lived but immensely prosperous golden age began.

With British efforts against the slave trade becoming more forceful, Seyyid Said had recognized early on that the trade would not last forever, and so in 1818 he introduced **clove trees** to Unguja and Pemba and forced landowners to plant them. The climate was ideal, and Zanzibar became the world's largest producer, providing four-fifths of global output. The sultan also cultivated trading relationships with the Western world: the United States opened a consulate in Stone Town in 1837, and European nations were swift to follow.

Seyyid Said was succeeded by **Sultan Majid**, and after a brief power struggle between him and his brother, the Omani empire was split into two: the Arabian half, and the vastly more prosperous African one centred on Zanzibar. In spite of the efforts of the British to stop it, the slave trade was now booming, as was the clove trade, and Omani control of the inland trade routes also made Zanzibar the logical base for European explorers of the "dark continent".

The age of exploration

Apart from a trip to Lake Nyasa by the Portuguese explorer Gaspar Bocarro in 1616, the first Europeans to travel through Tanzania were the German missionaries, **Johann Ludwig Krapf** and **Johannes Rebmann,** who in the 1840s tried to convert several tribes to Christianity, without much success. In 1848, Krapf – who considered Africans as "the fallen man, steeped in sin, living in darkness and [the] shadow of death" – moved inland to try his luck elsewhere, and became the first European to describe Mount Kilimanjaro (to the incredulity of the bigwigs back home, who ridiculed the idea of a snow-capped mountain on the Equator). Hot on his heels came a train of other explorers and missionaries, among them such Victorian heroes as Sir Richard Francis Burton, James Augustus Grant, Joseph Thomson, Samuel White Baker and John Hanning Speke. Many of them set out to locate **the source of the Nile** (see p.481 and p.529), a riddle that had baffled Europeans since Herodotus in the fifth century BC. The search for the Nile was not just an academic exercise, but had geo-political importance: whoever controlled the Nile's waters would control Egypt and, from 1869, the Suez Canal, giving quick access to India and the Far East. The "riddle of the Nile" was finally solved by the British explorer, **John Hanning Speke**, who reached the shore of Lake Victoria in 1858, and went on to sail down the great river, but the most famous explorers to have graced East Africa are a duo whose names have become inseparable: the journalist-turned-adventurer **Henry Morton Stanley**, and the missionary-turned-explorer **Dr David Livingstone**. Their famous "Dr Livingstone, I presume?" meeting took place in 1871 at Ujiji, on the shore of Lake Tanganyika in western Tanzania (see p.528).

Although Livingstone was careful about how he went around preaching the gospel of the Lord, he was very much an exception among a motley bunch of conceited missionaries who believed that Africans were primitive and inferior and therefore in need of being "civilized". But with competition heating up between rival European powers for new markets and natural resources, the supposedly backward nature of Africans and the handy excuse of wanting to stamp out the slave trade (in which Europeans had freely participated) gave them the perfect reason to begin the conquest of the continent by force.

German and British colonization

The **partition of Africa** was rendered official in a series of conferences and treaties in the 1880s between various European powers. Through the 1886 **Anglo-German Agreement**, finalized in 1890, Germany took nominal control of Tanganyika, while Britain gained Kenya, Uganda and Zanzibar.

The German colonization of Tanganyika

The arrival of the militaristic **Ngoni tribe** in the 1830s (see p.606) had plunged vast swathes of southern Tanganyika into chaos, while in the north the equally warlike **Maasai** (see box on pp.434–5) were busy carving out their own terrain. This turbulent state of affairs should have made the German conquest of Tanganyika an easy matter, but in fact their problems began the instant they arrived, when, in 1888, local slave traders, who were none too appreciative of Germany's intention to abolish their livelihoods and wrest away control of the caravan routes, rose up in arms. Led initially by a slaver named Abushiri ibn Salim al-Harthi – from whom the uprising got its name, the **Abushiri War** – the conflict dragged on for over a year before the Germans finally gained control.

With the coast subdued, the Germans set their sights inland, but immediately ran into opposition from those tribes whom they had failed to convince to sign over their land; a series of farcical treaties were cooked up by arch-colonist **Karl Peters**, whom locals knew as "the man with bloodstained hands", and who was later lauded as a "model colonial administrator" by Adolf Hitler.

In central Tanzania, two tribal chiefs in particular were able to take advantage of the crumbling status quo, and of Zanzibar's waning power, by taking military control of portions of the trade routes, which they used to exact tributes from passing caravans. The tributes in turn financed the purchase of arms on the coast, which enabled them to expand their budding empires. **Chief Mirambo** (see p.541) of the Nyamwezi built a short-lived empire between central Tanganyika and what is now Burundi, Rwanda and Uganda. Luckily for the Germans, Mirambo's empire disintegrated shortly after his death in 1884, but the more southerly Hehe tribe, under **Chief Mkwawa** (see p.571), were a formidable adversary to German rule, which they proved in 1891 by annihilating an attacking German force. Mkwawa's resistance only ended in 1898, when he killed himself rather than surrender to the surrounding German troops.

Mkwawa's suicide signalled a temporary lull in armed resistance to German rule until in 1905, frustrated with the harsh rule of the colonialists, a vast swath of central and southern Tanganyika rose up once more, in what became known as the **Maji Maji Uprising**. The war gets its name from a soothsayer named

Kinjikitile (see p.211), who claimed to have discovered a spring from which magic water (*maji*) flowed. If sprinkled on a person, he said, the water would protect the wearer from bullets.

This time using brutal scorched-earth and terror tactics, the German Schutztruppe finally crushed the uprising in 1907, and began the colonization proper of Tanganyika. Work included the construction of a railroad from their Indian Ocean capital of Dar es Salaam to Kigoma port on Lake Tanganyika, following almost exactly the route of one of the most infamous of nineteenth-century slave roads.

The railway arrived in Kigoma in February 1914, too late to be of much help to the Germans, however, as **World War I** was about to erupt. Although the war's main focus was Europe, the German troops posted in Tanganyika, ably led by Paul von Lettow-Vorbeck, began a guerrilla-style conflict against the British based in Kenya and Zanzibar, and Belgians in Burundi and Rwanda. Von Lettow-Vorbeck's purpose was not to defeat the numerically superior Allied forces, but to tie down resources that would have been more productively used back in Europe. The strategy worked, and Von Lettow-Vorbeck's force remained undefeated when, in 1918, the Armistice brought an end to the slaughter and forced his surrender.

The British Protectorate of Zanzibar

In 1870, Sultan Majid's successor, **Sultan Barghash**, inherited vast wealth – much of it squandered on opulent palaces and civic buildings that grace Stone Town today – but also an empire that had little real power. Omani control over the mainland slave routes was by now superficial, and political turbulence there saw the establishment of independent tribal kingdoms.

Barghash's accession coincided with a devastating cholera epidemic that killed 10,000 people in Stone Town alone. In April 1872, a violent cyclone swept across Zanzibar, destroying all but one ship in Stone Town's harbour (around three hundred in all), and levelling 85 percent of Unguja's clove plantations This string of disasters was compounded in 1873 when the sultan was forced by the British to ban the slave trade between the African mainland and Zanzibar (slavery itself was finally abolished in 1897). With both main sources of income in tatters, it became increasingly clear that Zanzibar was at the mercy of British.

Barghash tried briefly to reassert his authority on the mainland, but by 1882, European designs for the colonization of Africa were in full flow. Barghash's protests fell on deaf ears, and he retreated from international affairs, while Europe proceeded with the partition of Africa. Zanzibar's mainland possessions – with the exception of a six-kilometre coastal strip – were taken from it in 1886.

Barghash died in 1888 a bitter man, and was succeeded by his son, Khalifa bin Said, who had little choice but to acquiesce in whatever the Europeans wanted ed. After his death just two years later, Zanzibar was declared a **British Protectorate** on November 1, 1890. The sultanate was allowed to continue in a ceremonial capacity, but the real shots were called by British – quite literally, in August 1896, upon the death of Sultan Hamad bin Thuwaini bin Said. Two hours after the sultan's death, the palace complex in Stone Town was seized by Khalid, a son of Sultan Barghash, who, urged on by 2500 supporters, proclaimed himself sultan. The British, who preferred Thuwaini's cousin, Hamud ibn Mohammed, issued an ultimatum which Khalid ignored. At precisely 9.02am on August 27, the **shortest war in history** began when three British warships opened fire on the palace complex. By 9.40am the British had reduced two palaces to rubble, killed 500 people and forced the surrender of Khalid, who took refuge in the German consulate from where he fled into exile.

The road to Independence

At the end of World War I, the British were given control of Tanganyika, though the administration remained separate from that of Zanzibar, which was nominally still a sultanate. British rule in Tanganyika (1919–61) was relatively benign compared to the German period and the oppression of neighbouring Kenya, which ended with the Mau Mau Uprising in the 1950s. In Tanganyika, the British just picked up where the Germans had left off: the city of Dar es Salaam was expanded, agricultural "upcountry" towns like Arusha and Morogoro flourished, and the railway was extended to Mwanza on Lake Victoria. The five-decade British Protectorate over Zanzibar was similarly uneventful. Zanzibar's sultans were nothing more than puppets, and the real rulers set about consolidating their administration with a new judicial system, refinements to the rubber-stamping parliament and the installation of a sewerage system for Stone Town.

World War II was a major turning point in the history of Tanzania and of Africa. Many Tanzanians had been conscripted as soldiers and porters for the British and expected something in return when the war was over. Opposition to colonial rule began all across the continent and with the new world order now dominated by the United States and the Soviet Union, the European powers soon realized that change was inevitable.

In Tanganyika, the Independence movement was headed by **TANU**, the Tanganyika African National Union, formerly the Tanganyika African Association, founded in 1929. From 1954 onwards, TANU was led by **Julius Kambarage Nyerere** (see p.497), a mild-mannered former schoolteacher from Butiama in northern Tanganyika, and graduate of Edinburgh University. Professing a peaceful path to change inspired by Mahatma Gandhi, Nyerere's open-minded and down-to-earth style won TANU widespread support, and the grudging respect of the British, who, faced with the inevitability of Independence sooner or later, saw in Nyerere a figure that they could trust. Following a number of legislative elections in which TANU were kept at bay with a rigged system of "reserved seats", mounting tension finally forced free elections in August 1960 for 71 seats of the Tanganyika Legislative Council. TANU won all but one, Nyerere became chief minister, and in that capacity led the move towards **Tanganyikan Independence**, which was officially proclaimed on December 9, 1961.

Zanzibari Independence – and revolution

In Zanzibar, the situation was more complicated, as there were effectively two colonial overlords: the British, who wielded political and judicial power, and the Omanis, who still owned the land and the island's resources, and whose sultans retained their importance as heads of state. The first rumblings of **discontent** came in 1948, when African dockers and trade unionists publicly protested against both British and Arab domination. Britain eventually allowed the formation of political parties to dispute elections held in 1957 for the Legislative Council. Africans were represented by the **Afro-Shirazi Party (ASP)**, while the Arab minority supported the Zanzibar Nationalist Party (ZNP). Between 1959 and 1961 a series of increasingly rigged elections gave the ZNP, in coalition with the Zanzibar and Pemba People's Party (ZPPP), disproportionate representation in the council, while the ASP was consistently denied power. Heedless of the rising tension, the British instituted limited self-government in June 1963, and the following month another round of elections was held, which, again, saw the ASP lose, despite having polled 54 percent of the vote. Nonetheless, Britain went ahead with plans for Independence, and on December 10, 1963, the **Sultanate of Zanzibar** came into being.

African resentment of the Arab population on Zanzibar – who made up just twenty percent of the population but controlled most of the wealth and power – grew steadily until, on January 12, 1964, barely four weeks after Independence, **John Okello**, a Ugandan migrant labourer and self-styled Field Marshal, led six hundred armed supporters in a bloody **Revolution**. In one night of terror, some 12,000 Arabs and Indians were massacred, and all but one percent of Stone Town's Arab and Indian inhabitants fled the country. Among them was Zanzibar's last sultan, Jamshid ibn Abdullah, who ended up in exile in England. Despite having started the Revolution, Okello lacked the support to create a government, and the ASP's leader, Sheikh Abeid Amani Karume made himself Prime Minister of the Revolutionary Council of the **People's Republic of Zanzibar and Pemba**.

The United Republic of Tanzania

As President of Tanganyika, Nyerere's first moves were to promote a sense of national consciousness: Kiswahili was made the official language and was to be taught in every school, while tribal chiefdoms – a potential source of divisive conflict – were abolished. In 1962 Tanganyika adopted a republican constitution, and elections returned Nyerere as president. The following year, Tanganyika became a **one-party state** under TANU, although voters were given choice of candidates in subsequent elections.

The chaos of the Zanzibari Revolution coincided with the height of the Cold War, and came shortly after Nyerere had survived an army mutiny in January 1964, for which he had recourse to help from British marines. Feeling threatened by the possibility of extremists taking power in Zanzibar, Nyerere sought to defuse the threat through an **Act of Union** between Tanganyika and Zanzibar, which would give him the power to intervene militarily in Zanzibar. Karume, for his part, was in a quandary, as the exodus of Arabs and Indians after the bloody revolution instantly devastated Zanzibar's economy, and few international organizations were willing to help a left-wing regime that had come to power through such violent means. The solution, which he soon came to regret, was to accept Nyerere's overtures for the Act of Union, which was signed on April 26, 1964, bringing into existence the **United Republic of Tanzania**. Nyerere became Union president and Karume one of two vice-presidents, and Zanzibar retained political and economic autonomy, a separate administration and constitution and its own president and judicial system while gaining 50 of the 169 seats in the Tanzanian National Assembly. In spite of these concessions, Karume came to view the Union as a mainland plot to take over the island, and even now – four decades down the road – few people on either side are happy with the Marriage.

Ujamaa

As first President of the Union, Nyerere faced huge challenges. The entire country was one of the poorest on earth, with just twelve doctors and 120 university graduates to its name. Life expectancy was 35, and 85 percent of the adult population was illiterate. The outside world was willing to help out, but the inevitable strings would compromise Tanzania's independence. The task of developing the country was made harder as over ninety percent of the population lived in remote rural settlements.

In February 1967, at the height of an extended drought, Nyerere delivered a famous speech that became known as the **Arusha Declaration** (see p.381), in which he laid out his vision of self-reliant, non-Marxist "African socialism" for Tanzania: "The development of a country is brought about by people, not by money. Money, and the wealth it represents, is the result and not the basis of development...The biggest requirement is hard work. Let us go to the villages and talk to our people and see whether or not it is possible for them to work harder."

In practice, those noble ideals translated into "villagization": the resettlement of rural households into centralized and collective **Ujamaa villages**, *ujamaa* being the Kiswahili word for togetherness, familyhood and unity. Until 1972 the resettlement programme was voluntary, and around twenty percent of the population had moved. This, however, wasn't enough, so **forcible resettlement** started and by 1977 over thirteen million people, or about eighty per cent of the population, resided in some eight thousand Ujamaa villages.

Unfortunately, the policy was an **economic disaster**. Vast areas of formerly productive land were left untended and the communal system proved to be more fertile for corruption and embezzlement than for agriculture. Yet the policy did have its successes: access to clean water, health care and schools was vastly improved, and by the 1980s adult literacy had soared to over ninety percent. Equally important, throwing everyone together in the same, sinking boat, forged a strong and peaceful sense of **national identity** that completely transcended tribal lines, and created a nation of people justifiably proud of their peaceful and friendly relations with each other, and with outsiders. Tanzania, particularly the mainland, is one of few African countries wholly unaffected by ethnic or religious conflict, and is unique in having a population which takes pride in both its tribal and national identity.

Depression, collapse and conciliation

By the mid-1970s, both mainland Tanzania and Zanzibar were in a terrible state. *Ujamaa*, while forging a healthy sense of national identity, had completely wrecked the country's economy, and by 1979 Tanzania's jails contained more political prisoners than in Apartheid South Africa. Over on Zanzibar, Karume, who had courted the USSR, Cuba and China for help in establishing state-run plantations (many of which now lie abandoned), had brought about a similar result. Politically, too, Zanzibar was a mess. Karume became increasingly paranoid and dictatorial. He deported Asians whom he believed were "plotting" to take over the economy, elections were banned, arbitrary arrests and human-rights abuses became commonplace and there were even allegations that Karume himself had arranged the murder of leading politicians and businessmen in the late 1960s. In April 1972, after two previous attempts on his life, an **assassin's bullet** finally found its mark. Karume's successor, Aboud Jumbe, was more moderate and favoured closer relations with the mainland.

Big changes came in 1977. The failure of *Ujamaa* to address Tanzania's economic problems had become glaringly apparent, and the same year the **East African Community** between Tanzania, Kenya and Uganda, founded in 1967, was finally buried when rock-bottom relations with capitalist Kenya closed the border between the two countries. With both sides of the Union increasingly isolated, closer ties between them seemed to be the way forward. In February 1977, Zanzibar's Afro-Shirazi Party merged with Tanganyika's TANU to form **Chama Cha Mapinduzi** (CCM - The Revolutionary Party), which remains in power today. Nyerere was the chairman, and Jumbe vice-chairman.

The Kagera War and the road to change

While relations with Kenya had been cut in 1977, things were no better with **Idi Amin**'s brutal dictatorship in Uganda. Things came to a head in October 1978, when Uganda invaded Tanzania's **Kagera Region** in the far northwest. Tanzania barely had an army worth the name, so it took a few months to train up a force of some 50,000 men, who responded, assisted by armed Ugandan exiles, with a counter-attack in January 1979. Much to the surprise of seasoned military observers, they completely routed the supposedly better-equipped and better-trained Ugandan army, and pushed on to Uganda's capital, Kampala, driving Idi Amin into exile. The war, although brief, was something that Tanzania could ill afford, and the estimated $500-million cost ensured further economic misery back home.

As Tanzania sank deeper into **debt** and resorted to international donors for aid, Nyerere found himself increasingly at odds with his stated socialist ideals. Far from being self-reliant, Tanzania was more dependent than ever. The economy had virtually collapsed, agriculture was barely sufficient for subsistence needs, the country was saddled with a crippling debt burden and one third of Tanzania's budget was now accounted for by loans from donor countries and the International Monetary Fund (IMF). With the donors now demanding economic liberalization and privatization, **Nyerere resigned** from the Union presidency in 1985. It was time for change.

The **1985 elections** ushered in a Union government headed by pragmatic reformer **Ali Hassan Mwinyi**, who began a ten-year tenure (he was re-elected in 1990) characterized by the wholesale desertion of Nyerere's *Ujamaa* policies, economic reforms and liberalization, the implementation of IMF-imposed austerity measures, and – inevitably – **corruption** on all levels. In 1992, the one-party political system was scrapped, setting the country on the path towards its first multiparty elections, held in 1995.

The multiparty era

Independent Tanzania's first multiparty elections – a condition of donor aid – were held in 1995. As usual, there were two polls: one for the Union parliament and presidency, the other for Zanzibar's separate executive. On the mainland, things passed off smoothly, with the ruling CCM and their presidential candidate, the rather dull party functionary and former journalist, **Benjamin Mkapa**, easily winning the race in a vote that was generally seen as free and fair. Zanzibar, however, was an entirely different matter.

Trouble on Zanzibar

While the 1995 Union vote passed off without a hitch, things could not have been more different on Zanzibar, where the CCM was pitted against the **Civic United Front** (CUF), which, supported mainly by Muslims, promoted looser ties with the mainland and the possible imposition of Islamic **sharia law**. The run-up to the elections was marred by unrest, and although polling itself was peaceful, violence erupted once again when CCM was declared victorious by the slenderest of margins. In the Zanzibari parliament, CCM won 26 seats, CUF 24 (including all twenty seats in Pemba). International observers reported serious discrepancies and yet, in spite of the controversy, **Salmin Amour** was reinaugurated as Zanzibari president, responding to his critics with police harassment and arbitrary arrests, causing around 10,000 CUF supporters to flee and the European Union to cut off aid.

The violence and chaos continued. CUF activists were charged with treason after speaking out against police harassment. Amnesty International adopted the accused as prisoners of conscience. Further arrests of CUF MPs followed in 1998, and international pressure mounted against the repeatedly postponed treason trial, which finally got under way in March 1999. Notwithstanding the impending trial, CUF announced the end of its boycott of parliament in August 1998 and agreed to recognize Amour as president who – as was becoming habitual with Zanzibar's embattled presidents – claimed that Zanzibar's troubles were being orchestrated by an external "plot". More arrests followed in 1999, despite which CCM and CUF signed a Commonwealth-brokered reconciliation pact to resolve their differences through peaceful means.

There were high hopes that the **October 2000 elections** would indeed be free and fair, and indeed the vote on the mainland again passed off peacefully enough, with CCM and the incumbent Union President, Benjamin Mkapa, winning another five-year mandate. But, in a virtual repeat of 1995, the Zanzibari elections turned out to be dangerous farce. The trouble began almost immediately after the votes had been cast, with both CUF and CCM claiming there had been irregularities, and international observers calling the vote a shambles. The new Zanzibari president, **Amani Karume** – son of Zanzibar's first president – attempted to defuse the tension by acquitting the treason trial suspects. The gesture was not enough to appease CUF, however, who felt they had been cheated once again, and demanded a re-run. Tensions increased when CUF issued a 90-day ultimatum in November calling for fresh elections, failing which, "extraordinary action" was promised.

In **January 2001**, just days before CUF's ultimatum was to expire and ignoring a police ban, mass demonstrations in Zanzibar and Dar es Salaam were held, and the ensuing violence saw the deaths of at least 26 demonstrators and one policeman. News footage clearly showed police brutality, but the Zanzibari government went on the offensive, blaming CUF for having started the violence, and publicly praising the police for their handling of the "heavily armed demonstrators". Mass arrests of CUF supporters were widely reported, as were allegations of intimidation, torture and rape, especially in the CUF stronghold of Pemba.

Public condemnation of the killings came from all sections of Tanzanian society and the government finally agreed to talks with the CUF. Much to everyone's surprise and delight this resulted in the **CCM-CUF Peace Accord** – known as the *Muafaka*, meaning simply "agreement" – on October 10, 2001, by which the Zanzibari government was to incorporate other parties, political detainees were to be released and the judiciary and Zanzibar Electoral Commission were to be reformed.

Benjamin Mkapa's rule

While **Benjamin Mkapa**'s presidency of the Union, which comes to an end in 2005, has largely been overshadowed by events in Zanzibar (see opposite), his tenure has so far seen a number of quiet but positive changes, continuing Ali Hassan Mwinyi's reformist policies.

The **economy** has further been opened to international investment (some say too much – Tanzania's gold mines, for example, all of which are controlled by foreign companies, pay a measly five percent in taxes on their output), and **tourism** is now one of the country's biggest earners. Mkapa has also been at pains to grapple with Tanzania's enormous **foreign debt**, and in so doing regain donor confidence. The strategy appeared to have paid off in 2001, when Tanzania qualified for the IMF's **Highly Indebted Poor Country** status, entitling it to a $3-billion write-off over the next twenty years, amounting to just over half of its total debt. Nonetheless, this concession by the world's rich countries still leaves Tanzania owing billions, unless the "donors" follow China's recent example and write off the entirety of the debts owed them.

Mkapa has also moved towards closer ties with Kenya and Uganda, which resulted in the resurrection of the **East African Union** in January 2001, whose 27-member legislative assembly is based in Arusha. At the same time, an East African Court of Justice was founded. **Multiparty politics** is developing slowly but surely, though none of the mainland opposition parties has anywhere near enough popular support to unseat CCM. The **media** too, at least outside election times, are remarkably free, and can be surprisingly critical of the government and individual politicians.

The future

The main social challenge facing the government is **poverty**; Tanzania remains one of the world's poorest countries, with the average annual per capita income in the range $200–300. **Corruption**, too, is rife at all levels of society, despite periodic crackdowns. The **economy**'s continuing reliance on donors is also a major concern, although the savings made through the IMF's debt rescheduling mean that more pressing **social concerns**, largely ignored since the end of *Ujamaa*, can now be addressed: education, water, health, the fight against HIV/AIDS, agriculture and rural roads are priorities. In 2001 Mkapa announced a five-year plan for universal primary education, something that had been achieved during Nyerere's tenure but that the political and economic turmoil of the 1980s and 1990s had reversed. The scheme makes primary education free and compulsory, though the five-year deadline seems unrealistic.

But the government's biggest problem is political. Although opposition parties are unlikely to make much impact in the **2005 elections** for the Union parliament and presidency, Zanzibar is an entirely different matter, and it's obvious that a completely free vote would see the election of a CUF president and parliament. To date, work is progressing on the implementation of the *Muafaka* accord, and both sides still appear committed to it. Though at some point the status of Zanzibar as part of the United Republic will have to be clarified, for now the Union appears to be safe. The real test will be in 2005, when Tanzania's third multiparty elections take place, and for the islands to have a real chance of lasting peace, both Zanzibar and Tanzania will have to continue working in the spirit of *Muafaka*.

Wildlife and habitats

Despite tremendous losses over the last century, Tanzania teems with wildlife and is considered to be one of the twelve most biodiverse nations on earth, with at least 310 mammalian species, 1100 varieties of birds, 1370 species of butterfly, 380 reptilian and amphibian species and over 10,000 distinct plants, a quarter of which are unique to the country.

Even outside the protective boundaries of the national parks and game reserves, it's possible to see a lot of **wildlife** if you travel fairly widely, including gazelles, antelopes, zebras, giraffes, monkeys and baboons – even hippos, buffaloes, crocodiles and elephants. On the reptile front, snakes are rarely sighted, but lizards skitter everywhere, and geckos can be seen clinging upside down on ceilings at night. Other innocuous denizens include giant millipedes up to thirty centimetres long, which live on rotten fruit. The country's **birdlife**, ranging from the thumb-sized cordon bleu to the ostrich, is astonishingly diverse and attracts ornithologists from all over the world as well as making converts of many visitors.

If this impression of abundant wildlife alarms you, rest assured that any **danger** is minimal. The big cats, for example, are hardly ever seen outside the parks and reserves. Buffaloes, though plentiful, are only really dangerous when solitary. The main species to be wary of are **hippos** and **crocodiles**, who inhabit many of the lakes and rivers, meaning you should always seek local advice before swimming in inland waters – sticking to a hotel pool or the ocean is your safest choice.

This introduction to Tanzania's habitats, mammals, birds, reptiles and amphibians complements the full-colour guide to "The Wildlife of East and Southern Africa" at the front of this book, which will prove useful in identifying the main species likely to be seen on safari. For more detailed coverage, a good full-length field guide is a must – some recommended **books** are listed on p.748.

Habitats

Tanzania contains a huge range of **habitats**, from scrub and bushland to a wide range of woodland including rainforests, lakes, rivers, swamps, marshes, mangroves and coral reefs. Tanzania has a higher percentage of protected wildlife areas than any other country on earth, with over a quarter of its surface area covered by national parks and game and forest reserves. Amazingly, Tanzania also spends eight times as much as the US on its national parks – no mean feat for such a poor country.

Savanna and semi-arid habitats

Savanna, consisting of patches of grassland, bushland and some lightly wooded areas, covers vast areas of Tanzania, most famously in the Serengeti. Nowadays largely protected by national parks and reserves, the **grasslands** owe a good part of their existence to human presence over the centuries: bush fires set by hunter-gatherers and cattle herders regularly cleared the land of scrub (and tsetse flies), and the trampling of cattle inhibited new growth, thereby making humans an integral part of the ecological balance. Over the last century, humans have been excluded from vast swathes of the country, and a new balance has yet to be found. Serengeti's famous wildebeest herds are now 1.7 million strong – compared with a few hundred thousand until the 1950s when the Maasai were evicted from the Serengeti – while other species have seen their numbers plummet.

In areas with more erratic rainfall, a thin scattering of flat-topped acacia trees, along with shorter acacias, occurs among the grassland, producing the archetypal imagery of the East African landscape. In drier areas, these wooded grasslands give way to the typical semi-arid flora of **thornbush and thicket**, characterized by an often impenetrably thick growth of stunted, thorny trees, which are grey for most of the year, but become green during the rainy season. Scaly-barked species such as acacia and euphorbia also occur. The true **desert** habitat around Lake Natron is drier still and plant life is very limited; many of the trees and bushes are dwarf, and large areas are bare, stony desert with a thin and patchy growth of desert grasses and perhaps a few bushes along dry watercourses.

Woodland and forest

It's estimated that 38 percent of Tanzania is covered by some form of **woodland**, including deciduous and evergreen woods, rainforests and high-altitude montane forest. Open deciduous woodland covers a large part of central Tanzania, and is known as **miombo** (the local name for the dominant *Brachystegia* tree species). Despite its dry appearance for much of the year, the woodlands are particularly rich in plants and animals and are the cornerstone for the migratory ecosystem of Selous and Mikumi, which stretches down as far as Mozambique. The pristine state of much of the *miombo* woodlands owes a lot to the presence of **tsetse flies**, which are vectors for sleeping sickness. Though wild animals have developed immunity to the disease, it strikes down livestock and humans with impunity, leaving areas of infestation largely unpopulated. For more information on the *miombo* environment, see p.280.

The most important areas of natural woodland are **rainforests**, at their most spectacular and diverse along the isolated ranges of the ancient **Eastern Arc Mountains** (see p.343), which include North and South Pare, East and West Usambara, Uluguru and Udzungwa. The isolated nature of the forests over millions of years has enabled the evolution of an incredible diversity of plants and animals, and one place in particular – Amani Nature Reserve in East Usambara – fully deserves its unofficial tag of the Galapagos of Africa (see p.361).

At higher altitude, generally over 1500m, the rainforest gradually gives way to cloudy **montane forests**. Reaching 2900m, these are characteristically interspersed with meadows of grasses, which add to their conservation value. The **main highland forest areas** are to be found on Mount Kilimanjaro and Mount Meru. Higher up, beyond the tree line, the so-called **Afro-Alpine zone** bears strong similarities to those of other high East African mountains, and includes giant heather, protea and groundsel and desolate high-altitude tundra: see p.338 for a full description.

Inland wetlands

Tanzania has more **inland waters** than any other country in Africa, ranging from enormous freshwater and caustic salt-rimmed soda lakes in the Rift Valley, to both permanent and seasonal rivers scattered with water pools, marshes and swamps.

There are several **permanent rivers**, the main ones being the Ruvuma, Ruaha/Rufiji, Wami and Pangani. All drain eastwards into the Indian Ocean. Their permanent nature makes them extremely favourable dry-season habitats for wildlife, when the surrounding savanna and woodlands become too dry. Particularly rich are: the section of the Great Ruaha as it flows through Ruaha National Park; the estuary of the Ruvuma, now protected as part of Mnazi Bay-Ruvuma Estuary Marine Park; the Wami estuary, part of Saadani Game Reserve; the Kilombero Valley; and the Rufiji, as it flows through the northern part of Selous Game Reserve. **Seasonal rivers**, which only flow during the rains, are also known as sand rivers; permanent vegetation along their banks, and water pools in their beds during the dry seasons (which are sometimes deliberately excavated by wild animals such as elephants) are particularly good places for seeing wildlife.

Where rivers pass through flat land, **marshes and swamps** dominate, and are exceptionally rich for wildlife, especially birds, whether in the rains when water levels are at their height, or in the dry season when the waters drain into permanent water pools. Two superb and easily visited areas for seeing these habitats are Selous Game Reserve and Tarangire National Park.

In the far west, three big **freshwater lakes** – Africa's Great Lakes – dominate the scene, both ecologically and, for humans, economically. Lake Victoria, in the northwest, is the world's second-largest freshwater lake, and the main source of the River Nile; sadly, the lake has become a perfect example of catastrophic environmental damage caused by man, having been the scene of the mass extinction of hundreds of fish species in the last few decades (see p.475). Still, the lake retains its beauty, and a good deal of terrestrial and avian wildlife, particularly at Rubondo Island National Park. In the west, Lake Tanganyika occupies a deep Rift Valley fissure, making it the world's second-deepest lake. It contains an amazing profusion of fish species, especially the tiny and very colourful cichlids. Even richer is Lake Nyasa in the southwest, another deep Rift Valley lake, which contains over four hundred cichlid species – one third of the world total – many of which are unique. Apart from their fish life, the lakes also mark the eastern boundary of central and west African flora and fauna, and their shores contain many plant and animal species absent elsewhere in Tanzania, most famously Lake Tanganyika's chimpanzees.

Most of Tanzania's other inland water bodies are shallow **soda lakes**, occupying Rift Valley depressions that over the ages have been filled with sediment, making them extremely shallow. Their alkalinity isn't overly conducive to wildlife, though they are important as drinking points, especially during and after the rains when the water is fresher. Their most spectacular inhabitants are lesser flamingos, usually in flocks of tens of thousands, for whom the soda-loving algal blooms in the lakes are the staple food.

The coast

The islands of the Zanzibar and Mafia archipelagos, and the narrow, low-lying coastal strip itself between the shore and higher ground inland, receive ample rainfall, as their weather patterns follow the monsoon cycle of the western Indian Ocean. As a result, they contain a range of rich habitats, including coastal plain, forest and woodland, beaches, sandbanks and mudflats, mangrove swamps and – offshore – some of the finest coral reef systems on earth.

Large areas of the **coastal plain** are covered in moist, tree-scattered grasslands, and higher areas – ideally placed to break rainclouds as they roll in from the ocean – are covered by **coastal forests**, which at Amani Nature Reserve

African Wildlife Foundation (AWF) ⓦwww.awf.org. A huge US NGO sometimes criticized for not doing nearly as much as its vast corporate income would seem to permit. Their "African Heartlands" programme promotes "conservation management partnerships" on land outside parks and reserves.

East African Wildlife Society ⓦwww.eawildlife.org. An influential body involved in the movement to ban the ivory trade (achieved in 1989, now under threat again), and active in other areas such as forest protection. Individual membership entitles you to an annual subscription to their excellent magazine *Swara* and costs £35/$65.

Friends of Conservation (FOC) ⓦwww.friendsofconservation.com. An international organization whose objectives include wildlife monitoring programmes, anti-poaching support, re-creation of habitat, rhino translocation and education of locals and visitors.

Frontier ⓦwww.frontier.ac.uk. This organization has paying volunteers – usually gap-year students – working in worldwide environmental projects. Their Tanzanian involvement included much of the research that led to the establishment of Mafia Island and Mnazi Bay-Ruvuma Estuary marine parks. They're also involved in the Eastern Arc mountains.

Jane Goodall Institute ⓦwww.jane-goodall.org. Behind the self-mythologizing style of the self-proclaimed protector of Africa's chimpanzees lies some serious and laudable work, including the on-going study of Gombe's chimps.

Tanzania Wildlife Protection Fund (TWPF) Ivory Room, Nyerere Rd, PO Box 1994 Dar es Salaam ☎022/286 6377, ℱ022/286 3496. An NGO with close government ties supporting research and the management and development of wildlife resources. They publish the excellent quarterly, *Tanzania Wildlife*.

Wildlife Conservation Society of Tanzania (WCST) Headquarters in Dar, see "libraries", p.116. An energetic Tanzanian NGO heavily involved in the research and protection of Important Bird Areas and forests, notably the Uluguru and Udzungwa mountains, and Pugu Hills. Annual overseas membership costs $30, and gets you two issues of their *Miombo* newsletter and use of their library in Dar.

are among the world's richest. However, the extent of the forests has declined massively over the last century, due to commercial logging, clearance for agriculture and ensuing soil exhaustion and uncontrolled fires. Nonetheless, a good many coastal forests survive, albeit in isolated patches. On the beach itself, tall **coconut palms** and the rather weedy-looking **casuarina** (known as whistling pine) dominate the high-tide line.

Most of the coastline, though, is not the white sandy beaches of the holiday brochures, but humid and silty **mangrove swamps** (see p.166 and p.183), which play a vital part in offshore marine ecology by acting as gigantic filters for fresh water washed in by rivers, and as impediments to coastal erosion. The largest tract is in the Rufiji delta, but all the coastal tidal creeks and estuaries are more or less bordered by mangroves (*mkoko* in Kiswahili). There are also areas of saline grassland on the landward side of some of the mangrove thickets. Although fun to travel through by boat, mangrove forests are not noted for their faunal diversity, although the mangrove trees themselves – characterized by spiky aerial roots through which they breathe – are uniquely adapted to their salty, water-logged environment. One unusual animal you're bound to see is the **mudskipper**, a fish on the evolutionary road to becoming an amphibian.

C

CONTEXTS | Wildlife and habitats

Far and away the coast's richest habitat, and the country's most colourful, are **coral reefs** which form a fringing barrier along much of the shore between Kenya and Mozambique and also surround the offshore islands of Zanzibar and Mafia. Corals, which only thrive in warm, shallow tropical waters, are a strange mix of animal and mineral: the coral that we know as jewellery is actually an external skeleton (exoskeleton) excreted by coral polyps (microscopic animals). Growing together in colonies of billions, the excretions of these polyps eventually forms gigantic reefs, which provide a perfect habitat for all kinds of marine life, from micro-organisms, sea cucumbers, sea stars and crustaceans, to a dazzling array of fish, dolphins, sea turtles and whales.

Corals however are very vulnerable to small changes in ocean temperature. The 1997–98 El Niño event, which fractionally increased ocean temperatures, in places killed up to ninety percent of corals. Tanzania's reefs are recovering well, and much of the coast, but especially Pemba, Unguja and Mafia, offer some extraordinarily inspiring snorkelling and diving.

Wildlife

The **cross-references** given below to pages with roman numerals lead to our colour guide to "The Wildlife of East and Southern Africa" at the front of this book.

Mammals

Tanzania has 310 species of **mammals**, of which 30 are endangered and 13 are endemic, meaning that they occur here and nowhere else. The majority are vegetarian grazers, browsers and foragers at the lower end of the food chain – animals such as monkeys, rodents and antelopes. The big predators are fewer in species and tend to be the dominant topic of conversation at game lodges. Tour operators make a big song and dance of the **Big Five** – elephant, rhino, buffalo, lion and leopard or cheetah – and in consequence some safari-goers feel short-changed if they fail to see these emblematic species. But don't ignore the less glamorous animals: there can be just as much satisfaction in spotting a shy, uncommon antelope or in quietly observing a herd of gazelle. And once you get the bug, you'll be looking out for a lone-striped hyena rather than the common and gregarious spotted version, or for a serval cat rather than a cheetah.

Primates

Tanzania contains dozens of primate species. One you're certain to see almost anywhere with a few trees, is the small and delicately-built **vervet monkey** (p.000), which has no difficulty adjusting to the presence of humans and, if possible, their food. Vervets are characterized by long tails, black faces, white cheek tufts and grey fur, and are perfectly adapted to a life on the prowl for fruits, leaves, insects and just about anything else small and tasty. The males have pale blue genitalia. Their main predators are leopards and large eagles, hence their constant and nervous skyward glances.

Almost as common in certain areas, notably on the coast and in lowland rainforests, are agile **blue monkeys** (p.000), whose predilection for agricultural crops makes them a pest. Other than colour, the species is very similar to smaller **redtail monkeys** (the tails are actually orange), from whom they diverged only recently; male blue monkeys who fail to gather their own "harem" can be accepted into redtail troops, and hybrids of the two species are common enough. Their main predator is the crowned eagle.

The beautiful, leaf-eating and effortlessly acrobatic **black-and-white colobus monkeys** (p.000), with attractive bushy white tails, can be seen all across northern Tanzania's forests, albeit in isolated habitats. They are usually found high in the tree canopy, swinging from tree to tree in family groups and they rarely descend to the ground. Anatomically, they're distinguished by their lack of thumbs. Rare colobus offshoots include several isolated populations of **red colobus monkeys**, notably in the Udzungwa Mountains, in Zanzibar's Jozani Forest, in northwestern Selous and at Gombe and Mahale.

If you stay in a game lodge, you're quite likely to see **bushbabies** (galagos) at night, as they frequent dining rooms and verandahs. There are two species, the cat-sized greater galago and the kitten-sized lesser galago. Both are very cute, with sensitive, inquisitive fingers and large eyes and ears to aid them in their hunt for insects and small animals.

Chimpanzees live right across Africa's tropical rainforest belt, from the Gambia and Sierra Leone to Lake Tanganyika, and are the stars of Tanzania's primates; there are several communities at Gombe Stream and Mahale Mountains national parks on the east shore of Lake Tanganyika, and a translocated population on Lake Victoria's Rubondo Island. Chimpanzees are our closest living relatives, sharing 95 percent of our genes, and exert an irresistible fascination. Like us, too, they're intelligent and complex (sometimes temperamental) social creatures who feel and share emotions, and are able to adapt to different environments and foods, pass on knowledge learned from experience and make and use simple tools, like probes for fishing ants and termites from their nests. They also hunt in a human way, use plants medicinally, raid each other's communities and sometimes descend into states of war. Their **communities** consist of fifteen to eighty individuals, dominated by "alpha males", whose dominance depends not so much on physical strength as an ability to form and keep strategic alliances with other males. Chimps are endangered, their African population having dropped from two million a century ago to around 200,000 today. Continuing worries are the on-going loss of tropical forests outside the parks, subsistence hunting and the killing of mothers to capture infants for the pet trade, entertainment industry and – notoriously – biomedical research.

Equally gregarious are **baboons** (p.000), which you'll see wherever you go on safari. There are two species in Tanzania: yellow baboons in the centre and south, and the slightly larger olive baboons in the north. Like chimps, baboons form complex, hierarchical and highly territorial troops of between twenty and a hundred individuals. Rank and precedence, physical strength and kin ties all determine an individual's position in this mini-society led by a dominant male. The days are dictated by the need to forage and hunt (baboons will consume almost anything, from a fig tree's entire crop to a baby antelope). Grooming is a fundamental part of the social glue during times of relaxation. Large males can be somewhat intimidating in size and manner, and should always be treated with wary respect, as they're quite capable of mauling humans: never feed or tease them.

Rodents and hyraxes

Rodents aren't likely to make a strong impression on safari, unless you're lucky enough to do some night game drives – or preferably walks; Tarangire is a great place for this. In that case you may see the bristling back end of a **crested porcupine** (p.xix) or the frenzied leaps of a **spring hare** (p.xix), dazzled by headlights or a torch. In rural areas off the beaten track you occasionally see hunters taking home **giant rats** or **cane rats** – shy, vegetarian animals, which make good eating. Tanzania has several species of **squirrel**, the most spectacular of which are the giant forest squirrel – with its splendid bush of a tail – and the nocturnal flying squirrel – which actually glides, rather than flies, from tree to tree, on membranes between its outstretched limbs. Very widespread are the two species of ground squirrel – striped and unstriped – which are often seen dashing along the track in front of the vehicle.

The bucktoothed, furry **rock hyraxes** (p.xxiii), which you're certain to see on the kopjes and around the lodges of the Serengeti, look like they should be rodents, but in fact are technically ungulates (hoofed mammals) and form a classificatory level entirely their own. Incredibly, their closest living relatives, apart from tree hyraxes, are elephants. Present-day hyraxes are pygmies compared with some of their prehistoric ancestors, which were as big as a bear in some cases. Rock hyraxes live in busy, vocal colonies of twenty or thirty females and young, plus a male. Away from the lodges, they're timid in the extreme – not surprising in view of the wide range of predators that will take them. The related **tree hyraxes**, as is obvious, prefer trees; they're also common around Serengeti's lodges.

Predators and scavengers

Tanzania's carnivores are some of the most exciting and easily recognizable animals you'll see. Although often portrayed as fearsome hunters, pulling down plains game after a chase, many species do a fair bit of scavenging and all are content to eat smaller fry when conditions dictate or the opportunity arises.

Of the large cats, **lions** (p.xxii) are the easiest to find. Lazy, gregarious and physically large – up to 1.8 metres in length, not counting the tail, and up to a metre high at the shoulder – they rarely make much effort to hide or to move away, except on occasions when a large number of tourist vehicles intrude, or if elephants are passing through. They can be seen in nearly all the parks and reserves. Especially good photo-ops are in the Serengeti, where they form particularly large prides; at Ngorongoro, where you may well see them hunting; and at Mikumi and Ruaha. Normally, lions hunt co-operatively and at night, preferring to kill very young, old or sick animals, and make a kill roughly once in every three attacks. When they don't kill their own prey, they will steal the kills of cheetahs or hyenas. "Man-eating" lions appear from time to time, and though usually one-off feline misfits, there are two regions that have had persistent trouble with man-eaters for decades: Kondoa, north of Dodoma, and around Tunduru in the far south.

Leopards (p.xxii) may be the most feared animals in Tanzania. Intensely secretive, alert and wary, they live all across the country except in the most treeless zones. Their unmistakable call, likened to a big saw being pulled back and forth, is unforgettable. Solitary and mainly active at night, they're difficult to see by day, when they rest up in trees or thick bush. They also sometimes survive on the outskirts of towns and villages, carefully preying on different domestic animals to avoid a routine. They tolerate nearby human habitation and rarely kill people unless provoked. For the most part, leopards live off any small animals that come their way, including small mammals, primates and birds, pouncing from an ambush and dragging the kill up into a tree where it may be consumed over several days, away from the attentions of scavengers. The spots on a leopard vary from individual to individual, but are always in the form of rosettes.

While the leopard hunts by stealth, the **cheetah** (p.xxii) uses speed. Often confused with leopards because of their spots, once you get to know them, they're impossible to confuse: more lightly built, more finely spotted, with small heads, long legs and distinctive "tears" under their eyes. Unlike leopards, which are arboreal, cheetahs prefer open ground where they can hunt. Hunting is normally a solitary activity, down to eyesight and an incredible burst of speed that can take the animal to 100kph for a few seconds. Cheetahs are most common in the Serengeti and as they hunt by day, they're highly sensitive to human presence, and careless driving and noisy tourists will ruin their chances of success. Never drive directly at a cheetah (do a series of zigzags instead), pause frequently as you approach, keep quiet, don't crowd around and don't move or start engines when they're stalking prey.

Other large Tanzanian cats include the beautiful part-spotted, part-striped **serval** (p.xxiii), found in most of the parks, though its nocturnal nature means it's usually seen scavenging around lodges at night. Up to 100cm long including the tail, it uses its large ears to locate and approach prey – game birds, bustards, rodents, hares, snakes or frogs – before pouncing. The heavily-built grey-black **civet** resembles a large, terrestrial genet. It was formerly kept in captivity for its musk (once a part of the raw material for perfume), which is secreted from glands near the tail. Being nocturnal, they're infrequently seen, but are predictable creatures, wending their way along the same paths at the same time night after night, preying on small animals or looking for insects and fruit. Also nocturnal but much rarer is the aggressive, tuft-eared **caracal** (p.xxii), a kind of lynx that favours drier zones like Mkomazi and Tarangire.

The biggest carnivore after the lion is the **spotted hyena** (p.xxi); it's also, apart from the lion, the meat-eater you will most often see, especially in the Serengeti. Although considered a scavenger *par excellence*, the spotted hyena – with its distinctive sloping back, limping gait and short, broad muzzle – is also a formidable hunter, most often found where antelopes and zebras are present. In fact, their success rate at hunting, in packs and at speeds up to 50kph, is twice that of some specialized predators. Exceptionally efficient consumers, with strong teeth and jaws, spotted hyenas eat virtually every part of their prey in a matter of minutes, including bones and hide and, where habituated to humans, often steal shoes, unwashed pans and refuse from tents and villages. Although they can be seen by day, they are most often active at night – when they issue their unnerving, whooping cries. Socially, hyenas form territorial groups of up to eighty animals. These so-called clans are dominated by females, who are larger than males and compete with each other for rank. Curiously, female hyenas' genitalia are hard to distinguish from males', leading to a popular misconception that they are hermaphroditic. Not surprisingly, in view of all their attributes, the hyena is a key figure in mythology and folklore, usually as a limping, heartless bad guy, or as a symbol of duplicitous cunning. In comparison with the spotted hyena, you're not very likely to see a **striped hyena**. A usually solitary animal, it's slighter and much rarer than its spotted relative, though occasionally glimpsed very early in the morning. You have reasonable odds of seeing them at Tarangire, and at Ruaha, which marks their southernmost extent.

The unusual and rather magnificent **African hunting dogs** (p.xx), also called wild dogs or "painted wolves" (in Latin, *Lycaon pictus*), have disappeared from much of their historical range in Africa. Their remaining strongholds are at Mikumi, Selous and Ruaha, and there are smaller and more endangered populations at Mkomazi and Tarangire. Canine distemper and rabies have played as big a role in their decline as human predation and habitat disruption.

They are efficient pack hunters, running their prey in relays to exhaustion before tearing it apart, and live in groups of up to forty animals, with ranges of almost 800 square kilometres.

The commonest members of the dog family in Tanzania are the **jackals** (p.xx), one of few mammalian species in which mating couples stay together for life. The black-backed or silver-backed jackal and the similar side-striped jackal, can be seen just about anywhere, usually in pairs. The golden jackal is most likely to be seen in the Serengeti. All three species are scavengers, feeding off grubs and the remains of kills made by predators. **Bat-eared foxes** (p.xx) live in burrows in the plains, and while not uncommon, are rarely seen as they're most active at dawn and dusk. Their very large ears make them unmistakable.

Among smaller predators, the unusual **honey badger** or **ratel** (p.xx) is related to the European badger and has a reputation for defending itself extremely fiercely. Primarily an omnivorous forager, it will tear open bee hives (to which it is led by a small bird, the honey-guide; see p.464), its thick, loose hide rendering it impervious to their stings. The solitary and nocturnal **genets** (p.xxi) are reminiscent of slender, elongated black-and-white cats, with spotted coats and ringed tails. They were once domesticated around the Mediterranean, but cats proved better mouse-hunters, and in fact genets are related to mongooses. They're frequently seen after dark around national park lodges. Most species of **mongoose** (p.xxi), attractive animals with elongated bodies and long tails, are also tolerant of humans and, even when disturbed out in the bush, can usually be observed for some time before disappearing. Their snake-fighting reputation is greatly overplayed: in practice they are mostly social foragers, fanning out through the bush, rooting for anything edible – mostly invertebrates, eggs, lizards and frogs. The most common are the dwarf, banded and black-tipped (also called slender mongoose), the latter often seen darting across tracks as you approach. Rarer are the marsh mongoose (frequent at Gombe) and white-tailed mongoose (also Gombe, and Serengeti).

Elephants

African **elephants** (p.xxiii), larger than their Asian cousins and rarely domesticated, are found throughout Tanzania, and almost all the big plains and mountain parks have their populations. These are the most engaging of animals to watch, perhaps because their interactions, behaviour patterns and personalities have so many human parallels. They lead complex, interdependent social lives, growing from helpless infancy, through self-conscious adolescence, to adulthood. Babies are born with other cows in close attendance, after a 22-month gestation. The calves suckle for two to three years, from the mother's two breasts between her front legs. Elephants' basic family units are composed of a group of related females, tightly protecting their babies and young and led by a venerable matriarch. It's the matriarch that's most likely to bluff a charge – though occasionally she may get carried away and tusk a vehicle or person. Bush mythology has it that elephants become embarrassed and ashamed after killing a human, covering the body with sticks and grass. They certainly pay much attention to the disposal of their own dead relatives, often dispersing the bones, spending time near the remains, and returning to the site for several years. Old animals die in their seventies or eighties, when their last set of teeth wears out and they can no longer feed.

Seen in the flesh, elephants seem even bigger than you would imagine – you'll need little persuasion from those flapping, warning ears to back off if you're too close – but are surprisingly graceful, silent animals on their padded, carefully placed feet. In a matter of moments, a large herd can merge into the trees and disappear, their presence betrayed only by the noisy cracking of branches as they strip trees and uproot saplings. Relatively quiet they may be to our ears, but recent research has discovered that vibrations from stamping elephant feet can be picked up 50km away, and are almost certainly a form of communication, complementing their equally remarkable language of very low frequency rumbles.

Until the 1950s, elephants inhabited almost ninety percent of Tanzania, but their range now covers just half that original area. Apart from habitat loss, elephant populations also suffered from **ivory poachers**, especially in the 1970s and 1980s, when three quarters of the national population were massacred. The more peaceful 1990s managed to bring their Tanzanian population back to a healthy 100,000, of which 60,000 or so are concentrated in Selous Game Reserve. Although the population continues to grow steadily, an abiding worry is that pressure to open up the ivory trade – in 1999 Zimbabwe, Botswana and Namibia resumed trading in ivory – may also reopen the floodgates to poachers.

Rhinos

The rhino is one of world's oldest mammalian species, having appeared on earth some 50–60 million years ago, shortly after the demise of the dinosaurs. Nowadays, it's also one of the most critically endangered, due to catastrophic poaching for their valuable horns in the 1970s and 1980s, which completely wiped out the populations at Tarangire, Mikumi and Mkomazi. There are five species worldwide, the Tanzanian one being the hook-lipped or **black rhinoceros** (p.xxiv). The name is a misnomer, having been given in counterpoint to the white rhino, where "white" was a mistranslation of the Afrikaans for "wide", referring to its lip: the white rhino's broad lip is suitable to grazing, whereas the black rhino's is adapted for browsing. Both species are actually greyish in colour.

Until the mid-1970s, black rhinos were a fairly common sight in many Tanzanian parks and reserves. In the 1960s, for example, the Selous contained over 3000, some with long upper horns over a metre in length. Today, the Selous **population** is barely 150, accounting for three quarters of Tanzania's total (which had started the 1960s at around 10,000). The driving force behind the poaching, which began in earnest in the 1970s, was (and is) the high price for rhino horn on the black market. The horn is actually an agglomeration of hair, and has long been used to make status-symbol dagger handles in Arabia and an aphrodisiac medicine in Far Eastern countries. Contributing factors to the decline are their long gestation period (15–18 months), the fact than only one calf is born, that females only come on heat every five years or so, and that the calves take a year to two to be weaned, and remain dependent on their mothers until the age of five, when the next calf comes along.

The **location** and size of most surviving populations is, understandably, a closely guarded secret, and the only rhino that can readily be visited by tourists are fewer than a dozen at Ngorongoro Crater, and a handful on Rubondo Island.

Hippos

Hippopotamuses (p.xxv) are among the most impressive of Africa's creatures – lugubrious pink monsters that weigh up to three tons and measure up to four metres from their whiskered chins to their stubby tails. Despite their ungainly appearance they're highly adaptable and found wherever rivers or freshwater lakes and pools are deep enough for them to submerge in and also have a surrounding of suitable grazing grass. They are supremely adapted to long periods in water, a necessity as they need to protect their hairless skin from dehydration; their pinkish colour is a natural secretion that acts as a sun-block. In the water, their clumsy feet become supple paddles, and they can remain completely submerged for six minutes, and for hours on end with just their nostrils, eyes and ears protruding. They communicate underwater with clicks, pulses, croaks and whines, and at the surface with grunts, snorts and aggressive displays of fearsome dentition. After dark, and sometimes on wet and overcast days, hippos leave the water to spend the whole night grazing, their stumpy legs carrying them up to 10km in one session.

Hippos are reckoned to be responsible for more human deaths in Africa than any other animal except malarial mosquitoes. Deaths mainly occur on the water, when boats accidentally steer into hippo pods, but they can be aggressive on dry land, too, especially if you're between them and water. They can run at 30kph if necessary, and their enormous bulk and long incisors advocate extreme caution. Yet if they pass through a campground at night, nary a guy rope is twanged.

Zebras

Zebras (p.xxiv) are closely related to horses and, together with wild asses, form the equid family. Burchell's zebra is the only species in Tanzania, and is found throughout the country. In Serengeti and Tarangire, zebras gather in migrating herds up to several hundred thousand strong, along with wildebeest and other grazers. Socially, they're organized into family groups of up to fifteen individuals led by a stallion. The stripes appear to be a defence mechanism for confusing predators: bunched up in a jostling herd, the confusion of stripes makes it very difficult to single out an individual to chase; the stripes are also said to confuse tsetse flies.

Pigs

The commonest wild pig in Tanzania is the comical **warthog** (p.xxv). Quick of movement and nervous, warthogs are notoriously hard to photograph as they're generally on the run through the bush, often with the young in single file, tails erect like antennae, though you can catch them browsing in a kneeling position. They shelter in holes in the ground, usually old aardvark burrows, and live in family groups generally consisting of a mother and her litter of two to four piglets, or occasionally two or three females and their young. Boars join the group only to mate, and are distinguishable from sows by their longer tusks, and the warts below their eyes, which are thought to be defensive pads to protect their heads during often violent fights.

Also common but rarely seen is the nocturnal **bushpig**, which inhabits forest and dense thickets close to rivers and marshes. They're brownish in colour, resemble European boars, and weigh up to 80kg.

Giraffes

Tanzania's national symbol, and the world's tallest mammal (up to five metres), is the **giraffe** (p.xxv), found wherever there are trees. The species in Tanzania is the irregularly patterned Maasai giraffe. Both sexes have horns, but can be distinguished by the shorter height of the females, and by the tufts of hair over their horns. Daylight hours are spent browsing on the leaves of trees too high for other species; acacia and combretum are favourites. Non-territorial, they gather in loose leaderless herds, with bulls testing their strength while in bachelor herds. When a female comes into oestrus, which can happen at any time of year, the dominant male mates with her. She will give birth after a gestation of approximately fourteen months. Over half of all young, however, fall prey to lions or hyenas in their early years. Oddly, despite the great length of their necks, they're supported by only seven vertebrae – the same as humans.

Antelopes and other ruminants

This category of mammals includes buffalo and all the antelopes – exemplified by the two-toed cud-chewers illustrated on pp.xxvi–xxxii of our colour wildlife guide.

The fearsome African or Cape **buffalo** (p.xxvi), with its massive flattened horns and 800kg bulk, is a common and much-photographed animal, closely related to the domestic cow. They live in herds of several hundred, which can swell to over a thousand in times of drought. Though untroubled by close contact with humans or vehicles, they are one of Africa's most dangerous animals when alone: you don't have to read the papers in Tanzania for long before finding an example of buffaloes goring a farmer. Their preferred habitat is swamp and marsh, though they have also adapted to life in highland forests. Buffaloes are often accompanied by **oxpeckers** and **cattle egrets**, who hitch rides on the backs of buffalo and other game. They have a symbiotic relationship with their hosts, feeding off parasites such as ticks and blood-sucking flies. The oxpeckers also have an alarm call that warns their hosts of danger like lurking predators.

The rather ungainly, long-faced hartebeest family (p.xxvi), with its distinctive S-shaped horns, has three representatives in Tanzania: the reddish **Liechtenstein's hartebeest** is the most common, especially in *miombo* and acacia woodland; the paler **Coke's hartebeest**, with a longer, narrower head, is rarely found in the north; the **topi** is seen in the Serengeti and Katavi (p.xxvi)

Large herds of white-bearded **wildebeest** or gnu (p.xxvi) are particularly associated with the Serengeti; their spectacular annual migration is described in the box on p.457. The blue wildebeest (or brindled gnu) of central and southern Tanzania lack beards and are paler in colour. The strong shoulders and comparatively puny hindquarters of both species lend them an ungainly appearance, but the light rear end is useful for their wild and erratic bucking when attacked. Calves begin walking within minutes – a necessity when predators are always on the lookout.

Of the **gazelles**, the most obvious are **Thomson's** ("Tommies") and the larger **Grant's** (both p.xxvii), easily seen at the roadside in many parts of Tanzania. The **gerenuk** (p.xxvii) is an unusual browsing gazelle able to nibble from bushes standing on its hind legs (its name is Somali for "giraffe-necked"); in Tanzania, its range is restricted to the semi-arid north, around Lake Natron, Longido, Mkomazi and a few in Tarangire. The **impala** (p.xxviii), a metre high, is common throughout Tanzania and seen either in breeding herds of females, calves and one male, or in bachelor herds. They're seldom far from cover and, when panicked, the herd "explodes" in all directions, confusing predators. Only males have horns.

The **Bohor reedbuck** (p.xxviii) has a patchy distribution, and is easily confused with impala. Only males have horns; short, ringed and forward-curving. Their preferred habitat is long grass and reedbeds near swamps, where they're easily concealed. Mountain reedbuck are similar, and can be seen at Ngorongoro. The related brownish-grey **common waterbuck** (p.xxviii) is easier to find and has a wide distribution; they have a distinctive white ring around their rump, and are seen in mixed herds controlled by a dominant male. Like reedbucks, they're often seen near water, in which they can seek refuge from predators.

Two of the world's smallest antelopes are quite easily seen in Tanzania. **Kirk's dikdik** (p.xxix) is a miniature antelope found all over the country, measuring no more than 40cm in height (4kg in weight), and are most active in the morning and evening. Usually seen in monogamous pairs (the males are horned, the females are slightly larger), their territories are marked by piles of droppings and secretions deposited on grass stems. Their name mimics their whistling alarm call when fleeing. The forest-loving **suni** antelope is even daintier, measuring up to 32cm in height, but rare and with a scattered distribution: you have very good odds on seeing them on Prison Island in Zanzibar, and a reasonable chance at Zanzibar's Jozani Forest, the Pugu Hills near Dar, in the Udzungwa Mountains and on Rubondo Island where they've been introduced.

Other small Tanzanian antelopes – all fairly widespread but nowhere common – include the surprisingly aggressive **steinbok** (p.xxxii) which, despite a height of only 50cm, defends itself furiously against attackers (best seen at Tarangire), and the grey and shaggy **klipspringer** (Afrikaans for "stone jumper"; p.xxxii), whose hooves are wonderfully adapted for scaling near-vertical cliffs. They're both grazers and browsers, and like dikdiks are monogamous, giving birth to one offspring each year; their territory is marked by secretions from glands near the eyes. Klipspringers can easily be seen at Ruaha, Tarangire and Manyara, and sometimes in Udzungwa.

The **duikers** (Dutch for "diver", referring to their plunging into the bush) are larger – the **common duiker** (p.xxix) is around 60cm high – though they appear smaller because of their shorter forelimbs. It's found throughout the country in many habitats, but most duikers are more choosy and prefer plenty of dense cover and thicket. Their isolation from other communities means that they've evolved into several subspecies which still confuse taxonomists: the most common family is that of the **blue duiker** (sometimes called Abbot's duiker), which ranges from Mount Rungwe in the south to the world's largest population in the forests of Kilimanjaro. Rarer subspecies include the tiny **Ader's duiker** on Zanzibar (Chumbe Island and Jozani Forest); the **Pemba blue duiker** (Ngesi Forest on Pemba Island); a relict population of blue duikers on Juani Island in the Mafia archipelago; **red duikers** (Kilimanjaro and Udzungwa) and **grey duikers** (Gombe and Kilimanjaro).

Tanzania's big antelopes are the *Tragelaphinae* – twisted-horn bushbuck types – and the *Hippotraginae* – horse-like antelopes. The **bushbuck** itself (p.xxx) is nocturnal, solitary and notoriously shy – a loud crashing through the undergrowth and a flash of a chestnut rump are all most people witness. The **sitatunga** is semi-aquatic by nature, found in Tanzania only in remote corners of the Lake Victoria shoreline, notably Rubondo Island, where they are easy to see. Common throughout the country is the huge, cow-like **eland** (p.xxx), which weighs 600–900kg and has a distinctive dewlap. Females are reddish, males are grey; and both have corkscrew-like horns. The elegant **striped kudu** are not uncommon but very localized, and their preference for dense bush makes them hard to see; your best chance is at dawn or dusk. There are two species, both browsers: greater kudu (p.xxx), with eight to ten lateral stripes, are best seen at Selous, Mikumi and Saadani; the smaller lesser kudu (p.xxx), which has more stripes, can be seen in Mkomazi and Tarangire. Both can be seen at Ruaha. The spiralled horns of the male greater kudus can grow up to 180cm, and have long been used by local people for making musical instruments.

The horse-like antelopes include the imposing **fringe-eared oryx** (p.xxxi), which is present in small numbers throughout the country but best seen at Tarangire, and whose long straight horns may explain the unicorn myth. They live in herds of up to forty animals, and are migratory. The massive **roan ante-**

lope (p.xxxi), with their backward-sweeping horns, large ears and black-and-white faces, has a more restricted range (mainly central and western Tanzania, especially Katavi, Ruaha and Mahale); it's often seen close to water in the mornings. Related are **sable antelope** (p.xxxi), with their handsome curved and swept-back horns. Males are black with white bellies and face markings; females are all brown. They thrive in *miombo* woodland, making them regular sightings at Mikumi, Selous, Ruaha, Mahale and Katavi. There's also a lighter and smaller subspecies at Saadani on the coast, which was formerly classed as a separate species.

Marine mammals

Of the three main marine mammals of the western Indian Ocean, the most easily seen are **dolphins**, which need no introduction. They're most easily seen off Kizimkazi in Zanzibar, though the as-yet unknown psychological effects of dozens of tourists chasing them around day after day may put you off. **Whales**, both humpback and sperm, pass along the coast from October to December on their vast migrations around the world's oceans, and – if you're exceptionally lucky – can be heard singing when you're diving. The rarest of all of Tanzania's mammals, even rarer than the rhino, is the **dugong**, the original mermaid prototype which resembles a cross between a seal and walrus. The mermaid legend probably had something to do with the dugong's habit of floating around on its back, letting a pair of bobbing and rather ample breasts work their magic on the mariners of yore. Their only known breeding ground in Tanzanian waters lies between the mainland and Mafia Archipelago, but the population there is believed to be on the brink of extinction.

Other mammals

That much-loved dictionary leader, the **aardvark**, is one of Africa's – indeed the world's – strangest mammals, a solitary termite-eater weighing up to 70kg. Its name, Afrikaans for "earth pig", is an apt description, as it holes up during the day in large burrows, excavated with remarkable speed and energy, and emerges at night to visit termite mounds within a radius of up to 5km. It's most likely to be common in bush country well scattered with tall termite spires. **Ground pangolins** are equally unusual – nocturnal, scale-covered mammals, resembling armadillos and feeding on ants and termites. Under attack, they roll into a ball.

In wooded areas, insectivorous **elephant shrews** are worth looking out for, simply because they are so weird (the elephant bit refers to their trunk-like snout). They're extremely adaptable, as their habitat ranges from the semi-desert around Lake Natron to the lush forests of Amani, Gombe, Jozani and Udzungwa. Tanzania's many **bats** will usually be a mere flicker over a waterhole at twilight, or sometimes a flash across the headlights at night. The only bats you can normally observe in any decent way are fruit bats hanging from their roosting sites by day; there are visitable roosts on Chole Island in the Mafia Archipelago, at Misali and Makoongwe islands off Pemba Island and in Pemba Island's Ngesi Forest (the endemic Pemba flying fox or Mega Bat). For more "traditional" bat viewing, visit the incredible colonies of the Amboni Caves near Tanga.

Reptiles and amphibians

There is only one species of crocodile in Tanzania – the large **Nile crocodile**, which can reach six metres or more in length. You'll see them on the flat sandy shores of most of Tanzania's rivers and lakes. Although they mostly live off fish, they are also dangerous opportunists, seizing the unwary with disconcerting speed. Once caught, either by the mouth or after being tossed into the water by a flick of their powerful tails, the victim is spun underwater to drown it, before massive jaws make short work of the carcass.

Tanzania has many species of **snakes**, some of them quite common, but your chances of seeing a wild specimen are remote. In Tanzania, as all over Africa, snakes are both revered and reviled and, while they frequently have symbolic significance for local people, that is quite often forgotten in the rush to hack them to bits when found. All in all, snakes have a very hard time surviving in Tanzania: their turnover is high and their speed of exit from the scene when humans show up is remarkable. If you want to see them, wear boots and walk softly. If you want to avoid them completely, tread firmly and they'll flee on detecting your vibrations. The exception is the **puff adder**, which relies on camouflage to get within striking distance of prey, but will only bite when threatened (or stood on); around ten percent of its bites are fatal. Other common **poisonous species** include black mambas (fast, agile and arboreal; properly called black-mouthed mambas, they're actually green otherwise), the boomslang, the spitting cobra and blotched forest cobra, night adder, bush snake and bush viper. Common **non-poisonous species** of snakes include the constricting African python (a favoured partner of the Sukuma tribe's dance societies; see p.486), the egg-eating snake and the sand boa.

Tortoises are quite frequently encountered on park roads in the morning or late afternoon. Some, like the leopard tortoise, can be quite large, up to 50cm in length, while the hinged tortoise (which not only retreats inside its shell but shuts the door, too) is much smaller – up to 30cm. In rocky areas, look out for the unusual pancake tortoise, a flexible-shelled species that can put on quite a turn of speed but, when cornered in its fissure in the rocks, will inflate to wedge itself inextricably to avoid capture. Terrapins or turtles of several species are common in ponds and slow-flowing streams. On the coast, **sea turtles** breed and it's not unusual to see them from boats during snorkelling trips, though their populations have declined drastically and all three nesting species – the Olive Ridley, green, and hawksbill – are now endangered. Trade in turtle products (including "tortoiseshell") is illegal in Tanzania and internationally.

Lizards are common everywhere, harmless, often colourful and always amusing to watch. The commonest are **rock agamas**, the males often seen in courting "plumage", with brilliant orange heads and blue bodies, ducking and bobbing at each other. They live in loose colonies often near human habitation; one hotel may have hundreds, its neighbours none. The biggest lizards, **Nile monitors**, grow to nearly two metres in length and are often seen near water. From a distance, as they race off, they look like speeding baby crocodiles. The other common monitor, the smaller **Savanna monitor**, is less handsomely marked and often well camouflaged in its favoured bushy habitat.

A large, docile lizard you may come across is the **plated lizard**, an intelligent, mild-mannered reptile often found around coastal hotels, looking for scraps from the kitchen or pool terrace. At night on the coast, the translucent little aliens on the ceiling are **geckos**, catching moths and other insects. Recent research concluded that their gravity-defying ability is due to countless microscopic hairs on their padded toes whose adhesiveness functions at an atomic level. By day, their minuscule relatives, the day geckos (velvet grey and yellow), patrol coastal walls. In the highlands you may come across prehistoric-looking three-horned **Jackson's chameleons** creeping through the foliage, and there are several other species in this part of the country.

Night is usually the best time for spotting members of the **amphibian** world, though unless you make an effort to track down the perpetrators of the frog chorus down by the lodge water pump, you'll probably only come across the odd toad. There are, however, dozens of species of frogs and tree frogs, including the diminutive and unique Kihansi spray toad, whose discovery in the spray at the bottom of a waterfall in 1996 scuppered the profitability of a hydroelectric dam, which now has to divert part of its flow to keep the toads moist

Birds

Tanzania boasts one of Africa's highest counts of **bird species**, with over 1100 recorded so far (compared with around 300 for Britain and 600 for North America). This huge variety, spread across 75 families and very roughly split across northern and southern Tanzania, is made possible by the lack of climatic extremes, and a wide range of habitats in every conceivable altitudinal range, from montane forest to semi-desert, lakes, rivers and estuaries.

Nearly eighty percent of Tanzania's birds are thought to breed in the country. The remainder are **migratory species**, breeding during the northern summer but wintering in tropical Africa. Many of these are familiar British summer visitors, such as swallows, nightingales and whitethroats, which have to negotiate or skirt the inhospitable Sahara on their migration. The extent of the migration is astonishing: an estimated six billion birds make the journey each year.

No surprise, then, that Tanzania is a superb place for **bird-watching**, whether you're a novice or a dyed-in-the-wool twitcher, so make a point of bringing binoculars. Even on a standard wildlife safari, taking in all or some of the major game-viewing areas, the birds provide a superb added attraction. The keenest independent bird-watchers can expect to encounter over three hundred species in a ten-day trip, while some of the organized tour groups can hope for a hundred more.

Many bird-watchers are attracted to Tanzania by the large number of rare species: some forty **endemics** (of which 26 are endangered), meaning that they are found only in Tanzania and often only in one or two locations, and many more **near-endemics** confined to East Africa. Pretty much every location has a few endemics or near-endemics, but three places stand out in particular: the Kilombero floodplain of central Tanzania, which recently gave three new species to science; the ancient and disjointed East African Arc Mountains (see p.343), especially in the western Udzungwas (see p.298) and at Amani Nature Reserve near the coast (see p.361); and Tarangire National Park and its adjacent conservation area in the north, whose count recently topped 550 species.

It's impossible to give an adequate rundown of the main bird species, but the following are some of the more frequently seen and easily identified species. For a full list, consult the comprehensive and constantly worked at ⊛home.no.net/stenil1/TZbirdatlas/tzatlas.htm, or get hold of a dedicated birding guidebook to Tanzania or East Africa; see p.748. A good source of information is the *African Bird Club* ⊛www.africanbirdclub.org, who publish an excellent regular bulletin and occasional monographs and itineraries. For practical advice, see "Birding" in Basics on p.54.

Large walking birds

Several species of large, terrestrial (or partly terrestrial) birds are regularly seen on safari. The flightless **ostrich** is found in dry, open plains and semi-desert in the far north, namely Tarangire, Ngorongoro, Serengeti and around Lake Natron. At up to 2.5m high, it's the world's biggest bird and one of the fastest when need be. The females are neutral in colour, whilst courting males wow the ladies with their naked pink necks and thighs. Contrary to popular belief, they don't bury their heads in the sand, but do hide them in their plumage while resting.

The large, long-tailed **secretary bird** is also easily identified, and gets its name from its head quills, which resemble pens propped behind its ears. It's often seen in dry, open bush and wooded country, usually in pairs, and feeds on beetles, grasshoppers, reptiles and rodents.

The **marabou stork** is another easy one to spot – large and exceptionally ugly, up to 1.2m in height and with a bald head, long pointed funnel-like beak and dangling, pink throat pouch. The marabou flies with its head and neck retracted (unlike other storks) and is often seen in dry areas, including towns, where it feeds on small animals, carrion and refuse. If you're lucky, you'll see them roosting in trees.

Another reasonably common walking bird is the **ground hornbill**. This impressive creature lives in open country and is the largest hornbill by far, black with red face and wattles, bearing a distinct resemblance to a turkey. It's not uncommon to come across pairs, or sometimes groups, of ground hornbills, trailing through the scrub on the lookout for small animals. They nest among rocks or in tree stumps. The Maasai say their calls resemble humans talking.

Not really walking birds, but usually seen in flocks on the ground before scattering ahead of your advance in a low swooping flight, are several species of **guinea fowl**. These game birds have rather comical and brightly coloured heads, and a luxurious covering of royal blue feathers, often spotted white. The **vulturine guinea fowl** is found in very arid areas, while the **helmeted guinea fowl**, found in wetter areas, has a bony yellow skull protrusion (hence its name).

The world's heaviest flying bird, the greyish-brown **Kori bustard**, is also frequently seen; males weigh up to 12kg. Another commonly seen ground-lover is the **black-bellied bustard**. Both distinctive and elegant is the **crowned crane**, its head topped with a stunning halo-like array of yellow plumes. They're often seen feeding on cultivated fields or in marshy areas; Lake Victoria is a good place.

Flamingos and ibises

Many visitors to Tanzania are astounded by their first sight of **flamingos** – a sea of pink on a soda-encrusted Rift Valley lake (Natron and Manyara are the best places). There are two species: the greater flamingo, and the much more common lesser flamingo, which can usually be seen in flocks of tens of thousands, and sometimes several hundred thousand strong. The **lesser flamingo** is smaller, pinker and with a darker bill than its greater relative. The Rift Valley population – which only nests at Lake Natron but migrates to feed, notably to Lake Manyara and, most famously, at Kenya's Lake Nakuru – numbers several million, and is one of only three groups in Africa. Flocks can leave or arrive at an area in a very short period of time, the movements depending on all sorts of factors including the water's alkalinity and the presence of algal blooms, so sighting big flocks is impossible to predict. Lesser flamingos feed by filtering suspended aquatic food, mainly blue-green diatom algae that occur in huge concentrations on the shallow soda lakes of the Rift.

Greater flamingos may occur in their thousands but are considerably fewer in number than the lesser, and are bottom feeders, filtering small invertebrates as well as algae. Although greaters tend to be less nomadic than their relatives, they are more likely to move away from the Rift Valley lakes to smaller water bodies and even the coast.

The most widely distributed **ibis** species (stork-like birds with down-curved bills) is the **sacred ibis**, which occurs near water and human settlements. It has a white body with black head and neck, and black tips to the wings. Also frequently encountered is the **hadada ibis**, a bird of wooded streams, cultivated areas and parks in northern Tanzania. It's brown with a green-bronze sheen to the wings, and calls noisily in flight.

Water birds

Most large water bodies, apart from the extremely saline lakes, support several migratory species of **ducks, geese, herons, storks** and **egrets**. The commonest large heron is the black-headed heron, which can sometimes be found far from water. Mainly grey with a black head and legs, the black heron can be seen "umbrella-fishing" along coastal creeks and marsh shores: it cloaks its head with its wings while fishing, which is thought to cut down surface reflection from the water, allowing the bird to see its prey more easily. The **hammerkop** or hammer-headed stork is a brown, heron-like bird with a sturdy bill and mane of brown feathers, which gives it a top-heavy, slightly prehistoric appearance in flight, like a miniature pterodactyl. Hammerkops are widespread near water and build large, conspicuous nests that are often taken over by other animals, including owls, geese, ducks, monitor lizards or snakes. Another common stork is the **saddlebill**, sporting an elegant red bill with a yellow "saddle" and black banding.

Birds of prey

Tanzania abounds with **birds of prey** (raptors) – kites, vultures, eagles, harriers, hawks and falcons. Altogether, over a hundred species have been recorded in the country, several of which are difficult to miss.

Six species of **vulture** range over the plains and bushlands of Tanzania and are often seen soaring in search of a carcass. All the species can occur together, and birds may travel vast distances to feed. The main differences are in feeding behaviour: the lappet-faced vulture, for example, pulls open carcasses; the African white-backed feeds mainly on internal organs; the hooded vulture picks the bones.

Two other birds of prey that are firmly associated with East Africa are the **bateleur**, an acrobatic eagle that is readily identified by its silver wings, black body, chestnut red tail, stumpy body shape and wedge-shaped tail; and the elegant **fish eagle**, generally found in pairs near water, often along lakeshores.

Go-away birds and turacos

These distinctive, related families are found only in Africa. Medium-sized and with long tails, most **go-away birds** and **turacos** have short rounded wings. They are not excellent fliers, but are very agile in their movements along branches and through vegetation. Many species are colourful and display a crest. Turacos are generally green or violet in colour, and all are confined to thickly wooded and forest areas. Open-country species, such as the widely distributed and common **white-bellied go-away bird** (go-aways are named after their call), are white or grey in colour.

Rollers, shrikes and kingfishers

A family of very colourful and noticeable birds of the African bush, **rollers** perch on exposed bushes and telegraph wires. They take their name from their impressive courtship flights – a fast dive with a rolling and rocking motion, accompanied by raucous calls. Many have a sky-blue underbody and sandy-coloured back; long tail streamers are a distinctive feature of several Kenyan species. The **lilac-breasted roller** is common and conspicuous.

Shrikes are found throughout Tanzania. Fierce hunters with sharply hooked bills, they habitually sit on prominent perches, and take insects, reptiles and small birds. Particularly rare is the **Uluguru bush-shrike**, found only in the Uluguru Mountains.

There are around a dozen species of colourful **kingfishers** found in Tanzania, ranging in size from the tiny **African pygmy kingfisher**, which feeds on insects and is generally found near water, to the **giant kingfisher**, a shy fish-eating species of wooded streams in the west of the country. Several species eat insects rather than fish and they can often be seen perched high in trees or on open posts in the bush where they wait to pounce on passing prey. One of the more common is the **malachite kingfisher**, which stays true to its roots by catching small fish: it swallows its prey head first after killing it by whacking it against branches.

Hornbills

Named for their long, heavy bills, surmounted by a casque or bony helmet, **hornbills** generally have black and white plumage. Their flight consists of a series of alternate flaps and glides. When in flight, hornbills may be heard before they are seen, the beaten wings making a "whooshing" noise as air rushes through the flight feathers. Many species have bare areas of skin on the face and throat and around the eyes, with the bill and the casque often brightly coloured, their colours changing with the age of the bird. Most hornbills are omnivorous, but tending largely to eat fruit. Several species are common open-country birds, including the silvery-cheeked and red-billed hornbills. Hornbills have interesting breeding habits: the male generally incarcerates the female in a hollow tree, leaving a hole through which he feeds her while she incubates the eggs and rears the young. The unusual ground hornbill is covered on p.738 under "Large walking birds".

Sunbirds and starlings

Sunbirds are bright, buzzy, active birds, feeding on nectar from flowering plants, and distributed throughout Tanzania, wherever there are flowers, flowering trees and bushes. Over forty species have been recorded in the country, with many confined to discrete types of habitat. Males are brightly coloured and usually identifiable, but many of the drabber females require very careful observation to identify them. A particularly rare species is the **Amani sunbird**, which can be seen in small flocks at Amani Nature Reserve.

The glorious orange and blue **starlings** which are a common feature of bushland habitats – usually seen feeding on the ground – belong to one of three species. The **superb starling** is the most widespread of these, found everywhere from remote national parks to gardens in Arusha, and often quite tame. It can be identified by the white band above its orange breast. Of the thirty-odd other starling species present there is a handful of near-endemics, including Kenrick's, Hildebrandt's, Fischer's and Abbott's.

Weavers and whydahs

These small birds are some of the commonest and most widespread of all Tanzanian birds. Most male **weavers** have some yellow in the plumage, whereas the females are rather dull and sparrow-like. In fact, many species appear superficially very similar; distinctions are based on their range and preferred type of habitat. Weavers nest in colonies and weave their nests, many situated close to water or human habitation, into elongated shapes which can be used to help in the identification of the species. Unique to the Kilombero floodplain in central Tanzania is the **Kilombero weaver**, while the **Usambara weaver** is endemic to the Usambara Mountains, and the best place for the rufous-tailed weaver is Tarangire.

Whydahs are also known as widowbirds. The **paradise whydah** has extremely ornate tail feathers, with the central pair of tail feathers flattened and twisted into the vertical. Male paradise whydahs are mainly black in colour, and perform a strange bouncing display flight to attract females.

Adapted from the Rough Guide to Kenya by Richard Trillo,
with additional material from Tony Stones and Tony Pinchuck

C

CONTEXTS | Wildlife and habitats

Books

There's woefully little published about Tanzania, other than glossy coffee-table tomes on wildlife or Maasai. Locally produced books are mostly in Kiswahili, a notable exception being the output of Zanzibar's Gallery Publications, owned by photographer Javed Jafferji. Apart from these publications, a handful of other English-language works do trickle onto the market each year, mostly self-published collections of oral fables and proverbs with very limited distribution – snap them up wherever you can, as specific titles are often simply impossible to track down in Tanzania.

Tanzania's best **bookshops**, which can also order titles for you, are A Novel Idea in Dar es Salaam and the Zanzibar Gallery in Stone Town. These and other bookshops are mentioned in the "Listings" sections at the end of town accounts throughout this guide. You can usually also find a decent selection of stuff in the gift shops of larger beach hotels and safari lodges. Most of the UK, US and Zanzibar-published books reviewed below can also be bought online through ⓦwww.amazon.co.uk or ⓦwww.amazon.com. For other titles, it's a matter of trying your luck in Tanzania. Books marked with a star are highly recommended.

Travel and general accounts

★ **Peter Matthiessen** *The Tree Where Man Was Born* (Harvill, UK/NAL-Dutton, US). Wanderings and musings of the Zen-thinking polymath in Kenya and northern Tanzania. Enthralling for its detail on nature, society, culture and prehistory, and beautifully written, this is a gentle, appetizing introduction to the land and its people.

★ **George Monbiot** *No Man's Land* (Picador, UK). A journey through Kenya and Tanzania providing shocking exposés of Maasai dispossession and a major criticism of the wildlife conservation movement.

Shiva Naipaul *North of South* (Penguin, UK). A fine but caustic account of Naipaul's travels in Kenya, Tanganyika and Zambia. Always readable and sometimes hilarious, the insights make up for the occasionally angst-ridden social commentary and some passages that widely miss the mark.

Explorers' accounts

Copies of nineteenth-century explorers' journals are often difficult to track down unless they've been recently reprinted. Apart from the following, ask your bookshop for anything on or by David Livingstone, John Hanning Speke, Verney Lovett Cameron, James Elton, Samuel White Baker or Johann Krapf.

Richard Francis Burton *The Lake Regions of Central Africa: From Zanzibar to Lake Tanganyika* (Narrative Press, US); *Zanzibar: City, Island and Coast* (o/p). Entertaining but often bigoted accounts of the explorer's adventures.

Henry Morton Stanley *Autobiography of...* (Narrative Press, US). Subtitled *The Making of a 19th-Century Explorer*, this is a suitably bombastic autobiography by the famous explorer. The title of his bestseller, *How I Found Livingstone*

(Epaulet, US), needs no explanation.

Joseph Thomson *Through Maasailand: To the Central African Lakes and Back* (1885, 2 vols; Frank Cass/available in the US through International Specialized Book Services). A bestseller at the time,

Thomson was the originator of "Maasai-itis" and the nonsense that has been written about them ever since. To his credit, he was one of few explorers to have preferred the power of friendly relations with the locals to that of the gun.

Coffee-table books

★ **Mitsuaki Iwago** *Serengeti* (Thames and Hudson, UK/Chronicle, US). Simply the best volume of wildlife photography ever assembled, this makes most glossies look feeble. If any aesthetic argument were needed to preserve the parks and animals, this is the book to use.

★ **Javed Jafferji** *Images of Zanzibar* (Gallery, Zanzibar). Superb photos by Zanzibar's leading photographer.

Javed Jafferji and Gemma Pitcher *Safari Living* (Gallery, Zanzibar). A photographic tribute to Tanzania's top safari lodges and

camps. By the same authors are *Recipes from the Bush*, a collection of posh nosh; *Zanzibar Style*, inspiring eye-candy for budding interior decorators; and *Zanzibar Style: Recipes*.

★ **Javed Jafferji and Graham Mercer** *Tanzania: African Eden* (Gallery, Zanzibar). Very much a brochure in book form but stunningly beautiful, with over 200 photos from all over the country, many taken over the air.

Jonathan and Angela Scott *Mara Serengeti: A Photographer's Paradise* (Fountain Press, UK). A lush photo book on the Serengeti and Kenya's Maasai Mara.

History

Extremely little of a non-academic nature has been written about the history of mainland Tanzania; most of what's available covers Zanzibar and the Swahili coast.

Africa in general

Christopher Hibbert *Africa Explored: Europeans in the Dark Continent 1769–1889* (Penguin, UK). An entertaining read, devoted in large part to the "discovery" of East and Central Africa.

★ **John Iliffe** *Africans: the History of a Continent* (Cambridge UP,

UK). Available in abridged form in Tanzania, this is the standard and recommended overview of Africa's history.

Roland Oliver and J.D. Fage *A Short History of Africa* (Penguin, UK/Viking, US). Dated, but still the standard paperback introduction.

Tanzania and East Africa

Aga Khan Trust for Culture *Zanzibar: A Plan for the Historic Stone Town* (Gallery, Zanzibar). Hefty but entertaining academic tome covering Stone Town's architecture and history in great detail.

★ **British Institute in Eastern Africa** *Azania* (BIEA, Kenya/London). Annual academic journal containing a wealth of research articles, abstracts and book reviews about all aspects of East African archeology. Subscribe through ⊛britac3.britac.ac.uk/institutes/eafrica.

Heinrich Brode *Tippu Tip & the Story of his Career* (Gallery, Zanzibar). The semi-autobiographical story of East Africa's most notorious slave trader.

G.S.P. Freeman-Grenville *The East African Coast* (UK only: Oxford UP o/p). A fascinating series of accounts from the first to the nineteenth century – vivid and often extraordinary.

★ **Richard Hall** *Empires of the Monsoon* (HarperCollins, UK). A recommended sweep across the history of the western Indian Ocean.

John Iliffe *A Modern History of Tanganyika* (Cambridge UP, UK). A mammoth work and the definitive textbook on mainland Tanzania's history.

★ **I.N. Kimambo and A.J. Temu** (eds) *A History of Tanzania* (Kapsel, Tanzania). A comprehensive round-up from various authors, and the only one widely available in Tanzania. The modern period finishes at Ujamaa (1967), making it a little dated, but it's still a great resource.

★ **Alan Moorehead** *The White Nile* (Penguin, UK/Harper Perennial, US). A riveting account of the search for the source and European rivalries for control in the region. Good for a quick portrayal of nineteenth-century European attitudes towards Africa, with plenty of contemporary quotes and extracts from explorers' journals.

Kevin Patience *Zanzibar: Slavery and the Royal Navy; Zanzibar and The Bububu Railway; Zanzibar and the Loss of HMS Pegasus; Zanzibar and the Shortest War in History; Königsberg – A German East African Raider* (all self-published, ⊛dspace.dial.pipex.com/javatour/books/patience.htm). Various short, informative and pleasurable reads about Zanzibar. Most are available in Zanzibar and Dar.

★ **Emily Reute** *Memoirs of an Arabian Princess from Zanzibar* (Gallery, Zanzibar). The extraordinary memoirs of the runaway Princess Salme, who eloped in the 1860s with a German merchant.

Abdul Sheriff *Slaves, Spices and Ivory in Zanzibar* (James Currey, UK/Ohio University, US). Covers the immensely profitable eighteenth- and nineteenth-century slave trade. Abdul Sheriff is also editor of *Zanzibar under Colonial Rule* (James Currey, UK) and *Historical Zanzibar – Romance of the Ages* (HSP, UK).

★ **Gideon S. Were and Derek A. Wilson** *East Africa through a Thousand Years* (Evans Brothers, Kenya/UK). An authoritative sweep, including the cultures and traditions of several tribes, and illustrated with plenty of black-and-white photos, etchings and drawings.

Tanzania's people

Aside from the glossy and usually very superficial coffee-table splashes on the Maasai, decent material on any of Tanzania's tribes is difficult to come by, and there's no general overview.

Gregory H. Maddox (ed) *The Gogo: History, Customs and Traditions* (M.E. Sharpe, UK/US). Covers most facets of central Tanzania's Gogo tribe, including very detailed histories of separate clans, and transcriptions of songs.

★ **Sarah Mirza and Margaret Strobel** *Three Swahili Women* (Indiana UP, UK/US). Born between 1890 and 1920 into different social backgrounds, these biographies of three women document enormous changes from the most important of neglected viewpoints.

★ **David Read** *Barefoot over the Serengeti* (self-published, Kenya). No colonial rose-tint here – the author tells of his early Kenyan childhood and later upbringing in northern Tanzania with his Maasai friend. Contains fascinating tales of both colonial and later life told in a riveting matter-of-fact way and is a superb source of information on Maasai culture.

A. Roberts (ed) *Tanzania Before 1900* (East African Publishing House, o/p). An exhaustive book containing accounts on the histories of Sambaa, Hehe, Nyiha, Fipa, Kimbu and Nyamwezi peoples.

Frans Wijsen and Ralph Tanner *Seeking a Good Life* (Paulines, Kenya). Religion and society among the Sukuma of northern Tanzania, with a Christian undertone.

The arts

Most works dealing with the arts cover the whole continent.

★ **Anon** *Tribute to George Lilanga* (East African Movies, Tanzania). Gorgeously illustrated tome collecting many works by one of Tanzania's leading Tingatinga painters.

Susan Denyer *African Traditional Architecture* (Africana, UK/Holmes & Meier, US). Useful and interesting, with hundreds of photos (most of them old) and detailed line drawings.

★ **Yves Goscinny (ed)** *Art in Tanzania* (East African Movies, Tanzania). A gloriously illustrated annual catalogue for Dar es Salaam's Art in Tanzania exhibition of contemporary artists' work: fantastic and inspiring stuff, from Tingatinga to the brilliant woodcarvings of Bagamoyo's artists.

★ **Jens Jahn** *Tanzania – Meisterwerke Afrikanischer Skulptur* (Haus der Kulturen der Welt, Germany). Even if you don't read German, this mammoth work is a must; blissfully comprehensive on all kinds of traditional Tanzanian woodcarving. It's also available at the German Embassy in Dar.

Uwe Rau and Mwalim A. Mwalim *The Doors of Zanzibar* (Gallery, Zanzibar/HSP, UK). Gorgeously illustrated glossy tome.

Frank Willett *African Art* (Thames & Hudson o/p). An accessible volume; good value, with a generous illustrations-to-text ratio.

Geoffrey Williams *African Designs from Traditional Sources* (Dover). A designer's and enthusiast's sourcebook, from the copyright-free publishers.

Fiction and poetry

Tanzanian literature in English is a rare animal indeed, as most popular fiction published in Tanzania is written in Kiswahili; books go out of print quickly, too, so snap up anything you find.

Poetry

The oldest form of written poetry in Tanzania is from the coast. Inland, poetry in the sense of written verse is a recent form. But oral folk literature was often relayed in the context of music, rhythm and dance.

Ali A. Jahadmy *Anthology of Swahili Poetry* (Heinemann o/p). Rather wooden translations of classical compositions, and pertinent background.

Jonathan Kariara and Ellen Kitonga (eds) *An Introduction to East African Poetry* (Oxford UP). An accessible collection categorized into broad subjects like "love and marriage", and "yesterday, today and tomorrow".

★ **Shaaban Robert (tr. Clement Ndulute)** *The Poetry of Shaaban Robert* (Dar es Salaam UP, Tanzania). The only English translation of works by Tanzania's foremost poet, with the Kiswahili original on facing pages; a great tool if you're learning the language.

Various *Summons* (Tanzania Publishing House, Tanzania). The only collection of modern Tanzanian poetry written originally in English, offering an intimate insight into the concerns of post-Independence Tanzania.

Oral traditions and proverbs

Oral traditions are one of the jewels of Africa, encapsulating every aspect of myth, morals and reality with ogres, flying trees, strange worlds and lots of talking animals, who symbolize all manner of vices and virtues – the hare is invariably cunning, the hyena greedy and stupid, the elephant powerful but gullible, the lion a show-off. Anthologies of transcribed stories are extremely thin on the ground, so buy what you can.

George Bateman *Zanzibar Tales: Told by the Natives of East Africa* (Gallery, Zanzibar). A delightful collection of fables and legends first published in 1908.

★ **Naomi Kipury** *Oral literature of the Maasai* (East African Educational Publishers, Kenya). A lovely selection of transcribed narratives, proverbs, songs and poetry.

Amir A. Mohamed *Zanzibar Ghost Stories* (Good Luck, Zanzibar). A collection of weird and wonderful ghost stories from Zanzibar. Available in Zanzibar only.

O. Mtuweta H. Tesha *Famous Chagga Stories* (Twenty First Century Enterprises, Tanzania). A short but sweet collection, giving a pleasant insight into Tanzania's most prosperous tribe.

Criston S. Mwakasaka *The Oral Literature of the Banyakyusa* (Kenya Literature Bureau, Kenya). Tales and proverbs from southern Tanzania.

★ **R.A. Mwombeki and G.B. Kamanzi** *Folk Tales from Buhaya* (self-published, Tanzania). A hugely enjoyable collection of over sixty stories, representative of many other African oral traditions: a flying tree, ogres, and the classic tale of how hare managed to get it on with leopardess. Wonderful stuff.

Kiswahili proverbs

Proverbs (*methali*) are an important part of daily life, and find all sorts of uses. Proverbial knowledge is respected, and speakers who allude to appropriate proverbs at the right time are much lauded. The following is a selection that you might find useful yourself. The pithier ones also find their way onto kangas – the cotton wraps worn by women – which are used to display a woman's disapproval of her husband's actions, as a reminder of a woman's worth, or as a declaration of tenderness from a lover who gave the kanga as a present.

Asifuye mvuwa imemnyea.	He who praises rain has been rained on.
Atangaye na jua hujuwa.	He who wanders around by day a lot, learns a lot.
Fadhila ya punda ni mateke.	Gratitude of a donkey is a kick.
Fumbo mfumbe mjinga mwerevu huligangua.	Put a riddle to a fool, a clever person will solve it.
Haba na haba, hujaza kibaba.	Little and little, fills the measure.
Haraka haraka haina baraka.	Hurry hurry has no blessings.
Hata ukinichukia la kweli nitakwambia.	Hate me, but I won't stop telling you the truth.
Heri kujikwa kidole kuliko ulimi.	Better to stumble with toe than tongue.
Kila ndege huruka na mbawa zake.	Every bird flies with its own wings.
Kizuri chajiuza kibaya chajitembeza.	A good thing sells itself, a bad one advertises itself.
Maji ya kifufu ni bahari ya chungu.	Water in a coconut shell is like an ocean to an ant.
Mchumia juani, hilla kivulini.	He who earns his living in the sun, eats in the shade.
Mgeni ni kuku mweupe	A stranger is like a white fowl (i.e noticeable)
Mjinga akierevuka mwerevu yupo mashakani.	When a fool becomes enlightened, the wise man is in trouble.
Moyo wa kupenda hauna subira.	A heart deep in love has no patience.
Mtumai cha ndugu hufa masikini.	He who relies on his relative's property, dies poor.
Mwenye pupa hadiriki kula tamu.	A hasty person misses the sweet things (because they cannot wait for the fruit to ripen).
Nazi mbovu harabu ya nzima.	A rotten coconut in a heap spoils its neighbours.
Pekepeke za jirani, hazinitoi ndani.	Unwarranted spying by a neighbour does not take me out of my house.
Penye nia ipo njia.	Where there's a will there's a way.
Tulia tuishi wazuri haweshi.	Calm down and live with me, pretty ones are never in short supply.
Ulimi unauma kuliko meno.	The tongue hurts more than the teeth.

Guidebooks and field guides

Many of the following are readily available in Arusha and in safari lodges. Outstandingly helpful **guidebooks** to individual parks are published by the parks authority, TANAPA. There's also a series of guidebooks to Ngorongoro published by the Ngorongoro Conservation Area Authority. All can easily be found in Tanzania.

Mammals

Jean Dorst and Pierre Dandelot *Collins Field Guide: Larger Mammals of Africa* (HarperCollins, UK). Readable and accessible with lively illustrations, though it tends to favour classifying many races as separate species.

★ **Richard Estes and Daniel Otte** *The Safari Companion: A*

Guide to Watching African Mammals (Chelsea Green Pub Co, UK). Beautifully illustrated, especially detailed on social behaviour.

D. Hoskings and M. Withers *Collins Field Guide: Handbook to East African Mammals* (HarperCollins, UK). Handy, pocket-sized and readily available in Tanzania.

Birds

★ **Ber van Perlo** *Collins Illustrated Checklist of the Birds of East and Southern Africa* (HarperCollins, UK). An essential pocket guide, providing clear colour illustrations and distribution maps for every species in East Africa, though little by way of descriptive text.

Dave Richards *Photographic Guide to the Birds of East Africa* (New Holland, UK). Over three hundred colour photos.

John Williams *The Field Guide to the Birds of East Africa* (Collins, UK).

The most commonly used book on safari, also available in German, but now outdated.

★ **Nigel Wheatley** *Where to Watch Birds in Africa* (Helm, UK/Princeton UP, US). Tight structure and plenty of useful detail make this a must-have for serious birders in Africa.

Zimmerman, Turner and Pearson *A Field Guide to the Birds of Kenya and Northern Tanzania* (Helm, UK). Comprehensive coverage in hardback.

Flora

Michael Blundell *Wild Flowers of East Africa* (HarperCollins, UK). The most readily available botanical com-

panion for a safari, part of the Collins Field Guide series.

Scuba-diving and snorkelling

★ **Anton Koornhof** *The Dive Sites of East Africa* (New Holland, UK). Highly recommended if you're at all taken by snorkelling or diving, beautifully illustrated and with thoughtful sections on environmental matters.

Ewald Lieske and Robert Myers *Coral Reef Fishes: Caribbean, Indian Ocean, and Pacific Ocean* (Princeton University Press, US). Another beautifully illustrated guide, although not everything applies to Tanzania.

Music

Music is very much part of Tanzanian life and with 129 officially recognized tribes and an open attitude to influences from abroad, the country presents an extremely broad and rich musical panorama. On the coast, Islamic influences find expression in *taarab*, a blend of Bantu drum rhythms and Indian and Arabian chamber orchestras, while brassy Cuban beats underlie the lively sounds of Dar es Salaam's dance bands, dreadlocked rastas groove along to home-grown reggae, church choirs sing the praises of the Lord through translated European hymns, and rappers evoke urban woes over Stateside backing tracks and breakbeats. But all these are contemporary genres. Much older – and musically often much more sophisticated – is *ngoma*, or traditional music, which, although gradually disappearing, can still be heard all over the country if you're patient in your quest.

Ngoma ya kiasili – traditional music

Music, songs and dance play a vital role in traditional culture, not least in providing a sense of continuity from the past to the present, as can be seen in the Kiswahili name for traditional music, **ngoma ya kiasili** – "music of the ancestors". Traditional music is also a cohesive social force: *ngomas* involve everyone present, whether as singers, dancers or instrumentalists, or in combination.

Ngoma – as it's generally known – is often drum-based (the word *ngoma* also means drum), and tends to keep to its roots, hence giving each tribe's musical output a distinctive sound. The **lyrics**, often poetry that makes full use of tribal riddles, proverbs and metaphoric language, change according to the occasion, and are used to transmit all kinds of information from reciting family histories and advising youngsters of their responsibilities, to informing newly-weds of the pains and joys of married life and to seeking the intervention of the spirits of the deceased to bring rain.

The powerful **hypnotic quality** characteristic of many Tanzanian musical traditions (the Maasai and Gogo are superb examples) is not merely aesthetic, but has its purpose: the mesmerizing rhythms of work songs help reduce fatigue, while the ethereal rhythms and intricate harmonies of ritual dances aim to bring the living and the dead together and communicate in a mental limbo. This astonishing shifting of the senses can be done for all sorts of reasons: at funerals, for the living to accompany the departed to the spirit world, or for warriors preparing for battle to come into direct contact with their proud history of success in war. But the underlying idea is that of **continuity**, that a person is never completely "dead" until forgotten by the living – a crucial concept for understanding the basis of virtually every traditional African society.

Despite damaging outside influences, to a large extent Tanzania's traditional values remain unchanged, though the structures of traditional societies themselves are changing fast. Increasingly bereft of its original context, traditional music is gradually disappearing, albeit nowhere near as fast as in neighbouring

Kenya. Nevertheless, even the most "Westernized" tribes, like the Chagga, still prefer traditional music for special events like weddings and, nowadays, baptisms and other Christian and Muslim ceremonies. It's only in remote areas that you're likely to come across traditional festivities, but if you're patient and reasonably adventurous in your travels, you'll be able to witness something more authentic than the usual tourist fare and listen to some of the most extraordinary sounds you'll ever hear.

There is another way of getting to hear traditional music. Though the *Ujamaa* period of the 1960s and 1970s (see p.718) destroyed a good deal of the old ways, it also limited radio airtime for non-Tanzanian music, with the result that sound engineers from Radio Tanzania Dar es Salaam (RTD) set off to record traditional music. The result is a priceless **archive** housed at their headquarters in Dar es Salaam, of which almost eighty recordings – covering almost as many tribes – are for sale; see p.109 for more details. Although the recordings aren't perfect in terms of acoustics, they're a national treasure and the following are some highlights. There are several full-length **soundclips**, plus a mass of cultural information on several of these tribes, at ⓦwww.bluegecko.org/kenya.

Gogo

Central Tanzania's **Gogo** are among Africa's most skilled musicians. At the heart of their musical repertoire, known in Kigogo as *sawosi*, is the **mbira** (or *marimba ya mkono*), a hand-held xylophone with strung metal tongues that resound in a small wooden resonator when struck. The *mbira*, examples of which can be bought in the souvenir emporiums of Arusha and Dar es Salaam, provides a light but insistent bassline, which becomes immensely complex when several musicians are playing (several rhythms at a time, not quite overlapping and known as polyrhythm). Interwoven with equally polyrhythmic singing, and the plaintive voices of one-stringed *zeze* fiddles, the result is both beautiful and haunting. For more information, see "The Music of the Gogo" on p.252.

Kuria

The music of the **Kuria**, who straddle the border with Kenya, is characterized by one of Africa's largest lyres, the *litungu* (or *iritungu*), which has a distinctly metallic and incredibly deep timbre, with the resonant buzzing of the strings providing the hypnotic impetus. The musical tradition remains strong, even if the elaborate trappings that were once employed – such as giant "clogs" worn by dancers – have become museum pieces. See also p.496.

Luguru (Ruguru)

The instrumental genius of Luguru women – one of very few matriarchal societies remaining in Africa – has entered something akin to folklore in Tanzania. RTD has one outstanding recording for sale. The dominant instrument is a kind of flute, whose constant rising and falling immediately captures the imagination. You might be able to see a live performance of Luguru music in the Uluguru Mountains near Morogoro; see p.278.

Luo

The Luo are the largest tribe on Lake Victoria's Kenyan shore, but a minority also live on the Tanzanian side around Musoma and between Bunda and

Ukerewe Island. Despite having been almost wholly converted to Christianity, the Luo still play traditional music and instruments. They are best known for the *nyatiti*, a double-necked eight-string lyre with a skin resonator which is also struck on one neck with a metal ring tied to the toe. It produces a tight, resonant sound, and is used to generate sometimes long and remarkably complex hypnotic rhythms. Originally used in fields to relieve workers' tiredness, a typical piece begins at a moderate pace, and quickens progressively throughout, over which the musician sings. The lyrics cover all manner of subjects, from politics and change since the *wazungu* arrived, to moral fables and age-old legends. Look out also for recordings of the *onand* (accordion) and *orutu* (a single-stringed fiddle).

Maasai

The nomadic cattle-herding traditions of the **Maasai** precluded the carrying of large instruments, meaning that their music is entirely vocal (with the exception of kudu horns blown during one or two ceremonies). The result, similar to the music of other pastoral peoples in Kenya, Sudan and Ethiopia, is an astonishing multipart singing, sometimes with women included in the chorus. The best are the polyphonic songs of the *morani* warriors, where each man sings part of a rhythm, often produced in his throat, which together with the calls of his companions creates an incredibly complex rhythm (the buzzing from the vocal chords themselves are hypnotic to the singers). The songs are usually competitive, expressed through the singers leaping as high as they can, or bragging about how they killed a lion or rustled cattle from a neighbouring tribe. The Maasai have retained much of their traditional culture, so singing is still very much used in traditional ceremonies, most spectacularly in the *eunoto* circumcision ceremony in which boys are initiated into manhood to begin their ten- to fifteen-year stint as *morani*. See also box on p.432.

Mafia Island

In Kilindoni town on Mafia Island, the whole place stops for a **monthly celebration** during the full moon, when musicians and dancers, followed by the crowd, wends its way through town. Particular dances to ask about include the *Msanja* in the south (mainly for women), and *Mdatu* in the north, in which dancers compete in mock fights for attentions of a woman. There are sadly no recordings of Mafia Island's music at RTD.

Makonde

RTD has a couple of tapes of the powerfully rhythmical drumming of the **Makonde** (see p.232), but they're best known for the visual aspect of their dances, especially the *Sindimba*, in which the protagonist – a masked dancer embodying a spirit called *Mapiko* – performs on stilts to the terrified delight of the kids.

Nyasa (Nyanja)

Over on Lake Nyasa, musical groups from various districts in **Mbamba Bay** (see p.602) compete in a series of musical contests (*mashindano*) in the dance season, roughly at the end of the harvest following the long rains. The music is quite unlike anything else in Tanzania, with weirdly wonderful rasping pipes accompanied by big drums. When not competing, the groups practise in the evenings – visitors are welcome, but keep your camera away unless given permission to take photos.

Sukuma

In similarly competitive vein, the **Sukuma** on the opposite side of Tanzania, around Lake Victoria, also have an annual cycle of dance competitions, with roots in a nineteenth-century dispute between two witchdoctors about whose medicine was more powerful. They resolved to test the strength of their skills by trying to influence the crowd to favour one or another group of competing musicians and dancers; for more information, see p.486.

Zanzibar

The influence of Arabic and Indian music is particularly evident on the coast, especially Zanzibar, where taarab (see p.754) is the dominant form. Yet *ngoma* does exist, though, being of spiritual or supernatural significance, is rarely performed in public. There are many styles, but the one you're most likely to come across is **chakatcha**, in which drums provide a fine rhythmic base for dancing. Other dances worth enquiring about include *msondo, beni, bomu, kyaso, gonga, lelemama, msewe, tukulanga* and *kirumbizi*; DJ Yusuf Mahmoud, the music and performing arts director of the annual ZIFF festival (see p.642), is an excellent contact. **Unyago**, traditionally played for girls' initiation ceremonies, has been popularized by the *taarab* singer Bi Kidude. If you're around during Ramadan, the drumming and singing you might hear between midnight and 4am is **daku**, which urges people to take their last meal of the night before the next day's fast begins.

Popular music

Nowadays, *ngoma* has all but disappeared from the street and other popular venues. Taking its place is **popular music**: jazz or dance, Christian kwaya gospel, reggae, rap and hip-hop, and *taarab* on the coast and on Zanzibar.

C

CONTEXTS

Dance music – Muziki wa dansi

For most people, Tanzania's most enjoyable musical genre is what's locally known as *jazzi* or **muziki wa dansi** – dance music. The usual line-up includes several electric guitars and basses, drums, synthesizers and a lead singer (usually also a guitarist). Band sizes can be big – anything up to thirty members – a necessity given the almost nightly performances, and the all-too-frequent defections of musicians to rival bands.

Congolese and **Cuban** rhythms and styles have had an especially pervasive influence on the scene since its inception in the 1930s, especially Cuba's pre-Revolution big bands and Congo's enormously successful Afro-Cuban brand, and styles like rumba, cha-cha-cha, salsa, marimba, soukous, kwasa kwasa and *ndombolo* are recognized everywhere.

Most bands are known by two names: their proper name, like African Stars, and their *mtindo*, or dance style, which for African Stars is Twanga Pepeta. What follows is a brief rundown of the most popular bands; for an exhaustive round-up, see Volume 1 of the encyclopedic *Rough Guide to World Music*. See also ⊛http://members.aol.com/dpaterson, which has lots more information on East African music, with articles by Rough Guide contributors Doug Paterson and Werner Graebner.

The Congo connection

The **Congolese influence** began in between the wars, when 78s of Cuban rumba began to make their way into East Africa. These shellac recordings made a huge impression on Congolese and Tanzanian musicians, and started a marriage that is still going strong today. The scene was especially lively in Congo, which was quick to adapt the new Latin rhythms to a more African beat and style, and in time it was Congolese recordings that were wending their way into Tanzania.

The Congo connection reached its height in the 1970s, after a number of Congolese musicians had fled their war-torn country to settle in East Africa. The greatest of the lot – gathering the cream of Congo's expatriate musicians – was **Maquis du Zaïre**, founded in eastern Zaïre in 1970, and which later became **Orchestre Maquis Original**. Their first *mtindo*, Kamanyola bila jasho, aptly describes their cool, laid-back style: it means "dance Kamanyola without sweating". After the death of their charismatic lead singer and saxophonist, Chinyama Chiaza, in 1985, the band began to disintegrate. Many of its musicians went off to form their own bands, of which – since the demise of **Bana Marquis** in 1999 – there's now only one survivor, **Kilimanjaro Connection**, whose arrangements include rhythms borrowed from traditional Tanzanian *ngomas*.

Although the Congolese period was dominated by big bands, a couple of remarkable individual musicians still perform under their own names: **Remmy Ongala**, much loved for his powerful political and social lyrics over driving guitar riffs, and Marquis' former lead guitarist, **Nguza Mbangu "Viking"**, who plays in his own Nguza Group.

OTTU Jazz Band and DDC Mlimani Park Orchestra

A possible throw-back to traditional *ngomas* and their competing dance societies is the habit of Tanzanian dance bands to come in rival pairs. In the early 1980s, Orchestra Safari Sound sparred off with Maquis, while in the late 1980s, and throughout much of the 1990s, the big rivals were Ottu Jazz and Mlimani Park.

OTTU Jazz Band is Tanzania's longest-established band (their nickname is *baba ya muziki* – father of music), having been formed in 1964 as NUTA Jazz, the acronym for the National Union of Tanzanian Workers. The band changed its name to Juwata in 1977, after the defection of various band members, and takes its present name from the Organization of Tanzanian Trade Unions. Under their *mtindo* of Msondo (a kind of drum and a style of music performed during girls' initiations), they reached their first peak of fame in the 1970s, and have provided the model for a welter of copycat bands ever since. Their music now, as then, is dominated by supremely fluid guitar licks and rough, brassy horns, and although the vocals can get lost at times, is still the most danceable live music you'll hear in Dar.

Their big rivals are **DDC Mlimani Park Orchestra**, who have been strong since 1978 after a number of musicians from Juwata defected. Despite suffering waves of defections themselves over the years, Mlimani Park – under their *mtindo* of Sikinde (the name of a Zaramo *ngoma*) – produced a string of hits in the 1980s (the best known is *Neema*, "My comforter"), and their tight, cohesive sound, blissful harmonies and famously poetic lyrics have made them one of Tanzania's best-loved bands.

African Stars and African Revolution

The latest big name Congo-style bands are African Stars and African Revolution. **African Stars**, better known by their *mtindo*, Twanga Pepeta, are forthright about their Congolese influences, and play a version of whatever *ndombolo* style is currently making waves in Kinshasa. From the same stable are **African Revolution**, catering for a more upmarket crowd. Their output, under the *mtindo* Tam Tam, is virtually indistinguishable from **Mchinga Sound**.

Taarab and Kidumbak

A millennium of contact and intermarriage with cultures from around the Indian Ocean and Arabia has made a perfect synthesis of Zanzibari and coastal music, which combines traditional African forms – especially drumming – with Islamic, Indian and even Far Eastern elements.

Taarab (*tarab, tarabu*) is the quintessential music of the East African coast, from Somalia in the north to Mozambique in the south. It's actually barely a century old, but has roots stretching way back to pre-Islamic Arabia, Persia and India – something easily discernible in its sound. The soloist – in Zanzibar usually female – sings in a high-pitched and distinctly Arab-influenced nasal twang, and is accompanied by an orchestra of up to fifty musicians, often dressed in full European-style dinner suits. The main instruments are cellos and violins, Arab lutes (*udi*), the Egyptian *qanun* (a 72-strong zither called *taishokoto*), *zumari* (*nay*) clarinets and sometimes drums (*dumbak*). Most groups nowadays also include accordions, electric guitars and synthesizers, all in all lending modern *taarab* an uncannily "Sonic the Hedgehog goes to Bollywood" kind of quality. No coincidence – modern *taarab* is also influenced by Indian movie scores, and by a touch of Latin imported from Congo's dance music.

Taarab is usually performed at weddings and other social gatherings, when the poetic lyrics – composed in Kiswahili and laced with Arabic – come into their own. Dealing with love, jealousy and relationships, they are often composed especially for the occasion. Some of the songs, called *mipasho*, are requested by one person specifically to criticize or upbraid another, and although the "accused" is never named, his or her identity is easily understood by the parties involved.

The doyenne of Zanzibari *taarab* was the hugely influential **Siti Bint Saad**, Zanzibar's first female *taarab* singer and also the first to perform in Kiswahili rather than Arabic. In so doing, she did more than anyone else to popularize *taarab* across the social spectrum, reaching the peak of her fame in the 1930s and 1940s, when her voice became synonymous with Swahili culture.

Equally beloved, and still going strong after a career now spanning eight decades, is **Bi Kidude** (real name Fatuma Binti Baraka), who began her career in the 1920s under the tutelage of Siti Bint Saad. Like her mentor, Bi Kidude was not afraid to broach controversial topics in her songs, including the abuse of women, and as her fame grew, she did away with the veil that she and Siti Bint Saad had been obliged to wear for public performances. Old age has done nothing to temper her independence: she has recently experimented with *taarab* and jazz/dance fusion, and has also popularized drum-based *unyago*, which was formerly reserved for girls' initiation ceremonies. With her deep, bluesy and mesmerizing voice, the "little granny" (her nickname) is a giant among African musicians.

The main *taarab* orchestras, all based in Stone Town (see p.641 for a list of venues), are the traditionalist **Nadi Ikhwaan Safaa** (Akhwan Safaa; nicknamed Malindi *taarab*), founded in 1905, who remain close to the Arabic roots of *taarab*; **East African Melody**, whose raunchy *rusha roho* wedding lyrics – sung mainly by women – and modern style invariably cause a stir; and **Culture Music Club** (Mila na Utamaduni), the largest and most successful Zanzibari orchestra, who began life in the Afro-Shirazi Party in the years before Independence. Another band worth seeking out are **G-Clef Taarab Band**, who like East African Melody, excel in thinly veiled *mipasho* lyrics.

Hiring a full *taarab* orchestra is an expense that most cannot afford. A cheaper alternative is a smaller **Kidumbak** orchestra, which features more drums (*dumbak*; hence the name) and a peculiar bass made from a tea chest, giving it a much more African feel. **Makame Fakis**, the leader of Sina Chuki Kidumbak, is the main exponent of this genre.

Rap, hip-hop and reggae

Hip-hop and rap are the poorer cousins of the thriving dance-band scene, although each of these styles has been blossoming over the last few years, especially in Dar, Arusha, Mwanza and Mbeya. The scene is always changing with groups forming and disbanding almost constantly, while others give up music permanently for lack of proper funding. As a result much of the music remains underground and performances are difficult to locate, not helped by the fact that even the big names only perform a dozen times or so a year.

The ones to look out for in **hip-hop** are **Underground Souls** – who released their first single *Battlefield* in 1998, which became an instant success – and **Sos-B**, who had a similar baptism with their single *KKZ* (*Kukuru kakara zako*). Another popular combo, **Afro Reign**, were founded in 1995 and combine rap in both English and Kiswahili with R&B. For hardcore **rap**, the granddaddies are **Kwanza Unit** ("First Unit"), formed by veterans K.B.C. and Rhymson around 1990. Other crews worth checking out include **E-Attack**, **Mabaga Fresh**, the youthful **Hardblasters**, **Mr II**, the **De-Plow-MaTz**, **Gangstas With Matatizo (GWM)**, fronted by two sons of the renowned traditional music expert, Edward Makala, and **Ngoni Tribe**, whose *Manung'ayembe* managed to annoy a whole lot of people by equating single women with ugly whores.

But rap isn't only a man's game: mingling modern preoccupations with stylish delivery is **Lady Jay Dee**, who sometimes sings with the all-female crew, **Unique Sisters**, who've had a string of national successes, including one number in Japanese. Another female success is Witness Mwaijaga, aka **Bad Gear**, whose first hit, *Unanisuuza*, caused a bit of a fluster: there are three kinds of man: "the one who loves you, the one who beats you, and the one who will only 'open your beer'".

In Zanzibar, the leading exponent is **DJ Cool Para**, who pioneered a blend of *taarab* and rap dubbed Taa-Rap in the 1990s. The other big name crew – the line-up including Cool Para at times as well as female singers – are **Struggling Islanders**. Also worth tracking down is **Chronic G**, experimenting with a fusion of rap and a traditional Pemban dance called *msewe*. Details of upcoming rap and hip-hop events, if any, are posted on ❾www.africanhiphop.com, which also carries a round-up of crews that have been most active over the last year or so.

Reggae is surprisingly underrepresented, perhaps because of years of government disapproval. The official distrust of reggae was based on the fact that rastafarians smoke marijuana as part of their religion, which to the simple and always sober President Nyerere was plain immoral. The story goes that during the celebrations for Zimbabwe's independence, Nyerere refused to shake hands with Bob Marley. Come evening, Marley's rendition of *Africa Unite* was persuasion enough, and Nyerere got on stage to shake hands with the great musician, to huge applause. The government hasn't bothered with crackdowns on reggae since 1995. The main outfit in Tanzania is Roots & Culture, founded in 1983 and fronted by Jah Kimbute, Jhiko Man (Ras Jhiko) and Ras Inno.

Kwaya

With its roots mostly in American gospel and European hymns, **kwaya** ("choir") is perhaps the least "Tanzanian" of the popular music styles, though if the blaring wattage from mobile tape vendors is any indication, *kwaya* cassettes far outsell other musical genres. The best make superb use of traditional *ngoma* rhythms, vocal power and instruments; the worst use horribly synthesized tinny backing tracks – no fun if you're stuck on a bus blasting it out.

Each *kwaya* forms part of a church community; Sunday Mass is the best time and place for listening to it live, usually marked by plenty of uplifting singing, sometimes of Latin hymns in Kiswahili, more often totally African, all interspersed by fiery admonitions from the preacher. The cassettes can be bought everywhere, especially on Sundays outside churches.

Discography

Three good **compilations** worth seeking out are: *Music from Tanzania and Zanzibar* (CD 2 vols: Caprice, CAP 21554 & 21573); *The Music of Kenya and Tanzania – The Rough Guide* (CD: World Music Network, RGNET 1007); and *Zanzibar: Music of Celebration* (CD: Topic Records, TSCD917).

Ngoma ya kiasili

One performer that doesn't quite fit into any category is Hukwe Zawose (CDs: *Tanzania Yetu and Meteso*, Triple Earth; *The Art of Hukwe Zawose*, JVC; *Chibite*, RealWorld), who plays a modernized form of traditional Gogo *mbira* music.

The best place for buying **cassettes** of traditional *ngoma* is RTD in Dar es Salaam (see p.109), who have almost eighty different tapes for sale at Tsh1000 a pop. Dozens of playable, full-length recordings of Maasai, Kuria and Luo *ngoma* can be heard at ⓦwww.bluegecko.org/kenya.

Gogo *Tanzanie: chants des Wagogo et des Kuria* (CD: Maison des Cultures du Monde/Auvidis, 1992).

Iraqw *Safari Ingi* (CD: ⓦwww.leopardmannen.no/hanssen/safari.htm).

Maasai *Music of the Maasai* (CD: Hans Johnson, ⓔmaasaiboy@hotmail.com).

Sukuma *Tanzania: Music of the Farmer Composers of Sukumaland* (CD: Multicultural Media, MCM3013).

Various *Ouganda, Kenya, Tanzanie – Musiques de Cérémonies* (CD: Nonesuch, 7559-72063-2); *Maisha: Musiques de Tanzanie* (CD: Musique du Monde, 92546-2).

Taarab and kidumbak

Bi Kidude *Zanzibar* (CD: RetroAfric, RETRO12CD).

Culture Musical Club *The Music of Zanzibar* (CD: Globestyle, CDORB 041); *Spices of Zanzibar* (CD: Network Medien, 24.210); *Bashraf: Taarab Instrumentals from Zanzibar* (CD: Dizim, 4509).

Ikhwaan Safaa *The Music of Zanzibar: Ikhwani Safaa Musical Club* (CD: Globestyle, CDORB 033).

Kidumbak Kalcha *Ng'ambo – The other side of Zanzibar* (CD: Dizim, 4501).

Jazz and muziki wa dansi

The best place for buying cassettes of dance classics is RTD in Dar es Salaam (see p.109), which has close to a hundred recordings for sale.

Bana Maquis *Leila* (CD: Dakar Sound, 2002968).

Mbaraka Mwinshehe & The Morogoro Jazz Band *Masimango* (CD: Dizim, AAD, 69–72).

Mlimani Park Orchestra *Sikinde* (CD, cassette: Africassette/World Music Network, AC 9402); *Sungi* (CD: Popular African Music, PAM 403).

Orchestre Makassy *Agwaya* (LP: Virgin V2236; o/p); *The Greatest Hits of "Makassy"* (Editions Makassy (AI Records, EMKLP 01).

Remmy Ongala & Orchestre Super Matimila *Nalilia Mwana* (CD: WOMAD, 010); *Songs for the Poor Man* (CD: Real World/Womad

Select, WSCD0002); *The Kershaw Sessions* (CD: Strange Roots, ROOTCD004).

Shikamoo Jazz Band *Chela Chela Vol. 1* (CD: RetroAfric, Retro 9CD).

Tatunane *Bongoland* (CD: Amanda Music, AMA 9504); *Tanzanian Beat* (CD: King Record, KICC 5221).

Various *Dada Kidawa – Classic Tanzanian Hits from the 1960s* (CD: Original Music, OMCD 032); *The Tanzania Sound* (CD: Original Music, OMCD 018); *Musiki wa Dansi: Afropop Hits from Tanzania* (CD: World Music Network/Africassette, AC9403); *The Tanzania Sound* (CD: Original Music, OMCD018).

Rap and hip-hop

It's difficult to find particular recordings; just throw a few names at the tape vendors in the streets and see what they come up with.

Kwanza Unit *Kwanzanians* (CD: ⓦwww.africanhiphop.com).

Language

Language

A beginner's guide to Kiswahili

K iswahili is a Bantu language, incorporating thousands of foreign words – the majority of them Arabic – and is, perhaps surprisingly, one of the easiest languages to learn. It's pronounced exactly as it's written, with the stress nearly always on the penultimate syllable. Even with limited knowledge you can make yourself understood and people are delighted if you make the effort, though you'll rarely have problems in tourist areas with English. Zanzibar is acknowledged as being the source of the "standard" dialect of Kiswahili that is spoken throughout East Africa.

Phrasebooks and language courses

The best phrasebook is the **Rough Guide Swahili Phrasebook**. A good dictionary, available in Zanzibar, is the two-volume edition published by Oxford University Press, available in Arusha and Dar es Salaam. In Tanzania, language courses can be arranged in Arusha (see p.391), Bagamoyo (see p.149), Dar es Salaam (see p.116), Morogoro (p.274), Stone Town (see p.644) and Iringa (see p.569).

Pronunciation

Once you get the hang of voicing every syllable, pronunciation is easy. Each vowel is syllabic, and odd-looking combinations of consonants are often pronounced as one syllable, too. **Shauri** (advice) for example, is pronounced "sha-oor-i". Nothing is silent.

You'll often come across an "m" which is almost always pronounced as one syllable with what follows it. Just add a bit of an "m" sound at the beginning: eg **mboga** (vegetables) is pronounced "mmmb-oga". Don't say "erm-boga" or "mer-boga" – you'll be misunderstood. The letter "n" can precede a number of others and gives a nasal quality.

For memorizing, it often helps to ignore the first letter or syllable. Thousands of nouns, for example, start with "ki" (singular) and "vy" (plural), and they're all in the same noun class.

A as in Arthur
B as in bed
C doesn't exist on its own
CH as in church, but often sounds like a "t", a "dj", or a "ky"
D as in donkey
DJ as in pyjamas

DH like a cross between dhow and thou
E between the "e" in Edward and "ai" in ailing
F as in fan
G as in good
GH at the back of the throat, like a growl; nearly an "r"

H as in harmless, sometimes contracted from KH as in loch
I like the "e" in evil
J as in jug
K as in kiosk, sometimes like soft "t" or "ch"
KH a "k" but breathier
L as in lullaby, but often pronounced "r"
M as in Martian
MN one syllable, eg mnazi (coconut), "mna-zi"
N as in nonsense
NG as in wrong, but sometimes pronounced with no "g" sound at all
O as in orange, never as in "open" or "do"
P as in penguin

Q doesn't exist (except in early romanized texts; now "k")
R as in rapid, or rolled as in the French *rapide*
S as in Samson
T as in tiny
TH as in thanks, never like the "th" in them
U as in lute
V as in victory
W as in wobble
X doesn't exist
Y as in you
Z as in zero

Noun classes put people off Kiswahili. They are something like the genders in French or Latin in that you alter each adjective according to the class of noun. In Kiswahili you add a prefix to the word. Each class covers certain areas of meaning and usually has a prefix letter associated with most of its nouns. For example, words beginning "ki" or "ch" (singular), and "vi" or "vy" (plural) are in the general class of "things", notably smallish things (eg **kitoto** – small child, infant). Words beginning "m" in the singular and "wa" in the plural are people (eg **mtu/watu** – person/people; **mtalii/watalii** – tourist/s). Words beginning "m" (singular) and "mi" (plural) are often trees and plants (eg **mti, miti** – tree/s), or have connections with life. Most abstract nouns begin with "u" (eg **uhuru** – freedom, **utoto** – childhood). There are seven or eight classes (and plurals for each), but this gives you some idea.

Prefixes get added to adjectives, so you get **kiti kizuri** – a good chair; **mtu mzuri** – a good person; **miti mizuri** – lovely trees. Really correct Kiswahili, with everything agreeing, isn't much spoken except on the coast, and you can get away with murder. But once you've grasped the essential building blocks – the root meanings and the prefixes, suffixes and infixes of one or two letters which turn them into words – it becomes a very creative language to learn.

Although nouns are relatively complicated, the **verb** system is reasonably simple. You begin with a prefix for the person, then a marker for the tense (or just "ku-" for the infinitive), and then the verb root. So from the verb **ku-taka** (to want), you get **ni-na-taka** – I want, **u-li-taka** – you wanted, and **wa-ta-taka** – they will want. The present marker "na" isn't really a tense marker but a little connective, the best translation of which is really "with". Negatives are a bit more difficult: in principle, you add "ha-" at the beginning, but in the present you take away the tense marker and change the last letter to "i", so the negative of **tu-na-jua** ("we know") is **ha-tu-ju-i** ("we don't know"); also, the "ha-" gets merged into the singular person prefixes, as shown below.

Personal prefixes

I **ni-** (sometimes omitted in the present; negative **si-**). Eg: **najua** "I know", **sijui** "I don't know"
you (sing) **u-** (negative **hu-**)
he or she **a-** (negative **ha-**)

we **tu-** (negative **hatu-**)
you (pl) **m-** (negative **ham-**)
they (people or animals) **wa-** (negative **hawa-**)

Third person prefixes for inanimate objects are usually the same as their noun prefixes, but are i- (singular) and zi- (plural) for the common nouns in the N-class. However, for people and animals, regardless of the class, they are always a- and wa-

Pronouns

I, me – **mimi**
you (sing.) – **wewe**
he, she, him, her – **yeye**

we, us – **sisi**
you (pl.) – **ninyi**
they, them – **wao**

Verbs

There are a few exceptions and irregularities, but the **verb system** is basically straightforward and makes conversational Kiswahili a realistic goal even for convinced non-linguists. With irregular verbs (indicated below), the "ku" of the infinitive stays with the root.

to want – **ku-taka**
to come – **kuja** (irregular)
to go – **kwenda** (irregular)
to eat – **kula** (irregular)
to drink – **kunywa** (irregular)
to sleep – **ku-lala**
to be tired – **ku-choka**
to dream – **ku-otandoto**
to stay – **ku-kaa**
to say, speak – **ku-sema**
to see, to meet – **ku-ona, ku-onana**
to look – **ku-tazama**
to hear – **ku-sikia**
to buy – **ku-nunua**
to know – **ku-jua**

to think – **ku-fikiri**
to like/love – **ku-penda** (to love is irregular)
to be able (can) – **ku-weza**
to give – **ku-pa**
to bring – **ku-leta**
to be/become – **ku-wa**
to come from – **ku-toka**
to have – **ku-wa na** (litt. "to be with")
to play – **ku-cheza**
to drink – **kunywa** (irregular)
to be happy – **furai** (abbreviated to nafrai)
to write – **ku-andika**
to read – **ku-soma**
to do – **ku-fanya**

Tenses

present tense – **-na-**
past tense – **-li-**

future tense – **-ta-**
just past, or still going on – **-me-**

Examples of pronouns, verbs and tenses

she wanted – **a-li-taka**
I'm tired – **ni-me-choka**
we will sleep – **tu-ta-lala**
did you hear? – **u-li-sikia?**
they like... – **wa-na-penda...**
are you (pl.) going? – **m-na-enda?**
has he come? – **a-me-kuja?**
have they gone? – **wa-me-kwenda?**
she said... – **a-li-sema...**

can I...? – **ni-na-weza...?**
I will bring – **ni-ta-leta**
we are staying (at/in)... – **tu-na-kaa...**
I know – **ni-na-jua**
For the present tense of "to have", you can say **mimi nina gari** (I am with a car/I have a car) or just **nina gari, una gari, ana gari,** etc.

Words and phrases

The words and phrases listed here are all in common usage but Kiswahili (like English) is far from being a homogeneous language, so don't be surprised if you sometimes get funny looks. And, for lack of space for explanation, there are a number of apparent inconsistencies; just ignore them unless you intend to learn the language seriously. These phrases should make you understood at least.

Greetings

Hello – **Jambo** or **Hujambo** (multi-purpose greeting, means "problems?"); reply **Jambo** or **Sijambo** ("no problems"). Used mainly by tourists – if you want to distinguish yourself, use **Habari**

How are things? – **Habari?** ("news?"); can be qualified, eg. **Habari gani?** ("your news?"), **Habari yako?** ("what news?"), **Habari za kazi?** ("news of work?") or **Habari za safari?** ("news of the safari?"). Reply **mzuri** ("good"), **mzuri sana** ("very good"), or other adjective

"I show my respect" (said to an elder) **Shikamoo** (**Shikamooni** when greeting several), usually qualified by a title (**Shikamoo baba** for a man, **-mama** mother, **-bibi** grandmother, **-babu** grandfather, **-mzee** sir); reply **Marahaba**

What's up? (informal) – **Vipi?** Reply **Poa!** ("cool!") or **Fresh!** (ditto)

Peace be on you (spoken on the coast) – **Salaam alek**; reply **Wa alek issalaam**

Hello? May I come in? (said on knocking or entering) – **Hodi!**

Come in, enter, welcome (also said when offering something) – **Karibu**

Goodbye – **Kwaheri** (**Kwaherini** when speaking to several people); literally "with blessings"

Good night (when leaving) – **Usiku mwema**

Sleep well – **Lala salama**

Come back again – **Rudi tena**

We shall meet again – **Tutaonana**

Thank you – **Asante** (**asanteni** when speaking to several people)

My name is/I am called... – **Jina langu/Nina itwa...**

Where are you from? – **Unatoka wapi?**

I am from... – **Ninatoka...**

I'm British/American/German/French/Italian – **Mimi Mwingereza/Mwamerika/ Mjerumani/Mfaransa/Mwitalia**

yes – **ndio** (lit. "it is so"), or **naam** (especially on the coast)

no – **hapana** (a general negative); **la** (especially on the coast)

I don't understand – **Sifahamu/Sielewi**

Do you speak English? – **Unasema kingereza?**

I don't speak Kiswahili, but... – **Sisemi kiswahili, lakini...**

How do you say... in Kiswahili? – **Unasemaje kwa kiswahili...?**

Could you repeat that? – **Sema tena** (lit. "speak again")

I don't know – **Sijui**

friend – **rafiki**

If God wills it – **Mungu akipenda**, or **Inshallah** (Arabic)

Praise God – **Alhamdullilah** (Arabic, on coast), **Tunamshukuru mwenyezi Mungu**

OK – **sawa** or **sawa sawa**

please – **tafadhali**

Excuse me (let me through) – **Hebu**

sorry, pardon – **samahani**

No problem – **Hakuna matata/wasiwasi**

It's nothing – **Si kitu**

really? – **I say?** (one of the funnier English loan words)

I want to take a photo – **nataka piga picha**

May I take your picture – **nikupige picha?**

child – **mtoto** (pl. **watoto**)

father – **baba** (also used for a man)

mother – **mama** (also used for a woman)

grandfather – **babu** (also used for an old man or elder)

grandmother – **bibi** (also used for an old woman or elder)

mister – **bwana**

sir – **mzee** (a term of respect for an old or important man); pl. **wazee**

teacher (also a term of respect) – **mwalimu**

Basics

very – sana
why? – kwa nini?
because... – kwa sababu...
who? – nani?
what? – nini?
which? – gani?
and/with – na
or – au
(it) is/(they) are – ni
isn't it? – siyo?

good, pretty – -zuri (with a prefix at the front)
bad – -baya (ditto)
not bad – si mbaya
clean, fine, cool – safi
big – -kubwa
small – -dogo
a lot of – -ingi
mine – langu
maybe – labda
exactly – kabisa (used as positive emphasis)

Getting around

where (is)? – iko wapi?
when? – lini?
vehicle – gari (pl. magari)
taxi – teksi
bicycle – baiskeli
bus – basi (pl. mabasi)
communal minibus – daladala
train – treni
ferry – kivuko
boat/ship – chombo/meli
canoe (usually a dugout) – mtumbwi
outrigger (with sail) – ngalawa
trading dhow (large and uncommon) – jahazi
trading dhow (smaller) – mashua
plane – ndege
station – stesheni
bus stand – kituo cha mabasi
ferry terminal – kivukoni
ticket tout – manamba
petrol – petroli
road, path – njia/ndia
highway – barabara
roundabout – keeplefti (from old English
   signs)
on foot/walking – kwa miguu

When does it leave? – Inaondoka lini?
When will we arrive? – Tutafika lini?
Wait!/Hang on a moment! – Ngoja!/Ngoja
   kidogo!
slowly – pole pole
fast, quickly – haraka
Stop! – Simama!
Where are you going? – Unaenda wapi?
To where? – Mpaka wapi?
From where? – Kutoka wapi?
How many kilometres? – Kilometa ngapi?
I'm going to... – Nenda...
Move along, squeeze up a little –
   Songa!/Songa kidogo!
Let's go – Twende
Keep on going – Twende tuu
straight ahead – moja kwa moja
right – kulia
left – kushoto
up – juu
down – chini
I want to get off here – Nataka kushuka
   hapa
The car has broken down – Gari imevunjika

Health and toiletries

I'm ill – Mimi mgonjwa
doctor – daktari
hospital – hospitali
Where is the bathroom? – Iko wapi choo?
Insect – dudu
insect repellent – dawa ya wadudu

laundry – kufuliwa
medicine – dawa; dawa baridi is Western
   medicine: dawa kali is traditional medicine
razor – sembe
soap – sabuni

Shopping

shop - **duka**
street vendor - **machinga**
business, commerce - **biashara**
open - **fungua**
closed - **funga**
money - **pesa**
How much? (quantity) - **Ngapi?**
How much? (price) - **Pesa ngapi?, Bei gani?**
  or **Shillingi ngapi?**

That's too much - **Mingi zaidi**
expensive - **ghali sana**
cheap - **rahisi**
Reduce the price! - **Punguza kidogo!**
Give me (can I have?)... - **Nipe...**
I want... - **Nataka...**
May I have... - **Naomba...** (more polite)
I don't want... - **Sitaki...**
I don't want to do business - **Sitaki biashara**

Accommodation

Where can I stay? - **Naweza kukaa wapi?**
Can I stay here? - **Naweza kukaa hapa?**
room/s - **chumba/vyumba**
Do you have a room? - **Hini chumba hapa?**
I want a room for two nights - **Nataka
  chumba kwa wasiku mbili**

bed - **kitanda** (pl. **vitanda**)
toilet, bathroom - **choo, bafu**
hot/cold water - **maji moto/baridi**
en-suite room - **self container**
Where's the bathroom? - **Iko wapi choo?**

Food and drink

food - **chakula**
restaurant - **hoteli**
tea house (very basic restaurant) - **mgahawa**
table - **meza**
Is there any...? - **Iko...?** or **Kuna...?**
Yes, there is... - **Iko...** or **Kuna...**
No, there isn't - **Haiko...** or **Hakuna...**

half portion - **nusu**
again/more - **tena**
enough - **tosha/basi**
grilled - **choma**
boiled - **mchemsho**
enjoy your food - **kufurahia chakula**

Food items

andazi - doughnut
chai - tea
chipsi - chips
chipsi mayai - chip omelette
chumvi - salt
irio - maize mashed with beans
kababu - miniature kebabs
kamba - prawns
kamba coach - lobster
kitumbua - rice cake
kondo - lamb
kuku - chicken
mahindi - maize cob
maini - liver

mantabali - "Zanzibari pizza" – like a
  spring roll
matoke - banana stew
mayai - eggs
mboga - vegetables
mishkaki - grilled goatmeat skewers
mtama - millet
ngisi - squid
nyama - meat
pweza - octopus
samaki - fish
sambusa - samosa
sukari - sugar
uji - millet porridge

Fruit

chenza - tangerine
chongoma - Indian plum
chungwa - orange

dafu - young coconut (for drinking)
danzi - sour orange
doriani - durian

embe - mango
fenesi - jackfruit
gulabi - rose apple
korosho - cashew
kungu - Indian almond
kungumanga - pomegranate
limau - lemon
mratab - sapodilla
nanasi - pineapple
nazi - coconut
ndimu - lime
ndizi - banana

papai - papaya
pasheni - passion fruit
pea - avocado
pera - guava
sheli sheli - breadfruit
shoki-shoki - litchi
stafeli - custard apple
tende - date
tikiti - watermelon
tufaa jekenda - Malay apple
ukwaju - tamarind
zabibu - grape

Drinks

a drink - kinywaji
drinking water - maji ya kunywa
beer - bia (commercial); pombe (including local brews)
bottle - chupa
coconut juice - tuwi
coffee - kahawa
tea - chai

milk - maziwa
hot/cold (asked of sodas and beers) - moto/baridi
ice - barafu
coffee - kahawa
water - maji
milk - maziwa

Time, calendar and numbers

number - namba
What time is it? - Saa ngapi?
four o'clock - saa nne
quarter past - na robo
half past - na nusu
quarter to - kasa robo
minutes - dakika
yesterday - jana
today - leo
tomorrow - kesho
in two days - kesho kutwa
daytime - mchana
night time - usiku
dawn - alfajiri
morning - asubuhi
last/this/next week - wiki iliopita/hii/ijayo
this year - mwaka huu
this month (lit. "moon") - mwezi huu
now - sasa
soon - sasa hivi
wait - ngoja
not yet - bado
Monday - jumatatu
Tuesday - jumanne
Wednesday - jumatano
Thursday - alhamisi
Friday - ijumaa

Saturday - jumamosi
Sunday - jumapili
1 - moja
2 - mbili
3 - tatu
4 - nne
5 - tano
6 - sita
7 - saba
8 - nane
9 - tisa
10 - kumi
11 - kumi na moja
12 - kumi na mbili
20 - ishirini
21 - ishirini na moja
30 - thelathini
40 - arbaini
50 - hamsini
60 - sitini
70 - sabaini
80 - themanini
90 - tisini
100 - mia or mia moja
121 - mia moja na ishirini na moja
1000 - elfu

Danger – **Hatari!**
Warning – **Angalia!/Onyo!**

Fierce dog! – **Mbwa mkali!** (lit. "hot dog!")
No entry! – **Hakuna njia!**

Animals

Animal is **mnyama** (plural **wanyama**) but most species' names are the same in singular and plural.

aardvark – **muhanga**
Abbot's duiker – **vinde**
African hunting dog – **mbwa mwitu**
baboon – **nyani**
bat-eared fox – **bweha masigio**
bee – **nyuki**
bird – **ndege**
black-and-white colobus – **mbega**
blue monkey – **nyabu**
buffalo – **nyati** or **mbogo**
bushbaby – **komba**
bushbuck – **mato**
bushpig – **ngubi**
cane rat – **ndeze**
caracal – **simbamangu**
cat – **paka**
cattle – **ng'ombe**
cheetah – **duma** or **ndoa ndoa**
chimpanzee – **soko**
civet – **fungo**
crocodile – **mamba**
dog – **mbwa**
donkey, ass – **punda**
duiker – **nsya**
eland – **pofu**
elephant – **tembo** or **ndovu**
elephant shrew – **sange**
gazelle – **swala**
genet – **kanu**
gerenuk – **swala twiga**
giraffe – **twiga**
goat – **mbuzi**
Grant's gazelle – **swala granti**
ground squirrel – **kindi**
hare – **sunguru**
hartebeest – **kongoni**
hippopotamus – **kiboko**
horse – **farasi**
hyena – **fisi**
impala – **swala pala**

insect – **dudu**
iringa red colobus – **ng'uluba**
jackal – **bweha**
klipspringer – **mbuzi mawe**
kudu – **tandala**
leopard – **chui**
lion – **simba**
lizard – **mjusi**
mongoose – **nguchiro**
monkey – **tumbili**
oryx – **choroa**
ostrich – **mbuni**
otter – **fisi maji**
pangolin – **kakakuona**
pig, hog – **nguruwe**
porcupine – **nungu**
ratel – **nyegere**
red duiker – **nfuno**
reedbuck – **tohe**
rhinoceros – **faru**
roan antelope – **korongo**
rock hyrax – **pimbi**
sable antelope – **pala hala**
safari ant – **siafu**
serval – **mondo**
shark – **papa**
sheep – **kondoo**
snake – **nyoka**
spring hare – **kamandegere**
steinbok, grysbok – **dondoo**
Suni antelope – **swangala**
Thompson's gazelle – **swala tomi**
topi – **nyamera**
tortoise – **kobe**
tree hyrax – **pembere**
vervet monkey – **tumbili**
warthog – **nigri**
waterbuck – **kuru**
wildebeest – **nyumbu**
zebra – **punda milia**

Glossary

These words are all in common usage. Remember, however, that plural forms often have different beginnings.

askari – security guard, soldier

banda – any kind of hut (usually round and thatched)

baraza – stone bench, a sitting or meeting place

benki – bank

boma – Maasai village; also colonial German headquarters

boriti – mangrove poles used in building

buibui – the black cover-all cloak and veil of Muslim women

chai – a tip or bribe, literally "tea"

choo – toilet

imam – the man who leads prayers in a mosque

kabila – tribe

kanga – (or khanga) printed cotton sheet used as a wrap, incorporating a proverb

kaniki – cotton cloth

kanisa – church

kaskazi – northeast monsoon, blows December–March

kitenge – double-paned cotton cloth

korongo – ditch or ravine

kusi – southwest monsoon, blows strongest June–September

mabati – corrugated metal used as roofing

majengo – buildings

makuti – palm-leaf thatch, used for roofing

malaika – angel

malaya – prostitute

maskini – the poor, beggars (Saidia maskini! – "Help the poor!")

mbuga – black cotton soil, impassable by motor vehicles in rains

mihrab – prayer niche set in a mosque's qibla wall facing Mecca

msikiti – mosque

mtaa – ward or neighbourhood; used for "street" in Dar es Salaam

mtalii – (pl. watalii) tourist

Mungu – God

murram – red or black clay soil road

mzungu – (pl. wazungu) white person

ngoma – dance, drum, music, celebration

ngoma ya kiasili – traditional music

panga – multipurpose machete

polisi – police

posta – post office

rondavel – round cottage or chalet

safari – journey of any kind

sahil – coast

semadari – traditional Zanzibari four-poster bed

serikali – government

shamba – small farm, plot

shule – school (skule on Zanzibar)

sigara – cigarettes

simu – telephone

soko – market

soko kuu – main market

Ulaya – Europe

Index

and small print

Index

Map entries are in colour

A

I

J

K

L

INDEX

Twenty Years of Rough Guides

In the summer of 1981, Mark Ellingham, Rough Guides' founder, knocked out the first guide on a typewriter, with a group of friends. Mark had been travelling in Greece after university, and couldn't find a guidebook that really answered his needs.There were heavyweight cultural guides on the one hand – good on museums and classical sites but not on beaches and tavernas – and on the other hand student manuals that were so caught up with how to save money that they lost sight of the country's significance beyond its role as a place for a cool vacation. None of the guides began to address Greece as a country, with its natural and human environment, its politics and its contemporary life.

Having no urgent reason to return home, Mark decided to write his own guide. It was a guide to Greece that tried to combine some erudition and insight with a thoroughly practical approach to travellers' needs. Scrupulously researched listings of places to stay, eat and drink were matched by careful attention to detail on everything from Homer to Greek music, from classical sites to national parks and from nude beaches to monasteries. Back in London, Mark and his friends got their Rough Guide accepted by a far-sighted commissioning editor at the publisher Routledge and it came out in 1982.

The Rough Guide to Greece was a student scheme that became a publishing phenomenon. The immediate success of the book – shortlisted for the Thomas Cook award – spawned a series that rapidly covered dozens of countries. The Rough Guides found a ready market among backpackers and budget travellers, but soon acquired a much broader readership that included older and less impecunious visitors. Readers relished the guides' wit and inquisitiveness as much as the enthusiastic, critical approach that acknowledges everyone wants value for money – but not at any price.

Rough Guides soon began supplementing the "rougher" information – the hostel and low-budget listings – with the kind of detail that independent-minded travellers on any budget might expect. These days, the guides – distributed worldwide by the Penguin group – include recommendations spanning the range from shoestring to luxury, and cover more than 200 destinations around the globe. Our growing team of authors, many of whom come to Rough Guides initially as outstandingly good letter-writers telling us about their travels, are spread all over the world, particularly in Europe, the US and Australia. As well as the travel guides, Rough Guides publishes a series of dictionary phrasebooks covering two dozen major languages, an acclaimed series of music guides running the gamut from Classical to World Music, a series of music CDs in association with World Music Network, and a range of reference books on topics as diverse as the Internet, Pregnancy and Unexplained Phenomena. Visit **www.roughguides.com** to see what's cooking.

Rough Guide Credits

Text editors: Gavin Thomas &
Clifton Wilkinson
Series editor: Mark Ellingham
Editorial: Martin Dunford, Jonathan Buckley,
Kate Berens, Ann-Marie Shaw, Helena Smith,
Olivia Swift, Ruth Blackmore, Geoff Howard,
Claire Saunders, Alexander Mark Rogers,
Polly Thomas, Joe Staines, Richard Lim,
Duncan Clark, Peter Buckley, Lucy Ratcliffe,
Alison Murchie, Matthew Teller,
Andrew Dickson, Fran Sandham (UK);
Andrew Rosenberg, Yuki Takagaki,
Richard Koss, Hunter Slaton (US)
Production: Susanne Hillen, Andy Hilliard,
Link Hall, Helen Prior, Julia Bovis,
Michelle Draycott, Katie Pringle, Zoë Nobes,
Rachel Holmes, Andy Turner

Cartography: Maxine Repath, Melissa Baker,
Ed Wright, Katie Lloyd-Jones
Cover art direction: Louise Boulton
Picture research: Sharon Martins,
Mark Thomas
Online: Kelly Martinez, Anja Mutic-Blessing,
Jennifer Gold, Audra Epstein,
Suzanne Welles, Cree Lawson (US)
Finance: John Fisher, Gary Singh,
Edward Downey, Mark Hall, Tim Bill
Marketing & Publicity: Richard Trillo,
Niki Smith, David Wearn, Chloë Roberts,
Demelza Dallow, Claire Southern (UK);
Simon Carloss, David Wechsler,
Kathleen Rushforth (US)
Administration: Tania Hummel,
Julie Sanderson

Publishing Information

This first edition published January 2003 by
Rough Guides Ltd,
80 Strand, London WC2R 0RL.
Penguin Putnam, Inc. 375 Hudson Street,
NY 10014, USA.
Distributed by the Penguin Group
Penguin Books Ltd,
80 Strand, London WC2R 0RL
Penguin Putnam, Inc.
375 Hudson Street, NY 10014, USA
Penguin Books Australia Ltd,
487 Maroondah Highway, PO Box 257,
Ringwood, Victoria 3134, Australia
Penguin Books Canada Ltd,
10 Alcorn Avenue, Toronto, Ontario,
Canada M4V 1E4
Penguin Books (NZ) Ltd,
182–190 Wairau Road, Auckland 10,
New Zealand
Typeset in Bembo and Helvetica to an
original design by Henry Iles.

Printed in Italy by LegoPrint S.p.A

© Jens Finke, 2003

800pp includes index
A catalogue record for this book is available
from the British Library

ISBN 1-85828-783-9

Help us update

We've gone to a lot of effort to ensure that
the first edition of **The Rough Guide to
Tanzania** is accurate and up-to-date.
However, things change – places get
"discovered", opening hours are notoriously
fickle, restaurants and rooms raise prices or
lower standards. If you feel we've got it
wrong or left something out, we'd like to
know, and if you can remember the address,
the price, the time, the phone number, so
much the better.

We'll credit all contributions, and send a
copy of the next edition (or any other Rough
Guide if you prefer) for the best letters.
Everyone who writes to us and isn't already a
subscriber will receive a copy of our full-
colour thrice-yearly newsletter. Please mark
letters: "**Rough Guide Tanzania Update**"
and send to: 80 Strand, London WC2R 0RL,
or Rough Guides, 4th Floor, 345 Hudson St,
New York, NY 10014. Or send an email to
mail@roughguides.com

Have your questions answered and tell
others about your trip at
www.roughguides.atinfopop.com.

Acknowledgements

First off, I am deeply indebted to all the Tanzanians I met during my travels, whose unfailingly warm welcome, unassuming pride and sensitivity, caused me to fall head over heels in love with them and with Tanzania. Asanteni sana kabisa warafiki! As a couple of wazee I once overheard said, Mambo? Fresh!

Special thanks go to Maria Helena Barreira for her patience in putting up with my physical and, at times, mental absence for over two years. Special thanks also to Richard Trillo, author of the *Rough Guide to Kenya*, for getting me to East Africa in the first place, and for permission to use some of his work in the chapters on Basics and Contexts. Bitter-sweet thanks go to my long-suffering but whip-wielding editors, Gavin Thomas, Clifton Wilkinson and Helena Smith, for their excellent work. In Tanzania, particular thanks go to Hyasintha Lucas Hamza and family in Kwebarabara for some enchanting experiences, Kathleen "Mobitel" Bluekins and "Lekker" Jef Vercammen at Via Via in Arusha, without whom Arusha wouldn't have been the same, the indefatigable "Mama" Rita Daneels, the truly regal King brothers Simon "Orchidman" and Hartley "what chainsaw?", also in Arusha, and to Samuel and Rene Lugemalila, for their spectacular rescue of my maps!

Thanks also, for all kinds of help, advice and information, to the following: Lorna Abungu, Anne Adams, John Addison, Kristin Adeler, Bagamoyo Young Artists Cooperative Society, Charlie Bailey, Ben Barker, Aimee Bessire, Gerald Bigurube, Emmanuel P. Chacha, Dr Felix Chami, Marie Cidosa, Fatema at Coastal Travels, Barbara Cole, Cynthia Critton, Alan Dixson, Stephane Dondeyne, Claire Durbin, Mark Fairweather, Stephen H. Fisher, Bruce Fox, Werner Graebner, Oliver Guenay, David Guthrie, Father Henschel, Meghan Hicks, Jorgen Holm, Lennie Holm, Iain at Trade Aid in Mikindani, Javed Jafferji, Joas Kahembe, Dr Samahani M. Kejeri, R. Kilenga, Elly Kimbwereza, Catherine Kimer, Mr Kisamo, Johannes Kleppe and family, Frowin Komba, A.S. Kyambile, Massimo Lancellotti, Dr Paul Lane, Stefan Larsson, James Lembeli, Henrik Lerdorf, Glenn Lewis, Peter Lindstrom, Stephen Laiser, Risberg Matz Lonnedal, Kazimoto Sylvester Lucas, Mary L. Lwoga, Dr Audax Z.P. Mabulla, Newton J. Maganga, "DJ" Yusuf Mahmoud, Heike Mailaender, Mustafa Makame, Jasper Malewa, Dr Bertram Mapunda, Dr Fidelis T. Masao, Namassona John Maukah, Linus Peter Mchina, Chief Wilfred Mirambo, Stephen Michael Mnong'one, Edward Mikundi, Akida Mohamed, Jan Mohamed, Danford Mpumilwa, Hussein M. Msangi, Sarah Mutagobe, Stanley Mwalembe, Michael P. Mwaseba, Lesikar Ole Ngila, Joseph John "Boke" Nyabasi, Katia Palazzo, Gary Palmer, Doug Paterson, the Peterson brothers at Dorobo, Richard Phillips, Sophie Pitcher, Dyreen and Peter Quinn, Dr John Wembah-Rashid, Yunus Rafiq, Mr Rogati and the mapping office at CDA, Bonny Sands, Corodius Sawe, Barbara Schachenmann, Christian Schmeling, Ali Seif, Leonard Sekibaha, David Selby, Gerald Adam Semgomba, Victor Shao, Bernard "Mr Passion" Shirima, Tom Ole Sikar, Anna Simbila, Paul Stockley, Miet van Spittael, Steven Spurgin, Tabora Regional Council, Jesuit Temba, Timo Voipio, Greg Welby, and Daniel Yamat.

Photo Credits

around the world

Alaska ★ Algarve ★ Amsterdam ★ Andalucía ★ Antigua & Barbuda ★
Argentina ★ Auckland Restaurants ★ Australia ★ Austria ★ Bahamas ★
Bali & Lombok ★ Bangkok ★ Barbados ★ Barcelona ★ Beijing ★ Belgium &
Luxembourg ★ Belize ★ Berlin ★ Big Island of Hawaii ★ Bolivia ★ Boston
★ Brazil ★ Britain ★ Brittany & Normandy ★ Bruges & Ghent ★ Brussels ★
Budapest ★ Bulgaria ★ California ★ Cambodia ★ Canada ★ Cape Town ★
The Caribbean ★ Central America ★ Chile ★ China ★ Copenhagen ★
Corsica ★ Costa Brava ★ Costa Rica ★ Crete ★ Croatia ★ Cuba ★ Cyprus ★
Czech & Slovak Republics ★ Devon & Cornwall ★ Dodecanese & East
Aegean ★ Dominican Republic ★ The Dordogne & the Lot ★ Dublin ★
Ecuador ★ Edinburgh ★ Egypt ★ England ★ Europe ★ First-time Asia ★
First-time Europe ★ Florence ★ Florida ★ France ★ French Hotels &
Restaurants ★ Gay & Lesbian Australia ★ Germany ★ Goa ★ Greece ★
Greek Islands ★ Guatemala ★ Hawaii ★ Holland ★ Hong Kong & Macau ★
Honolulu ★ Hungary ★ Ibiza & Formentera ★ Iceland ★ India ★ Indonesia
★ Ionian Islands ★ Ireland ★ Israel & the Palestinian Territories ★ Italy ★
Jamaica ★ Japan ★ Jerusalem ★ Jordan ★ Kenya ★ The Lake District ★
Languedoc & Roussillon ★ Laos ★ Las Vegas ★ Lisbon ★ London ★

in twenty years

London Mini Guide ★ London Restaurants ★ Los Angeles ★ Madeira ★ Madrid ★ Malaysia, Singapore & Brunei ★ Mallorca ★ Malta & Gozo ★ Maui ★ Maya World ★ Melbourne ★ Menorca ★ Mexico ★ Miami & the Florida Keys ★ Montréal ★ Morocco ★ Moscow ★ Nepal ★ New England ★ New Orleans ★ New York City ★ New York Mini Guide ★ New York Restaurants ★ New Zealand ★ Norway ★ Pacific Northwest ★ Paris ★ Paris Mini Guide ★ Peru ★ Poland ★ Portugal ★ Prague ★ Provence & the Côte d'Azur ★ Pyrenees ★ The Rocky Mountains ★ Romania ★ Rome ★ San Francisco ★ San Francisco Restaurants ★ Sardinia ★ Scandinavia ★ Scotland ★ Scottish Highlands & Islands ★ Seattle ★ Sicily ★ Singapore ★ South Africa, Lesotho & Swaziland ★ South India ★ Southeast Asia ★ Southwest USA ★ Spain ★ St Lucia ★ St Petersburg ★ Sweden ★ Switzerland ★ Sydney ★ Syria ★ Tanzania ★ Tenerife and La Gomera ★ Thailand ★ Thailand's Beaches & Islands ★ Tokyo ★ Toronto ★ Travel Health ★ Trinidad & Tobago ★ Tunisia ★ Turkey ★ Tuscany & Umbria ★ USA ★ Vancouver ★ Venice & the Veneto ★ Vienna ★ Vietnam ★ Wales ★ Washington DC ★ West Africa ★ Women Travel ★ Yosemite ★ Zanzibar ★ Zimbabwe

also look out for our maps,
phrasebooks, music guides
and reference books

Music Reference Guides

CD Guides

Mini Guides

Rough Guide Instrument Guides

Essential Tipbook Series

THE ROUGH GUIDE TO
Acoustic Guitar
THE ESSENTIAL TIPBOOK

THE ROUGH GUIDE TO
Clarinet
THE ESSENTIAL TIPBOOK

THE ROUGH GUIDE TO
Electric Guitar
THE ESSENTIAL TIPBOOK

THE ROUGH GUIDE TO
Flute
THE ESSENTIAL TIPBOOK

THE ROUGH GUIDE TO
Keyboards & Digital Piano
THE ESSENTIAL TIPBOOK

THE ROUGH GUIDE TO
Piano
THE ESSENTIAL TIPBOOK

THE ROUGH GUIDE TO
Reading Music & Basic Theory
THE ESSENTIAL TIPBOOK

THE ROUGH GUIDE TO
Saxophone
THE ESSENTIAL TIPBOOK

THE ROUGH GUIDE TO
Trumpet & Trombone
THE ESSENTIAL TIPBOOK

THE ROUGH GUIDE TO
Cello
THE ESSENTIAL TIPBOOK

THE ROUGH GUIDE TO
Drums
THE ESSENTIAL TIPBOOK

THE ROUGH GUIDE
Violin & Viola
THE ESSENTIAL TIPBOOK

"These Rough Guides are admirably informative. They are ideal for anyone wanting to learn or discover an instrument"
Julian Lloyd Webber

www.roughguides.com

Rough Guide Reference

Pocket History Series

"Solidly written, immaculately researched, Rough Guides are as near as modern guides get to essential"
Sunday Times, London

www.roughguides.com

The ideas expressed in this code were developed by and for independent travellers.

Learn About The Country You're Visiting

Start enjoying your travels before you leave by tapping into as many sources of information as you can.

The Cost Of Your Holiday

Think about where your money goes - be fair and realistic about how cheaply you travel. Try and put money into local peoples' hands; drink local beer or fruit juice rather than imported brands and stay in locally owned accommodation. Haggle with humour and not aggressively. Pay what something is worth to you and remember how wealthy you are compared to local people.

Embrace The Local Culture

Open your mind to new cultures and traditions - it will transform your experience. Think carefully about what's appropriate in terms of your clothes and the way you behave. You'll earn respect and be more readily welcomed by local people. Respect local laws and attitudes towards drugs and alcohol that vary in different countries and communities. Think about the impact you could have on them.

Exploring The World – The Travellers' Code

Being sensitive to these ideas means getting more out of your travels - and giving more back to the people you meet and the places you visit.

Minimise Your Environmental Impact

Think about what happens to your rubbish - take biodegradable products and a water filter bottle. Be sensitive to limited resources like water, fuel and electricity. Help preserve local wildlife and habitats by respecting local rules and regulations, such as sticking to footpaths and not standing on coral.

Don't Rely On Guidebooks

Use your guidebook as a starting point, not the only source of information. Talk to local people, then discover your own adventure!

Be Discreet With Photography

Don't treat people as part of the landscape, they may not want their picture taken. Ask first and respect their wishes.

We work with people the world over to promote tourism that benefits their communities, but we can only carry on our work with the support of people like you. For membership details or to find out how to make your travels work for local people and the environment, visit our website.

www.tourismconcern.org.uk

Tourism Concern
Campaigning for Ethical and Fairly Traded Tourism

NO TIME TO PACK?

When disaster or war strike, there is no time to pack your bags.

Every year hundreds of thousands of people in Africa are forced to flee their homes and literally run for their lives.

MEDAIR, specialising in emergency humanitarian aid, provides life-saving care to over 3 million victims of disaster and conflict worldwide, regardless of race, sex, religion or age.

But with MEDAIR it's life that counts, not statistics.

We're committed to making our assistance as personal as possible. That's why our programmes are made to suit individual needs, from healthcare, health education and trauma counselling, to reconstruction, food-distribution and improving water supplies.

Join us on the frontline
and see how you can help
by visiting www.MEDAIR.org
or e-mailing info@MEDAIR.org.uk

MEDAIR from survival to life
international humanitarian aid

ISO 9001
SGS

With thanks to Rough Guides for sponsoring this advertisement.

Don't bury your head in the sand!

Take cover!

with Rough Guide Travel Insurance